Crafting and Executing Strategy

THE QUEST FOR COMPETITIVE ADVANTAGE

Concepts and Cases

D1342141

Crafting and Executing Strategy

THE QUEST FOR COMPETITIVE ADVANTAGE

Concepts and Cases

EIGHTEENTH EDITION

Arthur A. Thompson
The University of Alabama

Margaret A. Peteraf
Dartmouth College

John E. Gamble
University of South Alabama

A. J. Strickland III
The University of Alabama

McGraw-Hill Irwin

McGraw-Hill
Irwin

CRAFTING & EXECUTING STRATEGY: CONCEPTS AND CASES: GLOBAL EDITION

Published by McGraw-Hill/Irwin, a business unit of The McGraw-Hill Companies, Inc., 1221 Avenue of the Americas, New York, NY, 10020. Copyright © 2012, 2010, 2008, 2007, 2005, 2003, 2001 by The McGraw-Hill Companies, Inc. All rights reserved. Printed in the United States of America. No part of this publication may be reproduced or distributed in any form or by any means, or stored in a database or retrieval system, without the prior written consent of The McGraw-Hill Companies, Inc., including, but not limited to, in any network or other electronic storage or transmission, or broadcast for distance learning.

Some ancillaries, including electronic and print components, may not be available to customers outside the United States.

This book is printed on acid-free paper.

1 2 3 4 5 6 7 8 9 0 DOW/DOW 1 0 9 8 7 6 5 4 3 2 1

ISBN 978-0-07-131700-9
MHID 0-07-131700-7

The ICMR cases contained in this text were compiled from published sources, and are intended to be used as a basis for class discussion rather than to illustrate either effective or ineffective handling of a management situation. To order copies or request permission to reproduce, call +91-8417-236667 or write to IBS Center for Management Research (ICMR), IFHE Campus, Donthanapally, Sankarapally Road, Hyderabad 501504, Andhra Pradesh, India or email: info@icmrindia.org

With respect to Ivey cases, Richard Ivey School of Business Foundation prohibits any form of reproduction, storage or transmission without its written permission. This material is not covered under authorization from any reproduction rights organization. To order copies or request permission to reproduce materials, contact Ivey Publishing, Richard Ivey School of Business Foundation, The University of Western Ontario, London, Ontario, Canada, N6A 3K7; phone (519) 661-3208, fax (519) 661-3882, e-mail cases@ivey.uwo.ca.

One time permission to reproduce Ivey Cases granted by Richard Ivey School of Business Foundation on 1-23-11.

Photo Credits

Chapter 1: page 55, © Yu Chu Di/Redlink/Redlink/Corbis; **Chapter 2:** page 90, © Jason Reed/Reuters/Corbis; page 90, Bloomberg via Getty Images; **Chapter 4:** page 160, Just Coffee Cooperative; **Chapter 5:** page 191, Courtesy of Walmart; page 203, Pichi Chuang/Reuters/Corbis; page 207, 2010 Toyota Motor Sales, USA, Inc.; **Chapter 6:** page 224, Amazon.com, Inc.; **Chapter 7:** page 282, MARK/epa/Corbis; page 285, Bloomberg Via Getty Images; **Chapter 8:** page 329, AP Photo/Mike Derer; **Chapter 9:** page 341, Courtesy of Apple; page 350, Aaron M. Sprecher/Corbis; page 353, CLARO CORTESIV/Reuters/Corbis; **Chapter 10:** page 383, AFP/Getty Images; page 387, Courtesy of Toyota; **Chapter 11:** page 417, Paulo Fridman/Corbis; page 426, Courtesy of Lincoln Electric; page 429, Bloomberg Via Getty Images

www.mhhe.com

To our families and especially our spouses:
Hasseline, Paul, and Kitty.

Arthur A. Thompson, Jr., earned his B.S. and Ph.D. degrees in economics from The University of Tennessee, spent three years on the economics faculty at Virginia Tech, and served on the faculty of The University of Alabama's College of Commerce and Business Administration for 24 years. In 1974 and again in 1982, Dr. Thompson spent semester-long sabbaticals as a visiting scholar at the Harvard Business School.

His areas of specialization are business strategy, competition and market analysis, and the economics of business enterprises. In addition to publishing over 30 articles in some 25 different professional and trade publications, he has authored or co-authored five textbooks and six computer-based simulation exercises. His textbooks and strategy simulations have been used at well over 1,000 college and university campuses worldwide.

Dr. Thompson and his wife of 49 years have two daughters, two grandchildren, and a Yorkshire Terrier.

Margaret A. Peteraf is the Leon E. Williams Professor of Management at the Tuck School of Business at Dartmouth College. She is an internationally recognized scholar of strategic management, with a long list of publications in top management journals. She has earned myriad honors and prizes for her contributions, including the 1999 Strategic Management Society Best Paper Award recognizing the deep influence of her work on the field of Strategic Management. Professor Peteraf is on the Board of Directors of the Strategic Management Society and has been elected as a Fellow of the Society. She served previously as a member of the Academy of Management's Board of Governors and as Chair of the Business Policy and Strategy Division of the Academy. She has also served in various editorial roles and is presently on 9 editorial boards, including the *Strategic Management Journal,* the *Academy of Management Review,* and *Organization Science.* She has taught in Executive Education programs in various programs around the world and has won teaching awards at the MBA and Executive level.

Professor Peteraf earned her Ph.D., M.A., and M.Phil. at Yale University and held previous faculty appointments at Northwestern University's Kellogg Graduate School of Management and at the University of Minnesota's Carlson School of Management.

John E. Gamble is currently a Professor of Management in the Mitchell College of Business at the University of South Alabama. His teaching specialty at USA is strategic management and he also conducts a course in strategic management in Germany, which is sponsored by the University of Applied Sciences in Worms.

Dr. Gamble's research interests center on strategic issues in entrepreneurial, health care, and manufacturing settings. His work has been published in various scholarly journals and he is the author or co-author of more than 50 case studies published in an assortment of strategic management and strategic marketing texts. He has done consulting on industry and market analysis for clients in a diverse mix of industries.

Professor Gamble received his Ph.D. in management from The University of Alabama in 1995. Dr. Gamble also has a Bachelor of Science degree and a Master of Arts degree from The University of Alabama.

Dr. A. J. (Lonnie) Strickland is the Thomas R. Miller Professor of Strategic Management at the Culverhouse School of Business at The University of Alabama. He is a native of North Georgia, and attended the University of Georgia, where he received a Bachelor of Science degree in math and physics; Georgia Institute of Technology, where he received a Master of Science in industrial management; and Georgia State University, where he received his Ph.D. in business administration.

Lonnie's experience in consulting and executive development is in the strategic management arena, with a concentration in industry and competitive analysis. He has developed strategic planning systems for numerous firms all over the world. He served as Director of Marketing and Strategy at Bell-South, has taken two companies to the New York Stock Exchange, is one of the founders and directors of American Equity Investment Life Holding (AEL), and serves on numerous boards of directors. He is a very popular speaker in the area of Strategic Management.

Lonnie and his wife, Kitty, have been married for 44 years; they have two children, and two grandchildren. Each summer Lonnie and his wife live on their private game reserve in South Africa where they enjoy taking their friends on safaris.

PREFACE

The defining trait of this 18th edition is an invigorated and much sharpened presentation of the material in each of the 12 chapters, with an as up-to-date and engaging discussion of the core concepts and analytical tools as you will find anywhere. Complementing the text chapters is a fresh, engrossing collection of 24 cases with unusual ability to work magic in the classroom. We are confident you will find the text chapters in this edition squarely on target, clearly written, peppered with fresh examples, and compelling. Together with a power-house lineup of high-interest cases, this is a text sure to ignite your students' interest in strategy, translate their enthusiasm into learning achievements, and enable you to shine in the classroom.

This edition represents one of our most important and thoroughgoing revisions ever. The newest member of the author team, Margie Peteraf, led a thorough reexamination of every paragraph on every page of the 17th-edition chapters. The overriding objectives were to inject new perspectives and the best academic thinking, strengthen linkages to the latest research findings, modify the coverage and exposition as needed to ensure squarely on-target content, and give every chapter a major facelift. While this 18th edition retains the 12-chapter structure of the prior edition, every chapter has been totally refreshed. Coverage was trimmed in some areas and expanded in others. New material has been added here and there. The presentations of some topics were recast, others fine-tuned, and still others left largely intact. As with past editions, scores of new examples have been added, along with fresh Illustration Capsules, to make the content come alive and to provide students with a ringside view of strategy in action. The result is a major step forward in terms of punch, up-to-date coverage, clarity, and classroom effectiveness. But none of the changes have altered the fundamental character that has driven the text's success over three decades. The chapter content continues to be solidly mainstream and balanced, mirroring *both* the penetrating insight of academic thought and the pragmatism of real-world strategic management. And, as always, we have taken great care to keep the chapters very reader-friendly and exceptionally teachable.

A differentiating feature of this text has always been the tight linkage between the content of the chapters and the cases. The lineup of cases that accompany the 18th edition is outstanding in this respect—a truly appealing mix of strategically relevant and thoughtfully crafted cases, certain to engage students and sharpen their skills in applying the concepts and tools of strategic analysis. Many involve high-profile companies that the students will immediately recognize and relate to; all are framed around key strategic issues and serve to add depth and context to the topical content of the chapters. We are confident that you will be impressed with how well these cases work in the classroom and the amount of student interest they will spark.

For some years now, growing numbers of strategy instructors at business schools worldwide have been transitioning from a purely text-case course structure to a more robust and energizing text-case-simulation course structure.

Incorporating a competition-based strategy simulation has the strong appeal of providing class members with *an immediate and engaging opportunity to apply the concepts and analytical tools covered in the chapters and to become personally involved in crafting and executing a strategy for a virtual company that they have been assigned to manage and that competes head-to-head with companies run by other class members.* Two widely used and pedagogically effective online strategy simulations, *The Business Strategy Game* and *GLO-BUS,* are optional companions for this text. Both simulations were created by this text's senior author and, like the cases, are closely linked to the content of each chapter in the text. The Exercises for Simulation Participants, found at the end of each chapter, provide clear guidance to class members in applying the concepts and analytical tools covered in the chapters to the issues and decisions that they have to wrestle with in managing their simulation company.

Through our experiences as business school faculty members, we fully understand the assessment demands on faculty teaching strategic management and business policy courses. In many institutions, capstone courses have emerged as the logical home for assessing student achievement of program learning objectives. The 18th edition includes a set of Assurance of Learning Exercises at the end of each chapter that link to the specific learning objectives appearing at the beginning of each chapter and highlighted throughout the text. *An important new instructional feature of the 18th edition is the linkage of selected chapter-end Assurance of Learning Exercises and four cases to the publisher's Web-based assignment and assessment platform called Connect.* Your students will be able to use the online Connect supplement to (1) complete an Assurance of Learning Exercise for each of the 12 chapters, (2) complete chapter-end quizzes, and (3) enter their answers to a select number of the suggested assignment questions for 4 of 24 cases in this edition. All of the Connect exercises are automatically graded, thereby enabling you to easily assess the learning that has occurred.

In addition, both of the companion strategy simulations have a built-in Learning Assurance Report that quantifies how well each member of your class performed on nine skills/learning measures *versus tens of thousands of other students worldwide* who completed the simulation in the past 12 months. We believe the chapter-end Assurance of Learning Exercises, the all-new online and automatically graded Connect exercises, and the Learning Assurance Report generated at the conclusion of *The Business Strategy Game* and *GLO-BUS* simulations provide you with easy-to-use, empirical measures of student learning in your course. All can be used in conjunction with other instructor-developed or school-developed scoring rubrics and assessment tools to comprehensively evaluate course or program learning outcomes and measure compliance with AACSB accreditation standards.

Taken together, the various components of the 18th-edition package and the supporting set of instructor resources provide you with enormous course design flexibility and a powerful kit of teaching/learning tools. We've done our very best to ensure that the elements constituting the 18th edition will work well for you in the classroom, help you economize on the time needed to be well prepared for each class, and cause students to conclude that your course is one of the very best they have ever taken—from the standpoint of both enjoyment and learning.

REVITALIZED AND EFFECTIVE CONTENT: THE SIGNATURE OF THE 18TH EDITION

Our objective in undertaking a major revision of this text was to ensure that its content was current, with respect to both scholarship and managerial practice, and was presented in as clear and compelling a fashion as possible. We established five criteria for meeting this objective, namely, that the final product must:

- Explain core concepts in language that students can grasp and provide first-rate examples of their relevance and use by actual companies.
- Thoroughly describe the tools of strategic analysis, how they are used, and where they fit into the managerial process of crafting and executing strategy.
- Incorporate the latest developments in the theory and practice of strategic management in every chapter to keep the content solidly in the mainstream of contemporary strategic thinking.
- Focus squarely on what every student needs to know about crafting, implementing, and executing business strategies in today's market environments.
- Provide an attractive set of contemporary cases that involve headline strategic issues and give students ample opportunity to apply what they've learned from the chapters.

We believe the 18th edition measures up on all five criteria. Chapter discussions cut straight to the chase about what students really need to know. At the same time, our explanations of core concepts and analytical tools are covered in enough depth to make them understandable and usable, since a shallow explanation carries little punch and almost no instructional value. Chapter content is driven by the imperative of including well-settled strategic management principles, fresh examples that illustrate the principles through the practices of real-world companies, recent research findings and contributions to the literature on strategic management, and the latest thinking of prominent academics and practitioners. There's a logical flow from one chapter to the next, as well as an unparalleled set of cases with which to drive the lessons home. And we have worked hard to hammer home the whys and hows of successfully crafting and executing strategy in an engaging, cogent, and convincing fashion.

Six standout features strongly differentiate this text and the accompanying instructional package from others in the field:

1. *Our coverage of the resource-based theory of the firm in the 18th edition is unsurpassed by any other leading strategy text.* RBV principles and concepts are prominently and comprehensively integrated into our coverage of crafting both single-business and multibusiness strategies. In Chapters 3 through

8 it is repeatedly emphasized that a company's strategy must be matched *not only* to its external market circumstances *but also* to its internal resources and competitive capabilities. Moreover, an RBV perspective is thoroughly integrated into the presentation on strategy execution (Chapters 10, 11, and 12) to make it unequivocally clear how and why the tasks of assembling intellectual capital and building core competencies and competitive capabilities are absolutely critical to successful strategy execution and operating excellence.

2. *Our coverage of the relational view, which focuses on cooperative strategies and the role that interorganizational activity can play in the pursuit of competitive advantage, is similarly unsurpassed by other leading texts.* The topics of alliances, joint ventures, franchising, and other types of cooperative and collaborative relationships are featured prominently in a number of chapters and are integrated into other material throughout the text as well. We show how strategies of this nature can contribute to the success of single business companies as well as multibusiness enterprises. And while we begin with coverage of such topics with respect to firms operating in domestic markets, we extend our discussion of this material to the international realm as well.

3. *Our coverage of business ethics, core values, social responsibility, and environmental sustainability is unsurpassed by any other leading strategy text.* In this new edition, we have embellished the highly important chapter "Ethics, Corporate Social Responsibility, Environmental Sustainability, and Strategy" with fresh content so that it can better fulfill the important functions of (1) alerting students to the role and importance of ethical and socially responsible decision making and (2) addressing the accreditation requirement of the AACSB International that business ethics be visibly and thoroughly embedded in the core curriculum. Moreover, discussions of the roles of values and ethics are integrated into portions of other chapters to further reinforce why and how considerations relating to ethics, values, social responsibility, and sustainability should figure prominently into the managerial task of crafting and executing company strategies.

4. *The caliber of the case collection in the 18th edition is truly top-notch* from the standpoints of student appeal, teachability, and suitability for drilling students in the use of the concepts and analytical treatments in Chapters 1 through 12. The 24 cases included in this edition are the very latest, the best, and the most on target that we could find. The ample information about the cases in the Instructor's Manual makes it effortless to select a set of cases each term that will capture the interest of students from start to finish.

5. *The text is paired with the publisher's trailblazing Web-based assignment and assessment platform called Connect.* This will enable professors to gauge class members' prowess in accurately completing (a) selected chapter-end exercises, (b) chapter-end quizzes, and (c) the creative author-developed exercises for seven of the cases in this edition.

6. *Two cutting-edge and widely used strategy simulations—The Business Strategy Game and GLO-bus—are optional companions to the 18th edition.* These give you unmatched capability to employ a text-case-simulation model of course delivery.

ORGANIZATION, CONTENT, AND FEATURES OF THE 18TH-EDITION TEXT CHAPTERS

The following rundown summarizes the noteworthy features and topical emphasis in this new edition:

- Although Chapter 1 continues to focus on the central questions of *"What is strategy?"* and *"Why is it important?"* the presentation of this material has been sharpened considerably, with more concise definitions of the key concepts and significant updating to improve the currency of the material. We introduce students to the primary approaches to building competitive advantage and the key elements of business-level strategy. Following Henry Mintzberg's process approach, we explain why a company's strategy is partly planned and partly reactive and why a strategy and its environment tend to co-evolve over time. We discuss the importance of a viable business model that outlines the company's customer value proposition and its profit formula, framing this discussion in terms of key elements of value, price, and cost. We show how the mark of a winning strategy is its ability to pass three tests: (1) the *fit test* (for internal and external fit), (2) the *competitive advantage test,* and (3) the *performance test.* And we explain why good company performance depends upon good strategy execution as well as a sound strategy. In short, this brief chapter is a perfect accompaniment for your opening-day lecture on what the course is all about and why it matters.

- Chapter 2 delves more deeply into the managerial process of actually crafting and executing a strategy—it makes a great assignment for the second day of class and provides a smooth transition into the heart of the course. The focal point of the chapter is the five-step managerial process of crafting and executing strategy: (1) forming a strategic vision of where the company is headed and why, (2) developing strategic as well as financial objectives with which to measure the company's progress, (3) crafting a strategy to achieve these targets and move the company toward its market destination, (4) implementing and executing the strategy, and (5) monitoring progress and making corrective adjustments as needed. Students are introduced to such core concepts as strategic visions, mission statements and core values, the balanced scorecard, strategic intent, and business-level versus corporate-level strategies. There's a robust discussion of why *all managers are on a company's strategy-making, strategy-executing team* and why a company's strategic plan is a collection of strategies devised by different managers at different levels in the organizational hierarchy. The chapter winds up with a section on how to exercise good corporate governance and examines the conditions that led to recent high-profile corporate governance failures.

- Chapter 3 sets forth the now-familiar analytical tools and concepts of industry and competitive analysis and demonstrates the importance of tailoring strategy to fit the circumstances of a company's industry and competitive environment. The standout feature of this chapter is a presentation of Michael Porter's "five-forces model of competition" *that has long been the clearest, most straightforward discussion of any text in the field.* This edition also provides expanded coverage of a company's macro-environment to enable students to conduct what some call *Pestel analysis* of *p*olitical, *e*conomic, *s*ocial, *t*echnological, *e*nvironmental, and *l*egal factors.

- Chapter 4 presents the resource-based view of the firm and convincingly argues why a company's strategy must be built around its most competitively valuable resources and capabilities. We provide students with a simple taxonomy for identifying a company's resources and capabilities and frame our discussion of how a firm's resources and capabilities can provide a sustainable competitive advantage with the *VRIN model*. We introduce the notion of a company's *dynamic capabilities* and cast SWOT analysis as a simple, easy-to-use way to assess a company's overall situation in terms of its ability to seize market opportunities and ward off external threats. There is solid coverage of value chain analysis, benchmarking, and competitive strength assessments—standard tools for appraising a company's relative cost position and customer value proposition vis-à-vis rivals. *An important feature of this chapter is a table showing how key financial and operating ratios are calculated and how to interpret them;* students will find this table handy in doing the number crunching needed to evaluate whether a company's strategy is delivering good financial performance.

- Chapter 5 deals with the basic approaches used to compete successfully and gain a competitive advantage over market rivals. This discussion is framed around the five generic competitive strategies—low-cost leadership, differentiation, best-cost provider, focused differentiation, and focused low cost. We emphasize that regardless of a company's choice, competitive success depends upon a company's capacity to deliver more customer value—one way or another. We provide a fuller treatment of *cost drivers* and *uniqueness drivers* as the keys to bringing down a company's cost and enhancing its differentiation, respectively, in support of this overall goal.

- Chapter 6 continues the theme of competitive strategies for single-business firms with its spotlight on *strategic actions (offensive and defensive) and their timing,* including blue-ocean strategies and first-mover advantages and disadvantages. It also serves to segue into the material covered in the next two chapters (on international and diversification strategies) by introducing the topic of *strategies that alter a company's scope of operations.* The chapter features sections on the strategic benefits and risks of horizontal mergers and acquisitions, vertical integration, and outsourcing of certain value chain activities. The concluding section of this chapter covers the advantages and drawbacks of using strategic alliances and cooperative arrangements to alter a company's scope of operations, with some pointers on how to make strategic alliances work.

- Chapter 7 explores the full range of strategy options for expanding a company's geographic scope and competing in foreign markets: export strategies, licensing, franchising, establishing a wholly owned subsidiary via acquisition or "greenfield" venture, and alliance strategies. In the 18th edition, we've added new coverage of topics such as Porter's *Diamond of National Advantage;* the choice between *multidomestic, global, and transnational strategies; profit sanctuaries* and cross-border strategic moves; and *the quest for competitive advantage via sharing, transferring, or accessing valuable resources and capabilities across national borders.* The chapter concludes with a discussion of the special issues of competing in the markets of developing countries and the strategies that local companies can use to defend against global giants.

- Chapter 8 introduces the topic of corporate-level strategy—a topic of concern for multibusiness companies pursuing diversification. This chapter begins by explaining why successful diversification strategies must create shareholder value and lays out the three essential tests that a strategy must pass to achieve this goal *(the industry attractiveness, cost-of-entry, and better-off tests)*. We discuss alternative means of entering new businesses (acquisition, internal start-up, or joint venture) and offer a method for discerning which choice is a firm's best option. Then we turn our attention to a comparison of related versus unrelated diversification strategies, showing that they differ in terms of the nature of their critical resources *(specialized versus general parenting capabilities)* and whether they can exploit cross-business strategic fit for competitive gain. The chapter's analytical spotlight is trained on the techniques and procedures for assessing the strategic attractiveness of a diversified company's business portfolio—the relative attractiveness of the various industries the company has diversified into, the company's competitive strength in each of its lines of business, and the extent to which there is *strategic fit* and *resource fit* among its different businesses. The chapter concludes with a brief survey of a company's four main postdiversification strategy alternatives: (1) sticking closely with the existing business lineup, (2) broadening the diversification base, (3) divesting some businesses and retrenching to a narrower diversification base, and (4) restructuring the makeup of the company's business lineup.

- Chapter 9 reflects the very latest in the literature on (1) a company's duty to operate according to ethical standards, (2) a company's obligation to demonstrate socially responsible behavior and corporate citizenship, and (3) why more companies are limiting strategic initiatives to those that meet the needs of consumers in a manner that protects natural resources and ecological support systems needed by future generations. The discussion includes approaches to ensuring consistent ethical standards for companies with international operations. The contents of this chapter will definitely give students some things to ponder and will help to make them more *ethically aware* and conscious of *why all companies should conduct their business in a socially responsible and sustainable manner.* Chapter 9 has been written as a stand-alone chapter that can be assigned in the early, middle, or late part of the course.

- Chapter 10 begins a three-chapter module on executing strategy (Chapters 10 to 12), anchored around a pragmatic, compelling conceptual framework. Chapter 10 presents an overview of this 10-step framework and then develops the first three pieces of it: (1) *staffing the organization* with capable managers and employees, (2) *marshaling the resources and building the organizational capabilities* required for successful strategy execution, and (3) *creating a strategy-supportive organizational structure* and structuring the work effort. We discuss three approaches to building and strengthening a company's capabilities, ranging from internal development to acquisitions to collaborative arrangements, and consider outsourcing as an option for structuring the work effort. We argue for matching a company's organizational structure to its strategy execution requirements, describe four basic types of organizational structures (simple, functional, multidivisional, and matrix), and discuss centralized versus decentralized decision making. We conclude with some further perspectives on facilitating collaboration with external partners and structuring the company's work effort.

- Chapter 11 covers five important topics concerning strategy execution: (1) *allocating ample resources* to strategy-critical activities, (2) ensuring that *policies and procedures* facilitate rather than impede strategy execution, (3) employing *process management tools* and adopting *best practices* to drive continuous improvement in the performance of value chain activities, (4) installing *information and operating systems* that enable company personnel to better carry out their strategic roles proficiently, and (5) tying *rewards and incentives* directly to good strategy execution and the achievement of performance targets.

- Chapter 12 concludes the text with a discussion of corporate culture and leadership in relation to good strategy execution. The recurring theme throughout the final three chapters is that implementing strategy entails figuring out the specific actions, behaviors, and conditions that are needed for a smooth strategy-supportive operation and then following through to get things done and deliver results. The goal here is to ensure that students understand that the strategy-executing phase is a make-things-happen and make-them-happen-right kind of managerial exercise—one that is critical for achieving operating excellence and reaching the goal of strong company performance.

We have done our best to ensure that the 12 chapters convey the best thinking of academics and practitioners in the field of strategic management and hit the bull's-eye in topical coverage for senior- and MBA-level strategy courses. The ultimate test of the text, of course, is the positive pedagogical impact it has in the classroom. If this edition sets a more effective stage for your lectures and does a better job of helping you persuade students that the discipline of strategy merits their rapt attention, then it will have fulfilled its purpose.

THE CASE COLLECTION

The 24-case lineup in this edition is flush with interesting companies and valuable lessons for students in the art and science of crafting and executing strategy. There's a good blend of cases from a length perspective—close to one-fifth are under 15 pages yet offer plenty for students to chew on; about one-fourth are medium-length cases; and the remainder are detail-rich cases that call for more sweeping analysis.

At least 16 of the 24 cases involve companies, products, people, or activities that students will have heard of, know about from personal experience, or can easily identify with. The lineup includes at least eight cases that will provide students with insight into the special demands of competing in industry environments where technological developments are an everyday event, product life cycles are short, and competitive maneuvering among rivals comes fast and furious. Seventeen of the cases involve situations in which company resources and competitive capabilities play as large a role in the strategy-making, strategy-executing scheme of things as industry and competitive conditions do. All cases in the lineup either involve companies operating outside the United States or competing in globally competitive industries; these cases, in conjunction with the globalized content of the text chapters, provide abundant material for linking the study of strategic management tightly to the ongoing globalization of the world economy. You'll also find 3 cases dealing with the strategic problems of family-owned or relatively small entrepreneurial businesses and 20 cases involving public companies and situations on which students can do further research on the Internet.

THE TWO STRATEGY SIMULATION SUPPLEMENTS:
THE BUSINESS STRATEGY GAME AND *GLO-BUS*

The Business Strategy Game and *GLO-BUS: Developing Winning Competitive Strategies*—two competition-based strategy simulations that are delivered online and that feature automated processing and grading of performance—are being marketed by the publisher as companion supplements for use with the 18th edition (and other texts in the field).

- *The Business Strategy Game* is the world's most popular strategy simulation, having been used in courses involving over 600,000 students at more than 700 university campuses in over 40 countries.
- *GLO-BUS*, a somewhat simpler strategy simulation introduced in 2004, has been used at more than 400 university campuses worldwide in courses involving over 120,000 students.

How the Strategy Simulations Work

In both *The Business Strategy Game (BSG)* and *GLO-BUS*, class members are divided into teams of one to five persons and assigned to run a company that competes head-to-head against companies run by other class members.

- In *BSG*, team members run an athletic footwear company, producing and marketing both branded and private-label footwear.
- In *GLO-BUS*, team members operate a digital camera company that designs, assembles, and markets entry-level digital cameras and upscale, multifeatured cameras.

In both simulations, companies compete in a global market arena, selling their products in four geographic regions—Europe-Africa, North America, Asia-Pacific, and Latin America. Each management team is called upon to craft a strategy for their company and make decisions relating to plant operations, workforce compensation, pricing and marketing, social responsibility/citizenship, and finance.

Company co-managers are held accountable for their decision making. Each company's performance is scored on the basis of earnings per share, return on equity investment, stock price, credit rating, and image rating. Rankings of company performance, along with a wealth of industry and company statistics, are available to company co-managers after each decision round to use in making strategy adjustments and operating decisions for the next competitive round. You can be certain that the market environment, strategic issues, and operating challenges that company co-managers must contend with are *very tightly linked* to what your class members will be reading about in the text chapters. The circumstances that co-managers face in running their simulation company embrace the very concepts, analytical tools, and strategy options they encounter in the text chapters (this is something you can quickly confirm by skimming through some of the Exercises for Simulation Participants that appear at the end of each chapter).

We suggest that you schedule 1 or 2 practice rounds and anywhere from 4 to 10 regular (scored) decision rounds (more rounds are better than fewer rounds). Each decision round represents a year of company operations and will entail roughly two hours of time for company co-managers to complete. In traditional 13-week, semester-long courses, there is merit is scheduling one decision round per week. In courses that run 5 to 10 weeks, it is wise to schedule two decision rounds per week for the last several weeks of the term (sample course schedules are provided for courses of varying length and varying numbers of class meetings).

When the instructor-specified deadline for a decision round arrives, the simulation server automatically accesses the saved decision entries of each company, determines the competitiveness and buyer appeal of each company's product offering relative to the other companies being run by students in your class, and then awards sales and market shares to the competing companies, geographic region by geographic region. The unit sales volumes awarded to each company *are totally governed by:*

- How its prices compare against the prices of rival brands.
- How its product quality compares against the quality of rival brands.
- How its product line breadth and selection compare.
- How its advertising effort compares.
- And so on, for a total of 11 competitive factors that determine unit sales and market shares.

The competitiveness and overall buyer appeal of each company's product offering *in comparison to the product offerings of rival companies* is all-decisive—this algorithmic feature is what makes *BSG* and *GLO-BUS* "competition-based" strategy simulations. Once each company's sales and market shares are awarded based on the competitiveness of its respective overall product offering, the various company and industry reports detailing the outcomes of the decision round are then generated. Company co-managers can access the results of the decision round 15 to 20 minutes after the decision deadline.

The Compelling Case for Incorporating Use of a Strategy Simulation

There are *three exceptionally important benefits* associated with using a competition-based simulation in strategy courses taken by seniors and MBA students:

- *A three-pronged text-case-simulation course model delivers significantly more teaching-learning power than the traditional text-case model.* Using *both* cases and a strategy simulation to drill students in thinking strategically and applying what they read in the text chapters is a stronger, more effective means of helping them connect theory with practice and develop better business judgment. What cases do that a simulation cannot is give class members broad exposure to a variety of companies and industry situations and insight into the kinds of strategy-related problems managers face. But what a competition-based strategy simulation does far better than case analysis is thrust class members squarely into *an active, hands-on managerial role* where they are totally responsible for assessing market conditions, determining how to respond to the actions of competitors, forging a long-term direction and strategy for their company, and making all kinds of operating decisions. Because they are held fully accountable for their decisions and their company's performance, *co-managers are strongly motivated* to dig deeply into company operations, probe for ways to be more cost-efficient and competitive, and ferret out strategic moves and decisions calculated to boost company performance. *Consequently, incorporating both case assignments and a strategy simulation to develop the skills of class members in thinking strategically and applying the concepts and tools of strategic analysis turns out to be more pedagogically powerful than relying solely on case assignments—there's stronger retention of the lessons learned and better achievement of course learning objectives.*

To provide you with quantitative evidence of the learning that occurs with using *The Business Strategy Game* or *GLO-BUS,* there is a built-in Learning Assurance Report showing how well each class member performs on nine skills/learning measures versus tens of thousands of students worldwide who have completed the simulation in the past 12 months.

- *The competitive nature of a strategy simulation arouses positive energy and steps up the whole tempo of the course by a notch or two.* Nothing sparks class excitement quicker or better than the concerted efforts on the part of class members at each decision round to achieve a high industry ranking and avoid the perilous consequences of being outcompeted by other class members. Students really enjoy taking on the role of a manager, running their own company, crafting strategies, making all kinds of operating decisions, trying to outcompete rival companies, and getting immediate feedback on the resulting company performance. Lots of back-and-forth chatter occurs when the results of the latest simulation round become available and co-managers renew their quest for strategic moves and actions that will strengthen company performance. Co-managers become *emotionally invested* in running their company and figuring out what strategic moves to make to boost their company's performance. Interest levels climb. All this stimulates learning and causes students to see the practical relevance of the subject matter and the benefits of taking your course.

As soon as your students start to say "Wow! Not only is this fun but I am learning a lot," *which they will,* you have won the battle of engaging students in the subject matter and moved the value of taking your course to a much higher plateau in the business school curriculum. This translates into *a livelier, richer learning experience from a student perspective and better instructor-course evaluations.*

- *Use of a fully automated online simulation reduces the time instructors spend on course preparation, course administration, and grading.* Since the simulation exercise involves a 20- to 30-hour workload for student teams (roughly 2 hours per decision round times 10 to 12 rounds, plus optional assignments), simulation adopters often compensate by trimming the number of assigned cases from, say, 10 to 12 to perhaps 4 to 6. This significantly reduces the time instructors spend reading cases, studying teaching notes, and otherwise getting ready to lead class discussion of a case or grade oral team presentations. Course preparation time is further cut because you can use several class days to have students meet in the computer lab to work on upcoming decision rounds or a three-year strategic plan (in lieu of lecturing on a chapter or covering an additional assigned case). Not only does use of a simulation permit assigning fewer cases, but it also permits you to eliminate at least one assignment that entails considerable grading on your part. Grading one less written case or essay exam or other written assignment saves enormous time. With *BSG* and *GLO-BUS,* grading is effortless and takes only minutes; once you enter percentage weights for each assignment in your online grade book, a suggested overall grade is calculated for you. You'll be pleasantly surprised—and quite pleased—at how little time it takes to gear up for and to administer *The Business Strategy Game* or *GLO-BUS*.

In sum, incorporating use of a strategy simulation turns out to be *a win-win proposition for both students and instructors.* Moreover, a very convincing argument can be made that a competition-based strategy simulation is *the single most effective teaching/learning tool that instructors can employ to teach the discipline of business and competitive strategy, to make learning more enjoyable, and to promote better achievement of course learning objectives.*

A Bird's-Eye View of *The Business Strategy Game*

The setting for *The Business Strategy Game (BSG)* is the global athletic footwear industry (there can be little doubt in today's world that a globally competitive strategy simulation is *vastly superior* to a simulation with a domestic-only setting). Global market demand for footwear grows at the rate of 7 to 9 percent annually for the first five years and 5 to 7 percent annually for the second five years. However, market growth rates vary by geographic region—North America, Latin America, Europe-Africa, and Asia-Pacific.

Companies begin the simulation producing branded and private-label footwear in two plants, one in North America and one in Asia. They have the option to establish production facilities in Latin America and Europe-Africa, either by constructing new plants or by buying previously constructed plants that have been sold by competing companies. Company co-managers exercise control over production costs on the basis of the styling and quality they opt to manufacture, plant location (wages and incentive compensation vary from region to region), the use of best practices and Six Sigma programs to reduce the production of defective footwear and to boost worker productivity, and compensation practices.

All newly produced footwear is shipped in bulk containers to one of four geographic distribution centers. All sales in a geographic region are made from footwear inventories in that region's distribution center. Costs at the four regional distribution centers are a function of inventory storage costs, packing and shipping fees, import tariffs paid on incoming pairs shipped from foreign plants, and exchange rate impacts. At the start of the simulation, import tariffs average $4 per pair in Europe-Africa, $6 per pair in Latin America, and $8 in the Asia-Pacific region. However, the Free Trade Treaty of the Americas allows tariff-free movement of footwear between North America and Latin America. Instructors have the option to alter tariffs as the game progresses.

Companies market their brand of athletic footwear to footwear retailers worldwide and to individuals buying online at the company's Web site. Each company's sales and market share in the branded footwear segments hinge on its competitiveness on 11 factors: attractive pricing, footwear styling and quality, product line breadth, advertising, use of mail-in rebates, appeal of celebrities endorsing a company's brand, success in convincing footwear retailers to carry its brand, number of weeks it takes to fill retailer orders, effectiveness of a company's online sales effort at its Web site, and customer loyalty. Sales of private-label footwear hinge solely on being the low-price bidder.

All told, company co-managers make as many as 53 types of decisions each period that cut across production operations (up to 10 decisions per plant, with a maximum of four plants), plant capacity additions/sales/upgrades (up to 6 decisions per plant), worker compensation and training (3 decisions per plant), shipping (up to 8 decisions per plant), pricing and marketing (up to 10 decisions in four geographic regions), bids to sign celebrities (2 decision entries per bid), financing of company operations (up to 8 decisions), and corporate social responsibility and environmental sustainability (up to 6 decisions).

Each time company co-managers make a decision entry, an assortment of on-screen calculations instantly shows the projected effects on unit sales, revenues, market shares, unit costs, profit, earnings per share, ROE, and other operating statistics. The on-screen calculations help team members evaluate the relative merits of one decision entry versus another and put together a promising strategy.

Companies can employ any of the five generic competitive strategy options in selling branded footwear—low-cost leadership, differentiation, best-cost provider, focused low cost, and focused differentiation. They can pursue essentially the same strategy worldwide or craft slightly or very different strategies for the Europe-Africa, Asia-Pacific, Latin America, and North America markets. They can strive for competitive advantage based on more advertising, a wider selection of models, more appealing styling/quality, bigger rebates, and so on.

Any well-conceived, well-executed competitive approach is capable of succeeding, provided it is not overpowered by the strategies of competitors or defeated by the presence of too many copycat strategies that dilute its effectiveness. The challenge for each company's management team is to craft and execute a competitive strategy that produces good performance on five measures: earnings per share, return on equity investment, stock price appreciation, credit rating, and brand image.

All activity for *The Business Strategy Game* takes place at www.bsg-online.com.

A Bird's-Eye View of *GLO-BUS*

The industry setting for *GLO-BUS* is the digital camera industry. Global market demand grows at the rate of 8 to 10 percent annually for the first five years and 4 to 6 percent annually for the second five years. Retail sales of digital cameras are seasonal, with about 20 percent of consumer demand coming in each of the first three quarters of each calendar year and 40 percent coming during the big fourth-quarter retailing season.

Companies produce entry-level and upscale, multifeatured cameras of varying designs and quality in a Taiwan assembly facility and ship assembled cameras directly to retailers in North America, Asia-Pacific, Europe-Africa, and Latin America. All cameras are assembled as retail orders come in and are shipped immediately upon completion of the assembly process—companies maintain no finished-goods inventories, and all parts and components are delivered on a just-in-time basis (which eliminates the need to track inventories and simplifies the accounting for plant operations and costs). Company co-managers exercise control over production costs on the basis of the designs and components they specify for their cameras, workforce compensation and training, the length of warranties offered (which affects warranty costs), the amount spent for technical support provided to buyers of the company's cameras, and their management of the assembly process.

Competition in each of the two product market segments (entry-level and multifeatured digital cameras) is based on 10 factors: price, camera performance and quality, number of quarterly sales promotions, length of promotions in weeks, size of the promotional discounts offered, advertising, number of camera models, size of retail dealer network, warranty period, and amount/caliber of technical support provided to camera buyers. Low-cost leadership, differentiation strategies, best-cost provider strategies, and focus strategies are all viable competitive options. Rival companies can strive to be the clear market leader in either entry-level cameras or upscale multifeatured cameras or both. They can focus on one or two geographic regions or strive for geographic balance. They can pursue essentially the same strategy worldwide or craft slightly or very different strategies for the Europe-Africa, Asia-Pacific, Latin America, and North America markets. Just as with *The Business Strategy Game,* almost any well-conceived, well-executed competitive approach is capable of succeeding, *provided it is not overpowered by the strategies of competitors or defeated by the presence of too many copycat strategies that dilute its effectiveness.*

Company co-managers make 49 types of decisions each period, ranging from R&D, camera components, and camera performance (10 decisions) to production operations and worker compensation (15 decisions) to pricing and marketing (15 decisions) to the financing of company operations (4 decisions) to corporate social responsibility (5 decisions). *Each time participants make a decision entry, an assortment of on-screen calculations instantly shows the projected effects on unit sales, revenues, market shares, unit costs, profit, earnings per share, ROE, and other operating statistics. These on-screen calculations help team members evaluate the relative merits of one decision entry versus another and stitch the separate decisions into a cohesive and promising strategy.* Company performance is judged on five criteria: earnings per share, return on equity investment, stock price, credit rating, and brand image.

All activity for *GLO-BUS* occurs at www.glo-bus.com.

Administration and Operating Features of the Two Simulations

The Internet delivery and user-friendly designs of both *BSG* and *GLO-BUS* make them incredibly easy to administer, even for first-time users. And the menus and controls are so similar that you can readily switch between the two simulations or use one in your undergraduate class and the other in a graduate class. If you have not yet used either of the two simulations, you may find the following of particular interest:

- Setting up the simulation for your course is done online and takes about 10 to 15 minutes. Once setup is completed, no other administrative actions are required beyond those of moving participants to a different team (should the need arise) and monitoring the progress of the simulation (to whatever extent desired).

- Participant's Guides are delivered electronically to class members at the Web site—students can read the guide on their monitors or print out a copy, as they prefer.

- There are 2- to 4-minute Video Tutorials scattered throughout the software (including each decision screen and each page of each report) that provide on-demand guidance to class members who may be uncertain about how to proceed.

- Complementing the Video Tutorials are detailed and clearly written Help sections explaining "all there is to know" about (a) each decision entry and the relevant cause-effect relationships, (b) the information on each page of the

Industry Reports, and (c) the numbers presented in the Company Reports. *The Video Tutorials and the Help screens allow company co-managers to figure things out for themselves, thereby curbing the need for students to ask the instructor "how things work."*

- Built-in chat capability on each screen enables company co-managers to collaborate online in the event that a face-to-face meeting to review results and make decision entries is not convenient (or feasible, as is usually the case for class members taking an online course). Company co-managers can also use their cell phones to talk things over while online looking at the screens.

- Both simulations are quite suitable for use in distance-learning or online courses (and are currently being used in such courses on numerous campuses).

- Participants and instructors are notified via e-mail when the results are ready (usually about 15 to 20 minutes after the decision round deadline specified by the instructor/game administrator).

- Following each decision round, participants are provided with a complete set of reports—a six-page Industry Report, a one-page Competitive Intelligence report for each geographic region that includes strategic group maps and bulleted lists of competitive strengths and weaknesses, and a set of Company Reports (income statement, balance sheet, cash flow statement, and assorted production, marketing, and cost statistics).

- Two "open-book" multiple-choice tests of 20 questions are built into each simulation. The quizzes, which you can require or not as you see fit, are taken online and automatically graded, with scores reported instantaneously to participants and automatically recorded in the instructor's electronic grade book. Students are automatically provided with three sample questions for each test.

- Both simulations contain a three-year strategic plan option that you can assign. Scores on the plan are automatically recorded in the instructor's online grade book.

- At the end of the simulation, you can have students complete online peer evaluations (again, the scores are automatically recorded in your online grade book).

- Both simulations have a Company Presentation feature that enables each team of company co-managers to easily prepare PowerPoint slides for use in describing their strategy and summarizing their company's performance in a presentation to either the class, the instructor, or an "outside" board of directors.

- *A Learning Assurance Report provides you with hard data concerning how well your students performed vis-à-vis students playing the simulation worldwide over the past 12 months.* The report is based on nine measures of student proficiency, business know-how, and decision-making skill and can also be used in evaluating the extent to which your school's academic curriculum produces the desired degree of student learning insofar as accreditation standards are concerned.

For more details on either simulation, please consult Section 2 of the Instructor's Manual accompanying this text or register as an instructor at the simulation Web sites (www.bsg-online.com and www.glo-bus.com) to access even more comprehensive information. You should also consider signing up for one of the webinars that the simulation authors conduct several times each month (sometimes several times weekly) to demonstrate how the software works, walk you through the various features and menu options, and answer any questions. You have an open invitation to call the senior author of this text at (205) 722-9145 to arrange a personal demonstration or talk about how one of the simulations might work in one of your courses. We think you'll be quite impressed with the cutting-edge capabilities that have been programmed into *The Business Strategy Game* and *GLO-BUS,* the simplicity with which both simulations can be administered, and their exceptionally tight connection to the text chapters, core concepts, and standard analytical tools.

RESOURCES AND SUPPORT MATERIALS FOR THE 18TH EDITION

For Students

Key Points Summaries   At the end of each chapter is a synopsis of the core concepts, analytical tools, and other key points discussed in the chapter. These chapter-end synopses, along with the core concept definitions and margin notes scattered throughout each chapter, help students focus on basic strategy principles, digest the messages of each chapter, and prepare for tests.

Two Sets of Chapter-End Exercises   Each chapter concludes with two sets of exercises. The *Assurance of Learning Exercises* can be used as the basis for class discussion, oral presentation assignments, short written reports, and substitutes for case assignments. The *Exercises for Simulation Participants* are designed expressly for use by adopters who have incorporated use of a simulation and want to go a step further in tightly and explicitly connecting the chapter content to the simulation company their students are running. The questions in both sets of exercises (along with those Illustration Capsules that qualify as "mini-cases") can be used to round out the rest of a 75-minute class period should your lecture on a chapter last for only 50 minutes.

A Value-Added Web Site   The student section of the Online Learning Center (OLC) at Web site www.mhhe.com/thompson contains a number of helpful aids:

- Ten-question self-scoring chapter tests that students can take to measure their grasp of the material presented in each of the 12 chapters.
- The "Guide to Case Analysis," containing sections on what a case is, why cases are a standard part of courses in strategy, preparing a case for class discussion, doing a written case analysis, doing an oral presentation, and using financial ratio analysis to assess a company's financial condition. We suggest having students read this guide before the first class discussion of a case.
- PowerPoint slides for each chapter.

The *Connect*™ *Management* Web-Based Assignment and Assessment Platform   Beginning with this edition, we have taken advantage of the publisher's innovative *Connect*™ assignment and assessment platform and created several features that simplify the task of assigning and grading three types of exercises for students:

- There are self-scoring chapter tests consisting of 20 multiple-choice questions that students can take to measure their grasp of the material presented in each of the 12 chapters.
- There are author-developed Assurance of Learning Exercises for each of the 12 chapters that drill students in the use and application of the concepts and tools of strategic analysis.
- The *Connect*™ platform also includes author-developed Case Exercises for 4 of the 24 cases in this edition that require students to work through answers to a select number of the assignment questions for the case; these exercises have multiple components and include calculating assorted financial ratios to assess a company's financial performance and balance sheet strength, identifying a company's strategy, doing five-forces and driving-forces analysis, doing a SWOT analysis, and recommending actions to improve company performance. The content of these case exercises is tailored to match the circumstances presented in each case, calling upon students to do whatever strategic thinking and strategic analysis are called for to arrive at pragmatic, analysis-based action recommendations for improving company performance.

All of the *Connect*™ exercises are automatically graded (with the exception of a few exercise components that entail student entry of essay answers), thereby simplifying the task of evaluating each class member's performance and monitoring the learning outcomes. The progress-tracking function built into the *Connect*™ *Management* system enables you to:

- View scored work immediately and track individual or group performance with assignment and grade reports.
- Access an instant view of student or class performance relative to learning objectives.
- Collect data and generate reports required by many accreditation organizations, such as AACSB or EQUIS.

For Instructors

Online Learning Center (OLC)   In addition to the student resources, the instructor section of www.mhhe.com/thompson includes an Instructor's Manual and other support materials. Your McGraw-Hill representative can arrange delivery of instructor support materials in a format-ready Standard Cartridge for Blackboard, WebCT, and other Web-based educational platforms.

Instructor's Manual   The accompanying IM contains:

- A section on suggestions for organizing and structuring your course.
- Sample syllabi and course outlines.
- A set of lecture notes on each chapter.
- Answers to the chapter-end Assurance of Learning Exercises.
- A copy of the test bank.
- A comprehensive case teaching note for each of the 24 cases. These teaching notes are filled with suggestions for using the case effectively, have very thorough, analysis-based answers to the suggested assignment questions for the case, and contain an epilog detailing any important developments since the case was written.

Test Bank and EZ Test Online   There is a test bank containing over 900 multiple-choice questions and short-answer/essay questions. It has been tagged with AACSB and Bloom's Taxonomy criteria. All of the test bank questions are also accessible within a computerized test bank powered by McGraw-Hill's flexible electronic testing program EZ Test Online (www.eztestonline.com). Using EZ Test Online allows you to create paper and online tests or quizzes. With EZ Test Online, instructors can select questions from multiple McGraw-Hill test banks or author their own and then either print the test for paper distribution or give it online.

PowerPoint Slides   To facilitate delivery preparation of your lectures and to serve as chapter outlines, you'll have access to approximately 500 colorful and professional-looking slides displaying core concepts, analytical procedures, key points, and all the figures in the text chapters.

Instructor's Resource CD   All of our instructor supplements are available on disk; the disk set includes the complete Instructor's Manual, computerized test bank (EZ Test), accompanying PowerPoint slides, and the Digital Image Library with all of the figures from the text. It is a useful aid for compiling a syllabus and daily course schedule, preparing customized lectures, and developing tests on the text chapters.

The Business Strategy Game* and *GLO-BUS Online Simulations
Using one of the two companion simulations is a powerful and constructive way of emotionally connecting students to the subject matter of the course. We know of no more effective way to arouse the competitive energy of students and prepare them for the challenges of real-world business decision making than to have them match strategic wits with classmates in running a company in head-to-head competition for global market leadership.

ACKNOWLEDGMENTS

We heartily acknowledge the contributions of the case researchers whose case-writing efforts appear herein and the companies whose cooperation made the cases possible. To each one goes a very special thank-you. We cannot overstate the importance of timely, carefully researched cases in contributing to a substantive study of strategic management issues and practices. From a research standpoint, strategy-related cases are invaluable in exposing the generic kinds of strategic issues that companies face, in forming hypotheses about strategic behavior, and in drawing experience-based generalizations about the practice of strategic management. From an instructional standpoint, strategy cases give students essential practice in diagnosing and evaluating the strategic situations of companies and organizations, in applying the concepts and tools of strategic analysis, in weighing strategic options and crafting strategies, and in tackling the challenges of successful strategy execution. Without a continuing stream of fresh, well-researched, and well-conceived cases, the discipline of strategic management would lose its close ties to the very institutions whose strategic actions and behavior it is aimed at explaining. There's no question, therefore, that first-class case research constitutes a valuable scholarly contribution to the theory and practice of strategic management.

   A great number of colleagues and students at various universities, business acquaintances, and people at McGraw-Hill provided inspiration, encouragement, and counsel during the course of this project. Like all text authors in the strategy field, we are intellectually indebted to the many academics whose research and writing have blazed new trails and advanced the discipline of strategic management. In addition, we'd like to thank the following reviewers who provided seasoned advice and splendid suggestions for improving the chapters in this 18th edition:

Joan H. Bailar, Lake Forest Graduate School of Management
David Blair, University of Nebraska at Omaha
Jane Boyland, Johnson & Wales University
William J. Donoher, Missouri State University
Stephen A. Drew, Florida Gulf Coast University
Jo Ann Duffy, Sam Houston State University
Alan Ellstrand, University of Arkansas
Susan Fox-Wolfgramm, Hawaii Pacific University
Rebecca M. Guidice, University of Nevada–Las Vegas
Mark Hoelscher, Illinois State University
Sean D. Jasso, University of California–Riverside
Xin Liang, University of Minnesota–Duluth
Paul Mallette, Colorado State University
Dan Marlin, University of South Florida–St. Petersburg
Raza Mir, William Paterson University
Mansour Moussavi, Johnson & Wales University
James D. Spina, University of Maryland
Monica A. Zimmerman, West Chester University

We also express our thanks to Dennis R. Balch, Jeffrey R. Bruehl, Edith C. Busija, Donald A. Drost, Randall Harris, Mark Lewis Hoelscher, Phyllis Holland, James W. Kroeger, Sal Kukalis, Brian W. Kulik, Paul Mallette, Anthony U. Martinez, Lee Pickler, Sabine Reddy, Thomas D. Schramko, V. Seshan, Charles Strain, Sabine Turnley, S. Stephen Vitucci, Andrew Ward, Sibin Wu, Lynne Patten, Nancy E. Landrum, Jim Goes, Jon Kalinowski, Rodney M. Walter, Judith D. Powell, Seyda Deligonul, David Flanagan, Esmerlda Garbi, Mohsin Habib, Kim Hester, Jeffrey E. McGee, Diana J. Wong, F. William Brown, Anthony F. Chelte, Gregory G. Dess, Alan B. Eisner, John George, Carle M. Hunt, Theresa Marron-Grodsky, Sarah Marsh, Joshua D. Martin, William L. Moore, Donald Neubaum, George M. Puia, Amit Shah, Lois M. Shelton, Mark Weber, Steve Barndt, J. Michael Geringer, Ming-Fang Li, Richard Stackman, Stephen Tallman, Gerardo R. Ungson, James Boulgarides, Betty Diener, Daniel F. Jennings, David Kuhn, Kathryn Martell, Wilbur Mouton, Bobby Vaught, Tuck Bounds, Lee Burk, Ralph Catalanello, William Crittenden, Vince Luchsinger, Stan Mendenhall, John Moore, Will Mulvaney, Sandra Richard, Ralph Roberts, Thomas Turk, Gordon Von Stroh, Fred Zimmerman, S. A. Billion, Charles Byles, Gerald L. Geisler, Rose Knotts, Joseph Rosenstein, James B. Thurman, Ivan Able, W. Harvey Hegarty, Roger Evered, Charles B. Saunders, Rhae M. Swisher, Claude I. Shell, R. Thomas Lenz, Michael C. White, Dennis Callahan, R. Duane Ireland, William E. Burr II, C. W. Millard, Richard Mann, Kurt Christensen, Neil W. Jacobs, Louis W. Fry, D. Robley Wood, George J. Gore, and William R. Soukup. These reviewers provided valuable guidance in steering our efforts to improve earlier editions.

We owe a special debt of gratitude to Catherine Maritan, for her detailed comments on a number of chapters, and to Richard S. Shreve and Anant K. Sundaram, who gave us sage advice regarding the material in Chapter 9. We'd like to thank the following students of the Tuck School of Business for their assistance with the chapter revisions: C. David Morgan, Amy E. Florentino, John R. Moran, Mukund Kulashakeran, Jeffrey L. Boyink, Jonathan D. Keith, Anita Natarajan, Alison F. Connolly, and Melissa E. Vess. And we'd like to acknowledge the help of Dartmouth students Catherine Wu, Jack McNeily, and Jenna Pfeffer, as well as Feldberg librarians Karen Sluzenski and Sarah J. Buckingham and Tuck staff members Annette Lyman, Mary Biathrow, Doreen Aher, and Karen H. Summer.

As always, we value your recommendations and thoughts about the book. Your comments regarding coverage and contents will be taken to heart, and we always are grateful for the time you take to call our attention to printing errors, deficiencies, and other shortcomings. Please e-mail us at athompso@cba.ua.edu, margaret.a.peteraf@tuck.dartmouth.edu, jgamble@usouthal.edu, or astrickl@cba.ua.edu.

Arthur A. Thompson

Margaret A. Peteraf

John E. Gamble

A. J. Strickland

Chapter Structure and Organization

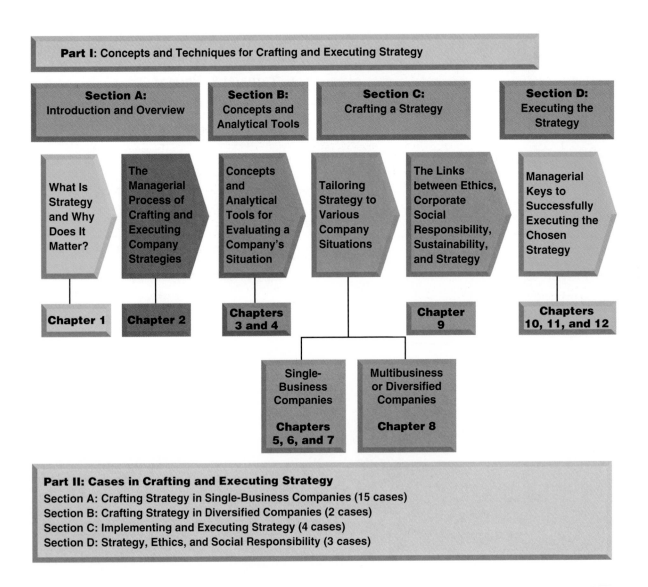

Part I: Concepts and Techniques for Crafting and Executing Strategy

Section A:
Introduction and Overview

Section B:
Concepts and Analytical Tools

Section C:
Crafting a Strategy

Section D:
Executing the Strategy

What Is Strategy and Why Does It Matter?

The Managerial Process of Crafting and Executing Company Strategies

Concepts and Analytical Tools for Evaluating a Company's Situation

Tailoring Strategy to Various Company Situations

The Links between Ethics, Corporate Social Responsibility, Sustainability, and Strategy

Managerial Keys to Successfully Executing the Chosen Strategy

Chapter 1

Chapter 2

Chapters 3 and 4

Chapter 9

Chapters 10, 11, and 12

Single-Business Companies

Chapters 5, 6, and 7

Multibusiness or Diversified Companies

Chapter 8

Part II: Cases in Crafting and Executing Strategy

Section A: Crafting Strategy in Single-Business Companies (15 cases)
Section B: Crafting Strategy in Diversified Companies (2 cases)
Section C: Implementing and Executing Strategy (4 cases)
Section D: Strategy, Ethics, and Social Responsibility (3 cases)

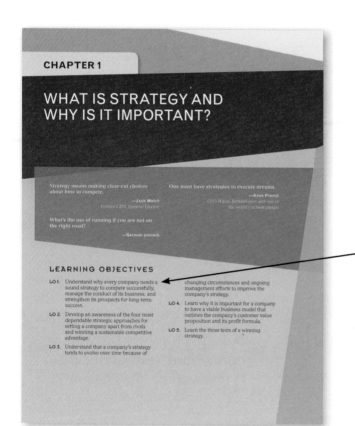

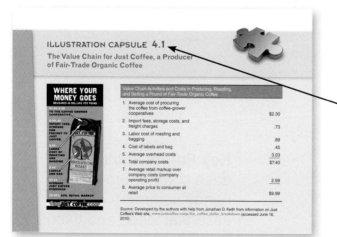

Learning Objectives are listed at the beginning of each chapter; corresponding numbered indicators in the margins show where learning objectives are covered in the text.

Illustration Capsules appear in boxes throughout each chapter to provide in-depth examples, connect the text presentation to real-world companies, and convincingly demonstrate "strategy in action." Some are appropriate for use as mini-cases.

Margin Notes define core concepts and call attention to important ideas and principles.

pany. The answer to the question "Where do we want to go from here?" lies within management's vision of the company's future direction—what new customer groups and customer needs to endeavor to satisfy and what new capabilities to build or acquire. The question "How are we going to get there?" challenges managers to craft and execute a strategy capable of moving the company in the intended direction.

Developing clear answers to the question "How are we going to get there?" is the essence of managing strategically. Rather than relying on the status quo as a road map and dealing with new opportunities or threats as they emerge, managing strategically involves developing a full-blown game plan that spells out the competitive moves and business approaches that will be employed to compete successfully, attract and please customers, conduct operations, achieve targeted levels of performance, and grow the business. Thus, a company's strategy is all about *how*:

- *How* to outcompete rivals.
- *How* to respond to changing economic and market conditions and capitalize on growth opportunities.
- *How* to manage each functional piece of the business (e.g., R&D, supply chain activities, production, sales and marketing, distribution, finance, and human resources).
- *How* to improve the company's financial and market performance.

CORE CONCEPT

A company's **strategy** consists of the competitive moves and business approaches that managers are employing to compete successfully, improve performance, and grow the business.

The specific elements that constitute management's answer to the question "How are we going to get there?" define a company's business strategy. Thus, a company's **strategy** is management's *action plan* for competing successfully and operating profitably, based on an integrated array of considered choices.[1] The crafting of a strategy represents a managerial commitment to pursuing a particular set of actions. In choosing a strategy, management is in effect saying, "Among all the many different business approaches and ways of competing we could have chosen, we have decided to employ this particular combination of approaches in moving the company in the intended direction, strengthening its market position and competitiveness, and boosting performance." The strategic choices a company

---

22   **Part 1**   Concepts and Techniques for Crafting and Executing Strategy

Figure 2.1   **The Strategy-Making, Strategy-Executing Process**

Stage 1	Stage 2	Stage 3	Stage 4	Stage 5
Developing a strategic vision, mission, and values	Setting objectives	Crafting a strategy to achieve the objectives and move the company along the intended path	Executing the strategy	Monitoring developments, evaluating performance, and initiating corrective adjustments

Revise as needed in light of the company's actual performance, changing conditions, new opportunities, and new ideas

Figure 2.1 displays this five-stage process, which we examine next in some detail.

STAGE 1: DEVELOPING A STRATEGIC VISION, A MISSION, AND A SET OF CORE VALUES

Figures scattered throughout the chapters provide conceptual and analytical frameworks.

KEY POINTS

The strategic management process consists of five interrelated and integrated stages:

1. *Developing a strategic vision* of the company's future, a *mission* that defines the company's current purpose, and a set of *core values* to guide the pursuit of the vision and mission. This managerial step provides direction for the company, motivates and inspires company personnel, aligns and guides actions throughout the organization, and communicates to stakeholders management's aspirations for the company's future.

2. *Setting objectives* to convert the vision and mission into performance targets and using the targeted results as yardsticks for measuring the company's performance. Objectives need to spell out *how much* of *what kind* of performance *by when*. Two broad types of objectives are required: *financial objectives* and *strategic objectives*. A *balanced-scorecard* approach provides a popular method for linking financial objectives to specific, measurable strategic objectives.

3. *Crafting a strategy* to achieve the objectives and move the company along the strategic course that management has charted. Crafting deliberate strategy calls for strategic analysis, based on the business model. Crafting emergent strategy is a learning-by-doing process involving experimentation. Who participates in the process of crafting strategy depends on (1) whether the process is emergent or deliberate and (2) the level of strategy concerned. Deliberate strategies are mostly top-down, while emergent strategies are bottom-up, although both cases require two-way interaction between different types of managers. In large, diversified companies, there are four levels of strategy, each of which involves a corresponding level of management: corporate strategy (multibusiness strategy), business strategy (strategy for individual businesses that compete in a single industry), functional-area strategies within each business (e.g., marketing, R&D, logistics), and operating strategies (for key operating units, such as manufacturing plants). Thus, strategy making is an inclusive, collaborative activity involving not only senior company executives but also the heads of major business divisions, functional-area managers, and operating managers on the frontlines. The larger and more diverse the operations of an enterprise, the more points of strategic initiative it has and the more levels of management that play a significant strategy-making role.

Key Points at the end of each chapter provide a handy summary of essential ideas and things to remember.

EXERCISES FOR SIMULATION PARTICIPANTS

LO 1

1. Which of the five competitive forces is creating the strongest competitive pressures for your company?
2. What are the "competitive weapons" that rival companies in your industry can use to gain sales and market share? See Table 3.2 to help you identify possible competitive tactics. (You may be able to think of others.)
3. What are the factors affecting the intensity of rivalry in the industry in which your company is competing. Use Figure 3.4 and the accompanying discussion to help you pinpoint the specific factors most affecting competitive intensity. Would you characterize the rivalry among the companies in your industry as brutal, strong, moderate, or relatively weak? Why?

LO 2

4. Are there any factors driving change in the industry in which your company is competing? What impact will these drivers of change have? How will they change demand or supply? Will they cause competition to become more or less intense? Will they act to boost or squeeze profit margins? List at least two actions your company should consider taking in order to combat any negative impacts of the factors driving change.

LO 3

5. Draw a strategic group map showing the market positions of the companies in your industry. Which companies do you believe are in the most attractive position on the map? Which companies are the most weakly positioned? Which companies do you believe are likely to try to move to a different position on the strategic group map?

LO 4

6. What do you see as the key factors for being a successful competitor in your industry? List at least three.

ENDNOTES

[1] For a more extended discussion of the problems with the life-cycle hypothesis, see Michael E. Porter, *Competitive Strategy: Techniques for Analyzing Industries and Competitors* (New York: Free Press, 1980), pp. 157–62.
[2] The five-forces model of competition is the creation of Professor Michael Porter of the Harvard Business School. See Michael E. Porter, "How Competitive Forces Shape Strategy," *Harvard Business Review* 57, no. 2 (March–April 1979), pp. 137–45; Porter, *Competitive Strategy*, chap. 1; and Porter's most recent discussion of the model, "The Five Competitive Forces That Shape Strategy," *Harvard Business Review* 86, no. 1 (January 2008), pp. 78–93.
[3] For a discussion of how a company's actions to counter the moves of rival firms tend to escalate competitive pressures, see Pamela J. Derfus, Patrick G. Maggitti, Curtis M. Grimm, and Ken G. Smith, "The Red Queen Effect: Competitive Actions and Firm Performance," *Academy of Management Journal* 51, no. 1 (February 2008), pp. 61–80.
[4] Many of these indicators of whether rivalry produces intense competitive pressures are based on Porter, *Competitive Strategy*, pp. 17–21.
[5] Porter, *Competitive Strategy*, p. 7; Porter, "The Five Competitive Forces That Shape Strategy," p. 81.
[6] The role of entry barriers in shaping the strength of competition in a particular market has long been a standard topic in the literature of microeconomics. For a discussion of how entry barriers affect competitive pressures associated with potential entry, see J. S. Bain, *Barriers to New Competition* (Cambridge, MA: Harvard University Press, 1956); F. M. Scherer, *Industrial Market Structure and Economic Performance*

Exercises at the end of each chapter, linked to learning objectives, provide a basis for class discussion, oral presentations, and written assignments. Several chapters have exercises that qualify as mini-cases.

Twenty-four cases detail the strategic circumstances of actual companies and provide practice in applying the concepts and tools of strategic analysis.

Atlassian: Supporting the World with Legendary Service

CASE 5

Tatiana Zalan[1]
University of South Australia, Australia

Olga Muzychenko
University of Adelaide, Australia

Sam Burshtein
Swinburne University of Technology, Australia

INTRODUCTION

In late February 2009, Mike Cannon-Brookes and Scott Farquhar, co-founders of Atlassian Software, a global technology company, were sipping beer on the deck of their office in downtown Sydney. Only days ago Mike was chosen by the World Economic Forum from a world-wide pool of 5,000 candidates as one of the 230 Young Global Leaders for his professional accomplishments, commitment to society and potential to contribute to shaping the future of the world. Mike and Scott, both in their late 20s, had all the reasons to feel proud that their efforts had been validated. Starting in 2002 as a consulting business, the founders, then fresh IT graduates, soon realised that they needed an issue and task tracking tool enabling them to manage their own consulting projects effectively. JIRA, Atlassian's first product, was soon to be followed by several other team collaboration products.

By 2009, Atlassian had become one of Australia's fastest growing technology ventures, had revenues of $35 million (nearly all of them outside Australia), in excess of 15,000 customers in some 110 countries and nearly 200 employees worldwide, with offices in Sydney, San Francisco, Amsterdam, Kuala Lumpur and Poland. Throughout the years Atlassian remained highly profitable and privately owned with no institutional or venture capital investment and spent 40% of its revenues on R&D. The company was equally well known for its transparent, vibrant and informal, yet highly professional culture. It received a sweep of industry and business awards (see Exhibit 1—Atlassian's awards), and in 2006, Mike and Scott became the youngest entrepreneurs to ever win the prestigious Ernst & Young's Entrepreneur of the Year Award for Australia.

Nevertheless, the current revenues and customer base were still a far cry from the founders' intent to grow a $100 million company with 50,000 customers worldwide. As Mike and Scott pondered the future of Atlassian, they wondered whether they could scale the business in a way that did not diminish the creative vitality, enthusiasm, and customer focus that had gotten them so far.

ATLASSIAN'S EARLY YEARS

The Founders

Mike and Scott met in 1998 as recipients of the prestigious Business IT Co-op Scholarship at the University of New South Wales (UNSW). The program was set up by industry and the UNSW to provide financial reward and industrial training for undergraduate students in the disciplines of Commerce, Science and Engineering.

Apart from this licensed copy, none of the material protected by the copyright notice can be reproduced or used in any form either electronic or mechanical, including photocopying, recording or by any other information recording or retrieval system, without prior written permission from the owner(s) of the copyright.
© NelsonJournals Publishing 2011.

Web site: www.mhhe.com/thompson The student portion of the Web site features the "Guide to Case Analysis," with special sections on what a case is, why cases are a standard part of courses in strategy, preparing a case for class discussion, doing a written case analysis, doing an oral presentation, and using financial ratio analysis to assess a company's financial condition. In addition, there are 10-question self-scoring chapter tests and a select number of PowerPoint slides for each chapter.

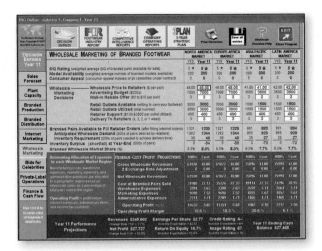

The Business Strategy Game or *GLO-BUS* **Simulation Exercises** Either one of these text supplements involves teams of students managing companies in a head-to-head contest for global market leadership. Company co-managers have to make decisions relating to product quality, production, workforce compensation and training, pricing and marketing, and financing of company operations. The challenge is to craft and execute a strategy that is powerful enough to deliver good financial performance despite the competitive efforts of rival companies. Each company competes in America, Latin America, Europe-Africa, and Asia-Pacific.

BRIEF CONTENTS

PART ONE Concepts and Techniques for Crafting and Executing Strategy

Section A: Introduction and Overview

1 What Is Strategy and Why Is It Important? 50

2 Charting a Company's Direction: Vision and Mission, Objectives, and Strategy 68

Section B: Core Concepts and Analytical Tools

3 Evaluating a Company's External Environment 96

4 Evaluating a Company's Resources, Capabilities, and Competitiveness 138

Section C: Crafting a Strategy

5 The Five Generic Competitive Strategies: Which One to Employ? 182

6 Strengthening a Company's Competitive Position: Strategic Moves, Timing, and Scope of Operations 214

7 Strategies for Competing in International Markets 250

8 Corporate Strategy: Diversification and the Multibusiness Company 292

9 Ethics, Corporate Social Responsibility, Environmental Sustainability, and Strategy 338

Section D: Executing the Strategy

10 Building an Organization Capable of Good Strategy Execution: People, Capabilities, and Structure 374

11 Managing Internal Operations: Actions That Promote Good Strategy Execution 406

12 Corporate Culture and Leadership: Keys to Good Strategy Execution 436

PART TWO Cases in Crafting and Executing Strategy

Section A: Crafting Strategy in Single-Business Companies

1   Afrigator: A Killer Start-up in Africa   C-2

2   Competition in Energy Drinks, Sports Drinks, and Vitamin-Enhanced Beverages   C-17

3   Competition in the Golf Equipment Industry in 2009   C-30

4   Dell Inc. in 2008: Can It Overtake Hewlett-Packard as the Worldwide Leader in Personal Computers?   C-51

5   Atlassian: Supporting the World with Legendary Service   C-81

6   Nintendo's Strategy in 2009: The Ongoing Battle with Microsoft and Sony   C-95

7   TomTom: New Competition Everywhere!   C-107

8   Apple Inc. in 2010   C-122

9   Google's Strategy in 2010   C-136

10   Research In Motion: Managing Explosive Growth   C-156

11   Problems at China Airlines   C-172

12   Canadian Solar   C-189

13   Cemex's Cost of 'Globalised' Growth—The Cash Crunch?   C-212

14   Corona Beer: Challenges of International Expansion   C-228

15   Globalization of Komatsu: Digging Out of Trouble   C-239

Section B: Crafting Strategy in Diversified Companies

16   PepsiCo's Diversification Strategy in 2008   C-255

17   Adidas in 2009: Has Corporate Restructuring Increased Shareholder Value?   C-271

Section C: Implementing and Executing Strategy

18   Robin Hood   C-286

19   Shangri-La Hotels   C-288

20   Toyota Motor Company: Losing Its Quality Edge?   C-304

21   Starbucks' Strategy and Internal Initiatives to Return to Profitable Growth   C-326

Section D: Strategy, Ethics and Social Responsibility

22   Rhino Capture in Kruger National Park   C-361

23   Coca-Cola India's Corporate Social Responsibility Strategy   C-377

24   Detecting Unethical Practices at Supplier Factories: The Monitoring and Compliance Challenges   C-396

Indexes

Company   I1

Name   I12

Subject   I18

TABLE OF CONTENTS

PART ONE Concepts and Techniques for Crafting and Executing Strategy

Section A: Introduction and Overview

1 WHAT IS STRATEGY AND WHY IS IT IMPORTANT? 50

What Do We Mean by *Strategy*? 52

Strategy and the Quest for Competitive Advantage 53
Why a Company's Strategy Evolves over Time 57
A Company's Strategy Is Partly Proactive and Partly Reactive 58

The Relationship between a Company's Strategy and Its Business Model 59

What Makes a Strategy a Winner? 60

Why Crafting and Executing Strategy Are Important Tasks 62

Good Strategy + Good Strategy Execution = Good Management 62

The Road Ahead 63

ILLUSTRATION CAPSULES

1.1 McDonald's Strategy in the Quick-Service Restaurant Industry 55
1.2 Microsoft and Red Hat Linux: Two Contrasting Business Models 61

2 CHARTING A COMPANY'S DIRECTION: VISION AND MISSION, OBJECTIVES, AND STRATEGY 68

What Does the Strategy-Making, Strategy-Executing Process Entail? 69

Stage 1: Developing a Strategic Vision, a Mission, and a Set of Core Values 70

Developing a Strategic Vision 70
Communicating the Strategic Vision 71
Crafting a Mission Statement 74
Linking the Vision and Mission with Company Values 75

Stage 2: Setting Objectives 76

What Kinds of Objectives to Set 76

Stage 3: Crafting a Strategy 81

Strategy Making Involves Managers at All Organizational Levels   81
A Strategic Vision + Objectives + Strategy = A Strategic Plan   85

Stage 4: Executing the Strategy   86

Stage 5: Evaluating Performance and Initiating Corrective Adjustments   87

Corporate Governance: The Role of the Board of Directors in the Strategy-Crafting, Strategy-Executing Process   88

ILLUSTRATION CAPSULES

2.1   Examples of Strategic Visions—How Well Do They Measure Up?   73
2.2   Royal Dutch Shell Mission, Core Values, and Business Principles   77
2.3   Examples of Company Objectives   80
2.4   Corporate Governance Failures at Fannie Mae and Freddie Mac   90

Section B: Core Concepts and Analytical Tools

3 EVALUATING A COMPANY'S EXTERNAL ENVIRONMENT   96

The Strategically Relevant Components of a Company's Macro-Environment   98

Thinking Strategically about a Company's Industry and Competitive Environment   100

Question 1: Does the Industry Offer Attractive Opportunities for Growth?   101

Question 2: What Kinds of Competitive Forces Are Industry Members Facing, and How Strong Are They?   102

Competitive Pressures Created by the Rivalry among Competing Sellers   102
Competitive Pressures Associated with the Threat of New Entrants   107
Competitive Pressures from the Sellers of Substitute Products   111
Competitive Pressures Stemming from Supplier Bargaining Power   112
Competitive Pressures Stemming from Buyer Bargaining Power and Price Sensitivity   115
Is the Collective Strength of the Five Competitive Forces Conducive to Good Profitability?   118

Question 3: What Factors Are Driving Industry Change, and What Impacts Will They Have?   120

Analyzing Industry Dynamics   120
Identifying an Industry's Drivers of Change   120
Assessing the Impact of the Factors Driving Industry Change   124
Developing a Strategy That Takes the Changes in Industry Conditions into Account   125

Question 4: How Are Industry Rivals Positioned—Who Is Strongly Positioned and Who Is Not?   125

Using Strategic Group Maps to Assess the Market Positions of Key Competitors   126
What Can Be Learned from Strategic Group Maps?   127

Question 5: What Strategic Moves Are Rivals Likely to Make Next?   128

Question 6: What Are the Key Factors for Future Competitive Success?   130

Question 7: Does the Industry Offer Good Prospects for Attractive Profits?   131

ILLUSTRATION CAPSULES

3.1   Comparative Market Positions of Selected Retail Chains: A Strategic Group Map Example   127

4 EVALUATING A COMPANY'S RESOURCES, CAPABILITIES, AND COMPETITIVENESS   138

Question 1: How Well Is the Company's Present Strategy Working?   140

Question 2: What are the Company's Competitively Important Resources and Capabilities?   141

Identifying the Company's Resources and Capabilities   144
Determining Whether a Company's Resources and Capabilities Are Potent Enough to Produce a Sustainable Competitive Advantage   147

Question 3: Is the Company Able to Seize Market Opportunities and Nullify External Threats?   150

Identifying a Company's Internal Strengths   151
Identifying Company Weaknesses and Competitive Deficiencies   152
Identifying a Company's Market Opportunities   152
Identifying the Threats to a Company's Future Profitability   153
What Do the SWOT Listings Reveal?   155

Question 4: Are the Company's Prices and Costs Competitive with Those of Key Rivals, and Does It Have an Appealing Customer Value Proposition?   156

The Concept of a Company Value Chain   157
The Value Chain System for an Entire Industry   161
Benchmarking: A Tool for Assessing Whether the Costs and Effectiveness of a Company's Value Chain Activities Are in Line   162
Strategic Options for Remedying a Disadvantage in Costs or Effectiveness   163
Translating Proficient Performance of Value Chain Activities into Competitive Advantage   166

Question 5: Is the Company Competitively Stronger or Weaker than Key Rivals?   168

Strategic Implications of Competitive Strength Assessments   172

Question 6: What Strategic Issues and Problems Merit Front-Burner Managerial Attention?   173

ILLUSTRATION CAPSULES

4.1   The Value Chain for Just Coffee, a Producer of Fair-Trade Organic Coffee   160

4.2   Benchmarking and Ethical Conduct   164

Section C: Crafting a Strategy

5 THE FIVE GENERIC COMPETITIVE STRATEGIES: WHICH ONE TO EMPLOY? 182

The Five Generic Competitive Strategies 183

Low-Cost Provider Strategies 185

The Two Major Avenues for Achieving a Cost Advantage 185
The Keys to Being a Successful Low-Cost Provider 190
When a Low-Cost Provider Strategy Works Best 192
Pitfalls to Avoid in Pursuing a Low-Cost Provider Strategy 193

Broad Differentiation Strategies 193

Managing the Value Chain to Create the Differentiating Attributes 194
Delivering Superior Value via a Broad Differentiation Strategy 197
When a Differentiation Strategy Works Best 199
Pitfalls to Avoid in Pursuing a Differentiation Strategy 199

Focused (Or Market Niche) Strategies 201

A Focused Low-Cost Strategy 201
A Focused Differentiation Strategy 201
When a Focused Low-Cost or Focused Differentiation Strategy Is Attractive 202
The Risks of a Focused Low-Cost or Focused Differentiation Strategy 203

Best-Cost Provider Strategies 205

When a Best-Cost Provider Strategy Works Best 206
The Big Risk of a Best-Cost Provider Strategy 207

The Contrasting Features of the Five Generic Competitive Strategies: A Summary 208

Successful Competitive Strategies Are Resource-Based 210

ILLUSTRATION CAPSULES

5.1 How Walmart Managed Its Value Chain to Achieve a Huge Low-Cost Advantage over Rival Supermarket Chains 191
5.2 Vizio's Focused Low-Cost Strategy 203
5.3 Nestlé Nespresso's Focused Differentiation Strategy in the Coffee Industry 204
5.4 Toyota's Best-Cost Provider Strategy for Its Lexus Line 207

6 STRENGTHENING A COMPANY'S COMPETITIVE POSITION: STRATEGIC MOVES, TIMING, AND SCOPE OF OPERATIONS 214

Going on the Offensive—Strategic Options to Improve a Company's Market Position 215

Choosing the Basis for Competitive Attack 216
Choosing Which Rivals to Attack 218
Blue-Ocean Strategy—A Special Kind of Offensive 219

Defensive Strategies—Protecting Market Position and Competitive Advantage   220

    Blocking the Avenues Open to Challengers   220
    Signaling Challengers That Retaliation Is Likely   221

Timing a Company's Offensive and Defensive Strategic Moves   221

    The Potential for First-Mover Advantages   221
    The Potential for First-Mover Disadvantages or Late-Mover Advantages   223
    To Be a First Mover or Not   224

Strengthening a Company's Market Position via Its Scope of Operations   225

Horizontal Merger and Acquisition Strategies   226

    Why Mergers and Acquisitions Sometimes Fail to Produce Anticipated Results   229

Vertical Integration Strategies   229

    The Advantages of a Vertical Integration Strategy   231
    The Disadvantages of a Vertical Integration Strategy   233
    Weighing the Pros and Cons of Vertical Integration   234

Outsourcing Strategies: Narrowing the Scope of Operations   235

    The Big Risk of Outsourcing Value Chain Activities   236

Strategic Alliances and Partnerships   237

    Why and How Strategic Alliances Are Advantageous   240
    Capturing the Benefits of Strategic Alliances   241
    The Drawbacks of Strategic Alliances and Partnerships   242
    How to Make Strategic Alliances Work   243

ILLUSTRATION CAPSULES

6.1   Amazon.com's First-Mover Advantage in Online Retailing   224

6.2   Clear Channel Communications: Using Mergers and Acquisitions to Become a Global Market Leader in Radio Broadcasting   230

7 STRATEGIES FOR COMPETING IN INTERNATIONAL MARKETS   250

Why Companies Decide to Enter Foreign Markets   252

Why Competing across National Borders Makes Strategy Making More Complex   253

    Cross-Country Variation in Factors That Affect Industry Competitiveness   253
    Locating Value Chain Activities for Competitive Advantage   255
    The Impact of Government Policies and Economic Conditions in Host Countries   256
    The Risks of Adverse Exchange Rate Shifts   257
    Cross-Country Differences in Demographic, Cultural, and Market Conditions   259

The Concepts of Multidomestic Competition and Global
Competition   260

Strategic Options for Entering and Competing in International
Markets   262

   Export Strategies   262
   Licensing Strategies   263
   Franchising Strategies   263
   Acquisition Strategies   264
   Greenfield Venture Strategies   264
   Alliance and Joint Venture Strategies   265

Competing Internationally: The Three Main Strategic
Approaches   268

   Multidomestic Strategy—Think Local, Act Local   269
   Global Strategy—Think Global, Act Global   271
   Transnational Strategy—Think Global, Act Local   272

The Quest for Competitive Advantage in the International Arena   273

   Using Location to Build Competitive Advantage   273
   *Sharing and Transferring Resources and Capabilities across Borders to
   Build Competitive Advantage   275*
   Using Cross-Border Coordination for Competitive Advantage   277

Profit Sanctuaries and Cross-Border Strategic Moves   277

   Using Cross-Market Subsidization to Wage a Strategic Offensive   279
   Using Cross-Border Tactics to Defend against International Rivals   280

Strategies for Competing in the Markets of Developing Countries   280

   Strategy Options for Competing in Developing-Country Markets   281

Defending against Global Giants: Strategies for Local Companies
in Developing Countries   284

ILLUSTRATION CAPSULES

7.1   Four Examples of Cross-Border Strategic Alliances   267

7.2   Yum! Brands' Strategy for Becoming the Leading Food Service
      Brand in China   282

7.3   How Ctrip Successfully Defended against International Rivals to
      Become China's Largest Online Travel Agency   285

8 CORPORATE STRATEGY: DIVERSIFICATION AND THE MULTIBUSINESS COMPANY   292

When to Diversify   294

Building Shareholder Value: The Ultimate Justification for
Diversifying   295

Strategies for Entering New Businesses   296

   Acquisition of an Existing Business   296
   Internal Development   297

Joint Ventures 298
Choosing a Mode of Entry 298

Choosing the Diversification Path: Related versus Unrelated Businesses 300

Strategic Fit and Diversification into Related Businesses 300

Identifying Cross-Business Strategic Fit along the Value Chain 304
Strategic Fit, Economies of Scope, and Competitive Advantage 306

Diversification into Unrelated Businesses 307

Building Shareholder Value via Unrelated Diversification 308
The Path to Greater Shareholder Value through Unrelated Diversification 310
The Drawbacks of Unrelated Diversification 311
Inadequate Reasons for Pursuing Unrelated Diversification 312

Combination Related-Unrelated Diversification Strategies 313

Evaluating the Strategy of a Diversified Company 313

Step 1: Evaluating Industry Attractiveness 314
Step 2: Evaluating Business-Unit Competitive Strength 317
Step 3: Checking the Competitive Advantage Potential of Cross-Business Strategic Fit 321
Step 4: Checking for Resource Fit 322
Step 5: Ranking the Performance Prospects of Business Units and Assigning a Priority for Resource Allocation 325
Step 6: Crafting New Strategic Moves to Improve Overall Corporate Performance 326

ILLUSTRATION CAPSULE

8.1 Managing Diversification at Johnson & Johnson: The Benefits of Cross-Business Strategic Fit 329

9 ETHICS, CORPORATE SOCIAL RESPONSIBILITY, ENVIRONMENTAL SUSTAINABILITY, AND STRATEGY 338

What Do We Mean by *Business Ethics*? 339

Where Do Ethical Standards Come From—Are They Universal or Dependent on Local Norms? 340

The School of Ethical Universalism 340
The School of Ethical Relativism 342
Ethics and Integrative Social Contracts Theory 345

How and Why Ethical Standards Impact the Tasks of Crafting and Executing Strategy 346

What are the Drivers of Unethical Strategies and Business Behavior? 348

Why Should Company Strategies be Ethical? 352

The Moral Case for an Ethical Strategy 354
The Business Case for Ethical Strategies 354

Strategy, Corporate Social Responsibility, and Environmental Sustainability   356

What Do We Mean by Corporate Social Responsibility?   356
What Do We Mean by Sustainability and Sustainable Business Practices?   362
Crafting Corporate Social Responsibility and Sustainability Strategies   364
The Moral Case for Corporate Social Responsibility and Environmentally Sustainable Business Practices   365
The Business Case for Corporate Social Responsibility and Environmentally Sustainable Business Practices   366

ILLUSTRATION CAPSULES

9.1   Many of Apple's Suppliers Flunk the Ethics Test   341
9.2   Investment Fraud at Bernard L. Madoff Investment Securities and Stanford Financial Group   350
9.3   How General Electric's Top Management Built a Culture That Fuses High Performance with High Integrity   353
9.4   John Deere's Approach to Corporate Social Responsibility   359

Section D: Executing the Strategy

10   BUILDING AN ORGANIZATION CAPABLE OF GOOD STRATEGY EXECUTION: PEOPLE, CAPABILITIES, AND STRUCTURE   374

A Framework for Executing Strategy   376

The Principal Components of the Strategy Execution Process   377

Building an Organization Capable of Good Strategy Execution: Where to Begin   379

Staffing the Organization   381

Putting Together a Strong Management Team   381
Recruiting, Training, and Retaining Capable Employees   382

Building and Strengthening Core Competencies and Competitive Capabilities   385

Three Approaches to Building and Strengthening Capabilities   385
Upgrading Employee Skills and Knowledge Resources   389
Strategy Execution Capabilities and Competitive Advantage   390

Organizing the Work Effort With a Supportive Organizational Structure   390

Deciding Which Value Chain Activities to Perform Internally and Which to Outsource   391
Aligning the Firm's Organizational Structure with Its Strategy   393
Determining How Much Authority to Delegate   397
Facilitating Collaboration with External Partners and Strategic Allies   400
Further Perspectives on Structuring the Work Effort   401

ILLUSTRATION CAPSULES

10.1 How General Electric Develops a Talented and Deep Management Team 383

10.2 Toyota's Legendary Production System: A Capability That Translates into Competitive Advantage 387

11 MANAGING INTERNAL OPERATIONS: ACTIONS THAT PROMOTE GOOD STRATEGY EXECUTION 406

Allocating Resources to the Strategy Execution Effort 407

Instituting Policies and Procedures That Facilitate Strategy Execution 409

Using Process Management Tools to Strive for Continuous Improvement 411

How the Process of Identifying and Incorporating Best Practices Works 411
Business Process Reengineering, Total Quality Management, and Six Sigma Quality Programs: Tools for Promoting Operating Excellence 413
Capturing the Benefits of Initiatives to Improve Operations 419

Installing Information and Operating Systems 420

Instituting Adequate Information Systems, Performance Tracking, and Controls 422

Tying Rewards and Incentives to Strategy Execution 423

Incentives and Motivational Practices That Facilitate Good Strategy Execution 424
Striking the Right Balance between Rewards and Punishment 425
Linking Rewards to Strategically Relevant Performance Outcomes 427

ILLUSTRATION CAPSULES

11.1 Whirlpool's Use of Six Sigma to Promote Operating Excellence 417

11.2 What Companies Do to Motivate and Reward Employees 426

11.3 Nucor Corporation: Tying Incentives Directly to Strategy Execution 429

12 CORPORATE CULTURE AND LEADERSHIP: KEYS TO GOOD STRATEGY EXECUTION 436

Instilling a Corporate Culture That Promotes Good Strategy Execution 437

Identifying the Key Features of a Company's Corporate Culture 438
Company Cultures Can Be Strongly or Weakly Embedded 443
Why Corporate Cultures Matter to the Strategy Execution Process 445
Healthy Cultures That Aid Good Strategy Execution 446
Unhealthy Cultures That Impede Good Strategy Execution 448
Changing a Problem Culture: The Role of Leadership 450

Leading the Strategy Execution Process 454

Staying on Top of How Well Things Are Going 455

Putting Constructive Pressure on Organizational Units to Execute the Strategy Well and Achieve Operating Excellence 455
Leading the Process of Making Corrective Adjustments 457

A Final Word on Leading the Process of Crafting and Executing Strategy 458

ILLUSTRATION CAPSULE

12.1 The Corporate Cultures at Google and Alberto-Culver 439

PART TWO Cases in Crafting and Executing Strategy

Section A: Crafting Strategy in Single-Business Companies

1 Afrigator: A Killer Start-up in Africa C-2
Debapratim Purkayastha, IBS Center for Management Research
Syeda Maseeha Qumer, IBS Center for Management Research

2 Competition in Energy Drinks, Sports Drinks, and Vitamin-Enhanced Beverages C-17
John E. Gamble, University of South Alabama

3 Competition in the Golf Equipment Industry in 2009 C-30
John E. Gamble, University of South Alabama

4 Dell Inc. in 2008: Can It Overtake Hewlett-Packard as the Worldwide Leader in Personal Computers? C-51
Arthur A. Thompson, The University of Alabama
John E. Gamble, University of South Alabama

5 Atlassian: Supporting the World with Legendary Service C-81
Tatiana Zalan, University of South Australia, Australia
Olga Muzychenko, University of Adelaide, Australia
Sam Burshtein, Swinburne University of Technology, Australia

6 Nintendo's Strategy in 2009: The Ongoing Battle with Microsoft and Sony C-95
Lou Marino, The University of Alabama
Sally Sarrett, The University of Alabama

7 TomTom: New Competition Everywhere! C-107
Alan N. Hoffman, Rotterdam School of Management, Erasmus University and Bentley University

8 Apple Inc. in 2010 C-122
Lou Marino, The University of Alabama
John E. Gamble, University of South Alabama

9 Google's Strategy in 2010 C-136
John E. Gamble, University of South Alabama

10   Research In Motion: Managing Explosive Growth   C-156
Rod White, University of Western Ontario
Paul Beamish, University of Western Ontario
Daina Mazutis, University of Western Ontario

11   Problems at China Airlines   C-172
Debapratim Purkayastha, IBS Center for Management Research
Hadiya Faheem, IBS Center for Management Research
Monjori Samanta, IBS Center for Management Research

12   Canadian Solar   C-189
Jordan Mitchell, University of Western Ontario
Paul W. Beamish, University of Western Ontario

13   Cemex's Cost of 'Globalised' Growth—The Cash Crunch?   C-212
M.V. Vivek Gonela, IBSCDC
Saradhi Kumar Gonela, IBSCDC
Nagendra V. Chowdary, IBSCDC

14   Corona Beer: Challenges of International Expansion   C-228
Ashok Som, ESSEC Business School

15   Globalization of Komatsu: Digging Out of Trouble   C-239
Nadine Khayat, INSEAD
J. Stewart Black, INSEAD

Section B: Crafting Strategy in Diversified Companies

16   PepsiCo's Diversification Strategy in 2008   C-255
John E. Gamble, University of South Alabama

17   Adidas in 2009: Has Corporate Restructuring Increased Shareholder Value?   C-271
John E. Gamble, University of South Alabama

Section C: Implementing and Executing Strategy

18   Robin Hood   C-286
Joseph Lampel, New York University

19   Shangri-La Hotels   C-288
Dennis Campbell, Harvard Business School
Brent Kazan, Harvard Business School

20   Toyota Motor Company: Losing Its Quality Edge?   C-304
Debapratim Purkayastha, IBS Center for Management Research
Syeda Maseeha Qumer, IBS Center for Management Research

21   Starbucks' Strategy and Internal Initiatives to Return to Profitable Growth   C-326
Arthur A. Thompson, The University of Alabama
Amit J. Shah, Frostburg State University

Section D: Strategy, Ethics and Social Responsibility

22   Rhino Capture in Kruger National Park   C-361
        A. J. Strickland, The University of Alabama
        William E. Mixon, The University of Alabama MBA Candidate

23   Coca-Cola India's Corporate Social Responsibility Strategy   C-377
        Debapratim Purkayastha, IBS Center for Management Research
        Hadiya Faheem, IBS Center for Management Research

24   Detecting Unethical Practices at Supplier Factories: The Monitoring
     and Compliance Challenges   C-396
        Arthur A. Thompson, The University of Alabama

INDEXES

Company   I1

Name   I12

Subject   I18

PART 1

Concepts and Techniques for Crafting and Executing Strategy

CHAPTER 1

WHAT IS STRATEGY AND WHY IS IT IMPORTANT?

Strategy means making clear-cut choices about how to compete.

—Jack Welch
Former CEO, General Electric

What's the use of running if you are not on the right road?

—German proverb

One must have strategies to execute dreams.

—Azim Premji
CEO Wipro Technologies and one of the world's richest people

LEARNING OBJECTIVES

LO 1. Understand why every company needs a sound strategy to compete successfully, manage the conduct of its business, and strengthen its prospects for long-term success.

LO 2. Develop an awareness of the four most dependable strategic approaches for setting a company apart from rivals and winning a sustainable competitive advantage.

LO 3. Understand that a company's strategy tends to evolve over time because of

changing circumstances and ongoing management efforts to improve the company's strategy.

LO 4. Learn why it is important for a company to have a viable business model that outlines the company's customer value proposition and its profit formula.

LO 5. Learn the three tests of a winning strategy.

In any given year, a group of companies will stand out as the top performers, in terms of metrics such as profitability, sales growth, or growth in shareholder value. Some of these companies will find that their star status fades quickly, due to little more than a fortuitous constellation of circumstances, such as being in the right business at the right time. But other companies somehow manage to rise to the top and stay there, year after year, pleasing their customers, shareholders, and other stakeholders alike in the process. Companies such as Apple, Google, Coca-Cola, Procter & Gamble, McDonald's, and Microsoft come to mind—but long-lived success is not just the province of U.S. companies. Diverse kinds of companies, both large and small, from many different countries have been able to sustain strong performance records, including Sweden's IKEA (in home furnishings), Australia's BHP Billiton (in mining), Korea's Hyundai Heavy Industries (in shipbuilding and construction), Mexico's America Movil (in telecommunications), and Japan's Nintendo (in video game systems).

What can explain the ability of companies like these to beat the odds and experience prolonged periods of profitability and growth? Why is it that some companies, like Southwest Airlines and Walmart, continue to do well even when others in their industry are faltering? Why can some companies survive and prosper even through economic downturns and industry turbulence?

Many factors enter into a full explanation of a company's performance, of course. Some come from the external environment; others are internal to the firm. But only one thing can account for the kind of long-lived success records that we see in the world's greatest companies—and that is a cleverly crafted and well executed *strategy,* one that facilitates the capture of emerging opportunities, produces enduringly good performance, is adaptable to changing business conditions, and can withstand the competitive challenges from rival firms.

In this opening chapter, we define the concept of strategy and describe its many facets. We will explain what is meant by a competitive advantage, discuss the relationship between a company's strategy and its business model, and introduce you to the kinds of competitive strategies that can give a company an advantage over rivals in attracting customers and earning above-average profits. We will look at what sets a winning strategy apart from others and why the caliber of a company's strategy determines whether it will enjoy a competitive advantage over other firms or be burdened by competitive disadvantage. By the end of this chapter, you will have a clear idea of why the tasks of crafting and executing strategy are core management functions and why excellent execution of an excellent strategy is the most reliable recipe for turning a company into a standout performer over a long-term horizon.

WHAT DO WE MEAN BY *STRATEGY*?

LO 1

Understand why
every company
needs a sound
strategy to compete
successfully,
manage the conduct
of its business,
and strengthen its
prospects for long-
term success.

In moving a company forward, managers of all types of organizations—small family-owned businesses, rapidly growing entrepreneurial firms, not-for-profit organizations, and the world's leading multinational corporations—face the same three central questions:

- What is our present situation?
- Where do we want to go from here?
- How are we going to get there?

The first question, *"What is our present situation?"* prompts managers to evaluate industry conditions, the company's current financial performance and market standing, its resources and capabilities, its competitive strengths and weaknesses, and changes taking place in the business environment that might affect the company. The answer to the question *"Where do we want to go from here?"* lies within management's vision of the company's future direction—what new customer groups and customer needs to endeavor to satisfy and what new capabilities to build or acquire. The question *"How are we going to get there?"* challenges managers to craft and execute a strategy capable of moving the company in the intended direction.

Developing clear answers to the question *"How are we going to get there?"* is the essence of managing strategically. Rather than relying on the status quo as a road map and dealing with new opportunities or threats as they emerge, managing strategically involves developing a full-blown game plan that spells out the competitive moves and business approaches that will be employed to compete successfully, attract and please customers, conduct operations, achieve targeted levels of performance, and grow the business. Thus, a company's strategy is all about *how:*

- *How* to outcompete rivals.
- *How* to respond to changing economic and market conditions and capitalize on growth opportunities.
- *How* to manage each functional piece of the business (e.g., R&D, supply chain activities, production, sales and marketing, distribution, finance, and human resources).
- *How* to improve the company's financial and market performance.

CORE CONCEPT

A company's **strategy**
consists of the competi-
tive moves and business
approaches that managers
are employing to compete
successfully, improve performance, and grow the
business.

The specific elements that constitute management's answer to the question *"How are we going to get there?"* define a company's business strategy. Thus, a company's **strategy** is management's *action plan* for competing successfully and operating profitably, based on an integrated array of considered choices.[1] The crafting of a strategy represents a managerial commitment to pursuing a particular set of actions. In choosing a strategy, management is in effect saying, "Among all the many different business approaches and ways of competing we could have chosen, we have decided to employ this particular combination of approaches in moving the company in the intended direction, strengthening its market position and competitiveness, and boosting performance." The strategic choices a company makes are seldom easy decisions and often involve difficult trade-offs—but that does not excuse failure to pursue a concrete course of action.[2]

In most industries, there are many different avenues for outcompeting rivals and boosting company performance, thus giving managers considerable freedom in choosing the specific elements of their company's strategy.[3] Consequently, some companies strive to improve their performance by employing strategies aimed at achieving lower costs than rivals, while others pursue strategies aimed at achieving product superiority or personalized customer service or quality dimensions that rivals cannot match. Some companies opt for wide product lines, while others concentrate their energies on a narrow product lineup. Some position themselves in only one part of the industry's chain of production/distribution activities (preferring to be just in manufacturing or wholesale distribution or retailing), while others are partially or fully integrated, with operations ranging from components production to manufacturing and assembly to wholesale distribution and retailing. Some competitors deliberately confine their operations to local or regional markets; others opt to compete nationally, internationally (several countries), or globally (all or most of the major country markets worldwide). Some companies decide to operate in only one industry, while others diversify broadly or narrowly into related or unrelated industries.

There is no shortage of opportunity to fashion a strategy that both tightly fits a company's own particular situation and is discernibly different from the strategies of rivals. In fact, competitive success requires a company's managers to make strategic choices about the key building blocks of its strategy that differ from the choices made by competitors— not 100 percent different but at least different in several important respects. A strategy stands a better chance of succeeding when it is predicated on actions, business approaches, and competitive moves aimed at appealing to buyers *in ways that set a company apart from rivals.* Simply trying to mimic the strategies of the industry's successful companies rarely works. Rather, every company's strategy needs to have some distinctive element that draws in customers and produces a competitive edge. Strategy, at its essence, is about competing differently—doing what rival firms *don't* do or what rival firms *can't* do.[4]

> Strategy is about competing differently from rivals— doing what competitors *don't* do or, even better, doing what they *can't* do! Every strategy needs a distinctive element that attracts customers and produces a competitive edge.

A company's strategy provides direction and guidance, in terms of not only what the company *should* do but also what it *should not* do. Knowing what not to do can be as important as knowing what to do, strategically. At best, making the wrong strategic moves will prove a distraction and a waste of company resources. At worst, it can bring about unintended long-term consequences that put the company's very survival at risk.

Figure 1.1 illustrates the broad types of actions and approaches that often characterize a company's strategy in a particular business or industry. For a more concrete example of the specific actions constituting a firm's strategy, see Illustration Capsule 1.1, describing McDonald's strategy in the quick-service restaurant industry.

Strategy and the Quest for Competitive Advantage

The heart and soul of any strategy is the actions and moves in the marketplace that managers are taking to gain a competitive edge over rivals. A creative, distinctive strategy that sets a company apart from rivals and

> **CORE CONCEPT**
>
> A company achieves **sustainable competitive advantage** when it can meet customer needs more effectively or efficiently than rivals and when the basis for this is durable, despite the best efforts of competitors to match or surpass this advantage.

Figure 1.1 Identifying a Company's Strategy—What to Look For

Actions to gain sales and market share via more performance features, more appealing design, better quality or customer service, wider product selection, or other such actions

Actions to strengthen the firm's bargaining position with suppliers, distributors, and others

Actions to gain sales and market share with lower prices based on lower costs

Actions to upgrade, build, or acquire competitively important resources and capabilities

THE PATTERN OF ACTIONS AND BUSINESS APPROACHES THAT DEFINE A COMPANY'S STRATEGY

Actions to enter new product or geographic markets or to exit existing ones

Actions and approaches used in managing R&D, production, sales and marketing, finance, and other key activities

Actions to capture emerging market opportunities and defend against external threats to the company's business prospects

Actions to strengthen competitiveness via strategic alliances and collaborative partnerships

Actions to strengthen market standing and competitiveness by acquiring or merging with other companies

provides a competitive advantage is a company's most reliable ticket for earning above-average profits. Competing in the marketplace on the basis of a competitive advantage tends to be more profitable than competing with no advantage. And a company is almost certain to earn significantly higher profits when it enjoys a competitive advantage as opposed to when it is hamstrung by competitive disadvantage.

Competitive advantage comes from an ability to meet customer needs more *effectively,* with products or services that customers value more highly, or more *efficiently,* at lower cost. Meeting customer needs more effectively can translate into the ability to command a higher price (e.g., Godiva chocolate), which can improve profits by boosting revenues. Meeting customer needs more cost-effectively can translate into being able to charge lower prices and achieve higher sales volumes (e.g., Walmart), thereby improving profits on the revenue side as well as the cost side. Furthermore, if a company's competitive edge holds promise for being sustainable (as opposed to just temporary), then so much the better for both the strategy and the company's future profitability. What makes a competitive advantage **sustainable** (or durable), as opposed to temporary, are elements of the strategy that give buyers *lasting reasons to prefer* a company's products or services over those of competitors—reasons that competitors are unable to nullify or overcome despite their best efforts.

LO 2

Develop an awareness of the four most-dependable strategic approaches for setting a company apart from rivals and winning a sustainable competitive advantage.

ILLUSTRATION CAPSULE 1.1

McDonald's Strategy in the Quick-Service Restaurant Industry

In 2010, McDonald's was setting new sales records despite a global economic slowdown and declining consumer confidence in the United States. More than 60 million customers visited one of McDonald's 32,000 restaurants in 117 countries each day, which allowed the company to record 2009 revenues and earnings of more than $22.7 billion and $6.8 billion, respectively. McDonald's performance in the marketplace made it one of only two companies listed on the Dow Jones Industrial Average (the other was Walmart Stores, Inc.) that actually increased in share value in spite of the economic meltdown. The company's sales were holding up well amid the ongoing economic uncertainty in early 2010, with global sales as measured in constant currencies increasing by more than 4 percent in the first quarter. Its combined operating margin had risen to nearly 30 percent. The company's success was a result of its well-conceived and executed Plan-to-Win strategy that focused on "being better, not just bigger." Key initiatives of the Plan-to-Win strategy included:

- *Improved restaurant operations.* McDonald's global restaurant operations improvement process involved employee training programs ranging from on-the-job training for new crew members to college-level management courses offered at the company's Hamburger University. The company also sent nearly 200 high-potential employees annually to its McDonald's Leadership Institute to build the leadership skills needed by its next generation of senior managers. McDonald's commitment to employee development earned the company a place on *Fortune*'s list of Top 25 Global Companies for Leaders in 2010. The company also trained its store managers to closely monitor labor, food, and utility costs.

- *Affordable pricing.* In addition to tackling operating costs in each of its restaurants, McDonald's kept its prices low by closely scrutinizing administrative costs and other corporate expenses. McDonald's saw the poor economy in the United States as an opportunity to renegotiate its advertising contracts with newspapers and television networks in early 2009. The company also began to replace its company-owned vehicles with more fuel-efficient models when gasoline prices escalated dramatically in the United States during 2008. However, McDonald's did not choose to sacrifice product quality in order to offer lower prices. The company implemented extensive supplier monitoring programs to ensure that its suppliers did not change product specifications to lower costs. For example, the company's chicken breasts were routinely checked for weight when arriving from suppliers' production facilities. The company's broad approach to minimizing non-value-adding expenses allowed it to offer more items on its Dollar Menu in the United States, its Ein Mal Eins menu in Germany, and its 100 Yen menu in Japan.

- *Wide menu variety and beverage choices.* McDonald's has expanded its menu beyond the popular-selling Big Mac and Quarter Pounder to include such new, healthy quick-service items as grilled chicken salads, chicken snack wraps, and premium chicken sandwiches in the United States, Lemon Shrimp Burgers in Germany, and Ebi shrimp wraps in Japan. The company has also added an extensive line of premium coffees that include espressos,

(continued)

cappuccinos, and lattes sold in its McCafe restaurant locations in the United States, Europe, and the Asia/Pacific region. McDonald's latte was judged "as good [as] or better" than lattes sold by Starbucks or Dunkin' Donuts in a review by the *Chicago Tribune*'s Good Eating and Dining staff in December 2008.

- *Convenience and expansion of dining opportunities.* The addition of McCafes helped McDonald's increase same store sales by extending traditional dining hours. Customers wanting a midmorning coffee or an afternoon snack helped keep store traffic high after McDonald's had sold its last Egg McMuffin, McGriddle, or chicken biscuit and before the lunch crowd arrived to order Big Macs, Quarter Pounders, chicken sandwiches, or salads. The company also extended its drive-thru hours to 24 hours in more than 25,000 locations in cities around the world where consumers tended to eat at all hours of the day and night. At many high-traffic locations in the United States, double drive-thru lanes were added to serve customers more quickly.

- *Ongoing restaurant reinvestment and international expansion.* With more than 14,000 restaurants in the United States, the focus of McDonald's expansion of units was in rapidly growing emerging markets such as Russia and China. The company opened 125 new restaurants in China and 40 new restaurants in Russia in 2008. The company also refurbished about 10,000 of its locations in the United States between 2004 and 2008 as a part of its McCafe rollout and as a way to make its restaurants pleasant places for both customers to dine and employees to work.

Sources: Janet Adamy, "McDonald's Seeks Way to Keep Sizzling," *Wall Street Journal Online,* March 10, 2009; various annual reports; various company press releases.

Four of the most frequently used and dependable strategic approaches to setting a company apart from rivals, building strong customer loyalty, and winning a competitive advantage are:

1. *Striving to be the industry's low-cost provider, thereby aiming for a cost-based competitive advantage over rivals.* Walmart and Southwest Airlines have earned strong market positions because of the low-cost advantages they have achieved over their rivals and their consequent ability to underprice competitors. These advantages in meeting customer needs *efficiently* have translated into volume advantages, with Walmart as the world's largest discount retailer and Southwest as the largest U.S. air carrier, based on the number of domestic passengers.[5]

2. *Outcompeting rivals on the basis of differentiating features, such as higher quality, wider product selection, added performance, value-added services, more attractive styling, and technological superiority.* Successful adopters of differentiation strategies include Apple (innovative products), Johnson & Johnson in baby products (product reliability), Rolex (top-of-the-line prestige), and Mercedes (engineering design). These companies have achieved a competitive advantage because of their ability to meet customer needs more effectively than rivals can, thus driving up their customers' willingness to pay higher prices. One way to sustain this type of competitive advantage is to be sufficiently innovative to thwart the efforts of clever rivals to copy or closely imitate the product offering.

3. *Focusing on a narrow market niche and winning a competitive edge by doing a better job than rivals of serving the special needs and tastes of buyers in the niche.* Firms using a focus strategy can achieve an advantage through either greater efficiency in serving the niche or greater effectiveness in meeting the special needs. Prominent companies that enjoy competitive success in a specialized market niche include eBay in online auctions, Jiffy Lube International

in quick oil changes, McAfee in virus protection software, and The Weather Channel in cable TV.

4.   *Aiming to offer the lowest (best) prices for differentiated goods that at least match the features and performance of higher-priced rival brands.* This is known as a *best-cost provider strategy,* and it rests on the ability to be the most cost-effective provider of an upscale product or service. This option is a hybrid strategy that blends elements of the previous approaches. Target is an example of a company that is known for its hip product design (a reputation it built by featuring cheap-chic designers such as Isaac Mizrahi), as well as a more appealing shopping ambience than other "big-box" discounters, such as Walmart and Kmart. It offers the perfect illustration of a best-cost provider strategy.

Winning a *sustainable* competitive edge over rivals with any of the above four strategies generally hinges as much on building competitively valuable expertise and capabilities that rivals cannot readily match as it does on having a distinctive product offering. Clever rivals can nearly always copy the attributes of a popular product or service, but for rivals to match the experience, know-how, and specialized capabilities that a company has developed and perfected over a long period of time is substantially harder to do and takes much longer. FedEx, for example, has superior capabilities in next-day delivery of small packages. Walt Disney has hard-to-beat capabilities in theme park management and family entertainment. In recent years, Apple has demonstrated impressive product innovation capabilities in digital music players, smart phones, and e-readers. Hyundai has become the world's fastest-growing automaker as a result of its advanced manufacturing processes and unparalleled quality control system. Ritz Carlton and Four Seasons have uniquely strong capabilities in providing their hotel guests with an array of personalized services. Each of these capabilities has proved hard for competitors to imitate or best.

The tight connection between competitive advantage and profitability means that the quest for sustainable competitive advantage always ranks center stage in crafting a strategy. The key to successful strategy making is to come up with one or more strategy elements that act as a magnet to draw customers and that produce a lasting competitive edge over rivals. Indeed, what separates a powerful strategy from a run-of-the-mill or ineffective one is management's ability to forge a series of moves, both in the marketplace and internally, that sets the company apart from its rivals, tilts the playing field in the company's favor by giving buyers reason to prefer its products or services, and produces a sustainable competitive advantage over rivals. The bigger and more sustainable the competitive advantage, the better are a company's prospects for winning in the marketplace and earning superior long-term profits relative to its rivals. Without a strategy that leads to competitive advantage, a company risks being outcompeted by stronger rivals and locked into mediocre financial performance.

Why a Company's Strategy Evolves over Time

The appeal of a strategy that yields a sustainable competitive advantage is that it offers the potential for an enduring edge over rivals. However, managers of every company must be willing and ready to modify the strategy in response to changing market conditions, advancing technology, the fresh moves of competitors, shifting buyer needs, emerging market opportunities, and new ideas for improving the strategy. In some industries, conditions change at a fairly slow pace, making it feasible for the major components of a good strategy to remain in place for long

LO 3

Understand that a company's strategy tends to evolve over time because of changing circumstances and ongoing management efforts to improve the company's strategy.

periods. But in industries where industry and competitive conditions change frequently and in sometimes dramatic ways, the life cycle of a given strategy is short. Industry environments characterized by high-velocity change require companies to repeatedly adapt their strategies.[6] For example, companies in industries with rapid-fire advances in technology like medical equipment, electronics, and wireless devices often find it essential to adjust key elements of their strategies several times a year, sometimes even finding it necessary to "reinvent" their approach to providing value to their customers.

Regardless of whether a company's strategy changes gradually or swiftly, the important point is that the task of crafting strategy is not a one-time event but always a work in progress. Adapting to new conditions and constantly evaluating what is working well enough to continue and what needs to be improved are normal parts of the strategy-making process, resulting in an *evolving strategy.*[7]

> Changing circumstances and ongoing management efforts to improve the strategy cause a company's strategy to evolve over time—a condition that makes the task of crafting strategy *a work in progress*, not a one-time event.

A Company's Strategy Is Partly Proactive and Partly Reactive

The evolving nature of a company's strategy means that the typical company strategy is a blend of (1) *proactive* actions to improve the company's financial performance and secure a competitive edge and (2) *adaptive* reactions to unanticipated developments and fresh market conditions. In most cases, much of a company's current strategy flows from previously initiated actions and business approaches that are working well enough to merit continuation and from newly launched initiatives aimed at boosting financial performance and edging out rivals. This part of management's action plan for running the company is its **deliberate strategy,** consisting of strategy elements that are both planned and realized as planned (while other planned strategy elements may not work out).

> A company's strategy is shaped partly by management analysis and choice and partly by the necessity of adapting and learning by doing.

But managers must always be willing to supplement or modify the proactive strategy elements with as-needed reactions to unanticipated conditions. Inevitably, there will be occasions when market and competitive conditions take an unexpected turn that calls for some kind of strategic reaction or adjustment. Hence, *a portion of a company's strategy is always developed on the fly,* coming as a response to fresh strategic maneuvers on the part of rival firms, unexpected shifts in customer requirements, fast-changing technological developments, newly appearing market opportunities, a changing political or economic climate, or other unanticipated happenings in the surrounding environment. Under conditions of high uncertainty, strategy elements are more likely to emerge from experimentation, trial-and-error, and adaptive learning processes than from a proactive plan. These unplanned, reactive, and adaptive strategy adjustments make up the firm's **emergent strategy,** consisting of the new strategy elements that emerge as changing conditions warrant. A company's strategy in toto (its *realized* strategy) thus tends to be a *combination* of proactive and reactive elements, with certain strategy elements being *abandoned* because they have become obsolete or ineffective—see Figure 1.2.[8] A company's realized strategy can be observed in the pattern of its actions over time—a far better indicator than any of its strategic plans on paper or public pronouncements about its strategy.

> **CORE CONCEPTS**
>
> A company's **proactive (or deliberate) strategy** consists of strategy elements that are both planned and realized as planned; its **reactive (or emergent) strategy** consists of new strategy elements that emerge as changing conditions warrant.

Figure 1.2   **A Company's Strategy Is a Blend of Proactive Initiatives and Reactive Adjustments**

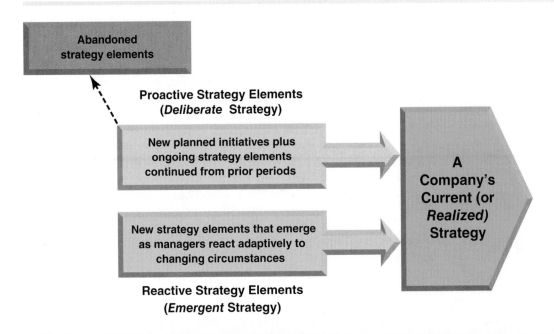

THE RELATIONSHIP BETWEEN A COMPANY'S STRATEGY AND ITS BUSINESS MODEL

LO 4

Learn why it is important for a company to have a viable business model that outlines the company's customer value proposition and its profit formula.

Closely related to the concept of strategy is the company's **business model.** A company's business model is management's blueprint for delivering a valuable product or service to customers in a manner that will generate ample revenues to cover costs and yield an attractive profit.[9] It is management's story line for how the strategy will be a moneymaker. Without the ability to deliver good profitability, the strategy is not viable and the survival of the business is in doubt.

The two crucial elements of a company's business model are (1) its *customer value proposition* and (2) its *profit formula.* The customer value proposition lays out the company's approach to satisfying buyer wants and needs at a price customers will consider a good value. The greater the value provided (V) and the lower the price (P), the more attractive the value proposition is to customers. The profit formula describes the company's approach to determining a cost structure that will allow for acceptable profits, given the pricing tied to its customer value proposition. More specifically, a company's profit formula depends on three basic elements: V—the *value* provided to customers, in terms of how effectively the goods or services of the company meet customers' wants and needs; P—the *price* charged to customers; and C—the company's *costs.* The lower the costs (C), given the customer value proposition ($V - P$), the greater the ability of the business model to be a moneymaker. Thus

CORE CONCEPT

A company's **business model** sets forth the economic logic for making money in a business, given the company's strategy. It describes two critical elements: (1) the customer value proposition and (2) the profit formula.

the profit formula reveals how efficiently a company can meet customer wants and needs and deliver on the value proposition.

Magazines and newspapers employ a business model keyed to delivering information and entertainment they believe readers will find valuable and a profit formula aimed at securing sufficient revenues from subscriptions and advertising to more than cover the costs of producing and delivering their products to readers. Mobile phone providers, satellite radio companies, and broadband providers also employ a subscription-based business model. The business model of network TV and radio broadcasters entails providing free programming to audiences but charging advertising fees based on audience size. Gillette's business model in razor blades involves selling a "master product"—the razor—at an attractively low price and then making money on repeat purchases of razor blades that can be produced very cheaply and sold at high profit margins. Printer manufacturers like Hewlett-Packard, Lexmark, and Epson pursue much the same business model as Gillette—selling printers at a low (virtually break-even) price and making large profit margins on the repeat purchases of printer supplies, especially ink cartridges.

The nitty-gritty issue surrounding a company's business model is whether it can execute its customer value proposition profitably. Just because company managers have crafted a strategy for competing and running the business, this does not automatically mean that the strategy will lead to profitability—it may or it may not. The relevance of a company's business model is to clarify *how the business will (1) provide customers with value and (2) generate revenues sufficient to cover costs and produce attractive profits.*[10] Illustration Capsule 1.2 discusses the contrasting buisness models of Microsoft and Redhat.

WHAT MAKES A STRATEGY A WINNER?

Three tests can be applied to determine whether a strategy is a *winning strategy:*

LO 5

Learn the three tests of a winning strategy.

1. ***The Fit Test:*** *How well does the strategy fit the company's situation?* To qualify as a winner, a strategy has to be well matched to industry and competitive conditions, a company's best market opportunities, and other pertinent aspects of the business environment in which the company operates. No strategy can work well unless it exhibits good *external fit* and is in sync with prevailing market conditions. At the same time, a winning strategy has to be tailored to the company's resources and competitive capabilities and be supported by a complementary set of functional activities (i.e., activities in the realms of supply chain management, operations, sales and marketing, and so on). That is, it must also exhibit *internal fit* and be compatible with a company's ability to execute the strategy in a competent manner. Unless a strategy exhibits good fit with both the external and internal aspects of a company's overall situation, it is likely to be an underperformer and fall short of producing winning results. Winning strategies also exhibit *dynamic fit* in the sense that they evolve over time in a manner that maintains close and effective alignment with the company's situation even as external and internal conditions change.[11]

A **winning strategy** must pass three tests:

1. The Fit Test
2. The Competitive Advantage Test
3. The Performance Test

ILLUSTRATION CAPSULE 1.2

Microsoft and Red Hat Linux: Two Contrasting Business Models

The strategies of rival companies are often predicated on strikingly different business models. Consider, for example, the business models for Microsoft and Red Hat Linux in operating system software for PCs. Microsoft's business model—sell proprietary code software and give service away free—is a proven money maker that generates billions in profits annually. On the other hand, the jury is still out on Red Hat's business model of selling subscriptions to open-source software to large corporations and deriving substantial revenues from the sales of technical support, training, consulting, software customization, and engineering to generate revenues sufficient to cover costs and yield a profit. Red Hat's fiscal 2010 revenues of $748 million and net income of $87 million are quite meager in comparison.

	Microsoft	Red Hat
Customer value proposition	• Employ a cadre of highly skilled programmers to develop proprietary code for the Windows operating system and software package. • Keep the source code hidden so as to keep the inner-workings of the software proprietary. • Provide a modest level of technical support to users at no cost. • Sell the Windows operating system and software package to personal computer PC makers and to PC users at relatively attractive prices.	• Rely on the collaborative efforts of volunteer programmers from all over the world who contribute bits and pieces of code to improve and polish the Linux system. • Collect and test enhancements and new applications submitted by the open-source community of volunteer programmers. Linux's originator, Linus Torvalds, and a team of 300-plus Red Hat engineers and software developers evaluate which incoming submissions merit inclusion in new releases of Red Hat Linux. • Make the source code open and available to all users, allowing them to create a customized version of Linux.
Profit formula	*Revenue generation:* • Strive to maintain a 90 percent or more market share of the 350 million PCs sold annually worldwide. • Charge licensing fees to PC makers and users ranging from $50 to $100 per installation. • Keep rejuvenating revenues by periodically introducing next-generation software versions with features that will induce PC users to upgrade the operating system on previously purchased PCs to the new version. *Profit margin:* • Most of Microsoft's costs arise on the front end in developing the software and are thus "fixed"; the variable costs of producing and packaging the CDs provided to users are only a couple of dollars per copy—once the break-even volume is reached, Microsoft's revenues from additional sales are almost pure profit.	*Revenue generation:* • Market the upgraded and tested family of Red Hat Linux products to large enterprises and charge them a subscription fee that includes 24/7 support within one hour in seven languages. Provide subscribers with updated versions of Red Hat Linux every 12–18 months to maintain the subscriber base. • Capitalize on the specialized expertise required to use Linux in multiserver, multiprocessor applications by providing fees-based training, consulting, software customization, and client-directed engineering to Red Hat Linux users. Red Hat offers Linux certification training programs at all skill levels at more than 60 global locations—Red Hat certification in the use of Linux is considered the best in the world. *Profit margin:* • Most of Red Hat's development costs arise from the evaluation and integration of new submissions for modifications to Linux; the company also incurs substantial variable costs related to its customer service, training, consulting, software customization, and client-directed engineering activities. The company's profit margin is dependent on sufficient subscription revenues and consulting fees to cover the costs of these activities.

Source: Company documents and information posted on their Web sites.

2. ***The Competitive Advantage Test:*** *Can the strategy help the company achieve a sustainable competitive advantage?* Strategies that fail to achieve a durable competitive advantage over rivals are unlikely to produce superior performance for more than a brief period of time. Winning strategies enable a company to achieve a competitive advantage over key rivals that is long-lasting. The bigger and more durable the competitive advantage, the more powerful it is.

3. ***The Performance Test:*** *Is the strategy producing good company performance?* The mark of a winning strategy is strong company performance. Two kinds of performance indicators tell the most about the caliber of a company's strategy: (1) profitability and financial strength and (2) competitive strength and market standing. Above-average financial performance or gains in market share, competitive position, or profitability are signs of a winning strategy.

Strategies that come up short on one or more of the above tests are plainly less appealing than strategies passing all three tests with flying colors. Managers should use the same questions when evaluating either proposed or existing strategies. New initiatives that don't seem to match the company's internal and external situations should be scrapped before they come to fruition, while existing strategies must be scrutinized on a regular basis to ensure they have good fit, offer a competitive advantage, and are contributing to above-average performance or performance improvements.

WHY CRAFTING AND EXECUTING STRATEGY ARE IMPORTANT TASKS

Crafting and executing strategy are top-priority managerial tasks for a very big reason. A clear and reasoned strategy is management's prescription for doing business, its road map to competitive advantage, its game plan for pleasing customers, and its formula for improving performance. High-achieving enterprises are nearly always the product of astute, creative, proactive strategy making. Companies don't get to the top of the industry rankings or stay there with illogical strategies, copy-cat strategies, or timid attempts to try to do better. Only a handful of companies can boast of hitting home runs in the marketplace due to lucky breaks or the good fortune of having stumbled into the right market at the right time with the right product. And even then, unless they subsequently craft a strategy that capitalizes on their luck, building in what's working and discarding the rest, success of this sort will be fleeting. So there can be little argument that a company's strategy matters—and matters a lot.

The chief executive officer of one successful company put it well when he said:

> In the main, our competitors are acquainted with the same fundamental concepts and techniques and approaches that we follow, and they are as free to pursue them as we are. More often than not, the difference between their level of success and ours lies in the relative thoroughness and self-discipline with which we and they develop and execute our strategies for the future.

Good Strategy + Good Strategy Execution = Good Management

Crafting and executing strategy are thus core management functions. Among all the things managers do, nothing affects a company's ultimate success or failure more fundamentally than how well its management team charts the company's direction, develops competitively effective strategic moves and business approaches, and pursues what needs to be done internally to produce good day-in, day-out strategy execution and operating excellence. Indeed, *good strategy and good strategy execution are the most telling signs of good management.* Managers don't deserve a gold star for designing a potentially brilliant strategy but failing to put the organizational means in place to carry it out in high-caliber fashion. Competent execution of a mediocre strategy scarcely merits enthusiastic applause for management's efforts either. The rationale for using the twin standards of good strategy making and good strategy execution to determine whether a company is well managed is therefore compelling: *The better conceived a company's strategy and the more competently it is executed, the more likely that the company will be a standout performer in the marketplace.* In stark contrast, a company that lacks clear-cut direction, has a flawed strategy, or can't execute its strategy competently is a company whose financial performance is probably suffering, whose business is at long-term risk, and whose management is sorely lacking.

> How well a company performs is directly attributable to the caliber of its strategy and the proficiency with which the strategy is executed.

THE ROAD AHEAD

Throughout the chapters to come and the accompanying case collection, the spotlight is trained on the foremost question in running a business enterprise: *What must managers do, and do well, to make a company a winner in the marketplace?* The answer that emerges, and that becomes the message of this book, is that doing a good job of managing inherently requires good strategic thinking and good management of the strategy-making, strategy-executing process.

The mission of this book is to provide a solid overview of what every business student and aspiring manager needs to know about crafting and executing strategy. We will explore what good strategic thinking entails, describe the core concepts and tools of strategic analysis, and examine the ins and outs of crafting and executing strategy. The accompanying cases will help build your skills both in diagnosing how well the strategy-making, strategy-executing task is being performed and in prescribing actions for how the strategy in question or its execution can be improved. In the process, we hope to convince you that first-rate capabilities in crafting and executing strategy are basic to managing successfully and are skills every manager needs to possess.

As you tackle the following pages, ponder the following observation by the essayist and poet Ralph Waldo Emerson: "Commerce is a game of skill which many people play, but which few play well." If the content of this book helps you become a savvy player and equips you to succeed in business, then your journey through these pages will indeed be time well spent.

KEY POINTS

The tasks of crafting and executing company strategies are the heart and soul of managing a business enterprise and winning in the marketplace. The key points to take away from this chapter include the following:

1. A company's strategy is the *game plan* management is using to stake out a market position, conduct its operations, attract and please customers, compete successfully, and achieve the desired performance targets.

2. The central thrust of a company's strategy is undertaking moves to build and strengthen the company's long-term competitive position and financial performance by *competing differently* from rivals and gaining a sustainable competitive advantage over them.

3. A company achieves a sustainable competitive advantage when it can meet customer needs more effectively or efficiently than rivals and when the basis for this is durable, despite the best efforts of competitors to match or surpass this advantage.

4. A company's strategy typically evolves over time, emerging from a blend of (1) proactive and deliberate actions on the part of company managers to improve the strategy and (2) reactive, as-needed adaptive responses to unanticipated developments and fresh market conditions.

5. A company's business model is management's story line for how the strategy will be a moneymaker. It contains two crucial elements: (1) the *customer value proposition*—a plan for satisfying customer wants and needs at a price customers will consider good value, and (2) the *profit formula*—a plan for a cost structure that will enable the company to deliver the customer value proposition profitably. In effect, a company's business model sets forth the economic logic for making money in a particular business, given the company's current strategy.

6. A winning strategy will pass three tests: (1) *Fit* (external, internal, and dynamic consistency), (2) *Competitive Advantage* (durable competitive advantage), and (3) *Performance* (outstanding financial and market performance).

7. Crafting and executing strategy are core management functions. How well a company performs and the degree of market success it enjoys are directly attributable to the caliber of its strategy and the proficiency with which the strategy is executed.

ASSURANCE OF LEARNING EXERCISES

LO 1, LO 2

1. Go to www.ikea.com, choose your country, and click on the About Ikea section, and explore Ikea's latest Yearly Summary and Other Facts & Figures to see if you can identify the key elements of Ikea's strategy. Use the framework provided in Figure 1.1 to help identify these key elements. What approach toward winning a competitive advantage does Ikea seem to be pursuing?

LO 1, LO 2, LO 5

2. On the basis of what you know about the quick-service restaurant industry, does McDonald's strategy as described in Illustration Capsule 1.1 seem to be well matched to industry and competitive conditions? Does the strategy seem to be keyed to having a cost-based advantage, offering differentiating features, serving the unique needs of a narrow market niche, or being the best-cost provider? What is there about the action elements of McDonald's strategy that is consistent with its approach to competitive advantage? From the information provided, which tests of a winning strategy does McDonald's strategy pass?

LO 3, LO 4

3. Go to www.redhat.com and check whether the company's recent financial reports indicate that its business model is working. Is the company sufficiently profitable to validate its business model and strategy? Is its revenue stream from selling training and consulting and engineering services growing or declining as a percentage of total revenues? Does your review of the company's recent financial performance suggest that its business model and strategy are changing? Read the company's latest statement about its business model and about why it is pursuing the subscription approach (as compared to Microsoft's approach of selling copies of its operating software directly to PC manufacturers and individuals).

EXERCISE FOR SIMULATION PARTICIPANTS

This chapter discusses three questions that must be answered by managers of organizations of all sizes:

- What is our present situation?
- Where do we want to go from here?
- How are we going to get there?

After you read the Participant's Guide or Player's Manual for the strategy simulation exercise that you will participate in this academic term, you and your co-managers should come up with brief one- or two-paragraph answers to these three questions *before* entering your first set of decisions. While the management team's answer to the first of the three questions can be developed from your reading of the manual, the second and third questions will require a collaborative discussion among the members of your company's management team about how you intend to manage the company you have been assigned to run.

LO 1, LO 2

1. *What is our company's current situation?* A substantive answer to this question should cover the following issues:

   - Is your company in a good, average, or weak competitive position vis-à-vis rival companies?
   - Does your company appear to be in sound financial condition?
   - What problems does your company have that need to be addressed?

LO 3, LO 5

2. *Where do we want to take the company during the time we are in charge?* A complete answer to this question should say something about each of the following:

   - What goals or aspirations do you have for your company?
   - What do you want the company to be known for?
   - What market share would you like your company to have after the first five decision rounds?

- By what amount or percentage would you like to increase total profits of the company by the end of the final decision round?
- What kinds of performance outcomes will signal that you and your co-managers are managing the company in a successful manner?

LO 3, LO 4

3. *How are we going to get there?* Your answer should cover these issues:

- Which of the basic strategic and competitive approaches discussed in this chapter do you think makes the most sense to pursue?
- What kind of competitive advantage over rivals will you try to achieve?
- How would you describe the company's business model?
- What kind of actions will support these objectives?

ENDNOTES

[1] Jan Rivkin, "An Alternative Approach to Making Strategic Choices," Harvard Business School, 9-702-433, 2001.

[2] Costas Markides, "What Is Strategy and How Do You Know If You Have One?" *Business Strategy Review* 15, no. 2 (Summer 2004), pp. 5–6. See also David J. Collis and Michael F. Rukstad, "Can You Say What Your Strategy Is?" *Harvard Business Review* 86, no. 4 (April 2008), pp. 82–90.

[3] For a discussion of the different ways that companies can position themselves in the marketplace, see Michael E. Porter, "What Is Strategy?" *Harvard Business Review* 74, no. 6 (November–December 1996), pp. 65–67.

[4] Ibid.

[5] Walmartstores.com/download/2230.pdf; Southwest Airlines Fact Sheet, July 16, 2009.

[6] For more on the strategic challenges posed by high-velocity changes, see Shona L. Brown and Kathleen M. Eisenhardt, *Competing on the Edge: Strategy as Structured Chaos* (Boston, MA: Harvard Business School Press, 1998), chap. 1.

[7] For an excellent discussion of strategy as a dynamic process involving continuous, unending creation and re-creation of strategy, see Cynthia A. Montgomery, "Putting Leadership Back into Strategy," *Harvard Business Review* 86, no. 1 (January 2008), pp. 54–60.

[8] See Henry Mintzberg and Joseph Lampel, "Reflecting on the Strategy Process," *Sloan Management Review* 40, no. 3 (Spring 1999), pp. 21–30; Henry Mintzberg and J. A. Waters, "Of Strategies, Deliberate and Emergent," *Strategic Management Journal* 6 (1985), pp. 257–72; Costas Markides, "Strategy as Balance: From 'Either-Or' to 'And,'" *Business Strategy Review* 12, no. 3 (September 2001), pp. 1–10.

[9] Mark W. Johnson, Clayton M. Christensen, and Henning Kagermann, "Reinventing Your Business Model," *Harvard Business Review* 86, no. 12 (December 2008), pp. 52–53; Joan Magretta, "Why Business Models Matter," *Harvard Business Review* 80, no. 5 (May 2002), p. 87.

[10] For further discussion of the meaning and role of a company's customer value proposition and profit proposition, see W. Chan Kim and Renée Mauborgne, "How Strategy Shapes Structure," *Harvard Business Review* 87, no. 9 (September 2009), pp. 74–75.

[11] For a discussion of the three types of fit, see Rivkin, "An Alternative Approach to Making Strategic Choices." For an example of managing internal fit dynamically, See M. Peteraf and R. Reed, "Managerial Discretion and Internal Alignment under Regulatory Constraints and Change," *Strategic Management Journal* 28 (2007), pp. 1089–1112.

CHAPTER 2

CHARTING A COMPANY'S DIRECTION: VISION AND MISSION, OBJECTIVES, AND STRATEGY

The vision we have . . . determines what we do and the opportunities we see or don't see.

—Charles G. Koch
CEO of Koch Industries, the second-largest privately held company in the U.S.

If you don't know where you are going, any road will take you there.

—Cheshire Cat to Alice
Lewis Carroll, Alice in Wonderland

A good goal is like a strenuous exercise—it makes you stretch.

—Mary Kay Ash
Founder of Mary Kay Cosmetics

LEARNING OBJECTIVES

LO 1. Grasp why it is critical for company managers to have a clear strategic vision of where a company needs to head and why.

LO 2. Understand the importance of setting both strategic and financial objectives.

LO 3. Understand why the strategic initiatives taken at various organizational levels must be tightly coordinated to achieve companywide performance targets.

LO 4. Become aware of what a company must do to achieve operating excellence and to execute its strategy proficiently.

LO 5. Become aware of the role and responsibility of a company's board of directors in overseeing the strategic management process.

Crafting and executing strategy are the heart and soul of managing a business enterprise. But exactly what is involved in developing a strategy and executing it proficiently? What are the various components of the strategy-making, strategy-executing process and to what extent are company personnel—aside from senior management—involved in the process? In this chapter we present an overview of the ins and outs of crafting and executing company strategies. Special attention will be given to management's direction-setting responsibilities—charting a strategic course, setting performance targets, and choosing a strategy capable of producing the desired outcomes. We will also explain why strategy making is a task for a company's entire management team and discuss which kinds of strategic decisions tend to be made at which levels of management. The chapter concludes with a look at the roles and responsibilities of a company's board of directors in the strategy-making, strategy-executing process and how good corporate governance protects shareholder interests and promotes good management.

WHAT DOES THE STRATEGY-MAKING, STRATEGY-EXECUTING PROCESS ENTAIL?

The process of crafting and executing a company's strategy consists of five interrelated managerial stages:

1. *Developing a strategic vision* of the company's long-term direction, a *mission* that describes the company's purpose, and a set of *values* to guide the pursuit of the vision and mission.
2. *Setting objectives* and using them as yardsticks for measuring the company's performance and progress.
3. *Crafting a strategy* to achieve the objectives and move the company along the strategic course that management has charted.
4. *Executing the chosen strategy* efficiently and effectively.
5. *Monitoring developments, evaluating performance, and initiating corrective adjustments* in the company's vision and mission, objectives, strategy, or execution in light of actual experience, changing conditions, new ideas, and new opportunities.

Figure 2.1   The Strategy-Making, Strategy-Executing Process

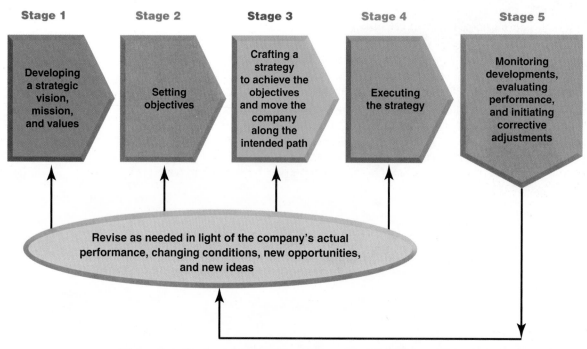

Figure 2.1 displays this five-stage process, which we examine next in some detail.

STAGE 1: DEVELOPING A STRATEGIC VISION, A MISSION, AND A SET OF CORE VALUES

LO 1

Grasp why it is critical for company managers to have a clear strategic vision of where a company needs to head and why.

Very early in the strategy-making process, a company's senior managers must wrestle with the issue of what directional path the company should take. Can the company's prospects be improved by changing its product offerings and/or the markets in which it participates and/or the customers it caters to and/or the technologies it employs? Deciding to commit the company to one path versus another pushes managers to draw some carefully reasoned conclusions about whether the company's present strategic course offers attractive opportunities for growth and profitability or whether changes of one kind or another in the company's strategy and long-term direction are needed.

Developing a Strategic Vision

Top management's views and conclusions about the company's long-term direction and what product-customer-market-technology mix seems optimal for the road ahead constitute a **strategic vision** for the company. A strategic vision delineates management's aspirations for the business, providing a panoramic view of "where we are going" and a convincing rationale for why this makes good business sense for the company. A strategic vision thus points an organization in a particular direction, charts a strategic path for it to follow in preparing for the future, and builds commitment to the future course of action. A clearly articulated strategic vision communicates management's aspirations to stakeholders and helps steer the energies of company personnel in a common direction.

Well-conceived visions are *distinctive* and *specific* to a particular organization; they avoid generic, feel-good statements like "We will become a global leader and the first choice of customers in every market we serve"—which could apply to hundreds of organizations.[1] And they are not the product of a committee charged with coming up with an innocuous but well-meaning one-sentence vision that wins consensus approval from various stakeholders. Nicely worded vision statements with no specifics about the company's product-market-customer-technology focus fall well short of what it takes for a vision to measure up.

A sampling of vision statements currently in use shows a range from strong and clear to overly general and generic. A surprising number of the vision statements found on company Web sites and in annual reports are vague and unrevealing, saying very little about the company's future direction. Some could apply to almost any company in any industry. Many read like a public relations statement—high-sounding words that someone came up with because it is fashionable for companies to have an official vision statement.[2] But the real purpose of a vision statement is to serve as a management tool for giving the organization a sense of direction. Like any tool, it can be used properly or improperly, either clearly conveying a company's future strategic path or not.

For a strategic vision to function as a valuable managerial tool, it must convey what management wants the business to look like and provide managers with a reference point in making strategic decisions and preparing the company for the future. It must say something definitive about how the company's leaders intend to position the company beyond where it is today. Table 2.1 provides some dos and don'ts in composing an effectively worded vision statement. Illustration Capsule 2.1 provides a critique of the strategic visions of several prominent companies.

> **CORE CONCEPT**
>
> A **strategic vision** describes management's aspirations for the future and delineates the company's strategic course and long-term direction.

Communicating the Strategic Vision

Effectively communicating the strategic vision down the line to lower-level managers and employees is as important as the strategic soundness of the long-term direction top management has chosen. Company personnel can't be expected to unite behind managerial efforts to get the organization moving in the intended direction until they understand why the strategic course that management has charted is reasonable and beneficial. It is particularly important for executives to provide a compelling rationale for a dramatically *new* strategic vision and company direction. When company personnel don't understand or accept the need for redirecting organizational efforts, they are prone to resist change. Hence, reiterating the basis for the new direction, addressing employee concerns head-on, calming fears, lifting spirits, and providing updates and progress reports as events unfold all become part of the task in mobilizing support for the vision and winning commitment to needed actions.

> An effectively communicated vision is a tool for enlisting the commitment of company personnel to actions that move the company forward in the intended direction.

Winning the support of organization members for the vision nearly always means putting "where we are going and why" in writing, distributing the statement organizationwide, and having executives personally explain the vision and its

Table 2.1   **Wording a Vision Statement—the Dos and Don'ts**

The Dos	The Don'ts
Be graphic. Paint a clear picture of where the company is headed and the market position(s) the company is striving to stake out.	**Don't be vague or incomplete.** Never skimp on specifics about where the company is headed or how the company intends to prepare for the future.
Be forward-looking and directional. Describe the strategic course that management has charted and the kinds of product-market-customer-technology changes that will help the company prepare for the future.	**Don't dwell on the present.** A vision is not about what a company once did or does now; it's about "where we are going."
Keep it focused. Be specific enough to provide managers with guidance in making decisions and allocating resources.	**Don't use overly broad language.** All-inclusive language that gives the company license to head in almost any direction, pursue almost any opportunity, or enter almost any business must be avoided.
Have some wiggle room. Language that allows some flexibility is good. The directional course may have to be adjusted as market-customer-technology circumstances change, and coming up with a new vision statement every one to three years signals rudderless management.	**Don't state the vision in bland or uninspiring terms.** The best vision statements have the power to motivate company personnel and inspire shareholder confidence about the company's direction and business outlook.
Be sure the journey is feasible. The path and direction should be within the realm of what the company can pursue and accomplish; over time, a company should be able to demonstrate measurable progress in achieving the vision.	**Don't be generic.** A vision statement that could apply to companies in any of several industries (or to any of several companies in the same industry) is incapable of giving a company its own unique identity.
Indicate why the directional path makes good business sense. The directional path should be in the long-term interests of stakeholders (especially shareowners, employees, and customers).	**Don't rely on superlatives only.** Visions that claim the company's strategic course is one of being the "best" or "the most successful" or "a recognized leader" or the "global leader" usually shortchange the essential and revealing specifics about the path the company is taking to get there.
Make it memorable. To give the organization a sense of direction and purpose, the vision needs to be easily communicated. Ideally, it should be reducible to a few choice lines or a memorable "slogan" (like Henry Ford's famous vision of "a car in every garage").	**Don't run on and on.** Vison statements that are overly long tend to be unfocused and meaningless. A vision statement that is not short and to-the-point will tend to lose its audience.

Sources: John P. Kotter, *Leading Change* (Boston: Harvard Business School Press, 1996), p. 72; Hugh Davidson, *The Committed Enterprise* (Oxford: Butterworth Heinemann, 2002), chap. 2; and Michel Robert, *Strategy Pure and Simple II* (New York: McGraw-Hill, 1992), chaps. 2, 3, and 6.

> Strategic visions become real only when the vision statement is imprinted in the minds of organization members and then translated into hard objectives and strategies.

rationale to as many people as feasible. *A strategic vision can usually be stated adequately in one to two paragraphs, and managers should be able to explain it to company personnel and outsiders in 5 to 10 minutes.* Ideally, executives should present their vision for the company in a manner that reaches out and grabs people. An engaging and convincing strategic vision has enormous motivational value—for the same reason that a stonemason is more inspired by building a great cathedral for the ages than simply laying stones to create floors and walls. When managers articulate a vivid and compelling case for where the company is headed, organization members begin to say "This is interesting and has a lot of merit. I want to be involved and do my part to help make it happen." The more that a vision evokes positive support and excitement, the greater its impact in terms of arousing a committed organizational effort and getting company personnel to move in a common direction.[3] Thus executive ability to paint a convincing and inspiring picture of a company's journey and destination is an important element of effective strategic leadership.

ILLUSTRATION CAPSULE 2.1

Examples of Strategic Visions—How Well Do They Measure Up?

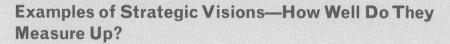

Vision Statement	Effective Elements	Shortcomings
Samsung Samsung is dedicated to developing innovative technologies and efficient processes that create new markets, enrich people's lives, and continue to make Samsung a digital leader.	• Directional • Focused • Flexible • Desirable • Easy to communicate	• Bland or uninspiring
UBS We are determined to be the best global financial services company. We focus on wealth and asset management, and on investment banking and securities businesses. We continually earn recognition and trust from clients, shareholders, and staff through our ability to anticipate, learn and shape our future. We share a common ambition to succeed by delivering quality in what we do. Our purpose is to help our clients make financial decisions with confidence. We use our resources to develop effective solutions and services for our clients. We foster a distinctive, meritocratic culture of ambition, performance and learning as this attracts, retains and develops the best talent for our company. By growing both our client and our talent franchises, we add sustainable value for our shareholders.	• Focused • Feasible • Desirable	• Not forward-looking • Bland or uninspiring • Hard to communicate
Caterpillar Be the global leader in customer value.	• Directional • Desirable • Easy to communicate	• Vague or incomplete • Could apply to many companies in many industries

Sources: Company documents and Web sites (accessed April 23, 2010, June 6, 2010, and February 4, 2011).

Expressing the Essence of the Vision in a Slogan   The task of effectively conveying the vision to company personnel is assisted when management can capture the vision of where to head in a catchy or easily remembered slogan. A number of organizations have summed up their vision in a brief phrase:

- Levi Strauss & Company: "We will clothe the world by marketing the most appealing and widely worn casual clothing in the world."
- Nike: "To bring innovation and inspiration to every athlete in the world."
- Mayo Clinic: "The best care to every patient every day."
- Scotland Yard: "To make London the safest major city in the world."
- Greenpeace: "To halt environmental abuse and promote environmental solutions."

Creating a short slogan to illuminate an organization's direction and purpose helps rally organization members to hurdle whatever obstacles lie in the company's path and maintain their focus.

The Payoffs of a Clear Vision Statement   A well-conceived, forcefully communicated strategic vision pays off in several respects: (1) It crystallizes senior executives' own views about the firm's long-term direction; (2) it reduces the risk of rudderless decision making; (3) it is a tool for winning the support of organization members for internal changes that will help make the vision a reality; (4) it provides a beacon for lower-level managers in setting departmental objectives and crafting departmental strategies that are in sync with the company's overall strategy; and (5) it helps an organization prepare for the future. When management is able to demonstrate significant progress in achieving these five benefits, the first step in organizational direction setting has been successfully completed.

Crafting a Mission Statement

The defining characteristic of a strategic vision is what it says about the company's *future strategic course*—"the direction we are headed and our aspirations for the future." In contrast, a **mission statement** describes the enterprise's *current business and purpose*—"who we are, what we do, and why we are here." The mission statements that one finds in company annual reports or posted on company Web sites are typically quite brief; some do a better job than others of conveying what the enterprise is all about. Consider for example, the mission statement of Sony:

> Sony is committed to developing a wide range of innovative products and multimedia services that challenge the way consumers access and enjoy digital entertainment. By ensuring synergy between businesses within the organization, Sony is constantly striving to create exciting new worlds of entertainment that can be experienced on a variety of different products.

Note that Sony's mission statement does a good job of conveying "who we are, what we do, and why we are here," but it says nothing about the company's long-term direction.

Another example of a well-stated mission statement with ample specifics about what the organization does is that of the Nestlé Research Center:

> At Nestlé, we believe that research can help us make better food so that people live a better life.
>
> Good Food is the primary source of Good Health throughout life. We strive to bring consumers foods that are safe, of high quality and provide optimal nutrition to meet physiological needs. In addition to Nutrition, Health and Wellness, Nestlé products bring consumers the vital ingredients of taste and pleasure.
>
> As consumers continue to make choices regarding foods and beverages they consume, Nestlé helps provide selections for all individual taste and lifestyle preferences.
>
> Research is a key part of our heritage at Nestlé and an essential element of our future. We know there is still much to discover about health, wellness and the role of food in our lives, and we continue to search for answers to bring consumers Good Food for Good Life.

Microsoft's grandiloquent mission statement—"To help people and businesses throughout the world realize their full potential"—says so little

The distinction between a strategic vision and a mission statement is fairly clear-cut: A **strategic vision** portrays a company's aspirations for its *future* ("where we are going"), whereas a company's **mission** describes its *purpose* and its *present* business ("who we are, what we do, and why we are here").

about the customer needs it is satisfying that it could be applied to almost any firm. A well-conceived mission statement should employ language specific enough to give the company its own identity.

Ideally, a company mission statement is sufficiently descriptive to:

- Identify the company's product or services.
- Specify the buyer needs it seeks to satisfy.
- Identify the customer groups or markets it is endeavoring to serve.
- Specify its approach to pleasing customers.
- Give the company its own identity.

Not many company mission statements fully reveal *all* these facets of the business or employ language specific enough to give the company an identity that is distinguishably different from those of other companies in much the same business or industry. A few companies have worded their mission statements so obscurely as to mask what they are all about. Occasionally, companies couch their mission in terms of making a profit. This is misguided. Profit is more correctly an *objective* and a *result* of what a company does. Moreover, earning a profit is the obvious intent of every commercial enterprise. Such companies as BMW, McDonald's, Shell Oil, Procter & Gamble, Nintendo, and Nokia are each striving to earn a profit for shareholders; but plainly the fundamentals of their businesses are substantially different when it comes to "who we are and what we do." It is management's answer to "make a profit doing what and for whom?" that reveals the substance of a company's true mission and business purpose.

Linking the Vision and Mission with Company Values

The **values** of a company (sometimes called *core values*) are the beliefs, traits, and behavioral norms that management has determined should guide the pursuit of its vision and mission. They relate to such things as fair treatment, integrity, ethical behavior, innovativeness, teamwork, top-notch quality, superior customer service, social responsibility, and community citizenship. Many companies have developed a statement of values to emphasize the expectation that the values be reflected in the conduct of company operations and the behavior of company personnel.

Most companies have identified four to eight core values. At FedEx, the six core values concern people (valuing employees and promoting diversity), service (putting customers at the heart of all it does), innovation (inventing services and technologies to improve what it does), integrity (managing with honesty, efficiency, and reliability), and loyalty (earning the respect of the FedEx people, customers, and investors every day, in everything it does). Samsung embraces five values—giving employees opportunities to reach their full potential; an unyielding passion for excellence; anticipating change in market needs and demands; operating in an ethical way; and being a socially and environmentally responsible corporate citizen—in its quest to be among the world's leading consumer electronics companies.

Do companies practice what they preach when it comes to their professed values? Sometimes no, sometimes yes—it runs the gamut. At one extreme are

> **CORE CONCEPT**
>
> A well-conceived **mission statement** conveys a company's *purpose* in language specific enough to give the company its own identity.

> **CORE CONCEPT**
>
> A company's **values** are the beliefs, traits, and behavioral norms that company personnel are expected to display in conducting the company's business and pursuing its strategic vision and mission.

companies with window-dressing values; the values are given lip service by top executives but have little discernible impact on either how company personnel behave or how the company operates. Such companies have value statements because they are in vogue and make the company look good. At the other extreme are companies whose executives are committed to infusing the company with the desired character, traits, and behavioral norms so that they are ingrained in the company's corporate culture—the core values thus become an integral part of the company's DNA and what makes it tick. At such value-driven companies, executives "walk the talk" and company personnel are held accountable for displaying the stated values.

At companies where the stated values are real rather than cosmetic, managers connect values to the pursuit of the strategic vision and mission in one of two ways. In companies with long-standing values that are deeply entrenched in the corporate culture, senior managers are careful to craft a vision, mission, and strategy that match established values; they also reiterate how the value-based behavioral norms contribute to the company's business success. If the company changes to a different vision or strategy, executives take care to explain how and why the core values continue to be relevant. In new companies or companies having unspecified values, top management has to consider what values, behaviors, and business conduct should characterize the company and then draft a value statement that is circulated among managers and employees for discussion and possible modification. A final value statement that incorporates the desired behaviors and traits and that connects to the vision and mission is then officially adopted. Some companies combine their vision, mission, and values into a single statement or document, circulate it to all organization members, and in many instances post the vision, mission, and value statement on the company's Web site. Illustration Capsule 2.2 describes how core values and business principles drive the company's mission and approach to conducting business at Royal Dutch Shell.

STAGE 2: SETTING OBJECTIVES

LO 2

Understand the importance of setting both strategic and financial objectives.

The managerial purpose of setting **objectives** is to convert the vision and mission into specific performance targets. Well-stated objectives are *specific, quantifiable* or *measurable,* and contain a *deadline for achievement.* As Bill Hewlett, cofounder of Hewlett-Packard, shrewdly observed, "You cannot manage what you cannot measure. . . . And what gets measured gets done."[4] Concrete, measurable objectives are managerially valuable for three reasons: (1) They focus efforts and align actions throughout the organization, (2) they serve as *yardsticks* for tracking a company's performance and progress, and (3) they provide motivation and inspire employees to greater levels of effort. Ideally, managers should develop challenging yet achievable objectives that *stretch* an organization to perform at its full potential.

What Kinds of Objectives to Set

Two very distinct types of performance targets are required: those relating to financial performance and those relating to strategic performance. **Financial objectives** communicate management's targets for financial

CORE CONCEPT

Objectives are an organization's performance targets—the specific results management wants to achieve.

ILLUSTRATION CAPSULE 2.2

Royal Dutch Shell Mission, Core Values, and Business Principles

The mission of the Shell Group is to engage efficiently, responsibly and profitably in oil, gas, chemicals and other selected businesses and to participate in the search for and development of other sources of energy to meet evolving customer needs and the world's growing demand for energy. Our shared core values of honesty, integrity and respect for people underpin all the work we do and are the foundation of our Business Principles. The Business Principles drive the behavior expected of every employee in every Shell company in the conduct of its business at all times and living by them is crucial to our continued success.

OUR VALUES

Shell employees share a set of core values—honesty, integrity and respect for people. We also firmly believe in the fundamental importance of trust, openness, teamwork and professionalism, and pride in what we do.

OUR BUSINESS PRINCIPLES

1. **Economic:** Long-term profitability is essential to achieving our business goals and to our continued growth. It is a measure both of efficiency and of the value that customers place on Shell products and services. It supplies the necessary corporate resources for the continuing investment that is required to develop and produce future energy supplies to meet customer needs. Without profits and a strong financial foundation, it would not be possible to fulfill our responsibilities.

2. **Competition:** Shell companies support free enterprise. We seek to compete fairly and ethically and within the framework of applicable competition laws; we will not prevent others from competing freely with us.

3. **Business Integrity:** Shell companies insist on honesty, integrity and fairness in all aspects of our business and expect the same in our relationships with all those with whom we do business. The direct or indirect offer, payment, soliciting or acceptance of bribes in any form is unacceptable. Facilitation payments are also bribes and must not be made. Employees must avoid conflicts of interest between their private activities and their part in the conduct of company business. Employees must also declare to their employing company potential conflicts of interest. All business transactions on behalf of a Shell company must be reflected accurately and fairly in the accounts of the company in accordance with established procedures and are subject to audit and disclosure.

4. **Political Activities:** Shell companies act in a socially responsible manner within the laws of the countries in which we operate in pursuit of our legitimate commercial objectives. Shell companies do not make payments to political parties, organizations or their representatives. Shell companies do not take part in party politics. However, when dealing with governments, Shell companies have the right and the responsibility to make our position known on any matters, which affect us, our employees, our customers, our shareholders or local communities in a manner, which is in accordance with our values and the Business Principles.

5. **Health, Safety, Security and the Environment:** Shell companies have a systematic approach to health, safety, security and environmental management in order to achieve continuous performance improvement. To this end, Shell companies manage these matters as critical business activities, set standards and targets for improvement, and measure, appraise and report performance externally. We continually look for ways to reduce the environmental impact of our operations, products and services.

6. **Local Communities:** Shell companies aim to be good neighbors by continuously improving the ways in which we contribute directly or indirectly to the general well-being of the communities within which we work. We manage the social impacts of our business activities carefully and work with others to enhance the benefits to local communities, and to mitigate any negative impacts from our activities. In addition, Shell companies take a constructive interest in societal matters, directly or indirectly related to our business.

7. **Communication and Engagement:** Shell companies recognise that regular dialogue and engagement with our stakeholders is essential.

We are committed to reporting of our performance by providing full relevant information to
legitimately interested parties, subject to any
overriding considerations of business confidentiality. In our interactions with employees,
business partners and local communities, we

seek to listen and respond to them honestly and
responsibly.

8. **Compliance:** We comply with all applicable
laws and regulations of the countries in which
we operate.

Source: Information posted at www.shell.com/home/content/aboutshell/who_we_are/our_values/sgbp/ (accessed March 15, 2011).

performance. **Strategic objectives** are related to a company's marketing standing
and competitive vitality. Examples of commonly used financial and strategic
objectives include the following:

Financial Objectives	Strategic Objectives
• An *x* percent increase in annual revenues	• Winning an *x* percent market share
• Annual increases in after-tax profits *of x* percent	• Achieving lower overall costs than rivals
• Annual increases in earnings per share of *x* percent	• Overtaking key competitors on product performance or quality or customer service
• Annual dividend increases of *x* percent	• Deriving *x* percent of revenues from the sale of new products introduced within the past five years
• Profit margins of *x* percent	
• An *x* percent return on capital employed (ROCE) or return on shareholders' equity investment (ROE)	• Having broader or deeper technological capabilities than rivals
	• Having a wider product line than rivals
• Increased shareholder value—in the form of an upward-trending stock price	• Having a better-known or more powerful brand name than rivals
• Bond and credit ratings of *x*	• Having stronger national or global sales and distribution capabilities than rivals
• Internal cash flows of *x* dollars to fund new capital investment	• Consistently getting new or improved products to market ahead of rivals

The importance of setting and achieving financial objectives is intuitive. Without adequate profitability and financial strength, a company's
long-term health and ultimate survival are jeopardized. Furthermore,
subpar earnings and a weak balance sheet alarm shareholders and creditors and put the jobs of senior executives at risk. However, good financial
performance, by itself, is not enough.

The Balanced Scorecard: Improved Strategic Perfor-
mance Fosters Better Financial Performance

A com-
pany's financial performance measures are really *lagging indicators* that
reflect the results of past decisions and organizational activities.[5] But a
company's past or current financial performance is not a reliable indicator of its future prospects—poor financial performers often turn things
around and do better, while good financial performers can fall upon hard
times. The best and most reliable *leading indicators* of a company's future
financial performance and business prospects are strategic outcomes that
indicate whether the company's competitiveness and market position are

CORE CONCEPT

Financial objectives relate
to the financial performance
targets management
has established for the
organization to achieve.
Strategic objectives
relate to target outcomes
that indicate a company is
strengthening its market
standing, competitive
vitality, and future business
prospects.

stronger or weaker. The accomplishment of strategic objectives signals that the company is well positioned to sustain or improve its performance. For instance, if a company is achieving ambitious strategic objectives such that its competitive strength and market position are on the rise, then there's reason to expect that its *future* financial performance will be better than its current or past performance. If a company begins to lose competitive strength and fails to achieve important strategic objectives, then its ability to maintain its present profitability is highly suspect.

Consequently, utilizing a performance measurement system that strikes a *balance* between financial objectives and strategic objectives is optimal.[6] Just tracking a company's financial performance overlooks the fact that what ultimately enables a company to deliver better financial results from its operations is the achievement of strategic objectives that improve its competitiveness and market strength. Indeed, *the surest path to boosting company profitability* quarter after quarter and year after year *is to relentlessly pursue strategic outcomes* that strengthen the company's market position and produce a growing competitive advantage over rivals.

The most widely used framework for balancing financial objectives with strategic objectives is known as the **Balanced Scorecard.**[7] This is a method for linking financial performance objectives to specific strategic objectives that derive from a company's business model. It provides a company's employees with clear guidelines about how their jobs are linked to the overall objectives of the organization, so they can contribute most productively and collaboratively to the achievement of these goals. In 2008, nearly 60 percent of global companies used a balanced-scorecard approach to measuring strategic and financial performance.[8] Examples of organizations that have adopted a balanced-scorecard approach to setting objectives and measuring performance include UPS, UK Ministry of Defense, Caterpillar, Daimler AG, Hilton Hotels, and Siemens AG.[9] Illustration Capsule 2.3 provides selected strategic and financial objectives of three prominent companies.

> **CORE CONCEPT**
>
> The **Balanced Scorecard** is a tool that is widely used to help a company achieve its *financial objectives* by linking them to specific *strategic objectives* derived from the company's business model.

The Merits of Setting Stretch Objectives   Ideally, managers ought to use the objective-setting exercise as a tool for *stretching an organization to perform at its full potential and deliver the best possible results.* Challenging company personnel to go all out and deliver "stretch" gains in performance pushes an enterprise to be more inventive, to exhibit more urgency in improving both its financial performance and its business position, and to be more intentional and focused in its actions. Stretch objectives spur exceptional performance and help build a firewall against contentment with modest gains in organizational performance.

Why Both Short-Term and Long-Term Objectives Are Needed   A company's set of financial and strategic objectives should include both near-term and longer-term performance targets. Short-term (quarterly or annual) objectives focus attention on delivering performance improvements in the current period and satisfy shareholder expectations for near-term progress. Longer-term targets (three to five years off) force managers to consider what to do *now* to put the company in position to perform better later. Long-term objectives are critical for achieving optimal long-term performance and stand as a barrier to a nearsighted management philosophy and an undue focus on short-term results. When trade-offs have to be made between achieving long-run objectives and achieving short-run objectives, long-run objectives should

YUM! BRANDS (KFC, PIZZA HUT, TACO BELL, LONG JOHN SILVER'S)

Increase operating profit derived from international operations from 65% in 2010 to 75% in 2010; Increase operating profit derived from operations in emerging markets from 48% in 2010 to 60 percent in 2015; increase number of KFC units in Africa from 655 in 2010 to 2,100 in 2020; increase KFC revenues in Africa from $865 million in 2010 to $1.94 billion in 2014; increase number of KFC units in India from 101 in 2010 to 1,250 in 2020; increase number of KFC units in Vietnam from 87 in 2010 to 500 in 2020; increase number of KFC units in Russia from 150 in 2010 to 500 in 2020; open 100+ new Taco Bell units in international markets in 2015; increase annual cash flows from operations from $1.5 billion in 2010 to $2+ billion in 2015.

MICROSOFT

On a broad level, deliver end-to-end experiences that connect users to information, communications, entertainment, and people in new and compelling ways across their lives at home, at work, and the broadest-possible range of mobile scenarios. Given the dramatic changes in the way people interact with technology, as touch, gestures, handwriting, and speech recognition become a normal part of how we control devices, focus on making technology more accessible and simpler to use, which will create opportunities to reach new markets and deliver new kinds of computing experiences.

More specifically, grow revenue in the PC Division slightly faster than the overall PC market fueled especially by emerging market trends. Launch Office 2010 for the business market and promote adoption followed by a 2011 launch of the WindowsPhone 7 in the Entertainment and Devices Division. Grow annuity revenue between 4–6% in the Server and Tools Business segment. Target overall gross margin increases of 1% fueled in part by improved operational efficiency. Operating expenses are targeted at $26.1–$26.3 billion for the year with projected capital spending at $2 billion.

MCDONALD'S

Reinvest $2.4 billion in the business; 50% of this will be spent on opening 1,000 new restaurants around the world, including roughly 500 in Asia Pacific, 250 in Europe, and 150 in the U.S. The other half will be allocated toward "re-imagining" the décor and menu of over 2,000 existing locations. Re-imagining has a direct positive impact on sales as market share increases after re-imagining restaurants in the U.S., France and Australia demonstrate. Continue to expand refranchising; 80% of restaurants have been refranchised and this will be augmented by 200–300 restaurants in the next year. Focus on menu choice with a balance of familiar and popular core products as well as new items to keep products relevant.

Developed with C. David Morgan.

Sources: www.yum.com/investors/; "Microsoft Annual Report" www.microsoft.com/msft/reports/default.mspx (accessed April 23, 2010); "Microsoft Third Quarter Earnings Call," www.microsoft.com/msft/earnings/fy10/earn_rel_q3_10.mspx (accessed April 30, 2010); Thompson Reuters Street Events, "MCD – Q4 2009 McDonald's Corporate Earnings Conference Call," www.streetevents.com, January 2010 (transcribed version of Webcast accessed April 30, 2010, through InvesText database).

take precedence (unless the achievement of one or more short-run performance targets has unique importance).

The Need for Objectives at All Organizational Levels   Objective setting should not stop with top management's establishing of companywide performance targets. Company objectives need to be broken down into performance targets for each of the organization's separate businesses, product lines, functional departments, and individual work units. Company performance can't reach full potential unless each organizational unit sets and pursues performance targets that contribute directly to the desired companywide outcomes and results. Objective-setting is thus a *top-down process* that must extend to the lowest organizational levels. And it means that each organizational unit must take care to set performance targets that support—rather than conflict with or negate—the achievement of companywide strategic and financial objectives.

The ideal situation is a team effort in which each organizational unit strives to produce results in its area of responsibility that contribute to the achievement of the company's performance targets and strategic vision. Such consistency signals that organizational units know their strategic role and are on board in helping the company move down the chosen strategic path and produce the desired results.

STAGE 3: CRAFTING A STRATEGY

The task of stitching a strategy together entails addressing a series of hows: *how* to grow the business, *how* to please customers, *how* to outcompete rivals, *how* to respond to changing market conditions, *how* to manage each functional piece of the business, *how* to develop needed capabilities, and *how* to achieve strategic and financial objectives. It also means choosing among the various strategic alternatives—proactively searching for opportunities to do new things or to do existing things in new or better ways.[10] The faster a company's business environment is changing, the more critical it becomes for its managers to be good entrepreneurs in diagnosing the direction and force of the changes under way and in responding with timely adjustments in strategy. Strategy makers have to pay attention to early warnings of future change and be willing to experiment with dare-to-be-different ways to establish a market position in that future. When obstacles appear unexpectedly in a company's path, it is up to management to adapt rapidly and innovatively. *Masterful strategies come from doing things differently from competitors where it counts—out-innovating them, being more efficient, being more imaginative, adapting faster—rather than running with the herd.* Good strategy making is therefore inseparable from good business entrepreneurship. One cannot exist without the other.

LO 3

Understand why the strategic initiatives taken at various organizational levels must be tightly coordinated to achieve companywide performance targets.

Strategy Making Involves Managers at All Organizational Levels

A company's senior executives obviously have important strategy-making roles. The chief executive officer (CEO), as captain of the ship, carries the mantles of chief direction setter, chief objective setter, chief strategy maker, and chief strategy implementer for the total enterprise. Ultimate responsibility for *leading* the strategy-making, strategy-executing process rests with the CEO. In some enterprises the CEO or owner functions as strategic visionary and chief architect of strategy, personally deciding what the key elements of the company's strategy will be, although others may well assist with data gathering and analysis and the CEO may seek the advice of senior executives or board members. A CEO-centered approach to strategy development is characteristic of small owner-managed companies and sometimes large corporations that were founded by the present CEO or that have a CEO with strong strategic leadership skills. Steve Jobs at Apple, Andrea Jung at Avon, Carlos Ghosn at Nissan, and Howard Schultz at Starbucks are prominent examples of corporate CEOs who have wielded a heavy hand in shaping their company's strategy.

Even here, however, it is a mistake to view strategy making as a *top* management function, the exclusive province of owner-entrepreneurs, CEOs, other senior executives, and board members. The more a company's operations cut across different products, industries, and geographic areas, the more that headquarters executives have little option but to delegate considerable strategy-making authority to down-the-line managers in charge of particular subsidiaries, divisions, product lines, geographic sales offices, distribution centers, and plants. On-the-scene managers who oversee specific operating units can be reliably counted on to have more detailed command of the strategic issues and choices for the particular operating unit under their supervision—knowing the prevailing market and competitive conditions, customer requirements and expectations, and all the other relevant aspects affecting the several strategic options available. Managers with day-to-day familiarity of, and authority over, a specific operating unit thus have a big edge over headquarters executives in making wise strategic choices for their operating unit.

Take, for example, a company like General Electric, a $183 billion global corporation with 325,000 employees, operations in some 100 countries, and businesses that include jet engines, lighting, power generation, electric transmission and distribution equipment, housewares and appliances, medical equipment, media and entertainment, locomotives, security devices, water purification, and financial services. While top-level headquarters executives may well be personally involved in shaping GE's *overall* strategy and fashioning *important* strategic moves, it doesn't follow that a few senior executives in GE's headquarters have either the expertise or a sufficiently detailed understanding of all the relevant factors to wisely craft all the strategic initiatives taken for hundreds of subsidiaries and thousands of products. They simply cannot know enough about the situation in every GE organizational unit to decide on every strategy detail and direct every strategic move made in GE's worldwide organization. Rather, it takes involvement on the part of GE's whole management team—top executives, business group heads, the heads of specific business units and product categories, and key managers in plants, sales offices, and distribution centers—to craft the thousands of strategic initiatives that end up constituting the whole of GE's strategy.

The *level* of strategy also has a bearing on who participates in crafting strategy. In diversified companies, where multiple businesses have to be managed, the strategy-making task involves four distinct levels of strategy. Each of these involves different facets of the company's overall strategy and calls for the participation of different types of managers, as shown in Figure 2.2.

1. *Corporate strategy* is strategy at the multibusiness level—how to achieve a competitive edge through a multibusiness, multimarket strategy. It concerns

> **CORE CONCEPT**
>
> In most companies, crafting and executing strategy is a *collaborative team effort* in which every manager has a role for the area he or she heads. It is flawed thinking to view crafting and executing strategy as something only high-level managers do.

Figure 2.2   A Company's Strategy-Making Hierarchy

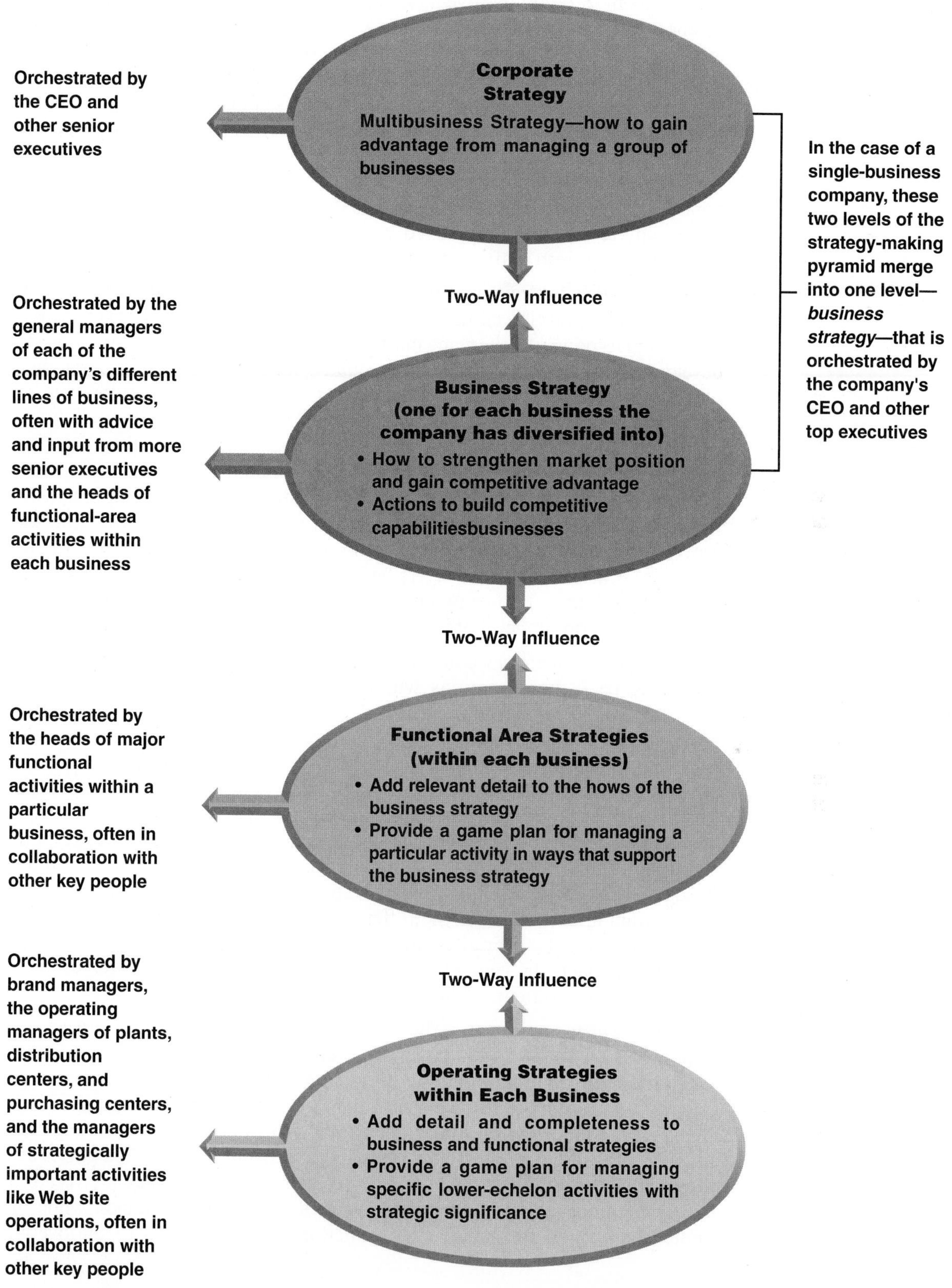

Orchestrated by the CEO and other senior executives

Corporate Strategy

Multibusiness Strategy—how to gain advantage from managing a group of businesses

In the case of a single-business company, these two levels of the strategy-making pyramid merge into one level— *business strategy*—that is orchestrated by the company's CEO and other top executives

Two-Way Influence

Orchestrated by the general managers of each of the company's different lines of business, often with advice and input from more senior executives and the heads of functional-area activities within each business

Business Strategy (one for each business the company has diversified into)

• How to strengthen market position and gain competitive advantage
• Actions to build competitive capabilitiesbusinesses

Two-Way Influence

Orchestrated by the heads of major functional activities within a particular business, often in collaboration with other key people

Functional Area Strategies (within each business)

• Add relevant detail to the hows of the business strategy
• Provide a game plan for managing a particular activity in ways that support the business strategy

Two-Way Influence

Orchestrated by brand managers, the operating managers of plants, distribution centers, and purchasing centers, and the managers of strategically important activities like Web site operations, often in collaboration with other key people

Operating Strategies within Each Business

• Add detail and completeness to business and functional strategies
• Provide a game plan for managing specific lower-echelon activities with strategic significance

how to boost the combined performance of *the set of businesses* the company has diversified into and the means of capturing cross-business synergies and turning them into competitive advantage. It addresses the questions of what businesses to hold or divest, which new markets to enter, and what mode of entry to employ (e.g., through an acquisition, strategic alliance, or franchising). It concerns the *scope* of the firm and thus includes diversification strategies, vertical integration strategies, and geographic expansion strategies. Senior corporate executives normally have lead responsibility for devising corporate strategy and for choosing among whatever recommended actions bubble up from the organization below. Key business-unit heads may also be influential regarding issues related to the businesses they head. Major strategic decisions are usually reviewed and approved by the company's board of directors. We will look deeper into crafting corporate strategy in Chapter 8.

2. *Business strategy* is strategy at the level of a single line of business—one that competes in a relatively well-defined industry or market domain. The key focus is on crafting responses to changing market circumstances and initiating actions to develop strong competitive capabilities, build competitive advantage, strengthen market position, and enhance performance. Orchestrating the development of business-level strategy is typically the responsibility of the manager in charge of the business, although corporate-level managers may be influential. The business head has at least two other strategy-related roles: (1) seeing that lower-level strategies are well conceived, consistent, and adequately matched to the overall business strategy and (2) getting major business-level strategic moves approved by corporate-level officers and keeping them informed of emerging strategic issues. In diversified companies, business-unit heads have the additional obligation of making sure business-level objectives and strategy conform to corporate-level objectives and strategy themes.

3. *Functional-area strategies* concern the actions and approaches employed in managing particular functions within a business—like R&D, production, sales and marketing, customer service, and finance. A company's marketing strategy, for example, represents the managerial game plan for running the sales and marketing part of the business. A company's product development strategy represents the game plan for keeping the company's product lineup in tune with what buyers are looking for. The primary role of functional strategies is to flesh out the details of a company's business strategy. Lead responsibility for functional strategies within a business is normally delegated to the heads of the respective functions, with the general manager of the business having final approval. Since the different functional-level strategies must be compatible with the overall business strategy and with one another to have beneficial impact, the general business manager may at times exert stronger influence on the content of the functional strategies.

4. *Operating strategies* concern the relatively narrow strategic initiatives and approaches for managing key operating units (e.g., plants, distribution centers, purchasing centers) and specific operating activities with strategic significance (e.g., quality control, materials purchasing, brand management, Internet sales). A distribution center manager of a company promising customers speedy delivery must have a strategy to ensure that finished goods are rapidly turned around and shipped out to customers once they are received from the company's manufacturing facilities. Operating strategies, while of limited scope, add further detail to functional strategies and to the overall

business strategy. Lead responsibility for operating strategies is usually delegated to frontline managers, subject to review and approval by higher-ranking managers.

Even though operating strategy is at the bottom of the strategy-making hierarchy, its importance should not be downplayed. A major plant that fails in its strategy to achieve production volume, unit cost, and quality targets can damage the company's reputation for quality products and undercut the achievement of company sales and profit objectives. Frontline managers are thus an important part of an organization's strategy-making team. One cannot reliably judge the strategic importance of a given action simply by the strategy level or location within the managerial hierarchy where it is initiated.

In single-business enterprises, the corporate and business levels of strategy making merge into one level—business strategy—because the strategy for the whole company involves only one distinct line of business. Thus a single-business enterprise has three levels of strategy: business strategy for the company as a whole, functional-area strategies for each main area within the business, and operating strategies undertaken by lower-echelon managers to flesh out strategically significant aspects of the company's business and functional-area strategies. Proprietorships, partnerships, and owner-managed enterprises may have only one or two strategy-making levels since their strategy-making process can be handled by just a few key people. The larger and more diverse the operations of an enterprise, the more points of strategic initiative it has and the more levels of management that have a significant strategy-making role.

The overall point is this: Regardless of the type of enterprise and whether the strategy is primarily deliberate or primarily emergent, crafting strategy involves managers in various positions and at various organizational levels. And while managers farther down in the managerial hierarchy obviously have a narrower, more specific strategy-making role than managers closer to the top, the important understanding is that in most of today's companies *every company manager typically has a strategy-making role—ranging from minor to major—for the area he or she heads.* Hence any notion that an organization's strategists are at the top of the management hierarchy and that midlevel and frontline personnel merely carry out the strategic directives of senior managers needs to be cast aside. In companies with wide-ranging operations, it is far more accurate to view strategy making as a *collaborative team effort* involving managers (and sometimes other key employees) down through the whole organizational hierarchy. A valuable strength of collaborative strategy making is that the team of people charged with crafting the strategy include the very people who will also be charged with implementing and executing it. Giving people an influential stake in crafting the strategy they must later help execute not only builds motivation and commitment but also enhances accountability at multiple levels of management—the excuse of "It wasn't my idea to do this" won't fly.

> In most companies, crafting strategy is a *collaborative team effort* that includes managers in various positions and at various organizational levels. Crafting strategy is rarely something only high-level executives do.

A Strategic Vision + Objectives + Strategy = A Strategic Plan

Developing a strategic vision and mission, setting objectives, and crafting a strategy are basic direction-setting tasks. They map out where a company is headed, its purpose, the targeted strategic and financial outcomes, the basic business model,

CORE CONCEPT

A company's **strategic plan** lays out its future direction and business purpose, performance targets, and strategy.

CORE CONCEPT

A company exhibits **strategic intent** when it relentlessly pursues an exceptionally ambitious strategic objective, committing to do whatever it takes to achieve the goals.

and the competitive moves and internal action approaches to be used in achieving the desired business results. Together, they constitute a **strategic plan** for coping with industry conditions, outcompeting rivals, meeting objectives, and making progress toward the strategic vision.[11] Typically, a strategic plan includes a commitment to allocate resources to the plan and specifies a time period for achieving goals (usually three to five years).

In some companies, the strategic plan is focused around achieving exceptionally bold strategic objectives—stretch goals requiring resources that are well beyond the current means of the company. This type of strategic plan is more the expression of a **strategic intent** to rally the organization through an *unshakable—often obsessive—commitment* to do whatever it takes to acquire the resources and achieve the goals. Nike's strategic intent during the 1960s was to overtake Adidas—an objective far beyond Nike's means at the time. Starbucks strategic intent is to make the Starbucks brand the world's most recognized and respected brand.

In companies that do regular strategy reviews and develop explicit strategic plans, the strategic plan usually ends up as a written document that is circulated to most managers and perhaps selected employees. Near-term performance targets are the part of the strategic plan most often spelled out explicitly and communicated to managers and employees. A number of companies summarize key elements of their strategic plans in the company's annual report to shareholders, in postings on their Web sites, or in statements provided to the business media, whereas others, perhaps for reasons of competitive sensitivity, make only vague, general statements about their strategic plans.[12] In small, privately owned companies, it is rare for strategic plans to exist in written form. Small-company strategic plans tend to reside in the thinking and directives of owners/executives, with aspects of the plan being revealed in meetings and conversations with company personnel, and in the understandings and commitments among managers and key employees about where to head, what to accomplish, and how to proceed.

STAGE 4: EXECUTING THE STRATEGY

LO 4

Become aware of what a company must do to achieve operating excellence and to execute its strategy proficiently.

Managing the implementation of a strategy is an operations-oriented, make-things-happen activity aimed at performing core business activities in a strategy-supportive manner. It is easily the most demanding and time-consuming part of the strategy management process. Converting strategic plans into actions and results tests a manager's ability to direct organizational action, motivate people, build and strengthen company competencies and competitive capabilities, create and nurture a strategy-supportive work climate, and meet or beat performance targets. Initiatives to put the strategy in place and execute it proficiently have to be launched and managed on many organizational fronts.

Management's action agenda for executing the chosen strategy emerges from assessing what the company will have to do to achieve the targeted financial and strategic performance. Each company manager has to think through the answer to "What has to be done in my area to execute my piece of the strategic plan, and what actions should I take to get the process under way?" How much internal change is needed depends on how much of the strategy is new, how far internal practices and competencies deviate from what the strategy requires, and how well the present work climate/culture supports good strategy execution. Depending on the amount of internal change involved, full implementation and proficient execution of company strategy (or important new pieces thereof) can take several months to several years.

In most situations, managing the strategy execution process includes the following principal aspects:

- Staffing the organization with the needed skills and expertise.
- Building and strengthening strategy-supporting resources and competitive capabilities.
- Organizing the work effort along the lines of best practice.
- Allocating ample resources to the activities critical to strategic success.
- Ensuring that policies and procedures facilitate rather than impede effective strategy execution.
- Installing information and operating systems that enable company personnel to carry out their roles effectively and efficiently.
- Motivating people and tying rewards and incentives directly to the achievement of performance objectives.
- Creating a company culture and work climate conducive to successful strategy execution.
- Exerting the internal leadership needed to propel implementation forward and drive continuous improvement of the strategy execution processes.

Good strategy execution requires diligent pursuit of operating excellence. It is a job for a company's whole management team. Success hinges on the skills and cooperation of operating managers who can push for needed changes in their organizational units and consistently deliver good results. Management's handling of the strategy implementation process can be considered successful if things go smoothly enough that the company meets or beats its strategic and financial performance targets and shows good progress in achieving management's strategic vision.

STAGE 5: EVALUATING PERFORMANCE AND INITIATING CORRECTIVE ADJUSTMENTS

The fifth component of the strategy management process—monitoring new external developments, evaluating the company's progress, and making corrective adjustments—is the trigger point for deciding whether to continue or change the company's vision and mission, objectives, strategy, and/or strategy execution methods.[13] As long as the company's strategy continues to pass the three tests of a winning strategy (good fit, competitive advantage, strong performance), company executives may well decide to stay the course. Simply fine-tuning the strategic plan and continuing with efforts to improve strategy execution are sufficient.

However, whenever a company encounters disruptive changes in its environment, questions need to be raised about the appropriateness of its direction and strategy. If a company experiences a downturn in its market position or

A company's vision and mission, objectives, strategy, and approach to strategy execution are never final; managing strategy is an ongoing process.

persistent shortfalls in performance, then company managers are obligated to ferret out the causes—do they relate to poor strategy, poor strategy execution, or both?—and take timely corrective action. A company's direction, objectives, and strategy have to be revisited anytime external or internal conditions warrant. It is to be expected that a company will modify its strategic vision, direction, objectives, and strategy over time.

Likewise, it is not unusual for a company to find that one or more aspects of its strategy execution are not going as well as intended. Proficient strategy execution is always the product of much organizational learning. It is achieved unevenly—coming quickly in some areas and proving nettlesome in others. It is both normal and desirable to periodically assess strategy execution to determine which aspects are working well and which need improving. Successful strategy execution entails vigilantly searching for ways to improve and then making corrective adjustments whenever and wherever it is useful to do so.

CORPORATE GOVERNANCE: THE ROLE OF THE BOARD OF DIRECTORS IN THE STRATEGY-CRAFTING, STRATEGY-EXECUTING PROCESS

LO 5

Become aware of the role and responsibility of a company's board of directors in overseeing the strategic management process.

Although senior managers have *lead responsibility* for crafting and executing a company's strategy, it is the duty of a company's board of directors to exercise strong oversight and see that the five tasks of strategic management are conducted in a manner that is in the best interests of shareholders and other stakeholders.[14] A company's board of directors has four important obligations to fulfill:

1. *Critically appraise the company's direction, strategy, and business approaches.* Board members must ask probing questions and draw on their business acumen to make independent judgments about whether strategy proposals have been adequately analyzed and whether proposed strategic actions appear to have greater promise than alternatives. Asking incisive questions is usually sufficient to test whether the case for management's proposals is compelling and to exercise vigilant oversight. However, when the company's strategy is failing or is plagued with faulty execution, and certainly when there is a precipitous collapse in profitability, board members have a duty to be more proactive, expressing their concerns about the validity of the strategy and/or operating methods, initiating debate about the company's strategic path, having one-on-one discussions with key executives and other board members, and perhaps directly intervening as a group to alter the company's executive leadership and, ultimately, its strategy and business approaches.

2. *Evaluate the caliber of senior executives' strategic leadership skills.* The board is always responsible for determining whether the current CEO is doing a good job of strategic leadership.[15] The board must also evaluate the leadership skills of other senior executives, since the board must elect a successor when the incumbent CEO steps down, either going with an insider

or deciding that an outsider is needed. Evaluation of senior executives' skills is enhanced when outside directors visit company facilities and talk with company personnel to personally evaluate whether the strategy is on track, how well the strategy is being executed, and how well issues and problems are being addressed. Independent board members at GE visit operating executives at each major business unit once a year to assess the company's talent pool and stay abreast of emerging strategic and operating issues affecting the company's divisions.

3. *Institute a compensation plan for top executives that rewards them for actions and results that serve stakeholder interests—especially those of shareholders.* A basic principle of corporate governance is that the owners of a corporation (the shareholders) delegate managerial control to a team of executives who are compensated for their efforts on behalf of the owners. In their role as an *agent* of shareholders, corporate managers have a clear and unequivocal duty to make decisions and operate the company in accord with shareholder interests. (This does not mean disregarding the interests of other stakeholders—employees, suppliers, the communities in which the company operates, and society at large.) Most boards of directors have a compensation committee, composed entirely of directors from *outside* the company, to develop a salary and incentive compensation plan that rewards senior executives for boosting the company's *long-term* performance and growing the economic value of the enterprise on behalf of shareholders; the compensation committee's recommendations are presented to the full board for approval. But during the past 10 to 15 years, many boards of directors have done a poor job of ensuring that executive salary increases, bonuses, and stock option awards are tied tightly to performance measures that are truly in the long-term interests of shareholders. Rather, compensation packages at many companies have increasingly rewarded executives for short-term performance improvements that led to undue risk taking and compensation packages that, in the view of many people, were obscenely large. This has proved damaging to long-term company performance and has worked against shareholder interests—witness the huge loss of shareholder wealth that occurred at many financial institutions in 2008–2009 because of executive risk taking in subprime loans, credit default swaps, and collateralized mortgage securities in 2006–2007. As a consequence, the need to overhaul and reform executive compensation has become a hot topic in both public circles and corporate boardrooms. Illustration Capsule 2.4 discusses how weak governance at the U.S. mortgage companies Fannie Mae and Freddie Mac allowed opportunistic senior managers to boost their compensation while making decisions that imperiled the futures of the companies they managed.

4. *Oversee the company's financial accounting and financial reporting practices.* While top executives, particularly the company's CEO and CFO (chief financial officer), are primarily responsible for seeing that the company's financial statements fairly and accurately report the results of the company's operations, board members have a fiduciary duty to protect shareholders by exercising oversight of the company's financial practices. In addition, corporate boards must ensure that generally acceptable accounting principles are properly used in preparing the company's financial statements and that proper financial controls are in place to

Corporate Governance Failures at Fannie Mae and Freddie Mac

Executive compensation in the financial services industry during the mid-2000s ranks high among examples of failed corporate governance. Corporate governance at the U.S. government-sponsored mortgage giants Fannie Mae and Freddie Mac was particularly weak. The politically appointed boards at both enterprises failed to understand the risks of the subprime loan strategies being employed, did not adequately monitor the decisions of the CEO, did not exercise effective oversight of the accounting principles being employed (which led to inflated earnings), and approved executive compensation systems that allowed management to manipulate earnings to receive lucrative performance bonuses. The audit and compensation committees at Fannie Mae were particularly ineffective in protecting shareholder interests, with the audit committee allowing the company's financial officers to audit reports prepared under their direction and used to determine performance bonuses. Fannie Mae's audit committee also was aware of management's use of questionable accounting practices that reduced losses and recorded one-time gains to achieve financial targets linked to bonuses. In addition, the audit committee failed to investigate formal charges of accounting improprieties filed by a manager in the U.S. Office of the Controller.

Fannie Mae's compensation committee was equally ineffective. The committee allowed the company's CEO, Franklin Raines, to select the consultant employed to design the mortgage firm's executive compensation plan and agreed to a tiered bonus plan that would permit Raines and other senior managers to receive maximum bonuses without great difficulty. The compensation plan allowed Raines to earn performance-based bonuses of $52 million and total compensation of $90 million between 1999 and 2004. Raines was forced to resign in December 2004 when the U.S. Office of Federal Housing Enterprise Oversight found that Fannie Mae executives had fraudulently inflated earnings to receive bonuses linked to financial performance. Securities and Exchange Commission investigators also found evidence of improper accounting at Fannie Mae and required the company to restate its earnings between 2002 and 2004 by $6.3 billion.

Poor governance at Freddie Mac allowed its CEO and senior management to manipulate financial data to receive performance-based compensation as well. Freddie Mac CEO Richard Syron received 2007 compensation of $19.8 million while the mortgage company's share price declined from a high of $70 in 2005 to $25 at year-end 2007. During Syron's tenure as CEO, the company became embroiled in a multibillion-dollar accounting scandal, and Syron personally disregarded internal reports dating to 2004 that cautioned of an impending financial crisis at the company. Forewarnings within Freddie Mac and by federal regulators and outside industry observers proved to be correct, with loan underwriting policies at Freddie Mac and Fannie Mae leading to combined losses at the two firms in 2008 of more than $100 billion. The price of

(continued)

Freddie Mac's shares had fallen to below $1 by the time of Syron's resignation in September 2008.

Both organizations were placed into a conservatorship under the direction of the U.S. government in September 2008 and were provided bailout funds of nearly $60 billion by April 2009. In May 2009, Fannie Mae requested another $19 billion of the $200 billion committed by the U.S. government to cover the operating losses of the two government-sponsored mortgage firms. By June 2010, the bill for bailing out the two enterprises had risen to $145 billion, with the expectation that still more aid would be required to get them back on sound financial footing.

Sources: "Adding Up the Government's Total Bailout Tab," *New York Times Online,* February 4, 2009; Eric Dash, "Fannie Mae to Restate Results by $6.3 Billion because of Accounting," *New York Times Online,* December 7, 2006; Annys Shin, "Fannie Mae Sets Executive Salaries," *Washington Post,* February 9, 2006, p. D4; Scott DeCarlo, Eric Weiss, Mark Jickling, James R. Cristie, *Fannie Mae and Freddie Mac: Scandal in U.S. Housing* (Nova, 2006), pp. 266–86; "Chaffetz, Conyers, Smith, Issa and Bachus Call for FOIA to Apply to Fannie-Freddie," June 17, 2010 (June 2010 Archives), http://chaffetz.house.gov/2010/06/ (accessed June 24, 2010).

prevent fraud and misuse of funds. Virtually all boards of directors have an audit committee, always composed entirely of *outside directors* (*inside directors* hold management positions in the company and either directly or indirectly report to the CEO). The members of the audit committee have lead responsibility for overseeing the decisions of the company's financial officers and consulting with both internal and external auditors to ensure that financial reports are accurate and that adequate financial controls are in place. Faulty oversight of corporate accounting and financial reporting practices by audit committees and corporate boards during the early 2000s resulted in the investigation of more than 20 major corporations between 2000 and 2002. The investigations of such well-known companies as Global Crossing, Enron, Qwest Communications, Parmalat, and WorldCom found that upper management had employed fraudulent or unsound accounting practices to artificially inflate revenues, overstate assets, and reduce expenses.

Every corporation should have a strong, independent board of directors that (1) is well informed about the company's performance, (2) guides and judges the CEO and other top executives, (3) has the courage to curb management actions the board believes are inappropriate or unduly risky, (4) certifies to shareholders that the CEO is doing what the board expects, (5) provides insight and advice to management, and (6) is intensely involved in debating the pros and cons of key decisions and actions.[16] Boards of directors that lack the backbone to challenge a strong-willed or "imperial" CEO or that rubber-stamp almost anything the CEO recommends without probing inquiry and debate (perhaps because the board is stacked with the CEO's cronies) abdicate their duty to represent and protect shareholder interests.

Effective corporate governance requires the board of directors to oversee the company's strategic direction, evaluate its senior executives, handle executive compensation, and oversee financial reporting practices.

KEY POINTS

The strategic management process consists of five interrelated and integrated stages:

1. *Developing a strategic vision* of the company's future, a *mission* that defines the company's current purpose, and a set of *core values* to guide the pursuit of the vision and mission. This managerial step provides direction for the company, motivates and inspires company personnel, aligns and guides actions throughout the organization, and communicates to stakeholders management's aspirations for the company's future.

2. *Setting objectives* to convert the vision and mission into performance targets and using the targeted results as yardsticks for measuring the company's performance. Objectives need to spell out *how much* of *what kind* of performance *by when.* Two broad types of objectives are required: *financial objectives* and *strategic objectives.* A *balanced-scorecard* approach provides a popular method for linking financial objectives to specific, measurable strategic objectives.

3. *Crafting a strategy* to achieve the objectives and move the company along the strategic course that management has charted. Crafting deliberate strategy calls for strategic analysis, based on the business model. Crafting emergent strategy is a learning-by-doing process involving experimentation. Who participates in the process of crafting strategy depends on (1) whether the process is emergent or deliberate and (2) the level of strategy concerned. Deliberate strategies are mostly top-down, while emergent strategies are bottom-up, although both cases require two-way interaction between different types of managers. In large, diversified companies, there are four levels of strategy, each of which involves a corresponding level of management: corporate strategy (multibusiness strategy), business strategy (strategy for individual businesses that compete in a single industry), functional-area strategies within each business (e.g., marketing, R&D, logistics), and operating strategies (for key operating units, such as manufacturing plants). Thus, strategy making is an inclusive, collaborative activity involving not only senior company executives but also the heads of major business divisions, functional-area managers, and operating managers on the frontlines. The larger and more diverse the operations of an enterprise, the more points of strategic initiative it has and the more levels of management that play a significant strategy-making role.

4. *Executing the chosen strategy* and converting the strategic plan into action. Managing the execution of strategy is an operations-oriented, make-things-happen activity aimed at shaping the performance of core business activities in a strategy-supportive manner. Management's handling of the strategy implementation process can be considered successful if things go smoothly enough that the company meets or beats its strategic and financial performance targets and shows good progress in achieving management's strategic vision.

5. *Monitoring developments, evaluating performance, and initiating corrective adjustments* in light of actual experience, changing conditions, new ideas, and new opportunities. This stage of the strategy management process is the trigger point for deciding whether to continue or change the company's vision and mission, objectives, strategy, and/or strategy execution methods.

The sum of a company's strategic vision and mission, objectives, and strategy constitutes a *strategic plan* for coping with industry conditions, outcompeting rivals, meeting objectives, and making progress toward the strategic vision. A company whose strategic plan is based around ambitious *stretch goals* that require an unwavering commitment to do whatever it takes to achieve them is said to have *strategic intent.*

Boards of directors have a duty to shareholders to play a vigilant role in overseeing management's handling of a company's strategy-making, strategy-executing process. This entails four important obligations: (1) Critically appraise the company's direction, strategy, and strategy execution, (2) evaluate the caliber of senior executives' strategic leadership skills, (3) institute a compensation plan for top executives that rewards them for actions and results that serve stakeholder interests—*especially those of shareholders,* and (4) ensure that the company issues accurate financial reports and has adequate financial controls.

ASSURANCE OF LEARNING EXERCISES

LO 1

1. Using the information in Table 2.1, critique the adequacy and merit of the following vision statements, listing effective elements and shortcomings. Rank the vision statements from best to worst once you complete your evaluation.

Vision Statement	Effective Elements	Shortcomings
BASF We are "The Chemical Company" successfully operating in all major markets. • Our customers view BASF as their partner of choice. • Our innovative products, intelligent solutions and services make us the most competent worldwide supplier in the chemical industry. • We generate a high return on assets. • We strive for Sustainable Development. • We welcome change as an opportunity. • We, the employees of BASF, together ensure our success.		
Hilton Hotels Corporation Our vision is to be the first choice of the world's travelers. Hilton intends to build on the rich heritage and strength of our brands by: • Consistently delighting our customers • Investing in our team members • Delivering innovative products and services • Continuously improving performance • Increasing shareholder value • Creating a culture of pride • Strengthening the loyalty of our constituents		
Bank of China To be customer's premier bank.		

(continued)

Vision Statement	Effective Elements	Shortcomings

Rio Tinto

Our vision of being the global mining leader means maintaining or achieving sector leadership, including operational excellence, sustainable development, exploration and innovation.

Chevron

To be *the* global energy company most admired for its people, partnership and performance. Our vision means we:

- provide energy products vital to sustainable economic progress and human development throughout the world;
- are people and an organization with superior capabilities and commitment;
- are the partner of choice;
- deliver world-class performance;
- earn the admiration of all our stakeholders—investors, customers, host governments, local communities and our employees—not only for the goals we achieve but how we achieve them.

Source: Company Web sites and annual reports.

LO 2

2. Review the analyst presentations and other reports at the company investor relations Web sites for Intel (www.intc.com), Lufthansa (http://investor-relations.lufthansa.com), and Tata Motors (http://ir.tatamotors.com) to find some examples of strategic and financial objectives. Make a list of four objectives for each company, and indicate which of these are strategic and which are financial.

LO 5

3. Go to www.dell.com/leadership, and read the sections dedicated to Dell's board of directors and corporate governance. Is there evidence of effective governance at Dell in regard to (1) accurate financial reports and controls, (2) a critical appraisal of strategic action plans, (3) evaluation of the strategic leadership skills of the CEO, and (4) executive compensation?

EXERCISES FOR SIMULATION PARTICIPANTS

LO 1, LO 2, LO 3

1. Meet with your co-managers and prepare a strategic vision statement for your company. It should be at least one sentence long and no longer than a brief paragraph. When you are finished, check to see if your vision statement is in compliance with the dos and don'ts set forth in Table 2.1. If not, revise it accordingly. What would be a good slogan that captures the essence of your strategic vision and that could be used to help communicate the vision to company personnel, shareholders, and other stakeholders?

2. What is your company's strategic intent? Write a sentence that expresses your company's strategic intent.

3. What are your company's financial objectives?

4. What are your company's strategic objectives?

5. What are the three or four key elements of your company's strategy?

ENDNOTES

[1] For a more in-depth discussion of the challenges of developing a well-conceived vision, as well as some good examples, see Hugh Davidson, *The Committed Enterprise: How to Make Vision and Values Work* (Oxford: Butterworth Heinemann, 2002), chap. 2; W. Chan Kim and Renée Mauborgne, "Charting Your Company's Future," *Harvard Business Review* 80, no. 6 (June 2002), pp. 77–83; James C. Collins and Jerry I. Porras, "Building Your Company's Vision," *Harvard Business Review* 74, no. 5 (September–October 1996), pp. 65–77; Jim Collins and Jerry Porras, *Built to Last: Successful Habits of Visionary Companies* (New York: HarperCollins, 1994), chap. 11; Michel Robert, *Strategy Pure and Simple II: How Winning Companies Dominate Their Competitors* (New York: McGraw-Hill, 1998), chaps. 2, 3 and 6.

[2] Davidson, *The Committed Enterprise,* pp. 20 and 54.

[3] Ibid., pp. 36, 54.

[4] As quoted in Charles H. House and Raymond L. Price, "The Return Map: Tracking Product Teams," *Harvard Business Review* 60, no. 1 (January–February 1991), p. 93.

[5] Robert S. Kaplan and David P. Norton, *The Strategy-Focused Organization* (Boston: Harvard Business School Press, 2001), p. 3. Also see Robert S. Kaplan and David P. Norton, *The Balanced Scorecard: Translating Strategy into Action* (Boston: Harvard Business School Press, 1996), chap. 1.

[6] Kaplan and Norton, p.7. Also see Kevin B. Hendricks, Larry Menor, and Christine Wiedman, "The Balanced Scorecard: To Adopt or Not to Adopt," *Ivey Business Journal* 69, no. 2 (November–December 2004), pp. 1–7; Sandy Richardson, "The Key Elements of Balanced Scorecard Success," *Ivey Business Journal*

69, no. 2 (November–December 2004), pp.7–9.

[7] Kaplan and Norton, *The Balanced Scorecard.*

[8] Information posted on the Web site of Bain and Company, www.bain.com (accessed May 27, 2009).

[9] Information posted on the Web site of Balanced Scorecard Institute, http://www.balancedscorecard.org/ (accessed May 27, 2009).

[10] For a fuller discussion of strategy as an entrepreneurial process, see Henry Mintzberg, Bruce Ahlstrand, and Joseph Lampel, *Strategy Safari: A Guided Tour through the Wilds of Strategic Management* (New York: Free Press, 1998), chap. 5. Also see Bruce Barringer and Allen C. Bluedorn, "The Relationship between Corporate Entrepreneurship and Strategic Management," *Strategic Management Journal* 20 (1999), pp. 421–44; Jeffrey G. Covin and Morgan P. Miles, "Corporate Entrepreneurship and the Pursuit of Competitive Advantage," *Entrepreneurship: Theory and Practice* 23, no. 3 (Spring 1999), pp. 47–63; David A. Garvin and Lynned C. Levesque, "Meeting the Challenge of Corporate Entrepreneurship," *Harvard Business Review* 84, no. 10 (October 2006), pp. 102–12.

[11] For an excellent discussion of why a strategic plan needs to be more than a list of bullet points and should in fact tell an engaging, insightful, stage-setting story that lays out the industry and competitive situation as well as the vision, objectives, and strategy, see Gordon Shaw, Robert Brown, and Philip Bromiley, "Strategic Stories: How 3M Is Rewriting Business Planning," *Harvard Business Review* 76, no. 3 (May–June 1998), pp. 41–50.

[12] In many companies, there is often confusion or ambiguity about exactly what a company's strategy is; see David J. Collis and Michael G. Rukstad, "Can You Say What Your Strategy Is?" *Harvard Business Review* 86, no. 4 (April 2008), pp. 82–90.

[13] For an excellent discussion of why effective strategic leadership on the part of senior executives involves continuous re-creation of a company's strategy, see Cynthia A. Montgomery, "Putting Leadership Back into Strategy," *Harvard Business Review* 86, no. 1 (January 2008), pp. 54–60.

[14] For a timely and insightful discussion of the strategic and leadership functions of a company's board of directors, see Jay W. Lorsch and Robert C. Clark, "Leading from the Boardroom," *Harvard Business Review* 86, no. 4 (April 2008), pp. 105–11.

[15] For a deeper discussion of this function, see Stephen P. Kaufman, "Evaluating the CEO," *Harvard Business Review* 86, no. 10 (October 2008), pp. 53–57.

[16] For a discussion of what it takes for the corporate governance system to function properly, see David A. Nadler, "Building Better Boards," *Harvard Business Review* 82, no. 5 (May 2004), pp. 102–5; Cynthia A. Montgomery and Rhonda Kaufman, "The Board's Missing Link," *Harvard Business Review* 81, no. 3 (March 2003), pp. 86–93; John Carver, "What Continues to Be Wrong with Corporate Governance and How to Fix It," *Ivey Business Journal* 68, no. 1 (September–October 2003), pp. 1–5. See also Gordon Donaldson, "A New Tool for Boards: The Strategic Audit," *Harvard Business Review* 73, no. 4 (July–August 1995), pp. 99–107.

CHAPTER 3

EVALUATING A COMPANY'S EXTERNAL ENVIRONMENT

Analysis is the critical starting point of strategic thinking.

—Kenichi Ohmae
Consultant and Author

Things are always different—the art is figuring out which differences matter.

—Laszlo Birinyi
Investments Manager

In essence, the job of a strategist is to understand and cope with competition.

—Michael Porter
Harvard Business School professor and Cofounder of Monitor Consulting

LEARNING OBJECTIVES

LO 1. Gain command of the basic concepts and analytical tools widely used to diagnose the competitive conditions in a company's industry.

LO 2. Learn how to diagnose the factors shaping industry dynamics and to forecast their effects on future industry profitability.

LO 3. Become adept at mapping the market positions of key groups of industry rivals.

LO 4. Understand why in-depth evaluation of a business's strengths and weaknesses in relation to the specific industry conditions it confronts is an essential prerequisite to crafting a strategy that is well-matched to its external situation.

n Chapter 1, we learned that one of the three central questions that managers must address in evaluating their business prospects is "What's the company's present situation?" Two facets of a company's situation are especially pertinent: (1) competitive conditions in the industry in which the company operates—its external environment; and (2) the company's resources and organizational capabilities—its internal environment.

Insightful diagnosis of a company's external and internal environments is a prerequisite for managers to succeed in crafting a strategy that is an excellent *fit* with the company's situation—the first test of a winning strategy. As depicted in Figure 3.1, the task of crafting a strategy should always begin with an appraisal of the company's external environment and internal environment (as a basis for deciding on a long-term direction and developing a strategic vision), then move toward an evaluation of the most promising alternative strategies and business models, and culminate in choosing a specific strategy.

This chapter presents the concepts and analytical tools for zeroing in on those aspects of a company's external environment that should be considered in making strategic choices about where and how to compete. Attention centers on the competitive arena in which a company operates, the drivers of market change, the market positions of rival companies, and the factors that determine competitive success. In Chapter 4 we explore the methods of evaluating a company's internal circumstances and competitive capabilities.

Figure 3.1   **From Thinking Strategically about the Company's Situation to Choosing a Strategy**

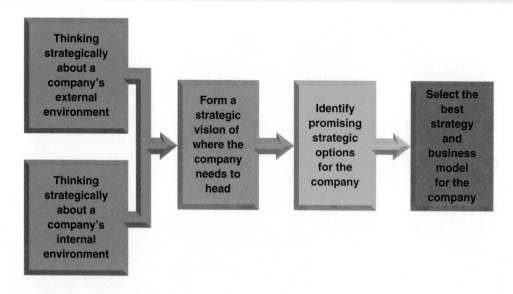

THE STRATEGICALLY RELEVANT COMPONENTS OF A COMPANY'S MACRO-ENVIRONMENT

Every company operates in a larger environment that goes well beyond just the industry in which it operates; this **"macro-environment"** includes seven principal components: population demographics; societal values and lifestyles; political, legal, and regulatory factors; the natural environment and ecological factors; technological factors; general economic conditions; and global forces. Each of these components has the potential to affect the firm's more immediate industry and competitive environment, although some are likely to have a more important effect than others (see Figure 3.2). Since macroeconomic factors affect different industries in different ways and to different degrees, it is important for managers to determine which of these represent the most *strategically relevant factors* outside the firm's industry boundaries. By *strategically relevant,* we mean important enough to have a bearing on the decisions the company ultimately makes about its direction, objectives, strategy, and business model. Strategically relevant influences coming from the outer ring of the external environment can sometimes have a high impact on a company's business situation and have a very significant impact on the company's direction and strategy. For example, the strategic opportunities of cigarette producers to grow their businesses are greatly reduced by antismoking ordinances, the decisions of governments to impose higher cigarette taxes, and the growing cultural stigma attached to smoking. Motor vehicle companies must adapt their strategies to customer concerns about high gasoline prices and to environmental concerns about

CORE CONCEPT

The **macro-environment** encompasses the broad environmental context in which a company's industry is situated.

Figure 3.2 The Components of a Company's Macro-Environment

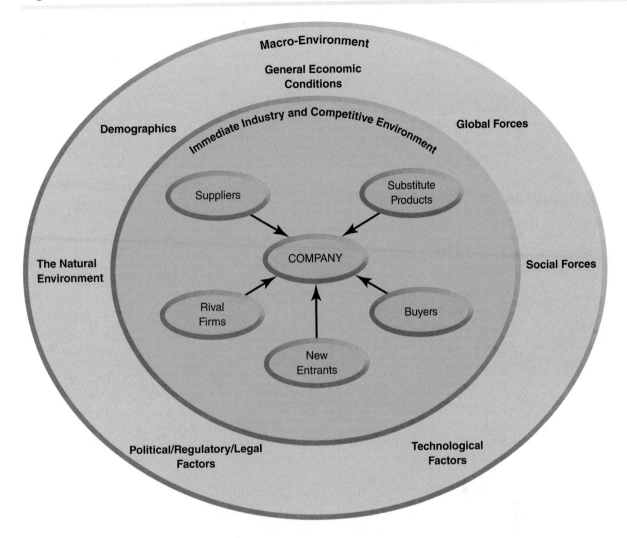

carbon emissions. Companies in the food processing, restaurant, sports, and fitness industries have to pay special attention to changes in lifestyles, eating habits, leisure-time preferences, and attitudes toward nutrition and fitness in fashioning their strategies. Table 3.1 provides a brief description of the components of the macro-environment and some examples of the industries or business situations that they might affect.

Happenings in the outer ring of the environment may occur rapidly or slowly, with or without advance warning. As company managers scan the external environment, they must be alert for potentially important outer-ring developments, assess their impact and influence, and adapt the company's direction and strategy as needed. However, the factors and forces in a company's environment having the *biggest* strategy-shaping impact typically pertain to the company's immediate industry and competitive environment—competitive pressures, the actions of rival firms, buyer behavior, supplier-related considerations, and so on. Consequently, it is on a company's industry and competitive environment that we concentrate the bulk of our attention in this chapter.

Table 3.1   **The Seven Components of the Macro-Environment**

Component	Description
Demographics	Demographics includes the size, growth rate, and age distribution of different sectors of the population. It includes the geographic distribution of the population, the distribution of income across the population, and trends in these factors. Population demographics can have large implications for industries such as health care, where costs and service needs vary with demographic factors such as age and income distribution.
Social forces	Social forces include the societal values, attitudes, cultural factors, and lifestyles that impact businesses. Social forces vary by locale and change over time. An example includes the attitudes toward gender roles and diversity in the workforce. Another example is the trend toward healthier lifestyles, which can shift spending toward exercise equipment and health clubs and away from alcohol and snack foods.
Political, legal, and regulatory factors	These factors include political policies and processes, as well as the regulations and laws with which companies must comply. Examples include labor laws, antitrust laws, tax policy, regulatory policies, the political climate, and the strength of institutions such as the court system. Some political factors, such as banking deregulation, are industry-specific. Others, such as minimum wage legislation, affect certain types of industries (low-wage, labor-intensive industries) more than others.
Natural environment	This includes ecological and environmental forces such as weather, climate, climate change, and associated factors like water shortages. These factors can directly impact industries such as insurance, farming, energy production, and tourism. They may have an indirect but substantial effect on other industries such as transportation and utilities.
Technological factors	Technological factors include the pace of technological change and technical developments that have the potential for wide-ranging effects on society, such as genetic engineering, the rise of the Internet, and changes in communication technologies. They include activities and institutions involved in creating new knowledge and controlling the use of technology, such as R&D consortia, university-sponsored technology incubators, patent and copyright laws, and government control over the Internet. Technological change can encourage the birth of new industries, such as those based on nanotechnology, and disrupt others, such as the recording industry.
Global forces	Global forces include conditions and changes in global markets, including political events and policies toward international trade. They also include sociocultural practices and the institutional environment in which global markets operate. Global forces influence the degree of international trade and investment through such mechanisms as trade barriers, tariffs, import restrictions, and trade sanctions. Their effects are often industry-specific, such as import restrictions on steel.
General economic conditions	General economic conditions include economic factors at the local, state, national, or international level that affect firms and industries. These include the rate of economic growth, unemployment rates, inflation rates, interest rates, trade deficits or surpluses, savings rates, and per capita domestic product. Economic factors also include conditions in the markets for stocks and bonds, which can affect consumer confidence and discretionary income. Some industries, such as construction, are particularly vulnerable to economic downturns but are positively affected by factors such as low interest rates. Others, such as discount retailing, may benefit when general economic conditions weaken, as consumers become more price-conscious.

THINKING STRATEGICALLY ABOUT A COMPANY'S INDUSTRY AND COMPETITIVE ENVIRONMENT

To gain a deep understanding of a company's industry and competitive environment, managers do not need to gather all the information they can find and spend lots of time digesting it. Rather, they can focus more directly on using some well-defined concepts and analytical tools to get clear answers to seven questions:

1. Does the industry offer attractive opportunities for growth?
2. What kinds of competitive forces are industry members facing, and how strong is each force?
3. What factors are driving changes in the industry, and what impact will these changes have on competitive intensity and industry profitability?
4. What market positions do industry rivals occupy—who is strongly positioned and who is not?
5. What strategic moves are rivals likely to make next?
6. What are the key factors for competitive success in the industry?
7. Does the industry offer good prospects for attractive profits?

Analysis-based answers to these seven questions provide managers with the understanding needed to craft a strategy that fits the company's external situation and positions the company to best meet its competitive challenges. The remainder of this chapter is devoted to describing the methods of obtaining solid answers to the seven questions and explaining how the nature of a company's industry and competitive environment weighs upon the strategic choices of company managers.

QUESTION 1: DOES THE INDUSTRY OFFER ATTRACTIVE OPPORTUNITIES FOR GROWTH?

Answering the question of whether or not an industry will offer the prospect of attractive profits begins with a consideration of whether it offers good opportunities for growth. Growth, of course, cannot guarantee profitability—a lesson that too many firms that have pursued growth for growth's sake have learned the hard way. But it is an indicator of how much customers value the industry's products (or services) and whether the industry demand is strong enough to support profitable sales growth.

Key economic indicators of an industry's growth prospects include market size, in terms of overall unit sales and sales volume, as well as the industry growth rate. Assessing the market size and growth rate will depend, however, on whether the industry is defined broadly or narrowly, in terms of its product or service characteristics. For example, the freight transport industry is far more inclusive than the air freight industry, and market size will vary accordingly. Market size and growth rates will also depend on where the geographic boundary lines are drawn (local, regional, national, or global). In addition, market size and growth rates often vary markedly by region (e.g., Europe versus Asia) and by demographic market segment (e.g., Gen Y versus baby boomers). Looking at the market in a variety of ways can help managers assess the various opportunities for growth and its limits.

One reason for differences among industries in the size of the market and the rate of growth stems from what is known as the "industry life cycle." This is the notion that industries commonly follow a general pattern of development and maturation, consisting of four stages: emergence, rapid growth, maturity, and decline.[1] The size of a market and its growth rate, then, depend on which stage of the life cycle best characterizes the industry in question.

QUESTION 2: WHAT KINDS OF COMPETITIVE FORCES ARE INDUSTRY MEMBERS FACING, AND HOW STRONG ARE THEY?

LO 1

Gain command of the basic concepts and analytical tools widely used to diagnose the competitive conditions in a company's industry.

The character and strength of the competitive forces operating in an industry are never the same from one industry to another. Far and away the most powerful and widely used tool for systematically diagnosing the principal competitive pressures in a market is the *five-forces model of competition.*[2] This model holds that the competitive forces affecting industry profitability go beyond rivalry among competing sellers and include pressures stemming from four coexisting sources. As depicted in Figure 3.3, the five competitive forces include (1) competition from *rival sellers,* (2) competition from *potential new entrants* to the industry, (3) competition from producers of *substitute products,* (4) *supplier* bargaining power, and (5) *customer* bargaining power.

Using the five-forces model to determine the nature and strength of competitive pressures in a given industry involves building the picture of competition in three steps:

- *Step 1:* For each of the five forces, identify the different parties involved, along with the specific factors that bring about competitive pressures.
- *Step 2:* Evaluate how strong the pressures stemming from each of the five forces are (strong, moderate to normal, or weak).
- *Step 3:* Determine whether the strength of the five competitive forces, overall, is conducive to earning attractive profits in the industry.

Competitive Pressures Created by the Rivalry among Competing Sellers

The strongest of the five competitive forces is often the market maneuvering for buyer patronage that goes on among rival sellers of a product or service. In effect, *a market is a competitive battlefield* where the contest among competitors is ongoing and dynamic. Each competing company endeavors to deploy whatever means in its business arsenal it believes will attract and retain buyers, strengthen its market position, and yield good profits. The challenge is to craft a competitive strategy that, at the very least, allows a company to hold its own against rivals and that, ideally, *produces a competitive edge over rivals.* But when one firm deploys a strategy or makes a new strategic move that produces good results, its rivals typically respond with offensive or defensive countermoves of their own. This pattern of action and reaction, move and countermove, produces a continually evolving competitive landscape where the market battle ebbs and flows, sometimes takes unpredictable twists and turns, and produces winners and losers.[3]

Competitive battles among rival sellers can assume many forms that extend well beyond lively price competition. For example, rivalrous firms may resort to such marketing tactics as special sales promotions, heavy advertising, rebates, or low-interest-rate financing to drum up additional sales. Active rivals may race one another to differentiate their products by offering better performance

Figure 3.3   The Five-Forces Model of Competition: A Key Analytical Tool

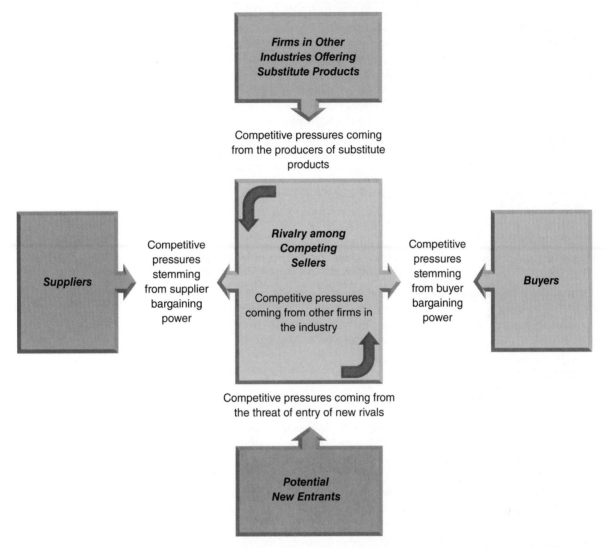

Sources: Adapted from Michael E. Porter, "How Competitive Forces Shape Strategy," *Harvard Business Review* 57, no. 2 (March–April 1979), pp. 137–45, and Michael E. Porter, "The Five Competitive Forces That Shape Strategy," *Harvard Business Review* 86, no. 1 (January 2008), pp. 80–86.

features or higher quality or improved customer service or a wider product selection. Rivals may also compete through the rapid introduction of next-generation products, frequent introduction of new or improved products, and efforts to build stronger dealer networks, establish positions in foreign markets, or otherwise expand distribution capabilities and market presence. Table 3.2 provides a sampling of the types of competitive weapons available to rivals, along with their primary effects.

The intensity of rivalry varies from industry to industry and depends on a number of identifiable factors. Figure 3.4 summarizes these factors, identifying those that intensify or weaken rivalry among direct competitors in an industry. A brief explanation of why these factors affect the degree of rivalry is in order:[4]

Table 3.2   **Common "Weapons" for Competing with Rivals**

Types of Competitive Weapons	Primary Effects
Price discounting, clearance sales, "blowout" sales	Lowers price (P), acts to boost total sales volume and market share, lowers profit margins per unit sold when price cuts are big and/or increases in sales volume are relatively small
Couponing, advertising items on sale	Acts to increase unit sales volume and total revenues, lowers price (P), increases unit costs (C), may lower profit margins per unit sold ($P - C$)
Advertising product or service characteristics, using ads to enhance a company's image or reputation	Boosts buyer demand, increases product differentiation and perceived value (V), acts to increase total sales volume and market share, may increase unit costs (C) and/or lower profit margins per unit sold
Innovating to improve product performance and quality	Acts to increase product differentiation and value (V), boosts buyer demand, acts to boost total sales volume, likely to increase unit costs (C)
Introducing new or improved features, increasing the number of styles or models to provide greater product selection	Acts to increase product differentiation and value (V), strengthens buyer demand, acts to boost total sales volume and market share, likely to increase unit costs (C)
Increasing customization of product or service	Acts to increase product differentiation and value (V), increases switching costs, acts to boost total sales volume, often increases unit costs (C)
Building a bigger, better dealer network	Broadens access to buyers, acts to boost total sales volume and market share, may increase unit costs (C)
Improving warranties, offering low-interest financing	Acts to increase product differentiation and value (V), increases unit costs (C), increases buyer costs to switch brands, acts to boost total sales volume and market share

- *Rivalry is stronger in markets where buyer demand is growing slowly or declining, and it is weaker in fast-growing markets.* Rapidly expanding buyer demand produces enough new business for all industry members to grow without using volume-boosting sales tactics to draw customers away from rival enterprises. But in markets where buyer demand is growing only 1 to 2 percent or is shrinking, companies anxious (or perhaps desperate) to gain more business typically employ price discounts, sales promotions, and other tactics to boost their sales volumes, sometimes to the point of igniting a fierce battle for market share.

- *Rivalry increases as it becomes less costly for buyers to switch brands.* The less expensive it is for buyers to switch their purchases from the seller of one brand to the seller of another brand, the easier it is for sellers to steal customers away from rivals. But the higher the costs buyers incur to switch brands, the less prone they are to brand switching. Switching costs include not only monetary costs but also the time, inconvenience, and psychological costs involved in switching brands. For example distributors and retailers may not switch to the brands of rival manufacturers because they are hesitant to sever long-standing supplier relationships, incur any technical support costs or retraining expenses in making the switchover, go to the trouble of testing the quality and reliability of the rival brand, or devote resources to marketing the new brand (especially if the brand is not well known).

- *Rivalry increases as the products of rival sellers become more alike, and it diminishes as the products of industry rivals become more strongly differentiated.* When the offerings of rivals are identical or weakly differentiated, buyers have less reason to be brand-loyal—a condition that makes it easier for rivals to convince

Figure 3.4 Factors Affecting the Strength of Rivalry

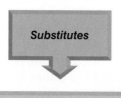

Substitutes

Suppliers

**Rivalry among Competing Sellers:
How strong is seller-related competition?**

Rivalry is stronger when:

- Buyer demand is growing slowly
- Buyer demand is falling off and sellers find themselves with excess capacity and/or inventory
- Buyer costs to switch brands are low
- The products of industry members are commodities or else weakly differentiated
- The firms in the industry have high fixed costs or high storage costs
- Competitors are numerous or are of roughly equal size and competitive strength
- Rivals have diverse objectives, strategies, and/or countries of origin
- Rivals have emotional stakes in the business or face high exit barriers

Rivalry is weaker when:

- Buyer demand is growing rapidly
- Buyer costs to switch brands are high
- The products of rival sellers are strongly differentiated and customer loyalty is high
- Fixed and storage costs are low
- Sales are concentrated among a few large sellers
- Industry members are relatively homogeneous in size, strength, objectives, strategy, and country of origin
- Exit barriers are low

Buyers

New Entrants

buyers to switch to their offerings. And since the brands of different sellers have comparable attributes, buyers can shop the market for the best deal and switch brands at will. On the other hand, strongly differentiated product offerings among rivals breed high brand loyalty on the part of buyers—because many buyers view the attributes of certain brands as more appealing or better suited to their needs. Strong brand attachments make it tougher for sellers to draw customers away from rivals. Unless meaningful numbers of buyers are open to considering new or different product attributes being offered by rivals, the high degree of brand loyalty that accompanies strong product differentiation works against fierce rivalry among competing sellers. *The degree of product differentiation also affects switching costs.* When the offerings of rivals are identical or weakly differentiated, it is usually easy and inexpensive for buyers to switch their purchases from one seller to another. But in the case of strongly differentiated brands with quite different features and functionality (like rival brands of cell phones), buyers may be reluctant to go through the brand-switching hassle.

- *Rivalry is more intense when there is unused production capacity, especially if the industry's product has high fixed costs or high storage costs.* Whenever a market is oversupplied (such that sellers have unutilized production capacity and/or too much inventory), the result is a "buyer's market" that intensifies rivalry perhaps even to the point of threatening the survival of competitively weak firms. A similar effect occurs when a product is perishable, seasonal, or costly to hold in inventory, since firms often engage in aggressive price cutting to ensure that they are not left with unwanted or costly inventories. Likewise, whenever fixed costs account for a large fraction of total cost so that unit costs are significantly lower at full capacity, firms come under significant pressure to cut prices to boost sales whenever they are operating below full capacity. Unused capacity imposes a significant cost-increasing penalty because there are fewer units over which to spread fixed costs. The pressure of high fixed or high storage costs can push rival firms into price concessions, special discounts, rebates, and other volume-boosting competitive tactics.

- *Rivalry intensifies as the number of competitors increases and as competitors become more equal in size and competitive strength.* The greater the number of competitors, the higher the probability that one or more companies will be busily engaged in a strategic offensive intended to enhance their market standing, thereby heating up competition and putting new pressures on rivals to respond with offensive or defensive moves of their own. In addition, when rivals are of comparable size and competitive strength, they can usually compete on a fairly equal footing—an evenly matched contest tends to be fiercer than a contest in which one or more industry members have commanding market shares and substantially greater resources and capabilities than their much smaller rivals.

- *Rivalry often becomes more intense—as well as more volatile and unpredictable—as the diversity of competitors increases in terms of long-term directions, objectives, strategies, and countries of origin.* A diverse group of sellers often contains one or more mavericks willing to try novel or rule-breaking market approaches, thus generating a livelier and less predictable competitive environment. Globally competitive markets usually boost the intensity of rivalry, especially when aggressors having lower costs or products with more attractive features are intent on gaining a strong foothold in new country markets.

- *Rivalry is stronger when high exit barriers keep unprofitable firms from leaving the industry.* In industries where the assets cannot easily be sold or transferred to other uses, where workers are entitled to job protection, or where owners are committed to remaining in business for personal reasons, failing firms tend to hold on longer than they might otherwise—even when they are bleeding red ink. This increases rivalry in two ways. Firms that are losing ground or in financial trouble often resort to deep price discounting that can trigger a price war and destabilize an otherwise attractive industry. In addition, high exit barriers result in an industry being more overcrowded than it would otherwise be, and this boosts rivalry and forces the weakest companies to scramble (often pushing them into desperate maneuvers of all kinds) to win sufficient sales and revenues to stay in business.

Rivalry can be characterized as *cutthroat* or *brutal* when competitors engage in protracted price wars or habitually undertake other aggressive strategic moves that prove mutually destructive to profitability. Rivalry can be considered *fierce* to *strong* when the battle for market share is so vigorous that the profit margins of most industry members are squeezed to bare-bones levels. Rivalry can be characterized as *moderate* or *normal* when the maneuvering among industry members, while lively and healthy, still allows most industry members to earn acceptable profits. Rivalry is *weak* when most companies in the industry are relatively well satisfied with their sales growth and market shares, rarely undertake offensives to steal customers away from one another, and—because of weak competitive forces—earn consistently good profits and returns on investment.

Competitive Pressures Associated with the Threat of New Entrants

New entrants to a market bring new production capacity, the desire to establish a secure place in the market, and sometimes substantial resources. Just how serious the competitive threat of entry is in a particular market depends on two classes of factors: *barriers to entry* and the *expected reaction of incumbent firms to new entry.*[5]

Industry incumbents that are willing and able to launch strong defensive maneuvers to maintain their positions can make it hard for a new entrant to gain a sufficient market foothold to survive and eventually become profitable. Entry candidates may have second thoughts if they conclude that existing firms are likely to give newcomers a hard time by offering price discounts (especially to the very customer groups a newcomer is seeking to attract), spending more on advertising, running frequent sales promotions, adding attractive new product features (to match or beat the newcomer's product offering), or providing additional services to customers. Such defensive maneuvers on the part of incumbents raise an entrant's costs and risks and have to be considered likely if one or more incumbents have previously tried to strongly contest the entry of new firms into the marketplace.

A barrier to entry exists whenever it is hard for a newcomer to break into the market and/or the economics of the business put a potential entrant at a disadvantage. The most widely encountered such barriers that entry candidates must hurdle include the following:[6]

- *Sizable economies of scale in production, distribution, advertising, or other areas of operation.* When incumbent companies enjoy cost advantages associated with large-scale operations, outsiders must either enter on a large scale (a costly and perhaps risky move) or accept a cost disadvantage and consequently lower profitability.

- *Significant cost advantages held by existing firms due to experience and learning curve effects.* In many industries, incumbent firms are favored by learning-based cost savings that accrue from experience in performing certain activities such as manufacturing or new product development or inventory management. This gives incumbent firms a first-mover advantage over new entrants that may be difficult to overcome.

- *Other cost advantages enjoyed by industry incumbents.* Existing industry members may also have other types of cost advantages that are hard for a newcomer to replicate. These can stem from (1) preferential access to raw materials, components, or other inputs, (2) cost savings accruing from patents or proprietary technology, (3) favorable locations, and (4) low fixed costs (because they have older facilities that have been mostly depreciated). The bigger the cost advantages of industry incumbents, the more risky it becomes for outsiders to attempt entry (since they will have to accept thinner profit margins or even losses until the cost disadvantages can be overcome).

- *Strong brand preferences and high degrees of customer loyalty.* The stronger the attachment of buyers to established brands, the harder it is for a newcomer to break into the marketplace. In such cases, a new entrant must have the financial resources to spend enough on advertising and sales promotion to overcome customer loyalties and build its own clientele. Establishing brand recognition and building customer loyalty can be a slow and costly process. In addition, if it is difficult or costly for a customer to switch to a new brand, a new entrant may have to offer buyers a discounted price or an extra margin of quality or service. Such barriers discourage new entry because they act to boost financial requirements and lower expected profit margins for new entrants.

- *Strong "network effects" in customer demand.* In industries where buyers are more attracted to a product when there are many other users of the product, there are said to be "network effects," since demand is higher the larger the network of users. Video game systems are an example, since users prefer to have the same systems as their friends so that they can play together on systems they all know and share games. When incumbents have a larger base of users, new entrants with comparable products face a serious disadvantage in attracting buyers.

- *High capital requirements.* The larger the total dollar investment needed to enter the market successfully, the more limited the pool of potential entrants. The most obvious capital requirements for new entrants relate to manufacturing facilities and equipment, introductory advertising and sales promotion campaigns, working capital to finance inventories and customer credit, and sufficient cash to cover start-up costs.

- *The difficulties of building a network of distributors or dealers and securing adequate space on retailers' shelves.* A potential entrant can face numerous distribution channel challenges. Wholesale distributors may be reluctant to take on a product that lacks buyer recognition. Retailers must be recruited and convinced to give a new brand ample display space and an adequate trial period. When existing sellers have strong, well-functioning distributor-dealer networks, a newcomer has an uphill struggle in squeezing its way into existing distribution channels. Potential entrants sometimes have to "buy" their way into wholesale or retail channels by cutting their prices to provide dealers and distributors with higher markups and profit margins or by giving them big advertising and promotional allowances. As a consequence, a potential entrant's own profits may be squeezed unless and until its product gains enough consumer acceptance that distributors and retailers are anxious to carry it.

- *Restrictive government policies.* Regulated industries like cable TV, telecommunications, electric and gas utilities, radio and television broadcasting, liquor retailing, and railroads entail government-controlled entry. Government agencies can also limit or even bar entry by requiring licenses and permits, such as the medallion required to drive a taxicab in New York City. Government-mandated safety regulations and environmental pollution standards also create entry barriers because they raise entry costs. In international markets, host governments commonly limit foreign entry and must approve all foreign investment applications. National governments commonly use tariffs and trade restrictions (anti-dumping rules, local content requirements, quotas, etc.) to raise entry barriers for foreign firms and protect domestic producers from outside competition.

The threat of entry changes as the industry's prospects grow brighter or dimmer and as entry barriers rise or fall. For example, in the pharmaceutical industry the expiration of a key patent on a widely prescribed drug virtually guarantees that one or more drug makers will enter with generic offerings of their own. Use of the Internet for shopping is making it much easier for e-tailers to enter into competition against some of the best-known retail chains. Moreover, new strategic actions by incumbent firms to increase advertising, strengthen distributor-dealer relations, step up R&D, or improve product quality can erect higher roadblocks to entry.

> High entry barriers and weak entry threats today do not always translate into high entry barriers and weak entry threats tomorrow.

Additional Entry Threat Considerations There are two additional factors that need to be considered in evaluating whether the threat of entry is strong or weak. The first concerns how attractive the growth and profit prospects are for new entrants. *Rapidly growing market demand and high potential profits act as magnets, motivating potential entrants to commit the resources needed to hurdle entry barriers.*[7] When growth and profit opportunities are sufficiently attractive, certain types of entry barriers are unlikely to provide an effective entry deterrent. At most, they limit the pool of candidate entrants to enterprises with the requisite competencies and resources and with the creativity to fashion a strategy for competing with incumbent firms. Hence, *the best test of whether potential entry is a strong or weak competitive force in the marketplace is to ask if the industry's growth and profit prospects are strongly attractive to potential entry candidates with sufficient expertise and resources to hurdle prevailing entry barriers.* When the answer is no, potential entry is a weak competitive force. When the answer is yes, then potential entry adds significantly to competitive pressures in the marketplace.

A second factor concerns the pool of potential entrants and their capabilities in relation to the particular entry barriers in place. Companies with sizable financial resources, proven competitive capabilities, and a respected brand name may be able to marshal the resources to hurdle certain types of entry barriers rather easily, while small start-up enterprises may find the same entry barriers insurmountable. Thus, how hard it will be for potential entrants to compete on a level playing field is always relative to the financial resources and competitive capabilities of likely entrants. The big take-away is this: *Whether an industry's entry barriers ought to be considered high or low depends on the resources and capabilities possessed by the pool of potential entrants.*[8] As a rule, the bigger the pool of entry candidates that have what it takes, the stronger is the threat of entry.

> The threat of entry is stronger when entry barriers are low, when incumbent firms are unable or unwilling to vigorously contest a newcomer's entry, and when there's a sizable pool of entry candidates with resources and capabilities well suited for competing in the industry.

For example, when Honda opted to enter the U.S. lawn mower market in competition against Toro, Snapper, Craftsman, John Deere, and others, it was easily able to hurdle entry barriers that would have been formidable to other newcomers because it had long-standing expertise in gasoline engines; its well-known reputation for quality and durability in automobiles gave it instant credibility with homeowners. In fact, the strongest competitive pressures associated with potential entry frequently come not from outsiders but from current industry participants with strong capabilities looking for growth opportunities. *Existing industry members are often strong candidates to enter market segments or geographic areas where they currently do not have a market presence.* Companies already well established in certain product categories or geographic areas often possess the resources, competencies, and competitive capabilities to hurdle the barriers of entering a different market segment or new geographic area.

Figure 3.5 summarizes the factors that cause the overall competitive threat from potential new entrants to be strong or weak.

Figure 3.5   Factors Affecting the Threat of Entry

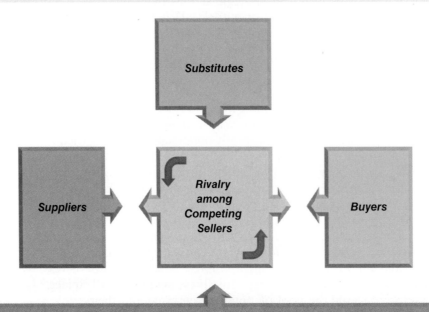

Potential New Entrants

How strong are the competitive pressures coming from the threat of entry of new rivals?

Entry threats are stronger when:
- Entry barriers are low
- Industry members are unwilling or unable to strongly contest the entry of newcomers
- There is a large pool of potential entrants, some of which have the capabilities to overcome high entry barriers
- Existing industry members are looking to expand their market reach by entering product segments or geographic areas where they do not have a presence
- Buyer demand is growing rapidly and newcomers can expect to earn attractive profits without inviting a strong reaction from incumbents

Entry threats are weaker when:
- Entry barriers are high
  - High economies of scale
  - Significant experience-based cost advantages
  - Other cost advantages held by industry members (e.g., access to inputs, technology, favorable location) or low fixed costs
  - Strong product differentiation and brand loyalty
  - Strong network effects
  - High capital requirements
  - Limited new access to distribution channels
  - Restrictive government policies
- Industry members are willing and able to contest new entry
- Industry outlook is risky and uncertain, discouraging entry

Competitive Pressures from the Sellers of Substitute Products

Companies in one industry come under competitive pressure from the actions of companies in a closely adjoining industry whenever buyers view the products of the two industries as good substitutes. For instance, the producers of sugar experience competitive pressures from the sales and marketing efforts of the makers of sucralose and aspartame. Newspapers are struggling to maintain their relevance to subscribers who can watch the news on any of numerous TV channels and use Internet sources to get information about sports results, stock quotes, and job opportunities. The retailers of music CDs are experiencing competitive pressure from downloadable digital music on sites such as iTunes.

As depicted in Figure 3.6, whether the competitive pressures from substitute products are strong, moderate, or weak depends on three factors:

1. *Whether substitutes are readily available.* The presence of readily available substitutes creates competitive pressure by placing a ceiling on the prices industry members can charge without giving customers an incentive to switch to substitutes and risking sales erosion.[9] This price ceiling, at the same time, puts a lid on the profits that industry members can earn unless they find ways to cut costs.

2. *Whether buyers view the substitutes as attractively priced in relation to their quality, performance, and other relevant attributes.* In deciding whether to switch to a substitute product, customers compare its performance, features, ease of use, and other attributes as well as price to see if the substitute offers more value for the money than the industry's product. The users of paper cartons constantly weigh the price/performance trade-offs with plastic containers and metal cans, for example.

3. *Whether the costs that buyers incur in switching to the substitutes are low or high.* Low switching costs make it easier for the sellers of attractive substitutes to lure buyers to their offerings; high switching costs deter buyers from purchasing substitute products.[10] Typical switching costs include the time and inconvenience involved in switching, payments for technical help in making the changeover, the cost of any additional equipment needed, employee retraining costs, the cost of testing the quality and reliability of the substitute, and the psychological costs of severing old supplier relationships and establishing new ones.

Before assessing the competitive pressures coming from substitutes, company managers must identify the substitutes, which is less easy than it sounds since it involves (1) determining where the industry boundaries lie and (2) figuring out which other products or services can address the same basic customer needs as those produced by industry members. Deciding on the industry boundaries is necessary for determining which firms are direct rivals and which produce substitutes. This is a matter of perspective—there are no hard-and-fast rules, other than to say that other brands of the same basic product constitute rival products and not substitutes.

As a rule, *the lower the price of substitutes, the higher their quality and performance; and the lower the user's switching costs, the more intense the competitive pressures posed by substitute products.* Other market indicators of the competitive strength of substitute products include (1) whether the sales of substitutes are growing faster than the sales of the industry being analyzed (a sign that the

Figure 3.6   Factors Affecting Competition from Substitute Products

Firms in Other Industries Offering Substitute Products

How strong are competitive pressures coming from substitute products from outside the industry?

Competitive pressures from substitutes are stronger when:

- Good substitutes are readily available or new ones are emerging
- Substitutes are attractively priced
- Substitutes have comparable or better performance features
- Buyers have low costs in switching to substitutes

Competitive pressures from substitutes are weaker when:

- Good substitutes are not readily available or don't exist
- Substitutes are higher-priced relative to the performance they deliver
- Buyers have high costs in switching to substitutes

Signs That Competition from Substitutes Is Strong

- Sales of substitutes are growing faster than sales of the industry being analyzed
- Producers of substitutes are moving to add new capacity
- Profits of the producers of substitutes are on the rise

Suppliers   →   *Rivalry among Competing Sellers*   ←   **Buyers**

New Entrants

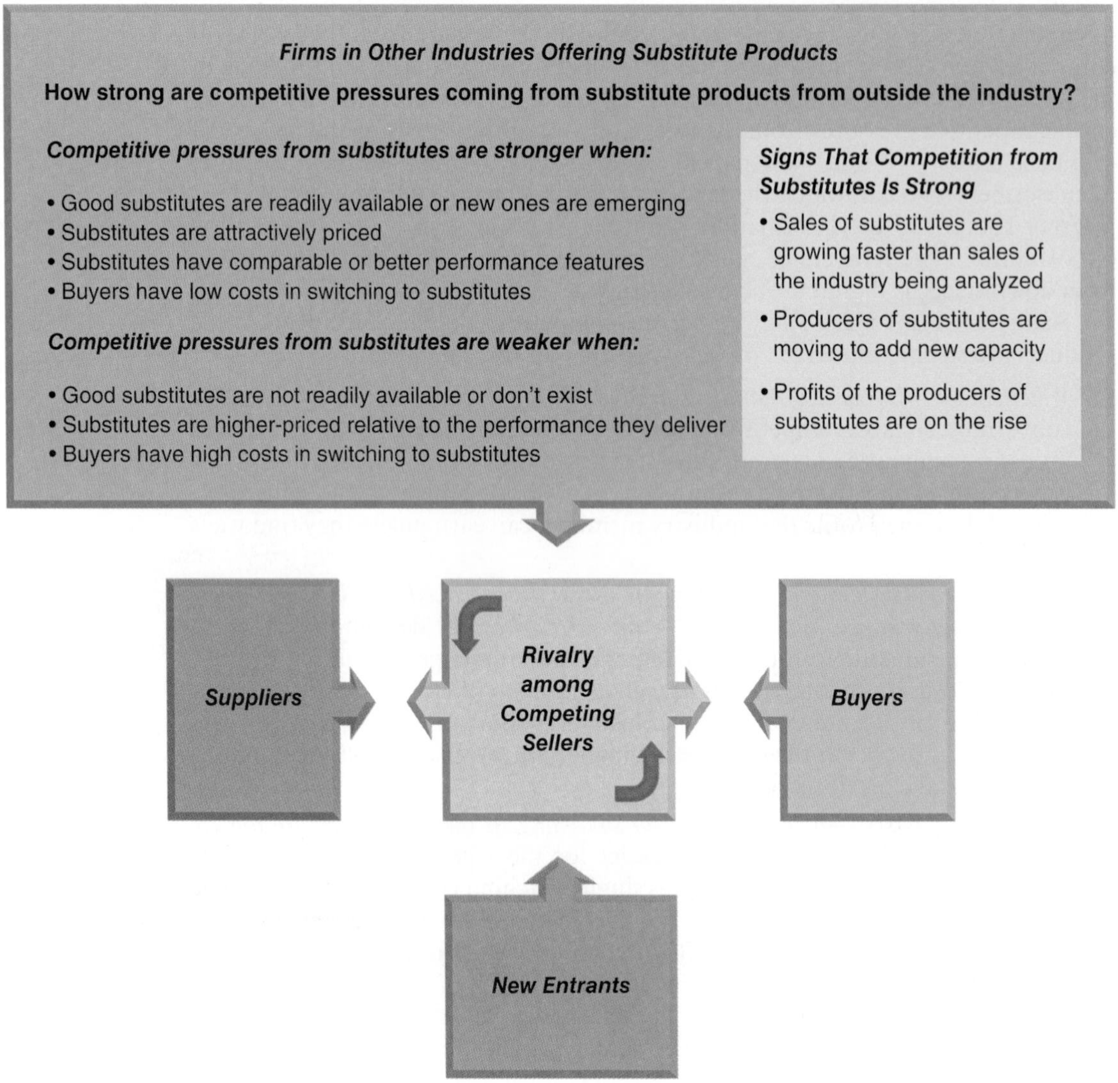

sellers of substitutes may be drawing customers away from the industry in question), (2) whether the producers of substitutes are moving to add new capacity, and (3) whether the profits of the producers of substitutes are on the rise.

Competitive Pressures Stemming from Supplier Bargaining Power

Whether the suppliers of industry members represent a weak or strong competitive force depends on the degree to which suppliers have sufficient *bargaining power* to influence the terms and conditions of supply in their favor. Suppliers with strong bargaining power can erode industry profitability by charging industry members higher prices, passing costs on to them, and limiting their opportunities to find better deals. For instance, Microsoft and Intel, both of whom supply PC makers with essential components, have been known to use their dominant market status not only to charge PC makers premium prices but also to leverage PC makers in other ways. The bargaining power of these two companies over their customers is so great that both companies have faced antitrust charges on numerous occasions. Before a legal agreement ending the practice, Microsoft pressured PC makers to load only Microsoft products on the screens of new computers that come with factory-loaded software. Intel has also defended against antitrust charges but continues to give PC makers who use the biggest percentages of Intel chips in their PC models top priority in filling orders for newly introduced Intel chips. Being on Intel's list of preferred customers helps a PC maker get an allocation of the first production runs of Intel's latest chips and thus get new PC models to market ahead of rivals. Microsoft's and Intel's pressuring of PC makers has helped them maintain their dominant positions in their industries.

Small-scale retailers often must contend with the power of manufacturers whose products enjoy well-known brand names, since consumers expect to find these products on the shelves of the retail stores where they shop. This provides the manufacturer with a degree of pricing power and often the ability to push hard for favorable shelf displays. Similarly, the operators of franchised units of such chains as McDonald's, KFC, Pizza Hut, 7-Eleven, Mr. Rooter, and Radisson Hotels must frequently agree to source some of their supplies from the franchisor at prices and terms favorable to that franchisor. Supplier bargaining power is also a competitive factor in industries where unions have been able to organize the workforce (which supplies labor). Air pilot unions, for example, have employed their bargaining power to increase pilots' wages and benefits in the air transport industry.

As shown in Figure 3.7, a variety of factors determines the strength of suppliers' bargaining power:[11]

- *Whether suppliers' products are in short supply.* Suppliers of items in short supply have pricing power and bargaining leverage, whereas a surge in the available supply of particular items shifts the bargaining power to the industry members.
- *Whether suppliers provide a differentiated input that enhances the performance or quality of the industry's product.* The more differentiated and valuable a particular input is in terms of enhancing the performance or quality of the products of industry members, the more bargaining leverage and pricing power suppliers have.
- *Whether the item being supplied is a standard item or a commodity that is readily available from a host of suppliers.* The suppliers of commodities (like copper or steel reinforcing rods or shipping cartons) are in a weak position to demand a premium price or insist on other favorable terms because industry members can readily obtain essentially the same item at the same price from many other suppliers eager to win their business.
- *Whether it is difficult or costly for industry members to switch their purchases from one supplier to another.* The higher the switching costs of industry members, the stronger the bargaining power of their suppliers. Low switching costs limit supplier bargaining power by enabling industry members to change suppliers if any one supplier attempts to raise prices by more than the costs of switching.
- *Whether there are good substitutes available for the suppliers' products.* The ready availability of substitute inputs lessens the bargaining power of suppliers by reducing the dependence of industry members on the suppliers. The better

Figure 3.7   **Factors Affecting the Bargaining Power of Suppliers**

Suppliers

How strong are the competitive pressures stemming from supplier bargaining power?

Supplier bargaining power is stronger when:

- Supplier products/services are in short supply (which gives suppliers leverage in setting prices)
- Supplier products/services are differentiated
- Supplier products/services are critical to industry members' production processes
- Industry members incur high costs in switching their purchases to alternative suppliers
- There are no good substitutes for what the suppliers provide
- Suppliers are not dependent on the industry for a large portion of their revenues
- The supplier industry is more concentrated than the industry it sells to and is dominated by a few large companies

Supplier bargaining power is weaker when:

- There is a surge in the availability of supplies
- The item being supplied is a "commodity" that is readily available from many suppliers at the going market price
- Industry members' switching costs to alternative suppliers are low
- Good substitutes for supplier products/services exist
- Industry members account for a big fraction of suppliers' sales
- The number of suppliers is large relative to the number of industry members and there are no suppliers with large market shares
- Industry members have the potential to integrate backward into the business of suppliers and to self-manufacture their own requirements

Substitutes

Rivalry among Competing Sellers

Buyers

New Entrants

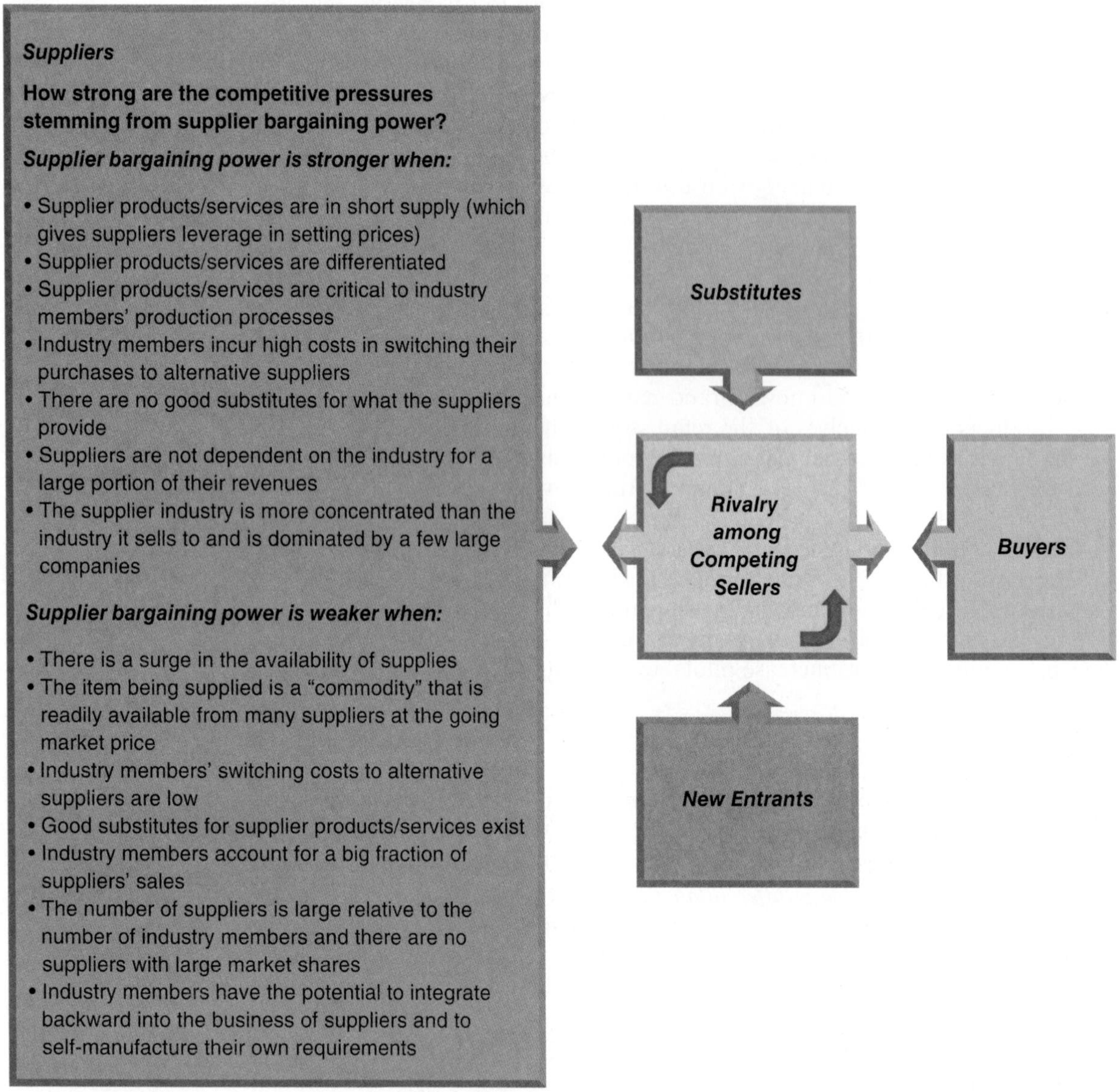

the price and performance characteristics of the substitute inputs, the weaker the bargaining power of suppliers.

- *Whether industry members account for a sizable fraction of suppliers' total sales.* As a rule, suppliers have less bargaining leverage when their sales to members of the industry constitute a big percentage of their total sales. In such cases, the well-being of suppliers is closely tied to the well-being of their major customers. Suppliers have a big incentive to protect and enhance the competitiveness of their major customers via reasonable prices, exceptional quality, and ongoing advances in the technology of the items supplied.
- *Whether the supplier industry is dominated by a few large companies and whether it is more concentrated than the industry it sells to.* Suppliers with sizable market

shares and strong demand for the items they supply generally have sufficient bargaining power to charge high prices and deny requests from industry members for lower prices or other concessions.

- *Whether it makes good economic sense for industry members to integrate backward and self-manufacture items they have been buying from suppliers.* The make-or-buy issue generally boils down to whether suppliers who specialize in the production of particular parts or components and make them in volume for many different customers have the expertise and scale economies to supply as-good or better components at a lower cost than industry members could achieve via self-manufacture. Frequently, it is difficult for industry members to self-manufacture parts and components more economically than they can obtain them from suppliers who specialize in making such items. For instance, most producers of outdoor power equipment (lawn mowers, rotary tillers, leaf blowers, etc.) find it cheaper to source the small engines they need from outside manufacturers that specialize in small-engine manufacture than to make their own engines, because the quantity of engines they need is too small to justify the investment in manufacturing facilities, master the production process, and capture scale economies. Specialists in small-engine manufacture, by supplying many kinds of engines to the whole power equipment industry, can obtain a big-enough sales volume to fully realize scale economies, become proficient in all the manufacturing techniques, and keep costs low. As a rule, suppliers are safe from the threat of self-manufacture by their customers *until* the volume of parts a customer needs becomes large enough for the customer to justify backward integration into self-manufacture of the component.

In identifying the degree of supplier power in an industry, it is important to recognize that different types of suppliers are likely to have different amounts of bargaining power. Thus, the first step is for managers to identify the different types of suppliers, paying particular attention to those that provide the industry with important inputs. The next step is to assess the bargaining power of each type of supplier separately. Figure 3.7 summarizes the conditions that tend to make supplier bargaining power strong or weak.

Competitive Pressures Stemming from Buyer Bargaining Power and Price Sensitivity

Whether buyers are able to exert strong competitive pressures on industry members depends on (1) the degree to which buyers have bargaining power and (2) the extent to which buyers are price-sensitive. Buyers with strong bargaining power can limit industry profitability by demanding price concessions, better payment terms, or additional features and services that increase industry members' costs. Buyer price sensitivity limits the profit potential of industry members by restricting the ability of sellers to raise prices without losing revenue.

The strength of buyers as a competitive force depends on a set of factors that predict the degree of bargaining power and price sensitivity, which may vary according to buyer group (e.g., wholesalers, large retail chains, small retailers, consumers). Retailers tend to have greater bargaining power over industry sellers if they have influence over the purchase decisions of the end user or if they are critical in providing sellers with access to the end user. For example, large retail chains like Walmart, Carrefour, Metro AG, Tesco, and Woolworths typically have considerable negotiating leverage in purchasing products from manufacturers because of manufacturers' need for broad retail exposure and the most appealing shelf locations. Retailers may stock two or three competing brands of a product but rarely all competing brands, so competition among rival manufacturers for visibility on the shelves of popular multistore retailers gives such retailers significant bargaining strength. Major supermarket chains like Walmart, Ahold, Kroger, Aldi, and Carrefour have sufficient bargaining power to demand promotional allowances and lump-sum payments (called slotting fees) from food products manufacturers in return for stocking certain brands or putting them in the best shelf locations. Motor vehicle manufacturers have strong bargaining power in negotiating to buy original-equipment tires from Goodyear, Michelin, Bridgestone/Firestone, Continental, and Pirelli not only because they buy in large quantities but also because tire makers believe they gain an advantage in supplying replacement tires to vehicle owners if their tire brand is original equipment on the vehicle.

In contrast, individual consumers rarely have any real bargaining power in negotiating price concessions or other favorable terms with sellers. While an individual with other purchase options may refuse to buy a high-priced item, her actions will have no discernible   effect on industry profitability. As a buyer group, however, consumers can limit the profit potential of an industry for the same reasons that other buyer groups exert competitive pressure. These reasons are discussed below and summarized in Figure 3.8:[12]

- *Buyers' bargaining power is greater when their costs of switching to competing brands or substitutes are relatively low.* Buyers who can readily switch brands have more leverage than buyers who have high switching costs. Switching costs limit industry profitability, in essence, by putting a cap on how much producers can raise price or reduce quality before they will lose the buyer's business.

- *Buyer power increases when industry goods are standardized or differentiation is weak.* In such circumstances, buyers make their selections on the basis of price, which increases price competition among vendors. When products are differentiated, buyers' options are more limited and they are less focused on obtaining low prices, which may signal poor quality.

- *Buyers have more power when they are large and few in number relative to the number of sellers.* The smaller the number of buyers, the more sellers have to compete for their business and the less easy it is for sellers to find alternative buyers when a customer is lost to a competitor. The prospect of losing a customer not easily replaced often makes a seller more willing to grant concessions of one kind or another. The larger the buyer, the more important their business is to the seller and the more sellers will be willing to grant concessions.

- *Buyer power increases when buyer demand is weak and industry members are scrambling to sell more units.* Weak or declining demand creates a "buyers' market," in which bargain-hunting buyers are able to press for better deals and special treatment; conversely, strong or rapidly growing demand creates a "sellers' market" and shifts bargaining power to sellers.

- *Buyers gain leverage if they are well informed about sellers' products, prices, and costs.* The more information buyers have, the better bargaining position they are in. The mushrooming availability of product information on the Internet is giving added bargaining power to consumers. Buyers can easily use the Internet to compare prices and features of vacation packages, shop for the best interest rates on mortgages and loans, and find the best prices on big-ticket items such as digital cameras. Bargain hunters can shop around for the best deal on the Internet and use that information to negotiate better deals

Figure 3.8 Factors Affecting the Bargaining Power of Buyers

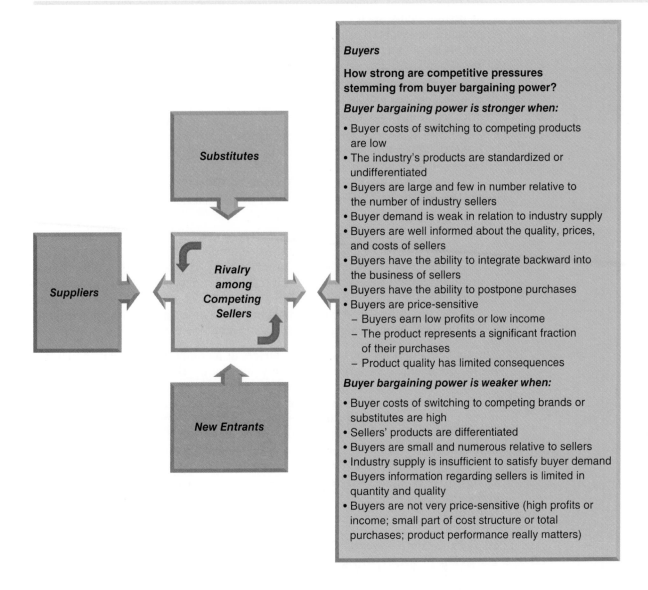

Buyers

How strong are competitive pressures stemming from buyer bargaining power?

Buyer bargaining power is stronger when:

- Buyer costs of switching to competing products are low
- The industry's products are standardized or undifferentiated
- Buyers are large and few in number relative to the number of industry sellers
- Buyer demand is weak in relation to industry supply
- Buyers are well informed about the quality, prices, and costs of sellers
- Buyers have the ability to integrate backward into the business of sellers
- Buyers have the ability to postpone purchases
- Buyers are price-sensitive
  - Buyers earn low profits or low income
  - The product represents a significant fraction of their purchases
  - Product quality has limited consequences

Buyer bargaining power is weaker when:

- Buyer costs of switching to competing brands or substitutes are high
- Sellers' products are differentiated
- Buyers are small and numerous relative to sellers
- Industry supply is insufficient to satisfy buyer demand
- Buyers information regarding sellers is limited in quantity and quality
- Buyers are not very price-sensitive (high profits or income; small part of cost structure or total purchases; product performance really matters)

from local retailers; this method is becoming commonplace in buying new and used motor vehicles.

- *Buyers' bargaining power is greater when they pose a credible threat of integrating backward into the business of sellers.* Companies like Anheuser-Busch, Coors, and Heinz have integrated backward into metal can manufacturing to gain bargaining power in obtaining the balance of their can requirements from otherwise powerful metal can manufacturers. Retailers gain bargaining power by stocking and promoting their own private-label brands alongside manufacturers' name brands.

- *Buyer leverage increases if buyers have discretion to delay their purchases or perhaps even not make a purchase at all.* Consumers often have the option to delay purchases of durable goods, such as major appliances, or discretionary goods, such as hot tubs and home entertainment centers, if they are not happy with the prices offered. Business customers may also be able to defer their purchases of certain items, such as plant equipment or maintenance services. This puts pressure on sellers to provide concessions to buyers so that the sellers can keep their sales numbers from dropping off.

- *Buyer price sensitivity increases when buyers are earning low profits or have low income.* Price is a critical factor in the purchase decisions of low-income consumers and companies that are barely scraping by. In such cases, their high price sensitivity limits the ability of sellers to charge high prices.
- *Buyers are more price-sensitive if the product represents a large fraction of their total purchases.* When a purchase eats up a large portion of a buyer's budget or represents a significant part of his or her cost structure, the buyer cares more about price than might otherwise be the case. When the item is a small fraction of total purchases, buyers are less likely to feel that negotiating or shopping for a better deal is worth the time and trouble.
- *Buyers are more price-sensitive if product performance has limited consequences.* When product performance has limited consequences for the buyer, then purchase decisions are based mostly on price. On the other hand, when product quality is important, such as when it materially affects the quality of an intermediate buyer's goods, then price becomes a less important factor. Price is particularly unimportant to intermediate buyers when a good has the potential to pay for itself by reducing a buyer's other production costs.

The starting point for the analysis of buyers as a competitive force is to identify the different types of buyers along the value chain—then proceed to analyzing the bargaining power and price sensitivity of each type separately. Overall, buyers exert strong competitive pressures and force industry profitability downward if the majority of industry member sales are made to buyer groups that have either strong bargaining power or high price sensitivity. Buyers are able to exert only moderate competitive pressures on sellers when the majority of sellers' revenues come from buyers with intermediate levels of power or price sensitivity. Competitive pressures exerted by buyers are weak when a big portion of sellers' sales revenues comes from buyers with weak bargaining power and price sensitivity.

Is the Collective Strength of the Five Competitive Forces Conducive to Good Profitability?

Assessing whether each of the five competitive forces gives rise to strong, moderate, or weak competitive pressures sets the stage for evaluating whether, overall, the strength of the five forces is conducive to good profitability. Is the state of competition in the industry stronger than "normal"? Can companies in this industry reasonably expect to earn decent profits in light of the prevailing competitive forces? Are some of the competitive forces sufficiently powerful to undermine industry profitability?

The most extreme case of a "competitively unattractive" industry occurs when all five forces are producing strong competitive pressures: Rivalry among sellers is vigorous, low entry barriers allow new rivals to gain a market foothold, competition from substitutes is intense, and both suppliers and buyers are able to exercise considerable leverage. Fierce to strong competitive pressures coming from all five directions drive industry profitability to unacceptably low levels, frequently producing losses for many industry members and forcing some out of business. But an industry can be competitively unattractive without all five competitive forces being strong. In fact, intense competitive pressures *from just one or two* of the five forces may suffice to destroy the conditions for good profitability and prompt some companies to exit the business.

As a rule, *the strongest competitive forces determine the extent of the competitive pressure on industry profitability.*[13] Thus, in evaluating the strength of the five forces overall and their effect on industry profitability, managers should look to the strongest forces. Having more than one strong force will not worsen the effect on industry profitability, but it does mean that the industry has multiple competitive challenges with which to cope. In that sense, an industry with three to five strong forces is even more "unattractive" as a place to compete. Especially intense competitive conditions seem to be the norm in tire manufacturing, apparel, and commercial airlines, three industries where profit margins have historically been thin.

> **CORE CONCEPT**
>
> The strongest of the five forces determines how strong the forces of competition are overall and the extent of the downward pressure on an industry's level of profitability.

In contrast, when the overall impact of the five competitive forces is moderate to weak, an industry is "attractive" in the sense that the *average* industry member can reasonably expect to earn good profits and a nice return on investment. The ideal competitive environment for earning superior profits is one in which both suppliers and customers are in weak bargaining positions, there are no good substitutes, high barriers block further entry, and rivalry among present sellers generates only limited competitive pressures. Weak competition is the best of all possible worlds for also-ran companies because even they can usually eke out a decent profit—if a company can't make a decent profit when competition is weak, then its business outlook is indeed grim.

In most industries, the collective strength of the five competitive forces is somewhere near the middle of the two extremes of very intense and very weak, typically ranging from slightly stronger than normal to slightly weaker than normal and typically allowing well-managed companies with sound strategies to earn moderately attractive profits.

Matching Company Strategy to Competitive Conditions

Working through the five-forces model step by step not only aids strategy makers in assessing whether the intensity of competition allows good profitability but also promotes sound strategic thinking about how to better match company strategy to the specific competitive character of the marketplace. Effectively matching a company's business strategy to prevailing competitive conditions has three aspects:

> A company's strategy is increasingly effective the more it provides some insulation from competitive pressures, shifts the competitive battle in the company's favor, and positions firms to take advantage of attractive growth opportunities.

1. Pursuing avenues that shield the firm from as many of the different competitive pressures as possible.
2. Initiating actions calculated to shift the competitive forces in the company's favor by altering the underlying factors driving the five forces.
3. Spotting attractive arenas for expansion, where competitive pressures in the industry are somewhat weaker.

But making headway on these three fronts first requires identifying competitive pressures, gauging the relative strength of each of the five competitive forces, and gaining a deep enough understanding of the state of competition in the industry to know which strategy buttons to push.

QUESTION 3: WHAT FACTORS ARE DRIVING INDUSTRY CHANGE, AND WHAT IMPACTS WILL THEY HAVE?

LO 2

Learn how to diagnose the factors shaping industry dynamics and to forecast their effects on future industry profitability.

While it is critical to understand the nature and intensity of the competitive forces in an industry, it is just as important to understand that the intensity of these forces and the level of an industry's attractiveness are fluid and subject to change. All industries are affected by new developments and ongoing trends that alter industry conditions, some more speedily than others. Many of these changes are important enough to require a strategic response. Since the five competitive forces have such significance for an industry's profit potential, it is critical that managers remain alert to the changes most likely to affect the strength of the five forces. Environmental scanning for changes of this nature will enable managers to forecast changes in the expected profitability of the industry and to adjust their company's strategy accordingly.

Changes that affect the competitive forces in a positive manner may present opportunities for companies to reposition themselves to take advantage of these forces. Changes that affect the five forces negatively may require a defensive strategic response. Regardless of the direction of change, managers will be able to react in a more timely fashion, with lower adjustment costs, if they have advance notice of the coming changes. Moreover, with early notice, managers may be able to influence the direction or scope of environmental change and improve the outlook.

Analyzing Industry Dynamics

CORE CONCEPT

Dynamic industry analysis involves determining how the **drivers of change** are affecting industry and competitive conditions.

Managing under changing conditions begins with a strategic analysis of the industry dynamics. This involves three steps: (1) identifying the **drivers of change**, (2) assessing whether the drivers of change are, individually or collectively, acting to make the industry more or less attractive, and (3) determining what strategy changes are needed to prepare for the impacts of the anticipated change. All three steps merit further discussion.

Identifying an Industry's Drivers of Change

While many types of environmental change can affect industries in one way or another, it is important to focus on the most powerful agents of change—those with the biggest influence in reshaping the industry landscape and altering competitive conditions. Many drivers of change originate in the outer ring of the company's external environment (see Figure 3.2), but others originate in the company's more immediate industry and competitive environment. Although some drivers of change are unique and specific to a particular industry situation, most drivers of industry and competitive change fall into one of the following categories:[14]

- *Changes in an industry's long-term growth rate.* Shifts in industry growth up or down are a key driver of industry change, affecting the balance between industry supply and buyer demand, entry and exit, and the character and strength of competition. Whether demand is growing or declining is one of the key factors influencing the intensity of rivalry in an industry, as explained earlier. But the strength of this effect will depend on how changes in the industry growth rate affect entry and exit in the industry. If entry barriers are low, then growth in demand will attract new entrants, increasing the number of industry rivals. If exit barriers are low, then shrinking demand will induce exit, resulting in fewer remaining rivals. Since the numbers of firms in an industry also affects the strength of rivalry, these secondary effects via entry and exit would counteract the more direct effects of the change in demand on rivalry. Depending on how much entry or exit takes place, the net result might be that the overall force of rivals remains the same. A change in the long-term growth rate may affect industry conditions in other ways as well. For example, if growth prospects induce the entry of a large, established firm with ambitious growth goals, the intensity of rivalry may increase markedly due to the added diversity or changes in the size mix of incumbents. The exact effect of growth rate changes will vary depending on the specific industry situation. In analyzing the effects of any change driver, managers need to keep in mind the various factors that influence the five forces.

- *Increasing globalization.* Globalization can be precipitated by the blossoming of consumer demand in more and more countries and by the actions of government officials in many countries to reduce trade barriers or open up once-closed markets to foreign competitors, as is occurring in many parts of Europe, Latin America, and Asia. Significant differences in labor costs among countries give manufacturers a strong incentive to locate plants for labor-intensive products in low-wage countries and use these plants to supply market demand across the world. Wages in China, India, Singapore, Mexico, and Brazil, for example, are about one-fourth those in the United States, Germany, and Japan. Because globalization is a complex phenomenon that affects different industries in different ways, analyzing its effects on industry dynamics is a challenging task that requires a consideration of how each of the five forces may be affected. For example, globalization increases the diversity and number of competitors, and this in turn increases the force of rivalry in an industry. At the same time, the lowering of trade barriers increases the threat of entry, putting further pressure on industry profitability. On the other hand, globalization is likely to weaken supplier power by increasing the number of suppliers and increasing the possibility of substituting cheap labor for other inputs. The specific effects vary by industry and will impact some industries more than others. Globalization is very much a driver of industry change in such industries as motor vehicles, steel, petroleum, personal computers, video games, public accounting, and textbook publishing.

- *Changes in who buys the product and how they use it.* Shifts in buyer demographics and the ways products are used can greatly alter industry and competitive conditions. Longer life expectancies and growing percentages of relatively well-to-do retirees, for example, are driving demand growth in such industries as health care, prescription drugs, recreational living, and vacation travel. This is the most common effect of changes in buyer demographics, and it affects industry rivalry, as observed above. But other effects are possible as well. Dell's "buy direct" strategy lessened the buyer power of big-box middlemen in the PC industry by cutting out the intermediate buyers and selling directly to end users. Buyer power increased in the pharmaceutical industry when large health care insurers and other large payers created lists of approved drugs, reducing the role of individual (powerless) doctors in the choice process.

- *Technological change.* Advances in technology can cause disruptive change in an industry by introducing substitutes that offer buyers an irresistible price/performance combination. At the least, this increases the power of substitutes; it may change the business landscape in more fundamental ways if it has a devastating effect on demand. Technological change can also impact the manufacturing process in an industry. This might lead to greater economies of scale, for example, which would increase industry entry barriers. Or it could lead to greater product differentiation, as did the introduction of "mass-customization" techniques. Increasing product differentiation tends to lower buyer power, increase entry barriers, and reduce rivalry—all of which have positive implications for industry profitability.

- *Emerging new Internet capabilities and applications.* The emergence of high-speed Internet service and Voice-Over-Internet-Protocol technology, along with an ever-growing series of Internet applications, provides a special case of technological change that has been a major driver of change in industry after industry. It has reshaped many aspects of the business landscape and can affect the five forces in various ways. The ability of companies to reach consumers via the Internet increases the number of rivals a company faces and often escalates rivalry by pitting pure online sellers against combination brick-and-click sellers against pure brick-and-mortar sellers (increasing diversity and size mix). The Internet gives buyers increasing power through unprecedented ability to research the product offerings of competitors and shop the market for the best value (making buyers better informed). Widespread use of e-mail has forever eroded the business of providing fax services and the first-class-mail delivery revenues of government postal services worldwide (substitute power). Video-conferencing via the Internet erodes the demand for business travel (increasing rivalry in the travel market). The Internet of the future will feature faster speeds, dazzling applications, and over a billion connected gadgets performing an array of functions, thus driving further industry and competitive changes. But Internet-related impacts vary from industry to industry. The challenges here are to assess precisely how emerging Internet developments are altering a particular industry's landscape and to factor these impacts into the strategy-making equation.

- *Product and marketing innovation.* An ongoing stream of product innovations tends to alter the pattern of competition in an industry by attracting more first-time buyers, rejuvenating industry growth, and/or increasing product differentiation, with concomitant effects on rivalry, entry threat, and buyer power. Product innovation has been a key driving force in such industries as digital cameras, golf clubs, video games, toys, and prescription drugs. Similarly, when firms are successful in introducing *new ways* to market their products, they can spark a burst of buyer interest, widen industry demand, increase or lower entry barriers, and increase product differentiation—any or all of which can alter the competitiveness of an industry.

- *Entry or exit of major firms.* The entry of one or more foreign companies into a geographic market once dominated by domestic firms nearly always changes the balance between demand and supply and shakes up competitive conditions by adding diversity. Likewise, when an established domestic firm from another industry attempts entry either by acquisition or by launching its own start-up venture, it usually applies its skills and resources in some innovative fashion that pushes competition in new directions. Entry by a major firm thus often produces a new ball game, with greater rivalry as the result. Similarly, exit of a major firm changes the competitive structure by reducing the number of market leaders and increasing the dominance of the leaders who remain. The primary effect is on the degree of rivalry in the industry, through changes in industry concentration.

- *Diffusion of technical know-how across more companies and more countries.* As knowledge about how to perform a particular activity or execute a particular manufacturing technology spreads, products tend to become more commodity-like. This increases the intensity of rivalry, buyer power, and the threat of entry into an industry, as described earlier.

- *Improvements in cost and efficiency in closely adjoining markets.* Big changes in the costs of substitute producers can dramatically alter the state of competition by changing the price/performance trade-off between an industry's products and that of substitute goods. For example, lower production costs and longer-life products have allowed the makers of super-efficient, fluorescent-based spiral lightbulbs to cut deeply into the sales of incandescent lightbulbs. This has occurred because the spiral lightbulbs, despite being priced two to three times higher than incandescent bulbs, are still far cheaper to use because of their energy-saving efficiency (as much as $50 per bulb) and longer lives (up to eight years between replacements).

- *Reductions in uncertainty and business risk.* Many companies are hesitant to enter industries with uncertain futures or high levels of business risk, and firms already in these industries may be cautious about making aggressive capital investments to expand—often because it is unclear how much time and money it will take to overcome various technological hurdles and achieve acceptable production costs (as is the case in the infant solar power industry). Likewise, firms entering foreign markets where demand is just emerging or where political conditions are volatile may be cautious and limit their downside exposure by using less risky strategies. Over time, however, diminishing risk levels and uncertainty tend to stimulate new entry and capital investments on the part of growth-minded companies seeking new opportunities. This can dramatically alter industry and competitive conditions by increasing rivalry, as the numbers of firms in the industry and their diversity increases.

- *Regulatory influences and government policy changes.* Changes in regulations and government policies can affect competitive conditions in industries in a variety of ways. For example, regulatory actions can affect barriers to entry directly, as they have in industries such as airlines, banking, and broadcasting. Regulations regarding product quality, safety, and environmental protection can affect entry barriers more indirectly, by altering capital requirements or economies of scale. Government actions can also affect rivalry through antitrust policies, as they have in soft-drink bottling, where exclusive territorial rights were granted, and in automobile parts, where a loosening of restrictions led to increasing supplier power.[15] In international markets, host governments can affect industry rivalry or supplier and buyer power by opening their domestic markets to foreign participation or closing them to protect domestic companies.

- *Changing societal concerns, attitudes, and lifestyles.* Emerging social issues and changing attitudes and lifestyles can be powerful instigators of industry change. Growing concerns about global warming have emerged as a major driver of change in the energy industry, changing the rate of industry growth in different sectors. The greater attention and care being given to household pets has driven growth across the whole pet industry. Changes in the industry growth rate, as we have seen, can affect the intensity of industry rivalry and entry conditions.

Table 3.3 lists these 12 most common drivers of change. That there are so many different *potential* drivers of change explains why a full understanding of all types of change drivers is a fundamental part of analyzing industry dynamics. However, for each industry no more than three or four of these drivers are likely to be powerful enough to qualify as the *major determinants* of why and how an industry's competitive conditions are changing. The true analytical task is to evaluate the forces of industry and competitive change carefully enough to separate major factors from minor ones.

Assessing the Impact of the Factors Driving Industry Change

Just identifying the factors driving industry change is not sufficient, however. The second, and more important, step in dynamic industry analysis is to determine whether the prevailing change drivers, on the whole, are acting to make the industry environment more or less attractive. Answers to three questions are needed:

1. Overall, are the factors driving change causing demand for the industry's product to increase or decrease?
2. Is the collective impact of the drivers of change making competition more or less intense?
3. Will the combined impacts of the change drivers lead to higher or lower industry profitability?

Getting a handle on the collective impact of the factors driving industry change requires looking at the likely effects of each factor separately, since the drivers of change may not all be pushing change in the same direction. For example, one change driver may be acting to spur demand for the industry's product while

Table 3.3   **The Most Common Drivers of Industry Change**

1. Changes in the long-term industry growth rate
2. Increasing globalization
3. Changes in who buys the product and how they use it
4. Technological change
5. Emerging new Internet capabilities and applications
6. Product and marketing innovation
7. Entry or exit of major firms
8. Diffusion of technical know-how across companies and countries
9. Improvements in efficiency in adjacent markets
10. Reductions in uncertainty and business risk
11. Regulatory influences and government policy changes
12. Changing societal concerns, attitudes, and lifestyles

another is working to curtail demand. Whether the net effect on industry demand is up or down hinges on which driver of change is the more powerful. Similarly, the effects of the drivers of change on each of the five forces should be looked at individually first, and then collectively, to view the overall effect. In summing up the overall effect of industry change on the five forces, it is important to recall that it is the *strongest* of the five forces that determines the degree of competitive pressure on industry profitability and therefore the industry's profit potential. The key question, then, is whether a new strong force is emerging or whether forces that are strong presently are beginning to weaken.

> The most important part of dynamic industry analysis is to determine whether the collective impact of the change drivers will be to increase or decrease market demand, make competition more or less intense, and lead to higher or lower industry profitability.

Developing a Strategy That Takes the Changes in Industry Conditions into Account

The third step in the strategic analysis of industry dynamics—where the real payoff for strategy making comes—is for managers to draw some conclusions about *what strategy adjustments will be needed to deal with the impacts of the changes in industry conditions.* The value of analyzing industry dynamics is to gain better understanding of what strategy adjustments will be needed to cope with the drivers of industry change and the impacts they are likely to have on competitive intensity and industry profitability. Indeed, without understanding the forces driving industry change and the impacts these forces will have on the character of the industry environment and on the company's business over the next one to three years, managers are ill-prepared to craft a strategy tightly matched to emerging conditions. To the extent that managers are unclear about the drivers of industry change and their impacts, or if their views are off-base, the chances of making astute and timely strategy adjustments are slim. So dynamic industry analysis is not something to take lightly; it has practical value and is basic to the task of thinking strategically about where the industry is headed and how to prepare for the changes ahead.

> Dynamic industry analysis, when done properly, pushes company managers to think about what's around the corner and what the company needs to be doing to get ready for it.

QUESTION 4: HOW ARE INDUSTRY RIVALS POSITIONED—WHO IS STRONGLY POSITIONED AND WHO IS NOT?

Since competing companies commonly sell in different price/quality ranges, emphasize different distribution channels, incorporate product features that appeal to different types of buyers, have different geographic coverage, and so on, it stands to reason that some companies enjoy stronger or more attractive market positions than other companies. Understanding which companies are strongly positioned and which are weakly positioned is an integral part of analyzing an industry's competitive structure. The best technique for revealing the market positions of industry competitors is **strategic group mapping**.[16]

LO 3

Become adept at mapping the market positions of key groups of industry rivals.

CORE CONCEPT

A **strategic group** is a cluster of industry rivals that have similar competitive approaches and market positions.

Using Strategic Group Maps to Assess the Market Positions of Key Competitors

A **strategic group** consists of those industry members with similar competitive approaches and positions in the market.[17] Companies in the same strategic group can resemble one another in any of several ways: They may have comparable product-line breadth, sell in the same price/quality range, emphasize the same distribution channels, use essentially the same product attributes to appeal to similar types of buyers, depend on identical technological approaches, or offer buyers similar services and technical assistance.[18] An industry contains only one strategic group when all sellers pursue essentially identical strategies and have similar market positions. At the other extreme, an industry may contain as many strategic groups as there are competitors when each rival pursues a distinctively different competitive approach and occupies a substantially different market position.

The procedure for constructing a *strategic group map* is straightforward:

- Identify the competitive characteristics that differentiate firms in the industry. Typical variables are price/quality range (high, medium, low), geographic coverage (local, regional, national, global), product-line breadth (wide, narrow), degree of service offered (no frills, limited, full), use of distribution channels (retail, wholesale, Internet, multiple), degree of vertical integration (none, partial, full), and degree of diversification into other industries (none, some, considerable).

- Plot the firms on a two-variable map using pairs of these differentiating characteristics.

- Assign firms occupying about the same map location to the same strategic group.

- Draw circles around each strategic group, making the circles proportional to the size of the group's share of total industry sales revenues.

This produces a two-dimensional diagram like the one for the retail chain store industry in Illustration Capsule 3.1.

Several guidelines need to be observed in creating strategic group maps.[19]

CORE CONCEPT

Strategic group mapping is a technique for displaying the different market or competitive positions that rival firms occupy in the industry.

First, the two variables selected as axes for the map should *not* be highly correlated; if they are, the circles on the map will fall along a diagonal and reveal nothing more about the relative positions of competitors than would be revealed by comparing the rivals on just one of the variables. For instance, if companies with broad product lines use multiple distribution channels while companies with narrow lines use a single distribution channel, then looking at broad versus narrow product lines reveals just as much about industry positioning as looking at single versus multiple distribution channels; that is, one of the variables is redundant.

Second, the variables chosen as axes for the map should reflect key approaches to offering value to customers and expose big differences in how rivals position themselves to compete in the marketplace. This, of course, means analysts must identify the characteristics that differentiate rival firms and use these differences as variables for the axes and as the basis for deciding which firm belongs in which strategic group. Third, the variables used as axes don't have to be either quantitative or continuous; rather, they can be discrete variables, defined in terms of distinct classes and combinations. Fourth, drawing the sizes of the circles on the map proportional to the combined sales of the firms in each strategic group allows the map to reflect the relative sizes of each strategic

ILLUSTRATION CAPSULE 3.1

Comparative Market Positions of Selected Retail Chains: A Strategic Group Map Example

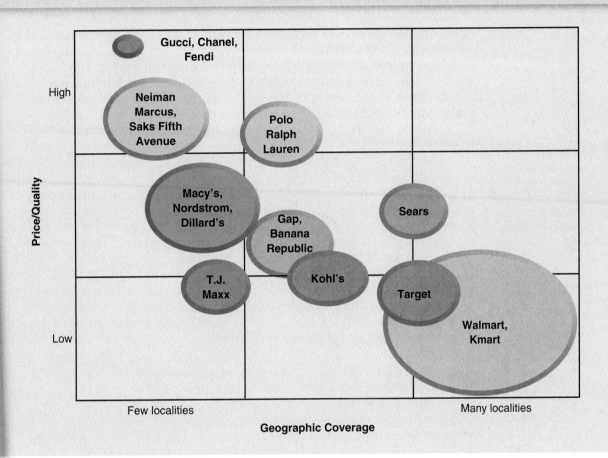

Note: Circles are drawn roughly proportional to the sizes of the chains, based on revenues.

group. Fifth, if more than two good variables can be used as axes for the map, then it is wise to draw several maps to give different views of the relationships among the competitive positions present in the industry's structure—there is not necessarily one best map for portraying how competing firms are positioned.

What Can Be Learned from Strategic Group Maps?

Strategic group maps are revealing in several respects. The most important has to do with identifying which industry members are close rivals and which are distant rivals. Firms in the same strategic group are the closest rivals; the next closest rivals are in the immediately adjacent groups. Often, firms in strategic groups that are far apart on the map hardly compete at all. For instance, Walmart's clientele, merchandise selection, and pricing points are much too different to justify calling Walmart a close

> Strategic group maps reveal which companies are close competitors and which are distant competitors.

127

competitor of Neiman Marcus or Saks Fifth Avenue. For the same reason, Timex is not a meaningful competitive rival of Rolex.

The second thing to be gleaned from strategic group mapping is that *not all positions on the map are equally attractive.*[20] Two reasons account for why some positions can be more attractive than others:[21]

1. *Prevailing competitive pressures in the industry and drivers of change favor some strategic groups and hurt others.* Discerning which strategic groups are advantaged and disadvantaged requires scrutinizing the map in light of what has been learned from the prior analyses of competitive forces and industry dynamics. Quite often the strength of competition varies from group to group—there's little reason to believe that all firms in an industry feel the same degrees of competitive pressure, since their strategies and market positions may well differ in important respects. For instance, in the ready-to-eat cereal industry, there are significantly higher entry barriers (capital requirements, brand loyalty, etc.) for the strategic group comprising the large branded-cereal makers than for the group of generic-cereal makers or the group of small natural-cereal producers. Furthermore, industry dynamics may affect different groups in different ways. For example, the long-term growth in demand may be increasing for some strategic groups and shrinking for others—as is the case in the news industry, where Internet news services and cable news networks are gaining ground at the expense of newspapers and network television. The industry driving forces of emerging Internet capabilities and applications, changes in who buys the product and how they use it, and changing societal concerns, attitudes, and lifestyles are making it increasingly difficult for traditional media to increase audiences and attract new advertisers.

2. *Profit prospects vary from strategic group to strategic group.* The profit prospects of firms in different strategic groups can vary from good to poor because of differing growth rates for the principal buyer segments served by each group, differing degrees of competitive rivalry within strategic groups, differing pressures from potential entrants to each group, differing degrees of exposure to competition from substitute products outside the industry, differing degrees of supplier or customer bargaining power from group to group, and differing impacts from the industry's drivers of change.

> Some strategic groups are more favorably positioned than others because they confront weaker competitive forces and/or because they are more favorably impacted by the drivers of industry change.

Thus, part of strategic group map analysis always entails drawing conclusions about where on the map is the "best" place to be and why. Which companies/strategic groups are destined to prosper because of their positions? Which companies/strategic groups seem destined to struggle because of their positions? What accounts for why some parts of the map are better than others?

QUESTION 5: WHAT STRATEGIC MOVES ARE RIVALS LIKELY TO MAKE NEXT?

Unless a company pays attention to the strategies and situations of competitors and has some inkling of what moves they will be making, it ends up flying blind into competitive battle. As in sports, scouting the opposition is an essential part of game plan development. **Competitive intelligence** about rivals' strategies, their latest actions and announcements, their financial performance, their strengths and weaknesses, and the thinking and leadership styles of their executives is valuable for anticipating the strategic moves competitors are likely to make next. Having good information about the strategic direction and likely moves of key competitors allows a company to prepare defensive countermoves, to craft its own strategic moves with some confidence about what market maneuvers to expect from rivals in response, and to exploit any openings that arise from competitors' missteps.

> Good **competitive intelligence** helps managers avoid the damage to sales and profits that comes from being caught napping by the surprise moves of rivals.

One indicator of the types of moves a rival is likely to make is its financial performance—how much pressure it is under to improve. Rivals with good financial performance are likely to continue their present strategy with only minor fine-tuning. Poorly performing rivals are virtually certain to make fresh strategic moves. Ambitious rivals looking to move up in the industry ranks are strong candidates for launching new strategic offensives to pursue emerging market opportunities and exploit the vulnerabilities of weaker rivals.

Other good clues about what actions a specific company is likely to undertake can often be gleaned from what its management is saying in company press releases, information posted on the company's Web site (especially the presentations management has recently made to securities analysts), and such public documents as annual reports and other financial reports. (Figure 1.1 in Chapter 1 indicates what to look for in identifying a company's strategy.) Many companies have a competitive intelligence unit that sifts through the available information to construct up-to-date strategic profiles of rivals—their current strategies, resources, competitive capabilities, and competitive shortcomings. Such profiles are typically updated regularly and made available to managers and other key personnel.

There are several useful questions that company managers can pose to help predict the likely actions of important rivals:

1. Which competitors have strategies that are producing good results—and thus are likely to make only minor strategic adjustments?

2. Which competitors are losing ground in the marketplace or otherwise struggling to come up with a good strategy—and thus are strong candidates for altering their prices, improving the appeal of their product offerings, moving to a different part of the strategic group map, and otherwise adjusting important elements of their strategy?

3. Which competitors are poised to gain market share, and which ones seem destined to lose ground?

4. Which competitors are likely to rank among the industry leaders five years from now? Do the up-and-coming competitors have strong ambitions and the resources needed to overtake the current industry leader?

5. Which rivals badly need to increase their unit sales and market share? What strategic options are they most likely to pursue: lowering prices, adding new models and styles, expanding their dealer networks, entering additional geographic markets, boosting advertising to build better brand-name awareness, acquiring a weaker competitor, or placing more emphasis on direct sales via their Web sites?

6. Which rivals are likely to enter new geographic markets or make major moves to substantially increase their sales and market share in a particular geographic region?

7. Which rivals are strong candidates to expand their product offerings and enter new product segments where they do not currently have a presence?

8. Which rivals are good candidates to be acquired? Which rivals may be looking to make an acquisition and are financially able to do so?

To succeed in predicting a competitor's next moves, company strategists need to have a good understanding of each rival's situation, its pattern of behavior in the past, how its managers think, and what the rival's best strategic options are. Doing the necessary detective work can be time-consuming, but scouting competitors well enough to anticipate their next moves allows managers to prepare effective countermoves (perhaps even beat a rival to the punch) and to take rivals' probable actions into account in crafting their own best course of action.

QUESTION 6: WHAT ARE THE KEY FACTORS FOR FUTURE COMPETITIVE SUCCESS?

An industry's **key success factors (KSFs)** are those competitive factors that affect industry members' ability to survive and prosper in the marketplace—the particular strategy elements, product attributes, operational approaches, resources, and competitive capabilities that spell the difference between being a strong competitor and a weak competitor—and between profit and loss. KSFs by their very nature are so important to competitive success that *all firms* in the industry must pay close attention to them or risk becoming an industry laggard or failure. To indicate the significance of KSFs another way, how well the elements of a company's strategy measure up against an industry's KSFs determines just how financially and competitively successful that company will be. Identifying KSFs, in light of the prevailing and anticipated industry and competitive conditions, is therefore always a top priority in analytical and strategy-making considerations. Company strategists need to understand the industry landscape well enough to separate the factors most important to competitive success from those that are less important.

Key success factors vary from industry to industry, and even from time to time within the same industry, as drivers of change and competitive conditions change. But regardless of the circumstances, an industry's key success factors can always be deduced by asking the same three questions:

1. On what basis do buyers of the industry's product choose between the competing brands of sellers? That is, what product attributes and service characteristics are crucial?

2. Given the nature of competitive rivalry and the competitive forces prevailing in the marketplace, what resources and competitive capabilities must a company have to be competitively successful?

3. What shortcomings are almost certain to put a company at a significant competitive disadvantage?

Only rarely are there more than five key factors for competitive success. When there appear to be more, usually some are of greater importance

CORE CONCEPT

Key success factors are the strategy elements, product and service attributes, operational approaches, resources, and competitive capabilities with the greatest impact on competitive success in the marketplace.

than others. Managers should therefore bear in mind the purpose of identifying key success factors—to determine which factors are most important to competitive success—and resist the temptation to label a factor that has only minor importance as a KSF. Compiling a list of every factor that matters even a little bit defeats the purpose of concentrating management attention on the factors truly critical to long-term competitive success.

In the beer industry, for example, although there are many types of buyers (wholesale, retail, end consumer), it is most important to understand the preferences and buying behavior of the beer drinkers. Their purchase decisions are driven by price, taste, convenient access, and marketing. Thus the KSFs include a *strong network of wholesale distributors* (to get the company's brand stocked and favorably displayed in retail outlets, bars, restaurants, and stadiums, where beer is sold) and *clever advertising* (to induce beer drinkers to buy the company's brand and thereby pull beer sales through the established wholesale/retail channels). Because there is a potential for strong buyer power on the part of large distributors and retail chains, competitive success depends on some mechanism to offset that power, of which advertising (to create demand pull) is one. Thus the KSFs also include *superior product differentiation* (as in microbrews) or *superior firm size and branding capabilities* (as in national brands). The KSFs also include *full utilization of brewing capacity* (to keep manufacturing costs low and offset the high advertising, branding, and product differentiation costs).

Correctly diagnosing an industry's KSFs raises a company's chances of crafting a sound strategy. The key success factors of an industry point to those things that every firm in the industry needs to attend to in order to retain customers and weather the competition. If the company's strategy cannot deliver on the key success factors of its industry, it is unlikely to earn enough profits to remain a viable business. The goal of strategists, however, should be to do more than just meet the KSFs, since all firms in the industry need to clear this bar to survive. The goal of company strategists should be to design a strategy that allows it to compare favorably vis-à-vis rivals on each and every one of the industry's KSFs and that aims at being *distinctively better* than rivals on one (or possibly two) of the KSFs.

LO 4

Understand why in-depth evaluation of a business's strengths and weaknesses in relation to the specific industry conditions it confronts is an essential prerequisite to crafting a strategy that is well-matched to its external situation.

QUESTION 7: DOES THE INDUSTRY OFFER GOOD PROSPECTS FOR ATTRACTIVE PROFITS?

The final step in evaluating the industry and competitive environment is to use the results of the analyses performed in answering Questions 1 to 6 to determine whether the industry presents the company with strong prospects for attractive profits. The important factors on which to base a conclusion include:

- The industry's growth potential.
- Whether strong competitive forces are squeezing industry profitability to subpar levels.
- Whether industry profitability will be favorably or unfavorably affected by the prevailing drivers of change in the industry (i.e., whether the industry growth potential and competition appear destined to grow stronger or weaker).

- Whether the company occupies a stronger market position than rivals (one more capable of withstanding negative competitive forces) and whether this is likely to change in the course of competitive interactions.
- How well the company's strategy delivers on the industry key success factors.

As a general proposition, if a company can conclude that its overall profit prospects are above average in the industry, then the industry environment is basically attractive *(for that company)*; if industry profit prospects are below average, conditions are unattractive *(for the company)*. However, it is a mistake to think of a particular industry as being equally attractive or unattractive to all industry participants and all potential entrants.[22] Attractiveness is relative, not absolute, and conclusions one way or the other have to be drawn from the perspective of a particular company. For instance, a favorably positioned competitor may see ample opportunity to capitalize on the vulnerabilities of weaker rivals even though industry conditions are otherwise somewhat dismal. And even if an industry has appealing potential for growth and profitability, a weak competitor (one that may be part of an unfavorably positioned strategic group) may conclude that having to fight a steep uphill battle against much stronger rivals holds little promise of eventual market success or good return on shareholder investment. Similarly, industries attractive to insiders may be unattractive to outsiders because of the difficulty of challenging current market leaders with their particular resources and competencies or because they have more attractive opportunities elsewhere.

> The degree to which an industry is attractive or unattractive is not the same for all industry participants and all potential entrants.

When a company decides an industry is fundamentally attractive and presents good opportunities, a strong case can be made that it should invest aggressively to capture the opportunities it sees and to improve its long-term competitive position in the business. When a strong competitor concludes an industry is becoming less attractive, it may elect to simply protect its present position, investing cautiously if at all and looking for opportunities in other industries. A competitively weak company in an unattractive industry may see its best option as finding a buyer, perhaps a rival, to acquire its business.

KEY POINTS

Thinking strategically about a company's external situation involves probing for answers to the following seven questions:

1. *Does the industry offer attractive opportunities for growth?* Industries differ significantly on such factors as market size and growth rate, geographic scope, life-cycle stage, the number and sizes of sellers, industry capacity, and other conditions that describe the industry's demand-supply balance and opportunities for growth. Identifying the industry's basic economic features and growth potential sets the stage for the analysis to come, since they play an important role in determining an industry's potential for attractive profits.

2. *What kinds of competitive forces are industry members facing, and how strong is each force?* The strength of competition is a composite of five forces: (1) competitive pressures stemming from the competitive jockeying among industry rivals, (2) competitive pressures associated with the market inroads

being made by the sellers of substitutes, (3) competitive pressures associated with the threat of new entrants into the market, (4) competitive pressures stemming from supplier bargaining power, and (5) competitive pressures stemming from buyer bargaining. The nature and strength of the competitive pressures have to be examined force by force and their collective strength must be evaluated. The strongest forces, however, are the ultimate determinant of the intensity of the competitive pressure on industry profitability. Working through the five-forces model aids strategy makers in assessing how to insulate the company from the strongest forces, identify attractive arenas for expansion, or alter the competitive conditions so that they offer more favorable prospects for profitability.

3. *What factors are driving changes in the industry, and what impact will these changes have on competitive intensity and industry profitability?* Industry and competitive conditions change because of a variety of forces, some coming from the industry's macro-environment and others originating within the industry. The most common change drivers include changes in the long-term industry growth rate, increasing globalization, changing buyer demographics, technological change, Internet-related developments, product and marketing innovation, entry or exit of major firms, diffusion of know-how, efficiency improvements in adjacent markets, reductions in uncertainty and business risk, government policy changes, and changing societal factors. Once an industry's change drivers have been identified, the analytical task becomes one of determining whether they are acting, individually and collectively, to make the industry environment more or less attractive. Are the change drivers causing demand for the industry's product to increase or decrease? Are they acting to make competition more or less intense? Will they lead to higher or lower industry profitability?

4. *What market positions do industry rivals occupy—who is strongly positioned and who is not?* Strategic group mapping is a valuable tool for understanding the similarities, differences, strengths, and weaknesses inherent in the market positions of rival companies. Rivals in the same or nearby strategic groups are close competitors, whereas companies in distant strategic groups usually pose little or no immediate threat. The lesson of strategic group mapping is that some positions on the map are more favorable than others. The profit potential of different strategic groups varies due to strengths and weaknesses in each group's market position. Often, industry competitive pressures and change drivers favor some strategic groups and hurt others.

5. *What strategic moves are rivals likely to make next?* Scouting competitors well enough to anticipate their actions can help a company prepare effective countermoves (perhaps even beating a rival to the punch) and allows managers to take rivals' probable actions into account in designing their own company's best course of action. Managers who fail to study competitors risk being caught unprepared by the strategic moves of rivals.

6. *What are the key factors for competitive success?* An industry's key success factors (KSFs) are the particular strategy elements, product attributes, operational approaches, resources, and competitive capabilities that all industry members must have in order to survive and prosper in the industry. KSFs vary by industry and may vary over time as well. For any industry, however, they can be deduced by answering three basic questions: (1) On what basis do buyers of the industry's product choose between the competing brands of

sellers, (2) what resources and competitive capabilities must a company have to be competitively successful, and (3) what shortcomings are almost certain to put a company at a significant competitive disadvantage? Correctly diagnosing an industry's KSFs raises a company's chances of crafting a sound strategy.

7. *Does the outlook for the industry present the company with sufficiently attractive prospects for profitability?* The last step in industry analysis is summing up the results from answering questions 1 to 6. If the answers reveal that a company's overall profit prospects in that industry are above average, then the industry environment is basically attractive *for that company;* if industry profit prospects are below average, conditions are unattractive for them. What may look like an attractive environment for one company may appear to be unattractive from the perspective of a different company.

Clear, insightful diagnosis of a company's external situation is an essential first step in crafting strategies that are well matched to industry and competitive conditions. To do cutting-edge strategic thinking about the external environment, managers must know what questions to pose and what analytical tools to use in answering these questions. This is why this chapter has concentrated on suggesting the right questions to ask, explaining concepts and analytical approaches, and indicating the kinds of things to look for.

ASSURANCE OF LEARNING EXERCISES

LO 1, LO 2

1. Prepare a brief analysis of the bottled water industry using the information provided on industry trade association Web sites. On the basis of information provided on these Web sites, draw a five-forces diagram for the bottled water industry and briefly discuss the nature and strength of each of the five competitive forces. What factors are driving change in the industry?

LO 1, LO 3

2. Based on the strategic group map in Illustration Capsule 3.1, who are Nordstrom's closest competitors? Between which two strategic groups is competition the strongest? Why do you think no retail chains are positioned in the upper right corner of the map? Which company/strategic group faces the weakest competition from the members of other strategic groups?

LO 1, LO 4

3. Using your knowledge as a bottled water consumer and your analysis of the five forces in that industry (from question 1), describe the key success factors for the bottled water industry. Your list should contain no more than six industry KSFs. In deciding on your list, it's important to distinguish between factors critical for the success of *any* firm in the industry and factors that pertain only to specific companies.

EXERCISES FOR SIMULATION PARTICIPANTS

LO 1

1. Which of the five competitive forces is creating the strongest competitive pressures for your company?

2. What are the "competitive weapons" that rival companies in your industry can use to gain sales and market share? See Table 3.2 to help you identify possible competitive tactics. (You may be able to think of others.)

3. What are the factors affecting the intensity of rivalry in the industry in which your company is competing. Use Figure 3.4 and the accompanying discussion to help you pinpoint the specific factors most affecting competitive intensity. Would you characterize the rivalry among the companies in your industry as brutal, strong, moderate, or relatively weak? Why?

LO 2

4. Are there any factors driving change in the industry in which your company is competing? What impact will these drivers of change have? How will they change demand or supply? Will they cause competition to become more or less intense? Will they act to boost or squeeze profit margins? List at least two actions your company should consider taking in order to combat any negative impacts of the factors driving change.

LO 3

5. Draw a strategic group map showing the market positions of the companies in your industry. Which companies do you believe are in the most attractive position on the map? Which companies are the most weakly positioned? Which companies do you believe are likely to try to move to a different position on the strategic group map?

LO 4

6. What do you see as the key factors for being a successful competitor in your industry? List at least three.

ENDNOTES

[1] For a more extended discussion of the problems with the life-cycle hypothesis, see Michael E. Porter, *Competitive Strategy: Techniques for Analyzing Industries and Competitors* (New York: Free Press, 1980), pp. 157–62.
[2] The five-forces model of competition is the creation of Professor Michael Porter of the Harvard Business School. See Michael E. Porter, "How Competitive Forces Shape Strategy," *Harvard Business Review* 57, no. 2 (March–April 1979), pp. 137–45; Porter, *Competitive Strategy*, chap. 1; and Porter's most recent discussion of the model, "The Five Competitive Forces That Shape Strategy," *Harvard Business Review* 86, no. 1 (January 2008), pp. 78–93.
[3] For a discussion of how a company's actions to counter the moves of rival firms tend to escalate competitive pressures, see Pamela J. Derfus, Patrick G. Maggitti, Curtis M.Grimm, and Ken G. Smith, "The Red Queen Effect: Competitive Actions and Firm Performance," *Academy of Management Journal* 51, no. 1 (February 2008), pp. 61–80.
[4] Many of these indicators of whether rivalry produces intense competitive pressures are based on Porter, *Competitive Strategy*, pp. 17–21.
[5] Porter, *Competitive Strategy*, p. 7; Porter, "The Five Competitive Forces That Shape Strategy," p. 81.
[6] The role of entry barriers in shaping the strength of competition in a particular market has long been a standard topic in the literature of microeconomics. For a discussion of how entry barriers affect competitive pressures associated with potential entry, see J. S. Bain, *Barriers to New Competition* (Cambridge, MA: Harvard University Press, 1956); F. M. Scherer, *Industrial Market Structure and Economic Performance*

(Chicago: Rand McNally, 1971), pp. 216–20, 226–33; Porter, *Competitive Strategy*, pp. 7–17; Porter, "The Five Competitive Forces That Shape Strategy," pp. 80–82.

[7] For a good discussion of this point, see George S. Yip, "Gateways to Entry," *Harvard Business Review* 60, no. 5 (September–October 1982), pp. 85–93.

[8] C. A. Montgomery and S. Hariharan, "Diversified Expansion by Large Established Firms," *Journal of Economic Behavior & Organization* 15, no. 1 (January 1991), pp. 71–89.

[9] Porter, "How Competitive Forces Shape Strategy," p. 142; Porter, *Competitive Strategy*, pp. 23–24.

[10] Porter, *Competitive Strategy*, p. 10.

[11] Ibid., pp. 27–28.

[12] Ibid., pp. 24–27.

[13] Porter, "The Five Competitive Forces That Shape Strategy," p. 80.

[14] Most of the candidate driving forces described here are based on the discussion in Porter, *Competitive Strategy*, pp. 164–83.

[15] D. Yoffie, "Cola Wars Continue: Coke and Pepsi in 2006," Harvard Business School case 9-706-447, rev. April 2, 2007; B. C. Lynn, "How Detroit Went Bottom-Up," *American Prospect*, October 2009, pp. 21–24.

[16] Porter, *Competitive Strategy*, chap. 7.

[17] Ibid., pp. 129–30.

[18] For an excellent discussion of how to identify the factors that define strategic groups, see Mary Ellen Gordon and George R. Milne, "Selecting the Dimensions That Define Strategic Groups: A Novel Market-Driven Approach," *Journal of Managerial Issues* 11, no. 2 (Summer 1999), pp. 213–33.

[19] Porter, *Competitive Strategy*, pp. 152–54.

[20] For other benefits of strategic group analysis, see Avi Fiegenbaum and Howard Thomas, "Strategic Groups as Reference Groups: Theory, Modeling and Empirical Examination of Industry and Competitive Strategy," *Strategic Management Journal* 16 (1995), pp. 461–76; S. Ade Olusoga, Michael P. Mokwa, and Charles H. Noble, "Strategic Groups, Mobility Barriers, and Competitive Advantage," *Journal of Business Research* 33 (1995), pp. 153–64.

[21] Porter, *Competitive Strategy*, pp. 130, 132–38, and 152–55.

[22] B. Wernerfelt and C. Montgomery, "What Is an Attractive Industry?" *Management Science* 32, no. 10 (October 1986), pp. 1223–30.

CHAPTER 4

EVALUATING A COMPANY'S RESOURCES, CAPABILITIES, AND COMPETITIVENESS

> Before executives can chart a new strategy, they must reach common understanding of the company's current position.
>
> **—W. Chan Kim and Renée Mauborgne**
> *Consultants and INSEAD Professors*

> You have to learn to treat people as a resource ... you have to ask not what do they cost, but what is the yield, what can they produce?
>
> **—Peter F. Drucker**
> *Business Thinker and Management Consultant*

> Organizations succeed in a competitive marketplace over the long run because they can do certain things their customers value better than can their competitors.
>
> **—Robert Hayes, Gary Pisano, and David Upton**
> *Harvard Business School Professors*

> Only firms who are able to continually build new strategic assets faster and cheaper than their competitors will earn superior returns over the long term.
>
> **—C. C. Markides and P. J. Williamson**
> *London Business School Professors and Consultants*

LEARNING OBJECTIVES

LO 1. Learn how to take stock of how well a company's strategy is working.

LO 2. Understand why a company's resources and capabilities are central to its strategic approach and how to evaluate their potential for giving the company a competitive edge over rivals.

LO 3. Discover how to assess the company's strengths and weaknesses in light of market opportunities and external threats.

LO 4. Grasp how a company's value chain activities can affect the company's cost structure, degree of differentiation, and competitive advantage.

LO 5. Understand how a comprehensive evaluation of a company's competitive situation can assist managers in making critical decisions about their next strategic moves.

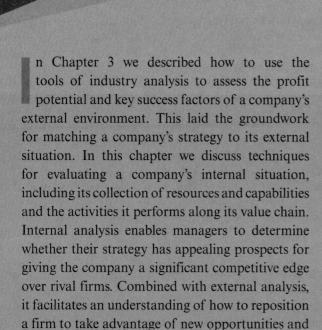

n Chapter 3 we described how to use the tools of industry analysis to assess the profit potential and key success factors of a company's external environment. This laid the groundwork for matching a company's strategy to its external situation. In this chapter we discuss techniques for evaluating a company's internal situation, including its collection of resources and capabilities and the activities it performs along its value chain. Internal analysis enables managers to determine whether their strategy has appealing prospects for giving the company a significant competitive edge over rival firms. Combined with external analysis, it facilitates an understanding of how to reposition a firm to take advantage of new opportunities and to cope with emerging competitive threats. The analytical spotlight will be trained on six questions:

1. How well is the company's present strategy working?

2. What are the company's competitively important resources and capabilities?

3. Is the company able to take advantage of market opportunities and overcome external threats to its external well-being?

4. Are the company's prices and costs competitive with those of key rivals, and does it have an appealing customer value proposition?

5. Is the company competitively stronger or weaker than key rivals?

6. What strategic issues and problems merit front-burner managerial attention?

In probing for answers to these questions, five analytical tools—resource and capability analysis, SWOT analysis, value chain analysis, benchmarking, and competitive strength assessment—will be used. All five are valuable techniques for revealing a company's competitiveness and for helping company managers match their strategy to the company's own particular circumstances.

QUESTION 1: HOW WELL IS THE COMPANY'S PRESENT STRATEGY WORKING?

LO 1

Learn how to take stock of how well a company's strategy is working.

In evaluating how well a company's present strategy is working, the best way to start is with a clear view of what the strategy entails. Figure 4.1 shows the key components of a single-business company's strategy. The first thing to examine is the company's competitive approach. What moves has the company made recently to attract customers and improve its market position—for instance, has it cut prices, improved the design of its product, added new features, stepped up advertising, entered a new geographic market (domestic or foreign), or merged with a competitor? Is it striving for a competitive advantage based on low costs or an appealingly different or better product offering? Is it concentrating on serving a broad spectrum of customers or a narrow market niche? The company's functional strategies in R&D, production, marketing, finance, human resources, information technology, and so on further characterize company strategy, as do any efforts to establish competitively valuable alliances or partnerships with other enterprises.

The two best indicators of how well a company's strategy is working are (1) whether the company is achieving its stated financial and strategic objectives and (2) whether the company is an above-average industry performer. Persistent shortfalls in meeting company performance targets and weak performance relative to rivals are reliable warning signs that the company has a weak strategy or suffers from poor strategy execution or both. Other indicators of how well a company's strategy is working include:

- Whether the firm's sales are growing faster than, slower than, or about the same pace as the market as a whole, thus resulting in a rising, eroding, or stable market share.
- Whether the company is acquiring new customers at an attractive rate as well as retaining existing customers.
- Whether the firm's profit margins are increasing or decreasing and how well its margins compare to rival firms' margins.
- Trends in the firm's net profits and return on investment and how they compare to the same trends for other companies in the industry.
- Whether the company's overall financial strength and credit rating are improving or declining.
- How shareholders view the company on the basis of trends in the company's stock price and shareholder value (relative to the stock price trends at other companies in the industry).
- Whether the firm's image and reputation with its customers are growing stronger or weaker.
- How well the company stacks up against rivals on technology, product innovation, customer service, product quality, delivery time, price, getting newly developed products to market quickly, and other relevant factors on which buyers base their choices.
- Whether key measures of operating performance (such as days of inventory, employee productivity, unit cost, defect rate, scrap rate, order-filling accuracy, delivery times, and warranty costs) are improving, remaining steady, or deteriorating.

Figure 4.1 Identifying the Components of a Single-Business Company's Strategy

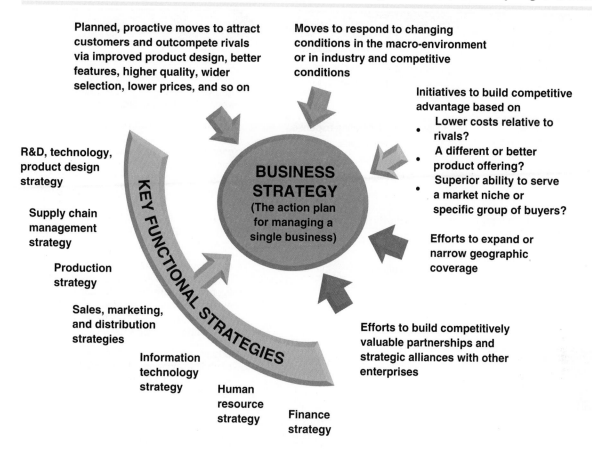

The stronger a company's current overall performance, the less likely the need for radical changes in strategy. The weaker a company's financial performance and market standing, the more its current strategy must be questioned. Weak performance is almost always a sign of weak strategy, weak execution, or both.

Evaluating how well a company's strategy is working should include quantitative as well as qualitative assessments. Table 4.1 provides a compilation of the financial ratios most commonly used to evaluate a company's financial performance and balance sheet strength.

> The stronger a company's financial performance and market position, the more likely it has a well-conceived, well-executed strategy.

QUESTION 2: WHAT ARE THE COMPANY'S COMPETITIVELY IMPORTANT RESOURCES AND CAPABILITIES?

Regardless of how well the strategy is working, it is important for managers to understand the underlying reasons. Clearly, this is critical if strategy changes are needed. But even when the strategy is working well, this can help managers to bolster a

Table 4.1   Key Financial Ratios: How to Calculate Them and What They Mean

Ratio	How Calculated	What It Shows
Profitability Ratios		
1. Gross profit margin	$$\frac{\text{Revenues} - \text{Cost of goods sold}}{\text{Revenues}}$$	Shows the percentage of revenues available to cover operating expenses and yield a profit. Higher is better, and the trend should be upward.
2. Operating profit margin (or return on sales)	$$\frac{\text{Revenues} - \text{Operating expenses}}{\text{Revenues}}$$ _or_ $$\frac{\text{Operating income}}{\text{Revenues}}$$	Shows how much profit is earned on each dollar of sales, before paying interest charges and income taxes. Earnings before interest and taxes is known as _EBIT_ in financial and business accounting. Higher is better, and the trend should be upward.
3. Net profit margin (or net return on sales)	$$\frac{\text{Profits after taxes}}{\text{Revenues}}$$	Shows after-tax profits per dollar of sales. Higher is better, and the trend should be upward.
4. Return on total assets	$$\frac{\text{Profits after taxes} + \text{Interest}}{\text{Total assets}}$$	A measure of the return on total investment in the enterprise. Interest is added to after-tax profits to form the numerator, since total assets are financed by creditors as well as by stockholders. Higher is better, and the trend should be upward.
5. Return on stockholder's equity	$$\frac{\text{Profits after taxes}}{\text{Total stockholders' equity}}$$	Shows the return stockholders are earning on their investment in the enterprise. A return in the 12% to 15% range is "average," and the trend should be upward.
6. Return on invested capital	$$\frac{\text{Profits after taxes}}{\text{Long-term debt} + \text{total equity}}$$	Shows how effectively a company uses the monetary capital invested in its operations and the returns to those investments. Higher is better, and the trend should be upward.
7. Earnings per share	$$\frac{\text{Profits after taxes}}{\text{Number of shares of common stock outstanding}}$$	Shows the earnings for each share of common stock outstanding. The trend should be upward, and the bigger the annual percentage gains, the better.
Liquidity Ratios		
1. Current ratio	$$\frac{\text{Current assets}}{\text{Current liabilities}}$$	Shows a firm's ability to pay current liabilities using assets that can be converted to cash in the near term. The ratio should definitely be higher than 1.0; a ratio of 2.0 or higher is better still.
2. Working capital	Current assets − Current liabilities	Shows the cash available for a firm's day-to-day operations. Bigger amounts are better because the company has more internal funds available to (1) pay its current liabilities on a timely basis and (2) finance inventory expansion, additional accounts receivable, and a larger base of operations without resorting to borrowing or raising more equity capital.

(Continued)

Ratio	How Calculated	What It Shows
Leverage Ratios		
1. Debt-to-assets ratio	$$\dfrac{\text{Total debt}}{\text{Total assets}}$$	Measures the extent to which borrowed funds have been used to finance the firm's operations. A low fraction or ratio is better—a high fraction indicates overuse of debt and greater risk of bankruptcy.
2. Long-term debt-to-capital ratio	$$\dfrac{\text{Long-term debt}}{\text{Long-term debt } + \text{Total stockholders' equity}}$$	An important measure of creditworthiness and balance sheet strength. It indicates the percentage of capital investment that has been financed by creditors and bondholders. A ratio below 0.25 is usually preferable since monies invested by stockholders account for 75% or more of the company's total capital. The lower the ratio, the greater the capacity to borrow additional funds. A debt-to capital ratio above 0.50 and certainly above 0.75 indicates a heavy and perhaps excessive reliance on debt, lower creditworthiness, and weak balance sheet strength.
3. Debt-to-equity ratio	$$\dfrac{\text{Total debt}}{\text{Total stockholders' equity}}$$	Should usually be less than 1.0. A high ratio (especially above 1.0) signals excessive debt, lower creditworthiness, and weaker balance sheet strength.
4. Long-term debt-to-equity ratio	$$\dfrac{\text{Long-term debt}}{\text{Total stockholders' equity}}$$	Shows the balance between debt and equity in the firm's *long-term* capital structure. A low ratio indicates greater capacity to borrow additional funds if needed.
5. Times-interest-earned (or coverage) ratio	$$\dfrac{\text{Operating income}}{\text{Interest expenses}}$$	Measures the ability to pay annual interest charges. Lenders usually insist on a minimum ratio of 2.0, but ratios above 3.0 signal better creditworthiness.
Activity Ratios		
1. Days of inventory	$$\dfrac{\text{Inventory}}{\text{Cost of goods sold} \div 365}$$	Measures inventory management efficiency. Fewer days of inventory are usually better.
2. Inventory turnover	$$\dfrac{\text{Cost of goods sold}}{\text{Inventory}}$$	Measures the number of inventory turns per year. Higher is better.
3. Average collection period	$$\dfrac{\text{Accounts receivable}}{\text{Total sales} \div 365}$$ *or* $$\dfrac{\text{Accounts receivable}}{\text{Average daily sales}}$$	Indicates the average length of time the firm must wait after making a sale to receive cash payment. A shorter collection time is better.
Other Important Measures of Financial Performance		
1. Dividend yield on common stock	$$\dfrac{\text{Annual dividends per share}}{\text{Current market price per share}}$$	A measure of the return to owners received in the form of dividends.

(Continued)

Ratio	How Calculated	What It Shows
2. Price-earnings ratio	$\dfrac{\text{Current market price per share}}{\text{Earnings per share}}$	A P/E ratio above 20 indicates strong investor confidence in a firm's outlook and earnings growth. Firms whose future earnings are at risk or likely to grow slowly typically have ratios below 12.
3. Dividend payout ratio	$\dfrac{\text{Annual dividends per share}}{\text{Earnings per share}}$	Indicates the percentage of after-tax profits paid out as dividends.
4. Internal cash flow	After tax profits + Depreciation	A quick and rough estimate of the cash a company's business is generating after payment of operating expenses, interest, and taxes. Such amounts can be used for dividend payments or funding capital expenditures.
5. Free cash flow	After tax profits + Depreciation − Capital Expenditures − Dividends	A quick and rough estimate of the cash a company's business is generating after payment of operating expenses, interest, taxes, dividends, and desirable reinvestments in the business. The larger a company's free cash flow, the greater is its ability to internally fund new strategic initiatives, repay debt, make new acquisitions, repurchase shares of stock, or increase dividend payments.

CORE CONCEPT

A company's resources and capabilities represent its **competitive assets** and are big determinants of its competitiveness and ability to succeed in the marketplace.

LO 2

Understand why a company's resources and capabilities are central to its strategic approach and how to evaluate their potential for giving the company a competitive edge over rivals.

successful strategy and avoid harmful missteps. How well a strategy works depends a great deal on the relative strengths and weaknesses of a company's resources and capabilities. A company's resources and capabilities are its **competitive assets** and determine whether its competitive power in the marketplace will be impressively strong or disappointingly weak. Companies with minimal or only ordinary competitive assets nearly always are relegated to a trailing position in the industry.

Resource and capability analysis provides managers with a powerful tool for sizing up the company's competitive assets and determining whether they can provide the foundation necessary for competitive success in the marketplace. This is a two step process. The first step is for managers to identify the company's resources and capabilities so that they have a better idea of what they have to work with in crafting the company's competitive strategy. The second step is to examine the company's resources and capabilities more closely to ascertain which of them are the most competitively valuable and to determine whether the best of them can help the firm attain a sustainable competitive advantage over rival firms.[1] This step involves applying the *four tests of a resource's competitive power.*

Identifying the Company's Resources and Capabilities

A firm's resources and capabilities are the fundamental building blocks of its competitive strategy. In crafting strategy, it is essential for managers to be able to recognize a resource or an organizational capability for what it is and to know how to take stock of the company's full complement of resources and capabilities.

To do a good job with this, managers and strategists need to start with a basic understanding of what these terms mean.

In brief, a **resource** is a productive input or competitive asset that is owned or controlled by the firm. Firms have many different types of resources at their disposal that vary not only in kind but in quality as well. Some are higher-quality than others, and some are more competitively valuable, having greater potential to give a firm a competitive advantage over its rivals. For example, a company's brand is a resource, as is an R&D team—yet some brands such as Coca-Cola and Danone are well known, with enduring value, while others have little more name recognition than generic products. In similar fashion, some R&D teams are far more innovative and productive than others due to the outstanding talents of the individual team members, the team's composition, and its chemistry.

A **capability** is the capacity of a firm to perform some activity proficiently. Capabilities also vary in form, quality, and competitive importance, with some being more competitively valuable than others. Apple's product innovation capabilities are widely recognized as being far superior to those of its competitors; BMW is known for its engineering capabilities; PepsiCo is admired for its marketing and brand management capabilities.

> **Resource and capability analysis** is a powerful tool for sizing up a company's competitive assets and determining if they can support a sustainable competitive advantage over market rivals.

> **CORE CONCEPT**
>
> A **resource** is a competitive asset that is owned or controlled by a company; a **capability** is the capacity of a firm to perform some activity proficiently.

Types of Company Resources   A useful way to identify a company's resources is to look for them within categories, as shown in Table 4.2. Broadly speaking, resources can be divided into two main categories:

Table 4.2   Types of Company Resources

Tangible Resources

- *Physical resources:* ownership of or access rights to natural resources (such as mineral deposits); state-of-the-art manufacturing plants, equipment, and/or distribution facilities; land and real estate; the locations of stores, manufacturing plants, or distribution centers, including the overall pattern of their physical locations

- *Financial resources:* cash and cash equivalents; marketable securities; other financial assets such as the borrowing capacity of the firm (as indicated from its balance sheet and credit rating)

- *Technological assets:* patents, copyrights, and trade secrets; production technology, stock of other technologies, technological processes

- *Organizational resources:* IT and communication systems (servers, workstations, etc.); other planning, coordination, and control systems; the company's organizational design and reporting structure

Intangible Resources

- *Human assets and intellectual capital:* the experience, cumulative learning, and tacit knowledge of employees; the education, intellectual capital, and know-how of specialized teams and work groups; the knowledge of key personnel concerning important business functions (e.g., skills in keeping operating costs low, improving product quality, and providing customer service); managerial talent; the creativity and innovativeness of certain personnel

- *Brands, company image, and reputational assets:* brand names, trademarks, product image, buyer loyalty and goodwill; company image, reputation for quality, service, and reliability; reputation with suppliers and partners for fair dealing

- *Relationships:* alliances or joint ventures that provide access to technologies, specialized know-how, or geographic markets; partnerships with suppliers that reduce costs and/or enhance product quality and performance; networks of dealers or distributors; the trust established with various partners

- *Company culture and incentive system:* the norms of behavior, business principles, and ingrained beliefs within the company; the attachment of personnel to the company's ideals; the compensation system and the motivation level of company personnel

tangible and **intangible** resources. Although *human resources* make up one of the most important parts of a company's resource base, we include them in the intangible category to emphasize the role played by the skills, talents, and knowledge of a company's human resources.

Tangible resources are the most easily identified, since tangible resources are those that can be touched or quantified readily. Obviously, they include various types of *physical resources* such as manufacturing facilities and mineral resources, but they also include a company's *financial resources, technological resources,* and *organizational resources* such as the company's communication and control systems.

Intangible resources are harder to discern, but they are often among the most important of a firm's competitive assets. They include various sorts of *human assets and intellectual capital,* as well as a company's *brands, image, and reputational assets.* While intangible resources have no material existence on their own, they are often embodied in something material. Thus the skills and knowledge resources of a firm are embodied in its managers and employees; a company's brand name is embodied in the company logo or product labels. Other important kinds of intangible resources include a company's *relationships* with suppliers, buyers, or partners of various sorts, and the *company's culture and incentive system.* A more detailed listing of the various types of tangible and intangible resources is provided in Table 4.2.

Listing a company's resources category by category can prevent managers from inadvertently overlooking some company resources that might be competitively important. At times, it can be difficult to decide exactly how to categorize certain types of resources. For example, resources such as a work group's specialized expertise in developing innovative products can be considered to be technological assets or human assets or intellectual capital and knowledge assets; the work ethic and drive of a company's workforce could be included under the company's human assets or its culture and incentive system. In this regard, it is important to remember that *it is not exactly how a resource is categorized that matters but, rather, that all of the company's different types of resources are included in the inventory.* The real purpose of using categories in identifying a company's resources is to ensure that none of a company's resources go unnoticed when sizing up the company's competitive assets.

Identifying Capabilities

Organizational capabilities are more complex entities than resources; indeed, they are built up through the use of resources and draw on some combination of the firm's resources as they are exercised.[2] Virtually all organizational capabilities are *knowledge-based, residing in people and in a company's intellectual capital or in organizational processes and systems, which embody tacit knowledge.* For example, Nestlé's brand management capabilities draw on the knowledge of the company's brand managers, the expertise of its marketing department, and the company's relationships with retailers, since brand building is a cooperative activity requiring retailer support. The capability in video game design for which Electronic Arts is known derives from the creative talents and technological expertise of its highly talented game developers, the company's culture of creativity, and a compensation system that generously rewards talented developers for creating best-selling video games.

Because of their complexity, capabilities are harder to categorize than resources and more challenging to search for as a result. There are, however, two approaches that can make the process of uncovering and identifying a firm's capabilities more systematic. The first method takes the completed listing of a firm's resources as its starting point. Since capabilities are built from resources and utilize resources as they are exercised, a firm's resources can provide a strong set of clues about the types of capabilities the firm is likely to have accumulated. This approach simply involves looking over the firm's resources and considering whether (and to what extent) the firm has built up any related capabilities. So, for example, a fleet of trucks, the latest RFID tracking technology, and a set of large automated distribution centers may be indicative of sophisticated capabilities in logistics and distribution. R&D teams composed of top scientists with expertise in genomics may suggest organizational capabilities in developing new gene therapies or in biotechnology more generally.

The second method of identifying a firm's capabilities takes a functional approach. Many capabilities relate to fairly specific functions; these draw on a limited set of resources and typically involve a single department or organizational unit. Capabilities in injection molding or continuous casting or metal stamping are manufacturing-related; capabilities in direct selling, promotional pricing, or database marketing all connect to the sales and marketing functions; capabilities in basic research, strategic innovation, or new product development link to a company's R&D function. This approach requires managers to survey the various functions a firm performs to find the different capabilities associated with each function.

A problem with this second method is that many of the most important capabilities of firms are inherently *cross-functional*. Cross-functional capabilities draw on a number of different kinds of resources and are generally multidisciplinary in nature—they spring from the effective collaboration among people with different expertise working in different organizational units. An example is the capability for fast-cycle, continuous product innovation that comes from teaming the efforts of groups with expertise in market research, new product R&D, design and engineering, advanced manufacturing, and market testing. Cross-functional capabilities and other complex capabilities involving numerous linked and closely integrated competitive assets are sometimes referred to as **resource bundles.** Although resource bundles are not as easily pigeonholed as other types of resources and capabilities, they can still be identified by looking for company activities that link different types of resources, functions, and departmental units. It is important not to miss identifying a company's resource bundles, since they can be the most competitively important of a firm's competitive assets. Unless it includes a company's cross-functional capabilities and resource bundles, no identification of a company's resources and capabilities can be considered complete.

> **CORE CONCEPT**
>
> A **resource bundle** is a linked and closely integrated set of competitive assets centered around one or more cross-functional capabilities.

Determining Whether a Company's Resources and Capabilities Are Potent Enough to Produce a Sustainable Competitive Advantage

To determine the strategic relevance and competitive power of a firm's resources and capabilities, it is necessary to go beyond merely identifying a company's resources and capabilities. The second step in resource and capability analysis is designed to ascertain which of a company's resources and capabilities are competitively valuable and to what extent they can support a company's quest for a sustainable competitive advantage over market rivals. This involves probing the *caliber* of a firm's competitive assets relative to those of its competitors.[3] When a company has competitive assets that are central to its strategy and superior to those of rival firms, it has a competitive advantage over other firms. If this advantage proves durable despite the best efforts of competitors to overcome it, then the company is said to have a ***sustainable* competitive advantage.** While it may be difficult for a company to achieve a sustainable competitive advantage, it is an important strategic objective because it imparts a potential for attractive and long-lived profitability.

The Four Tests of a Resource's Competitive Power

The competitive power of a resource or capability is measured by how many of the following four tests it can pass.[4] The first two tests determine whether a resource or capability can support a competitive advantage. The last two determine whether the competitive advantage can be sustained in the face of active competition.

> **CORE CONCEPT**
>
> A ***sustainable* competitive advantage** is an advantage over market rivals that persists despite efforts of the rivals to overcome it.

1. *Is the resource (or capability) competitively valuable?* To be competitively valuable, a resource or capability must be directly relevant to the company's strategy, making the company a more effective competitor, able to exploit market opportunities and ward off external threats. Unless the resource contributes to the effectiveness of the company's strategy, it cannot pass this first test. An indicator of its effectiveness is whether the resource enables the company to strengthen its business model through a better customer value proposition and/or profit formula. Companies have to guard against contending that something they do well is necessarily competitively valuable. Apple's operating system for its PCs is by most accounts a world beater (compared to Windows Vista and Windows 7), but Apple has failed miserably in converting its strength in operating system design into competitive success in the global PC market—it is an also-ran with a paltry 3 to 5 percent market share worldwide.

2. *Is the resource rare—is it something rivals lack?* Resources and capabilities that are common among firms and widely available cannot be a source of competitive advantage. All makers of branded cereals have valuable marketing capabilities and brands, since the key success factors in the ready-to-eat cereal industry demand this. They are not rare. The brand strength of Pillsbury, however, is uncommon and has provided General Mills with greater market share as well as the opportunity to benefit from brand extensions like Pillsbury Grands! Biscuits, Pillsbury Ready to Bake! Cookies, and Pillsbury Simply . . . Cookies. A resource or capability is considered rare if it is held by only a small number of firms in an industry or specific competitive domain. Thus, while general management capabilities are not rare in an absolute sense, they are relatively rare in some of the less developed regions of the world and in some business domains.

3. *Is the resource hard to copy?* If a resource or capability is both valuable and rare, it will be competitively superior to comparable resources of rival firms. As such, it is a source of competitive advantage for the company. The more difficult and more costly it is for competitors to imitate, the more likely that it can also provide a *sustainable* competitive advantage. Resources tend to be difficult to copy when they are unique (a fantastic real estate location, patent-protected technology, an unusually talented and motivated labor force), when they must be built over time in ways that are difficult to imitate (a well-known brand name, mastery of a complex process technology, a global network of dealers and distributors), and when they entail financial outlays or large-scale operations that few industry members can undertake. Imitation is also difficult for resources that

reflect a high level of *social complexity* (company culture, interpersonal relationships among the managers or R&D teams, trust-based relations with customers or suppliers) and *causal ambiguity,* a term that signifies the hard-to-disentangle nature of the complex resources, such as a web of intricate processes enabling new drug discovery. Hard-to-copy resources and capabilities are important competitive assets, contributing to the longevity of a company's market position and offering the potential for sustained profitability.

4. *Can the resource be trumped by different types of resources and capabilities—are there good substitutes available for the resource?* Even resources and capabilities that are valuable, rare, and hard to copy can lose much of their competitive power if rivals have other types of resources and capabilities that are of equal or greater competitive power. A company may have the most technologically advanced and sophisticated plants in its industry, but any efficiency advantage it enjoys may be nullified if rivals are able to produce equally good products at lower cost by locating their plants in countries where wage rates are relatively low and a labor force with adequate skills is available.

> **CORE CONCEPTS**
>
> **Social complexity** and **causal ambiguity** are two factors that inhibit the ability of rivals to imitate a firm's most valuable resources and capabilities. Causal ambiguity makes it very hard to figure out how a complex resource contributes to competitive advantage and therefore exactly what to imitate.

The vast majority of companies are not well endowed with standout resources or capabilities, capable of passing all four tests with high marks. Most firms have a mixed bag of resources—one or two quite valuable, some good, many satisfactory to mediocre. Resources and capabilities that are valuable pass the first of the four tests. As key contributors to the efficiency and effectiveness of the strategy, they are relevant to the firm's competitiveness but are no guarantee of competitive advantage. They may offer no more than competitive parity with competing firms.

Passing both of the first two tests requires more—it requires resources and capabilities that are not only valuable but also rare. This is a much higher hurdle that can be cleared only by resources and capabilities that are *competitively superior.* Resources and capabilities that are competitively superior are the company's true strategic assets.[5] They provide the company with a competitive advantage over its competitors, if only in the short run.

To pass the last two tests, a resource must be able to maintain its competitive superiority in the face of competition. It must be resistant to imitative attempts and efforts by competitors to find equally valuable substitute resources. Assessing the availability of substitutes is the most difficult of all the tests since substitutes are harder to recognize, but the key is to look for resources or capabilities held by other firms that *can serve the same function* as the company's core resources and capabilities.[6]

Very few firms have resources and capabilities that can pass these tests, but those that do enjoy a sustainable competitive advantage with far greater profit potential. Walmart is a notable example, with capabilities in logistics and supply chain management that have surpassed those of its competitors for over 30 years. Lincoln Electric Company, less well known but no less notable in its achievements, has been the world leader in welding products for over 100 years as a result of its unique piecework incentive system for compensating production workers and the unsurpassed worker productivity and product quality that this system has fostered.

A Company's Resources and Capabilities Must Be Managed Dynamically

Even companies like Walmart and Lincoln Electric cannot afford to rest on their laurels. Rivals that are initially unable to replicate a key resource may develop better and better substitutes over time. Resources and capabilities can depreciate like other assets if they are managed with benign neglect. Disruptive environmental change can also destroy the value of key strategic assets, turning resources and capabilities "from diamonds to rust."[7] Some resources lose their clout quickly when there are rapid changes in technology, customer preferences, distribution channels, or other competitive factors.

> A company requires a dynamically evolving portfolio of resources and capabilities to sustain its competitiveness and help drive improvements in its performance.

For a company's resources and capabilities to have *durable* value, they must be continually refined, updated, and sometimes augmented with altogether new kinds of expertise. Not only are rival companies endeavoring to sharpen and recalibrate their capabilities, but customer needs and expectations are also undergoing constant change. Organizational capabilities grow stale unless they are kept freshly honed and on the cutting edge.[8] A company's resources and capabilities are far more competitively potent when they are (1) in sync with changes in the company's own strategy and its efforts to achieve a resource-based competitive advantage and (2) fully supportive of company efforts to attract customers and combat competitors' newly launched offensives to win bigger sales and market shares. Management's challenge in managing the firm's resources and capabilities dynamically has two elements: attending to ongoing recalibration of existing competitive assets and casting a watchful eye for opportunities to develop totally new kinds of capabilities.

The Role of Dynamic Capabilities   Companies that know the importance of recalibrating and upgrading their most valuable resources and capabilities ensure that these activities are done on a continual basis. By incorporating these activities into their routine managerial functions, they gain the experience necessary to be able to do them consistently well. At that point, their ability to freshen and renew their competitive assets becomes a capability in itself—a **dynamic capability.** A dynamic capability is the ability to modify or augment the company's existing resources and capabilities.[9] This includes the capacity to improve existing resources and capabilities incrementally, in the way that 3M continually upgrades the R&D resources driving its product innovation strategy. It also includes the capacity to add new resources and capabilities to the company's competitive asset portfolio. An example is Pfizer's acquisition capabilities, which have enabled it to replace degraded resources such as expiring patents with newly acquired capabilities in biotechnology.

CORE CONCEPT

A **dynamic capability** is the capacity of a company to modify its existing resources and capabilities or create new ones.

QUESTION 3: IS THE COMPANY ABLE TO SEIZE MARKET OPPORTUNITIES AND NULLIFY EXTERNAL THREATS?

An essential element in evaluating a company's overall situation entails examining the company's resources and competitive capabilities in terms of the degree to which they enable it to pursue its best market opportunities and defend against the external threats to its future well-being. The simplest and most easily applied tool for conducting this examination is widely known as *SWOT analysis*, so named because it zeros in on a company's internal **S**trengths and **W**eaknesses, market **O**pportunities, and external **T**hreats. Just as important, a first-rate SWOT analysis provides the basis for crafting a strategy that capitalizes on the company's resource strengths, overcomes its resource weaknesses, aims squarely at capturing the company's best opportunities, and defends against the threats to its future well-being.

Identifying a Company's Internal Strengths

A *strength* is something a company is good at doing or an attribute that enhances its competitiveness in the marketplace. A company's strengths depend on the quality of its resources and capabilities. Resource and capability analysis provides a way for managers to assess the quality objectively. While resources and capabilities that pass the four tests of sustainable competitive advantage are among the company's greatest strengths, other types can be counted among the company's strengths as well. A capability that is not potent enough to produce a sustainable advantage over rivals may yet enable a series of temporary advantages if used as a basis for entry into a new market or market segment. A resource bundle that fails to match those of top-tier competitors may still allow a company to compete successfully against the second tier.

Assessing a Company's Competencies—What Activities Does It Perform Well?   One way to appraise the degree of a company's strengths has to do with the company's competence level in performing key pieces of its business—such as supply chain management, R&D, production, distribution, sales and marketing, and customer service. Which activities does it perform especially well? And are there any activities it performs better than rivals? A company's proficiency in conducting different facets of its operations can range from a mere competence in performing an activity to a core competence to a distinctive competence.

A **competence** is an internal activity an organization performs with proficiency—a capability, in other words. A **core competence** is a proficiently performed internal activity that is *central* to a company's strategy and competitiveness. Ben & Jerry's Ice Cream, a subsidiary of Unilever, has a core competence in creating unusual flavors of ice cream and marketing them with catchy names like Chunky Monkey, Chubby Hubby, Cherry Garcia, Karamel Sutra, Imagine Whirled Peace, and Phish Food. A core competence is a more competitively valuable company strength than a competence because of the activity's key role in the company's strategy and the contribution it makes to the company's market success and profitability. Often, core competencies can be leveraged to create new markets or new product demand, as the engine behind a company's growth. 3M Corporation has a core competence in product innovation—its record of introducing new products goes back several decades and new product introduction is central to 3M's strategy of growing its business.

A **distinctive competence** is a competitively valuable activity that a company *performs better than its rivals.* A distinctive competence thus signifies greater proficiency than a core competence. Because a distinctive competence represents a level of proficiency that rivals do not have, it qualifies as a *competitively superior strength* with competitive advantage potential. This is particularly true when the distinctive competence enables

LO 3

Discover how to assess the company's strengths and weaknesses in light of market opportunities and external threats.

SWOT analysis is a simple but powerful tool for sizing up a company's strengths and weaknesses, its market opportunities, and the external threats to its future well-being.

Basing a company's strategy on its most competitively valuable resource and capability strengths gives the company its best chance for market success.

CORE CONCEPT

A **competence** is an activity that a company has learned to perform with proficiency—a capability, in other words.

CORE CONCEPT

A **core competence** is an activity that a company performs proficiently that is also central to its strategy and competitive success.

CORE CONCEPT

A **distinctive competence** is a competitively important activity that a company performs better than its rivals—it thus represents *a competitively superior internal strength.*

CORE CONCEPT

A company's **strengths** represent its competitive assets; its **weaknesses** are shortcomings that constitute competitive liabilities.

a company to deliver standout value to customers (in the form of lower prices, better product performance, or superior service). For instance, Apple has a distinctive competence in product innovation, as exemplified by its iPod, iPhone, and iPad products.

The conceptual differences between a competence, a core competence, and a distinctive competence draw attention to the fact that a company's strengths and competitive assets are not all equal.[10] Some competencies merely enable market survival because most rivals have them—indeed, not having a competence or capability that rivals have can result in competitive disadvantage. If an apparel company does not have the competence to produce its apparel items very cost-efficiently, it is unlikely to survive given the intensely price-competitive nature of the apparel industry. Every Web retailer requires a basic competence in designing an appealing and user-friendly Web site. Core competencies are *competitively* more important strengths than competencies because they are central to the company's strategy. Distinctive competencies are even more competitively important. Because a distinctive competence is a competitively valuable capability that is unmatched by rivals, it can propel the company to greater market success and profitability. A distinctive competence is thus potentially the mainspring of a company's success—unless it is trumped by other, even more powerful types of competencies that rivals hold.

Identifying Company Weaknesses and Competitive Deficiencies

A **weakness,** or *competitive deficiency,* is something a company lacks or does poorly (in comparison to others) or a condition that puts it at a competitive disadvantage in the marketplace. A company's internal weaknesses can relate to (1) inferior or unproven skills, expertise, or intellectual capital in competitively important areas of the business; (2) deficiencies in competitively important physical, organizational, or intangible assets; or (3) missing or competitively inferior capabilities in key areas. *Company weaknesses are thus internal shortcomings that constitute competitive liabilities.* Nearly all companies have competitive liabilities of one kind or another. Whether a company's internal weaknesses make it competitively vulnerable depends on how much they matter in the marketplace and whether they are offset by the company's strengths.

Table 4.3 lists many of the things to consider in compiling a company's strengths and weaknesses. Sizing up a company's complement of strengths and deficiencies is akin to constructing a *strategic balance sheet,* where strengths represent *competitive assets* and weaknesses represent *competitive liabilities.* Obviously, the ideal condition is for the company's competitive assets to outweigh its competitive liabilities by an ample margin—a 50-50 balance is definitely not the desired condition!

Identifying a Company's Market Opportunities

Market opportunity is a big factor in shaping a company's strategy. Indeed, managers can't properly tailor strategy to the company's situation without first identifying its market opportunities and appraising the growth and profit potential each one holds. Depending on the prevailing circumstances, a company's opportunities can be plentiful or scarce, fleeting or lasting, and can range from wildly attractive (an absolute "must" to pursue) to marginally interesting (because of the high risks or questionable profit potentials) to unsuitable (because the company's strengths are ill-suited to successfully capitalizing on the opportunities). A sampling of potential market opportunities is shown in Table 4.3.

Newly emerging and fast-changing markets sometimes present stunningly big or "golden" opportunities, but it is typically hard for managers at one company to peer into "the fog of the future" and spot them much ahead of managers at other companies.[11] But as the fog begins to clear, golden opportunities are nearly always seized rapidly—and the companies that seize them are usually those that have been actively waiting, staying alert with diligent market reconnaissance, and preparing themselves to capitalize on shifting market conditions by patiently assembling an arsenal of competitively valuable resources—talented personnel, technical know-how, strategic partnerships, and a war chest of cash to finance aggressive action when the time comes.[12] In mature markets, unusually attractive market opportunities emerge sporadically, often after long periods of relative calm—but future market conditions may be more predictable, making emerging opportunities easier for industry members to detect.

> A company is well advised to pass on a particular market opportunity unless it has or can acquire the competencies needed to capture it.

In evaluating a company's market opportunities and ranking their attractiveness, managers have to guard against viewing every *industry* opportunity as a *company* opportunity. Not every company is equipped with the competencies to successfully pursue each opportunity that exists in its industry. Some companies are more capable of going after particular opportunities than others, and a few companies may be hopelessly outclassed. *The market opportunities most relevant to a company are those that match up well with the company's competitive assets, offer the best growth and profitability, and present the most potential for competitive advantage.*

Identifying the Threats to a Company's Future Profitability

Often, certain factors in a company's external environment pose *threats* to its profitability and competitive well-being. Threats can stem from the emergence of cheaper or better technologies, rivals' introduction of new or improved products, the entry of lower-cost foreign competitors into a company's market stronghold, new regulations that are more burdensome to a company than to its competitors, vulnerability to a rise in interest rates or tight credit conditions, the potential of a hostile takeover, unfavorable demographic shifts, adverse changes in foreign exchange rates, political upheaval in a foreign country where the company has facilities, and the like. A list of potential threats to a company's future profitability and market position is shown in Table 4.3.

External threats may pose no more than a moderate degree of adversity (all companies confront some threatening elements in the course of doing business), or they may be so imposing as to make a company's situation and outlook quite tenuous. On rare occasions, market shocks can give birth to a *sudden-death* threat that throws a company into an immediate crisis and a battle to survive. Many of the world's major airlines were plunged into an unprecedented financial crisis by the perfect storm of 9/11, rising prices for jet fuel, mounting competition

Table 4.3   **What to Look For in Identifying a Company's Strengths, Weaknesses, Opportunities, and Threats**

Potential Strengths and Competitive Assets	Potential Weaknesses and Competitive Deficiencies
• Competencies that are well matched to industry key success factors • Strong financial condition; ample financial resources to grow the business • Strong brand-name image/company reputation • Attractive customer base • Proprietary technology/superior technological skills/ important patents • Superior intellectual capital • Skills in advertising and promotion • Strong bargaining power over suppliers or buyers • Product innovation capabilities • Proven capabilities in improving production processes • Good supply chain management capabilities • Good customer service capabilities • Superior product quality • Wide geographic coverage and/or strong global distribution capability • Alliances/joint ventures that provide access to valuable technology, competencies, and/or attractive geographic markets • A product that is strongly differentiated from those of rivals • Cost advantages over rivals • Core competencies in _____ • A distinctive competence in _____ • Resources that are hard to copy and for which there are no good substitutes	• Competencies that are not well-matched to industry key success factors • In the wrong strategic group • Losing market share because _____ • Lack of attention to customer needs • Weak balance sheet, short on financial resources to grow the firm, too much debt; • Higher overall unit costs relative to those of key competitors • Weak or unproven product innovation capabilities • A product/service with ho-hum attributes or features inferior to the offerings of rivals • Too narrow a product line relative to rivals • Weak brand image or reputation • Weaker dealer network than key rivals and/or lack of adequate global distribution capability • Behind on product quality, R&D, and/or technological know-how • Lack of management depth • Inferior intellectual capital relative to rivals • Plagued with internal operating problems or obsolete facilities • Too much underutilized plant capacity • No well-developed or proven core competencies • No distinctive competencies or competitively superior resources • Resources that are readily copied or for which there are good substitutes • No clear strategic direction
Potential Market Opportunities	Potential External Threats to a Company's Future Profitability
• Openings to win market share from rivals • Sharply rising buyer demand for the industry's product • Serving additional customer groups or market segments • Expanding into new geographic markets • Expanding the company's product line to meet a broader range of customer needs • Utilizing existing company skills or technological know-how to enter new product lines or new businesses • Online sales via the Internet • Integrating forward or backward • Falling trade barriers in attractive foreign markets • Acquiring rival firms or companies with attractive technological expertise or capabilities • Entering into alliances or joint ventures to expand the firm's market coverage or boost its competitive capability • Openings to exploit emerging new technologies	• Increasing intensity of competition among industry rivals—may squeeze profit margins • Slowdowns in market growth • Likely entry of potent new competitors • Loss of sales to substitute products • Growing bargaining power of customers or suppliers • Vulnerability to industry driving forces • Shift in buyer needs and tastes away from the industry's product • Adverse demographic changes that threaten to curtail demand for the industry's product • Adverse economic conditions that threaten critical suppliers or distributers • Changes in technology—particularly disruptive technology that can undermine the company's distinctive competencies • Restrictive foreign trade policies • Costly new regulatory requirements • Tight credit conditions • Rising prices on energy or other key inputs

from low-fare carriers, shifting traveler preferences for low fares as opposed to lots of in-flight amenities, and higher labor costs. Similarly, the global economic crisis that began with the mortgage lenders, banks, and insurance companies has produced shock waves from which few industries have been insulated, causing even strong performers like General Electric to falter. While not all crises can be anticipated, it is management's job to identify the threats to the company's future prospects and to evaluate what strategic actions can be taken to neutralize or lessen their impact.

> Simply making lists of a company's strengths, weaknesses, opportunities, and threats is not enough; the payoff from SWOT analysis comes from the conclusions about a company's situation and the implications for strategy improvement that flow from the four lists.

What Do the SWOT Listings Reveal?

SWOT analysis involves more than making four lists. The two most important parts of SWOT analysis are *drawing conclusions* from the SWOT listings about the company's overall situation and *translating these conclusions into strategic actions* to better match the company's strategy to its internal strengths and market opportunities, to correct important weaknesses, and to defend against external threats. Figure 4.2 shows the steps involved in gleaning insights from SWOT analysis.

Figure 4.2   The Steps Involved in SWOT Analysis: Identify the Four Components of SWOT, Draw Conclusions, Translate Implications into Strategic Actions

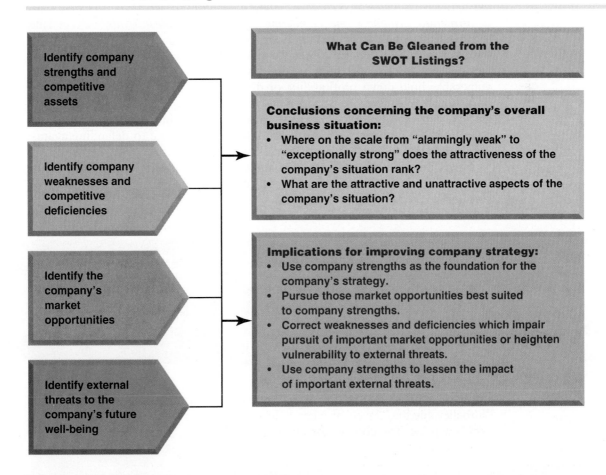

Just what story the SWOT listings tell about the company's overall situation is often revealed in the answers to the following set of questions:

- What aspects of the company's situation are particularly attractive?
- What aspects are of the most concern?
- All things considered, where on a scale of 1 to 10 (where 1 is alarmingly weak and 10 is exceptionally strong) do the company's overall situation and future prospects rank?
- Are the company's internal strengths and competitive assets powerful enough to enable it to compete successfully?
- Are the company's weaknesses and competitive deficiencies mostly inconsequential and readily correctable, or could one or more prove fatal if not remedied soon?
- Do the company's strengths and competitive assets outweigh its weaknesses and competitive liabilities by an attractive margin?
- Does the company have attractive market opportunities that are well suited to its internal strengths? Does the company lack the competitive assets to pursue any of the most attractive opportunities?
- Are the threats alarming, or are they something the company appears able to deal with and defend against?

The final piece of SWOT analysis is to translate the diagnosis of the company's situation into actions for improving the company's strategy and business prospects. *A company's internal strengths should always serve as the basis of its strategy— placing heavy reliance on a company's best competitive assets is the soundest route to attracting customers and competing successfully against rivals.*[13] As a rule, strategies that place heavy demands on areas where the company is weakest or has unproven competencies are suspect and should be avoided. Plainly, managers have to look toward correcting competitive weaknesses that make the company vulnerable, hold down profitability, or disqualify it from pursuing an attractive opportunity. Furthermore, strategy has to be aimed squarely at capturing those market opportunities that are most attractive and suited to the company's collection of competencies. How much attention to devote to defending against external threats to the company's market position and future performance hinges on how vulnerable the company is, whether there are attractive defensive moves that can be taken to lessen their impact, and whether the costs of undertaking such moves represent the best use of company competitive assets.

QUESTION 4: ARE THE COMPANY'S PRICES AND COSTS COMPETITIVE WITH THOSE OF KEY RIVALS, AND DOES IT HAVE AN APPEALING CUSTOMER VALUE PROPOSITION?

Company managers are often stunned when a competitor cuts its price to "unbelievably low" levels or when a new market entrant comes on strong with a very low price. The competitor may not, however, be "dumping" (an economic term for selling at prices that are below cost), buying its way into the market with a super-low price, or waging a desperate move to gain sales—it may simply have substantially lower costs. One of the most telling signs of whether a company's business position is strong or precarious is whether its prices and costs can remain competitive with industry rivals. For a company to retain its market share, its costs must be *in line* with those of close rivals selling similar quality products.

While less common, new entrants can also storm the market with a product that ratchets the quality level up so high that customers will abandon competing sellers even if they have to pay more for the new product. With its vastly greater storage capacity and lightweight, cool design, Apple's iPod left other makers of portable digital music players in the dust when it was first introduced. By introducing new models with even more attractive features, Apple has continued its worldwide dominance of this market. Apple's new iPad appears to be doing the same in the market for e-readers and tablet PCs.

Regardless of where on the quality spectrum a company competes, it must also remain competitive in terms of its customer value proposition in order to stay in the game. Tiffany's value proposition, for example, remains attractive to customers who want customer service, the assurance of quality, and a high-status brand despite the availability of cut-rate diamond jewelry online. Target's customer value proposition has withstood the Walmart low-price juggernaut by attention to product design, image, and attractive store layouts in addition to efficiency.

The value provided to the customer depends on how well a customer's needs are met for the price paid. How well customer needs are met depends on the perceived quality of a product or service as well as other, more tangible attributes. The greater the amount of customer value that the company can offer profitably compared to its rivals, the less vulnerable it will be to competitive attack. For managers, the key is to keep close track of how *cost effectively* the company can deliver value to customers relative to its competitors. If they can deliver the same amount of value with lower expenditures (or more value at the same cost), they will maintain a competitive edge.

Two analytical tools are particularly useful in determining whether a company's prices, costs, and customer value proposition are competitive: value chain analysis and benchmarking.

The Concept of a Company Value Chain

Every company's business consists of a collection of activities undertaken in the course of designing, producing, marketing, delivering, and supporting its product or service. All the various activities that a company performs internally combine to form a **value chain**—so called because the underlying intent of a company's activities is to do things that ultimately *create value for buyers.*

As shown in Figure 4.3, a company's value chain consists of two broad categories of activities: the *primary activities* that are foremost in creating value for customers and the requisite *support activities* that facilitate and enhance the performance of the primary activities.[14] The exact nature of the primary and secondary activities that make up a company's value chain

LO 4

Grasp how a company's value chain activities can affect the company's cost structure, degree of differentiation, and competitive advantage.

The higher a company's costs are above those of close rivals, the more competitively vulnerable it becomes.

The greater the amount of customer value that a company can offer profitably relative to close rivals, the less competitively vulnerable it becomes.

CORE CONCEPT

A company's **value chain** identifies the primary activities that create customer value and the related support activities.

vary according to the specifics of a company's business; hence, the listing of the primary and support activities in Figure 4.3 is illustrative rather than definitive. For example, the primary value-creating activities for a manufacturer of bakery goods, such as Grupo Bimbo, include supply chain management, baking and packaging operations, distribution, and sales and marketing but are unlikely to include service. Its support activities include quality control as well as product R&D, human resource management, and administration. For a department store retailer, such as Saks Fifth Avenue, customer service is included among its primary activities, along with merchandise selection and buying, store layout and product display, and advertising; its support activities include site selection, hiring and training, and store maintenance, plus the usual assortment of administrative activities. For a hotel chain like Marriot, the primary activities and costs are in site selection and construction, reservations, operation of its hotel properties, and marketing; principal support activities include accounting, hiring and training hotel staff, supply chain management, and general administration.

With its focus on value-creating activities, the value chain is an ideal tool for examining how a company delivers on its customer value proposition. It permits a deep look at the company's cost structure and ability to offer low prices. It reveals the emphasis that a company places on activities that enhance differentiation and support higher prices, such as service and marketing. Note that there is also a profit margin component to the value chain; this is because profits are necessary to compensate the company's owners/shareholders and investors, who bear risks and provide capital. Tracking the profit margin along with the value-creating activities is critical because unless an enterprise succeeds in delivering customer value profitably (with a sufficient return on invested capital), it can't survive for long. This is the essence of a sound business model.

Illustration Capsule 4.1 shows representative costs for various activities performed by Just Coffee, a cooperative producer and roaster of fair-trade organic coffee.

Comparing the Value Chains of Rival Companies   The primary purpose of value chain analysis is to facilitate a comparison, activity-by-activity, of how effectively and efficiently a company delivers value to its customers, relative to its competitors. Segregating the company's operations into different types of primary and secondary activities is the first step in this comparison. The next is to do the same for the company's most significant competitors.

Even rivals in the same industry may differ significantly in terms of the activities they perform. For instance, the "operations" component of the value chain for a manufacturer that makes all of its own parts and components and assembles them into a finished product differs from the "operations" of a rival producer that buys the needed parts and components from outside suppliers and only performs assembly operations. How each activity is performed may affect a company's relative cost position as well as its capacity for differentiation. Thus, even a simple comparison of how the activities of rivals' value chains differ can be revealing of competitive differences.

A Company's Primary and Secondary Activities Identify the Major Components of Its Internal Cost Structure   Each activity in the value chain gives rise to costs and ties up assets. For a company to remain competitive, it is critical for it to perform its activities cost-effectively,

Figure 4.3 A Representative Company Value Chain

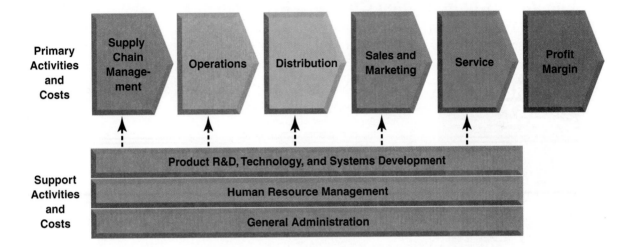

PRIMARY ACTIVITIES

- **Supply Chain Management**—Activities, costs, and assets associated with purchasing fuel, energy, raw materials, parts and components, merchandise, and consumable items from vendors; receiving, storing, and disseminating inputs from suppliers; inspection; and inventory management.

- **Operations**—Activities, costs, and assets associated with converting inputs into final product form (production, assembly, packaging, equipment maintenance, facilities, operations, quality assurance, environmental protection).

- **Distribution**—Activities, costs, and assets dealing with physically distributing the product to buyers (finished goods warehousing, order processing, order picking and packing, shipping, delivery vehicle operations, establishing and maintaining a network of dealers and distributors).

- **Sales and Marketing**—Activities, costs, and assets related to sales force efforts, advertising and promotion, market research and planning, and dealer/distributor support.

- **Service**—Activities, costs, and assets associated with providing assistance to buyers, such as installation, spare parts delivery, maintenance and repair, technical assistance, buyer inquiries, and complaints.

SUPPORT ACTIVITIES

- **Product R&D, Technology, and Systems Development**—Activities, costs, and assets relating to product R&D, process R&D, process design improvement, equipment design, computer software development, telecommunications systems, computer-assisted design and engineering, database capabilities, and development of computerized support systems.

- **Human Resources Management**—Activities, costs, and assets associated with the recruitment, hiring, training, development, and compensation of all types of personnel; labor relations activities; and development of knowledge-based skills and core competencies.

- **General Administration**—Activities, costs, and assets relating to general management, accounting and finance, legal and regulatory affairs, safety and security, management information systems, forming strategic alliances and collaborating with strategic partners, and other "overhead" functions.

Source: Based on the discussion in Michael E. Porter, *Competitive Advantage* (New York: Free Press, 1985), pp. 37–43.

ILLUSTRATION CAPSULE 4.1

The Value Chain for Just Coffee, a Producer of Fair-Trade Organic Coffee

WHERE YOUR MONEY GOES
— MEASURED IN DOLLARS PER POUND —

$1.91-3.00
TO THE COFFEE GROWER COOPERATIVE.

$.60-.85
IMPORT FEES, STORAGE AND FREIGHT TO JUST COFFEE.

$.89
LABOR COST OF ROASTING AND BAGGING

$.45
LABELS AND BAG

$3.03
AVERAGE JUST COFFEE OVERHEAD

30-40% AVG. RETAIL MARKUP

Value Chain Activities and Costs in Producing, Roasting, and Selling a Pound of Fair-Trade Organic Coffee	
1. Average cost of procuring the coffee from coffee-grower cooperatives	$2.30
2. Import fees, storage costs, and freight charges	.73
3. Labor cost of roasting and bagging	.89
4. Cost of labels and bag	.45
5. Average overhead costs	3.03
6. Total company costs	$7.40
7. Average retail markup over company costs (company operating profit)	2.59
8. Average price to consumer at retail	$9.99

Source: Developed by the authors with help from Jonathan D. Keith from information on Just Coffee's Web site, www.justcoffee.coop/the_coffee_dollar_breakdown (accessed June 16, 2010).

regardless of which it chooses to emphasize. Once the major value chain activities are identified, the next step is to evaluate the company's cost competitiveness using what accountants call *activity-based costing* to determine the costs of performing each value chain activity (and assets required, including working capital).[15] The degree to which a company's costs should be disaggregated into specific activities depends on how valuable it is to develop cost data for narrowly defined activities as opposed to broadly defined activities. Generally speaking, cost estimates are needed at least for each broad category of primary and secondary activities, but finer classifications may be needed if a company discovers that it has a cost disadvantage vis-à-vis rivals and wants to pin down the exact source or activity causing the disadvantage. Quite often, there are links between activities such that the manner in which one activity is done can affect the costs of performing other activities. For instance, how an automobile is designed has a huge impact on the number of different parts and components, their respective manufacturing costs, and the expense of assembling the various parts and components into a finished product.

The combined costs of all the various activities in a company's value chain define the company's internal cost structure. Further, the cost of each activity contributes to whether the company's overall cost position relative to rivals is favorable or unfavorable. But a company's own internal costs are insufficient to assess whether its costs are competitive with those of rivals. Cost and price differences among competing companies can have their origins in activities performed by suppliers or by distribution allies involved in getting the product to the final customer or end user of the product, in which case the company's entire value chain system becomes relevant.

The Value Chain System for an Entire Industry

A company's value chain is embedded in a larger system of activities that includes the value chains of its suppliers and the value chains of whatever wholesale distributors and retailers it utilizes in getting its product or service to end users. This *value chain system* has implications that extend far beyond the company's costs. It can affect attributes like product quality that enhance differentiation and have importance for the company's customer value proposition as well as its profitability.[16] Suppliers' value chains are relevant because suppliers perform activities and incur costs in creating and delivering the purchased inputs utilized in a company's own value-creating activities. The costs, performance features, and quality of these inputs influence a company's own costs and product differentiation capabilities. Anything a company can do to help its suppliers' drive down the costs of their value chain activities or improve the quality and performance of the items being supplied can enhance its own competitiveness—a powerful reason for working collaboratively with suppliers in managing supply chain activities.[17]

> A company's cost competitiveness depends not only on the costs of internally performed activities (its own value chain) but also on costs in the value chains of its suppliers and distribution channel allies.

Similarly, the value chains of a company's distribution channel partners are relevant because (1) the costs and margins of a company's distributors and retail dealers are part of the price the ultimate consumer pays and (2) the activities that distribution allies perform affect sales volumes and customer satisfaction. For these reasons, companies normally work closely with their distribution allies (who are their direct customers) to perform value chain activities in mutually beneficial ways. For instance, motor vehicle manufacturers have a competitive interest in working closely with their automobile dealers to promote higher sales volumes and better customer satisfaction with dealers' repair and maintenance services. Producers of bathroom fixtures are heavily dependent on the sales and promotional activities of their distributors and building supply retailers and on whether distributors/retailers operate cost-effectively enough to be able to sell at prices that lead to attractive sales volumes.

As a consequence, *accurately assessing a company's competitiveness entails scrutinizing the nature and costs of value chain activities throughout the entire value chain system for delivering its products or services to end-use customers.* A typical industry value chain system that incorporates the value chains of suppliers and forward channel allies (if any) is shown in Figure 4.4. As was the case with company value chains, the specific activities constituting industry value chains also vary significantly. The primary value chain system activities in the pulp and paper industry (timber farming, logging, pulp mills, and papermaking) differ from the primary value chain system activities in the home appliance industry (parts and components manufacture, assembly, wholesale distribution, retail sales). The value chain system in the soft-drink industry (syrup manufacture, bottling and can filling, wholesale distribution, advertising, and retail merchandising) differs from that in the computer software industry (programming, disk loading, marketing, distribution).

Figure 4.4   Representative Value Chain System for an Entire Industry

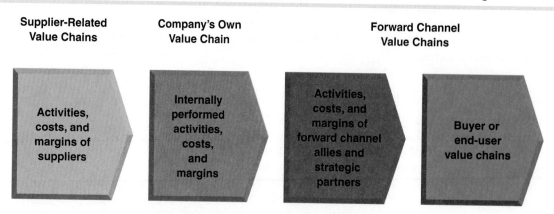

Source: Based in part on the single-industry value chain displayed in Michael E. Porter, *Competitive Advantage* (New York: Free Press, 1985), p. 35.

Benchmarking: A Tool for Assessing Whether the Costs and Effectiveness of a Company's Value Chain Activities Are in Line

Once a company has developed good estimates for the costs and effectiveness of each of the major activities in its own value chain and has sufficient data relating to the value chain activities of suppliers and distribution allies, then it is ready to explore how it compares on these dimensions with key rivals. This is where benchmarking comes in. **Benchmarking** entails comparing how different companies perform various value chain activities—how inventories are managed, how products are assembled, how fast the company can get new products to market, how customer orders are filled and shipped—and then making cross-company comparisons of the costs and effectiveness of these activities.[18] The objectives of benchmarking are to identify the best practices in performing an activity, to learn how other companies have actually achieved lower costs or better results in performing benchmarked activities, and to take action to improve a company's competitiveness whenever benchmarking reveals that its costs and results of performing an activity are not on a par with what other companies have achieved.

CORE CONCEPT

Benchmarking is a potent tool for improving a company's own internal activities that is based on learning how other companies perform them and borrowing their "best practices."

Xerox became one of the first companies to use benchmarking in 1979 when Japanese manufacturers began selling midsize copiers in the United States for $9,600 each—less than Xerox's production costs.[19] Xerox management suspected its Japanese competitors were dumping, but it sent a team of line managers to Japan, including the head of manufacturing, to study competitors' business processes and costs. With the aid of Xerox's joint venture partner in Japan, Fuji-Xerox, which knew the competitors well, the team found that Xerox's costs were excessive due to gross inefficiencies in the company's manufacturing processes and business practices. The findings triggered a major internal effort at Xerox to become cost-competitive and prompted Xerox to begin benchmarking 67 of its key work processes against companies identified as employing the best practices. Xerox quickly decided not to restrict its benchmarking efforts to its office equipment rivals but to extend them to any company regarded as "world class" in performing *any activity* relevant to Xerox's business. Other companies quickly picked up on Xerox's approach. Toyota managers got their idea for just-in-time inventory deliveries by studying how U.S. supermarkets replenished their shelves. Southwest Airlines reduced the turnaround time of its aircraft at each scheduled stop by studying pit crews on the auto racing circuit. Over 80 percent of Fortune 500 companies reportedly use benchmarking for comparing themselves against rivals on cost and other competitively important measures.

The tough part of benchmarking is not whether to do it but rather how to gain access to information about other companies' practices and costs. Sometimes benchmarking can be accomplished by collecting information from published reports, trade groups, and industry research firms or by talking to knowledgeable industry analysts, customers, and suppliers. Sometimes field trips to the facilities of competing or noncompeting companies can be arranged to observe how things are done, ask questions, compare practices and processes, and perhaps exchange data on productivity, staffing levels, time requirements, and other cost components—but the problem here is that such companies, even if they agree to host facilities tours and answer questions, are unlikely to share competitively sensitive cost information. Furthermore, comparing one company's costs to another's costs may not involve comparing apples to apples if the two companies employ different cost accounting principles to calculate the costs of particular activities.

> Benchmarking the costs of company activities against rivals provides hard evidence of whether a company is cost-competitive.

However, a third and fairly reliable source of benchmarking information has emerged. The explosive interest of companies in benchmarking costs and best practices has prompted numerous consulting firms and business organizations (e.g., Accenture, A.T. Kearney, Benchnet—The Benchmarking Exchange, Best Practices LLC, and the Strategic Planning Institute's Council on Benchmarking and Best Practices, LLC) to gather benchmarking data, distribute information about best practices, and provide comparative cost data without identifying the names of particular companies. Having an independent group gather the information and report it in a manner that disguises the names of individual companies protects competitively sensitive data and lessens the potential for unethical behavior on the part of company personnel in gathering their own data about competitors. Illustration Capsule 4.2 presents a widely recommended code of conduct for engaging in benchmarking.

Strategic Options for Remedying a Disadvantage in Costs or Effectiveness

Examining the costs of a company's own value chain activities and comparing them to rivals' indicates who has how much of a cost advantage or disadvantage and which cost components are responsible. Similarly, much can be learned by comparisons at the activity level of how effectively a company delivers on its value proposition relative to its competitors and which elements in its value chain system are responsible. Such information is vital in strategic actions to eliminate a cost disadvantage, deliver more customer value, enhance differentiation, and improve profitability. Such information can also help a company to recognize and reinforce activities in which it has a comparative advantage and to find

ILLUSTRATION CAPSULE 4.2

Benchmarking and Ethical Conduct

Because discussions between benchmarking partners can involve competitively sensitive data, conceivably raising questions about possible restraint of trade or improper business conduct, many benchmarking organizations urge all individuals and organizations involved in benchmarking to abide by a code of conduct grounded in ethical business behavior. One of the most widely used codes of conduct is the one developed by APQC (formerly the American Productivity and Quality Center) and advocated by the Qualserve Benchmarking Clearinghouse; it is based on the following principles and guidelines:

- Avoid discussions or actions that could lead to or imply an interest in restraint of trade, market and/or customer allocation schemes, price fixing, dealing arrangements, bid rigging, or bribery. Don't discuss costs with competitors if costs are an element of pricing.

- Refrain from the acquisition of trade secrets from another by any means that could be interpreted as improper, including the breach of any duty to maintain secrecy. Do not disclose or use any trade secret that may have been obtained through improper means or that was disclosed by another in violation of duty to maintain its secrecy or limit its use.

- Be willing to provide to your benchmarking partner the same type and level of information that you request from that partner.

- Communicate fully and early in the relationship to clarify expectations, avoid misunderstanding, and establish mutual interest in the benchmarking exchange.

- Be honest and complete with the information submitted.

- The use or communication of a benchmarking partner's name with the data obtained or practices observed requires the prior permission of the benchmarking partner.

- Honor the wishes of benchmarking partners regarding how the information that is provided will be handled and used.

- In benchmarking with competitors, establish specific ground rules up front. For example, "We don't want to talk about things that will give either of us a competitive advantage, but rather we want to see where we both can mutually improve or gain benefit."

- Check with legal counsel if any information-gathering procedure is in doubt. If uncomfortable, do not proceed. Alternatively, negotiate and sign a specific nondisclosure agreement that will satisfy the attorneys representing each partner.

- Do not ask competitors for sensitive data or cause benchmarking partners to feel they must provide data to continue the process.

- Use an ethical third party to assemble and "blind" competitive data, with inputs from legal counsel in direct competitor sharing. (Note: When cost is closely linked to price, sharing cost data can be considered to be the same as sharing price data.)

- Any information obtained from a benchmarking partner should be treated as internal, privileged communications. If "confidential" or proprietary material is to be exchanged, then a specific agreement should be executed to specify the content of the material that needs to be protected, the duration of the period of protection, the conditions for permitting access to the material, and the specific handling requirements necessary for that material.

Sources: APQC, www.apqc.org; Qualserve Benchmarking Clearinghouse, www.awwa.org (accessed October 8, 2010).

new avenues for enhancing its competitiveness through lower costs, greater differentiation, or a more attractive customer value proposition. There are three main areas in a company's total value chain system where company managers can try to improve its efficiency and effectiveness: (1) a company's own activity segments, (2) suppliers' part of the overall value chain, and (3) the distribution channel portion of the chain.

Improving the Efficiency and Effectiveness of Internally Performed Value Chain Activities Managers can pursue any of several strategic approaches to reduce the costs of internally performed value chain activities and improve a company's cost competitiveness:[20]

1. Implement the use of best practices throughout the company, particularly for high-cost activities.
2. Redesign the product and/or some of its components to eliminate high-cost components or facilitate speedier and more economical manufacture or assembly—computer chip makers regularly design around the patents held by others to avoid paying royalties; automakers have substituted lower-cost plastic and rubber for metal at many exterior body locations.
3. Relocate high-cost activities (such as manufacturing) to geographic areas like Southeast Asia or Latin America or eastern Europe where they can be performed more cheaply.
4. See if certain internally performed activities can be outsourced from vendors or performed by contractors more cheaply than they can be done in-house.
5. Shift to lower-cost technologies and/or invest in productivity-enhancing, cost-saving technological improvements (robotics, flexible manufacturing techniques, state-of-the-art information systems).
6. Stop performing activities that add little or no customer value. Examples include seldom-used customer services, employee training programs that are of marginal value, and maintaining large raw-material or finished-goods inventories.

How successfully a company competes depends on more than low costs. It also depends on how effectively it delivers value to the customer and on its ability to differentiate itself from rivals. To improve the effectiveness of its customer value proposition and enhance differentiation, there are several approaches a manager can take:[21]

1. Implement the use of best practices for quality throughout the company, particularly for high-value activities (those that are important for creating value for the customer).
2. Adopt best practices and technologies that spur innovation, improve design, and enhance creativity.
3. Implement the use of best practices in providing customer service.
4. Reallocate resources to devote more to activities that will have the biggest impact on the value delivered to the customer and that address buyers' most important purchase criteria.
5. For intermediate buyers (distributors or retailers, for example), gain an understanding of how the activities the company performs impact the buyer's value chain. Improve the effectiveness of company activities that have the greatest impact on the efficiency or effectiveness of the buyer's value chain.
6. Adopt best practices for signaling the value of the product and for enhancing customer perceptions.

Improving the Efficiency and Effectiveness of Supplier-Related Value Chain Activities Improving the efficiency and effectiveness of the value chain activities of suppliers can also address a company's competitive weaknesses with respect to costs and differentiation. On the cost side, a company can gain savings in suppliers' part of the overall value chain by pressuring suppliers for lower prices, switching to lower-priced substitute inputs, and collaborating closely with suppliers to identify mutual cost-saving opportunities.[22] For example, just-in-time deliveries from suppliers can lower a company's inventory and internal logistics costs and may also allow suppliers to economize on their warehousing, shipping, and production scheduling costs—a win-win outcome for both. In a few instances, companies may find that it is cheaper to integrate backward into the business of high-cost suppliers and make the item in-house instead of buying it from outsiders.

Similarly, a company can enhance its differentiation by working with or through its suppliers to do so. Some methods include selecting and retaining suppliers who meet higher-quality standards, coordinating with suppliers to enhance design or other features desired by customers, providing incentives to encourage suppliers to meet higher-quality standards, and assisting suppliers in their efforts to improve. Fewer defects in parts from suppliers not only improve quality and enhance differentiation throughout the value chain system but can lower costs as well since there is less waste and disruption to the production processes.

Improving the Efficiency and Effectiveness of Distribution-Related Value Chain Activities

Taking actions aimed at improvements with respect to the forward or downstream portion of the value chain system can also help to remedy a company's competitive disadvantage with respect to either costs or differentiation. Any of three means can be used to achieve better cost competitiveness in the forward portion of the industry value chain: (1) Pressure distributors, dealers, and other forward channel allies to reduce their costs and markups so as to make the final price to buyers more competitive with the prices of rivals; (2) collaborate with forward channel allies to identify win-win opportunities to reduce costs—a chocolate manufacturer, for example, learned that by shipping its bulk chocolate in liquid form in tank cars instead of as 10-pound molded bars, it could not only save its candy-bar manufacturing customers the costs associated with unpacking and melting but also eliminate its own costs of molding bars and packing them; and (3) change to a more economical distribution strategy, including switching to cheaper distribution channels (perhaps direct sales via the Internet) or perhaps integrating forward into company-owned retail outlets.

The means to enhance differentiation through activities at the forward end of the value chain system include (1) engaging in cooperative advertising and promotions with forward allies (dealers, distributors, retailers, etc.), (2) creating exclusive arrangements with downstream sellers or other mechanisms that increase their incentives to enhance delivered customer value, and (3) creating and enforcing standards for downstream activities and assisting in training channel partners in business practices. Harley-Davidson, for example, enhances the shopping experience and perceptions of buyers by selling through retailers that sell Harley-Davidson motorcycles exclusively and meet Harley-Davidson standards.

Translating Proficient Performance of Value Chain Activities into Competitive Advantage

Value chain analysis and benchmarking are not only useful for identifying and remedying competitive disadvantages; they can also be used to uncover and strengthen competitive advantages. A company's value-creating activities can offer a competitive advantage in one of two ways: (1) They can contribute to greater efficiency and lower costs relative to competitors, or (2) they can provide a basis for differentiation, so customers are willing to pay relatively more for the company's goods and services. A company that does a *first-rate job* of managing its value chain activities *relative to competitors* stands a good chance of profiting from its competitive advantage.

Achieving a cost-based competitive advantage requires determined management efforts to be cost-efficient in performing value chain activities. Such efforts have to be ongoing and persistent, and they have to involve each and every value chain activity. The goal must be continuous cost reduction, not a one-time or on-again–off-again effort. Companies whose managers are truly committed to low-cost performance of value chain activities and succeed in engaging company personnel to discover innovative ways to drive costs out of the business have a real chance of gaining a durable low-cost edge over rivals. It is not as easy as it seems to imitate a company's low-cost practices. Companies like Nucor Steel, Ryanair, and Carrefour have been highly successful in managing their values chains in a low-cost manner.

Ongoing and persistent efforts are also required for a competitive advantage based on differentiation. Superior reputations and brands are built up slowly over time, through continuous investment and activities that deliver consistent, reinforcing messages. Differentiation based on quality requires vigilant management of activities for quality assurance throughout the value chain. While the basis for differentiation (e.g., status, design, innovation, customer service, reliability, image) may vary widely among companies pursuing a differentiation advantage, companies that succeed do so on the basis of a commitment to coordinated value chain activities aimed purposefully at this objective. Examples include Chopin Vodka (status), IKEA (design), FedEx (reliability), 3M (innovation), Louis Vuitton (image), and Ritz Carlton (customer service).

How Activities Relate to Resources and Capabilities   There is a close relationship between the value-creating activities that a company performs and its resources and capabilities. An organizational capability or competence implies a *capacity* for action; in contrast, a value-creating activity *is* the action. With respect to resources and capabilities, activities are "where the rubber hits the road." When companies engage in a value-creating activity, they do so by drawing on specific company resources and capabilities that underlie and enable the activity. For example, brand-building activities depend on human resources, such as experienced brand managers (including their knowledge and expertise in this arena), as well as organizational capabilities in advertising and marketing. Cost-cutting activities may derive from organizational capabilities in inventory management, for example, and resources such as inventory tracking systems.

Because of this correspondence between activities and supporting resources and capabilities, value chain analysis can complement resource and capability analysis as tools for assessing a company's competitive advantage. Resources and capabilities that are *both valuable and rare* provide a company with *what it takes* for competitive advantage. For a company with competitive assets of this sort, the potential is there. When these assets are deployed in the form of a value-creating activity, that potential is realized due to their competitive superiority. Resource analysis is one tool for identifying competitively superior resources and capabilities. But their value and the competitive superiority of that value can only be assessed objectively *after* they are deployed. Value chain analysis and benchmarking provide the type of data needed to make that objective assessment.

There is also a dynamic relationship between a company's activities and its resources and capabilities. Value-creating activities are more than just the embodiment of a resource's or capability's potential. They also contribute to the formation and development of capabilities. The road to competitive advantage begins with management efforts to build organizational expertise in performing certain competitively important value chain activities. With consistent practice and continuous investment of company resources, these activities rise to the level of a reliable organizational capability or a competence. To the extent that top management makes the growing capability a cornerstone of the company's strategy, this capability becomes a core competence for the company. Later, with further organizational learning and gains in proficiency, the core competence may evolve into a distinctive competence, giving the company superiority over rivals in performing an important value chain activity. Such superiority, if it gives the company significant competitive clout in the marketplace, can produce an attractive competitive edge over rivals. Whether the resulting competitive advantage is on the cost side or on the differentiation side (or both) will depend on the company's choice of which types of competence-building activities to engage in over this time period, as shown in Figure 4.5.

> Performing value chain activities in ways that give a company the capabilities to either outmatch rivals on differentiation or beat them on costs will help the company to secure a competitive advantage.

QUESTION 5: IS THE COMPANY COMPETITIVELY STRONGER OR WEAKER THAN KEY RIVALS?

LO 5

Understand how a comprehensive evaluation of a company's competitive situation can assist managers in making critical decisions about their next strategic moves.

Resource and capability analysis together with value chain analysis and benchmarking will reveal whether a company has a competitive advantage over rivals on the basis of *individual* resources, capabilities, and activities. These tools can also be used to assess the competitive advantage attributable to a *bundle* of resources and capabilities. Resource bundles can sometimes pass the four tests of a resource's competitive power even when the individual components of the resource bundle cannot. For example, although Callaway Golf Company's engineering capabilities and market research capabilities are matched relatively well by rivals Cobra Golf and Ping Golf, the company's bundling of resources used in its product development process (including cross-functional development systems, technological capabilities, knowledge of consumer preferences, and a collaborative organizational culture) gives it a competitive advantage that has allowed it to remain the largest seller of golf equipment for more than a decade.

Resource analysis and value chain/benchmarking analysis of the company's resources, capabilities, and activities (both as individual entities and as bundles) are necessary for determining whether the company is competitively stronger or weaker than key rivals. But they are not sufficient for gaining a complete picture

Figure 4.5   Translating Company Performance of Value Chain Activities into Competitive Advantage

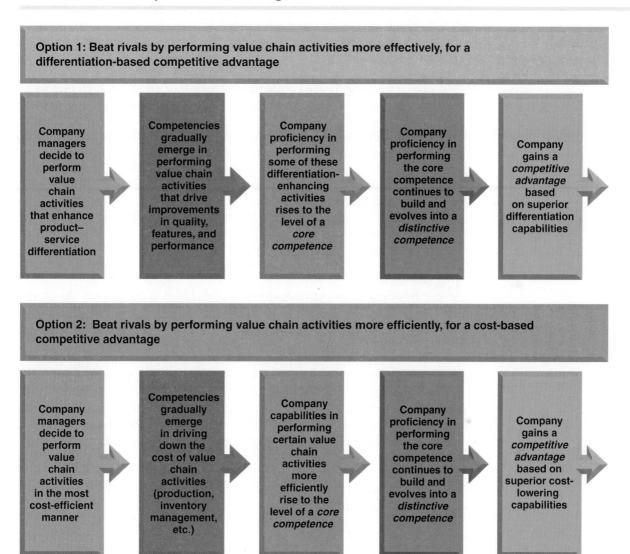

Option 1: Beat rivals by performing value chain activities more effectively, for a differentiation-based competitive advantage

Company managers decide to perform value chain activities that enhance product–service differentiation
→ Competencies gradually emerge in performing value chain activities that drive improvements in quality, features, and performance
→ Company proficiency in performing some of these differentiation-enhancing activities rises to the level of a *core competence*
→ Company proficiency in performing the core competence continues to build and evolves into a *distinctive competence*
→ Company gains a *competitive advantage* based on superior differentiation capabilities

Option 2: Beat rivals by performing value chain activities more efficiently, for a cost-based competitive advantage

Company managers decide to perform value chain activities in the most cost-efficient manner
→ Competencies gradually emerge in driving down the cost of value chain activities (production, inventory management, etc.)
→ Company capabilities in performing certain value chain activities more efficiently rise to the level of a *core competence*
→ Company proficiency in performing the core competence continues to build and evolves into a *distinctive competence*
→ Company gains a *competitive advantage* based on superior cost-lowering capabilities

of a company's competitive situation. A more comprehensive assessment needs to be made of the company's *overall* competitive strengths and weaknesses since a competitive advantage along one part of its value chain can be overwhelmed by competitive disadvantages along other parts of the chain. In making an overall assessment of a company's competitiveness, the answers to two questions are of particular interest: First, how does the company rank relative to competitors on each of the important factors that determine market success? Second, all things considered, does the company have a *net* competitive advantage or disadvantage versus major competitors?

An easy-to-use method for answering these two questions involves developing quantitative strength ratings for the company and its key competitors on each industry key success factor and each competitively pivotal resource and capability. Much of the information needed for doing a competitive strength assessment comes from previous analyses. Industry and five-forces analyses reveal the key success factors and competitive forces that separate industry winners from losers. Analyzing benchmarking data and scouting key competitors provide a basis for judging the competitive strength of rivals on such factors as cost, key product attributes, customer service, image and reputation, financial strength, technological skills, distribution capability, and other resources and capabilities. Resource and capability analysis reveals which factors are competitively important, given the external situation. Together with value chain analysis, it also shines a light on the competitive strengths of the company. That is, it reveals whether the company or its rivals have the advantage with respect to competitively important resources, capabilities, and activities. The four tests of a resource's competitive power indicate, further, whether any of these advantages are sustainable. SWOT analysis provides a more comprehensive and forward-looking picture of the company's overall situation by surveying the entire set of its strengths and weaknesses in relation to rivals and the external environment.

Step 1 in doing a competitive strength assessment is to make a list of the industry's key success factors and most telling measures of competitive strength or weakness (6 to 10 measures usually suffice). Step 2 is to assign weights to each of the measures of competitive strength based on their perceived importance—it is highly unlikely that the different measures are equally important. In an industry where the products/services of rivals are virtually identical, for instance, having low unit costs relative to rivals is nearly always the most important determinant of competitive strength. In an industry with strong product differentiation, the most significant measures of competitive strength may be brand awareness, brand image and reputation, product attractiveness, and distribution capability. A weight could be as high as 0.75 (maybe even higher) in situations where one particular competitive variable is overwhelmingly decisive, or a weight could be as low as 0.20 when two or three strength measures are more important than the rest. Lesser competitive strength indicators can carry weights of 0.05 or 0.10. Whether the differences between the importance weights are big or little, *the sum of the weights must add up to 1.*

Step 3 is to rate the firm and its rivals on each competitive strength measure. Numerical rating scales (e.g., from 1 to 10) are best to use, although ratings of stronger (+), weaker (−), and about equal (=) may be appropriate when information is scanty and assigning numerical scores conveys false precision. Step 4 is to multiply each strength rating by its importance weight to obtain weighted strength scores (a strength rating of 4 times a weight of 0.20 gives a weighted strength score of 0.80). Step 5 is to sum the weighted scores on each measure to get overall weighted competitive strength ratings for each company. Step 6 is to use the overall strength ratings to draw conclusions about the size and extent of the company's net competitive advantage or disadvantage and to take specific note of areas of strength and weakness.

Table 4.4 provides an example of competitive strength assessment in which a hypothetical company (ABC Company) competes against two rivals. In the

Table 4.4 A Representative Weighted Competitive Strength Assessment

Key Success Factor/Strength Measure	Importance Weight	Competitive Strength Assessment (Rating scale: 1 = very weak; 10 = very strong)					
		ABC Co.		Rival 1		Rival 2	
		Strength Rating	Weighted Score	Strength Rating	Weighted Score	Strength Rating	Weighted Score
Quality/product performance	0.10	8	0.80	5	0.50	1	0.10
Reputation/image	0.10	8	0.80	7	0.70	1	0.10
Manufacturing capability	0.10	2	0.20	10	1.00	5	0.50
Technological skills	0.05	10	0.50	1	0.05	3	0.15
Dealer network/distribution capability	0.05	9	0.45	4	0.20	5	0.25
New product innovation capability	0.05	9	0.45	4	0.20	5	0.25
Financial resources	0.10	5	0.50	10	1.00	3	0.30
Relative cost position	0.30	5	1.50	10	3.00	1	0.30
Customer service capabilities	0.15	5	0.75	7	1.05	1	0.15
Sum of importance weights	**1.00**						
Overall weighted competitive strength rating			**5.95**		**7.70**		**2.10**

example, relative cost is the most telling measure of competitive strength, and the other strength measures are of lesser importance. The company with the highest rating on a given measure has an implied competitive edge on that measure, with the size of its edge reflected in the difference between its weighted rating and rivals' weighted ratings. For instance, Rival 1's 3.00 weighted strength rating on relative cost signals a considerable cost advantage versus ABC Company (with a 1.50 weighted score on relative cost) and an even bigger cost advantage against Rival 2 (with a weighted score of 0.30). The measure-by-measure ratings reveal the competitive areas where a company is strongest and weakest, and against whom.

The overall competitive strength scores indicate how all the different strength measures add up—whether the company is at a net overall competitive advantage or disadvantage against each rival. The higher a company's *overall weighted strength rating,* the stronger its *overall competitiveness* versus rivals. The bigger the difference between a company's overall weighted rating and the scores of *lower-rated* rivals, the greater is its implied *net competitive advantage.* Thus, Rival 1's overall weighted score of 7.70 indicates a greater net competitive advantage over Rival 2 (with a score of 2.10) than over ABC Company (with a score of 5.95). Conversely, the bigger the difference between a company's overall rating and the scores of *higher-rated* rivals, the greater its implied *net competitive disadvantage.* Rival 2's score of 2.10 gives it a smaller net competitive disadvantage against ABC Company (with an overall score of 5.95) than against Rival 1 (with an overall score of 7.70).

> High weighted competitive strength ratings signal a strong competitive position and possession of competitive advantage; low ratings signal a weak position and competitive disadvantage.

Strategic Implications of Competitive Strength Assessments

Competitive strength assessments provide useful conclusions about a company's competitive situation. The ratings show how a company compares against rivals, factor by factor (or capability by capability), thus revealing where it is strongest and weakest, and against whom. Moreover, the overall competitive strength score indicates how all the different factors add up—whether the company is at a net competitive advantage or disadvantage against each rival. The firm with the largest overall competitive strength rating enjoys the strongest competitive position, with the size of its net competitive advantage reflected by how much its score exceeds the scores of rivals.

In addition, the strength ratings provide guidelines for designing wise offensive and defensive strategies. For example, if ABC Co. wants to go on the offensive to win additional sales and market share, such an offensive probably needs to be aimed directly at winning customers away from Rival 2 (which has a lower overall strength score) rather than Rival 1 (which has a higher overall strength score). Moreover, while ABC has high ratings for technological skills (a 10 rating), dealer network/distribution capability (a 9 rating), new product innovation capability (a 9 rating), quality/product performance (an 8 rating), and reputation/image (an 8 rating), these strength measures have low importance weights—meaning that ABC has strengths in areas that don't translate into much competitive clout in the marketplace. Even so, it outclasses Rival 2 in all five areas, plus it enjoys substantially lower costs than Rival 2 (ABC has a 5 rating on relative cost position versus a 1 rating for Rival 2)—and relative cost position carries the highest importance weight of all the strength measures. ABC also has greater competitive strength than Rival 3 as concerns customer service capabilities (which carries the second-highest importance weight). Hence, because ABC's strengths are in the very areas where Rival 2 is weak, ABC is in a good position to attack Rival 2—it may well be able to persuade a number of Rival 2's customers to switch their purchases over to ABC's product.

> A company's competitive strength scores pinpoint its strengths and weaknesses against rivals and point directly to the kinds of offensive/defensive actions it can use to exploit its competitive strengths and reduce its competitive vulnerabilities.

But ABC should be cautious about cutting price aggressively to win customers away from Rival 2, because Rival 1 could interpret that as an attack by ABC to win away Rival 1's customers as well. And Rival 1 is in far and away the best position to compete on the basis of low price, given its high rating on relative cost in an industry where low costs are competitively important (relative cost carries an importance weight of 0.30). Rival 1's very strong relative cost position vis-à-vis both ABC and Rival 2 arms it with the ability to use its lower-cost advantage to thwart any price cutting on ABC's part; clearly ABC is vulnerable to any retaliatory price cuts by Rival 1—Rival 1 can easily defeat both ABC and Rival 2 in a price-based battle for sales and market share. If ABC wants to defend against its vulnerability to potential price cutting by Rival 1, then it needs to aim a portion of its strategy at lowering its costs.

The point here is that a competitively astute company should utilize the strength scores in deciding what strategic moves to make—what strengths to exploit in winning business away from rivals, which rivals to attack, and which competitive weaknesses to try to correct. When a company has important competitive strengths in areas where one or more rivals are weak, it makes sense to consider offensive moves to exploit rivals' competitive weaknesses. When a company has important competitive weaknesses in areas where one or more rivals are strong, it makes sense to consider defensive moves to curtail its vulnerability.

QUESTION 6: WHAT STRATEGIC ISSUES AND PROBLEMS MERIT FRONT-BURNER MANAGERIAL ATTENTION?

The final and most important analytical step is to zero in on exactly what strategic issues company managers need to address—and resolve—for the company to be more financially and competitively successful in the years ahead. This step involves drawing on the results of both industry analysis and the evaluations of the company's own competitiveness. The task here is to get a clear fix on exactly what strategic and competitive challenges confront the company, which of the company's competitive shortcomings need fixing, what obstacles stand in the way of improving the company's competitive position in the marketplace, and what specific problems merit front-burner attention by company managers.

The "worry list" of issues and problems that have to be wrestled with can include such things as:

- *How* to stave off market challenges from new foreign competitors.
- *How* to combat the price discounting of rivals.
- *How* to reduce the company's high costs and pave the way for price reductions.
- *How* to sustain the company's present rate of growth in light of slowing buyer demand.
- *Whether* to expand the company's product line.
- *Whether* to correct the company's competitive deficiencies by acquiring a rival company with the missing strengths.
- *Whether* to expand into foreign markets rapidly or cautiously.
- *Whether* to reposition the company and move to a different strategic group.
- *What to do* about growing buyer interest in substitute products.
- *What to do* to combat the aging demographics of the company's customer base.

The worry list thus always centers on such concerns as "how to ... ," "what to do about ... ," and "whether to... ." The purpose of the worry list is to identify the specific issues/problems that management needs to address, not to figure out what specific actions to take. Deciding what to do—which strategic actions to take and which strategic moves to take—comes later (when it is time to craft the strategy and choose among the various strategic alternatives).

If the items on the worry list are relatively minor—which suggests that the company's strategy is mostly on track and reasonably well matched to the company's overall situation, company managers seldom need to go much beyond fine-tuning the present strategy. If, however, the issues and problems confronting the company are serious and indicate the present strategy is not well suited for the road ahead, the task of crafting a better strategy has got to go to the top of management's action agenda.

> Zeroing in on the strategic issues a company faces and compiling a "worry list" of problems and roadblocks creates a strategic agenda of problems that merit prompt managerial attention.

> Actually deciding on a strategy and what specific actions to take is what comes *after* developing the list of strategic issues and problems that merit front-burner management attention.

> A good strategy must contain ways to deal with all the strategic issues and obstacles that stand in the way of the company's financial and competitive success in the years ahead.

    b. How can Just Coffee respond to this type of competitive threat? Does it have any valuable competitive assets that can help it respond, or will it need to acquire new ones. Would your answer change the company's value chain in any way?

LO 1

2. Using the information in Table 4.1 and the financial statement information for Avon Products below, calculate the following ratios for Avon for both 2008 and 2009:

    a. Gross profit margin

    b. Operating profit margin

    c. Net profit margin.

    d. Times interest earned coverage

    e. Return on shareholders' equity

    f. Return on assets

    g. Debt-to-equity ratio

    h. Days of inventory

    i. Inventory turnover ratio

    j. Average collection period

Based on these ratios, did Avon's financial performance improve, weaken, or remain about the same from 2008 to 2009?

Consolidated Statements of Income for Avon Products, Inc., 2008–2009 (in millions, except per-share data)

	Years ended December 31	
	2009	**2008**
Net sales	$10,284.7	$10,588.9
Other revenue	98.1	101.2
Total revenue	10,382.8	10,690.1
Costs, expenses, and other:		
Cost of sales	3,888.3	3,949.1
Selling, general and administrative expenses	5,476.3	5,401.7
Operating profit	1,018.2	1,339.3
Interest expense	104.8	100.4
Interest income	(20.2)	(37.1)
Other expense, net	7.1	37.7
Total other expenses	91.7	101.0
Income before taxes	926.5	1,238.3
Income taxes	298.3	362.7
Net income	628.2	875.6

(Continued)

| | Years ended December 31 | |
	2009	2008
Net income attributable to noncontrolling interests	(2.4)	(.3)
Net income attributable to Avon	$ 625.8	$ 875.3
Earnings per share:		
Basic	$ 1.45	$ 2.04
Diluted	$ 1.45	$ 2.03

Consolidated Balance Sheets for Avon Products, Inc., 2008–2009 (in millions, except per-share data)

	As of Dec. 31, 2009	As of Dec. 31, 2008
Assets		
Cash and cash equivalents	$ 1,311.6	$ 1,104.7
Accounts receivable (less allowances of $165.5 and $127.9)	779.7	687.8
Inventories	1,067.5	1,007.9
Prepaid expenses and other	1,030.5	756.5
Total current assets	4,189.3	3,556.9
Property, plant, and equipment, at cost		
Land	144.3	85.3
Buildings and improvements	1,048.1	1,008.1
Equipment	1,506.9	1,346.5
Total property, plant, and equipment, at cost	2,699.3	2,439.9
Less accumulated depreciation	(1,169.7)	(1,096.0)
Net property, plant, and equipment	1,529.6	1,343.9
Other assets	1,113.8	1,173.2
Total assets	$ 6,832.7	$ 6,074.0
Liabilities and Shareholders' Equity		
Debt maturing within 1 year	$ 138.1	$1,031.4
Accounts payable	754.7	724.3
Accrued compensation	291.0	234.4
Other accrued liabilities	697.1	581.9
Sales and taxes other than income	259.2	212.2
Income taxes	134.7	128.0
Total current liabilities	2,274.8	2,912.2
Long-term debt	2,307.8	1,456.2
Employee benefit plans	588.9	665.4
Long-term income taxes	173.8	168.9
Other liabilities	174.8	159.0
Total liabilities	$ 5,520.1	$ 5,361.7
Commitments and contingencies		

(Continued)

[9] The concept of dynamic capabilities was introduced by D. Teece, G. Pisano, and A. Shuen, "Dynamic Capabilities and Strategic Management," *Strategic Management Journal* 18, no. 7 (1997), pp. 509–33. Other important contributors to the concept include K. Eisenhardt and J. Martin, "Dynamic Capabilities: What Are They?" *Strategic Management Journal* 21, nos. 10–11 (2000), pp. 1105–21; M. Zollo and S. Winter, "Deliberate Learning and the Evolution of Dynamic Capabilities," *Organization Science* 13 (2002), pp. 339–51; C. Helfat et al., *Dynamic Capabilities: Understanding Strategic Change in Organizations* (Malden, MA: Blackwell, 2007).

[10] For a more extensive discussion of how to identify and evaluate the competitive power of a company's capabilities, see David W. Birchall and George Tovstiga, "The Strategic Potential of a Firm's Knowledge Portfolio," *Journal of General Management* 25, no. 1 (Autumn 1999), pp. 1–16; Nick Bontis, Nicola C. Dragonetti, Kristine Jacobsen, and Goran Roos, "The Knowledge Toolbox: A Review of the Tools Available to Measure and Manage Intangible Resources," *European Management Journal* 17, no. 4 (August 1999), pp. 391–401. Also see David Teece, "Capturing Value

from Knowledge Assets: The New Economy, Markets for Know-How, and Intangible Assets," *California Management Review* 40, no. 3 (Spring 1998), pp. 55–79.

[11] Donald Sull, "Strategy as Active Waiting," *Harvard Business Review* 83, no. 9 (September 2005), pp. 121–22.

[12] Ibid., pp. 124–26.

[13] See M. Peteraf, "The Cornerstones of Competitive Advantage: A Resource-Based View," *Strategic Management Journal,* March 1993, pp. 179–91.

[14] The value chain concept was developed and articulated by Michael Porter in his 1985 best-seller, *Competitive Advantage* (New York: Free Press).

[15] For discussions of the accounting challenges in calculating the costs of value chain activities, see John K. Shank and Vijay Govindarajan, *Strategic Cost Management* (New York: Free Press, 1993), especially chaps. 2–6, 10, and 11; Robin Cooper and Robert S. Kaplan, "Measure Costs Right: Make the Right Decisions," *Harvard Business Review* 66, no. 5 (September–October 1988), pp. 96–103; Joseph A. Ness and Thomas G. Cucuzza, "Tapping the Full Potential of ABC," *Harvard Business Review* 73, no. 4 (July–August 1995), pp. 130–38.

[16] Porter, *Competitive Advantage,* p. 34.

[17] The strategic importance of effective supply chain management is discussed in Hau L. Lee, "The Triple-A Supply Chain," *Harvard Business Review* 82, no. 10 (October 2004), pp. 102–12.

[18] For more details, see Gregory H. Watson, *Strategic Benchmarking: How to Rate Your Company's Performance Against the World's Best* (New York: Wiley, 1993); Robert C. Camp, *Benchmarking: The Search for Industry Best Practices That Lead to Superior Performance* (Milwaukee: ASQC Quality Press, 1989); Dawn Iacobucci and Christie Nordhielm, "Creative Benchmarking," *Harvard Business Review* 78 no. 6 (November–December 2000), pp. 24–25.

[19] Jeremy Main, "How to Steal the Best Ideas Around," *Fortune,* October 19, 1992, pp. 102–3.

[20] Some of these options are discussed in more detail in Porter, *Competitive Advantage,* chap. 3.

[21] Porter discusses options such as these in *Competitive Advantage,* chap. 4.

[22] An example of how Whirlpool Corporation transformed its supply chain from a competitive liability to a competitive asset is discussed in Reuben E. Stone, "Leading a Supply Chain Turnaround," *Harvard Business Review* 82, no. 10 (October 2004), pp. 114–21.

	Years ended December 31	
	2009	2008
Net income attributable to noncontrolling interests	(2.4)	(.3)
Net income attributable to Avon	$ 625.8	$ 875.3
Earnings per share:		
Basic	$ 1.45	$ 2.04
Diluted	$ 1.45	$ 2.03

Consolidated Balance Sheets for Avon Products, Inc., 2008–2009 (in millions, except per-share data)

	As of Dec. 31, 2009	As of Dec. 31, 2008
Assets		
Cash and cash equivalents	$ 1,311.6	$ 1,104.7
Accounts receivable (less allowances of $165.5 and $127.9)	779.7	687.8
Inventories	1,067.5	1,007.9
Prepaid expenses and other	1,030.5	756.5
Total current assets	4,189.3	3,556.9
Property, plant, and equipment, at cost		
Land	144.3	85.3
Buildings and improvements	1,048.1	1,008.1
Equipment	1,506.9	1,346.5
Total property, plant, and equipment, at cost	2,699.3	2,439.9
Less accumulated depreciation	(1,169.7)	(1,096.0)
Net property, plant, and equipment	1,529.6	1,343.9
Other assets	1,113.8	1,173.2
Total assets	$ 6,832.7	$ 6,074.0
Liabilities and Shareholders' Equity		
Debt maturing within 1 year	$ 138.1	$1,031.4
Accounts payable	754.7	724.3
Accrued compensation	291.0	234.4
Other accrued liabilities	697.1	581.9
Sales and taxes other than income	259.2	212.2
Income taxes	134.7	128.0
Total current liabilities	2,274.8	2,912.2
Long-term debt	2,307.8	1,456.2
Employee benefit plans	588.9	665.4
Long-term income taxes	173.8	168.9
Other liabilities	174.8	159.0
Total liabilities	$ 5,520.1	$ 5,361.7
Commitments and contingencies		

(Continued)

Shareholders' equity

Common stock, par value $.25—authorized 1,500 shares; issued 740.9 and 739.4 shares	$ 186.1	$ 185.6
Additional paid-in capital	1,941.0	1,874.1
Retained earnings	4,383.9	4,118.9
Accumulated other comprehensive loss	(692.6)	(965.9)
Treasury stock, at cost (313.4 and 313.1 shares)	(4,545.8)	(4,537.8)
Total Avon shareholders' equity	1,272.6	674.9
Noncontrolling interest	40.0	37.4
Total shareholders' equity	**$ 1,312.6**	**$ 712.3**
Total liabilities and shareholders' equity	**$ 6,832.7**	**$ 6,074.0**

Source: Avon Products, Inc., 2009 10-K.

LO 3

3. Prepare a SWOT analysis for Singapore Airlines after reviewing the company's latest Annual Reports, Financial Results, Analyst Briefings, and Operating Statistics at its Web site (www.singaporeair.com). Using the steps in Figure 4.2, create a list of important company strengths and competitive assets, weaknesses and competitive deficiencies, market opportunities, and threats to the company's future well-being. Also, summarize your conclusions concerning the company's overall business situation and implications for improving the company's strategy.

EXERCISES FOR SIMULATION PARTICIPANTS

LO 1

1. Using the formulas in Table 4.1 and the data in your company's latest financial statements, calculate the following measures of financial performance for your company:

   a. Operating profit margin

   b. Return on total assets

   c. Current ratio

   d. Working capital

   e. Long-term debt-to-capital ratio

   f. Price-earnings ratio

LO 1

2. On the basis of your company's latest financial statements and all the other available data regarding your company's performance that appear in the Industry Report, list the three measures of financial performance on which

your company did "best" and the three measures on which your company's financial performance was "worst."

LO 1, LO 2, LO 3, LO 4, LO 5

3. What hard evidence can you cite that indicates your company's strategy is working fairly well (or perhaps not working so well, if your company's performance is lagging that of rival companies)?

LO 3

4. What internal strengths and weaknesses does your company have? What external market opportunities for growth and increased profitability exist for your company? What external threats to your company's future well-being and profitability do you and your co-managers see? What does the preceding SWOT analysis indicate about your company's present situation and future prospects—where on the scale from "exceptionally strong" to "alarmingly weak" does the attractiveness of your company's situation rank?

LO 2, LO 3

5. Does your company have any core competencies? If so, what are they?

LO 4

6. What are the key elements of your company's value chain? Refer to Figure 4.3 in developing your answer.

LO 5

7. Using the methodology presented in Table 4.4, do a weighted competitive strength assessment for your company and two other companies that you and your co-managers consider to be very close competitors.

ENDNOTES

[1] In recent years, considerable research has been devoted to the role a company's resources and competitive capabilities play in determining its competitiveness, shaping its strategy, and impacting its profitability. Following the trailblazing article by Birger Wernerfelt, "A Resource-Based View of the Firm," *Strategic Management Journal* 5, no. 5 (September–October 1984), pp. 171–80, the findings and conclusions have merged into what is now referred to as the resource-based view of the firm. Other very important contributions include Jay Barney, "Firm Resources and Sustained Competitive Advantage," *Journal of Management* 17, no. 1 (1991), pp. 99–120; Margaret A. Peteraf, "The Cornerstones of Competitive Advantage: A Resource-Based View," *Strategic Management Journal* 14, no. 3 (March 1993), pp. 179–91; Birger Wernerfelt, "The Resource-Based View of the Firm: Ten Years After," *Strategic Management Journal* 16, no. 3 (March 1995), pp. 171–74. A full-blown overview of the resource-based view of the firm, in its most current form, is

presented in Jay B. Barney and Delwyn N. Clark, *Resource-Based Theory: Creating and Sustaining Competitive Advantage* (New York: Oxford University Press, 2007).
[2] A more detailed explanation of the relationship between resources and capabilities can be found in R. Amit and P. Schoemaker, "Strategic Assets and Organizational Rent," *Strategic Management Journal* 14 (1993), pp. 33–46.
[3] See, for example, Jay B. Barney, "Looking Inside for Competitive Advantage," *Academy of Management Executive* 9, no. 4 (November 1995), pp. 49–61; Christopher A. Bartlett and Sumantra Ghoshal, "Building Competitive Advantage through People," *MIT Sloan Management Review* 43, no. 2 (Winter 2002), pp. 34–41; Danny Miller, Russell Eisenstat, and Nathaniel Foote, "Strategy from the Inside Out: Building Capability-Creating Organizations," *California Management Review* 44, no. 3 (Spring 2002), pp. 37–54.
[4] See Barney , "Firm Resources and Sustained Competitive Advantage," pp. 105–9; M. Peteraf and J. Barney, "Unraveling the Resource-Based

Tangle," *Managerial and Decision Economics* 24, no. 4 (June–July 2003), pp. 309–23.
[5] See Amit and Schoemaker, Strategic Assets and Organizational Rent, for more on the power of strategic assets to improve a company's profitability.
[6] For a discussion of how to recognize powerful substitute resources, see Margaret A. Peteraf and Mark E. Bergen, "Scanning Dynamic Competitive Landscapes: A Market-Based and Resource-Based Framework," *Strategic Management Journal* 24 (2003), pp. 1027–42.
[7] See C. Montgomery, "Of Diamonds and Rust: A New Look at Resources," in C. Montgomery (ed.), *Resource-Based and Evolutionary Theories of the Firm* (Boston: Kluwer Academic, 1995), pp. 251–68.
[8] For a good discussion of what happens when a company's capabilities grow stale and obsolete, see D. Leonard-Barton, "Core Capabilities and Core Rigidities: A Paradox in Managing New Product Development," *Strategic Management Journal* 13 (Summer 1992), pp. 111–25; Montgomery, "Of Diamonds and Rust."

[9] The concept of dynamic capabilities was introduced by D. Teece, G. Pisano, and A. Shuen, "Dynamic Capabilities and Strategic Management," *Strategic Management Journal* 18, no. 7 (1997), pp. 509–33. Other important contributors to the concept include K. Eisenhardt and J. Martin, "Dynamic Capabilities: What Are They?" *Strategic Management Journal* 21, nos. 10–11 (2000), pp. 1105–21; M. Zollo and S. Winter, "Deliberate Learning and the Evolution of Dynamic Capabilities," *Organization Science* 13 (2002), pp. 339–51; C. Helfat et al., *Dynamic Capabilities: Understanding Strategic Change in Organizations* (Malden, MA: Blackwell, 2007).

[10] For a more extensive discussion of how to identify and evaluate the competitive power of a company's capabilities, see David W. Birchall and George Tovstiga, "The Strategic Potential of a Firm's Knowledge Portfolio," *Journal of General Management* 25, no. 1 (Autumn 1999), pp. 1–16; Nick Bontis, Nicola C. Dragonetti, Kristine Jacobsen, and Goran Roos, "The Knowledge Toolbox: A Review of the Tools Available to Measure and Manage Intangible Resources," *European Management Journal* 17, no. 4 (August 1999), pp. 391–401. Also see David Teece, "Capturing Value

from Knowledge Assets: The New Economy, Markets for Know-How, and Intangible Assets," *California Management Review* 40, no. 3 (Spring 1998), pp. 55–79.

[11] Donald Sull, "Strategy as Active Waiting," *Harvard Business Review* 83, no. 9 (September 2005), pp. 121–22.

[12] Ibid., pp. 124–26.

[13] See M. Peteraf, "The Cornerstones of Competitive Advantage: A Resource-Based View," *Strategic Management Journal,* March 1993, pp. 179–91.

[14] The value chain concept was developed and articulated by Michael Porter in his 1985 best-seller, *Competitive Advantage* (New York: Free Press).

[15] For discussions of the accounting challenges in calculating the costs of value chain activities, see John K. Shank and Vijay Govindarajan, *Strategic Cost Management* (New York: Free Press, 1993), especially chaps. 2–6, 10, and 11; Robin Cooper and Robert S. Kaplan, "Measure Costs Right: Make the Right Decisions," *Harvard Business Review* 66, no. 5 (September–October 1988), pp. 96–103; Joseph A. Ness and Thomas G. Cucuzza, "Tapping the Full Potential of ABC," *Harvard Business Review* 73, no. 4 (July–August 1995), pp. 130–38.

[16] Porter, *Competitive Advantage,* p. 34.

[17] The strategic importance of effective supply chain management is discussed in Hau L. Lee, "The Triple-A Supply Chain," *Harvard Business Review* 82, no. 10 (October 2004), pp. 102–12.

[18] For more details, see Gregory H. Watson, *Strategic Benchmarking: How to Rate Your Company's Performance Against the World's Best* (New York: Wiley, 1993); Robert C. Camp, *Benchmarking: The Search for Industry Best Practices That Lead to Superior Performance* (Milwaukee: ASQC Quality Press, 1989); Dawn Iacobucci and Christie Nordhielm, "Creative Benchmarking," *Harvard Business Review* 78 no. 6 (November–December 2000), pp. 24–25.

[19] Jeremy Main, "How to Steal the Best Ideas Around," *Fortune,* October 19, 1992, pp. 102–3.

[20] Some of these options are discussed in more detail in Porter, *Competitive Advantage,* chap. 3.

[21] Porter discusses options such as these in *Competitive Advantage,* chap. 4.

[22] An example of how Whirlpool Corporation transformed its supply chain from a competitive liability to a competitive asset is discussed in Reuben E. Stone, "Leading a Supply Chain Turnaround," *Harvard Business Review* 82, no. 10 (October 2004), pp. 114–21.

CHAPTER 5

THE FIVE GENERIC COMPETITIVE STRATEGIES

Which One to Employ?

> I'm spending my time trying to understand our competitive position and how we're serving customers.
>
> **—Lou Gerstner**
> *Former CEO credited with IBM's turnaround*

> Competitive strategy is about being different. It means deliberately choosing to perform activities differently or to perform different activities than rivals to deliver a unique mix of value.
>
> **—Michael E. Porter**
> *Harvard Business School professor and Cofounder of Monitor Consulting*

> The essence of strategy lies in creating tomorrow's competitive advantages faster than competitors mimic the ones you possess today.
>
> **—Gary Hamel and C. K. Prahalad**
> *Professors, authors, and consultants*

LEARNING OBJECTIVES

LO 1. Understand what distinguishes each of the five generic strategies and why some of these strategies work better in certain kinds of industry and competitive conditions than in others.

LO 2. Gain command of the major avenues for achieving a competitive advantage based on lower costs.

LO 3. Learn the major avenues to a competitive advantage based on differentiating a company's product or service offering from the offerings of rivals.

LO 4. Recognize the attributes of a best-cost provider strategy and the way in which some firms use a hybrid strategy to go about building a competitive advantage and delivering superior value to customers.

There are several basic approaches to competing successfully and gaining a competitive advantage over rivals, but they all involve the capacity to deliver more customer value than rivals can. Superior value can mean a good product at a lower price, a superior product that is worth paying more for, or a best-value offering that represents an attractive combination of price, features, quality, service, and other appealing attributes. But whatever form delivering superior value takes, it nearly always requires performing value chain activities differently than rivals and building competitively valuable resources and capabilities that rivals cannot readily match or trump.

This chapter describes the five *generic competitive strategy options*. Which of the five to employ is a company's first and foremost choice in crafting an overall strategy and beginning its quest for competitive advantage.

THE FIVE GENERIC COMPETITIVE STRATEGIES

A company's competitive strategy *deals exclusively with the specifics of management's game plan for competing successfully*—its specific efforts to please customers, its offensive and defensive moves to counter the maneuvers of rivals, its responses to shifting market conditions, its initiatives to strengthen its market position, and the specific kind of competitive advantage it is trying to achieve. The chances are remote that any two companies—even companies in the same industry—will employ competitive strategies that are exactly alike in every detail. Why? Because managers at different companies always have a slightly different spin on how best to deal with competitive pressures and industry driving forces, what future market conditions will be like, and what strategy specifics make the most sense for their particular company in light of the company's strengths and weaknesses, its most promising market opportunities, and the external threats to its future well-being.

LO 1

Understand what distinguishes each of the five generic strategies and why some of these strategies work better in certain kinds of industry and competitive conditions than in others.

However, when one strips away the details to get at the real substance, the two factors that most distinguish one competitive strategy from another boil down to (1) whether a company's market target is broad or narrow and (2) whether the company is pursuing a competitive advantage linked to low costs or product differentiation. As shown in Figure 5.1, these two factors give rise to five competitive strategy options for staking out a market position, operating the business, and delivering value to customers:[1]

1. *A low-cost provider strategy:* striving to achieve lower overall costs than rivals on products that attract a broad spectrum of buyers.

2. *A broad differentiation strategy:* seeking to differentiate the company's product offering from rivals' with attributes that will appeal to a broad spectrum of buyers.

3. *A focused (or market niche) low-cost strategy:* concentrating on a narrow buyer segment and outcompeting rivals on costs, thus being in position to win buyer favor by means of a lower-priced product offering.

4. *A focused (or market niche) differentiation strategy:* concentrating on a narrow buyer segment and outcompeting rivals with a product offering that meets the specific tastes and requirements of niche members better than the product offerings of rivals.

5. *A best-cost provider strategy:* giving customers *more value for the money* by offering upscale product attributes at a lower cost than rivals. Being the "best-cost" producer of an upscale product allows a company to underprice rivals whose products have similar upscale attributes. This option is a *hybrid* strategy that *blends elements of differentiation and low-cost strategies* in a unique way.

The remainder of this chapter explores the ins and outs of these five generic competitive strategies and how they differ.

Figure 5.1   The Five Generic Competitive Strategies: Each Stakes Out a Different Market Position

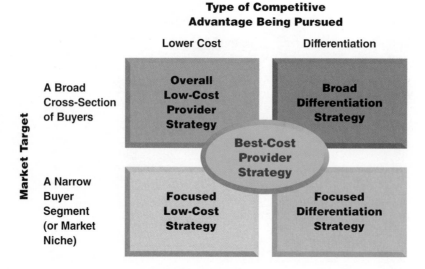

Source: This is an author-expanded version of a three-strategy classification discussed in Michael E. Porter, *Competitive Strategy* (New York: Free Press, 1980), pp. 35–40.

LOW-COST PROVIDER STRATEGIES

LO 2

Gain command of the major avenues for achieving a competitive advantage based on lower costs.

Striving to be the industry's overall low-cost provider is a powerful competitive approach in markets with many price-sensitive buyers. A company achieves **low-cost leadership** when it becomes the industry's lowest-cost provider rather than just being one of perhaps several competitors with comparatively low costs. A low-cost provider's strategic target is to have lower costs than rivals on products of comparable quality. In striving for a cost advantage over rivals, company managers must take care to incorporate features and services that buyers consider essential—*a product offering that is too frills-free sabotages the attractiveness of the company's product and can turn buyers off even if it is cheaper than competing products.* For maximum effectiveness, a low-cost provider needs to pursue cost-saving approaches that are difficult for rivals to copy. When it is relatively easy or inexpensive for rivals to imitate the low-cost firm's methods, then any resulting cost advantage evaporates too quickly to gain a very valuable edge in the marketplace.

CORE CONCEPT

A **low-cost leader**'s basis for competitive advantage is lower overall costs than competitors. Successful low-cost leaders are exceptionally good at finding ways to drive costs out of their businesses and still provide a product or service that buyers find acceptable.

A low-cost advantage over rivals has enormous competitive power, sometimes enabling a company to achieve faster rates of growth (by using price cuts to draw customers away from rivals) and frequently helping to boost a company's profitability. A company can translate a low-cost advantage over rivals into attractive profit performance in either of two ways:

1. By using its lower-cost edge to underprice competitors and attract price-sensitive buyers in great enough numbers to increase total profits.
2. By refraining from using price cuts to steal sales away from rivals (which runs the risk of starting a price war) and, instead, charging a price roughly equal to those of other low-priced rivals. While this strategy will not increase the company's market share, it will enable the company to earn a bigger profit margin per unit sold (because the company's costs per unit are below the unit costs of rivals) and thereby propel it to higher total profits and return on investment than rivals are able to earn.

While many companies are inclined to exploit a low-cost advantage by attacking rivals with lower prices (in hopes that the expected gains in sales and market share will lead to higher total profits), this strategy can backfire if rivals respond with retaliatory price cuts of their own (in order to protect their customer base) and the aggressor's price cuts fail to produce sales gains that are big enough to offset the profit erosion associated with charging a lower price. The bigger the risk that rivals will respond with matching price cuts, the more appealing it becomes to employ the second option for using a low-cost advantage to achieve higher profitability.

A low-cost advantage over rivals can translate into better profitability than rivals attain.

The Two Major Avenues for Achieving a Cost Advantage

To achieve a low-cost edge over rivals, a firm's cumulative costs across its overall value chain must be lower than competitors' cumulative costs. There are two ways to accomplish this:[2]

1. Do a better job than rivals of performing value chain activities more cost-effectively.

2. Revamp the firm's overall value chain to eliminate or bypass some cost-producing activities.

Let's look at each of the two approaches to securing a cost advantage.

Cost-Efficient Management of Value Chain Activities

CORE CONCEPT

A **cost driver** is a factor that has a strong influence on a company's costs.

For a company to do a more cost-efficient job of managing its value chain than rivals, managers must launch a concerted, ongoing effort to ferret out cost-saving opportunities in every part of the value chain. No activity can escape cost-saving scrutiny, and all company personnel must be expected to use their talents and ingenuity to come up with innovative and effective ways to keep costs down. All avenues for performing value chain activities at a lower cost than rivals have to be explored. Particular attention, however, needs to be paid to a set of factors known as **cost drivers,** which have an especially strong effect on a company's costs and which managers can use as levers to push costs down. (Figure 5.2 provides a list of important cost drivers.) Cost-cutting methods that demonstrate an effective use of the cost drivers include:

1. *Striving to capture all available economies of scale.* Economies of scale stem from an ability to lower unit costs by increasing the scale of operation, and they can affect the unit costs of many activities along the value chain, including manufacturing, R&D, advertising, distribution, and general administration. For example, PepsiCo and Anheuser-Busch have the ability to afford the $3 million cost of a 30-second Super Bowl ad because the cost of such an ad can be spread out over the hundreds of millions of units they sell. In contrast, a small company with a sales volume of only 1 million units would find the $3 million cost of a Super Bowl ad prohibitive—just one ad would raise costs over $2 per unit even if the ad was unusually effective and caused sales volume to jump 25 percent, to 1.25 million units. Similarly, a large manufacturing plant can be more economical to operate than a smaller one. In global industries, making separate products for each country market instead of selling a mostly standard product worldwide tends to boost unit costs because of lost time in model changeover, shorter production runs, and inability to reach the most economic scale of production for each country model.

2. *Taking full advantage of experience and learning-curve effects.* The cost of performing an activity can decline over time as the learning and experience of company personnel build. Learning/experience economies can stem from debugging and mastering newly introduced technologies, using the experiences and suggestions of workers to install more efficient plant layouts and assembly procedures, and the added speed and effectiveness that accrues from repeatedly picking sites for and building new plants, retail outlets, or distribution centers. Aggressively managed low-cost providers pay diligent attention to capturing the benefits of learning and experience and to keeping these benefits proprietary to whatever extent possible.

3. *Trying to operate facilities at full capacity.* Whether a company is able to operate at or near full capacity has a big impact on units costs when

Figure 5.2   Cost Drivers: The Keys to Driving Down Company Costs

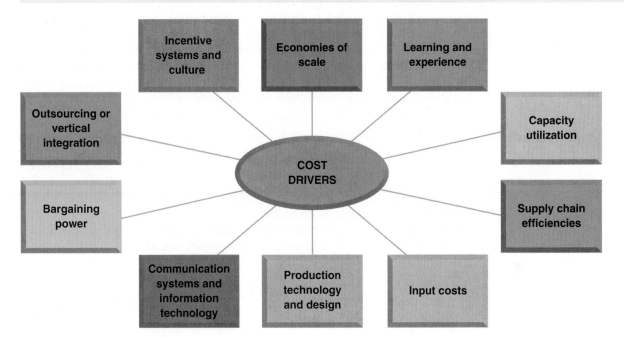

Sources: Adapted by the authors from M. Porter, *Competitive Advantage: Creating and Sustaining Competitive Advantage* (New York: Free Press, 1985).

its value chain contains activities associated with substantial fixed costs. Higher rates of capacity utilization allow depreciation and other fixed costs to be spread over a larger unit volume, thereby lowering fixed costs per unit. The more capital-intensive the business and the higher the fixed costs relative to total costs, the greater the unit-cost penalty for underutilizing existing capacity.

4. *Improving supply chain efficiency.* Partnering with suppliers to streamline the ordering and purchasing process, to reduce inventory carrying costs via just-in-time inventory practices, to economize on shipping and materials handling, and to ferret out other cost-saving opportunities is a much-used approach to cost reduction. A company with a distinctive competence in cost-efficient supply chain management can sometimes achieve a sizable cost advantage over less adept rivals.

5. *Using lower cost inputs wherever doing so will not entail too great a sacrifice in quality.* Some examples include lower-cost raw materials or component parts, nonunion labor "inputs," and lower rental fees due to differences in location. If the costs of certain factors are "too high," a company may even design the high-cost inputs out of the product altogether.

6. *Using the company's bargaining power vis-à-vis suppliers or others in the value chain system to gain concessions.* Home Depot, for example, has sufficient bargaining clout with suppliers to win price discounts on large-volume purchases. PepsiCo similarly uses its bargaining power to win concessions from supermarkets, mass merchandisers, and other forward channel allies.

7. *Using communication systems and information technology to achieve operating efficiencies.* For example, data sharing, starting with customer orders and going all the way back to components production, coupled with the use of enterprise resource planning (ERP) and manufacturing execution system (MES) software, can greatly reduce production times and labor costs. Numerous companies now have online systems and software that turn formerly time-consuming and labor-intensive tasks like purchasing, inventory management, invoicing, and bill payment into speedily performed mouse clicks.

8. *Employing advanced production technology and process design to improve overall efficiency.* Examples range from highly automated robotic production technology to computer-assisted design (CAD) techniques to design for manufacture (DFM) procedures that enable more integrated and efficient production. Dell's highly automated PC assembly plant in Austin, Texas, is a prime example of the use of advanced product and process technologies. Other manufacturers have pioneered the use of production or processing technology that eliminates the need for costly investments in facilities or equipment and that requires fewer employees. Companies can also achieve substantial efficiency gains through process innovation or through approaches such as business process management, business process reengineering, and total quality management that aim to coordinate production activities and drive continuous improvement in productivity and quality.[3] Procter & Gamble is an example of a company known for its successful application of business process reengineering techniques.

9. *Being alert to the cost advantages of outsourcing or vertical integration.* Outsourcing the performance of certain value chain activities can be more economical than performing them in-house if outside specialists, by virtue of their expertise and volume, can perform the activities at lower cost. Indeed, outsourcing has, in recent years, become a widely used cost reduction approach. On the other hand, there can be times when integrating into the activities of either suppliers or distribution channel allies can lower costs through greater production efficiencies, reduced transaction costs, or a better bargaining position.

10. *Motivating employees through incentives and company culture.* A company's incentive system can encourage not only greater worker productivity but also cost-saving innovations that come from worker suggestions. The culture of a company can also spur worker pride in productivity and continuous improvement. Companies that are well known for their cost-reducing incentive systems and culture include Nucor Steel, which characterizes itself as a company of "11,900 teammates," Southwest Airlines, and Walmart.

In addition to the above means of performing value chain activities more efficiently than rivals, managers can also achieve important cost savings by deliberately opting for an inherently economical strategy. For instance, a company can often open up a significant cost advantage over rivals by:

• Having lower specifications for purchased materials, parts, and components than do rivals. Thus, a maker of personal computers can use the cheapest hard drives, microprocessors, monitors, and other components so as to end up with lower production costs than rival PC makers.

• Stripping frills and features from its product offering that are not highly valued by price-sensitive or bargain-hunting buyers. Deliberately restricting the company's product offering to "the essentials" can help a company cut costs associated with snazzy attributes and a full lineup of options and extras. Activities and costs can also be eliminated by offering buyers fewer services.

- Offering a limited product line as opposed to a full product line. Pruning slow-selling items from the product lineup and being content to meet the needs of most buyers rather than all buyers can eliminate activities and costs associated with numerous product versions and wide selection.

- Distributing the company's product only through low-cost distribution channels and avoiding high-cost distribution channels.

- Choosing to use the most economical method for delivering customer orders (even if it results in longer delivery times).

The point here is that a low-cost provider strategy entails not only performing value chain activities cost-effectively but also judiciously choosing cost-saving strategic approaches.

Revamping the Value Chain System to Lower Costs
Dramatic cost advantages can often emerge from redesigning the company's value chain system in ways that eliminate costly work steps and entirely bypass certain cost-producing value chain activities. While using communication technologies and information systems or business process reengineering to drive down costs often involves activities that span the value chain system, other approaches to revamping the value chain system can include:

- *Selling direct to consumers and bypassing the activities and costs of distributors and dealers.* To circumvent the need for distributors-dealers, a company can (1) create its own direct sales force (which adds the costs of maintaining and supporting a sales force but which may well be cheaper than utilizing independent distributors and dealers to access buyers) and/or (2) conduct sales operations at the company's Web site (incurring costs for Web site operations and shipping may be a substantially cheaper way to make sales to customers than going through distributor-dealer channels). Costs in the wholesale/retail portions of the value chain frequently represent 35 to 50 percent of the price final consumers pay, so establishing a direct sales force or selling online may offer big cost savings.

- *Coordinating with suppliers to bypass the need to perform certain value chain activities, speed up their performance, or otherwise increase overall efficiency.* Examples include having suppliers combine particular parts and components into preassembled modules, thus permitting a manufacturer to assemble its own product in fewer work steps and with a smaller workforce, and sharing real-time sales information to lower costs through improved inventory management. At Walmart, some items supplied by manufacturers are delivered directly to retail stores rather than being routed through Walmart's distribution centers and delivered by Walmart trucks; in other instances, Walmart unloads incoming shipments from manufacturers' trucks arriving at its distribution centers directly onto outgoing Walmart trucks headed to particular stores without ever moving the goods into the distribution center. Many supermarket chains have greatly reduced in-store meat butchering and cutting activities by shifting to meats that are cut and packaged at the meatpacking plant and then delivered to their stores in ready-to-sell form.

- *Reducing materials handling and shipping costs by having suppliers locate their plants or warehouses close to the company's own facilities.* Having suppliers locate their plants or warehouses very close to a company's own plant facilitates just-in-time deliveries of parts and components to the exact work station where they will be utilized in assembling the company's product. This not only lowers incoming shipping costs but also curbs or eliminates the need for a company to build and operate storerooms for incoming parts and components and have plant personnel move the inventories to the work stations as needed for assembly.

Illustration Capsule 5.1 describes how Walmart has managed its value chain in the retail grocery portion of its business to achieve a dramatic cost advantage over rival supermarket chains and become the world's biggest grocery retailer.

Examples of Companies That Revamped Their Value Chains to Reduce Costs

Nucor Corporation, the most profitable steel producer in the United States and one of the largest steel producers worldwide, drastically revamped the value chain process for manufacturing steel products by using relatively inexpensive electric arc furnaces where scrap steel and directly reduced iron ore are melted and then sent to a continuous caster and rolling mill to be shaped into steel bars, steel beams, steel plate, and sheet steel. Using electric arc furnaces to make new steel products by recycling scrap steel eliminated many of the steps used by traditional steel mills that made their steel products from iron ore, coke, limestone, and other ingredients using costly coke ovens, basic oxygen blast furnaces, ingot casters, and multiple types of finishing facilities—plus Nucor's value chain system required far few employees. As a consequence, Nucor was able to make steel with a far lower capital investment, a far smaller workforce, and far lower operating costs than traditional steel mills. Nucor's strategy to replace the traditional steelmaking value chain with its simpler, quicker value chain approach has made it one of the lowest-cost producers of steel in the world and enabled Nucor to take huge volumes of sales and market share away from traditional steel companies and earn attractive profits. (Nucor has reported profits for every quarter in every year during the 1966–2008 period—a remarkable accomplishment in a mature and cyclical industry notorious for poor profitability.) While the recession-plagued year of 2009 was not a good one for Nucor, it returned to profits quickly in 2010.

Southwest Airlines has achieved considerable cost savings by reconfiguring the traditional value chain of commercial airlines, thereby allowing it to offer travelers dramatically lower fares. Its mastery of fast turnarounds at the gates (about 25 minutes versus 45 minutes for rivals) allows its planes to fly more hours per day. This translates into being able to schedule more flights per day with fewer aircraft, allowing Southwest to generate more revenue per plane on average than rivals. Southwest does not offer assigned seating, baggage transfer to connecting airlines, or first-class seating and service, thereby eliminating all the cost-producing activities associated with these features. The company's fast and user-friendly online reservation system facilitates e-ticketing and reduces staffing requirements at telephone reservation centers and airport counters. Its use of automated check-in equipment reduces staffing requirements for terminal check-in.

The Keys to Being a Successful Low-Cost Provider

To succeed with a low-cost provider strategy, company managers have to scrutinize each cost-creating activity and determine what factors cause costs to be high or low. Then they have to use this knowledge to streamline or reengineer how activities are performed, exhaustively pursuing cost efficiencies throughout the value chain. Normally, low-cost producers try to engage all company personnel in continuous cost improvement efforts, and they strive to operate with exceptionally small corporate staffs to keep administrative costs to a minimum. Many successful low-cost

How Walmart Managed Its Value Chain to Achieve a Huge Low-Cost Advantage over Rival Supermarket Chains

Walmart has achieved a very substantial cost and pricing advantage over rival supermarket chains both by revamping portions of the grocery retailing value chain and by outmanaging its rivals in efficiently performing various value chain activities. Its cost advantage stems from a series of initiatives and practices:

- Instituting extensive information sharing with vendors via online systems that relay sales at its checkout counters directly to suppliers of the items, thereby providing suppliers with real-time information on customer demand and preferences (creating an estimated 6 percent cost advantage). It is standard practice at Walmart to collaborate extensively with vendors on all aspects of the purchasing and store delivery process to squeeze out mutually beneficial cost savings. Procter & Gamble, Walmart's biggest supplier, went so far as to integrate its enterprise resource planning (ERP) system with Walmart's.

- Pursuing global procurement of some items and centralizing most purchasing activities so as to leverage the company's buying power (creating an estimated 2.5 percent cost advantage).

- Investing in state-of-the-art automation at its distribution centers, efficiently operating a truck fleet that makes daily deliveries to Walmart's stores, and putting other assorted cost-saving practices into place at its headquarters, distribution centers, and stores (resulting in an estimated 4 percent cost advantage).

- Striving to optimize the product mix and achieve greater sales turnover (resulting in about a 2 percent cost advantage).

- Installing security systems and store operating procedures that lower shrinkage rates (producing a cost advantage of about 0.5 percent).

- Negotiating preferred real estate rental and leasing rates with real estate developers and owners of its store sites (yielding a cost advantage of 2 percent).

- Managing and compensating its workforce in a manner that produces lower labor costs (yielding an estimated 5 percent cost advantage).

Altogether, these value chain initiatives give Walmart an approximately 22 percent cost advantage over Kroger, Safeway, and other leading supermarket chains. With such a sizable cost advantage, Walmart has been able to underprice its rivals and rapidly become the world's leading supermarket retailer.

Sources: Developed by the authors from information at www.walmart.com and in Marco Iansiti and Roy Levien, "Strategy as Ecology," *Harvard Business Review* 82, no. 3 (March 2004), p. 70.

leaders also use benchmarking to keep close tabs on how their costs compare with those of rivals and firms performing comparable activities in other industries.

But while low-cost providers are champions of frugality, they seldom hesitate to spend aggressively on resources and capabilities *that promise to drive costs out of the business.* Indeed, having resources or capabilities of this type and ensuring that they remain competitively superior is essential for achieving competitive advantage as a low-cost provider. Walmart, one of the world's foremost

Success in achieving a low-cost edge over rivals comes from out-managing rivals in finding ways to perform value chain activities faster, more accurately, and more cost-effectively.

low-cost providers, has been an early adopter of state-of-the-art technology throughout its operations—its distribution facilities are an automated showcase, it has developed sophisticated online systems to order goods from suppliers and manage inventories, it equips its stores with cutting-edge sales-tracking and checkout systems, and it sends daily point-of-sale data to 4,000 vendors, *but Walmart carefully estimates the cost savings of new technologies before it rushes to invest in them.* By continuously investing in complex technologies that are hard for rivals to match, Walmart has sustained its competitive advantage for over 30 years.

Other companies noted for their successful use of low-cost provider strategies include Haier in home appliances, Toyota in automobiles, Bata in footwear, and Acer in computers.

When a Low-Cost Provider Strategy Works Best

A low-cost provider strategy becomes increasingly appealing and competitively powerful when:

1. *Price competition among rival sellers is vigorous.* Low-cost providers are in the best position to compete offensively on the basis of price, to use the appeal of lower price to grab sales (and market share) from rivals, to win the business of price-sensitive buyers, to remain profitable despite strong price competition, and to survive price wars.

2. *The products of rival sellers are essentially identical and readily available from many eager sellers.* Look-alike products and/or overabundant product supply set the stage for lively price competition; in such markets, it is the less efficient, higher-cost companies whose profits get squeezed the most.

3. *There are few ways to achieve product differentiation that have value to buyers.* When the differences between product attributes or brands do not matter much to buyers, buyers are nearly always very sensitive to price differences and market share winners will tend to be those with the lowest-priced brands.

4. *Most buyers use the product in the same ways.* With common user requirements, a standardized product can satisfy the needs of buyers, in which case low selling price, not features or quality, becomes the dominant factor in causing buyers to choose one seller's product over another's.

5. *Buyers incur low costs in switching their purchases from one seller to another.* Low switching costs give buyers the flexibility to shift purchases to lower-priced sellers having equally good products or to attractively priced substitute products. A low-cost leader is well positioned to use low price to induce its customers not to switch to rival brands or substitutes.

6. *Buyers are large and have significant power to bargain down prices.* Low-cost providers have partial profit-margin protection in bargaining with high-volume buyers, since powerful buyers are rarely able to bargain price down past the survival level of the next most cost-efficient seller.

7. *Industry newcomers use introductory low prices to attract buyers and build a customer base.* A low-cost provider can use price cuts of its own to make it harder for a new rival to win customers. Moreover, the pricing power of a low-cost provider acts as a barrier for new entrants.

As a rule, the more price-sensitive buyers are, the more appealing a low-cost strategy becomes. A low-cost company's ability to set the industry's price floor and still earn a profit erects protective barriers around its market position.

Pitfalls to Avoid in Pursuing a Low-Cost Provider Strategy

Perhaps the biggest mistake a low-cost provider can make to spoil the profitability of its low-cost advantage is getting carried away with overly aggressive price cutting to win sales and market share away from rivals. *Higher unit sales and market shares do not automatically translate into higher total profits.* A low-cost/low-price advantage results in superior profitability only if (1) prices are cut by less than the size of the unit cost advantage or (2) the added gains in unit sales are large enough to bring in a bigger total profit despite lower margins per unit sold. A company with a 5 percent per-unit cost advantage cannot cut prices 20 percent, end up with a volume gain of only 10 percent, and still expect to earn higher profits!

A lower price improves total profitability only if the price cuts lead to total revenues that are big enough to *more than cover* all the added costs associated with selling more units. When the incremental gains in total revenues flowing from a lower price exceed the incremental increases in total costs associated with a higher sales volume, then cutting price is a profitable move. But if a lower selling price results in revenue gains that are smaller than the increases in total costs, company profits end up lower than before and the price cut ends up reducing profits rather than raising them.

A second pitfall of a low-cost provider strategy is failing to emphasize avenues of cost advantage that can be kept proprietary or that relegate rivals to playing catch-up. The real value of a cost advantage depends on its sustainability. Sustainability, in turn, hinges on whether the company achieves its cost advantage in ways difficult for rivals to copy or otherwise overcome.

A third pitfall is becoming too fixated on cost reduction. Low cost cannot be pursued so zealously that a firm's offering ends up being too features-poor to generate buyer appeal. Furthermore, a company driving hard to push its costs down has to guard against misreading or ignoring increased buyer interest in added features or service, declining buyer sensitivity to price, or new developments that start to alter how buyers use the product. Otherwise, it risks losing market ground if buyers start opting for more upscale or feature-rich products.

Even if these mistakes are avoided, a low-cost provider strategy still entails risk. An innovative rival may discover an even lower-cost value chain approach. Important cost-saving technological breakthroughs may suddenly emerge. And if a low-cost provider has heavy investments in its present means of operating, then it can prove very costly to quickly shift to the new value chain approach or a new technology.

> A low-cost provider is in the best position to win the business of price-sensitive buyers, set the floor on market price, and still earn a profit.

> Reducing price does not lead to higher total profits unless the incremental gain in total revenues exceeds the incremental increase in total costs.

> A low-cost provider's product offering must always contain enough attributes to be attractive to prospective buyers—low price, by itself, is not always appealing to buyers.

BROAD DIFFERENTIATION STRATEGIES

Differentiation strategies are attractive whenever buyers' needs and preferences are too diverse to be fully satisfied by a standardized product offering. Successful product differentiation requires careful study of buyers' needs and behaviors to learn what buyers consider important, what they think has value, and what they are

LO 3

Learn the major
avenues to a
competitive
advantage based
on differentiating a
company's product
or service offering
from the offerings
of rivals.

willing to pay for.[4] Then the trick is for a company to incorporate certain buyer-desired attributes into its product offering such that its offering will not only appeal to a broad range of buyers but also be different enough to stand apart from the product offerings of rivals—in regard to the latter, a strongly differentiated product offering is always preferable to a weakly differentiated one. A differentiation strategy calls for a customer value proposition that is *unique.* The strategy achieves its aim when an attractively large number of buyers find the customer value proposition appealing and become strongly attached to a company's differentiated attributes.

Successful differentiation allows a firm to do one or more of the following:

- Command a premium price for its product.
- Increase unit sales (because additional buyers are won over by the differentiating features).
- Gain buyer loyalty to its brand (because some buyers are strongly bonded to the differentiating features of the company's product offering).

Differentiation enhances profitability whenever a company's product can command a sufficiently higher price or produce sufficiently bigger unit sales *to more than cover the added costs of achieving the differentiation.* Company differentiation strategies fail when buyers don't value the brand's uniqueness and/or when a company's approach to differentiation is easily copied or matched by its rivals.

Companies can pursue differentiation from many angles: a unique taste (Red Bull); multiple features (Microsoft Office, the iPhone); superior service (FedEx); engineering design and performance (Mercedes, BMW); prestige and distinctiveness (Rolex); product reliability (Johnson & Johnson in baby products); quality manufacture (Michelin in tires, Honda in automobiles); technological leadership (3M Corporation in bonding and coating products); a full range of services (ING in banking, investments, and insurance); wide product selection (Ikea, Amazon.com); and high fashion design (Gucci and Chanel).

Managing the Value Chain to Create the Differentiating Attributes

Differentiation is not something hatched in marketing and advertising departments, nor is it limited to the catchalls of quality and service. Differentiation opportunities can exist in activities all along an industry's value chain. The most systematic approach that managers can take, however, involves focusing on the **uniqueness drivers,** a set of factors—analogous to cost drivers—that are particularly effective in creating differentiation. Figure 5.3 contains a list of important uniqueness drivers. Ways that managers can enhance differentiation based on these drivers include the following:

1. *Striving to create superior product features, design, and performance.* This applies to the physical and well as functional attributes of a product, including features such as expanded end uses and applications, added user safety, greater recycling capability, or enhanced environmental protection. Design features can be important in enhancing the aesthetic appeal of a product. Ducati's motorcycles, for example, are prized for their designs and have been exhibited in the Guggenheim art museum in New York City.[5]

CORE CONCEPT

The essence of a **broad differentiation strategy** is to offer unique product attributes that a wide range of buyers find appealing and worth paying for.

CORE CONCEPT

A **uniqueness driver** is a factor that can have a strong differentiating effect.

Figure 5.3   Uniqueness Drivers: The Keys to Creating a Differentiation Advantage

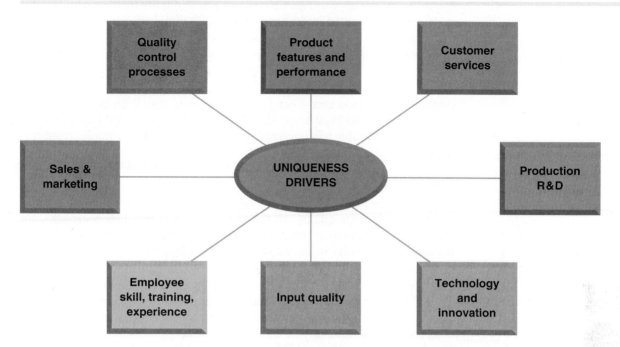

Source: Adapted from M. Porter, *Competitive Advantage: Creating and Sustaining Competitive Advantage* (New York: Free Press, 1985).

2. *Improving customer service or adding additional services.* Better customer services, in areas such as delivery, returns, and repair, can be as important in creating differentiation as superior product features. Examples include superior technical assistance to buyers, higher-quality maintenance services, more and better product information provided to customers, more and better training materials for end users, better credit terms, quicker order processing, or greater customer convenience.

3. *Pursuing production R&D activities.* Engaging in production R&D may permit custom-order manufacture at an efficient cost, provide wider product variety and selection through product "versioning," improve product quality, or make production methods safer for the environment. Many manufacturers have developed flexible manufacturing systems that allow different models and product versions to be made on the same assembly line. Being able to provide buyers with made-to-order products can be a potent differentiating capability.

4. *Striving for innovation and technological advances.* Successful innovation is the route to more frequent first-on-the-market victories and is a powerful differentiator. If the innovation proves hard to replicate, through patent protection or other means, it can provide a company with a first mover advantage that is sustainable.

5. *Pursuing continuous quality improvement.* Perceived quality differences can be an important differentiator in the eyes of customers. Quality control processes can be applied throughout the value chain, including postsale customer service activities. They can reduce product defects, prevent premature product failure, extend product life, make it economical to offer longer warranty

coverage, improve economy of use, result in more end-user convenience, or enhance product appearance. Companies whose quality management systems meet certification standards, such as the ISO 9001 standards, can enhance their reputation for quality with customers.

6. *Increasing the intensity of marketing and sales activities.* Marketing and advertising can have a tremendous effect on the value perceived by buyers and therefore their willingness to pay more for the company's offerings. They can create differentiation even when little tangible differentiation exists otherwise. For example, blind taste tests show that even the most loyal Pepsi or Coke drinkers have trouble telling one cola drink from another.[6] Brands create customer loyalty, which increases the perceived "cost" of switching to another product. Brand management activities are therefore also important in supporting differentiation.

7. *Seeking out high-quality inputs.* Input quality can ultimately spill over to affect the performance or quality of the company's end product. Starbucks, for example, gets high ratings on its coffees partly because it has very strict specifications on the coffee beans purchased from suppliers.

8. *Improving employee skill, knowledge, and experience through human resource management activities.* Hiring, training, and retaining highly skilled and experienced employees is important since such employees are often the source of creative, innovative ideas that are behind new product development. Moreover, they are essential to performing differentiating activities such as design, engineering, marketing, and R&D. Company culture and reward systems can help unleash the potential contribution of high-value employees to a differentiation strategy.

Managers need keen understanding of the sources of differentiation and the activities that drive uniqueness to evaluate various differentiation approaches and design durable ways to set their product offering apart from rival brands.

Revamping the Value Chain System to Increase Differentiation
Just as pursuing a cost advantage can involve the entire value chain system, the same is true for a differentiation advantage. Activities performed upstream by suppliers or downstream by distributors and retailers can have a meaningful effect on customers' perceptions of a company's offerings and its value proposition. Approaches to enhancing differentiation through changes in the value chain system include:[7]

- *Coordinating with channel allies to enhance customer perceptions of value.* Coordinating with downstream partners such as distributors, dealers, brokers, and retailers can contribute to differentiation in a variety of ways. Methods that companies use to influence the value chain activities of their channel allies include setting standards for downstream partners to follow, providing them with templates to standardize the selling environment or practices, training channel personnel, or cosponsoring promotions and advertising campaigns. Coordinating with retailers is important for enhancing the buying experience and building a company's image. Coordinating with distributors or shippers can mean quicker delivery to customers, more accurate order filling, and/or lower shipping costs. The Coca-Cola Company considers coordination with its bottler/distributors so important that it has at times taken over a troubled bottler for the purpose of improving its management and upgrading its plant and equipment before releasing the product to the market.[8]

- *Coordinating with suppliers to better address customer needs.* Collaborating with suppliers can also be a powerful route to a more effective differentiation strategy. Coordinating and collaborating with suppliers can improve many dimensions affecting product features and quality. This is particularly true for companies that only engage in assembly operations, such as Dell in PCs and Ducati in motorcycles. Close coordination with suppliers can also enhance differentiation by speeding up new product development cycles or speeding delivery to end customers. Strong relationships with suppliers can also mean that the company's supply requirements are prioritized when industry supply is insufficient to meet overall demand.

Delivering Superior Value via a Broad Differentiation Strategy

Differentiation strategies depend on meeting customer needs in unique ways or creating new needs, through activities such as innovation or persuasive advertising. The objective is to offer customers something that rivals can't—at least in terms of the level of satisfaction. There are four basic routes to achieving this aim.

The first route is to incorporate product attributes and user features that *lower the buyer's overall costs* of using the company's product. This is the least obvious and most overlooked route to a differentiation advantage. It is a differentiating factor since it can help business buyers be more competitive in their markets and more profitable. Producers of materials and components often win orders for their products by reducing a buyer's raw-material waste (providing cut-to-size components), reducing a buyer's inventory requirements (providing just-in-time deliveries), using online systems to reduce a buyer's procurement and order processing costs, and providing free technical support. This route to differentiation can also appeal to individual consumers who are looking to economize on their overall costs of consumption. Making a company's product more economical for a buyer to use can be done by incorporating energy-efficient features (energy-saving appliances and lightbulbs help cut buyers' utility bills; fuel-efficient vehicles cut buyer costs for gasoline) and/or by increasing maintenance intervals and product reliability so as to lower buyer costs for maintenance and repairs.

A second route is to incorporate *tangible* features that increase customer satisfaction with the product, such as product specifications, functions, and styling. This can be accomplished by including attributes that add functionality, enhance the design, expand the range of uses, save time for the user, are more reliable, or make the product cleaner, safer, quieter, simpler to use, portable, more convenient, or longer-lasting than rival brands. Mobile phone manufacturers are in a race to introduce next-generation devices capable of being used for more purposes and having simpler menu functionality.

A third route to a differentiation-based competitive advantage is to incorporate *intangible* features that enhance buyer satisfaction in noneconomic ways. Toyota's Prius appeals to environmentally conscious motorists not only because these drivers want to help reduce global carbon dioxide emissions but also because they identify with the image conveyed. Rolls-Royce, Ralph Lauren, Tiffany, Rolex, and Prada have differentiation-based competitive advantages linked to buyer desires for status, image, prestige, upscale fashion, superior craftsmanship, and the finer things in life.

Differentiation can be based on *tangible* or *intangible* attributes.

Intangibles that contribute to differentiation can extend beyond product attributes to the reputation of the company and to customer relations or trust.

The fourth route is to *signal the value* of the company's product offering to buyers. Typical signals of value include a high price (in instances where high price implies high quality and performance), more appealing or fancier packaging than competing products, ad content that emphasizes a product's standout attributes, the quality of brochures and sales presentations, the luxuriousness and ambience of a seller's facilities (important for high-end retailers and for offices or other facilities frequented by customers). They make potential buyers aware of the professionalism, appearance, and personalities of the seller's employees and/or make potential buyers realize that a company has prestigious customers. Signaling value is particularly important (1) when the nature of differentiation is based on intangible features and is therefore subjective or hard to quantify, (2) when buyers are making a first-time purchase and are unsure what their experience with the product will be, and (3) when repurchase is infrequent and buyers need to be reminded of a product's value.

Regardless of the approach taken, achieving a successful differentiation strategy requires, first, that the company have strengths in capabilities, such as customer service, marketing, brand management, and technology, that can create and support differentiation. That is, the resources, competencies, and value chain activities of the company must be well matched to the requirements of the strategy. For the strategy to result in competitive advantage, the company's competencies must also be sufficiently unique in delivering value to buyers that they help set its product offering apart from those of rivals. They must be competitively superior. There are numerous examples of companies that have differentiated themselves on the basis of distinctive competencies and capabilities. Apple has set itself apart from rivals on the basis of its capabilities to develop innovative new products and speed next-generation products to market ahead of competitors. When a major new event occurs, many people turn to Sky News and BBC because they have the capability to devote more airtime to breaking news stories and get reporters on the scene very quickly. Avon has differentiated itself from other cosmetics and personal care companies by assembling a sales force numbering in the hundreds of thousands that gives it a direct sales capability—its sales associates personally demonstrate products to interested buyers, take their orders on the spot, and deliver the items to buyers' homes.

The most successful approaches to differentiation are those that are hard or expensive for rivals to duplicate. Indeed, this is the route to a sustainable differentiation advantage. While resourceful competitors can, in time, clone almost any tangible product attribute, socially complex intangible attributes, such as company reputation, long-standing relationships with buyers, and image are much harder to imitate. Differentiation that creates switching costs that lock in buyers also provides a route to sustainable advantage. For example, if a buyer makes a substantial investment in learning to use one type of system, that buyer is less likely to switch to a competitor's system. (This has kept many users from switching away from Microsoft Office products, despite the fact that there are other applications with superior features.) As

> Easy-to-copy differentiating features cannot produce sustainable competitive advantage.

a rule, differentiation yields a longer-lasting and more profitable competitive edge when it is based on a well-established brand image, patent-protected product innovation, complex technical superiority, a reputation for superior product quality and reliability, relationship-based customer service, and unique competitive capabilities. Such differentiating attributes are generally tougher and take longer for rivals to match, and buyers widely perceive them as offering superior value.

When a Differentiation Strategy Works Best

Differentiation strategies tend to work best in market circumstances where:

- *Buyer needs and uses of the product are diverse.* Diverse buyer preferences present competitors with a bigger window of opportunity to do things differently and set themselves apart with product attributes that appeal to particular buyers. For instance, the diversity of consumer preferences for menu selection, ambience, pricing, and customer service gives restaurants exceptionally wide latitude in creating a differentiated product offering. Similar opportunities exist for the publishers of magazines, the makers of motor vehicles, and the manufacturers of cabinetry and countertops.

- *There are many ways to differentiate the product or service that have value to buyers.* There's plenty of room for retail apparel competitors to stock different styles and quality of apparel merchandise but very little room for the makers of paper clips or copier paper or sugar to set their products apart. Likewise, the sellers of different brands of gasoline or orange juice have little differentiation opportunity compared to the sellers of high-definition TVs or patio furniture or breakfast cereal. Basic commodities, such as chemicals, mineral deposits, and agricultural products, provide few opportunities for differentiation.

- *Few rival firms are following a similar differentiation approach.* The best differentiation approaches involve trying to appeal to buyers on the basis of attributes that rivals are not emphasizing. A differentiator encounters less head-to-head rivalry when it goes its own separate way in creating uniqueness and does not try to outdifferentiate rivals on the very same attributes. When many rivals are all claiming "ours tastes better than theirs" or "ours gets your clothes cleaner than theirs," the most likely result is weak brand differentiation and "strategy overcrowding"— competitors end up chasing much the same buyers with much the same product offerings.

- *Technological change is fast-paced and competition revolves around rapidly evolving product features.* Rapid product innovation and frequent introductions of next-version products not only provide space for companies to pursue separate differentiating paths but also heighten buyer interest. In video game hardware and video games, golf equipment, PCs, and smartphones, competitors are locked into an ongoing battle to set themselves apart by introducing the best next-generation products; companies that fail to come up with new and improved products and distinctive performance features quickly lose out in the marketplace. In U.S. network TV broadcasting, NBC, ABC, CBS, Fox, and several others are always scrambling to develop a lineup of TV shows that will win higher audience ratings and pave the way for charging higher advertising rates and boosting ad revenues.

Pitfalls to Avoid in Pursuing a Differentiation Strategy

Differentiation strategies can fail for any of several reasons. *A differentiation strategy is always doomed when competitors are able to quickly copy most or all of the appealing product attributes a company comes up with.* Rapid imitation means that no rival achieves differentiation, since whenever one firm introduces some aspect of uniqueness that strikes the fancy of buyers, fast-following copycats quickly reestablish similarity. This is

> Any differentiating feature that works well is a magnet for imitators, although imitation attempts are not always successful.

differentiation strategy aimed at many buyer groups and market segments). Successful use of a focused differentiation strategy depends on the existence of a buyer segment that is looking for special product attributes or seller capabilities and on a firm's ability to stand apart from rivals competing in the same target market niche.

Companies like Godiva Chocolates, Rolls-Royce, Haägen-Dazs, and W. L. Gore (the maker of Gore-Tex) employ successful differentiation-based focused strategies targeted at upscale buyers wanting products and services with world-class attributes. Indeed, most markets contain a buyer segment willing to pay a big price premium for the very finest items available, thus opening the strategic window for some competitors to pursue differentiation-based focused strategies aimed at the very top of the market pyramid. Ferrari markets its 1,500 cars sold in North America each year to a list of just 20,000 highly affluent car enthusiasts. Only the highest echelon of this exclusive group were contacted by Ferrari for a chance to put their names on the waiting list for one of the 29 $1.9 million FXX models planned for sale in North America.

Another successful focused differentiator is "fashion food retailer" Trader Joe's, a 300-store, 25-state chain that is a combination gourmet deli and food warehouse. Customers shop Trader Joe's as much for entertainment as for conventional grocery items—the store stocks out-of-the-ordinary culinary treats like raspberry salsa, salmon burgers, and jasmine fried rice, as well as the standard goods normally found in supermarkets. What sets Trader Joe's apart is not just its unique combination of food novelties and competitively priced grocery items but also its capability to turn an otherwise mundane grocery excursion into a whimsical treasure hunt that is just plain fun. Illustration Capsule 5.3 describes Nestlé's focused differentiation strategy for Nespresso.

When a Focused Low-Cost or Focused Differentiation Strategy Is Attractive

A focused strategy aimed at securing a competitive edge based either on low cost or differentiation becomes increasingly attractive as more of the following conditions are met:

- The target market niche is big enough to be profitable and offers good growth potential.
- Industry leaders do not see that having a presence in the niche is crucial to their own success—in which case focusers can often escape battling head to head against some of the industry's biggest and strongest competitors.
- It is costly or difficult for multisegment competitors to put capabilities in place to meet the specialized needs of buyers constituting the target market niche and at the same time satisfy the expectations of their mainstream customers.
- The industry has many different niches and segments, thereby allowing a focuser to pick a competitively attractive niche suited to its most valuable resources and capabilities. Also, with more niches there is more room for focusers to avoid each other in competing for the same customers.
- Few, if any, other rivals are attempting to specialize in the same target segment—a condition that reduces the risk of segment overcrowding.
- The focuser has a reservoir of customer goodwill and loyalty (accumulated from having catered to the specialized needs and preferences of niche members over many years) that it can draw on to help stave off ambitious challengers looking to horn in on its business.

Overdif
and ove
can be f
mistake

ILLUSTRATION CAPSULE 5.2

Vizio's Focused Low-Cost Strategy

California-based Vizio, Inc., designs flat-panel LCD and plasma TVs that range in size from 20 to 55 inches and are sold only by big-box discount retailers such as Walmart, Sam's Club, Costco Wholesale, and Best Buy. If you've shopped for a flat-panel TV recently, you've probably noticed that Vizio is among the lowest-priced brands and that its picture quality is surprisingly good considering the price. The company is able to keep its cost low by only designing TVs and then sourcing its production to a limited number of contract manufacturers in Taiwan. In fact, 80 percent of its production is handled by a company called AmTran Technology. Such a dependence on a supplier can place a buyer in a precarious situation by making it vulnerable to price increases or product shortages, but Vizio has countered this possible threat by making AmTran a major stockholder. AmTran Technology owns a 23 percent stake in Vizio and earns about 80 percent of its revenues from its sales of televisions to Vizio. Vizio's close relationship with its major supplier and its focus on a single product category sold through limited distribution channels allows it to offer its customers deep price discounts.

Vizio's first major account was landed in 2003 when it approached buyers for Costco with a 46-inch plasma TV whose wholesale price was half that of the next lowest-price competitor. Within two months, Costco was carrying Vizio flat-panel TVs in 320 of its warehouse stores in the United States. In October 2007, Vizio approached buyers for Sam's Club with a 20-inch LCD TV that could be sold at retail for under $350. The price and quality of the 20-inch TV led Sam's Club buyers to place an order for 20,000 TVs for March 2008 delivery. By 2009, Vizio had become the largest seller of flat-panel HDTVs in the United States, with a market share of 21.6 percent.

Sources: "Picture Shift: U.S. Upstart Takes On TV Giants in Price War," *Wall Street Journal,* April 15, 2008, p. A1; Vizio, Inc., "Vizio Achieves #1 LCD HDTV Ranking in North America and #1 Ranking in U.S. Flat Panel HDTV Shipments," press release, May 11, 2009.

The advantages of focusing a company's entire competitive effort on a single market niche are considerable, especially for smaller and medium-size companies that may lack the breadth and depth of resources to tackle going after a broad customer base with a "something for everyone" lineup of models, styles, and product selection. YouTube has become a household name by concentrating on short video clips posted online. Papa John's and Domino's Pizza have created impressive businesses by focusing on the home delivery segment. Porsche and Ferrari have done well catering to wealthy sports car enthusiasts.

The Risks of a Focused Low-Cost or Focused Differentiation Strategy

Focusing carries several risks. One is the chance that competitors will find effective ways to match the focused firm's capabilities in serving the target niche—perhaps by coming up with products or brands specifically designed to appeal to buyers in the target niche or by developing expertise and capabilities that offset the focuser's strengths. In the lodging business, large chains like Accor have launched multibrand strategies that allow them to compete effectively in several

Nestlé Nespresso's Focused Differentiation Strategy in the Coffee Industry

Nestlé's strategy in the gourmet coffee industry has allowed its Nespresso brand of espresso coffee to become the fastest growing billion dollar brand in its broad lineup of chocolates and confectionery, bottled waters, coffee, ready-to-eat cereals, frozen food, dairy products, ice cream, and baby foods. The Nespresso concept was developed in 1986 to allow consumers to create a perfect cup of espresso coffee, equal to that of a skilled barista, with the use of a proprietary line of coffee makers designed to accommodate Nespresso's single-serving coffee capsules. Nespresso capsules are available in 16 different roasts and aromatic profiles and can be purchased online at Nestlé's Nespresso Club Web site, in any of Nestlé's 200 lavish Nespresso boutiques located in the world's most exclusive shopping districts, and in select upscale retailers across the globe. Nespresso coffee machines are designed for ease-of-use while having advanced technological features that maximize the aroma of the coffee and automate the entire process even down to creating a thick and creamy froth from cold milk for cappuccinos. Nespresso coffee makers also set standards for aesthetics with classic, sleek models, avant-garde models, and retro-modern models.

The ease-of-use of the stylish Nespresso coffee makers and the high quality coffee selected by Nestlé for its single-serving coffee pods allow coffee drinkers with little experience in preparing gourmet coffees to master great-tasting lattes, cappuccinos, and espresso drinks. Nespresso was sold in more than 50 countries in 2011 and had averaged annual growth in revenues of 30 percent since 2000 to reach sales of more than $3 billion Swiss Francs in 2010.

Nestlé's focused differentiation strategy for Nespresso includes the following primary elements:

- **Unsurpassed product quality and proven coffee expertise**—Through its unique business model, Nespresso has the ability to guarantee highest quality at every stage of the coffee value chain. Nespresso's team of passionate green coffee experts, agronomists, and supply partners regularly crisscross the globe in search of highest quality beans from specialty farms in the finest countries of origin. They in turn work with a variety of other Nespresso coffee experts including coffee sensory, aroma and flavor experts who create the exquisite Nespresso Grand Crus at state-of-the-art coffee production facilities in Orbe and Avenches, Switzerland.

- **Unstoppable drive for innovation and distinctive design**—Obsessed about innovation, compulsive about the fine details and passionate about the fusion between technology and design, the Nespresso in-house Research and Development Team has pioneered many award winning machine innovations and cutting edge designs, in collaboration with external design and machine experts. These breakthroughs have resulted in more than 1,700 patents.

- **Inspirational, iconic global reputation of the brand**—Nespresso is continually infusing itself with original ideas, flavors and innovations from around the world to define its own unique lifestyle. Its journey toward becoming an iconic brand has made it a well recognized, loved and respected reference for highest quality around the world. Through Nespresso's network of more than 200 exclusive boutiques in key cities around the world, coffee lovers can come together to experience the brand with all senses, such as tasting Nespresso's luxurious coffees or learning more about the coffee countries of origin. These stylish sanctuaries are the perfect destinations for people who love the very best coffee.

- **Global brand community thanks to direct customer relationships**—Much of the success Nespresso has enjoyed in recent years can be attributed to the privileged relationships the brand has developed with its consumers and the reciprocal enthusiasm consumers have consistently shown for the brand. Currently, more than 50% of all new Nespresso Club Members first experience the brand through existing members. Between 2001 and 2009, the number of Nespresso Club Members worldwide has jumped from 600,000 to more than 6 million.

- **Exclusive routes-to-market**—The unique Nespresso business model enables the company to maintain direct relationships with its customers

(continued)

through three channels: a global Internet boutique available 24/7 at http://www.nespresso.com; a global retail boutique network, which gives consumers the opportunity to experience the brand with all senses; and Customer Relationship Centers which help consumers connect with friendly coffee specialists by phone.

- **Expertise in Sustainable Quality development**—Nespresso and its key suppliers work closely with more than 30,000 farmers who are part of the AAA Sustainable Quality™ Program to ensure they are implementing farming practices that lead to highest quality beans and economic viability, whilst respecting the environment. Coffee farmers who are part of the program are rewarded not only with higher compensation but also with a long-term partnership with Nespresso. Approximately 50% of the coffee Nespresso buys is AAA Sustainable Quality™.

Source: Nestlé press releases, June 9, 2009, September 21, 2009 and August 11, 2010.

lodging segments simultaneously. Accor has 120 Sofitel luxury hotels on all five continents that offer business travelers and vacationers elegant accommodations and world-class service; its 15 Thalassa sea & spa resorts are among the finest resorts in the Mediterranean; Pullman, MGallery, and Grand Mercure offer travelers upscale amenities in prime locations around the world; Novotel and Mercure midscale hotels are located in nearly 50 countries and offer a comfortable setting and personalized service to business and leisure travelers; ibis is the worldwide economy hotel brand of Accor with 879 hotels in 45 countries; and its Etap hotels in Europe, its Formule1 hotels in the southern hemisphere, and Motel 6 hotels in the U.S. and Canada offer budget-minded travelers affordable rates and comfortable rooms. Multibrand strategies are attractive to large companies like Accor precisely because they enable a company to enter a market niche and siphon business away from companies that employ a focused strategy.

A second risk of employing a focused strategy is the potential for the preferences and needs of niche members to shift over time toward the product attributes desired by the majority of buyers. An erosion of the differences across buyer segments lowers entry barriers into a focuser's market niche and provides an open invitation for rivals in adjacent segments to begin competing for the focuser's customers. A third risk is that the segment may become so attractive that it is soon inundated with competitors, intensifying rivalry and splintering segment profits.

BEST-COST PROVIDER STRATEGIES

Best-cost provider strategies stake out a middle ground between pursuing a low-cost advantage and a differentiation advantage and between appealing to the broad market as a whole and a narrow market niche—see Figure 5.1. Such a middle ground allows a company to aim squarely at the sometimes great mass of value-conscious buyers looking for a good to very good product or service at an economical price. Value-conscious buyers frequently shy away from both cheap low-end products and expensive high-end products, but they are quite willing to pay a "fair" price for extra

CORE CONCEPT

Best-cost provider strategies are a *hybrid* of low-cost provider and differentiation strategies that aim at providing desired quality/features/performance/service attributes while beating rivals on price.

LO 4

Recognize the attributes of a best-cost provider strategy and the way in which some firms use a hybrid strategy to go about building a competitive advantage and delivering superior value to customers.

features and functionality they find appealing and useful. The essence of a best-cost provider strategy is giving customers more *value for the money* by satisfying buyer desires for appealing features/performance/quality/service and charging a lower price for these attributes compared to rivals with similar caliber product offerings.[10] From a competitive-positioning standpoint, best-cost strategies are thus a *hybrid,* balancing a strategic emphasis on low cost against a strategic emphasis on differentiation (desirable features delivered at a relatively low price).

To profitably employ a best-cost provider strategy, a company *must have the resources and capabilities to incorporate attractive or upscale attributes into its product offering at a lower cost than rivals.* When a company can incorporate appealing features, good to excellent product performance or quality, or more satisfying customer service into its product offering *at a lower cost than rivals,* then it enjoys "best-cost" status—it is the low-cost provider of a product or service with *desirable attributes.* A best-cost provider can use its low-cost advantage to underprice rivals whose products or services have similarly desirable attributes and still earn attractive profits. It is usually not difficult to entice buyers away from rivals with an equally good product at a more economical price.

Being a best-cost provider is different from being a low-cost provider because the additional attractive attributes entail additional costs (which a low-cost provider can avoid by offering buyers a basic product with few frills). Moreover, the two strategies aim at a distinguishably different market target. *The target market for a best-cost provider is value-conscious buyers*—buyers who are looking for appealing extras and functionality at an appealingly low price. Value-hunting buyers (as distinct from *price-conscious buyers* looking for a basic product at a bargain-basement price) often constitute a very sizable part of the overall market. Normally, value-conscious buyers are willing to pay a "fair" price for extra features, but they shy away from paying top dollar for items having all the bells and whistles. It is the desire to cater to *value-conscious buyers* as opposed to *budget-conscious buyers* that sets a best-cost provider apart from a low-cost provider—the two strategies aim at distinguishably different market targets.

When a Best-Cost Provider Strategy Works Best

A best-cost provider strategy works best in markets where product differentiation is the norm and there is an attractively large number of value-conscious buyers who prefer midrange products to cheap, basic products or expensive top-of-the-line products. A best-cost provider needs to position itself near the middle of the market with either a medium-quality product at a below-average price or a high-quality product at an average or slightly higher price. The objective is to provide the *best value* for better-quality, differentiated products. Best-cost provider strategies also work well in recessionary times when great masses of buyers become value-conscious and are attracted to economically priced products and services with appealing attributes. *But unless a company has the resources, know-how, and capabilities to incorporate upscale product or service attributes at a lower cost than rivals, adopting a best-cost strategy is ill-advised*—a winning strategy must always be matched to a company's most valuable resources and capabilities.

Illustration Capsule 5.4 describes how Toyota has applied the principles of the best-cost provider strategy in producing and marketing its Lexus brand.

ILLUSTRATION CAPSULE 5.4
Toyota's Best-Cost Provider Strategy for Its Lexus Line

Toyota Motor Company is widely regarded as a low-cost producer among the world's motor vehicle manufacturers. Despite its emphasis on product quality, Toyota has achieved low-cost leadership because it has developed considerable skills in efficient supply chain management and low-cost assembly capabilities and because its models are positioned in the low-to-medium end of the price spectrum, where high production volumes are conducive to low unit costs. But when Toyota decided to introduce its new Lexus models to compete in the luxury-car market segment, it employed a classic best-cost provider strategy. Toyota took the following four steps in crafting and implementing its Lexus strategy:

- Designing an array of high-performance characteristics and upscale features into the Lexus models to make them comparable in performance and luxury to other high-end models and attractive to Mercedes, BMW, Audi, Jaguar, Cadillac, and Lincoln buyers.

- Transferring its capabilities in making high-quality Toyota models at low cost to making premium-quality Lexus models at costs below other luxury-car makers. Toyota's supply chain capabilities and low-cost assembly know-how allowed it to incorporate high-tech performance features and upscale quality into Lexus models at substantially less cost than Mercedes, BMW, and other luxury-vehicle makers have been able to achieve in producing their models.

- Using its relatively lower manufacturing costs to underprice comparable Mercedes, BMW, Audi, and Jaguar models. Toyota believed that with its cost advantage it could price attractively equipped Lexus cars low enough to draw price-conscious buyers away from comparable high-end brands. Toyota's pricing policy also allowed it to induce Toyota, Honda, Ford, or GM owners desiring more luxury to switch to a Lexus. Lexus's pricing advantage has typically been quite significant. For example, in 2009 the Lexus RX 350, a midsize SUV, carried a sticker price in the $38,000 to $48,000 range (depending on how it was equipped), whereas comparable Mercedes M-class SUVs had price tags in the $45,000 to $63,000 range and a comparable BMW X5 SUV could range anywhere from $47,000 to $65,000.

- Establishing a new network of Lexus dealers, separate from Toyota dealers, dedicated to providing a level of personalized, attentive customer service unmatched in the industry.

Toyota's best-cost strategy has resulted in growing sales of Lexus models (now over 400,000 vehicles annually). Lexus has consistently ranked first in the widely watched J. D. Power & Associates quality survey, and Lexus owners enjoy both top-notch dealer service and product quality.

The Big Risk of a Best-Cost Provider Strategy

A company's biggest vulnerability in employing a best-cost provider strategy is getting squeezed between the strategies of firms using low-cost and high-end differentiation strategies. Low-cost providers may be able to siphon customers away with the appeal of a lower price (despite less appealing product attributes). High-end differentiators may be able to steal customers away with the appeal of better product attributes (even though their products carry a higher price tag). Thus, to be successful, a best-cost provider must offer buyers *significantly* better product attributes in order to justify a price above what low-cost leaders are charging. Likewise, it has to achieve significantly lower costs in providing upscale features so that it can outcompete high-end differentiators on the basis of a *significantly* lower price.

THE CONTRASTING FEATURES OF THE FIVE GENERIC COMPETITIVE STRATEGIES: A SUMMARY

Deciding which generic competitive strategy should serve as the framework on which to hang the rest of the company's strategy is not a trivial matter. Each of the five generic competitive strategies *positions* the company differently in its market and competitive environment. Each establishes a central theme for how the company will endeavor to outcompete rivals. Each creates some boundaries or guidelines for maneuvering as market circumstances unfold and as ideas for improving the strategy are debated. Each points to different ways of experimenting and tinkering with the basic strategy—for example, employing a low-cost leadership strategy means experimenting with ways that costs can be cut and value chain activities can be streamlined, whereas a broad differentiation strategy means exploring ways to add new differentiating features or to perform value chain activities differently if the result is to add value for customers in ways they are willing to pay for. Each entails differences in terms of product line, production emphasis, marketing emphasis, and means of maintaining the strategy, as shown in Table 5.1.

Thus a choice of which generic strategy to employ spills over to affect many aspects of how the business will be operated and the manner in which value chain activities must be managed. Deciding which generic strategy to employ is perhaps the most important strategic commitment a company makes—it tends to drive the rest of the strategic actions a company decides to undertake.

Table 5.1   Distinguishing Features of the Five Generic Competitive Strategies

	Low-Cost Provider	Broad Differentiation	Focused Low-Cost Provider	Focused Differentiation	Best-Cost Provider
Strategic target	• A broad cross-section of the market.	• A broad cross-section of the market.	• A narrow market niche where buyer needs and preferences are distinctively different.	• A narrow market niche where buyer needs and preferences are distinctively different.	• Value-conscious buyers. • A middle market range.
Basis of competitive strategy	• Lower overall costs than competitors.	• Ability to offer buyers something attractively different from competitors' offerings.	• Lower overall cost than rivals in serving niche members.	• Attributes that appeal specifically to niche members.	• Ability to offer better goods at attractive prices.

(Continued)

	Low-Cost Provider	Broad Differentiation	Focused Low-Cost Provider	Focused Differentiation	Best-Cost Provider
Product line	• A good basic product with few frills (acceptable quality and limited selection).	• Many product variations, wide selection; emphasis on differentiating features.	• Features and attributes tailored to the tastes and requirements of niche members.	• Features and attributes tailored to the tastes and requirements of niche members.	• Items with appealing attributes; assorted features; better quality, not best.
Production emphasis	• A continuous search for cost reduction without sacrificing acceptable quality and essential features.	• Build in whatever differentiating features buyers are willing to pay for; strive for product superiority.	• A continuous search for cost reduction for products that meet basic needs of niche members.	• Small-scale production or custom-made products that match the tastes and requirements of niche members.	• Build in appealing features and better quality at lower cost than rivals.
Marketing emphasis	• Low prices, good value. • Try to make a virtue out of product features that lead to low cost.	• Tout differentiating features. • Charge a premium price to cover the extra costs of differentiating features.	• Communicate attractive features of a budget-priced product offering that fits niche buyers' expectations.	• Communicate how product offering does the best job of meeting niche buyers' expectations.	• Tout delivery of *best* value. • Either deliver comparable features at a lower price than rivals or else match rivals on prices and provide better features.
Keys to maintaining the strategy	• Economical prices, good value. • Strive to manage costs down, year after year, in every area of the business.	• Stress constant innovation to stay ahead of imitative competitors. • Concentrate on a few key differentiating features.	• Stay committed to serving the niche at the lowest overall cost; don't blur the firm's image by entering other market segments or adding other products to widen market appeal.	• Stay committed to serving the niche better than rivals; don't blur the firm's image by entering other market segments or adding other products to widen market appeal.	• Unique expertise in simultaneously managing costs down while incorporating upscale features and attributes.
Resources and capabilities required	• Capabilities for driving costs out of the value chain system. • *Examples:* large-scale automated plants, an efficiency-oriented culture, bargaining power.	• Capabilities concerning quality, design, intangibles, and innovation. • *Examples:* marketing capabilities, R&D teams, technology.	• Capabilities to lower costs on niche goods. • *Examples:* lower input costs for the specific product desired by the niche, batch production capabilities.	• Capabilities to meet the highly specific needs of niche members. • *Examples:* custom production, close customer relations.	• Capabilities to simultaneously deliver lower cost and higher-quality/ differentiated features. • *Examples:* TQM practices, mass customization.

Successful Competitive Strategies Are Resource-Based

A company's competitive strategy is unlikely to succeed unless it is predicated on leveraging a competitively valuable collection of resources and capabilities that match the strategy.

For a company's competitive strategy to succeed in delivering good performance and the intended competitive edge over rivals, it has to be underpinned by an appropriate set of resources, know-how, and competitive capabilities. To succeed in employing a low-cost provider strategy, a company has to have the resources and capabilities needed to keep its costs below those of its competitors; this means having the expertise to cost-effectively manage value chain activities better than rivals and/or having the innovative capability to bypass certain value chain activities being performed by rivals. Successful focused strategies require the capability to do an outstanding job of satisfying the needs and expectations of niche buyers. Success in employing a best-cost strategy requires the resources and capabilities to simultaneously incorporate desirable product or service attributes and deliver them at a lower cost than rivals. To succeed in strongly differentiating its product in ways that are appealing to buyers, a company must have the resources and capabilities to incorporate unique attributes into its product offering that a broad range of buyers will find appealing and worth paying for, This is easier said than done because, given sufficient time, competitors can clone almost any product feature buyers find quite appealing. Hence, long-term differentiation success is usually dependent on having a hard-to-imitate portfolio of resource capabilities (like patented technology; strong, socially complex skills in product innovation; expertise in relationship-based customer service) that allow a company to sustain its differentiation-based competitive advantage. Likewise, sustaining the competitive edge inherent in any generic strategy depends on resources, capabilities, and competences that rivals have a hard time duplicating and for which there are no good substitutes.

KEY POINTS

The key points to take away from this chapter include the following:

1. Deciding which of the five generic competitive strategies to employ—overall low-cost, broad differentiation, focused low-cost, focused differentiation, or best-cost—is perhaps the most important strategic commitment a company makes. It tends to drive the remaining strategic actions a company undertakes and sets the whole tone for pursuing a competitive advantage over rivals.

2. In employing a low-cost provider strategy and trying to achieve a low-cost advantage over rivals, a company must do a better job than rivals of cost-effectively managing value chain activities and/or it must find innovative ways to eliminate cost-producing activities. Low-cost provider strategies work particularly well when the products of rival sellers are virtually identical or very weakly differentiated and supplies are readily available from eager sellers, when there are not many ways to differentiate that have value to buyers, when many buyers are price-sensitive and shop the market for the lowest price, and when buyer switching costs are low.

3. Broad differentiation strategies seek to produce a competitive edge by incorporating tangible and intangible attributes that set a company's product/service offering apart from rivals in ways that buyers consider valuable and worth

paying for. Successful differentiation allows a firm to (1) command a premium price for its product, (2) increase unit sales (because additional buyers are won over by the differentiating features), and/or (3) gain buyer loyalty to its brand (because some buyers are strongly attracted to the differentiating features and bond with the company and its products). Differentiation strategies work best when diverse buyer preferences open up windows of opportunity to strongly differentiate a company's product offering from those of rival brands, in situations where few other rivals are pursuing a similar differentiation approach, and in circumstances where companies are racing to bring out the most appealing next-generation product. A differentiation strategy is doomed when competitors are able to quickly copy most or all of the appealing product attributes a company comes up with, when a company's differentiation efforts fail to interest many buyers, and when a company overspends on efforts to differentiate its product offering or tries to overcharge for its differentiating extras.

4. A focused strategy delivers competitive advantage either by achieving lower costs than rivals in serving buyers constituting the target market niche or by developing a specialized ability to offer niche buyers an appealingly differentiated offering that meets their needs better than rival brands do. A focused strategy based on either low cost or differentiation becomes increasingly attractive when the target market niche is big enough to be profitable and offers good growth potential, when it is costly or difficult for multisegment competitors to put capabilities in place to meet the specialized needs of the target market niche and at the same time satisfy the expectations of their mainstream customers, and when few other rivals are attempting to specialize in the same target segment.

5. Best-cost provider strategies combine a strategic emphasis on low cost with a strategic emphasis on more than minimal quality, service, features, or performance. The aim is to create competitive advantage by giving buyers *more value for the money for midrange products*—an approach that entails (1) matching close rivals on key quality/service/features/performance attributes, (2) beating them on the costs of incorporating such attributes into the product or service, and (3) charging a more economical price. A best-cost provider strategy works best in markets with large numbers of value-conscious buyers desirous of purchasing appealingly good products and services for less money.

6. In all cases, competitive advantage depends on having competitively superior resources and capabilities that are a good match for the chosen generic strategy. A sustainable advantage depends on maintaining that competitive superiority with resources, capabilities, and value chain activities that rivals have trouble matching and for which there are no good substitutes.

ASSURANCE OF LEARNING EXERCISES

LO 1, LO 2

1. Haier is the world's fourth largest appliance manufacturer and one of China's 100 largest companies. The company's four leading product categories—refrigerators, refrigerating cabinets, air conditioners, and washing machines—hold over 30 percent market shares and are available in 12 of the top

15 chain stores in Europe and 10 leading chains stores in the U.S. Review its Corporate Profile at http://www.haier.com/abouthaier/corporateprofile/ and list specific elements of its low cost provider strategy that have yielded its advantage in the marketplace.

LO 3

2. Stihl is the world's leading manufacturer and marketer of chain saws, with annual sales exceeding $2 billion. With innovations dating to its 1929 invention of the gasoline-powered chain saw, the company holds over 1,000 patents related to chain saws and outdoor power tools. The company's chain saws, leaf blowers, and hedge trimmers sell at price points well above competing brands and are sold only by its network of over 8,000 independent dealers. The company boasts in its advertisements that its products are rated number one by consumer magazines and are *not* sold at Lowe's or Home Depot. How does Stihl's choice of distribution channels and advertisements contribute to its differentiation strategy?

LO 3

3. Explore BMW's Web site (www.bmw.com), and then click on the link for www.bmwgroup.com. The site you find provides an overview of the company's key functional areas, including research and development and production activities (see the page headings). Under Research and Development, click on Innovation & Technology and explore the links at the sidebar to better understand the types of resources and capabilities that underlie BMW's approach to innovation. Also review the statements under Production focusing on automobile production worldwide and sustainable production. How do the resources, capabilities, and activities of BMW contribute to its differentiation strategy and the unique position in the industry that it has achieved?

EXERCISES FOR SIMULATION PARTICIPANTS

LO 1, LO 2, LO 3, LO 4

1. Which one of the five generic competitive strategies best characterizes your company's strategic approach to competing successfully?
2. Which rival companies appear to be employing a low-cost provider strategy?
3. Which rival companies appear to be employing a broad differentiation strategy?
4. Which rival companies appear to be employing some type of focused strategy?
5. Which rival companies appear to be employing a best-cost provider strategy?
6. What is your company's action plan to achieve a sustainable competitive advantage over rival companies? List at least three (preferably more) specific kinds of decision entries on specific decision screens that your company has made or intends to make to win this kind of competitive edge over rivals.

ENDNOTES

[1] This classification scheme is an adaptation of a narrower three-strategy classification presented in Michael E. Porter, *Competitive Strategy: Techniques for Analyzing Industries and Competitors* (New York: Free Press, 1980). For a discussion of the different ways that companies can position themselves in the marketplace, see Michael E. Porter, "What Is Strategy?" *Harvard Business Review* 74, no. 6 (November–December 1996), pp. 65–67.

[2] M. Porter, *Competitive Advantage: Creating and Sustaining Superior Performance* (New York: Free Press, 1985), p. 97.

[3] Michael Hammer and James Champy were the main proponents of business process reengineering. See M. Hammer and J. Champy, *Reengineering the Corporation: A Manifesto for Business Revolution,* rev. and updated (New York: HarperBusiness, 2003).

[4] For a discussion of how unique industry positioning and resource combinations are linked to consumers' perspectives of value and their willingness to pay more for differentiated products or services, see Richard L. Priem, "A Consumer Perspective on Value Creation," *Academy of Management Review* 32, no. 1 (2007), pp. 219–35.

[5] G. Gavetti, "Ducati," Harvard Business School case 9-701-132, rev. March 8, 2002.

[6] http://jrscience.wcp.muohio.edu/nsfall01/FinalArticles/Final-IsitWorthitBrandsan.html.

[7] This section expands on the section on value chain linkages found in Porter, *Competitive Advantage,* p. 125.

[8] D. Yoffie, "Cola Wars Continue: Coke and Pepsi in 2006," Harvard Business School case 9-706-447.

[9] Porter, *Competitive Advantage,* pp. 160–62.

[10] For an excellent discussion of best-cost provider strategies, see Peter J. Williamson and Ming Zeng, "Value-for-Money Strategies for Recessionary Times," *Harvard Business Review* 87, no. 3 (March 2009), pp. 66–74.

LO 1

Learn whether
and when to
pursue offensive or
defensive strategic
moves to improve a
company's market
position.

but to try to whittle away at a strong rival's competitive advantage. Companies like Walmart, Apple, and Google play hardball, aggressively pursuing competitive advantage and trying to reap the benefits of a leading market share, superior profit margins, and more rapid growth, as well as the reputational rewards of being known as a winning company on the move.[1] The best offensives tend to incorporate several principles: (1) focusing relentlessly on building competitive advantage and then striving to convert it into sustainable advantage (as described in Chapter 4), (2) creating and deploying company resources in ways that cause rivals to struggle to defend themselves, (3) employing the element of surprise as opposed to doing what rivals expect and are prepared for, and (4) displaying a strong bias for swift, decisive, and overwhelming actions to overpower rivals.[2]

Choosing the Basis for Competitive Attack

As a rule, challenging rivals on competitive grounds where they are strong is an uphill struggle.[3] Offensive initiatives that exploit competitor weaknesses stand a far better chance of succeeding than do those that challenge competitor strengths, especially if the weaknesses represent important vulnerabilities and if weak rivals can be caught by surprise with no ready defense.[4]

The best offensives
use a company's most
competitively potent
resources to attack rivals
in the areas where they
are weakest.

Strategic offensives should, as a general rule, be based on exploiting a company's strongest strategic assets—its most valuable resources and capabilities, such as a better-known brand name, a more efficient production or distribution system, greater technological capability, or a superior reputation for quality. But a consideration of the company's strengths should not be made without also considering the rival's strengths and weaknesses. A strategic offensive should be based on those areas of strength where the company has its greatest competitive advantage over the targeted rivals. If a company has especially good customer service capabilities, it can make special sales pitches to the customers of those rivals that provide subpar customer service. Aggressors with a recognized brand name and strong marketing skills can launch efforts to win customers away from rivals with weak brand recognition. There is considerable appeal in emphasizing sales to buyers in geographic regions where a rival has a weak market share or is exerting less competitive effort. Likewise, it may be attractive to pay special attention to buyer segments that a rival is neglecting or is weakly equipped to serve.

Sometimes a company's
best strategic option is
to seize the initiative, go
on the attack, and launch
a strategic offensive
to improve its market
position.

Ignoring the need to tie a strategic offensive to a company's resources where they are competitively stronger than rivals' is like going to war with a popgun—the prospects for success are dim. For instance, it is foolish for a company with relatively high costs to employ a price-cutting offensive— price-cutting offensives are best left to financially strong companies whose costs are relatively low in comparison to those of the companies being attacked. Likewise, it is ill-advised to pursue a product innovation offensive without having competitively superior expertise in R&D, new product development, and speeding new products to market.

The principal offensive strategy options include the following:

1. *Using a cost-based advantage to attack competitors on the basis of price or value.* A price-cutting offensive can involve offering customers an equally good or better product at a lower price or offering a low-priced, lower-quality product that gives customers more value for the money. This is the classic offensive for improving a company's market position vis-à-vis rivals, but it works well only

under certain circumstances. Lower prices can produce market share gains if competitors don't respond with price cuts of their own and if the challenger convinces buyers that its product offers them a better value proposition. However, such a strategy increases total profits only if the gains in additional unit sales are enough to offset the impact of lower prices and thinner margins per unit sold. Price-cutting offensives are generally successful only when a company *first achieves a cost advantage and then hits competitors with a lower price.*[5] Walmart's rise to dominance in discount retailing and supermarkets was based on just this type of strategic offensive. Ryanair also used this strategy successfully against rivals such as British Air and Aer Lingus, by first cutting costs to the bone and then targeting leisure passengers who care more about low price than in-flight amenities and service.[6] While some companies have used price-cutting offensives as a means of obtaining the cost advantages associated with greater market share (economies of scale or experience), this has proved to be a highly risky strategy. More often than not, such price-cutting offensives are met with retaliatory attacks that can mire the entire industry in a costly price war.

2. *Leapfrogging competitors by being the first adopter of next-generation technologies or being first to market with next-generation products.* In technology-based industries, the opportune time to overtake an entrenched competitor is when there is a shift to the next generation of the technology. Microsoft got its next-generation Xbox 360 to market a full 12 months ahead of Sony's PlayStation 3 and Nintendo's Wii, helping it convince video gamers to buy an Xbox rather than wait for the new PlayStation 3 and Wii to hit the market. This type of offensive strategy is high-risk, however, since it requires costly investment at a time when consumer reactions to the new technology are yet unknown.

3. *Pursuing continuous product innovation to draw sales and market share away from less innovative rivals.* Ongoing introductions of new and improved products can put rivals under tremendous competitive pressure, especially when rivals' new product development capabilities are weak. But such offensives can be sustained only if a company has sufficient product innovation skills to keep its pipeline full and maintain buyer enthusiasm for its new and better product offerings.

4. *Adopting and improving on the good ideas of other companies (rivals or otherwise).*[7] The idea of warehouse-type home improvement centers did not originate with Home Depot cofounders Arthur Blank and Bernie Marcus; they got the "big-box" concept from their former employer Handy Dan Home Improvement. But they were quick to improve on Handy Dan's business model and take Home Depot to the next plateau in terms of product line breadth and customer service. Casket maker Hillenbrand greatly improved its market position by adapting Toyota's production methods to casket making. Offense-minded companies are often quick to take any good idea (not nailed down by a patent or other legal protection), make it their own, and then aggressively apply it to create competitive advantage for themselves.

5. *Using hit-and-run or guerrilla warfare tactics to grab sales and market share from complacent or distracted rivals.* Options for "guerrilla offensives" include occasional lowballing on price (to win a big order or steal a key account from a rival), surprising key rivals with sporadic but intense bursts of promotional activity (offering a special trial offer for new customers to draw them away

from rival brands), or undertaking special campaigns to attract buyers away from rivals plagued with a strike or problems in meeting buyer demand.[8] Guerrilla offensives are particularly well suited to small challengers that have neither the resources nor the market visibility to mount a full-fledged attack on industry leaders and that may not merit a full retaliatory response from larger rivals.[9]

6. *Launching a preemptive strike to secure an advantageous position that rivals are prevented or discouraged from duplicating.*[10] What makes a move preemptive is its one-of-a-kind nature—whoever strikes first stands to acquire competitive assets that rivals can't readily match. Examples of preemptive moves include (1) securing the best distributors in a particular geographic region or country; (2) obtaining the most favorable sites in terms of customer demographics, cost characteristics, or access to transportation, raw-material supplies, or low-cost inputs; (3) tying up the most reliable, high-quality suppliers via exclusive partnerships, long-term contracts, or acquisition; and (4) moving swiftly to acquire the assets of distressed rivals at bargain prices. To be successful, a preemptive move doesn't have to totally block rivals from following; it merely needs to give a firm a prime position that is not easily replicated or circumvented.

How long it takes for an offensive to yield good results varies with the competitive circumstances.[11] It can be short if buyers respond immediately (as can occur with a dramatic cost-based price cut, an imaginative ad campaign, or an especially appealing new product). Securing a competitive edge can take much longer if winning consumer acceptance of an innovative product will take some time or if the firm may need several years to debug a new technology, put new production capacity in place, or develop and perfect new competitive capabilities. But how long it takes for an offensive move to improve a company's market standing (and whether it can do so) also depends on whether market rivals recognize the threat and begin a counterresponse. And whether rivals will respond depends on whether they are capable of making an effective response and if they believe that a counterattack is worth the expense and the distraction.[12]

Choosing Which Rivals to Attack

Offensive-minded firms need to analyze which of their rivals to challenge as well as how to mount the challenge. The following are the best targets for offensive attacks:[13]

• *Market leaders that are vulnerable.* Offensive attacks make good sense when a company that leads in terms of size and market share is not a true leader in terms of serving the market well. Signs of leader vulnerability include unhappy buyers, an inferior product line, a weak competitive strategy with regard to low-cost leadership or differentiation, strong emotional commitment to an aging technology the leader has pioneered, outdated plants and equipment, a preoccupation with diversification into other industries, and mediocre or declining profitability. Toyota's massive product recalls in the U.S. during 2009 and 2010 due to safety concerns presented other car companies with a prime opportunity to attack a vulnerable and distracted market leader. GM and Ford used incentives and low-financing offers aimed at winning over Toyota buyers to increase their market share during this period. Offensives to erode the positions of vulnerable market leaders have real promise when the challenger is also able to revamp its value chain or innovate to gain a fresh cost-based or differentiation-based competitive advantage.[14] To be judged successful, attacks on leaders don't have to result in making the aggressor the new leader; a challenger may "win" by simply becoming a stronger runner-up. Caution is well advised in challenging strong market leaders—there's a significant risk of squandering valuable resources in a futile effort or precipitating a fierce and profitless industrywide battle for market share.

- *Runner-up firms with weaknesses in areas where the challenger is strong.* Runner-up firms are an especially attractive target when a challenger's resources and capabilities are well suited to exploiting their weaknesses.

- *Struggling enterprises that are on the verge of going under.* Challenging a hard-pressed rival in ways that further sap its financial strength and competitive position can weaken its resolve and hasten its exit from the market. In this type of situation, it makes sense to attack the rival in the market segments where it makes the most profits, since this will threaten its survival the most.

- *Small local and regional firms with limited capabilities.* Because small firms typically have limited expertise and resources, a challenger with broader and/or deeper capabilities is well positioned to raid their biggest and best customers—particularly those that are growing rapidly, have increasingly sophisticated requirements, and may already be thinking about switching to a supplier with more full-service capability.

Blue-Ocean Strategy—A Special Kind of Offensive

A **blue-ocean strategy** seeks to gain a dramatic and durable competitive advantage by abandoning efforts to beat out competitors in existing markets and, instead, inventing a new industry or distinctive market segment that renders existing competitors largely irrelevant and allows a company to create and capture altogether new demand.[15] This strategy views the business universe as consisting of two distinct types of market space. One is where industry boundaries are defined and accepted, the competitive rules of the game are well understood by all industry members, and companies try to outperform rivals by capturing a bigger share of existing demand; in such markets, lively competition constrains a company's prospects for rapid growth and superior profitability since rivals move quickly to either imitate or counter the successes of competitors. The second type of market space is a "blue ocean" where the industry does not really exist yet, is untainted by competition, and offers wide-open opportunity for profitable and rapid growth if a company can come up with a product offering and strategy that allows it to create new demand.

> **CORE CONCEPT**
>
> A **blue-ocean strategy** is based on discovering or inventing new industry segments that create altogether new demand, thereby positioning the firm in uncontested market space offering superior opportunities for profitability and growth.

A terrific example of such wide-open or blue-ocean market space is the online auction industry that eBay created and now dominates. Other examples of companies that have achieved competitive advantages by creating blue-ocean market spaces include Starbucks in the U.S. espresso bar industry, FedEx in overnight package delivery, and Cirque du Soleil in live entertainment. Cirque du Soleil "reinvented the circus" by creating a distinctively different market space for its performances (Las Vegas nightclubs and theater-type settings) and pulling in a whole new group of customers—adults and corporate clients—who were willing to pay several times more than the price of a conventional circus ticket to have an "entertainment experience" featuring sophisticated clowns and star-quality acrobatic acts in a comfortable atmosphere. Companies that create blue-ocean market spaces can usually sustain their initial competitive advantage without encountering a major competitive challenge for 10 to 15 years because of high barriers to imitation and the strong brand-name awareness that a blue-ocean strategy can produce.

Zipcar Inc. is presently using a blue-ocean strategy to compete against entrenched rivals in the rental-car industry. It rents cars by the hour or day (rather than by the week) to members who pay a yearly fee for access to cars parked in designated spaces located conveniently throughout large cities. By allowing drivers under 25 years of age to rent cars and by targeting city dwellers who need to supplement their use of public transportation with short-term car rentals, Zipcar entered uncharted waters in the rental-car industry, growing rapidly in the process. Founded in 2000, Zipcar filed to go public in mid-2010.

DEFENSIVE STRATEGIES—PROTECTING MARKET POSITION AND COMPETITIVE ADVANTAGE

Good defensive strategies can help protect a competitive advantage but rarely are the basis for creating one.

In a competitive market, all firms are subject to offensive challenges from rivals. The purposes of defensive strategies are to (1) lower the risk of being attacked, (2) weaken the impact of any attack that occurs, and (3) influence challengers to aim their efforts at other rivals. While defensive strategies usually don't enhance a firm's competitive advantage, they can definitely help fortify the firm's competitive position, protect its most valuable resources and capabilities from imitation, and defend whatever competitive advantage it might have. Defensive strategies can take either of two forms: actions to block challengers and actions to signal the likelihood of strong retaliation.

Blocking the Avenues Open to Challengers

The most frequently employed approach to defending a company's present position involves actions that restrict a challenger's options for initiating a competitive attack. There are any number of obstacles that can be put in the path of would-be challengers.[16] A defender can participate in alternative technologies as a hedge against rivals attacking with a new or better technology. A defender can introduce new features, add new models, or broaden its product line to close off gaps and vacant niches to opportunity-seeking challengers. It can thwart the efforts of rivals to attack with a lower price by maintaining economy-priced options of its own. It can try to discourage buyers from trying competitors' brands by lengthening warranties, offering free training and support services, developing the capability to deliver spare parts to users faster than rivals can, providing coupons and sample giveaways to buyers most prone to experiment, and making early announcements about impending new products or price changes to induce potential buyers to postpone switching. It can challenge the quality or safety of rivals' products. Finally, a defender can grant volume discounts or better financing terms to dealers

There are many ways to throw obstacles in the path of would-be challengers.

and distributors to discourage them from experimenting with other suppliers, or it can convince them to handle its product line *exclusively* and force competitors to use other distribution outlets.

Signaling Challengers That Retaliation Is Likely

The goal of signaling challengers that strong retaliation is likely in the event of an attack is either to dissuade challengers from attacking at all or to divert them to less threatening options. Either goal can be achieved by letting challengers know the battle will cost more than it is worth. Signals to would-be challengers can be given by:[17]

- Publicly announcing management's commitment to maintaining the firm's present market share.
- Publicly committing the company to a policy of matching competitors' terms or prices.
- Maintaining a war chest of cash and marketable securities.
- Making an occasional strong counterresponse to the moves of weak competitors to enhance the firm's image as a tough defender.

Signaling is most likely to be an effective defensive strategy if the signal is accompanied by a credible commitment to follow through.

TIMING A COMPANY'S OFFENSIVE AND DEFENSIVE STRATEGIC MOVES

When to make a strategic move is often as crucial as *what* move to make. Timing is especially important when **first-mover advantages** or **disadvantages** exist.[18] Under certain conditions, being first to initiate a strategic move can have a high payoff in the form of a competitive advantage that later movers can't dislodge. Moving first is no guarantee of success, however, since first movers also face some significant disadvantages. Indeed, there are circumstances in which it is more advantageous to be a fast follower or even a late mover. Because the timing of strategic moves can be consequential, it is important for company strategists to be aware of the nature of first-mover advantages and disadvantages and the conditions favoring each type.[19]

> **CORE CONCEPT**
>
> Because of **first-mover advantages** and **disadvantages,** competitive advantage can spring from *when* a move is made as well as from *what* move is made.

The Potential for First-Mover Advantages

Market pioneers and other types of first movers typically bear greater risks and greater development costs than firms that move later. If the market responds well to its initial move, the pioneer will benefit from a monopoly position (by virtue of being first to market) that enables it to recover its investment costs and make an attractive profit. If the firm's pioneering move gives it a competitive advantage that can be sustained even after other firms enter the market space, its first-mover advantage will be greater still. The extent of this type of advantage, however, will

> **LO 2**
>
> Recognize when being a first mover or a fast follower or a late mover is most advantageous.

depend on whether and how fast follower firms can piggyback on the pioneer's success and either imitate or improve on its move.

The conditions that favor first-mover advantages, then, are those that slow the moves of follower firms or prevent them from imitating the success of the first mover. There are six such conditions in which first-mover advantages are most likely to arise:

1. *When pioneering helps build a firm's reputation with buyers and creates brand loyalty.* A firm's reputation can insulate it from competition when buyer uncertainty about product quality keeps the firm's customers from trying competitors' offerings and when new buyers minimize their risk by choosing on the basis of reputation. Similarly, customer loyalty to an early mover's brand can create a tie that binds, limiting the success of later entrants' attempts to poach from the early mover's customer base and steal market share.

2. *When a first mover's customers will thereafter face significant switching costs.* Switching costs limit the ability of late movers to lure away the customers of early movers by making it expensive for a customer to switch to another company's product or service. Switching costs can arise for a number of reasons. They may be due to the time a consumer invests in learning how to use a specific company's product. They may arise from an investment in complementary products that are also brand-specific. They can also arise from certain types of loyalty programs or long-term contracts that give customers greater incentives to remain with an initial provider.

3. *When property rights protections thwart rapid imitation of the initial move.* In certain types of industries, property rights protections in the form of patents, copyrights, and trademarks prevent the ready imitation of an early mover's initial moves. First-mover advantages in pharmaceuticals, for example, are heavily dependent on patent protections, and patent races in this industry are common. In other industries, however, patents provide limited protection and can frequently be circumvented. Property rights protections also vary among nations, since they are dependent on a country's legal institutions and enforcement mechanisms.

4. *When an early lead enables the first mover to move down the learning curve ahead of rivals.* When there is a steep learning curve and when learning can be kept proprietary, a first mover can benefit from volume-based cost advantages that grow ever larger as its experience accumulates and its scale of operations increases. This type of first-mover advantage is self-reinforcing and, as such, can preserve a first mover's competitive advantage over long periods of time. Honda's advantage in small multiuse motorcycles has been attributed to such an effect, as has the long-lived advantage of Lincoln Electric Company in arc welders, which are used in industries such as construction and shipbuilding.

5. *When a first mover can set the technical standard for the industry.* In many technology-based industries, the market will converge around a single technical standard. By establishing the industry standard, a first mover can gain a powerful advantage that, like experienced-based advantages, builds over time. The greater the importance of technical standards in an industry, the greater the advantage of being the one to set the standard and the more firmly the first mover will be entrenched. The lure of such an advantage, however, can result in standard wars among early movers, as each strives to set the industry standard. The key to winning such wars is to enter early on the

basis of strong fast-cycle product development capabilities, gain the support of key customers and suppliers, employ penetration pricing, and make allies of the producers of complementary products.

To sustain any advantage that may initially accrue to a pioneer, a first mover needs to be a fast learner and continue to move aggressively to capitalize on any initial pioneering advantage. It helps immensely if the first mover has deep financial pockets, important competitive capabilities, and astute managers. What makes being a first mover strategically important is not being the first company to do something but, rather, being the first competitor to put together the precise combination of features, customer value, and sound revenue/cost/profit economics that gives it an edge over rivals in the battle for market leadership.[20] If the marketplace quickly takes to a first mover's innovative product offering, the first mover must have large-scale production, marketing, and distribution capabilities if it is to take full advantage of its market lead. If technology is advancing at a torrid pace, a first mover cannot hope to sustain its lead without having strong capabilities in R&D, design, and new product development, along with the financial strength to fund these activities.

Illustration Capsule 6.1 describes how Amazon.com achieved a first-mover advantage in online retailing.

The Potential for First-Mover Disadvantages or Late-Mover Advantages

There are circumstances when first movers face significant disadvantages and when it is actually better to be an adept follower than a first mover. First-mover disadvantages *(or late-mover advantages)* arise in the following four instances:

1. *When pioneering is more costly than imitating, and only negligible experience or learning-curve benefits accrue to the leader.* Such conditions allow a follower to end up with lower costs than the first mover and either win customers away with lower prices or benefit from more profitable production.

2. *When the products of an innovator are somewhat primitive and do not live up to buyer expectations.* In this situation, a clever follower can study customers' reactions to the pioneer's products and win disenchanted buyers away from the leader with better-performing products. Moreover, the first mover may find itself saddled with a negative reputation that retards its ability to recover from its early missteps.

3. *When rapid market evolution gives fast followers the opening to leapfrog a first mover's products with more attractive next-version products.* Industries characterized by fast-paced changes in either technology or buyer needs and expectations may present opportunities for second movers to improve on the pioneer's products and offer customers a more attractive value proposition as a result.

4. *When market uncertainties make it difficult to ascertain what will eventually succeed.* Under these conditions, first movers are likely to make numerous mistakes that later movers can avoid and learn from. Even if the pioneer manages to please early adopters, it may turn out that the needs of early adopters are very different from mass-market needs. Late movers may find it far more advantageous to wait until these needs are clarified and then focus on satisfying the mass market's demand.

ILLUSTRATION CAPSULE 6.1

Amazon.com's First-Mover Advantage in Online Retailing

Amazon.com's path to becoming the world's largest online retailer began in 1994 when Jeff Bezos, a Manhattan hedge fund analyst at the time, noticed that the number of Internet users was increasing by 2,300 percent annually. Bezos saw the tremendous growth as an opportunity to sell products online that would be demanded by a large number of Internet users and could be easily shipped. Bezos launched the online bookseller Amazon.com in 1995. The start-up's revenues soared to $148 million in 1997, $610 million in 1998, and $1.6 billion in 1999. Bezos' business plan—hatched while on a cross-country trip with his wife in 1994—made him *Time* magazine's Person of the Year in 1999.

The volume-based and reputational benefits of Amazon.com's early entry into online retailing had delivered a first-mover advantage, but between 2000 and 2009 Bezos undertook a series of additional strategic initiatives to solidify the company's number-one ranking in the industry. Bezos undertook a massive building program in the late-1990s that added five new warehouses and fulfillment centers totaling $300 million. The additional warehouse capacity was added years before it was needed, but Bezos wanted to move preemptively against potential rivals and ensure that, as demand continued to grow, the company could continue to offer its customers the best selection, the lowest prices, and the cheapest and most convenient delivery. The company also expanded its product line to include sporting goods, tools, toys, grocery items, electronics, and digital music downloads, giving it another means of maintaining its experience

and scale-based advantages. Amazon.com's 2008 revenues of $19.2 billion made it the world's largest Internet retailer; Jeff Bezos' shares in Amazon.com made him the 110th-wealthiest person in the world in 2009, with an estimated net worth of $8.2 billion.

Moving down the learning curve in Internet retailing was not an entirely straightforward process for Amazon.com. Bezos commented in a *Fortune* article profiling the company, "We were investors in every bankrupt, 1999-vintage e-commerce startup. Pets.com, living.com, kozmo.com. We invested in a lot of high-profile flameouts." He went on to specify that although the ventures were a "waste of money," they "didn't take us off our own mission." Bezos also suggested that gaining advantage as a first mover is "taking a million tiny steps—and learning quickly from your missteps."

Sources: Mark Brohan, "The Top 500 Guide," *Internet Retailer,* June 2009 (accessed at www.internetretailer.com on June 17, 2009); Josh Quittner, "How Jeff Bezos Rules the Retail Space," *Fortune,* May 5, 2008, pp. 126–34.

To Be a First Mover or Not

In weighing the pros and cons of being a first mover versus a fast follower versus a late mover, it matters whether the race to market leadership in a particular industry is a marathon or a sprint. In marathons, a slow mover is not unduly penalized—first-mover advantages can be fleeting, and there's ample time for fast followers and sometimes even late movers to play catch-up.[21] Thus the speed at which the pioneering innovation is likely to catch on matters considerably as companies struggle with whether to pursue a particular emerging market opportunity aggressively (as a first mover or fast follower) or cautiously (as a late mover). For instance, it took 18 months for 10 million users to sign up for Hotmail, 5.5 years for worldwide mobile phone use to grow from 10 million to 100 million, and close to 10 years for the number of at-home broadband subscribers to reach 100 million worldwide. The lesson here is that there is a market penetration curve for every emerging opportunity; typically, the curve has an inflection point at which all the pieces of the business model fall into place, buyer demand explodes, and the market takes off. The inflection point can come early on a fast-rising curve (as with use of e-mail) or farther on up a slow-rising curve (as with the use of broadband). Any company that seeks competitive advantage by being a first mover thus needs to ask some hard questions:

- Does market takeoff depend on the development of complementary products or services that currently are not available?
- Is new infrastructure required before buyer demand can surge?
- Will buyers need to learn new skills or adopt new behaviors? Will buyers encounter high switching costs in moving to the newly introduced product or service?
- Are there influential competitors in a position to delay or derail the efforts of a first mover?

When the answers to any of these questions are yes, then a company must be careful not to pour too many resources into getting ahead of the market opportunity—the race is likely going to be more of a 10-year marathon than a 2-year sprint.[22] On the other hand, if the market is a winner-take-all type of market, where powerful first-mover advantages insulate early entrants from competition and prevent later movers from making any headway, then it may be best to move quickly despite the risks.

STRENGTHENING A COMPANY'S MARKET POSITION VIA ITS SCOPE OF OPERATIONS

Apart from considerations of competitive moves and their timing, there is another set of managerial decisions that can affect the strength of a company's market position. These decisions concern the scope of a company's operations—the breadth of its activities and the extent of its market reach. Decisions regarding the **scope of the firm** focus on which activities a firm will perform internally and which it will not. For example, should Spanish fashion retailer Zara design the apparel items it sells in its stores? Should it die its own fabrics and carry out all of its manufacturing needs internally? Should it handle all of its logistics rather than outsource distribution? Scope decisions also concern which segments of the market to serve—decisions that can include geographic market segments as well as product and service segments. Should Zara increase its number of retail locations in North America? Should it make all of its product line available in all stores rather than vary its product assortment by location? Should it expand its product offerings to include accessories, lingerie, and home furnishings?

Decisions such as these, in essence, determine where the boundaries of a firm lie and the degree to which the operations within those boundaries cohere. They also have much to do with the direction and extent of a business's growth. In this

CORE CONCEPT

The **scope of the firm** refers to the range of activities which the firm performs internally, the breadth of its product and service offerings, the extent of its geographic market presence, and its mix of businesses.

CORE CONCEPT

Horizontal scope is the range of product and service segments that a firm serves within its focal market.

CORE CONCEPT

Vertical scope is the extent to which a firm's internal activities encompass one, some, many, or all of the activities that make up an industry's entire value chain system, ranging from raw-material production to final sales and service activities.

chapter, we introduce the topic of company scope and discuss different types of scope decisions in relation to a company's business-level strategy. In the next two chapters, we develop two additional dimensions of a firm's scope. Chapter 7 focuses on international expansion—a matter of extending the company's geographic scope into foreign markets. Chapter 8 takes up the topic of corporate strategy, which concerns diversifying into a mix of different businesses. Scope issues are at the very heart of corporate-level strategy.

Several dimensions of firm scope have relevance for business-level strategy in terms of their capacity to strengthen a company's position in a given market. These include the firm's **horizontal scope,** which is the range of product and service segments that the firm serves within its market. Mergers and acquisitions involving other market participants provide a means for a company to expand its horizontal scope. Expanding the firm's vertical scope by means of vertical integration can also affect the success of its market strategy. **Vertical scope** is the extent to which the firm engages in the various activities that make up the industry's entire value chain system, from initial activities such as raw-material production all the way to retailing and after-sales service activities. Outsourcing decisions concern another dimension of scope since they involve narrowing the firm's boundaries with respect to its participation in value chain activities. We discuss the pros and cons of each of these options in the sections that follow. Since strategic alliances and partnerships provide an alternative to vertical integration and acquisition strategies and are sometimes used to facilitate outsourcing, we conclude this chapter with a discussion of the benefits and challenges associated with cooperative arrangements of this sort.

HORIZONTAL MERGER AND ACQUISITION STRATEGIES

LO 3

Become aware of the strategic benefits and risks of expanding a company's horizontal scope through mergers and acquisitions.

Mergers and acquisitions are much-used strategic options; for example, the total worldwide value of mergers and acquisitions completed in 2008 and 2009 was approximately $5 trillion.[23] A *merger* is the combining of two or more companies into a single corporate entity, with the newly created company often taking on a new name. An *acquisition* is a combination in which one company, the acquirer, purchases and absorbs the operations of another, the acquired. The difference between a merger and an acquisition relates more to the details of ownership, management control, and financial arrangements than to strategy and competitive advantage. The resources and competitive capabilities of the newly created enterprise end up much the same whether the combination is the result of acquisition or merger.

Horizontal mergers and acquisitions, which involve combining the operations of firms within the same general industry, provide an effective means for firms to rapidly increase the scale and horizontal scope of their core business. For example, Microsoft has used an aggressive acquisition strategy to extend its software business into new segments and strengthen its technological capabilities in this domain. Mergers between airlines, such as the 2010 United-Continental merger, have increased their scale of operations and extended their reach geographically. Companies from developing economies are increasingly expanding their businesses through cross-border acquisitions, as we discuss in the following chapter on international strategy.

Combining the operations of two companies, via merger or acquisition, is an attractive strategic option for strengthening the resulting company's competitiveness and opening up avenues of new market opportunity. Increasing a company's horizontal scope can strengthen its business and increase its profitability in five ways: (1) by improving the efficiency of its operations, (2) by heightening its product differentiation, (3) by reducing market rivalry, (3) by increasing the company's bargaining power over suppliers and buyers, and (5) by enhancing its flexibility and dynamic capabilities (discussed in Chapter 4).

To achieve these benefits, horizontal merger and acquisition strategies typically are aimed at any of five outcomes:[24]

1. *Increasing the company's scale of operations and market share.* Many mergers and acquisitions are undertaken with the objective of transforming two or more high-cost companies into one lean competitor with significantly lower costs. When a company acquires another company in the same industry, there's usually enough overlap in operations that less efficient plants can be closed or distribution and sales activities partly combined and downsized. Likewise, it is usually feasible to squeeze out cost savings in administrative activities, again by combining and downsizing such administrative activities as finance and accounting, information technology, human resources, and so on. The combined companies may also be able to reduce supply chain costs because of greater bargaining power over common suppliers and closer collaboration with supply chain partners. By helping to consolidate the industry and remove excess capacity, such combinations can also reduce industry rivalry and improve industry profitability.

2. *Expanding a company's geographic coverage.* One of the best and quickest ways to expand a company's geographic coverage is to acquire rivals with operations in the desired locations. If there is some geographic overlap, then one benefit is being able to reduce costs by eliminating duplicate facilities in those geographic areas where undesirable overlap exists. Since a company's size increases with its geographic scope, another benefit is increased bargaining power with the company's suppliers or buyers. For companies whose business customers require national or international coverage, a broader geographic scope can provide differentiation benefits while also enhancing the company's bargaining power. Food products companies like Nestlé, Kraft, Unilever, and Procter & Gamble have made acquisitions an integral part of their strategies to expand internationally in order to serve key customers such as Walmart on a global basis. Greater geographic coverage can also contribute to product differentiation by enhancing a company's name recognition and brand awareness. Banks like Deutsche Bank and Bank of America have used acquisition strategies to establish a market presence and gain name recognition in an ever-growing number of states and localities.

3. *Extending the company's business into new product categories.* Many times a company has gaps in its product line that need to be filled in order to offer customers a more effective product bundle or the benefits of one-stop-shopping.[25] For example, customers might prefer to acquire a suite of software applications from a single vendor that can offer more integrated solutions to the company's problems. Acquisition can be a quicker and more potent way to broaden a company's product line than going through the exercise of introducing a company's own new product to fill the gap. Expanding

into additional market segments or product categories can offer companies benefits similar to those gained by expanding geographically: greater product differentiation, bargaining power, and efficiencies. It can also reduce rivalry by helping to consolidate an industry. Coca-Cola has increased the effectiveness of the product bundle it provides to retailers by acquiring Minute Maid (juices and juice drinks), Odwalla (juices), Hi-C (ready-to-drink fruit beverages), and Glaceau, the maker of VitaminWater. By entering the low-cost segment of the rental-car industry with its 2010 acquisition of Dollar Thrifty (whose brands include Dollar Rent a Car and Thrifty Rent a Car), Hertz can benefit from greater scale and stronger bargaining power over its suppliers.

4. *Gaining quick access to new technologies or complementary resources and capabilities.* By making acquisitions to bolster a company's technological know-how or to expand its skills and capabilities, a company can bypass a time-consuming and expensive internal effort to build desirable new resources and organizational capabilities. From 2000 through April 2009, Cisco Systems purchased 85 companies to give it more technological reach and product breadth, thereby enhancing its standing as the world's biggest provider of hardware, software, and services for building and operating Internet networks. By acquiring technologies and other resources and capabilities that complement its own set, a company can gain many of the types of benefits available from extending its horizontal scope. Among them is the greater flexibility and dynamic capabilities that spring from greater innovativeness and the ability to compete on the basis of a more effective bundle of resources.

5. *Leading the convergence of industries whose boundaries are being blurred by changing technologies and new market opportunities.* In fast-cycle industries or industries whose boundaries are changing, companies can use acquisition strategies to hedge their bets about the direction that an industry will take, increase their capacity to meet changing demands, and respond flexibly to changing buyer needs and technological demands. Such acquisitions add to a company's dynamic capabilities by bringing together the resources and products of several different companies and enabling the company to establish a strong position in the consolidating markets. Microsoft has made a series of acquisitions that have enabled it to launch Microsoft TV Internet Protocol Television (IPTV). Microsoft TV allows broadband users to use their home computers or Xbox game consoles to watch live programming, see video on demand, view pictures, and listen to music. News Corporation has also prepared for the convergence of media services with the purchase of satellite TV companies that include SKY Italia, British Sky Broadcasting, Sky Deutschland, Asia's TATA SKY, and FOXTEL in Australia and New Zealand to complement its media holdings in TV broadcasting (the Fox network and TV stations in various countries), cable TV (Fox News, Fox Sports, and FX), filmed entertainment (Twentieth Century Fox and Fox studios), newspapers, magazines, and book publishing.

Numerous companies have employed a horizontal acquisition strategy to catapult themselves from the ranks of the unknown into positions of market leadership. In 1998, Wells Fargo & Company became the 10th-largest bank in the United States as a result of the merger between Wells Fargo and Norwest Corporation. Although it was still only a network of small midwestern banks at that time, it continued to grow via acquisition over the next decade, pursuing a business model based on selling a full range of financial services to an ever-larger base of customers.

New opportunity presented itself, however, in the wake of the 2008 financial crisis. By acquiring troubled Wachovia Bank (which operated primarily in the Southeast and parts of the Atlantic Coast), Wells Fargo & Company was able to double its size and transform itself into a nationwide bank with global presence. By 2010, it was the fourth-largest bank in the United States, with $1.2 trillion in assets and over 10,000 branch banks. Moreover, its reputation had grown along with it; it was listed by *Fortune* magazine as the world's 14th "Most Admired Company in 2009," was among *Barron's* "World's 25 Most Respected Companies," and was on *Forbes's* list of the "Top 100 Best Companies in the World."

Illustration Capsule 6.2 describes how Clear Channel Worldwide has used acquisitions to build a leading global position in radio broadcasting.

Why Mergers and Acquisitions Sometimes Fail to Produce Anticipated Results

All too frequently, mergers and acquisitions do not produce the hoped-for outcomes.[26] Cost savings may prove smaller than expected. Gains in competitive capabilities may take substantially longer to realize or, worse, may never materialize at all. Efforts to mesh the corporate cultures can stall due to formidable resistance from organization members. Managers and employees at the acquired company may argue forcefully for continuing to do things the way they were done before the acquisition. Key employees at the acquired company can quickly become disenchanted and leave; the morale of company personnel who remain can drop to disturbingly low levels because they disagree with newly instituted changes. Differences in management styles and operating procedures can prove hard to resolve. The managers appointed to oversee the integration of a newly acquired company can make mistakes in deciding which activities to leave alone and which activities to meld into their own operations and systems.

A number of mergers/acquisitions have been notably unsuccessful. Ford's $2.5 billion acquisition of Jaguar was a failure, as was its $2.5 billion acquisition of Land Rover (both were sold to India's Tata Motors in 2008 for $2.3 billion). Daimler AG, the maker of Mercedes-Benz and Smart cars, entered into a high-profile merger with Chrysler only to dissolve it in 2007, taking a loss of $30 billion. A number of recent mergers and acquisitions have yet to live up to expectations—prominent examples include Oracle's acquisition of Sun Microsystems, the Fiat-Chrysler deal, Bank of America's acquisition of Merrill Lynch, and the merger of Sprint and Nextel in the mobile phone industry. Antitrust concerns on the part of regulatory authorities have prevented the successful conclusion of other mergers and acquisitions. Coca-Cola, for example, failed to win approval in 2009 for its proposed $2.4 billion acquisition of Huiyuan Juice Group under China's new antimonopoly law.

VERTICAL INTEGRATION STRATEGIES

Expanding the firm's vertical scope by means of a vertical integration strategy provides another way to strengthen the company's position in its core market. A **vertically integrated firm** is one that participates in multiple segments or stages of an industry's overall value chain. A good example of a vertically integrated

ILLUSTRATION CAPSULE 6.2

Clear Channel Communications: Using Mergers and Acquisitions to Become a Global Market Leader in Radio Broadcasting

In 2009, Clear Channel Communications was among the worldwide leaders in radio broadcasting. Clear Channel owned and operated more than 1,000 radio stations in the United States and operated an additional 240 radio stations in Australia, New Zealand, and Mexico. The company, which was founded in 1972 by Lowry Mays and Billy Joe McCombs, got its start by acquiring an unprofitable country-music radio station in San Antonio, Texas. Over the next 10 years, Mays learned the radio business and slowly bought other radio stations in a variety of states. Going public in 1984 helped the company raise the equity capital needed to continue acquiring radio stations in additional geographic markets.

By 1998, Clear Channel had used acquisitions to build a leading position in radio stations. Domestically, it owned, programmed, or sold airtime for 69 AM radio stations and 135 FM stations in 48 local markets in 24 states. Clear Channel's big move was to begin expanding internationally by acquiring interests in radio station properties in a variety of countries. In October 1999, Clear Channel made a major acquisition that expanded its horizontal scope significantly: It acquired AM-FM, Inc., and changed its name to Clear Channel Communications. The AM-FM, Inc., acquisition gave Clear Channel operations in 32 countries, including 830 radio stations.

Additional acquisitions were completed during the 2000–2003 period. The emphasis was on buying radio broadcasting properties with operations in many of the same local markets, which made it feasible to (1) cut costs by sharing facilities and staffs, (2) improve programming, and (3) sell advertising to customers in packages that not only helped Clear Channel's advertising clients distribute their messages more effectively but also allowed the company to combine its sales activities, achieving significant cost savings and boosting profit margins. In 2008, Clear Channel sought a buyer for 288 of its 1,005 radio stations that operated in small markets. Its remaining 717 radio stations all operated in the top-100 markets in the United States.

Sources: www.clearchannel.com (accessed May 2008); *BusinessWeek,* October 19, 1999, p. 56.

LO 4

Learn the advantages and disadvantages of extending the company's scope of operations via vertical integration.

firm is Maple Leaf Foods, a major Canadian producer of fresh and processed meats whose best-selling brands include Maple Leaf and Schneiders. Maple Leaf Foods participates in hog and poultry production, with company-owned hog and poultry farms; it has its own meat-processing and -rendering facilities; it packages its products and distributes them from company-owned distribution centers; and it conducts marketing, sales, and customer service activities for its wholesale and retail buyers but does not otherwise participate in the final stage of the meat processing vertical chain—the retailing stage.

A vertical integration strategy can expand the firm's range of activities *backward* into sources of supply and/or *forward* toward end users. When Tiffany & Co, a manufacturer and retailer of fine jewelry, began sourcing, cutting, and polishing its own diamonds, it integrated backward along the diamond supply chain. Mining giant De Beers Group and Canadian miner Aber Diamond integrated forward when they entered the diamond retailing business.

A firm can pursue vertical integration by starting its own operations in other stages of the vertical activity chain, by acquiring a company already performing the activities it wants to bring in-house, or by entering into a strategic alliance or joint venture. Vertical integration strategies can aim at *full integration* (participating in all stages of the vertical chain) or *partial integration* (building positions in selected stages of the vertical chain). Firms can also engage in *tapered integration* strategies, which involve a mix of in-house and outsourced activity in any given stage of the vertical chain. Oil companies, for instance, supply their refineries with oil from their own wells as well as with oil that they purchase from other producers—they engage in tapered backward integration. Since Boston Beer Company, the maker of Samuel Adams, sells most of its beer through distributors but also operates brew-pubs, it practices tapered forward integration.

The Advantages of a Vertical Integration Strategy

Under the right conditions, a vertical integration strategy can add materially to a company's technological capabilities, strengthen the firm's competitive position, and boost its profitability.[27] But it is important to keep in mind that vertical integration has no real payoff strategywise or profitwise unless it produces cost savings and/or differentiation benefits sufficient to justify the extra investment.

Integrating Backward to Achieve Greater Competitiveness

It is harder than one might think to generate cost savings or improve profitability by integrating backward into activities such as parts and components manufacture (which could otherwise be purchased from suppliers with specialized expertise in making these parts and components). For backward integration to be a cost-saving and profitable strategy, a company must be able to (1) achieve the same scale economies as outside suppliers and (2) match or beat suppliers' production efficiency with no drop-off in quality. Neither outcome is a slam dunk. To begin with, a company's in-house requirements are often too small to reach the optimum size for low-cost operation—for instance, if it takes a minimum production volume of 1 million units to achieve mass-production economies and a company's in-house requirements are just 250,000 units, then it falls far short of being able to capture the scale economies of outside suppliers (which may readily find buyers for 1 million or more units). Furthermore, matching the production efficiency of suppliers is fraught with problems when suppliers have considerable production experience of their own, when the technology they employ has elements that are hard to master, and/or when substantial R&D expertise is required to develop next-version parts and components or keep pace with advancing technology in parts/components production.

But that said, there are still occasions when a company can improve its cost position and competitiveness by performing a broader range of vertical chain activities in-house rather than having certain of these activities performed by outside suppliers. When the item being supplied is a major cost component, when there is a sole supplier, or when suppliers have outsized profit margins, vertical integration can lower costs by limiting supplier power. Vertical integration can also lower costs by facilitating the coordination of production flows and avoiding bottleneck problems. Furthermore, when a company has proprietary know-how that it wants to keep from rivals, then in-house performance of value-adding activities related to this know-how is beneficial even if such activities could be performed by outsiders. Apple recently decided to integrate backward

> **CORE CONCEPT**
>
> A **vertically integrated firm** is one that performs value chain activities along several portions or stages of an industry's overall value chain, which begins with the production of raw materials or initial inputs and culminates in final sales and service to the end consumer.

> **CORE CONCEPT**
>
> **Backward integration** involves performing industry value chain activities previously performed by suppliers or other enterprises engaged in earlier stages of the industry value chain; **forward integration** involves performing industry value chain activities closer to the end user.

into producing its own chips for iPhones, chiefly because chips are a major cost component, they have big profit margins, and in-house production would help coordinate design tasks and protect Apple's proprietary iPhone technology. International Paper Company backward integrates into pulp mills that it sets up nearby its paper mills (outside suppliers are generally unwilling to make a site-specific investment for a buyer) and reaps the benefits of coordinated production flows, energy savings, and transportation economies.

Backward vertical integration can produce a differentiation-based competitive advantage when performing activities internally contributes to a better-quality product/service offering, improves the caliber of customer service, or in other ways enhances the performance of the final product. On occasion, integrating into more stages along the vertical added-value chain can add to a company's differentiation capabilities by allowing it to build or strengthen its core competencies, better master key skills or strategy-critical technologies, or add features that deliver greater customer value. Spanish clothing maker Inditex has backward integrated into fabric making, as well as garment design and manufacture, for its successful Zara brand. By tightly controlling the process and postponing dyeing until later stages, Zara can respond quickly to changes in fashion trends and supply its customers with the hottest items. NewsCorp backward integrated into film studios (Twentieth Century Fox) and TV program production to ensure access to high-quality content for its TV stations (and to limit supplier power).

Integrating Forward to Enhance Competitiveness

Like backward integration, forward integration can lower costs by increasing efficiency and bargaining power. In addition, it can allow manufacturers to gain better access to end users, strengthen brand awareness, and increase product differentiation. Automakers, for example, have forward integrated into the lending business in order to exercise more control and make auto loans a more attractive part of the car-buying process. Forward integration can also enable companies to make the end users' purchasing experience a differentiating feature. For example, Ducati and Harley motorcycles both have company-owned retail stores that are essentially little museums, filled with iconography, that provide an environment conducive to selling not only motorcycles and gear but memorabilia, clothing, and other items featuring the brand. Insurance companies and brokerages have the ability to make consumers' interactions with local agents and office personnel a differentiating feature by focusing on building relationships.

In many industries, independent sales agents, wholesalers, and retailers handle competing brands of the same product; having no allegiance to any one company's brand, they tend to push whatever earns them the biggest profits. An independent insurance agency, for example, represents a number of different insurance companies and tries to find the best match between a customer's insurance requirements and the policies of alternative insurance companies. Under this arrangement, it's possible for an agent to develop a preference for one company's policies or underwriting practices and neglect other represented insurance companies. An insurance company may conclude, therefore, that it is better off integrating forward and setting up its own local offices. Likewise, some tire manufacturers (such as Goodyear) have integrated forward into tire retailing to exert better control over sales force/customer interactions. A number of consumer-goods manufacturers, like Coach, Ralph Lauren, and Samsonite, have integrated forward into retailing so as to move seconds, overstocked items, and slow-selling merchandise through their own branded factory outlet stores.

Some producers have opted to integrate forward by selling directly to customers at the company's Web site. Bypassing regular wholesale/retail channels in favor of direct sales and Internet retailing can have appeal if it reinforces the brand and enhances consumer satisfaction or if it lowers distribution costs, produces a relative cost advantage over certain rivals, and results in lower selling prices to end users. In addition, sellers are compelled to include the Internet as a retail channel when a sufficiently large number of buyers in an industry prefer to make purchases online. However, a company that is vigorously pursuing online sales to consumers at the same time that it is also heavily promoting sales to consumers through its network of wholesalers and retailers is competing directly against its distribution allies. Such actions constitute *channel conflict* and create a tricky route to negotiate. A company that is actively trying to expand online sales to consumers is signaling *a weak strategic commitment to its dealers* and *a willingness to cannibalize dealers' sales and growth potential.* The likely result is angry dealers and loss of dealer goodwill. Quite possibly, a company may stand to lose more sales by offending its dealers than it gains from its own online sales effort. Consequently, in industries where the strong support and goodwill of dealer networks is essential, companies may conclude that it is important to avoid channel conflict and that their Web sites should be designed to partner with dealers rather than compete against them.

The Disadvantages of a Vertical Integration Strategy

Vertical integration has some substantial drawbacks beyond the potential for channel conflict.[28] The most serious drawbacks to vertical integration include the following concerns:

- Vertical integration raises a firm's capital investment in the industry, *increasing business risk.* What if industry growth and profitability go sour?

- Vertically integrated companies are often *slow to embrace technological advances* or more efficient production methods when they are saddled with older technology or facilities. A company that obtains parts and components from outside suppliers can always shop the market for the latest and best parts and components, whereas a vertically integrated firm that is saddled with older technology or facilities that make items it no longer needs is looking at the high costs of premature abandonment.

- Integrating backward into parts and components manufacture *can impair a company's operating flexibility* when it comes to changing out the use of certain parts and components. It is one thing to design out a component made by a supplier and another to design out a component being made in-house (which can mean laying off employees and writing off the associated investment in equipment and facilities). Most of the world's automakers, despite their expertise in automotive technology and manufacturing, have concluded that purchasing many of their key parts and components from manufacturing specialists results in higher quality, lower costs, and greater design flexibility than does the vertical integration option.

- Vertical integration potentially results in *less flexibility in accommodating shifting buyer preferences* when a new product design doesn't include parts and components that the company makes in-house. Integrating forward or backward locks a firm into relying on its own in-house activities and sources of supply.

- Vertical integration *may not enable a company to realize economies of scale* if its production levels are below the minimum efficient scale. Small companies in particular are likely to suffer a cost disadvantage by producing in-house when suppliers of many small companies can realize scale economies that a small company cannot attain on its own.

- Vertical integration poses all kinds of *capacity matching problems.* In motor vehicle manufacturing, for example, the most efficient scale of operation for making axles is different from the most economic volume for radiators and different yet again for both engines and transmissions. Building the capacity to produce just the right number of axles, radiators, engines, and transmissions in-house—and doing so at the lowest unit costs for each—is much easier said than done. If internal capacity for making transmissions is deficient, the difference has to be bought externally. If internal capacity for radiators proves excessive, customers need to be found for the surplus. And if by-products are generated—as occurs in the processing of many chemical products—they require arrangements for disposal. Consequently, integrating across several production stages in ways that achieve the lowest feasible costs can be a monumental challenge.

- Integration forward or backward often calls for *radical new skills and business capabilities.* Parts and components manufacturing, assembly operations, wholesale distribution and retailing, and direct sales via the Internet represent different kinds of businesses, operating in different types of industries, with different key success factors. Managers of a manufacturing company should consider carefully whether it makes good business sense to invest time and money in developing the expertise and merchandising skills to integrate forward into wholesaling or retailing. Many manufacturers learn the hard way that company-owned wholesale/retail networks present many headaches, fit poorly with what they do best, and don't always add the kind of value to their core business they thought they would.

In today's world of close working relationships with suppliers and efficient supply chain management systems, *very few businesses can make a case for integrating backward into the business of suppliers* to ensure a reliable supply of materials and components or to reduce production costs. The best materials and components suppliers stay abreast of advancing technology and are adept in improving their efficiency and keeping their costs and prices as low as possible. A company that pursues a vertical integration strategy and tries to produce many parts and components in-house is likely to find itself very hard-pressed to keep up with technological advances and cutting-edge production practices for each part and component used in making its product.

Weighing the Pros and Cons of Vertical Integration

All in all, therefore, a strategy of vertical integration can have both important strengths and weaknesses. The tip of the scales depends on (1) whether vertical integration can enhance the performance of strategy-critical activities in ways that lower cost, build expertise, protect proprietary know-how, or increase differentiation; (2) the impact of vertical integration on investment costs, flexibility and response times, and the administrative costs of coordinating operations across more vertical chain activities; and (3) how difficult it will be for the company to acquire the set of skills and capabilities needed to operate in another stage of the vertical chain. *Vertical integration strategies have merit according to which capabilities and value-adding activities truly need to be performed in-house and which can be performed better or cheaper by outsiders.* Without solid benefits, integrating forward or backward is not likely to be an attractive strategy option.

OUTSOURCING STRATEGIES: NARROWING THE SCOPE OF OPERATIONS

In contrast to vertical integration strategies, outsourcing strategies narrow the scope of a business's operations (and the firm's boundaries, in terms of what activities are performed internally). **Outsourcing** involves a conscious decision to forgo attempts to perform certain value chain activities internally and instead to farm them out to outside specialists.[29] Many PC makers, for example, have shifted from assembling units in-house to outsourcing the entire assembly process to manufacturing specialists because enterprises that assemble many brands of PCs are better able to bargain down the prices of PC components (by buying in very large volumes) and because they have greater expertise in performing assembly tasks more cost-effectively. Nike has outsourced most of its manufacturing-related value chain activities so that it can concentrate on marketing and managing its brand.

> **CORE CONCEPT**
>
> **Outsourcing** involves farming out certain value chain activities to outside vendors.

Outsourcing certain value chain activities can be advantageous whenever:

- *An activity can be performed better or more cheaply by outside specialists.* A company should generally *not* perform any value chain activity internally that can be performed more efficiently or effectively by outsiders—the chief exception occurs when a particular activity is strategically crucial and internal control over that activity is deemed essential.

- *The activity is not crucial to the firm's ability to achieve sustainable competitive advantage and won't hollow out its core competencies.* Outsourcing of support activities such as maintenance services, data processing and data storage, fringe-benefit management, and Web site operations has become commonplace. Colgate-Palmolive, for instance, has been able to reduce its information technology operational costs by more than 10 percent per year through an outsourcing agreement with IBM. A number of companies have outsourced their call center operations to foreign-based contractors that have access to lower-cost labor supplies and can employ lower-paid call center personnel to respond to customer inquiries or requests for technical support.

- *It streamlines company operations in ways that improve organizational flexibility and speed time to market.* Outsourcing gives a company the flexibility to switch suppliers in the event that its present supplier falls behind competing suppliers. To the extent that its suppliers can speedily get next-generation parts and components into production, then a company can get its own next-generation product offerings into the marketplace quicker. Moreover, seeking out new suppliers with the needed capabilities already in place is frequently quicker, easier, less risky, and cheaper than hurriedly retooling internal operations to replace obsolete capabilities or trying to install and master new technologies.

> **LO 5**
>
> Become aware of the conditions that favor farming out certain value chain activities to outside parties.

- *It reduces the company's risk exposure to changing technology and/or buyer preferences.* When a company outsources certain parts, components, and services, its suppliers must bear the burden of incorporating state-of-the-art technologies and/or undertaking redesigns and upgrades to accommodate a company's plans to introduce next-generation products. If what a supplier provides falls out of favor with buyers, or is designed out of next-generation products, or rendered unnecessary by technological change, it is the supplier's business that suffers rather than a company's own internal operations.

- *It allows a company to assemble diverse kinds of expertise speedily and efficiently.* A company can nearly always gain quicker access to first-rate capabilities and expertise by employing suppliers who already have them in place than it can by trying to build them from scratch with its own company personnel.

- *It allows a company to concentrate on its core business, leverage its key resources, and do even better what it already does best.* A company is better able to heighten its own competitively valuable capabilities when it concentrates its full resources and energies on performing those activities internally that it can perform better than outsiders and/or that it needs to have under its direct control. Coach, for example, devotes its energy to designing new styles of ladies handbags and leather accessories, opting to outsource handbag production to 40 contract manufacturers in 15 countries. Hewlett-Packard, IBM, and others have sold manufacturing plants to suppliers and then contracted to purchase the output.

The Big Risk of Outsourcing Value Chain Activities

The biggest danger of outsourcing is that a company will farm out too many or the wrong types of activities and thereby hollow out its own capabilities.[30] For example, in recent years, companies anxious to reduce operating costs have opted to outsource such strategically important activities as product development, engineering design, and sophisticated manufacturing tasks—the very capabilities that underpin a company's ability to lead sustained product innovation. While these companies may have been able to lower their operating costs by outsourcing these functions to outsiders that can perform them more cheaply, *their ability to lead the development of innovative new products has been weakened in the process.* For example, nearly every U.S. brand of laptop and cell phone (with the notable exception of Apple) is not only manufactured but designed in Asia.[31] It is strategically dangerous for a company to be dependent on outsiders for competitive capabilities that over the long run determine its market success. Companies like IBM, Dell, American Express, and Bank of America are alert to the danger of farming out the performance of strategy-critical value chain activities and generally only outsource relatively mundane functions: IBM outsources customer support operations, Dell outsources manufacturing, American Express outsources IT functions, and BoA outsources human resource management.

> A company must guard against outsourcing activities that hollow out the resources and capabilities that it needs to be a master of its own destiny.

Another risk of outsourcing comes from the lack of direct control. It may be difficult to monitor, control, and coordinate the activities of outside parties by mean of contracts and arm's-length transactions alone; unanticipated problems may arise that cause delays or cost overruns and become hard to resolve amicably. Moreover, contract-based outsourcing can be problematic because outside parties lack incentives to make investments specific to the needs of the outsourcing company's value chain.

STRATEGIC ALLIANCES AND PARTNERSHIPS

Strategic alliances and cooperative partnerships provide one way to gain some of the benefits offered by vertical integration, outsourcing, and horizontal mergers and acquisitions while minimizing the associated problems. Companies frequently engage in cooperative strategies as an alternative to vertical integration or horizontal mergers and acquisitions. Increasingly, companies are also employing strategic alliances and partnerships to extend their scope of operations via international expansion and diversification strategies, as we describe in Chapters 7 and 8. Strategic alliances and cooperative arrangements are now a common means of narrowing a company's scope of operations as well, serving as a useful way to manage outsourcing (in lieu of traditional, purely price-oriented contracts).

LO 6

Understand when and how strategic alliances can substitute for horizontal mergers and acquisitions or vertical integration and how they can facilitate outsourcing.

For example, oil and gas companies engage in considerable vertical integration—but Shell Oil Company and Pemex (Mexico's state-owned petroleum company) have found that joint ownership of their Deer Park Refinery in Texas lowers their investment costs and risks in comparison to going it alone. The colossal failure of the Daimler-Chrysler merger formed an expensive lesson for Daimler AG about what can go wrong with horizontal mergers and acquisitions; its 2010 strategic alliance with Renault-Nissan may allow the two companies to achieve jointly the global scale required for cost competitiveness in cars and trucks while avoiding the type of problems that so plagued Daimler-Chrysler. Many companies employ strategic alliances to manage the problems that might otherwise occur with outsourcing—Cisco's system of alliances guards against loss of control, protects its proprietary manufacturing expertise, and enables the company to monitor closely the assembly operations of its partners while devoting its energy to designing new generations of the switches, routers, and other Internet-related equipment for which it is known.

Companies in all types of industries and in all parts of the world have elected to form strategic alliances and partnerships to complement their own strategic initiatives and strengthen their competitiveness in domestic and international markets—the very same goals that motivate vertical integration, horizontal mergers and acquisitions, and outsourcing initiatives. This is an about-face from times past, when the vast majority of companies were content to go it alone, confident that they already had or could independently develop whatever resources and know-how were needed to be successful in their markets. But in today's world, large corporations—even those that are successful and financially strong—have concluded that it doesn't always make good strategic and economic sense to be *totally independent* and *self-sufficient* with regard to each and every skill, resource, and capability they may need. When a company needs to strengthen its competitive position, whether through greater differentiation, efficiency improvements, or a stronger bargaining position, the fastest and most effective route may be to partner with other enterprises having similar goals and complementary capabilities; moreover, partnering offers greater flexibility should a company's resource requirements or goals later change.

A **strategic alliance** is a formal agreement between two or more separate companies in which there is strategically relevant collaboration of some sort, joint contribution of resources, shared risk, shared control, and

CORE CONCEPT

A **strategic alliance** is a formal agreement between two or more separate companies in which they agree to work cooperatively toward some common objective.

mutual dependence. Often, alliances involve cooperative marketing, sales or distribution, joint production, design collaboration, or projects to jointly develop new technologies or products. They can vary in terms of their duration and the extent of the collaboration; some are intended as long-term arrangements, involving an extensive set of cooperative activities, while others are designed to accomplish more limited, short-term objectives.

CORE CONCEPT

A **joint venture** is a type of strategic alliance in which the partners set up an independent corporate entity that they own and control jointly, sharing in its revenues and expenses.

Collaborative arrangements may entail a contractual agreement, but they commonly stop short of formal ownership ties between the partners (although sometimes an alliance member will secure minority ownership of another member). A special type of strategic alliance involving ownership ties is the **joint venture.** A joint venture entails forming a new corporate entity that is jointly owned by two or more companies that agree to share in the revenues, expenses, and control of the newly formed entity. Since joint ventures involve setting up a mutually owned business, they tend to be more durable but also riskier than other arrangements. In other types of strategic alliances, the collaboration between the partners involves a much less rigid structure in which the partners retain their independence from one another. If a strategic alliance is not working out, a partner can choose to simply walk away or reduce its commitment to collaborating at any time.

Five factors make an alliance "strategic," as opposed to just a convenient business arrangement:[32]

1. It helps build, sustain, or enhance a core competence or competitive advantage.
2. It helps block a competitive threat.
3. It increases the bargaining power of alliance members over suppliers or buyers.
4. It helps open up important new market opportunities.
5. It mitigates a significant risk to a company's business.

Strategic cooperation is a much-favored approach in industries where new technological developments are occurring at a furious pace along many different paths and where advances in one technology spill over to affect others (often blurring industry boundaries). Whenever industries are experiencing high-velocity technological advances in many areas simultaneously, firms find it virtually essential to have cooperative relationships with other enterprises to stay on the leading edge of technology and product performance even in their own area of specialization.

It took a $3.2 billion joint venture involving the likes of Sprint-Nextel, Clearwire, Intel, Time Warner Cable, Google, Comcast, and Bright House Networks to roll out next-generation 4G wireless services based on Sprint's and Clearwire's WiMax mobile networks, with the objective of reaching 100 metropolitan areas and 120 million people by the end of 2010. WiMax was an advanced Wi-Fi technology that allowed people to browse the Internet at speeds as great as 10 times faster than other cellular Wi-Fi technologies. The venture was a necessity for Sprint-Nextel and Clearwire since they lacked the financial resources to handle the rollout on their own. The appeal of the partnership for Time Warner, Comcast, and Bright House was the ability to bundle the sale of wireless services to their cable customers, while Intel had the chip sets for WiMax and hoped that WiMax would become the dominant wireless Internet format. Google's interest in the alliance was to strengthen its lead in desktop search on wireless devices.

Clear Channel Communications has entered into a series of partnerships to provide a multiplatform launchpad for artists like Taylor Swift, Phoenix, and Sara Bareilles. In 2008, they launched iHeartRadio on the iPhone, leveraging their relationships with record labels, artists, TV music channels, and media companies to rake in $175 million in digital revenue as compared to $50 million earned by Pandora in the same period. In 2010, they partnered with MySpace, Hulu, and the artist management company 19 Entertainment for "If I Can Dream," an original reality series where unsigned musicians and actors share a "Real World"-style house in Los Angeles and document their attempts at stardom. Clear Channel has helped promote the show by conducting exclusive radio interviews and performances with the talent, which in turn has helped the show become a top-30 weekly program on Hulu.[33]

Since 2003, Samsung Electronics, a global electronics company headquartered in South Korea, has entered into more than 30 major strategic alliances involving such companies as Sony, Nokia, Intel, Microsoft, Dell, Toshiba, Lowe's, IBM, Hewlett-Packard, and Disney Automation; the alliances involved joint investments, technology transfer arrangements, joint R&D projects, and agreements to supply parts and components—all of which facilitated Samsung's strategic efforts to globalize its business and secure its position as a leader in the worldwide electronics industry. Microsoft collaborates very closely with independent software developers to ensure that their programs will run on the next-generation versions of Windows. Genentech, a leader in biotechnology and human genetics, has formed R&D alliances with over 30 companies to boost its prospects for developing new cures for various diseases and ailments. United Airlines, American Airlines, Continental, Delta, and Northwest created an alliance to form Orbitz, an Internet travel site that enabled them to compete head to head against Expedia and Travelocity and, further, gave them more economical access to travelers and vacationers shopping online for airfares, rental cars, lodging, cruises, and vacation packages.

Toyota has forged long-term strategic partnerships with many of its suppliers of automotive parts and components, both to achieve lower costs and to improve the quality and reliability of its vehicles. In 2008, when Chrysler found itself unable to build hybrid SUVs and trucks using its Two Mode technological innovation (because it lacked the economies of scale necessary to produce proprietary components at a reasonable cost), it entered into a strategic alliance with Nissan whereby Nissan would build Chrysler vehicles with the hybrid technology and Chrysler would take over the production of certain Nissan truck models. Daimler AG has been entering a variety of alliances to lower its risks and improve its prospects in electric cars, where it lacks key capabilities. Its equity-based strategic partnership with Tesla Motors, for example, will allow Daimler to use proven technology to bring its electric vehicles to market quickly, while helping Tesla learn how to mass produce its electric cars. Daimler's 2010 joint venture with Chinese car maker BYD is intended to help Daimler make and sell electric cars for the Chinese market.

Studies indicate that large corporations are commonly involved in 30 to 50 alliances and that a number have hundreds of alliances. One study estimated that corporate revenues coming from activities involving strategic alliances have more than doubled since 1995.[34] Another study reported that the typical large corporation relied on alliances for 15 to 20 percent of its revenues, assets, or income.[35] Companies that have formed a host of alliances have a need to manage their alliances like a portfolio—terminating those that no longer serve a useful purpose or that have produced meager results, forming promising new alliances, and restructuring certain existing alliances to correct performance problems and/or redirect the collaborative effort.[36]

Company use of alliances is quite widespread.

Why and How Strategic Alliances Are Advantageous

The most common reasons companies enter into strategic alliances are to expedite the development of promising new technologies or products, to overcome deficits in their own technical and manufacturing expertise, to bring together the personnel and expertise needed to create desirable new skill sets and capabilities, to improve supply chain efficiency, to share the risks of high-stake, risky ventures, to gain economies of scale in production and/or marketing, and to acquire or improve market access through joint marketing agreements.[37] Manufacturers frequently pursue alliances with parts and components suppliers to gain the efficiencies of better supply chain management and to speed new products to market. By joining forces in components production and/or final assembly, companies may be able to realize cost savings not achievable with their own small volumes. Allies can learn much from one another in performing joint research, sharing technological know-how, and collaborating on complementary new technologies and products—sometimes enough to enable them to pursue other new opportunities on their own.[38] In industries where technology is advancing rapidly, alliances are all about fast cycles of learning, staying abreast of the latest developments, gaining quick access to the latest round of technological know-how, and developing dynamic capabilities. In bringing together firms with different skills and knowledge bases, alliances open up learning opportunities that help partner firms better leverage their own resources and capabilities.[39]

> The best alliances are highly selective, focusing on particular value-creating activities, whether within or across industry boundaries, and on obtaining a specific competitive benefit. They enable a firm to build on its strengths and to learn.

There are several other instances in which companies find strategic alliances particularly valuable. As we explain in the next chapter, a company that is racing for *global market leadership* needs alliances to:[40]

- *Get into critical country markets quickly* and accelerate the process of building a potent global market presence.

- *Gain inside knowledge about unfamiliar markets and cultures through alliances with local partners.* For example, U.S., European, and Japanese companies wanting to build market footholds in the fast-growing Chinese market have pursued partnership arrangements with Chinese companies to help get products through the customs process, to help guide them through the maze of government regulations, to supply knowledge of local markets, to provide guidance on adapting their products to better match the buying preferences of Chinese consumers, to set up local manufacturing capabilities, and to assist in distribution, marketing, and promotional activities.

- *Access valuable skills and competencies* that are concentrated in particular geographic locations (such as software design competencies in the United States, fashion design skills in Italy, and efficient manufacturing skills in Japan and China).

A company that is racing to *stake out a strong position in an industry of the future* needs alliances to:[41]

- *Establish a stronger beachhead* for participating in the target industry.
- *Master new technologies and build new expertise and competencies* faster than would be possible through internal efforts.
- *Open up broader opportunities* in the target industry by melding the firm's own capabilities with the expertise and resources of partners.

Capturing the Benefits of Strategic Alliances

The extent to which companies benefit from entering into alliances and partnerships seems to be a function of six factors:[42]

1. *Picking a good partner.* A good partner must bring complementary strengths to the relationship. To the extent that alliance members have nonoverlapping strengths, there is greater potential for synergy and less potential for coordination problems and conflict. In addition, a good partner needs to share the company's vision about the overall purpose of the alliance and to have specific goals that either match or complement those of the company. Strong partnerships also depend on good chemistry among key personnel and compatible views about how the alliance should be structured and managed.

2. *Being sensitive to cultural differences.* Cultural differences among companies can make it difficult for their personnel to work together effectively. Cultural differences can be problematic among companies from the same country, but when the partners have different national origins, the problems are often magnified. Unless there is respect among all the parties for company cultural differences, including those stemming from different local cultures and local business practices, productive working relationships are unlikely to emerge.

3. *Recognizing that the alliance must benefit both sides.* Information must be shared as well as gained, and the relationship must remain forthright and trustful. Many alliances fail because one or both partners grow unhappy with what they are learning. Also, if either partner plays games with information or tries to take advantage of the other, the resulting friction can quickly erode the value of further collaboration. Open, trustworthy behavior on both sides is essential for fruitful collaboration.

4. *Ensuring that both parties live up to their commitments.* Both parties have to deliver on their commitments for the alliance to produce the intended benefits. The division of work has to be perceived as fairly apportioned, and the caliber of the benefits received on both sides has to be perceived as adequate. Such actions are critical for the establishment of trust between the parties; research has shown that trust is an important factor in fostering effective strategic alliances.[43]

5. *Structuring the decision-making process so that actions can be taken swiftly when needed.* In many instances, the fast pace of technological and competitive changes dictates an equally fast decision-making process. If the parties get bogged down in discussions or in gaining internal approval from higher-ups, the alliance can turn into an anchor of delay and inaction.

6. *Managing the learning process and then adjusting the alliance agreement over time to fit new circumstances.* One of the keys to long-lasting success is adapting the nature and structure of the alliance to be responsive to shifting market conditions, emerging technologies, and changing customer requirements. Wise allies are quick to recognize the merit of an evolving collaborative arrangement, where adjustments are made to accommodate changing market conditions and to overcome whatever problems arise in establishing an effective working relationship. Most alliances encounter troubles of some kind within a couple of years—those that are flexible enough to evolve are better able to recover.[44]

Most alliances that aim at sharing technology or providing market access turn out to be temporary, lasting only a few years. This is not necessarily an indicator of failure, however. Strategic alliances can be terminated after a few years simply because they have fulfilled their purpose; indeed, many alliances are intended to be of limited duration, set up to accomplish specific short-term objectives. Longer-lasting collaborative arrangements, however, may provide even greater strategic benefits. Alliances are more likely to be long-lasting when (1) they involve collaboration with partners that do not compete directly, (2) a trusting relationship has been established, and (3) both parties conclude that continued collaboration is in their mutual interest, perhaps because new opportunities for learning are emerging.

The Drawbacks of Strategic Alliances and Partnerships

While strategic alliances provide a way of obtaining the benefits of vertical integration, mergers and acquisitions, and outsourcing, they also suffer from some of the same drawbacks. Culture clash and integration problems due to different management styles and business practices can interfere with the success of an alliance, just as they can with vertical integration or horizontal mergers and acquisitions. Anticipated gains may fail to materialize due to an overly optimistic view of the synergies or a poor fit in terms of the combination of resources and capabilities. When outsourcing is conducted via alliances, there is no less risk of becoming dependent on other companies for essential expertise and capabilities—indeed, this may be the Achilles' heel of such alliances.

Moreover, there are additional pitfalls to collaborative arrangements. The greatest danger is that a partner will gain access to a company's proprietary knowledge base, technologies, or trade secrets, enabling the partner to match the company's core strengths and costing the company its hard-won competitive advantage. This risk is greatest when the alliance is among industry rivals or when the alliance is for the purpose of collaborative R&D, since this type of partnership requires an extensive exchange of closely held information.

The question for managers is when to engage in a strategic alliance and when to choose an alternative means of meeting their objectives. The answer to this question depends on the relative advantages of each method and the circumstances under which each type of organizational arrangement is favored.

The principle advantages of strategic alliances over vertical integration or horizontal mergers/acquisitons are threefold:

1. They lower investment costs and risks for each partner by facilitating resource pooling and risk sharing. This can be particularly important when investment needs and uncertainty are high, such as when a dominant technology standard has not yet emerged.

2. They are more flexible organizational forms and allow for a more adaptive response to changing conditions. Flexibility is key when environmental conditions or technologies are changing rapidly. Moreover, strategic alliances under such circumstances may enable the development of each partner's dynamic capabilities.

3. They are more rapidly deployed—a critical factor when speed is of the essence. Speed is of the essence when there is a winner-take-all type of competitive situation, such as the race for a dominant technological design or a race down a steep experience curve, where there is a large first-mover advantage.

The key advantages of using strategic alliances rather than arm's-length transactions to manage outsourcing are (1) the increased ability to exercise control over the partners' activities and (2) a greater willingness for the partners to make relationship-specific investments. Arm's-length transactions discourage such investments since they imply less commitment and do not build trust.

On the other hand, there are circumstances when other organizational mechanisms are preferable to partnering. Mergers and acquisitions are especially suited for situations in which strategic alliances or partnerships do not go far enough in providing a company with access to needed resources and capabilities.[45] Ownership ties are more permanent than partnership ties, allowing the operations of the merger/acquisition participants to be tightly integrated and creating more in-house control and autonomy. Other organizational mechanisms are also preferable to alliances when there is limited property rights protection for valuable know-how and when companies fear being taken advantage of by opportunistic partners.

While it is important for managers to understand when strategic alliances and partnerships are most likely (and least likely) to prove useful, it is also important to know how to manage them.

How to Make Strategic Alliances Work

A surprisingly large number of alliances never live up to expectations. A recent article reported that even though the number of strategic alliances increases by about 25 percent annually, about 60 to 70 percent of alliances continue to fail each year.[46] The success of an alliance depends on how well the partners work together, their capacity to respond and adapt to changing internal and external conditions, and their willingness to renegotiate the bargain if circumstances so warrant. A successful alliance requires real in-the-trenches collaboration, not merely an arm's-length exchange of ideas. Unless partners place a high value on the skills, resources, and contributions each brings to the alliance and the cooperative arrangement results in valuable win-win outcomes, it is doomed.

While the track record for strategic alliances is poor on average, many companies have learned how to manage strategic alliances successfully and routinely defy these averages. Samsung Group, which includes Samsung Electronics and had worldwide sales of $117.8 billion in 2009, successfully manages an ecosystem of over 1,300 partnerships that enable productive activities from global procurement to local marketing to collaborative R&D. Samsung Group takes a systematic approach to managing its partnerships and devotes considerable resources to this enterprise. In 2008, for example, it established a Partner Collaboration and Enhancement Office under the direct control of its CEO. Samsung Group supports its partners with financial help as well as training and development resources to ensure that its alliance partners' technical, manufacturing, and management capabilities remain globally competitive. As a result, some of its equipment providers have emerged as the leading firms in their industries while contributing to Samsung's competitive advantage in the global TV market.

Companies that have greater success in managing their strategic alliances and partnerships often credit the following factors:

- *They create a system for managing their alliances.* Companies need to manage their alliances in a systematic fashion, just as they manage other functions. This means setting up a process for managing the different aspects of alliance management from partner selection to alliance termination procedures. To ensure that the system is followed on a routine basis by all company managers, many companies create a set of explicit procedures, process templates, manuals, or the like.

- *They build relationships with their partners and establish trust.* Establishing strong interpersonal relationships is a critical factor in making strategic alliances work since they facilitate opening up channels of communication, coordinating activity, aligning interests, and building trust. Cultural sensitivity is a key part of this, particularly for cross-border alliances. Accordingly, many companies include cultural sensitivity training for their managers as a part of their alliance management program.

- *They protect themselves from the threat of opportunism by setting up safeguards.* There are a number of means for preventing a company from being taken advantage of by an untrustworthy partner or unwittingly losing control over key assets. Contractual safeguards, including noncompete clauses, can provide some protection. But if the company's core assets are vulnerable to being appropriated by partners, it may be possible to control their use and strictly limit outside access. Cisco Systems, for example, does not divulge the source code for its designs to its alliance partners, thereby controlling the initiation of all improvements and safeguarding its innovations from imitation.

- *They make commitments to their partners and see that their partners do the same.* When partners make credible commitments to a joint enterprise, they have stronger incentives for making it work and are less likely to "free-ride" on the efforts of other partners. Because of this, equity-based alliances tend to be more successful than nonequity alliances.[47]

- *They make learning a routine part of the management process.* There are always opportunities for learning from a partner, but organizational learning does not take place automatically. Moreover, whatever learning takes place cannot add to a company's knowledge base unless the learning is incorporated into the company's routines and practices. Particularly when the purpose of an alliance is to improve a company's knowledge assets and capabilities, it is important for the company to learn thoroughly and rapidly about its partners' technologies, business practices, and organizational capabilities and then transfer valuable ideas and practices into its own operations promptly.

Finally, managers should realize that alliance management is an organizational capability, much like any other. It develops over time, out of effort, experience, and learning. For this reason, it is wise to begin slowly, with simple alliances, designed to meet limited, short-term objectives. Short-term partnerships that are successful often become the basis for much more extensive collaborative arrangements. Even when strategic alliances are set up with the hope that they will become long-term engagements, they have a better chance of succeeding if they are phased in so that the partners can learn how they can work together most fruitfully.

KEY POINTS

1. Once a company has settled on which of the five generic competitive strategies to employ, attention turns to how strategic choices regarding (1) competitive actions, (2) timing, and (3) scope of operations can complement its competitive approach and maximize the power of its overall strategy.

2. Strategic offensives should, as a general rule, be grounded in a company's strategic assets. The best offensives use a company's resource and capability strengths to attack rivals in the competitive areas where they are comparatively weakest.

3. Companies have a number of offensive strategy options for improving their market positions: using a cost-based advantage to attack competitors on the basis of price or value, leapfrogging competitors with next-generation technologies, pursuing continuous product innovation, adopting and improving the best ideas of others, using hit-and-run tactics to steal sales away from unsuspecting rivals, and launching preemptive strikes. A blue-ocean type of offensive strategy seeks to gain a dramatic and durable competitive advantage by abandoning efforts to beat out competitors in existing markets and, instead, inventing a new industry or distinctive market segment that renders existing competitors largely irrelevant and allows a company to create and capture altogether new demand.

4. The purposes of defensive strategies are to lower the risk of being attacked, weaken the impact of any attack that occurs, and influence challengers to aim their efforts at other rivals. Defensive strategies to protect a company's position usually take one of two forms: (1) actions to block challengers and (2) actions to signal the likelihood of strong retaliation.

5. The timing of strategic moves also has competitive relevance and is especially important when first-mover advantages or disadvantages exist. Company managers are obligated to carefully consider the advantages or disadvantages that attach to being a first mover versus a fast follower versus a wait-and-see late mover.

6. Decisions concerning the scope of a company's operations—which activities a firm will perform internally and which it will not—can also affect the strength of a company's market position. The *scope of the firm* refers to the range of its activities, the breadth of its product and service offerings, the extent of its geographic market presence, and its mix of businesses. Companies can expand their scope horizontally (more broadly within their focal market) or vertically (up or down the chain of value-adding activities that start with raw-material production and end with sales and service to the end consumer). Horizontal mergers and acquisitions (combinations of market rivals) provide a means for a company to expand its horizontal scope. Vertical integration expands a firm's vertical scope.

7. Horizontal mergers and acquisitions can strengthen a firm's competitiveness in five ways: (1) by improving the efficiency of its operations, (2) by heightening its product differentiation, (3) by reducing market rivalry, (3) by increasing the company's bargaining power over suppliers and buyers, and (5) by enhancing its flexibility and dynamic capabilities.

8. Vertical integration, forward or backward, makes strategic sense only if it strengthens a company's position via either cost reduction or creation of a differentiation-based advantage. Otherwise, the drawbacks of vertical integration (increased investment, greater business risk, increased vulnerability to technological changes, less flexibility in making product changes, and the potential for channel conflict) are likely to outweigh any advantages.

9. Outsourcing involves farming out pieces of the value chain formerly performed in-house to outside vendors, thereby narrowing the scope of the firm. Outsourcing can enhance a company's competitiveness whenever (1) an activity can be performed better or more cheaply by outside specialists; (2) having the activity performed by others won't hollow out the outsourcing company's core competencies; (3) it streamlines company operations in ways that improve organizational flexibility, speed decision making, and cut cycle time; (4) it reduces the company's risk exposure; (5) it allows a company to access capabilities more quickly and improves its ability to innovate; and (6) it permits a company to concentrate on its core business and focus on what it does best.

10. Strategic alliances and cooperative partnerships provide one way to gain some of the benefits offered by vertical integration, outsourcing, and horizontal mergers and acquisitions while minimizing the associated problems. They serve as an alternative to vertical integration and mergers and acquisitions; they serve as a supplement to outsourcing, allowing more control relative to outsourcing via arm's-length transactions.

11. Companies that manage their alliances well generally (1) create a system for managing their alliances, (2) build relationships with their partners and establish trust, (3) protect themselves from the threat of opportunism by setting up safeguards, (4) make commitments to their partners and see that their partners do the same, and (5) make learning a routine part of the management process.

ASSURANCE OF LEARNING EXERCISES

LO 2

1. Has Nintendo's timing of strategic moves made it an early-mover or a fast-follower? Could Nintendo's introduction of the Wii be characterized as a Blue Ocean strategy? You may rely on your knowledge of the video game industry and information provided at Nintendo's Investor Relations Web site (www.nintendo.co.jp) to provide justification for your answers to these questions.

LO 4

2. Go to www.bridgstone.co.jp/english/ir, and review information about Bridgestone Corporation's tire and raw-material operations under the About Bridgestone and IR Library links. To what extent is the company vertically integrated? What segments of the vertical chain has the company chosen to enter? What are the benefits and liabilities of Bridgestone's vertical integration strategy?

LO 5, LO 6

3. Go to www.google.com, and do a search on "outsourcing." Identify at least two companies in different industries that have entered into outsourcing agreements with firms with specialized services. In addition, describe what value chain activities the companies have chosen to outsource. Do any of these outsourcing agreements seem likely to threaten any of the companies' competitive capabilities? Are the companies using strategic alliances to manage their outsourcing?

EXERCISES FOR SIMULATION PARTICIPANTS

LO 1

1. What offensive strategy options does your company have? Identify at least two offensive moves that your company should seriously consider to improve the company's market standing and financial performance.

LO 2

2. What options for being a first mover does your company have? Do any of these first-mover options hold competitive advantage potential?

LO 1

3. What defensive strategy moves should your company consider in the upcoming decision round? Identify at least two defensive actions that your company has taken in a past decision round.

LO 3

4. Does your company have the option to merge with or acquire other companies? If so, which rival companies would you like to acquire or merge with?

LO 4

5. Is your company vertically integrated? Explain.

LO 5, LO 6

6. Is your company able to engage in outsourcing? If so, what do you see as the pros and cons of outsourcing? Are strategic alliances involved? Explain.

ENDNOTES

[1] An insightful discussion of aggressive offensive strategies is presented in George Stalk, Jr., and Rob Lachenauer, "Hardball: Five Killer Strategies for Trouncing the Competition," *Harvard Business Review* 82, no. 4 (April 2004), pp. 62–71. For a discussion of offensive strategies to enter attractive markets where existing firms are making above-average profits, see David J. Bryce and Jeffrey H. Dyer, "Strategies to Crack Well-Guarded Markets," *Harvard Business Review* 85, no. 5 (May 2007), pp.

84–92. A discussion of offensive strategies particularly suitable for industry leaders is presented in Richard D'Aveni, "The Empire Strikes Back: Counterrevolutionary Strategies for Industry Leaders," *Harvard Business Review* 80, no. 11 (November 2002), pp. 66–74.
[2] George Stalk, "Playing Hardball: Why Strategy Still Matters," *Ivey Business Journal* 69, no.2 (November–December 2004), pp. 1–2. See K. G. Smith, W. J. Ferrier, and C. M. Grimm, "King of the Hill: Dethroning the

Industry Leader," *Academy of Management Executive* 15, no. 2 (May 2001), pp. 59–70; also see W. J. Ferrier, K. G. Smith, and C. M. Grimm, "The Role of Competitive Action in Market Share Erosion and Industry Dethronement: A Study of Industry Leaders and Challengers," *Academy of Management Journal* 42, no. 4 (August 1999), pp. 372–88.
[3] For a discussion of how to wage offensives against strong rivals, see David B. Yoffie and Mary Kwak, "Mastering Balance: How to Meet and Beat a Stronger Opponent," *California*

Management Review 44, no. 2 (Winter 2002), pp. 8–24.

[4] Stalk, "Playing Hardball," pp. 1–2.

[5] Ian C. MacMillan, Alexander B. van Putten, and Rita Gunther McGrath, "Global Gamesmanship," *Harvard Business Review* 81, no. 5 (May 2003), pp. 66–67; also see Ashkay R. Rao, Mark E. Bergen, and Scott Davis, "How to Fight a Price War," *Harvard Business Review* 78, no. 2 (March–April 2000), pp. 107–16.

[6] D. B. Yoffie and M. A. Cusumano, "Judo Strategy—The Competitive Dynamics of Internet Time," *Harvard Business* Review 77, no. 1 (January–February 1999), pp. 70–81.

[7] Stalk and Lachenauer, "Hardball: Five Killer Strategies," p. 64.

[8] For an interesting study of how small firms can successfully employ guerrilla-style tactics, see Ming-Jer Chen and Donald C. Hambrick, "Speed, Stealth, and Selective Attack: How Small Firms Differ from Large Firms in Competitive Behavior," *Academy of Management Journal* 38, no. 2 (April 1995), pp. 453–82. Other discussions of guerrilla offensives can be found in Ian MacMillan, "How Business Strategists Can Use Guerrilla Warfare Tactics," *Journal of Business Strategy* 1, no. 2 (Fall 1980), pp. 63–65; William E. Rothschild, "Surprise and the Competitive Advantage," *Journal of Business Strategy* 4, no. 3 (Winter 1984), pp. 10–18; Kathryn R. Harrigan, *Strategic Flexibility* (Lexington, MA: Lexington Books, 1985), pp. 30–45; Liam Fahey, "Guerrilla Strategy: The Hit-and-Run Attack," in Liam Fahey (ed.), *The Strategic Management Planning Reader* (Englewood Cliffs, NJ: Prentice Hall, 1989), pp. 194–97.

[9] Yoffie and Cusumano, "Judo Strategy." See also D. B. Yoffie and M. Kwak, "Mastering Balance: How to Meet and Beat a Stronger Opponent," *California Management Review* 44, no. 2 (Winter 2002), pp. 8–24.

[10] The use of preemptive strike offensives is treated comprehensively in Ian MacMillan, "Preemptive Strategies," *Journal of Business Strategy* 14, no. 2 (Fall 1983), pp. 16–26.

[11] Ian C. MacMillan, "How Long Can You Sustain a Competitive Advantage?" in Liam Fahey (ed.), *The Strategic Planning Management Reader* (Englewood Cliffs, NJ: Prentice Hall, 1989), pp. 23–24.

[12] For a discussion of competitors' reactions, see Kevin P. Coyne and John Horn, "Predicting Your Competitor's Reactions," *Harvard Business Review* 87 no. 4 (April 2009), pp. 90–97.

[13] Philip Kotler, *Marketing Management,* 5th ed. (Englewood Cliffs, NJ: Prentice Hall, 1984), p. 400.

[14] Michael E. Porter, *Competitive Advantage* (New York: Free Press, 1985), p. 518.

[15] W. Chan Kim and Renée Mauborgne, "Blue Ocean Strategy," *Harvard Business Review* 82, no. 10 (October 2004), pp. 76–84.

[16] Porter, *Competitive Advantage,* pp. 489–94.

[17] Ibid., pp. 495–97. The list here is selective; Porter offers a greater number of options.

[18] Ibid., pp. 232–33.

[19] For research evidence on the effects of pioneering versus following, see Jeffrey G. Covin, Dennis P. Slevin, and Michael B. Heeley, "Pioneers and Followers: Competitive Tactics, Environment, and Growth," *Journal of Business Venturing* 15, no. 2 (March 1999), pp. 175–210; Christopher A. Bartlett and Sumantra Ghoshal, "Going Global: Lessons from Late-Movers," *Harvard Business Review* 78, no. 2 (March–April 2000), pp. 132–45.

[20] Gary Hamel, "Smart Mover, Dumb Mover," *Fortune,* September 3, 2001, p. 195.

[21] Ibid., p.192; Costas Markides and Paul A. Geroski, Racing to be 2nd: Conquering the Industries of the Future," *Business Strategy Review* 15, no. 4 (Winter 2004), pp. 25–31.

[22] For a more extensive discussion, see Fernando Suarez and Gianvito Lanzolla, "The Half-Truth of First-Mover Advantage," *Harvard Business Review* 83, no. 4 (April 2005), pp. 121–27.

[23] Henry Gibbon, "Worldwide M&A Declines 28% to US$2trn," *Acquisitions Monthly,* January 2010 (issue 303), pp. 4–11.

[24] For an excellent review of the strategic objectives of various types of mergers and acquisitions and the managerial challenges that different kinds of mergers and acquisitions present, see Joseph L. Bower, "Not All M&As Are Alike—and That Matters," *Harvard Business Review* 79, no. 3 (March 2001), pp. 93–101.

[25] O. Chatain and P. Zemsky, "The Horizontal Scope of the Firm: Organizational Tradeoffs vs. Buyer-Supplier Relationships," *Management Science* 53, no. 4 (April 2007), pp. 550–65.

[26] For a more expansive discussion, see Jeffrey H. Dyer, Prashant Kale, and Harbir Singh, "When to Ally and When to Acquire," *Harvard Business Review* 82, no. 4 (July–August 2004), pp. 109–10.

[27] See Kathryn R. Harrigan, "Matching Vertical Integration Strategies to Competitive Conditions," *Strategic Management Journal* 7, no. 6 (November–December 1986), pp. 535–56; for a more extensive discussion of the advantages and disadvantages of vertical integration, see John Stuckey and David White, "When and When Not to Vertically Integrate," *Sloan Management Review* (Spring 1993), pp. 71–83.

[28] The resilience of vertical integration strategies despite the disadvantages is discussed in Thomas Osegowitsch and Anoop Madhok, "Vertical Integration Is Dead, or Is It?" *Business Horizons* 46, no. 2 (March–April 2003), pp. 25–35.

[29] For a good overview of outsourcing strategies, see Ronan McIvor, "What Is the Right Outsourcing Strategy for Your Process?" *European Management Journal* 26, no. 1 (February 2008), pp. 24–34.

[30] For a good discussion of the problems that can arise from outsourcing, see Gary P. Pisano and Willy C. Shih, "Restoring American Competitiveness," *Harvard Business Review* 87, no. 7–8 (July–August 2009), pp. 114–25; Jérôme Barthélemy, "The Seven Deadly Sins of Outsourcing," *Academy of Management Executive* 17, no. 2 (May 2003), pp. 87–100.

[31] Pisano and Shih, "Restoring American Competitivness," pp. 116–17.

[32] Jason Wakeam, "The Five Factors of a Strategic Alliance," *Ivey Business Journal* 68, no 3 (May–June 2003), pp. 1–4.

[33] *Advertising Age,* May 24, 2010, p. 14.

[34] Salvatore Parise and Lisa Sasson, "Leveraging Knowledge Management across Strategic Alliances," *Ivey Business Journal* 66, no. 4 (March–April 2002), p. 42.

[35] David Ernst and James Bamford, "Your Alliances Are Too Stable," *Harvard Business Review* 83, no. 6 (June 2005), p.133.

[36] An excellent discussion of the portfolio approach to managing multiple alliances and how to restructure a faltering alliance is presented in Ernst and Bamford, "Your Alliances Are Too Stable," pp. 133–41.

[37] Michael E. Porter, *The Competitive Advantage of Nations* (New York: Free Press, 1990), p. 66. For a discussion of how to realize the advantages of strategic partnerships, see Nancy J. Kaplan and Jonathan Hurd, "Realizing the Promise of Partnerships," *Journal of Business Strategy* 23, no. 3 (May–June 2002), pp. 38–42; Parise and Sasson, "Leveraging Knowledge Management across Strategic Alliances," pp. 41-47; Ernst and Bamford, "Your Alliances Are Too Stable," pp. 133–41; and Jonathan Hughes and Jeff Weiss, "Simple Rules for Making Alliances Work," *Harvard Business Review* 85, no. 11 (November 2007), pp. 122–31.

[38] For a discussion of how to raise the chances that a strategic alliance will produce strategically important outcomes, see M. Koza and A. Lewin, "Managing Partnerships and Strategic Alliances: Raising the Odds of Success," *European Management Journal* 18, no. 2 (April 2000), pp. 146–51.

[39] A. Inkpen, "Learning, Knowledge Acquisition, and Strategic Alliances," *European Management Journal* 16, no. 2 (April 1998), pp. 223–29.

[40] Yves L. Doz and Gary Hamel, *Alliance Advantage: The Art of Creating Value through Partnering* (Boston: Harvard Business School Press), chap. 1.

[41] Ibid.

[42] Ibid., chaps. 4–8; Patricia Anslinger and Justin Jenk, "Creating Successful Alliances," *Journal of Business Strategy* 25, no. 2 (2004), pp. 18–23; Rosabeth Moss Kanter, "Collaborative Advantage: The Art of the Alliance," *Harvard Business Review* 72, no. 4 (July–August 1994), pp. 96–108; Joel Bleeke and David Ernst, "The Way to Win in Cross-Border Alliances," *Harvard Business Review* 69, no. 6 (November–December 1991), pp. 127–35; Gary Hamel, Yves L. Doz, and C. K. Prahalad, "Collaborate with Your Competitors—and Win," *Harvard Business Review* 67, no. 1 (January–February 1989), pp. 133–39; Hughes and Weiss, "Simple Rules for Making Alliances Work."

[43] J. B. Cullen, J. L. Johnson, and T. Sakano, "Success through Commitment and Trust: The Soft Side of Strategic Alliance Management," *Journal of World Business* 35, no. 3 (Fall 2000), pp. 223–40; T. K. Das and B. S. Teng, "Between Trust and Control: Developing Confidence in Partner Cooperation in Alliances," *Academy of Management Review* 23, no. 3 (July 1998), pp. 491–512.

[44] K. M. Eisenhardt and C. B. Schoonhoven, "Resource-Based View of Strategic Alliance Formation: Strategic and Social Effects in Entrepreneurial Firms," *Organization Science* 7, no. 2 (March–April 1996), pp. 136–50; M. Zollo, J. J. Reuer, and H. Singh, "Interorganizational Routines and Performance in Strategic Alliances," *Organization Science* 13, no. 6 (November–December 2002), pp. 701–13.

[45] The pros and cons of mergers/acquisitions versus strategic alliances are described in Dyer, Kale, and Singh, "When to Ally and When to Acquire," pp. 109–15.

[46] Hughes and Weiss, "Simple Rules for Making Alliances Work," p. 122.

[47] Y. G. Pan and D. K. Tse, "The Hierarchical Model of Market Entry Modes," *Journal of International Business Studies* 31, no. 4 (2000), pp. 535–54.

CHAPTER 7

STRATEGIES FOR COMPETING IN INTERNATIONAL MARKETS

We're not going global because we want to or because of any megalomania, but because it's really necessary. . . . The costs are so enormous today that you really need to have worldwide revenues to cover them.

—Rupert Murdoch
CEO of the media conglomerate News Corporation

Globalization [provides] a long-lasting competitive advantage. If we build a new gas turbine, in 18 months our competitors also have one. But building a global company is not so easy to copy.

—Percy Barnevik
Former CEO of the Swiss-Swedish industrial corporation ABB

Capital, technology, and ideas flow these days like quicksilver across national boundaries.

—Robert H. Waterman, Jr.
Internationally recognized expert on management practices

LEARNING OBJECTIVES

LO 1. Develop an understanding of the primary reasons companies choose to compete in international markets.

LO 2. Learn how and why differing market conditions across countries and industries make crafting international strategy a complex undertaking.

LO 3. Learn about the major strategic options for entering and competing in foreign markets.

LO 4. Gain familiarity with the three main strategic approaches for competing internationally.

LO 5. Understand how international companies go about building competitive advantage in foreign markets.

Any company that aspires to industry leadership in the 21st century must think in terms of global, not domestic, market leadership. The world economy is globalizing at an accelerating pace as ambitious growth-minded companies race to build stronger competitive positions in the markets of more and more countries, as countries previously closed to foreign companies open up their markets, as companies in developing countries gain competitive strength, and as advances in information technology and communication shrink the importance of geographic distance. The forces of globalization are changing the competitive landscape in many industries, offering companies attractive new opportunities but at the same time introducing new competitive threats. Companies in industries where these forces are greatest are therefore under considerable pressure to come up with a strategy for competing successfully in foreign markets.

This chapter focuses on strategy options for expanding beyond domestic boundaries and competing in the markets of either a few or a great many countries. In the process of exploring these issues, we will introduce such concepts as multidomestic, global, and transnational strategies; the Porter diamond of national advantage; and cross-country differences in cultural, demographic, and market conditions. The chapter also includes sections on strategy options for entering and competing in foreign markets; the importance of locating value chain operations in the most advantageous countries; and the special circumstances of competing in such developing markets as China, India, Brazil, Russia, and eastern Europe.

WHY COMPANIES DECIDE TO ENTER FOREIGN MARKETS

LO 1

Develop an understanding of the primary reasons companies choose to compete in international markets.

A company may opt to expand outside its domestic market for any of five major reasons:

1. *To gain access to new customers.* Expanding into foreign markets offers potential for increased revenues, profits, and long-term growth and becomes an especially attractive option when a company's home markets are mature and nearing saturation levels. Companies often expand internationally to extend the life cycle of their products, as Honda has done with its classic 50-cc motorcycle, the Honda cub (which is still selling well in developing markets, more than 50 years after it was first introduced in Japan). A larger target market also offers companies the opportunity to earn a return on large investments more rapidly. This can be particularly important in R&D-intensive industries, where development is fast-paced or competitors imitate innovations rapidly.

2. *To achieve lower costs through economies of scale, experience, and increased purchasing power.* Many companies are driven to sell in more than one country because domestic sales volume alone is not large enough to fully capture economies of scale in product development, manufacturing, or marketing. Similarly, firms expand internationally to increase the rate at which they accumulate experience and move down the learning curve. International expansion can also lower a company's input costs through greater pooled purchasing power. The relatively small size of country markets in Europe and limited domestic volume explains why companies like Michelin, BMW, and Nestlé long ago began selling their products all across Europe and then moved into markets in North America and Latin America.

3. *To further exploit its core competencies.* A company with competitively valuable resources and capabilities can often extend a market-leading position in its home market into a position of regional or global market leadership by leveraging these resources further. Nokia's competencies and capabilities in mobile phones have propelled it to global market leadership in the wireless telecommunications business. Walmart is capitalizing on its considerable expertise in discount retailing to expand into China, Latin America, Japan, South Korea, and the United Kingdom; Walmart executives believe the company has tremendous growth opportunities in China. Companies can often leverage their resources internationally by replicating a successful business model, using it as a basic blueprint for international operations, as Starbucks and McDonald's have done.[1]

4. *To gain access to resources and capabilities located in foreign markets.* An increasingly important motive for entering foreign markets is to acquire resources and capabilities that cannot be accessed as readily in a company's home market. Companies often enter into cross-border alliances or joint ventures, for example, to gain access to resources and capabilities that complement their own or to learn from their partners.[2] Cross-border acquisitions are commonly made for similar reasons.[3] In other cases, companies choose to establish operations in other countries to utilize local distribution networks, employ low-cost human resources, or acquire technical knowledge. In a few

cases, companies in industries based on natural resources (e.g., oil and gas, minerals, rubber, and lumber) find it necessary to operate in the international arena because attractive raw-material supplies are located in many different parts of the world.

5. *To spread its business risk across a wider market base.* A company spreads business risk by operating in many different countries rather than depending entirely on operations in a few countries. Thus, when a company with operations across much of the world encounters economic downturns in certain countries, its performance may be bolstered by buoyant sales elsewhere.

In addition, companies that are the suppliers of other companies often expand internationally when their major customers do so, to meet their needs abroad and retain their position as a key supply chain partner. Automotive parts suppliers, for example, have followed automobile manufacturers abroad, and retail goods suppliers have followed large retailers into foreign markets.

WHY COMPETING ACROSS NATIONAL BORDERS MAKES STRATEGY MAKING MORE COMPLEX

Crafting a strategy to compete in one or more countries of the world is inherently more complex because of (1) factors that affect industry competitiveness that vary from country to country, (2) the potential for location-based advantages in certain countries, (3) different government policies and economic conditions that make the business climate more favorable in some countries than in others, (4) the risks of adverse shifts in currency exchange rates, and (5) cross-country differences in cultural, demographic, and market conditions.

LO 2

Learn how and why differing market conditions across countries and industries make crafting international strategy a complex undertaking.

Cross-Country Variation in Factors That Affect Industry Competitiveness

Certain countries are known for their strengths in particular industries. For example, Chile has competitive strengths in industries such as copper, fruit, fish products, paper and pulp, chemicals, and wine. Japan is known for competitive strength in consumer electronics, automobiles, semiconductors, steel products, and specialty steel. Where industries are more likely to develop competitive strength depends on a set of factors that describe the nature of each country's business environment and vary across countries. Because strong industries are made up of strong firms, the strategies of firms that expand internationally are usually grounded in one or more of these factors. The four major factors are summarized in a framework known as the *Diamond of National Advantage* (see Figure 7.1).[4]

Demand Conditions
The demand conditions in an industry's home market include the relative size of the market and the nature of domestic buyers' needs and wants. Industry sectors that are larger and more important in their home market tend to attract more resources and grow faster than others. Demanding domestic buyers for an industry's products spur greater innovativeness and improvements in quality. Such conditions foster the development of stronger

Figure 7.1 The Diamond of National Advantage

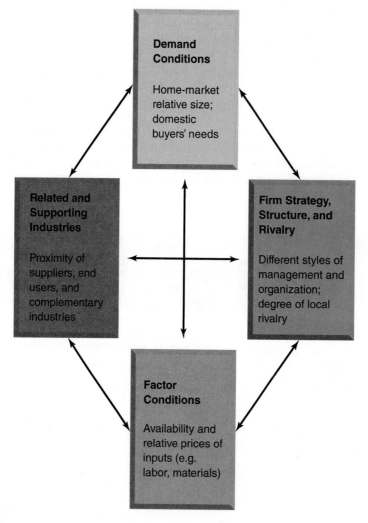

Source: Adapted from M. Porter, "The Competitive Advantage of Nations," *Harvard Business Review,* March–April 1990, pp. 73–93.

industries, with firms that are capable of translating a home-market advantage into a competitive advantage in the international arena.

Factor Conditions Factor conditions describe the availability, quality, and cost of raw materials and other inputs (called *factors*) that firms in an industry require to produce their products and services. The relevant factors vary from industry to industry but can include different types of labor, technical or managerial knowledge, land, financial capital, and natural resources. Elements of a country's infrastructure may be included as well, such as its transportation, communication, and banking system. For instance, in India there are efficient, well-developed national channels for distributing trucks, scooters, farm equipment, groceries, personal care items, and other packaged products to the country's 3 million retailers, whereas in China distribution is primarily local and there is a limited national network for distributing most products. Competitively strong industries and firms develop where relevant factor conditions are favorable.

Related and Supporting Industries   Robust industries often develop as part of a cluster of related industries, including suppliers of components and capital equipment, end users, and the makers of complementary products, including those that are technologically related. The sports car makers Ferrari and Maserati, for example, are located in an area of Italy known as the "engine technological district" that includes other firms involved in racing, such as Ducati Motorcycles, along with hundreds of small suppliers. The advantage to firms that develop as part of a related-industry cluster comes from the close collaboration with key suppliers and the greater knowledge sharing throughout the cluster, resulting in greater efficiency and innovativeness.

Firm Strategy, Structure, and Rivalry   Different country environments foster the development of different styles of management, organization, and strategy. For example, strategic alliances are a more common strategy for firms from Asian or Latin American countries, which emphasize trust and cooperation in their organizations, than for firms from North American, where individualism is more influential. In addition, countries vary in terms of the competitiveness of their industries. Fierce competitive conditions in home markets tend to hone domestic firms' competitive capabilities and ready them for competing internationally.

For an industry in a particular country to become competitively strong, all four factors must be favorable for that industry. When they are, the industry is likely to contain firms that are capable of competing successfully in the international arena. Thus the diamond framework can be used to reveal the answers to several questions that are important for competing on an international basis. First, it can help predict where foreign entrants into an industry are most likely to come from. This can help managers prepare to cope with new foreign competitors, since the framework also reveals something about the basis of the new rivals' strengths. Second, it can reveal the countries in which foreign rivals are likely to be weakest and thus help managers decide which foreign markets to enter first. And third, because it focuses on the attributes of a country's business environment that allow firms to flourish, it reveals something about the advantages of conducting particular business activities in that country. Thus the diamond framework is an aid to deciding where to locate different value chain activities most beneficially—a topic that we address next.

Locating Value Chain Activities for Competitive Advantage

Increasingly, companies are locating different value chain activities in different parts of the world to exploit location-based advantages that vary from country to country. This is particularly evident with respect to the location of manufacturing activities. Differences in wage rates, worker productivity, energy costs, environmental regulations, tax rates, inflation rates, and the like, create sizable variations in manufacturing costs from country to country. By locating its plants in certain countries, firms in some industries can reap major manufacturing cost advantages because of lower input costs (especially labor), relaxed government regulations, the proximity of suppliers and technologically related industries, or unique natural resources. In such cases, the low-cost countries become principal production sites, with most of the output being exported to markets in other parts of the world. Companies that build production facilities in low-cost countries (or that source their products from contract manufacturers in these countries) gain a competitive advantage over rivals with plants in countries where costs are higher. The competitive role of low manufacturing costs is most evident in low-wage countries like China, India, Pakistan, Cambodia, Vietnam, Mexico, Brazil, Guatemala, the Philippines, and several countries in Africa and eastern Europe that have become production havens for manufactured goods with high labor content (especially textiles and apparel). Hourly compensation for production workers in 2007 averaged about $0.81 in China versus about $1.10 in the Philippines, $2.92 in Mexico, $5.96 in Brazil, $6.58 in Taiwan, $7.91 in Hungary, $8.27 in Portugal, $19.75 in Japan, $24.59 in the United States, $28.91 in Canada, $37.66 in Germany, and $48.56 in Norway.[5] China is fast becoming the manufacturing capital of the world—virtually all of the world's major manufacturing companies now have facilities in China.

For other types of value chain activities, input quality or availability are more important considerations. Tiffany entered the mining industry in Canada to access diamonds that could be certified as "conflict free" and not associated with either the funding of African wars or unethical mining conditions. Many U.S. companies locate call centers in countries such as India and Ireland, where English is spoken and the workforce is well educated. Other companies locate R&D activities in countries where there are prestigious research institutions and well-trained scientists and engineers. Likewise, concerns about short delivery times and low shipping costs make some countries better locations than others for establishing distribution centers.

The Impact of Government Policies and Economic Conditions in Host Countries

Cross-country variations in government policies and economic conditions affect both the opportunities available to a foreign entrant and the risks of operating within that country. The governments of some countries are anxious to attract foreign investments and go all out to create a business climate that outsiders will view as favorable. A good example is Ireland, which has one of the world's most pro-business environments. Ireland offers companies very low corporate tax rates, has a government that is responsive to the needs of industry, and aggressively recruits high-tech manufacturing facilities and international companies. Ireland's policies were a major factor in Intel's decision to locate a $2.5 billion chip manufacturing plant in Ireland that employs over 4,000 people. Governments anxious to spur economic growth, create more jobs, and raise living standards for their citizens usually enact policies aimed at stimulating business innovation and capital investment. They may provide incentives such as reduced taxes, low-cost loans, site location and site development assistance, and government-sponsored training for workers to encourage companies to construct production and distribution facilities. When new business-related issues or developments arise, pro-business governments make a practice of seeking advice and counsel from business leaders. When tougher business-related regulations are deemed appropriate, they endeavor to make the transition to more costly and stringent regulations somewhat business-friendly rather than adversarial.

On the other hand, governments sometimes enact policies that, from a business perspective, make locating facilities within a country's borders less attractive. For example, the nature of a company's operations may make it particularly costly to achieve compliance with a country's environmental regulations. Some governments, desirous of discouraging foreign imports, provide subsidies and low-interest loans to domestic companies (to enable them to better compete against foreign companies), enact deliberately burdensome procedures and requirements for imported goods to pass customs inspection (to make it harder for imported goods to compete against the products of local businesses), and impose tariffs or quotas on the imports of certain goods (also to help protect local businesses from foreign competition). They may also specify that a certain percentage of the parts and components used in manufacturing a product be obtained from local suppliers, require prior approval of capital spending projects, limit withdrawal of funds from the country, and require minority (sometimes majority) ownership of foreign company operations by local companies or investors. Sometimes foreign companies wanting only to sell their products in a country face a web of regulations regarding technical standards and product certification. Political leaders in some countries may be openly hostile to or suspicious of companies from certain foreign countries operating within their borders. Moreover, there are times when a government may place restrictions on exports to ensure adequate local supplies and regulate the prices of imported and locally produced goods. Such government actions make a country's business climate less attractive and in some cases may be sufficiently onerous as to discourage a company from locating production or distribution facilities in that country or maybe even selling its products in that country.

The decision about whether to enter a particular country must take into account the degree of political and economic risk. **Political risks** stem from government hostility to foreign business, weak governments, and political instability. In industries that a government deems critical to the national welfare, there is sometimes a risk that the government will nationalize the industry and expropriate the assets of foreign companies. In 2010, for example, Ecuador threatened to expropriate the holdings of all foreign oil companies that refused to sign new contracts giving the state control of all production. Other political risks include the loss of investments due to war or political unrest, regulatory changes that create operating uncertainties, security risks due to terrorism, and corruption. **Economic risks** are intertwined with political risks but also stem from factors such as inflation rates and the stability of a country's monetary system. The threat of piracy and lack of protection for intellectual property are important sources of economic risk. Another is fluctuations in the value of different currencies—a factor that we discuss in more detail next.

CORE CONCEPTS

Political risks stem from instability or weakness in national governments and hostility to foreign business. **Economic risks** stem from the stability of a country's monetary system, economic and regulatory policies, lack of property rights protections, and risks due to exchange rate fluctuation.

The Risks of Adverse Exchange Rate Shifts

When companies produce and market their products and services in many different countries, they are subject to the impacts of sometimes favorable and sometimes unfavorable changes in currency exchange rates. The rates of exchange between different currencies can vary by as much as 20 to 40 percent annually, with the changes occurring sometimes gradually and sometimes swiftly. Sizable shifts in exchange rates, which tend to be hard to predict because of the variety of factors involved and the uncertainties surrounding when and by how much these factors will change, shuffle the global cards of which countries represent the low-cost manufacturing locations and which rivals have the upper hand in the marketplace.

To understand the economic risks associated with fluctuating exchange rates, consider the case of a U.S. company that has located manufacturing facilities in Brazil (where the currency is reals—pronounced "ray-alls") and that exports most of the Brazilian-made goods to markets in the European Union (where the currency is euros). To keep the numbers simple, assume that the exchange rate is 4 Brazilian reals for 1 euro and that the product being made in Brazil has a manufacturing cost of 4 Brazilian reals (or 1 euro). Now suppose that for some reason the exchange rate shifts from 4 reals per euro to 5 reals per euro (meaning that the real has declined in value and that the euro is stronger). Making the product in Brazil is now more cost-competitive because a Brazilian good costing 4 reals to produce has fallen to only 0.8 euro at the new exchange rate (4 reals divided by 5 reals per euro = 0.8 euro) and this clearly puts the producer of the Brazilian-made good *in a better position to compete* against the European makers of the same good. On the other hand, should the value of the Brazilian real grow stronger in relation to the euro—resulting in an exchange rate of 3 reals to 1 euro—the same Brazilian-made good formerly costing 4 reals (or 1 euro) to produce now has a cost of 1.33 euros (4 reals divided by 3 reals per euro = 1.33 euros) and this puts the producer of the Brazilian-made good in a weaker competitive position vis-à-vis European producers of the same good. Clearly, the attraction of manufacturing a good in Brazil and selling it in Europe is far greater when the euro is strong (an exchange rate of 1 euro for 5 Brazilian reals) than when the euro is weak and exchanges for only 3 Brazilian reals.

But there is one more piece to the story. When the exchange rate changes from 4 reals per euro to 5 reals per euro, not only is the cost competitiveness of the Brazilian manufacturer stronger relative to European manufacturers of the same item but the Brazilian-made good that formerly cost 1 euro and now costs

Fluctuating exchange rates pose significant economic risks to a company's competitiveness in foreign markets. Exporters are disadvantaged when the currency of the country where goods are being manufactured grows stronger relative to the currency of the importing country.

only 0.8 euro can also be sold to consumers in the European Union for a lower euro price than before. In other words, the combination of a stronger euro and a weaker real acts to *lower the price of Brazilian-made goods* in all the countries that are members of the European Union, and this is likely to *spur sales of the Brazilian-made good in Europe and boost Brazilian exports to Europe.* Conversely, should the exchange rate shift from 4 reals per euro to 3 reals per euro—which makes the Brazilian manufacturer less cost competitive with European manufacturers of the same item—the Brazilian-made good that formerly cost 1 euro and now costs 1.33 euros will sell for a higher price in euros than before, thus weakening the demand of European consumers for Brazilian-made goods and acting to reduce Brazilian exports to Europe. Thus *Brazilian exporters are likely to experience (1) rising demand for their goods in Europe whenever the Brazilian real grows weaker relative to the euro and (2) falling demand for their goods in Europe whenever the real grows stronger relative to the euro.*

Insofar as U.S.-based manufacturers are concerned, declines in the value of the U.S. dollar against foreign currencies act to reduce or eliminate whatever cost advantage foreign manufacturers might have over U.S. manufacturers and can even prompt foreign companies to establish production plants in the United States. Likewise, a weak euro versus other currencies enhances the cost competitiveness of companies manufacturing goods in Europe for export to foreign markets; a strong euro versus other currencies weakens the cost competitiveness of

European plants that manufacture goods for export. The growing strength of the euro relative to the U.S. dollar has encouraged a number of European manufacturers such as Volkswagen, Fiat, and Airbus to shift production from European factories to new facilities in the United States. Also, the weakening dollar caused Chrysler to discontinue its contract manufacturing agreement with an Austrian firm for assembly of minivans and Jeeps sold in Europe. Beginning in 2008, Chrysler's vehicles sold in Europe were exported from its factories in Illinois and Missouri. The weak dollar was also a factor in Ford's and GM's recent decisions to begin exporting U.S.-made vehicles to China and Latin America.

Domestic companies facing competitive pressure from lower-cost imports are benefited when their government's currency grows *weaker* in relation to the currencies of the countries where the lower-cost goods are being made.

It is important to note that *currency exchange rates are rather unpredictable,* swinging first one way and then another way, so the competitiveness of any company's facilities in any country is partly dependent on whether exchange rate changes over time have a favorable or unfavorable cost impact. Companies producing goods in one country for export abroad always improve their cost competitiveness when the country's currency grows weaker relative to currencies of the countries where the goods are being exported to, and they find their cost competitiveness eroded when the local currency grow stronger. On the other hand, domestic companies that are under pressure from lower-cost imported goods become more cost competitive when their currency grows weaker in relation to the currencies of the countries where the imported goods are made—in other words, a U.S. manufacturer views a weaker U.S. dollar as a *favorable exchange rate shift* because such shifts help make its costs more competitive than those of foreign rivals.

Cross-Country Differences in Demographic, Cultural, and Market Conditions

Differing population sizes, income levels, and other demographic factors give rise to considerable differences in market size and growth rates from country to country. Less than 20 percent of the populations of Brazil, India, and China have annual purchasing power equivalent to $25,000. Middle-class consumers represent a much smaller portion of the population in these and other developing countries than in North America, Japan, and much of western Europe—China's middle class numbers about 300 million out of a population of 1.35 billion.[6] At the same time, in developing markets like India, China, Brazil, and Malaysia, market growth potential is far higher than it is in the more mature economies of Britain, Denmark, Canada, and Japan. The potential for market growth in automobiles is explosive in China, where 2009 sales of new vehicles amounted to 13.6 million, surpassing U.S. sales of 10 million and making China the world's largest market.[7] Owing to widely differing population demographics and income levels, there is a far bigger market for luxury automobiles in the United States and Germany than in Argentina, India, Mexico, China, and Thailand.

Buyer tastes for a particular product or service sometimes differ substantially from country to country. In France consumers prefer top-loading washing machines, while in most other European countries consumers prefer front-loading machines. Soups that appeal to Swedish consumers are not popular in Malaysia. Italian coffee drinkers prefer espressos, but in North America the preference is for mild-roasted coffees. Sometimes, product designs suitable in one country are inappropriate in another because of differing local standards—for example, in the United States electrical devices run on 110-volt electric systems, but in some

European countries the standard is a 240-volt electric system, necessitating the use of different electrical designs and components. Cultural influences can also affect consumer demand for a product. For instance, in South Korea, many parents are reluctant to purchase PCs even when they can afford them because of concerns that their children will be distracted from their schoolwork by surfing the Web, playing PC-based video games, and becoming Internet "addicts."[8]

Consequently, companies operating in an international marketplace have to wrestle with *whether and how much to customize their offerings in each different country market to match the tastes and preferences of local buyers or whether to pursue a strategy of offering a mostly standardized product worldwide.* While making products that are closely matched to local tastes makes them more appealing to local buyers, customizing a company's products country by country may have the effect of raising production and distribution costs due to the greater variety of designs and components, shorter production runs, and the complications of added inventory handling and distribution logistics. Greater standardization of a multinational company's product offering, on the other hand, can lead to scale economies and learning curve effects, thus contributing to the achievement of a low-cost advantage. *The tension between the market pressures to localize a company's product offerings country by country and the competitive pressures to lower costs is one of the big strategic issues that participants in foreign markets have to resolve.*

THE CONCEPTS OF MULTIDOMESTIC COMPETITION AND GLOBAL COMPETITION

In crafting a strategy to compete on an international basis, it is essential for managers to recognize that the pattern of international competition varies in important ways from industry to industry.[9] At one extreme is **multidomestic competition,** in which there's so much cross-country variation in market conditions and in the companies contending for leadership that the market contest among rivals in one country is localized and not closely connected to the market contests in other countries. The standout features of multidomestic competition are that (1) buyers in different countries are attracted to different product attributes, (2) sellers vary from country to country, and (3) industry conditions and competitive forces in each national market differ in important respects. Take the banking industry in Poland, Mexico, and Australia as an example—the requirements and expectations of banking customers vary among the three countries, the lead banking competitors in Poland differ from those in Mexico or Australia, and the competitive battle going on among the leading banks in Poland is unrelated to the rivalry taking place in Mexico or Australia. Thus, with multidomestic competition, rival firms battle for national championships and winning in one country does not necessarily signal the ability to fare well in other countries. In multidomestic competition, the power of a company's strategy and capabilities in one country has little impact on its competitiveness in other countries where it operates. Moreover, any competitive advantage a company secures in one country is largely confined to that country; the spillover effects to other countries are minimal to nonexistent.

CORE CONCEPT

Multidomestic competition exists when the competition among rivals in each country market is localized and not closely connected to the competition in other country markets—there is no world market, just a collection of self-contained local markets.

Industries characterized by multidomestic competition include radio and TV broadcasting, consumer banking, life insurance, apparel, metals fabrication, many types of food products (coffee, cereals, breads, canned goods, frozen foods), and retailing.

At the other extreme is **global competition,** in which prices and competitive conditions across country markets are strongly linked and the term *global* has true meaning. In a globally competitive industry, much the same group of rival companies competes in many different countries but especially in countries where sales volumes are large and where having a competitive presence is strategically important to building a strong global position in the industry. Thus, a company's competitive position in one country both affects and is affected by its position in other countries. In global competition, a firm's overall competitive advantage grows out of its entire worldwide operations; the competitive advantage it creates at its home base is supplemented by advantages growing out of its operations in other countries (having plants in low-wage countries, being able to transfer expertise from country to country, having the capability to serve customers that also have multinational operations, and having brand-name recognition in many parts of the world). Rival firms in globally competitive industries vie for worldwide leadership. Global competition exists in motor vehicles, television sets, tires, cell phones, personal computers, copiers, watches, digital cameras, bicycles, and commercial aircraft.

> **CORE CONCEPT**
>
> **Global competition** exists when competitive conditions across national markets are linked strongly enough to form a true world market and when leading competitors compete head to head in many different countries.

An industry can have segments that are globally competitive and segments in which competition is country by country.[10] In the hotel/motel industry, for example, the low- and medium-priced segments are characterized by multidomestic competition—competitors mainly serve travelers within the same country. In the business and luxury segments, however, competition is more globalized. Companies like Nikki (owned by Japan Airlines), Marriott, Sheraton, and Hilton have hotels at many international locations, use worldwide reservation systems, and establish common quality and service standards to gain marketing advantages in serving businesspeople and other travelers who make frequent international trips. In lubricants, the marine engine segment is globally competitive—ships move from port to port and require the same oil everywhere they stop. Brand reputations in marine lubricants have a global scope, and successful marine engine lubricant producers (ExxonMobil, BP Amoco, and Shell) operate globally. In automotive motor oil, however, multidomestic competition dominates—countries have different weather conditions and driving patterns, production of motor oil is subject to limited scale economies, shipping costs are high, and retail distribution channels differ markedly from country to country. Thus, domestic firms—like Quaker State and Pennzoil in the United States and Castrol in Great Britain—can be leaders in their home markets without competing globally.

It is also important to recognize that an industry can be in transition from multidomestic competition to global competition. In a number of today's industries—beer and major home appliances are prime examples—leading domestic competitors have begun expanding into more and more foreign markets, often acquiring local companies or brands and integrating them into their operations. As some industry members start to build global brands and a global presence, other industry members find themselves pressured to follow the same strategic path—especially if establishing multinational operations results in important scale economies and a powerhouse brand name. As the industry consolidates to fewer players, such that many of the same companies find themselves in head-to-head competition in more and more country markets, global competition begins to replace multidomestic competition.

At the same time, consumer tastes in a number of important product categories are converging across the world. Less diversity of tastes and preferences opens the way for companies to create global brands and sell essentially the same products in almost all countries of the world. Even in industries where consumer tastes remain fairly diverse, companies are learning to use "custom mass production" to economically create different versions of a product and thereby satisfy the tastes of people in different countries.

In addition to taking the obvious cultural and political differences between countries into account, a company must shape its strategic approach to competing in foreign markets according to whether its industry is characterized by multidomestic competition, global competition, or some combination, depending on differences among industry sectors and on how the industry is evolving.

STRATEGIC OPTIONS FOR ENTERING AND COMPETING IN INTERNATIONAL MARKETS

LO 3

Learn about the major strategic options for entering and competing in foreign markets.

Once a company decides to expand beyond its domestic borders it must consider the question of how to enter foreign markets. There are six primary strategic options for doing so:

1. Maintain a national (one-country) production base and export goods to foreign markets.
2. License foreign firms to produce and distribute the company's products abroad.
3. Employ a franchising strategy.
4. Establish a wholly owned subsidiary in the foreign market by acquiring a foreign company.
5. Create a wholly owned foreign subsidiary from the ground up via a "greenfield" venture.
6. Rely on strategic alliances or joint ventures to partner with foreign companies.

Which option to employ depends on a variety of factors, including the nature of the firm's strategic objectives, whether the firm has the full range of resources and capabilities needed to operate abroad, country-specific factors such as trade barriers, and the transaction costs involved (the costs of contracting with a partner and monitoring its compliance with the terms of the contract, for example). The options vary considerably regarding the level of investment required and the associated risks, but higher levels of investment and risk generally provide the firm with the benefits of greater ownership and control.

Export Strategies

Using domestic plants as a production base for exporting goods to foreign markets is an excellent initial strategy for pursuing international sales. It is a conservative way to test the international waters. The amount of capital needed to begin exporting is often quite minimal; existing production capacity may well be sufficient to make goods for export. With an export strategy, a manufacturer can limit its involvement in foreign markets by contracting with foreign wholesalers experienced in importing to handle the entire distribution and marketing function in their countries or regions of the world. If it is more advantageous to maintain control over these functions, however, a manufacturer can establish its own distribution and sales organizations in some or all of the target foreign markets. Either way, a home-based production and export strategy helps the firm minimize its direct investments in foreign countries. Such strategies have been favored traditionally by Chinese, Korean, and Italian companies—products are designed and manufactured at home and then distributed through local channels in the importing countries; the primary functions performed abroad relate chiefly to establishing a network of distributors and perhaps conducting sales promotion and brand awareness activities.

Whether an export strategy can be pursued successfully over the long run hinges on whether its advantages for the company continue to outweigh its disadvantages. This depends in part on the relative cost competitiveness of the home-country production base. In some industries, firms gain additional scale economies and learning curve benefits from centralizing production in one or several giant plants whose output capability exceeds demand in any one country market; exporting is one obvious way to capture such economies. However, an export strategy is vulnerable when (1) manufacturing costs in the home country are substantially higher than in foreign countries where rivals have plants, (2) the costs of shipping the product to distant foreign markets are relatively high, or (3) adverse shifts occur in currency exchange rates. The disadvantages of export strategies can also swell due to high tariffs and other trade barriers, inadequate control over marketing or distribution, and an inability to tap into location advantages available elsewhere, such as skilled low-cost labor.

Licensing Strategies

Licensing makes sense when a firm with valuable technical know-how, an appealing brand, or a unique patented product has neither the internal organizational capability nor the resources to enter foreign markets. Licensing also has the advantage of avoiding the risks of committing resources to country markets that are unfamiliar, politically volatile, economically unstable, or otherwise risky. By licensing the technology, trademark, or production rights to foreign-based firms, the firm does not have to bear the costs and risks of entering foreign markets on its own, yet it is able to generate income from royalties. The big disadvantage of licensing is the risk of providing valuable technological know-how to foreign companies and thereby losing some degree of control over its use; monitoring licensees and safeguarding the company's proprietary know-how can prove quite difficult in some circumstances. But if the royalty potential is considerable and the companies to whom the licenses are being granted are trustworthy and reputable, then licensing can be a very attractive option. Many software and pharmaceutical companies use licensing strategies.

Franchising Strategies

While licensing works well for manufacturers and owners of proprietary technology, franchising is often better suited to the international expansion efforts of service and retailing enterprises. McDonald's, Yum! Brands (the parent of Pizza Hut,

KFC, and Taco Bell), the UPS Store, Jani-King International (the world's largest commercial cleaning franchisor), Roto-Rooter, 7-Eleven, and Hilton Hotels have all used franchising to build a presence in foreign markets. Franchising has much the same advantages as licensing. The franchisee bears most of the costs and risks of establishing foreign locations; a franchisor has to expend only the resources to recruit, train, support, and monitor franchisees. The big problem a franchisor faces is maintaining quality control; foreign franchisees do not always exhibit strong commitment to consistency and standardization, especially when the local culture does not stress the same kinds of quality concerns. Another problem that can arise is whether to allow foreign franchisees to make modifications in the franchisor's product offering so as to better satisfy the tastes and expectations of local buyers. Should McDonald's allow its franchised units in Japan to modify Big Macs slightly to suit Japanese tastes? Should the franchised Pizza Hut units in China be permitted to substitute spices that appeal to Chinese consumers? Or should the same menu offerings be rigorously and unvaryingly required of all franchisees worldwide?

Acquisition Strategies

Acquisition strategies have the advantages of a high level of control as well as speed, which can be a significant factor when a firm wants to enter a foreign market at a relatively large scale. When a strong presence in the market or local economies of scale are a significant competitive factor in the market, these advantages may make acquiring a large local firm preferable to most other entry modes. Similarly, when entry barriers are high—whether in the form of trade barriers, access to a local distribution network, or building key relationships with local constituents and officials—an acquisition may be the only route to overcoming such hurdles. Acquisition may also be the preferred entry strategy if the strategic objective is to gain access to the core capabilities or well-guarded technologies of a foreign firm.

At the same time, acquisition strategies have their downside as a foreign entry strategy. Acquisition strategies are always costly, since it is necessary to pay a premium over the share-price value of a company in order to acquire control. This can saddle the acquiring company with a good deal of debt, increasing its risk of bankruptcy and limiting its other investment options. Acquiring a foreign firm can be particularly tricky due to the challenge of international negotiations, the burden of foreign legal and regulatory requirements, and the added complexity of postacquisition integration efforts when companies are separated by distance, culture, and language.[11] While the potential benefits of a cross-border acquisition can be high, the risk of failure is high as well.

Greenfield Venture Strategies

CORE CONCEPT

A **greenfield venture** is a subsidiary business that is established by setting up the entire operation from the ground up.

A **greenfield venture** strategy is one in which the company creates a subsidiary business in the foreign market by setting up the entire operation (plants, distribution system, etc.) from the ground up. Like acquisition strategies, greenfield ventures have the advantage of high control, but to an even greater degree since starting from scratch allows the company to set up every aspect of the operation to its specifications. Since organizational change is notoriously difficult and hampered by a variety of inertial factors, it is much harder to fine-tune the operations of an acquired firm to this degree—particularly a foreign firm. Entering a foreign market from the ground up provides a firm with another potential advantage: It enables the company to *learn by doing* how to operate in the foreign market and how to best serve local needs, navigate the local politics, and compete most effectively against local rivals. This is not to say, however, that the company needs to acquire all the knowledge and experience needed from the ground up; in building its operation, the company can avail itself of local managerial talent and know-how by simply hiring experienced local managers who understand the local market conditions, local buying habits, local competitors, and local ways of doing business. By assembling a management team that also includes senior managers from the parent company (preferably with considerable international experience), the parent company can transfer technology, business practices, and the corporate culture into the new foreign subsidiary and ensure that there is a conduit for the flow of information between the corporate office and local operations.

Greenfield ventures in foreign markets also pose a number of problems, just as other entry strategies do. They represent a costly capital investment, subject to a high level of risk. They require numerous other company resources as well, diverting them from other uses. They do not work well in countries without strong, well-functioning markets and institutions that protect the rights of foreign investors and provide other legal protections.[12] Moreover, an important disadvantage of greenfield ventures relative to other means of international expansion is that they are the slowest entry route—particularly if the objective is to achieve a sizable market share. On the other hand, successful greenfield ventures may offer higher returns to compensate for their high risk and slower path.

Alliance and Joint Venture Strategies

Collaborative agreements with foreign companies in the form of strategic alliances or joint ventures are widely used as a means of entering foreign markets.[13] Often they are used in conjunction with another entry strategy, such as exporting, franchising, or establishing a greenfield venture. Historically, firms in industrialized nations that wanted to export their products and market them in less developed countries sought alliances with local companies in order to do so—such arrangements were often necessary to win approval for entry from the host country's government. Companies wanting to set up a manufacturing operation abroad often had to do so via a joint venture with a foreign firm. Over the last 20 years, those types of restrictions have been lifted in countries such as India and China, and companies have been able to enter these markets via more direct means.[14]

Today, a more important reason for using strategic alliances and joint ventures as a vehicle for international expansion is that they facilitate resource and risk sharing. When firms need access to complementary resources to succeed abroad, when the venture requires substantial investment, and when the risks are high, the attraction of such strategies grows. A company can benefit immensely from a foreign partner's familiarity with local government regulations, its knowledge of the buying habits and product preferences of consumers, its distribution channel relationships, and so on. Both Japanese and American companies are actively forming alliances with European companies to better compete in the 27-nation European Union and to capitalize on emerging but risky opportunities in the countries of eastern Europe. Similarly, many U.S. and European companies

> Collaborative strategies involving alliances or joint ventures with foreign partners are a popular way for companies to edge their way into the markets of foreign countries.

are allying with Asian companies in their efforts to enter markets in China, India, Thailand, Indonesia, and other Asian countries where they lack local knowledge and uncertainties abound. Many foreign companies, of course, are particularly interested in strategic partnerships that will strengthen their ability to gain a foothold in the U.S. market.

Another potential benefit of a collaborative strategy is the learning and added expertise that come from performing joint research, sharing technological know-how, studying one another's manufacturing methods, and understanding how to tailor sales and marketing approaches to fit local cultures and traditions. Indeed, by learning from the skills, technological know-how, and capabilities of alliance partners and implanting the knowledge and know-how of these partners in its own personnel and organization, a company can upgrade its capabilities and become a stronger competitor in its home market. DaimlerChrysler's strategic alliance with Mitsubishi, for example, was motivated by a desire to learn from Mitsubishi's technological strengths in small-size vehicles in order to improve the performance of its loss-making "smart car" division.[15]

> Cross-border alliances enable a growth-minded company to widen its geographic coverage and strengthen its competitiveness in foreign markets; at the same time, they offer flexibility and allow a company to retain some degree of autonomy and operating control.

Many companies believe that cross-border alliances and partnerships are a better strategic means of gaining the above benefits (as compared to acquiring or merging with foreign-based companies to gain much the same benefits) because they allow a company to preserve its independence (which is not the case with a merger), retain veto power over how the alliance operates, and avoid using scarce financial resources to fund acquisitions. Furthermore, an alliance offers the flexibility to readily disengage once its purpose has been served or if the benefits prove elusive, whereas an acquisition is a more permanent sort of arrangement (although the acquired company can, of course, be divested).[16]

Illustration Capsule 7.1 provides four examples of cross-border strategic alliances.

The Risks of Strategic Alliances with Foreign Partners   Alliances and joint ventures with foreign partners have their pitfalls, however. Cross-border allies typically have to overcome language and cultural barriers and figure out how to deal with diverse operating practices. The transaction costs of working out a mutually agreeable arrangement and monitoring partner compliance with the terms of the arrangement can be high. The communication, trust building, and coordination costs are not trivial in terms of management time.[17] Often, partners soon discover they have conflicting objectives and strategies, deep differences of opinion about how to proceed, and/or important differences in corporate values and ethical standards. Tensions build up, working relationships cool, and the hoped-for benefits never materialize.[18] It is not unusual for there to be little personal chemistry among some of the key people on whom success or failure of the alliance depends—the rapport such personnel need to work well together may never emerge. And even if allies are able to develop productive personal relationships, they can still have trouble reaching mutually agreeable ways to deal with key issues or resolve differences. Occasionally, the egos of corporate executives can clash. An alliance between Northwest Airlines and KLM Royal Dutch Airlines resulted in a bitter feud among both companies' top officials (who, according to some reports, refused to speak to each other).[19] Plus there is the thorny problem of getting alliance partners to sort through issues and reach decisions fast enough to stay abreast of rapid advances in technology or fast-changing market conditions.

One worrisome problem with alliances or joint ventures is that a firm may risk losing some of its competitive advantage if an alliance partner is given full access to

ILLUSTRATION CAPSULE 7.1
Four Examples of Cross-Border Strategic Alliances

1. The engine of General Motors' growth strategy in Asia is its three-way joint venture with Wulung, a Chinese producer of mini-commercial vehicles, and SAIC (Shanghai Automotive Industrial Corporation), China's largest automaker. The success of the SAIC-GM-Wulung Automotive Company is also GM's best hope for financial recovery since it emerged from bankruptcy on July 10, 2009. While GM lost $4.8 billion overall before interest and taxes during the last six months of 2009, its international operations (everything except North America and Europe) earned $1.2 billion. Its Chinese joint ventures accounted for approximately one-third of that profit, due in part to the roaring success of the no-frills Wulung Sunshine, a lightweight minivan that has become China's best-selling vehicle. In 2010, General Motors' sales in China topped its U.S. sales—the first time that sales in a foreign market have done so in the 102-year history of the company. GM is now positioning its Chinese joint venture to serve as a springboard for the company's expansion in India, with the possibility of launching a product to rival the Tata Nano there. When GM's president of international operations, Timothy E. Lee, was asked about GM's ability to compete in India, he replied, "When you harvest from your partnerships the collective wisdom of other cultures, it's incredible what you can do."

2. The European Aeronautic Defense and Space Company (EADS) was formed by an alliance of aerospace companies from Britain, Spain, Germany, and France that included British Aerospace, Daimler-Benz Aerospace, and Aerospatiale. The objective of the alliance was to create a European aircraft company capable of competing with U.S.-based Boeing Corp. The alliance has proved highly successful, infusing its commercial airline division, Airbus, with the know-how and resources needed to compete head to head with Boeing for world leadership in large commercial aircraft (those designed for over 100 passengers).

3. Cisco, the worldwide leader in networking components, entered into a strategic alliance with Finnish telecommunications firm Nokia Siemens Networks to develop communications networks capable of transmitting data either across the Internet or by mobile technologies. Nokia Siemens Networks itself was created through a 2006 international joint venture between German-based Siemens AG and the Finnish communications giant Nokia. The Cisco–Nokia Siemens alliance was created to better position both companies for convergence among Internet technologies and wireless communication devices that was expected to dramatically change how both computer networks and wireless telephones would be used.

4. Verio, a subsidiary of Japan-based NTT Communications and one of the leading global providers of Web hosting services and IP data transport, operates with the philosophy that in today's highly competitive and challenging technology market, companies must gain and share skills, information, and technology with technology leaders across the world. Believing that no company can be all things to all customers in the Web hosting industry, Verio executives have developed an alliance-oriented business model that combines the company's core competencies with the skills and products of best-of-breed technology partners. Verio's strategic partners include Accenture, Cisco Systems, Microsoft, Sun Microsystems, Oracle, Arsenal Digital Solutions (a provider of worry-free tape backup, data restore, and data storage services), Internet Security Systems (a provider of firewall and intrusion detection systems), and Mercantec (which develops storefront and shopping cart software). Verio's management believes that its portfolio of strategic alliances allows it to use innovative, best-of-class technologies in providing its customers with fast, efficient, accurate data transport and a complete set of Web hosting services. An independent panel of 12 judges recently selected Verio as the winner of the Best Technology Foresight Award for its efforts in pioneering new technologies.

Developed with Mukund Kulashekaran.

Sources: Company Web sites and press releases; Yves L. Doz and Gary Hamel, *Alliance Advantage: The Art of Creating Value through Partnering* (Boston: Harvard Business School Press, 1998); Joanne Muller, "Can China Save GM?" *Forbes.com,* May 10, 2010, www.forbes.com/forbes/2010/0510/global-2000-10-automobiles-china-detroit-whitacre-save-gm.html; "GM's First-Half China Sales Surge Past the U.S.," *Bloomberg Businessweek,* July 2, 2010, www.businessweek.com/news/2010-07-02/gm-s-first-half-china-sales-surge-past-the-u-s-.html; Nandini Sen Gupta, "General Motors May Drive in Nano Rival with Chinese Help," *Economic Times,* May 31, 2010, http://economictimes.indiatimes.com/articleshow/5992589.cms.

its proprietary technological expertise or other unique and competitively valuable capabilities. There is a natural tendency for allies to struggle to collaborate effectively in competitively sensitive areas, thus spawning suspicions on both sides about forthright exchanges of information and expertise. It requires many meetings of many people working in good faith over a period of time to iron out what is to be shared, what is to remain proprietary, and how the cooperative arrangements will work.

Even if a collaborative arrangement proves to be a win-win proposition for both parties, a company has to guard against becoming overly dependent on foreign partners for essential expertise and competitive capabilities. If a company is aiming for global market leadership and needs to develop capabilities of its own, then at some juncture a cross-border merger or acquisition may have to be substituted for cross-border alliances and joint ventures. One of the lessons about cross-border alliances is that they are more effective in helping a company establish a beachhead of new opportunity in world markets than they are in enabling a company to achieve and sustain global market leadership.

When a Cross-Border Alliance May Be Unnecessary   Experienced multinational companies that market in 50 to 100 or more countries across the world find less need for entering into cross-border alliances than do companies in the early stages of globalizing their operations.[20] Multinational companies make it a point to develop senior managers who understand how "the system" works in different countries, plus they can avail themselves of local managerial talent and know-how by simply hiring experienced local managers and thereby detouring the hazards of collaborative alliances with local companies. If a multinational enterprise with considerable experience in entering the markets of different countries wants to detour the hazards of allying with local businesses, it can simply assemble a capable management team consisting of both senior managers with considerable international experience and local managers. The role of its own in-house managers with international business savvy is to transfer technology, business practices, and the corporate culture into the company's operations in the new country market and to serve as conduits for the flow of information between the corporate office and local operations. The role of local managers is to contribute needed understanding of the local market conditions, local buying habits, and local ways of doing business and, often, to head up local operations.

Hence, one cannot automatically presume that a company needs the wisdom and resources of a local partner to guide it through the process of successfully entering the markets of foreign countries. Indeed, experienced multinationals often discover that local partners do not always have adequate local market knowledge—much of the so-called experience of local partners can predate the emergence of current market trends and conditions and sometimes their operating practices can be archaic.[21]

COMPETING INTERNATIONALLY: THE THREE MAIN STRATEGIC APPROACHES

Broadly speaking, a firm's **international strategy** is simply its strategy for competing in two or more countries simultaneously. Typically, a company will start to compete internationally by entering just one or perhaps a select few foreign markets, selling its products or services in countries where there is a ready market for them. But as it expands further internationally, it will have to confront head-on the conflicting pressures of local responsiveness versus efficiency gains from standardizing and integrating operations globally. Moreover, it will have to consider whether the markets abroad are characterized by multidomestic competition, global competition, or some mix. The issue of whether and how to vary the company's competitive approach to fit specific market conditions and buyer preferences in each host country or whether to employ essentially the same strategy in all countries is perhaps the foremost strategic issue that companies must address when they operate in two or more foreign markets.[22] Figure 7.2 shows a company's three options for resolving this issue: a *multidomestic, global,* or *transnational* strategy.

Multidomestic Strategy—Think Local, Act Local

A **multidomestic strategy** is one based on differentiating products and services on a country-by-country or regional basis to meet differing buyer needs and to address divergent local market conditions. It is a good choice for companies that compete primarily in industries characterized by multidomestic competition. This type of strategy involves having plants produce different product versions for different local markets and adapting marketing and distribution to fit local customs, cultures, regulations, and market requirements. Castrol, a specialist in oil lubricants, produces over 3,000 different formulas of lubricants to meet the requirements of different climates, vehicle types and uses, and equipment applications that characterize different country markets. In the food products industry, it is common for companies to vary the ingredients in their products and sell the localized versions under local brand names to cater to country-specific tastes and eating preferences.

In essence, a multidomestic strategy represents a **think-local, act-local** approach to international strategy. A think-local, act-local approach is possible only when decision making is decentralized, giving local managers considerable latitude for crafting and executing strategies for the country markets they are responsible for. Giving local managers decision-making authority allows them to address specific market needs and respond swiftly to local changes in demand. It also enables them to focus their competitive efforts, stake out attractive market positions vis-à-vis local competitors, react to rivals' moves in a timely fashion, and target new opportunities as they emerge.

A think-local, act-local approach to strategy making is most appropriate when the need for local responsiveness is high due to significant cross-country differences in demographic, cultural, and market conditions and when the potential for efficiency gains from standardization is limited, as depicted in Figure 7.2. Consider, for example, the wide variation in refrigerator usage and preference around the world. Northern Europeans want large refrigerators because they tend to shop once a week in supermarkets; southern Europeans prefer small refrigerators because they shop daily. In parts of Asia refrigerators are a status symbol and may be placed in the living room, leading to preferences for stylish designs and

LO 4

Gain familiarity with the three main strategic approaches for competing internationally.

CORE CONCEPT

An **international strategy** is a strategy for competing in two or more countries simultaneously.

CORE CONCEPT

A **multidomestic strategy** is one in which a company varies its product offering and competitive approach from country to country in an effort to be responsive to differing buyer preferences and market conditions. It is a **think-local, act-local** type of international strategy, facilitated by decision making decentralized to the local level.

Figure 7.2   **Three Approaches for Competing Internationally**

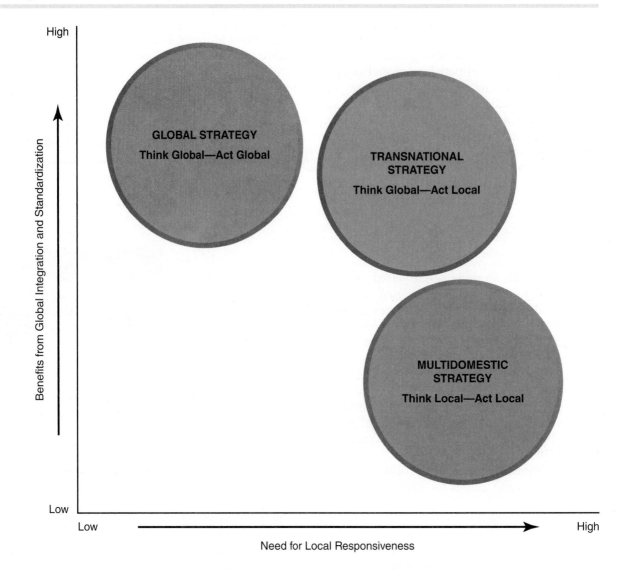

colors—in India bright blue and red are popular colors. In other Asian countries household space is constrained, and many refrigerators are only 4 feet high so that the top can be used for storage. If the minimum efficient scale for producing refrigerators is relatively low, there would be little reason to forgo the benefits of meeting these varying needs precisely in favor of a standardized, one-size-fits-all approach to production.

Despite their obvious benefits, think-local, act-local strategies have three big drawbacks:

1. They hinder transfer of a company's capabilities, knowledge, and other resources across country boundaries, since the company's efforts are not integrated or coordinated across country boundaries. This can make the company less innovative overall.

2. They raise production and distribution costs due to the greater variety of designs and components, shorter production runs for each product version, and complications of added inventory handling and distribution logistics.

3. They are not conducive to building a single, worldwide competitive advantage. When a company's competitive approach and product offering vary from country to country, the nature and size of any resulting competitive edge also tends to vary. At the most, multidomestic strategies are capable of producing a group of local competitive advantages of varying types and degrees of strength.

Global Strategy—Think Global, Act Global

A **global strategy** contrasts sharply with a multidomestic strategy in that it takes a standardized, globally integrated approach to producing, packaging, selling, and delivering the company's products and services worldwide. Companies employing a global strategy sell the same products under the same brand names everywhere, utilize much the same distribution channels in all countries, and compete on the basis of the same capabilities and marketing approaches worldwide. Although the company's strategy or product offering may be adapted in very minor ways to accommodate specific situations in a few host countries, the company's fundamental competitive approach (low cost, differentiation, best cost, or focused) remains very much intact worldwide and local managers stick close to the global strategy.

A **think-global, act-global** strategic theme prompts company managers to integrate and coordinate the company's strategic moves worldwide and to expand into most, if not all, nations where there is significant buyer demand. It puts considerable strategic emphasis on building a *global* brand name and aggressively pursuing opportunities to transfer ideas, new products, and capabilities from one country to another.[23] Global strategies are characterized by relatively centralized value chain activities, such as production and distribution. While there may be more than one manufacturing plant and distribution center to minimize transportation costs, for example, they tend to be few in number. Achieving the efficiency potential of a global strategy requires that resources and best practices be shared, value chain activities be integrated, and capabilities be transferred from one location to another as they are developed. These objectives are best facilitated through centralized decision making and strong headquarters control.

Because a global strategy cannot accommodate varying local needs, it is an appropriate strategic choice when there are pronounced efficiency benefits from standardization and when buyer needs are relatively homogeneous across countries and regions. A globally standardized and integrated approach is especially beneficial when high volumes significantly lower costs due to economies of scale or added experience (moving the company further down a learning curve). It can also be advantageous if it allows the firm to replicate a successful business model on a global basis efficiently or engage in higher levels of R&D by spreading the fixed costs and risks over a higher-volume output. It is a fitting response to industry conditions marked by global competition.

CORE CONCEPT

A **global strategy** is one in which a company employs the same basic competitive approach in all countries where it operates, sells much the same products everywhere, strives to build global brands, and coordinates its actions worldwide with strong headquarters control. It represents a **think-global, act-global** approach.

The drawbacks of global strategies are several: (1) They do not enable firms to address local needs as precisely as locally based rivals can, (2) they are less responsive to changes in local market conditions, either in the form of new opportunities or competitive threats, (3) they raise transportation costs and may involve higher tariffs, and (4) they involve higher coordination costs due to the more complex task of managing a globally integrated enterprise.

Transnational Strategy—Think Global, Act Local

A **transnational strategy** (sometimes called *glocalization*) incorporates elements of both a globalized and a localized approach to strategy making. This type of middle-ground strategy is called for when there are relatively high needs for local responsiveness as well as appreciable benefits to be realized from standardization, as Figure 7.2 suggests. A transnational strategy encourages a company to **think global, act local** to balance these competing objectives.

Often, companies implement a transnational strategy with mass-customization techniques that enable them to address local preferences in an efficient, semi-standardized manner. Both McDonald's and KFC have discovered ways to customize their menu offerings in various countries without compromising costs, product quality, and operating effectiveness. When it first opened Disneyland Paris, Disney learned the hard way that a global approach to its international theme parks would not work; it has since adapted elements of its strategy to accommodate local preferences even though much of its strategy still derives from a globally applied formula. Otis Elevator found that a transnational strategy delivers better results than a global strategy when competing in countries like China where local needs are highly differentiated. In 2000, it switched from its customary single-brand approach to a multibrand strategy aimed at serving different segments of the market. By 2009, it had doubled its market share in China and increased its revenues sixfold.[24]

> **CORE CONCEPT**
>
> A **transnational strategy** is a **think-global, act-local** approach that incorporates elements of both multidomestic and global strategies.

A transnational strategy is far more conducive than other strategies to transferring and leveraging subsidiary skills and capabilities. But, like other approaches to competing internationally, transnational strategies also have significant drawbacks:

1. They are the most difficult of all international strategies to implement due to the added complexity of varying the elements of the strategy to situational conditions.

2. They place large demands on the organization due to the need to pursue conflicting objectives simultaneously.

3. Implementing the strategy is likely to be a costly and time-consuming enterprise, with an uncertain outcome.

Table 7.1 provides a summary of the pluses and minuses of the three approaches to competing internationally.

Table 7.1   **Advantages and Disadvantages of Multidomestic, Global, and Transnational Approaches**

	Advantages	Disadvantages
Multidomestic (think local, act local)	• Can meet the specific needs of each market more precisely • Can respond more swiftly to localized changes in demand • Can target reactions to the moves of local rivals • Can respond more quickly to local opportunities and threats	• Hinders resource and capability sharing or cross-market transfers • Higher production and distribution costs • Not conducive to a worldwide competitive advantage
Transnational (think global, act local)	• Offers the benefits of both local responsiveness and global integration • Enables the transfer and sharing of resources and capabilities across borders • Provides the benefits of flexible coordination	• More complex and harder to implement • Conflicting goals may be difficult to reconcile and require trade-offs • Implementation more costly and time-consuming
Global (think global, act global)	• Lower costs due to scale and scope economies • Greater efficiencies due to the ability to transfer best practices across markets • More innovation from knowledge sharing and capability transfer • The benefit of a global brand and reputation	• Unable to address local needs precisely • Less responsive to changes in local market conditions • Higher transportation costs and tariffs • Higher coordination and integration costs

THE QUEST FOR COMPETITIVE ADVANTAGE IN THE INTERNATIONAL ARENA

There are three important ways in which a firm can gain competitive advantage (or offset domestic disadvantages) by expanding outside its domestic market.[25] First, it can use location to lower costs or achieve greater product differentiation. Second, it can transfer competitively valuable resources, competencies, and capabilities from one country to another or share them across international borders to extend and deepen its competitive advantages. And third, it can benefit from cross-border coordination in ways that a domestic-only competitor cannot.

LO 5

Understand how international companies go about building competitive advantage in foreign markets.

Using Location to Build Competitive Advantage

To use location to build competitive advantage, a company must consider two issues: (1) whether to concentrate each activity it performs in a few select countries or to disperse performance of the activity to many nations, and (2) in which countries to locate particular activities.[26]

When to Concentrate Activities in a Few Locations   It is advantageous for a company to concentrate its activities in a limited number of locations when:

- *The costs of manufacturing or other activities are significantly lower in some geographic locations than in others.* For example, much of the world's athletic footwear is manufactured in Asia (China and Korea) because of low labor costs; much of the production of circuit boards for PCs is located in Taiwan because of both low costs and the high-caliber technical skills of the Taiwanese labor force.

- *There are significant scale economies in production or distribution.* The presence of significant economies of scale in components production or final assembly means that a company can gain major cost savings from operating a few ultra-efficient plants as opposed to a host of small plants scattered across the world. Achieving low-cost provider status often requires a company to have the largest worldwide manufacturing share (as distinct from brand share or market share), with production centralized in one or a few world-scale plants. Some companies even use such plants to manufacture units sold under the brand names of rivals to further boost production-related scale economies. Makers of digital cameras and LCD TVs located in Japan, South Korea, and Taiwan have used their scale economies to establish a low-cost advantage. Likewise, a company may be able to reduce its distribution costs by capturing scale economies associated with establishing large-scale distribution centers to serve major geographic regions of the world market (for example, North America, Latin America, Europe–Middle East, and Asia-Pacific).

> Companies that compete internationally can pursue competitive advantage in world markets by locating their value chain activities in whatever nations prove most advantageous.

- *There are sizable learning and experience benefits associated with performing an activity in a single location.* In some industries, a manufacturer can lower unit costs, boost quality, or master a new technology more quickly by concentrating production in a few locations. The greater the cumulative volume of production at a plant, the faster the buildup of learning and experience of the plant's workforce, thereby enabling quicker capture of the learning/experience benefits.

- *Certain locations have superior resources, allow better coordination of related activities, or offer other valuable advantages.* A research unit or a sophisticated production facility may be situated in a particular nation because of its pool of technically trained personnel. Samsung became a leader in memory chip technology by establishing a major R&D facility in Silicon Valley and transferring the know-how it gained back to its operations in South Korea. Companies also locate activities to benefit from proximity to a cluster of related and supporting industries, as discussed earlier. Cisco Systems, an international firm that sells networking and communications technology, such as routers, restricts its acquisitions to companies located in one of three well-known clusters of high-tech activity.[27] Where just-in-time inventory practices yield big cost savings and/or where an assembly firm has long-term partnering arrangements with its key suppliers, parts manufacturing plants may be located close to final assembly plants. A customer service center or sales office may be opened in a particular country to help cultivate strong relationships with pivotal customers located nearby.

When to Disperse Activities across Many Locations   There are several instances when dispersing activities is more advantageous than concentrating them. Buyer-related activities—such as distribution to dealers, sales and advertising, and after-sale service—usually must take place close to buyers. This means physically locating the capability to perform such activities in every country market where a firm has major customers (unless buyers in several adjoining countries can be served quickly from a nearby central location). For example, firms that make mining and oil-drilling equipment maintain operations in many locations around the world to support customers' needs for speedy equipment repair and technical assistance. The four biggest public accounting firms have offices in numerous countries to serve the foreign operations of their international corporate clients. Dispersing activities to many locations is also competitively advantageous when high transportation costs, diseconomies of large size, and trade barriers make it too expensive to operate from a central location. Many companies distribute their products from multiple locations to shorten delivery times to customers. In addition, it is strategically advantageous to disperse activities to hedge against the risks of fluctuating exchange rates, supply interruptions (due to strikes, mechanical failures, and transportation delays), and adverse political developments. Such risks are usually greater when activities are concentrated in a single location.

As discussed earlier, there are a variety of reasons for locating different value chain activities in different countries—all having to do with location-based advantages that vary from country to country. While the classic reason for locating an activity in a particular country is low cost, input quality and availability are also important considerations.[28] Such activities as materials procurement, parts manufacture, finished-goods assembly, technology research, and new product development can frequently be decoupled from buyer locations and performed wherever advantage lies. Components can be made in Mexico; technology research done in Frankfurt; new products developed and tested in Phoenix; and assembly plants located in Spain, Brazil, Taiwan, or South Carolina. Capital can be raised in whatever country it is available on the best terms.

Sharing and Transferring Resources and Capabilities across Borders to Build Competitive Advantage

When a company has competitively valuable resources and capabilities, it may be able to mount a resource-based strategic offensive to enter additional country markets. If a company's resources retain their value in foreign contexts, then entering new markets can extend the company's resource-based competitive advantage over a broader domain. For example, companies have used powerful brand names such as Rolex, Chanel, and Tiffany to extend their differentiation-based competitive advantages into markets far beyond their home-country origins. In each of these cases, the luxury brand name represents a valuable resource that is *shared among all of the company's international operations* and allows the company to command a higher willingness to pay from its customers in each country.

Transferring resources and capabilities across borders provides another means to extend a company's competitive advantage internationally. For example, if a firm learns how to assemble its product more efficiently at its Brazilian plant, the accumulated expertise can be quickly communicated to assembly plants in other world locations. Whirlpool, the leading global manufacturer of home appliances, with 69 manufacturing and technology research centers around the world and sales in nearly every country, uses an online global information technology platform to quickly and effectively transfer key product innovations and improved production techniques both across national borders and across its various appliance brands.

Sharing or transferring resources and capabilities across borders provides a way for a company to leverage its core competencies more fully and extend its competitive advantages into a wider array of geographic markets. Thus a technology-based competitive advantage in one country market may provide a similar basis for advantage in other country markets (depending on local market conditions). But since sharing or transferring valuable resources across borders is a very cost-effective means of extending a company's competitive advantage, these activities can also contribute to a company's competitive advantage on the costs side, giving multinational companies a powerful edge over domestic-only rivals. Since valuable resources and capabilities (such as brands, technologies, and production capabilities) are often developed at very high cost, deploying them abroad spreads the fixed development cost over greater output, thus lowering the company's unit costs. The cost of transferring already developed resources and capabilities is low by comparison. And even if the resources and capabilities need to be fully replicated in the foreign market or adapted to local conditions, this can usually be done at low additional cost relative to the initial investment in capability building.

Consider the case of Walt Disney's theme parks as an example. The success of the theme parks in the United States derives in part from core resources such as the Disney brand name and characters like Mickey Mouse that have universal appeal and worldwide recognition. These resources can be freely shared with new theme parks as Disney expands internationally. Disney can replicate its theme parks in new countries cost-effectively since it has already borne the costs of developing its core resources, park attractions, basic park design, and operating capabilities. The cost of replicating its theme parks abroad should be relatively low, even if they need to be adapted to a variety of local country conditions. By expanding internationally, Disney is able to enhance its competitive advantage over local theme park rivals. It does so by leveraging the differentiation advantage conferred by resources such as the Disney name and the park attractions. And by moving into new foreign markets, it augments its competitive advantage worldwide through the efficiency gains that come from cross border resource sharing and low-cost capability transfer and business model replication.

Sharing and transferring resources and capabilities across country borders may also contribute to the development of broader or deeper competencies and capabilities—ideally helping a company achieve *dominating depth* in some competitively valuable area. For example, an international company that consistently incorporates the same differentiating attributes in its products worldwide has enhanced potential to build a global brand name with significant power in the marketplace. The reputation for quality that Honda established worldwide began in motorcycles but enabled the company to command a position in both automobiles and outdoor power equipment in multiple-country markets. A one-country customer base is often too small to support the resource buildup needed to achieve such depth; this is particularly true when the market is developing or protected and sophisticated resources have not been required. By deploying capabilities across a larger international domain, a company can gain the experience needed to upgrade them to a higher performance standard. And by facing a more challenging set of international competitors, a company may be spurred to develop a stronger set of competitive capabilities. Moreover, by entering international markets, firms may be able to augment their capability set by learning from international rivals, cooperative partners, or acquisition targets.

However, sharing and transferring resources and capabilities across borders cannot provide a guaranteed recipe for competitive success. Because lifestyles and buying habits differ internationally, resources that are valuable in one country may not have value in another. For example, brands that are popular in one country may not transfer well or may lack recognition in the new context and thus offer no advantage against an established local brand. In addition, whether a resource or capability can confer a competitive advantage abroad depends on the conditions of rivalry in each particular market. If the rivals in a foreign country market have superior resources and capabilities, then an entering firm may find itself at a competitive disadvantage even if it has a resource-based advantage domestically and can transfer the resources at low cost.

Using Cross-Border Coordination for Competitive Advantage

Companies that compete on an international basis have another source of competitive advantage relative to their purely domestic rivals: They are able to benefit from coordinating activities across different countries' domains.[29] For example, an international manufacturer can shift production from a plant in one country to a plant in another to take advantage of exchange rate fluctuations, to cope with components shortages, or to profit from changing wage rates or energy costs. Production schedules can be coordinated worldwide; shipments can be diverted from one distribution center to another if sales rise unexpectedly in one place and fall in another. By coordinating their activities, multinational companies may also be able to enhance their leverage with host-country governments or respond adaptively to changes in tariffs and quotas.

Efficiencies can also be achieved by shifting workloads from where they are unusually heavy to locations where personnel are underutilized. Whirlpool's efforts to link its product R&D and manufacturing operations in North America, Latin America, Europe, and Asia allowed it to accelerate the discovery of innovative appliance features, coordinate the introduction of these features in the appliance products marketed in different countries, and create a cost-efficient worldwide supply chain. Whirlpool's conscious efforts to integrate and coordinate its various operations around the world have helped it become a low-cost producer and also speed product innovations to market, thereby giving Whirlpool an edge over rivals worldwide.

PROFIT SANCTUARIES AND CROSS-BORDER STRATEGIC MOVES

Profit sanctuaries are country markets (or geographic regions) in which a company derives substantial profits because of its protected market position or unassailable competitive advantage. Japan, for example, is the chief profit sanctuary for most Japanese companies because trade barriers erected by the Japanese government effectively block foreign companies from competing for a large share of Japanese sales. Protected from the threat of foreign competition in

CORE CONCEPT

Profit sanctuaries are country markets that provide a company with substantial profits because of a protected market position or sustainable competitive advantage.

their home market, Japanese companies can safely charge somewhat higher prices to their Japanese customers and thus earn attractively large profits on sales made in Japan. Other profit sanctuaries may be protected because a company has an unassailable market position due to unrivaled and inimitable capabilities. In most cases, a company's biggest and most strategically crucial profit sanctuary is its home market, but multinational companies may also enjoy profit sanctuary status in other nations where they have a strong position based on some type of competitive advantage. Companies that compete worldwide are likely to have more profit sanctuaries than companies that compete in just a few country markets; a domestic-only competitor, of course, can have only one profit sanctuary at most (see Figure 7.3).

Figure 7.3   Profit Sanctuary Potential of Domestic-only, International, and Global Competitors

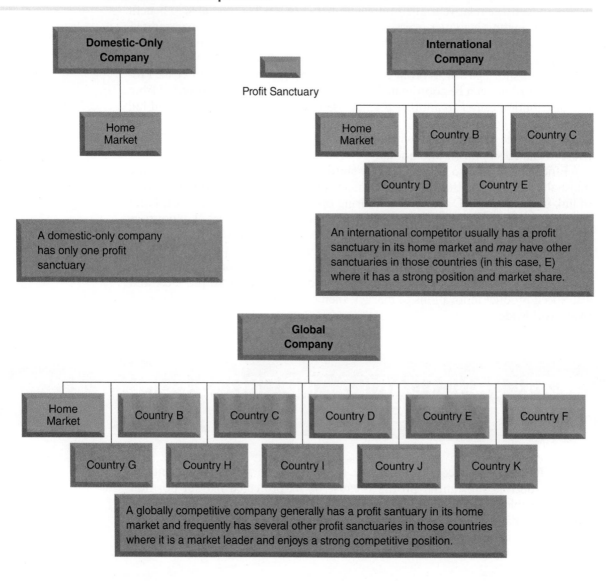

Domestic-Only Company

Home Market

Profit Sanctuary

International Company

Home Market   Country B   Country C

Country D   Country E

A domestic-only company has only one profit sanctuary

An international competitor usually has a profit sanctuary in its home market and *may* have other sanctuaries in those countries (in this case, E) where it has a strong position and market share.

Global Company

Home Market   Country B   Country C   Country D   Country E   Country F

Country G   Country H   Country I   Country J   Country K

A globally competitive company generally has a profit sanctuary in its home market and frequently has several other profit sanctuaries in those countries where it is a market leader and enjoys a strong competitive position.

Using Cross-Market Subsidization to Wage a Strategic Offensive

Profit sanctuaries are valuable competitive assets, providing the financial strength to support strategic offensives in selected country markets and fuel a company's race for world-market leadership. The added financial capability afforded by multiple profit sanctuaries gives an international competitor the financial strength to wage a market offensive against a domestic competitor whose only profit sanctuary is its home market. The international company has the flexibility of lowballing its prices or launching high-cost marketing campaigns in the domestic company's home market and grabbing market share at the domestic company's expense. Razor-thin margins or even losses in these markets can be subsidized with the healthy profits earned in its profit sanctuaries—a practice called **cross-market subsidization.** The international company can adjust the depth of its price cutting to move in and capture market share quickly, or it can shave prices slightly to make gradual market inroads (perhaps over a decade or more) so as not to threaten domestic firms precipitously and trigger protectionist government actions. If the domestic company retaliates with matching price cuts or increased marketing expenses, it exposes its entire revenue stream and profit base to erosion; its profits can be squeezed substantially and its competitive strength sapped, even if it is the domestic market leader.

> ### CORE CONCEPT
>
> **Cross-market subsidization**—supporting competitive offensives in one market with resources and profits diverted from operations in another market—can be a powerful competitive weapon.

When taken to the extreme, cut-rate pricing attacks by international competitors may draw charges of unfair dumping. A company is said to be dumping when it sells its goods in foreign markets at prices that are (1) well below the prices at which it normally sells in its home market or (2) well below its full costs per unit. Companies that engage in dumping usually keep their selling prices high enough to cover variable costs per unit, thereby limiting their losses on each unit to some percentage of fixed costs per unit.

Dumping can be a tempting strategy in either of two instances: (1) when selling goods abroad at below-market prices can allow a firm to avoid the high costs of idling plants, and (2) when temporary below-cost pricing can allow a company to make lasting market share gains by driving weak firms from the market. The first may be justified as a legitimate competitive practice, while the latter is usually viewed to be predatory in nature. A charge of unfair dumping is more easily defended when a company with unused production capacity discovers that it is cheaper to keep producing (as long as the selling prices cover average variable costs per unit) than it is to incur the costs associated with idle plant capacity. By keeping its plants operating at or near capacity, not only may a company be able to cover variable costs and earn a contribution to fixed costs, but it also may be able to use its below-market prices to draw price-sensitive customers away from foreign rivals. It is wise for companies pursuing such an approach to court these new customers and retain their business when prices later begin a gradual rise back to normal market levels.

Alternatively, a company may use below-market pricing to drive down the price so far in the targeted country that domestic firms are quickly put in dire financial straits or in danger of being driven out of business. However, using below-market pricing in this way *runs a high risk of host-government retaliation on behalf of the adversely affected domestic companies.* Almost all governments can be expected to retaliate against perceived dumping practices by imposing special tariffs on goods being imported from the countries of the guilty companies.

Indeed, as the trade among nations has mushroomed over the past 10 years, most governments have joined the World Trade Organization (WTO), which promotes fair-trade practices among nations and actively polices dumping. Companies based in France and China were recently found guilty of dumping laminate flooring at unreasonably low prices in Canada to the detriment of Canadian producers.[30] Companies deemed guilty of dumping frequently come under pressure from their government to cease and desist, especially if the tariffs adversely affect innocent companies based in the same country or if the advent of special tariffs raises the specter of an international trade war.

Using Cross-Border Tactics to Defend against International Rivals

Cross-border tactics can also be used as a means of defending against the strategic moves of strong international rivals with multiple profit sanctuaries of their own. If a company finds itself under competitive attack by an international rival in one country market, one way to respond is with a counterattack against one of the rival's key markets in a different country—preferably where the rival is least protected and has the most to lose. This is a possible option when rivals compete against one another in much the same markets around the world.

For companies with at least one profit sanctuary, having a presence in a rival's key markets can be enough to deter the rival from making aggressive attacks. The reason for this is that the combination of some market presence (even at small scale) and a profit sanctuary elsewhere can send a signal to the rival that the company could quickly ramp up production (funded by the profit sanctuary) to mount a competitive attack in that market if the rival attacks one of the company's key markets in another country.

When international rivals compete against one another in multiple-country markets, this type of deterrence effect can restrain them from taking aggressive action against one another due to the fear of a retaliatory response that might escalate the battle into a cross-border competitive war. **Mutual restraint** of this sort tends to stabilize the competitive position of multimarket rivals against one another. And while it may prevent each firm from making any major market share gains at the expense of its rival, it also prevents costly competitive battles that would be likely to erode the profitability of both companies without any compensating gain.

> **CORE CONCEPT**
>
> When the same companies compete against one another in multiple geographic markets, the threat of cross-border counterattacks may be enough to deter aggressive competitive moves and encourage **mutual restraint** among international rivals.

STRATEGIES FOR COMPETING IN THE MARKETS OF DEVELOPING COUNTRIES

Companies racing for global leadership have to consider competing in developing-economy markets like China, India, Brazil, Indonesia, Thailand, Poland, Russia, and Mexico—countries where the business risks are considerable but where the opportunities for growth are huge, especially as their economies develop and living standards climb toward levels in the industrialized world.[31]

With the world now comprising nearly 7 billion people—fully 40 percent of whom live in India and China, and hundreds of millions more live in other, less developed countries in Asia and Latin America—a company that aspires to world market leadership (or to sustained rapid growth) cannot ignore the market opportunities or the base of technical and managerial talent such countries offer. For example, in 2010 China was the world's second-largest economy (behind the United States), as measured by purchasing power. Its population of 1.4 billion people now consumes a quarter of the world's luxury products, due to the rapid growth of a wealthy class.[32] China is also the world's largest consumer of many commodities. China's growth in demand for consumer goods had made it the world's largest market for vehicles by 2009 and put it on track to become the world's largest market for luxury goods by 2014.[33] Thus, no company that aspires to global market leadership can afford to ignore the strategic importance of establishing competitive market positions in China, India, other parts of the Asia-Pacific region, Latin America, and eastern Europe. Illustration Capsule 7.2 describes Yum! Brands' strategy to increase its sales and market share in China.

Tailoring products to fit market conditions in a developing country like China, however, often involves more than making minor product changes and becoming more familiar with local cultures.[34] Ford's attempt to sell a Ford Escort in India at a price of $21,000—a luxury-car price, given that India's best-selling Maruti-Suzuki model sold at the time for $10,000 or less and that fewer than 10 percent of Indian households had an annual purchasing power greater than $20,000—met with a less-than-enthusiastic market response. McDonald's has had to offer vegetable burgers in parts of Asia and to rethink its prices, which are often high by local standards and affordable only by the well-to-do. Kellogg has struggled to introduce its cereals successfully because consumers in many less developed countries do not eat cereal for breakfast and changing habits is difficult and expensive. Single-serving packages of detergents, shampoos, pickles, cough syrup, and cooking oils are very popular in India because they allow buyers to conserve cash by purchasing only what they need immediately. Thus, many companies find that trying to employ a strategy akin to that used in the markets of developed countries is hazardous.[35] Experimenting with some, perhaps many, local twists is usually necessary to find a strategy combination that works.

Strategy Options for Competing in Developing-Country Markets

There are several options for tailoring a company's strategy to fit the sometimes unusual or challenging circumstances presented in developing-country markets:

- *Prepare to compete on the basis of low price.* Consumers in developing markets are often highly focused on price, which can give low-cost local competitors the edge unless a company can find ways to attract buyers with bargain prices as well as better products.[36] For example, when Unilever entered the market for laundry detergents in India, it realized that 80 percent of the population could not afford the brands it was selling to affluent consumers there. To compete against a very low-priced detergent made by a local company, Unilever developed a low-cost detergent (named Wheel), constructed new low-cost production facilities, packaged the detergent in single-use amounts so that it could be sold at a very low unit price, distributed the product to local merchants by handcarts, and crafted an economical marketing campaign that

Yum! Brands' Strategy for Becoming the Leading Food Service Brand in China

In 2010, Yum! Brands operated more than 37,000 restaurants in more than 110 countries. Its best-known brands were KFC, Taco Bell, Pizza Hut, A&W, and Long John Silver's. In 2009, its fastest growth in revenues came from its 3,369 restaurants in China, which recorded operating profits of $602 million during the year. KFC was the largest quick-service chain in China, with 2,870 units in 2009, while Pizza Hut was the largest casual-dining chain, with 450 units. Yum! Brands planned to open at least 500 new restaurant locations annually in China, including new Pizza Hut Home delivery units and East Dawning units, which had a menu offering traditional Chinese food. All of Yum! Brands' menu items for China were developed in its R&D facility in Shanghai.

In addition to adapting its menu to local tastes and adding new units at a rapid pace, Yum! Brands also adapted the restaurant ambience and decor to appeal to local consumer preferences and behavior. The company changed its KFC store formats to provide educational displays that supported parents' priorities for their children and to make KFC a fun place for children to visit. The typical KFC outlet in China averaged two birthday parties per day.

In 2009, Yum! Brands operated 60 KFC, Taco Bell, Pizza Hut, A&W, and Long John Silver's restaurants for every 1 million Americans. The company's more than 3,300 units in China represented only 2 restaurants per 1 million Chinese. Yum! Brands management believed that its strategy keyed to continued expansion in the number of units in China and additional menu refinements

would allow its operating profits from restaurants located in China to account for 40 percent of system-wide operating profits by 2017.

Sources: Yum! Brands 2009 10-K and other information posted at www.yum.com.

included painted signs on buildings and demonstrations near stores. The new brand quickly captured $100 million in sales and was the number-one detergent brand in India in 2008 based on dollar sales. Unilever later replicated the strategy in India with low-priced packets of shampoos and deodorants and in South America with a detergent brand named Ala.

- *Be prepared to modify aspects of the company's business model or strategy to accommodate local circumstances (but not to such an extent that the company loses the advantage of global scale and branding).*[37] For instance, when Dell entered China, it discovered that individuals and businesses were not accustomed to placing orders through the Internet (whereas over 50 percent

ILLUSTRATION CAPSULE 7.3

How Ctrip Successfully Defended against International Rivals to Become China's Largest Online Travel Agency

Ctrip has utilized a business model tailored to the Chinese travel market, its access to low-cost labor, and its unique understanding of customer preferences and buying habits to build scale rapidly and defeat foreign rivals such as Expedia and Travelocity in becoming the largest travel agency in China. The company was founded in 1999 with a focus on business travelers, since corporate travel accounts for the majority of China's travel bookings. The company also placed little emphasis on online transactions, since at the time there was no national ticketing system in China, most hotels did not belong to a national or international chain, and most consumers preferred paper tickets to electronic tickets. To overcome this infrastructure shortcoming, the company established its own central database of 5,600 hotels located throughout China and flight information for all major airlines operating in China. Ctrip set up a call center of 3,000 representatives that could use its proprietary database to provide travel information for up to 100,000 customers per day. Because most of its

transactions were not done over the Internet, the company hired couriers in all major cities in China to ride by bicycle or scooter to collect payments and deliver tickets to Ctrip's corporate customers. Ctrip also initiated a loyalty program that provided gifts and incentives to the administrative personnel who arranged travel for business executives. By 2009, Ctrip.com held 60 percent of China's online travel market and planned to enter the Taiwanese tourism market, having just acquired EzTravel, Taiwan's largest online travel site.* By April 2010, its market cap reached $5.34 billion and was creeping up rapidly on Expedia's market cap of $7.23 billion.**

*"Ctrip.com Acquires ezTravel," *China Hospitality News,* August 11, 2009, www.chinahospitalitynews.com/en/2009/08/11/12859-ctrip-com-acquires-eztravel/. ** Dennis Schaal, "Online Travel Powerhouses—Priceline, Expedia . . . and Ctrip?" *Tnooz.co: Talking Travel Tech,* April 1, 2010, www.tnooz.com/2010/04/01/news/online-travel-powerhouses-priceline-expedia-and-ctrip/.

Source: Based on information in Arindam K. Bhattacharya and David C. Michael, "How Local Companies Keep Multinationals at Bay," *Harvard Business Review 86,* no. 3 (March 2008), pp. 85–95.

2. *Utilize keen understanding of local customer needs and preferences to create customized products or services.* When developing-country markets are largely made up of customers with strong local needs, a good strategy option is to concentrate on customers who prefer a local touch and to accept the loss of the customers attracted to global brands.[42] A local company may be able to astutely exploit its local orientation—its familiarity with local preferences, its expertise in traditional products, its long-standing customer relationships. A small Middle Eastern cell phone manufacturer competes successfully against industry giants Nokia, Samsung, and Motorola by selling a model designed especially for Muslims—it is loaded with the Koran, alerts people at prayer times, and is equipped with a compass that points them toward Mecca. Shenzhen-based Tencent has become the leader in instant messaging in China through its unique understanding of Chinese behavior and culture.

3. *Take advantage of aspects of the local workforce with which large multinational companies may be unfamiliar.* Local companies that lack the technological capabilities of foreign entrants may be able to rely on their better

understanding of the local labor force to offset any disadvantage. Focus Media is China's largest outdoor advertising firm and has relied on low-cost labor to update its 130,000 LCD displays and billboards in 90 cities in a low-tech manner, while multinational companies operating in China use electronically networked screens that allow messages to be changed remotely. Focus uses an army of employees who ride to each display by bicycle to change advertisements with programming contained on a USB flash drive or DVD. Indian information technology firms such as Infosys Technologies and Satyam Computer Services have been able to keep their personnel costs lower than those of international competitors EDS and Accenture because of their familiarity with local labor markets. While the large internationals have focused recruiting efforts in urban centers like Bangalore and Delhi, driving up engineering and computer science salaries in such cities, local companies have shifted recruiting efforts to second-tier cities that are unfamiliar to foreign firms.

4. *Use acquisition and rapid-growth strategies to better defend against expansion-minded internationals.* With the growth potential of developing markets such as China, Indonesia, and Brazil obvious to the world, local companies must attempt to develop scale and upgrade their competitive capabilities as quickly as possible to defend against the stronger international's arsenal of resources. Most successful companies in developing markets have pursued mergers and acquisitions at a rapid-fire pace to build first a nationwide and then an international presence. Hindalco, India's largest aluminum producer, has followed just such a path to achieve its ambitions for global dominance. By acquiring companies in India first, it gained enough experience and confidence to eventually acquire much larger foreign companies with world-class capabilities.[43] When China began to liberalize its foreign trade policies, Lenovo (the Chinese PC maker) realized that its long-held position of market dominance in China could not withstand the onslaught of new international entrants such as Dell and HP. Its acquisition of IBM's PC business allowed Lenovo to gain rapid access to IBM's globally recognized PC brand, its R&D capability, and its existing distribution in developed countries. This has allowed Lenovo not only to hold its own against the incursion of global giants into its home market but to expand into new markets around the world.[44]

5. *Transfer company expertise to cross-border markets and initiate actions to contend on an international level.* When a company from a developing country has resources and capabilities suitable for competing in other country markets, launching initiatives to transfer its expertise to foreign markets becomes a viable strategic option.[45] Televisa, Mexico's largest media company, used its expertise in Spanish culture and linguistics to become the world's most prolific producer of Spanish-language soap operas. Jollibee Foods, a family-owned company with 56 percent of the fast-food business in the Philippines, combated McDonald's entry first by upgrading service and delivery standards and then by using its expertise in seasoning hamburgers with garlic and soy sauce and making noodle and rice meals with fish to open outlets catering to Asian residents in Hong Kong, the Middle East, and California. By continuing to upgrade its capabilities and learn from its experience in foreign markets, a company can sometimes transform itself into one capable of competing on a worldwide basis, as an emerging global giant.[46] Sundaram Fasteners of India began its foray into foreign markets as a supplier of radiator caps to

GM—an opportunity it pursued when GM first decided to outsource the production of this part. As a participant in GM's supplier network, the company learned about emerging technical standards, built its capabilities, and became one of the first Indian companies to achieve QS 9000 quality certification. With the expertise it gained and its recognition for meeting quality standards, Sundaram was then able to pursue opportunities to supply automotive parts in Japan and Europe.

KEY POINTS

1. Competing in international markets allows companies to (1) gain access to new customers, (2) achieve lower costs through greater scale economies, learning curve effects, or purchasing power, (3) leverage core competencies developed domestically in additional country markets, (4) gain access to resources and capabilities located outside a company's domestic market, and (5) spread business risk across a wider market base.

2. Companies electing to expand into international markets must consider five factors when evaluating strategy options: (1) cross-country variation in factors that affect industry competitiveness, (2) location-based drivers regarding where to conduct different value chain activities, (3) varying political and economic risks, (4) potential shifts in exchange rates, and (5) differences in cultural, demographic, and market conditions.

3. The strategies of firms that expand internationally are usually grounded in home-country advantages concerning demand conditions, factor conditions, related and supporting industries, and firm strategy, structure, and rivalry, as described by the Diamond of National Advantage framework.

4. The pattern of international competition varies in important ways from industry to industry. At one extreme is *multidomestic competition,* in which the market contest among rivals in one country is not closely connected to the market contests in other countries—there is no world market, just a collection of self-contained country (or maybe regional) markets. At the other extreme is *global competition,* in which competitive conditions across national markets are linked strongly enough to form a true world market, wherein leading competitors compete head to head in many different countries.

5. There are six strategic options for entering foreign markets. These include (1) maintaining a national (one-country) production base and exporting goods to foreign markets, (2) licensing foreign firms to produce and distribute the company's products abroad, (3) employing a franchising strategy, (4) establishing a wholly owned subsidiary by acquiring a foreign company, (5) creating a wholly owned foreign subsidiary from the ground up via a greenfield venture, and (6) using strategic alliances or other collaborative partnerships to enter a foreign market.

6. A company must choose among three alternative approaches for competing internationally: (1) a *multidomestic strategy,* which is a *think-local, act-local* approach to crafting international strategy; (2) a *global strategy*—a *think-global, act-global* approach; and (3) a combination *think-global, act-local* approach, known as a *transnational strategy.* A think-local, act-local, or multi-domestic, strategy is appropriate for industries or companies that must vary

their product offerings and competitive approaches from country to country in order to accommodate different buyer preferences and market conditions. The think-global, act-global approach that characterizes a global strategy works best when there are substantial cost benefits to be gained from taking a standardized and globally integrated approach and little need for local responsiveness. A transnational approach (think global, act local) is called for when there is a high need for local responsiveness as well as substantial benefits from taking a globally integrated approach. While this is the most challenging international strategy to implement, it can be used when it is feasible for a company to employ essentially the same basic competitive strategy in all markets but still customize its product offering and some aspect of its operations to fit local market circumstances.

7. There are three general ways in which a firm can gain competitive advantage (or offset domestic disadvantages) in international markets. One way involves locating various value chain activities among nations in a manner that lowers costs or achieves greater product differentiation. A second way draws on an international competitor's ability to extend or deepen its competitive advantage by cost-effectively sharing, replicating, or transferring its most valuable resources and capabilities across borders. A third concerns benefiting from cross-border coordination in ways that are unavailable to domestic-only competitors.

8. Profit sanctuaries are country markets in which a company derives substantial profits because of its protected market position. They are valuable competitive assets, providing companies with the financial strength to mount strategic offensives in selected country markets or to support defensive moves that can ward off mutually destructive competitive battles. They may be used to wage strategic offenses in international markets through *cross-subsidization*—a practice of supporting competitive offensives in one market with resources and profits diverted from operations in another market. They may be used defensively to encourage *mutual restraint* among competitors when there is international *multimarket competition* by signaling that each company has the financial capability for mounting a strong counterattack if threatened. For companies with at least one profit sanctuary, having a presence in a rival's key markets can be enough to deter the rival from making aggressive attacks.

9. Companies racing for global leadership have to consider competing in developing markets like China, India, Brazil, Indonesia, and Mexico—countries where the business risks are considerable but the opportunities for growth are huge. To succeed in these markets, companies often have to (1) compete on the basis of low price, (2) be prepared to modify aspects of the company's business model or strategy to accommodate local circumstances (but not so much that the company loses the advantage of global scale and global branding), and/or (3) try to change the local market to better match the way the company does business elsewhere. Profitability is unlikely to come quickly or easily in developing markets, typically because of the investments needed to alter buying habits and tastes, the increased political and economic risk, and/or the need for infrastructure upgrades. And there may be times when a company should simply stay away from certain developing markets until conditions for entry are better suited to its business model and strategy.

10. Local companies in developing-country markets can seek to compete against large multinational companies by (1) developing business models that exploit shortcomings in local distribution networks or infrastructure, (2) utilizing superior understanding of local customer needs and preferences or local relationships, (3) taking advantage of competitively important qualities of the local workforce with which large multinational companies may be unfamiliar, (4) using acquisition strategies and rapid-growth strategies to better defend against expansion-minded multinational companies, or (5) transferring company expertise to cross-border markets and initiating actions to compete on a global level.

ASSURANCE OF LEARNING EXERCISES

LO 2, LO 3, LO 4

1. Chile's largest producer of wine, Concha y Toro, chooses to compete in Europe, North America, the Caribbean, and Asia using an export strategy. Go to the Investor Relations section of the company's Web site (http://www. conchaytoro.com/the-company/investor-relations/) to review the company's press releases, annual reports, and presentations. Why does it seem that the company has avoided developing vineyards and wineries in wine growing regions outside of South America?

LO 3, LO 5

2. The Hero Group is among the 10 largest corporations in India, with 20 business segments and annual revenues of $3.2 billion in fiscal 2006. Many of the corporation's business units have utilized strategic alliances with foreign partners to compete in new product and geographic markets. Review the company's statements concerning its alliances and international business operations at www.herogroup.com/alliance.htm, and prepare a two-page report that outlines the group's successful use of international strategic alliances.

LO 2, LO 4, LO 5

3. Assume you are in charge of developing the strategy for an international company selling products in 50 different countries around the world. One of the issues you face is whether to employ a multidomestic strategy, a global strategy, or a transnational strategy.

   a. If your company's product is mobile phones, do you think it would make better strategic sense to employ a multidomestic strategy, a global strategy, or a transnational strategy? Why?

   b. If your company's product is dry soup mixes and canned soups, would a multidomestic strategy seem to be more advisable than a global strategy? Why?

   c. If your company's product is large home appliances such as washing machines, ranges, ovens, and refrigerators, would it seem to make more sense to pursue a multidomestic strategy, a global strategy, or a transnational strategy? Why?

   d. If your company's product is apparel and footwear, would a multidomestic strategy, a global strategy, or a transnational strategy seem to have more appeal? Why?

EXERCISES FOR SIMULATION PARTICIPANTS

The questions below are for simulation participants whose companies operate in an international market arena. If your company competes only in a single country, then skip the questions in this section.

LO 2

1. Does your company compete in a world-market arena characterized by multidomestic competition or global competition? Explain why.

LO 3, LO 4, LO 5

2. Which one of the following best describes the strategic approach your company is taking in trying to compete successfully on an international basis?

   • Think local, act local
   • Think global, act local
   • Think global, act global

   Explain your answer, and indicate two or three chief elements of your company's strategic approach to competing in two or more different geographic regions.

LO 2

3. To what extent, if any, have you and your co-managers adapted your company's strategy to take shifting exchange rates into account? In other words, have you undertaken any actions to try to minimize the impact of adverse shifts in exchange rates?

LO 2

4. To what extent, if any, have you and your co-managers adapted your company's strategy to take geographic differences in import tariffs or import duties into account?

ENDNOTES

[1] Sidney G. Winter and Gabriel Szulanski, "Replication as Strategy," *Organization Science* 12, no. 6 (November–December 2001), pp. 730–43; Sidney G. Winter and Gabriel Szulanski, "Getting It Right the Second Time," *Harvard Business Review* 80, no. 1 (January 2002), pp. 62–69.

[2] A. C. Inkpen and A. Dinur, "Knowledge Management Processes and International Joint Ventures," *Organization Science* 9, no. 4 (July–August 1998), pp. 454–68; P. Dussauge, B. Garrette, and W. Mitchell, "Learning from Competing Partners: Outcomes and Durations of Scale and Link Alliances in Europe, North America and Asia," *Strategic Management Journal* 21, no. 2 (February 2000), pp. 99–126; C. Dhanaraj, M. A. Lyles, H. K. Steensma et al., "Managing Tacit and Explicit Knowledge Transfer in IJVs: The Role of Relational Embeddedness and the Impact on

Performance," *Journal of International Business Studies* 35, no. 5 (September 2004), pp. 428–42; K. W. Glaister and P. J. Buckley, "Strategic Motives for International Alliance Formation," *Journal of Management Studies* 33, no. 3 (May 1996), pp. 301–32.

[3] J. Anand and B. Kogut, "Technological Capabilities of Countries, Firm Rivalry and Foreign Direct Investment," *Journal of International Business Studies* 28, no. 3 (1997), pp. 445–65; J. Anand and A. Delios, "Absolute and Relative Resources as Determinants of International Acquisitions," *Strategic Management Journal* 23, no. 2 (February 2002), pp. 119–35; A. Seth, K. Song, and A. Pettit, "Value Creation and Destruction in Cross-Border Acquisitions: An Empirical Analysis of Foreign Acquisitions of U.S. Firms," *Strategic Management Journal* 23, no. 10 (October 2002), pp. 921–40; J. Anand, L. Capron, and W. Mitchell, "Using

Acquisitions to Access Multinational Diversity: Thinking beyond the Domestic versus Cross-Border M&A Comparison," *Industrial & Corporate Change* 14, no. 2 (April 2005), pp. 191–224.

[4] M. Porter, "The Competitive Advantage of Nations," *Harvard Business Review*, March–April 1990, pp. 73–93.

[5] U.S. Department of Labor, "International Comparisons of Hourly Compensation Costs in Manufacturing in 2007," *Bureau of Labor Statistics Newsletter*, March 26, 2009, p. 8.

[6] "China's Middle Class Found Wanting for Happiness," *The Independent*, March 19, 2010, www.independent.co.uk/life-style/house-and-home/chinas-middle-class-found-wanting-for-happiness-1924180.html.

[7] "China Car Sales 'Overtook the US' in 2009," *BBC News*, January 11, 2010, http://news.bbc.co.uk/2/hi/8451887.stm.

[8] Sangwon Yoon, "South Korea Targets Internet Addicts; 2 Million Hooked," *Valley News,* April 25, 2010, p. C2.

[9] Michael E. Porter, *The Competitive Advantage of Nations* (New York: Free Press, 1990), pp. 53–54.

[10] Ibid., p. 61.

[11] K.E. Meyer, M. Wright, and S. Pruthi, "Institutions, Resources, and Entry Strategies in Emerging Economies," *Strategic Management Journal* 30, no. 5 (2009), pp. 61–80; E. Pablo, "Determinants of Cross-Border M&As in Latin America," *Journal of Business Research* 62, no. 9 (2009), pp. 861–67; R. Olie, "Shades of Culture and Institutions in International Mergers," *Organization Studies* 15, no. 3 (1994), pp. 381–406.

[12] Meyer et al., "Institutions, Resources, and Entry Strategies in Emerging Economies."

[13] See Yves L. Doz and Gary Hamel, *Alliance Advantage* (Boston: Harvard Business School Press, 1998), especially chaps. 2–4; Joel Bleeke and David Ernst, "The Way to Win in Cross-Border Alliances," *Harvard Business Review* 69, no. 6 (November –December 1991), pp. 127–33; Gary Hamel, Yves L. Doz, and C. K. Prahalad, "Collaborate with Your Competitors—and Win," *Harvard Business Review* 67, no. 1 (January–February 1989), pp. 134–35; Porter, *The Competitive Advantage of Nations,* p. 66.

[14] N. Kumar and A. Chadha, "India's Outward Foreign Direct Investments in Steel Industry in a Chinese Comparative Perspective," *Industrial and Corporate Change* 18, no. 2 (2009), pp. 249–67; R. Chittoor, S. Ray, P. Aulakh, and M. B. Sarkar, "Strategic Responses to Institutional Changes: 'Indigenous Growth' Model of the Indian Pharmaceutical Industry," *Journal of International Management* 14 (2008), pp. 252–69.

[15] F. Froese and L. Goeritz, "Integration Management of Western Acquisitions in Japan," *Asian Business and Management* 6 (2007) pp. 95–114.

[16] For a discussion of the pros and cons of alliances versus acquisitions, see Jeffrey H. Dyer, Prashant Kale, and Harbir Singh, "When to Ally and When to Acquire," *Harvard Business Review* 82, no. 7–8 (July–August 2004), pp. 109–15.

[17] For additional discussion of company experiences with alliances and partnerships, see Doz and Hamel, *Alliance Advantage,* chaps. 2–7; and Rosabeth Moss Kanter, "Collaborative Advantage: The Art of the Alliance," *Harvard Business Review* 72, no. 4 (July–August 1994), pp. 96–108.

[18] Jeremy Main, "Making Global Alliances Work," *Fortune,* December 19, 1990, p. 125.

[19] Details are reported in Shawn Tully, "The Alliance from Hell," *Fortune,* June 24, 1996, pp. 64–72.

[20] C. K. Prahalad and K. Lieberthal, "The End of Corporate Imperialism," *Harvard Business Review,* 81, no. 8 (August 2003), pp.109–117.

[21] Ibid.

[22] For an in-depth discussion of the challenges of crafting strategies suitable for a world in which both production and markets are globalizing, see Pankaj Ghemawat, "Managing Differences: The Central Challenge of Global Strategy," *Harvard Business Review* 85, no. 3 (March 2007), pp. 59–68.

[23] For more details on the merits of and opportunities for cross-border transfer of successful strategy experiments, see C. A. Bartlett and S. Ghoshal, *Managing across Borders: The Transnational Solution,* 2nd ed. (Boston: Harvard Business School Press, 1998), pp. 79–80 and chap. 9. Also see Pankaj Ghemawat, "Managing Differences: The Central Challenge of Global Strategy," *Harvard Business Review* 85, no. 3 (March 2007), pp. 58–68.

[24] Lynn S. Paine, "The China Rules," *Harvard Business Review* 88, no. 6 (June 2010) pp. 103–8.

[25] Porter, *The Competitive Advantage of Nations,* pp. 53–55.

[26] Ibid., pp. 55–58.

[27] A. Inkpen, A. Sundaram, and K. Rockwood, "Cross-Border Acquisitions of U.S. Technology Assets," *California Management Review* 42, no. 3 (Spring 2000), pp. 50–71.

[28] Porter, *The Competitive Advantage of Nations,* p. 57.

[29] C. K. Prahalad and Yves L. Doz, *The Multinational Mission* (New York: Free Press, 1987), pp. 58–60; Ghemawat, "Managing Differences," pp. 58–68.

[30] Canadian International Trade Tribunal, findings issued June 16, 2005, and posted at www.citt-tcce.gc.ca (accessed September 28, 2005).

[31] This point is discussed at greater length in Prahalad and Lieberthal, "The End of Corporate Imperialism," pp. 68–79; also see David J. Arnold and John A. Quelch, "New Strategies in Emerging Markets," *Sloan Management Review* 40, no. 1 (Fall 1998), pp. 7–20. For a more extensive discussion of strategy in emerging markets, see C. K. Prahalad, *The Fortune at the Bottom of the Pyramid: Eradicating Poverty through Profits* (Upper Saddle River, NJ: Wharton, 2005), especially chaps. 1–3.

[32] "Is a Luxury Good Consumption Tax Useful?" *Beijing Review.com.cn,* June 18, 2010, www.bjreview.com.cn/print/txt/2010-06/18/content_280191.htm; "GM's First-Half China

Sales Surge Past the U.S.," *Bloomberg Businessweek,* July 2, 2010, http://businessweek.com/news/2010-07-02/gm-s-first-half-china-sales-surge-past-the-u-s-.html.

[33] Joanne Muller, "Can China Save GM?" *Forbes.com,* May 10, 2010, www.forbes.com/forbes/2010/0510/global-2000-10-automobiles-china-detroit-whitacre-save-gm.html; "Is a Luxury Good Consumption Tax Useful?"

[34] Prahalad and Lieberthal, "The End of Corporate Imperialism," pp. 72–73.

[35] Tarun Khanna, Krishna G. Palepu, and Jayant Sinha, "Strategies That Fit Emerging Markets," *Harvard Business Review* 83, no. 6 (June 2005), p. 63; Arindam K. Bhattacharya and David C. Michael, "How Local Companies Keep Multinationals at Bay," *Harvard Business Review* 86, no. 3 (March 2008), pp. 94–95.

[36] Prahalad and Lieberthal, "The End of Corporate Imperialism," p. 72.

[37] Khanna, Palepu, and Sinha, "Strategies That Fit Emerging Markets," pp. 73–74.

[38] Ibid., p. 74.

[39] Ibid., p. 76.

[40] The results and conclusions from a study of 134 local companies in 10 emerging markets are presented in Tarun Khanna and Krishna G. Palepu, "Emerging Giants: Building World-Class Companies in Developing Countries," *Harvard Business Review* 84, no. 10 (October 2006), pp. 60–69; also, an examination of strategies used by 50 local companies in emerging markets is discussed in Arindam K. Bhattacharya and David C. Michael, "How Local Companies Keep Multinationals at Bay," pp. 85–95.

[41] Steve Hamm, "Tech's Future," *BusinessWeek,* September 27, 2004, p. 88.

[42] Niroj Dawar and Tony Frost, "Competing with Giants: Survival Strategies for Local Companies in Emerging Markets," *Harvard Business Review* 77, no. 1 (January–February 1999), p. 122; see also Guitz Ger, "Localizing in the Global Village: Local Firms Competing in Global Markets," *California Management Review* 41, no. 4 (Summer 1999), pp. 64–84; Khanna and Palepu, "Emerging Giants," pp. 63–66.

[43] N. Kumar, "How Emerging Giants Are Rewriting the Rules of M&A," *Harvard Business Review,* May 2009, pp. 115–21.

[44] H. Rui and G. Yip, "Foreign Acquisitions by Chinese Firms: A Strategic Intent Perspective," *Journal of World Business* 43 (2008), pp. 213–26.

[45] Dawar and Frost, "Competing with Giants," p. 124.

[46] Ibid., p. 126; Khanna and Palepu, "Emerging Giants," pp. 60–69.

CHAPTER 8

CORPORATE STRATEGY

Diversification and the Multibusiness Company

> Fit between a parent and its businesses is a two-edged sword: A good fit can create value; a bad one can destroy it.
>
> **—Andrew Campbell,**
> *Michael Gould, and Marcus Alexander*

> Make winners out of every business in your company. Don't carry losers.
>
> **—Jack Welch**
> *Former CEO, General Electric*

> We are quite pragmatic. If a business does not contribute to our overall vision, it has to go.
>
> **—Richard Wambold**
> *CEO, Pactiv*

> I think our biggest achievement to date has been bringing back to life an inherent Disney synergy that enables each part of our business to draw from, build upon, and bolster the others.
>
> **—Michael Eisner**
> *Former CEO, Walt Disney Company*

LEARNING OBJECTIVES

LO 1. Understand when and how business diversification can enhance shareholder value.

LO 2. Gain an understanding of how related diversification strategies can produce cross-business strategic fit capable of delivering competitive advantage.

LO 3. Become aware of the merits and risks of corporate strategies keyed to unrelated diversification.

LO 4. Gain command of the analytical tools for evaluating a company's diversification strategy.

LO 5. Understand a diversified company's four main corporate strategy options for solidifying its diversification strategy and improving company performance.

n this chapter, we move up one level in the strategy-making hierarchy, from strategy making in a single-business enterprise to strategy making in a diversified enterprise. Because a diversified company is a collection of individual businesses, the strategy-making task is more complicated. In a one-business company, managers have to come up with a plan for competing successfully in only a single industry environment—the result is what we labeled in Chapter 2 as *business strategy* (or *business-level strategy*). But in a diversified company, the strategy-making challenge involves assessing multiple industry environments and developing a *set* of business strategies, one for each industry arena in which the diversified company operates. And top executives at a diversified company must still go one step further and devise a companywide or *corporate strategy* for improving the attractiveness and performance of the company's overall business lineup and for making a rational whole out of its diversified collection of individual businesses.

In most diversified companies, corporate-level executives delegate considerable strategy-making authority to the heads of each business, usually giving them the latitude to craft a business strategy suited to their particular industry and competitive circumstances and holding them accountable for producing good results. But the task of crafting a diversified company's overall or corporate strategy falls squarely in the lap of top-level executives and involves four distinct facets:

1. *Picking new industries to enter and deciding on the mode of entry.* The first concerns in diversifying are what new industries to get into and whether to enter by starting a new business from the ground up, acquiring a company already in the target industry, or forming a joint venture or strategic alliance with another company.

2. *Pursuing opportunities to leverage cross-business value chain relationships and strategic fit into competitive advantage.* A company that diversifies into businesses with competitively important value chain matchups (pertaining to common technology, supply chain logistics, production, distribution channels, and/or customers) gains competitive advantage potential not open to a company that diversifies into businesses whose value chains are totally unrelated and that require totally different resources and capabilities. Capturing this competitive advantage potential requires capitalizing on such cross-business opportunities as transferring skills or technology from one business to another, reducing costs via sharing common facilities and resources, utilizing the company's well-known brand names and distribution muscle to increase the sales of newly acquired products, and encouraging knowledge-sharing and collaborative activity among the businesses.

3. *Establishing investment priorities and steering corporate resources into the most attractive*

business units. A diversified company's different businesses are usually not equally attractive from the standpoint of investing additional funds. It is incumbent on corporate management to (a) decide on the priorities for investing capital in the company's different businesses, (b) channel resources into areas where earnings potentials are higher and away from areas where they are lower, and (c) divest business units that are chronically poor performers or are in an increasingly unattractive industry. Divesting poor performers and businesses in unattractive industries frees up unproductive investments either for redeployment to promising business units or for financing attractive new acquisitions.

4. *Initiating actions to boost the combined performance of the corporation's collection of businesses.* Corporate strategists must craft moves to improve the overall performance of the corporation's business lineup and sustain increases in shareholder value. Strategic options for diversified corporations include (a) sticking closely with the existing business lineup and pursuing opportunities presented by these businesses, (b) broadening the scope of diversification by entering additional industries, (c) divesting some businesses and retrenching to a narrower collection of diversified businesses with better overall performance prospects, and (d) restructuring the entire company by divesting some businesses and acquiring others so as to put a whole new face on the company's business lineup.

The demanding and time-consuming nature of these four tasks explains why corporate executives generally refrain from becoming immersed in the details of crafting and executing business-level strategies, preferring instead to delegate lead responsibility for business strategy and business-level operations to the heads of each business unit.

In the first portion of this chapter we describe the various means a company can use to become diversified, and we explore the pros and cons of related versus unrelated diversification strategies. The second part of the chapter looks at how to evaluate the attractiveness of a diversified company's business lineup, decide whether the company has a good diversification strategy, and identify ways to improve its future performance. In the chapter's concluding section, we survey the strategic options open to already diversified companies.

WHEN TO DIVERSIFY

As long as a company has its hands full trying to capitalize on profitable growth opportunities in its present industry, there is no urgency to pursue diversification. But the opportunities for profitable growth are often limited in mature industries and declining markets. A company may also encounter diminishing market opportunities and stagnating sales if its industry becomes competitively unattractive and unprofitable. A company's growth prospects may dim quickly if demand for the industry's product is eroded by the appearance of alternative technologies, substitute products, or fast-shifting buyer preferences. Consider, for example, how digital cameras have virtually destroyed the business of companies dependent on making camera film and doing film processing, how iPods and other brands of digital music players (as well as online music stores) have affected the revenues of retailers of music CDs, and how the mushrooming use of cell phones and Internet-based voice communication have diminished demand for landline-based telecommunication services and eroded the revenues of such once-dominant long-distance providers as AT&T, British Telecommunications, and NTT in Japan. Under conditions such as these, diversification into new industries always merits strong consideration—particularly if the resources and capabilities of a company can be employed more fruitfully in other industries.[1]

A company becomes a prime candidate for diversifying under the following four circumstances:[2]

1. When it spots opportunities for expanding into industries whose technologies and products complement its present business.

2. When it can leverage its collection of resources and capabilities by expanding into businesses where these resources and capabilities are valuable competitive assets.

3. When diversifying into additional businesses opens new avenues for reducing costs via cross-business sharing or transfer of competitively valuable resources and capabilities.

4. When it has a powerful and well-known brand name that can be transferred to the products of other businesses and thereby used as a lever for driving up the sales and profits of such businesses.

BUILDING SHAREHOLDER VALUE: THE ULTIMATE JUSTIFICATION FOR DIVERSIFYING

Diversification must do more for a company than simply spread its business risk across various industries. In principle, diversification cannot be considered a success unless it results in *added long-term economic value for shareholders*—value that shareholders cannot capture on their own by purchasing stock in companies in different industries or investing in mutual funds so as to spread their investments across several industries.

For there to be reasonable expectations of producing added long-term shareholder value, a move to diversify into a new business must pass three tests:[3]

1. *The industry attractiveness test.* The industry to be entered must be attractive enough to yield consistently good returns on investment. Whether an industry is attractive depends chiefly on the presence of industry and competitive conditions that are conducive to earning as-good or better profits and return on investment than the company is earning in its present business(es). It is hard to justify diversifying into an industry where profit expectations are *lower* than those in the company's present businesses.

2. *The cost-of-entry test.* The cost of entering the target industry must not be so high as to erode the potential for good profitability. Industry attractiveness is not a sufficient reason for a firm to diversify into an industry. In fact, the more attractive an industry's prospects are for growth and long-term profitability, the more expensive the industry can be to get into. Entry barriers for start-up companies are likely to be high in attractive industries; were barriers

LO 1

Understand when and how business diversification can enhance shareholder value.

low, a rush of new entrants would soon erode the potential for high profitability. And buying a well-positioned company in an appealing industry often entails a high acquisition cost that makes passing the cost-of-entry test less likely. Since the owners of a successful and growing company usually demand a price that reflects their business's profit prospects, it's easy for such an acquisition to fail the cost-of-entry test.

3. *The better-off test.* Diversifying into a new business must offer potential for the company's existing businesses and the new business to perform better together under a single corporate umbrella than they would perform operating as independent, stand-alone businesses—an effect known as **synergy.** For example, let's say that company A diversifies by purchasing company B in another industry. If A and B's consolidated profits in the years to come prove no greater than what each could have earned on its own, then A's diversification won't provide its shareholders with added value. Company A's shareholders could have achieved the same $1 + 1 = 2$ result by merely purchasing stock in company B. Diversification does not result in added long-term value for shareholders unless it produces a $1 + 1 = 3$ effect where the businesses *perform better together* as part of the same firm than they could have performed as independent companies.

CORE CONCEPT

Creating added value for shareholders via diversification requires building a multibusiness company where the whole is greater than the sum of its parts—an outcome known as **synergy.**

Diversification moves must satisfy all three tests to grow shareholder value over the long term. Diversification moves that can pass only one or two tests are suspect.

STRATEGIES FOR ENTERING NEW BUSINESSES

The means of entering new businesses can take any of three forms: acquisition, internal start-up, or joint ventures with other companies.

Acquisition of an Existing Business

Acquisition is a popular means of diversifying into another industry. Not only is it quicker than trying to launch a brand-new operation, but it also offers an effective way to hurdle such entry barriers as acquiring technological know-how, establishing supplier relationships, becoming big enough to match rivals' unit costs, having to spend large sums on introductory advertising and promotions, and securing adequate distribution. Acquisitions are also commonly employed to access resources and capabilities that are complementary to those of the acquiring firm and that cannot be developed readily internally. Buying an ongoing operation allows the acquirer to move directly to the task of building a strong market position in the target industry, rather than getting bogged down in trying to develop the knowledge, experience, scale of operation, and market reputation necessary for a start-up entrant to become an effective competitor.

However, acquiring an existing business can prove quite expensive. The costs of acquiring another business include not only the acquisition price but also the costs of negotiating and completing the purchase transaction and the costs of integrating the business into the diversified company's portfolio. If the company to be acquired is a successful company, the acquisition price will include a hefty *premium* over the preacquisition value of the company. For example, the $5.8 billion that Xerox paid to acquire Affiliated Computer Services in 2010 included a 38 percent premium over the service company's market value.[4] Premiums are paid in order to convince the shareholders and managers of the target company that it is in their financial interests to approve the deal. The average premium in deals between U.S. companies rose to 56 percent in 2009, but it is more often in the 30 to 40 percent range.[5]

The big dilemma an acquisition-minded firm faces is whether to pay a premium price for a successful company or to buy a struggling company at a bargain price.[6] If the buying firm has little knowledge of the industry but ample capital, it is often better off purchasing a capable, strongly positioned firm—even if its current owners demand a premium price. However, when the acquirer sees promising ways to transform a weak firm into a strong one and has the resources, the know-how, and the patience to do it, a struggling company can be the better long-term investment.

While acquisitions offer an enticing means for entering a new business, many fail to deliver on their promise.[7] Realizing the potential gains from an acquisition requires a successful integration of the acquired company into the culture, systems, and structure of the acquiring firm. This can be a costly and time-consuming operation. Acquisitions can also fail to deliver long-term shareholder value if the acquirer overestimates the potential gains and pays a premium in excess of the realized gains. High integration costs and excessive price premiums are two reasons that an acquisition might fail the cost-of-entry test. Firms with significant experience in making acquisitions are better able to avoid these types of problems.[8]

> **CORE CONCEPT**
>
> An **acquisition premium** is the amount by which the price offered exceeds the preacquisition market value of the target company.

Internal Development

Internal development of new businesses has become an increasingly important means for companies to diversify and is often referred to as **corporate venturing** or *new venture development.* It involves building a new business from scratch. Although building a new business from the ground up is generally a time-consuming and uncertain process, it avoids the pitfalls associated with entry via acquisition and may allow the firm to realize greater profits in the end. It may offer a viable means of entering a new or emerging industry where there are no good acquisition candidates.

Entering a new business via internal development also poses some significant hurdles. An internal new venture not only has to overcome industry entry barriers but also has to invest in new production capacity, develop sources of supply, hire and train employees, build channels of distribution, grow a customer base, and so on. The risks associated with internal start-ups are substantial, and the likelihood of failure is often high. Moreover, the culture, structures, and organizational systems of some companies may impede innovation and make it difficult for corporate entrepreneurship to flourish.

Generally, internal development of a new business has appeal only when (1) the parent company already has in-house most or all of the skills and resources it needs to piece together a new business and compete effectively; (2) there is ample time to launch the business; (3) the internal cost of entry is lower than the cost of entry via acquisition; (4) the targeted industry is populated with many relatively

> **CORE CONCEPT**
>
> **Corporate venturing** (or *new venture development*) is the process of developing new businesses as an outgrowth of a company's established business operations. It is also referred to as *corporate entrepreneurship* or *intrapreneurship* since it requires entrepreneurial-like qualities within a larger enterprise.

small firms such that the new start-up does not have to compete head to head against larger, more powerful rivals; (5) adding new production capacity will not adversely impact the supply-demand balance in the industry; and (6) incumbent firms are likely to be slow or ineffective in responding to a new entrant's efforts to crack the market.[9]

Joint Ventures

Joint ventures entail forming a new business that is owned jointly by two or more companies. Entering a new business via joint venture can be useful in at least three types of situations.[10] First, a joint venture is a good vehicle for pursuing an opportunity that is too complex, uneconomical, or risky for one company to pursue alone. Second, joint ventures make sense when the opportunities in a new industry require a broader range of competencies and know-how than a company can marshal. Many of the opportunities in satellite-based telecommunications, biotechnology, and network-based systems that blend hardware, software, and services call for the coordinated development of complementary innovations and the tackling of an intricate web of financial, technical, political, and regulatory factors simultaneously. In such cases, pooling the resources and competencies of two or more companies is a wiser and less risky way to proceed. Third, companies sometimes use joint ventures to diversify into a new industry when the diversification move entails having operations in a foreign country—several governments require foreign companies operating within their borders to have a local partner that has minority, if not majority, ownership in the local operations. Aside from fulfilling host-government ownership requirements, companies usually seek out a local partner with expertise and other resources that will aid the success of the newly established local operation.

However, as discussed in Chapters 6 and 7, partnering with another company—in the form of either a joint venture or a collaborative alliance—has significant drawbacks due to the potential for conflicting objectives, disagreements over how to best operate the venture, culture clashes, and so on. Joint ventures are generally the least durable of the entry options, usually lasting only until the partners decide to go their own ways.

Choosing a Mode of Entry

The choice of how best to enter a new business—whether through internal development, acquisition, or joint venture—depends on the answers to four important questions:

- Does the company have all of the resources and capabilities it requires to enter the business through internal development or is it lacking some critical resources?
- Are there entry barriers to overcome?
- Is speed an important factor in the firm's chances for successful entry?
- Which is the least costly mode of entry, given the company's objectives?

The Question of Critical Resources and Capabilities   If a firm has all the resources it needs to start up a new business or will be able to easily purchase or lease any missing resources, it may choose to enter the business via internal development. However, if missing critical resources cannot be easily purchased or leased, a firm wishing to enter a new business must obtain these missing resources through either acquisition or joint venture. Bank of America acquired Merrill Lynch in 2008 to obtain critical investment banking resources and capabilities that it lacked. The acquisition of these additional capabilities complemented Bank of America's strengths in corporate banking and opened up new business opportunities for Bank of America. Firms often acquire other companies as a way to enter foreign markets where they lack local marketing knowledge, distribution capabilities, and relationships with local suppliers or customers. McDonald's acquisition of Burghy, Italy's only national hamburger chain, offers an example.[11] If there are no good acquisition opportunities or if the firm wants to avoid the high cost of acquiring and integrating another firm, it may choose to enter via joint venture. This type of entry mode has the added advantage of spreading the risk of entering a new business, which is particularly attractive when uncertainty is high. DeBeers's joint venture with the luxury goods company LVMH provided DeBeers with the complementary marketing capabilities it needed to enter the diamond retailing business, as well as partner to share the risk.

The Question of Entry Barriers The second question to ask is whether entry barriers would prevent a new entrant from gaining a foothold and succeeding in the industry. If entry barriers are low and the industry is populated by small firms, internal development may be the preferred mode of entry. If entry barriers are high, the company may still be able to enter with ease if it has the requisite resources and capabilities for overcoming high barriers. For example, entry barriers due to reputational advantages may be surmounted by a diversified company with a widely known and trusted corporate name. But if the entry barriers cannot be overcome readily, then the only feasible entry route may be through acquisition of a well-established company. While entry barriers may also be overcome with a strong complementary joint venture, this mode is the more uncertain choice due to the lack of industry experience.

The Question of Speed Speed is another determining factor in deciding how to go about entering a new business. Acquisition is a favored mode of entry when speed is of the essence, as is the case in rapidly changing industries where fast movers can secure long-term positioning advantages. Speed is important in industries where early movers gain experience-based advantages that grow ever larger over time as they move down the learning curve and in technology-based industries where there is a race to establish an industry standard or leading technological platform. But in other cases it can be better to enter a market after the uncertainties about technology or consumer preferences have been resolved and learn from the missteps of early entrants. In these cases, joint venture or internal development may be preferred.

The Question of Comparative Cost The question of which mode of entry is most cost-effective is a critical one, given the need for a diversification strategy to pass the cost-of-entry test. Acquisition can be a high-cost mode of entry due to the need to pay a premium over the share price of the target company. When the premium is high, the price of the deal will exceed the worth of the acquired company as a stand-alone business by a substantial amount. Moreover, the true cost of an acquisition must include the *transaction costs* of identifying and evaluating potential targets, negotiating a price, and completing other aspects of

CORE CONCEPT

Transaction costs are the costs of completing a business agreement or deal of some sort, over and above the price of the deal. They can include the costs of searching for an attractive target, the costs of evaluating its worth, bargaining costs, and the costs of completing the transaction.

deal making. In addition, the true cost must take into account the costs of integrating the acquired company into the parent company's portfolio of businesses.

Strategic alliances and other types of partnerships may provide a way to conserve on such entry costs. But even here, there are organizational coordination costs and transaction costs that must be considered, including settling on the terms of the arrangement. If the partnership doesn't proceed smoothly and is not founded on trust, these costs may be significant. In making the choice about how to proceed, the firm should also consider the possibility of even simpler arrangements. If the objective is simply to leverage a brand name and company logo, for example, a strategic alliance centered on licensing may be the lowest-cost alternative. Licensing is particularly attractive if the company lacks other resources and capabilities that are needed for an entry move. Harley-Davidson, for example, has chosen to license its brand name to makers of apparel as an alternative to entering the apparel industry, for which it is ill suited.

CHOOSING THE DIVERSIFICATION PATH: RELATED VERSUS UNRELATED BUSINESSES

CORE CONCEPT

Related businesses possess competitively valuable cross-business value chain and resource matchups; **unrelated businesses** have dissimilar value chains and resource requirements, with no competitively important cross-business relationships at the value chain level.

Once a company decides to diversify, it faces the choice of whether to diversify into **related businesses, unrelated businesses,** or some mix of both. Businesses are said to be *related* when their value chains exhibit competitively important cross-business relationships. By this, we mean that there is a close correspondence between the businesses in terms of how they perform *key* value chain activities and the resources and capabilities each needs to perform those activities. The big appeal of related diversification is to build shareholder value by leveraging these cross-business relationships into competitive advantages, thus allowing the company as a whole to perform better than just the sum of its individual businesses. Businesses are said to be *unrelated* when the resource requirements and key value chain activities are so dissimilar that no competitively important cross-business relationships exist.

The next two sections explore the ins and outs of related and unrelated diversification.

STRATEGIC FIT AND DIVERSIFICATION INTO RELATED BUSINESSES

A related diversification strategy involves building the company around businesses where there is *strategic fit with respect to key value chain activities and competitive assets.* **Strategic fit** exists whenever one or more activities constituting the value chains of different businesses are sufficiently similar as to present opportunities for cross-business sharing or transferring of the resources and capabilities that enable these activities.[12] Prime examples of such opportunities include:

- *Transferring specialized expertise, technological know-how, or other competitively valuable capabilities from one business's value chain to another's.*

- *Combining the related value chain activities of separate businesses into a single operation to achieve lower costs.* For instance, it is often feasible to manufacture the products of different businesses in a single plant, use the same warehouses for shipping and distribution, or have a single sales force for the products of different businesses (because they are marketed to the same types of customers).

- *Exploiting common use of a well-known brand name that connotes excellence in a certain type of product range.* For example, Yamaha's name in motorcycles gave the company instant credibility and recognition in entering the personal-watercraft business, allowing it to achieve a significant market share without spending large sums on advertising to establish a brand identity for the WaveRunner. Sony's name in consumer electronics made it easier for Sony to enter the market for video games with its PlayStation console and lineup of PlayStation video games. Apple's well-known and highly popular iPods gave the firm instant credibility and name recognition in launching its iPhones and iPads.

- *Sharing other resources that support corresponding value chain activities of the businesses, such as relationships with suppliers or a dealer network.* After acquiring Marvel Comics in 2009, the Walt Disney Company saw to it that Marvel's iconic characters, such as Spiderman, Iron Man, and the Black Widow, were shared with many of the other Disney businesses, including its theme parks, retail stores, and video game business. (Disney's characters, starting with Mickey Mouse, have always been among the most valuable of its resources.)

- *Engaging in cross-business collaboration and knowledge sharing to create new competitively valuable resources and capabilities.*

Related diversification is based on value chain matchups with respect to *key* value chain activities—those that play a central role in each business's strategy and that link to its industry's key success factors. Such matchups facilitate the sharing or transfer of the competitively important resources and capabilities that enable the performance of these activities and underlie each business's quest for competitive advantage. By facilitating the sharing or transferring of such important competitive assets, related diversification can boost each business's prospects for competitive success.

The resources and capabilities that are leveraged in related diversification are *specialized resources and capabilities.* By this, we mean that they have very *specific* applications; their use is restricted to a limited range of business contexts in which these applications are competitively relevant. Because they are adapted for particular applications, specialized resources and capabilities must be utilized by certain kinds of businesses operating in specific types of industries to have value; they have limited utility outside this specific range of industry and business applications. This is in contrast to *generalized resources and capabilities* (such as general management capabilities, human resource management capabilities, and

LO 2

Gain an understanding of how related diversification strategies can produce cross-business strategic fit capable of delivering competitive advantage.

CORE CONCEPT

Strategic fit exists when the value chains of different businesses present opportunities for cross-business resource transfer, lower costs through combining the performance of related value chain activities or resource sharing, cross-business use of a potent brand name, and cross-business collaboration to build stronger competitive capabilities.

general accounting services), which can be applied usefully across a wide range of industry and business types.

L'Oréal is the world's largest beauty products company, with more than $25 billion in revenues and a successful strategy of related diversification built upon leveraging a highly specialized set of resources and capabilities. These include 18 dermatologic and cosmetic research centers, R&D capabilities and scientific knowledge concerning skin and hair care, patents and secret formulas for hair and skin care products, and robotic applications developed specifically for testing the safety of hair and skin care products. These resources and capabilities are highly valuable for businesses focused on products for human skin and hair—they are *specialized* to such applications, and, in consequence, they are of little or no value beyond this restricted range of applications. To leverage these resources in a way that maximizes their potential value, L'Oréal has diversified into cosmetics, hair care products, skin care products, and fragrances (but not food, transportation, industrial services, or any application area far from the narrow domain in which its specialized resources are competitively relevant). L'Oréal's businesses are related to one another on the basis of its value-generating specialized resources and capabilities and the cross-business linkages among the value chain activities that they enable.

Corning's most competitively valuable resources and capabilities are specialized to applications concerning fiber optics and specialty glass and ceramics. Over the course of its 150-year history, it has developed an unmatched understanding of fundamental glass science and related technologies in the field of optics. Its capabilities now span a variety of sophisticated technologies and include expertise in domains such as custom glass composition, specialty glass melting and forming, precision optics, high-end transmissive coatings, and opto-mechanical materials. Corning has leveraged these specialized capabilities into a position of global leadership in five related market segments: display technologies based on glass substrates, environmental technologies using ceramic substrates and filters, optical fibers and cables for telecommunications, optical biosensors for drug discovery, and specialty materials employing advanced optics and specialty glass solutions. The market segments into which Corning has diversified are all related by their reliance on Corning's specialized capability set and by the many value chain activities that they have in common as a result.

General Mills has diversified into a closely related set of food businesses on the basis of its capabilities in the realm of "kitchen chemistry" and food production technologies. Its businesses include General Mills cereals, Pillsbury and Betty Crocker baking products, yogurts, organic foods, dinner mixes, canned goods, and snacks. Earlier it had diversified into restaurant businesses on the mistaken notion that all food businesses were related. As a result of exiting these businesses in the mid-1990s, the company was able to improve its overall profitability and strengthen its position in its remaining businesses. The lesson from its experience—and a takeaway for the managers of any diversified company—is that it is not product relatedness that defines a well-crafted related diversification strategy. Rather, the businesses must be related in terms of their key value chain activities and the specialized resources and capabilities that enable these activities.[13] An example is Citizen Holdings Company, whose products appear to be different (watches, miniature card calculators, handheld televisions) but are related in terms of their common reliance on miniaturization know-how and advanced precision technologies.[14]

While companies pursuing related diversification strategies may also have opportunities to share or transfer their *generalized* resources and capabilities (e.g. information systems; human resource management practices; accounting and tax services; budgeting, planning, and financial reporting systems; expertise in legal and regulatory affairs; and fringe-benefit management systems), the most competitively valuable opportunities for resource sharing or transfer always come from leveraging their specialized resources and capabilities. The reason for this is that specialized resources and capabilities drive the key value-creating activities that both connect the businesses (at points where there is strategic fit) and link to the key success factors in the markets where they are competitively relevant. Figure 8.1 illustrates the range of opportunities to share and/or transfer specialized resources and capabilities among the value chain activities of related businesses. It is important to recognize that even though generalized resources and capabilities may be shared by multiple business units, such resource sharing alone cannot form the backbone of a strategy keyed to related diversification.

CORE CONCEPT

Related diversification involves sharing or transferring *specialized* resources and capabilities. **Specialized resources and capabilities** have very specific applications and their use is limited to a restricted range of industry and business types, in contrast to **generalized resources and capabilities** that can be widely applied and can be deployed across a broad range of industry and business types.

Figure 8.1   Related Businesses Provide Opportunities to Benefit from Competitively Valuable Strategic Fit

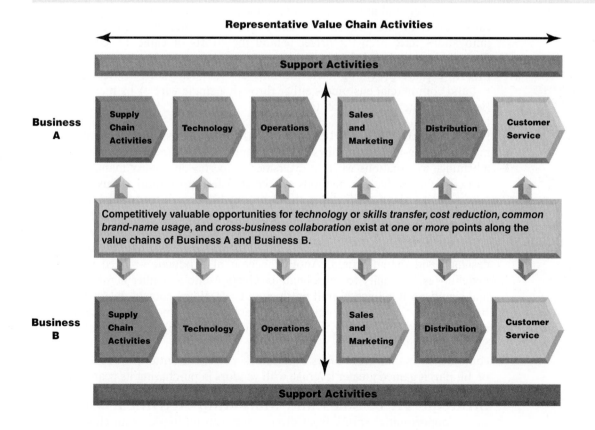

Identifying Cross-Business Strategic Fit along the Value Chain

Cross-business strategic fit can exist anywhere along the value chain—in R&D and technology activities, in supply chain activities and relationships with suppliers, in manufacturing, in sales and marketing, in distribution activities, or in customer service activities.[15]

Strategic Fit in Supply Chain Activities   Businesses that have strategic fit with respect to supply chain activities can perform better together because of the potential for skills transfer in procuring materials, the sharing of capabilities in logistics, the benefits of added collaboration with common supply chain partners, and/or added leverage with shippers in securing volume discounts on incoming parts and components. Dell Computer's strategic partnerships with leading suppliers of microprocessors, circuit boards, disk drives, memory chips, flat-panel displays, wireless capabilities, long-life batteries, and other PC-related components have been an important element of the company's strategy to diversify into servers, data storage devices, networking components, and LCD TVs—products that include many components common to PCs and that can be sourced from the same strategic partners that provide Dell with PC components.

Strategic Fit in R&D and Technology Activities   Businesses with technology-sharing benefits can perform better together than apart because of potential cost savings in R&D, potentially shorter times in getting new products to market, and more innovative products or processes. Moreover, technological advances in one business can lead to increased sales for both. Technological innovations have been the driver behind the efforts of cable TV companies to diversify into high-speed Internet access (via the use of cable modems) and, further, to explore providing local and long-distance telephone service to residential and commercial customers either through a single wire or by means of VoIP (voice over Internet protocol) technology.

Manufacturing-Related Strategic Fit   Cross-business strategic fit in manufacturing-related activities can represent an important source of competitive advantage in situations where a diversifier's expertise in quality manufacture and cost-efficient production methods can be transferred to another business. When Emerson Electric diversified into the chain-saw business, it transferred its expertise in low-cost manufacture to its newly acquired Beaird-Poulan business division; the transfer drove Beaird-Poulan's new strategy—to be the low-cost provider of chain-saw products—and fundamentally changed the way Beaird-Poulan chain saws were designed and manufactured. Another benefit of production-related value chain matchups is the ability to consolidate production into a smaller number of plants and significantly reduce overall production costs. When snowmobile maker Bombardier diversified into motorcycles, it was able to set up motorcycle assembly lines in the same manufacturing facility where it was assembling snowmobiles. When Smucker's acquired Procter & Gamble's Jif peanut butter business, it was able to combine the manufacture of its own Smucker's peanut butter products with those of Jif, plus it gained greater leverage with vendors in purchasing its peanut supplies.

Strategic Fit in Sales and Marketing Activities   Various cost-saving opportunities spring from diversifying into businesses with closely related sales and marketing activities. When the products are sold directly to the same customers, sales costs can often be reduced by using a single sales force and avoiding having two different salespeople call on the same customer. The products of related businesses can be promoted at the same Web site and included in the same media ads and sales brochures. After-sale service and repair organizations for the products of closely related businesses can often be consolidated into a single operation. There may be opportunities to reduce costs by consolidating order processing and billing and using common promotional tie-ins. When global power-tool maker Black & Decker acquired Vector Products, it was able to use its own global sales force and distribution facilities to sell and distribute the newly acquired Vector power inverters, vehicle battery chargers, and rechargeable spotlights because the types of customers that carried its power tools (discounters like Walmart and Target, home centers, and hardware stores) also stocked the types of products produced by Vector.

A second category of benefits arises when different businesses use similar sales and marketing approaches; in such cases, there may be competitively valuable opportunities to transfer selling, merchandising, advertising, and product differentiation skills from one business to another. Procter & Gamble's product lineup includes Folgers coffee, Tide laundry detergent, Crest toothpaste, Ivory soap, Charmin toilet tissue, Gillette razors and blades, Duracell batteries, Oral-B toothbrushes, and Head & Shoulders shampoo. All of these have different competitors and different supply chain and production requirements, but they all move through the same wholesale distribution systems, are sold in common retail settings to the same shoppers, are advertised and promoted in much the same ways, and require the same marketing and merchandising skills.

Distribution-Related Strategic Fit Businesses with closely related distribution activities can perform better together than apart because of potential cost savings in sharing the same distribution facilities or using many of the same wholesale distributors and retail dealers to access customers. When Conair Corporation acquired Allegro Manufacturing's travel bag and travel accessory business in 2007, it was able to consolidate its own distribution centers for hair dryers and curling irons with those of Allegro, thereby generating cost savings for both businesses. Likewise, since Conair products and Allegro's neck rests, ear plugs, luggage tags, and toiletry kits were sold by the same types of retailers (discount stores, supermarket chains, and drugstore chains), Conair was able to convince many of the retailers not carrying Allegro products to take on the line.

Strategic Fit in Customer Service Activities Opportunities for cost savings from sharing resources or for greater differentiation through skills transfer can come from strategic fit with respect to customer service activities, just as they do along other points of the value chain. For example, cost savings may come from consolidating after-sale service and repair organizations for the products of closely related businesses into a single operation. Likewise, different businesses can often use the same customer service infrastructure. For instance, an electric utility that diversifies into natural gas, water, appliance sales and repair services, and home security services can use the same customer data network, the same customer call centers and local offices, the same billing and customer accounting systems, and the same customer service infrastructure to support all of its products and services. Through the transfer of best practices in customer service across a set of related businesses or through sharing resources such as proprietary information about customer preferences, a multibusiness company can create a differentiation advantage through higher-quality customer service.

Strategic Fit, Economies of Scope, and Competitive Advantage

What makes related diversification an attractive strategy is the opportunity to convert cross-business strategic fit into a competitive advantage over business rivals whose operations do not offer comparable strategic-fit benefits. The greater the relatedness among a diversified company's businesses, the bigger a company's window for converting strategic fit into competitive advantage via (1) transferring skills or knowledge, (2) combining related value chain activities to achieve lower costs, (3) leveraging the use of a well-respected brand name or other differentiation-enhancing resources, and (4) using cross-business collaboration and knowledge sharing to create new resources and capabilities and drive innovation.

The Path to Competitive Advantage and Economies of Scope

Sharing or transferring valuable specialized assets among the company's businesses can help each business perform its value chain activities more proficiently. This translates into competitive advantage for the businesses in one or two basic ways: (1) The businesses can contribute to greater efficiency and lower costs relative to their competitors, and/or (2) they can provide a basis for differentiation so that customers are willing to pay relatively more for the businesses' goods and services. In either or both of these ways, a firm with a well-executed related diversification strategy can boost the chances of its businesses attaining a competitive advantage.

> **CORE CONCEPT**
>
> **Economies of scope** are cost reductions that flow from operating in multiple businesses (a *larger scope* of operation), whereas *economies of scale* accrue from a *larger-size* operation.

Related businesses often present opportunities to eliminate or reduce the costs of performing certain value chain activities; such cost savings are termed **economies of scope**—a concept distinct from *economies of scale.* Economies of *scale* are cost savings that accrue directly from a larger-size operation; for example, unit costs may be lower in a large plant than in a small plant, lower in a large distribution center than in a small one, lower for large-volume purchases of network advertising than for small-volume purchases. Economies of *scope,* however, stem directly from resource sharing, facilitated by strategic fit along the value chains of related businesses. Such economies are open only to a multibusiness enterprise that enables its businesses to share technology, perform R&D together, use common manufacturing or distribution facilities, share a common sales force or distributor-dealer network, use the same established brand name, and/or share other commonly employed resources and capabilities. *The greater the cross-business economies associated with resource sharing and strategic fit, the greater the potential for a related diversification strategy to yield a competitive advantage based on lower costs than those of rivals.*

From Competitive Advantage to Added Profitability and Gains in Shareholder Value

The competitive advantage potential that flows from economies of scope and the capture of other strategic-fit benefits is what enables a company pursuing related diversification to achieve $1 + 1 = 3$ financial performance and the hoped-for gains in shareholder value. The strategic and business logic is compelling: Capturing the benefits of strategic fit along the value chains of its related businesses gives a diversified company a clear path to achieving competitive advantage over undiversified competitors and competitors whose own diversification efforts don't offer equivalent strategic-fit benefits.[16] Such competitive advantage potential provides a company with a dependable basis for earning profits and a return on investment that exceeds what the company's businesses could earn as stand-alone enterprises. Converting the competitive advantage potential into greater profitability is what fuels $1 + 1 = 3$ gains in shareholder value—the necessary outcome for satisfying the better-off test and proving the business merit of a company's diversification effort.

There are four things to bear in mind here:

> Diversifying into related businesses where competitively valuable strategic-fit benefits can be captured puts a company's businesses in position to perform better financially as part of the company than they could have performed as independent enterprises, thus providing a clear avenue for boosting shareholder value.

1. Capturing cross-business strategic-fit benefits via a strategy of related diversification builds shareholder value in ways that shareholders cannot undertake by simply owning a portfolio of stocks of companies in different industries.

2. The capture of cross-business strategic-fit benefits is possible only via a strategy of related diversification.

3. The benefits of cross-business strategic fit come from the transferring or sharing of competitively valuable resources and capabilities among the businesses—resources and capabilities that are *specialized* to certain applications and have value only in specific types of industries and businesses.

4. The benefits of cross-business strategic fit are not automatically realized when a company diversifies into related businesses; *the benefits materialize only after management has successfully pursued internal actions to capture them.*

DIVERSIFICATION INTO UNRELATED BUSINESSES

An unrelated diversification strategy discounts the merits of pursuing cross-business strategic fit and, instead, focuses squarely on entering and operating businesses in industries that allow the company as a whole to increase its earnings. Companies that pursue a strategy of unrelated diversification generally exhibit a willingness to diversify into *any industry* where senior managers see an opportunity to realize consistently good financial results. Such companies are frequently labeled *conglomerates* because their business interests range broadly across diverse industries. Companies that pursue unrelated diversification nearly always enter new businesses by acquiring an established company rather than by forming a start-up subsidiary within their own corporate structures or participating in joint ventures.

> **LO 3**
>
> Become aware of the merits and risks of corporate strategies keyed to unrelated diversification.

With a strategy of unrelated diversification, the emphasis is on satisfying the attractiveness and cost-of-entry tests and each business's prospects for good financial performance. Thus, with an unrelated diversification strategy, company managers spend much time and effort screening acquisition candidates and evaluating the pros and cons of keeping or divesting existing businesses, using such criteria as:

- Whether the business can meet corporate targets for profitability and return on investment.
- Whether the business is in an industry with attractive growth potential.
- Whether the business is big enough to contribute *significantly* to the parent firm's bottom line.

But the key to successful unrelated diversification is to go beyond these considerations and ensure that the strategy passes the better-off test as well. This test requires more than just growth in revenues; it requires *growth in profits*—beyond what could be achieved by a mutual fund or a holding company that owns the businesses without adding any value. Unless the different businesses are more profitable together under the corporate umbrella than they are apart as independent businesses, *the strategy cannot create economic value for shareholders.* And unless it does so, there is *no real justification for unrelated diversification,* since top executives have a fiduciary responsibility to maximize long-term shareholder value.

Building Shareholder Value via Unrelated Diversification

Given the absence of cross-business strategic fit with which to create competitive advantages, building economic shareholder value via unrelated diversification ultimately hinges on the ability of the parent company to improve its businesses via other means. Critical to this endeavor is the role that the parent company plays *as a corporate parent.* To the extent that a company has strong *parenting capabilities*—capabilities that involve nurturing, guiding, grooming, and governing constituent businesses—a corporate parent can propel its businesses forward and help them gain ground over their market rivals. Corporate parents also contribute to the competitiveness of their unrelated businesses by sharing or transferring *generalized resources and capabilities* across the businesses—competitive assets that have utility in any type of industry and that can be leveraged across a wide range of business types as a result. Examples of the kinds of generalized resources that a corporate parent leverages in unrelated diversification include the corporation's reputation, credit rating, and access to financial markets; governance mechanisms; a corporate ethics program; a central data and communications center; shared administrative resources such as public relations and legal services; and common systems for functions such as budgeting, financial reporting, and quality control.

The three principal ways in which a parent company can further the prospects of its unrelated businesses and increase long-term economic shareholder value are discussed below.

Astute Corporate Parenting   An effective way for a diversified company to improve the performance of its otherwise unrelated businesses is through astute corporate parenting. *Corporate parenting* refers to the role that a diversified corporation plays in nurturing its component businesses through the provision of top management expertise, disciplined control, financial resources, and other types of generalized resources and capabilities such as long-term planning systems, business development skills, management development processes, and incentive systems.[17]

One of the most important ways that corporate parents contribute to the success of their businesses is by offering high-level oversight and guidance.[18] The top executives of a large diversified corporation have among them many years of accumulated experience in a variety of business settings and can often contribute expert problem-solving skills, creative strategy suggestions, and first-rate advice and guidance on how to improve competitiveness and financial performance to the heads of the company's various business subsidiaries; this is especially true in the case of newly acquired businesses. Particularly astute high-level guidance from corporate executives can help the subsidiaries perform better than they would otherwise be able to do through the efforts of the business-unit heads alone.[19]

The outstanding leadership of Royal Little, the founder of Textron, was a major reason that the company became an exemplar of the unrelated diversification strategy while he was CEO. Little's bold moves transformed the company from its origins as a small textile manufacturer into a global powerhouse known for its Bell helicopters, Cessna aircraft, and host of other strong brands in a wide array of industries. Norm Wesley, CEO of the conglomerate Fortune Brands from 1999 to 2007, is similarly credited with driving the sharp rise in the company's stock price while he was at the helm. Fortune Brands is now the $7 billion maker of products ranging from spirits (e.g., Jim Beam bourbon and rye, Gilbey's gin and vodka, Courvoisier cognac) to golf products (e.g., Titleist golf balls and clubs, FootJoy golf shoes and apparel, Scotty Cameron putters) to hardware (e.g., Moen faucets, American Lock security devices, Therma-Tru doors).

Corporate parents can also create added value for their businesses by providing them with other types of generalized or parenting resources that lower the operating costs of the individual businesses or that enhance their operating effectiveness. The administrative resources located at a company's corporate head-quarters are a prime example. They typically include legal services, accounting expertise and tax services, and other elements of the administrative infrastructure, such as risk management capabilities, information technology resources, and resources concerning public relations and corporate communications. Providing individual business with such types of generalized and support resources and capabilities creates value by lowering companywide overhead costs, since each business would otherwise have to duplicate the centralized activities.

Corporate brands that do not connote any specific type of product are another type of generalized corporate resource that can be shared among unrelated businesses. GE's brand is an example, having been applied to businesses as diverse as financial services (GE Capital), medical imaging (GE medical diagnostics), and lighting (GE lightbulbs). Corporate brands that are applied in this fashion are sometimes called *umbrella brands*. Utilizing a well-known corporate name (GE) in a diversified company's individual businesses has potential not only to lower costs (by spreading the fixed cost of developing and maintaining the brand over many businesses) but also to enhance each business's customer value proposition by linking its products to a name that consumers trust. In similar fashion, a corporation's reputation for well-crafted products, for product reliability, or for trustworthiness can lead to greater customer willingness to purchase the products of a wider range of a diversified company's businesses. Incentive systems, financial control systems, and a company's culture are other types of generalized corporate resources that may prove useful in enhancing the daily operations of a diverse set of businesses.

Judicious Cross-Business Allocation of Financial Resources

Widely diversified firms may also be able to create added value by serving as an internal capital market and allocating surplus cash flows from some businesses to fund the capital requirements of other businesses. This can be particularly important when interest rates are high or credit is unusually tight (such as in the wake of the worldwide banking crisis that began in 2008) or in economies with less well developed capital markets. Under these conditions, an unrelated diversifier with strong financial resources can add value by shifting funds from business units generating excess cash (more than they need to fund their own operating requirements and new capital investment opportunities) to other, cash-short businesses with appealing growth prospects. A parent company's ability to function as its own internal capital market enhances overall corporate performance and boosts shareholder value to the extent that its top managers have better access to information about investment opportunities internal to the firm than do external financiers and can avoid the costs of external borrowing.

Acquiring and Restructuring Undervalued Companies

One way for parent companies to add value to unrelated businesses is by acquiring weakly performing companies at a bargain price and then *restructuring* their operations (and perhaps their strategies) in ways that produce sometimes dramatic increases in profitability. **Restructuring** refers to overhauling and streamlining the operations of a business—combining plants with excess capacity, selling off redundant or underutilized assets, reducing unnecessary expenses, revamping its product offerings, instituting new sales and marketing approaches, consolidating administrative functions to reduce overhead costs, instituting new financial controls and accounting systems, and otherwise improving the operating efficiency and profitability of a company. Restructuring sometimes involves transferring seasoned managers to the newly acquired business, either to replace the top layers of management or to step in temporarily until the business is returned to profitability or is well on its way to becoming a major market contender.

> **CORE CONCEPT**
>
> **Restructuring** refers to overhauling and streamlining the activities of a business—combining plants with excess capacity, selling off underutilized assets, reducing unnecessary expenses, and otherwise improving the productivity and profitability of a company.

Restructuring is often undertaken when a diversified company acquires a new business that is performing well below levels that the corporate parent believes are achievable. Diversified companies that have capabilities in restructuring (sometimes called *turnaround capabilities*) are often able to significantly boost the performance of weak businesses in a relatively wide range of industries. Newell Rubbermaid (whose diverse product line includes Sharpie pens, Levolor window treatments, Bernzomatic propane torches, Goody hair accessories, Aprica strollers and car seats, Calphalon cookware, and Lenox power and hand tools) developed such a strong set of turnaround capabilities that the company was said to "Newellize" the businesses it acquired.

Successful unrelated diversification strategies based on restructuring require the parent company to have considerable expertise in identifying underperforming target companies and in negotiating attractive acquisition prices so that each acquisition passes the cost-of-entry test. The capabilities in this regard of Lords James Hanson and Gordon White, who headed up the storied British conglomerate Hanson Trust, played a large part in Hanson's impressive record of profitability through the early 1990s.

The Path to Greater Shareholder Value through Unrelated Diversification

For a strategy of unrelated diversification to produce companywide financial results above and beyond what the businesses could generate operating as stand-alone entities, corporate executives must:

- Do a superior job of diversifying into new businesses that can produce consistently good earnings and returns on investment (to satisfy the attractiveness test).

- Do an excellent job of negotiating favorable acquisition prices (to satisfy the cost-of-entry test).

- Do a superior job of corporate parenting via high-level managerial oversight and resource sharing, financial resource allocation and portfolio management, or restructuring underperforming businesses (to satisfy the better-off test).

The best corporate parents understand the nature and value of the kinds of resources at their command and know how to leverage them effectively across their businesses. Those that are able to create more value in their businesses than other diversified companies have what is called a **parenting advantage**.[20] When a corporation has a parenting advantage, its top executives have the best chance of being able to craft and execute an unrelated diversification strategy that can satisfy all three tests and truly enhance long-term economic shareholder value.

CORE CONCEPT

A diversified company has a **parenting advantage** when it is more able than other companies to boost the combined performance of its individual businesses through high-level guidance, general oversight, and other corporate-level contributions.

The Drawbacks of Unrelated Diversification

Unrelated diversification strategies have two important negatives that undercut the pluses: very demanding managerial requirements and limited competitive advantage potential.

Demanding Managerial Requirements Successfully managing a set of fundamentally different businesses operating in fundamentally different industry and competitive environments is a very challenging and exceptionally difficult proposition.[21] Consider, for example, that corporations like General Electric and Berkshire Hathaway have dozens of business subsidiaries making hundreds and sometimes thousands of products. While headquarters executives can glean information about the industry from third-party sources, ask lots of questions when making occasional visits to the operations of the different businesses, and do their best to learn about the company's different businesses, they still remain heavily dependent on briefings from business-unit heads and on "managing by the numbers"—that is, keeping a close track on the financial and operating results of each subsidiary. Managing by the numbers works well enough when business conditions are normal and the heads of the various business units are capable of consistently meeting their numbers. But the problem comes when things start to go awry in a business due to exceptional circumstances and corporate management has to get deeply involved in the problems of a business it does not know all that much about. Because every business tends to encounter rough sledding at some juncture, unrelated diversification is thus a somewhat risky strategy from a managerial perspective.[22] Just one or two unforeseen problems or big strategic mistakes (like misjudging the importance of certain competitive forces, not recognizing that a newly acquired business has some serious resource deficiencies and/or competitive shortcomings, or being too optimistic about turning around a struggling subsidiary) can cause a precipitous drop in corporate earnings and crash the parent company's stock price.

Hence, competently overseeing a set of widely diverse businesses can turn out to be much harder than it sounds. In practice, comparatively few companies have proved that they have top management capabilities that are up to the task. There are far more companies whose corporate executives have failed at delivering consistently good financial results with an unrelated diversification strategy than there are companies with corporate executives who have been successful.[23] Unless a company truly has a parenting advantage, the odds are that the result of unrelated diversification will be 1 + 1 = 2 or less.

Limited Competitive Advantage Potential The second big negative is that *unrelated diversification offers a limited potential for competitive advantage beyond what each individual business can generate on its own.* Unlike

Relying solely on the expertise of corporate executives to wisely manage a set of unrelated businesses is *a much weaker foundation for enhancing shareholder value* than is a strategy of related diversification.

a related diversification strategy, unrelated diversification provides no cross-business strategic-fit benefits that allow each business to perform its key value chain activities in a more efficient and effective manner. A cash-rich corporate parent pursuing unrelated diversification can provide its subsidiaries with much-needed capital, may achieve economies of scope in activities relying on generalized corporate resources, and may even offer some managerial know-how to help resolve problems in particular business units, but otherwise it has little to offer in the way of enhancing the competitive strength of its individual business units. In comparison to the highly specialized resources that facilitate related diversification, the generalized resources that support unrelated diversification tend to be relatively low value, for the simple reason that they are more common. Unless they are of exceptionally high quality (such as GE's world-renowned general management capabilities), resources and capabilities that are generalized in nature are less likely to provide a source of competitive advantage for diversified companies. *Without the competitive advantage potential of strategic fit in strategically important value chain activities, consolidated performance of an unrelated group of businesses stands to be little more than the sum of what the individual business units could achieve if they were independent, in most circumstances.*

Inadequate Reasons for Pursuing Unrelated Diversification

When firms pursue an unrelated diversification strategy for the wrong reasons, the odds are that the result will be 1 + 1 = 2 or less. Rationales for unrelated diversification that are not likely to increase shareholder value include the following:

- *Risk reduction.* Managers sometimes pursue unrelated diversification in order to reduce risk by spreading the company's investments over a set of truly diverse industries whose technologies and markets are largely disconnected. But this cannot create long-term shareholder value since the company's shareholders can more flexibly (and more efficiently) reduce their exposure to risk by investing in a diversified portfolio of stocks and bonds.
- *Growth.* While unrelated diversification may enable a company to achieve rapid or continuous growth, firms that pursue growth for growth's sake are unlikely to maximize shareholder value. While growth can bring more attention and prestige to a firm from greater visibility and higher industry rankings, only profitable growth—the kind that comes from creating added value for shareholders—can justify a strategy of unrelated diversification.
- *Stabilization.* In a broadly diversified company, there's a chance that market downtrends in some of the company's businesses will be partially offset by cyclical upswings in its other businesses, thus producing somewhat less earnings volatility. In actual practice, however, there's no convincing evidence that the consolidated profits of firms with unrelated diversification strategies are more stable or less subject to reversal in periods of recession and economic stress than the profits of firms with related diversification strategies.
- *Managerial motives.* Unrelated diversification can provide benefits to managers such as higher compensation (which tends to increase with firm size and degree of diversification) and reduced employment risk. Diversification for these reasons is far more likely to reduce shareholder value than to increase it.

Because unrelated diversification strategies *at their best* have only a limited potential for creating long-term economic value for shareholders, it is essential that managers not compound this problem by taking a misguided approach toward unrelated diversification, in pursuit of objectives that are more likely to destroy shareholder value than create it.

COMBINATION RELATED-UNRELATED DIVERSIFICATION STRATEGIES

There's nothing to preclude a company from diversifying into both related and unrelated businesses. Indeed, in actual practice the business makeup of diversified companies varies considerably. Some diversified companies are really *dominant-business enterprises*—one major "core" business accounts for 50 to 80 percent of total revenues and a collection of small related or unrelated businesses accounts for the remainder. Some diversified companies are *narrowly diversified* around a few (two to five) related or unrelated businesses. Others are *broadly diversified* around a wide-ranging collection of related businesses, unrelated businesses, or a mixture of both. And a number of multibusiness enterprises have diversified into unrelated areas but have a collection of related businesses within each area—thus giving them a business portfolio consisting of *several unrelated groups of related businesses.* There's ample room for companies to customize their diversification strategies to incorporate elements of both related and unrelated diversification, as may suit their own competitive asset profile and strategic vision. *Combination related-unrelated diversification strategies have particular appeal for companies with a mix of valuable competitive assets, covering the spectrum from generalized to specialized resources and capabilities.*

Figure 8.2 shows the range of alternatives for companies pursuing diversification.

EVALUATING THE STRATEGY OF A DIVERSIFIED COMPANY

Strategic analysis of diversified companies builds on the concepts and methods used for single-business companies. But there are some additional aspects to consider and a couple of new analytical tools to master. The procedure for evaluating the pluses and minuses of a diversified company's strategy and deciding what actions to take to improve the company's performance involves six steps:

LO 4

Gain command of the analytical tools for evaluating a company's diversification strategy.

1. Assessing the attractiveness of the industries the company has diversified into, both individually and as a group.
2. Assessing the competitive strength of the company's business units and determining which are strong contenders in their respective industries.

Figure 8.2   **Strategy Alternatives for a Company Pursuing Diversification**

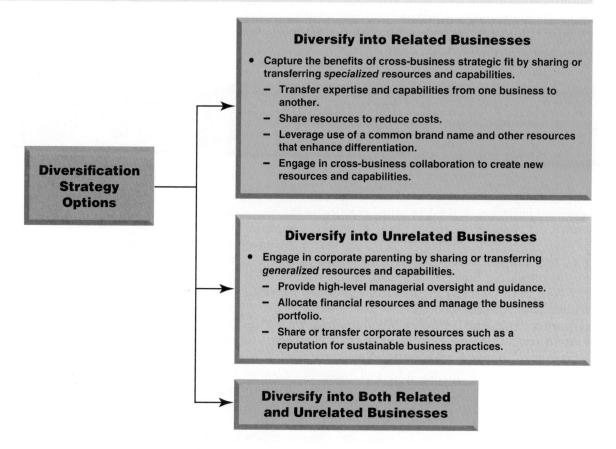

3. Checking the competitive advantage potential of cross-business strategic fit among the company's various business units.
4. Checking whether the firm's resources fit the requirements of its present business lineup.
5. Ranking the performance prospects of the businesses from best to worst and determining what the corporate parent's priority should be in allocating resources to its various businesses.
6. Crafting new strategic moves to improve overall corporate performance.

The core concepts and analytical techniques underlying each of these steps merit further discussion.

Step 1: Evaluating Industry Attractiveness

A principal consideration in evaluating a diversified company's business makeup and the caliber of its strategy is the attractiveness of the industries in which it has business operations. Answers to several questions are required:

1. *Does each industry the company has diversified into represent a good market for the company to be in?* Ideally, each industry in which the firm operates will pass the attractiveness test.
2. *Which of the company's industries are most attractive, and which are least attractive?* Comparing the attractiveness of the industries and ranking them

from most to least attractive is a prerequisite to wise allocation of corporate resources across the various businesses.

3. *How appealing is the whole group of industries in which the company has invested?* The answer to this question points to whether the group of industries holds promise for attractive growth and profitability. A company whose revenues and profits come chiefly from businesses in relatively unattractive industries probably needs to look at divesting businesses in unattractive industries and entering industries that qualify as highly attractive.

The more attractive the industries (both individually and as a group) a diversified company is in, the better its prospects for good long-term performance.

Calculating Industry Attractiveness Scores for Each Industry into Which the Company Has Diversified
A simple and reliable analytical tool involves calculating quantitative industry attractiveness scores, which can then be used to gauge each industry's attractiveness, rank the industries from most to least attractive, and make judgments about the attractiveness of all the industries as a group.

Assessing industry attractiveness involves a consideration of the conditions of each business's macro-environment as well as its competitive environment—the very same factors that are used to evaluate the strategy of a single-business company, as discussed in Chapter 3. Key indicators of industry attractiveness thus include:

- Social, political, regulatory, and environmental factors
- Seasonal and cyclical factors
- Industry uncertainty and business risk
- Market size and projected growth rate
- Industry profitability
- The intensity of competition (five forces)
- Emerging opportunities and threats

In addition, it is critically important to consider those aspects of industry attractiveness that pertain *specifically* to a company's diversification strategy. This involves looking at all the industries in which the company has invested to assess their resource requirements and to consider whether there is good cross-industry strategic fit. The following measures are typically used to gauge industry attractiveness from this multibusiness perspective:

- *The presence of cross-industry strategic fit.* The more an industry's value chain and resource requirements match up well with the value chain activities of other industries in which the company has operations, the more attractive the industry is to a firm pursuing related diversification.
- *Resource requirements.* Industries having resource requirements that match those of the parent company or are otherwise within the company's reach are more attractive than industries in which capital and other resource requirements could strain corporate financial resources and organizational capabilities.

After a set of attractiveness measures that suit a diversified company's circumstances has been identified, each attractiveness measure is assigned a weight reflecting its relative importance in determining an industry's attractiveness—it is weak methodology to assume that the various attractiveness measures are equally important. The intensity of competition in an industry should nearly always carry a high weight (say, 0.20 to 0.30). Strategic-fit considerations should be assigned a high weight in the case of companies with related diversification strategies; but for companies with an unrelated diversification strategy, strategic fit with other industries may be dropped from the list of attractiveness measures altogether. The importance weights must add up to 1.

Next, each industry is rated on each of the chosen industry attractiveness measures, using a rating scale of 1 to 10 (where a *high* rating signifies *high* attractiveness and a *low* rating signifies *low* attractiveness). *Keep in mind here that the more intensely competitive an industry is, the lower the attractiveness rating for that industry.* Likewise, the more the resource requirements associated with being in a particular industry are beyond the parent company's reach, the lower the attractiveness rating. On the other hand, the presence of good cross-industry strategic fit should be given a very high attractiveness rating, since there is good potential for competitive advantage and added shareholder value. Weighted attractiveness scores are then calculated by multiplying the industry's rating on each measure by the corresponding weight. For example, a rating of 8 times a weight of 0.25 gives a weighted attractiveness score of 2.00. The sum of the weighted scores for all the attractiveness measures provides an overall industry attractiveness score. This procedure is illustrated in Table 8.1.

Interpreting the Industry Attractiveness Scores   Industries
with a score much below 5 probably do not pass the attractiveness test. If a company's industry attractiveness scores are all above 5, it is probably fair to conclude that the group of industries the company operates in is attractive as a whole. But the group of industries takes on a decidedly lower degree of attractiveness as the number of industries with scores below 5 increases, especially if industries with low scores account for a sizable fraction of the company's revenues.

Table 8.1   Calculating Weighted Industry Attractiveness Scores*

Industry Attractiveness Measure	Importance Weight	Industry A Rating/ Score	Industry B Rating/ Score	Industry C Rating/ Score	Industry D Rating/ Score
Market size and projected growth rate	0.10	8/0.80	5/0.50	7/0.70	3/0.30
Intensity of competition	0.25	8/2.00	7/1.75	3/0.75	2/0.50
Emerging opportunities and threats	0.10	2/0.20	9/0.90	4/0.40	5/0.50
Cross-industry strategic fit	0.20	8/1.60	4/0.80	8/1.60	2/0.40
Resource requirements	0.10	9/0.90	7/0.70	10/1.00	5/0.50
Seasonal and cyclical influences	0.05	9/0.45	8/0.40	10/0.50	5/0.25
Societal, political, regulatory, and environmental factors	0.05	10/0.50	7/0.35	7/0.35	3/0.15
Industry profitability	0.10	5/0.50	10/1.00	3/0.30	3/0.30
Industry uncertainty and business risk	0.05	5/0.25	7/0.35	10/0.50	1/0.05
Sum of the assigned weights	1.00				
Overall weighted industry attractiveness scores		**7.20**	**6.75**	**5.10**	**2.95**

*Rating scale: 1 = very unattractive to company; 10 = very attractive to company.

For a diversified company to be a strong performer, a substantial portion of its revenues and profits must come from business units with relatively high attractiveness scores. It is particularly important that a diversified company's principal businesses be in industries with a good outlook for growth and above-average profitability. Having a big fraction of the company's revenues and profits come from industries with slow growth, low profitability, or intense competition tends to drag overall company performance down. Business units in the least attractive industries are potential candidates for divestiture, unless they are positioned strongly enough to overcome the unattractive aspects of their industry environments or they are a strategically important component of the company's business makeup.

The Difficulties of Calculating Industry Attractiveness Scores There are two hurdles to using this method of evaluating industry attractiveness. One is deciding on appropriate weights for the industry attractiveness measures, since they have a subjective component; different analysts may have different views about which weights are appropriate for the different attractiveness measures. The second hurdle is gaining sufficient command of the industry to assign more accurate and objective ratings. Generally, a company can come up with the statistical data needed to compare its industries on such factors as market size, growth rate, seasonal and cyclical influences, and industry profitability. Cross-industry fit and resource requirements are also fairly easy to judge. But the attractiveness measure on which judgment weighs most heavily is intensity of competition. It is not always easy to conclude whether competition in one industry is stronger or weaker than in another industry because of the different types of competitive influences that prevail and the differences in their relative importance. In the event that the available information is too skimpy to confidently assign a rating value to an industry on a particular attractiveness measure, then it is usually best to use a score of 5, which avoids biasing the overall attractiveness score either up or down.

But despite the hurdles, calculating industry attractiveness scores is a systematic and reasonably reliable method for ranking a diversified company's industries from most to least attractive—numbers like those shown for the four industries in Table 8.1 help pin down the basis for judging which industries are more attractive and to what degree.

Step 2: Evaluating Business-Unit Competitive Strength

The second step in evaluating a diversified company is to appraise how strongly positioned each of its business units is in its respective industry. Doing an appraisal of each business unit's strength and competitive position in its industry not only reveals its chances for industry success but also provides a basis for ranking the units from competitively strongest to competitively weakest and sizing up the competitive strength of all the business units as a group.

Calculating Competitive Strength Scores for Each Business Unit Quantitative measures of each business unit's competitive strength can be calculated using a procedure similar to that for measuring industry attractiveness.

The following factors are used in quantifying the competitive strengths of a diversified company's business subsidiaries:

Using relative market share to measure competitive strength is analytically superior to using straight-percentage market share.

- *Relative market share.* A business unit's *relative market share* is defined as the ratio of its market share to the market share held by the largest rival firm in the industry, with market share measured in unit volume, not dollars. A 10 percent market share, for example, does not signal much competitive strength if the leader's share is 50 percent (a 0.20 relative market share), but a 10 percent share is actually quite strong if the leader's share is only 12 percent (a 0.83 relative market share)—this why a company's relative market share is a better measure of competitive strength than a company's market share based on either dollars or unit volume.
- Costs relative to competitors' costs.
- Ability to match or beat rivals on key product attributes.
- Brand image and reputation.
- Other competitively valuable resources and capabilities.
- Ability to benefit from strategic fit with the company's other businesses.
- Ability to exercise bargaining leverage with key suppliers or customers.
- Caliber of alliances and collaborative partnerships with suppliers and/or buyers.
- Profitability relative to competitors. Above-average profitability is a signal of competitive advantage, while below-average profitability usually denotes competitive disadvantage.

After settling on a set of competitive strength measures that are well matched to the circumstances of the various business units, weights indicating each measure's importance need to be assigned. A *case can be made for using different weights* for different business units whenever the importance of the strength measures differs significantly from business to business, but otherwise it is simpler just to go with a single set of weights and avoid the added complication of multiple weights. As before, the importance weights must add up to 1. Each business unit is then rated on each of the chosen strength measures, using a rating scale of 1 to 10 (where a *high* rating signifies competitive *strength* and a *low* rating signifies competitive *weakness*). In the event that the available information is too skimpy to confidently assign a rating value to a business unit on a particular strength measure, then it is usually best to use a score of 5, which avoids biasing the overall score either up or down. Weighted strength ratings are calculated by multiplying the business unit's rating on each strength measure by the assigned weight. For example, a strength score of 6 times a weight of 0.15 gives a weighted strength rating of 0.90. The sum of the weighted ratings across all the strength measures provides a quantitative measure of a business unit's overall market strength and competitive standing. Table 8.2 provides sample calculations of competitive strength ratings for four businesses.

Interpreting the Competitive Strength Scores

Business units with competitive strength ratings above 6.7 (on a scale of 1 to 10) are strong market contenders in their industries. Businesses with ratings in the 3.3-to-6.7 range have moderate competitive strength vis-à-vis rivals. Businesses with ratings below 3.3 are in competitively weak market positions. If a diversified company's business units all have competitive strength scores above 5, it is fair to conclude that its business units are all fairly strong market contenders in their respective industries.

Table 8.2   **Calculating Weighted Competitive Strength Scores for a Diversified Company's Business Units***

Competitive Strength Measure	Importance Weight	Business A in Industry A Rating/ Score	Business B in Industry B Rating/ Score	Business C in Industry C Rating/ Score	Business D in Industry D Rating/ Score
Relative market share	0.15	10/1.50	1/0.15	6/0.90	2/0.30
Costs relative to competitors' costs	0.20	7/1.40	2/0.40	5/1.00	3/0.60
Ability to match or beat rivals on key product attributes	0.05	9/0.45	4/0.20	8/0.40	4/0.20
Ability to benefit from strategic fit with company's other businesses	0.20	8/1.60	4/0.80	8/0.80	2/0.60
Bargaining leverage with suppliers/ buyers; caliber of alliances	0.05	9/0.45	3/0.15	6/0.30	2/0.10
Brand image and reputation	0.10	9/0.90	2/0.20	7/0.70	5/0.50
Competitively valuable capabilities	0.15	7/1.05	2/0.30	5/0.75	3/0.45
Profitability relative to competitors	0.10	5/0.50	1/0.10	4/0.40	4/0.40
Sum of the assigned weights	1.00				
Overall weighted competitive strength scores		**7.85**	**2.30**	**5.25**	**3.15**

*Rating scale: 1 = very weak; 10 = very strong.

But as the number of business units with scores below 5 increases, there's reason to question whether the company can perform well with so many businesses in relatively weak competitive positions. This concern takes on even more importance when business units with low scores account for a sizable fraction of the company's revenues.

Using a Nine-Cell Matrix to Simultaneously Portray Industry Attractiveness and Competitive Strength   The industry attractiveness and business strength scores can be used to portray the strategic positions of each business in a diversified company. Industry attractiveness is plotted on the vertical axis and competitive strength on the horizontal axis. A nine-cell grid emerges from dividing the vertical axis into three regions (high, medium, and low attractiveness) and the horizontal axis into three regions (strong, average, and weak competitive strength). As shown in Figure 8.3, high attractiveness is associated with scores of 6.7 or greater on a rating scale of 1 to 10, medium attractiveness to scores of 3.3 to 6.7, and low attractiveness to scores below 3.3. Likewise, high competitive strength is defined as scores greater than 6.7, average strength as scores of 3.3 to 6.7, and low strength as scores below 3.3. *Each business unit is plotted on the nine-cell matrix according to its overall attractiveness score and strength score, and then it is shown as a "bubble."* The size of each bubble is scaled to the percentage of revenues the business generates relative to total corporate revenues. The bubbles in Figure 8.3 were located on the grid using the four industry attractiveness scores from Table 8.1 and the strength scores for the four business units in Table 8.2.

The locations of the business units on the attractiveness-strength matrix provide valuable guidance in deploying corporate resources to the various business units. In general, *a diversified company's prospects for good overall performance are*

Figure 8.3   A Nine-Cell Industry Attractiveness–Competitive Strength Matrix

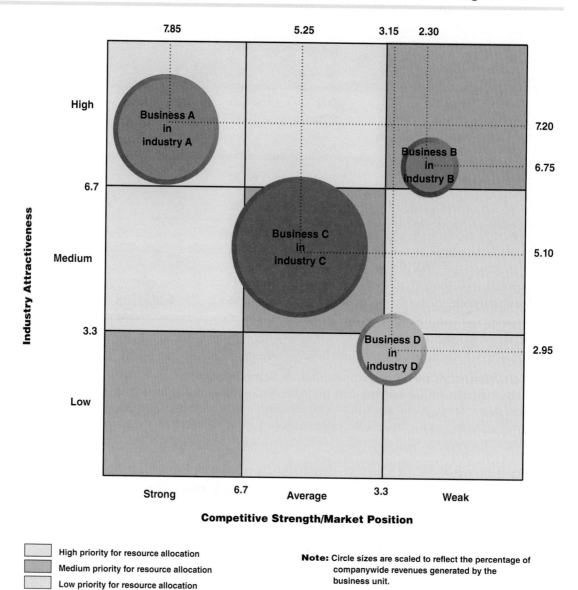

enhanced by concentrating corporate resources and strategic attention on those business units having the greatest competitive strength and positioned in highly attractive industries—specifically, businesses in the three cells in the upper left portion of the attractiveness-strength matrix, where industry attractiveness and competitive strength/market position are both favorable. The general strategic prescription for businesses falling in these three cells (for instance, business A in Figure 8.3) is "grow and build," with businesses in the high-strong cell standing first in line for resource allocations by the corporate parent.

Next in priority come businesses positioned in the three diagonal cells stretching from the lower left to the upper right (businesses B and C in Figure 8.3). Such businesses usually merit medium or intermediate priority in the parent's resource allocation ranking. However, some businesses in the medium-priority diagonal cells may have brighter or dimmer prospects than others. For example, a small business in the upper right cell of the matrix (like business B), despite being in a highly attractive industry, may occupy too weak a competitive position in its industry to justify the investment and resources needed to turn it into a strong market contender and shift its position leftward in the matrix over time. If, however, a business in the upper right cell has attractive opportunities for rapid growth and a good potential for winning a much stronger market position over time, it may merit a high claim on the corporate parent's resource allocation ranking and be given the capital it needs to pursue a grow-and-build strategy—the strategic objective here would be to move the business leftward in the attractiveness-strength matrix over time.

Businesses in the three cells in the lower right corner of the matrix (like business D in Figure 8.3) typically are weak performers and have the lowest claim on corporate resources. Most such businesses are good candidates for being divested (sold to other companies) or else managed in a manner calculated to squeeze out the maximum cash flows from operations—the cash flows from low-performing/low-potential businesses can then be diverted to financing expansion of business units with greater market opportunities. In exceptional cases where a business located in the three lower right cells is nonetheless fairly profitable (which it might be if it is in the low-average cell) or has the potential for good earnings and return on investment, the business merits retention and the allocation of sufficient resources to achieve better performance.

The nine-cell attractiveness-strength matrix provides clear, strong logic for why a diversified company needs to consider both industry attractiveness and business strength in allocating resources and investment capital to its different businesses. A good case can be made for concentrating resources in those businesses that enjoy higher degrees of attractiveness and competitive strength, being very selective in making investments in businesses with intermediate positions on the grid, and withdrawing resources from businesses that are lower in attractiveness and strength unless they offer exceptional profit or cash flow potential.

Step 3: Checking the Competitive Advantage Potential of Cross-Business Strategic Fit

While this step can be bypassed for diversified companies whose businesses are all unrelated (since, by design, strategic fit is lacking), a high potential for converting strategic fit into competitive advantage is central to concluding just how good a company's related diversification strategy is. Checking the competitive advantage potential of cross-business strategic fit involves searching for and evaluating how much benefit a diversified company can gain from cross-business resource and value chain matchups.

But more than just strategic-fit identification is needed. The real test is what competitive value can be generated from strategic fit. To what extent can cost savings be realized? How much competitive value will come from cross-business transfer of skills, technology, or intellectual capital? Will transferring a potent brand name to the products of other businesses increase sales significantly? Will cross-business collaboration to create or strengthen competitive capabilities lead to significant gains in the marketplace or in financial performance? Without significant strategic fit and

> The greater the value of cross-business strategic fit in enhancing a company's performance in the marketplace or on the bottom line, the more competitively powerful is its strategy of related diversification.

Figure 8.4 **Identifying the Competitive Advantage Potential of Cross-Business Strategic Fit**

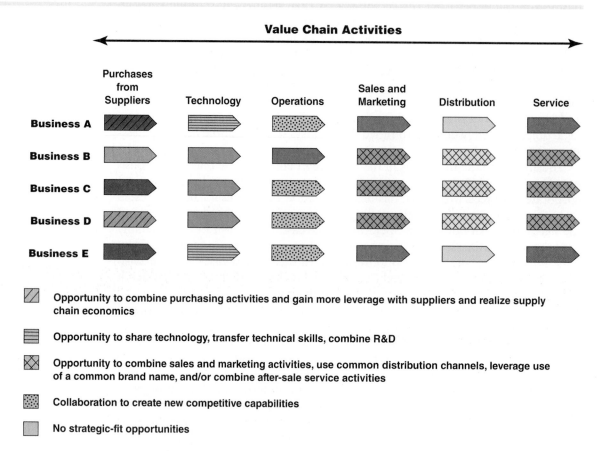

Value Chain Activities

Purchases from Suppliers | Technology | Operations | Sales and Marketing | Distribution | Service

Business A
Business B
Business C
Business D
Business E

Opportunity to combine purchasing activities and gain more leverage with suppliers and realize supply chain economics

Opportunity to share technology, transfer technical skills, combine R&D

Opportunity to combine sales and marketing activities, use common distribution channels, leverage use of a common brand name, and/or combine after-sale service activities

Collaboration to create new competitive capabilities

No strategic-fit opportunities

dedicated company efforts to capture the benefits, one has to be skeptical about the potential for a diversified company's businesses to perform better together than apart.

Figure 8.4 illustrates the process of comparing the value chains of a company's businesses and identifying opportunities to exploit competitively valuable cross-business strategic fit.

Step 4: Checking for Resource Fit

The businesses in a diversified company's lineup need to exhibit good **resource fit.** In firms with a related diversification strategy, resource fit exists when the firm's businesses strengthen its overall mix of resources and capabilities and when the businesses have matching resource requirements at points along their value chains that are critical for the businesses' market success. In companies pursuing unrelated diversification, resource fit exists when the parent company has capabilities *as a corporate parent* of unrelated businesses, resources of a general nature that it can share or transfer to its component businesses, and corporate resources sufficient to support its entire group of businesses without being spread too thin. Resource fit in terms of a sufficiency

CORE CONCEPT

A diversified company exhibits **resource fit** when its businesses add to a company's overall resource strengths and have matching resource requirements and/or when the parent company has adequate corporate resources to support its businesses' needs and add value.

of corporate resources to manage and support the entire enterprise is also relevant for related diversifiers and companies pursuing a mixed diversification strategy; Firms pursuing related diversification can also benefit from leveraging the resources of the corporate parent.

Financial Resource Fit

One dimension of resource fit concerns whether a diversified company can generate the internal cash flows sufficient to fund the capital requirements of its businesses, pay its dividends, meet its debt obligations, and otherwise remain financially healthy. While additional capital can usually be raised in financial markets, it is important for a diversified firm to have a healthy **internal capital market** that can support the financial requirements of its business lineup. The greater the extent to which a diversified company is able to fund investment in its businesses through internally generated cash flows rather than from equity issues or borrowing, the more powerful its financial resource fit and the less dependent the firm is on external financial resources. This can provide an important competitive advantage over single business rivals when credit market conditions are tight, as they have been in the United States and abroad in recent years.

A *portfolio approach* to ensuring financial fit among a firm's businesses is based on the fact that different businesses have different cash flow and investment characteristics. For example, business units in rapidly growing industries are often **cash hogs**—so labeled because the cash flows they are able to generate from internal operations aren't big enough to fund their expansion. To keep pace with rising buyer demand, rapid-growth businesses frequently need sizable annual capital investments—for new facilities and equipment, for new product development or technology improvements, and for additional working capital to support inventory expansion and a larger base of operations. A business in a fast-growing industry becomes an even bigger cash hog when it has a relatively low market share and is pursuing a strategy to become an industry leader.

In contrast, business units with leading market positions in mature industries may be **cash cows**—businesses that generate substantial cash surpluses over what is needed to adequately fund their operations. Market leaders in slow-growth industries often generate sizable positive cash flows *over and above what is needed for growth and reinvestment* because their industry-leading positions tend to enable them to earn attractive profits and because the slow-growth nature of their industry often entails relatively modest annual investment requirements. Cash cows, although not always attractive from a growth standpoint, are valuable businesses from a financial resource perspective. The surplus cash flows they generate can be used to pay corporate dividends, finance acquisitions, and provide funds for investing in the company's promising cash hogs.

Viewing a diversified group of businesses as a collection of cash flows and cash requirements (present and future) is a major step forward in understanding what the financial ramifications of diversification are and why having businesses with good financial resource fit can be important. For instance, *a diversified company's businesses exhibit good financial resource fit when the excess cash generated by its cash cow businesses is sufficient to fund the investment requirements of*

> **CORE CONCEPT**
>
> A strong **internal capital market** allows a diversified company to add value by shifting capital from business units generating *free cash flow* to those needing additional capital to expand and realize their growth potential.

> **CORE CONCEPT**
>
> A **cash hog** business generates cash flows that are too small to fully fund its operations and growth and requires cash infusions to provide additional working capital and finance new capital investment.

> **CORE CONCEPT**
>
> A **cash cow** business generates cash flows over and above its internal requirements, thus providing a corporate parent with funds for investing in cash hog businesses, financing new acquisitions, or paying dividends.

promising cash hog businesses. Ideally, investing in promising cash hog businesses over time results in growing the hogs into self-supporting *star businesses* that have strong or market-leading competitive positions in attractive, high-growth markets and high levels of profitability. Star businesses are often the cash cows of the future—when the markets of star businesses begin to mature and their growth slows, their competitive strength should produce self-generated cash flows more than sufficient to cover their investment needs. The "success sequence" is thus cash hog to young star (but perhaps still a cash hog) to self-supporting star to cash cow. While the practice of viewing a diversified company in terms of cash cows and cash hogs has declined in popularity, it illustrates one approach to analyzing financial resource fit and allocating financial resources across a portfolio of different businesses.

Aside from cash flow considerations, there are two other factors to consider in assessing whether a diversified company's businesses exhibit good financial fit:

- *Does the company have adequate financial strength to fund its different businesses and maintain a healthy credit rating?* A diversified company's strategy fails the resource-fit test when the company's financial resources are stretched across so many businesses that its credit rating is impaired. Severe financial strain sometimes occurs when a company borrows so heavily to finance new acquisitions that it has to trim way back on capital expenditures for existing businesses and use the big majority of its financial resources to meet interest obligations and to pay down debt. Many of the world's largest banks (e.g., Royal Bank of Scotland, Citigroup, HSBC) recently found themselves so undercapitalized and financially overextended that they were forced to sell off some of their business assets to meet regulatory requirements and restore public confidence in their solvency.

- *Do any of the company's individual businesses not contribute adequately to achieving companywide performance targets?* A business exhibits poor financial fit with the company if it soaks up a disproportionate share of the company's financial resources, makes subpar bottom-line contributions, is too small to make a material earnings contribution, or is unduly risky (such that the financial well-being of the whole company could be jeopardized in the event it falls on hard times).

Nonfinancial Resource Fit   Just as a diversified company must have adequate financial resources to support its various individual businesses, it must also have a big-enough and deep-enough pool of managerial, administrative, and competitive capabilities to support all of its different businesses. The following two questions help reveal whether a diversified company has sufficient nonfinancial resources:

- *Does the company have (or can it develop) the specific resources and capabilities needed to be successful in each of its businesses?*[24] Sometimes a diversified company's resources and capabilities are poorly matched to the resource requirements of one or more businesses it has diversified into. For instance, BTR, a multibusiness company in Great Britain, discovered that the company's resources and managerial skills were quite well suited for parenting its industrial manufacturing businesses but not for parenting its distribution businesses (National Tyre Services and Texas-based Summers Group). As a result, BTR decided to divest its distribution businesses and focus exclusively on diversifying around small industrial manufacturing.[25] For companies pursuing related diversification strategies, a mismatch between the company's competitive assets and the key success factors of an industry can be serious enough to warrant divesting businesses in that industry or not acquiring a new business. In contrast, when a company's resources and capabilities are a good match with the key success factors of industries it is not presently in, it makes sense to take a hard look at acquiring companies in these industries and expanding the company's business lineup.

- *Are the company's resources being stretched too thinly by the resource requirements of one or more of its businesses?* A diversified company must guard against overtaxing its resources and capabilities, a condition that can arise when (1) it goes on an acquisition spree and management is called on to assimilate and oversee many new businesses very quickly or (2) it lacks sufficient resource depth to do a creditable job of transferring skills and competencies from one of its businesses to another. The broader the diversification, the greater the concern about whether the company has sufficient managerial depth to cope with the diverse range of operating problems its wide business lineup presents. Plus, the more a company's diversification strategy is tied to transferring its existing know-how or technologies to new businesses, the more it has to develop a big-enough and deep-enough resource pool to supply these businesses with sufficient capability to create competitive advantage.[26] Otherwise, its competitive assets end up being thinly spread across many businesses, and the opportunity for competitive advantage slips through the cracks.

Step 5: Ranking the Performance Prospects of Business Units and Assigning a Priority for Resource Allocation

Once a diversified company's strategy has been evaluated from the perspective of industry attractiveness, competitive strength, strategic fit, and resource fit, the next step is to rank the performance prospects of the businesses from best to worst and determine which businesses merit top priority for resource support and new capital investments by the corporate parent.

The most important considerations in judging business-unit performance are sales growth, profit growth, contribution to company earnings, and return on capital invested in the business. Sometimes, cash flow is a big consideration. As a rule, the prior analyses, taken together, signal which business units are likely to be strong performers on the road ahead and which are likely to be laggards. And it is a short step from ranking the prospects of business units to drawing conclusions about whether the company as a whole is capable of strong, mediocre, or weak performance in upcoming years.

The rankings of future performance generally determine what priority the corporate parent should give to each business in terms of resource allocation. *Business subsidiaries with the brightest profit and growth prospects and solid strategic and resource fit generally should head the list for corporate resource support.* More specifically, corporate executives must be diligent in steering resources out of low-opportunity areas into high-opportunity areas. Divesting marginal businesses is one of the best ways of freeing unproductive assets for redeployment. Surplus funds from cash cows also can be used to finance the range of chief strategic and financial options shown in Figure 8.5. Ideally, a company will have enough funds to do what is needed, both strategically and financially. If not,

Figure 8.5   **The Chief Strategic and Financial Options for Allocating a Diversified Company's Financial Resources**

strategic uses of corporate resources should usually take precedence unless there is a compelling reason to strengthen the firm's balance sheet or divert financial resources to pacify shareholders.

Step 6: Crafting New Strategic Moves to Improve Overall Corporate Performance

LO 5

Understand a diversified company's four main corporate strategy options for solidifying its diversification strategy and improving company performance.

The diagnosis and conclusions flowing from the five preceding analytical steps set the agenda for crafting strategic moves to improve a diversified company's overall performance. Corporate strategy options once a company has diversified boil down to four broad categories of actions (see Figure 8.6):

1. Sticking closely with the existing business lineup and pursuing the opportunities these businesses present.
2. Broadening the company's business scope by making new acquisitions in new industries.
3. Divesting some businesses and retrenching to a narrower base of business operations.
4. Restructuring the company's business lineup with a combination of divestitures and new acquisitions to put a whole new face on the company's business makeup.

Sticking Closely with the Existing Business Lineup The option of sticking with the current business lineup makes sense when the company's present businesses offer attractive growth opportunities and can be counted on to create economic value for shareholders. As long as the company's set of existing businesses puts it in good position for the future and these businesses

Figure 8.6   A Company's Four Main Strategic Alternatives After It Diversifies

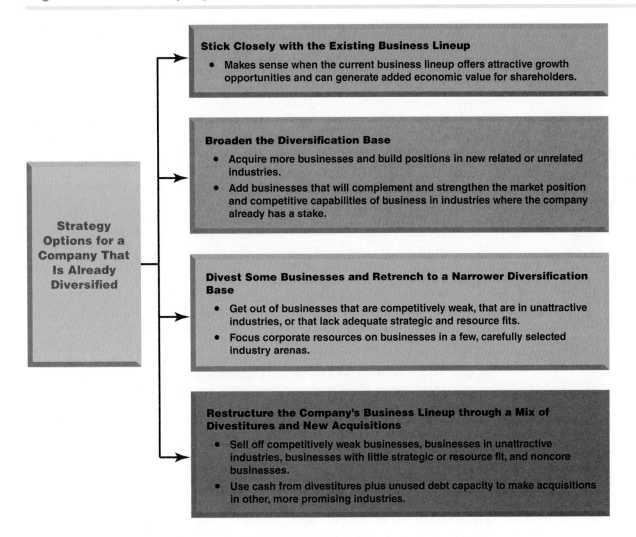

Stick Closely with the Existing Business Lineup

- Makes sense when the current business lineup offers attractive growth opportunities and can generate added economic value for shareholders.

Broaden the Diversification Base

- Acquire more businesses and build positions in new related or unrelated industries.
- Add businesses that will complement and strengthen the market position and competitive capabilities of business in industries where the company already has a stake.

Divest Some Businesses and Retrench to a Narrower Diversification Base

- Get out of businesses that are competitively weak, that are in unattractive industries, or that lack adequate strategic and resource fits.
- Focus corporate resources on businesses in a few, carefully selected industry arenas.

Restructure the Company's Business Lineup through a Mix of Divestitures and New Acquisitions

- Sell off competitively weak businesses, businesses in unattractive industries, businesses with little strategic or resource fit, and noncore businesses.
- Use cash from divestitures plus unused debt capacity to make acquisitions in other, more promising industries.

Strategy Options for a Company That Is Already Diversified

have good strategic and resource fit, then rocking the boat with major changes in the company's business mix is unnecessary. Corporate executives can concentrate their attention on getting the best performance from each of the businesses, steering corporate resources into areas of greatest potential and profitability. The specifics of "what to do" to wring better performance from the present business lineup have to be dictated by each business's circumstances and the preceding analysis of the corporate parent's diversification strategy.

However, in the event that corporate executives are not entirely satisfied with the opportunities they see in the company's present set of businesses and conclude that changes in the company's direction and business makeup are in order, they can opt for any of the three other strategic alternatives that follow.

Broadening a Diversified Company's Business Base   Diversified companies sometimes find it desirable to build positions in new industries, whether related or unrelated. There are several motivating factors. One is the potential for transferring resources and capabilities to other related or complementary businesses. A second is rapidly changing conditions in one or more of a company's core businesses brought on by technological, legislative, or new product innovations that alter buyer preferences and resource requirements. For instance, the passage of legislation in the United States allowing banks, insurance companies, and stock brokerages to enter each other's businesses spurred a raft of acquisitions and mergers to create full-service financial enterprises capable of meeting the multiple financial needs of customers.

A third, and often very important, motivating factor for adding new businesses is to complement and strengthen the market position and competitive capabilities of one or more of the company's present businesses. Procter & Gamble's acquisition of Gillette strengthened and extended P&G's reach into personal care and household products—Gillette's businesses included Oral-B toothbrushes, Gillette razors and razor blades, Duracell batteries, and Braun shavers and small appliances. Cisco Systems built itself into a worldwide leader in networking systems for the Internet by making 130 technology-based acquisitions between 1993 and 2008 to extend its market reach from routing and switching into IP telephony, home networking, wireless LAN, storage networking, network security, broadband, and optical and broadband systems.

Another important avenue for expanding the scope of a diversified company is to grow by extending the operations of existing businesses into additional country markets. Expanding a company's geographic scope may offer an exceptional competitive advantage potential by facilitating the full capture of economies of scale and learning/experience curve effects. In some businesses, the volume of sales needed to realize full economies of scale and/or benefit fully from experience and learning curve effects exceeds the volume that can be achieved by operating within the boundaries of just one or several country markets, especially small ones.

Illustration Capsule 8.1 describes how Johnson & Johnson has used acquisitions to diversify far beyond its well-known Band-Aid and baby care businesses and become a major player in pharmaceuticals, medical devices, and medical diagnostics.

Divesting Some Businesses and Retrenching to a Narrower Diversification Base

Retrenching to a narrower diversification base is usually undertaken when top management concludes that its diversification strategy has ranged too far afield and that the company can improve long-term performance by concentrating on building stronger positions in a smaller number of core businesses and industries. Hewlett-Packard spun off its testing and measurement businesses into a stand-alone company called Agilent Technologies so that it could better concentrate on its PC, workstation, server, printer and peripherals, and electronics businesses.

But there are other important reasons for divesting one or more of a company's present businesses. Sometimes divesting a business has to be considered because market conditions in a once-attractive industry have badly deteriorated. A business can become a prime candidate for divestiture because it lacks adequate strategic or resource fit, because it is a cash hog with questionable long-term potential, or because it is weakly positioned in its industry with little prospect the corporate parent can realize a decent return on its investment in the business. Sometimes a company acquires businesses that, down the road, just do not work out as expected even though management has tried all it can think of to make them profitable. Subpar performance by some business units is bound to occur,

ILLUSTRATION CAPSULE 8.1

Managing Diversification at Johnson & Johnson: The Benefits of Cross-Business Strategic Fit

Johnson & Johnson (J&J), once a consumer products company known for its Band-Aid line and its baby care products, has evolved into a $61 billion diversified enterprise consisting of some 250-plus operating companies organized into three divisions: pharmaceuticals, medical devices and diagnostics, and consumer health care products. Over the past decade J&J has made acquisitions totaling more than $50 billion; about 10 to 15 percent of J&J's annual growth in revenues has come from acquisitions. Much of the company's recent growth has been in the pharmaceutical division, which in 2009 accounted for 36 percent of J&J's revenues and 41 percent of its operating profits.

While each of J&J's business units sets its own strategies and operates with its own finance and human resource departments, corporate management strongly encourages cross-business cooperation and collaboration, believing that many of the advances in 21st-century medicine will come from applying advances in one discipline to another. J&J's drug-coated stent grew out of a discussion between a drug researcher and a researcher in the company's stent business. The innovative product helps prevent infection after cardiac procedures. (When stents are inserted to prop open arteries following angioplasty, the drug coating helps prevent infection.) A gene technology database compiled by the company's gene research lab was shared with personnel from the diagnostics division, who developed a test that the drug researchers used to predict which patients would most benefit from an experimental cancer therapy. J&J's liquid Band-Aid product (a liquid coating applied to hard-to-cover places like fingers and knuckles) is based on a material used in a wound-closing product sold by the company's hospital products company. Scientists from three separate business units worked collaboratively toward the development of an absorbable patch that would stop bleeding on contact. The development of the instant clotting patch was expected to save the lives of thousands of accident victims since uncontrolled bleeding was the number-one cause of death due to injury.

J&J's corporate management maintains that close collaboration among people in its diagnostics, medical devices, and pharmaceutical businesses—where numerous examples of cross-business strategic fit exist—gives J&J an edge on competitors, most of whom cannot match the company's breadth and depth of expertise.

Sources: Amy Barrett, "Staying on Top," *BusinessWeek,* May 5, 2003, pp. 60–68; Johnson & Johnson 2007 Annual Report; www. jnj.com (accessed July 29, 2010).

thereby raising questions of whether to divest them or keep them and attempt a turnaround. Other business units, despite adequate financial performance, may not mesh as well with the rest of the firm as was originally thought. For instance, PepsiCo divested its group of fast-food restaurant businesses to focus its resources on its core soft-drink and snack-food businesses, where their resources and capabilities could add more value.

On occasion, a diversification move that seems sensible from a strategic-fit standpoint turns out to be a poor *cultural fit.*[27] Several pharmaceutical companies had just this experience. When they diversified into cosmetics and perfume, they discovered their personnel had little respect for the "frivolous" nature of such products compared to the far nobler task of developing miracle drugs to cure the ill. The absence of shared values and cultural compatibility between the medical research and chemical-compounding expertise of the pharmaceutical companies and the fashion/marketing orientation of the cosmetics business was the undoing of what otherwise was diversification into businesses with technology-sharing potential, product-development fit, and some overlap in distribution channels.

There's evidence indicating that pruning businesses and narrowing a firm's diversification base improves corporate performance.[28] A useful guide to determine whether or when to divest a business subsidiary is to ask, "If we were not in this business today, would we want to get into it now?"[29] When the answer is no or probably not, divestiture should be considered. Another signal that a business should become a divestiture candidate is whether it is worth more to another company than to the present parent; in such cases, shareholders would be well served if the company sells the business and collects a premium price from the buyer for whom the business is a valuable fit.[30]

Selling a business outright to another company is far and away the most frequently used option for divesting a business. But sometimes a business selected for divestiture has ample resources and capabilities to compete successfully on its own. In such cases, a corporate parent may elect to spin the unwanted business off as a financially and managerially independent company, either by selling shares to the investing public via an initial public offering or by distributing shares in the new company to existing shareholders of the corporate parent.

> **Diversified companies need to divest low-performing businesses or businesses that don't fit in order to concentrate on expanding existing businesses and entering new ones where opportunities are more promising.**

Restructuring a Diversified Company's Business Lineup through a Mix of Divestitures and New Acquisitions

If there is a serious mismatch between the company's resources and the type of diversification it has pursued, then a **companywide restructuring** effort may be called for. Restructuring a diversified company on a companywide basis *(corporate restructuring)* involves divesting some businesses and acquiring others so as to put a whole new face on the company's business lineup.[31] Performing radical surgery on a company's group of businesses may also be an appealing strategy alternative when its financial performance is being squeezed or eroded by:

CORE CONCEPT

> **Companywide restructuring** *(corporate restructuring)* involves divesting some businesses and acquiring others so as to put a whole new face on the company's business lineup.

- Too many businesses in slow-growth, declining, low-margin, or otherwise unattractive industries (a condition indicated by the number and size of businesses with industry attractiveness ratings below 5 and located on the bottom half of the attractiveness-strength matrix—see Figure 8.3).
- Too many competitively weak businesses (a condition indicated by the number and size of businesses with competitive strength ratings below 5 and located on the right half of the attractiveness-strength matrix).
- Ongoing declines in the market shares of one or more major business units that are falling prey to more market-savvy competitors.
- An excessive debt burden with interest costs that eat deeply into profitability.
- Ill-chosen acquisitions that haven't lived up to expectations.

Companywide restructuring can also be mandated by the emergence of new technologies that threaten the survival of one or more of a diversified company's important businesses. On occasion, corporate restructuring can be prompted by special circumstances—such as when a firm has a unique opportunity to make an acquisition so big and important that it has to sell several existing business units to finance the new acquisition or when a company needs to sell off some businesses in order to raise the cash for entering a potentially big industry with wave-of-the-future technologies or products.

Candidates for divestiture in a corporate restructuring effort typically include not only weak performers or those in unattractive industries but also business units that lack strategic fit with the businesses to be retained, businesses that are cash hogs or that lack other types of resource fit, and businesses incompatible with the company's revised diversification strategy (even though they may be profitable or in an attractive industry). As businesses are divested, corporate restructuring generally involves aligning the remaining business units into groups with the best strategic fit and then redeploying the cash flows from the divested business to either pay down debt or make new acquisitions to strengthen the parent company's business position in the industries it has chosen to emphasize.[32]

Over the past decade, corporate restructuring has become a popular strategy at many diversified companies, especially those that had diversified broadly into many different industries and lines of business. In 2008, GE's CEO Jeffrey Immelt announced that GE would spin off its industrial division, which included GE appliances, lighting, and various industrial businesses. Earlier, he had led GE's withdrawal from the insurance business by divesting several companies and spinning off others. He further restructured GE's business lineup with two other major initiatives: (1) spending $10 billion to acquire British-based Amersham and extend GE's Medical Systems business into diagnostic pharmaceuticals and biosciences, thereby creating a $15 billion business designated as GE Healthcare, and (2) acquiring the entertainment assets of debt-ridden French media conglomerate Vivendi Universal Entertainment and integrating its operations into GE's NBC division, thereby creating a broad-based $13 billion media business positioned to compete against Walt Disney, Time Warner, Fox, and Viacom.

KEY POINTS

1. The purpose of diversification is to build shareholder value. Diversification builds shareholder value when a diversified group of businesses can perform better under the auspices of a single corporate parent than they would as independent, stand-alone businesses—the goal is to achieve not just a $1 + 1 = 2$ result but, rather, to realize important $1 + 1 = 3$ performance benefits. Whether getting into a new business has potential to enhance shareholder value hinges on whether a company's entry into that business can pass the attractiveness test, the cost-of-entry test, and the better-off test.

2. Entry into new businesses can take any of three forms: acquisition, internal start-up, or joint venture/strategic partnership. The choice of which is best depends on the firm's resources and capabilities, the industry's entry barriers, the importance of speed, and the relative costs.

3. There are two fundamental approaches to diversification—into related businesses and into unrelated businesses. The rationale for *related* diversification is to benefit from *strategic fit:* Diversify into businesses with matchups along their respective value chains, and then capitalize on the strategic fit by sharing or transferring the resources and capabilities that enable the matching value chain activities in order to gain competitive advantage.

4. *Unrelated* diversification strategies surrender the competitive advantage potential of strategic fit at the value chain level in return for the potential that can be realized from superior corporate parenting. An outstanding corporate parent can benefit its businesses through (1) providing high-level oversight and making available other corporate resources, (2) allocating financial resources across the business portfolio, and (3) restructuring underperforming acquisitions.

5. Related diversification provides a stronger foundation for creating shareholder value than unrelated diversification, since the *specialized resources and capabilities* that are leveraged in related diversification tend to be more valuable competitive assets than the *generalized resources and capabilities* underlying unrelated diversification, which in most cases are relatively common and easier to imitate.

6. Analyzing how good a company's diversification strategy is consists of a six-step process:

   Step 1: *Evaluate the long-term attractiveness of the industries into which the firm has diversified.* Industry attractiveness needs to be evaluated from three angles: the attractiveness of each industry on its own, the attractiveness of each industry relative to the others, and the attractiveness of all the industries as a group.

   Step 2: *Evaluate the relative competitive strength of each of the company's business units.* The purpose of rating the competitive strength of each business is to gain a clear understanding of which businesses are strong contenders in their industries, which are weak contenders, and the underlying reasons for their strength or weakness. The conclusions about industry attractiveness can be joined with the conclusions about competitive strength by drawing an industry attractiveness–competitive strength matrix that helps identify the prospects of each business and what priority each business should be given in allocating corporate resources and investment capital.

   Step 3: *Check for cross-business strategic fit.* A business is more attractive strategically when it has value chain relationships with the company's other business units that offer potential to (1) realize economies of scope or cost-saving efficiencies, (2) transfer technology, skills, know-how, or other resource capabilities from one business to another, (3) leverage use of a trusted brand name or other resources that enhance differentiation, and (4) build new resources and competitive capabilities via cross-business collaboration. Cross-business strategic fit represents a significant avenue for producing competitive advantage beyond what any one business can achieve on its own.

   Step 4: *Check whether the firm's resource mix fits the resource requirements of its present business lineup.* In firms with a related diversification strategy, resource fit exists when the company's businesses add to its overall resource position and when they have matching resource requirements at the value chain level. In companies pursuing unrelated diversification, resource fit exists when the parent company has generalized resources that can add value to its component businesses and when it has corporate resources sufficient to support its entire group of businesses without spreading itself too thin. When there is financial resource fit among the businesses of any type of diversified company, the company can generate internal cash flows sufficient to fund the capital requirements of its businesses, pay its dividends, meet its debt obligations, and otherwise remain financially healthy.

Step 5: *Rank the performance prospects of the businesses from best to worst, and determine what the corporate parent's priority should be in allocating resources to its various businesses.* The most important considerations in judging business-unit performance are sales growth, profit growth, contribution to company earnings, and the return on capital invested in the business. Normally, strong business units in attractive industries have significantly better performance prospects than weak businesses or businesses in unattractive industries. Business subsidiaries with the brightest profit and growth prospects and solid strategic and resource fit generally should head the list for corporate resource support.

Step 6: *Crafting new strategic moves to improve overall corporate performance.* This step entails using the results of the preceding analysis as the basis for devising actions to strengthen existing businesses, make new acquisitions, divest weak-performing and unattractive businesses, restructure the company's business lineup, expand the scope of the company's geographic reach into new markets around the world, and otherwise steer corporate resources into the areas of greatest opportunity.

7. Once a company has diversified, corporate management's task is to manage the collection of businesses for maximum long-term performance. There are four different strategic paths for improving a diversified company's performance: (1) sticking with the existing business lineup, (2) broadening the firm's business base by diversifying into additional businesses or geographic markets, (3) retrenching to a narrower diversification base by divesting some of its present businesses, and (4) restructuring the company's business lineup with a combination of divestitures and new acquisitions to put a whole new face on the company's business makeup.

ASSURANCE OF LEARNING EXERCISES

LO 1, LO 2

1. See if you can identify the value chain relationships that make the businesses of the following companies related in competitively relevant ways. In particular, you should consider whether there are cross-business opportunities for (1) transferring skills/technology, (2) combining related value chain activities to achieve economies of scope, and/or (3) leveraging the use of a well-respected brand name or other resources that enhance differentiation.

OSI Restaurant Partners

- Outback Steakhouse
- Carrabba's Italian Grill

- Roy's Restaurant (Hawaiian fusion cuisine)
- Bonefish Grill (market-fresh fine seafood)
- Fleming's Prime Steakhouse & Wine Bar

L'Oréal

- Maybelline, Lancôme, Helena Rubinstein, Kiehl's, Garner, and Shu Uemura cosmetics
- L'Oréal and Soft Sheen/Carson hair care products
- Redken, Matrix, L'Oréal Professional, and Kerastase Paris professional hair care and skin care products
- Ralph Lauren and Giorgio Armani fragrances
- Biotherm skincare products
- La Roche–Posay and Vichy Laboratories dermocosmetics

Johnson & Johnson

- Baby products (powder, shampoo, oil, lotion)
- Band-Aids and other first-aid products
- Women's health and personal care products (Stayfree, Carefree, Sure & Natural)
- Neutrogena and Aveeno skin care products
- Nonprescription drugs (Tylenol, Motrin, Pepcid AC, Mylanta, Monistat)
- Prescription drugs
- Prosthetic and other medical devices
- Surgical and hospital products
- Acuvue contact lenses

LO 2, LO 3

2. Peruse the business group listings for United Technologies shown below and listed at its Web site (www.utc.com). How would you characterize the company's corporate strategy? related diversification, unrelated diversification, or a combination related-unrelated diversification strategy? Explain your answer.

- Carrier—the world's largest provider of air-conditioning, heating, and refrigeration solutions.
- Hamilton Sundstrand—technologically advanced aerospace and industrial products.
- Otis—the world's leading manufacturer, installer and maintainer of elevators, escalators and moving walkways.
- Pratt & Whitney—designs, manufactures, services and supports aircraft engines, industrial gas turbines and space propulsion systems.
- Sikorsky—a world leader in helicopter design, manufacture and service.
- UTC Fire & Security—fire and security systems developed for commercial, industrial and residential customers.
- UTC Power—a full-service provider of environmentally advanced power solutions.

LO 1, LO 2, LO 3

3. The Walt Disney Company is in the following businesses:

   - Theme parks
   - Disney Cruise Line
   - Resort properties
   - Movie, video, and theatrical productions (for both children and adults)
   - Television broadcasting (ABC, Disney Channel, Toon Disney, Classic Sports Network, ESPN and ESPN2, E!, Lifetime, and A&E networks)
   - Radio broadcasting (Disney Radio)
   - Musical recordings and sales of animation art
   - Anaheim Mighty Ducks NHL franchise
   - Anaheim Angels major-league baseball franchise (25 percent ownership)
   - Books and magazine publishing
   - Interactive software and Internet sites
   - The Disney Store retail shops

   Based on the above listing, would you say that Walt Disney's business lineup reflects a strategy of related diversification, unrelated diversification, or a combination of related and unrelated diversification? Be prepared to justify and explain your answer in terms of the nature of Disney's shared or transferred resources and capabilities and the extent to which the value chains of Disney's different businesses seem to have competitively valuable cross-business relationships.

   If need be, visit the company's Web site (http://corporate.disney.go.com/index.html?ppLink=pp_wdig) to obtain additional information about its business lineup and strategy.

EXERCISES FOR SIMULATION PARTICIPANTS

LO 1, LO 2, LO 3

1. In the event that your company had the opportunity to diversify into other products or businesses of your choosing, would you opt to pursue related diversification, unrelated diversification, or a combination of both? Explain why.

LO 1, LO 2

2. What specific resources and capabilities does your company possess that would make diversifying into related businesses attractive? Indicate what kinds of strategic-fit benefits could be captured by transferring these resources and competitive capabilities to newly acquired related businesses.

LO 1, LO 2

3. If your company opted to pursue a strategy of related diversification, what industries or product categories could it diversify into that would allow it to achieve economies of scope? Name at least two or three such industries or product categories, and indicate the specific kinds of cost savings that might accrue from entry into each.

LO 1, LO 2

4. If your company opted to pursue a strategy of related diversification, what industries or product categories could it diversify into that would allow it to capitalize on using its present brand name and corporate image to good advantage in the newly entered businesses or product categories? Name at least two or three such industries or product categories, and indicate *the specific benefits* that might be captured by transferring your company's brand name to each.

ENDNOTES

[1] For a more detailed discussion of when diversification makes good strategic sense, see Constantinos C. Markides, "To Diversify or Not to Diversify," *Harvard Business Review* 75, no. 6 (November–December 1997), pp. 93–99.

[2] For a discussion of how hidden opportunities within a corporation's existing asset base may offer growth to corporations with declining core businesses, see Chris Zook, "Finding Your Next Core Business," *Harvard Business Review* 85, no. 4 (April 2007), pp. 66–75.

[3] Michael E. Porter, "From Competitive Advantage to Corporate Strategy," *Harvard Business Review* 45, no. 3 (May–June 1987), pp. 46–49.

[4] Rita Nazareth, "CEOs Paying 56% M&A Premium Shows Stocks May Be Cheap (Update3)," *Bloomberg.com,* December 21, 2009, www.bloomberg.com/apps/news?pid=20603037&sid=ahPoIYY.zgQ.

[5] Ibid.

[6] Michael E. Porter, *Competitive Strategy: Techniques for Analyzing Industries and Competitors* (New York: Free Press, 1980), pp. 354–55.

[7] A. Shleifer and R. Vishny, "Takeovers in the 60s and the 80s—Evidence and Implications," *Strategic Management Journal* 12 (Winter 1991), pp. 51–59; T. Brush, "Predicted Change in Operational Synergy and Post-Acquisition Performance of Acquired Businesses," *Strategic Management Journal* 17, no. 1(1996), pp. 1–24; J. P. Walsh, "Top Management Turnover Following Mergers and Acquisitions," *Strategic Management Journal* 9, no. 2 (1988), pp. 173–83; A. Cannella and D. Hambrick, "Effects of Executive Departures on the Performance of Acquired Firms," *Strategic Management Journal* 14 (Summer 1993), pp.137–52; R. Roll, "The Hubris Hypothesis of Corporate Takeovers," *Journal of Business* 59, no. 2 (1986), pp. 197–216; P. Haspeslagh and D. Jemison, *Managing Acquisitions* (New York: Free Press, 1991).

[8] M. L. A. Hayward, "When Do Firms Learn from Their Acquisition Experience? Evidence from 1990–1995," *Strategic Management Journal* 23, no. 1 (2002), pp. 21–29; G. Ahuja and R. Katila, "Technological Acquisitions and the Innovation Performance of Acquiring Firms: A Longitudinal Study," *Strategic Management Journal* 22, no. 3 (2001), pp. 197–220; H. Barkema and F. Vermeulen,

"International Expansion through Start-Up or Acquisition: A Learning Perspective," *Academy of Management Journal* 41, no. 1 (1998), pp. 7–26.

[9] Haspeslagh and Jemison, *Managing Acquisitions,* pp. 344–45.

[10] Yves L. Doz and Gary Hamel, *Alliance Advantage: The Art of Creating Value through Partnering* (Boston: Harvard Business School Press, 1998), chaps. 1 and 2.

[11] J. Glover, "The Guardian," March 23, 1996, www.mcspotlight.org/media/press/guardpizza_23mar96.html.

[12] Michael E. Porter, *Competitive Advantage* (New York: Free Press, 1985), pp. 318–19 and pp. 337–53; Porter, "From Competitive Advantage to Corporate Strategy," pp. 53–57. For an empirical study supporting the notion that strategic fit enhances performance (provided the resulting combination is competitively valuable and difficult to duplicate by rivals), see Constantinos C. Markides and Peter J. Williamson, "Corporate Diversification and Organization Structure: A Resource-Based View," *Academy of Management Journal* 39, no. 2 (April 1996), pp. 340–67.

[13] David J. Collis and Cynthia A. Montgomery, "Creating Corporate Advantage," *Harvard Business Review* 76, no. 3 (May–June 1998), pp. 72–80; Markides and Williamson, "Corporate Diversification and Organization Structure."

[14] Markides and Williamson, "Corporate Diversification and Organization Structure."

[15] For a discussion of the strategic significance of cross-business coordination of value chain activities and insight into how the process works, see Jeanne M. Liedtka, "Collaboration across Lines of Business for Competitive Advantage," *Academy of Management Executive* 10, no. 2 (May 1996), pp. 20–34.

[16] For a discussion of what is involved in actually capturing strategic-fit benefits, see Kathleen M. Eisenhardt and D. Charles Galunic, "Coevolving: At Last, a Way to Make Synergies Work," *Harvard Business Review* 78, no. 1 (January–February 2000), pp. 91–101; Constantinos C. Markides and Peter J. Williamson, "Related Diversification, Core Competences and Corporate Performance," *Strategic Management Journal* 15 (Summer 1994), pp. 149–65.

[17] A. Campbell, M. Goold, and M. Alexander, "Corporate Strategy: The Quest for Parenting Advantage," *Harvard Business Review* 73, no. 2 (March–April 1995), pp. 120–32.

[18] C. Montgomery and B. Wernerfelt, "Diversification, Ricardian Rents, and Tobin-Q," *RAND Journal of Economics* 19, no. 4 (1988), pp. 623–32.

[19] Ibid.

[20] Ibid.

[21] For a review of the experiences of companies that have pursued unrelated diversification successfully, see Patricia L. Anslinger and Thomas E. Copeland, "Growth through Acquisitions: A Fresh Look," *Harvard Business Review* 74, no. 1 (January–February 1996), pp. 126–35.

[22] Of course, management may be willing to assume the risk that trouble will not strike before it has had time to learn the business well enough to bail it out of almost any difficulty. But there is research that shows this is very risky from a financial perspective; see, for example, M. Lubatkin and S. Chatterjee, "Extending Modern Portfolio Theory," *Academy of Management Journal* 37, no.1(February 1994), pp. 109–36.

[23] For research evidence of the failure of broad diversification and trend of companies to focus their diversification efforts more narrowly, see Lawrence G. Franko, "The Death of Diversification? The Focusing of the World's Industrial Firms, 1980–2000," *Business Horizons* 47, no. 4 (July–August 2004), pp. 41–50.

[24] For an excellent discussion of what to look for in assessing this type of strategic fit, see Campbell, Goold, and Alexander, "Corporate Strategy: The Quest for Parenting Advantage."

[25] Ibid., p. 128.

[26] A good discussion of the importance of having adequate resources, as well as upgrading corporate resources and capabilities, can be found in David J. Collis and Cynthia A. Montgomery, "Competing on Resources: Strategy in the 90s," *Harvard Business Review* 73, no. 4 (July–August 1995), pp. 118–28.

[27] Peter F. Drucker, *Management: Tasks, Responsibilities, Practices,* (New York: Harper & Row, 1974), p. 709.

[28] See, for, example, Constantinos C. Markides, "Diversification, Restructuring, and Economic Performance," *Strategic*

Management Journal 16 (February 1995), pp. 101–18.

[29] Drucker, *Management: Tasks, Responsibilities, Practices,* p. 94.

[30] Collis and Montgomery, "Creating Corporate Advantage."

[31] For a discussion of why divestiture needs to be a standard part of any company's diversification strategy, see Lee Dranikoff, Tim Koller, and Anton Schneider, "Divestiture: Strategy's Missing Link," *Harvard Business Review* 80, no. 5 (May 2002), pp. 74–83.

[32] Evidence that restructuring strategies tend to result in higher levels of performance is contained in Markides, "Diversification, Restructuring, and Economic Performance."

CHAPTER 9

ETHICS, CORPORATE SOCIAL RESPONSIBILITY, ENVIRONMENTAL SUSTAINABILITY, AND STRATEGY

Business is the most important engine for social change in our society.

—Lawrence Perlman
Former CEO of Ceridian Corporation

It takes many good deeds to build a good reputation and only one bad one to lose it.

—Benjamin Franklin
American Statesman, Inventor, and Philosopher

Corporations are economic entities, to be sure, but they are also social institutions that must justify their existence by their overall contribution to society.

—Henry Mintzberg, Robert Simons, and Kunal Basu
Professors

Companies have to be socially responsible or shareholders pay eventually.

—Warren Shaw
Former CEO of LGT Asset Management

LEARNING OBJECTIVES

LO 1. Understand how the standards of ethical behavior in business relate to the ethical standards and norms of the larger society and culture in which a company operates.

LO 2. Recognize conditions that can give rise to unethical business strategies and behavior.

LO 3. Gain an understanding of the costs of business ethics failures.

LO 4. Gain an understanding of the concepts of corporate social responsibility and environmental sustainability and of how companies balance these duties with economic responsibilities to shareholders.

Clearly, a company has a responsibility to make a profit and grow the business—in capitalistic or market economies, management's fiduciary duty to create value for shareholders is not a matter for serious debate. Just as clearly, a company and its personnel also have a duty to obey the law and play by the rules of fair competition. But does a company have a duty to go beyond legal requirements and operate according to the ethical norms of the societies in which it operates—should all company personnel be held to some standard of ethical conduct? And does a company have a duty or obligation to contribute to the betterment of society independent of the needs and preferences of the customers it serves? Should a company display a social conscience and devote a portion of its resources to bettering society? How far should a company go in protecting the environment, conserving natural resources for use by future generations, and ensuring that its operations do not ultimately endanger the planet?

The focus of this chapter is to examine what link, if any, there should be between a company's efforts to craft and execute a winning strategy and its duties to (1) conduct its activities in an ethical manner, (2) demonstrate socially responsible behavior by being a committed corporate citizen and directing corporate resources to the betterment of employees, the communities in which it operates, and society as a whole, and (3) adopt business practices that conserve natural resources, protect the interests of future generations, and preserve the well-being of the planet.

WHAT DO WE MEAN BY *BUSINESS ETHICS*?

Ethics concerns principles of right or wrong conduct. **Business ethics** is the application of ethical principles and standards to the actions and decisions of business organizations and the conduct of their personnel.[1] Ethical principles in business are not materially different from ethical principles in general because business actions have to be judged in the context of society's standards of right and wrong. There is not a special set of ethical standards applicable only to business situations. If dishonesty is considered unethical and immoral, then dishonest behavior in business— whether it relates to customers, suppliers, employees, shareholders, competitors, government, or society—qualifies as equally unethical and immoral. If being ethical entails not deliberately harming others, then

CORE CONCEPT

Business ethics is the application of general ethical principles to the actions and decisions of businesses and the conduct of their personnel.

recalling a defective or unsafe product is ethically necessary. If society deems bribery unethical, then it is unethical for company personnel to make payoffs to government officials or bestow gifts and other favors on prospective customers to win or retain business. In short, ethical behavior in business situations requires adhering to generally accepted norms about right or wrong conduct. As a consequence, company managers have an obligation—indeed, a duty—to observe ethical norms when crafting and executing strategy.

WHERE DO ETHICAL STANDARDS COME FROM—ARE THEY UNIVERSAL OR DEPENDENT ON LOCAL NORMS?

LO 1

Understand how the standards of ethical behavior in business relate to the ethical standards and norms of the larger society and culture in which a company operates.

Notions of right and wrong, fair and unfair, ethical and unethical are present in all societies and cultures. But there are three distinct schools of thought about the extent to which ethical standards travel across cultures and whether multinational companies can apply the same set of ethical standards in any and all locations where they operate. Illustration Capsule 9.1 describes the difficulties Apple has faced in trying to enforce a common set of ethical standards across its vast global supplier network.

The School of Ethical Universalism

According to the school of **ethical universalism,** the most important concepts of what is right and what is wrong are *universal* and transcend culture, society, and religion.[2] For instance, being truthful (or not being deliberately deceitful) strikes a chord of what's right in the peoples of all nations. Likewise, demonstrating integrity of character, not cheating, and treating people with courtesy and respect are concepts that resonate with people of virtually all cultures and religions. In most societies, people would concur that it is unethical for companies to knowingly expose workers to toxic chemicals and hazardous materials or to sell products known to be unsafe or harmful to the users.

Common moral agreement about right and wrong actions and behaviors across multiple cultures and countries gives rise to universal ethical standards that apply to members of all societies, all companies, and all businesspeople. These universal ethical principles set forth the traits and behaviors that are considered virtuous and that a good person is supposed to believe in and to display. Thus, adherents of the school of ethical universalism maintain it is entirely appropriate to expect all businesspeople to conform to these universal ethical standards.[3]

The strength of ethical universalism is that it draws on the collective views of multiple societies and cultures to put some clear boundaries on what constitutes ethical business behavior and what constitutes unethical business behavior regardless of the country or culture in which a company's personnel are conducting activities. This means that in those instances where basic moral standards really do not vary significantly according to local cultural beliefs, traditions, or religious convictions, a multinational company can develop a code

CORE CONCEPT

The school of **ethical universalism** holds that common understandings across multiple cultures and countries about what constitutes right and wrong give rise to universal ethical standards that apply to members of all societies, all companies, and all businesspeople.

ILLUSTRATION CAPSULE 9.1

Many of Apple's Suppliers Flunk the Ethics Test

Apple requires its suppliers to comply with the company's Supplier Code of Conduct as a condition of being awarded contracts. To ensure compliance, Apple has a supplier monitoring program that includes audits of supplier factories, corrective action plans, and verification measures. In the company's 24-page 2010 Progress Report on Supplier Responsibility, Apple reported that in 2009 it conducted 102 audits of supplier facilities in such countries as China, the Czech Republic, Malaysia, the Philippines, Singapore, South Korea, Taiwan, Thailand, and the United States; 80 of these audits were first-time audits and 22 were repeat audits.

Apple distinguishes among the seriousness of infractions, designating "core violations" as those that go directly against the core principles of its Supplier Code of Conduct and must be remedied immediately. During the 2009 audits, 17 such violations were discovered, including 3 cases of underage labor, 8 cases involving excessive recruitment fees, 3 cases of improper hazardous waste disposal, and 3 cases of deliberately falsified audit records. Apple responded by ensuring that immediate corrective actions were taken, placing violators on probation, and planning to audit them again in a year's time.

While all six of Apple's final assembly manufacturers had high compliance scores—on average, registering well above 90 percent compliance on all issues—other suppliers did not fare so well on the 2009 audits. At 60 of the audited facilities, workers were required to work more than 60 hours per week more than 50 percent of the time—Apple sets a maximum of 60 hours per week (except in unusual or emergency circumstances). In 65 of the audited facilities, workers were found to have been required to work more than six consecutive days a week at least once per month—Apple requires at least one day of rest per seven days of work (except in unusual or emergency circumstances).

At 48 facilities, Apple found that overtime wages had been calculated improperly, resulting in underpayment of overtime compensation. Apple

auditors discovered that at 24 facilities workers were being paid less than the specified minimum wage and that at 45 facilities wage deductions were used to discipline employees. At 57 of the audited facilities, worker benefits (for such things as retirement, sick leave, or maternity leave) were below the legally required amounts.

Apple requires suppliers to provide a safe working environment and to eliminate physical hazards to employees where possible. But the 2009 audits revealed that workers were not wearing appropriate protective personal equipment at 49 facilities. Violations were found at 70 facilities where workers were improperly trained, where unlicensed workers were operating equipment, and where required inspections of equipment were not being conducted. Apple auditors found that 44 facilities had failed to conduct environmental impact assessments, 11 facilities did not have permits for air emissions, and 4 facilities did not meet the conditions specified in their emission permits. Moreover, the audits revealed that 55 supplier facilities did not have any personnel assigned to ensuring compliance with Apple's Supplier Code of Conduct.

For Apple, the audits represent a starting point for bringing its suppliers into compliance, through greater scrutiny, education and training of suppliers' personnel, and incentives. Apple collects quarterly data to hold its suppliers accountable for their actions and makes procurement decisions based, in part, on these numbers. Suppliers that are unable to meet Apple's high standards of conduct ultimately end up losing Apple's business.

Sources: Apple's 2010 Progress Report on Supplier Responsibility; Dan Moren, "Apple Releases 2010 Report on Supplier Responsibility," *Macworld.com,* February 23, 2010, www.macworld.com/article/146653/2010/02/suppliers_2010.htm (accessed July 1, 2010); Andrew Morse and Nick Wingfield, "Apple Audits Labor Practices: Company Says Suppliers Hired Underage Workers, Violated Other Core Policies," *Wall Street Journal Online,* March 1, 2010, http://online.wsj.com/article/SB10001424 052748704231304575091920704104154.html (accessed July 1, 2010); Nicholas Kolakowski, "Apple Finds Violations during 2009 Supplier and Manufacturer Audit," *eWeek.com,* March 1, 2010, www.eweek.com/c/a/Mobile-and-Wireless/Apple-Finds-Violations-During-2009-Supplier-and-Manufacturer-Audit-522622/ (accessed July 1, 2010).

of ethics that it applies more or less evenly across its worldwide operations.[4] It can avoid the slippery slope that comes from having different ethical standards for different company personnel depending on where in the world they are working.

The School of Ethical Relativism

CORE CONCEPT

The school of **ethical relativism** holds that differing religious beliefs, customs, and behavioral norms across countries and cultures give rise to *multiple sets of standards concerning what is ethically right or wrong.* These differing standards mean that whether business-related actions are right or wrong depends on the prevailing local ethical standards.

Apart from a select set of universal moral prescriptions—like being truthful and trustworthy—that apply in every society and business circumstance, there are meaningful variations in the ethical standards by which different societies judge the conduct of business activities. Indeed, differing religious beliefs, social customs, traditions, and behavioral norms frequently give rise to different standards about what is fair or unfair, moral or immoral, and ethically right or wrong. The school of **ethical relativism** holds that when there are cross-country or cross-cultural differences in what is deemed ethical or unethical in business situations, it is appropriate for local moral standards to take precedence over what the ethical standards may be in a company's home market. The thesis is that what constitutes ethical or unethical behavior on the part of local businesspeople is properly governed by local ethical standards rather than the standards that prevail in other locations.[5] Consider the following examples.

The Use of Underage Labor In industrialized nations, the use of underage workers is considered taboo. Social activists are adamant that child labor is unethical and that companies should neither employ children under the age of 18 as full-time employees nor source any products from foreign suppliers that employ underage workers. Many countries have passed legislation forbidding the use of underage labor or, at a minimum, regulating the employment of people under the age of 18. However, in India, Bangladesh, Botswana, Sri Lanka, Ghana, Somalia, and more than 100 other countries, it is customary to view children as potential, even necessary, workers.[6] Many poverty-stricken families cannot subsist without the income earned by young family members; sending their children to school instead of having them work is not a realistic option. In 2006, the International Labor Organization estimated that 191 million children ages 5 to 14 were working around the world.[7] If such children are not permitted to work—due to pressures imposed by activist groups in industrialized nations—they may be forced to go out on the streets begging or to seek work in parts of the "underground" economy such as drug trafficking and prostitution.[8] So if all businesses in countries where employing underage workers is common succumb to the pressures of activist groups and government organizations to stop employing underage labor, then have they served the best interests of the underage workers, their families, and society in general?

The Payment of Bribes and Kickbacks A particularly thorny area facing multinational companies is the degree of cross-country variability in paying bribes.[9] In many countries in eastern Europe, Africa, Latin America, and Asia, it is customary to pay bribes to government officials in order to win a government contract, obtain a license or permit, or facilitate an administrative ruling.[10] Likewise, in many countries it is normal to make payments to prospective customers in order to win or retain their business. In some developing nations, it is difficult for any company, foreign or domestic, to move goods through customs without paying off low-level officials.[11] A *Wall Street Journal* article reported that

30 to 60 percent of all business transactions in eastern Europe involved paying bribes and the costs of bribe payments averaged 2 to 8 percent of revenues.[12] Some people stretch to justify the payment of bribes and kickbacks on grounds that bribing government officials to get goods through customs or giving kickbacks to customers to retain their business or win new orders is simply a payment for services rendered, in the same way that people tip for service at restaurants.[13] But while this is a clever rationalization, it rests on moral quicksand.

Companies that forbid the payment of bribes and kickbacks in their codes of ethical conduct and that are serious about enforcing this prohibition face a particularly vexing problem in countries where bribery and kickback payments are an entrenched local custom.[14] Refusing to pay bribes or kickbacks in these countries (so as to comply with the company's code of ethical conduct) is very often tantamount to losing business to competitors willing to make such payments—an outcome that penalizes ethical companies and ethical company personnel (who may suffer lost sales commissions or bonuses). On the other hand, the payment of bribes or kickbacks not only undercuts the company's code of ethics but also risks breaking the law. U.S. companies are prohibited by the Foreign Corrupt Practices Act (FCPA) from paying bribes to government officials, political parties, political candidates, or others in all countries where they do business. The Organization for Economic Cooperation and Development (OECD) has antibribery standards that criminalize the bribery of foreign public officials in international business transactions—as of 2009, the 30 OECD members and 8 nonmember countries had adopted these standards.[15] In 2008, Siemens, one of the world's largest corporations and headquartered in Munich, Germany, was fined $1.6 billion by the U.S. and German governments for bribing foreign officials to help it secure huge public works contracts around the world. Investigations revealed that Siemens created secret offshore bank accounts and used middlemen posing as consultants to deliver suitcases filled with cash, paying an estimated $1.4 billion to over 4,000 well-placed government officials in Asia, Africa, Europe, the Middle East, and Latin America between 2001 and 2007. An estimated 300 Siemens sales employees, executives, and board members were being investigated in 2009 for their roles in the scheme. The evidence gathered indicated that such bribes were a core element of Siemens' strategy and business model.

Penalizing companies for overseas bribes is becoming more widespread internationally. The Serious Fraud Office (SFO) in London held a landmark investigation in December 2009 of DePuy International, a subsidiary of Johnson & Johnson, for bribing Greek officials to purchase products. This comes after DePuy was fined over $311 million by the U.S. government for kickbacks to U.S. surgeons in 2007.[16]

Ethical Relativism Equates to Multiple Sets of Ethical Standards The existence of varying ethical norms such as those cited above explains why the adherents of ethical relativism maintain that there are few absolutes when it comes to business ethics and thus few ethical absolutes for consistently judging a company's conduct in various countries and markets. Indeed, ethical relativists argue that while there are some general moral prescriptions that apply regardless of the business circumstance, there are plenty of situations where ethical norms must be contoured to fit the local customs, traditions, and notions of fairness shared by the parties involved. They argue that a "one-size-fits-all" template for judging the ethical appropriateness of business actions and the behaviors of company personnel simply does not exist—in other

Under ethical relativism, there can be no one-size-fits-all set of authentic ethical norms against which to gauge the conduct of company personnel.

words, ethical problems in business cannot be fully resolved without appealing to the shared convictions of the parties in question.[17] While European and American managers may want to impose standards of business conduct that give heavy weight to such core human rights as personal freedom, individual security, political participation, and the ownership of property, managers in China may have a much weaker commitment to these kinds of human rights. Japanese managers may prefer ethical standards that show respect for the collective good of society. Muslim managers may wish to apply ethical standards compatible with the teachings of Mohammed. Clearly, there is some merit in the school of ethical relativism's view that what is deemed right or wrong, fair or unfair, moral or immoral, ethical or unethical in business situations depends partly on the context of each country's local customs, religious traditions, and societal norms. Hence, there is a kernel of truth in the argument that businesses need some room to tailor their ethical standards to fit local situations. A company has to be very cautious about exporting its home-country values and ethics to foreign countries where it operates—"photocopying" ethics is disrespectful of other cultures and neglects the important role of moral free space (in which there is room to accommodate local ethical standards).

Pushed to the Extreme, Ethical Relativism Breaks Down

While the ethical relativism rule of "When in Rome, do as the Romans do" appears reasonable, it nonetheless presents a big problem—when the envelope starts to be pushed, as will inevitably be the case, *it is tantamount to rudderless ethical standards.* Consider, for instance, the following example: In 1992, the owners of the *SS United States,* an aging luxury ocean liner constructed with asbestos in the 1940s, had the liner towed to Turkey, where a contractor had agreed to remove the asbestos for $2 million (versus a far higher cost in the United States, where asbestos removal safety standards were much more stringent).[18] When Turkish officials blocked the asbestos removal because of the dangers to workers of contracting cancer, the owners had the liner towed to the Black Sea port of Sevastopol, in the Crimean Republic, where the asbestos removal standards were quite lax and where a contractor had agreed to remove more than 500,000 square feet of carcinogenic asbestos for less than $2 million. There are no moral grounds for arguing that exposing workers to carcinogenic asbestos is ethically correct, regardless of what a country's law allows or the value the country places on worker safety.

A company that adopts the principle of ethical relativism and holds company personnel to local ethical standards necessarily assumes that what prevails as local morality is an adequate guide to ethical behavior. This can be ethically dangerous—it leads to the conclusion that if a country's culture is accepting of bribery or environmental degradation or exposing workers to dangerous conditions (toxic chemicals or bodily harm), then so much the worse for honest people and environmental protection and safe working conditions. Such a position is morally unacceptable. Even though bribery of government officials in China is a common practice, when Lucent Technologies found that managers in its Chinese operations had bribed government officials, it fired the entire senior management team.[19]

Moreover, from a global markets perspective, ethical relativism results in a maze of conflicting ethical standards for multinational companies wanting to address the very real issue of which ethical standards to enforce companywide. It is a slippery slope indeed to resolve such ethical diversity without any kind of higher-order moral compass. Imagine, for example, that a multinational company (in the name of ethical relativism) permits company personnel to pay bribes and kickbacks in countries where such payments are customary but forbids them to make such payments in countries where bribes and kickbacks are considered unethical or illegal. Or that the company says it is appropriate to use child labor in its plants in countries where underage labor is acceptable but inappropriate to employ child labor at the remainder of its plants. Having thus adopted conflicting ethical standards for operating in different countries, company managers have little moral basis for enforcing any ethical standards companywide—rather, the clear message to employees would be that the company has no ethical standards or principles of its own. This is scarcely strong moral ground to stand on.

> Codes of conduct based on ethical relativism can be *ethically dangerous* for multinational companies by creating a maze of conflicting ethical standards.

Ethics and Integrative Social Contracts Theory

Social contract theory provides a middle position between the opposing views of universalism (that the same set of ethical standards should apply everywhere) and relativism (that ethical standards vary according to local custom).[20] According to **integrated social contracts theory,** universal ethical principles or norms based on the collective views of multiple cultures and societies combine to form a "social contract" that all individuals, groups, organizations and businesses in all situations have a duty to observe. *Within the boundaries of this social contract,* local cultures or groups can specify what other actions may or may not be ethically permissible. While this system leaves some "moral free space" for the people in a particular country (or local culture or even a company) to make specific interpretations of what other actions may or may not be permissible, universal ethical norms always take precedence. Thus, local ethical standards can be *more* stringent than the universal ethical standards, but never less so.

Hence, while firms, industries, professional associations, and other business-relevant groups are "contractually obligated" to society to observe universal ethical norms, they have the discretion to go beyond these universal norms and specify other behaviors that are out of bounds and place further limitations on what is considered ethical. For example, both the legal and medical professions have standards regarding what kinds of advertising are ethically permissible that extend beyond the universal norm that advertising not be false or misleading. Similarly, food products companies are beginning to establish ethical guidelines for judging what is and is not appropriate advertising for food products that are inherently unhealthy and may cause dietary or obesity problems for people who eat them regularly or consume them in large quantities.

The strength of integrated social contracts theory is that it accommodates the best parts of ethical universalism and ethical relativism. It is indisputable that cultural differences impact how business is conducted in various parts of the world and that these cultural differences sometimes give rise to different ethical norms. But it is just as indisputable that some ethical norms are more authentic or universally applicable than others, meaning that in many instances of cross-country differences one side may be more "ethically correct" than another. In such instances, resolving cross-cultural differences over what is ethically permissible entails applying the rule that *universal or "first-order" ethical norms override the*

> **CORE CONCEPT**
>
> According to **integrated social contracts theory,** universal ethical principles based on the collective views of multiple societies form a "social contract" that all individuals and organizations have a duty to observe in all situations. *Within the boundaries of this social contract,* local cultures or groups can specify what additional actions may or may not be ethically permissible.

local or "second-order" ethical norms. A good example is the payment of bribes and kickbacks. Yes, bribes and kickbacks seem to be common in some countries, but does this justify paying them? Just because bribery flourishes in a country does not mean it is an authentic or legitimate ethical norm. Virtually all of the world's major religions (e.g., Buddhism, Christianity, Confucianism, Hinduism, Islam, Judaism, Sikhism, and Taoism) and all moral schools of thought condemn bribery and corruption.[21] Therefore, a multinational company might reasonably conclude that the right ethical standard is one of refusing to condone bribery and kickbacks on the part of company personnel no matter what the local custom is and no matter what the sales consequences are.

Granting an automatic preference to local-country ethical norms presents vexing problems to multinational company managers when the ethical standards followed in a foreign country are lower than those in its home country or are in conflict with the company's code of ethics. Sometimes—as with bribery and kickbacks—there can be no compromise on what is ethically permissible and what is not. *This is precisely what integrated social contracts theory maintains—adherence to universal or "first-order" ethical norms should always take precedence over local or "second-order" norms.* Consequently, integrated social contracts theory offers managers in multinational companies clear guidance in resolving cross-country ethical differences: Those parts of the company's code of ethics that involve universal ethical norms must be enforced worldwide, but *within* these boundaries there is room for ethical diversity and opportunity for host-country cultures to exert *some* influence in setting their own moral and ethical standards. Such an approach avoids the discomforting case of a self-righteous multinational company trying to operate as the standard bearer of moral truth and imposing its interpretation of its code of ethics worldwide no matter what. And it avoids the equally disturbing case for a company's ethical conduct to be no higher than local ethical norms in situations where local ethical norms permit practices that are generally considered immoral or when local norms clearly conflict with a company's code of ethical conduct.

> According to integrated social contracts theory, adherence to universal or "first-order" ethical norms should always take precedence over local or "second-order" norms.

HOW AND WHY ETHICAL STANDARDS IMPACT THE TASKS OF CRAFTING AND EXECUTING STRATEGY

Many companies have acknowledged their ethical obligations in official codes of ethical conduct and statements of company values. In the United States, for example, the Sarbanes-Oxley Act, passed in 2002, requires that companies whose stock is publicly traded have a code of ethics or else explain in writing to the Securities and Exchange Commission (SEC) why they do not. But there's a big difference between having a code of ethics that serves merely as public window dressing and having ethical standards that truly paint the white lines for a company's actual strategy and business conduct.[22] *The litmus test of whether a company's code of ethics is cosmetic is the extent to which it is embraced in crafting strategy and in operating the business day to day.*

It is up to senior executives to walk the talk and make a point of considering three sets of questions whenever a new strategic initiative is under review:

- Is what we are proposing to do fully compliant with our code of ethical conduct? Are there any areas of ambiguity that may be of concern?

- Is it apparent that this proposed action is in harmony with our core values? Are any conflicts or potential problems evident?

- Is there anything in the proposed action that could be considered ethically objectionable? Would our stakeholders, our competitors, the SEC, or the media view this action as ethically objectionable?

Unless questions of this nature are posed—either in open discussion or by force of habit in the minds of strategy makers—there's room for strategic initiatives to become disconnected from the company's code of ethics and stated core values. If a company's executives believe strongly in living up to the company's ethical standards, they will unhesitatingly reject strategic initiatives and operating approaches that don't measure up. However, in companies with a cosmetic approach to ethics, any strategy-ethics-values linkage stems mainly from a desire to avoid the risk of embarrassment and possible disciplinary action should strategy makers be held accountable for approving a strategic initiative that is deemed by society to be unethical and perhaps illegal.

While most company managers are careful to ensure that a company's strategy is within the bounds of what is legal, evidence indicates they are not always so careful to ensure that all elements of their strategies and operating activities are within the bounds of what is considered ethical. In recent years, there have been revelations of ethical misconduct on the part of managers at such companies as Enron, Tyco International, HealthSouth, Adelphia, Royal Dutch/Shell, Parmalat (an Italy-based food products company), Rite Aid, Mexican oil giant Pemex, AIG, Citigroup, several leading brokerage houses, mutual fund companies, investment banking firms, and a host of mortgage lenders. Much of the crisis in residential real estate that emerged in the United States in 2007–2008 stemmed from consciously unethical strategies at certain banks and mortgage companies to boost the fees they earned on processing home mortgage applications by deliberately lowering lending standards and finding ways to secure mortgage approvals for home buyers who lacked sufficient income to make their monthly mortgage payments. Once these lenders earned their fees on the so-called subprime loans (a term used for high-risk mortgage loans to home buyers with dubious qualifications to repay the loans), they secured the assistance of investment banking firms to bundle those and other mortgages into collateralized debt obligations (CDOs), found means of having the CDOs assigned triple-A bond ratings, and auctioned them to unsuspecting investors, who later suffered huge losses when the high-risk borrowers began to default on their loan payments (government authorities later forced some of the firms that auctioned off these CDOs to repurchase them at the auction price and bear the losses themselves).

The consequences of crafting strategies that cannot pass the test of moral scrutiny are manifested in sizable fines, devastating public relations hits, sharp drops in stock prices that cost shareholders billions of dollars, and criminal indictments and convictions of company executives. The fallout from all these scandals has resulted in heightened management attention to legal and ethical considerations in crafting strategy.

WHAT ARE THE DRIVERS OF UNETHICAL STRATEGIES AND BUSINESS BEHAVIOR?

LO 2

Recognize conditions that can give rise to unethical business strategies and behavior.

Confusion over conflicting ethical standards may suggest one reason for the lack of an effective moral compass in business dealings and why certain elements of a company's strategy may be unethical. But apart from this, three main drivers of unethical business behavior stand out:[23]

- Faulty oversight that implicitly allows the overzealous pursuit of personal gain, wealth, and self-interest.

- Heavy pressures on company managers to meet or beat short-term performance targets.

- A company culture that puts profitability and business performance ahead of ethical behavior.

Faulty Oversight and the Overzealous Pursuit of Personal Gain, Wealth, and Self-Interest   People who are obsessed with wealth accumulation, greed, power, status, and their own self-interest often push ethical principles aside in their quest for personal gain. Driven by their ambitions, they exhibit few qualms in skirting the rules or doing whatever is necessary to achieve their goals. A general disregard for business ethics can prompt all kinds of unethical strategic maneuvers and behaviors at companies. According to a civil complaint filed by the Securities and Exchange Commission, the chief executive officer (CEO) of Tyco International, a well-known $35.6 billion manufacturing and services company, conspired with the company's chief financial officer (CFO) to steal more than $170 million, including a company-paid $2 million birthday party for the CEO's wife held on an island off the coast of Italy, a $7 million Park Avenue apartment for his wife, and secret interest-free loans to finance personal investments and purchase lavish artwork, yachts, estate jewelry, and vacation homes. Tyco's CEO and CFO were further charged with conspiring to reap more than $430 million from sales of stock, using questionable accounting to hide their actions, and engaging in deceptive accounting practices to distort the company's financial condition from 1995 to 2002. In 2005, both Tyco executives were convicted on multiple counts of looting the company and sent to jail.

Responsible corporate governance and oversight by the company's corporate board is necessary to guard against self-dealing and the manipulation of information to disguise such actions by a company's managers. **Self-dealing** occurs when managers take advantage of their position to further their own private interests rather than those of the firm. As discussed in Chapter 2, the duty of the corporate board (and its compensation and audit committees in particular) is to guard against such actions. A strong, independent board is necessary to have proper oversight of the company's financial practices and to hold top managers accountable for their actions.

A particularly egregious example of the lack of proper oversight is the case of Enron Corporation, a former diversified energy company that has become a symbol of corporate corruption and fraud. Andrew Fastow, Enron's chief financial officer (CFO), set himself up as the manager of one of Enron's off-the-books partnerships and as the part-owner of another, allegedly earning extra compensation of $30 million for his owner-manager roles in the two part-nerships; Enron's board of directors agreed to suspend the company's con-flict-of-interest rules designed to protect the company from this very kind of executive self-dealing. Although *Fortune* magazine had named Enron "America's Most Innovative Company" for six years running, in the end it turned out that Enron's real creativity was in its accounting practices. Enron's eventual downfall resulted not only in the company's bankruptcy in 2001 but also in the dissolution of its auditor, Arthur Andersen, which was one of the top-five accounting firms at the time.

Illustration Capsule 9.2 discusses the more recent multibillion-dollar Ponzi schemes perpetrated at Bernard L. Madoff Investment Securities and alleged at Stanford Financial Group.

CORE CONCEPT

Self-dealing occurs when managers take advantage of their position to further their own private interests rather than those of the firm.

Heavy Pressures on Company Managers to Meet or Beat Short-Term Earnings Targets

Performance expectations of Wall Street analysts and investors create enormous pressure on management to do whatever it takes to deliver good financial results each and every quarter. Executives at high-performing companies know that investors will see the slightest sign of a slowdown in earnings growth as a red flag and drive down the company's stock price. In addition, slowing growth or declining profits could lead to a downgrade of the company's credit rating if it has used lots of debt to finance its growth. The pressure to "never miss a quarter"—so as not to upset the expectations of analysts, investors, and creditors—prompts nearsighted managers to engage in short-term maneuvers to make the numbers, regardless of whether these moves are really in the best long-term interests of the company. Sometimes the pressure induces company personnel to continue to stretch the rules until the limits of ethical conduct are overlooked.[24] Once ethical boundaries are crossed in efforts to "meet or beat their numbers," the threshold for making more extreme ethical compromises becomes lower.

Several top executives at the former telecommunications company WorldCom were convicted of concocting a fraudulent $11 billion accounting scheme to hide costs and inflate revenues and profit over several years; the scheme was said to have helped the company keep its stock price propped up high enough to make additional acquisitions, support its nearly $30 billion debt load, and allow executives to cash in on their lucrative stock options. HealthSouth's chief financial managers were convicted of overstating the company's earnings by $1.4 billion between 1996 and 2002 in an attempt to hide the company's slowing growth from investors. A 2007 internal investigation at Dell Computer found that executives had engaged in a scheme to manipulate the company's accounting data to meet investors' quarterly earnings expectations. The fraudulent accounting practices inflated the company's earnings by $150 million between 2002 and 2006. The executives were terminated by Dell Computer in 2007.

Company executives often feel pressured to hit financial performance targets because their compensation depends heavily on the company's performance. During the late 1990s, it became fashionable for boards of directors to grant lavish bonuses, stock option awards, and other compensation benefits to executives for meeting specified performance targets. So outlandishly large were these rewards that executives had strong personal incentives to bend the rules and engage in behaviors that allowed the targets to be met. Much of the accounting manipulation at the root of recent corporate scandals has entailed situations in which executives benefited enormously from misleading accounting or other shady activities that

Investment Fraud at Bernard L. Madoff Investment Securities and Stanford Financial Group

Bernard Madoff engineered the largest investment scam in history to accumulate a net worth of more than $800 million and build a reputation as one of Wall Street's most savvy investors—he was appointed to various Securities and Exchange Commission panels, invited to testify before Congress on investment matters, made chairman of Nasdaq, and befriended by some of the world's most influential people. Madoff deceived Wall Street and investors with a simple Ponzi scheme that promised investors returns that would beat the market by 400 to 500 percent. The hedge funds, banks, and wealthy individuals that sent Bernard L. Madoff Investment Securities billions to invest on their behalf were quite pleased when their statements arrived showing annual returns as high as 45 percent. But, in fact, the portfolio gains shown on these statements were fictitious. Funds placed with Bernard Madoff were seldom, if ever, actually invested in any type of security—the money went to cover losses in his legitimate stock-trading business, fund periodic withdrawals of investors' funds, and support Madoff's lifestyle (including three vacation homes, a $7 million Manhattan condominium, yachts, and luxury cars).

For decades, the Ponzi scheme was never in danger of collapse because most Madoff investors were so impressed with the reported returns that they seldom made withdrawals from their accounts, and when they did withdraw funds Madoff used the monies being deposited by new investors to cover the payments. Madoff's deception came to an end in late 2008 when the dramatic drop in world stock prices caused so many of Madoff's investors to request withdrawals of their balances that there was not nearly enough new money coming in to cover the amounts being withdrawn. As with any Ponzi scheme, the first investors to ask Madoff for their funds were paid, but those asking later were left empty-handed. All told, more than 1,300 account holders lost about $65 billion when Bernard Madoff admitted to the scam in December 2008. As of late October 2009, investigators had located assets of only about $1.4 billion to return to Madoff account holders. Madoff was sentenced to 150 years in prison for his crimes.

Increased oversight at the Securities and Exchange Commission after the December 2008

Madoff confession led to the June 2009 indictment of R. Allen Stanford and five others who were accused of running an investment scheme similar to that perpetrated by Bernard Madoff. Stanford was alleged to have defrauded more than 30,000 Stanford Financial Group account holders out of $7 billion through the sale of spurious certificates of deposit (CDs). The CDs marketed by Stanford Financial Group were issued by the company's Antiguan subsidiary, Stanford International Bank, and carried rates that were as much as three to four times greater than the CD rates offered by other financial institutions. Stanford claimed that the Stanford International Bank was able to provide such exceptional yields because of its investment in a globally diversified portfolio of stocks, bonds, commodities, and alternative investments and because of the tax advantages provided by the bank's location in Antigua. All the investments made by Stanford International Bank were said to be safe and liquid financial instruments monitored by more than 20 analysts and audited by Antiguan regulators. In fact, the deposits were invested in much riskier private equity placements and real estate investments and were subject to severe fluctuations in value. The statements provided to CD holders were alleged by prosecutors to be based on fabricated performance and phony financial statements.

Federal prosecutors also alleged that deposits of at least $1.6 billion were diverted into undisclosed personal loans to Allen Stanford. At the time of Stanford's indictment, he ranked 605th on *Forbes* magazine's list of the world's wealthiest persons, with an estimated net worth of

$2.2 billion. Stanford was a notable sports enthusiast and philanthropist—he supported a cricket league in Antigua and professional golf tournaments in the United States and contributed millions to the St. Jude Children's Research Hospital and museums in Houston and Miami.

Stanford also pledged $100 million to support programs aimed at slowing global warming. In May 2009, Stanford Investment Bank disclosed that it owed $7.2 billion to about 28,000 account holders. Its total assets at the time stood at $1 billion, including $46 million in cash.

Developed with C. David Morgan.

Sources: James Bandler, Nicholas Varchaver, and Doris Burke, "How Bernie Did It," *Fortune Online,* April 30, 2009 (accessed July 7, 2009); Duncan Greenberg, "Billionaire Responds to SEC Probe," *Forbes Online,* February 13, 2009 (accessed July 9, 2009); Katie Benner, "Stanford Scandal Sets Antigua on Edge," *Fortune Online,* February 25, 2009 (accessed July 9, 2009); Alyssa Abkowitz, "The Investment Scam-Artist's Playbook," *Fortune Online,* February 25, 2009 (accessed July 9, 2009); Kathryn Glass, "Stanford Bank Assets Insufficient to Repay Depositors," *Fox Business.com,* May 15, 2009 (accessed July 9, 2009); Bill McQuillen, Justin Blum, and Laurel Brubaker Calkins, "Allen Stanford Indicted by U.S. in $7 Billion Scam," *Bloomberg.com,* June 19, 2009 (accessed July 9, 2009); Jane J. Kim, "The Madoff Fraud: SIPC Sets Payouts in Madoff Scandal," *Wall Street Journal* (Eastern Edition), October 29, 2009, p. C4.

allowed them to hit the numbers and receive incentive awards ranging from $10 million to $100 million.

The fundamental problem with **short-termism**—the tendency for managers to focus excessive attention on short-term performance objectives—is that it doesn't create value for customers or improve the firm's competitiveness in the marketplace; that is, it sacrifices the activities that are the most reliable drivers of higher profits and added shareholder value in the long run. Cutting ethical corners in the name of profits carries exceptionally high risk for shareholders—the steep stock price decline and tarnished brand image that accompany the discovery of scurrilous behavior leave shareholders with a company worth much less than before—and the rebuilding task can be arduous, taking both considerable time and resources.

> **CORE CONCEPT**
>
> **Short-termism** is the tendency for managers to focus excessively on short-term performance objectives at the expense of longer-term strategic objectives. It has negative implications for the likelihood of ethical lapses as well as company performance in the longer run.

A Company Culture That Puts Profitability and Business Performance Ahead of Ethical Behavior

When a company's culture spawns an ethically corrupt or amoral work climate, people have a company-approved license to ignore "what's right" and engage in any behavior or employ any strategy they think they can get away with.[25] At such companies, unethical people are given free reign, and otherwise honorable people may succumb to the many opportunities around them to engage in unethical practices. A perfect example of a company culture gone awry on ethics is Enron.[26]

Enron's leaders encouraged company personnel to focus on the current bottom line and to be innovative and aggressive in figuring out how to grow current earnings—regardless of the methods. Enron's annual "rank and yank" performance evaluation process, in which the lowest-ranking 15 to 20 percent of employees were let go, made it abundantly clear that bottom-line results were what mattered most. The name of the game at Enron became devising clever ways to boost revenues and earnings, even if this sometimes meant operating outside established policies. In fact, outside-the-lines behavior was celebrated if it generated profitable new business.

A high-performance/high-rewards climate came to pervade the Enron culture, as the best workers (determined by who produced the best bottom-line results) received impressively large incentives and bonuses (amounting to as much as

$1 million for traders and even more for senior executives). On Car Day at Enron, an array of luxury sports cars arrived for presentation to the most successful employees. Understandably, employees wanted to be seen as part of Enron's star team and partake in the benefits granted to Enron's best and brightest employees. The high monetary rewards, the ambitious and hard-driving people whom the company hired and promoted, and the competitive, results-oriented culture combined to give Enron a reputation not only for trampling competitors at every opportunity but also for internal ruthlessness. The company's super-aggressiveness and win-at-all-costs mindset nurtured a culture that gradually and then more rapidly fostered the erosion of ethical standards, eventually making a mockery of the company's stated values of integrity and respect. When it became evident in fall 2001 that Enron was a house of cards propped up by deceitful accounting and a myriad of unsavory practices, the company imploded in a matter of weeks—one of the biggest bankruptcies of all time, costing investors $64 billion in losses.

More recently, a team investigating an ethical scandal at oil giant Royal Dutch/ Shell Group that resulted in the payment of $150 million in fines found that an ethically flawed culture was a major contributor to why managers made rosy forecasts that they couldn't meet and why top executives engaged in maneuvers to mislead investors by overstating Shell's oil and gas reserves by 25 percent (equal to 4.5 billion barrels of oil). The investigation revealed that top Shell executives knew that a variety of internal practices, together with unrealistic and unsupportable estimates submitted by overzealous, bonus-conscious managers in Shell's exploration and production group, were being used to overstate reserves. An e-mail written by Shell's top executive for exploration and production (who was caught up in the ethical misdeeds and later forced to resign) said, "I am becoming sick and tired of lying about the extent of our reserves issues and the downward revisions that need to be done because of our far too aggressive/optimistic bookings."[27]

In contrast, when high ethical principles are deeply ingrained in the corporate culture of a company, culture can function as a powerful mechanism for communicating ethical behavioral norms and gaining employee buy-in to the company's moral standards, business principles, and corporate values. In such cases, the ethical principles embraced in the company's code of ethics and/or in its statement of corporate values are seen as integral to the company's identity, self-image, and ways of operating. Stories of former and current moral heroes are kept in circulation, and the deeds of company personnel who display ethical values and are dedicated to walking the talk are celebrated at internal company events. The message that ethics matters—and matters a lot—resounds loudly and clearly throughout the organization and in its strategy and decisions. Illustration Capsule 9.3 discusses GE's approach to building a culture that combines demands for high performance with expectations for ethical conduct.

WHY SHOULD COMPANY STRATEGIES BE ETHICAL?

There are two reasons why a company's strategy should be ethical: (1) because a strategy that is unethical is morally wrong and reflects badly on the character of the company personnel and (2) because an ethical strategy can be good business and serve the self-interest of shareholders.

GE's CEO, Jeffrey Immelt, has made it a priority to foster a culture built on high ethical standards. The company's heavy reliance on financial controls and performance-based reward systems—which are necessary because of GE's broad multinational diversification—could easily tempt managers at all levels to cut corners, engage in unethical sales tactics, inaccurately record revenues or expenses, or participate in corrupt practices prevalent in the many emerging markets where GE competes. Immelt and GE's other top managers clearly recognize that without a strong ethical culture, there would be little to deter the company's thousands of managers across the globe from pursuing the many types of unethical behavior that would, on the surface, boost performance.

The first step in establishing an ethical culture at GE was for its top management to forcefully communicate the company's principles that should guide decision making. Jeffrey Immelt begins and ends each annual meeting of the company's 220 officers and 600 senior managers with a recitation of the company's fundamental ethical principles. Immelt and GE's other managers are careful to not violate these principles themselves or give implied consent for others to skirt these principles, since human nature makes subordinates at all levels ever vigilant for the signs of hypocrisy in the actions of higher-ups. The importance of walking the talk justifies GE's "one strike and you're out" standard for its top management. For example, a high-level manager in an emerging market was terminated for failing to conduct required diligence on a third-party vendor known for its shady business practices, including the payment of bribes to local officials. Another executive was fired from GE for agreeing to a large and important Asian customer's request to falsify supplier documents that were used by regulatory agencies.

With so many ethical standards prevailing in the more than 100 countries where GE operates, the company has turned to global ethical standards rather than allowing local cultures to shape business behavior. The company's global standards cover such topics as how to best evaluate suppliers' environmental records and working conditions in its manufacturing businesses and how to avoid money-laundering schemes or aiding and abetting financial services customers engaged in tax evasion or accounting fraud. Operating-level managers are formally responsible for ensuring ethical compliance in their divisions and are required to submit quarterly tracking reports to GE's corporate offices on key indicators such as spills, accident rates, and violation notices. Managers of operating units falling in the bottom quartile on the quarterly assessments are required to submit plans for improving the ethical shortcomings. GE also evaluates the ethical performance of its 4,000 managers who are responsible for profit centers or are key contributors on business teams.

GE's approach to culture building also includes instilling such principles into the behavior of the company's 300,000-plus employees with no managerial responsibility. Employees are provided training to help them understand the company's ethical principles and how those principles can help them make decisions in the ethical gray areas that arise while making everyday decisions. In Immelt's words, "At a time when many people are more cynical than ever about business, GE must seek to earn this high level of trust every day, employee by employee."* GE also allows employees to lodge anonymous complaints about ethics compliance; the complaints are evaluated by more than 500 employees around the world with either full-time or part-time ombudsperson capacity. About 20 percent of the

(Continued)

1,500 concerns lodged annually lead to serious discipline. Hourly employees are also included in annual assessments of ethical performance and are rewarded through bonuses, promotions, or recognition for identifying or resolving ethical issues at the operating level.

* *General Electric*, "The Spirit and the Letter," January 2008, www.ge.com/citizenship/reporting/spirit_and_letter.jsp.

Developed with C. David Morgan.

Source: Based on the discussion of GE's culture-building process by the company's former legal counsel in Ben W. Heineman, Jr., "Avoiding Integrity Land Mines," *Harvard Business Review* 85, no. 4 (April 2007), pp. 100–8.

The Moral Case for an Ethical Strategy

Managers do not dispassionately assess what strategic course to steer. Ethical strategy making generally begins with managers who themselves have strong moral character (i.e., who are trustworthy, have integrity, and truly care about conducting the company's business in an honorable manner). Managers with high ethical principles are usually advocates of a corporate code of ethics and strong ethics compliance, and they are genuinely committed to upholding corporate values and ethical business principles. They demonstrate their commitment by displaying the company's stated values and living up to its business principles and ethical standards. They understand there's a big difference between adopting value statements and codes of ethics and ensuring that they are followed strictly in a company's actual strategy and business conduct. As a consequence, ethically strong managers consciously opt for strategic actions that can pass the strictest moral scrutiny—they display no tolerance for strategies with ethically controversial components.

LO 3

Gain an understanding of the costs of business ethics failures.

The Business Case for Ethical Strategies

In addition to the moral reasons for adopting ethical strategies, there may be solid business reasons. Pursuing unethical strategies and tolerating unethical conduct not only damages a company's reputation but also may result in a wide-ranging set of other costly consequences. Figure 9.1 shows the types of costs a company can incur when unethical behavior on its part is discovered, the wrongdoings of company personnel are headlined in the media, and it is forced to make amends for its behavior. The more egregious are a company's ethical violations, the higher the costs and the bigger the damage to its reputation (and to the reputations of the company personnel involved). In high-profile instances, the costs of ethical misconduct can easily run into the hundreds of millions and even billions of dollars, especially if they provoke widespread public outrage and many people were harmed. The penalties levied on executives caught in wrongdoing can skyrocket as well, as the 150-year prison term sentence of financier Bernie Madoff illustrates.

Conducting business in an ethical fashion is not only morally right—it is in a company's enlightened self-interest.

The fallout of ethical misconduct on the part of a company goes well beyond the costs of making amends for the misdeeds. Rehabilitating a company's shattered reputation is time-consuming and costly. Customers shun companies known for their shady behavior. Companies known to have engaged in unethical conduct have difficulty in recruiting and retaining talented employees; indeed, many people take a company's ethical reputation into account when deciding whether to accept a job

Figure 9.1   The Costs Companies Incur When Ethical Wrongdoing Is Found Out

Visible Costs	Internal Administrative Costs	Intangible or Less Visible Costs
• Government fines and penalties • Civil penalties arising from class-action lawsuits and other litigation aimed at punishing the company for its offense and the harm done to others • The costs to shareholders in the form of a lower stock price (and possibly lower dividends)	• Legal and investigative costs incurred by the company • The costs of providing remedial education and ethics training to company personnel • Costs of taking corrective actions • Administrative costs associated with ensuring future compliance	• Customer defections • Loss of reputation • Lost employee morale and higher degrees of employee cynicism • Higher employee turnover • Higher recruiting costs and difficulty in attracting talented employees • Adverse effects on employee productivity • The costs of complying with often harsher government regulations

Source: Adapted from Terry Thomas, John R. Schermerhorn, and John W. Dienhart, "Strategic Leadership of Ethical Behavior," *Academy of Management Executive* 18, no. 2 (May 2004), p. 58.

offer.[28] Most ethically upstanding people are repulsed by a work environment where unethical behavior is condoned; they don't want to get entrapped in a compromising situation, nor do they want their personal reputations tarnished by the actions of an unsavory employer. Creditors are usually unnerved by the unethical actions of a borrower because of the potential business fallout and subsequent risk of default on loans.

All told, a company's unethical behavior risks doing considerable damage to shareholders in the form of lost revenues, higher costs, lower profits, lower stock prices, and a diminished business reputation. To a significant degree, therefore, ethical strategies and ethical conduct are *good business*. Most companies understand the value of operating in a manner that wins the approval of suppliers, employees, investors, and society at large. Most businesspeople recognize the risks and adverse fallout attached to the discovery of unethical behavior. Hence, companies have an incentive to employ strategies that can pass the test of being ethical. Even if a company's managers are not of strong moral character and personally committed to high ethical standards, they have good reason to operate within ethical bounds, if only to (1) avoid the risk of embarrassment, scandal, and possible disciplinary action for unethical conduct on their part and (2) escape being held accountable for unethical behavior by personnel under their supervision and their own lax enforcement of ethical standards.

> Shareholders suffer major damage when a company's unethical behavior is discovered. Making amends for unethical business conduct is costly, and it takes years to rehabilitate a tarnished company reputation.

STRATEGY, CORPORATE SOCIAL RESPONSIBILITY, AND ENVIRONMENTAL SUSTAINABILITY

LO 4

Gain an understanding of the concepts of corporate social responsibility and environmental sustainability and of how companies balance these duties with economic responsibilities to shareholders.

The idea that businesses have an obligation to foster social betterment, a much-debated topic in the past 50 years, took root in the 19th century when progressive companies in the aftermath of the industrial revolution began to provide workers with housing and other amenities. The notion that corporate executives should balance the interests of all stakeholders—shareholders, employees, customers, suppliers, the communities in which they operated, and society at large—began to blossom in the 1960s. Some years later, a group of chief executives of America's 200 largest corporations, calling themselves the Business Roundtable, came out in strong support of the concept of **corporate social responsibility:**[29]

> Balancing the shareholder's expectations of maximum return against other priorities is one of the fundamental problems confronting corporate management. The shareholder must receive a good return but the legitimate concerns of other constituencies (customers, employees, communities, suppliers and society at large) also must have the appropriate attention. . . . [Leading managers] believe that by giving enlightened consideration to balancing the legitimate claims of all its constituents, a corporation will best serve the interest of its shareholders.

Today, corporate social responsibility (CSR) is a concept that resonates in western Europe, the United States, Canada, and such developing nations as Brazil and India.

What Do We Mean by *Corporate Social Responsibility?*

CORE CONCEPT

Corporate social responsibility (CSR) refers to a company's *duty* to operate in an honorable manner, provide good working conditions for employees, encourage workforce diversity, be a good steward of the environment, and actively work to better the quality of life in the local communities where it operates and in society at large.

The essence of socially responsible business behavior is that a company should balance strategic actions to benefit shareholders against the *duty* to be a good corporate citizen. The underlying thesis is that company managers should display a *social conscience* in operating the business and specifically take into account how management decisions and company actions affect the well-being of employees, local communities, the environment, and society at large.[30] Acting in a socially responsible manner thus encompasses more than just participating in community service projects and donating monies to charities and other worthy social causes. Demonstrating social responsibility also entails undertaking actions that earn trust and respect from all stakeholders—operating in an honorable and ethical manner, striving to make the company a great place to work, demonstrating genuine respect for the environment, and trying to make a difference in bettering society. As depicted in Figure 9.2, corporate responsibility programs commonly include the following elements:

- *Making efforts to employ an ethical strategy and observe ethical principles in operating the business.* A sincere commitment to observing ethical principles is a necessary component of a CSR strategy simply because unethical conduct is incompatible with the concept of good corporate citizenship and socially responsible business behavior.

Figure 9.2   **The Five Components of a Corporate Social Responsibility Strategy**

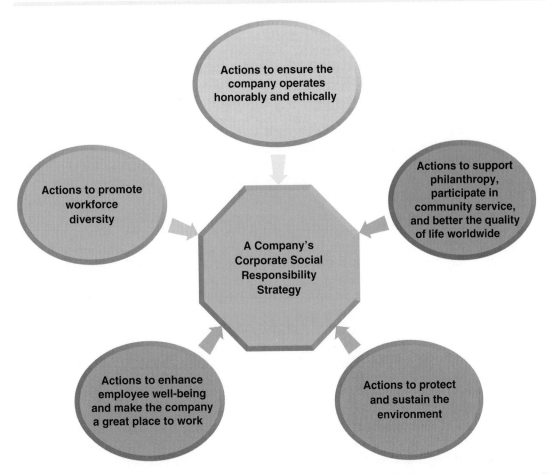

Source: Adapted from material in Ronald Paul Hill, Debra Stephens, and Iain Smith, "Corporate Social Responsibility: An Examination of Individual Firm Behavior," *Business and Society Review* 108, no. 3 (September 2003), p. 348.

- *Making charitable contributions, supporting community service endeavors, engaging in broader philanthropic initiatives, and reaching out to make a difference in the lives of the disadvantaged.* Some companies fulfill their philanthropic obligations by spreading their efforts over a multitude of charitable and community activities—for instance, Microsoft and Johnson & Johnson support a broad variety of community, art, and social welfare programs. Others prefer to focus their energies more narrowly. McDonald's, for example, concentrates on sponsoring the Ronald McDonald House program (which provides a home away from home for the families of seriously ill children receiving treatment at nearby hospitals). British Telecom gives 1 percent of its profits directly to communities, largely for education—teacher training, in-school workshops, and digital technology. Leading prescription drug maker GlaxoSmithKline and other pharmaceutical companies either donate or heavily discount medicines for distribution in the least developed nations. Companies frequently reinforce their philanthropic efforts by encouraging employees to support charitable causes and participate in community affairs, often through programs that match employee contributions.

- *Taking actions to protect the environment and, in particular, to minimize or eliminate any adverse impact on the environment stemming from the company's own business activities.* Social responsibility as it applies to environmental protection entails actively striving to be a good steward of the environment. This means using the best available science and technology to reduce environmentally harmful aspects of the company's operations *below the levels required by prevailing environmental regulations.* It also means putting time and money into improving the environment in ways that extend past a company's own industry boundaries—such as participating in recycling projects, adopting energy conservation practices, and supporting efforts to clean up local water supplies. Retailers like Walmart and Home Depot in the United States and B&Q in the United Kingdom have pressured their suppliers to adopt stronger environmental protection practices in order to lower the carbon footprint of their entire supply chains.[31]

- *Taking actions to create a work environment that enhances the quality of life for employees.* Numerous companies exert extra effort to enhance the quality of life for their employees, both at work and at home. This can include on-site day care, flexible work schedules, workplace exercise facilities, special leaves for employees to care for sick family members, work-at-home opportunities, career development programs and education opportunities, special safety programs, and the like.

- *Taking actions to build a workforce that is diverse with respect to gender, race, national origin, and other aspects that different people bring to the workplace.* Most large companies in the United States have established workforce diversity programs, and some go the extra mile to ensure that their workplaces are attractive to ethnic minorities and inclusive of all groups and perspectives. At some companies, the diversity initiative extends to suppliers—sourcing items from small businesses owned by women or ethnic minorities, for example. The pursuit of workforce diversity can be good business. At Coca-Cola, where strategic success depends on getting people all over the world to become loyal consumers of the company's beverages, efforts to build a public persona of inclusiveness for people of all races, religions, nationalities, interests, and talents have considerable strategic value.

The particular combination of socially responsible endeavors a company elects to pursue defines its **corporate social responsibility (CSR) strategy.** Illustration Capsule 9.4 describes John Deere's approach to corporate social responsibility—an approach that corresponds closely to the description in Figure 9.2. But the specific components emphasized in a CSR strategy vary from company to company and are typically linked to a company's core values. General Mills, for example, builds its CSR strategy around the theme of "nourishing lives" to emphasize its commitment to good nutrition as well as philanthropy, community building, and environmental protection.[32] Starbucks' CSR strategy includes four main elements (ethical sourcing, community service, environmental stewardship, and farmer support), all of which have touch points with the way that the company procures its coffee—a key aspect of its product differentiation strategy.[33] Some companies use other terms, such as *corporate citizenship, corporate responsibility,* or *sustainable responsible business (SRB)* to characterize their CSR initiatives.

> **CORE CONCEPT**
>
> A company's **CSR strategy** is defined by the specific combination of socially beneficial activities the company opts to support with its contributions of time, money, and other resources.

ILLUSTRATION CAPSULE 9.4

John Deere's Approach to Corporate Social Responsibility

Principal Components of John Deere's Corporate Social Responsibility Strategy	Specific Actions to Execute the Strategy
Adhering to the core values of integrity, quality commitment, and innovation *Integrity* means telling the truth, keeping our word, and treating others with fairness and respect. *Quality* means delivering the value customers, employees, shareholders, and other business partners expect every day. *Commitment* means doing our best to meet expectations over the long run. *Innovation* means inventing, designing, and developing breakthrough products and services that customers want to buy from John Deere.	• Committing to ethical behavior and fair dealing in all relationships • Providing Business Conduct Guidelines that show employees how they are expected to carry out company business • Creating an Office of Corporate Compliance to ensure ethical and fair business practices are maintained throughout global operations • Instituting a 24-hour hotline for confidential anonymous reporting of ethical violations • Offering employees professional guidance when they feel they are operating in complicated or ambiguous business and cultural situations
Engaging in philanthropy and community betterment	• Supporting agricultural development in resource-poor countries • Providing increased access to financing for the rural poor in Africa (in partnership with Opportunity International) • Helping start *BackPack* programs in the U.S. to supply supplemental food for school-age children • Supporting a variety of higher educational programs and such programs as Junior Achievement, FFA, and the National 4-H Council • Instituting an employee matching gift program
Conserving resources and sustaining the environment	• Establishing ambitious greenhouse-gas reduction goals to be achieved over the next 5 to 10 years • Mandating the use of recycling and waste reduction practices across all company operations • Implementing a worldwide Environmental Management System geared to ISO14001 standards • Helping to develop long-term comprehensive climate change strategies through EPS's Climate Leaders Program • Designing products to conserve water, encourage biofuel development, and support sustainable agriculture
Supporting and enhancing the workforce	• Maintaining effective workplace safety programs—more than 1,000 awards from the U.S. National Safety Council • Providing programs to promote employee health and wellness and work-life balance • Establishing global occupational health programs keyed to local health issues and infrastructure

(Continued)

Principal Components of John Deere's Corporate Social Responsibility Strategy	Specific Actions to Execute the Strategy
	• Helping employees with career development through mentoring, coaching, and a programmatic approach • Creating a continuous learning environment with extensive training opportunities and a tuition reimbursement program
Promoting diversity and inclusiveness	• Creating an inclusive culture in which employees of all backgrounds can develop their leadership potential • Providing training and tools designed to make work teams more diverse, productive, and effective • Sponsoring employee networks that bring together people from around the world with shared interests, gender, ethnicity, or skills • Encouraging diversity within the company's dealer and supplier base • Supporting minority education programs and collegiate diversity initiatives

Source: Information posted at www.deere.com (accessed July 8, 2010).

Although there is wide variation in how companies devise and implement a CSR strategy, communities of companies concerned with corporate social responsibility (such as CSR Europe) have emerged to help companies share best CSR practices. Moreover, a number of reporting standards have been developed, including ISO 26000—a new internationally recognized standard for social responsibility produced by the International Standards Organization (ISO).[34] Companies that exhibit a strong commitment to corporate social responsibility are often recognized by being included on lists such as *Corporate Responsibility* magazine's "100 Best Corporate Citizens" or *Corporate Knights* magazine's "Global 100 Most Sustainable Corporations."

Corporate Social Responsibility and the Triple Bottom Line

CSR initiatives undertaken by companies are frequently directed at improving the company's "triple bottom line"—a reference to three types of performance metrics: *economic, social, environmental.* The goal is for a company to succeed simultaneously in all three dimensions, as illustrated in Figure 9.3.[35] The three dimensions of performance are often referred to in terms of the "three pillars" of "people, planet, and profit." The term *people* refers to the various social initiatives that make up CSR strategies, such as corporate giving, community involvement, and company efforts to improve the lives of its internal and external stakeholders. *Planet* refers to a firm's ecological impact and environmental practices. The term *profit* has a broader meaning with respect to the triple bottom line than it does otherwise. It encompasses not only the profit a firm earns for its shareholders but also the economic impact that the company has on society more generally, in terms of the overall value that it creates and the overall costs that it imposes on society. For example, Procter & Gamble's Swiffer cleaning system, one of the company's best-selling products, not only offers an earth-friendly design but also outperforms less ecologically friendly alternatives in terms of its broader economic impact: It

Figure 9.3   The Triple Bottom Line: Excelling on Three Measures of Company Performance

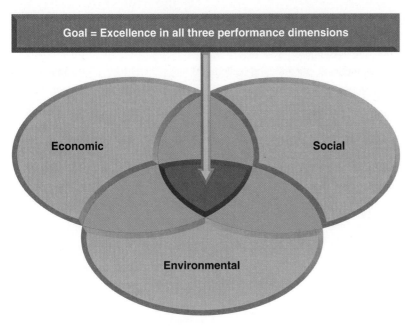

Source: Developed with help from Amy E.Florentino.

reduces demands on municipal water sources, saves electricity that would be needed to heat mop water, and doesn't add to the amount of detergent making its way into waterways and waste treatment facilities. Nike sees itself as bringing people, planet, and profits into balance by producing innovative new products in a more sustainable way, recognizing that sustainability is key to its future profitability.

Many companies now make a point of citing the beneficial outcomes of their CSR strategies in press releases and issue special reports for consumers and investors to review. Staples, the world's largest office products company, makes reporting an important part of its commitment to corporate responsibility; the company posts a "Staples Soul Report" on its Web site that describes its initiatives and accomplishments in the areas of diversity, environment, community, and ethics. Triple-bottom-line (TBL) reporting is emerging as an increasingly important way for companies to make the results of their CSR strategies apparent to stakeholders and for stakeholders to hold companies accountable for their impact on society. The use of standard reporting frameworks and metrics, such as those developed by the Global Reporting Initiative, promotes greater transparency and facilitates benchmarking CSR efforts across firms and industries.

Investment firms have created mutual funds comprising companies that are excelling on the basis of the triple bottom line in order to attract funds from environmentally and socially aware investors. The Dow Jones Sustainability World Index is made up of the top 10 percent of the 2,500 companies listed in the Dow Jones World Index in terms of economic performance, environmental performance, and social performance. Companies are evaluated in these three performance areas, using indicators such as corporate governance, climate change mitigation, and labor practices. Table 9.1 shows a sampling of the companies selected for the Dow Jones Sustainability World Index in 2009 and 2010.

Table 9.1 **A Selection of Companies Recognized for Their Triple Bottom Line Performance in 2009 and 2010**

Name	Market Sector	Country
Johnson & Johnson	Health care and pharmaceuticals	United States
PepsiCo	Food and beverages	United States
adidas	Athletic footwear, apparel, and equipment	Germany
Intel	Technology	United States
Unilever	Food and beverages	Netherlands
Samsung	Electronics	Korea
Nokia	Technology	Finland
Caterpillar	Machinery and equipment	United States
Roche AG	Health care	Switzerland
Air France–KLM	Travel and leisure	France
3M	Adhesives and abrasives	United States
Procter & Gamble	Consumer goods	United States
Sony	Electronics	Japan
BMW	Automobiles and parts	Germany
Novartis	Health care	Switzerland
IBM	Technology	United States
CEMIG	Utilities	Brazil
Cisco Systems	Technology	United States
General Electric	Technology	United States
Coca-Cola	Beverages	United States

Sources: Dow Jones indexes, STOXX Limited, and SAM Group, www.sustainability-indexes.com/07_htmle/indexes/djsiworld_ supersectorleaders.html, www.sustainability-indexes.com/07_htmle/publications/factsheets.html (accessed July 5, 2010).

What Do We Mean by *Sustainability* and *Sustainable Business Practices?*

The term *sustainability* is used in a variety of ways. In many firms, it is synonymous with corporate social responsibility; it is seen by some as a term that is gradually replacing CSR in the business lexicon. Indeed, sustainability reporting and TBL reporting are often one and the same, as illustrated by the Dow Jones Sustainability Index, which tracks the same three types of performance measures that constitute the triple bottom line.

More often, however, the term takes on a more focused meaning, concerned with the relationship of a company to its *environment* and its use of *natural resources,* including land, water, air, plants, animals, minerals, fossil fuels, and biodiversity. It is widely recognized that the world's natural resources are finite and are being consumed and degraded at rates that threaten their capacity for renewal. Since corporations are the biggest users of natural resources, managing and maintaining these resources is critical for the long-term economic interests of corporations.

For some companies, this issue has direct and obvious implications for the continued viability of their business model and strategy. Pacific Gas and Electric has begun measuring the full carbon footprint of its supply chain to become not only "greener" but a more efficient energy producer.[36] Beverage companies such as Coca-Cola and PepsiCo are having to rethink their business models because of the prospect of future worldwide water shortages. For other companies, the connection is less direct, but all companies are part of a business ecosystem whose economic health depends on the availability of natural resources. In response, most major companies have begun to change *how* they do business, emphasizing the use of **sustainable business practices,** defined as those capable of meeting the needs of the present without compromising the ability to meet the needs of the future.[37] Many have also begun to incorporate a consideration of environmental sustainability into their strategy-making activities.

Environmental sustainability strategies entail deliberate and concerted actions to operate businesses in a manner that protects natural resources and ecological support systems, guards against outcomes that will ultimately endanger the planet, and is therefore sustainable for centuries.[38] One aspect of environmental sustainability is keeping use of the Earth's natural resources within levels that can be replenished via the use of sustainable business practices. In the case of some resources (like crude oil, fresh water, and the harvesting of edible fish from the oceans), scientists say that use levels either are already unsustainable or will be soon, given the world's growing population and propensity to consume additional resources as incomes and living standards rise. Another aspect of sustainability concerns containing the adverse effects of greenhouse gases and other forms of air pollution so as to reduce global warming and other undesirable climate and atmospheric changes. Other aspects of sustainability include greater reliance on sustainable energy sources, greater use of recyclable materials, the use of sustainable methods of growing foods (so as to reduce topsoil depletion and the use of pesticides, herbicides, fertilizers, and other chemicals that may be harmful to human health or ecological systems), habitat protection, environmentally sound waste management practices, and increased attempts to decouple environmental degradation and economic growth (according to many scientists, economic growth has historically been accompanied by declines in the well-being of the environment).

Unilever, a diversified producer of processed foods, personal care, and home cleaning products, is among the many committed corporations pursuing sustainable business practices. The company tracks 11 sustainable agricultural indicators in its processed-foods business and has launched a variety of programs to improve the environmental performance of its suppliers. Examples of such programs include special low-rate financing for tomato suppliers choosing to switch to water-conserving irrigation systems and training programs in India that have allowed contract cucumber growers to reduce pesticide use by 90 percent while improving yields by 78 percent. Unilever has also reengineered many internal processes to improve the company's overall performance on sustainability measures. For example, the company's factories have reduced water usage by 63 percent and total waste by 67 percent since 1995 through the implementation of sustainability initiatives. Unilever has also redesigned packaging for many of

CORE CONCEPT

Sustainable business practices are those that meet the needs of the present without compromising the ability to meet the needs of the future.

CORE CONCEPT

A company's **environmental sustainability strategy** consists of its deliberate actions to protect the environment, provide for the longevity of natural resources, maintain ecological support systems for future generations, and guard against ultimate endangerment of the planet.

its products to conserve natural resources and reduce the volume of consumer waste. For example, the company's Suave shampoo bottles were reshaped to save almost 150 tons of plastic resin per year, which is the equivalent of 15 million fewer empty bottles making it to landfills annually. As the producer of Lipton Tea, Unilever is the world's largest purchaser of tea leaves; the company has committed to sourcing all of its tea from Rainforest Alliance Certified farms by 2015, due to their comprehensive triple-bottom-line approach toward sustainable farm management.

Crafting Corporate Social Responsibility and Sustainability Strategies

While CSR and environmental sustainability strategies take many forms, those that both provide valuable social benefits *and* fulfill customer needs in a superior fashion may also contribute to a company's competitive advantage.[39] For example, while carbon emissions may be of some concern for financial institutions such as Wells Fargo, Toyota's sustainability strategy for reducing carbon emissions has produced both competitive advantage and environmental benefits. Its Prius hybrid electric- and gasoline-powered automobile is not only among the least polluting automobiles but is also the best-selling hybrid vehicle in the United States; it has earned the company the loyalty of fuel-conscious buyers and given Toyota a green image. Green Mountain Coffee Roasters' commitment to protect the welfare of coffee growers and their families (in particular, making sure they receive a fair price) also meets its customers' wants and needs. In its dealings with suppliers at small farmer cooperatives in Peru, Mexico, and Sumatra, Green Mountain pays "fair-trade" prices for coffee beans (in 2009, the fair-trade prices were a minimum of $1.26 per pound for conventional coffee versus market prices of $0.65 per pound). Green Mountain also purchases about 29 percent of its coffee directly from farmers so as to cut out intermediaries and see that farmers realize a higher price for their efforts—coffee is the world's second most heavily traded commodity after oil, requiring the labor of some 20 million people, most of whom live at the poverty level.[40] Its consumers are aware of these efforts and purchase Green Mountain coffee, in part, to encourage such practices.

CSR strategies and environmental sustainability strategies are more likely to contribute to a company's competitive advantage if they are linked to a company's competitively important resources and capabilities or value chain activities. Thus, it is common for companies engaged in natural resource extraction, electric power production, forestry and paper products, motor vehicles, and chemical production to place more emphasis on addressing environmental concerns than, say, software and electronics firms or apparel manufacturers. Companies whose business success is heavily dependent on high employee morale or attracting and retaining the best and brightest employees are somewhat more prone to stress the well-being of their employees and foster a positive, high-energy workplace environment that elicits the dedication and enthusiastic commitment of employees, thus putting real meaning behind the claim "Our people are our greatest asset." Ernst & Young, one of the four largest global accounting firms, stresses its "People First" workforce diversity strategy that is all about respecting differences, fostering individuality, and promoting inclusiveness so that its more than 144,000 employees in 140 countries

> CSR strategies and environmental sustainability strategies that both provide valuable social benefits *and* fulfill customer needs in a superior fashion can lead to competitive advantage. Corporate social agendas that address only social issues may help boost a company's reputation for corporate citizenship but are unlikely to improve its competitive strength in the marketplace.

can feel valued, engaged, and empowered in developing creative ways to serve the firm's clients. As a service business, Marriot's most competitively important resource is also people. Thus its social agenda includes providing 180 hours of paid classroom and on-the-job training to the chronically unemployed. Ninety percent of the graduates from the job training program take jobs with Marriott, and about two-thirds of those remain with Marriott for more than a year. At Whole Foods Market, an $8 billion supermarket chain specializing in organic and natural foods, its environmental sustainability strategy is evident in almost every segment of its company value chain and is a big part of its differentiation strategy. The company's procurement policies encourage stores to purchase fresh fruits and vegetables from local farmers and screen processed-food items for more than 400 common ingredients that the company considers unhealthy or environmentally unsound. Spoiled food items are sent to regional composting centers rather than landfills, and all cleaning products used in its stores are biodegradable. The company also has created the Animal Compassion Foundation to develop natural and humane ways of raising farm animals and has converted all of its vehicles to run on biofuels.

Not all companies choose to link their corporate environmental or social agendas to their value chain, their business model, or their industry. For example, Chick-Fil-A, an Atlanta-based fast-food chain with over 1,400 outlets in 38 states, has a charitable foundation that funds two scholarship programs and supports 12 foster homes as well as a summer camp for some 1,900 campers.[41] However, unless a company's social responsibility initiatives become part of the way it operates its business every day, the initiatives are unlikely to catch fire and be fully effective. As an executive at Royal Dutch/Shell put it, corporate social responsibility "is not a cosmetic; it must be rooted in our values. It must make a difference to the way we do business."[42] The same is true for environmental sustainability initiatives.

The Moral Case for Corporate Social Responsibility and Environmentally Sustainable Business Practices

The moral case for why businesses should act in a manner that benefits all of the company's stakeholders—not just shareholders—boils down to "It's the right thing to do." Ordinary decency, civic-mindedness, and contributions to the well-being of society should be expected of any business.[43] In today's social and political climate, most business leaders can be expected to acknowledge that socially responsible actions are important and that businesses have a duty to be good corporate citizens. But there is a complementary school of thought that business operates on the basis of an implied social contract with the members of society. According to this contract, society grants a business the right to conduct its business affairs and agrees not to unreasonably restrain its pursuit of a fair profit for the goods or services it sells. In return for this "license to operate," a business is obligated to act as a responsible citizen, do its fair share to promote the general welfare, and avoid doing any harm. Such a view clearly puts a moral burden on a company to take corporate citizenship into consideration and do what's best for shareholders within the confines of discharging its duties to operate honorably, provide good working conditions to employees, be a good environmental steward, and display good corporate citizenship.

> Every action a company takes can be interpreted as a statement of what it stands for.

The Business Case for Corporate Social Responsibility and Environmentally Sustainable Business Practices

Whatever the moral arguments for socially responsible business behavior and environmentally sustainable business practices, it has long been recognized that it is in the enlightened self-interest of companies to be good citizens and devote some of their energies and resources to the betterment of employees, the communities in which they operate, and society in general. In short, there are reasons why the exercise of social and environmental responsibility may be good business:

- *Such actions can lead to increased buyer patronage.* A strong visible social responsibility or environmental sustainability strategy may give a company an edge in differentiating itself from rivals and in appealing to consumers who prefer to do business with companies that are good corporate citizens. The Body Shop, Puma, Ben & Jerry's, and Patagonia have definitely expanded their customer bases because of their visible and well-publicized activities as socially conscious companies. More and more companies are also recognizing the cash register payoff of social responsibility strategies that reach out to people of all cultures and demographics (women, retirees, and ethnic groups).

- *A strong commitment to socially responsible behavior reduces the risk of reputation-damaging incidents.* Companies that place little importance on operating in a socially responsible manner are more prone to scandal and embarrassment. Consumer, environmental, and human rights activist groups are quick to criticize businesses whose behavior they consider to be out of line, and they are adept at getting their message into the media and onto the Internet. Pressure groups can generate widespread adverse publicity, promote boycotts, and influence like-minded or sympathetic buyers to avoid an offender's products. Research has shown that product boycott announcements are associated with a decline in a company's stock price.[44] When a major oil company suffered damage to its reputation on environmental and social grounds, the CEO repeatedly said that the most negative impact the company suffered—and the one that made him fear for the future of the company—was that bright young graduates were no longer attracted to working for the company.[45] For many years, Nike received stinging criticism for not policing sweatshop conditions in the Asian factories that produced Nike footwear, causing Nike cofounder and former CEO Phil Knight to observe that "Nike has become synonymous with slave wages, forced overtime, and arbitrary abuse."[46] In 1997, Nike began an extensive effort to monitor conditions in the 800 factories of the contract manufacturers that produced Nike shoes. As Knight said, "Good shoes come from good factories and good factories have good labor relations." Nonetheless, Nike has continually been plagued by complaints from human rights activists that its monitoring procedures are flawed and that it is not doing enough to correct the plight of factory workers. As this suggests, a damaged reputation is not easily repaired.

- *Socially responsible actions and sustainable business practices can lower costs and enhance employee recruiting and workforce retention.* Companies with

> The higher the public profile of a company or its brand, the greater the scrutiny of its activities and the higher the potential for it to become a target for pressure group action.

deservedly good reputations for social responsibility and sustainable business practices are better able to attract and retain employees, compared to companies with tarnished reputations. Some employees just feel better about working for a company committed to improving society.[47] This can contribute to lower turnover, better worker productivity, and lower costs for staff recruitment and training. For example, Starbucks is said to enjoy much lower rates of employee turnover because of the company's socially responsible practices as well as superior employee benefits and management efforts to make Starbucks a great place to work. Making a company a great place to work pays dividends in recruitment of talented workers, more creativity and energy on the part of workers, higher worker productivity, and greater employee commitment to the company's business mission/vision and success in the marketplace. Sustainable business practices are often concomitant with greater operational efficiencies. For example, when a U.S. manufacturer of recycled paper, taking eco-efficiency to heart, discovered how to increase its fiber recovery rate, it saved the equivalent of 20,000 tons of waste paper—a factor that helped the company become the industry's lowest-cost producer.[48]

- *Opportunities for revenue enhancement may also come from CSR and environmental sustainability strategies.* The drive for sustainability and social responsibility can spur innovative efforts that in turn lead to new products and opportunities for revenue enhancement. Electric cars such as the Chevy Volt and the Tesler Roadster are one example. In many cases, the revenue opportunities are tied to a company's core products. PepsiCo and Coca-Cola, for example, have expanded into the juice business to offer a healthier alternative to their carbonated beverages. GE has created a profitable new business in wind turbines. In other cases, revenue enhancement opportunities come from innovative ways to reduce waste and use the by-products of a company's production. Tyson Foods now produces jet fuel for B52 bombers from the vast amount of animal waste resulting from its meat product business. Staples has become one of the largest nonutility corporate producers of renewable energy in the United States due to its installation of solar power panels in all of its outlets (and sale of what it does not consume in renewable energy credit markets).

- *Well-conceived CSR strategies and sustainable business practices are in the best long-term interest of shareholders.* Social responsibility strategies and strategies to promote environmental sustainability can work to the advantage of shareholders in several ways. They help avoid or preempt legal and regulatory actions that could prove costly and otherwise burdensome. In addition, when CSR and sustainability strategies increase buyer patronage, offer revenue-enhancing opportunities, lower costs, increase productivity, and reduce the risk of reputation-damaging incidents, they contribute to the total value created by a company and improve its profitability. In this manner, well-conceived socially and environmentally responsible strategies can enhance shareholder value even as they address the needs of other company stakeholders. While some question whether addressing social needs is truly in the interest of a company's shareholders, the answer depends on how well such strategies are crafted and whether they contribute to the success of the company's business model. A review of 135 studies indicated there is a positive, but small, correlation between good corporate behavior and good financial

> Socially responsible strategies that create value for customers and lower costs can improve company profits and shareholder value at the same time that they address other stakeholder interests.

performance; only 2 percent of the studies showed that dedicating corporate resources to social responsibility harmed the interests of shareholders.[49] Another indicator is the performance of mutual funds dedicated to socially responsible investments (SRIs) relative to other types of funds. The longest-running SRI index, the Domini 400, has continued to perform competitively, slightly outperforming the S&P 500 (the top-500 firms in the Standard and Poor's Index).[50] Similarly, the Dow Jones Sustainability Index has performed comparably to the Dow Jones Large Cap and Total Market Indexes.[51]

In sum, companies that take social responsibility and environmental sustainability seriously can improve their business reputations and operational efficiency while also reducing their risk exposure and encouraging loyalty and innovation. Overall, companies that take special pains to protect the environment (beyond what is required by law), are active in community affairs, and are generous supporters of charitable causes and projects that benefit society are more likely to be seen as good investments and as good companies to work for or do business with. Shareholders are likely to view the business case for social responsibility as a strong one, particularly when it results in the creation of more customer value, greater productivity, lower operating costs, and lower business risk—all of which should increase firm profitability and enhance shareholder value even as the company's actions address broader stakeholder interests.

> There's little hard evidence indicating shareholders are disadvantaged in any meaningful way by a company's actions to be socially responsible.

Companies are, of course, sometimes rewarded for bad behavior—a company that is able to shift environmental and other social costs associated with its activities onto society as a whole can reap large short-term profits. The major cigarette producers for many years were able to earn greatly inflated profits by shifting the health-related costs of smoking onto others and escaping any responsibility for the harm their products caused to consumers and the general public. Only recently have they been facing the prospect of having to pay high punitive damages for their actions. Unfortunately, the cigarette makers are not alone in trying to evade paying for the social harms of their operations for as long as they can. Calling a halt to such actions usually hinges on (1) the effectiveness of activist social groups in publicizing the adverse consequences of a company's social irresponsibility and marshaling public opinion for something to be done, (2) the enactment of legislation or regulations to correct the inequity, and (3) widespread actions on the part of socially conscious buyers to take their business elsewhere.

KEY POINTS

1. Ethics concerns standards of right and wrong. Business ethics concerns the application of ethical principles and standards to the actions and decisions of business organizations and the conduct of their personnel. Ethical principles in business are not materially different from ethical principles in general.

2. There are three schools of thought about ethical standards for companies with international operations:

   • According to the *school of ethical universalism,* common understandings across multiple cultures and countries about what constitutes right and wrong behaviors give rise to universal ethical standards that apply to members of all societies, all companies, and all businesspeople.

- According to the *school of ethical relativism,* different societal cultures and customs have divergent values and standards of right and wrong. Thus, what is ethical or unethical must be judged in the light of local customs and social mores and can vary from one culture or nation to another.

- According to the *integrated social contracts theory,* universal ethical principles or norms based on the collective views of multiple cultures and societies combine to form a "social contract" that all individuals in all situations have a duty to observe. Within the boundaries of this social contract, local cultures or groups can specify what additional actions are not ethically permissible. However, when local ethical norms are more permissive than the universal norms, universal norms always take precedence.

3. Confusion over conflicting ethical standards may provide one reason why some company personnel engage in unethical strategic behavior. But three other factors prompt unethical business behavior: (1) faulty oversight that implicitly sanctions the overzealous pursuit of wealth and personal gain, (2) heavy pressures on company managers to meet or beat short-term earnings targets, and (3) a company culture that puts profitability and good business performance ahead of ethical behavior. In contrast, culture can function as a powerful mechanism for promoting ethical business conduct when high ethical principles are deeply ingrained in the corporate culture of a company.

4. Business ethics failures can result in three types of costs: (1) visible costs, such as fines, penalties, and lower stock prices, (2) internal administrative costs, such as legal costs and costs of taking corrective action, and (3) intangible costs, such as customer defections and damage to the company's reputation.

5. The term *corporate social responsibility* concerns a company's *duty* to operate in an honorable manner, provide good working conditions for employees, encourage workforce diversity, be a good steward of the environment, and support philanthropic endeavors in local communities where it operates and in society at large. The particular combination of socially responsible endeavors a company elects to pursue defines its corporate social responsibility (CSR) strategy.

6. The triple bottom line refers to company performance in three realms: economic, social, environmental. Increasingly, companies are reporting their performance with respect to all three performance dimensions.

7. *Sustainability* is a term that is used in various ways, but most often it concerns a firm's relationship to the environment and its use of natural resources. Sustainable business practices are those capable of meeting the needs of the present without compromising the world's ability to meet future needs. A company's environmental sustainability strategy consists of its deliberate actions to protect the environment, provide for the longevity of natural resources, maintain ecological support systems for future generations, and guard against ultimate endangerment of the planet.

8. CSR strategies and environmental sustainability strategies that both provide valuable social benefits *and* fulfill customer needs in a superior fashion can lead to competitive advantage.

9. The moral case for social responsibility boils down to a simple concept: It's the right thing to do. There are also solid reasons why CSR and environmental sustainability strategies may be good business—they can be conducive to greater buyer patronage, reduce the risk of reputation-damaging incidents, provide opportunities for revenue enhancement, and lower costs. Well-crafted CSR and environmental sustainability strategies are in the best long-term interest of shareholders, for the reasons above and because they can avoid or preempt costly legal or regulatory actions.

ASSURANCE OF LEARNING EXERCISES

LO 1, LO 4

1. Ikea is widely known for its commitment to business ethics and environmental sustainability. After reviewing the About Ikea section of its Web site (http://www.ikea.com/ms/en_US/about_ikea/index.html), prepare a list of 10 specific policies and programs that help the company achieve its vision of creating a better everyday life for people around the world.

LO 4

2. Review Microsoft's statements about its corporate citizenship programs at www.microsoft.com/about/corporatecitizenship. How does the company's commitment to global citizenship provide positive benefits for its stakeholders? How does Microsoft plan to improve social and economic empowerment in developing countries through its Unlimited Potential program? Why is this important to Microsoft shareholders?

LO4

3. Go to www.nestle.com, and read the company's latest sustainability report. What are Nestlé's key sustainable environmental policies? How is the company addressing social needs? How do these initiatives relate to the company's principles, values, and culture and its approach to competing in the food industry?

EXERCISES FOR SIMULATION PARTICIPANTS

LO 1

1. Is your company's strategy ethical? Why or why not? Is there anything that your company has done or is now doing that could legitimately be considered "shady" by your competitiors?

LO 4

2. In what ways, if any, is your company exercising corporate social responsibility and good corporate citizenship? What are the elements of your company's CSR strategy? Are there any changes to this strategy that you would suggest?

LO 3, LO 4

3. If some shareholders complained that you and your co-managers have been spending too little or too much on corporate social responsibility, what would you tell them?

LO 4

4. Is your company striving to conduct its business in an environmentally sustainable manner? What specific *additional* actions could your company take that would make an even greater contribution to environmental sustainability?

LO4

5. In what ways is your company's environmental sustainability strategy in the best long-term interest of shareholders? Does it contribute to your company's competitive advantage or profitability?

ENDNOTES

[1] James E. Post, Anne T. Lawrence, and James Weber, *Business and Society: Corporate Strategy, Public Policy, Ethics,* 10th ed. (Burr Ridge, IL: McGraw-Hill Irwin, 2002), p. 103.

[2] For research on what are the universal moral values (six are identified—trustworthiness, respect, responsibility, fairness, caring, and citizenship), see Mark S. Schwartz, "Universal Moral Values for Corporate Codes of Ethics," *Journal of Business Ethics* 59, no. 1 (June 2005), pp. 27–44.

[3] See Mark. S. Schwartz, "A Code of Ethics for Corporate Codes of Ethics," *Journal of Business Ethics* 41, nos. 1–2 (November–December 2002), pp. 27–43.

[4] Ibid., pp. 29–30.

[5] T. L. Beauchamp and N. E. Bowie, *Ethical Theory and Business* (Upper Saddle River, NJ: Prentice-Hall, 2001), p. 17.

[6] Based on information in U.S. Department of Labor, "The Department of Labor's 2002 Findings on the Worst Forms of Child Labor," 2003, accessible at www.dol.gov/ILAB/media/reports.

[7] U.S. Department of Labor, "The Department of Labor's 2006 Findings on the Worst Forms of Child Labor," 2006, www.dol.gov/ilab/programs/ocft/PDF/2006OCFTreport.pdf; ibid., p. 17.

[8] W. M. Greenfield, "In the Name of Corporate Social Responsibility," *Business Horizons* 47, no. 1 (January–February 2004), p. 22.

[9] For a study of why such factors as low per-capita income, lower disparities in income distribution, and various cultural factors are often associated with a higher incidence of bribery, see Rajib Sanyal, "Determinants of Bribery in International Business: The Cultural and Economic Factors," *Journal of Business Ethics* 59, no. 1 (June 2005), pp. 139–45.

[10] For data relating to bribe-paying frequency in 30 countries, see Transparency International, *2007 Global Corruption Report,* p. 332, and *2008 Global Corruption Report,* p. 306, www.globalcorruptionreport.org.

[11] Thomas Donaldson and Thomas W. Dunfee, "When Ethics Travel: The Promise and Peril of Global Business Ethics," *California Management Review* 41, no. 4 (Summer 1999), p. 53.

[12] John Reed and Erik Portanger, "Bribery, Corruption Are Rampant in Eastern Europe, Survey Finds," *Wall Street Journal,* November 9, 1999, p. A21.

[13] For a study of "facilitating" payments to obtain a favor (such as expediting an administrative process, obtaining a permit or license, or avoiding an abuse of authority), which are sometimes condoned as unavoidable or are excused on grounds of low wages and lack of professionalism among public officials, see Antonio Argandoña, "Corruption and Companies: The Use of Facilitating Payments," *Journal of Business Ethics* 60, no. 3 (September 2005), pp. 251–64.

[14] Donaldson and Dundee, "When Ethics Travel," p. 59.

[15] See "OECD Convention on Combating Bribery of Foreign Public Officials in International Business Transactions," www.oecd.org/document/21/0,3343, en_2649_34859_2017813_1_1_1_1,00.html (accessed May 22, 2009).

[16] Michael Peel, "Landmark Bribery Case Goes to Trial," *Financial Times,* December 2, 2009, p. 4 (retrieved December 27, 2009, from ABI/INFORM Global, document ID:1913325051).

[17] Thomas Donaldson and Thomas W. Dunfee, *Ties That Bind: A Social Contracts Approach to Business Ethics* (Boston: Harvard Business School Press, 1999), pp. 35 and 83.

[18] Based on a report in M. J. Satchell, "Deadly Trade in Toxics," *U.S. News & World Report,* March 7, 1994, p. 64, and cited in Donaldson and Dunfee, "When Ethics Travel," p. 46.

[19] R. Chen and C. Chen, "Chinese Professional Managers and the Issue of Ethical Behavior," *Ivey Business Journal* 69, no. 5 (May/June 2005), pp. 1–5.

[20] Two of the definitive treatments of integrated social contracts theory as applied to ethics are Thomas Donaldson and Thomas W. Dunfee, "Towards a Unified Conception of Business Ethics: Integrative Social Contracts Theory," *Academy of Management Review* 19, no. 2 (April 1994), pp. 252–84, and Donaldson and Dunfee, *Ties That Bind,* especially chaps. 3, 4, and 6. See also Andrew Spicer, Thomas W. Dunfee, and Wendy J. Bailey, "Does National

Context Matter in Ethical Decision Making? An Empirical Test of Integrative Social Contracts Theory," *Academy of Management Journal* 47, no. 4 (August 2004), p. 610.

[21] P. M. Nichols, "Outlawing Transnational Bribery through the World Trade Organization," *Law and Policy in International Business* 28, no. 2 (1997), pp. 321–22.

[22] For an overview of widely endorsed guidelines for creating codes of conduct, see Lynn Paine, Rohit Deshpandé, Joshua D. Margolis, and Kim Eric Bettcher, "Up to Code: Does Your Company's Conduct Meet World-Class Standards?" *Harvard Business Review* 83, no. 12 (December 2005), pp. 122–33.

[23] For survey data on what managers say about why they sometimes behave unethically, see John F. Veiga, Timothy D. Golden, and Kathleen Dechant, "Why Managers Bend Company Rules," *Academy of Management Executive* 18, no. 2 (May 2004), pp. 84–89.

[24] For more details, see Ronald R. Sims and Johannes Brinkmann, "Enron Ethics (Or: Culture Matters More than Codes)," *Journal of Business Ethics* 45, no. 3 (July 2003), pp. 244–46.

[25] Veiga, Golden, and Dechant, "Why Managers Bend Company Rules," p. 36.

[26] The following account is based largely on the discussion and analysis in Sims and Brinkmann, "Enron Ethics," pp. 245–52. Perhaps the definitive book-length account of the corrupt Enron culture is Kurt Eichenwald, *Conspiracy of Fools: A True Story* (New York: Broadway Books, 2005).

[27] Chip Cummins and Almar Latour, "How Shell's Move to Revamp Culture Ended in Scandal," *Wall Street Journal,* November 2, 2004, p. A14.

[28] Archie B. Carroll, "The Four Faces of Corporate Citizenship," *Business and Society Review* 100/101 (September 1998), p. 6.

[29] Business Roundtable, "Statement on Corporate Responsibility," October 1981, p. 9.

[30] For an argument that the concept of corporate social responsibility is not viable because of the inherently conflicted nature of a corporation, see Timothy M. Devinney, "Is the Socially Responsible Corporation a Myth? The Good, the Bad, and the Ugly of Corporate Social Responsibility," *Academy*

of *Management Perspectives* 23, no. 2 (May 2009), pp. 44–56.

[31] Sarah Roberts, Justin Keeble, and David Brown, "The Business Case for Corporate Citizenship" (study conducted by Arthur D. Little for the World Economic Forum), p. 3, www.afic.am (accessed June 9, 2009). A revised and more wide-ranging version of this study can be found at www.bitc.org.uk/document.rm?id = 5253.

[32] "General Mills' 2010 Corporate Social Responsibility Report Highlights New and Longstanding Achievements in the Areas of Health, Community, and Environment" (CSR press release), *CSRwire*, April 15, 2010, www.csrwire.com/press_releases/29347-General-Mills-2010- Corporate-Social-Responsibility-report-now-available.html.

[33] Arthur A. Thompson and Amit J. Shah, "Starbucks' Strategy and Internal Initiatives to Return to Profitable Growth," a case study appearing in the Cases section of this text.

[34] Adrian Henriques, "ISO 26000: A New Standard for Human Rights?" Institute for Human Rights and Business, March 23, 2010, www.institutehrb.org/blogs/guest/iso_26000_a_new_standard_for_human_rights.html?gclid = CJih7NjN2alCFVs65Qo-drVOdyQ (accessed July 7, 2010).

[35] Gerald I. J. M. Zetsloot and Marcel N. A. van Marrewijk, "From Quality to Sustainability," *Journal of Business Ethics* 55 (2004), pp. 79–82.

[36] Tilde Herrera, "PG&E Claims Industry First with Supply Chain Footprint Project," *GreenBiz.com,* June 30, 2010, www.greenbiz.com/news/2010/06/30/pge-claims-industry-first-supply-chain-carbon-footprint-project.

[37] This definition is based on the Brundtland Commission's report, which described sustainable development in a like manner: United Nations General Assembly, "Report of the World Commission on Environment and Development: Our Common Future," 1987, www.un-documents.net/wced-ocf.htm, transmitted to the General Assembly as an annex to document A/42/427—"Development and International Co-operation: Environment" (retrieved February 15, 2009).

[38] See, for example, Robert Goodland, "The Concept of Environmental Sustainability," *Annual Review of Ecology and Systematics* 26 (1995), pp. 1–25; J. G. Speth, *The Bridge at the End of the World: Capitalism, the Environment, and Crossing from Crisis to Sustainability* (New Haven, CT: Yale University Press, 2008).

[39] For an excellent discussion of crafting corporate social responsibility strategies capable of contributing to a company's competitive advantage, see Michael E. Porter and Mark R. Kramer, "Strategy & Society: The Link between Competitive Advantage and Corporate Social Responsibility," *Harvard Business Review* 84, no. 12 (December 2006), pp. 78–92.

[40] World Business Council for Sustainable Development, "Corporate Social Responsibility: Making Good Business Sense," January 2000, p. 7, www.wbscd.ch (accessed October 10, 2003). For a discussion of how companies are connecting social initiatives to their core values, see David Hess, Nikolai Rogovsky, and Thomas W. Dunfee, "The Next Wave of Corporate Community Involvement: Corporate Social Initiatives," *California Management Review* 44, no. 2 (Winter 2002), pp. 110–25. See also Susan Ariel Aaronson, "Corporate Responsibility in the Global Village: The British Role Model and the American Laggard," *Business and Society Review* 108, no. 3 (September 2003), p. 323.

[41] www.chick-fil-a.com (accessed June 1, 2009).

[42] N. Craig Smith, "Corporate Responsibility: Whether and How," *California Management Review* 45, no. 4 (Summer 2003), p. 63.

[43] For an excellent discussion of the social responsibilities that corporations have in emerging countries where many people live in poverty, see Jeb Brugmann and C. K. Pralahad, "Cocreating Business's New Social Compact," *Harvard Business Review* 85, no. 2 (February 2007), pp. 80–90.

[44] Wallace N. Davidson, Abuzar El-Jelly, and Dan L. Worrell, "Influencing Managers to Change Unpopular Corporate Behavior

through Boycotts and Divestitures: A Stock Market Test," *Business and Society* 34, no. 2 (1995), pp. 171–96.

[45] Ibid., p. 3.

[46] Tom McCawley, "Racing to Improve Its Reputation: Nike Has Fought to Shed Its Image as an Exploiter of Third-World Labor Yet It Is Still a Target of Activists," *Financial Times,* December 2000, p. 14; Smith, "Corporate Responsibility," p. 61.

[47] Smith, "Corporate Responsibility," p. 63; see also World Economic Forum, "Findings of a Survey on Global Corporate Leadership," www.weforum.org/corporatecitizenship (accessed October 11, 2003).

[48] Roberts, Keeble, and Brown, "The Business Case for Corporate Citizenship," p. 6.

[49] Joshua D. Margolis and Hillary A. Elfenbein, "Doing Well by Doing Good: Don't Count on It," *Harvard Business Review* 86, no. 1 (January 2008), pp. 19–20. Of some 80 studies that examined whether a company's social performance is a good predictor of its financial performance, 42 concluded yes, 4 concluded no, and the remainder reported mixed or inconclusive findings. See Smith, "Corporate Responsibility," p. 65; Lee E. Preston and Douglas P. O'Bannon, "The Corporate Social-Financial Performance Relationship," *Business and Society* 36, no. 4 (December 1997), pp. 419–29; Ronald M. Roman, Sefa Hayibor, and Bradley R. Agle, "The Relationship between Social and Financial Performance: Repainting a Portrait," *Business and Society* 38, no. 1 (March 1999), pp. 109–25; Joshua D. Margolis and James P. Walsh, *People and Profits* (Mahwah, NJ: Lawrence Erlbaum, 2001).

[50] "Performance and Socially Responsible Investments," *The Social Investment Forum,* 2009, www.socialinvest.org/resources/performance.cfm (accessed November 15, 2009).

[51] Glenn Cheney, "Sustainability Looms as a Bigger Issue," *Accounting Today,* May 18, 2009, www.accessmylibrary.com/article-1G1-199972817/sustainability-looms-bigger-issue.html (accessed November 15, 2009).

CHAPTER 10

BUILDING AN ORGANIZATION CAPABLE OF GOOD STRATEGY EXECUTION

People, Capabilities, and Structure

> Strategies most often fail because they aren't executed well.
>
> **—Larry Bossidy and Ram Charan**
> *CEO Honeywell International, author and consultant*

> People are not your most important asset. The right people are.
>
> **—Jim Collins**
> *Professor and author*

> Of all the things I've done, the most vital is coordinating the talents of those who work for us and pointing them toward a certain goal.
>
> **—Walt Disney**
> *Founder of the Disney Company*

LEARNING OBJECTIVES

LO 1. Gain an understanding of what managers must do to execute strategy successfully.

LO 2. Learn why hiring, training, and retaining the right people constitute a key component of the strategy execution process.

LO 3. Understand that good strategy execution requires continuously building and upgrading the organization's resources and capabilities.

LO 4. Gain command of what issues to consider in establishing a strategy-supportive organizational structure and organizing the work effort.

LO 5. Become aware of the pros and cons of centralized and decentralized decision making in implementing the chosen strategy.

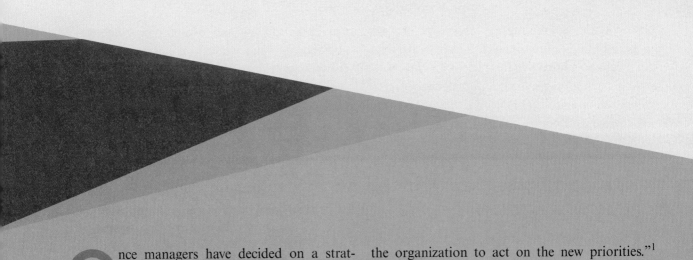

Once managers have decided on a strategy, the emphasis turns to converting it into actions and good results. Putting the strategy into place and getting the organization to execute it well call for different sets of managerial skills. Whereas crafting strategy is largely a market-driven and resource-driven activity, executing strategy is an operations-driven activity revolving around the management of people and business processes. Whereas successful strategy making depends on strategic vision, solid industry and competitive analysis, and shrewd market positioning, successful strategy execution depends on doing a good job of working with and through others; allocating resources; building and strengthening competitive capabilities; creating an appropriate organizational structure; instituting strategy-supportive policies, processes, and systems; motivating and rewarding people; and instilling a discipline of getting things done. Executing strategy is an action-oriented, make-things-happen task that tests a manager's ability to direct organizational change, achieve continuous improvement in operations and business processes, create and nurture a strategy-supportive culture, and consistently meet or beat performance targets.

Experienced managers are emphatic in declaring that it is a whole lot easier to develop a sound strategic plan than it is to execute the plan and achieve the desired outcomes. According to one executive, "It's been rather easy for us to decide where we wanted to go. The hard part is to get the organization to act on the new priorities."[1] In a recent study of 1,000 companies, government agencies, and not-for-profit organizations in over 50 countries, 60 percent of employees rated their organizations poor in terms of strategy implementation.[2] *Just because senior managers announce a new strategy doesn't mean that organization members will embrace it and move forward enthusiastically to implement it.* Senior executives cannot simply direct immediate subordinates to abandon old ways and take up new ways, and they certainly cannot expect the needed actions and changes to occur in rapid-fire fashion and still lead to the desired outcomes. Some managers and employees may be skeptical about the merits of the strategy, seeing it as contrary to the organization's best interests, unlikely to succeed, or threatening to their departments or careers. Moreover, employees may have misconceptions about the new strategy or have different ideas about what internal changes are needed to execute it. Long-standing attitudes, vested interests, inertia, and ingrained organizational practices don't melt away when managers decide on a new strategy and begin efforts to implement it—especially if only a few people have been involved in crafting the strategy or if the rationale for strategic change requires quite a bit of salesmanship. It takes adept managerial leadership to convincingly communicate a new strategy and the reasons for it, overcome pockets of doubt and disagreement, secure the commitment and enthusiasm of key personnel, gain agreement on how to implement the strategy, and move forward to get all the pieces into place. Company personnel must understand—in their heads and hearts—why a new strategic direction is necessary and where the new strategy is taking them.[3] Instituting change is, of course, easier when the problems with the old strategy have become obvious and/or the company has spiraled into a financial crisis.

But the challenge of successfully implementing new strategic initiatives goes well beyond managerial adeptness in overcoming resistance to change. What really makes executing strategy a tougher, more time-consuming management challenge than crafting strategy are the wide array of managerial activities that must be attended to and the number of bedeviling issues that must be worked out. It takes first-rate "managerial smarts" to zero in on what exactly needs to be done to put new strategic initiatives in place and, further, how best to get these things done in a timely manner that yields good results. Demanding people-management skills and perseverance are required to get a variety of initiatives launched and moving and to integrate the efforts of many different work groups into a smoothly functioning whole. Depending on how much consensus building and organizational change is involved, the process of implementing strategy changes can take several months to several years. To achieve *real proficiency* in executing the strategy can take even longer.

Like crafting strategy, *executing strategy is a job for a company's whole management team, not just a few senior managers.* While the chief executive officer and the heads of major units (business divisions, functional departments, and key operating units) are ultimately responsible for seeing that strategy is executed successfully, the process typically affects every part of the firm—all value chain activities and all work groups. Top-level managers must rely on the active support and cooperation of middle and lower managers to institute whatever new operating practices are needed in the various functional areas and operating units to achieve proficient strategy execution. It is middle and lower-level managers who ultimately must ensure that work groups and frontline employees do a good job of performing strategy-critical value chain activities and produce operating results that allow companywide performance targets to be met. In consequence, strategy execution requires every manager to think through the answer to the question: *"What does my area have to do to implement its part of the strategic plan, and what should I do to get these things accomplished efficiently and effectively?"*

CORE CONCEPT

Good strategy execution requires a *team effort.* All managers have strategy-executing responsibility in their areas of authority, and all employees are active participants in the strategy execution process.

A FRAMEWORK FOR EXECUTING STRATEGY

LO 1

Gain an understanding of what managers must do to execute strategy successfully.

Executing strategy entails figuring out the specific techniques, actions, and behaviors that are needed for a smooth strategy-supportive operation—and then following through to get things done and deliver results. The idea is to make things happen and make them happen right. The first step in implementing strategic change is for management to communicate the case for organizational change so clearly and persuasively to organization members that a determined commitment takes hold throughout the ranks to find ways to put the strategy into place, make it work, and meet performance targets. The ideal condition is for managers to arouse enough enthusiasm for the strategy to turn the implementation process into a companywide crusade. Management's handling of the strategy implementation process can be considered successful if and when the company achieves the targeted strategic and financial performance and shows good progress in making its strategic vision a reality.

The specifics of how to execute a strategy—the exact items that need to be placed on management's action agenda—always need to be customized to fit the particulars of a company's situation. The hot buttons for successfully executing a low-cost provider strategy are different from those for executing a high-end differentiation strategy. Implementing a new strategy for a struggling company in the midst of a financial crisis is a different job from that of making minor improvements to strategy execution in a company that is doing relatively well. Moreover, some managers are more adept than others at using particular approaches to achieving the desired kinds of organizational changes. Hence, there's no definitive managerial recipe for successful strategy execution that cuts across all company situations and all types of strategies or that works for all types of managers. Rather, the specific actions required to implement a strategy—the "to-do list" that constitutes management's action agenda—always represent management's judgment about how best to proceed in light of prevailing circumstances.

The Principal Components of the Strategy Execution Process

Despite the need to tailor a company's strategy-executing approaches to the particulars of its situation, certain managerial bases must be covered no matter what the circumstances. Ten basic managerial tasks crop up repeatedly in company efforts to execute strategy (see Figure 10.1):

1. Staff the organization with managers and employees capable of executing the strategy well.
2. Build the organizational capabilities required for successful strategy execution.
3. Create a strategy-supportive organizational structure.
4. Allocate sufficient budgetary (and other) resources to the strategy execution effort.
5. Institute policies and procedures that facilitate strategy execution.
6. Adopt best practices and business processes that drive continuous improvement in strategy execution activities.
7. Install information and operating systems that enable company personnel to carry out their strategic roles proficiently.
8. Tie rewards and incentives directly to the achievement of strategic and financial targets.
9. Instill a corporate culture that promotes good strategy execution.
10. Exercise the internal leadership needed to propel strategy implementation forward.

How well managers perform these 10 tasks has a decisive impact on whether the outcome of the strategy execution effort is a spectacular success, a colossal failure, or something in between.

Figure 10.2   **Building an Organization Capable of Proficient Strategy Execution: Three Types of Paramount Actions**

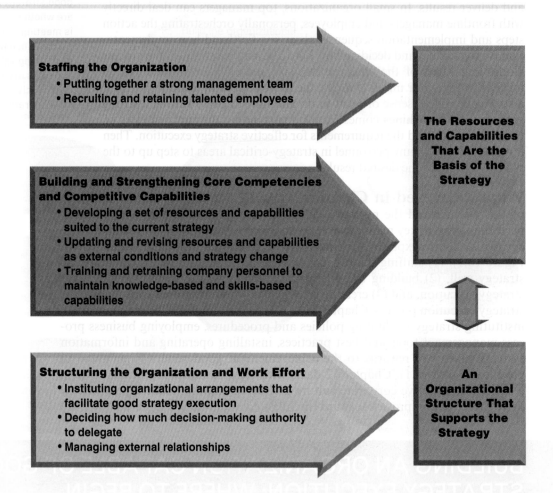

Structuring the organization and work effort is another critical aspect of building an organization capable of good strategy execution. An organization structure that is well matched to the strategy can help facilitate its implementation; one that is not well suited can lead to higher bureaucratic costs and communication or coordination breakdowns. As shown in Figure 10.2, three types of organization-building actions are paramount:

- *Staffing the organization:* putting together a strong management team, and recruiting and retaining employees with the needed experience, technical skills, and intellectual capital.

- *Building and strengthening core competencies and competitive capabilities:* developing proficiencies in performing strategy-critical value chain activities and updating them to match changing market conditions and customer expectations.

- *Structuring the organization and work effort:* organizing value chain activities and business processes, establishing lines of authority and reporting relationships, deciding how much decision-making authority to delegate to lower-level managers and frontline employees, and managing external relationships.

STAFFING THE ORGANIZATION

No company can hope to perform the activities required for successful strategy execution without attracting and retaining talented managers and employees with suitable skills and intellectual capital.

LO 2

Learn why hiring, training, and retaining the right people constitute a key component of the strategy execution process.

Putting Together a Strong Management Team

Assembling a capable management team is a cornerstone of the organization-building task.[5] While different strategies and company circumstances sometimes call for different mixes of backgrounds, experiences, management styles, and know-how, *the most important consideration is to fill key managerial slots with smart people who are clear thinkers, capable of figuring out what needs to be done, good at managing people, and skilled in delivering good results.*[6] The task of implementing challenging strategic initiatives must be assigned to executives who have the skills and talents to turn their decisions into results that meet or beat the established performance targets. Without a smart, capable, results-oriented management team, the implementation process is likely to be hampered by missed deadlines, misdirected or wasteful efforts, and managerial ineptness.[7] Weak executives are serious impediments to getting optimal results because they are unable to differentiate between ideas that have merit and those that are misguided—the caliber of work done under their supervision usually suffers accordingly.[8] In contrast, managers with strong strategy-implementing capabilities have a talent for asking tough, incisive questions; they know enough about the details of the business to be able to ensure the soundness of the decisions of the people around them, and they can discern whether the resources people are asking for to put the strategy in place make sense. They are good at getting things done through others, partly by making sure they have the right people under them and that these people are put in the right jobs.[9] They consistently follow through on issues, monitor progress carefully, make adjustments when needed, and keep important details from slipping through the cracks. In short, they understand how to drive organizational change, and they have the managerial skills and discipline requisite for first-rate strategy execution.

> Putting together a talented management team with the right mix of experiences, skills, and abilities to get things done is one of the first strategy-implementing steps.

Sometimes a company's existing management team is up to the task; at other times it may need to be strengthened or expanded by promoting qualified people from within or by bringing in outsiders whose experiences, talents, and leadership styles better suit the situation. In turnaround and rapid-growth situations, and in instances when a company doesn't have insiders with the requisite know-how, filling key management slots from the outside is a fairly standard organization-building approach. In addition, it is important to ferret out and replace managers who, for whatever reasons, either do not buy into the case for making organizational changes or do not see ways to make things better.[10] For a management team to be truly effective at strategy execution, it must be composed of managers who recognize that organizational changes are needed and who are ready to get on with the process. Weak executives and die-hard resisters have to be replaced or sidelined, perhaps by shifting them to areas where they cannot hamper new strategy execution initiatives.

The overriding aim in building a management team should be to assemble a *critical mass* of talented managers who can function as agents of change and further the cause of first-rate strategy execution. Every manager's success is enhanced (or limited) by the quality of his or her managerial colleagues and the degree to which they freely exchange ideas, debate ways to make operating improvements, and join forces to tackle issues and solve problems.[11] When a first-rate manager enjoys the help and support of other first-rate managers, it's possible to create a managerial whole that is greater than the sum of individual efforts—talented managers who work well together as a team can produce organizational results that are dramatically better than what one or two star managers acting individually can achieve.[12]

Illustration Capsule 10.1 describes General Electric's widely acclaimed approach to developing a top-caliber management team.

Recruiting, Training, and Retaining Capable Employees

Assembling a capable management team is not enough. Staffing the organization with the right kinds of people must go much deeper than managerial jobs in order for strategy-critical value chain activities to be performed competently. *The quality of an organization's people is always an essential ingredient of successful strategy execution—knowledgeable, engaged employees are a company's best source of creative ideas for the nuts-and-bolts operating improvements that lead to operating excellence.* Companies like Google, Microsoft, McKinsey & Company, Cisco Systems, Amazon.com, Procter & Gamble, PepsiCo, Nike, Electronic Data Systems (EDS), Goldman Sachs, and Intel make a concerted effort to recruit the best and brightest people they can find and then retain them with excellent compensation packages, opportunities for rapid advancement and professional growth, and interesting assignments. Having a pool of "A players" with strong skill sets and lots of brainpower is essential to their business.

> In many industries, adding to a company's talent base and building intellectual capital are more important to good strategy execution than additional investments in capital projects.

Microsoft makes a point of hiring the very brightest and most talented programmers it can find and motivating them with both good monetary incentives and the challenge of working on cutting-edge software design projects. McKinsey & Company, one of the world's premier management consulting firms, recruits only cream-of-the-crop MBAs at the nation's top-10 business schools; such talent is essential to McKinsey's strategy of performing high-level consulting for the world's top corporations. The leading global accounting firms screen candidates not only on the basis of their accounting expertise but also on whether they possess the people skills needed to relate well with clients and colleagues. Southwest Airlines goes to considerable lengths to hire people who can have fun and be fun on the job; it uses special interviewing and screening methods to gauge whether applicants for customer-contact jobs have outgoing personality traits that match its strategy of creating a high-spirited, fun-loving, in-flight atmosphere for passengers. Southwest Airlines is so selective that only about 3 percent of the people who apply are offered jobs.

In high-tech companies, the challenge is to staff work groups with gifted, imaginative, and energetic people who can bring life to new ideas quickly and inject into the organization what one Dell executive calls "hum."[13] The saying "People are our most important asset" may seem trite, but it fits high-technology companies precisely. Besides checking closely for functional and technical skills, Dell tests

How General Electric Develops a Talented and Deep Management Team

General Electric (GE) is widely considered to be one of the best-managed companies in the world, partly because of its concerted effort to develop outstanding managers. It ranked number one among the best companies for leadership in the most recent global survey conducted by the Hay Group. For starters, GE strives to hire talented people with high potential for executive leadership; it then goes to great lengths to expand the leadership, business, and decision-making capabilities of all its managers. The company spends about $1 billion annually on training and education programs. In 2009, all of its 191 most-senior executives had spent at least 12 months in training and professional development during their first 15 years at GE.

Four key elements undergird GE's efforts to build a talent-rich stable of managers:

1. GE makes a practice of transferring managers across divisional, business, or functional lines for sustained periods of time. Such transfers allow managers to develop relationships with colleagues in other parts of the company, help break down insular thinking in business "silos," promote the sharing of cross-business ideas and best practices, and build a mindset open and adaptive to international markets. There is an enormous emphasis at GE on transferring ideas and best practices from business to business and making GE a "boundaryless" company.

2. In selecting executives for key positions, GE is strongly disposed to candidates who exhibit what are called the four E's—enormous personal *energy,* the ability to *energize* others, *edge* (a GE code word for instinctive competitiveness and the ability to make tough decisions in a timely fashion—saying yes or no, and not maybe), and *execution* (the ability to carry things through to fruition). Considerable attention is also paid to problem-solving ability, experience in multiple functions or businesses, and experience in driving business growth (as indicated by good market instincts, in-depth knowledge of particular markets, customer touch, and technical understanding).

3. All managers are expected to be proficient at what GE calls *workout*—a process in which managers and employees come together to confront issues as soon as they come up, pinpoint the root cause of the issues, and bring about quick resolutions so that the business can move forward. Workout is GE's way of training its managers to diagnose what to do and how to do it.

4. Each year GE sends about 10,000 newly hired and longtime managers to its John F. Welch Leadership Development Center (generally regarded as one of the best corporate training centers in the world) for a three-week course on the company's Six Sigma quality initiative. GE's Leadership Development Center also offers advanced courses for senior managers that may focus on a single management topic for a month. All classes involve managers from different GE businesses and different parts of the world. Some of the most valuable learning comes between formal class sessions when GE managers from different businesses trade ideas about how to improve processes and better serve the customer. This knowledge sharing not only spreads best practices throughout the organization but also improves each GE manager's knowledge.

One of the keys to the success of the management development process at GE is its ability to be adapted to a changing environment: "It's a constant evolution," according to Chief Learning Officer Susan Peters.* Under the leadership of Jack Welch, GE's CEO from 1980 to 2001, training activities were

(Continued)

focused around cost cutting, efficiency, and deal making. His successor, Jeffrey Immelt, adapted the focus of development programs to drive toward new goals of risk taking, innovation, and customer focus. Recently, GE has tackled the ascendancy of emerging markets by increased focus on global capability development, including the development of the China Learning Center in Shanghai. This has had a visible impact on the organization: In the last seven years the proportion of non-U.S. executives has doubled, from 15 percent to more than 30.

As a key part of talent development, talent assessment and feedback are approached with characteristic GE energy. Each of GE's 85,000 managers and professionals is graded in an annual process that divides them into five tiers: the top 10 percent, the next 15 percent, the middle 50 percent, the next 15 percent, and the bottom 10 percent. Everyone in the top tier gets stock awards, nobody in the fourth tier gets shares of stock, and most of those in the fifth tier become candidates for being weeded out. Business heads are pressured to wean out "C" players. CEO Jeffrey Immelt personally reviews the performance reviews of the top-600 employees each year, as part of GE's intensive, months-long performance review process.

* D. Brady, "Can GE Still Manage?" *Bloomberg BusinessWeek,* April 25, 2010, pp. 26–32.

Developed with Jeffrey L. Boyink.

Sources: GE Web site (accessed June 2010); Hewitt Associates, "Managing Leadership in Turbulent Times—Why and How the Global Top Companies for Leaders Optimize Leadership Talent in Emerging Markets" (White Paper), www.hewittassociates.com/_ MetaBasicCMAssetCache_/Assets/Articles/2009/Managing_Leadership_Turbulent_Times_033009.pdf; D. Brady, "Can GE Still Manage?" *Bloomberg BusinessWeek,* April 25, 2010, pp. 26–32; "Hay Group Study Identifies Best Companies for Leadership," *Bloomberg BusinessWeek.com,* February 18, 2010, www.greatleadershipbydan.com/2010/02/bloomberg-businessweekcomhay-group.html.

> The best companies make a point of recruiting and retaining talented employees—the objective is to make the company's entire workforce (managers and rank-and-file employees) a genuine competitive asset.

applicants for their tolerance of ambiguity and change, their capacity to work in teams, and their ability to learn on the fly. Companies like Amazon.com, Google, and Cisco Systems have broken new ground in recruiting, hiring, cultivating, developing, and retaining talented employees—almost all of whom are in their 20s and 30s. Cisco goes after the top 10 percent, raiding other companies and endeavoring to retain key people at the companies it acquires. Cisco executives believe that a cadre of star engineers, programmers, managers, salespeople, and support personnel is the backbone of the company's efforts to execute its strategy and remain the world's leading provider of Internet infrastructure products and technology.

The practices listed below are common among companies dedicated to recruiting, training, and retaining the most capable people they can find:

1. Spending considerable effort on screening and evaluating job applicants—selecting only those with suitable skill sets, energy, initiative, judgment, aptitude for learning, and personality traits that mesh well with the company's work environment and culture.

2. Putting employees through training programs that continue throughout their careers.

3. Providing promising employees with challenging, interesting, and skill-stretching assignments.

4. Rotating people through jobs that span functional and geographic boundaries. Providing people with opportunities to gain experience in a variety of international settings is increasingly considered an essential part of career development in multinational or global companies.

5. Making the work environment stimulating and engaging so that employees will consider the company a great place to work. Progressive companies work hard at creating an environment in which employees are made to feel that their views and suggestions count.

6. Striving to retain talented, high-performing employees via promotions, salary increases, performance bonuses, stock options and equity ownership, fringe-benefit packages, and other perks.

7. Coaching average performers to improve their skills and capabilities, while weeding out underperformers and benchwarmers.

BUILDING AND STRENGTHENING CORE COMPETENCIES AND COMPETITIVE CAPABILITIES

High among the organization-building priorities in the strategy execution process is the need to build and strengthen competitively valuable core competences and capabilities. As explained in Chapter 4, a company's ability to perform the value-creating activities that express its strategy derives from its resources and capabilities. In the course of crafting strategy, managers identify the resources and capabilities that will enable the firm's strategy. In executing the strategy, managers deploy those resources and capabilities in the form of value-creating activities. But the first step is to ensure that the necessary resources and capabilities are in place and that they are renewed, upgraded, or augmented, as needed.

> **LO 3**
>
> Understand that good strategy execution requires continuously building and upgrading the organization's resources and capabilities.

If the strategy being implemented is new, company managers may have to acquire new resources, significantly broaden or deepen certain capabilities, or even add entirely new competencies in order to put the strategic initiatives in place and execute them proficiently. But even if the strategy has not changed materially, good strategy execution involves refreshing and strengthening the firm's resources and capabilities to keep them in top form. Moreover, it involves augmenting and modifying them to keep pace with evolving market needs and competitive conditions.

Three Approaches to Building and Strengthening Capabilities

Building core competencies and competitive capabilities is a time-consuming, managerially challenging exercise. While some assistance can be gotten from discovering how best-in-industry or best-in-world companies perform a particular activity, trying to replicate and then improve on the competencies and capabilities of others is, however, much easier said than done—for the same reasons that one is unlikely to ever become a good golfer just by studying what Tiger Woods does.

> Building new competencies and capabilities is a multistage process that occurs over a period of months and years. It is not something that is accomplished overnight.

With deliberate effort, well-orchestrated organizational actions, and continued practice, however, it is possible for a firm to become proficient at capability building despite the difficulty. Indeed, by making capability-building activities a routine part of their strategy execution endeavors, some firms are able to develop *dynamic capabilities* that assist them in managing resource and capability change, as discussed in Chapter 4. The most common approaches to capability building include (1) internal development, (2) acquiring capabilities through mergers and acquisitions, and (3) accessing capabilities via collaborative partnerships.[14]

Developing Capabilities Internally   Capabilities develop incrementally along an evolutionary development path as organizations search for solutions to their problems. The process is a complex one, since capabilities are the product of bundles of skills and know-how that are integrated into organizational routines and deployed within activity systems through the combined efforts of teams and work groups that are often cross-functional in nature, spanning a variety of departments and locations. For instance, the capability of speeding new products to market involves the collaborative efforts of personnel in R&D, engineering and design, purchasing, production, marketing, and distribution. Similarly, the capability to provide superior customer service is a team effort among people in customer call centers (where orders are taken and inquiries are answered), shipping and delivery, billing and accounts receivable, and after-sale support. The process of building a capability begins when managers set an objective of developing a particular capability and organize activity around that objective.[15] Managers can ignite the process by having high aspirations and setting "stretch goals" for the organization.[16]

Because the process is incremental, the first step is to develop the *ability* to do something, however imperfectly or inefficiently. This entails selecting people with the requisite skills and experience, upgrading or expanding individual abilities as needed, and then molding the efforts of individuals into a collaborative effort to create an organizational ability. At this stage, progress can be fitful since it depends on experimentation, active search for alternative solutions, and learning through trial and error.[17]

As experience grows and company personnel learn how to perform the activities consistently well and at an acceptable cost, the ability evolves into a tried-and-true competence or capability. Getting to this point requires a continual investment of resources and systematic efforts to improve processes and solve problems creatively as they arise. Improvements in the functioning of a capability come from task repetition and the resulting learning by doing of individuals and teams.[18] But the process can be accelerated by making learning a more deliberate endeavor and providing the incentives that will motivate company personnel to achieve the desired ends.[19] This can be critical to successful strategy execution when market conditions are changing rapidly.

> A company's capabilities must be continually refreshed and renewed to remain aligned with changing customer expectations, altered competitive conditions, and new strategic initiatives.

It is generally much easier and less time-consuming to update and remodel a company's existing capabilities as external conditions and company strategy change than it is to create them from scratch. Maintaining capabilities in top form may simply require exercising them continually and fine-tuning them as necessary. Refreshing and updating capabilities require only a limited set of modifications to a set of routines that is otherwise in place. Phasing out an existing capability takes significantly less effort than adding a brand-new one. Replicating a company capability, while not an easy process, still begins with an established template.[20] Even the process of augmenting a capability may require less effort if it involves the recombination of well-established company capabilities and draws on existing company resources.[21] Companies like Cray in large computers and Honda in gasoline engines, for example, have leveraged the expertise of their talent pool by frequently re-forming high-intensity teams and reusing key people on special projects designed to augment their capabilities. Canon combined miniaturization capabilities that it developed in producing calculators with its existing capabilities in precision optics to revolutionize the 35-mm camera market.[22] Toyota, en route to overtaking General Motors as the global leader in motor vehicles, has aggressively upgraded its capabilities in fuel-efficient hybrid engine technology and constantly fine-tuned its famed Toyota Production System to enhance its already proficient capabilities in manufacturing top-quality vehicles at relatively low costs—see Illustration Capsule 10.2.

ILLUSTRATION CAPSULE 10.2

Toyota's Legendary Production System: A Capability That Translates into Competitive Advantage

The heart of Toyota's strategy in motor vehicles is to outcompete rivals by manufacturing world-class, quality vehicles at lower costs and selling them at competitive price levels. Executing this strategy requires top-notch manufacturing capability and super-efficient management of people, equipment, and materials. Toyota began conscious efforts to improve its manufacturing competence over 50 years ago. Through tireless trial and error, the company gradually took what started as a loose collection of techniques and practices and integrated them into a full-fledged process that has come to be known as the Toyota Production System (TPS). The TPS drives all plant operations and the company's supply chain management practices. TPS is grounded in the following principles, practices, and techniques:

- *Use just-in-time delivery of parts and components to the point of vehicle assembly.* The idea here is to cut out all the bits and pieces of transferring materials from place to place and to discontinue all activities on the part of workers that don't add value (particularly activities where nothing ends up being made or assembled).

- *Develop people who can come up with unique ideas for production improvements.* Toyota encourages employees at all levels to question existing ways of doing things—even if this means challenging a boss on the soundness of a directive. Former Toyota president Katsuaki Watanabe encouraged the company's employees to "pick a friendly fight." Also, Toyota doesn't fire its employees who, at first, have little judgment for improving work flows; instead, the company gives them extensive training to become better problem solvers.

- *Emphasize continuous improvement.* Workers are expected to use their heads and develop better ways of doing things, rather than mechanically follow instructions. Toyota managers tout messages such as "Never be satisfied" and "There's got to be a better way." Another mantra at Toyota is that the *T* in TPS also stands for "Thinking." The thesis is that a work environment where people have to think generates the wisdom to spot opportunities for making tasks

simpler and easier to perform, increasing the speed and efficiency with which activities are performed, and constantly improving product quality.

- *Empower workers to stop the assembly line when there's a problem or a defect is spotted.* Toyota views worker efforts to purge defects and sort out the problem immediately as critical to the whole concept of building quality into the production process. According to TPS, "If the line doesn't stop, useless defective items will move on to the next stage. If you don't know where the problem occurred, you can't do anything to fix it."

- *Deal with defects only when they occur.* TPS philosophy holds that when things are running smoothly, they should not be subject to control; if attention is directed to fixing problems that are found, quality control along the assembly line can be handled with fewer personnel.

- *Ask yourself "Why?" five times.* While errors need to be fixed whenever they occur, the value of asking "Why?" five times enables identifying the root cause of the error and correcting it so that the error won't recur.

- *Organize all jobs around human motion to create a production/assembly system with no wasted effort.* Work organized in this fashion is called "standardized work" and people are trained to observe standardized work procedures (which include supplying parts to each process on the

(Continued)

387

assembly line at the proper time, sequencing the work in an optimal manner, and allowing workers to do their jobs continuously in a set sequence of subprocesses).

- *Find where a part is made cheaply, and use that price as a benchmark.*

The TPS utilizes a unique vocabulary of terms (such as *kanban, takt-time, jikoda, kaizen, heijunka, monozukuri, poka yoke,* and *muda*) that facilitates precise discussion of specific TPS elements. In 2003, Toyota established its Global Production Center to efficiently train large numbers of shop-floor experts in the latest TPS methods and better operate an increasing number of production sites worldwide. Since then, additional upgrades and refinements have been introduced, some in response to the large number of defects in Toyota vehicles that surfaced in 2009–2010.

There's widespread agreement that Toyota's ongoing effort to refine and improve on its renowned TPS gives it important manufacturing capabilities that are the envy of other motor vehicle manufacturers. Not only have such auto manufacturers as Ford, Daimler, Volkswagen, and General Motors attempted to emulate key elements of TPS, but elements of Toyota's production philosophy have been adopted by hospitals and postal services.

Sources: Information posted at www.toyotageorgetown.com; Hirotaka Takeuchi, Emi Osono, and Norihiko Shimizu, "The Contradictions That Drive Toyota's Success," *Harvard Business Review* 86, no. 6 (June 2008), pp. 96–104; Taiichi Ohno, *Toyota Production System: Beyond Large-Scale Production* (New York: Sheridan, 1988).

Managerial actions to develop core competencies and competitive capabilities generally take one of two forms: either strengthening the company's base of skills, knowledge, and intellect or coordinating and integrating the efforts of the various work groups and departments. Actions of the first sort can be undertaken at all managerial levels, but actions of the second sort are best orchestrated by senior managers who not only appreciate the strategy-executing significance of strong capabilities but also have the clout to enforce the necessary cooperation and coordination among individuals, groups, departments, and external allies.[23]

Acquiring Capabilities through Mergers and Acquisitions

Sometimes a company can refresh and strengthen its competencies by acquiring another company with attractive resources and capabilities.[24] An acquisition aimed at building a stronger portfolio of competencies and capabilities can be every bit as valuable as an acquisition aimed at adding new products or services to the company's lineup of offerings. The advantage of this mode of acquiring new capabilities is primarily one of speed, since developing new capabilities internally can take many years of effort. Capabilities-motivated acquisitions are essential (1) when a market opportunity can slip by faster than a needed capability can be created internally and (2) when industry conditions, technology, or competitors are moving at such a rapid clip that time is of the essence.

At the same time, acquiring capabilities in this way is not without difficulty. Capabilities involve tacit knowledge and complex routines that cannot be transferred readily from one organizational unit to another. This may limit the extent to which the new capability can be utilized. For example, the Newell Company acquired Rubbermaid in part for its famed product innovation capabilities. Transferring these capabilities to other parts of the Newell organization proved easier said than done, however, contributing to a slump in the firm's stock prices that lasted for some time. Integrating the capabilities of two firms involved in a merger or acquisition may pose an additional challenge, particularly if there are underlying incompatibilities in their supporting systems or processes. Moreover, since internal fit is important, there is always the risk that under new management the acquired capabilities may not be as productive as they had been. In a worst-case scenario, the acquisition process may end up damaging or destroying the very capabilities that were the object of the acquisition in the first place.

Accessing Capabilities through Collaborative Partnerships

Another method of acquiring capabilities from an external source is to access them via collaborative partnerships with suppliers, competitors, or other companies having the cutting-edge expertise. There are three basic ways to pursue this course of action:

1. *Outsource the function requiring the capabilities to a key supplier or another provider.* Whether this is a wise move depends on what can be safely delegated to outside suppliers or allies versus what internal capabilities are key to the company's long-term success. As discussed in Chapter 6, outsourcing has the advantage of conserving resources so that the firm can focus its energies on those activities most central to its strategy. It may be a good choice for firms that are too small and resource-constrained to execute all the parts of their strategy internally.

2. *Collaborate with a firm that has complementary resources and capabilities in a joint venture, strategic alliance, or other type of partnership established for the purpose of achieving a shared strategic objective.* This requires launching initiatives to identify the most attractive potential partners and to establish collaborative working relationships. Since the success of the venture will depend on how well the partners work together, potential partners should be selected as much for their management style, culture, and goals as for their resources and capabilities.

3. *Engage in a collaborative partnership for the purpose of learning how the partner does things, internalizing its methods and thereby acquiring its capabilities.* Since this method involves an abuse of trust, it not only puts the cooperative venture at risk but also encourages the firm's partner to treat the firm similarly or refuse further dealings with the firm.

Upgrading Employee Skills and Knowledge Resources

Good strategy execution also requires that employees have the skills and knowledge resources they will need to perform their tasks well. Employee training thus plays an important role in the strategy execution process. Training and retraining are important when a company shifts to a strategy requiring different skills, competitive capabilities, and operating methods. Training is also strategically important in organizational efforts to build skills-based competencies. And it is a key activity in businesses where technical know-how is changing so rapidly that a company loses its ability to compete unless its employees have cutting-edge knowledge and expertise. Successful strategy implementers see to it that the training function is both adequately funded and effective. If the chosen strategy calls for new skills, deeper technological capability, or the building and using of new capabilities, training should be placed near the top of the action agenda.

The strategic importance of training has not gone unnoticed. Over 600 companies have established internal "universities" to lead the training effort, facilitate continuous organizational learning, and help upgrade company capabilities. Many companies conduct orientation sessions for new employees, fund an assortment of competence-building training programs, and reimburse employees for tuition and other expenses associated with obtaining additional college education, attending professional development courses, and earning professional certification of one kind or another. A number of companies offer online, just-in-time training courses to employees around the clock. Increasingly, employees at all levels are expected to take an active role in their own professional development and assume responsibility for keeping their skills up to date and in sync with the company's needs.

Strategy Execution Capabilities and Competitive Advantage

As firms get better at executing their strategies, they develop capabilities in the domain of strategy execution much as they build other organizational capabilities. Superior strategy execution capabilities allow companies to get the most from their organizational resources and competitive capabilities. In this way they contribute to the success of a firm's business model. But excellence in strategy execution can also be a more direct source of competitive advantage, since more efficient and effective strategy execution can lower costs and permit firms to deliver more value to customers. Superior strategy execution capabilities may also enable a company to react more quickly to market changes and beat other firms to the market with new products and services. This can allow a company to profit from a period of uncontested market dominance.

> Superior strategy execution capabilities are the only source of sustainable competitive advantage when strategies are easy for rivals to copy.

Because strategy execution capabilities are socially complex capabilities that develop with experience over long periods of time, they are hard to imitate. And there is no substitute for good strategy execution. (Recall the tests of resource advantage from Chapter 4.) As such, they may be as important a source of sustained competitive advantage as the capabilities that drive a firm's strategies. Indeed, they may be a far more important avenue for securing a competitive edge over rivals in situations where it is relatively easy for rivals to copy promising strategies. In such cases, the only way for firms to achieve lasting competitive advantage is to outexecute their competitors.

ORGANIZING THE WORK EFFORT WITH A SUPPORTIVE ORGANIZATIONAL STRUCTURE

LO 4

Gain command of what issues to consider in establishing a strategy-supportive organizational structure and organizing the work effort.

There are few hard-and-fast rules for organizing the work effort to support good strategy execution. Every firm's organization chart is partly a product of its particular situation, reflecting prior organizational patterns, varying internal circumstances, executive judgments about reporting relationships, and the politics of who gets which assignments. Moreover, every strategy is grounded in its own set of organizational capabilities and value chain activities. But some considerations in organizing the work effort are common to all companies. These are summarized in Figure 10.3 and discussed in the following sections.

Figure 10.3 Structuring the Work Effort to Promote Successful Strategy Execution

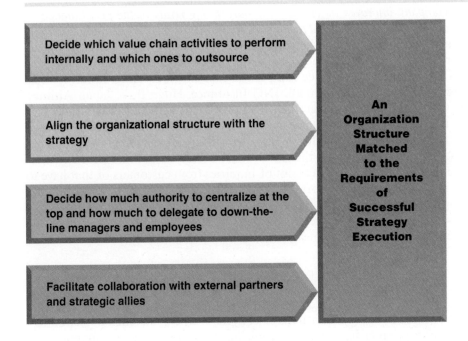

Deciding Which Value Chain Activities to Perform Internally and Which to Outsource

The advantages of a company's having an outsourcing component in its strategy were discussed in Chapter 6, but there is also a need to consider the role of outsourcing in executing the strategy. Aside from the fact that another company (because of its experience, scale of operations, and specialized know-how) may be able to perform certain value chain activities better or cheaper than a company can perform them internally, outsourcing can also sometimes make a positive contribution to better strategy execution. Managers too often spend inordinate amounts of time, mental energy, and resources haggling with functional support groups or other internal bureaucracies over needed services, leaving less time for them to devote to performing strategy-critical activities in the most proficient manner.

> Wisely choosing which activities to perform internally and which to outsource can lead to several strategy-executing advantages—lower costs, heightened strategic focus, less internal bureaucracy, speedier decision making, and a better arsenal of organizational capabilities.

One way to reduce such distractions is to outsource the performance of assorted administrative support functions and perhaps even selected primary value chain activities to outside vendors, thereby enabling the company to concentrate its full energies on performing the value chain activities that are at the core of its strategy, where it can create unique value. For example, E. & J. Gallo Winery outsources 95 percent of its grape production, letting farmers take on weather-related and other grape-growing risks while it concentrates its efforts on wine production and sales.[25] Broadcom, a global leader in chips for broadband communication systems, outsources the manufacture of its chips to Taiwan Semiconductor, thus freeing company personnel to focus their full energies on R&D, new chip design, and marketing. Nike concentrates on design, marketing, and distribution while outsourcing virtually all production of its shoes and sporting apparel.

Such heightened focus on performing strategy-critical activities can yield three important execution-related benefits:

- *The company improves its chances for outclassing rivals in the performance of strategy-critical activities and turning a core competence into a distinctive competence.* At the very least, the heightened focus on performing a select few value chain activities should promote more effective performance of those activities. This could materially enhance competitive capabilities by either lowering costs or improving quality. Whirlpool, ING Insurance, Hugo Boss, Japan Airlines, and Chevron have outsourced their data processing activities to computer service firms, believing that outside specialists can perform the needed services at lower costs and equal or better quality. A relatively large number of companies outsource the operation of their Web sites to Web design and hosting enterprises. Many business that get a lot of inquiries from customers or that have to provide 24/7 technical support to users of their products across the world have found that it is considerably less expensive to outsource these functions to specialists (often located in foreign countries where skilled personnel are readily available and worker compensation costs are much lower) than to operate their own call centers.

- *The streamlining of internal operations that flows from outsourcing often serves to decrease internal bureaucracies, flatten the organizational structure, speed internal decision making, and shorten the time it takes to respond to changing market conditions.*[26] In consumer electronics, where advancing technology drives new product innovation, organizing the work effort in a manner that expedites getting next-generation products to market ahead of rivals is a critical competitive capability. The world's motor vehicle manufacturers have found that they can shorten the cycle time for new models by outsourcing the large majority of their parts and components from independent suppliers and then working closely with their vendors to swiftly incorporate new technology and better integrate individual parts and components to form engine cooling systems, transmission systems, and electrical systems.

- *Partnerships can add to a company's arsenal of capabilities and contribute to better strategy execution.* By building, continually improving, and then leveraging partnerships, a company enhances its overall organizational capabilities and strengthens its competitive assets—assets that deliver more value to customers and consequently pave the way for competitive success. Soft-drink and beer manufacturers cultivate their relationships with their bottlers and distributors to strengthen access to local markets and build loyalty, support, and commitment for corporate marketing programs, without which their own sales and growth are weakened. Similarly, fast-food enterprises like McDonald's and KFC find it essential to work hand in hand with franchisees on outlet cleanliness, consistency of product quality, in-store ambience, courtesy and friendliness of store personnel, and other aspects of store operations. Unless franchisees continuously deliver sufficient customer satisfaction to attract repeat business, a fast-food chain's sales and competitive standing will suffer quickly. Companies like Boeing, Aerospatiale, Vodafone, and Dell have learned that their central R&D groups cannot begin to match the innovative capabilities of a well-managed network of supply chain partners.[27]

However, as was emphasized in Chapter 6, a company must guard against going overboard on outsourcing and becoming overly dependent on outside suppliers.

A company cannot be the master of its own destiny unless it maintains expertise and resource depth in performing those value chain activities that underpin its long-term competitive success.[28] As a general rule, therefore, it is the strategically less important activities—like handling customer inquiries and providing technical support, doing the payroll, administering employee benefit programs, providing corporate security, managing stockholder relations, maintaining fleet vehicles, operating the company's Web site, conducting employee training, and managing an assortment of information and data processing functions—for which outsourcing makes the most strategic sense.

Aligning the Firm's Organizational Structure with Its Strategy

The design of the firm's **organizational structure** is a critical aspect of the strategy execution process. The organizational structure comprises the formal and informal arrangement of tasks, responsibilities, and lines of authority and communication by which the firm is administered.[29] It specifies the linkages among parts of the organization, the reporting relationships, the direction of information flows, and the decision-making processes. It is a key factor in strategy implementation since it exerts a strong influence on how well managers can coordinate and control the complex set of activities involved.[30]

> **CORE CONCEPT**
>
> A firm's **organizational structure** comprises the formal and informal arrangement of tasks, responsibilities, lines of authority, and reporting relationships by which the firm is administered.

A well-designed organizational structure is one in which the various parts (e.g., decision-making rights, communication patterns) are aligned with one another and also matched to the requirements of the strategy. With the right structure in place, managers can orchestrate the various aspects of the implementation process with an even hand and a light touch. Without a supportive structure, strategy execution is more likely to become bogged down by administrative confusion, political maneuvering, and bureaucratic waste.

Good organizational design may even contribute to the firm's ability to create value for customers and realize a profit. By enabling lower bureaucratic costs and facilitating operational efficiency, it can lower a firm's operating costs. By facilitating the coordination of activities within the firm, it can improve the capability-building process, leading to greater differentiation and/or lower costs. Moreover, by improving the speed with which information is communicated and activities are coordinated, it can enable the firm to beat rivals to the market and profit from a period of unrivaled advantage.

Making Strategy-Critical Activities the Main Building Blocks of the Organizational Structure

In any business, some activities in the value chain are always more critical to successful strategy execution than others. For instance, a ski apparel manufacturer must be good at styling and design, low-cost manufacturing, distribution (convincing an attractively large number of retailers to stock and promote the company's brand), and marketing and advertising (building a brand image that generates buzz and appeal among ski enthusiasts). In discount stock brokerage, the strategy-critical activities are fast access to information, accurate order execution, efficient record keeping and transactions processing, and good customer service. In specialty chemicals, the critical activities are R&D, product innovation, getting new products onto the market quickly, effective marketing, and expertise in assisting customers.

Where such is the case, it is important for management to build its organizational structure around proficient performance of these activities, making them the centerpieces or main building blocks in the enterprise's organizational structure.

The rationale for making strategy-critical activities the main building blocks in structuring a business is compelling: If activities crucial to strategic success are to have the resources, decision-making influence, and organizational impact they need, they have to be centerpieces in the organizational scheme. Making them the focus of structuring efforts will also facilitate their coordination and promote good internal fit—an essential attribute of a winning strategy, as summarized in Chapter 1. To the extent that implementing a new strategy entails new or altered key activities or capabilities, different organizational arrangements may be required.[31]

Matching Type of Organizational Structure to Strategy Execution Requirements

Organizational structures can be classified into a limited number of standard types. The type that is most suitable for a given firm will depend on the firm's size and complexity as well as its strategy. As firms grow and their needs for structure evolve, their structural form is likely to evolve from one type to another. The four basic types are the *simple structure,* the *functional structure,* the *multidivisional structure,* and the *matrix structure,* as described below.

1. Simple Structure   A **simple structure** is one in which a central executive (often the owner-manager) handles all major decisions and oversees the operations of the organization with the help of a small staff.[32] Simple structures are also known as *line-and-staff structures,* since a central administrative staff supervises line employees who conduct the operations of the firm, or *flat structures,* since there are few levels of hierarchy.[33] It is characterized by limited task specialization; few rules; informal relationships; minimal use of training, planning, and liaison devices; and a lack of sophisticated support systems. It has all the advantages of simplicity, including low administrative costs, ease of coordination, flexibility, quick decision making, adaptability, and responsiveness to change.[34] Its informality and lack of rules may foster creativity and heightened individual responsibility.

Simple organizational structures are typically employed by small firms and entrepreneurial start-ups. The simple structure is the most common type of organizational structure since small firms are the most prevalent type of business. As an organization grows, however, this structural form becomes inadequate to the demands that come with size and complexity. In response, growing firms tend to alter their organizational structure from a simple structure to a functional structure.

2. Functional Structure   A **functional structure** is one that is organized along functional lines, where a function represents a major step in the firm's value chain, such as R&D, engineering and design, manufacturing, sales and marketing, logistics, and customer service. Each functional unit is supervised by functional line managers who report to the chief executive officer and a corporate staff. This arrangement allows functional managers to focus on their area of responsibility, leaving it to the CEO and headquarters to provide direction and ensure that their activities are coordinated and integrated. Functional structures

CORE CONCEPT

A **simple structure** consists of a central executive who handles all major decisions and oversees all operations with the help of a small staff.

Simple structures are also called *line-and-staff* structures or *flat* structures.

CORE CONCEPT

A **functional structure** is organized into functional departments, with departmental managers who report to the CEO and small corporate staff.

are also known as *departmental structures,* since the functional units are commonly called departments, and *unitary structures* or *U-forms,* since a single unit is responsible for each function.

In large organizations, functional structures lighten the load on top management, relative to simple structures, and make for a more efficient use of managerial resources. Their primary advantage, however, is due to greater task specialization, which promotes learning, enables the realization of scale economies, and offers productivity advantages not otherwise available. Their disadvantage is that the departmental boundaries can inhibit the flow of information and limit the opportunities for cross-functional cooperation and coordination.

It is generally agreed that some type of functional structure is the best organizational arrangement when a company is in just one particular business (regardless of which of the five generic competitive strategies it opts to pursue). For instance, a technical instruments manufacturer may be organized around research and development, engineering, supply chain management, assembly, quality control, marketing, and technical services. A discount retailer, such as Metro, Walmart, and Tesco, may organize around such functional units as purchasing, warehousing and distribution, store operations, advertising and sales, merchandising, and customer service. Functional structures can also be appropriate for firms with high-volume production, products that are closely related, and a limited degree of vertical integration. For example, General Motors now manages all of its brands (e.g., Cadillac, Oldsmobile, Chevrolet, Buick) under a common functional structure designed to promote technical transfer and capture economies of scale.[35]

As firms continue to grow, they often become more diversified and complex, placing a greater burden on top management. At some point, the centralized control that characterizes the functional structure becomes a liability, and the advantages of functional specialization begin to break down. To resolve these problems and address a growing need for coordination across functions, firms generally turn to the multidivisional structure.

3. Multidivisional Structure A **multidivisional structure** is a decentralized structure consisting of a set of operating divisions organized along market, customer, product, or geographic lines, and a central corporate headquarters, which monitors divisional activities, allocates resources, performs assorted support functions, and exercises overall control. Since each division is essentially a business, the divisions typically operate as independent profit centers (i.e., with profit/loss responsibility) and are organized internally along functional lines.[36] Division managers oversee day-to-day operations and the development of business-level strategy, while corporate executives attend to overall performance and corporate strategy, the elements of which were described in Chapter 8. Multidivisional structures are also called *divisional structures* or *M-forms,* in contrast with the U-form (functional) structure.

Multidivisional structures are common among companies pursuing some form of diversification strategy or global strategy, with operations in a number of businesses or countries. When the strategy is one of unrelated diversification, as in a conglomerate or holding company, the divisions generally represent separate industries. When the strategy is based on related diversification, the divisions may be organized according to markets, customer groups, product lines, geographic regions, or technologies. In this arrangement, the

> Functional structures are also called *departmental* structures, *unitary* structures, or *U-forms.*

CORE CONCEPT

A **multidivisional structure** is a decentralized structure consisting of a set of operating divisions organized along business, product, customer group, or geographic lines, and a central corporate headquarters that allocates resources, provides support functions, and monitors divisional activities.

Multidivisional structures are also called *divisional* structures or *M-forms*.

decision about where to draw the divisional lines depends foremost on the nature of the relatedness and the strategy-critical building blocks, in terms of which businesses have key value chain activities in common. For example, a company selling closely related products to business customers as well as two types of end consumers—online buyers and in-store buyers—may organize its divisions according to customer groups since the value chains involved in serving the three groups differ. Another company may organize by product line due to commonalities in product development and production within each product line. Multidivisional structures are also common among vertically integrated firms. There the major building blocks are often divisional units performing one or more of the major processing steps along the value chain (e.g., raw-material production, components manufacture, assembly, wholesale distribution, retail store operations).

Multidivisional structures offer significant advantages over functional structures in terms of facilitating the management of a complex and diverse set of operations.[37] Putting business-level strategy in the hands of division managers while leaving corporate strategy to top executives reduces the potential for information overload and improves the quality of decision making in each domain. This also minimizes the costs of coordinating divisionwide activities while enhancing top management's ability to control a diverse and complex operation. Moreover, multidivisional structures can help align individual incentives with the goals of the corporation and spur productivity by encouraging competition for resources among the different divisions.

But a divisional business-unit structure can also present some problems to a company pursuing related diversification, because having independent business units—each running its own business in its own way—inhibits cross-business collaboration and the capture of cross-business synergies. To solve this type of problem, firms turn to more complex structures, such as the matrix structure.

4. Matrix Structure   A **matrix structure** is a combination structure in which the organization is organized along two or more dimensions at once (e.g., business, geographic area, value chain function) for the purpose of enhancing cross-unit communication, collaboration, and coordination. In essence, it overlays one type of structure onto another type. Matrix structures are managed through multiple reporting relationships, so a middle manager may report to several bosses. For instance, in a matrix structure based on product line, region, and function, a sales manager for plastic containers in Georgia might report to the manager of the plastics division, the head of the southeast sales region, and the head of marketing.

Matrix organizational structures have evolved from the complex, overformalized structures that were popular in the 60s, 70s and 80s but often produced inefficient, unwieldy bureaucracies. The modern incarnation of the matrix structure is generally a more flexible arrangement, with a single primary reporting relationship that can be overlaid with a temporary secondary reporting relationship as need arises. For example, a software company that is organized into functional departments (software design, quality control, customer relations) may assign employees from those departments to different projects on a temporary basis, so an employee reports to a project manager as well as to his or her primary boss (the functional department head) for the duration of a project.

Matrix structures are also called *composite structures* or *combination structures*. They are often used for project-based, process-based, or team-based management.

CORE CONCEPT

A **matrix structure** is a structure that combines two or more organizational forms, with multiple reporting relationships. It is used to foster cross-unit collaboration.

Such approaches are common in businesses involving projects of limited duration, such as consulting, architecture, and engineering services. The type of close cross-unit collaboration that a flexible matrix structure supports is also needed to build competitive capabilities in strategically important activities, such as speeding new products to market, that involve employees scattered across several organizational units.[38] Capabilities-based matrix structures that combine process departments (like new product development) with more traditional functional departments provide a solution.

An advantage of matrix structures is that they facilitate the sharing of plant and equipment, specialized knowledge, and other key resources—they lower costs by enabling the realization of economies of scope. They also have the advantage of flexibility in form and may allow for better oversight since supervision is provided from more than one perspective. A disadvantage is that they add an additional layer of management, thereby increasing bureaucratic costs and decreasing response time to new situations.[39] In addition, there is a potential for confusion among employees due to dual reporting relationships and divided loyalties. While there is some controversy over the utility of matrix structures, the modern approach to matrix structures does much to minimize their disadvantages.[40]

> Matrix structures are also called *composite* structures or *combination* structures.

Determining How Much Authority to Delegate

On average, larger companies with more complex organizational structures are more decentralized in their decision making than smaller firms with simple structures—by necessity and by design. Under any organizational structure, however, there is still room for considerable variation in how much authority top managers retain and how much is delegated to down-the-line managers and employees. In executing strategy, then, companies must decide how much authority to delegate to the managers of each organizational unit—especially the heads of divisions, functional departments, and other operating units—and how much decision-making latitude to give individual employees in performing their jobs. The two extremes are to *centralize decision making* at the top (the CEO and a few close lieutenants) or to *decentralize decision making* by giving managers and employees considerable decision-making latitude in their areas of responsibility. As shown in Table 10.1, the two approaches are based on sharply different underlying principles and beliefs, with each having its pros and cons.

> **LO 5**
>
> Become aware of the pros and cons of centralized and decentralized decision making in implementing the chosen strategy.

Centralized Decision Making: Pros and Cons *In a highly centralized organizational structure, top executives retain authority for most strategic and operating decisions and keep a tight rein on business-unit heads, department heads, and the managers of key operating units; comparatively little discretionary authority is granted to frontline supervisors and rank-and-file employees.* The command-and-control paradigm of centralized structures is based on the underlying assumptions that frontline personnel have neither the time nor the inclination to direct and properly control the work they are performing and that they lack the knowledge and judgment to make wise decisions about how best to do it—hence the need for managerially prescribed policies and procedures, close supervision, and tight control. The thesis underlying authoritarian structures is that strict enforcement of detailed procedures backed by rigorous managerial oversight is the most reliable way to keep the daily execution of strategy on track.

One advantage of an authoritarian structure is tight control by the manager in charge—it is easy to know who is accountable when things do not go well.

Table 10.1   **Advantages and Disadvantages of Centralized versus Decentralized Decision Making**

Centralized Organizational Structures	Decentralized Organizational Structures
Basic Tenets	**Basic Tenets**
• Decisions on most matters of importance should be in the hands of top-level managers who have the experience, expertise, and judgment to decide what is the best course of action. • Lower-level personnel have neither the knowledge, the time, nor the inclination to properly manage the tasks they are performing. • Strong control from the top is a more effective means for coordinating company actions.	• Decision-making authority should be put in the hands of the people closest to, and most familiar with, the situation. • Those with decision-making authority should be trained to exercise good judgment. • A company that draws on the combined intellectual capital of all its employees can outperform a command-and-control company.
Chief Advantages	**Chief Advantages**
• Fixes accountability through tight control from the top. • Eliminates goal conflict among those with differing perspectives or interests. • Allows for quick decision making and strong leadership under crisis situations.	• Encourages company employees to exercise initiative and act responsibly. • Promotes greater motivation and involvement in the business on the part of more company personnel. • Spurs new ideas and creative thinking. • Allows fast response to market change. • May entail fewer layers of management.
Primary Disadvantages	**Primary Disadvantages**
• Lengthens response times by those closest to the market conditions because they must seek approval for their actions. • Does not encourage responsibility among lower-level managers and rank-and-file employees. • Discourages lower-level managers and rank-and-file employees from exercising any initiative.	• Top management lacks "full control"—higher-level managers may be unaware of actions taken by empowered personnel under their supervision. • Puts the organization at risk if empowered employees happen to make "bad" decisions. • Can impair cross-unit collaboration.

This structure can also reduce goal conflict among managers from different parts of the organization who may have different perspectives, incentives, and objectives. For example, a manager in charge of an engineering department may be more interested in pursuing a new technology than is a marketing manager who doubts that customers will value the technology as highly. Another advantage of a command-and-control structure is that it can enable a more uniform and swift response to a crisis situation that affects the organization as a whole.

But there are some serious disadvantages as well. Hierarchical command-and-control structures make a large organization with a complex structure sluggish in responding to changing market conditions because of the time it takes for the review/approval process to run up all the layers of the management bureaucracy. Furthermore, to work well, centralized decision making requires top-level managers to gather and process whatever information is relevant to the decision. When the relevant knowledge resides at lower organizational levels (or is technical, detailed, or hard to express in words), it is difficult and time-consuming to get all the facts and nuances in front of a high-level executive located far from the scene of the action—full understanding of the situation cannot be readily copied from one mind to another. Hence, centralized decision making is often impractical—the larger the company and the more scattered its operations, the more that decision-making authority must be delegated to managers closer to the scene of the action.

Decentralized Decision Making: Pros and Cons

In a highly decentralized organization, decision-making authority is pushed down to the lowest organizational level capable of making timely, informed, competent decisions. The objective is to put adequate decision-making authority in the hands of the people closest to and most familiar with the situation and train them to weigh all the factors and exercise good judgment. Decentralized decision making means, for example, that employees with customer contact are empowered to do what it takes to please customers. At Starbucks, for example, employees are encouraged to exercise initiative in promoting customer satisfaction—there's the oft-repeated story of a store employee who, when the computerized cash register system went offline, enthusiastically offered free coffee to waiting customers.[41]

> The ultimate goal of decentralized decision making is to put authority in the hands of those persons or teams closest to and most knowledgeable about the situation.

The case for empowering down-the-line managers and employees to make decisions regarding daily operations and strategy execution is based on the belief that a company that draws on the combined intellectual capital of all its employees can outperform a command-and-control company.[42] The challenge in a decentralized system is in maintaining adequate control. With decentralized decision making, top management maintains control by determining the limits to authority for each type of position, installing companywide strategic control systems, holding people accountable for their decisions, instituting compensation incentives that reward people for doing their jobs in a manner that contributes to good company performance, and creating a corporate culture where there's strong peer pressure on individuals to act responsibly.[43]

Decentralized organization structures have much to recommend them. Pushing decision-making authority down to subordinate managers, work teams, and individual employees shortens organizational response times and spurs new ideas, creative thinking, innovation, and greater involvement on the part of all company personnel. Moreover, in worker-empowered structures, jobs can be defined more broadly, several tasks can be integrated into a single job, and people can direct their own work. Fewer layers of managers are needed because deciding how to do things becomes part of each person's or team's job. Today's online communication systems and smart phones make it easy and relatively inexpensive for people at all organizational levels to have direct access to data, other employees, managers, suppliers, and customers. They can access information quickly (via the Internet or company network), readily check with superiors or whomever else as needed, and take responsible action. Typically, there are genuine gains in morale and productivity when people are provided with the tools and information they need to operate in a self-directed way.

But decentralization also has some disadvantages. Top managers lose an element of control over what goes on (since empowered subordinates have authority to act on their own) and may thus be unaware of actions being taken by personnel under their supervision. Such lack of control can put a company at risk in the event that empowered employees make unwise decisions. Moreover, because decentralization gives organizational units the authority to act independently, there is risk of too little collaboration and coordination between different organizational units.

Many companies have concluded that the advantages of decentralization outweigh the disadvantages. Over the past 15 to 20 years, there's been a decided shift from authoritarian multilayered hierarchical structures to flatter, more decentralized structures that stress employee empowerment. This shift reflects a strong and growing consensus that authoritarian, hierarchical organizational structures are not well suited to implementing and executing strategies in an era when extensive information and instant communication are the norm and when a big fraction of the organization's most valuable assets consists of intellectual capital and resides in the knowledge and capabilities of its employees.

Capturing Cross-Business Strategic Fit in a Decentralized Structure

Diversified companies striving to capture the benefits of synergy between separate businesses have to beware of giving business-unit heads full rein to operate independently. Cross-business strategic fit typically has to be captured either by enforcing close cross-business collaboration or by centralizing performance of functions requiring close coordination at the corporate level.[44] For example, if businesses with overlapping process and product technologies have their own independent R&D departments—each pursuing its own priorities, projects, and strategic agendas—it's hard for the corporate parent to prevent duplication of effort, capture either economies of scale or economies of scope, or encourage more collaborative R&D efforts. Where the potential for cross-business R&D synergies exist, the best solution is usually to centralize the R&D function and have a coordinated corporate R&D effort that serves the interests of both the individual businesses and the company as a whole. Likewise, centralizing the related activities of separate businesses makes sense when there are opportunities to share a common sales force, use common distribution channels, rely on a common field service organization, use common e-commerce systems, and so on.

> Efforts to decentralize decision making and give company personnel some leeway in conducting operations must be tempered with the need to maintain adequate control and cross-unit coordination.

Facilitating Collaboration with External Partners and Strategic Allies

Organizational mechanisms—whether formal or informal—are also required to ensure effective working relationships with each major outside constituency involved in strategy execution. Strategic alliances, outsourcing arrangements, joint ventures, and cooperative partnerships present immediate opportunities and open the door to future possibilities, but little of value can be realized without active management of the relationship. Unless top management sees that constructive organizational bridge building with strategic partners occurs and that productive working relationships emerge, the value of cooperative relationships is lost and the company's power to execute its strategy is weakened. If close working relationships with suppliers are crucial, then supply chain management must enter into considerations regarding how to create an effective organizational structure. If distributor/dealer/franchisee relationships are important, someone must be assigned the task of nurturing the relationships with forward channel allies. If working in parallel with providers of complementary products and services contributes to enhanced organizational capability, then cooperative organizational arrangements have to be put in place and managed to good effect.

Building organizational bridges with external allies can be accomplished by appointing "relationship managers" with responsibility for making particular strategic partnerships or alliances generate the intended benefits. Relationship managers have many roles and functions: getting the right people together, promoting good rapport, seeing that plans for specific activities are developed and carried out, helping adjust internal organizational procedures and communication systems, ironing out operating dissimilarities, and nurturing interpersonal cooperation. Multiple cross-organization ties have to be established and kept open to ensure proper communication and coordination.[45] There has to be enough information sharing to make the relationship work and periodic frank discussions of conflicts, trouble spots, and changing situations.

Organizing and managing a network structure provides another mechanism for encouraging more effective collaboration and cooperation among external partners. A **network structure** is the arrangement linking a number of independent organizations involved in some common undertaking. A well-managed network structure typically includes one firm in a more central role, with the responsibility of ensuring that the right partners are included and the activities across the network are coordinated. The high-end Italian motorcycle company Ducati operates in this manner, assembling its motorcycles from parts obtained from a hand-picked integrated network of parts suppliers.

> **CORE CONCEPT**
>
> A **network structure** is the arrangement linking a number of independent organizations involved in some common undertaking.

Further Perspectives on Structuring the Work Effort

All organization designs have their strategy-related strengths and weaknesses. To do a good job of matching structure to strategy, strategy implementers first have to pick a basic design and modify it as needed to fit the company's particular business lineup. They must then (1) supplement the design with appropriate coordinating mechanisms (cross-functional task forces, special project teams, self-contained work teams, and so on) and (2) institute whatever networking and communications arrangements it takes to support effective execution of the firm's strategy. Some companies may avoid setting up "ideal" organizational arrangements because they do not want to disturb existing reporting relationships or because they need to accommodate other situational idiosyncrasies, yet they must still work toward the goal of building a competitively capable organization.

The ways and means of developing stronger core competencies and organizational capabilities (or creating altogether new ones) have to fit a company's own circumstances. Not only do different companies and executives tackle the capabilities-building challenge in different ways, but the task of building different capabilities requires different organizing techniques. Thus, generalizing about how to build capabilities has to be done cautiously. What can be said unequivocally is that building a capable organization entails a process of consciously knitting together the efforts of individuals and groups. Organizational capabilities emerge from establishing and nurturing cooperative working relationships among people and groups to perform activities in a more efficient, value-creating fashion. While an appropriate organizational structure can facilitate this, organization building is a task in which senior management must be deeply involved. Indeed, effectively managing both internal organization processes and external collaboration to create and develop competitively valuable organizational capabilities remains a top challenge for senior executives in today's companies.

KEY POINTS

1. Executing strategy is an action-oriented, operations-driven activity revolving around the management of people and business processes. The way for managers to start in implementing a new strategy is with *a probing assessment of what the organization must do differently to carry out the strategy successfully.* They should then consider *precisely how to make the necessary internal changes* as rapidly as possible.

2. Good strategy execution requires a *team effort.* All managers have strategy-executing responsibility in their areas of authority, and all employees are active participants in the strategy execution process.

3. Ten managerial tasks crop up repeatedly in company efforts to execute strategy: (1) staffing the organization well, (2) building the necessary organizational capabilities, (3) creating a supportive organizational structure, (4) allocating sufficient resources, (5) instituting supportive policies and procedures, (6) adopting processes for continuous improvement, (7) installing systems that enable proficient company operations, (8) tying incentives to the achievement of desired targets, (9) instilling the right corporate culture, and (10) exercising internal leadership.

4. The two best signs of good strategy execution are whether a company is meeting or beating its performance targets and performing value chain activities in a manner that is conducive to companywide operating excellence. *Shortfalls in performance signal weak strategy, weak execution, or both.*

5. Building an organization capable of good strategy execution entails three types of organization-building actions: (1) *staffing the organization*—assembling a talented management team, and recruiting and retaining employees with the needed experience, technical skills, and intellectual capital; (2) *building and strengthening core competencies and competitive capabilities*—developing proficiencies in performing strategy-critical value chain activities and updating them to match changing market conditions and customer expectations; and (3) *structuring the organization and work effort*—instituting organizational arrangements that facilitate good strategy execution, deciding how much decision-making authority to delegate, and managing external relationships.

6. Building core competencies and competitive capabilities is a time-consuming, managerially challenging exercise that can be approached in three ways: (1) developing capabilities internally, (2) acquiring capabilities through mergers and acquisitions, and (3) accessing capabilities via collaborative partnerships.

7. In building capabilities internally, the first step is to develop the *ability* to do something, through experimentation, active search for alternative solutions, and learning by trial and error. As experience grows and company personnel learn how to perform the activities consistently well and at an acceptable cost, the ability evolves into a tried-and-true capability. The process can be accelerated by making learning a more deliberate endeavor and providing the incentives that will motivate company personnel to achieve the desired ends.

8. As firms get better at executing their strategies, they develop capabilities in the domain of strategy execution. Superior strategy execution capabilities allow companies to get the most from their organizational resources and competitive capabilities. But excellence in strategy execution can also be a more direct source of competitive advantage, since more efficient and effective strategy execution can lower costs and permit firms to deliver more value to customers. Superior

strategy execution capabilities are hard to imitate and have no good substitutes. As such, they can be an important source of *sustainable* competitive advantage. Any time rivals can readily duplicate successful strategies, making it impossible to *outstrategize* rivals, the chief way to achieve lasting competitive advantage is to *outexecute* them.

9. Structuring the organization and organizing the work effort in a strategy-supportive fashion has four aspects: (1) deciding which value chain activities to perform internally and which ones to outsource; (2) aligning the firm's organizational structure with its strategy; (3) deciding how much authority to centralize at the top and how much to delegate to down-the-line managers and employees; and (4) facilitating the necessary collaboration and coordination with external partners and strategic allies.

10. To align the firm's organizational structure with its strategy, it is important to make strategy-critical activities the main building blocks. There are four basic types of organizational structures: the simple structure, the functional structure, the multidivisional structure, and the matrix structure. Which is most appropriate depends on the firm's size, complexity, and strategy.

ASSURANCE OF LEARNING EXERCISES

LO 2, LO 3

1. Review the Careers link on L'Oréal's worldwide corporate Web site (go to www.loreal.com and click on the company's worldwide corporate Web site option). The section provides extensive information about personal development, international learning opportunities, integration of new hires into existing teams, and other areas of management development. How do the programs discussed help L'Oréal to hire good people and build core competencies and competitive capabilities? Please use the chapter's discussions of recruiting, training, and retaining capable employees and building core competencies and competitive capabilities as a guide for preparing your answer.

LO 3

2. Using Google or your university library's access to EBSCO, InfoTrac, or other online databases, search for FedEx's February 2011 acquisition of India's AFL Pvt. Ltd. and its affiliate, Unifreight India Pvt. How does the acquisition help build and strengthen FedEx's competencies and competitive capabilities? What specific capabilities gained through the acquisition will make FedEx a stronger competitor in India?

LO 5

3. Using Google Scholar or your university library's access to EBSCO, InfoTrac, or other online databases, do a search for recent writings on decentralized decision making and employee empowerment. According to the articles you find in the various management journals, what are the conditions under which decision making should be pushed down to lower levels of management?

EXERCISES FOR SIMULATION PARTICIPANTS

LO 5

1. How would you describe the organization of your company's top management team? Is some decision making decentralized and delegated to individual managers? If so, explain how the decentralization works. Or are decisions made more by consensus, with all co-managers having input? What do you see as the advantages and disadvantages of the decision-making approach your company is employing?

LO 3

2. What specific actions have you and your co-managers taken to develop core competencies or competitive capabilities that can contribute to good strategy execution and potential competitive advantage? If no actions have been taken, explain your rationale for doing nothing.

LO 1, LO 4

3. What value chain activities are most crucial to good execution of your company's strategy? Does your company have the ability to outsource any value chain activities? If so, have you and your co-managers opted to engage in outsourcing? Why or why not?

ENDNOTES

[1] As quoted in Steven W. Floyd and Bill Wooldridge, "Managing Strategic Consensus: The Foundation of Effective Implementation," *Academy of Management Executive* 6, no. 4 (November 1992), p. 27.

[2] As cited in Gary L. Neilson, Karla L. Martin, and Elizabeth Powers, "The Secrets of Successful Strategy Execution," *Harvard Business Review* 86, no. 6 (June 2008), pp. 61–62.

[3] Jack Welch with Suzy Welch, *Winning* (New York: HarperBusiness, 2005), p. 135.

[4] For an excellent and very pragmatic discussion of this point, see Larry Bossidy and Ram Charan, *Execution: The Discipline of Getting Things Done* (New York: Crown Business, 2002), chap. 1.

[5] For an insightful discussion of how important staffing an organization with the right people is, see Christopher A. Bartlett and Sumantra Ghoshal, "Building Competitive Advantage through People," *MIT Sloan Management Review* 43, no. 2 (Winter 2002), pp. 34–41.

[6] The importance of assembling an executive team that has an exceptional ability to gauge what needs to be done and an instinctive talent for figuring out how to get it done is discussed in Justin Menkes, "Hiring for Smarts," *Harvard Business Review* 83, no. 11 (November 2005), pp. 100–9, and Justin Menkes, *Executive Intelligence* (New York: HarperCollins, 2005), especially chaps. 1 to 4.

[7] See Bossidy and Charan, *Execution: The Discipline of Getting Things Done*, chap. 1.

[8] Menkes, *Executive Intelligence*, pp. 68, 76.

[9] Bossidy and Charan, *Execution: The Discipline of Getting Things Done*, chap. 5.

[10] Welch with Welch, *Winning*, pp. 141–42.

[11] Menkes, *Executive Intelligence*, pp. 65–71.

[12] Jim Collins, *Good to Great* (New York: HarperBusiness, 2001), p. 44.

[13] John Byrne, "The Search for the Young and Gifted," *BusinessWeek*, October 4, 1999, p. 108.

[14] See chapters 5 and 6 in Helfat et al., *Dynamic Capabilities: Understanding Strategic Change in Organizations* (Malden, MA: Blackwell, 2007); R. Grant, *Contemporary Strategy Analysis*, 6th ed. (Malden, MA: Blackwell, 2008).

[15] C. Helfat and M. Peteraf, "The Dynamic Resource-Based View: Capability Lifecycles," *Strategic Management Journal*, 24, no. 10 (October 2003), pp. 997–1010.

[16] G. Hamel and C. K. Prahalad, "Strategy as Stretch and Leverage," *Harvard Business Review* 71, no. 2 (March/April 1993), pp. 75–84.

[17] G. Dosi, R. Nelson, and S. Winter (eds.), *The Nature and Dynamics of Organizational Capabilities* (Oxford, England: Oxford University Press, 2001).

[18] C. Helfat and M. Peteraf, "The Dynamic Resource-Based View: Capability Lifecycles."

[19] S. Winter, "The Satisficing Principle in Capability Learning," *Strategic Management Journal* 21, nos. 10/11 (October/November 2000), pp. 981–96; M. Zollo and S. Winter, "Deliberate Learning and the Evolution of Dynamic Capa-

bilities," *Organization Science* 13, no. 3 (May/June 2002), pp. 339–51.

[20] G. Szulanski and S. Winter, "Getting It Right the Second Time," *Harvard Business Review* 80 (January 2002), pp. 62–69; S. Winter and G. Szulanski, "Replication as Strategy," *Organization Science* 12, no. 6 (November/December 2001), pp. 730–43.

[21] B. Kogut and U. Zander, "Knowledge of the Firm, Combinative Capabilities, and the Replication of Technology," *Organization Science* 3, no. 3 (August 1992), pp. 383–97.

[22] C. Helfat and R. Raubitschek, "Product Sequencing: Co-Evolution of Knowledge, Capabilities and Products," *Strategic Management Journal* 21, nos. 10/11 (October/November 2000), pp. 961–80.

[23] Robert H. Hayes, Gary P. Pisano, and David M. Upton, *Strategic Operations: Competing through Capabilities* (New York: Free Press, 1996), pp. 503–7. Also see Jonas Ridderstråle, "Cashing In on Corporate Competencies," *Business Strategy Review* 14, no. 1 (Spring 2003), pp. 27–38; Danny Miller, Russell Eisenstat, and Nathaniel Foote, "Strategy from the Inside Out: Building Capability-Creating Organizations," *California Management Review* 44, no. 3 (Spring 2002), pp. 37–55.

[24] S. Karim and W. Mitchell, "Path-Dependent and Path-Breaking Change: Reconfiguring Business Resources Following Business," *Strategic Management Journal* 21, nos. 10/11 (October/November 2000), pp. 1061–82; L. Capron, P. Dussague, and W. Mitchell,

"Resource Redeployment Following Horizontal Acquisitions in Europe and North America, 1988–1992," *Strategic Management Journal* 19, no. 7 (July 1998), pp. 631–62.

[25] J. B. Quinn, *Intelligent Enterprise* (New York: Free Press, 1992), p. 43.

[26] Ibid., pp. 33 and 89; J. B. Quinn and F. Hilmer, "Strategic Outsourcing," *McKinsey Quarterly* 1 (1995), pp. 48–70; Jussi Heikkilä and Carlos Cordon, "Outsourcing: A Core or Non-core Strategic Management Decision," *Strategic Change* 11, no. 3 (June–July 2002), pp. 183–93; and J. B. Quinn, "Strategic Outsourcing: Leveraging Knowledge Capabilities," *Sloan Management Review* 40, no. 4 (Summer 1999), pp. 9–21. A strong case for outsourcing is presented in C. K. Pralahad, "The Art of Outsourcing," *Wall Street Journal,* June 8, 2005, p. A13. For a discussion of why outsourcing initiatives fall short of expectations, see Jérôme Barthélemy, "The Seven Deadly Sins of Outsourcing," *Academy of Management Executive* 17, no. 2 (May 2003), pp. 87–98.

[27] Quinn, "Strategic Outsourcing: Leveraging Knowledge Capabilities," p. 17.

[28] Quinn, *Intelligent Enterprise,* pp. 39–40; also see Gary P. Pisano and Willy C. Shih, "Restoring American Competitiveness," *Harvard Business Review* 87, nos. 7–8 (July–August 2009), pp. 114–25; Barthélemy, "The Seven Deadly Sins of Outsourcing."

[29] A. Chandler, *Strategy and Structure* (Cambridge, MA: MIT Press, 1962).

[30] E. Olsen, S. Slater, and G. Hult, "The Importance of Structure and Process to Strategy Implementation," *Business Horizons* 48, no. 1 (2005), pp. 47–54; H. Barkema, J. Baum, and E. Mannix, "Management Challenges in a New Time", *Academy of Management Journal* 45, no. 5 (October 2002), pp. 916–30.

[31] The importance of matching organization design and structure to the particular requirements for good strategy execution was first brought to the forefront in a landmark study of 70 large corporations conducted by Professor Alfred Chandler of Harvard University. Chandler's research revealed that changes in an organization's strategy bring about new administrative problems that, in turn, require a new or refashioned structure for the new strategy to be successfully implemented and executed. He found that structure tends to follow the growth strategy of the firm—but often not until inefficiency and internal operating problems provoke a structural adjustment. The experiences of these firms followed a consistent sequential pattern: new strategy creation, emergence of new administrative problems, a decline in profitability and performance, a shift to a more appropriate organizational structure, and then recovery to more profitable levels and improved strategy execution. See Chandler, *Strategy and Structure.*

[32] H. Mintzberg, *The Structuring of Organizations* (Englewood Cliffs, NJ: Prentice Hall,1979); C. Levicki, *The Interactive Strategy Workout,* 2nd ed. (London: Prentice Hall,1999).

[33] Chandler, *Strategy and Structure.*

[34] Mintzberg, *The Structuring of Organizations.*

[35] Grant, *Contemporary Strategy Analysis.*

[36] Chandler, *Strategy and Structure.*

[37] O. Williamson, *Market and Hierarchies* (New York: Free Press, 1975); R. M. Burton and B. Obel, "A Computer Simulation Test of the M-Form Hypothesis," *Administrative Science Quarterly* 25 (1980), pp. 457–76.

[38] J. Baum and S. Wally, "Strategic Decision Speed and Firm Performance," *Strategic Management Journal* 24 (2003), pp. 1107–29.

[39] C. Bartlett and S. Ghoshal, "Matrix Management: Not a Structure, a Frame of Mind," *Harvard Business Review,* July–August 1990, pp. 138–45.

[40] M. Goold and A. Campbell, "Structured Networks: Towards the Well Designed Matrix," *Long Range Planning* 36, no. 5 (2003), pp. 427–39.

[41] Iain Somerville and John Edward Mroz, "New Competencies for a New World," in Frances Hesselbein, Marshall Goldsmith, and Richard Beckard (eds.), *The Organization of the Future* (San Francisco: Jossey-Bass, 1997), p. 70.

[42] The importance of empowering workers in executing strategy and the value of creating a great working environment are discussed in Stanley E. Fawcett, Gary K. Rhoads, and Phillip Burnah, "People as the Bridge to Competitiveness: Benchmarking the 'ABCs' of an Empowered Workforce," *Benchmarking: An International Journal* 11, no. 4 (2004), pp. 346–60.

[43] A discussion of the problems of maintaining adequate control over empowered employees and possible solutions is presented in Robert Simons, "Control in an Age of Empowerment," *Harvard Business Review* 73 (March–April 1995), pp. 80–88.

[44] For a discussion of the importance of cross-business coordination, see Jeanne M. Liedtka, "Collaboration across Lines of Business for Competitive Advantage," *Academy of Management Executive* 10, no. 2 (May 1996), pp. 20–34.

[45] Rosabeth Moss Kanter, "Collaborative Advantage: The Art of the Alliance," *Harvard Business Review* 72, no. 4 (July–August 1994), pp. 105–6.

CHAPTER 11

MANAGING INTERNAL OPERATIONS

Actions That Promote Good Strategy Execution

> True motivation comes from achievement, personal development, job satisfaction, and recognition.
>
> **—Frederick Herzberg**
> *Expert on motivation*

> Leadership almost always involves cooperative and collaborative activity that can occur only in a conducive context.
>
> **—Lt. General William G. Pagonis**
> *Retired U.S. Army officer and author*

> Note to salary setters: Pay your people the least possible and you'll get the same from them.
>
> **—Malcolm Forbes**
> *Late publisher of Forbes Magazine*

LEARNING OBJECTIVES

LO 1. Learn why resource allocation should always be based on strategic priorities.

LO 2. Understand how well-designed policies and procedures can facilitate good strategy execution.

LO 3. Learn how process management tools that drive continuous improvement in the performance of value chain activities can help an organization achieve superior strategy execution.

LO 4. Recognize the role of information and operating systems in enabling company personnel to carry out their strategic roles proficiently.

LO 5. Appreciate how and why the use of well-designed incentives and rewards can be management's single most powerful tool for promoting adept strategy execution and operating excellence.

In Chapter 10, we emphasized the importance of building organization capabilities and structuring the work effort so as to perform execution-critical value chain activities in a coordinated and competent manner. In this chapter, we discuss five additional managerial actions that promote good strategy execution:

- Allocating resources to the drive for good strategy execution.
- Instituting policies and procedures that facilitate strategy execution.
- Using process management tools to drive continuous improvement in how value chain activities are performed.
- Installing information and operating systems that enable company personnel to carry out their strategic roles proficiently.
- Using rewards and incentives to promote better strategy execution and the achievement of strategic and financial targets.

ALLOCATING RESOURCES TO THE STRATEGY EXECUTION EFFORT

Early in the process of implementing a new strategy, managers need to determine what resources (in terms of funding, people, etc.) will be required for good strategy execution and how they should be distributed across the various organizational units involved. A company's ability to marshal the resources needed to support new strategic initiatives has a major impact on the strategy execution process. Too little funding slows progress and impedes the efforts of organizational units to execute their pieces of the strategic plan proficiently. Too much funding wastes organizational resources and reduces financial performance. Both outcomes argue for managers to be deeply involved in reviewing budget proposals and directing the proper amounts of resources to strategy-critical organizational units. This includes carefully screening requests for more people and new facilities and equipment, approving those that hold promise for making a contribution to strategy execution and turning down those that don't. Should internal cash flows prove insufficient to fund the planned strategic initiatives, then management must raise additional funds through borrowing or selling additional shares of stock to willing investors.

LO 1

Learn why resource allocation should always be based on strategic priorities.

A change in strategy nearly always calls for budget reallocations and resource shifting. Previously important units having a lesser role in the new strategy may need downsizing. Units that now have a bigger strategic role may need more people, new equipment, additional facilities, and above-average increases in their operating budgets. Implementing a new strategy requires managers to take an active and sometimes forceful role in shifting resources, downsizing some functions and upsizing others, not only to amply fund activities with a critical role in the new strategy but also to avoid inefficiency and achieve profit projections. It requires putting enough resources behind new strategic initiatives to fuel their success and making the tough decisions to kill projects and activities that are no longer justified. Honda's strong support of R&D activities allowed it to develop the first motorcycle airbag, the first low-polluting four-stroke outboard marine engine, a wide range of ultra-low-emission cars, the first hybrid car (Honda Insight) in the U.S. market, and the first hydrogen fuel cell car (Honda Clarity). However, Honda managers had no trouble stopping production of the Honda Insight in 2006 when its sales failed to take off and then shifting resources to the development and manufacture of other promising hybrid models, including a totally redesigned Insight that was launched in the United States in 2009.

The funding requirements of good strategy execution must drive how capital allocations are made and the size of each unit's operating budget. Underfunding organizational units and activities pivotal to the strategy impedes successful strategy implementation.

Visible actions to reallocate operating funds and move people into new organizational units signal a determined commitment to strategic change and frequently are needed to catalyze the implementation process and give it credibility. Microsoft has made a practice of regularly shifting hundreds of programmers to new high-priority programming initiatives within a matter of weeks or even days. At Harris Corporation, where the strategy was to diffuse research ideas into areas that were commercially viable, top management regularly moved groups of engineers out of low-opportunity activities into its most promising new commercial venture divisions. Fast-moving developments in many markets are prompting companies to abandon traditional annual or semiannual budgeting and resource allocation cycles in favor of resource allocation processes supportive of more rapid adjustments in strategy.

A company's operating budget must be both *strategy-driven* (in order to amply fund the performance of key value chain activities) and *lean* (in order to operate as cost-efficiently as possible).

The bigger the change in strategy (or the more obstacles that lie in the path of good strategy execution), the bigger the resource shifts that will likely be required. Merely fine-tuning the execution of a company's existing strategy seldom requires big movements of people and money from one area to another. The desired improvements can usually be accomplished through above-average budget increases to organizational units launching new initiatives and below-average increases (or even small budget cuts) for the remaining organizational units. However, there are times when strategy changes or new execution initiatives need to be made without adding to total company expenses. In such circumstances, managers have to work their way through the existing budget line by line and activity by activity, looking for ways to trim costs and shift resources to higher-priority activities where new execution initiatives are needed. In the event that a company needs to make significant cost cuts during the course of launching new strategic initiatives, then managers have to be especially creative in finding ways to do more with less and execute the strategy more efficiently. Indeed, it is not unusual for strategy changes and the drive for good strategy execution to be conducted in a manner that entails achieving considerably higher levels of operating efficiency and, at the same time, making sure key activities are performed as effectively as possible.

Figure 11.1   How Policies and Procedures Facilitate Good Strategy Execution

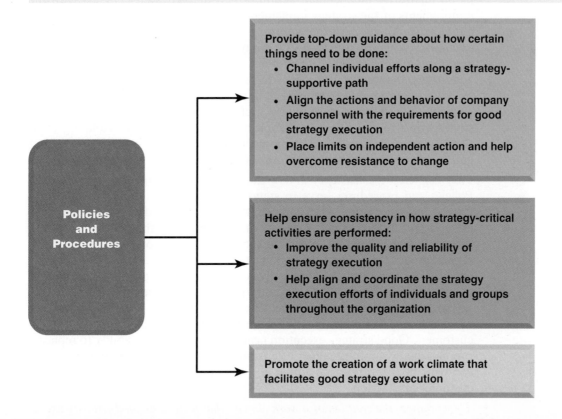

Policies and Procedures

Provide top-down guidance about how certain things need to be done:
- Channel individual efforts along a strategy-supportive path
- Align the actions and behavior of company personnel with the requirements for good strategy execution
- Place limits on independent action and help overcome resistance to change

Help ensure consistency in how strategy-critical activities are performed:
- Improve the quality and reliability of strategy execution
- Help align and coordinate the strategy execution efforts of individuals and groups throughout the organization

Promote the creation of a work climate that facilitates good strategy execution

INSTITUTING POLICIES AND PROCEDURES THAT FACILITATE STRATEGY EXECUTION

A company's policies and procedures can either support or obstruct good strategy execution. Any time a company moves to put new strategy elements in place or improve its strategy execution capabilities, some changes in work practices and the behavior of company personnel are usually required. Managers are thus well advised to examine whether existing policies and procedures support such changes and to proactively revise or discard those that are out of sync.

As shown in Figure 11.1, well-conceived policies and operating procedures facilitate strategy execution in three ways:

- *They provide top-down guidance regarding how things need to be done.* Policies and procedures provide company personnel with a set of guidelines for how to perform organizational activities, conduct various aspects of operations, solve problems as they arise, and accomplish particular tasks. In essence, they represent a store of organizational or managerial knowledge about efficient and effective ways of doing things. They clarify uncertainty about how to proceed in executing strategy and align the actions and behavior of company personnel

LO 2

Understand how well-designed policies and procedures can facilitate good strategy execution.

Well-conceived policies and procedures aid strategy execution; out-of-sync ones hinder effective execution.

with the requirements for good strategy execution. Moreover, they place limits on ineffective independent action. When they are well matched with the requirements of the strategy implementation plan, they channel the efforts of individuals along a path that supports the plan and facilitates good strategy execution. When existing ways of doing things are misaligned with strategy execution initiatives, actions and behaviors have to be changed. Under these conditions, the managerial role is to establish and enforce new policies and operating practices that are more conducive to executing the strategy appropriately. Policies are a particularly useful way to counteract tendencies for some people to resist change. People generally refrain from violating company policy or going against recommended practices and procedures without gaining clearance and having strong justification.

- *They help ensure consistency in how execution-critical activities are performed.* Policies and procedures serve to standardize the way that activities are performed and encourage strict conformity to the standardized approach. This is important for ensuring the quality and reliability of the strategy execution process. It helps align and coordinate the strategy execution efforts of individuals and groups throughout the organization—a feature that is particularly beneficial when there are geographically scattered operating units. For example, eliminating significant differences in the operating practices of different plants, sales regions, customer service centers, or the individual outlets in a chain operation helps a company deliver consistent product quality and service to customers. Good strategy execution nearly always entails an ability to replicate product quality and the caliber of customer service at every location where the company does business—anything less blurs the company's image and lowers customer satisfaction.

- *They promote the creation of a work climate that facilitates good strategy execution.* A company's policies and procedures help to set the tone of a company's work climate and contribute to a common understanding of "how we do things around here." Because discarding old policies and procedures in favor of new ones invariably alters the internal work climate, managers can use the policy-changing process as a powerful lever for changing the corporate culture in ways that produce a stronger fit with the new strategy. The trick here, obviously, is to come up with new policies or procedures that catch the immediate attention of company personnel, quickly shift their actions and behavior, and then become embedded in how things are done.

To ensure consistency in product quality and service behavior patterns, McDonald's policy manual spells out detailed procedures that personnel in each McDonald's unit are expected to observe. For example, "Cooks must turn, never flip, hamburgers. If they haven't been purchased, Big Macs must be discarded in 10 minutes after being cooked and French fries in 7 minutes. Cashiers must make eye contact with and smile at every customer." The upscale U.S. department store chain Nordstrom has a company policy of promoting only those people whose personnel records contain evidence of "heroic acts" to please customers—especially customers who may have made "unreasonable requests" that require special efforts. This induces store personnel to dedicate themselves to outstanding customer service, consistent with the requirements of executing a strategy based on exceptionally high service quality. To ensure that its R&D activities are responsive to customer needs and expectations, Hewlett-Packard requires its R&D people to make regular visits to customers to learn about their problems and learn their reactions to HP's latest new products.

One of the big policy-making issues concerns what activities need to be rigidly prescribed and what activities ought to allow room for independent action on the part of empowered personnel. Few companies need thick policy manuals to direct the strategy execution process or prescribe exactly how daily operations are to be conducted. Too much policy can be as much of a hindrance as wrong policy and as confusing as no policy. There is wisdom in a middle approach: *Prescribe enough policies to give organization members clear direction and to place reasonable boundaries on their actions; then empower them to act within these boundaries in whatever way they think makes sense.* Allowing company personnel to act with some degree of freedom is especially appropriate when individual creativity and initiative are more essential to good strategy execution than standardization and strict conformity. Instituting policies that facilitate strategy execution can therefore mean more policies, fewer policies, or different policies. It can mean policies that require things be done according to a strictly defined standard or policies that give employees substantial leeway to do activities the way they think best.

USING PROCESS MANAGEMENT TOOLS TO STRIVE FOR CONTINUOUS IMPROVEMENT

Company managers can significantly advance the cause of superior strategy execution by using various process management tools to drive continuous improvement in how internal operations are conducted. One of the most widely used and effective tools for gauging how well a company is executing pieces of its strategy entails benchmarking the company's performance of particular activities and business processes against "best-in-industry" and "best-in-world" performers.[1] It can also be useful to look at "best-in-company" performers of an activity if a company has a number of different organizational units performing much the same function at different locations. Identifying, analyzing, and understanding how top-performing companies or organizational units conduct particular value chain activities and business processes provides useful yardsticks for judging the effectiveness and efficiency of internal operations and setting performance standards for organizational units to meet or beat.

LO 3

Learn how process management tools that drive continuous improvement in the performance of value chain activities can help an organization achieve superior strategy execution.

How the Process of Identifying and Incorporating Best Practices Works

A **best practice** is a technique for performing an activity or business process that has been shown to consistently deliver superior results compared to other methods.[2] To qualify as a legitimate best practice, the technique must have a proven record in significantly lowering costs, improving quality or performance, shortening time requirements, enhancing safety, or delivering some other highly positive operating outcome. Best practices thus identify a path to operating excellence. For a best practice to be valuable and transferable, it must demonstrate success over time, deliver quantifiable and highly positive results, and be repeatable.

CORE CONCEPT

A **best practice** is a method of performing an activity that has been shown to consistently deliver superior results compared to other methods.

Figure 11.2　**From Benchmarking and Best-Practice Implementation to Operating Excellence**

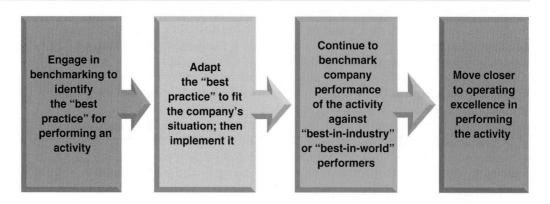

As discussed in Chapter 4, *benchmarking* is the backbone of the process of identifying, studying, and implementing best practices. A company's benchmarking effort looks outward to find best practices and then proceeds to develop the data for measuring how well a company's own performance of an activity stacks up against the best-practice standard. For individual managers, benchmarking involves being humble enough to admit that others have come up with world-class ways to perform particular activities yet wise enough to try to learn how to match, and even surpass, them. But, as shown in Figure 11.2, the payoff of benchmarking comes from adapting the top-notch approaches pioneered by other companies to the company's own operation and thereby boosting, perhaps dramatically, the proficiency with which strategy-critical value chain tasks are performed.

However, benchmarking is more complicated than simply identifying which companies are the best performers of an activity and then trying to imitate their approaches—especially if these companies are in other industries. Normally, the outstanding practices of other organizations have to be *adapted* to fit the specific circumstances of a company's own business, strategy, and operating requirements. Since each organization is unique, the telling part of any best-practice initiative is how well the company puts its own version of the best practice into place and makes it work.

Indeed, a best practice remains little more than another company's interesting success story unless company personnel buy into the task of translating what can be learned from other companies into real action and results. The agents of change must be frontline employees who are convinced of the need to abandon the old ways of doing things and switch to a best-practice mindset. *The more that organizational units use best practices in performing their work, the closer a company moves toward performing its value chain activities as effectively and efficiently as possible.* This is what excellent strategy execution is all about.

Legions of companies across the world now engage in benchmarking to improve their strategy execution efforts. Scores of trade associations and special-interest organizations have undertaken efforts to collect best-practice data relevant to a particular industry or business function and make their databases available online to members. Good examples include The Benchmarking Exchange (www.benchnet.com); Best Practices, LLC

> The more that organizational units use best practices in performing their work, the closer a company comes to achieving effective and efficient strategy execution.

(www.best-in-class.com); and the American Productivity and Quality Center (www.apqc.org). Benchmarking and best-practice implementation have clearly emerged as legitimate and valuable managerial tools for promoting operational excellence and enhancing strategy execution.

Business Process Reengineering, Total Quality Management, and Six Sigma Quality Programs: Tools for Promoting Operating Excellence

In striving for operating excellence, many companies have also come to rely on three other potent process management tools: business process reengineering, total quality management (TQM), and Six Sigma quality control techniques. Indeed, these three tools have become globally pervasive techniques for implementing strategies keyed to cost reduction, defect-free manufacture, superior product quality, superior customer service, and total customer satisfaction. The following sections describe how business process reengineering, TQM, and Six Sigma programs can contribute to top-notch strategy execution and operating excellence.

Business Process Reengineering Companies scouring for ways to improve their operations have sometimes discovered that the execution of strategy-critical activities is hindered by an organizational arrangement where pieces of the activity are performed in several different functional departments, with no one manager or group being accountable for optimal performance of the entire activity. This can easily occur in such inherently cross-functional activities as customer service (which can involve personnel in order filling, warehousing and shipping, invoicing, accounts receivable, after-sale repair, and technical support), new product development (which typically involves personnel in R&D, design and engineering, purchasing, manufacturing, and sales and marketing), and supply chain management (which cuts across such areas as purchasing, inventory management, manufacturing and assembly, warehousing, and shipping).

To address the suboptimal performance problems that can arise from this type of situation, many companies have opted to *reengineer the work effort,* pulling the pieces of strategy-critical activities out of different departments and creating a single department or work group to take charge of the whole process and perform it in a better, cheaper, and more strategy-supportive fashion. The use of cross-functional teams has been popularized by the practice of **business process reengineering,** which involves radically redesigning and streamlining the workflow (often enabled by cutting-edge use of online technology and information systems), with the goal of achieving quantum gains in performance of the activity.[3]

> **CORE CONCEPT**
>
> **Business process reengineering** involves radically redesigning and streamlining how an activity is performed, with the intent of achieving dramatic improvements in performance.

When done properly, business process reengineering can produce dramatic operating benefits. Hallmark reengineered its process for developing new greeting cards, creating teams of mixed-occupation personnel (artists, writers, lithographers, merchandisers, and administrators) to work on a single holiday or greeting card theme; the reengineered process speeded development times for new lines of greeting cards by up to 24 months, was more cost-efficient, and increased customer satisfaction.[4] In the order-processing section of General Electric's circuit breaker division, elapsed time from order receipt to delivery was cut from three weeks to three days by consolidating six production units into one, reducing a variety of former inventory and handling steps, automating the design system to replace a human custom-design process, and cutting the organizational layers between managers and workers from three to one. Productivity rose 20 percent in one year, and unit manufacturing costs dropped 30 percent. Northwest Water, a British utility, used process reengineering to eliminate 45 work depots that served as home bases to crews who installed and repaired water and sewage lines and equipment. Under the reengineered arrangement, crews worked directly from their vehicles, receiving assignments and reporting work completion from computer terminals in their trucks. Crew members became contractors to Northwest Water rather than employees, a move that not only eliminated the need for the work depots but also allowed Northwest Water to eliminate a big percentage of the bureaucratic personnel and supervisory organization that managed the crews.[5]

Reengineering of value chain activities has been undertaken at many companies in many industries all over the world, with excellent results at some firms.[6] At companies where it has produced only modest results, this is usually because of ineptness and/or lack of wholehearted commitment from the top. While business process reengineering has been criticized for its use by some companies as an excuse for downsizing, it has nonetheless proved itself as a useful tool for streamlining a company's work effort and moving closer to operational excellence. It has also inspired more technologically based approaches to integrating and streamlining business processes, such as *Enterprise Resource Planning,* a software-based system implemented with the help of consulting companies such as SAP (the leading provider of business software).

Total Quality Management Programs

Total quality management (TQM) is a philosophy of managing a set of business practices that emphasizes continuous improvement in all phases of operations, 100 percent accuracy in performing tasks, involvement and empowerment of employees at all levels, team-based work design, benchmarking, and total customer satisfaction.[7] While TQM concentrates on producing quality goods and fully satisfying customer expectations, it achieves its biggest successes when it is extended to employee efforts in *all departments*—for example, human resources, billing, accounting, and information systems—that may lack pressing, customer-driven incentives to improve. It involves reforming the corporate culture and shifting to a total quality/continuous improvement business philosophy that permeates every facet of the organization.[8] TQM aims at instilling enthusiasm and commitment to doing things right from the top to the bottom of the organization. Management's job is to kindle an organizationwide search for ways to improve, a search that involves all company personnel exercising initiative and using their ingenuity. TQM doctrine preaches that there's no such thing as "good enough" and that everyone has a responsibility to participate in continuous improvement. TQM is thus a race without a finish. Success comes from making little steps forward each day, a process that the Japanese call *kaizen.*

> **CORE CONCEPT**
>
> **Total quality management (TQM)** entails creating a total quality culture bent on continuously improving the performance of every task and value chain activity.

TQM takes a fairly long time to show significant results—very little benefit emerges within the first six months. The long-term payoff of TQM, if it comes, depends heavily on management's success in implanting a culture within which the TQM philosophy and practices can thrive. TQM is a managerial tool that has attracted numerous users and advocates over several decades, and it can deliver good results when used properly.

Six Sigma Quality Programs Six Sigma programs offer another way to drive continuous improvement in quality and strategy execution. This approach entails the use of advanced statistical methods to identify and remove the causes of defects (errors) and variability in performing an activity or business process. When performance of an activity or process reaches "Six Sigma quality," there are *no more than 3.4 defects per million iterations* (equal to 99.9997 percent accuracy).[9]

CORE CONCEPT

Six Sigma programs utilize advanced statistical methods to improve quality by reducing defects and variability in the performance of business processes.

There are two important types of Six Sigma programs. DMAIC (define, measure, analyze, improve, and control) is an improvement system for existing processes falling below specification and needing incremental improvement. The DMADV process of define, measure, analyze, design, and verify is used to develop *new* processes or products at Six Sigma quality levels. DMADV is sometimes referred to as a Design for Six Sigma, or DFSS. Both Six Sigma programs are overseen by personnel who have completed Six Sigma "master black belt" training and are executed by personnel who have earned Six Sigma "green belts" and Six Sigma "black belts." According to the Six Sigma Academy, personnel with black belts can save companies approximately $230,000 per project and can complete four to six projects a year.[10]

The statistical thinking underlying Six Sigma is based on the following three principles: All work is a process, all processes have variability, and all processes create data that explain variability.[11] To illustrate how these three principles drive the metrics of DMAIC, consider the case of a hypothetical janitorial company that wants to improve the caliber of work done by its cleaning crews and thereby improve customer satisfaction. The janitorial company's Six Sigma team can pursue quality enhancement and continuous improvement via the DMAIC process as follows:

- *Define.* Because Six Sigma is aimed at reducing defects, the first step is to define what constitutes a defect. Six Sigma team members might decide that leaving streaks on windows is a defect because it is a source of customer dissatisfaction.
- *Measure.* The next step is to collect data to find out why, how, and how often this defect occurs. This might include creating a process flow map of the specific ways that cleaning crews go about the task of cleaning a commercial customer's windows. Other metrics may include recording what tools and cleaning products the crews use to clean windows.
- *Analyze.* After the data are gathered and the statistics analyzed, the company's Six Sigma team may discover that the tools and window-cleaning techniques of certain employees are better than those of other employees because their tools and procedures leave no streaked windows—a "best practice" for avoiding window streaking is thus identified and documented.
- *Improve.* The Six Sigma team implements the documented best practice as a standard way of cleaning windows.
- *Control.* The company teaches new and existing employees the best-practice technique for window cleaning. Over time, there is significant improvement in customer satisfaction and increased business.

Six Sigma's DMAIC process is a particularly good vehicle for improving performance when there are *wide variations* in how well an activity is performed.[12] For instance, airlines striving to improve the on-time performance of their flights have more to gain from actions to curtail the number of flights that are late by more than 30 minutes than from actions to reduce the number of flights that are late by less than 5 minutes. Likewise, FedEx might have a 16-hour average delivery time for its overnight package service operation, but if the actual delivery time varies around the 16-hour average from a low of 12 hours to a high of 26 hours, such that 10 percent of its packages are delivered over 6 hours late, then it has a huge reliability problem of the sort that Six Sigma programs are well suited to address.

Since the mid-1990s, thousands of companies and nonprofit organizations around the world have used Six Sigma programs to promote operating excellence. Such manufacturers as Motorola, Caterpillar, DuPont, Xerox, Alcan Aluminum, BMW, Volkswagen, Nokia, Owens Corning, Boeing, and Emerson Electric have employed Six Sigma techniques to improve their strategy execution and increase production quality. General Electric (GE), one of the most successful companies implementing Six Sigma training and pursuing Six Sigma perfection across the company's entire operations, estimated benefits on the order of $10 billion during the first five years of implementation; its Lighting division, for example, cut invoice defects and disputes by 98 percent, while GE Capital Mortgage improved the chances of a caller reaching a "live" GE person from 76 to 99 percent.[13] Illustration Capsule 11.1 describes Whirlpool's use of Six Sigma in its appliance business.

Six Sigma is, however, not just a quality-enhancing tool for manufacturers. At one company, product sales personnel typically wined and dined customers to close their deals, but the costs of such entertaining were viewed as excessively high.[14] A Six Sigma project that examined sales data found that although face time with customers was important, wining, dining, and other types of entertainment were not. The data showed that regular face time helped close sales, but that time could be spent over a cup of coffee instead of golfing at a resort or taking clients to expensive restaurants. In addition, analysis showed that too much face time with customers was counterproductive. A regularly scheduled customer picnic was found to be detrimental to closing sales because it was held at a busy time of year, when customers preferred not to be away from their offices. Changing the manner in which prospective customers were wooed resulted in a 10 percent increase in sales. Six Sigma has also been used to improve processes in health care. A Milwaukee, Wisconsin, hospital used Six Sigma to improve the accuracy of administering the proper drug doses to patients. DMAIC analysis of the three-stage process by which prescriptions were written by doctors, filled by the hospital pharmacy, and then administered to patients by nurses revealed that most mistakes came from misreading the doctors' handwriting.[15] The hospital implemented a program requiring doctors to enter the prescription on the hospital's computers, which slashed the number of errors dramatically. Bank of America, Credit Suisse, Amazon.com, Philips, and Siemens also have reportedly used Six Sigma techniques successfully in their operations.

While many enterprises have used Six Sigma methods to improve the quality with which activities are performed, there is evidence that Six Sigma techniques can stifle innovation and creativity.[16] The essence of Six Sigma is to reduce variability in processes, but creative processes, by nature, include quite a bit of variability. In many instances, breakthrough innovations occur only after thousands of ideas have been abandoned and promising ideas have gone through multiple iterations and extensive prototyping. Google CEO Eric Schmidt has commented

ILLUSTRATION CAPSULE 11.1

Whirlpool's Use of Six Sigma to Promote Operating Excellence

Top management at Whirlpool Corporation (with 67 manufacturing and technology centers around the globe and sales in some 170 countries totaling $17 billion in 2009) has a vision of Whirlpool appliances in "Every Home . . . Everywhere with Pride, Passion, and Performance." One of management's chief objectives in pursuing this vision is to build unmatched customer loyalty to the Whirlpool brand. Whirlpool's strategy to win the hearts and minds of appliance buyers the world over has been to produce and market appliances with top-notch quality and innovative features that users will find appealing. In addition, Whirlpool's strategy has been to offer a wide selection of models (recognizing that buyer tastes and needs differ) and to strive for low-cost production efficiency, thereby enabling Whirlpool to price its products very competitively. Executing this strategy at Whirlpool's operations in North America (where it is the market leader), Latin America (where it is also the market leader), Europe (where it ranks third), and Asia (where it is number one in India and has a foothold with huge growth opportunities elsewhere) has involved a strong focus on continuous improvement, lean manufacturing capabilities, and a drive for operating excellence. To marshal the efforts of its 67,000 employees in executing the strategy successfully, management developed a comprehensive Operational Excellence program with Six Sigma as one of the centerpieces.

The Operational Excellence initiative, which began in the 1990s, incorporated Six Sigma techniques to improve the quality of Whirlpool products and, at the same time, lower costs and trim the time it took to get product innovations into the marketplace. The Six Sigma program helped Whirlpool save $175 million in manufacturing costs in its first three years.

To sustain the productivity gains and cost savings, Whirlpool embedded Six Sigma practices within each of its manufacturing facilities worldwide and instilled a culture based on Six Sigma and lean manufacturing skills and capabilities. In 2002, each of Whirlpool's operating units began taking the Six Sigma initiative to a higher level by first placing the needs of the customer at the center of every function—R&D, technology, manufacturing, marketing, and administrative support—and then striving to consistently improve quality levels while eliminating all unnecessary costs. The company systematically went through every aspect of its business with the view that company personnel should perform every activity at every level in a manner that delivers value to the customer and leads to continuous improvement on how things are done.

Whirlpool management believes that the company's Operational Excellence process has been a major contributor in sustaining the company's position as the leading global manufacturer and marketer of home appliances.

Source: www.whirlpool.com, accessed September 25, 2003, November 15, 2005, August 16, 2008, and July 9, 2010; Lexis-Nexis-Edgar Online, exhibit type: exhibit 99 - additional exhibits, filing date: June 21, 2010.

that the innovation process is "anti-Six Sigma" and that applying Six Sigma principles to those performing creative work at Google would choke off innovation at the company.[17]

James McNerney, a GE executive schooled in the constructive use of Six Sigma, became CEO at 3M Corporation and proceeded to institute a series of Six Sigma–based principles. McNerney's dedication to Six Sigma and his elimination of 8 percent of the company's workforce did cause 3M's profits to jump shortly after his arrival, but the application of Six Sigma in 3M's R&D and new product development activities soon proved to stifle innovation and new product introductions, undermining the company's long-standing reputation for innovation. 3M's researchers complained that the innovation process did not lend itself well to the extensive data collection and analysis required under Six Sigma and that too much time was spent completing reports that outlined the market potential and possible manufacturing concerns for projects in all stages of the R&D pipeline. Six Sigma rigidity and a freeze on 3M's R&D budget from McNerney's first year as CEO through 2005 was blamed for the company's drop from first to seventh place on the Boston Consulting Group's Most Innovative Companies list.[18]

A blended approach to Six Sigma implementation that is gaining in popularity pursues incremental improvements in operating efficiency, while R&D and other processes that allow the company to develop new ways of offering value to customers are given freer rein. Managers of these *ambidextrous organizations* are adept at employing continuous improvement in operating processes but allowing R&D to operate under a set of rules that allows for the development of breakthrough innovations. However, the two distinctly different approaches to managing employees must be carried out by tightly integrated senior managers to ensure that the separate and diversely oriented units operate with a common purpose. Ciba Vision, a global leader in contact lenses, has dramatically reduced operating expenses through the use of continuous improvement programs, while simultaneously and harmoniously developing new series of contact lens products that have allowed its revenues to increase by 300 percent over a 10-year period.[19] An enterprise that systematically and wisely applies Six Sigma methods to its value chain, activity by activity, can make major strides in improving the proficiency with which its strategy is executed without sacrificing innovation. As is the case with TQM, obtaining managerial commitment, establishing a quality culture, and fully involving employees are all of critical importance to the successful implementation of Six Sigma quality programs.[20]

The Difference between Business Process Reengineering and Continuous Improvement Programs like Six Sigma and TQM

Business process reengineering and continuous improvement efforts like TQM and Six Sigma both aim at improved productivity and reduced costs, better product quality, and greater customer satisfaction. The essential difference between business process reengineering and continuous improvement programs is that reengineering aims at *quantum gains* on the order of 30 to 50 percent or more, whereas programs like TQM and Six Sigma stress *incremental progress,* striving for inch-by-inch gains again and again in a never-ending stream. The two approaches to improved performance of value chain activities and operating excellence are not mutually exclusive; it makes sense to use them in tandem. Reengineering can be used first to produce a good basic design that yields quick, dramatic improvements in performing a business process. Total quality programs can then be used as a follow-on to reengineering and/or best-practice implementation, delivering gradual improvements over a longer period of time. Such a two-pronged approach to implementing operational excellence is like a marathon race in which you run the first 4 miles as fast as you can and then gradually pick up speed the remainder of the way.

Business process reengineering aims at one-time quantum improvement, while continuous improvement programs like TQM and Six Sigma aim at ongoing incremental improvements.

Capturing the Benefits of Initiatives to Improve Operations

The biggest beneficiaries of benchmarking and best-practice initiatives, reengineering, TQM, and Six Sigma are companies that view such programs not as ends in themselves but as tools for implementing company strategy more effectively. The skimpiest payoffs occur when company managers seize on them as something worth trying—novel ideas that could improve things. In most such instances, they result in strategy-blind efforts to simply manage better.

There's an important lesson here. Business process management tools all need to be linked to a company's strategic priorities to contribute effectively to improving the strategy's execution. Only strategy can point to which value chain activities matter and what performance targets make the most sense. Without a strategic framework, managers lack the context in which to fix things that really matter to business-unit performance and competitive success.

To get the most from initiatives to execute strategy more proficiently, managers must have a clear idea of what specific outcomes really matter. Is it high on-time delivery, lower overall costs, fewer customer complaints, shorter cycle times, a higher percentage of revenues coming from recently introduced products, or what? Benchmarking best-in-industry and best-in-world performance of most or all value chain activities provides a realistic basis for setting internal performance milestones and longer-range targets.

Once initiatives to improve operations are linked to the company's strategic priorities, then comes the managerial task of building a total quality culture that is genuinely committed to achieving the performance outcomes that strategic success requires.[21] Managers can take the following action steps to realize full value from TQM or Six Sigma initiatives and promote a culture of operating excellence: [22]

1. Visible, unequivocal, and unyielding commitment to total quality and continuous improvement, including a vision concerned with quality and specific, measurable objectives for increasing quality and making continuous improvement.

2. Nudging people toward quality-supportive behaviors by:
   a. Screening job applicants rigorously and hiring only those with attitudes and aptitudes right for quality-based performance.
   b. Providing quality training for most employees.
   c. Using teams and team-building exercises to reinforce and nurture individual effort (the creation of a quality culture is facilitated when teams become more cross-functional, multitask-oriented, and increasingly self-managed).
   d. Recognizing and rewarding individual and team efforts to improve quality regularly and systematically.
   e. Stressing prevention (doing it right the first time), not inspection (instituting ways to correct mistakes).

3. Empowering employees so that authority for delivering great service or improving products is in the hands of the doers rather than the overseers—*improving quality has to be seen as part of everyone's job.*

4. Using online systems to provide all relevant parties with the latest best practices, thereby speeding the diffusion and adoption of best practices throughout the organization. Online systems can also allow company personnel to exchange data and opinions about how to upgrade the prevailing best practices.

5. Emphasizing that performance can, and must, be improved because competitors are not resting on their laurels and customers are always looking for something better.

If the quality initiatives are linked to the strategic objectives and if all organization members buy into a supporting culture of operating excellence, then a company's continuous improvement practices become decidedly more conducive to proficient strategy execution.

> The purpose of using benchmarking, best practices, business process reengineering, TQM, and Six Sigma programs is to improve the performance of strategy-critical activities and thereby enhance strategy execution.

In sum, benchmarking, the adoption of best practices, business process reengineering, TQM, and Six Sigma techniques all need to be seen and used as part of a bigger-picture effort to execute strategy proficiently. Used properly, all of these tools are capable of improving the proficiency with which an organization performs its value chain activities. Not only do improvements from such initiatives add up over time and strengthen organizational capabilities, but they also help build a culture of operating excellence. All this lays the groundwork for gaining a competitive advantage.[23] While it is relatively easy for rivals to also implement process management tools, it is much more difficult and time-consuming for them to instill a deeply ingrained culture of operating excellence (as occurs when such techniques are religiously employed and top management exhibits lasting commitment to operational excellence throughout the organization).

INSTALLING INFORMATION AND OPERATING SYSTEMS

> **LO 4**
>
> Recognize the role of information and operating systems in enabling company personnel to carry out their strategic roles proficiently.

Company strategies can't be executed well without a number of internal systems for business operations. Southwest Airlines, Singapore Airlines, Lufthansa, British Airways, and other successful airlines cannot hope to provide passenger-pleasing service without a user-friendly online reservation system, an accurate and speedy baggage handling system, and a strict aircraft maintenance program that minimizes problems requiring at-the-gate service that delay departures. FedEx has internal communication systems that allow it to coordinate its over 80,000 vehicles in handling an average of 8.0 million packages a day. Its leading-edge flight operations systems allow a single controller to direct as many as 200 of FedEx's 664 aircraft simultaneously, overriding their flight plans should weather problems or other special circumstances arise. In addition, FedEx has created a series of e-business tools for customers that allow them to ship and track packages online, create address books, review shipping history, generate custom reports, simplify customer billing, reduce internal warehousing and inventory management costs, purchase goods and services from suppliers, and respond to quickly changing customer demands. All of FedEx's systems support the company's strategy of providing businesses and individuals with a broad array of package delivery services (from premium next-day to economical five-day deliveries) and enhancing its competitiveness against UPS and DHL.

Otis Elevator, the world's largest manufacturer of elevators, with some 2.3 million elevators and escalators installed worldwide, has a 24-hour remote electronic monitoring system that can detect when an elevator or escalator installed on a customer's site has any of 325 problems.[24] If the monitoring system detects a problem, it analyzes and diagnoses the cause and location, then makes the service call to an Otis mechanic at the nearest location, and helps the mechanic (who is equipped with a Web-enabled cell phone) identify the component causing the problem. The company's maintenance system helps keep outage times under three hours. All trouble-call data are relayed to design and manufacturing personnel, allowing them to quickly alter design specifications or manufacturing procedures when needed to correct recurring problems. All customers have online access to performance data on each of their Otis elevators and escalators.

Amazon.com ships customer orders of books, CDs, toys, and myriad other items from fully computerized warehouses with a capacity of over 17½ million square feet in 2010. The warehouses are so technologically sophisticated that they require about as many lines of code to run as Amazon's Web site does. Using complex picking algorithms, computers initiate the order-picking process by sending signals to workers' wireless receivers, telling them which items to pick off the shelves in which order. Computers also generate data on misboxed items, chute backup times, line speed, worker productivity, and shipping weights on orders. Systems are upgraded regularly, and productivity improvements are aggressively pursued. In 2003 Amazon turned their inventory over 20 times annually in an industry whose average was 15 turns; by 2009 its industry turnover had decreased to an unprecedented 12. Amazon's warehouse efficiency and cost per order filled was so low that one of the fastest-growing and most profitable parts of Amazon's business was using its warehouses to run the e-commerce operations of large retail chains such as Target.

Most telephone companies, electric utilities, and TV broadcasting systems have online monitoring systems to spot transmission problems within seconds and increase the reliability of their services. At eBay, there are systems for real-time monitoring of new listings, bidding activity, Web site traffic, and page views. Kaiser Permanente spent $3 billion to digitize the medical records of its 8.2 million members so that it could manage patient care more efficiently.[25] IBM makes extensive use of social software applications such as Lotus Connections to support its 1,796 online communities, having discovered that many of its employees depend on these tools to do their work.[26] In businesses such as public accounting and management consulting, where large numbers of professional staff need cutting-edge technical know-how, companies have developed systems that identify when it is time for certain employees to attend training programs to update their skills and know-how. Many companies have cataloged best-practice information on their intranets to promote faster transfer and implementation organizationwide.[27]

Well-conceived state-of-the-art operating systems not only enable better strategy execution but also strengthen organizational capabilities—sometimes enough to provide a competitive edge over rivals. For example, a company with a differentiation strategy based on superior quality has added capability if it has systems for training personnel in quality techniques, tracking product quality at each production step, and ensuring that all goods shipped meet quality standards. If the systems it employs are advanced systems that have not yet been adopted by rivals, the systems may provide the company with a competitive advantage as long as the costs of deploying the systems do not outweigh their benefits. Similarly, a company striving to be a low-cost provider is competitively stronger if it has an unrivaled benchmarking system that identifies opportunities to implement best practices and drive costs out of the business. Fast-growing companies get an important assist from having capabilities in place to recruit and train new employees in large numbers and from investing in infrastructure that gives them the capability to handle rapid growth as it occurs. It is nearly always better to put infrastructure and support systems in place before they are actually needed than to have to scramble to catch up to customer demand.

Instituting Adequate Information Systems, Performance Tracking, and Controls

Accurate and timely information about daily operations is essential if managers are to gauge how well the strategy execution process is proceeding. Information systems need to cover five broad areas: (1) customer data, (2) operations data, (3) employee data, (4) supplier/partner/collaborative ally data, and (5) financial performance data. All key strategic performance indicators must be tracked and reported in real time where possible. Long the norm, monthly profit-and-loss statements and monthly statistical summaries are fast being replaced with daily statistical updates and even up-to-the-minute performance monitoring, made possible by online technology. Most retail companies have automated online systems that generate daily sales reports for each store and maintain up-to-the-minute inventory and sales records on each item. Manufacturing plants typically generate daily production reports and track labor productivity on every shift. Many retailers and manufacturers have online data systems connecting them with their suppliers that monitor the status of inventories, track shipments and deliveries, and measure defect rates.

Real-time information systems permit company managers to stay on top of implementation initiatives and daily operations and to intervene if things seem to be drifting off course. Tracking key performance indicators, gathering information from operating personnel, quickly identifying and diagnosing problems, and taking corrective actions are all integral pieces of the process of managing strategy implementation and exercising adequate control over operations. A number of companies have recently begun creating "electronic scorecards" for senior managers that gather daily or weekly statistics from different databases about inventory, sales, costs, and sales trends; such information enables these managers to easily stay abreast of what's happening and make better on-the-spot decisions.[28] Telephone companies have elaborate information systems to measure signal quality, connection times, interrupts, wrong connections, billing errors, and other measures of reliability that affect customer service and satisfaction. British Petroleum (BP) has outfitted rail cars carrying hazardous materials with sensors and global-positioning systems (GPS) so that it can track the status, location, and other information about these shipments via satellite and relay the data to its corporate intranet. Companies that rely on empowered customer-contact personnel to act promptly and creatively in pleasing customers have installed online information systems that make essential customer data accessible to such personnel through a few keystrokes; this enables them to respond more effectively to customer inquiries and deliver personalized customer service.

Statistical information gives managers a feel for the numbers; briefings and meetings provide a feel for the latest developments and emerging issues; and personal contacts add a feel for the people dimension. All are good barometers.

> Having state-of-the-art operating systems, information systems, and real-time data is integral to superior strategy execution and operating excellence.

Managers must identify problem areas and deviations from plans before they can take action to get the organization back on course, by either improving the approaches to strategy execution or fine-tuning the strategy. Jeff Bezos, Amazon's CEO, is an ardent proponent of managing by the numbers. As he puts it, "Math-based decisions always trump opinion and judgment. The trouble with most corporations is that they make judgment-based decisions when data-based decisions could be made."[29]

Monitoring Employee Performance Information systems also provide managers with a means for monitoring the performance of empowered workers to see that they are acting within the specified limits.[30] Leaving empowered employees to their own devices in meeting performance standards without appropriate checks and balances can expose an organization to excessive risk.[31] Instances abound of employees' decisions or behavior having gone awry, sometimes costing a company huge sums or producing lawsuits aside from just generating embarrassing publicity.

Scrutinizing daily and weekly operating statistics is one of the important ways in which managers can monitor the results that flow from the actions of empowered subordinates without resorting to constant over-the-shoulder supervision; if the operating results flowing from the actions of empowered employees look good, then it is reasonable to assume that empowerment is working. But close monitoring of operating performance is only one of the control tools at management's disposal. Another valuable lever of control in companies that rely on empowered employees, especially in those that use self-managed work groups or other such teams, is peer-based control. Because peer evaluation is such a powerful control device, companies organized into teams can remove some layers of the management hierarchy and rely on strong peer pressure to keep team members operating between the white lines. This is especially true when a company has the information systems capability to monitor team performance daily or in real time.

TYING REWARDS AND INCENTIVES TO STRATEGY EXECUTION

LO 5

Appreciate how and why the use of well-designed incentives and rewards can be management's single most powerful tool for promoting adept strategy execution and operating excellence.

It is essential that company personnel be enthusiastically committed to executing strategy successfully and achieving performance targets. Company managers typically use an assortment of motivational techniques and rewards to enlist organizationwide commitment to executing the strategic plan. Indeed, a properly designed reward structure is management's most powerful tool for mobilizing organizational commitment to successful strategy execution. But incentives and rewards do more than just strengthen the resolve of company personnel to succeed—they also focus their attention on the accomplishment of specific strategy execution objectives. Not only do they spur the efforts of individuals to achieve those aims, but they also help to coordinate the activities of individuals throughout the organization by aligning their personal motives with the goals of the organization. In this manner, reward systems serve as an indirect type of control mechanism that conserves on the more costly control mechanism of supervisory oversight.

A properly designed reward structure is management's most powerful tool for mobilizing organizational commitment to successful strategy execution and aligning efforts throughout the organization with strategic priorities.

CORE CONCEPT

Financial rewards provide **high-powered incentives** when rewards are tied to specific outcome objectives.

To win employees' sustained, energetic commitment to the strategy execution process, management must be resourceful in designing and using motivational incentives—both monetary and nonmonetary. The more a manager understands what motivates subordinates and the more he or she relies on motivational incentives as a tool for achieving the targeted strategic and financial results, the greater will be employees' commitment to good day-in, day-out strategy execution and achievement of performance targets.[32]

Incentives and Motivational Practices That Facilitate Good Strategy Execution

Financial incentives generally head the list of motivating tools for gaining wholehearted employee commitment to good strategy execution and focusing attention on strategic priorities. They provide *high-powered* motivation for individuals to increase their efforts when rewards are tied to specific outcome objectives. A company's package of monetary rewards typically includes some combination of base-pay increases, performance bonuses, profit-sharing plans, stock awards, company contributions to employee 401(k) or retirement plans, and piecework incentives (in the case of production workers). But most successful companies and managers also make extensive use of nonmonetary incentives. Some of the most important nonmonetary approaches companies can use to enhance motivation are listed below:[33]

- *Provide attractive perks and fringe benefits.* The various options include full coverage of health insurance premiums, college tuition reimbursement, generous paid vacation time, on-site child care, on-site fitness centers, getaway opportunities at company-owned recreational facilities, personal concierge services, subsidized cafeterias and free lunches, casual dress every day, personal travel services, paid sabbaticals, maternity and paternity leaves, paid leaves to care for ill family members, telecommuting, compressed workweeks (four 10-hour days instead of five 8-hour days), flextime (variable work schedules that accommodate individual needs), college scholarships for children, and relocation services.

- *Give awards and other forms of public recognition to high performers, and celebrate the achievement of organizational goals.* Many companies hold award ceremonies to honor top-performing individuals, teams, and organizational units and to showcase company successes. This can help create healthy competition among units and teams within the company, but it can also create a positive esprit de corps among the organization as a whole. Other examples include special recognition at informal company gatherings or in the company newsletter, tangible tokens of appreciation for jobs well done, and frequent words of praise.

- *Rely on promotion from within whenever possible.* The practice of promoting from within helps bind workers to their employer, and employers to their workers, providing strong incentives for good performance. Moreover, promoting from within helps ensure that people in positions of responsibility have knowledge specific to the business, technology, and operations they are managing.

- *Invite and act on ideas and suggestions from employees.* Many companies find that their best ideas for nuts-and-bolts operating improvements come from the suggestions of employees. Moreover, research indicates that the moves of many companies to push decision making down the line and empower employees increases employees' motivation and satisfaction as well as their productivity. The use of self-managed teams has much the same effect.

- *Create a work atmosphere in which there is genuine caring and mutual respect among workers and between management and employees.* A "family" work environment where people are on a first-name basis and there is strong camaraderie promotes teamwork and cross-unit collaboration.

- *State the strategic vision in inspirational terms so that employees feel they are a part of something very worthwhile in a larger social sense.* There's strong motivating power associated with giving people a chance to be part of something exciting and personally satisfying. Jobs with noble purpose tend to inspire employees to give their all. As described in Chapter 9, this not only increases productivity but reduces turnover and lowers costs for staff recruitment and training as well.

- *Share information with employees about financial performance, strategy, operational measures, market conditions, and competitors' actions.* Broad disclosure and prompt communication send the message that managers trust their workers and regard them as valued partners in the enterprise. Keeping employees in the dark denies them information useful to performing their jobs, prevents them from being intellectually engaged, saps their motivation, and detracts from performance.

- *Maintain attractive office space and facilities.* A workplace environment that is attractive and comfortable usually has decidedly positive effects on employee morale and productivity. An appealing work environment is particularly important when workers are expected to spend long hours at work.

For specific examples of the motivational tactics employed by several prominent companies (many of which appear on *Fortune*'s list of the 100 best companies to work for in America), see Illustration Capsule 11.2.

Striking the Right Balance between Rewards and Punishment

Decisions on salary increases, incentive compensation, promotions, key assignments, and the ways and means of awarding praise and recognition are potent attention-getting, commitment-generating devices. Such decisions seldom escape the closest employee scrutiny, thus saying more about what is expected and who is considered to be doing a good job than virtually any other factor. While most approaches to motivation, compensation, and people management accentuate the positive, companies also combine positive rewards with the risk of punishment. At General Electric, McKinsey & Company, several global public accounting firms, and other companies that look for and expect top-notch individual performance, there's an "up-or-out" policy—managers and professionals whose performance is not good enough to warrant promotion are first denied bonuses and stock awards and eventually weeded out. A number of companies deliberately give employees heavy workloads and tight deadlines—personnel are pushed hard to achieve "stretch" objectives and are expected to put in long hours (nights and weekends if need be). At most companies, senior executives and key personnel in underperforming units are pressured to raise performance to acceptable levels and keep it there or risk being replaced.

ILLUSTRATION CAPSULE 11.2

What Companies Do to Motivate and Reward Employees

Companies have come up with an impressive variety of motivational and reward practices to help create a work environment that energizes employees and promotes better strategy execution. Here's a sampling of what companies are doing:

- Google has a sprawling 20-building headquarters complex known as the Googleplex where its several thousand employees have access to 19 cafes and 60 snack centers, unlimited ice cream, four gyms, heated swimming pools, ping-pong and pool tables, and community bicycles to go from building to building. Management built the Googleplex to be "a dream workplace" and a showcase for environmentally correct building design and construction.

- Lincoln Electric, widely known for its piecework pay scheme and incentive bonus plan, rewards individual productivity by paying workers for each nondefective piece produced. Workers have to correct quality problems on their own time—defects in products used by customers can be traced back to the worker who caused them. Lincoln's piecework plan motivates workers to pay attention to both quality and volume produced. In addition, the company sets aside a substantial portion of its profits above a specified base for worker bonuses. To determine bonus size, Lincoln Electric rates each worker on four equally important performance measures: (1) dependability, (2) quality, (3) output, and (4) ideas and cooperation. The higher a worker's merit rating, the higher the incentive bonus earned; the highest-rated workers in good profit years receive bonuses of as much as 110 percent of their piecework compensation.

- At JM Family Enterprises, a Toyota distributor in Florida, employees get attractive lease options on new Toyotas and enjoy on-site amenities such as a heated lap pool, a fitness center, a free nail salon, free prescriptions delivered by a "pharmacy concierge," and professionally made take-home dinners. Exceptionally high performers are flown to the Bahamas for cruises on the 172-foot company yacht.

- Wegmans, a family-owned grocer with 75 stores on the East Coast of the United States, provides employees with flexible schedules and benefits that include onsite fitness centers. The company's approach to managing people allows it to provide a very high level of customer service not found in other grocery chains. Employees ranging from cashiers to butchers to store managers are all treated equally and viewed as experts in their jobs. Employees receive 50 hours of formal training per year and are allowed to make decisions that they believe are appropriate for their jobs. The company's 2009 annual turnover rate is only 7 percent, which is less than one-half the 19 percent average turnover rate in the U.S. supermarket industry.

- Nordstrom, widely regarded for its superior in-house customer service experience, typically pays its retail salespeople an hourly wage higher than the prevailing rates paid by other department store chains plus a commission on each sale. Spurred by a culture that encourages salespeople to go all out to satisfy customers and to seek out and promote new fashion ideas, Nordstrom salespeople earn nearly 65 percent more than the average sales employee at competing stores. The typical Nordstrom salesperson earns nearly $38,900 per year, but top performers can earn salaries in the six figures.[34] Nordstrom's rules for employees are simple: "Rule #1: Use your good judgment in all situations. There will be no additional rules."

- At W. L. Gore (the maker of GORE-TEX), employees get to choose what project/team they work on, and each team member's compensation is based on other team members' rankings of his or her contribution to the enterprise.
- At Ukrop's Super Markets, a family-owned chain in Virginia, stores stay closed on Sunday; the company pays out 20 percent of pretax profits to employees in the form of quarterly bonuses;

and the company picks up the membership tab for employees if they visit their health club 30 times a quarter.
- At biotech leader Amgen, employees get 16 paid holidays, generous vacation time, tuition reimbursements up to $10,000, on-site massages, discounted car-wash services, and the convenience of shopping at on-site farmers' markets.

Sources: Fortune's lists of the 100 best companies to work for in America, 2002, 2004, 2005, 2008, 2009, and 2010; Jefferson Graham, "The Search Engine That Could," *USA Today,* August 26, 2003, p. B3; company Web sites (accessed June 2010).

As a general rule, it is unwise to take off the pressure for good individual and group performance or play down the adverse consequences of shortfalls in performance. There is no evidence that a no-pressure/no-adverse-consequences work environment leads to superior strategy execution or operating excellence. As the CEO of a major bank put it, "There's a deliberate policy here to create a level of anxiety. Winners usually play like they're one touchdown behind."[35] High-performing organizations nearly always have a cadre of ambitious people who relish the opportunity to climb the ladder of success, love a challenge, thrive in a performance-oriented environment, and find some competition and pressure useful to satisfy their own drives for personal recognition, accomplishment, and self-satisfaction.

However, if an organization's motivational approaches and reward structure induce too much stress, internal competitiveness, job insecurity, and fear of unpleasant consequences, the impact on workforce morale and strategy execution can be counterproductive. Evidence shows that managerial initiatives to improve strategy execution should incorporate more positive than negative motivational elements because when cooperation is positively enlisted and rewarded, rather than coerced by orders and threats (implicit or explicit), people tend to respond with more enthusiasm, dedication, creativity, and initiative.[36]

Linking Rewards to Strategically Relevant Performance Outcomes

To create a strategy-supportive system of rewards and incentives, a company must reward people for accomplishing results, not for just dutifully performing assigned tasks. To make the work environment results-oriented, managers need to focus jobholders' attention and energy on what to *achieve* as opposed to what to *do*. It is flawed management to tie incentives and rewards to satisfactory performance of duties and activities instead of desired business outcomes and company achievements.[37] In any job, performing assigned tasks is not equivalent to achieving intended outcomes. Diligently showing up for work and attending to one's job assignment does not, by itself, guarantee results. Employee productivity among employees at Best Buy's corporate headquarters rose by 35 percent after the company began to focus on the results of each employee's work rather than on employees' willingness to come to work early and stay late.

> Incentives must be based on accomplishing the right results, not on dutifully performing assigned tasks.

The key to creating a reward system that promotes good strategy execution is to make measures of good business performance and good strategy execution the *dominating basis* for designing incentives, evaluating individual and group efforts, and handing out rewards.

Ideally, performance targets should be set for every organizational unit, every manager, every team or work group, and perhaps every employee—targets that measure whether strategy execution is progressing satisfactorily. If the company's strategy is to be a low-cost provider, the incentive system must reward actions and achievements that result in lower costs. If the company has a differentiation strategy based on superior quality and service, the incentive system must reward such outcomes as Six Sigma defect rates, infrequent need for product repair, low numbers of customer complaints, speedy order processing and delivery, and high levels of customer satisfaction. If a company's growth is predicated on a strategy of new product innovation, incentives should be tied to factors such as the percentages of revenues and profits coming from newly introduced products.

Incentive compensation for top executives is typically tied to such financial measures as revenue and earnings growth, stock price performance, return on investment, and creditworthiness or to strategic measures such as market share growth. However, incentives for department heads, teams, and individual workers may be tied to performance outcomes more closely related to their strategic area of responsibility. In manufacturing, incentive compensation may be tied to unit manufacturing costs, on-time production and shipping, defect rates, the number and extent of work stoppages due to equipment breakdowns, and so on. In sales and marketing, there may be incentives for achieving dollar sales or unit volume targets, market share, sales penetration of each target customer group, the fate of newly introduced products, the frequency of customer complaints, the number of new accounts acquired, and customer satisfaction. Which performance measures to base incentive compensation on depends on the situation—the priority placed on various financial and strategic objectives, the requirements for strategic and competitive success, and what specific results are needed in different facets of the business to keep strategy execution on track.

Illustration Capsule 11.3 provides a vivid example of how one company has designed incentives linked directly to outcomes reflecting good execution.

Guidelines for Designing Effective Incentive Compensation Systems

As explained above, the first principle in designing an effective incentive compensation system is to tie rewards to performance outcomes directly linked to good strategy execution and targeted strategic and financial objectives. But for a company's reward system to truly motivate organization members, inspire their best efforts, and sustain high levels of productivity, it is equally important to observe the following additional guidelines in designing and administering the reward system:

- *Make the financial incentives a major, not minor, piece of the total compensation package.* Performance payoffs must be at least 10 to 12 percent of base salary to have much impact. Incentives that amount to 20 percent or more of total compensation are big attention-getters, likely to really drive individual or team efforts. Incentives amounting to less than 5 percent of total compensation have a comparatively weak motivational impact. Moreover, the payoff for high-performing individuals and teams must be meaningfully greater than the payoff for average performers, and the payoff for average performers meaningfully bigger than that for below-average performers.

- *Have incentives that extend to all managers and all workers, not just top management.* Lower-level managers and employees are just as likely as senior executives to be motivated by the possibility of lucrative rewards.

Nucor Corporation: Tying Incentives Directly to Strategy Execution

The strategy at Nucor Corporation, one of the three largest steel producers in the United States, is to be *the* low-cost producer of steel products. Because labor costs are a significant fraction of total cost in the steel business, successful implementation of Nucor's low-cost leadership strategy entails achieving lower labor costs per ton of steel than competitors' costs. Nucor management uses an incentive system to promote high worker productivity and drive labor costs per ton below rivals'. Each plant's workforce is organized into production teams (each assigned to perform particular functions), and weekly production targets are established for each team. Base-pay scales are set at levels comparable to wages for similar manufacturing jobs in the local areas where Nucor has plants, but workers can earn a 1 percent bonus for each 1 percent that their output exceeds target levels. If a production team exceeds its weekly production target by 10 percent, team members receive a 10 percent bonus in their next paycheck; if a team exceeds its quota by 20 percent, team members earn a 20 percent bonus. Bonuses, paid every two weeks, are based on the prior two weeks' actual production levels measured against the targets.

Nucor's piece-rate incentive plan has produced impressive results. The production teams put forth exceptional effort; it is not uncommon for most teams to beat their weekly production targets anywhere from 20 to 50 percent. When added to their base pay, the bonuses earned by Nucor workers make Nucor's work force among the highest-paid in the U.S. steel industry. From a management perspective, the incentive system has resulted in Nucor having labor productivity levels 10 to 20 percent above the average of the unionized workforces at several of its largest rivals, which in turn has given Nucor a significant labor cost advantage over most rivals.

After years of record-setting profits, Nucor struggled in the economic downturn of 2008–2010, along with the manufacturers and builders who buy its steel. But while bonuses have dwindled, Nucor showed remarkable loyalty to its production workers, avoiding layoffs by having employees get ahead on maintenance, perform work formerly done by contractors, and search for cost savings. Morale at the company has remained high and Nucor's CEO Daniel DiMicco has received thank-you notes from grateful employees by the basketful. As industry growth resumes, Nucor will have a well-trained workforce still in place, more committed than ever to achieving the kind of productivity for which Nucor is justifiably famous. When the turnaround comes, DiMicco has good reason to expect Nucor to be "first out of the box."

Sources: Company Web site (accessed July 2010); N. Byrnes, "Pain, but No Layoffs at Nucor," *Bloomberg Businessweek,* March 26, 2009.

- *Administer the reward system with scrupulous objectivity and fairness.* If performance standards are set unrealistically high or if individual/group performance evaluations are not accurate and well documented, dissatisfaction with the system will overcome any positive benefits.

- *Ensure that the performance targets each individual or team is expected to achieve involve outcomes that the individual or team can personally affect.* The role of incentives is to enhance individual commitment and channel behavior in beneficial directions. This role is not well served when the performance measures by which company personnel are judged are outside their arena of influence.

- *Keep the time between achieving the targeted performance outcome and the payment of the reward as short as possible.* Companies like Nucor Steel and Continental Airlines have discovered that weekly or monthly payments for good performance work much better than annual payments. Nucor pays weekly bonuses based on prior-week production levels, while Continental pays employees a bonus whenever actual on-time flight performance meets or beats the monthly on-time target. Annual bonus payouts work best for higher-level managers and for situations where the outcome target relates to overall company profitability or stock price performance.

- *Avoid rewarding effort rather than results.* While it is tempting to reward people who have tried hard yet fallen short of achieving performance targets because of circumstances beyond their control, it is ill advised. The problem with making exceptions for unknowable, uncontrollable, or unforeseeable circumstances is that once "good excuses" start to creep into justifying rewards for subpar results, the door is open for all kinds of reasons why actual performance has failed to match targeted performance. A "no excuses" standard is more even-handed, easier to administer, and more conducive to creating a results-oriented work climate.

> The unwavering standard for judging whether individuals, teams, and organizational units have done a good job must be whether they meet or beat performance targets that reflect good strategy execution.

Once an organization's incentive plan is designed, it must be communicated and explained. Everybody needs to understand how his or her incentive compensation is calculated and how individual/group performance targets contribute to organizational performance targets. The pressure to continuously improve strategy execution and achieve performance objectives should be unrelenting, with no loopholes for rewarding shortfalls in performance. People at all levels must be held accountable for carrying out their assigned parts of the strategic plan, and they must understand that their rewards are based on the caliber of results achieved. But with the pressure to perform should come meaningful rewards. Without an ample payoff, the system breaks down, and managers are left with the less workable options of issuing orders, trying to enforce compliance, and depending on the goodwill of employees.

KEY POINTS

1. Implementing and executing a new or different strategy calls for managers to identify the resource requirements of each new strategic initiative and then consider whether the current pattern of resource allocation and the budgets of the various subunits are suitable.

2. Company policies and procedures facilitate strategy execution when they are designed to fit the strategy and its objectives. Anytime a company alters its strategy, managers should review existing policies and operating procedures and replace those that are out of sync. Well conceived policies and procedures aid the task of strategy execution by (1) providing top-down guidance to company personnel regarding how certain things need to be done and

what the boundaries are on independent actions and decisions, (2) enforcing consistency in the performance of strategy-critical activities, thereby improving the quality of the strategy execution effort and aligning the actions of company personnel, however widely dispersed, and (3) promoting the creation of a work climate conducive to good strategy execution.

3. Competent strategy execution entails visible unyielding managerial commitment to best practices and continuous improvement. Benchmarking, best-practice adoption, business process reengineering, total quality management (TQM), and Six Sigma programs are important process management tools for promoting better strategy execution.

4. Company strategies can't be implemented or executed well without a number of support systems to carry on business operations. Real-time information systems and control systems further aid the cause of good strategy execution.

5. Strategy-supportive motivational practices and reward systems are powerful management tools for gaining employee commitment and focusing their attention on the strategy execution goals. The key to creating a reward system that promotes good strategy execution is to make measures of good business performance and good strategy execution the *dominating basis* for designing incentives, evaluating individual and group efforts, and handing out rewards. Positive motivational practices generally work better than negative ones, but there is a place for both. While financial rewards provide high-powered incentives, there's also place for nonmonetary incentives. For an incentive compensation system to work well, (1) the monetary payoff should be a major percentage of the compensation package, (2) the use of incentives should extend to all managers and workers, (3) the system should be administered with care and fairness, (4) each individual's performance targets should involve outcomes the person can personally affect, (5) rewards should promptly follow the determination of good performance, and (6) rewards should be given for results and not just effort.

ASSURANCE OF LEARNING EXERCISES

LO 3

1. Read some of the recent Six Sigma articles posted at isixsigma.com. Prepare a one-page report to your instructor detailing how Six Sigma is being used in various companies and what benefits these companies are reaping from Six Sigma implementation.

LO 3

2. Review the profiles and applications of the latest Malcolm Baldrige National Quality Award recipients at www.baldrige.nist.gov. What are the standout features of the companies' approaches to managing operations? What do you find impressive about the companies' policies and procedures, use of best practices, emphasis on continuous improvement, and use of rewards and incentives?

LO 4

3. Using Google or your university library's access to online business periodicals, search for articles discussing radio frequency identification (RFID) technology. Prepare a 1–2 page report that discusses how information systems that incorporate RFID technology provide more accurate and timely supplier data and have improved strategy execution at various companies.

LO 5

4. Consult the issue of *Fortune* containing the latest annual "100 Best Companies to Work For" (usually a late-January or early-February issue), or else go to www.fortune.com to access the list, and identify at least five compensation incentives and work practices that these companies use to enhance employee motivation and reward them for good strategic and financial performance. You should identify compensation methods and work practices that are different from those cited in Illustration Capsule 11.2.

EXERCISES FOR SIMULATION PARTICIPANTS

LO 1

1. Have you and your co-managers allocated ample resources to strategy-critical areas? If so, explain how these investments have contributed to good strategy execution and improved company performance.

LO 3

2. Is benchmarking data available in the simulation exercise in which you are participating? If so, do you and your co-managers regularly study the benchmarking data to see how well your company is doing? Do you consider the benchmarking information provided to be valuable? Why or why not? Cite three recent instances in which your examination of the benchmarking statistics has caused you and your co-managers to take corrective actions to boost company performance.

LO 2, LO 3, LO 4

3. What actions, if any, is your company taking to pursue continuous improvement in how it performs certain value chain activities?

LO 5

4. Does your company have opportunities to use incentive compensation techniques? If so, explain your company's approach to incentive compensation. Is there any hard evidence you can cite that indicates your company's use of incentive compensation techniques has worked? For example, have your company's compensation incentives actually increased productivity? Can you cite evidence indicating that the productivity gains have resulted in lower labor

costs? If the productivity gains have *not* translated into lower labor costs, is it fair to say that your company's use of incentive compensation is a failure?

LO 2, LO 3, LO 4

5. Are you and your co-managers consciously trying to achieve "operating excellence"? What are the indicators of operating excellence at your company? Based on these indicators, how well does your company measure up?

LO 3

6. What hard evidence can you cite that indicates your company's management team is doing a *better* or *worse* job of achieving operating excellence and executing your strategy than are the management teams at rival companies?

ENDNOTES

[1] For a discussion of the value of benchmarking in implementing and executing strategy, see Christopher E. Bogan and Michael J. English, *Benchmarking for Best Practices: Winning through Innovative Adaptation* (New York: McGraw-Hill, 1994) chaps. 2 and 6; Mustafa Ungan, "Factors Affecting the Adoption of Manufacturing Best Practices," *Benchmarking: An International Journal* 11, no. 5 (2004), pp. 504–20; Paul Hyland and Ron Beckett, "Learning to Compete: The Value of Internal Benchmarking," *Benchmarking: An International Journal* 9, no. 3 (2002), pp. 293–304; Yoshinobu Ohinata, "Benchmarking: The Japanese Experience," *Long-Range Planning* 27, no. 4 (August 1994), pp. 48–53.

[2] www.businessdictionary.com/definition/best-practice.html (accessed December 2, 2009).

[3] M. Hammer and J. Champy, *Reengineering the Corporation: A Manifesto for Business Revolution* (New York: Harper Collins Publishers, 1993), pp. 26–27.

[4] Information on the greeting card industry is posted at www.answers.com (accessed July 8, 2009), and "Reengineering: Beyond the Buzzword," *BusinessWeek*, May 24, 1993, www.businessweek.com (accessed July 8, 2009).

[5] Gene Hall, Jim Rosenthal, and Judy Wade, "How to Make Reengineering Really Work," *Harvard Business Review* 71, no. 6 (November–December 1993), pp. 119–31.

[6] For more information on business process reengineering and how well it has worked in various companies, see James Brian Quinn, *Intelligent Enterprise* (New York: Free Press, 1992), p. 162; Ann Majchrzak and Qianwei Wang, "Breaking the Functional Mind-Set in Process Organizations," *Harvard Business Review* 74, no. 5 (September–October 1996), pp. 93–99; Stephen L. Walston, Lawton. R. Burns, and John R. Kimberly, "Does Reengineering Really Work? An Examination of the Context and Outcomes of Hospital Reengineering Initiatives," *Health*

Services Research 34, no. 6 (February 2000), pp. 1363–88; Allessio Ascari, Melinda Rock, and Soumitra Dutta, "Reengineering and Organizational Change: Lessons from a Comparative Analysis of Company Experiences," *European Management Journal* 13, no. 1 (March 1995), pp. 1–13. For a review of why some company personnel embrace process reengineering and some don't, see Ronald J. Burke, "Process Reengineering: Who Embraces It and Why?" *TQM Magazine* 16, no. 2 (2004), pp. 114–19.

[7] For some of the seminal discussions of what TQM is and how it works, written by ardent enthusiasts of the technique, see M. Walton, *The Deming Management Method* (New York: Pedigree, 1986); J. Juran, *Juran on Quality by Design* (New York: Free Press, 1992); Philip Crosby, *Quality Is Free: The Act of Making Quality Certain* (New York: McGraw-Hill, 1979); S. George, *The Baldrige Quality System* (New York: Wiley, 1992). For a critique of TQM, see Mark J. Zbaracki, "The Rhetoric and Reality of Total Quality Management," *Administrative Science Quarterly* 43, no 3 (September 1998), pp. 602–36.

[8] For a discussion of the shift in work environment and culture that TQM entails, see Robert T. Amsden, Thomas W. Ferratt, and Davida M. Amsden, "TQM: Core Paradigm Changes," *Business Horizons* 39, no. 6 (November–December 1996), pp. 6–14.

[9] For easy-to-understand overviews of what Six Sigma is all about, see Peter S. Pande and Larry Holpp, *What Is Six Sigma?* (New York: McGraw-Hill, 2002); Jiju Antony, "Some Pros and Cons of Six Sigma: An Academic Perspective," *TQM Magazine* 16, no. 4 (2004), pp. 303–6; Peter S. Pande, Robert P. Neuman, and Roland R. Cavanagh, *The Six Sigma Way: How GE, Motorola and Other Top Companies Are Honing Their Performance* (New York: McGraw-Hill, 2000); Joseph Gordon and M. Joseph Gordon, Jr., *Six Sigma Quality for Business and Manufacture* (New York: Elsevier, 2002). For how Six Sigma can be

used in smaller companies, see Godecke Wessel and Peter Burcher, "Six Sigma for Small and Medium-Sized Enterprises," *TQM Magazine* 16, no. 4 (2004), pp. 264–72.

[10] Based on information posted at www.isixsigma.com (accessed November 4, 2002).

[11] Kennedy Smith, "Six Sigma for the Service Sector," *Quality Digest Magazine,* May 2003, www.qualitydigest.com (accessed September 28, 2003).

[12] Del Jones, "Taking the Six Sigma Approach," *USA Today,* October 31, 2002, p. 5B.

[13] Pande, Neuman, and Cavanagh, *The Six Sigma Way,* pp. 5–6.

[14] Smith, "Six Sigma for the Service Sector."

[15] Jones, "Taking the Six Sigma Approach," p. 5B.

[16] See, for example, "A Dark Art No More," *Economist* 385, no. 8550 (October 13, 2007), p. 10; Brian Hindo, "At 3M, a Struggle between Efficiency and Creativity," *BusinessWeek,* June 11, 2007, pp. 8–16.

[17] As quoted in "A Dark Art No More."

[18] Hindo, "At 3M, a Struggle between Efficiency and Creativity."

[19] For a discussion of approaches to pursuing radical or disruptive innovations while also seeking incremental gains in efficiency, see Charles A. O'Reilly and Michael L. Tushman, "The Ambidextrous Organization," *Harvard Business Review* 82, no. 4 (April 2004), pp. 74–81.

[20] Terry Nels Lee, Stanley E. Fawcett, and Jason Briscoe, "Benchmarking the Challenge to Quality Program Implementation," *Benchmarking: An International Journal* 9, no. 4 (2002), pp. 374–87.

[21] For a recent study documenting the imperatives of establishing a supportive culture, see Milan Ambrož, "Total Quality System as a Product of the Empowered Corporate Culture," *TQM Magazine* 16, no. 2 (2004), pp. 93–104. Research confirming the factors that are important in making TQM programs successful in both Europe and the United States is

presented in Nick A. Dayton, "The Demise of Total Quality Management," *TQM Magazine* 15, no. 6 (2003), pp. 391–96.

[22] Judy D. Olian and Sara L. Rynes, "Making Total Quality Work: Aligning Organizational Processes, Performance Measures, and Stakeholders," *Human Resource Management* 30, no. 3 (Fall 1991), pp. 310–11; Paul S. Goodman and Eric D. Darr, "Exchanging Best Practices Information through Computer-Aided Systems," *Academy of Management Executive* 10, no. 2 (May 1996), p. 7.

[23] Thomas C. Powell, "Total Quality Management as Competitive Advantage," *Strategic Management Journal* 16 (1995), pp. 15–37. See also Richard M. Hodgetts, "Quality Lessons from America's Baldrige Winners," *Business Horizons* 37, no. 4 (July–August 1994), pp. 74–79; Richard Reed, David J. Lemak, and Joseph C. Montgomery, "Beyond Process: TQM Content and Firm Performance," *Academy of Management Review* 21, no. 1 (January 1996), pp. 173–202.

[24] Based on information at www.otiselevator.com (accessed July 9, 2009).

[25] "The Web Smart 50," *BusinessWeek*, November 21, 2005, pp. 87–88.

[26] Aishah Mustapha, "Net Value: Social Software a New Way to Work," *The Edge Malaysia (Weekly),* February 16, 2009.

[27] Such systems speed organizational learning by providing fast, efficient communication, creating an organizational memory for collecting and retaining best-practice information, and permitting people all across the organization to exchange information and updated solutions. See Goodman and Darr, "Exchanging Best Practices Information through Computer-Aided Systems," pp. 7–17.

[28] "The Web Smart 50," pp. 85–90.

[29] Fred Vogelstein, "Winning the Amazon Way," *Fortune* 147, no. 10 (May 26, 2003), pp. 60–69.

[30] For a discussion of the need for putting appropriate boundaries on the actions of empowered employees and possible control and monitoring systems that can be used, see Robert Simons, "Control in an Age of Empowerment," *Harvard Business Review* 73 (March–April 1995), pp. 80–88.

[31] Ibid. Also see David C. Band and Gerald Scanlan, "Strategic Control through Core Competencies," *Long Range Planning* 28, no. 2 (April 1995), pp. 102–14.

[32] The importance of motivating and empowering workers so as to create a working environment that is highly conducive to good strategy execution is discussed in Stanley E. Fawcett, Gary K. Rhoads, and Phillip Burnah, "People as the Bridge to Competitiveness: Benchmarking the 'ABCs' of an Empowered Workforce," *Benchmarking: An International Journal* 11 no. 4 (2004), pp. 346–60.

[33] Jeffrey Pfeffer and John F. Veiga, "Putting People First for Organizational Success," *Academy of Management Executive* 13, no. 2 (May 1999), pp. 37–45; Linda K. Stroh and Paula M. Caliguiri, "Increasing Global Competitiveness through Effective People Management," *Journal of World Business* 33, no. 1 (Spring 1998), pp. 1–16; articles in *Fortune* on the 100 best companies to work for (various issues).

[34] Jenni Mintz, "Nordstrom Opening in Three Weeks: Company Plans 'Tailgate Party for Women' and Other Events", *Ventura County Star* (California), *McClatchy-Tribune Regional News,* August 12, 2008.

[35] As quoted in John P. Kotter and James L. Heskett, *Corporate Culture and Performance* (New York: Free Press, 1992), p. 91.

[36] Clayton M. Christensen, Matt Marx, and Howard Stevenson, "The Tools of Cooperation and Change," *Harvard Business Review* 84, no. 10 (October 2006), pp. 73–80.

[37] See Steven Kerr, "On the Folly of Rewarding A While Hoping for B," *Academy of Management Executive* 9, no. 1 (February 1995), pp. 7–14; S. Kerr and E. Davies, "Risky Business: The New Pay Game," *Fortune* 134, no. 2 (July 22, 1996) pp. 94–96; and Doran Twer, "Linking Pay to Business Objectives," *Journal of Business Strategy* 15, no. 4 (July–August 1994), pp. 15–18.

CHAPTER 12

CORPORATE CULTURE AND LEADERSHIP

Keys to Good Strategy Execution

> The biggest levers you've got to change a company are strategy, structure, and culture. If I could pick two, I'd pick strategy and culture.
>
> **—Wayne Leonard**
> *Chairman and CEO, Entergy Corporation*

> Success goes to those with a corporate culture that assures the ability to anticipate and meet customer demand.
>
> **—Tadashi Okamura**
> *Former Chairman and CEO of Toshiba Corporation*

> The soft stuff is always harder than the hard stuff.
>
> **—Roger Enrico**
> *Former CEO of PepsiCo*

LEARNING OBJECTIVES

LO 1. Be able to identify the key features of a company's corporate culture and appreciate the role of a company's core values and ethical standards in building corporate culture.

LO 2. Gain an understanding of how and why a company's culture can aid the drive for proficient strategy execution and operating excellence.

LO 3. Learn the kinds of actions management can take to change a problem corporate culture.

LO 4. Understand what constitutes effective managerial leadership in achieving superior strategy execution.

In the previous two chapters, we examined six of the managerial tasks that drive good strategy execution: building a capable organization, marshaling the needed resources and steering them to strategy-critical operating units, establishing appropriate policies and procedures, driving continuous improvement in value chain activities, creating the necessary operating systems, and providing the incentives needed to ensure employee commitment to the strategy execution process. In this chapter, we explore the two remaining managerial tasks that contribute to good strategy execution: creating a strategy-supportive corporate culture and exerting the internal leadership needed to drive the implementation of strategic initiatives forward and achieve higher plateaus of operating excellence.

INSTILLING A CORPORATE CULTURE THAT PROMOTES GOOD STRATEGY EXECUTION

Every company has its own unique culture. The character of a company's culture or work climate is a product of the core values and business principles that executives espouse, the standards of what is ethically acceptable and what is not, the work practices and norms of behavior that define "how we do things around here," the approach to people management and style of operating, the "chemistry" and the "personality" that permeates the work environment, and the stories that get told over and over to illustrate and reinforce the company's values, business practices, and traditions. The meshing together of shared values, beliefs, business principles, and traditions into a style of operating, behavioral norms, ingrained attitudes, and work atmosphere defines a company's **corporate culture.**[1] A company's culture is important because it influences the organization's actions and approaches to conducting business—in a very real sense, the culture is the company's automatic, self-replicating "operating system"—it can be thought of as the organizational DNA.[2] As we learned in Chapter 4, a superior corporate culture can also be a source of sustainable competitive advantage under some circumstances.

Corporate cultures vary widely. For instance, the bedrock of Walmart's culture is dedication to zealous pursuit of low costs and frugal operating practices, a strong work ethic, ritualistic headquarters meetings to exchange ideas and review problems, and company executives' commitment to visiting stores, listening to customers, and soliciting suggestions from employees. General Electric's culture is founded on a hard-driving, results-oriented atmosphere; extensive cross-business sharing of ideas, best practices, and learning; reliance on "workout sessions" to identify, debate, and resolve burning issues; a commitment to Six Sigma quality; and a globalized approach to operations. At U.S. upscale department store chain, Nordstrom, the corporate culture is centered on delivering exceptional service to customers—the company's motto is "Respond to unreasonable customer requests," and each out-of-the-ordinary request is seen as an opportunity for a "heroic" act by an employee that can further the company's reputation for unparalleled customer service. Nordstrom makes a point of promoting employees noted for their heroic acts and dedication to outstanding service; the company motivates its salespeople with a commission-based compensation system that enables Nordstrom's best salespeople to earn more than double what other department stores pay. Illustration Capsule 12.1 relates how Google and Albert-Culver describe their corporate cultures.

CORE CONCEPT

Corporate culture refers to the character of a company's internal work climate—as shaped by a system of *shared* values, beliefs, ethical standards, and traditions that define behavioral norms, ingrained attitudes, accepted work practices, and styles of operating.

Identifying the Key Features of a Company's Corporate Culture

LO 1

Be able to identify the key features of a company's corporate culture and appreciate the role of a company's core values and ethical standards in building corporate culture.

A company's corporate culture is mirrored in the character or "personality" of its work environment—the factors that underlie how the company tries to conduct its business and the behaviors that are held in high esteem. Some of these factors are readily apparent, and others operate quite subtly. The chief things to look for include the following:

- The values, business principles, and ethical standards that management preaches and *practices*—these are the key to a company's culture, but actions speak much louder than words here.
- The company's approach to people management and the official policies, procedures, and operating practices that provide guidelines for the behavior of company personnel.
- The atmosphere and spirit that pervades the work climate. Is the workplace vibrant and fun? Methodical and all business? Tense and harried? Highly competitive and politicized? Are people excited about their work and emotionally connected to the company's business, or are they just there to draw a paycheck? Is there an emphasis on empowered worker creativity, or do people have little discretion in how jobs are done?
- The way managers and employees interact and relate to one another—the reliance on teamwork and open communication, the extent to which there is good camaraderie, whether people are called by their first names, whether co-workers spend little or lots of time together outside the workplace, and what the dress codes are (the accepted styles of attire and whether there are casual days).
- The strength of peer pressure to do things in particular ways and conform to expected norms—what actions and behaviors are encouraged on a peer-to-peer basis?

ILLUSTRATION CAPSULE 12.1

The Corporate Cultures at Google and Alberto-Culver

Founded in 1998 by Larry Page and Sergey Brin, two Ph.D. students in computer science at Stanford University, Google has become world-renowned for its search engine technology. Google.com was the most frequently visited Internet site in 2009, attracting over 844 million unique visitors monthly from around the world. Google has some unique ways of operating, and its culture is also rather quirky. The company describes its culture as follows:

> Though growing rapidly, Google still maintains a small company feel. At lunchtime, almost everyone eats in the office café, sitting at whatever table has an opening and enjoying conversations with Googlers from different teams. Our commitment to innovation depends on everyone being comfortable sharing ideas and opinions. Every employee is a hands-on contributor, and everyone wears several hats. Because we believe that each Googler is an equally important part of our success, no one hesitates to pose questions directly to Larry or Sergey in our weekly all-hands ("TGIF") meetings—or spike a volleyball across the net at a corporate officer.
>
> We are aggressively inclusive in our hiring, and we favor ability over experience. We have offices around the world and dozens of languages are spoken by Google staffers, from Turkish to Telugu. The result is a team that reflects the global audience Google serves. When not at work, Googlers pursue interests from cross-country cycling to wine tasting, from flying to frisbee.
>
> As we continue to grow, we are always looking for those who share a commitment to creating search perfection and having a great time doing it.
>
> Our corporate headquarters, fondly nicknamed the Googleplex, is located in Mountain View, California. Today it's one of our many offices around the globe. While our offices are not identical, they tend to share some essential elements. Here are a few things you might see in a Google workspace:
>
> - Local expressions of each location, from a mural in Buenos Aires to ski gondolas in Zurich, showcasing each office's region and personality.
> - Bicycles or scooters for efficient travel between meetings; dogs; lava lamps; massage chairs; large inflatable balls.

> - Googlers sharing cubes, yurts and huddle rooms—and very few solo offices.
> - Laptops everywhere—standard issue for mobile coding, email on the go and note-taking.
> - Foosball, pool tables, volleyball courts, assorted video games, pianos, ping pong tables, and gyms that offer yoga and dance classes.
> - Grassroots employee groups for all interests, like meditation, film, wine tasting and salsa dancing.
> - Healthy lunches and dinners for all staff at a variety of cafés.
> - Break rooms packed with a variety of snacks and drinks to keep Googlers going.

The Alberto-Culver Company, with fiscal 2009 revenues of more than $1.4 billion, is the producer and marketer of Alberto VO5, TRESemmé, Motions, Soft & Beautiful, Just for Me, and Nexxus hair care products; St. Ives skin care products; and such brands as Molly McButter, Mrs. Dash, Sugar Twin, and Static Guard. Alberto-Culver brands are sold in more than 120 countries.

At the careers section of its Web site, the company described its culture in the following words:

> Building careers is as important to us as building brands. We believe that passionate people create powerful growth. We believe in a workplace built on values and believe our best people display those same values in their families and their communities. We believe in recognizing and rewarding accomplishment and celebrating our victories.
>
> We believe the best ideas work their way—quickly—up an organization, not down. We believe that we should take advantage of every ounce of your talent on teams and cross-functional activities, not just assign you to a box.
>
> We believe in open communication. We believe that you can improve what you measure, so we survey and spot check all the time. For that same reason, everyone has specific goals so that their expectations are in line with their managers' and the company's.
>
> We believe that victory is a team accomplishment. We believe in personal development. We believe if you talk with us you will catch our enthusiasm and want to be a part of the Alberto-Culver team.

Sources: Information posted at www.google.com and www.alberto.com (accessed June 30, 2010); S. McClellan, "Alberto Culver Launches Global Search: The Client's Annual U.S. Ad Spending Alone Touches $100 Mil.," *Adweek,* January 29, 2010, www.adweek.com/aw/content_display/news/account-activity/e3i68e64a3cf2727350dd0013083626e8ae.

- The actions and behaviors that are explicitly encouraged and rewarded by management in the form of compensation and promotion.
- The company's revered traditions and oft-repeated stories about "heroic acts" and "how we do things around here."
- The manner in which the company deals with external stakeholders (particularly vendors and local communities where it has operations)—whether it treats suppliers as business partners or prefers hard-nosed, arm's-length business arrangements, and the strength and genuineness of the commitment to corporate citizenship and environmental sustainability.

The values, beliefs, and practices that undergird a company's culture can come from anywhere in the organizational hierarchy, most often representing the business philosophy and managerial style of influential executives but also resulting from exemplary actions on the part of company personnel and consensus agreement about appropriate norms of behavior.[3] Typically, key elements of the culture originate with a founder or certain strong leaders who articulated them as a set of business principles, company policies, operating approaches, and ways of dealing with employees, customers, vendors, shareholders, and local communities where the company has operations. Over time, these cultural underpinnings take root, become embedded in how the company conducts its business, come to be accepted by company managers and employees alike, and then persist as new employees are encouraged to embrace the company values and adopt the implied attitudes, behaviors, and work practices.

The Role of Core Values and Ethics   The foundation of a company's corporate culture nearly always resides in its dedication to certain core values and the bar it sets for ethical behavior. The culture-shaping significance of core values and ethical behaviors accounts for one reason why so many companies have developed a formal values statement and a code of ethics. Many executives want the work climate at their companies to mirror certain values and ethical standards, partly because they are personally committed to these values and ethical standards but also because they are convinced that adherence to such values and ethical principles will promote better strategy execution, make the company a better performer, and improve its image.[4] And, not incidentally, strongly ingrained values and ethical standards reduce the likelihood of lapses in ethical and socially approved behavior that mar a company's reputation and put its financial performance and market standing at risk, as discussed in Chapter 9.

> A company's culture is grounded in and shaped by its core values and ethical standards.

As depicted in Figure 12.1, a company's stated core values and ethical principles have two roles in the culture-building process. First, a company that works hard at putting its stated core values and ethical principles into practice fosters a work climate in which company personnel share strongly held convictions about how the company's business is to be conducted. Second, the stated values and ethical principles provide company personnel with guidance about the manner in which they are to do their jobs—which behaviors and ways of doing things are approved (and expected) and which are out-of-bounds. These values-based and ethics-based cultural norms serve as yardsticks for gauging the appropriateness of particular actions, decisions, and behaviors, thus helping steer company personnel toward both doing things right and doing the right thing.

Figure 12.1   **The Two Culture-Building Roles of a Company's Core Values and Ethical Standards**

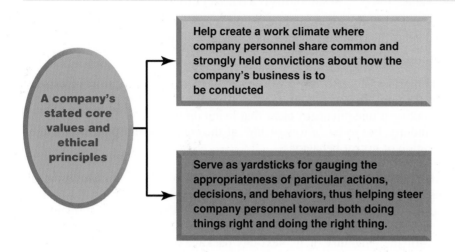

Transforming Core Values and Ethical Standards into Cultural Norms   Once values and ethical standards have been formally adopted, they must be institutionalized in the company's policies and practices and embedded in the conduct of company personnel. This can be done in a number of different ways.[5] Tradition-steeped companies with a rich folklore rely heavily on word-of-mouth indoctrination and the power of tradition to instill values and enforce ethical conduct. But most companies employ a variety of techniques, drawing on some or all of the following:

> A company's values statement and code of ethics communicate expectations of how employees should conduct themselves in the workplace.

1. Giving explicit attention to values and ethics in recruiting and hiring to screen out applicants who do not exhibit compatible character traits.

2. Incorporating the statement of values and the code of ethics into orientation programs for new employees and training courses for managers and employees.

3. Having senior executives frequently reiterate the importance and role of company values and ethical principles at company events and in internal communications to employees.

4. Using values statements and codes of ethical conduct as benchmarks for judging the appropriateness of company policies and operating practices.

5. Making the display of core values and ethical principles a big factor in evaluating each person's job performance—there's no better way to win the attention and commitment of company personnel than by using the degree to which individuals observe core values and ethical standards as a basis for compensation increases and promotion.

6. Making sure that managers, from the CEO down to frontline supervisors, are diligent in stressing the importance of ethical conduct and observance of core values. Line managers at all levels must give serious and continuous attention to the task of explaining how the values and ethical code apply in their areas.

7. Encouraging everyone to use his or her influence in helping enforce obser- vance of core values and ethical standards—strong peer pressure to exhibit core values and ethical standards is a deterrent to wayward behavior.

8. Periodically having ceremonial occasions to recognize individuals and groups who display the company values and ethical principles.

9. Instituting ethics enforcement procedures.

To deeply ingrain the stated core values and high ethical standards, companies must turn them into *strictly enforced cultural norms.* They must put a stake in the ground, making it unequivocally clear that living up to the company's values and ethical standards has to be "a way of life" at the company and that there will be little toleration of errant behavior.

The Role of Stories   Frequently, a significant part of a company's cul- ture is captured in the stories that get told over and over again to illustrate to newcomers the importance of certain values and the depth of commitment that various company personnel have displayed. One of the folktales at FedEx, world renowned for the reliability of its next-day package delivery guarantee, is about a deliveryman who had been given the wrong key to a FedEx drop box. Rather than leave the packages in the drop box until the next day when the right key was available, the deliveryman unbolted the drop box from its base, loaded it into the truck, and took it back to the station. There, the box was pried open and the con- tents removed and sped on their way to their destination the next day. Nordstrom keeps a scrapbook commemorating the heroic acts of its employees and uses it as a regular reminder of the above-and-beyond-the-call-of-duty behaviors that employees are encouraged to display. When a customer was unable to find a shoe she was looking for at Nordstrom, a salesman found the shoe at a competing store and had it shipped to her, at Nordstrom's expense.[6] At Frito-Lay, there are dozens of stories about truck drivers who went to extraordinary lengths in overcoming adverse weather conditions in order to make scheduled deliveries to retail custom- ers and keep store shelves stocked with Frito-Lay products. At Microsoft, there are stories of the long hours programmers put in, the emotional peaks and valleys in encountering and overcoming coding problems, the exhilaration of complet- ing a complex program on schedule, the satisfaction of working on cutting-edge projects, the rewards of being part of a team responsible for a popular new soft- ware program, and the tradition of competing aggressively. Such stories serve the valuable purpose of illustrating the kinds of behavior the company reveres and inspiring company personnel to perform similarly. Moreover, each retelling of a legendary story puts a bit more peer pressure on company personnel to display core values and do their part in keeping the company's traditions alive.

Perpetuating the Culture   Once established, company cultures are perpetuated in six important ways: (1) by screening and selecting new employees that will mesh well with the culture, (2) by systematic indoctrination of new members in the culture's fundamentals, (3) by the efforts of senior managers to reiterate core values in daily conversations and pronouncements, (4) by the telling and retelling of company legends, (5) by regular ceremonies honoring employees who display desired cultural behaviors, and (6) by visibly rewarding those who display cultural norms and penalizing those who don't.[7] *The more new employees a company is hiring, the more important it becomes to screen job applicants every bit as much for how well their values, beliefs, and personalities match up with the* *culture as for their technical skills and experience.* For example, a company that stresses operating with integrity and fairness has to hire people who themselves have integrity and place a high value on fair play. A company whose culture revolves around creativity, product innovation, and leading change has to screen new hires for their ability to think outside the box, generate new ideas, and thrive in a climate of rapid change and ambiguity. Southwest Airlines—whose two core values, "LUV" and fun, permeate the work environment and whose objective is to ensure that passengers have a positive and enjoyable flying experience—goes to considerable lengths to hire flight attendants and gate personnel who are witty, cheery, and outgoing and who display "whistle while you work" attitudes. Fast-growing companies risk creating a culture by chance rather than by design if they rush to hire employees mainly for their talents and credentials and neglect to screen out candidates whose values, philosophies, and personalities aren't a good fit with the organizational character, vision, and strategy being articulated by the company's senior executives.

As a rule, companies are careful to hire people who they believe will fit in and embrace the prevailing culture. And, usually, job seekers lean toward accepting jobs at companies where they feel comfortable with the atmosphere and the people they will be working with. Employees who don't fit in well at a company tend to leave quickly, while employees who thrive and are pleased with the work environment stay on, eventually moving up the ranks to positions of greater responsibility. The longer people stay at an organization, the more that they come to embrace and mirror the corporate culture—their values and beliefs tend to be molded by mentors, co-workers, company training programs, and the reward structure. Normally, employees who have worked at a company for a long time play a major role in indoctrinating new employees into the culture.

Forces That Cause a Company's Culture to Evolve However, cultures aren't static—just like strategy and organization structure, they evolve. New challenges in the marketplace, revolutionary technologies, and shifting internal conditions—especially eroding business prospects, an internal crisis, or top executive turnover—tend to breed new ways of doing things and, in turn, drive cultural evolution. An incoming CEO who decides to shake up the existing business and take it in new directions often triggers a cultural shift, perhaps one of major proportions. Likewise, diversification into new businesses, expansion into foreign countries, rapid growth that brings an influx of new employees, and merger with or acquisition of another company can all precipitate significant cultural change.

Company Cultures Can Be Strongly or Weakly Embedded

Company cultures vary widely in strength and influence. Some are strongly embedded and have a big influence on a company's operating practices and the behavior of company personnel. Others are weakly ingrained and have little effect on behaviors and how company activities are conducted.

Strong-Culture Companies The hallmark of a **strong-culture company** is the dominating presence of certain deeply rooted values, behavioral norms, and operating approaches that are widely shared and "regulate" the conduct of a company's business and the climate of its workplace.[8] Strong cultures emerge over a

CORE CONCEPT

In a **strong-culture company,** deeply rooted values and norms of behavior are widely shared and regulate the conduct of the company's business.

period of years (sometimes decades) and are never an overnight phenomenon. In strong-culture companies, senior managers make a point of reiterating the company's principles and values to organization members and explaining how they relate to its business environment. But, more importantly, the managers make a conscious effort to display these principles in their own actions and behavior—they walk the talk and *insist* that *company values and business principles be reflected in the decisions and actions taken by all company personnel.* An unequivocal expectation that company personnel will act and behave in accordance with the adopted values and ways of doing business leads to two important outcomes: (1) Over time, the values come to be widely shared by rank-and-file employees—people who dislike the culture tend to leave—and (2) individuals encounter strong peer pressure from co-workers to observe the culturally approved norms and behaviors. Hence, a strongly implanted corporate culture ends up having a powerful influence on behavior because so many company personnel are accepting of cultural traditions and because this acceptance is reinforced by both management expectations and co-worker peer pressure to conform to cultural norms.

Two factors contribute to the development of strong cultures: (1) a founder or strong leader who established core values, principles, and practices that are viewed as having contributed to the success of the company, and (2) a sincere, long-standing company commitment to operating the business according to these established traditions and values, thereby creating an internal environment that supports decision making based on cultural norms. Continuity of leadership, low workforce turnover, geographic concentration, and considerable organizational success all contribute to the emergence and sustainability of a strong culture.[9]

In strong-culture companies, values and behavioral norms are so ingrained that they can endure leadership changes at the top—although their strength can erode over time if new CEOs cease to nurture them or move aggressively to institute cultural adjustments. The cultural norms in a strong-culture company typically do not change much as strategy evolves, either because the culture constrains the choice of new strategies or because the dominant traits of the culture are somewhat strategy-neutral and compatible with evolving versions of the company's strategy.

Weak-Culture Companies

In direct contrast to strong-culture companies, weak-culture companies lack values and principles that are consistently preached or widely shared (sometimes because the company has had a series of CEOs with differing values and differing views about how the company's business ought to be conducted). As a consequence, few widely revered traditions and few culture-induced norms are evident in employee behavior or operating practices. Because top executives at a weak-culture company don't repeatedly espouse any particular business philosophy or exhibit long-standing commitment to particular values or behavioral norms, individuals encounter little pressure to do things in particular ways. A weak company culture breeds no strong employee allegiance to what the company stands for or to operating the business in well-defined ways. While individual employees may well have some bonds of identification with and loyalty toward their department, their colleagues, their union, or their immediate boss, there's neither passion about the company nor emotional commitment to what it is trying to accomplish—a condition that often results in many employees viewing their company as just a place to work and their job as just a way to make a living.

As a consequence, *weak cultures provide little or no assistance in executing strategy* because there are no traditions, beliefs, values, common bonds, or behavioral norms that management can use as levers to mobilize commitment to executing the chosen strategy. The only plus of a weak culture is that it does not usually pose a strong barrier to strategy execution, but the negative of not providing any support means that culture building has to be high on management's action agenda. Without a work climate that channels organizational energy in the direction of good strategy execution, managers are left with the options of either using compensation incentives and other motivational devices to mobilize employee commitment, supervising and monitoring employee actions more closely, or trying to establish cultural roots that will in time start to nurture the strategy execution process.

Why Corporate Cultures Matter to the Strategy Execution Process

Unlike weak cultures, strong cultures can have a powerful effect on the strategy execution process. This effect may be *positive or negative* since a company's present culture and work climate may or may not be compatible with what is needed for effective implementation and execution of the chosen strategy. When a company's present culture promotes attitudes, behaviors, and ways of doing things that are conducive to first-rate strategy execution, the culture functions as a valuable ally in the strategy execution process.

For example, a corporate culture characterized by frugality and thrift nurtures employee actions to identify cost-saving opportunities—the very behavior needed for successful execution of a low-cost leadership strategy. A culture built around such business principles as outstanding customer satisfaction, operating excellence, and employee empowerment promotes employee behaviors and an esprit de corps that facilitate execution of strategies keyed to high product quality and superior customer service. A culture in which taking initiative, exhibiting creativity, taking risks, and embracing change are the behavioral norms is conducive to successful execution of product innovation and technological leadership strategies.[10]

A culture that is grounded in actions, behaviors, and work practices that are conducive to good strategy implementation assists the strategy execution effort in three ways:[11]

1. *A culture that is well matched to the requirements of the strategy execution effort focuses the attention of employees on what is most important to this effort.* Moreover, it directs their behavior and serves as a guide to their decision making. In this manner, it can align the efforts and decisions of employees throughout the firm and minimize the need for direct supervision.

2. *Culture-induced peer pressure further induces company personnel to do things in a manner that aids the cause of good strategy execution.* The stronger the culture (the more widely shared and deeply held the values), the more effective peer pressure is in shaping and supporting the strategy execution effort. Research has shown that strong group norms can shape employee behavior even more powerfully than can financial incentives.[12]

3. *A company culture that is consistent with the requirements for good strategy execution can energize employees, deepen their commitment to execute the*

> **LO 2**
>
> Gain an understanding of how and why a company's culture can aid the drive for proficient strategy execution and operating excellence.

> A strong culture that encourages actions, behaviors, and work practices conducive to good strategy execution adds significantly to the power and effectiveness of a company's strategy execution effort.

strategy flawlessly, and enhance worker productivity in the process. When a company's culture is grounded in many of the needed strategy-executing behaviors, employees feel genuinely better about their jobs, the company they work for, and the merits of what the company is trying to accomplish. As a consequence, greater numbers of company personnel exhibit passion in their work and exert their best efforts to execute the strategy and achieve performance targets.

In sharp contrast, when a culture is in conflict with what is required to execute the company's strategy well, a strong culture becomes a hindrance to the success of the implementation effort.[13] Some of the very behaviors needed to execute the strategy successfully run contrary to the attitudes, behaviors, and operating practices embedded in the prevailing culture. Such a clash poses a real dilemma for company personnel. Should they be loyal to the culture and company traditions (to which they are likely to be emotionally attached) and thus resist or be indifferent to actions that will promote better strategy execution—a choice that will certainly weaken the drive for good strategy execution? Alternatively, should they go along with the strategy execution effort and engage in actions that run counter to the culture—a choice that will likely impair morale and lead to a less-than-wholehearted commitment to management's strategy execution efforts? Neither choice leads to desirable outcomes. Culture-bred resistance to the actions and behaviors needed for good strategy execution, particularly if strong and widespread, poses a formidable hurdle that must be cleared for a strategy's execution to get very far.

This says something important about the task of managing the strategy execution process: *Closely aligning corporate culture with the requirements for proficient strategy execution merits the full attention of senior executives.* The culture-building objective is to create a work climate and style of operating that mobilize the energy and behavior of company personnel squarely behind efforts to execute strategy competently. The more deeply that management can embed execution-supportive ways of doing things, the more that management can rely on the culture to automatically steer company personnel toward behaviors and work practices that aid good strategy execution and veer from doing things that impede it. Moreover, culturally astute managers understand that nourishing the right cultural environment not only adds power to their push for proficient strategy execution but also promotes strong employee identification with and commitment to the company's vision, performance targets, and strategy.

> It is in management's best interest to dedicate considerable effort to establishing a corporate culture that encourages behaviors and work practices conducive to good strategy execution.

Healthy Cultures That Aid Good Strategy Execution

A strong culture, provided it embraces execution-supportive attitudes, behaviors, and work practices, is definitely a healthy culture. Two other types of cultures exist that tend to be healthy and largely supportive of good strategy execution: high-performance cultures and adaptive cultures.

High-Performance Cultures Some companies have so-called high-performance cultures where the standout traits are a "can-do" spirit, pride in doing things right, no-excuses accountability, and a pervasive results-oriented work climate in which people go all out to meet or beat stretch objectives.[14] In high-performance cultures, there's a strong sense of involvement on the part of company personnel and emphasis on individual initiative and effort. Performance expectations are clearly delineated for the company as a whole, for each organizational unit, and for each individual. Issues and problems are promptly addressed; there's a razor-sharp focus on what needs to be done. The clear and unyielding expectation is that all company personnel, from senior executives to frontline employees, will display high-performance behaviors and a passion for making the company successful. Such a culture—supported by constructive pressure to achieve good results—is a valuable contributor to good strategy execution and operating excellence. Results-oriented cultures are permeated with a spirit of achievement and have a good track record in meeting or beating performance targets.[15]

The challenge in creating a high-performance culture is to inspire high loyalty and dedication on the part of employees, such that they are energized to put forth their very best efforts to do things right and be unusually productive. Managers have to take pains to reinforce constructive behavior, reward top performers, and purge habits and behaviors that stand in the way of high productivity and good results. They must work at knowing the strengths and weaknesses of their subordinates, so as to better match talent with task and enable people to make meaningful contributions by doing what they do best.[16] They have to stress learning from mistakes and building on strengths and must put an unrelenting emphasis on moving forward and making good progress—in effect, there has to be a disciplined, performance-focused approach to managing the organization.

Adaptive Cultures
The hallmark of adaptive corporate cultures is willingness on the part of organization members to accept change and take on the challenge of introducing and executing new strategies.[17] Company personnel share a feeling of confidence that the organization can deal with whatever threats and opportunities arise; they are receptive to risk taking, experimentation, innovation, and changing strategies and practices. The work climate is supportive of managers and employees at all ranks who propose or initiate useful change. Internal entrepreneurship on the part of individuals and groups is encouraged and rewarded. Senior executives seek out, support, and promote individuals who exercise initiative, spot opportunities for improvement, and display the skills to implement them. Managers openly evaluate ideas and suggestions, fund initiatives to develop new or better products, and take prudent risks to pursue emerging market opportunities. As in high-performance cultures, the company exhibits a proactive approach to identifying issues, evaluating the implications and options, and moving ahead quickly with workable solutions. Strategies and traditional operating practices are modified as needed to adjust to or take advantage of changes in the business environment.

But why is change so willingly embraced in an adaptive culture? Why are organization members not fearful of how change will affect them? Why does an adaptive culture not break down from the force of ongoing changes in strategy, operating practices, and approaches to strategy execution? The answers lie in two distinctive and dominant traits of an adaptive culture: (1) Any changes in operating practices and behaviors must *not* compromise core values and long-standing business principles (since they are at the root of the culture), and (2) the changes that are instituted must satisfy the legitimate interests of stakeholders—customers, employees, shareowners, suppliers, and the communities where the company operates.[18] In other words, what sustains an adaptive culture is that organization members

> As a company's strategy evolves, an adaptive culture is a definite ally in the strategy-implementing, strategy-executing process as compared to cultures that are resistant to change.

perceive the changes that management is trying to institute as *legitimate* and in keeping with the core values and business principles that form the heart and soul of the culture.[19] Not surprisingly, company personnel are usually more receptive to change when their employment security is not threatened and when they view new duties or job assignments as part of the process of adapting to new conditions. Should workforce downsizing be necessary, it is important that layoffs be handled humanely and employee departures be made as painless as possible.

Technology companies, software companies, and Internet-based companies are good illustrations of organizations with adaptive cultures. Such companies thrive on change—driving it, leading it, and capitalizing on it. Companies like Google, Intel, Cisco Systems, eBay, Amazon.com, and Apple cultivate the capability to act and react rapidly. They are avid practitioners of entrepreneurship and innovation, with a demonstrated willingness to take bold risks to create altogether new products, new businesses, and new industries. To create and nurture a culture that can adapt rapidly to shifting business conditions, they make a point of staffing their organizations with people who are flexible, who rise to the challenge of change, and who have an aptitude for adapting well to new circumstances.

In fast-changing business environments, a corporate culture that is receptive to altering organizational practices and behaviors is a virtual necessity. However, adaptive cultures work to the advantage of all companies, not just those in rapid-change environments. Every company operates in a market and business climate that is changing to one degree or another and that, in turn, requires internal operating responses and new behaviors on the part of organization members.

Unhealthy Cultures That Impede Good Strategy Execution

The distinctive characteristic of an unhealthy corporate culture is the presence of counterproductive cultural traits that adversely impact the work climate and company performance.[20] Five particularly unhealthy cultural traits are hostility to change, heavily politicized decision making, insular thinking, behaviors that are driven by greed and a disregard for ethical standards, and the presence of incompatible, clashing subcultures.

Change-Resistant Cultures   In contrast to adaptive cultures, change-resistant cultures—where skepticism about the importance of new developments and a fear of change are the norm—place a premium on not making mistakes, prompting managers to lean toward safe, conservative options intended to maintain the status quo, protect their power base, and guard the interests of their immediate work groups. When such companies encounter business environments with accelerating change, going slow on altering traditional ways of doing things can be a serious liability. Under these conditions, change-resistant cultures encourage a number of undesirable or unhealthy behaviors—viewing circumstances myopically, avoiding risks, not capitalizing on emerging opportunities, taking a lax approach to both product innovation and continuous improvement in performing value chain activities, and responding more slowly than is warranted to market change. In change-resistant cultures, word quickly gets around that proposals to do things differently face an uphill battle and that people who champion them may be seen as something of a nuisance. Executives who don't value managers or employees with initiative and new ideas put a damper on product innovation, experimentation, and efforts to improve. At the same time, change-resistant companies have little appetite for being first movers or fast followers, believing that being in the forefront of change is too risky and that acting too quickly increases vulnerability to costly mistakes. Hostility to change is most often found in companies with multilayered management bureaucracies that have enjoyed considerable market success in years past and that are wedded to the "We have done it this way for years" syndrome. Before filing bankruptcy in 2009, General Motors was a classic example of a company whose change-resistant bureaucracy was slow to adapt to fundamental changes in its markets, preferring to cling to the traditions, operating practices, and business approaches that had at one time made it the global industry leader.

Politicized Cultures What makes a politicized internal environment so unhealthy is that political infighting consumes a great deal of organizational energy, often with the result that what's best for the company takes a backseat to political maneuvering. In companies where internal politics pervades the work climate, empire-building managers jealously guard their decision-making prerogatives. They have their own agendas and operate the work units under their supervision as autonomous "fiefdoms"; the positions they take on issues are usually aimed at protecting or expanding their own turf. Collaboration with other organizational units is viewed with suspicion, and cross-unit cooperation occurs grudgingly. The support or opposition of politically influential executives and/or coalitions among departments with vested interests in a particular outcome tends to shape what actions the company takes. All this political maneuvering takes away from efforts to execute strategy with real proficiency and frustrates company personnel who are less political and more inclined to do what is in the company's best interests.

Insular, Inwardly Focused Cultures Sometimes a company reigns as an industry leader or enjoys great market success for so long that its personnel start to believe they have all the answers or can develop them on their own. There is a strong tendency to neglect what customers are saying and how their needs and expectations are changing. Such confidence in the correctness of its approach to business and an unflinching belief in the company's competitive superiority breeds arrogance, prompting company personnel to discount the merits of what outsiders are doing and the payoff from studying best-in-class performers. Insular thinking, internally driven solutions, and a must-be-invented-here mindset come to permeate the corporate culture. An inwardly focused corporate culture gives rise to managerial inbreeding and a failure to recruit people who can offer fresh thinking and outside perspectives. The big risk of insular cultural thinking is that the company can underestimate the capabilities and accomplishments of rival companies and overestimate its own progress—until its loss of market position makes the realities obvious.

Unethical and Greed-Driven Cultures Companies that have little regard for ethical standards or that are run by executives driven by greed and ego gratification are scandals waiting to happen, as discussed in Chapter 9. Executives exude the negatives of arrogance, ego, greed, and an "ends-justify-the-means" mentality in pursuing stretch revenue and profitability targets.[21] Senior managers wink at unethical behavior and may cross over the line to unethical (and sometimes criminal) behavior themselves. They are prone to adopt accounting principles that make financial performance look better than it really is. Legions of companies have fallen prey to unethical behavior and greed, most notably WorldCom, Enron, Quest, HealthSouth, Adelphia, Tyco, Parmalat, Rite Aid, Hollinger International, Refco, Marsh & McLennan, Siemens, Countrywide Financial, and Stanford Financial Group, with executives being indicted and/or convicted of criminal behavior.

Incompatible Subcultures   Although it is common to speak about corporate culture in the singular, it is not unusual for companies to have multiple cultures (or subcultures).[22] Values, beliefs, and practices within a company sometimes vary significantly by department, geographic location, division, or business unit. As long as the subcultures are compatible with the overarching corporate culture and are supportive of the strategy execution efforts, this is not problematic. Multiple cultures pose an unhealthy situation when they are composed of incompatible subcultures that embrace conflicting business philosophies, support inconsistent approaches to strategy execution, and encourage incompatible methods of people management. Clashing subcultures can prevent a company from coordinating its efforts to craft and execute strategy and can distract company personnel from the business of business. When incompatible subcultures encourage the emergence of warring factions within the company, they are not just unhealthy—they are downright poisonous.

Incompatible subcultures arise most commonly because of important cultural differences between a company's culture and that of a recently acquired company or because of a merger between companies with cultural differences. Companies with M&A experience are quite alert to the importance of cultural compatibility in making acquisitions and the need to integrate the cultures of newly acquired companies—cultural due diligence is often as important as financial due diligence in deciding whether to go forward on an acquisition or merger. On a number of occasions, companies decided to pass on acquiring particular companies because of culture conflicts they believed would be hard to resolve.

Changing a Problem Culture: The Role of Leadership

LO 3

Learn the kinds of actions management can take to change a problem corporate culture.

When a strong culture is unhealthy or otherwise out of sync with the actions and behaviors needed to execute the strategy successfully, the culture must be changed as rapidly as can be managed. While correcting a strategy-culture conflict can occasionally mean revamping a company's approach to strategy execution to better fit the company's culture, more usually it means altering aspects of the mismatched culture to better enable first-rate strategy execution. The more entrenched the mismatched or unhealthy aspects of a company culture, the more likely the culture will impede strategy execution and the greater the need for change.

Changing a problem culture is among the toughest management tasks because of the heavy anchor of ingrained behaviors and attitudes. It is natural for company personnel to cling to familiar practices and to be wary, if not hostile, to new approaches of how things are to be done. Consequently, it takes concerted management action over a period of time to root out unconstructive behaviors and replace them with new ways of doing things deemed more conducive to executing the strategy.

The single most visible factor that distinguishes successful culture-change efforts from failed attempts is competent leadership at the top. Great power is needed to force major cultural change and overcome the "springback" resistance of entrenched cultures—and great power is possessed only by the most senior executives, especially the CEO. However, while top management must be out front leading the effort, marshaling support for a new culture and instilling the desired cultural behaviors is a job for the whole management team. Middle managers and frontline supervisors play a key role in implementing the new work practices and operating approaches, helping win rank-and-file acceptance of and support for the desired behavioral norms.

As shown in Figure 12.2, the first step in fixing a problem culture is for top management to identify those facets of the present culture that are dysfunctional and pose obstacles to executing new strategic initiatives and meeting company performance targets. Second, managers must clearly define the desired new behaviors and features of the culture they want to create. Third, managers have to convince company personnel of why the present culture poses problems and why and how new behaviors and operating approaches will improve company performance—the case for cultural reform has to be persuasive. Fourth, and most important, all the talk about remodeling the present culture has to be followed swiftly by visible, forceful actions to promote the desired new behaviors and work practices—actions that company personnel will interpret as a determined top management commitment to bringing about a different work climate and new ways of operating.

Making a Compelling Case for Culture Change

The way for management to begin a major remodeling of the corporate culture is by selling company personnel on the need for new-style behaviors and work practices. This means making a compelling case for why the culture-remodeling efforts are in the organization's best interests and why company personnel should wholeheartedly join the effort to doing things somewhat differently. Skeptics and opinion leaders have to be convinced that all is not well with the status quo. This can be done by:

- Explaining why and how certain behavioral norms and work practices in the current culture pose obstacles to good execution of strategic initiatives.
- Explaining how new behaviors and work practices will be more advantageous and produce better results. Effective culture-change leaders are good at telling stories to describe the new values and desired behaviors and connect them to everyday practices.
- Citing reasons why the current strategy has to be modified, if the need for cultural change is due to a change in strategy. This includes explaining why the new strategic initiatives will bolster the company's competitiveness and performance and how a change in culture can help in executing the new strategy.

It is essential for the CEO and other top executives to talk personally to company personnel all across the company about the reasons for modifying work practices and culture-related behaviors. Senior officers and department heads have to play a lead role in explaining the need for a change in behavioral norms to those they manage—and the explanations will likely have to be repeated many times. For the culture-change effort to be successful, frontline supervisors and employee opinion leaders must be won over to the cause, which means convincing them of the merits of *practicing* and *enforcing* cultural norms at every level of the organization, from the highest to the lowest. Arguments for new ways of doing things and new work practices tend to be embraced more readily if employees understand how they will benefit company stakeholders (particularly customers, employees, and shareholders).

Figure 12.2   **Steps to Take in Changing a Problem Culture**

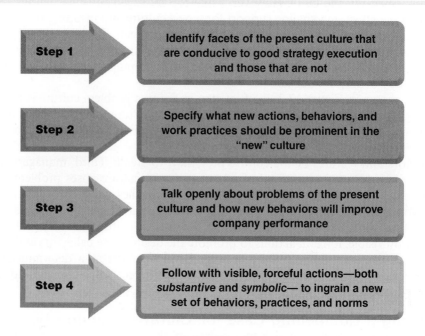

Until a large majority of employees accept the need for a new culture and agree that different work practices and behaviors are called for, there's more work to be done in selling company personnel on the whys and wherefores of culture change. Building widespread organizational support requires taking every opportunity to repeat the message of why the new work practices, operating approaches, and behaviors are good for company stakeholders.

Management's efforts to make a persuasive case for changing what is deemed to be a problem culture must be *followed quickly* by forceful, high-profile actions across several fronts. The actions to implant the new culture must be both substantive and symbolic.

Substantive Culture-Changing Actions   No culture change effort can get very far with just talk about the need for different actions, behaviors, and work practices. Company executives must give the culture-change effort some teeth by initiating *a series of actions* that company personnel will see as credible and unmistakably indicative of the seriousness of management's commitment to cultural change. The strongest signs that management is truly committed to instilling a new culture include:

- Replacing key executives who are stonewalling needed organizational and cultural changes.
- Promoting individuals who have stepped forward to advocate the shift to a different culture and who can serve as role models for the desired cultural behavior.
- Appointing outsiders with the desired cultural attributes to high-profile positions—bringing in new-breed managers sends an unmistakable message that a new era is dawning.
- Screening all candidates for new positions carefully, hiring only those who appear to fit in with the new culture.

- Mandating that all company personnel attend culture-training programs to learn more about the new work practices and to better understand the culture-related actions and behaviors that are expected.

- Designing compensation incentives that boost the pay of teams and individuals who display the desired cultural behaviors. Company personnel are much more inclined to exhibit the desired kinds of actions and behaviors when it is in their financial best interest to do so.

- Revising policies and procedures in ways that will help drive cultural change.

Executives must take care to launch enough companywide culture-change actions at the outset so as to leave no room for doubt that management is dead serious about changing the present culture and that a cultural transformation is inevitable. The series of actions initiated by top management must create lots of hallway talk across the whole company, get the change process off to a fast start, and be followed by unrelenting efforts to firmly establish the new work practices, desired behaviors, and style of operating as "standard."

Symbolic Culture-Changing Actions   There's also an important place for symbolic managerial actions to alter a problem culture and tighten the strategy-culture fit. The most important symbolic actions are those that top executives take to *lead by example.* For instance, if the organization's strategy involves a drive to become the industry's low-cost producer, senior managers must display frugality in their own actions and decisions: inexpensive decorations in the executive suite, conservative expense accounts and entertainment allowances, a lean staff in the corporate office, scrutiny of budget requests, few executive perks, and so on. At Walmart, all the executive offices are simply decorated; executives are habitually frugal in their own actions, and they are zealous in their efforts to control costs and promote greater efficiency. At Nucor, one of the world's low-cost producers of steel products, executives fly coach class and use taxis at airports rather than limousines. If the culture-change imperative is to be more responsive to customers' needs and to pleasing customers, the CEO can instill greater customer awareness by requiring all officers and executives to spend a significant portion of each week talking with customers about their needs. Top executives must be alert to the fact that company personnel will be watching their actions and decisions to see if their actions match their rhetoric. Hence, they need to make sure their current decisions and behaviors will be construed as consistent with the new-culture values and norms.[23]

Another category of symbolic actions includes holding ceremonial events to single out and honor people whose actions and performance exemplify what is called for in the new culture. A point is made of holding events to celebrate each culture-change success (and any other outcome that management would like to see happen again). Executives sensitive to their role in promoting strategy-culture fit make a habit of appearing at ceremonial functions to praise individuals and groups that exemplify the desired behaviors. They show up at employee training programs to stress strategic priorities, values, ethical principles, and cultural norms. Every group gathering is seen as an opportunity to repeat and ingrain values, praise good deeds, expound on the merits of the new culture, and cite instances of how the new work practices and operating approaches have worked to good advantage.

The use of symbols in culture building is widespread. Many universities give outstanding teacher awards each year to symbolize their commitment to good teaching and their esteem for instructors who display exceptional classroom talents. Numerous businesses have employee-of-the-month awards. The military has a long-standing custom of awarding ribbons and medals for exemplary actions. Avon awards an array of prizes ceremoniously to its beauty consultants for reaching various sales plateaus.

How Long Does It Take to Change a Problem Culture?   Planting and growing the seeds of a new culture require a determined effort by the chief executive and other senior managers. A sustained and persistent effort to reinforce the culture at every opportunity through both word and deed is required. Changing a problem culture is never a short-term exercise. It takes time for a new culture to emerge and prevail; overnight transformations simply don't occur. And it takes even longer for a new culture to become deeply embedded. The bigger the organization and the greater the cultural shift needed to produce an execution-supportive fit, the longer it takes. In large companies, fixing a problem culture and instilling a new set of attitudes and behaviors can take two to five years. In fact, it is usually tougher to reform an entrenched problematic culture than it is to instill a strategy-supportive culture from scratch in a brand new organization.

LEADING THE STRATEGY EXECUTION PROCESS

LO 4

Understand what constitutes effective managerial leadership in achieving superior strategy execution.

For an enterprise to execute its strategy in truly proficient fashion and approach operating excellence, top executives have to take the lead in the implementation/execution process and personally drive the pace of progress. The have to be out in the field, seeing for themselves how well operations are going, gathering information firsthand, and gauging the progress being made. Proficient strategy execution requires company managers to be diligent and adept in spotting problems, learning what obstacles lie in the path of good execution, and then clearing the way for progress—the goal must be to produce better results speedily and productively. There has to be constructive, but unrelenting, pressure on organizational units to (1) demonstrate excellence in all dimensions of strategy execution and (2) do so on a consistent basis—ultimately, that's what will enable a well-crafted strategy to achieve the desired performance results.

The strategy execution process must be driven by mandates to get things on the right track and show good results. The specifics of how to implement a strategy and deliver the intended results must start with understanding the requirements for good strategy execution. Afterward comes a diagnosis of the organization's preparedness to execute the strategic initiatives and decisions as to which of several ways to proceed to move forward and achieve the targeted results.[24] In general, leading the drive for good strategy execution and operating excellence calls for three actions on the part of the manager in charge:

- Staying on top of what is happening and closely monitoring progress.
- Putting constructive pressure on the organization to execute the strategy well and achieve operating excellence.
- Initiating corrective actions to improve strategy execution and achieve the targeted performance results.

Staying on Top of How Well Things Are Going

To stay on top of how well the strategy execution process is going, senior executives have to tap into information from a wide range of sources. In addition to talking with key subordinates and reviewing the latest operating results, watching the competitive reactions of rival firms, and visiting with key customers and suppliers to get their perspectives, they usually make regular visits to various company facilities and talk with many different company personnel at many different organization levels—a technique often labeled **managing by walking around (MBWA).** Most managers attach great importance to spending time with people at company facilities, asking questions, listening to their opinions and concerns, and gathering firsthand information about how well aspects of the strategy execution process are going. Facilities tours and face-to-face contacts with operating-level employees give executives a good grasp of what progress is being made, what problems are being encountered, and whether additional resources or different approaches may be needed. Just as important, MBWA provides opportunities to give encouragement, lift spirits, shift attention from the old to the new priorities, and create some excitement—all of which can boost strategy execution efforts.

> **CORE CONCEPT**
>
> **Management by walking around (MBWA)** is one of the techniques that effective leaders use to stay informed about how well the strategy execution process is progressing.

Jeff Bezos, Amazon.com's CEO, is noted for his practice of MBWA, firing off a battery of questions when he tours facilities and insisting that Amazon managers spend time in the trenches with their people to prevent getting disconnected from the reality of what's happening.[25] Walmart executives have had a long-standing practice of spending two to three days every week visiting Walmart's stores and talking with store managers and employees. Sam Walton, Walmart's founder, insisted, "The key is to get out into the store and listen to what the associates have to say." Jack Welch, the highly effective CEO of General Electric (GE) from 1980 to 2001, not only spent several days each month personally visiting GE operations and talking with major customers but also arranged his schedule so that he could spend time exchanging information and ideas with GE managers from all over the world who were attending classes at the company's leadership development center near GE's headquarters.

Many manufacturing executives make a point of strolling the factory floor to talk with workers and meeting regularly with union officials. Some managers operate out of open cubicles in big spaces populated with open cubicles for other personnel so that they can interact easily and frequently with co-workers. Managers at some companies host weekly get-togethers (often on Friday afternoons) to create a regular opportunity for information to flow freely between down-the-line employees and executives.

Putting Constructive Pressure on Organizational Units to Execute the Strategy Well and Achieve Operating Excellence

Managers have to be out front in mobilizing organizational energy behind the drive for good strategy execution and operating excellence. Part of the leadership task entails nurturing a results-oriented work climate, where performance standards are high and a spirit of achievement is pervasive. Successfully leading the effort to foster a results-oriented, high-performance culture generally entails such leadership actions and managerial practices as:

- *Treating employees as valued partners in the drive for operating excellence and good business performance.* Some companies symbolize the value of individual employees and the importance of their contributions by referring to them as cast members (Disney), crew members (McDonald's), partners (Starbucks), or associates (Walmart, W. L. Gore, and Marriott International). Very often, there is a strong company commitment to providing thorough training, offering attractive compensation and career opportunities, emphasizing promotion from within, providing a high degree of job security, and otherwise making employees feel well treated and valued.

- *Fostering an esprit de corps that energizes organization members.* The task here is to skillfully use people-management practices calculated to build morale, foster pride in doing things right, promote teamwork, create a strong sense of involvement on the part of company personnel, win their emotional commitment, and inspire them to do their best.[26]

- *Using empowerment to help create a fully engaged workforce.* Top executives must seek to engage the full organization in the strategy execution effort. A fully engaged workforce, one where individuals bring their best to work every day, is necessary to produce great results.[27] So is having a group of dedicated managers committed to making a difference in their organization. The two best things top-level executives can do to create a fully engaged organization are (1) delegate authority to middle and lower-level managers to get the implementation/execution process moving and (2) empower rank-and-file employees to act on their own initiative. Operating excellence requires that everybody contribute ideas, exercise initiative and creativity in performing his or her work, and have a desire to do things in the best possible manner.

- *Making champions out of the people who spearhead new ideas and/or turn in winning performances.* The best champions and change agents are persistent, competitive, tenacious, committed, and fanatical about seeing their ideas through to success. It is particularly important that people who champion an unsuccessful idea not be punished or sidelined but, rather, be encouraged to try again. Encouraging lots of "tries" is important, since many ideas won't pan out.

- *Setting stretch objectives and clearly communicating an expectation that company personnel are to give their best in achieving performance targets.* Stretch objectives—those beyond an organization's current capacities—can sometimes spur organization members to increase their resolve and redouble their efforts to execute the strategy flawlessly and ultimately reach the stretch objectives. When stretch objectives are met, the satisfaction of achievement and boost to employee morale can result in an even higher level of organizational drive.

- *Using the tools of benchmarking best practices, business process reengineering, TQM, and Six Sigma to focus attention on continuous improvement.* These are proven approaches to getting better operating results and facilitating better strategy execution.

- *Using the full range of motivational techniques and compensation incentives to inspire company personnel, nurture a results-oriented work climate, and enforce high-performance standards.* Managers cannot mandate innovative improvements by simply exhorting people to "be creative," nor can they make continuous progress toward operating excellence with directives to "try harder." Rather, they must foster a culture where innovative ideas and experimentation with new ways of doing things can blossom and thrive. Individuals and groups should be strongly encouraged to brainstorm, let their imaginations fly in all directions, and come up with proposals for improving how things are done. This means giving company personnel enough autonomy to stand out, excel, and contribute. And it means that the rewards for successful champions of new ideas and operating improvements should be large and visible.

• *Celebrating individual, group, and company successes.* Top management should miss no opportunity to express respect for individual employees and appreciation of extraordinary individual and group effort.[28] Companies like Avon, Tupperware, and McDonald's actively seek out reasons and opportunities to give pins, ribbons, buttons, badges, and medals for good showings by average performers—the idea being to express appreciation and give a motivational boost to people who stand out in doing ordinary jobs. General Electric and 3M Corporation make a point of ceremoniously honoring individuals who believe so strongly in their ideas that they take it on themselves to hurdle the bureaucracy, maneuver their projects through the system, and turn them into improved services, new products, or even new businesses.

While leadership efforts to instill a results-oriented, high-performance culture usually accentuate the positive, negative reinforcers abound too. Managers whose units consistently perform poorly must be replaced. Low-performing workers and people who reject the results-oriented cultural emphasis must be weeded out or at least employed differently. Average performers should be candidly counseled that they have limited career potential unless they show more progress in the form of additional effort, better skills, and improved ability to execute the strategy well and deliver good results.

Leading the Process of Making Corrective Adjustments

Since strategy execution takes place amid changing environmental and organizational circumstances, there is often a need for corrective adjustments. The process of making corrective adjustments in strategy execution varies according to the situation. In a crisis, taking remedial action fairly quickly is of the essence. But it still takes time to review the situation, examine the available data, identify and evaluate options (crunching whatever numbers may be appropriate to determine which options are likely to generate the best outcomes), and decide what to do. When the situation allows managers to proceed more deliberately in deciding when to make changes and what changes to make, most managers seem to prefer a process of incrementally solidifying commitment to a particular course of action.[29] The process that managers go through in deciding on corrective adjustments is essentially the same for both proactive and reactive changes: They sense needs, gather information, broaden and deepen their understanding of the situation, develop options and explore their pros and cons, put forth action proposals, strive for a consensus, and finally formally adopt an agreed-on course of action.[30] The time frame for deciding what corrective changes to initiate can be a few hours, a few days, a few weeks, or even a few months if the situation is particularly complicated.

Success in making corrective actions hinges on (1) a thorough analysis of the situation, (2) the exercise of good business judgment in deciding what actions to take, and (3) good implementation of the corrective actions that are initiated. Successful managers are skilled in getting an organization back on track rather quickly. They (and their staffs) are good at discerning what actions to take and in bringing them to a successful conclusion. Managers who struggle to show measurable progress in implementing corrective actions in a timely fashion are often candidates for being replaced.

The challenges of making the right corrective adjustments and leading a successful strategy execution effort are, without question, substantial.[31] Because each instance of executing strategy occurs under different organizational circumstances, the managerial agenda for executing strategy always needs to be situation-specific—there's no generic procedure to follow. But the job is definitely doable. Although there is no prescriptive answer to the question of exactly what to do, any of several courses of action may produce good results. And, as we said at the beginning of Chapter 10, executing strategy is an action-oriented, make-the-right-things-happen task that challenges a manager's ability to lead and direct organizational change, create or reinvent business processes, manage and motivate people, and achieve performance targets.

A FINAL WORD ON LEADING THE PROCESS OF CRAFTING AND EXECUTING STRATEGY

In practice, it is hard to separate leading the process of executing strategy from leading the other pieces of the strategy process. As we emphasized in Chapter 2, the job of crafting, implementing, and executing strategy consists of five inter-related and linked stages, with much looping and recycling to fine-tune and adjust the strategic vision, objectives, strategy, and implementation/execution approaches to fit one another and to fit changing circumstances. The process is continuous, and the conceptually separate acts of crafting and executing strategy blur together in real-world situations. The best tests of good strategic leadership are whether the company has a good strategy and business model, whether the strategy is being competently executed, and whether the enterprise is meeting or beating its performance targets. If these three conditions exist, then there is every reason to conclude that the company has good strategic leadership and is a well managed enterprise.

KEY POINTS

1. Corporate culture is the character of a company's internal work climate—as shaped by a system of *shared* values, beliefs, ethical standards, and traditions that in turn define behavioral norms, ingrained attitudes, accepted work practices, and styles of operating. A company's culture is important because it influences the organization's actions and approaches

to conducting business. In a very real sense, the culture is the company's organizational DNA.

2. The key features of a company's culture include the company's values and ethical standards, its approach to people management, its work atmosphere and company spirit, how its personnel interact, the behaviors awarded through incentives (both financial and symbolic), the traditions and oft-repeated "myths," and its manner of dealing with stakeholders.

3. A company's culture is grounded in and shaped by its core values and ethical standards. Core values and ethical principles serve two roles in the culture-building process: (1) They foster a work climate in which employees share common and strongly held convictions about how company business is to be conducted, and (2) they serve as yardsticks for gauging the appropriateness of particular actions, decisions, and behaviors, thus helping steer company personnel toward both doing things right and doing the right thing.

4. Company cultures vary widely in strength and influence. Some are strongly embedded and have a big impact on a company's practices and behavioral norms. Others are weak and have comparatively little influence on company operations.

5. Strong company cultures can have either positive or negative effects on strategy execution. When they are well matched to the behavioral requirements of the company's strategy implementation plan, they can be a powerful aid to strategy execution. A culture that is grounded in the types of actions and behaviors that are conducive to good strategy execution assists the effort in three ways:

    •   By focusing employee attention on the actions that are most important in the strategy execution effort.

    •   Through culture-induced peer pressure for employees to contribute to the success of the strategy execution effort.

    •   By energizing employees, deepening their commitment to the strategy execution effort, and increasing the productivity of their efforts

6. It is thus in management's best interest to dedicate considerable effort to establishing a strongly implanted corporate culture that encourages behaviors and work practices conducive to good strategy execution.

7. Strong corporate cultures that are conducive to good strategy execution are healthy cultures. So are high-performance cultures and adaptive cultures. The latter are particularly important in dynamic environments. Strong cultures can also be unhealthy. The five types of unhealthy cultures are (1) those that are change-resistant, (2) those that are characterized by heavily politicized decision making, (3) those that are insular and inwardly focused, (4) those that are ethically unprincipled and infused with greed, and (5) those that are composed of incompatible subcultures. All five impede good strategy execution.

8. Changing a company's culture, especially a strong one with traits that don't fit a new strategy's requirements, is a tough and often time-consuming challenge. Changing a culture requires competent leadership at the top. It requires making a compelling case for cultural change and employing both symbolic actions and substantive actions that unmistakably indicate serious commitment on the part of top management. The more that culture-driven

actions and behaviors fit what's needed for good strategy execution, the less managers must depend on policies, rules, procedures, and supervision to enforce what people should and should not do.

9. Leading the drive for good strategy execution and operating excellence calls for three actions on the part of the manager in charge:

   • Staying on top of what is happening and closely monitoring progress. This is often accomplished through managing by walking around (MBWA).

   • Putting constructive pressure on the organization to execute the strategy well and achieve operating excellence.

   • Initiating corrective actions to improve strategy execution and achieve the targeted performance results.

ASSURANCE OF LEARNING EXERCISES

LO 1, LO 2

1. Go to www.google.com. Click on the About Google link and then on the Corporate Info link. Under the Culture link, read what Google has to say about its culture. Also, in the "Our Philosophy" section, read "Ten things Google has found to be true." How do the "ten things" and Google's culture aid in management's attempts to execute the company's strategy?

LO 1, LO 2

2. Go to the Jobs section at www.intel.com, and see what Intel has to say about its culture under the links for Careers, Diversity, and The Workplace. Does what's on this Web site appear to be just recruiting propaganda, or does it convey the type of work climate that management is actually trying to create? Explain your answer.

LO 1, LO 2

3. Go to www.jnj.com, the Web site of Johnson & Johnson, and read the J&J Credo, which sets forth the company's responsibilities to customers, employees, the community, and shareholders. Then read the "Our Company" section. Why do you think the credo has resulted in numerous awards and accolades that recognize the company as a good corporate citizen?

LO 4

4. In the last couple of years, Liz Claiborne, Inc., has been engaged in efforts to turn around its faltering Mexx chain. Use your favorite browser to search for information on the turnaround plan at Mexx, and read at least two articles or reports on this subject. Describe in 1 to 2 pages the approach being taken to turn around the Mexx chain. In your opinion, have the managers involved been demonstrating the kind of internal leadership needed for superior strategy execution at Mexx? Explain your answer.

EXERCISES FOR SIMULATION PARTICIPANTS

LO 1, LO 2

1. If you were making a speech to company personnel, what would you tell them about the kind of corporate culture you would like to have at your company? What specific cultural traits would you like your company to exhibit? Explain.

LO 1

2. What core values would you want to ingrain in your company's culture? Why?

LO 3, LO 4

3. Following each decision round, do you and your co-managers make corrective adjustments in either your company's strategy or how well the strategy is being executed? List at least three such adjustments you made in the most recent decision round. What hard evidence (in the form of results relating to your company's performance in the most recent year) can you cite that indicates the various corrective adjustments you made either succeeded or failed to improve your company's performance?

LO 4

4. What would happen to your company's performance if you and your co-managers stick with the status quo and fail to make any corrective adjustments after each decision round?

ENDNOTES

[1] Jennifer A. Chatham and Sandra E. Cha, "Leading by Leveraging Culture," *California Management Review* 45, no. 4 (Summer 2003), pp. 20–34.

[2] Joanne Reid and Victoria Hubbell, "Creating a Performance Culture," *Ivey Business Journal* 69, no. 4 (March–April 2005), p. 1.

[3] John P. Kotter and James L. Heskett, *Corporate Culture and Performance* (New York: Free Press, 1992), p. 7. See also Robert Goffee and Gareth Jones, *The Character of a Corporation* (New York: HarperCollins, 1998).

[4] For several perspectives on the role and importance of core values and ethical behavior, see Joseph L. Badaracco, *Defining Moments: When Managers Must Choose between Right and Wrong* (Boston: Harvard Business School Press, 1997); Joe Badaracco and Allen P. Webb. "Business Ethics: A View from the Trenches," *California Management Review* 37, no. 2 (Winter 1995), pp. 8–28; Patrick E. Murphy, "Corporate Ethics Statements: Current Status and Future Prospects," *Journal of Business Ethics* 14 (1995), pp. 727–40; and Lynn Sharp Paine, "Managing for Organizational Integrity," *Harvard Business Review* 72, no. 2 (March–April 1994), pp. 106–17.

[5] For a study of the status of formal codes of ethics in large corporations, see Emily F. Carasco and Jang B. Singh, "The Content and Focus of the Codes of Ethics of the World's Largest Transnational Corporations," *Business and Society Review* 108, no. 1 (January 2003), pp. 71–94, and Patrick E. Murphy, "Corporate Ethics Statements: Current Status and Future Prospects," *Journal of Business Ethics* 14 (1995), pp. 727–40. For a discussion of the strategic benefits of formal statements of corporate values, see John Humble, David Jackson, and Alan Thomson, "The Strategic Power of Corporate Values," *Long Range Planning* 27, no. 6 (December 1994), pp. 28–42. An excellent discussion of whether one should assume that company codes of ethics are always ethical is presented in Mark S. Schwartz, "A Code of Ethics for Corporate Codes of Ethics," *Journal of Business Ethics* 41, nos. 1–2 (November–December 2002), pp. 27–43.

[6] Chatham and Cha, "Leading by Leveraging Culture."

[7] Kotter and Heskett, *Corporate Culture and Performance*, pp. 7–8.

[8] Terrence E. Deal and Allen A. Kennedy, *Corporate Cultures* (Reading, MA: Addison-Wesley, 1982), p. 22. See also Terrence E. Deal and Allen A. Kennedy, *The New Corporate Cultures: Revitalizing the Workplace after Downsizing, Mergers, and Reengineering* (Cambridge, MA: Perseus Publishing, 1999); Chatham and Cha, "Leading by Leveraging Culture."

[9] Vijay Sathe, *Culture and Related Corporate Realities* (Homewood, IL: Irwin, 1985).

[10] Avan R. Jassawalla and Hemant C. Sashittal, "Cultures That Support Product-Innovation Processes," *Academy of Management Executive* 16, no. 3 (August 2002), pp. 42–54.

[11] Kotter and Heskett, *Corporate Culture and Performance*, pp. 15–16. Also see Chatham and Cha, "Leading by Leveraging Culture."

[12] Chatham and Cha, "Leading by Leveraging Culture."

[13] Kotter and Heskett, *Corporate Culture and Performance*, p. 5.

[14] For a discussion of how to build a high-performance culture, see Reid and Hubbell, "Creating a Performance Culture," pp. 1–5.

[15] A strategy-supportive, high-performance culture can contribute to competitive advantage; see Jay B. Barney and Delwyn N. Clark, *Resource-Based Theory: Creating and Sustaining Competitive Advantage* (New York: Oxford University Press, 2007), chap. 4.

[16] Reid and Hubbell, "Creating a Performance Culture," pp. 2 and 5.

Afrigator: A Killer Start-up in Africa

Debapratim Purkayastha
IBS Center for Management Research

Syeda Maseeha Qumer
IBS Center for Management Research

"Afrigator is an extremely strong and recognized brand not just in Africa but globally. We are a market leader within our space, and through innovative products and services we are building trust and value for our brand because we continually engage our users. We have built up an extremely loyal user base that thrives on our ability to deliver new products that benefit them."[1]

—Justin Hartman, Managing Director & co-founder of Afrigator in 2009

INTRODUCTION

In December 2008, South Africa–based social media aggregator,[2] Afrigator, joined the Online Publishers Association[3] (OPA) of South Africa in order to achieve statistical insights for its core products, namely, Afrigator (www.afrigator.com) and Adgator (www.adgator.co.za). Within a month of joining, Afrigator had become the ninth largest publisher on the OPA with respect to total unique browsers, registering a growth rate of 1,079%, as measured by Nielson Online[4] (Refer to Exhibit 1 for Nielsen Online Rankings by Publisher.) Commenting on the achievement, Justin Hartman (Hartman), Managing Director of Afrigator, said, "Being ranked the ninth largest publisher in South Africa is a massive achievement for Afrigator. We joined the OPA because there was a growing need for us to provide detailed metrics and demographics to advertisers, but we didn't anticipate we'd be ranked this high so soon."[5]

Founded in 2007, Afrigator is the largest social media aggregator and blog directory[6] in Africa, built specifically for African consumers to publish and use content on the Web. It is the flagship product of Afrigator Internet (Pty) Ltd., a technology company based in Cape Town.

© 2010, IBS Center for Management Research. All rights reserved. This case was written by Syeda Maseeha Qumer, under the direction of Prof. Debapratim Purkayastha, IBS Center for Management Research. It was compiled from published sources, and is intended to be used as a basis for class discussion rather than to illustrate either effective or ineffective handling of a management situation.

To order copies, call +91-08417-236667/68 or write to IBS Center for Management Research (ICMR), IFHE Campus, Donthanapally, Sankarapally Road, Hyderabad 501 504, Andhra Pradesh, India or email: info@icmrindia.org.

ICMR
IBS Center for Management Research
www.icmrindia.org

Exhibit 1 **Nielsen Online Ranking by Publisher (by Total Unique Browsers)**

1	Media24
2	MSN
3	Independent Online
4	Avusa
5	Interface
6	MWEB
7	SuperSport Zone
8	MyBroadband.co.za
9	**Afrigator Internet**
10	Mail & Guardian Online

Data as of January 2009.
Source: Nielsen Online.

Besides Afrigator, the company's other products include Adgator, a blog advertising network, and Gatorpeeps, a micro-blogging site. Using Afrigator one can index blogs, podcasts and videocasts,[7] news feeds[8] and images and discover new sites in the Afrosphere. Basically, any site that publishes an RSS feed[9] can use Afrigator to market its content to the world. According to analysts, the site was created with the aim of building useful data for social media users and content generators in Africa and to provide a platform for African Web users to get African content into the limelight.

Analysts opined that the emergence of social media networks with features such as blogging and photo and video sharing had helped Afrigator find its audience and gain international recognition. With blogging and social networking becoming a norm in Africa and the continent recognizing the advantages of user generated content, the business of Afrigator would grow remarkably in the future, they said. To be more user friendly, the company planned to make improvements and add new features to its site in the future.

Analysts were of the view that though Afrigator had been able to make a significant impact on the African social media space, it had to overcome certain challenges in order to expand its reach in the future. According to them, the African continent faced socio-economic problems, low Internet penetration, infrastructural problems, language barriers, inadequate resources, and limited broadband connectivity. To enhance its global presence, Afrigator needed to overcome these barriers, they added. Talking about the future of Afrigator, Hartman said, "Afrigator has a long way to go to truly be successful and I have a long learning curve ahead of me but as it stands right now I wouldn't change it for the world. My life has changed so much in the last six months, I'm interacting with some of the most influential business minds in South Africa, I have a great team at my disposal, I am working on innovative ideas and I'm being tested on all levels every day of my life."[10]

BACKGROUND NOTE

Afrigator was co-founded by Hartman and Mike Stopforth[11] (Stopforth) on April 6, 2007. Since early 1997, Hartman had been involved with the media and the Internet industry and worked for various well-known national magazines and publications as well as media companies such as Media24, Synaptix (Pty) Ltd, CareerJunction, *True Love Magazine,* and *Finance Week.* After gaining considerable experience in website design, multimedia, and print design, Hartman established a web development company called Hartman Productions in October 2003. In February 2004, he started a web hosting[12] division of the company and offered clients the latest-technology web hosting using Windows and Unix packages[13] and reliable servers. In 2006, Hartman was involved in various Web 2.0[14] development projects which included a South African local search engine Grabble,[15] a free blogging platform, and two local blog and website directories. But the company shut down after running for over three years.

In August 2007, Hartman joined *The Times*[16] as the New Media Strategist and was responsible for conceptualizing, analyzing, and implementing web-based strategies for the company. Later, he worked as the Digital Innovation Manager at iLab,[17] a unit of Avusa Limited,[18] where he managed a small team of Web 2.0 specialists and built commercial applications for online media and the mobile community. In the meantime, Hartman was trying to develop Grabble into a news aggregator like Google News. Around this time, he met Stopforth, an entrepreneur, who suggested to him the idea of coming up with a social media aggregator just like Technorati, Inc.[19] for South African Web users. According to Stopforth, as there was a lack of quality information on the Web about Africa, developing a social media aggregator for information related to Africa would be beneficial. Stopforth offered to help Hartman. As Stopforth possessed social media skills and the business acumen required to run a social media business, Hartman decided to make him his business associate. As a result, they became partners and decided to go ahead with the development of a social media aggregator for African Web users.

As Hartman had the technical expertise and Stopforth the management skills, together they started a two-week intensive process of redesigning the Grabble aggregator into a social media aggregator and directory that would index blogs, podcasts, and videocasts. They wanted to create a product which bloggers and anyone who was interested in social media developments across Africa would enjoy using and where the best of user-generated content would be gathered and filtered. After developing the site, the duo approached Mark Forrester[20] (Forrester), a freelance Web designer from London, to design the Afrigator logo. Forrester's commitment and implementation of various ideas for developing Afrigator impressed them. They began to consider him more as a business partner than a service provider. Thereafter Forrester became a partner in Afrigator. After some time, Stiaan Pretorius[21] (Pretorius), a freelance Web developer, joined them. He was responsible for the development of the software platform of the site. The project was funded by all the four who played vital roles in its growth and development.

The social media aggregator was launched in April 2007 and its name was derived from the words AFRIcan blog aggreGATOR. Until November 2007, the site was in the Alpha development stage.[22]

In November 2007, Afrigator moved out of the Alpha development stage and launched its Beta version[23] with a host of new functionalities. In order to enter the social networking arena and differentiate themselves from competitors, the Afrigator team began to focus on turning the start-up into a social media aggregator instead of just aggregating blogs. Afrigator started aggregating not only blogs but also podcasts, videos,

and news. As part of the Beta version, a photos section which aggregated images was introduced (refer to Box I for some new features in the Beta version). The Beta version generated revenues for the company by creating various advertising options for advertisers. Talking about the launch of the Beta version, Hartman said, "The biggest issue we were faced with in being a social media aggregator was that we didn't feel we were living up to our mandate and this spurred us on to rethink our strategy considerably and redevelop the core functionality of the website. The other major issue we had to address was a revenue model. It's been a lot of fun working and developing this project. However, at some point we need to cover our costs in running the project and we also have some big plans for the future which require some money in the piggy bank."[24]

As mobile social networking was growing in Africa, Afrigator decided to launch a mobile platform for its site. Soon after its launch, in April 2007, Afrigator released its first mobile version called the Afrigator Mobile. In February 2008 an optimized mobile version of Afrigator was launched with a fast-loading interface that provided users with all the relevant social media in one place. Blogs, podcasts, news, and videos were integrated into the mobile site. In the same year, an optimized version of Afrigator for the Apple iPhone and iPod Touch[25] was launched.

Box I   **New Features in the Beta Version**

1. New website design and user interface.
2. Home page with latest blog posts, podcasts, videos, and a news box with the latest headlines from news sites in Africa.
3. Featured categories in all main sections for better filtering of content.
4. Blogs section with a breakdown of blogs signed up by country.
5. A new Author page which displayed an author's latest blog posts, podcasts, and videos/photos.
6. New Top 10 Posts featured on the Blogs page, calculated based on clicks generated by each post.
7. Revamped ranking system of blogs. To calculate the blog rankings, blog traffic, clicks on blog posts, and author ratings were taken into account.
8. Blog ranking displayed on the Author page with country-wise as well as overall ranking.
9. Search optimized and results displayed by blog posts, podcasts, and news items.
10. The functionality of the dashboard* optimized to give an overview of data accumulated from a blogger's website.
11. A "forgot password" function added.
12. Top Searches tag cloud removed to prevent spammers from abusing the system.

* A dashboard is a control panel of a blog where users could access weblog settings, account information, etc.
Source: http://blog.afrigator.com.

Exhibit II A Brief Note on Adgator and Gatorpeeps

ADGATOR

Launched on November 11, 2008, Adgator was a blog advertising network which allowed advertisers to target their ads across top blogs in South Africa. It connected advertisers with bloggers and vice versa. With more than 5.5 million page views every month as of October 2009, Adgator helped advertisers in **targeting popular blogs** as well as **category specific** niches depending on their budget and target market. It also helped bloggers monetize their blog by serving ads on a Cost Per Thousand (CPM)* basis with a 50%-50% revenue share.

One of the key features of Adgator was that it served the right ad to the right reader and helped advertisers communicate to a social media audience in Africa. Soon after its launch, Adgator was able to reach more than 1.7 million unique readers. The company planned to implement the Adgator blog ad network in Kenya and Nigeria in the first quarter of 2009.

GATORPEEPS

In May 2009, Afrigator launched its micro-blogging site Gatorpeeps. Gatorpeeps connected Afrigator users together through short updates and community interaction. Analysts referred to it as Africa's answer to Twitter. Gatorpeeps helped the vastly growing community of Africa to connect with each other. The launch of a micro-blogging platform was considered as a wise move as less than 5% of Afrigator users had Twitter accounts. Through Gatorpeeps, users could join several communities, view blog posts of friends, and include their latest blog posts. The character limit of a post (peep) on Gatorpeeps was about 140 characters.

Gatorpeeps offered multiple tools to enable users to integrate their peeps with other social networking platforms. It was connected to Twitter's API which meant peeps of a user on Gatorpeeps automatically appeared on his/her Twitter updates. Since the Twitter account was linked to other services like Facebook, my personal blog, Yahoo! etc., updates from Gatorpeeps would automatically be broadcast on the other platforms. The company planned to develop Gatorpeeps at a faster rate including as an SMS-based mobile offering. Some of the future development plans for Gatorpeeps included:

- Mobile web front-end
- Mobile apps for Symbian,† Windows Mobile, BlackBerry, and iPhone
- SMS integration
- Extending community functionality
- New ways to share links and photos via Gatorpeeps
- Plugins‡ and widgets§ for all environments
- Closer integration with Afrigator

* The Cost Per Thousand (CPM) is the amount an advertiser pays for every 1000 times a user views his/her ad and an impression is recorded (or) the cost per thousand page impressions.

† Symbian is an open source operating system designed for mobile devices and smartphones.

‡ A plugin is a program application that can be installed easily and used as part of a web browser.

§ A widget is a live update on a website or a web page which contains organized content or applications selected by the user.

Source: Compiled from various sources.

Since its launch, Afrigator had grown on an average at a rate of 300 new websites per month and it sent more than 12,000 unique users every day to member sites on Afrigator. The response from bloggers across the continent was overwhelming. As of 2008, Afrigator had over 1000 registered sites. Its estimated worth was about US$137,918.9. The daily ad revenues of the Afrigator were estimated to be about US$188.93.[26] In November 2008, the company launched a blog advertising network called the Adgator. This was followed by the launch of Gatorpeeps, a micro-blogging site, in May 2009 (refer to Exhibit II for a brief note on Adgator and Gatorpeeps).

FEATURES

Considered as a search engine for blogs, Afrigator aggregated blog content from all over the African continent and allowed users to publish and use content on the Web. It could be used to index blogs, podcasts, and video content and to discover new sites. Any site with an RSS feed could use Afrigator to index its content. Specially built for African consumers, Afrigator utilized social media tools and technologies to display the best digital content that Africa had to offer. It invited African publishers to submit their sites so that it could send traffic to them and scanned the Web for African-related tags and aggregated those contents on its site. "Afrigator is a very original site that goes beyond what Techmeme does in content . . . In some ways it's like what Technorati is trying to do with its move to multimedia, but better executed in this case . . . ," said reviewer Marshall Kirkpatrick, Vice President of Content Development at ReadWriteWeb, a weblog.[27]

According to analysts, Afrigator helped bloggers to popularize their blogs so that their content got noticed. With many blogs listed on the site, users got exposure to some good blogs and bloggers they might not have noticed otherwise, they said. For instance, the Top 45 Female African Bloggers list compiled by Afrigator was an eye opener for some Web users in Africa who, until then, had been unaware of the existence of such a large number of female bloggers.

The homepage of the site featured podcasts and videos along with the latest blog posts. The videos section of Afrigator was integrated with the YouTube[28] application so that users could provide

their YouTube account details and watch YouTube videos on the site. According to experts, the highlight of the site was its design and eye catching analytics display which included inbound links and a list of blog rolls.[29] Afrigator offered services for both readers and content providers (refer to Table I for features of Afrigator). It aggregated and divided content based on country channels, category, and content types. Based on the type, the content was further divided into several broad channels such as news, blogs, videos, and images. Users could access the content by keyword, country, and time.

Afrigator was equipped with user-friendly tools and interface which made surfing easier. The "Top Tags" and "Top Searches" features on the site revealed keywords which were popular on the blogosphere. The site used an OpenID system[30] which allowed users to operate with a single login at multiple websites. Users could log on to multiple websites using Afrigator's OpenID rather than create yet another account. Another interesting feature was that even bloggers who did not register on the site would have their content indexed as Afrigator could track blog posts even if bloggers had not registered on its site. Afrigator followed a unique blog ranking system based on page views,

Table I   **Features of Afrigator**

News Section	News section aggregated major news sites in Africa. It featured the latest aggregated news entries from leading publishers such as *ITWeb* and *The Times*. The News section was categorized into areas like "Breaking News," "World News," "Africa," and "Technology."
Blogs Section	The Blogs section featured the latest aggregated blog posts with various content filters such as Latest, Hottest, Mygator (your blogs posts), and view blog content by country. The Top 10 Blog Posts were featured on the Blogs pages which were ranked on the basis of clicks generated by each post.
Podcasts and Videos	The Podcasts section displayed podcasts from around the continent. The Videos section was integrated with YouTube application.
My Gator Area	MyGator was a dashboard featuring statistics related to blogs such as daily, weekly, and monthly page views and unique visitors. The statistics were displayed as graphs. With the help of this feature, bloggers can track their blogs' performance and view blog rankings.
Author Page	Author page featured an Author's latest blog posts, podcasts, videos, and photos.
Blog Rankings	The Afrigator blog ranking system was found on the Author page where users rated blog posts on a scale of 1 to 5. The page showed country-wise as well as overall ranking.
Channels & tag clouds	Each country was assigned a channel. This allowed users to filter content which was not relevant to their country and retain content of their choice. Tag clouds also helped in finding content relevant to a specific topic.
On-the-fly reader	This feature allowed users to read the blog post on Afrigator without having to visit the original post, thereby saving time and bandwidth.

Source: www.bandwidthblog.com/2007/11/28/afrigator-beta-launched/.

unique visits, and links from blog posts. The blog posts were arranged based on country channels and users could vote for blog posts they liked the most. The ranking system helped each blog in attracting a sizable amount of traffic.

BUSINESS MODEL

The business model of Afrigator was advertising-based with some of the top South African brands sponsoring sections on the site. This business model allowed Afrigator to generate revenues. Across the site, users could find a few well-placed advertising banners. Afrigator used a corporate reporting tool called AfriData which allowed advertisers to see what effect their brand had in the social as well as mainstream media. "The most visible is a standard advertising stream. But we are getting more creative and will be expanding our revenue streams in the next three months in a way that will really benefit consumers and bloggers," said Hartman.[31]

To improve the state of social media in the country, Afrigator monitored vast amounts of content and provided Africans with access to specific subjects of interest and allowed them to get involved with particular content types and publishers. Due to its functionality, it quickly established its presence in key markets such as South Africa, Egypt, Nigeria, and Kenya (refer to Table II for user percentage of Afrigator). According to analysts, Afrigator carved a niche for itself because of its local relevance and its ability to aggregate and filter an increasing number of social media sources around the world. According to Pretorius, "Afrigator is community driven in

that the user decides what is important, so content relevancy is democratic and dictated from a community perspective, which drives our appeal. Our most active countries are currently South Africa, Kenya, Nigeria, and Egypt. Then we have a general Africa category that is very active."[32]

In November 2008, in order to increase the relevance of its content and to make the services available on the site more accessible, Afrigator revamped its site both content-wise as well as in its functionality. It increased the site's focus on search so that users could find data faster and more easily. The redesign of Afrigator was based on the AfriGreater campaign, which asked bloggers to help identify ways in which Afrigator could improve its service. Talking about the site upgrade, Hartman said, "The company's strategy is to continually work on its service to ensure that we are appealing and remain the first choice of users. The Afrigator design upgrade moves it in line with the company's progressive attitude and reinforces its African identity. Users of this unique site will be as impressed with the fresh new look as they already are with its genuinely useful service."[33]

As part of the restructuring strategy, Afrigator introduced a three-step graphic to the registration and login pages which gave a brief introduction to the site. A search algorithm called Sphinx Search[34] was used, which cut the average search time from 4 seconds to roughly 0.01 seconds and returned relevant results. Users were able to view blogs on the home page depending on the country they were posted from. Earlier, the Afrigator home page displayed content aggregated from all over Africa, while the new version determined which country a reader was visiting from and provided content relevant to that particular country. For instance, when a user visited the site from a particular country in Africa he/she could find results relevant to that country whereas in the older version, they would have had to view all the entries irrespective of the country they signed in from. One of the important inclusions to the revamped service was user generated images and photographs. A new photos section was created on the site where users could view images from their country of interest.

With considerable improvements in its design and features, Afrigator began to make a mark on the social media industry in Africa. Experts opined that Afrigator was a well executed model of just

Table II **Geographic Location of Afrigator Users**

Country	% of Users
South Africa	73.7
Kenya	5.0
Nigeria	4.0
India	3.8
Egypt	3.2
UK	3.1
U.S.	2.3
Others	5.0

Source: www.alexa.com/siteinfo/afrigator.com.

the kind of service that any region or niche could use to aggregate and filter the increasing number of social media channels the world over. To expand its market presence, the company was looking for a potential investor with similar business interests.

ACQUISITION BY NASPERS

On September 7, 2008, MIH Print Africa (Pty) Ltd,[35] a division of Naspers Limited,[36] acquired a majority stake in Afrigator (refer to Exhibit III for the income statement of Naspers Limited). The reason behind the acquisition was to help Afrigator reach a wider audience, analysts said. According to them, the founders of Afrigator who were funding the project felt that managing the business was consuming a significant amount of their time and they had to compromise on their family life.

Experts opined that under the ownership of MIH Print Africa, Afrigator could market and develop its platform and become a technology focused company. Analysts opined that as MIH Print Africa had a presence all over Africa the acquisition would help Afrigator reach a large audience across the continent. Using MIH Print Africa's platform, Afrigator could develop new products in key markets such as South Africa, Egypt, and Nigeria, they said. "We could not have chosen a better partner in MIH Print Africa as their strategy for Africa aligns perfectly with ours and is an important development for the social media space across our continent—validating the importance of blogging and social media in Africa," said Hartman.[37]

Though the financial details of the deal were not disclosed, analysts speculated that the deal was rewarding for the founders. As per the deal, MIH Print Africa became a majority shareholder in Afrigator while Hartman, Pretorius, Stopforth, and Forrester retained a 25% share. Along with Pretorius, Hartman was to direct Afrigator's growth, while Stopforth was to play an advisory role. "We're hoping this deal will inspire and encourage more young African Internet entrepreneurs to pursue their business ideas. As with

Exhibit III   Naspers Limited: Income Statements

(Amounts in millions of US Dollars except per share data)	March 2009	March 2008	March 2007
Revenue	2,746.4	2,503.2	2,670.7
Cost of Goods Sold	1,392.4	1,314.9	1,459.5
Gross Profit	1,354.0	1,188.3	1,211.2
Gross Profit Margin	49.3%	47.5%	45.4%
SG&A Expense	955.8	717.0	710.2
Depreciation & Amortization	115.2	136.6	—
Operating Income	581.6	683.0	522.6
Operating Margin	21.2%	27.3%	19.6%
Non-operating Income	133.5	68.1	46.4
Non-operating Expenses	(31.4)	102.3	(51.5)
Income Before Taxes	491.3	643.5	471.1
Income Taxes	147.7	168.1	171.2
Net Income After Taxes	343.5	475.4	299.9
Continuing Operations	343.5	475.4	299.9
Discontinued Operations	13.1	19.6	0.0
Total Operations	356.6	495.0	299.9
Total Net Income	356.6	495.0	299.9
Net Profit Margin	13.0%	19.8%	11.2%
Diluted EPS from Total Net Income ($)	0.73	1.15	0.89
Dividends per Share	0.19	0.00	0.00

Source: www.hoovers.com/naspers.

anyone who has been following the rise of Afrigator, it comes as good news. This will mean a better Afrigator for the whole blogosphere to use,"said Stopforth.[38]

COMPETITORS

In Africa, the Internet penetration rate was growing steadily. As per the Internet World Statistics, the Internet penetration rate in Africa was about 6.7% as of June 2009. According to experts, the rise in Internet usage along with an increase in demand for consumer generated content had led to the emergence of many social media sites in Africa. Blogging was growing significantly with the number of bloggers in the continent estimated to be around 35,000 to 40,000 as of February 2009 (refer to Exhibit IV for a brief note on the social media scene in Africa). Strong blogging activity was noticed in countries such as Nigeria and Uganda and some of the mainstream publishers

Exhibit IV   **A Brief Note on Social Media in Africa**

In Africa, social networking is evolving rapidly due to the rise in Internet penetration, reduced information technology (IT) costs, and the increase in the number of Web users. Web communities with features such as blogging and photo and video sharing have sprung up all over the African continent. Social networking sites the world over are supporting the growth of social media applications in Africa by investing in several social media projects in the country. For instance, in 2008, Google organized a "Barcamp Africa"* at their headquarters in California and also launched a blog to document their operations in sub-Saharan Africa. Analysts opined that with international investments and improvements in the IT infrastructure, Africa will have a prominent online presence in the world in the future.

Over the years, the three biggest social media sites which have become successful in Africa are Afrigator (social media aggregator), Zoopy (content sharing service like YouTube/Flickr), and Ushahidi (an SMS crisis reporting and mapping web application from Kenya). Besides these three home grown social media sites, there are an increasing number of other social media applications such as Muti (local news site), Amatomu (blog aggregator), Sokwanele (an SMS/mapping application), and BlogSpirit (blog aggregator from Uganda), which are establishing their presence in Africa. According to experts, as Internet penetration in Africa was growing steadily along with an increase in demand for consumer generated content, more social media sites may emerge in the future. It was reported that the Internet penetration rate in the continent was about 6.7% as of June 2009 (Refer to Table for top Internet usage countries in Africa).

Table   **Africa—Top Internet Usage Countries (Data as of June 30, 2009)**

Country	Internet Users	Penetration	User Growth (2000–2009)	% Users in Africa
Egypt	12,568,900	15.9 %	2,693.1 %	18.7 %
Nigeria	11,000,000	7.4 %	5,400.0 %	16.3 %
Morocco	10,300,000	32.9 %	10,200.0 %	15.3 %
South Africa	4,590,000	9.4 %	91.3 %	6.8 %
Sudan	4,200,000	10.2 %	13,900.0 %	6.2 %
Algeria	4,100,000	12.0 %	8,100 %	6.1 %
Kenya	3,359,600	8.6 %	1,579.8 %	5.0 %
Tunisia	2,800,000	26.7 %	2,700.0 %	4.2 %
Uganda	2,500,000	7.7 %	6,150.0 %	3.7 %
Zimbabwe	1,421,000	12.5 %	2,742.0 %	2.1 %
Total for Africa	67,371,700	6.8%	1,392.4 %	3.9% (in World)
Rest of World	1,666,622,041	28.9%	367.5 %	96.1% (in World)

* BarCamp is a network of user generated open, participatory conferences wherein content is provided by participants.

Source: www.internetworldstats.com/stats1.htm.

(Continued)

Exhibit IV   *(Concluded)*

Africa has also witnessed a remarkable growth in the blogging arena. As of January 2008, there were about 4000 active South African blogs that received more than 10.5 million page views and over 1.8 million unique users each month. Places such as Cape Town and Johannesburg are considered the epicenters for blogging in South Africa, as they account for more than 75% of South Africa's active bloggers.

Experts are of the view that though Africa has been embracing the web technologies steadily, there were still a number of factors challenging the growth of the social media in the continent as of 2009. Lack of proper broadband and communications infrastructure was one of the major challenges. Electricity had reached only 5% of the continent's population and there were not enough gateways to the undersea cables to maintain Internet connectivity with other continents. Much of the African continent still communicated via satellite which was considered slow as well as expensive. Another problem relating to the development of the social media in Africa was lack of interconnectivity as more than 70% of Internet traffic within Africa was routed outside the continent, thereby driving up costs for social networking businesses. In South Africa, language was also a problem for social media applications as the country had about 11 official languages which made it difficult for social media operators to focus on any one particular language. Moreover, analysts felt that the socio-political environment in the country was quite unstable. With respect to IT, there was a huge digital divide as the black African community did not have access to computing resources compared to the whites. Owing to economic problems, the access to social media was almost non-existent for the black community, analysts said.

Analysts predicted that despite the problems, social media networks in South Africa would witness significant growth in the future as they were gaining popularity among young users. The government was also trying to make the Internet available for lower income groups as well. As of 2009, about 1.3 million South African users were into some kind of social networking, and this number was expected to exceed 4.5 million by 2013. It was reported that Internet usage in South Africa might double from 4.5 million in 2009 to over 9 million by 2013* (Refer to figure for the projected growth of social networking in South Africa).

Figure   **Projected Growth of Social Networking in South Africa (2008–2013)**

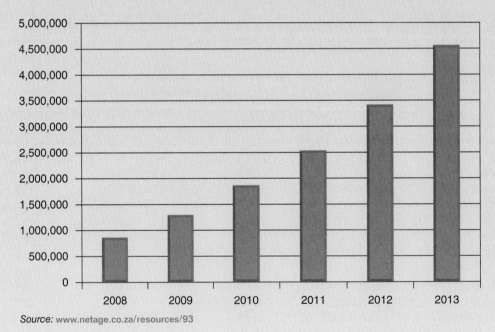

Source: www.netage.co.za/resources/93

* http://www.netage.co.za/resources/93.

Source: Compiled from various sources.

Table III   Top Web Start-Ups in Africa*

Amatomu	Amatomu, which means "reins" in Zulu, aggregates content from South African blogs. Backed by Mail & Guardian, it is considered one of Afrigator's biggest competitors. It features various widgets to integrate Amatomu's functionality into a user's blog.
Yola	Launched in 2007, Yola (earlier known as Synthasite) is a website builder and website hosting service. The application features widgets and templates to help web designers create professional web properties.
Blueworld	Blueworld is a social networking site which allows users to communicate through blogs, videos, and photos.
Zoopy	Zoopy is an online and mobile social media community and one of the first photo and video sharing networks in South Africa.
Muti	Muti is a social bookmarking site dedicated to content of interest to Africans or those interested in Africa. It is one of the first social media start-ups to come out of South Africa.
Vottle	Vottle is one of the largest free online classifieds site in Africa with several ad listings in various categories. It allows users to network online and allows them to buy and sell goods.
iBlog	iBlog is one of the biggest South African blogging communities and showcases thousands of bloggers. On iBlog, anyone can register and create their own blog.
MyGenius	MyGenius is a South Africa-based business networking and community website which allows users to promote themselves, build relationships, and collaborate with others.
iJol	iJol is a South Africa-based online events community which allows users to scan through a summary of events happening in their area.

* The list is not exhaustive.

Source: www.sagoodnews.co.za/science_technology/sas_top_10_web_start-ups_to_watch.html.

launched their own blogging platforms. Analysts considered blogs as a powerful networking medium compared to other traditional websites. For instance, the top 100 blogs in South Africa accounted for more than 1.7 million unique users and served over 5.6 million page views each month. "Currently Afrigator has around 6,000 blogs from Africa, so as you can see there is lots of room for growth in this space. It is a huge market," Hartman said.[39]

Experts were of the view that with the growth of social media channels in Africa, Afrigator would be facing some competition in the future (refer to Table III for some of the top Web start-ups in Africa). One of the biggest competitors of Afrigator was Amatomu which was launched two months prior to Afrigator. Amatomu was exclusively a blog aggregator. Analysts felt that Afrigator had a competitive edge over Amatomu because of its ability to localize content as well as to aggregate mainstream news. Talking about competition, Hartman said, "The fledgling aggregators we're seeing are largely very different to what we are doing and we don't see them

as competition. It is just a matter of bringing them on board. It is better to collaborate than to compete. However, where there is competition we welcome it, because this will drive improvement. Amatomu forced us to improve our product, and as a result, both services were strengthened. The winner in this scenario was the blogger who had even more choice and greater functionality."[40]

RESULTS

With content feeds from Nigeria to Uganda, Afrigator provided a platform for African citizens to popularize African content. Because of its ability to aggregate and filter social media sources around the world, Afrigator received international recognition and was compared with some major social media aggregators in the world. Consistent growth and a driving commitment to innovation made Afrigator one of the biggest social media aggregators in Africa, analysts said. Since its inception, Afrigator achieved considerable success with a steady 25% month-on-month growth

Table IV   **Afrigator Blog Statistics, 2007–2008**

	South Africa	Rest of Africa
Total Blogs	1,399	871
Total Blog Posts	104,600	89,120
Page View to Blogs	34,844,279	16,609,970
Unique Visitors to Blogs	16,797,281	7,777,751
Traffic sent to Blogs (June 16 2007–April 2008)	1,771,537	1,495,393

Source: www.slideshare.net/justinhartman/afrigator-social-media-stats.

rate despite limited broadband availability and slow Internet speeds in the continent.[41] Between April 2007 and April 2008, a total of 2,270 bloggers joined Afrigator and the total blog posts collected were about 193,720. In January 2008, as many as 10,427 articles were collected by Afrigator and the traffic sent to news sites was 44,102 clicks.[42] (Refer to Table IV for statistics related to Afrigator and Exhibit V for Monthly Traffic Sent to Blogs by Afrigator: 2007–2008).

Afrigator was reviewed by popular blogging sites such as ReadWriteWeb[43] which described it as "The best of African social media, in real time." The design of the site was termed as a "real highlight." Besides being featured on ReadWriteWeb, Afrigator also appeared on Go2Web20.net, VentureBeat, KillerStartups.com. It received press coverage in the *Financial Mail, Financial Week, The Sunday Times, The New York Times, The Times, Intelligence Magazine,* and *Bizcommunity.* "Being compared to major International websites like Technorati and Techmeme is a major achievement for us. Often Africa is forgotten about in the online space and this level of exposure just confirms that we are certainly moving in the right direction with Afrigator. I'm extremely excited about our future," Hartman said.[44]

In 2007, Afrigator was listed at #20 among 31 "top non-US startups to watch worldwide" by *Business 2.0.*[45] In December 2008, it was voted as one of the Top 10 International Products for 2008 by ReadWriteWeb.[46] For the recognition, Afrigator competed with popular Web 2.0 products such as Netvibes, Zoho, Google Reader, Feedburner, and Yahoo!. Afrigator also received a special mention in the Top 10 RSS and Syndication

Exhibit V   **Monthly Traffic Sent to Blogs by Afrigator, 2007–2008**

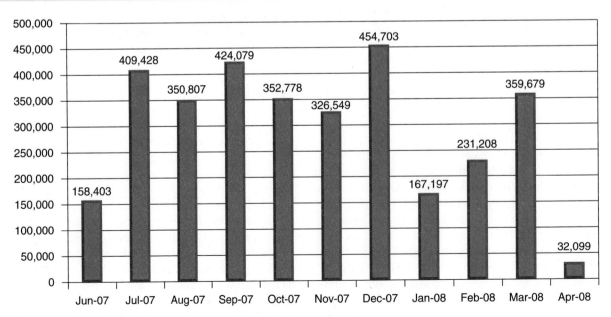

Source: www.slideshare.net/justinhartman/afrigator-social-media-stats.

Exhibit VI   Top International Products of 2008

Product	Country	Type of Business
Remember The Milk	Australia	Task- and time-management web application
Afrigator	**South Africa**	**Social media aggregator**
Zoho	India	Suite of online web applications
Netvibes	France	Personalized start page/personal web portal
Dopplr	Finland / U.K	Social networking service for sharing personal and business travel plans
Maxthon	China	Web browser
Xing	Germany	Social network for business professionals
FreshBooks	Canada	Online invoicing service
Mixi	Japan	Social networking website
Wuala	Switzerland	Online storage tool

Source: www.readwriteweb.com/archives/top_10_international_products_2008.php.

Products of 2008 listed by ReadWriteWeb (refer to Exhibit VI for Top 10 international products for 2008).

In December 2008, Afrigator became a member of OPA of South Africa and was ranked ninth in terms of total unique browsers. Adgator was ranked the eighth largest brand. According to the company, Adgator was largely responsible for the jump in rankings and was successful from the perspective of both blogger and advertiser. During the month of January 2009, Afrigator reached 628,878 unique browsers and registered 2,360,689 page views while serving more than 2.5 million advertisers.[47] The company forecast that both Adgator as well as Afrigator would continue to grow and climb the OPA rankings even further in the coming months "Since the launch of Adgator we've been quoting big numbers to advertisers and media planners and now, for the first time, there are audited statistics that really validate how big blogging has become in South Africa. We always knew it was a large network, and now we have the numbers to back us up," Hartman said.[48]

PARTNERSHIPS

On February 25, 2009, 24.com, one of the largest blogging platforms in Africa, announced its integration with Afrigator. The integration allowed bloggers of 24.com to sign up for Afrigator with a single click and get their blog posts indexed and included in Afrigator. They also received statistics related to their blogs such as page views and traffic and were able to view the latest blog posts and new members within the community. "Adding the country's largest blogging community to Afrigator effectively puts 24.com bloggers out into the wider world and lets them discover fellow bloggers, make new friends, and generally contribute toward the African zeitgeist," said Hartman.[49]

In February 2009, a South African national elections[50] site, http://www.saelections.co.za, was started to track news articles, twitter[51] streams, and inputs related to the elections from people across South Africa. In order to include the views of bloggers as well, *The Times,* which powered the site, approached Afrigator. Afrigator then built a special feed which gathered the opinions of bloggers from around South Africa. As a result, the new election site could gather more content, and also benefited the bloggers by sending more traffic from interested readers toward their blogging sites.

In August 2009, the U.S. government formed a partnership with Afrigator to set up a web page on Afrigator that would aggregate web content from Africa. The new page called the U.S. in Africa social media stream showcased all the latest developments the U.S. had undertaken in Africa. The social media stream covered all major social media websites such as Twitter, Flickr,[52] YouTube, and Afrigator. To showcase the work the U.S. government had done in Africa, Afrigator worked closely with the Department of

State, the South African Embassy, as well as the American government.

In September 2009, Afrigator teamed up with The Parlotones, one of South Africa's successful rock bands, to launch the pop group's new wine Giant Mistake. Afrigator created a social media stream to promote the wine. Though the company claimed that it would not get involved with something like promoting a wine, it said that it was doing so as it was an opportunity for the company to test its social stream functionality platform and develop it further. The social stream would track the happenings related to the popularity of the wine across Twitter, Afrigator, Flickr, You-Tube, and Digg.[53] A new feature which could track fans of the Parlotones was also introduced to the stream. Besides the ventures, Afrigator also planned to sponsor the 2009 South Africa Blog awards with R30,000 in prizes for the winning bloggers. The prize would be in the form of advertising. The winning blog would get R20,000[54] worth of advertising on Afrigator.com (approx 100,000 ads) and the best new blog would receive R10,000 (approx 50,000 ads) worth of advertising.[55]

OUTLOOK

Experts opined that in the future, Afrigator would evolve into the preferred choice of Web users who wanted to get a taste of the social networking scene in the African continent. The company planned to gain market share and leverage its existing user base in the future by making the site more useful to social media users and bloggers. Talking about the company's expansion plans, Hartman said, "Afrigator's success is dependent upon how representative we are within the African continent. We claim to be an African product but are still not representing every country within Africa. Currently our biggest markets are South Africa, Egypt, Nigeria, and Kenya, and these are growing very nicely; however, we want similar growth within other countries. We've realized that approaching Africa as a continent must be done systematically because there are far too many differences

between each country for us to really assume to understand each one."[56]

Afrigator planned to extend its reach in each country and enhance user interaction by localizing the site in accordance with the preferences and cultures of that particular country. Commenting on the importance of localization, Hartman said, "Then relevance and localization are very important. Where else could you go to find out what people are talking about in Africa? We have real people talking about real issues in Africa for Africa. Afrigator has given Africa a voice, and not a small voice. Now that we have resource we want to be on the ground in these countries, with people who understand the landscape and can help us embed the service into relationships and content networks."[57]

Afrigator also planned to focus on its mobile platform as statistics revealed that in Africa, mobile usage was close to 300 million as of 2008. Mobile social networking constituted more than 60% of mobile web traffic in South Africa. By developing its mobile platform, Afrigator wanted to differentiate itself through ease of use and integration with mobile communication. According to Hartman, "Mobile is a massive area that we're focusing on right now. It is our belief that if you can't [provide] a decent mobile offering within Africa then you're really missing the mark. If we do manage to make mobile work in Africa I believe our mobile offering will be much bigger than the Internet offering."[58]

Considered as a killer start-up by some analysts, Afrigator had a large number of users who could find loads of relevant and filtered information on the site. It planned to introduce some more features on its site in order to attract more visitors to it. Commenting on the company's future strategy, Hartman said, "The focus is to intensify on the innovative and creative ways we built the site, but to put some resource behind this. We have a great forward-looking strategy, which speaks strongly to viral and community driven growth. However, our growth will be strongly rooted in customer satisfaction. We realize that providing great service is crucial to customer retention."[59]

ENDNOTES

1 Mandy De Waal, "Afrigator Bytes," www.brandchannel.com, February 23, 2009.

2 Social media aggregation is the process of collecting content from multiple social network services. The task is generally carried out by a social network aggregator, which gathers all the content into a single location. Social media aggregators have no original content. They use content from blogs and other social networking sites to drive traffic from search engines to their aggregator sites. Some examples of social media aggregators are power.com, FriendFeed, Technorati, and Flock.

3 Online Publishers Association is an independent and not-for-profit trade association whose stated objective is to promote the online publishing industry and to advance the business interests of online content providers before the advertising community, the press, the government and the public.

4 Nielsen Online, a service of the global information and media company The Nielsen Company, provides comprehensive and independent analysis of online audiences, advertising, video, consumer-generated media, word of mouth, and consumer behavior.

5 Ismail Dhorat, "Afrigator Joins the Online Publishers Association," www.startupafrica.com, February 5, 2009.

6 Blog, short form for web log, is an online personal diary where an individual can share his/her thoughts on a specific topic. A blog directory contains a list of blogs which are grouped either by country, category, or content type.

7 A podcast is a digital multimedia file which can be downloaded over the Internet for playback on a portable audio digital player or a personal computer or a mobile device. Podcasts are distributed on the Internet using RSS feeds and are hosted by a podcaster. A Videocast is a podcast containing video files.

8 A news feed, also referred to as a web feed, is a data format used for providing users with frequently updated content. News feeds allow users to see the new content added on a website.

9 An RSS (Really Simple Syndication) feed is a type of web feed format used to publish blog entries, news, audio, and video content in a standardized format.

10 "Afrigator Turns Two Today… Somehow it Feels Like More!" http://justinhartman.com, April 3, 2009.

11 Mike Stopforth is an entrepreneur, writer, and speaker. He heads Cerebra, one of the leading social media consultancies in South Africa. He is also a columnist for the *Citizen Newspaper* (South Africa) and a member of the National Speakers Association of South Africa (NSASA) and an associate of the Institute of Technology Strategy and Innovation (ITSI). Besides, he is involved in a number of sideline projects including Afrigator.

12 Web hosting is a service which allows users to post web pages to the Internet. It follows a server/client model for distributing content.

13 Microsoft Windows and Unix are software operating systems.

14 Web 2.0 Technologies is a term used for advanced Internet technology and applications including blogs, wikis, and social networking sites.

15 Grabble was a South African search engine developed by Justin Hartman in 2006. At that time, Hartman developed a passion for search and was completely in awe of Google. This inspired him to start Grabble.

16 *The Times* is a popular daily newspaper in South Africa.

17 In March 2008, Avusa Limited launched a new commercial application, the iLab, to facilitate online, offline, and mobile innovation within the company.

18 Avusa Limited (earlier known as Johnnic Communications Limited) is one of the prominent media and entertainment groups in Africa.

19 Launched in 2002, Technorati, Inc. is a leading blog search engine which indexes millions of blog posts on the Web. It is based in San Francisco, U.S.

20 Mark Forrester obtained a Bachelor of Commerce Degree, majoring in Information Systems, from the University of Cape Town in 2003. He also holds a Digital Design Diploma from Hirt & Carter, a well-known design house in Cape Town.

21 Stiaan Pretorius is a freelance web developer and PHP programmer. He works for Ja! Productions, a company which aggregates and distributes user generated content, as their lead developer. He spends his spare time in improving and developing Afrigator.

22 The Alpha development is the second stage in the software development life cycle wherein a product attains basic structure and satisfies most of the software requirements but requires debugging. At this stage, the product is tested for preliminary functionality.

23 The Alpha development stage is followed by the Beta stage wherein a software product is released to users for software testing before its official release. It is a prototype of the product released to the public who provide feedback, so that any problem related to the product can be reported to the developers and fixed.

24 "Afrigator Launches Public Beta Site," http://blog.afrigator.com, January 10, 2008.

25 The iPhone, designed by Apple Inc., is a smartphone with advanced features such as Internet connectivity, e-mail facility, camera, and multimedia player. iPod is the company's very popular digital music player. An iPhone/iPod touch application is a set of software applications designed for end users for a particular purpose.

26 www.websiteoutlook.com/www.afrigator.com.

27 Simone Puterman, "Highest Praise for Afrigator by Top Global Tech Blog," www.bizcommunity.com, November 29, 2007.

28 YouTube, owned by Google Inc., is a video sharing website where users can upload, view, and share video clips.

29 A blog roll is a list of recommended blog links placed in the sidebar of a blog.

30 An OpenID system allows users to use an existing identity to sign into multiple websites instead of creating new passwords. The user password is accessible only to the identity provider who confirms the user's identity to the websites he/she visits.

31 Mandy De Waal, "Afrigator Takes on Africa," ww2.itweb.co.za, October 7, 2008.

32 Ibid.

33 "Facelift for Afrigator," www.bizcommunity.com, December 1, 2008.

34 The Sphinx Search is a full text search engine which provides fast and relevant search results. It has an indexing speed of up to 10 MB/sec on modern CPUs.

35 MIH Print Africa (Pty) Ltd, a subsidiary of MIH Holdings Ltd., is involved in printing and publishing of magazine and newspaper. It is owned by South Africa-based media company Naspers. The company's publications include True Love East Africa and Drum, Kick Off Nigeria, True Love West Africa, and a weekly soccer newspaper, Goal and a television magazineTV24 in Angola.

36 Founded in 1915, Naspers Limited is a multinational media company involved in the electronic media and print media businesses. It operates primarily in Africa, South America, Europe, China, India, Southeast Asia, and the U.S. It is based in Cape Town, South Africa.

37 "MIH Acquires Stake in Afrigator," http://blog.afrigator.com, September 5, 2008.

38 "Naspers Buys into Afrigator," http://marketing.bizcommunity.com, September 5, 2008.

39 De Waal, "Afrigator Bytes."

40 De Waal, "Afrigator Takes on Africa."

41 "Naspers Buys Controlling Stake in Afrigator," http://business.africanpath.com, September 6, 2008.

42 "Afrigator Social Media Stats," http://www.slideshare.net/justinhartman/afrigator-social-media-stats, April 2008.

43 Started in 2003, ReadWriteWeb is a blog which provides news, reviews, and analyses related to web technology trends, web apps, and social networking. It is among the world's top 20 blogs.

44 Puterman, "Highest Praise for Afrigator."

45 *Business 2.0* was a monthly magazine owned by Time, Inc. The publication was closed in October 2007 due to low profitability.

46 The "Top 10 International Products for 2008" selected by Read/WriteWeb were innovative products that were developed outside the U.S. in accordance with global web standards.

47 Ismail Dhorat, "Is Adgator No Longer Serving Paid Ads?" www.startupafrica.com, July 23, 2009.

48 Ismail Dhorat, "Afrigator Joins the Online Publishers Association," www.startupafrica.com, February 5, 2009.

49 Ismail Dhorat, "24.com Blogs are Now Integrated with Afrigator," www.startupafrica.com, February 25, 2009.

[50] South African national and provincial elections were held on April 22, 2009.
[51] Twitter is a free social networking and micro-blogging service which allows users to send and read short text-based messages known as tweets.
[52] Flickr, owned by Yahoo! Inc., is an online photo sharing and video hosting website.

[53] Digg is a U.S.-based social content website that shares news, entertainment, and videos from all over the Web.
[54] The rand (denoted by letter R) is the currency of South Africa. As of October 2009, one South Africa rand was approximately equal to 0.1371 U.S. dollars.

[55] Lester Hein, "Afrigator Sponsors the SA Blog Awards," http://blog.afrigator.com, March 16, 2009.
[56] De Waal, "Afrigator Bytes."
[57] De Waal, "Afrigator Takes on Africa."
[58] De Waal, "Afrigator Bytes."
[59] De Waal, "Afrigator Takes on Africa."

REFERENCES AND SUGGESTED READINGS

Ismail Dhorat, **"Is Adgator No Longer Serving Paid Ads?"** www.startupafrica.com, July 23, 2009.

"Afrigator Turns Two Today… Somehow it Feels Like More!" http://justinhartman.com, April 3, 2009.

Lester Hein, **"Afrigator Sponsors the SA Blog Awards,"** http://blog.afrigator.com, March 16, 2009.

Ismail Dhorat, **"24.com Blogs are Now Integrated with Afrigator,"** www.startupafrica.com, February 25, 2009.

Mandy De Waal, **"Afrigator Bytes,"** www.brandchannel.com, February 23, 2009.

Ismail Dhorat, **"Afrigator Joins the Online Publishers Association,"** www.startupafrica.com, February 5, 2009.

"Facelift for Afrigator," www.bizcommunity.com, December 1, 2008.

"Naspers Buys Controlling Stake in Afrigator," http://business.africanpath.com, September 6, 2008.

"MIH Acquires Stake in Afrigator," http://blog.afrigator.com, September 5, 2008.

"Naspers Buys into Afrigator," http://marketing.bizcommunity.com, September 5, 2008.

"Afrigator Social Media Stats," http://www.slideshare.net/justinhartman/afrigator-social-media-stats, April 2008.

"Afrigator Launches Public Beta Site," http://blog.afrigator.com, January 10, 2008.

Simone Puterman, **"Highest Praise for Afrigator by Top Global Tech Blog,"** www.bizcommunity.com, November 29, 2007.

Mandy De Waal, **"Afrigator Takes on Africa,"** ww2.itweb.co.za, October 7, 2008.

http://www.netage.co.za/resources/93.

www.websiteoutlook.com/www.afrigator.com.

http://afrigator.com/.

www.hoovers.com.

www.readwriteweb.com.

www.nielsen-online.com.

www.internetworldstats.com.

Competition in Energy Drinks, Sports Drinks, and Vitamin-Enhanced Beverages

John E. Gamble
University of South Alabama

Alternative beverages such as energy drinks, sports drinks, and vitamin-enhanced beverages were the stars of the beverage industry during the mid-2000s. Rapid growth in the category, coupled with premium prices and high profit margins made alternative beverages an important part of beverage companies' lineup of brands. Global beverage companies such as Coca-Cola and PepsiCo had relied on such beverages to sustain volume growth in mature markets where consumers were reducing their consumption of carbonated soft drinks. In addition, Coca-Cola, PepsiCo, and other beverage companies were intent on expanding the market for alternative beverages by introducing energy drinks, sports drinks, and vitamin drinks in more and more emerging international markets. Global beverage producers had not been the only ones to benefit from increasing consumer demand for alternative beverage choices. Entrepreneurs such as the founders of Red Bull GmbH, Rockstar, Inc., Hansen Natural Corporation (maker of Monster Energy), Living Essentials (maker of 5-Hour Energy), and Energy Brands (originator of glacéau vitaminwater) had become multimillionaires through their development and sale of alternative beverages.

However, the premium-priced alternative beverage market had been hit especially hard by the lingering economic downturn in the United States. Sales of sports drinks declined by 12.3 percent between 2008 and 2009, and sales of flavored and vitamin-enhanced waters had declined by 12.5 percent over the same period. The sales of energy drinks fared better, but 2009 segment sales exceeded sales in 2008 by only 0.2 percent. Industry analysts were undecided on what

percentage of the poor 2009 performance for alternative beverages was related to the overall economy and how much could be attributed to market maturity. Beverage producers had made various attempts at increasing the size of the market for alternative beverages by extending existing product lines and developing altogether new products. For example, PepsiCo had expanded its lineup of Amp Energy drinks to 12 flavors, expanded SoBe vitamin-enhanced beverages to 28 flavors and variations, and increased the Gatorade lineup to include dozens of flavors and variations. Beverage producers were also seeking additional growth by quickly launching concentrated two-ounce energy shots to garner a share of the new beverage category that originated with the development of Living Essentials' 5-Hour Energy. Some beverage producers were also moving to capture demand for new relaxation drinks that were designed to have a calming effect or help those with insomnia.

While attempting to expand the market for alternative beverages and increase sales and market share, beverage producers also were forced to contend with criticism from some that energy drinks, energy shots, and relaxation drinks presented health risks for consumers and that some producers' strategies promoted reckless behavior. Excessive consumption of high-caffeine-content beverages could produce arrhythmias and insomnia, while mixing alcohol with energy drinks could mask the consumer's level of intoxication and lead to increased risk-taking and other serious alcohol-related problems. In addition, many physicians warned consumers against consuming

Copyright © 2010 by John E. Gamble. All rights reserved.

relaxation drinks that contained the potentially harmful ingredients melatonin and kava. But as 2011 approached, the primary concern of most producers of energy drinks, sports drinks, and vitamin-enhanced beverages was how to best improve their competitive standing in the marketplace.

INDUSTRY CONDITIONS IN 2010

The global beverage industry was projected to grow from $1.58 trillion in 2009 to nearly $1.78 trillion in 2014 as beverage producers entered new geographic markets, developed new types of beverages, and continued to create demand for popular drinks. A great deal of industry growth was expected to result from steady growth in the purchasing power of consumers in developing countries, since the saturation rate for all types of beverages was high in developed countries. For example, market maturity and poor economic conditions caused the U.S. beverage industry to decline by 2.1 percent in 2008 and by 3.1 percent in 2009. The 2.3 percent decline in the volume sales of carbonated soft drinks marked the

Exhibit 1   Dollar Value and Volume Sales of the Global Beverage Industry, 2005–2009, with Forecasts for 2010–2014

Year	Dollar Value ($ billions)	Volume Sales (billions of liters)
2005	$1,428.4	391.8
2006	1,469.3	409.1
2007	1,514.1	427.3
2008	1,548.3	442.6
2009	1,581.7	458.3
2010*	1,618.4	474.9
2011*	1,657.6	492.1
2012*	1,696.1	508.4
2013*	1,736.5	525.8
2014*	1,775.3	542.5

*Forecast.

Source: Global Beverages Industry Profile, Datamonitor, March 2010.

fifth consecutive year that U.S. consumers had purchased fewer carbonated soft drinks than the year before. Industry analysts believed that while carbonated soft drinks would remain the most-consumed beverage in the United States for some time, annual sales would continue to decline as consumers developed preferences for bottled water, sports drinks, fruit juices, ready-to-drink tea, vitamin-enhanced beverages, energy drinks, ready-to-drink coffee, and other types of beverages.

As consumer preferences shifted during the 2000s, sports drinks, energy drinks, and vitamin-enhanced drinks had grown to become important segments within the industry in 2010. In addition, such alternative beverages tended to carry high price points, which made them attractive to both new entrants and established beverage companies such as the Coca-Cola Company and PepsiCo. Sports drinks and vitamin-enhanced beverages tended to carry retail prices that were 50 to 75 percent higher than similar-size carbonated soft drinks and bottled water, while energy drink pricing by volume might be as much as 400 percent higher than carbonated soft drinks. While the alternative beverage segment of the industry offered opportunities for bottlers, the poor economy had decreased demand for higher-priced beverages, with sales of sports drinks declining by 12.3 percent between 2008 and 2009 and the sales of flavored and vitamin-enhanced waters declining by 12.5 percent over the same period. The economy had also impacted the sales of energy drinks, but only by slowing the growth in volume sales to 0.2 percent between 2008 and 2009. Among all types of beverages, only energy drinks and ready-to-drink tea experienced volume growth between 2008 and 2009. Exhibits 1 and 2 present sales statistics for the global and U.S. beverage industry.

Worldwide dollar sales of alternative beverages (sports drinks, energy drinks, and vitamin-enhanced beverages) grew by more than 13 percent annually between 2005 and 2007 before slowing to about 6 percent annually between 2007 and 2009. Demand in the United States had contributed greatly to the worldwide growth in alternative beverage consumption, with the United States accounting for 42.3 percent of the industry's worldwide sales of $40.2 billion in 2009. In the United States, sports drinks accounted for

Exhibit 2   **U.S. Beverage Industry Volume Sales by Segment, 2009**

Category	Volume (millions of gallons)	Market Share	Growth	Share Point Change
Carbonated soft drinks	13,919.3	48.2%	−2.3%	+0.4
Bottled water	8,435.3	29.2	−2.7	+0.1
Fruit beverages	3,579.2	12.4	−3.7	−0.1
Sports drinks	1,157.8	4.0	−12.3	+0.4
Ready-to-drink tea	901.4	3.1	1.2	+0.1
Flavored or enhanced water	460.0	1.6	−12.5	−0.2
Energy drinks	354.5	1.2	0.2	0.0
Ready-to-drink coffee	51.5	0.2	−5.4	0.0
Total	28,859.0	100.0%	− 3.1%	0.0

Note: Totals may not match data reported by Datamonitor because of differences in research methods.
Source: Beverage Marketing Corporation, as reported in "A Market in Decline," *Beverage World,* April 2010, p. 52.

nearly 60 percent of alternative beverage sales in 2009, while vitamin-enhanced drinks and energy drinks accounted for about 23 percent and 18 percent of 2009 alternative beverage sales, respectively. Exhibit 3 presents alternative beverage dollar value and volume sales for 2005 through 2009 and forecasts for alternative beverage sales for 2010 through 2014. Exhibits 4–7 present statistics on the relative sizes of the regional markets for alternative beverages.

Exhibit 3   **Dollar Value and Volume Sales of the Global Market for Alternative Beverages, 2005–2009, with Forecasts for 2010–2014**

Year	Dollar Value ($ billions)	Volume (billions of liters)
2005	$27.7	9.4
2006	31.9	10.3
2007	35.5	11.1
2008	37.8	11.9
2009	40.2	12.7
2010*	42.8	13.5
2011*	45.5	14.4
2012*	48.0	15.1
2013*	50.8	16
2014*	53.5	16.8

*Forecast.
Source: Global Functional Drinks Industry Profile, Datamonitor, April 2010.

Even though energy drinks, sports drinks, and vitamin-enhanced drinks were all categorized as alternative beverages, the consumer profile varied substantially across the three types of beverages. While the profile of an energy drink consumer was a teenage boy, sports drinks were most frequently purchased by those who engaged in sports, fitness, or other strenuous activities such as outdoor manual labor jobs. It was quite common for teens to consume sports drinks after practicing or participating in school sports events and for manual laborers to consume sports drinks on hot days. Vitamin-enhanced beverages could substitute for sports drinks but were frequently purchased by adult consumers interested in increasing their intakes of vitamins. Even though enhanced waters offered potential benefits, there

Exhibit 4   **Geographic Share of the Alternative Beverages Market, 2009**

Country	Percentage
United States	42.3%
Asia-Pacific	31.5
Europe	22.2
Americas (excluding U.S.)	4.0
Total	100.0%

Source: Global Functional Drinks Industry Profile, Datamonitor, April 2010, and United States Functional Drinks Industry Profile, Datamonitor, April 2010.

Exhibit 5   **Dollar Value and Volume Sales of the U.S. Market for Alternative Beverages, 2005–2009, with Forecasts for 2010–2014**

Year	Dollar Value ($ billions)	Volume (billions of liters)
2005	$9.2	2.8
2006	12.4	3.3
2007	14.8	3.7
2008	15.9	4.0
2009	17.0	4.2
2010*	18.2	4.5
2011*	19.5	4.7
2012*	20.8	5.0
2013*	22.2	5.3
2014*	23.6	5.5

*Forecast.
Source: United States Functional Drinks Industry Profile, Datamonitor, April 2010.

were some features of enhanced waters that might cause consumers to limit their consumption of such products, including the need for sweeteners to disguise the taste of added vitamins and

Exhibit 6   **Volume Sales and Dollar Value of the Asia-Pacific Alternative Beverages Market, 2005–2009, Forecasts for 2010–2014**

Year	Dollar Value ($ billions)	Volume (billions of liters)
2005	$10.2	4.80
2006	10.7	5.10
2007	11.2	5.44
2008	12.0	5.81
2009	12.7	6.20
2010*	13.5	6.63
2011*	14.3	7.09
2012*	14.9	7.41
2013*	15.7	7.82
2014*	16.5	8.23

*Forecast.
Source: Asia-Pacific Functional Drinks Industry Profile, Datamonitor, April 2010.

Exhibit 7   **Volume Sales and Dollar Value of the European Alternative Beverages Market, 2005–2009, with Forecasts for 2010–2014**

Year	Dollar Value ($ billions)	Volume (billions of liters)
2005	$7.4	1.27
2006	7.8	1.34
2007	8.2	1.43
2008	8.6	1.51
2009	9.1	1.60
2010*	9.5	1.69
2011*	9.9	1.78
2012*	10.4	1.88
2013*	10.8	1.98
2014*	11.3	2.08

*Forecast.
Source: Europe Functional Drinks Industry Profile, Datamonitor, April 2010.

supplements. As a result, calorie counts for vitamin-enhanced beverages ranged from 20 calories per 16-ounce serving for Propel to 100 calories per 16-ounce serving for glacéau vitaminwater. In addition, some medical researchers had suggested that consumers would need to drink approximately 10 bottles of enhanced water each day to meet minimum dietary requirements for the vitamins promoted on the waters' labels.

Distribution and Sale of Alternative Beverages

Consumers could purchase most alternative beverages in supermarkets, supercenters, natural foods stores, wholesale clubs, and convenience stores. Convenience stores were a particularly important distribution channel for alternative beverages since sports drinks, vitamin-enriched drinks, and energy drinks were usually purchased for immediate consumption. In fact, convenience stores accounted for about 75 percent of energy drink sales in 2010. Although energy drinks were typically purchased in convenience stores, sports drinks and vitamin-enhanced beverages were also available in most delis and many restaurants, from vending machines, and sometimes at sporting events and other special events like concerts, outdoor festivals, and carnivals.

Pepsi-Cola and Coca-Cola's soft drink businesses aided the two companies in making alternative beverages available in supermarkets, supercenters, wholesale clubs, and convenience stores. Soft drink sales were important to all types of food stores since soft drinks made up a sizable percentage of the store's sales and since food retailers frequently relied on soft drink promotions to generate store traffic. Coca-Cola and Pepsi-Cola were able to encourage their customers to purchase items across its product line to ensure prompt and complete shipment of key soft drink products. Smaller producers typically used third parties like beer and wine distributors or food distributors to make sales and deliveries to supermarkets, convenience store buyers, and restaurants and delis. Most distributors made deliveries of alternative beverages to convenience stores and restaurants along with their regular scheduled deliveries of other foods and beverages.

Because of the difficulty for food service distributors to restock vending machines and provide alternative beverages to special events, Coca-Cola and Pepsi-Cola were able to dominate such channels since they could make deliveries of sports drinks and vitamin-enhanced drinks along with their deliveries of carbonated soft drinks. Coca-Cola and Pepsi-Cola's vast beverage distribution systems made it easy for the two companies to make Gatorade, SoBe, Powerade, and glacéau vitaminwater available anywhere Coke or Pepsi could be purchased.

Convenience stores were aggressive in pressing alternative beverage producers and food distributors for low prices and slotting fees. Most convenience stores carried only two to four brands of alternative beverages beyond what was distributed by Coca-Cola and PepsiCo, and required sellers to pay annual slotting fees in return for providing bottle facings on a cooler shelf. Food and beverage distributors usually allowed alternative beverage producers to negotiate slotting fees and any rebates directly with convenience store buyers.

There was not as much competition among producers of sports drinks and vitamin-enhanced drinks to gain shelf space in delis and restaurants, since volume was relatively low—making per unit distribution costs exceedingly high unless other beverages were delivered along with alternative beverages. PepsiCo and Coca-Cola were among the better-suited alternative beverage producers to economically distribute sports drinks and vitamin-enhanced beverages to restaurants, since they likely provided fountain drinks to such establishments. Exhibit 8 presents worldwide and regional market shares for the three largest producers of alternative beverages in 2009. Distributors for the leading energy drink brands sold in the United States are listed in Exhibit 9.

Suppliers to the Industry

The suppliers to the alternative beverage industry included the makers of such nutritive and non-nutritive ingredients as sugar, aspartame, fructose, glucose, natural and artificial flavoring,

Exhibit 8 **Worldwide and Regional Market Shares for the Three Largest Producers of Alternative Beverages, 2009**

Company	Worldwide	United States	Asia-Pacific	Europe
PepsiCo	26.5%	47.8%	12.4	12.9%
Coca-Cola	11.5	10.2	13.7	n.a.
Red Bull	7.0	10.6	n.a.	10.1
Others	55.0	31.5	73.9	77.0
Total	100.0%	100.0%	100.0%	100.0%

n.a. = Not available

Sources: Global Functional Drinks Industry Profile, Datamonitor, April 2010; United States Functional Drinks Industry Profile, Datamonitor, April 2010; Asia-Pacific Functional Drinks Industry Profile, Datamonitor, April 2010; and Europe Functional Drinks Industry Profile, Datamonitor, April 2010.

Exhibit 9   **Market Shares for the Leading Energy Drink Brands in the United States, 2006–2009**

Brand	Distributor	2006 (% of dollar sales)	2007 (% of dollar sales)	2008 (% of dollar sales)	2009 (% of dollar sales)
Red Bull	Independent	43%	35%	40%	40%
Monster	Coca-Cola	15	27	23	27
Rockstar	PepsiCo	11	11	12	8
NOS	Coca-Cola	n.a.	2	2	4
Amp	PepsiCo	4	5	8	3
DoubleShot	PepsiCo	n.a.	n.a.	2	3
Full Throttle	Coca-Cola	7	7	4	2
Others		20	13	9	13
Total		100%	100%	100%	100%

n.a. = Not available.

Sources: "2010 State of the Industry Report," *Beverage World,* April 2010; BevNET.com.

artificial colors, caffeine, taurine, glucuronolactone, niacin, sodium, potassium, chloride, and other nutritional supplements. Suppliers to the industry also included the manufacturers of aluminum cans, plastic bottles and caps, label printers, and secondary packaging suppliers. While unique supplements like taurine might be available from only a few sources, most packaging supplies needed for the production of alternative beverages were readily available for a large number of suppliers. The numerous suppliers of secondary packaging materials (e.g., cardboard boxes, shrink-wrap, six-pack rings, printed film or paper labels) aggressively competed for the business of large alternative beverage producers. All but the largest sellers of alternative beverages contracted procurement and production activities to contract bottlers who produced energy drinks and other alternative beverages to the sellers' specifications.

Key Competitive Capabilities in the Alternative Beverages Market

Product innovation had been among the most important competitive features of the alternative beverage industry since the introduction of Gatorade in 1967. Alternative beverages competed on the basis of differentiation from traditional drinks such as carbonated soft drinks or fruit juices and

were also positioned within their respective segments on the basis of differentiation. For example, all energy drink brands attempted to develop brand loyalty based on taste, the energy-boosting properties of their ingredients, and image. An energy drink's image was a factor of its brand name and packaging, clever ads, endorsements from celebrities and extreme sports athletes, and sponsorships of extreme sports events and music concerts. Differentiation among vitamin-enhanced beverages tended to center on brand name and packaging, advertising, unique flavors, and nutritional properties. Because of the importance of brand recognition, successful sellers of alternative beverages were required to possess well-developed brand-building skills. The industry's largest sellers were global food and beverage companies—having built respected brands in snack foods, soft drinks, and fruit juices prior to entering the alternative beverage industry.

Alternative beverage sellers also needed to have efficient distribution systems to supermarket and convenience store channels to be successful in the industry. It was imperative for alternative beverage distributors (whether direct store delivery by bottlers or delivery by third-parties) to maximize the number of deliveries per driver since distribution included high fixed costs for warehouses, trucks, handheld inventory tracking devices, and labor. It was also critical for distributors and sellers to provide on-time deliveries and offer responsive customer service to large customers. Also, volume and market share were key factors in keeping marketing expenses at an acceptable per-unit level.

Recent Trends in the Alternative Beverage Market

Despite the impact of the ongoing U.S. recession on the entire beverage industry, alternative beverage producers were optimistic about prospects for the industry. Demand was expected to grow worldwide as consumer purchasing power increased, and even though volume was down in the United States for sports drinks and vitamin-enhanced drinks, alternative beverages offered profit margins much higher than those of other beverages. Innovation in brands, flavors, and formulations was expected to be necessary for supporting premium pricing and volume increases. Industry analysts believed that such exotic flavors as cardamom, hibiscus, and cupuacu might prove to be hits in 2011 and 2012.

The emergence of two-ounce energy shots sold on convenience store counters had proved to be an important growth category for the industry. The category was created with the introduction of Living Essentials' 5-Hour Energy in 2004. 5-Hour Energy contained amino acids and taurine plus 2,000 percent of the daily requirement for vitamin B_6, 8,333 percent of the daily requirement for B_{12}, and 100 milligrams of caffeine (the equivalent of a cup of coffee). By comparison, the caffeine content of energy drinks ranged from 160 milligrams for Red Bull to 240 milligrams for Rockstar Punched. Unlike energy drinks that focused on teens, energy shots were targeted to office workers, parents, and other adults who might need a boost of energy during a demanding day. Red Bull, Coca-Cola's NOS, Hansen's Monster, PepsiCo's Amp, and Rockstar had all developed competing energy shots, but none were a serious threat to Living Essentials' 5-Hour Energy in 2010. 5-Hour Energy held an 85 percent market share in the category in 2009. Exhibit 10 presents annual revenues for the top five energy shot brands in the United States in 2009. Analysts believed that Europe, Australia, South America, and the Middle East were attractive markets for the expansion-minded makers of energy shots.

Unlike carbonated soft drinks, the caffeine content of energy shots and energy drinks was

Exhibit 10 **Annual Revenues for the Top Five Energy Shot Brands in the United States, 2009**

Brand	Revenues ($ millions)	Revenue Growth (2008–2009)
5-Hour Energy	$494.6	+58.6%
Stacker2 6-Hour Power	30.4	+32.9
Red Bull Energy Shot	22.1	n.a.
Monster Hitman	19.7	+611.7
NOS Energy Shot	11.8	−10.4

n.a. = Not available

Source: Beverage World 2010 State of the Industry Report, April 2010.

not regulated by the U.S. Food and Drug Administration and could contain as much caffeine as the producer thought appropriate. There was concern among some health professionals over the high caffeine content of energy drinks and the effects of large doses of caffeine on individuals, especially children. The most significant health problems related to high caffeine consumption were heart arrhythmia and insomnia. It was not unheard of for adults with heart arrhythmias to be admitted to emergency rooms after consuming three or more energy drinks in one day. Also, physicians attributed a New Mexico man's appendicitis and gallstones to excessive consumption of energy drinks. Physicians also warned that the combination of energy drinks and over-the-counter drugs such as NoDoz could cause seizures. However, clinical studies had shown that, in moderate doses, caffeine contributed to healthy weight loss, was an effective treatment for asthma and headaches and reduced the risk of Parkinson's disease, depression, colon cancer, and type 2 diabetes. As a precaution, Monster Energy placed the following warning on its labels: "Limit 3 cans per day, not recommended for children, pregnant women or people sensitive to caffeine."[1]

There was also concern over the tendency of some individuals to mix alcohol with energy drinks. It was not uncommon at all for partiers to use energy drinks as a mixer to help offset the depressive effects of alcohol and keep their energy levels high throughout the evening. It was estimated that more than 25 percent of college-age drinkers mixed alcohol with energy drinks. The frequency of the practice led MillerCoors to develop an alcohol energy drink that contained caffeine, taurine, guarana, and ginseng in addition to alcohol. Anheuser-Busch sold two similar drinks called Tilt and Bud Extra. Both companies removed the caffeine from the drinks after attorneys general in several states had written the U.S. Food and Drug Administration (FDA) to ask that the federal government force the removal of the products from the market. The attorneys general argued that the addition of caffeine to alcohol masked a drinker's level of intoxication and could lead to "increased risk-taking and other serious alcohol related problems such as traffic accidents, violence, sexual assault, and suicide."[2]

The relaxation drink niche within the alternative beverage industry also caused some concern among health professionals and members of law enforcement. Relaxation drinks such as Vacation in a Bottle (ViB) and Dream Water contained the hormone melatonin, which was produced by humans, plants, and animals and had many known and unknown effects on the human body. Melatonin had been associated with rapid-eye movement (REM) sleep and was used by some as a supplement to help treat insomnia. A Harvard Medical School sleep expert warned against the consumption of relaxation drinks by stating that hormones "should not be put in beverages, since the amount people drink often depends on thirst and taste rather than being taken only when needed like any other drug."[3] Kava and valerian root were two other common ingredients of relaxation drinks; the FDA warned against the use of kava and had not approved valerian root as a food additive.

Controversy also surrounded some relaxation drinks because of their association with the abuse of prescription cough syrup. The practice of mixing a prescription cough syrup whose ingredients included promethazine and codeine with Sprite or other carbonated soft drinks had become common in some inner-city areas, especially in southern U.S. states. The purple-colored cough syrup drink, which was commonly called "purple drank" or "sizzurp," was said to have been originated by Houston, Texas, disc jockey and rapper DJ Screw, who died from an overdose of purple drank in 2000. Purple drank was frequently mentioned in hip-hop and rap songs such as those performed by Three 6 Mafia, Eminem, Lil' Wyte, Lil Boosie, Mike Jones, Lil' Wayne, Ludacris, T.I., and Kanye West. The use of sizzurp was also a problem in professional sports, and possession of the controlled substances used to make sizzurp had led to the arrests of a number of professional athletes, including Green Bay Packers defensive lineman Johnny Jolly and former Oakland Raiders quarterback JaMarcus Russell. Legal authorities believed that the purple-colored relaxation drinks Drank and Purple Stuff attempted to exploit the street use of purple drank. Innovative Beverage Group, the maker of Drank, had built its marketing plan on product placements in rap and hip-hop videos and launched a competition in summer 2010 that would award prizes to those who wrote the best new rap songs about the company's product.

PROFILES OF THE LEADING ALTERNATIVE BEVERAGE PRODUCERS

PepsiCo

In 2010, PepsiCo was the world's fourth-largest food and beverage company, with 2009 sales of about $43 billion. The company's brands were sold in more than 200 countries and included such well-known names as Lay's, Tostitos, Cheetos, Mountain Dew, Pepsi, Doritos, Lipton Iced Tea, Tropicana, Aquafina, SoBe, Gatorade, Quaker, and Cracker Jack. The company held commanding market shares in many of the food and beverage categories where it competed. In 2009, it was the number one seller of beverages in the United States and its Frito-Lay division was four times as large as the next-largest seller of snacks in the United States. PepsiCo had upset Coca-Cola to become the largest seller of beverages in the United States, not by selling more carbonated soft drinks than Coke (Coca-Cola was the largest seller of carbonated soft drinks in 2009), but by leading in most other beverage categories. For example, Aquafina was the best-selling brand of water in the United States, Frappuccino was the number one brand of ready-to-drink coffee, Tropicana was ranked first in orange juice sales, and Gatorade held a commanding lead in sports drinks. The company's strength in noncarbonated beverages made it the world's largest seller of alternative beverages, with a global market share in 2009 of 26.5 percent. PepsiCo held more than a 2-to-1 worldwide market-share lead over industry runner-up, Coca-Cola, which had a global market share in alternative beverages of 11.5 percent in 2009. However, PepsiCo's greatest strength was in the United States, where it held a 47.8 percent share of the total alternative beverage market in 2009.

PepsiCo's best-selling alternative beverages included Gatorade (which held a 75 percent share of the $1.57 billion U.S. sports drink market), Propel, SoBe Lifewater, and Amp Energy. PepsiCo produced 12 flavors of Amp Energy drinks and two flavors of No Fear energy drinks. Its SoBe brand included both energy drinks and vitamin-enhanced drinks. In 2010, PepsiCo bottled and marketed 2 varieties of SoBe Adrenaline Rush energy drinks and 28 varieties of SoBe vitamin-enhanced beverages. PespiCo also marketed a line of DoubleShot Energy drinks that complemented its Starbucks Frappuccino drink line.

The company expanded its lineup of alternative drinks in 2009 with the launch of Charge,

a lemon-flavored energy drink containing L-carnitine; Rebuild, a black tea drink fortified with amino acids and antioxidants; Defend, a drink fortified with antioxidants and beta-alanine; and Bloodshot, a juice drink containing 150 percent of the daily recommended dosage of vitamins B and C. The company also had a multiyear distribution agreement with Rockstar to distribute Rockstar energy drinks in the United States and Canada.

A summary of PepsiCo's financial performance between 2007 and 2009 is presented in Exhibit 11.

The Coca-Cola Company

The Coca-Cola Company was the world's leading manufacturer, marketer, and distributor of nonalcoholic beverage concentrates, with 2009 revenues of nearly $31 billion and sales in more than 200 countries. The company was best known for Coca-Cola, which had been called the world's most valuable brand. Along with the universal appeal of the Coca-Cola brand, Coca-Cola's vast global distribution system—which included independent bottlers, bottlers partially owned by Coca-Cola, and company-owned bottlers—made

Exhibit 11 **Financial Summary for PepsiCo, 2007–2009 ($ millions, except per share information)**

	2009	2008	2007
Net revenue	$43,232	$43,251	$39,474
Cost of sales	20,099	20,351	18,038
Selling, general and administrative expenses	15,026	15,877	14,196
Amortization of intangible assets	63	64	58
Operating profit	8,044	6,959	7,182
Bottling equity income	365	374	560
Interest expense	(397)	(329)	(224)
Interest income	67	41	125
Income before income taxes	8,079	7,045	7,643
Provision for income taxes	2,100	1,879	1,973
Net income	5,979	5,166	5,670
Less: Net income attributable to noncontrolling interests	33	24	12
Net income attributable to PepsiCo	$5,946	$5,142	$5,658
Net income attributable to PepsiCo per common share			
Basic	$3.81	$3.26	$3.48
Diluted	$3.77	$3.21	$3.41

Source: PepsiCo, 2009 10-K report.

Coke an almost unstoppable international power-house. Coca-Cola, Diet Coke, Fanta, and Sprite all ranked among the top five best-selling nonalcoholic beverages worldwide in 2009.

The strength of the Coca-Cola brand also aided the company in gaining distribution for new beverages. In the United States, Coca-Cola produced, marketed, and distributed Minute Maid orange juice products, Dasani purified water, Powerade sports drinks, an assortment of energy drink brands, Fuze vitamin-enhanced beverages, Nestea ready-to-drink teas, and glacéau vitaminwater. The company also produced and sold country- and region-specific beverages such as Bonaqua sparkling water in Europe, Georgia ready-to-drink coffee in Japan, and Hugo fruit and milk protein drinks in Latin America.

Even though Coca-Cola was the worldwide leader in carbonated soft drink sales, it had struggled to build market share in alternative beverages and trailed PepsiCo by a significant margin worldwide in energy drinks, sports drinks, and vitamin-enhanced beverages. Asia was the only geographic market where Coca-Cola's sales of alternative beverages exceeded the sales of PepsiCo's energy drinks, sports drinks, and vitamin-enhanced beverages. As of 2009, Coca-Cola had yet to gain strong demand for its alternative beverages in Europe and, as a result, was not listed among the leading sellers of alternative beverages in that market. In the United States, Coca-Cola was the third-largest seller of alternative beverages, with its combined sales of Powerade, Full Throttle, NOS, Rehab, TaB, and Vault energy drinks; glacéau vitaminwater; and Fuze vitamin-enhanced drinks, falling just short of the sales of Red Bull energy drinks.

Much of the company's efforts to build market share in 2009 and 2010 centered on new-product development and the introduction of existing brands into new country markets. In 2009, Coca-Cola introduced glacéau vitaminwater in South Africa, France, South Korea, Japan, Belgium, Portugal, Hong Kong, China, and Sweden; in that same year it also launched Cascal, a fermented fruit drink, in the United States and Burn energy drink in India. The company had introduced its newly developed Gladiator energy drink in Latin America in 2008. Among Coca-Cola's greatest resources in the energy drink category was its multiyear distribution agreement with Hansen Natural Corporation to distribute Hansen's Monster energy drink in parts of the United States, Canada, and six European countries.

A summary of the Coca-Cola Company's financial performance between 2007 and 2009 is presented in Exhibit 12.

Red Bull GmbH

Red Bull was the world's number one seller of energy drinks, which made it the third-largest producer of alternative beverages worldwide and the number two seller of alternative beverages in the United States and Europe. Red Bull's distinctive taste and formula of vitamins, taurine, and caffeine launched the energy drink market in the Western world in the late 1990s. Energy drinks similar to Red Bull had been produced and marketed in Asia since the 1970s. In fact, Red Bull's formula was modeled after Krating Daeng, a popular energy drink sold in Thailand that was recommended as a jet lag remedy to Austrian businessman Dietrich Mateschitz. Mateschitz had been in Thailand to call on T.C. Pharmaceutical, which was a client of his employer at the time and the manufacturer or Krating Daeng. Mateschitz was so impressed with the flavor and energy-boosting capabilities of Krating Daeng that he left his job and formed a partnership with T.C. Pharmaceutical's founder in 1984 to market the drink in Europe. The energy drink's formula was modified slightly to better appeal to Western palates and was renamed Red Bull, which was the English translation of Krating Daeng. Red Bull was launched in Austria in 1987 and sold more than 1 million cans during the year. The company expanded into Hungary and Slovenia in 1992, Germany and the United Kingdom in 1994, and the United States in 1997. In 2010, the company exported its energy drinks to more than 160 countries and delivered to retailers by independent distributors.

The company's slogan, "Red Bull gives you wings," signaled its energy-boosting properties, and the company's endorsements involved almost every high-energy sport worldwide. In 2010, Red Bull sponsored not only athletes and teams competing in sports ranging from auto racing to freestyle biking to wakeboarding to snowboarding to golf but also a number of music events around the

Exhibit 12   Financial Summary for the Coca-Cola Company, 2007–2009 ($ millions)

	2009	2008	2007
Net operating revenues	$30,990	$31,944	$28,857
Cost of goods sold	11,088	11,374	10,406
Gross profit	19,902	20,570	18,451
Selling, general, and administrative expenses	11,358	11,774	10,945
Other operating charges	313	350	254
Operating income	8,231	8,446	7,252
Interest income	249	333	236
Interest expense	355	438	456
Equity income (loss)—net	781	(874)	668
Other income (loss)—net	40	39	219
Income before income taxes	8,946	7,506	7,919
Income taxes	2,040	1,632	1,892
Consolidated net income	6,906	5,874	6,027
Less: Net income attributable to noncontrolling interests	82	67	46
Net income	$ 6,824	$ 5,807	$ 5,981

Source: Coca-Cola Company, 2009 10-K report.

world featuring hip-hop, rap, and hard rock groups. In addition, Red Bull fielded company-sponsored soccer teams in New York City; Salzburg, Austria; Leipzig, Germany; and São Paulo, Brazil. The company owned the Salzburg, Austria, hockey team that played under the Red Bull name.

Red Bull also promoted a series of Flugtag (flight day) events held around the world, during which participants were encouraged to fly their homemade human-powered flying machines—most of which seemed more comically designed than flightworthy. Teams of five designed and piloted their crafts to the end of a 30-foot-high ramp positioned over a body of water. Each team was scored for flight distance, creativity, and showmanship to determine a winner. The appeal of attending the events for spectators was to watch the vast majority of the flying machines merely crash off the end of the ramp.

In 2010, the company produced Red Bull Energy Drink, Red Bull Sugarfree, Red Bull Cola, Red Bull Energy Shots. The privately held company did not disclose financial information to the public, but it did announce shipments of 3.906 billion cans in 2009 and shipments of 3.921 billion cans in 2008.

Hansen Natural Corporation

Hansen Natural Corporation developed and marketed a variety of alternative beverages including natural sodas, blended fruit juices, energy drinks, sports drinks, fruit juice smoothies, ready-to-drink teas, and vitamin-enhanced drinks. The Corona, California, company was founded in 1935 by Hubert Hansen to produce a line of natural sodas and fruit juices and was acquired by South Africans Rodney Sacks and Hilton Schlosberg in 1992 for $14.5 million. Under the leadership of Sacks and Schlosberg, Hansen's sales steadily grew from about $17 million in 1992 to $80 million in 2001. However, the company's sales skyrocketed after its launch of Monster Energy drinks in 2002. By 2004, the company's revenues had increased to $180 million and its profits had grown from $3 million in 2001 to $20 million in 2004. In 2009, Monster was the second-best-selling energy drink brand in the United States and the company's annual revenues and net earnings had grown to more than $1.3 billion and $208 million, respectively. A summary of the company's financial performance between 2005 and 2009 is presented in Exhibit 13.

Exhibit 13   Financial Summary for Hansen Natural Corporation, 2005–2009 ($ thousands, except per share information)

	2009	2008	2007	2006	2005
Gross sales	$1,309,335	$1,182,876	$1,025,795	$696,322	$415,417
Net sales	1,143,299	1,033,780	904,465	605,774	348,886
Gross profit	612,316	538,794	468,013	316,594	182,543
Gross profit as a percentage to net sales	53.6%	52.1%	51.7%	52.3%	52.3%
Operating income	337,309	163,591	230,986	158,579	103,443
Net income	$208,716	$108,032	$149,406	$97,949	$62,775
Net income per common share:					
Basic	$2.32	$1.17	$1.64	$1.09	$0.71
Diluted	$2.21	$1.11	$1.51	$0.99	$0.65
Cash, cash equivalents, and investments	$427,672	$375,513	$302,650	$136,796	$73,515
Total assets	800,070	761,837	544,603	308,372	163,890
Debt	206	959	663	303	525
Stockholders' equity	584,953	436,316	422,167	225,084	125,509

Source: Hansen Natural Corporation, 2009 10-K report.

In 2010, Hansen's energy drink lineup included Monster Energy, X-Presso Monster Hammer, Nitrous Monster Energy, Monster Hitman Energy Shooter, Hansen Energy Pro, and Lost Energy. The company also produced and sold Hansen's natural juices and iced tea; Peace Tea, Rumba, Samba, and Tango energy juices; Blue Sky natural sodas; SELF Beauty Elixir; and Vidration enhanced alternative beverages. Sales of Monster energy drinks accounted for approximately 90 percent of Hansen Natural Corporation's total revenues in 2009.

Hansen Natural's rapid success in the energy drink market came about in large part because of its decision in 2002 to match Red Bull on price while packaging Monster drinks in 16-ounce containers (nearly double the size of Red Bull's 8.3-ounce container). The company also imitated Red Bull's image-building and marketing approaches through eye-catching in-store promotions and point-of-sale materials and extreme sports endorsements in snowboarding, BMX, mountain biking, skiing, snowmobiling, skateboarding, and automobile and motorcycle racing. In addition, Hansen and Vans co-sponsored music festivals featuring hard rock and alternative bands.

Hansen Natural outsourced 100 percent of its production of energy drinks and other beverages to contract bottlers throughout the United States. Distribution of the company's energy drinks and other beverages in the United States was split between Anheuser-Busch and Coca-Cola. Coca-Cola also distributed Monster energy drinks in Great Britain, France, Belgium, the Netherlands, Luxembourg, and Monaco. Hansen Natural had also entered into distribution agreements with beverage producers in Mexico and Australia to make Monster energy drinks available in those countries. While its energy drinks were sold in supermarkets, convenience stores, bars, nightclubs, and restaurants, Hansen's other beverage brands were typically found only in health food stores.

Other Sellers

In addition to the industry's leading sellers of alternative beverages, there were hundreds of regional and specialty brands of energy drinks, sports drinks, and enhanced beverages in the United States and internationally. Most of these companies were privately held bottlers with distribution limited to either small geographic regions or specialty grocers and health food stores. In some cases, regional brands were produced by divisions of large corporations and might have a commanding market share in one particular country but limited distribution outside that market. For example, global pharmaceutical giant GlaxoSmithKline did not sell alternative beverages in North America or Asia, but its sales of Lucozade Energy, Lucozade Sport, and Lucozade Alert energy shot made it the second-largest seller of alternative beverages in Europe, with a 2009 market share of 11.4 percent. GlaxoSmithKline's sales of alternative beverages accounted for $1.3 billion of its 2009 annual revenues of $44.2 billion. The majority of the company's revenues came from the sale of prescription drugs and over-the-counter medicines and oral care products such as Contact, Nicorette gum, Tums, and Aquafresh. Japanese pharmaceutical company Otsuka Pharmaceutical was the third-largest seller of energy drinks, sports drinks, and vitamin-enhanced beverages in the Asia-Pacific region, with a 9.4 percent market share in 2009.

Other than Red Bull, Rockstar was the most noteworthy privately held alternative beverage company. The Las Vegas, Nevada–based company entered the energy drink market in 2001 using a strategy that would be imitated by Hansen's Monster brand a year later. Rockstar was packaged in a 16-ounce can and priced comparably to Red Bull's pricing for its 8.3-ounce can. Rockstar's image, like that of Red Bull and Monster, was built on extreme sports endorsements and hard rock promotions. Among the company's annually sponsored music festivals was the Mayhem Festival, which in 2010 included such musical acts as Rob Zombie, Five Finger Death Punch, Korn, In This Moment, Chimaira, and 3 Inches of Blood. The company also sponsored other hard rock and metal tours such as Taste of Chaos, the Warped Tour, and the Uproar Festival. In 2010, Rockstar energy drinks were available in 11 flavors and Rockstar energy shots were available in two flavors. Rockstar beverages were distributed in the United States and Canada by PepsiCo and were distributed in Australia, New Zealand, Japan, Germany, Switzerland, Finland, Spain, the Netherlands, and the United Kingdom through agreements with beverage distributors in those countries.

The number of brands competing in the sports drinks, energy drinks, and vitamin-enhanced beverage segments of the alternative beverage industry continued to grow each year. In 2009, 231 new vitamin-enhanced beverages were introduced in the United States. The relative maturity of the sports drink segment and the dominant market position held by Gatorade limited the number of new sports drink introductions to 51 in 2009. Launches of new energy drink brands had grown steadily from 172 in 2005 to 380 in 2008, but energy drink introductions fell to 138 in 2009 as the segment matured and financially squeezed consumers became more price conscious. Overall, the relative strength of the energy drink, enhanced beverage, and sports drink beverage segments would likely attract additional entrants over the next several years.

ENDNOTES

[1] Quoted in "Energy Boost a Bummer? Hospital Study Raises Alarm about Drinks," *Chattanooga Times Free Press*, April 9, 2009, p. E6.

[2] Quoted in "FDA Questions Safety of Alcoholic Energy Drinks," Associated Press, November 13, 2009.

[3] Quoted in "These Drinks'll Knock You Out!" *Daily News* (New York), February 7, 2010, p. 6.

Competition in the Golf Equipment Industry in 2009

John E. Gamble
University of South Alabama

It is not known with certainty when the game of golf originated, but historians believe it evolved from ball and stick games played throughout Europe in the Middle Ages. The first known reference to golf in historical documents was a 1452 decree by King James II of Scotland banning the game. The ban was instituted because King James believed his archers were spending too much time playing golf and not enough time practicing archery. King James III and King James IV reaffirmed the ban in 1471 and 1491, respectively, but King James IV ultimately repealed the ban in 1502 after he himself became hooked on the game. The game became very popular with royalty and commoners alike, with the Archbishop of St. Andrews decreeing in 1553 that the local citizenry had the right to play on the links of St. Andrews and King James VI declaring in 1603 that his subjects had the right to play golf on Sundays.

The first known international golf tournament was played in Leith, Scotland, in 1682 when Scotsmen George Patterson and James VII prevailed over two Englishmen. By the 1700s golf had become an established sport in the British Isles, complete with golfing societies, published official rules, regularly held tournaments, full-time equipment manufacturers, and equipment exports from Scotland to the American Colonies. The links of St. Andrews became a private golf society in 1754 and was bestowed the title of Royal & Ancient Golf Club of St. Andrews by King William IV in 1834. The first golf society in the United States was founded in Charleston, South Carolina, in 1786.

In the United States, golf was a game that interested primarily the wealthy until the arrival of televised tournaments in the 1950s and 1960s featuring the charismatic PGA Tour players Arnold Palmer, Gary Player, and Jack Nicklaus. Increased public awareness, rising household incomes, and a rise in the number of public golf courses helped golf become a game enjoyed by more than 27 million Americans by the late 1990s. Perhaps the greatest contributor to the golf's growth was the series of technological innovations in golf club design that made the game a little easier to play. The innovations in clubhead design by equipment manufacturers such as Callaway Golf, Ping Golf, and Taylor-Made Golf gave golfers of all skill levels added distance and accuracy and helped equipment sales grow to $2.9 billion by 2007.

Even though golf equipment industry sales at on-course and off-course golf shops totaled nearly $2.8 billion in 2008, the industry was in the midst of its worst-ever crisis in 2009. Equipment industry revenues had begun to decline as growth in the number of golfers stalled and rules put in place by golf's governing organizations to limit innovation in golf clubs had forced manufacturers to rely more on price to increase volume. In addition, the U.S recession that began in December 2007 and continued into 2009 had placed many industries in peril, but left industries relying on discretionary spending badly battered. Rounds played had not grown appreciably

Copyright © 2010 by John E. Gamble. All rights reserved.

between 2004 and 2007 and had declined by 1.8 percent during 2008 as Americans began shifting discretionary income from spending to savings. Sales of golf equipment declined by 5.7 percent during 2008 and it appeared that 2009 industry sales would decline by an additional 15 percent to 20 percent. The effects of technological limitations imposed by golf's governing organizations, a decline in the number of golf-

ers, and the worst economic conditions since the early 1980s had converged to force senior managers of the leading golf equipment manufacturers to rethink their strategies. Whatever new strategies that might unfold would have to stand up under the pressure of a possible protracted recession. Golf equipment retail sales, units sold, and average selling price by product category for 1997–2008 are presented in Exhibit 1.

Exhibit 1   **Retail Value, Units Sold, and Average Selling Price of Golf Equipment Sold by U.S. On-Course and Off-Course Pro Shops, 1997–2008 (retail value dollar amounts and units in millions)**

	Drivers and Woods		
Year	Retail Value (in Millions)	Units Sold (in Millions)	Average Selling Price
1997	$ 676.8	2.93	$ 231
1998	601.1	2.81	214
1999	583.8	2.91	201
2000	599.1	2.94	204
2001	626.6	2.99	210
2002	608.7	3.09	197
2003	660.4	3.28	201
2004	654.1	3.56	184
2005	792.2	4.76	166
2006	883.3	5.12	172
2007	877.7	5.03	174
2008	772.2	4.61	167

	Irons		
Year	Retail Value (in Millions)	Units Sold (in Millions)	Average Selling Price Per Club
1997	$ 533.4	7.12	$ 75
1998	485.4	6.87	71
1999	447.9	6.97	64
2000	475.3	7.14	67
2001	459.3	7.17	64
2002	456.4	7.42	62
2003	461.4	7.66	60
2004	482.6	8.06	60
2005	534.3	8.26	65
2006	570.7	8.35	68
2007	579.5	8.22	71
2008	544.5	7.61	72

(Continued)

Exhibit 1   *(Continued)*

	Putters		
Year	Retail Value (in Millions)	Units Sold (in Millions)	Average Selling Price
1997	$ 142.1	1.70	$ 83
1998	150.3	1.68	89
1999	160.1	1.68	95
2000	161.5	1.67	97
2001	167.2	1.65	101
2002	184.3	1.65	111
2003	195.2	1.60	122
2004	188.6	1.58	120
2005	188.4	1.56	121
2006	193.8	1.53	127
2007	190.0	1.46	130
2008	182.7	1.34	137

	Wedges		
Year	Retail Value (in Millions)	Units Sold (in Millions)	Average Selling Price
1997	$ 67.6	0.78	$ 86
1998	64.3	0.79	82
1999	65.0	0.81	80
2000	68.3	0.82	83
2001	69.4	0.82	85
2002	71.2	0.83	85
2003	77.0	0.88	87
2004	79.3	0.93	86
2005	87.5	0.99	89
2006	93.9	1.03	91
2007	95.6	1.07	90
2008	100.4	1.09	92

	Golf Balls		
Year	Retail Value (in Millions)	Units Sold (in Million Dozens)	Average Selling Price Per Dozen
1997	$ 458.7	19.97	$ 22.97
1998	487.4	20.06	24.30
1999	518.1	20.46	25.32
2000	530.8	20.80	25.52
2001	555.6	21.32	26.06
2002	529.9	20.81	25.46
2003	496.4	19.85	25.01
2004	506.3	19.98	25.34
2005	536.0	20.39	26.29
2006	539.0	20.45	26.35
2007	552.3	20.99	26.31
2008	536.3	19.87	26.98

(Continued)

Exhibit 1   *(Concluded)*

	Footwear		
Year	**Retail Value (in Millions)**	**Units Sold (in Million Pairs)**	**Average Selling Price**
1997	$ 214.3	2.48	$ 86
1998	204.3	2.43	84
1999	206.9	2.47	84
2000	220.8	2.52	88
2001	217.8	2.57	85
2002	211.7	2.68	79
2003	217.1	2.82	77
2004	234.4	3.00	78
2005	245.2	3.15	78
2006	257.7	3.24	80
2007	275.5	3.42	81
2008	281.9	3.35	84

	Gloves		
Year	**Retail Value (in Millions)**	**Units Sold (in Million Dozens)**	**Average Selling Price (Per Unit)**
1997	$ 156.7	1.28	$ 12.23
1998	160.6	1.28	12.56
1999	161.6	1.30	12.46
2000	165.4	1.32	12.53
2001	169.2	1.34	12.61
2002	163.7	1.34	12.26
2003	157.1	1.29	12.16
2004	159.3	1.32	12.11
2005	164.0	1.12	12.22
2006	168.4	1.13	12.45
2007	174.9	1.17	12.46
2008	172.2	1.13	12.73

	Golf Bags		
Year	**Retail Value (in Millions)**	**Units Sold (in Millions)**	**Average Selling Price**
1997	$ 171.8	1.37	$ 126
1998	165.6	1.32	125
1999	165.4	1.32	125
2000	165.1	1.31	126
2001	163.2	1.32	124
2002	153.4	1.32	116
2003	145.5	1.32	111
2004	146.8	1.34	110
2005	150.7	1.39	109
2006	158.5	1.41	112
2007	165.8	1.43	116
2008	162.6	1.36	120

Source: Golf Datatech.

Exhibit 2   Participation Rates for Selected Sports and Recreational Activities, 1998–2008, Various Years (in millions)

	1998	2000	2002	2004	2006	2008
Bicycle riding	43.5	43.1	39.7	40.3	35.6	44.7
Fishing	43.6	49.3	44.2	41.2	40.6	42.2
Golf	27.5	26.4	27.1	24.5	24.4	25.6
Hunting	17.3	19.1	19.5	17.7	17.8	18.8
Running	22.5	22.8	24.7	26.7	28.8	35.9
Swimming	58.2	60.7	53.1	53.4	56.5	63.5
Tennis	11.2	10.0	11.0	9.6	10.4	12.6
Workout at fitness club	26.5	24.1	28.9	31.8	37.0	39.3

Source: National Sporting Goods Association.

INDUSTRY CONDITIONS IN 2009

In 2008, approximately 25.6 million Americans played golf at least once per year—which was about 2 million less than the number of Americans playing golf in 1998. About 2 million Europeans played golf in 2008 and there were about 17 million golfers in Asia in 2008. About one-third of golfers were considered core golfers—those playing at least eight times per year and averaging 37 rounds per year. Industry sales were keyed to the number of core golfers since these frequent golfers accounted for 91 percent of rounds played each year and 87 percent of industry equipment sales, membership fees, and green fees. Even though core golfers might play once a week or more, only a small fraction of golfers might be confused for PGA touring professionals while on the course. The average score for adult male golfers on an 18-hole course was 96, with only 5 percent of adult male golfers regularly breaking a score of 80. The average score for adult female golfers was 108. Exhibit 2 provides the number of Americans playing golf during various years between 1998 and 2008. The exhibit also provides participation rates for other sports and recreational activities popular with adults. The number of golf rounds played for each year between 2001 and 2008 is presented in Exhibit 3.

Exhibit 3   Total Rounds of Golf Played in the United States, 2001–2008 (in millions)

Year	Rounds Played (in Millions)	Percent Change
2001	518.1	—
2002	502.4	−3.0%
2003	494.9	−1.5
2004	528.6	6.8
2005	528.1	−0.1
2006	532.3	0.8
2007	529.6	−0.5
2008	520.1	−1.8

Source: National Golf Foundation.

Limited Opportunities for Innovation in Clubface Design

The arrival of Tiger Woods to the PGA Tour in 1996 had inspired many to take up the game of golf, but most soon found that becoming a somewhat accomplished golfer was a highly demanding task. Developing a sound golf swing required regular instruction from a teaching professional, many hours of practice, and the patience to master all aspects of the game—driving the ball from the tee, long iron shots, short approach shots, hitting from the rough, chipping to the green, sand shots, and putting. Few adults had the leisure time to master all elements of the game simultaneously—for example, they might find they were hitting iron shots really well at a particular point in time, but were having trouble off the tee or botching chips and sand shots. Later they might be very pleased with their drives, but furious with their poor putting.

Golf equipment manufacturers had developed innovations at a rapid clip during the late 1990s and early 2000s to help make the game easier to play for recreational golfers. The size of the driver was increased to reduce the adverse effect of off-center hits, wedges were given more defined grooves to help improve accuracy on approach shots, and balls were redesigned to provide greater distance off the tee and better control on the green. The technological innovations proved to give golfers of modest skills an assist such that their bad shots were not quite so bad. The primary benefit of technologically advanced golf clubs and balls related to distance. Under no conditions would a poorly struck ball fly as far as a well-struck ball, but the loss of distance using modern equipment was not as great as what would be the case with older 1980s or early 1990s era equipment.

The advent of game improvement equipment was also a benefit to the world's elite professional golfers on the PGA Tour, the PGA European Tour, and the Ladies Professional Golf Association Tour (LPGA). The average driving distance on the PGA Tour had increased from 257 yards in 1980 to 290 yards in 2005. Also, it was not uncommon for touring professionals to hit the ball more than 320 yards off the tee and for women on the LPGA Tour to hit the ball as far as 290 yards. Tournament committees responded to the increased driving distance by lengthening the overall distance of the courses hosting professional tournaments. USGA officials believed that it was the organization's responsibility to limit golf club performance to protect historic golf courses that could not be lengthened because of space limitations. The USGA developed a Coefficient of Restitution (COR) measurement and limitation in 1998 that would defend against any "spring-like" effect that a high-tech driver clubface might deliver. The COR was calculated by firing a golf ball at a driver out of a cannon-like machine at 109 miles per hour. The speed that the ball returned to the cannon could not exceed 83 percent of its initial speed (90.47 miles per hour). The USGA called the ratio of incoming to outgoing velocity the coefficient of restitution (COR). Drivers that did not conform to the USGA 0.83 COR threshold were barred from use by recreational or professional golfers in the United States, Canada, and Mexico who intended to play by the USGA's Rules of Golf. The USGA refused to calculate handicaps for golfers who had used nonconforming equipment, but did not attempt to restrict the clubs' usage among players who did not choose to establish or maintain handicaps.

Golf club manufacturers disagreed that a "spring-like" effect could be produced by a metal golf club and believed the USGA's ruling that affected recreational as well as professional tournament golfers would discourage new golfers from taking up the game. Callaway Golf challenged the USGA's COR limitation in 2000 when it introduced for sale in the U.S. the ERC II driver with a COR of 0.86. The company's management believed that the 6–10 additional yards of carry achieved by recreational golfers using the ERC II posed no threat to the game of golf. Callaway Golf executives did concede that equipment limitations might be set for professional golfers, but saw no need to limit the performance of equipment used by recreational golfers who might gain more pleasure from hitting longer drives. Upon the announcement that Callaway Golf would make the club available to golfers in the United States, Arnold Palmer supported the company's decision by saying, "I think what Callaway is doing is just right. I have given a lot of thought to conforming and nonconforming clubs. If my daughter, who is a 100s shooter, can shoot 90 with a nonconforming driver, I can't imagine that there would be anything wrong with that."[1]

The ERC II was a failure in the United States since most core golfers did not want to purchase equipment that violated the USGA's Rules of Golf. The USGA clarified its purpose for barring products like the ERC II in 2002 by stating "the purpose of the Rules is to prevent an overreliance on technological advances rather than skill and to ensure that skill is the dominant element in determining success throughout the game."[2] Initially, the R&A chose only to place limitations on equipment used in elite competitive events, but came to an agreement with the USGA in 2006 to regulate driver performance for both professional golfers and recreational golfers. In order to arrive at a worldwide standard, the USGA scrapped the COR test for the R&A's Characteristic Time (CT) test. The CT test required that the golf ball remain in contact with the face of a driver for 239 microseconds, plus a test tolerance of 18 microseconds. Contact longer than 257 microseconds was considered evidence of a "spring-like" effect and would place a driver on the R&A's nonconforming list.

Once the USGA had successfully eliminated the possibility of a "spring-like" effect produced by a driver club face, it created additional rules regulating driver dimensions and other elements of driver performance. In 2004, the USGA ruled that driving clubs were not allowed to be larger than 5 inches by 5 inches and could not have a volume of more than 460 cubic centimeters. With clubhead size and clubface CT off limits, golf club manufacturers began to pursue innovations that would increase the clubface area capable of producing the maximum CT. Specifically, drivers offered by all golf club manufacturers produced the maximum CT rating allowed by the USGA and R&A, but the percentage of the surface area of the clubface producing the maximum CT might vary quite a bit between driver models and brands. Therefore, all club manufacturers were in a race to push the allowable CT area out to the perimeter of the clubface. This club-face performance characteristic was referred to as Moment of Inertia (MOI). Higher MOI drivers allowed golfers to hit the ball near the inside heel of the club or toward the outer toe of the club and still achieve a near-maximum driving distance. The USGA notified golf equipment manufacturers in 2005 that driver MOI had tripled over the past 15 years and, beginning in 2006, MOI would be limited to 5,900 g-cm^2 with a tolerance of 100 g-cm^2.

The USGA was also concerned about the performance of technologically advanced golf balls such as the Titleist Pro V1, which was introduced in 2000. The Pro V1, Callaway Golf Tour-i, Nike One, and a few other high-tech golf balls were designed to reduce spin when hit by a driver and increase spin when hit by a wedge during an approach shot. Low spin off the tee made the ball fly much farther than higher spinning balls,

while high spin on shorter shots allowed golfers to stop the ball quickly once it hit the green. Before the development of the Pro V1, golfers were required to make a choice—low spin off the tee (increased driving distance) and low spin into the green (poor distance control on the green) or high spin off the tee (shorter driving distance) and high spin into the green (good shot-stopping ability). In June 2005, the USGA asked all golf ball manufacturers to develop prototypes of golf balls that would fly 15–25 yards shorter than current models. USGA officials asked that these prototypes be submitted for evaluation by golf's governing body.

The USGA also believed that the tremendous spin that PGA Tour golfers achieved when hitting shots into the green was partly attributable to wedge technology. The combination of soft-cover golf balls like the Pro V1, Callaway Golf Tour-i, or Nike One and the precision milled grooves of the latest-technology wedges produced ample spin to stop shots near the hole, even when hit from deep rough. The USGA ruled in August 2008 that, beginning January 2010, golf equipment manufacturers must discontinue producing wedges with sharply squared groove edges on irons and wedges. The grooves of irons and wedges produced after January 2010 were required to have rounded edges to minimize spin. Under the new rule concerning groove shape, any remaining inventory of Callaway Golf Mack Daddy, Titleist Spin Milled, or Cleveland Zip Groove wedges would have to be removed from the market after 2009.

With all of the technological advances in golf club and golf ball design, there was little evidence that it was helping golfers achieve lower scores. The average score on the PGA Tour had declined only from 71.18 in 1990 to 71.07 in 2005 and with the exception of Tiger Woods, almost none of the longest drivers on the PGA Tour were at the top of the Tour's Money List. Technology also had a minimal effect on the scores of recreational golfers. The average men's handicap maintained with the USGA had declined from 16.3 in 1993 to just 15.0 in 2005, while the average women's handicap had declined from 29.9 in 1993 to 28.0 in 2005.

In a March 2006 PGA *Magazine* article focusing on the future of golf equipment, a teaching professional and PGA member argued against the USGA's position on innovation in golf equipment:[3]

> Technology has had a wonderful impact on golf, and although we see longer drives and some lower scores on the PGA Tour, what's the harm? . . . If the average golfer enjoys the game more by playing a little better through technology, that's a plus.

A 16-year PGA professional disagreed with the entire premise behind the USGA's technology limitations by commenting:[4]

> Today's high-tech equipment isn't making any courses obsolete for the average player. Maybe technology has made some courses too short for Tiger [Woods] and players on the PGA Tour, but technology has only helped most players gain more gratification from playing the game.

When asked about what impact USGA rulings might have on the health of the game of golf, the USGA's senior communications director commented:[5]

> In a nutshell, we are pleased overall with the state of our game. Growth, however, is not the yardstick by which we judge success or failure. . . . I would contend that we look at our role as one of governing the game responsibly and effectively so that all constituencies—tours, manufacturers, amateurs—enjoy a healthy climate in which to pursue a favorite and rewarding pastime that can be passed down from one generation to the next.

Decline in the Number of Golfers and Rounds Played

The decline in the number of golfers and the recent downturn in the number of rounds played were thought by industry analysts to result from a variety of factors. The overall difficulty of the game and the disappointment of many golfers that low scores didn't come quickly after taking up the sport were certainly factors in people leaving the game. A survey of golfers conducted in June 2003 by the National Golf Foundation found that limited time to practice and play golf was another closely related factor contributing to golf's decline. Golfers who were married with children were most likely to comment that job responsibilities, lack of free time, and family responsibilities prohibited them from playing golf on a more regular basis. Job responsibilities and lack of free time were also barriers to playing golf more frequently for married or single golfers who had no children. Older golfers who were either retired or who were working less than 40 hours per week were more likely to list heath concerns or injuries as a major reason for not playing golf more often. About 30 percent of survey respondents cited high golf fees as a barrier to playing more golf.

The Rise of Counterfeiting in the Golf Equipment Industry

In 2007, more than $600 billion worth of counterfeit goods were sold in countries throughout the world. Fake Rolex watches or Ralph Lauren Polo shirts had long been a problem, but by the mid-2000s counterfeiters were even making knockoffs of branded auto parts, shampoo, canned vegetables, and prescription drugs. It was estimated that 90 percent of the world's counterfeit merchandise originated in China and that counterfeit goods accounted for 15–20 percent of all products made in China. Interpol testified before U. S. Congress in 2005 that counterfeits were frequently illegally imported from China into Western countries by organized crime and terrorist groups such as al Qaeda and Hezbollah. Counterfeiting was an effective approach to funding the activities of organized crime and terrorist groups since fake brands were as profitable as drugs and there was very little risk of being prosecuted if caught.

Counterfeit clubs were a considerable threat to the industry since good counterfeits were nearly exact copies of legitimate products. The extraordinarily low prices that counterfeit clubs were offered at were too great a temptation for many bargain hunter golfers. In 2009, it was not unusual to see complete sets of new Callaway, TaylorMade, Ping, Titleist, Nike, or Cobra clubs that would retail for more than $2,000 sell on eBay or similar auction Web sites for $150 to $400. eBay sellers and others who dealt in counterfeit merchandise could purchase counterfeit sets complete with eight irons, a driver, two or three fairway woods, a putter, a golf bag, and a travel bag for as little as $100–$200 in China. Callaway Golf Company alerted visitors to its Web site to counterfeit clubs sold on eBay or other Internet sites with the warning: "A full set of authentic Callaway Golf clubs, depending on the models, will retail for $2,500–$3,000 or more. If the deal looks too good to be true, it probably is."[6]

The rise of counterfeiting in the golf equipment industry was attributable, to a large extent, to the decisions by golf executives to source clubheads and sometimes contract out assembly of golf clubs to manufacturers in China. Counterfeiters were able to make very accurate copies of branded golf clubs by enticing employees of contract manufacturers to steal clubhead molds that could be used to produce counterfeit clubheads. In some cases, contract manufacturers scheduled production runs after hours to produce black market clubs. Counterfeiters even copied the details of the packaging golf clubs were shipped in to better disguise the fakes. It was estimated that counterfeiters in China could produce golf clubs for less than $3 per club.

The golf equipment industry's six leading manufacturers created an alliance in December 2003 to identify and pursue counterfeiters and sellers of counterfeit clubs. TaylorMade Golf, Fortune Brands (parent of Titleist and Cobra Golf), Callaway Golf, Ping Golf, Cleveland Golf, and Nike Golf had successfully shut down many Internet auction sellers in the United States and Canada that listed counterfeit clubs and had gained cooperation from the Chinese government to confiscate counterfeit goods produced in that country. In 2008, a Chinese man was sentenced to three years and six months in jail and ordered to pay a $58,000 fine after being convicted of running an illegal operation selling counterfeit golf equipment during 2007. Chinese officials confiscated nearly 10,000 counterfeit golf clubs, accessories, and components from a Beijing counterfeiter in 2009 after evidence against the counterfeiter had been provided to the Chinese government by the golf industry anti-counterfeiting alliance.

The Recession of 2008 and 2009

The combined effect of the USGA and R&A performance limitations, the decline in the number of golfers, and international counterfeiting on the golf equipment industry was amplified by the U.S. recession that began in December 2007. A number of factors contributed to the recession, but the onset of the recession coincided with tumult in the credit and housing industries and a rapid increase in the average U.S. gasoline price, which jumped from less than $2.25 per gallon in early 2007 to more than $3.00 by year-end 2007; and to more than $4.00 per gallon in June 2008.[7] As average

monthly household expenditures for gasoline hit a near-record 4.0 percent of after-tax income in April 2008, many consumers saddled with increasing payments on adjustable rate mortgages and rising monthly payments on credit card bills or other growing expenses were forced to cut back on discretionary spending.[8] Rising unemployment quickly followed scaled-back discretionary spending with the unemployment rate growing from 5 percent in April 2008 to about 6 percent by the end of summer 2008 and to 9.5 percent in June 2009.[9] Some economists, including Lawrence Summers, President Barack Obama's top economic advisor, noted that based on historical patterns the loss of jobs accompanying the 2008–2009 recession was much worse that would be expected under economic rules of thumb. For example, the economy had contracted by only 2.5 percent between the beginning of the recession in December 2007 and June 2009, but more than 6.5 million Americans had lost their jobs during that time (a number equal to 4.7 percent of total U.S. employment).[10] With more than 500,000 additional Americans losing jobs each month and no sign that the $787 billion economic stimulus package passed by the House and Senate and signed by President Obama in February 2009 was bringing an end to the recession, many U.S. consumers cut back further on discretionary purchases to boost personal savings. The U.S. personal savings rate had increased from negative or near zero savings rates between 2005 and 2007 to 6.9 percent in May 2009.[11] Falling consumer confidence and the massive spending pullback by consumers fearful of losing their jobs impacted all industries, but hit the providers of nonessential goods and services the hardest.[12]

FORCES SHAPING COMPETITION IN THE GOLF EQUIPMENT INDUSTRY

Competitive Rivalry in the Golf Equipment Industry

Competitive rivalry in the golf equipment industry centered on technological innovations as allowed by the USGA and R&A, product performance, brand image, tour exposure, and price.

Product innovation, performance, image, tour exposure, and price were also the primary competitive variables at play in the golf ball segment of the industry. In 2009, most golf club manufacturers had met dimension, volume, CT, and MOI limits and were attempting to achieve differentiation in drivers by either lowering the center of gravity to increase launch angle or by offering clubs with adjustable features. For example, Nike Golf, Callaway Golf and Nickent Golf had introduced drivers utilizing square or other geometric shapes to position weight further behind the clubface to boost MOI and produce a higher launch angle. Some equipment manufacturers had looked to adjustability to differentiate their product lines from competing brands. Callaway Golf's I-Mix drivers introduced in 2008 allowed golfers to install different shafts into the driver head to produce different launch characteristics. TaylorMade's r9 and Nike's Dymo drivers utilized an interchangeable shaft that adjusted the clubhead launch angle and left/right face angle. Interchangeable and adjustable shafts were allowed under USGA rules that went into effect in January 2008 that permitted adjustable features to clubs provided that the adjustable feature was approved by the USGA during the design process.

Golf club manufacturers also relied heavily on endorsements from touring professionals to enhance their image with consumers. Most recreational golfers who watched televised golf tournaments or read golf magazines were very aware of what brands of clubs and golf balls their favorite touring professionals used. It was not at all unusual for recreational golfers to base purchase decisions on the equipment choices of successful golfers on the PGA Tour. Leading golf equipment companies had always struck endorsement deals with the game's best-known players, but the value of endorsement contracts had escalated since 2000. During the late 1990s, the PGA Tour's top-10 golfers could expect to earn between $250,000 and $400,000 annually through endorsement contracts. By 2007, the top-10 golfers on the PGA Tour all earned at least $4 million annually through endorsements and PGA Tour professionals ranked 40 to 70 on the Money List could expect anywhere from $450,000 to $800,000 in annual endorsement fees. Tiger Woods had led the PGA Tour in endorsement fees since his professional debut in 1996 when he earned over $12 million from product endorsements. Tiger Woods earned more than $80 million from endorsement contracts in 2009, which brought his career earnings from prize money, endorsements, and golf course design fees to $1 billion.

Suppliers to the Industry

Many club makers' manufacturing activities were restricted to club assembly since clubhead production was contracted out to investment casting houses located in Asia and shafts and grips were usually purchased from third-party suppliers. Casting houses like Advanced International Multitech Company in Taiwan produced clubheads to manufacturers' specifications and shipped the clubheads to the United States for assembly. In some cases, clubheads and shafts were also assembled by suppliers in China and shipped to the United States as fully assembled products ready for shipment to retailers.

Manufacturers were quite selective in establishing contracts with offshore casting houses since the quality of clubhead greatly affected consumers' perception of overall golf club quality and performance. Poor casting could result in clubheads that could easily break or fail to perform to the developers' expectations. In addition, it was important that golf equipment manufacturers perform background checks on suppliers and initiate security procedures to prevent finished clubheads and completed golf clubs from leaving the production facility and making it to the black market.

Differentiation based upon shaft performance became more important to golf club manufacturers as technological differences between brands of golf clubs decreased after the USGA limitation on clubhead size and performance was enacted. Most golf club manufacturers codeveloped modestly-sized lines of proprietary shafts with companies specializing in shaft design and manufacturing. The relatively narrow line of shafts bearing the club manufacturer's name was supplemented with branded shafts produced and marketed by companies such as Aldila, UST, Fujikura, or Graphite Designs. Even though third-party branded shafts were equally available to all manufacturers, they were important in attracting sales to skilled core golfers, since these golfers might have as strong a preference for a particular shaft as for a clubhead design. For example, the purchase decision made by a low handicap golfer considering two drivers might come down to which club could be ordered with a specific shaft. Grips had yet to prove to be a point of differentiation and few golfers showed a strong preference for one brand of grip over another.

Golf Equipment Retailers and the Distribution and Sale of Golf Equipment

Leading golf equipment manufacturers distributed their products through on-course pro shops, off-course pro shops such as Edwin Watts and Nevada Bob's, and online golf retailers such as Golfsmith.com and TGW.com. Most on-course pro shops sold only to members and carried few clubs since their members purchased golf clubs infrequently. Off-course pro shops accounted for the largest portion of retail golf club sales because they carried a wider variety of brands and marketed more aggressively than on-course shops. Off-course pro shops held an advantage over online retailers as well since golf equipment consumers could inspect clubs and try out demo models before committing to a purchase. Also, both on-course and off-course pro shops were able to offer consumers custom fitting and advice from a PGA professional or other individual with the training necessary to properly match equipment to the customer. Most consumers making online purchases had already decided on a brand and model and bought online to get a lower price or to avoid sales taxes. However, most of the top brands required online retailers to sell their equipment at the suggested retail price. Both online retailers and brick-and-mortar retailers were free to sell discontinued models at deep discounts, which was very appealing to golfers who did not mind purchasing models from the previous year.

Custom-fitting was offered by most manufacturers and large off-course pro shops with the use of specialized computer equipment. Common swing variables recorded and evaluated in determining the proper clubs for golfers included club-head speed, launch angle of the ball, back spin on the ball, side spin on the ball, ball flight pattern, ball flight carry distance, and roll distance. Custom-fitting had become very important as golf equipment companies expanded shaft flex

options. For example, the Callaway Golf I-Mix FT-9 and FT-iQ drivers could be ordered with any number of 70 different shafts produced by Aldila, Fujikura, Graffaloy, UST, Mitsubishi Rayon, Matrix, or Graphite Design shafts.

Pro shops generally chose to stock only equipment produced by leading manufacturers and did not carry less expensive, less technologically advanced equipment. Low-end manufacturers sold their products mainly through discounters, mass merchandisers, and large sporting goods stores. These retailers had no custom fitting capabilities and rarely had sales personnel knowledgeable about the performance features of the different brands and models of golf equipment carried in the store. The appeal of such retail outlets was low price, and such stores mainly attracted beginning golfers and occasional golfers who were unwilling to invest in more expensive equipment.

PROFILES OF THE LEADING MANUFACTURERS AND MARKETERS OF GOLF EQUIPMENT

Callaway Golf Company

Callaway Golf Company began to take form in 1983 when Ely Reeves Callaway, Jr., purchased a 50 percent interest in a Temecula, California, manufacturer and marketer of hickory shafted wedges and putters for $400,000. Ely Callaway knew from the outset that the company's prospects for outstanding profits were limited as long as its product line was restricted to reproductions of antique golf clubs. Callaway purchased the remaining 50 percent interest in the company and, in 1985, hired a team of aerospace and metallurgical engineers to design and produce the industry's most technologically advanced golf clubs. The company launched noteworthy product lines within a few years, but its revenues skyrocketed from less than $10 million to more than $500 million after its 1991 introduction of the Big Bertha stainless steel driver. The Big Bertha was revolutionary in that it was much larger than conventional wooden drivers and performed far better than wooden drivers when players made poor contact with the ball. The success of the Big Bertha driver set off a technology race in the industry, whereby Callaway Golf and its chief rivals launched innovations every 12–18 months that further improved the performance of metal drivers.

Also during Ely Callaway's tenure as CEO, the company acquired Odyssey, a leading brand of putters, in 1996 and began manufacturing and marketing golf balls in 2000. In February 2000, a survey of golf equipment company executives voted Callaway's Big Bertha driver the best golf product of the century by a two-to-one margin. The same group of executives called Ely Callaway the most influential golf trade person of the 1990s. Ely Callaway stepped down as president and CEO of the company in May 2001 after being diagnosed with pancreatic cancer. The company's performance began to decline soon after Ely Callaway's death in July 2001 and by 2003 had lost its number-one ranking in the driver and fairway wood segments of the industry.

In 2009, Callaway Golf was the second-largest seller of drivers and fairway woods. Its square geometric-shaped FT-iQ and traditional-shaped FT-9 driver lines featured titanium clubfaces, carbon composite shells and prepositioned weights that produced a draw, fade, or neutral ball path. Both the FT-iQ and the FT-9 were available with fixed shafts or any of its 70 I-Mix interchangeable shafts. The FT-9 and FTiQ drivers were priced at $399 and $499, respectively, with a fixed shaft or $400–$700 with a single I-Mix shaft. Each additional shaft ranged from $99 to $299. Callaway Golf also produced a fixed shaft Big Bertha Diablo driver that sold for $299 and a fixed shaft Hyper X driver line that sold for $199. The company's Big Bertha Diablo fairway woods sold for $179–$199 in retail stores, its X line of fairway woods were offered at $149–$169, and its FT fairway woods carried a retail price of $249–$299.

In the years following Ely Callaway's death, the company struggled with a series of issues beyond loss of market share of its flagship driver business. The company misread the market potential for hybrid clubs, which were substitutes for low-lofted, long irons. TaylorMade's Rescue was the first hybrid to gain a widespread appeal, but almost all manufacturers raced to quickly get hybrid clubs to the market. Callaway Golf's failure to get its hybrid club to market before 2005 caused it to lose significant sales as many golfers purchased TaylorMade, Adams Golf, and Cobra hybrid clubs to replace the 2-, 3-, and 4-irons in their bags. It was estimated that 31 percent of all golfers had purchased at least one hybrid club by 2007. In 2009, Callaway Golf's X line of hybrid clubs retailed from $99–$129, while its FT line of hybrids sold for $199.

As Callaway Golf struggled with its golf club business, its golf ball start-up also failed to perform to management's expectations. The company's golf ball business had lost $90 million between 2000 and 2002 and showed little hope of providing a return on its $170 million investment in a state-of-the-art golf ball plant. In 2003, Callaway Golf Company acquired bankrupt golf ball producer Top-Flite Golf for $125 million. The Top-Flite acquisition was executed to give Callaway Golf Company the volume necessary to achieve economies of scale in golf ball production since Top-Flite was the second largest seller of golf balls in the United States with a market share of 16.3 percent. About $175 million of Top-Flite's 2002 revenues were generated from the sale of golf balls. Top-Flite's sales of Top-Flite and Hogan branded golf clubs accounted for about $75 million of the company's $250 million total revenues in 2002.

Callaway Golf's integration of Top-Flite's golf ball operations proved to be more troublesome that management expected. Top-Flite had invested little in R&D over the years and the performance of its products had fallen substantially behind that of key industry rivals. Top-Flite golf balls sold at the lowest price points in the industry and had become known among golfers as "Rock-Flite" because of their hard covers and overall poor quality. The perception of poor quality and performance caused Top-Flite's market share to fall to 6.3 percent by 2006. Callaway branded golf balls, however, had grown to account for nearly 10 percent of industry sales by 2006. Callaway Golf's Tour-i golf ball was a technological equal to Titleist's Pro V1 and was used by such touring professionals as Phil Mickelson, Stuart Appleby, Morgan Pressel, and Ernie Els.

Callaway Golf launched a broad plan to resurrect the Top-Flite brand in 2007 that included the development of a new line of D2 golf balls that included some of the innovations found in the Tour-i line of golf balls. The company supported the launch of the D2 line with the "Rock Flite is Dead" advertising campaign that acknowledged the company's past reputation for poor quality and performance. The better-performing D2 line allowed Top-Flite to add 900 retailers who had previously not considered Top-Flite to be a legitimate brand. The strong sales for the Callaway Golf's technologically advanced Tour-i golf balls and the sales gains from the D2 line helped its golf ball division record its first profitable year in 2007. Profitability in the golf ball business was also achieved by moving production from Callaway Golf's production facilities in the United States to suppliers in China. Callaway Golf had closed its Carlsbad, California, golf ball plant in 2005 and, in 2008, closed one of its two remaining golf ball plants in the United States in order to outsource a larger percentage of its golf ball production requirements. The sales of Top-Flite and Callaway Golf branded golf balls made the company the second largest seller of golf balls in 2008.

Callaway Golf's Odyssey putter line had remained a bright spot for the company since its 1996 acquisition. From quarter to quarter during the late 1990s, Odyssey and Ping shifted spots as the industry's top-selling brand of putter. However, Callaway Golf's 2001 development of the innovative Odyssey 2-Ball putter gave it a decisive lead in the putter category of the golf equipment industry. Odyssey had a 35 percent market share in the putter category of the industry in 2007. It had retained its market-leading position through the development of new models of 2-Ball putters and a variety of conventional-looking models. Most Odyssey putters sold at price points between $100 and $170, but the company had offered a Black Series of Odyssey putters in 2009 that carried an average sales price of $270. The Black Series was intended to compete against Titleist's Scotty Cameron premium line of putters and had a 1.2 percent market share in 2007.

Callaway Golf became the industry leader in the iron segment with its 2000 introduction of the X-14 series of perimeter-weighted irons. Callaway remained the leader in the iron segment of the industry between 2002 and 2008 through continued innovation in perimeter-weighted irons. Its X-16, X-18, X-20, and X-22 model lines incrementally improved the performance of the popular X-14 line. The company also produced a composite construction FT line of irons that featured a titanium face welded to a proprietary metal frame and finished with a thermoplastic urethane cavity-back insert. Callaway's X-Forged irons were designed to compete against Titleist's blade-style irons that were popular with touring pros and the most skilled recreational golfers. Callaway Golf also produced a Big Bertha line of irons that featured a low center of gravity and produced a high launch angle. The low center of gravity and high launch angle benefited many women and senior men golfers with slower than average swing speeds. Callaway Golf irons covered all price points between $600 and $1,300 per 8-club set. The company had chosen to limit its endorsement contracts to 12 PGA Tour professionals and 5 LPGA Tour professionals in 2009.

Callaway Golf Company also designed and sold a Callaway Golf footwear line and received royalties from the sale of Callaway branded golf apparel, watches and clocks, travel gear, eyewear, and golf rangefinders. Discontinued apparel, footwear, accessories, and golf club models could be purchased online at Callaway Golf's www.callawaygolfpreowned.com Web site. New models of Callaway golf clubs could be purchased online at shop.callawaygolf.com. Order fulfillment for new clubs purchased online was made by a network of retailers who participated in Callaway Golf's Internet sales program. The company acquired uPlay, the maker of the uPro golf GPS system in 2009. Callaway's uPro GPS units retailed for $399 and were available at shop.callawaygolf.com and in on-course and off-course golf shops. A financial summary for Callaway Golf Company for the years 1997 to 2008 is presented in Exhibit 4. Exhibit 5 provides the company's revenues by product group for the period 1999 to 2008.

During the first six months of 2009, Callaway Golf's revenues had declined by 17 percent compared to the first six months of 2008. Its earnings per diluted share had declined from $0.58 in the second quarter of 2008 to $0.10 in the second quarter of 2009. A preferred equity offering during 2009 diluted second quarter 2009 earnings by $0.01 per share. The uPlay acquisition resulted in a second quarter 2009 charge of $0.05 per share.

Exhibit 4 **Callaway Golf Company, Financial Summary, 1997–2008 (in thousands, except per share amounts)**

	2008	2007	2006	2005	2004	2003	2002	2001	2000	1999	1998	1997
Net sales	$1,117,204	$1,124,591	$1,017,907	$998,093	$934,564	$814,032	$792,064	$816,163	$837,627	$719,038	$703,060	$848,941
Operating income	84,188	90,183	37,055	17,206	(24,702)	65,855	111,060	114,317	124,727	79,909	(40,139)	209,189
Operating income as a percent of sales	8%	8%	4%	2%	−3%	8%	14%	14%	15%	11%	−6%	25%
Pretax income	101,307	88,275	34,998	14,537	(23,713)	67,883	111,671	98,192	128,365	85,497	(38,899)	213,765
Pretax income as a percent of sales	9%	8%	3%	1%	−3%	8%	14%	12%	15%	12%	−6%	25%
Net income	$ 66,176	$ 54,587	$ 23,290	$ 13,284	($ 10,103)	$ 45,523	$ 69,446	$ 58,375	$ 80,999	$ 55,322	($ 25,564)	$132,704
Net income as a percent of sales	6%	5%	2%	1%	−1%	9%	9%	7%	10%	8%	−4%	16%
Fully diluted earnings per share	$ 1.04	$ 0.81	$ 0.34	$ 0.19	($ 0.15)	$ 0.68	$ 1.03	$ 0.82	$ 1.13	$ 0.78	($ 0.38)	$ 1.85
Shareholders' equity	$ 578,155	$ 568,230	$ 577,117	$596,048	$586,317	$589,383	$543,387	$514,349	$511,744	$499,934	$453,096	$481,425

Source: Callaway Golf Company annual reports.

Exhibit 5 **Callaway Golf Company's Net Sales by Product Group, 1999–2008 (in thousands)**

PRODUCT GROUP	2008	2007	2006	2005	2004	2003	2002	2001	2000	1999
Woods	$ 268.3	$ 305.9	$ 266.5	$241.3	$238.6	$252.4	$310.0	$ 392.9	$ 403.0	$ 429.0
Irons	308.5	309.6	288	316.5	259.1	280.7	243.5	248.9	299.9	221.3
Putters	101.7	109.1	102.7	109.3	—[1]	—[1]	—[1]	—[1]	—[1]	—[1]
Golf balls	223.1	213.1	214.8	214.7	231.3	78.4	66	54.9	34	—[2]
Accessories and other	215.6	186.9	145.9	116.3	205.6	202.5	172.6	119.5	100.8	68.7
Net Sales	$1,117.2	$1,124.6	$1,017.9	$998.1	$934.6	$814.0	$792.1	$816.20	$837.60	$719.00

[1] Net sales for putters included in Accessories and other for 1999–2004.
[2] Golf ball operations began in 2000.

Source: Callaway Golf Company annual reports

TaylorMade-adidas Golf

TaylorMade was founded in 1979 when Gary Adams mortgaged his home and began production of his "metalwoods" in an abandoned car dealership building in McHenry, Illinois. Both touring pros and golf retailers alike were skeptical of the new club design until they found that the metal woods actually hit the ball higher and farther than persimmon woods. By 1984, TaylorMade metalwoods were the number one wood on the PGA Tour and the company had grown to be the third largest golf equipment company in the United States. The company was acquired by France-based Salomon SA in 1984, which provided the capital necessary for the company to continue to develop innovative new lines of metal woods. The company also produced irons and putters, but the majority of TaylorMade's sales were derived from high-margin drivers and fairway woods.

TaylorMade's metalwood drivers were the most technologically advanced in the industry until Callaway Golf's 1991 introduction of the oversized Big Bertha metal wood. During the entire decade of the 1990s, TaylorMade fell further behind Callaway Golf in the technology race, but remained runner-up in the driver segment. TaylorMade and its parent were acquired by athletic footwear and apparel company adidas in 1997 and gained the lead in the market for drivers with its 2003 introduction of its 400 cc R580 driver. The company's R580 driver was 40ccs larger than Callaway's competing Great Big Bertha II driver and matched consumers' preference for the largest possible driver. TaylorMade expanded its lead over Callaway Golf in drivers with its 2004 introduction of its r5 series and r7 Quad drivers. The r7 Quad's moveable weight technology allowed users to use a special tool to move four tungsten weights with a total weight of 48 grams to ports in various positions in the clubhead to produce whatever bias the golfer found necessary on a given day. For example, a golfer who was struggling with a low fade could move the heaviest of the four weights to the toe of the clubhead to favor a high draw. The golfer could later move the weights to a different position if he or she experienced a different ball flight on a different day. The moveable weight system allowed golfers to have a single driver that could produce six ball flight paths.

In 2009, TaylorMade's latest-generation r9 driver combined the moveable weight system with interchangeable shafts that had different settings to adjust the face angle up and down and from left to right. The adjustable face allowed golfers to further refine their ball flight path higher or lower and by 75 yards left and right. The r9 carried a retail price of $500. TaylorMade offered drivers at four different price points, with two r9 sub-models selling for $400 and $300, two r7 models that included the moveable weight system, but not having an adjustable face or interchangeable shafts, selling for $300 and $200, and three non-adjustable Burner models selling at price points of $400, $300, and $200. As of 2009, TaylorMade's management had not chosen to develop a geometric-shaped driver—having commented in 2007 that square drivers did not offer any technological advantage over traditional-shaped drivers.

TaylorMade was also the leading seller of hybrid clubs. TaylorMade introduced its Rescue line of hybrid clubs in 1999, but the clubs did not become a huge success in the marketplace until 2002. In 2009, TaylorMade Rescue hybrid clubs sold at $160–$200, while its Burner Rescue hybrids sold at a retail price of $130. TaylorMade's r9 line of fairway woods also featured adjustable shafts and moveable weights and sold for $230–$300 in retail stores. TaylorMade's r7 fairway woods sold for $130–$180 and its Burner series of fairway woods also sold for $130–$180 at retail and did not have moveable weights.

TaylorMade success in drivers and hybrid clubs had not translated to iron sales with the company never challenging Callaway Golf for market share leadership in the category. In late 2005, the company introduced its r7 irons in hopes of repeating the success of the r7 driver in irons. The r7 irons were designed much like Callaway Golf's Fusion irons and Ping Rapture V2 irons with a titanium face mounted to a steel perimeter-weighted frame. The r7 irons also featured pre-positioned tungsten cartridges imbedded into the stainless steel clubhead to improve launch angles. The company also produced Burner and Tour Burner lines of perimeter-weighted irons, which competed with Callaway Golf X-22 irons, Ping i10 irons, and other perimeter-weighted irons. Its Burner Plus high trajectory irons competed with Callaway Golf Big Bertha Irons and Ping G5 and G10 irons. TaylorMade's Tour Preferred and TP MB Smoke forged irons that were targeted to low-handicap golfers and competed against Titleist irons, Callaway Golf X-Forged irons, and Ping

S57 irons. In 2008, TaylorMade irons covered all price points between $600 and $1,300 for an 8-club set. TaylorMade's combined sales of all three lines of irons gave it a 15.2 percent market share in the iron category of the industry in 2007.

TaylorMade was a weak competitor in the putter category of the golf equipment industry with a 14-model product line that had long been ignored by most golfers. The company's putters carried retail prices between $100 and $230 in 2009. As was the case with putters, TaylorMade wedges were not particularly well-regarded by core golfers. The company introduced a new line of forged Z groove wedges to better compete against Cleveland, Titleist, and Callaway Golf in the wedge category, but as of 2009, had made no real headway in capturing a larger share of the market for wedges. The retail price of Taylor-Made's wedges ranged from $70 to $120 in 2009.

The division's Maxfli golf ball business had produced consistently dismal results each year since its acquisition in 2002. Maxfli's Noodle sub-brand had become popular with price sensitive consumers and had sold more than 2 million dozen per year, but the Maxfli brand in total accounted for less than 5 percent of golf ball sales worldwide. TaylorMade sold the chronic money loser in 2008 to Dick's Sporting Goods, which also manufactured and marketed Slazenger and Walter Hagen branded golf equipment. At the time of the sale, Maxfli produced only one Maxfli branded golf ball model and the Noodle sub-brand. The terms of the sale allowed TaylorMade to retain the Noodle brand along with its newly introduced Taylor-Made TP Red and TP Black premium-priced golf balls and lower-priced TaylorMade Burner brand of golf balls. TaylorMade had not achieved any significant market success with its TP Red, TP Black, or Burner golf balls, but expected to eventually challenge Callaway Golf and Nike for the title of runner-up to golf ball leader, Titleist.

The sales of TaylorMade's adidas branded golf apparel and golf shoes had grown at compounded annual rates of 23.3 percent and 13.5 percent, respectively, between 2004 and 2008 through the continued introduction of new styles and exposure on the professional tours by such well-known golfers and Sergio Garcia, Natalie Gulbis, Paula Creamer, and Retief Goosen. In all, TaylorMade-adidas Golf had signed endorsement contracts with 70 golfers on the men's and women's professional tours. The company's endorsement contracts called for golfers to use a TaylorMade driver and 11 other TaylorMade clubs and wear either the company's apparel or shoes during tournaments. The heavy reliance on endorsements by touring professionals made adidas the most widely worn apparel brand on the professional tours. Some of its touring staff was also compensated to use TaylorMade's TP Red or TP Black golf balls during tournaments. TaylorMade also had limited contracts with an additional 40 golfers to use TaylorMade drivers during professional tournaments. Exhibit 6 presents net sales and operating profit

Exhibit 6   **Financial Summary for adidas Group's TaylorMade-adidas Golf Business Unit, 2004–2008 (in millions)**

TaylorMade-adidas Golf Financial Performance (in millions)					
	2008	**2007**	**2006**	**2005**	**2004**
Net sales	€812	€804	€856	€709	€633
Operating profit	78	65	73	50	60

Sales Contribution by Product Line (in millions)					
	2008	**2007**	**2006**	**2005**	**2004**
Metalwoods	€308	€338	€325	€319	€304
Apparel	162	145	197	99	70
Footwear	73	72	60	50	44
Other hardware*	268	249	274	255	215

* Other hardware includes irons, putters, golf balls, golf bags, gloves and other accessories.

Source: adidas Group annual reports, various years.

between 2004 and 2008 for TaylorMade-adidas Golf. The exhibit also presents the TaylorMade-adidas Golf division's sales by product category for 2004–2008. Its apparel segment included adidas Golf and Ashworth branded shirts, pants, and outerwear. The company outsourced 92 percent of its production of golf clubs and 96 percent of accessories such as golf balls and golf bags from suppliers in Asia to improve its operating margins. As of 2009, TaylorMade-adidas Golf did not offer consumers the option of purchasing clubs or apparel while visiting its Web site.

Titleist/Cobra Golf

Titleist golf balls were developed in 1932 after the founder of an Acushnet, Massachusetts, rubber deresinating company concluded that a bad putt during his round of golf was a result of a faulty ball rather than poor putting. Philip Young took the ball to a dentist's office to have it X-rayed and found that the core of the ball was indeed off-center. Young believed that the Acushnet Processing Company could develop and manufacture high quality golf balls and teamed with a fellow MIT graduate, Fred Bommer, to create the Titleist line of balls. Young and Bommer introduced their first Titleist golf ball in 1935 and by 1949 Titleist had become the most played ball on the PGA Tour.

Acushnet's acquisition of John Reuter, Jr., Inc. in 1958 and Golfcraft, Inc., in 1969 put Titleist into the golf club business. Titleist's Reuter Bulls Eye putter became a favorite on the PGA Tour during the 1960s and its AC-108 heel-toe weighted irons were among the most popular brands of irons during the early-1970s. The company's Pinnacle line of golf balls was developed in 1980 as a lower priced alternative to Titleist branded golf balls. In 1996, The Acushnet Company was acquired by tobacco and spirits producer and marketer American Brands. American Brands increased its presence in the golf equipment industry in 1985 when it acquired Foot-Joy, the number-one seller of golf gloves and shoes. In 1996 American Brands acquired Cobra Golf for $715 million. The company changed its name to Fortune Brands in 1997 when it completed its divestiture of tobacco businesses that began in 1994.

In 2008, Fortune Brands' golf division had become the world's largest seller of golf equipment with sales of $1.4 billion. Titleist was the number-one brand of golf balls with a 40 percent market share and annual sales approximating $650 million in 2008. Fortune Brands' Foot-Joy brand led the industry in the sale of golf shoes, golf gloves, and golf outerwear with a 60 percent market share and 2008 revenues of about $300 million. The remainder of the golf division's 2008 revenues were nearly equally divided between Cobra and Titleist branded golf clubs and accessories at about $200 million each.

Titleist golf balls were considered to be technologically superior to other brands by most golfers, although Callaway Golf's Tour-i and Nike One golf balls were considered equally impressive by industry analysts and golf retailers. Titleist's Pro V1 golf ball was the company's most advanced and expensive golf ball and was able to offer maximum distance along with spin rates that allowed low-handicap golfers to stop approach shots near the pin. Pro V1 was the number-one selling golf ball in the industry and accounted for about 22 percent of industry sales. A one dozen–sized box of Titleist Pro V1 golf balls carried a suggested retail price of $58. The remainder of Titleist's 40 percent market share in golf balls was made up of its lesser priced NXT and DT models and its value-priced Pinnacle sub-brand.

The company had remained the largest seller of golf balls since 1949 through a heavy reliance on endorsements by touring professionals and a long-running advertising campaign boasting Titleist's status as the "most played ball on the Tour."[13] More than 100 PGA Tour professionals had endorsement contracts with Titleist to play the Pro V1, which ensured that the Pro V1 would be played by at least 75 percent of the field in any PGA Tour event. Fifty of its tour staff members also endorsed Titleist golf clubs and Foot-Joy shoes and apparel. The company also compensated about 50 golfers on other professional tours to use Titleist golf balls during competitive events and gave free boxes of sample golf balls to top amateurs and club champions. The company also gave 15,000 two-ball packs to club professionals in 2007 to distribute to club members.

Titleist's line of golf clubs was targeted toward professional golfers and elite recreational players. The company's forged iron design was not that different from its AC-108 irons produced in the early 1970s and offered very little or no element of forgiveness for poorly struck shots. Titleist's market share in the iron category was less than 2.5 percent in 2007. The perception among even very good golfers that "I'm not good enough" to use Titleist irons had allowed the brand's market share to slowly erode from about 10 percent in 2002.[14] Fortune Brands' Cobra line of irons was designed to appeal to lesser skilled golfers and included many of the technological features found in Callaway Golf, Ping, and TaylorMade irons. Cobra produced four game improvement lines including two multi-material iron lines, a perimeter-weighted line, and a combination set of perimeter-weighted irons and hybrids. Cobra also produced a forged line for better players, but overall, held a modest 5 percent market share in 2007. Even though Cobra had signed endorsement contracts with rising PGA Tour stars like Camillo Villegas, J. B. Holmes, and Ian Poulter, core recreational golfers remained hesitant to abandon more widely used brands for Cobra's $500–$700 iron sets.

Cobra's chief manager was given control over Titleist's line of irons in 2007 to develop products for golfers who aspired to Titleist branded products, but were realistic about their abilities. Titleist's AP1 and AP2 line of irons that were introduced in 2008 retained the look of a forged iron, but offered some forgiveness for mis-hit shots. The company's Z Muscle forged irons were used by many of Titleists staff golfers playing on professional tours, while its Z Blend line of iron sets included a mix of more-difficult-to-hit forged irons and easier-to-hit perimeter-weighted irons. The new product lines carried retail prices between $700 and $1,000 and had not produced any discernable growth in sales by mid-2009.

Titleist offered one driver model—the 909, which came in a 440cc version and two 460cc versions. Titleist also produced two versions of its 909 fairway wood and a single line of hybrid clubs. Titleist drivers, fairway woods, and hybrids were popular choices with professionals and better recreational golfers. The 909 driver line carried a retail price of $400, while 909 fairway woods and hybrid clubs carried retail prices of $200 and $190, respectively. Fortune Brands' Cobra lines of drivers, fairway woods, and hybrids were targeted to golfers of an average skill level. King Cobra S9-1 driver featured a carbon composite top plate, tungsten weights near the rear of the clubhead, and a titanium clubface and came in five basic models that all met the USGA maximum

for size and CT. The King Cobra L5V driver was also a multi-material design that had an adjustable shaft with two face settings to alter the ball flight path and trajectory. King Cobra L5V drivers were sold at retail for $300, while most King Cobra S9-1 drivers sold at $200. The King Cobra S9-1 Pro line of drivers similar to the models used by Cobra's tour professionals carried a retail price of $400. Cobra S9-1 fairway woods retailed for $150–$200, while Cobra Baffler hybrid clubs sold in the $150–$180 price range.

Titleist's Vokey forged wedges were frequently used on the PGA Tour and were favorites of many low-handicap golfers. The Vokey wedge line was named for golf club craftsman Bob Vokey, and held a 22.5 percent share of the wedge category of the golf equipment industry in 2007. Vokey wedges were second in sales only to Cleveland Golf, which held a 24.8 percent market share in the category. Vokey spin milled wedge models accounted for one-half of Titleist's sales of wedges. All Vokey wedges carried a retail price of $110. Vokey spin milled wedges sold in 2009 did not conform to USGA groove dimension specifications that would go into effect in January 2010. The USGA ban on squared grooves had created a spike in demand for wedges in 2008 and 2009 as golfers rushed to purchase the technologically superior products before they were discontinued (see Exhibit 1).

As with its wedge line, Titleist's putter line was named after a famed club designer. The Titleist Scotty Cameron putter line held an approximately 10 percent share of the putter segment and was the most widely purchased premium putter brand. Titleist offered four Scotty Cameron putter models, which were all priced at $300. Cobra's wedges and putters were not widely used on the PGA Tour or among recreational golfers.

Titleist management's biggest concern in 2009 centered on the USGA's interest in lesser performing golf balls. In a special equipment issue of *Inside the USGA* published in October 2005, the editors worried openly that technology might endanger some of golf's most historic courses. The editors recalled how the wound rubber-cored Haskell ball that was developed in 1898 and was popularized during the early 1900s eventually "removed for consideration the Myopia Hunt Club, which hosted four U.S. Opens between 1898 and 1908."[15] The USGA editorial staff continued to speculate that the "confluence of golf science and commercial investment . . . accelerated by the injection of large amounts of capital" might possibly have the same effect on such championship courses as Merion or Oakland Hills.[16] Arguing against the concern, Titleist CEO Wally Uihlein attributed the overall scoring improvement among recreational and tournament golfers to "six contributing factors: (1) the introduction of low-spinning high performance golf balls, (2) the introduction of oversize, thin-faced drivers, (3) improved golf course conditioning and agronomy, (4) player physiology—they're bigger and stronger, (5) improved techniques and instruction, and (6) launch monitors and the customization of equipment."[17] Exhibit 7 presents net sales and operating profit between 2004 and 2008 for Fortune Brands' golf division.

Ping Golf

Perimeter weighting came about due to the poor putting of Karsten Solheim, a General Electric mechanical engineer, who took up golf at the age of 47 in 1954. Solheim designed a putter for himself that he found provided more "feel" when he struck the ball. Solheim moved much of the club head weight to the perimeter of the club face, which created a higher MOI and larger "sweet spot." In addition to perimeter weighting, Karsten Solheim also developed the investment-casting manufacturing process. This process allowed clubheads to be formed from molds, rather than forged from steel—the traditional manufacturing process.

Solheim made his putters by hand from 1959 until 1967 when he left GE and founded Karsten Manufacturing. By the 1970s, Karsten manufactured a full line of perimeter-weighted putters and irons that carried the Ping brand. Solheim named the brand Ping because of the sound the perimeter-weighted clubhead made when it struck the ball. Karsten Manufacturing's Ping line of putters and irons were thought to be among the most technologically advanced throughout the 1980s and reigned as the market leaders. Karsten Manufacturing was renamed Ping, Inc., in 1999.

Karsten Solheim was also the pioneer of custom fitting, with his fitting activities predating the official founding of the company. During

Exhibit 7 **Financial Summary for Fortune Brands' Golf Division, 2004–2008 (in millions)**

	2008	2007	2006	2005	2004
Net sales	$1,369	$1,400	$1,313	$1,266	$1,212
Operating profit	125	168	166	172	154

Source: Fortune Brands' annual reports, various years.

the 1960s, touring professionals would meet with Solheim to have him custom-fit putters to their body measurements and, by the 1970s, Solheim had developed a fitting system for irons. His system utilized the golfer's physical measurements, stance and swing, and ball flight to select irons with the optimal lie. The company's irons were sold in 12 color-coded lie configurations to best match recreational golfers' unique fit conditions. Ping invited retailers to 3-day training programs in its Phoenix plant to become better skilled at custom fitting and, in 2009, had provided retailers with 2,000 iron-fitting systems, 1,900 driver-fitting systems, and 2,000 putter-fitting systems.

Ping was an industry leader in the iron segment in 2009—frequently trading the number-one ranking with Callaway Golf. The company offered six lines of irons—the traditional blade S57 irons featured minimal perimeter weighting, the i15 line offered a medium degree of perimeter weighting, and the G15, G10, G5, and Rapture lines had expanded perimeter weighting. Like Callaway Golf FT irons and Taylor-Made r7 irons, the Rapture iron line featured a multi-material construction that included a tungsten sole, titanium face, and stainless steel frame. The G15, G10, G5, and Rapture iron lines produced a higher ball flight than other models and were intended for average golfers who were able to produce only modest amounts of club-head speed. The i15 was designed for better players looking for a moderate ball flight, while the S57 line was suitable for professionals and low-handicap recreational golfers. Ping irons ranged in price from $400 for an 8-club set of G5 irons to $1,225 for an 8-club set of Rapture irons. The company produced a broad line of putters and was a strong runner-up to Odyssey in the putter category of the industry. The majority of Ping's putter line sold in the $90 to $170 range, but its Redwood premium line of putters carried a retail price of $200. The Redwood putter line held a 1.2 percent market share in 2007.

Even though Ping had been known at one time for only its irons and putters, the privately owned company was the fourth largest seller of drivers behind TaylorMade, Callaway Golf, and Titleist/Cobra Golf. The company's 460cc G15 titanium driver was a popular choice for golfers who did not want to tinker with the TaylorMade r7 moveable weight system or did not like the carbon composite design of Callaway Golf's FT drivers. The suggested retail price of the Ping G15 driver was $300. Ping's $400 Rapture V2 driver included the use of tungsten weights to produce a higher launch angle than the G15, but was not a popular seller in 2009. Similarly, its fade-biased i15 driver introduced in fall 2009 had yet to catch on with recreational golfers. Like Callaway Golf, the company had failed to develop a hybrid until 2005 and was struggling to gain market share in the category in 2009. Its $100 G5, $130 G10, $160 G15, $190 i15, and $200 Rapture hybrid lines were most frequently purchased by golfers who had purchased either a Ping driver or Ping irons. Ping fairway woods were also frequently purchased by those owning a Ping driver. Ping G15 fairway woods sold for $200 in retail stores, while Ping i15 fairway woods and Rapture fairway woods typically sold at retail prices of $230 and $250, respectively. The company's wedges were not big sellers in the market. Ping Golf had endorsement contracts with 20 golfers on the PGA Tour and 12 LPGA Tour members, including LPGA Money List leader Lorena Ochoa. Ping Golf did not produce a golf ball in 2009.

Nike Golf

Nike seized upon the instant popularity of Tiger Woods in 1996 by signing the young star to a five year, $40 million contract to endorse Nike shoes and apparel. In 1999 Woods extended the contract for an additional five years for $90 million to endorse Nike's golf ball and golf clubs which would be launched in 2000 and 2002, respectively. Woods extended his contract with Nike a number of times after 1999 for undisclosed amounts,

but industry analysts suspected the value of Tiger Woods' endorsement contract with Nike exceeded $25 million per year in 2009.

Nike management's 1996 assessment of Tiger Woods' enduring worldwide popularity was on the mark with PGA tournament viewership doubling when Tiger Woods was in contention for a Sunday win. However, Woods' appeal with television viewers did not always translate into equipment sales. Nike's entry into the golf equipment industry had proven successful in terms of apparel and footwear sales, where it was the second leading seller of golf shoes behind Foot-Joy. Similarly, Nike Golf had achieved notable success in golf balls, with its Nike One, Juice, and Power Distance balls controlling about 10 percent of the market in 2008. However, Nike's sales of golf clubs had never grown to be more than about 2 percent to 3 percent of the market.

Much of Nike Golf's troubles in the marketplace had to do with the image it created when it entered the golf equipment industry in 2002. The company had produced a line of clubs endorsed by Tiger Woods, but any serious golfer watching a televised tournament could tell that the Nike clubs in Tiger's hands bore no resemblance to the poor performing Nike clubs on store shelves. To combat the perception that Nike was not a serious golf equipment manufacturer, the company introduced the improved Sumo and Dymo driver lines between 2006 and 2008 that were produced to the USGA limitations for MOI, volume, CT, and dimensions. The Nike Dymo's STR8-Fit adjustability feature was similar to the adjustability feature used by the TaylorMade r9 and the King Cobra L5V and could produce eight different ball flight paths. As of 2009 the Dymo had yet to catch on with a great number of golfers and the SasQuatch Sumo had proven to be a failure. Many golfers found the bright yellow color used in the SasQuatch Sumo paint scheme distracting. It was also common for golfers to comment that the sound made by the SasQuatch Sumo was too similar to that of an aluminum bat striking a baseball.

Nike Golf also signed 17 PGA Tour members in addition to Tiger Woods to endorse its clubs and golf balls in a further attempt to change opinions among core golfers that it was primarily a marketer of sporting goods and apparel. However, the poor performance of its hybrids, irons, wedges, and putters that were far inferior to those produced by other leading manufacturers may have reinforced the impression held by many golfers that Nike was not a serious golf equipment brand and overshadowed the recent improvement in its drivers. Nike's market share in drivers was estimated at less than 2 percent in 2008.

While Callaway Golf, TaylorMade, Ping, Titleist and Cobra Golf tightly controlled retail prices and allowed markdowns only when a new product line was introduced, Nike Golf equipment almost never sold at the suggested retail price. In 2009, the Nike SasQuatch Sumo 5900 that had a suggested retail price of $300 was sold by most retailers for $150. Its SasQuatch Sumo Square had a suggested retail price of $400, but

was usually listed at $200 in retail stores. Nike Dymo adjustable drivers had a suggested retail price of $300, but were typically sold for $200 in most on-course and off-course golf shops. Nike fairway woods carried retail prices of $100 to $150, while its hybrid clubs sold for $90. Nike Ignite, Sasquatch Sumo, and Slingshot irons sets carried list prices of $300 to $700, while its Victory Red line sold for $700 to $900. The name Victory Red was a reference to Tiger Woods' routine of wearing a red shirt on the last day of a tournament. Nike wedge models sold for $50 to $110. Nike putters ranged from $100 to $140. Nike One golf balls sold for $45 per dozen, while its other models carried retail prices between $18 and $22 per dozen.

ENDNOTES

[1] As quoted in "Callaway Golf Introduced ERC II Forged Titanium Driver—Its Hottest and Most Forgiving Driver Ever," *PR Newswire,* October 24, 2000.

[2] Joint Statements of Principles, USGA, http://www.usga.org/equipment/mission/joint_statement.html (accessed September 8, 2008).

[3] Ibid., p. 39.

[4] Ibid., p. 37.

[5] Ibid., pp. 43–44.

[6] http://www.callawaygolf.com/EN/customerservice.aspx?pid=9ways

[7] "Retail Gasoline Historical Prices," U.S. Department of Energy, http://www.eia.doe.gov/oil_gas/petroleum/data_publications/wrgp/mogas_history.html (accessed July 25, 2009).

[8] As cited in Amanda Logan and Christian E. Weller, "Running on Fumes," *American Progress,* June 30, 2008, http://www.americanprogress.org/issues/2008/06/gas_food.html (accessed July 28, 2009).

[9] "The Employment Situation: June 2009," U.S. Bureau of Labor Statistics, http://www.bls.gov/news.release/pdf/empsit.pdf (accessed July 26, 2009).

[10] As discussed in "Job Cuts Outpace DGP Fall," *The Wall Street Journal Online,* July 23, 2009, http://online.wsj.com/article/SB124830700226074069.html (accessed July 26, 2009).

[11] "Personal Income and Outlays, May 2009," Bureau of Economic Analysis, U.S. Department of Commerce, June 26, 2009, http://www.bea.gov/newsreleases/national/pi/pinewsrelease.htm (accessed July 28, 2009); and "Personal Income and Outlays, May 2007," Bureau of Economic Analysis, U.S. Department of Commerce, June 29, 2007, http://www.bea.gov/newsreleases/national/pi/2007/pi0507.htm (accessed July 28, 2009).

[12] The steep slide in consumer confidence in July 2009 was discussed in Peter A. McKay, "Confidence Data Rattle Markets,"

The Wall Street Journal Online, July 28, 2009, http://online.wsj.com/article/SB124877925179086469.html#mod=testMod (accessed July 28, 2009).

[13] Adam Schupak, "Pro V Is Still the 1," *GolfWeek,* February 19, 2007, accessed at www.golfweek.com/business/equipment/story/prov1_feature_021907 on August 29, 2008.

[14] Adam Schupak, "Iron Supplement," *GolfWeek,* February 18, 2008, accessed at www.golfweek.com/business/equipment/story/titleistap_news_021808 on August 28, 2008.

[15] As quoted in "Keeping Our Eye on the Ball," *Inside the USGA, Special Issue: Equipment,* October 2005, p. 1.

[16] Ibid., p. 9.

[17] As quoted in a reprint of "Mr. Titleist Talks," *Travel & Leisure Golf,* 2005, www.titleist.com.

Dell Inc. in 2008: Can It Overtake Hewlett-Packard as the Worldwide Leader in Personal Computers?

Arthur A. Thompson
The University of Alabama

John E. Gamble
University of South Alabama

In 1984, at the age of 19, Michael Dell invested $1,000 of his own money and founded Dell Computer with a simple vision and business concept—that personal computers (PCs) could be built to order and sold directly to customers. Michael Dell believed his approach to the PC business had two advantages: (1) Bypassing distributors and retail dealers eliminated the markups of resellers, and (2) building to order greatly reduced the costs and risks associated with carrying large stocks of parts, components, and finished goods. Between 1986 and 1993, the company worked to refine its strategy, build an adequate infrastructure, and establish market credibility against better-known rivals. In the mid-to-late 1990s, Dell's strategy started to click into full gear. By 2003, Dell's sell-direct and build-to-order business model and strategy had provided the company with the most efficient procurement, manufacturing, and distribution capabilities in the global PC industry and given Dell a substantial cost and profit margin advantage over rival PC vendors.

During 2004–2005, Dell overtook Hewlett-Packard (HP) to become the global market leader in PCs. But Dell's global leadership proved short-lived; HP, energized by a new CEO who engineered a revitalized strategy, dramatically closed the gap on Dell in 2006 and regained the global market share lead by a fairly wide margin in 2007—winning an 18.8 percent global share versus Dell's 14.9 percent. In the United States, Dell also struggled to fend off a resurgent HP during 2006–2007. Whereas Dell had a commanding 33.6 percent share of PC sales in the United States in 2005, comfortably ahead of HP (19.5 percent) and far outdistancing Apple, Acer, Toshiba, Gateway, and Lenovo/IBM, Dell's U.S. share had slipped to 28.0 percent by the end of 2007, while HP's share was up to 23.9 percent. Exhibit 1 shows the shifting domestic and global sales and market share rankings in PCs during 1998–2007.

Since the late 1990s, Dell had also been driving for industry leadership in servers. In the mid-to-late 1990s, a big fraction of the servers sold were proprietary machines running on customized Unix operating systems and carrying price tags ranging from $30,000 to $1 million or more. But a seismic shift in server technology, coupled with growing cost-consciousness on the part of server users, produced a radical shift away from more costly, proprietary, Unix-based servers during 1999–2004 to low-cost x86 machines that were based on standardized components and technology, ran on either Windows or Linux operating systems, and carried price tags below $10,000. Servers with these characteristics fit Dell's strategy and capabilities perfectly, and the company seized on the opportunity to use its considerable resources and capabilities in making low-cost, standard-technology PCs to go after the market for low- and mid-range x86 servers in a big way. During 2004–2007, Dell reigned as the number one domestic seller of x86 servers for Windows and Linux (based on unit volume), with just over a 30 percent market share (up from about 3–4 percent in the mid-1990s). Dell ranked number two in the world in x86 server shipments during this same period, with market shares in the 24–26 percent range, which put it in position to contend with HP for global market leadership.

Copyright © 2008 by Arthur A. Thompson and John E. Gamble. All rights reserved.

Exhibit 1   U.S. and Global Market Shares of Leading PC Vendors, 1998–2007

A. U.S. Market Shares of the Leading PC Vendors, 1998–2007

2007 Rank	Vendor	2007 Shipments (in 000s)	2007 Market Share	2006 Shipments (in 000s)	2006 Market Share	2005 Shipments (in 000s)	2005 Market Share	2004 Shipments (in 000s)	2004 Market Share	2002 Shipments (in 000s)	2002 Market Share	2000 Shipments (in 000s)	2000 Market Share	1998 Shipments (in 000s)	1998 Market Share
1	Dell	19,645	28.0%	20,472	31.2%	21,466	33.6%	19,296	33.7%	13,324	27.9%	9,645	19.7%	4,799	13.2%
2	Hewlett-Packard[1]	16,759	23.9	11,600	21.5	12,456	19.5	11,600	20.3	8,052	16.8	5,630	11.5	2,832	7.8
	Compaq[1]	—	—								—	7,761	15.9	6,052	16.7
3	Apple	4,081	5.8	3,109	4.7	2,555	4.0	1,935	3.3	1,693	3.5	n.a.	n.a.	n.a.	n.a.
4	Acer[2]	3,860	5.5	1,421	2.2	n.a.	n.a.	n.a.	n.a.	n.a.	n.a.	n.a.	n.a.	n.a.	n.a.
5	Toshiba	3,509	5.0	2,843	4.3	2,327	3.6	2,945	5.1	2,725	5.7	4,237	8.7	3,039	8.4
	Gateway	—	—	n.a.	n.a.	n.a.	n.a.								
	Lenovo/IBM[3]	n.a.	n.a.	n.a.	n.a.	n.a.	n.a.	2,932	5.0	2,531	5.3	2,668	5.5	2,983	8.2
	Others	22,235	31.7	23,350	35.7	25,070	39.2	24,425	33.6	19,514	40.8	18,959	38.8	16,549	45.6
	All vendors	70,088	100.0%	65,481	100.0%	63,874	100.0%	57,256	100.0%	47,839	100.0%	48,900	100.0%	36,254	100.0%

B. Worldwide Market Shares of the Leading PC Vendors, 1998–2007[4]

2007 Rank	Vendor	2007 Shipments (in 000s)	2007 Market Share	2006 Shipments (in 000ss)	2006 Market Share	2005 Shipments (in 000s)	2005 Market Share	2004 Shipments (in 000s)	2004 Market Share	2002 Shipments (in 000s)	2002 Market Share	2000 Shipments (in 000s)	2000 Market Share	1998 Shipments (in 000s)	1998 Market Share
1	Hewlett-Packard[1]	50,526	18.8%	38,838	16.5%	32,575	15.7%	28,063	15.8%	18,432	13.6%	10,327	7.4%	5,743	6.3%
—	Compaq[1]	—	—	—		—		—		—		17,399	12.5	13,266	14.5
2	Dell	39,993	14.9	39,094	16.6	37,755	18.2	31,771	17.9	20,672	15.2	14,801	10.6	7,770	8.5
3	Acer[2]	21,206	7.9	13,594	5.8	9,845	4.7	6,461	3.6	n.a.	n.a.	n.a.	n.a.	n.a.	n.a.
4	Lenovo/IBM[3]	20,224	7.5	16,609	7.1	12,979	6.2	10,492	5.9	8,292	6.2	9,308	6.7	7,946	8.7
5	Toshiba	10,936	4.1	9,292	3.9	7,234	3.5	n.a.	n.a.	n.a.	n.a.	n.a.	n.a.	n.a.	n.a.
	Others	126,075	46.9	117,971	50.1	107,450	51.7	100,693	52.7	73,237	54.9	80,640	58	50,741	55.5
	All Vendors	268,960	100.0%	235,397	100.0%	207,837	100.0%	177,480	100.0%	133,466	100.0%	139,057	100.0%	91,442	100.0%

n.a. = not available; sales and market shares for these companies in the years where n.a. appears are included in the "Others" category because the company was not in the top five in shipments or market share.

[1]Compaq was acquired by Hewlett-Packard in May 2002. The 2002 data for Hewlett-Packard include both Compaq-branded and Hewlett-Packard-branded PCs for the last three quarters of 2002 plus only Hewlett-Packard-branded PCs for Q1 2002. Compaq's worldwide PC shipments during Q1 2002 were 3,367,000; its U.S. PC shipments during Q1 2002 were 1,280,000 units. Compaq's line of PCs were later rebranded and absorbed into Hewlett-Packard PC offerings.

[2]Acer acquired Gateway in 2007. Data for Acer include shipments for Gateway starting in Q4 2007, and only Acer data for prior periods.

[3]Lenovo, a Chinese computer company, completed the acquisition of IBM's PC business in the second quarter of 2005 (the deal was made in December 2004). The numbers for Lenovo/IBM for 1998–2004 reflect sales of IBM branded PCs only; the numbers for 2005–2007 reflect their combined sales beginning in the second quarter of 2005. In 2007, Lenovo rebranded all IBM PCs as Lenovo.

[4]The worldwide market share data include branded shipments only and exclude sales of units carrying the brands of other PC producers and marketers; shipments of Compaq PCs for last three quarters of 2002 are included in 2002 figures for Hewlett-Packard due to HP's acquisition of Compaq.

Source: International Data Corporation.

In addition, Dell was making market inroads in other product categories. Its sales of data storage devices had grown to nearly $2.5 billion annually, aided by a strategic alliance with EMC, a leader in data storage. In 2001–2002, Dell began selling low-cost, data-routing switches—a product category where Cisco Systems was the dominant global leader. Starting in 2003, Dell began marketing Dell-branded printers and printer cartridges, product categories that provided global leader HP with the lion's share of its profits; as of 2008, Dell's sales of printers and printer supplies were believed to exceed $3 billion. Also in 2003, Dell began selling flat-screen LCD TVs and retail-store systems, including electronic cash registers, specialized software, services, and peripherals required to link retail-store checkout lanes to corporate information systems. Dell's MP3 player, the Dell DJ, was number two behind the Apple iPod. Dell added plasma screen TVs to its TV product line in 2004. Since the late 1990s, Dell had been marketing CD and DVD drives, printers, scanners, modems, monitors, digital cameras, memory cards, data storage devices, and speakers made by a variety of manufacturers.

So far, Dell's foray into new products and businesses had, in most cases, proved to be profitable—for a time, Dell sold handheld PC devices, an MP3 player (called the Dell DJ) that competed against the Apple iPod, and big-screen TVs, but these products were abandoned when profits proved elusive. According to Michael Dell, "We believe that all our businesses should make money. If a business doesn't make money, if you can't figure out how to make money in that business, you shouldn't be in that business."[1] Dell products were sold in more than 170 countries, but sales in 60 countries accounted for about 95 percent of total revenues.

COMPANY BACKGROUND

At age 12, Michael Dell was running a mail order stamp-trading business, complete with a national catalog, and grossing $2,000 a month. At 16 he was selling subscriptions to the *Houston Post,* and at 17 he bought his first BMW with money he had earned. He enrolled at the University of Texas in 1983 as a premed student (his parents wanted him to become a doctor), but he soon became immersed in computers and started selling PC components out of his college dormitory room. He bought random-access memory (RAM) chips and disk drives for IBM PCs at cost from IBM dealers, who at the time often had excess supplies on hand because they were required to order large monthly quotas from IBM. Dell resold the components through newspaper ads (and later through ads in national computer magazines) at 10–15 percent below the regular retail price.

By April 1984, sales were running about $80,000 per month. Dell decided to drop out of college and form a company, PCs Ltd., to sell both PC components and PCs under the brand name PCs Limited. He obtained his PCs by buying retailers' surplus stocks at cost, then powering them up with graphics cards, hard disks, and memory before reselling them. His strategy was to sell directly to end users; by eliminating the retail markup, Dell's new company was able to sell IBM clones (machines that copied the functioning of IBM PCs using the same or similar components) about 40 percent below the price of IBM's best-selling PCs. The discounting strategy was successful, attracting price-conscious buyers and generating rapid revenue growth. By 1985, the company was assembling its own PC designs with a few people working on six-foot tables. The company had 40 employees, and Michael Dell worked 18-hour days, often sleeping on a cot in his office. By the end of fiscal 1986, sales had reached $33 million.

During the next several years, however, PCs Limited was hampered by growing pains—specifically, a lack of money, people, and resources. Michael Dell sought to refine the company's business model; add needed production capacity; and build a bigger, deeper management staff and corporate infrastructure while at the same time keeping costs low. The company was renamed Dell Computer in 1987, and the first international offices were opened that same year. In 1988, Dell added a sales force to serve large customers, began selling to government agencies, and became a public company—raising $34.2 million in its first offering of common stock. Sales to large customers quickly became the dominant part of Dell's business. By 1990, Dell Computer had sales of $388 million, a market share of 2–3 percent, and an R&D staff of more than 150 people.

Michael Dell's vision was for Dell Computer to become one of the top three PC companies.

Thinking its direct sales business would not grow fast enough, in 1990–93, the company began distributing its computer products through Soft Warehouse Superstores (now CompUSA), Staples (a leading office products chain), Walmart, Sam's Club, and Price Club (which merged with Costco in 1993). Dell also sold PCs through Best Buy stores in 16 states and through Xerox in 19 Latin American countries. But when the company learned how thin its margins were in selling through such distribution channels, it realized it had made a mistake and withdrew from selling to retailers and other intermediaries in 1994 to refocus on direct sales. At the time, sales through retailers accounted for only about 2 percent of Dell's revenues.

In 1993, further problems emerged: Dell reportedly lost $38 million in risky foreign-currency hedging, quality difficulties arose with certain PC lines made by the company's contract manufacturers, profit margins declined, and buyers were turned off by the company's laptop PC models. To get laptop sales back on track, the company took a charge of $40 million to write off its laptop line and suspended sales of laptops until it could get redesigned models into the marketplace.

Because of higher costs and unacceptably low profit margins in selling to individuals and households, Dell did not pursue the consumer market aggressively until sales to individuals at the company's Internet site took off in 1996 and 1997. It became clear that PC-savvy individuals, who were buying their second and third computers, wanted powerful computers with multiple features; did not need much technical support; and liked the convenience of buying direct from Dell, ordering a PC configured exactly to their liking, and having it delivered to their door within a matter of days. In early 1997, Dell created an internal sales and marketing group dedicated to serving the individual consumer segment and introduced a product line designed especially for home and personal use.

By late 1997, Dell had become a low-cost leader among PC vendors by wringing greater and greater efficiency out of its direct sales and build-to-order business model. Since then, the company had continued driving hard to reduce its costs by closely partnering with key suppliers to drive costs out of its supply chain and by incorporating e-commerce technology and use of the Internet into its everyday business practices. Throughout 2002–2007, Dell was widely regarded as the lowest-cost producer among all the leading vendors of PCs and servers worldwide. Moreover, its products were highly regarded; in 2007, Dell products received more than 400 awards relating to design, quality, and innovation—this was the largest number of product awards for a single year in the company's history.

In its 2008 fiscal year, Dell posted revenues of $61.1 billion and profits of nearly $3.0 billion. It ranked number 34 on *Fortune*'s list of the 500 largest U.S. corporations for 2007. In 2008, Dell had approximately 88,200 employees worldwide, up from 16,000 at year-end 1997; more than 66 percent of Dell's employees were located in countries outside the United States, and this percentage was growing. The company's headquarters and main office complex was in Round Rock, Texas (an Austin suburb). Its name had been changed from Dell Computer to Dell Inc. in 2003 to reflect the company's growing business base outside of PCs. Exhibits 2 and 3 provide information about Dell's financial performance and geographic operations.

Michael Dell

In the company's early days Michael Dell hung around mostly with the company's engineers. He was so shy that some employees thought he was stuck up because he never talked to them. But people who worked with him closely described him as a likable young man who was slow to warm up to strangers.[2] He was a terrible public speaker and wasn't good at running meetings. But Lee Walker, a 51-year-old venture capitalist brought in by Michael Dell to provide much-needed managerial and financial experience during the company's organization-building years, became Michael Dell's mentor, built up his confidence, and was instrumental in turning him into a polished executive.[3] Walker served as the company's president and chief operating officer from 1986 to 1990; he had a fatherly image, knew everyone by name, and played a key role in implementing Michael Dell's marketing ideas. Under Walker's tutelage, Michael Dell became intimately familiar

Exhibit 2 Selected Financial Statement Data for Dell Inc., Fiscal Years 2000–2008 (in millions, except per share data)

	Fiscal Year Ended						
	February 1, 2008	February 2, 2007	February 3, 2006	January 28, 2005	January 30, 2004	February 1, 2002	January 28, 2000
Results of Operations							
Net revenue	$61,133	$57,420	$55,788	$49,121	$41,327	$31,168	$25,265
Cost of revenue	49,462	47,904	45,897	40,103	33,764	25,661	20,047
Gross margin	11,671	9,516	9,891	9,018	7,563	5,507	5,218
Gross profit margin	19.1%	16.6%	17.7%	18.4%	18.3%	17.7%	20.7%
Operating expenses:							
Selling, general and administrative[a]	7,538	5,948	5,051	4,352	3,604	2,784	2,387
Research, development and engineering[b]	693	498	458	460	434	452	374
Special charges	—	—	—	—	—	482	194
Total operating expenses	8,231	6,446	5,509	4,812	4,038	3,718	2,955
Total operating expenses as a % of net revenues	13.5%	11.2%	9.9%	9.8%	9.8%	10.4%[c]	10.9%[c]
Operating income	3,440	3,070	4,382	4,206	3,525	1,789	2,263
Operating profit margin	5.6%	5.3%	7.9%	8.6%	8.5%	5.7%	9.0%
Investment and other income (loss), net	387	275	26	197	186	(58)	188
Income before income taxes, extraordinary loss, and cumulative effect of change in accounting principle	3,827	3,345	4,608	4,403	3,711	1,731	2,451
Provision for income taxes	880	762	1,006	1,385	1,086	485	785
Net income	$ 2,947	$ 2,583	$ 3,602	$ 3,018	$ 2,625	$ 1,246	$ 1,666
Net profit margin	4.8%	5.8%	6.5%	6.1%	6.4%	4.0%	6.6%
Earnings per common share: Basic	$1.33	$1.15	$1.50	$1.20	$1.02	$0.48	$0.66
Diluted	$1.31	$1.14	$1.47	$1.18	$1.01	$0.46	$0.61
Weighted average shares outstanding: Basic	2,223	2,255	2,403	2,509	2,565	2,602	2,536
Diluted	2,247	2,271	2,449	2,568	2,619	2,726	2,728
Cash Flow and Balance Sheet Data							
Net cash provided by operating activities	$ 3,949	$ 3,969	$ 4,751	$ 5,821	$ 3,670	$ 3,797	$ 3,926
Cash, cash equivalents, and short-term investments	7,972	10,298	9,070	9,807	11,922	8,287	6,853
Total assets	27,561	25,635	23,252	23,215	19,311	13,535	11,560
Long-term debt	362	569	625	505	505	520	508
Total stockholders' equity	3,735	4,328	4,047	6,485	6,280	4,694	5,308

[a]Includes stock-based compensation expenses for fiscal years 2007 and 2008, pursuant to Statement of Financial Accounting Standards No. 123.

[b]Includes one-time in-process research and development charges of $83 million related to companies acquired by Dell during fiscal 2008.

[c]Excluding special charges.

Sources: Dell Inc., 10-K reports, 2002, 2005–2008.

Exhibit 3 Dell's Geographic Area Performance, Fiscal Years 2000–2008 (in millions)

	February 1, 2008	February 2, 2007	February 3, 2006	January 28, 2005	January 30, 2004	February 1, 2002	January 28, 2000
Net revenues							
Americas							
Business	$31,144	$29,311	$28,365	$25,289	$21,824	$ 17,275	$15,160
U.S. consumer	6,244	7,069	7,960	7,614	6,696	4,485	2,719
Total Americas	37,368	36,380	36,325	32,903	28,520	21,760	17,879
Europe/Middle East/Africa	15,267	13,682	12,887	10,753	8,472	6,429	5,590
Asia-Pacific/ Japan	8,498	7,358	6,576	5,465	4,335	2,979	1,796
Total net revenues	$61,133	$57,420	$55,788	$49,121	$41,444	$31,168	$25,265
Operating income							
Americas							
Business	$ 2,549	$ 2,388	$ 2,956	$ 2,534	$ 2,229	$ 1,482	$ 1,800
U.S. consumer	(59)	135	452	414	373	260	204
Total Americas	2,490	2,523	3,408	2,948	2,602	1,742	2,004
Europe/Middle East/Africa	1,009	583	871	815	614	377	359
Asia-Pacific/ Japan	471	332	524	443	309	152	94
Special charges	(530)	(368)	(421)	—	—	(482)	(194)
Total operating income	$ 3,440	$ 3,070	$ 4,382	$ 4,206	$ 3,525	$ 1,789	$ 2,263

Sources: Dell Inc., 10-K reports, 2002, 2005 and 2008; financial data posted at www.dell.com (accessed May 6, 2008).

with all parts of the business, overcame his shyness, learned to control his ego, and turned into a charismatic leader with an instinct for motivating people and winning their loyalty and respect.

When Walker had to leave the company in 1990 for health reasons, Dell turned to Morton Meyerson, former CEO and president of Electronic Data Systems, for advice and guidance on how to transform Dell Computer from a fast-growing medium-sized company into a billion-dollar enterprise. Though sometimes given to displays of impatience, Michael Dell usually spoke in a quiet, reflective manner and came across as a person with maturity and seasoned judgment far beyond his age. His prowess was based more on an astute combination of technical

knowledge and marketing know-how than on being a technological wizard. In 1992, at the age of 27, Michael Dell became the youngest CEO ever to head a Fortune 500 company; he was a billionaire at the age of 31.

By the late 1990s, Michael Dell had become one of the most respected executives in the PC industry. Journalists had described him as "the quintessential American entrepreneur" and "the most innovative guy for marketing computers." He was a much-sought-after speaker at industry and company conferences. His views and opinions about the future of PCs, the Internet, and e-commerce practices carried considerable weight both in the PC industry and among executives worldwide. Once pudgy and bespectacled, in early

2008, 43-year-old Michael Dell was physically fit, considered good-looking, wore contact lenses, ate only health foods, and lived in a three-story 33,000-square-foot home on a 60-acre estate in Austin, Texas, with his wife and four children. In 2008, he owned about 10 percent of Dell's common stock, worth about $4.3 billion.

Michael Dell was considered a very accessible CEO and a role model for young executives because he had done what many of them were trying to do. He delegated authority to subordinates, believing that the best results came from "turning loose talented people who can be relied upon to do what they're supposed to do." Business associates viewed Michael Dell as an aggressive personality, an extremely competitive risk taker who had always played close to the edge. He spent about 30 percent of his time traveling to company operations and meeting with customers. In a typical year, he would make two or three trips to Europe and two trips to Asia.

In mid-2004, Michael Dell, who had been the company's first and only CEO, transferred his title of CEO to Kevin Rollins, the company's president and chief operating officer. Dell remained as chairman of the board. Dell and Rollins had run the company for the past seven years under a shared leadership structure. The changes were primarily ones of title, not of roles or responsibilities. But when the company's performance stalled in 2006, Kevin Rollins was relieved of his responsibilities and Michael Dell reassumed the title of CEO (and continued in the role of chairman of the company's board of directors).

DELL'S STRATEGY AND BUSINESS MODEL

In orchestrating Dell Inc.'s rise to global prominence, company executives had come to believe strongly that four tenets were the key to delivering superior customer value:[4]

1. Selling direct to customers is the most efficient way to market the company's products because it eliminates wholesale and retail dealers that impede Dell's understanding of customer needs and expectations and that add unnecessary time and cost.

2. Allowing customers to purchase custom-built products and custom-tailored services is the most effective way to meet customer needs.

3. A highly efficient supply chain and manufacturing organization, grounded in the use of standardized technologies and selling direct, paves the way for a low-cost structure where cost savings can be passed along to customers in the form of lower prices.

4. Dell can deliver added value to customers by (1) researching all the technological options, (2) trying to determine which ones are "optimal" in the sense of delivering the best combination of performance and efficiency, and (3) being accountable to customers for helping them obtain the highest return on their investment in IT products and services. In almost all cases, non-proprietary, standardized technologies deliver the best value to customers.

With top management holding firmly to these tenets, Dell's strategy during the 2002–2007 period had seven core elements: (1) making build-to-order manufacturing progressively more cost-efficient, (2) partnering closely with suppliers to squeeze cost savings out of the supply chain, (3) using direct sales techniques to gain customers, (4) expanding into additional products and services to capture a bigger share of customers' IT spending, (5) providing good customer service and technical support, (6) keeping R&D and engineering activities focused squarely on better meeting the needs of customers, and (7) using standardized technologies in all product offerings.

The business model on which the strategy was predicated was straightforward: Continuously search for ways to reduce costs—the company's latest initiative was to reduce costs by $3 billion in 2008. Use the company's strong capabilities in supply chain management, low-cost manufacturing, and direct sales to grow sales and market share in both the PC and server segments and expand into product categories where Dell could provide added value to its customers in the form of lower prices. The standard pattern for entering new product categories was to identify an IT product with good margins; figure out how to build it (or else have it built by others) cheaply enough to be able to significantly underprice competitive products; market the new product to Dell's steadily growing customer base; and watch the market share points, incremental revenues, and incremental profits pile up.

Cost-Efficient Build-to-Order Manufacturing

Dell built the vast majority of its computers, workstations, and servers to order; only a small fraction was produced for inventory and shipped to wholesale or retail partners. Dell customers could order custom-equipped servers and workstations according to the needs of their applications. Desktop and laptop customers ordered whatever configuration of microprocessor speed, random-access memory, hard disk capacity, CD or DVD drives, fax/modem/wireless capabilities, graphics cards, monitor size, speakers, and other accessories they preferred. The orders were directed to the nearest factory. In 2008, Dell had assembly plants in Austin, Texas; Nashville, Tennessee; Winston-Salem, North Carolina; Limerick, Ireland; Xiamen, China; Penang, Malaysia; Hortolândia, Brazil; Chennai, India; and Lodz, Poland. In March 2008, the company announced that its desktop assembly plant in Austin, Texas, would be closed. The Winston-Salem plant was Dell's largest when it opened in 2005 and had the capacity to assemble 15,000 to 20,000 desktops per day—it could turn out a new PC every five seconds. Dell shipped about 140,000 products daily—about 1 every second. PCs, workstations, and servers were assembled at all locations; assembly of lower-volume products was concentrated in a more limited number of locations. All plants used much the same production systems and procedures. Typically, a plant had the capability to build and deliver a customer's order in three to five business days; however, the Winston-Salem plant could in most cases deliver orders to customers on the eastern coast of the United States in one to three business days. Dell believed in building its assembly plants close to customers because the labor costs to assemble a PC were about $10 whereas the logistics costs to move parts and ship a finished PC were about $40.[5]

Ongoing Improvements In Assembly Efficiency Until 1997, Dell operated its assembly lines in traditional fashion, with each worker performing a single operation. An order form accompanied each metal chassis across the production floor; drives, chips, and ancillary items were installed to match customer specifications. As a partly assembled PC arrived at a new workstation, the operator, standing beside a tall steel rack with drawers full of components, was instructed what to do by little red and green lights flashing beside the drawers. When the operator was finished, the component drawers were automatically replenished from the other side and the PC chassis glided down the line to the next workstation. However, Dell had reorganized its plants in 1997, shifting to "cell manufacturing" techniques whereby a team of workers operating at a group workstation (or cell) assembled an entire PC according to customer specifications. The shift to cell manufacturing reduced Dell's assembly times by 75 percent and doubled productivity per square foot of assembly space. Assembled computers were first tested and then loaded with the desired software, shipped, and typically delivered five to six business days after the order was placed.

Later, the cell manufacturing approach was gradually abandoned in favor of an even more efficient assembly-line approach that allowed workers to turn out close to 800 desktop PCs per hour on three assembly lines that took half the floor space of the cell manufacturing process, where production had run about 120 units per hour. Here the gains in assembly efficiency were achieved partly by redesigning the PCs to permit easier and faster assembly, partly by making innovations in the assembly process, and partly by reducing (by 50 percent) the number of times a computer was touched by workers during assembly and shipping. In 2005, it took about 66 minutes to assemble and test a PC. Moreover, just-in-time inventory practices that left pallets of parts sitting around everywhere had been tweaked to just-in-the-nick-of-time delivery by suppliers of the exact parts needed every couple of hours; double-decker conveyor belts moved parts and components to designated assembly points. Newly assembled PCs were routed on conveyors to shipping, where they were boxed and shipped to customers the same day.

Dell's new 750,000-square-foot plant in Winston-Salem featured a production layout that allowed computers to be tested as its components and software were installed. This "instantaneous build and test" operation permitted team members to identify and correct any problems on the spot rather than waiting until the PC was fully assembled. Workers at all Dell plants competed with one another to come up with more efficient assembly methods. Cost-saving assembly innovations pioneered in one Dell plant were quickly implemented worldwide.

Dell's latest cost-saving initiative was to move away from 100 percent configure-to-customer-order assembly to a mixture of fixed configurations (for components that rarely varied from order to order) and flexible configurations (for components that were subject to strong and varying customer preferences—like hard drive size, screen displays, amount of memory, graphics cards, type of microprocessor, and version of Windows operating system).

Dell was regarded as a world-class manufacturing innovator and a pioneer in how to mass-produce a customized product—its methods were routinely studied in business schools worldwide. Several of Dell's PC rivals—most notably Hewlett-Packard—had given up on trying to produce their own PCs as cheaply as Dell and shifted to outsourcing their PCs from contract manufacturers who specialized in PC assembly and often assembled a variety of PC brands. Dell management believed that its in-house manufacturing delivered about a 6 percent cost advantage versus outsourcing. Dell's build-to-order strategy meant that the company had only a tiny stock of finished goods inventories in-house and that, unlike competitors using the traditional value chain model, it did not have to wait for resellers to clear out their own inventories before it could push new models into the marketplace—resellers typically operated with 30 to 60 days inventory of prebuilt models (see Exhibit 4). Equally important was the fact that customers who bought from Dell got the

EXHIBIT 4   Comparative Value Chain Models of PC Vendors

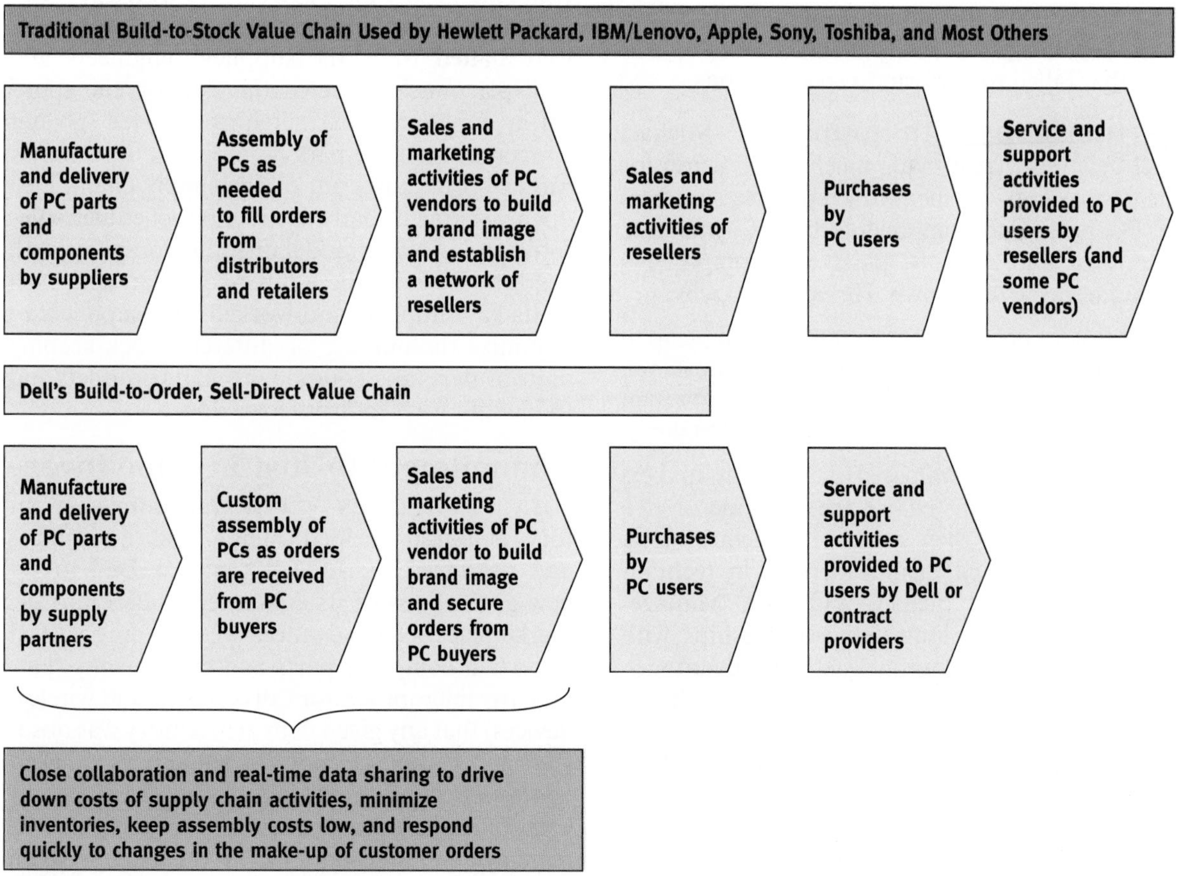

Traditional Build-to-Stock Value Chain Used by Hewlett Packard, IBM/Lenovo, Apple, Sony, Toshiba, and Most Others

Manufacture and delivery of PC parts and components by suppliers → Assembly of PCs as needed to fill orders from distributors and retailers → Sales and marketing activities of PC vendors to build a brand image and establish a network of resellers → Sales and marketing activities of resellers → Purchases by PC users → Service and support activities provided to PC users by resellers (and some PC vendors)

Dell's Build-to-Order, Sell-Direct Value Chain

Manufacture and delivery of PC parts and components by supply partners → Custom assembly of PCs as orders are received from PC buyers → Sales and marketing activities of PC vendor to build brand image and secure orders from PC buyers → Purchases by PC users → Service and support activities provided to PC users by Dell or contract providers

Close collaboration and real-time data sharing to drive down costs of supply chain activities, minimize inventories, keep assembly costs low, and respond quickly to changes in the make-up of customer orders satisfaction of having their computers custom-ized to their particular liking and pocketbook.

Quality Control

All assembly plants had the capability to run testing and quality control processes on components, parts, and subassem-blies obtained from suppliers, as well as on the finished products Dell assembled. Suppliers were urged to participate in a quality certification pro-gram that committed them to achieving defined quality specifications. Quality control activities were undertaken at various stages in the assem-bly process. In addition, Dell's quality control program included testing of completed units after assembly, ongoing production reliability audits, failure tracking for early identification of produc-tion and component problems associated with new models shipped to customers, and informa-tion obtained from customers through service and technical support programs. All of the com-pany's plants had been certified as meeting ISO 9001:2000 standards. But while Dell's quality control program was first-rate, it was not perfect; in fiscal year 2008, Dell incurred special warranty cost charges of $307 million to service or replace certain desktop models that included a vendor part that failed to perform to specifications.

Partnerships with Suppliers

Michael Dell believed that it made much better sense for the company to partner with reputable suppliers of PC parts and components than to integrate backward and get into parts and components manufacturing on its own. He explained why:

> If you've got a race with 20 players all vying to make the fastest graphics chip in the world, do you want to be the twenty-first horse, or do you want to evaluate the field of 20 and pick the best one?[6]

Dell management evaluated the various makers of each component; picked the best one or two as suppliers; and then stuck with them as long as they maintained their leadership in technol-ogy, performance, quality, and cost. Manage-ment believed that long-term partnerships with reputable suppliers had at least five advantages. First, using name-brand processors, disk drives, modems, speakers, and multimedia components enhanced the quality and performance of Dell's PCs. Because of varying performance among dif-ferent brands of components, the brand of the components was quite important to customers

concerned about performance and reliability. Sec-ond, because Dell partnered with suppliers for the long term and because it committed to purchase a specified percentage of its requirements from each supplier, Dell was assured of getting the vol-ume of components it needed on a timely basis even when overall market demand for a particular component temporarily exceeded the overall mar-ket supply. Third, Dell's long-run commitment to its suppliers made it feasible for suppliers to locate their plants or distribution centers within a few miles of Dell assembly plants, putting them in position to make deliveries daily or every few hours, as needed. Dell supplied data on inven-tories and replenishment needs to its suppliers at least once a day—hourly in the case of com-ponents being delivered several times daily from nearby sources.

Fourth, long-term supply partnerships facili-tated having some of the supplier's engineers assigned to Dell's product design teams and being treated as part of Dell. When new products were launched, suppliers' engineers were stationed in Dell's plants; if early buyers called with a problem related to design, further assembly and shipments were halted while the supplier's engineers and Dell personnel corrected the flaw on the spot.[7] Fifth, long-term partnerships enlisted greater cooperation on the part of suppliers to seek new ways to drive costs out of the supply chain. Dell openly shared its daily production schedules, sales forecasts, and new model introduction plans with vendors. Dell also did a three-year plan with each of its key suppliers and worked with suppliers to minimize the number of different stock-keeping units of parts and components in its products and to identify ways to drive costs down.

Commitment to Just-in-Time Inventory Practices

Dell's just-intime inven-tory emphasis yielded major cost advantages and shortened the time it took for Dell to get new generations of its computer models into the marketplace. New advances were coming so fast in certain computer parts and components (par-ticularly microprocessors, disk drives, and wireless devices) that any given item in inventory was obso-lete in a matter of months, sometimes quicker. Moreover, rapid-fire reductions in the prices of components were not unusual—for example, Intel regularly cut the prices on its older chips when it introduced newer chips, and it introduced new chip generations about every three months. In 2003–2004, component costs declined an average of 0.5 percent weekly.[8] Michael Dell explained the competitive and economic advantages of minimal component inventories:

> If I've got 11 days of inventory and my competitor has 80 and Intel comes out with a new chip, that means I'm going to get to market 69 days sooner. In the computer industry, inventory can be a pretty massive risk because if the cost of materials is going down 50 percent a year and you have two or three months of inventory versus 11 days, you've got a big cost disadvantage. And you're vulnerable to product transitions, when you can get stuck with obsolete inventory.[9]

For a growing number of parts and components, Dell's close partnership with suppliers was allowing it to operate with no more than two hours of inventory.

In fiscal year 1995, Dell averaged an inventory turn cycle of 32 days. By the end of fiscal 1997 (January 1997), the average was down to 13 days. In fiscal 1998, Dell's inventory averaged 7 days, which compared very favorably with a 14-day average at Gateway, a 23-day average at then industry leader Compaq, and the estimated industrywide average of over 50 days. In fiscal years 1999 and 2000, Dell operated with an average of six days' supply of production materials in inventory; the average dropped to five days' supply in fiscal year 2001, four days' supply in 2002, and 2.7 to four days' supply in fiscal years 2003–2007.

Dell's Direct Sales Strategy and Marketing Efforts

With thousands of phone, fax, and Internet orders daily and ongoing field sales force contact with customers, the company kept its finger on the market pulse, quickly detecting shifts in sales trends, design problems, and quality glitches. If the company got more than a few of the same complaints, the information was relayed immediately to design engineers who checked out the problem. When design flaws or components defects were found, the factory was notified and the problem corrected within a few days. Management believed Dell's ability to respond quickly gave it a significant advantage over PC makers that operated on the basis of large production runs of variously configured and equipped PCs and sold them through retail channels. Dell saw its direct sales approach as a totally customer-driven system, with the flexibility to transition quickly to new generations of components and PC models.

Web Site Strategy Dell's Web site was one of the world's highest volume Internet commerce sites, with nearly 500 million unique visitors, well over 1 billion visits, and close to 10 billion page requests annually. Dell began Internet sales at its Web site in 1995, almost overnight achieving sales of $1 million a day. Sales at its Web site reached $5 million daily in 1998, $35 million daily in 2000, and $60 million a day in 2004. By early 2003, over 50 percent of Dell's sales were Web-enabled—and the percentage trended upward through 2007. The revenues generated at the Web site were greater than those generated at Yahoo, Google, eBay, and Amazon combined.[10]

At the company's Web site, prospective buyers could review Dell's entire product line in detail, configure and price customized PCs, place orders, and track orders from manufacturing through shipping. The closing rate on sales at Dell's Web site was 20 percent higher than that on sales inquiries received via telephone. Management believed that enhancing www.dell.com to shrink transaction and order fulfillment times, increase accuracy, and provide more personalized content resulted in a higher degree of "e-loyalty" than traditional attributes like price and product selection.

Dell's Customer-Based Sales and Marketing Focus Whereas many technology companies organized their sales and marketing efforts around product lines, Dell was organized around customer groups. Dell had placed managers in charge of developing sales and service programs appropriate to the needs and expectations of each customer group. Until the early 1990s, Dell operated with sales and service programs aimed at just two market segments—high-volume corporate and governmental buyers and low-volume business and individual buyers. But as sales took off in 1995–1997, these segments were subdivided into finer, more homogeneous categories that by 2000 included global enterprise accounts, large and midsize companies (over 400 employees), small companies (under 400 employees), health care businesses (over 400 employees), federal government agencies, state and local government agencies, educational institutions, and individual consumers. Many of these customer segments were further subdivided—for instance, in education, there were separate sales and marketing programs for K–12 schools; higher education institutions; and personal-use purchases by faculty, staff, and students.

Dell had a field sales force that called on large business and institutional customers throughout the world. Dell's largest global enterprise accounts were assigned their own dedicated sales force—for example, Dell had a sales force of 150 people dedicated to meeting the needs of General Electric's facilities and personnel scattered across the world. Individuals and small businesses could place orders by telephone or at Dell's Web site. Dell had call centers in the United States, Canada, Europe, and Asia with toll-free lines; customers could talk with a sales representative about specific models, get information faxed or mailed to them, place an order, and pay by credit card. The Asian and European call centers were equipped with technology that routed calls from a particular country to a particular call center. Thus, for example, a customer calling from Lisbon, Portugal, was automatically directed to a Portuguese-speaking sales rep at the call center in Montpelier, France.

However, in some countries Dell's sell-direct-to-customers strategy put it at a disadvantage in appealing to small business customers and individual consumers, since most of these customers were reluctant to place orders by phone or over the Internet. Rivals in Japan and China who marketed PCs through retailers and other resellers were outselling Dell in the small business and household segments. According to an executive at Lenovo, one of Dell's biggest rivals in China, "It takes two years of a person's savings to buy a PC in China. And when two years of savings is at stake, the whole family wants to come out to a store to touch and try the machine."[11] To address the reluctance of households to buy direct from Dell, the head of Dell's consumer PC sales group in Japan installed 34 kiosks in leading electronics stores around Japan, allowing shoppers to test Dell computers, ask questions of staff, and place orders—close to half the sales were to people

who did not know about Dell prior to visiting the kiosk. The kiosks proved quite popular and were instrumental in boosting Dell's share of PC sales to consumers in Japan.

Inspired by the success of kiosks in Japan, in 2002 Dell began installing Dell Direct Store kiosks in a variety of U.S. retail settings as a hands-on complement to Internet and phone sales. The kiosk stores showcased Dell's newest notebook and desktop computers, plasma and LCD TVs, printers, and music players. The kiosks did not carry inventory, but customers could talk face-to-face with a knowledgeable Dell sales representative, inspect Dell's products, and order them on the Internet while at the kiosk. The kiosks were considered a success in getting consumers to try Dell products. More kiosks were added and, by December 2005, Dell had 145 Dell Direct Store kiosks in 20 states, within reach of more than 50 percent of the U.S. population.

Supplementing the Direct Sales Strategy with Sales at the Retail Stores of Select Partners

In fiscal 2006, Dell's share of PC sales to U.S. households dropped to 25.6 percent from 29.3 percent the prior year. In 2007, its share of the home or consumer market in the United States dropped even more precipitously, to 18.9 percent (see Exhibit 5). Sales to households weakened in other parts of the world market as well. The declines were partly due (1) to Hewlett-Packard's aggressive and successful efforts (mainly, lower pricing and better feature sets) to gain market share at Dell's expense and (2) to surging U.S. sales of Apple's PC models (see Exhibit 1), buoyed chiefly by consumer infatuation with Apple's iPod models and its new iPhone. Dell management responded to the unexpected and unprecedented falloff in sales to households by backing off on its almost 100 percent commitment to selling direct and forging partnerships with such retailers as Walmart, Staples, and Best Buy to begin offering select Dell PCs in retail stores. Similar initiatives to begin selling through retailers were taken in other parts of the world market. In Latin America, Dell forged retailing partnerships with Walmart and Pontofrio. Dell's retailing partners in Europe, the Middle East, and Africa included Carphone Warehouse, Carrefour, Tesco, and DSGi. In China, Japan, and other parts of the Asia-Pacific

Exhibit 5   **Trends in Dell's Market Shares in PCs and x86 Servers, 1994–2007**

Market Segment	Dell's Market Share								
	2007	2006	2005	2004	2002	2000	1998	1996	1994
Worldwide share by geographic area	14.9%	17.2%	18.2%	17.7%	14.9%	10.5%	8.0%	4.1%	2.7%
United States	29.3	31.3	33.6	33.1	28.0	18.4	12.0	6.4	4.2
Europe/Middle East/Africa	11.0	12.2	12.5	11.5	9.6	7.8	7.0	3.8	2.4
Asia-Pacific	8.9	8.8	8.2	7.0	4.8	3.4	2.4	1.3	0.3
Japan	14.0	14.2	12.3	11.3	7.7	4.0	3.0	1.6	1.1
Worldwide share by product									
Desktop PCs	15.0%	17.2%	18.2%	18.0%	14.8%	10.1%	7.8%	4.3%	3.0%
Notebook PCs	14.2	16.4	17.3	16.2	14.4	11.3	8.5	3.4	1.1
x86 Servers	25.0	25.6	26.3	24.8	21.7	15.4	9.7	3.4	3.1
U.S. segment share	29.3%	31.3%	33.1%	33.1%	28.0%	18.4%	12.0%	6.4%	4.2%
Education	40.7	43.8	44.6	44.3	34.9	26.2	11.0	3.9	1.1
Government	37.7	33.2	36.0	32.9	33.7	22.9	14.6	6.5	7.1
Home	18.9	25.6	29.3	29.7	22.7	6.5	3.5	2.1	1.2
Large business	43.3	43.7	43.3	44.2	39.9	31.3	21.6	11.2	6.9
Small/medium business	29.1	27.0	29.2	28.5	24.2	22.6	14.3	7.9	5.4

Source: Information posted at www.dell.com (accessed May 6, 2008).

region, Dell began selling its PCs at the stores of Gome (the leading consumer electronics retailer in China), Suning, Hontu, HiMart, Courts, Croma, Officeworks (104 stores in Australia), and Bic Camera. By mid-2008, Dell had its products available in 12,000 retail stores worldwide and planned to grow this number considerably.

So far, Dell management was pleased with the initial results of its shift to using retail stores as a way to supplement online and telephone sales to consumers and small businesses.

Expansion into New Products

In recent years, Dell had expanded its product offerings to include data storage hardware, switches, handheld PCs, printers, and printer cartridges, and software products in an effort to diversify its revenue stream and use its competitive capabilities in PCs and servers to pursue growth opportunities. Michael Dell explained

why Dell had decided to expand into products and services that complemented its sales of PCs and servers:

We tend to look at what is the next big opportunity all the time. We can't take on too many of these at once, because it kind of overloads the system. But we believe fundamentally that if you think about the whole market, it's about an $800 billion market, all areas of technology over time go through a process of standardization or commoditization. And we try to look at those, anticipate what's happening, and develop strategies that will allow us to get into those markets. In the server market in 1995 we had a 2 percent market, share; today we have over a 30 percent share; we're number 1 in the U.S. How did that happen? Well, first of all it happened because we started to have a high market share for desktops and notebooks. Then customers said, oh yes, we know Dell; those are the guys who have really good desktops and notebooks. So they have servers; yes, we'll test those; we'll test them around the periphery, maybe not in the most critical applications at first, but we'll test them here. [Then they discover] these are really good and Dell provides great support . . . and I think to some extent we've benefited from the fact that our competitors have underestimated the importance of value, and the power of the relationship and the service that we can create with the customer.

And, also, as a product tends to standardize there's not an elimination of the requirement for custom services; there's a reduction of it. So by offering some services, but not the services of the traditional proprietary computer company, we've been able to increase our share. And, in fact, what tends to happen is customers embrace the standards, because they know that's going to save them costs. Let me give you an example . . . about a year ago we entered into the data networking market. So we have Ethernet switches, layer 2 switches. So if you have PCs and servers, you need switches; every PC attaches to a switch; every server attaches to a switch. It's a pretty easy sale; switches go along with computer systems. We looked at this market and were able to come up with products that are priced about 2½ times less than the market leader today, Cisco, and as a result the business has grown very, very quickly. We shipped 1.8 million switch ports in a period of about a year, when most people would have said that's not going to work and come up with all kinds of reasons why we can't succeed.[12]

As Dell's sales of data-routing switches accelerated in 2001–2002 and Dell management mulled over whether to expand into other networking products and Internet gear, Cisco elected to discontinue supplying its switches to Dell for resale as of October 2002. Dell's family of Power-Connect switches—simple commodity-like products generally referred to as layer 2 switches in the industry—were about 75 percent cheaper than those made by Cisco as of 2005.

Senior Dell executives saw external storage devices as a growth opportunity because the company's corporate and institutional customers were making increasing use of high-speed data storage and retrieval devices. Dell's Power-Vault line of storage products had data protection and recovery features that made it easy for customers to add and manage storage and simplify consolidation. The PowerVault products used standardized technology and components (which were considerably cheaper than customized ones), allowing Dell to underprice rivals and drive down storage

costs for its customers by about 50 percent. Dell's competitors in storage devices included Hewlett-Packard and IBM.

Some observers saw Dell's 2003 entry into the printer market as a calculated effort to go after Hewlett-Packard's biggest and most profitable business segment and believed the Dell offensive was deliberately timed to throw a wrench into HP's efforts to resolve the many challenges of successfully merging its operations with those of Compaq. One of the reasons Dell had entered the market for servers back in 1995 was that Compaq Computer, then its biggest rival in PCs, had been using its lucrative profits on server sales to subsidize charging lower prices on Compaq computers and thus be more price-competitive against Dell's PCs—at the time Compaq was losing money on its desktop and notebook PC business. According to Michael Dell:

> Compaq had this enormous profit pool that they were using to fight against us in the desktop and notebook business. That was not an acceptable situation. Our product teams knew that the servers weren't that complicated or expensive to produce, and customers were being charged unfair prices.[13]

Dell management believed that in 2000–2002 HP was doing much the same thing in printers and printer products, where it had a dominant market share worldwide and generated about 75 percent of its operating profits. Dell believed that HP was using its big margins on printer products to subsidize selling its PCs at prices comparable to Dell's, even though Dell had costs that were about 8 percent lower than HP's. HP's PC operations were either in the red or barely in the black during most of 2000–2003, while Dell consistently had profit margins of 8 percent or more on PCs. Dell management believed the company's entry into the printer market would add value for its customers. Michael Dell explained:

> We think we can drive down the entire cost of owning and using printing products. If you look at any other market Dell has gone into, we have been able to significantly save money for customers. We know we can do that in printers; we have looked at the supply chain all the way through its various cycles and we know there are inefficiencies there. I think the price of the total offering when we include the printer and the supplies . . . can come down quite considerably.[14]

When Dell announced it had contracted with Lexmark to make printers and printer and toner cartridges for sale under the Dell label beginning in 2003, HP immediately discontinued supplying HP printers to Dell for resale at Dell's Web site. Dell had been selling Lexmark printers for two years and, since 2000, had resold about 4 million printers made by such vendors as HP, Lexmark, and other vendors to its customers. Lexmark designed and made critical parts for its printers but used offshore contract manufacturers for assembly. Gross profit margins on printers (sales minus cost of goods sold) were said to be in single digits in 2002–2004, but the gross margins on printer supplies were in the 50–60 percent range—brand-name ink cartridges for printers typically ran $25 to $35. As of fall 2005, Dell had sold more than 10 million printers and had an estimated 20 percent of the market for color network lasers and color inkjet printers in the United States.[15]

Dell executives believed the company's entry and market success in printer products had put added competitive pressure on Hewlett-Packard in the printer market and was partly responsible for HP's share of the printer market worldwide slipping from just under 50 percent to around 46 percent in 2004. To further keep the pricing pressure on HP in 2003, Dell had priced its storage and networking products below comparable HP products.

Exhibit 6 shows a breakdown of Dell's sales by product category. Exhibit 7 shows Dell's average revenues per unit sold for fiscal years 1998–2008. The declines were driven by steadily falling costs for components, Dell's ability to improve productivity and take costs out of its value chain, and Dell's strategy of passing along cost savings to its customers and trying to deliver more value to customers than its rivals did. However, the tiny increases in average revenues per unit in the past two fiscal years reflected slowing declines in components prices, a shift in the PC sales mix away from desktops to laptops (which carried higher price tags and thus yielded greater average revenues per unit sold), and Dell's more restrained pricing (to protect its operating and net profit margins from further erosion). In fiscal 2007–2008, unlike prior years, Dell had difficulty in lowering unit costs; out-of-proportion increases in operating expenses (see Exhibit 2) made it infeasible for Dell to cut prices and still preserve its operating profit margins. Top executives opted to maintain prices to keep the company's already

Exhibit 6　Dell's Revenues by Product Category, 2006–2008

Product Category	2008 Revenues (in Billions)	2008 % of Total Revenues	2007 Revenues (in Billions)	2007 % of Total Revenues	2006 Revenues (in Billions)	2006 % of Total Revenues
Desktop PCs	$19.6	32.1%	$19.8	34.5%	$21.6	38.7%
Mobility products (laptop PCs and workstations)	17.4	28.5	15.5	27.0	14.4	25.8
Software and peripherals (printers, monitors, TVs, projectors, ink and toner cartridges)	9.9	16.2	9.0	15.7	8.3	14.9
Servers and networking hardware	6.5	10.6	5.8	10.1	5.4	9.8
Consulting and enhanced services	5.3	8.8	5.1	8.9	4.2	7.5
Storage products	2.4	3.9	2.3	4.0	1.9	3.4
Totals	$61.1	100.1%	$57.4	100.2%	$55.8	100.1%

Note: Total revenue percentages may exceed 100% due to rounding up of revenue percentage data.
Source: Dell's 10-K report, fiscal 2008, p. 90.

Exhibit 7   Trend in Dell's Approximate Average Revenue per Unit Sold, Fiscal Years 1998–2008

Fiscal Year	Dell's Approximate Average Revenue Per Unit Sold
1998	$2,600
2000	2,250
2001	2,050
2002	1,700
2003	1,640
2004	1,590
2005	1,560
2006	1,500
2007	1,510
2008	1,540

Source: Company financial records and company postings at www.dell.com (accessed May 3, 2008).

lower operating profit margins from going down any further (see Exhibit 2); this left Dell vulnerable to HP's strategic offensive to regain sales and market share—an offensive that featured prices for HP products that were more in line with what Dell was charging.

Customer Service and Technical Support

Service became a feature of Dell's strategy in 1986 when the company began providing a year's free on-site service with most of its PCs after users complained about having to ship their PCs back to Austin for repairs. Dell began offering PC buyers the option of buying contracts for on-site repair services for a defined period (usually one to four years). Dell contracted with local service providers to handle customer requests for repairs; on-site service was provided on a four-hour basis to large customers and on a next-day basis to small customers. Dell generally contracted with third-party providers to make the necessary on-site service calls. Customers notified Dell when they had problems; such notices triggered two electronic dispatches—one to ship replacement parts from Dell's factory to the customer, and one to notify the contract service provider to prepare to make the needed repairs as soon as the

parts arrived.[16] Bad parts were returned so that Dell could determine what went wrong and how to prevent such problems from happening again (problems relating to faulty components or flawed components design were promptly passed along to the relevant supplier for correction). If business or institutional customers preferred to work with their own service provider, Dell supplied the provider of choice with training and spare parts needed to service the customers' equipment.

Later, Dell began offering contracts for CompleteCare accidental damage service. In 2006, Dell began using an online diagnostics tool called DellConnect to troubleshoot and resolve problems with a customer's computer while the customer was connected to Dell's Web site. In 2007, Dell launched a corporate blog called Direct-2Dell, a customer idea engine called IdeaStorm, and several online community forums for the purpose of better listening to and engaging with customers. Dell's online training programs featured more than 1,200 courses for consumer, business, and IT professionals. Over 50 percent of Dell's technical support and customer service activities were conducted via the Internet. Customers could also request technical support via a toll-free phone number and e-mail; Dell received more than 8 million phone calls and 500,000 to 600,000 e-mail messages annually requesting service and support.

Dell had 25 customer service centers worldwide in 2008 that were primarily engaged in handling technical support, requests for repairs, and other issues and inquiries. In a move to trim rising technical support and customer service costs in 2004–2005, Dell opted to move a large portion of its support services to countries where labor costs were low. But according to Dell's president of global services and chief information officer, "We did it way too quickly—we didn't move process management disciplines with it as effectively as we should have, and we wound up making some mistakes with the services experience."[17] The outcome was a sharp rise in customer complaints, especially among small business and individual customers who were most affected—a number of irritated Dell customers went so far as to post their horror stories at Web sites like IhateDell.net, and the resulting media publicity tarnished Dell's reputation for customer service among these buyers. To correct the service problems, Dell had moved many of its service centers back to countries where big numbers of its customers were located. Service processes were standardized worldwide, and best practices from all over the world were built into the standards. Dell's goal was to reach 90 percent customer satisfaction—where customers rated their service experience with Dell as "top notch" or "very satisfied"—as quickly as possible. In early 2008, Dell's customer satisfaction ratings were at 92 percent for Asia, at 90 percent in the Europe/Middle East/Africa region, and in the 80 percent range for the Americas (these ratings included all services for small, medium, and large customers).[18]

Premier Pages Dell had developed customized, password-protected Web sites called Premier Pages for more than 50,000 corporate, governmental, and institutional customers worldwide. These Premier Pages gave customers' personnel online access to information about all Dell products and configurations the company had purchased or that were currently authorized for purchase. Employees could use Premier Pages to (1) obtain customer-specific pricing for whatever machines and options the employee wanted to consider, (2) place an order online that would be routed electronically to higher-level managers for approval and then on to Dell for assembly and delivery, and (3) seek advanced help desk support. Customers could also search and sort all invoices and obtain purchase histories. These features eliminated paper invoices, cut ordering time, and reduced the internal labor customers needed to staff corporate purchasing and accounting functions. Customer use of Premier Pages had boosted the productivity of Dell salespeople assigned to these accounts by 50 percent. Dell was providing Premier Page service to additional customers annually and adding more features to further improve functionality.

Product Design Services One of Dell's latest services for large customers was making special-purpose products for such customers as Internet search providers, social networking sites, and big video content sites that might need 10,000 or more units to accommodate its requirements. Such customers did not want to pay for a general-purpose product with components or performance features it did not need. So Dell created a

group that had the capability to provide a big user with thousands of units of a product stripped of unnecessary features and equipped with whatever processor, memory, and disk drive suited the customer's needs. Dell personnel would visit with the customer, ascertain the customer's needs and preferences, provide a prototype within three weeks for evaluation and testing, make any additional changes within another two weeks for further testing and evaluation, and then be in volume production by the thousands of units within another three or four weeks—altogether about a nine-week design-to-production/delivery cycle.

Value-Added Services for Customers with Large IT Operations Dell kept close track of the purchases of its large global customers, country by country and department by department—and customers themselves found this purchase information valuable. Dell's sales and support personnel used their knowledge about a particular customer's needs to help that customer plan PC purchases, to configure the customer's PC networks, and to provide value-added services. For example, for its large customers Dell loaded software and placed ID tags on newly ordered PCs at the factory, thereby eliminating the need for the customer's IT personnel to unpack the PC, deliver it to an employee's desk, hook it up, place asset tags on the PC, and load the needed software—a process that could take several hours and cost $200–$300.[19] While Dell charged an extra $15 or $20 for the software-loading and asset-tagging services, the savings to customers were still considerable—one large customer reported savings of $500,000 annually from this service.[20]

In 2007 and early 2008, Dell spent about $2 billion to make a series of software-related acquisitions that gave it an altogether new value-added capability:

1. Everdream Corporation—Everdream was a leading provider of Software as a Service (SaaS) solutions, with operations in California and North Carolina. This acquisition enabled Dell to extend its capabilities to use the Internet to remotely manage global delivery of software solutions from servers, storage devices, and printers to desktop PCs, laptops, and other end-user devices. Dell

management believed that remote-service management of software products would help business customers of all sizes simplify their IT infrastructure—a value-added outcome that Dell was aggressively pursuing. Terms of the acquisition were not disclosed.

2. SilverBack Technologies Inc.—Silverback was a privately owned, Massachusetts-based company that had a delivery platform to remotely manage and monitor SaaS products. Such a platform was essential to Dell's strategy of simplifying customers' IT infrastructures by providing their personnel with desirable software applications on an as-needed basis via the Internet. Terms of the acquisition were not disclosed.

3. MessageOne Inc.—Acquired for $155 million, MessageOne was an industry leader in SaaS-enabled continuous e-mail service, e-mail archiving, and disaster recovery of e-mail messages. The MessageOne acquisition further enhanced Dell's strategy to use SaaS applications and remote software management tools to deliver configure-to-order IT services to commercial customers over the Internet.

4. EqualLogic—This company, acquired for $1.4 billion, was a leading provider of high-performance storage area network (SAN) solutions that made storing and processing data easier and cheaper. EqualLogic's technological capabilities allowed Dell to offer its customers a secure data storage solution that used the customer's existing IT infrastructure, could be installed in minutes, managed itself, and was easily expanded as needs increased.

5. ASAP Software—ASAP, acquired at a cost of $340 million, was a leading software solutions and licensing services provider, with expertise in software licensing and the management of IT assets. The ASAP acquisition expanded Dell's lineup of software offerings from 200 to 2,000.

6. The Networked Storage Company—Networked Storage was a leading IT consulting group that specialized in transitioning customers to proven, simplified, cost-efficient data storage solutions. Dell management saw this acquisition as an important element in its strategy to build the capability to offer Dell customers simple, cost-effective ways to manage their IT infrastructures. Terms of the acquisition were not disclosed.

Dell management saw all six acquisitions as greatly strengthening the company's capabilities to provide an altogether new value-added service to customers with sizable IT operations, all of whom were finding the tasks of managing and maintaining an IT infrastructure to be increasingly complex and costly. Executives at Dell believed that having greater capability than rivals to offer commercial customers simple, cost-effective ways to manage their IT operations would give Dell added competitiveness in marketing its lineup of product offerings to commercial enterprises worldwide. While Dell already was the sales leader in PCs sold to corporations and businesses in North America and Europe, extending its lead in these regions and growing sales and market share in the remaining parts of the world could make a material contribution not only to growing Dell's overall business but also to overtaking Hewlett-Packard as the global leader in PCs.

Enhanced Services and Support for Large Enterprises

Corporate customers paid Dell fees to provide on-site service and help with migrating to new information technologies. Service revenues had climbed from $1.7 billion in 2002 to about $5.3 billion in fiscal 2008. This portion of Dell's business was split between what Michael Dell called close-to-the-box services and management/professional services. Dell estimated that close-to-the-box support services for Dell products represented about a $50 billion market as of 2005, whereas the market for management/professional services (IT life-cycle services, deployment of new technology, and solutions for greater IT productivity) in 2005 was about $90 billion. The market for IT consulting and services was forecast to be in the $850–$900 billion range in 2011. For the most part, IT consulting services were becoming more standardized, driven primarily by growing hardware and software standardization, reduction in on-site service requirements (partly because of online diagnostic and support tools, growing ease of repair and maintenance, increased customer knowledge, and increased remote management capabilities), and declines in the skills and know-how that were required to perform service tasks on standardized equipment and install new, more standardized systems.

Dell's strategy in enhanced services, like its strategy in hardware products, was to bring down the cost of IT-related services for its large enterprise customers and free customers from "overpriced relationships" with such vendors as IBM, Sun Microsystems, and Hewlett-Packard that typically charged premium prices ($250 per hour) and realized hefty profits for their efforts.[21] According to Michael Dell, customers who bought the services being provided by Dell saved 40 to 50 percent over what they would have paid other providers of IT services.

The caliber of technical support and customer service that Dell provided to its large enterprise customers was highly regarded (despite the problems sometimes experienced by small businesses and individuals). In a 2005 survey of IT executives by *CIO* magazine, Dell was rated number one among leading vendors for providing "impeccable customer service" to large enterprises.

Providing Online Shoppers with Customer Reviews of Dell Products

Users of Dell products were encouraged to provide Dell with a review of their experiences with the products they had purchased. As part of the review process, customers were asked to provide a rating of the product using a 5-point scale that ran from 1 (poor) to 5 (excellent). Shoppers browsing through Dell's product offerings could view the average customer rating score for each product directly on the screen where the product details were displayed and could click on an adjacent link to read the accompanying reviews. In 2008, about 50,000 customer reviews of Dell products were posted and available for inspection.

Listening to Customers
In addition to using its sales and support mechanisms to stay close to customers, Dell periodically held regional forums that gave senior Dell personnel opportunities to listen to the company's biggest and most influential customers and discuss their emerging needs and expectations. The meeting agenda frequently included a presentation by Michael Dell, plus presentations by Dell's senior technologists on the direction of the latest technological developments and what the flow of technology really meant for customers, presentations on what new

and upgraded products Dell was planning to introduce, and breakout sessions on topics of current interest.

In February 2007, Dell began inviting customers to post their ideas for improving its products and services at a section of its Web site called IdeaStorm. As of April 2008, customers had posted more than 8,900 ideas, 45 of which had been implemented. Michael Dell believed that the Internet and the speed with which people worldwide were able to connect to the Internet via a growing number of devices had forever redefined what it means to listen to customers:

> Listening used to mean commissioning a customer survey. Now it means engaging directly with customers and critics and using those relationships to create a smarter business. Tapping into the ideas of our customers is like having an open source R&D lab.[22]

Customer-Driven Research and Development and Standardized Technology

Dell's R&D focus was to track and test new developments in components and software, ascertain which ones would prove most useful and cost-effective for customers, and then design them into Dell products. Management's philosophy was that it was Dell's job on behalf of its customers to sort out all the new technology coming into the marketplace and design products having the features, options, and solutions that were the most relevant for customers. Studies conducted by Dell's R&D personnel indicated that, over time, products incorporating standardized technology delivered about twice the performance per dollar of cost as products based on proprietary technology.

At the University of Buffalo, for example, Dell had installed a 5.6 teraflop cluster of about 2,000 Dell servers containing 4,000 microprocessors that constituted one of the most powerful supercomputers in the world and gave researchers the computing power needed to help decode the human genome. The cluster of servers, which were the same as those Dell sold to many other customers, had been installed in about 60 days at a cost of a few million dollars—far less than the cost of another vendor's supercomputer that used proprietary technology. Energy giant Amerada

Hess Corporation (now known as Hess Corporation), attracted by Dell's use of standardized and upgradable parts and components, installed a cluster of several hundred Dell workstations and allocated about $300,000 a year to upgrade and maintain it; the cluster replaced an IBM supercomputer that cost $1.5 million a year to lease and operate.

Dell's R&D unit also studied and implemented ways to control quality and to streamline the assembly process. In 2008, Dell had a portfolio of 1,954 U.S. patents and another 2,196 patent applications were pending. Dell's R&D group included about 4,000 engineers, and its annual budget for research, development, and engineering was in the $430–$500 million range before jumping to more than $600 million in fiscal 2008 (see Exhibit 2).

Other Elements of Dell's Business Strategy

Dell's strategy had three other elements that complemented its core strategy: entry into the white-box segment of the PC industry, advertising, and continuous pursuit of cost reduction initiatives.

Dell's Entry into the White-Box PC Segment
In 2002, Dell announced it would begin making so-called white-box (i.e., unbranded) PCs for resale under the private labels of retailers. PC dealers that supplied white-box PCs to small businesses and price-conscious individuals under the dealer's own brand name accounted for about one-third of total PC sales and about 50 percent of sales to small businesses. According to one industry analyst, "Increasingly, Dell's biggest competitor these days isn't big brand-name companies like IBM or HP; it's white-box vendors." Dell's thinking in entering the white-box PC segment was that it was cheaper to reach many small businesses through the white-box dealers that already served them than by using its own sales force and support groups to sell and service businesses with fewer than 100 employees. Dell believed that its low-cost supply chain and assembly capabilities would allow it to build generic machines cheaper than white-box resellers could buy components and assemble a customized machine. Management forecast that Dell would achieve $380 million in sales of white-box PCs in 2003 and would

generate profit margins equal to those on Dell-branded PCs. Some industry analysts were skeptical of Dell's move into white-box PCs because they expected white-box dealers to be reluctant to buy their PCs from a company that had a history of taking their clients. Others believed this was a test effort by Dell to develop the capabilities to take on white-box dealers in Asia and especially in China, where the sellers of generic PCs were particularly strong.

Advertising
Michael Dell was a firm believer in the power of advertising and frequently espoused its importance in the company's strategy. He insisted that the company's ads be communicative and forceful, not soft and fuzzy. The company regularly had prominent ads describing its products and prices in such leading computer publications as *PC Magazine* and *PC World*, as well as in *USA Today*, *The Wall Street Journal*, and other business publications. From time to time, the company ran ads on TV to promote its products to consumers and small businesses. Catalogs of about 25–30 pages describing Dell's latest desktop and laptop PCs, along with its printers and other offerings, were periodically mailed to consumers who had bought Dell products. Other marketing initiatives included printing newspaper inserts and sending newsletters and promotional pieces to customers via the Internet.

Continuous Pursuit of Cost Reduction Initiatives
Michael Dell had long been an ardent advocate of relentless efforts to improve efficiency and keeps costs as low as feasible. But during Kevin Rollins's tenure as CEO, Dell's cost edge over rivals had narrowed, and the company's profit margins had slipped as well (partly because fierce price competition was driving down the prices of many products that Dell sold faster than Dell was able to lower its costs per unit)—Exhibit 7 shows the downward trend in the average revenue Dell received from each unit sold. When he reassumed his role as CEO in 2007, Michael Dell announced that tighter controls over operating expenses would be implemented immediately and that management would begin an in-depth exploration of ways for improving Dell's cost-competitiveness, organizing operations more efficiently, and boosting profitability and cash flows. In May 2007, Dell announced an initiative

to reduce the global workforce headcount by 10 percent, or 8,800 people. By March 2008, a net of 3,200 jobs had been eliminated. However, the company had actually hired 2,100 more people to staff frontline operations and customer-facing activities; the net reduction of 3,200 people was achieved by cutting 5,300 personnel engaged in performing what Dell called non-frontline activities. The result was to increase the number of Dell employees engaged in frontline and customer-facing activities from 54 percent to 57 percent.

In March 2008, Dell executives announced that over the next three years the company would seek to achieve annualized savings of $3 billion via productivity improvements and cost-reduction efforts across all the company's value chain—design, supply chain logistics, materials, manufacturing, and other operating activities. Management reaffirmed its commitment to reducing the global employee headcount by 8,800 and achieving the related labor-cost savings. At the same time, Dell also put programs in place to reignite the company's revenue growth in five focus areas: global consumer products, sales to large enterprise customers, laptop computers, sales to small and medium enterprises, and sales in emerging countries.

THE INFORMATION TECHNOLOGY MARKETPLACE IN 2008

Analysts expected the worldwide IT industry to grow from $1.2 trillion in 2007 to $1.5 trillion in 2010, a compound growth rate of about 7.7 percent. Of that projected 2010 total, about $560 billion was expected to be for hardware (PCs, servers, storage devices, networking equipment, and printers and peripherals); $327 billion for software; and $613 billion for services. From 1980 to 2000, IT spending had grown at an average annual rate of 12 percent; thereafter, it had flattened—to a 1 percent decline in 2001, a 2.3 percent decline in 2002, a single-digit increase in 2003—then rose more briskly at rates in the 5–10 percent range in 2004, 2005, 2006 and 2007. The slowdown in IT spending in 2001–2007 compared to earlier years reflected a combination of factors: sluggish economic growth in many countries in 2001–2003;

overinvestment in IT in the 1995–1999 period; declining unit prices for many IT products (especially PCs and servers); and a growing preference for lower-priced, standard-component hardware that was good enough to perform a variety of functions using off-the-shelf Windows or Linux operating systems (as opposed to relying on proprietary hardware and customized Unix software). The selling points that appealed most to IT customers were standardization, flexibility, modularity, simplicity, economy of use, and value.

There were several driving forces contributing to increased global spending for information technology products and services starting in 2004.[23] One was the explosion of digital information and content. According to Forrester Research, the world's data doubled approximately every three years, a phenomenon that was expected to produce more than a sixfold increase in data between 2003 and 2010. A second force was the rapid expansion of search engine activity, e-mail, text messages, social networking Web sites like My Space and Facebook, blogs, and online video and images; these fed the worldwide demand for digital devices to create, store, share, and print the mushrooming volume of digital information and content. The third force was the rapidly growing demand for information technology products and services in emerging markets around the world—like Brazil, Russia, China, India, and several other countries in Southeast Asia and Eastern Europe—where over half of the world's population resided. At the same time, several other complicating factors were at work. Much of the growing volume of content lacked authentication and proper security, plus the content was increasingly global and mobile. And consumer expectations were changing—people wanted instantaneous access to content regardless of what kind of device they were using or where they happened to be, and their tolerance for complexity was low. All of these aspects of the global IT marketplace created huge opportunities for IT providers and huge challenges for IT users.

Exhibit 8 shows actual and projected PC sales for 1980–2012 as compiled by industry researcher International Data Corporation (IDC). According to Gartner Research, the billionth PC was shipped sometime in July 2002; of the billion PCs sold, an estimated 550 million were still in use. Forrester Research estimated that the numbers of

Exhibit 8   **Worldwide Shipments of PCs, Actual and Forecast, 1980–2012 (in millions)**

Year	PCs Shipped
1980	1
1985	11
1990	24
1995	58
2000	139
2001	133
2002	136
2003	153
2004	177
2005	208
2006	235
2007	269
2008*	302
2009*	335
2010*	368
2011*	398
2012*	426

*Forecast.

Source: International Data Corporation.

PCs in use worldwide would exceed 1 billion by the end of 2008 (up from 575 million in 2004) and would approach 1.3 billion by 2011 and 2.0 billion by 2016. With a world population of more than 6 billion, most industry participants believed there was ample opportunity for further growth in the PC market. Growth potential for PCs was particularly strong in Russia, China, India, several other Asian countries, and portions of Latin America (especially Brazil and Mexico). At the same time, forecasters expected full global build-out of the Internet to continue, which would require the installation of millions of servers.

HOW DELL'S STRATEGY PUT COMPETITIVE PRESSURE ON RIVALS

When the personal computer industry first began to take shape in the early 1980s, the founding companies manufactured many of the components themselves—disk drives, memory chips, graphics chips, microprocessors, motherboards, and software. Subscribing to a philosophy that mandated in-house development of key components, they built expertise in a variety of PC-related technologies and created organizational units to produce components as well as handle final assembly. While certain noncritical items were typically outsourced, if a computer maker was not at least partially vertically integrated and did not produce some components for its PCs, then it was not taken seriously as a manufacturer. But as the industry grew, technology advanced quickly in so many directions on so many parts and components that the early personal computer manufacturers could not keep pace as experts on all fronts. There were too many technologies and manufacturing intricacies to master for a vertically integrated manufacturer to keep its products on the cutting edge.

As a consequence, companies emerged that specialized in making particular components. Specialists could marshal enough R&D capability and resources to either lead the technological developments in their area of specialization or else quickly match the advances made by their competitors. Moreover, specialist firms could mass-produce the component and supply it to several computer manufacturers far cheaper than any one manufacturer could fund the needed component R&D and then make only whatever smaller volume of components it needed for assembling its own brand of PCs. Thus, in the early 1990s, such computer makers as Compaq Computer, IBM, Hewlett-Packard, Sony, Toshiba, and Fujitsu-Siemens began to abandon vertical integration in favor of a strategy of outsourcing most components from specialists and concentrating on efficient assembly and marketing their brand of computers. They adopted the build-to-stock value chain model shown in the top section of Exhibit 4. It featured arm's-length transactions between specialist suppliers, manufacturer/assemblers, distributors and retailers, and end users. However, a few others, most notably Dell and Gateway, employed a shorter value chain model, selling directly to customers and eliminating the time and costs associated with distributing through independent resellers. Building to order avoided (1) having to keep many differently equipped models on retailers' shelves to fill buyer requests for one or another configuration of options and components, and (2) having to clear out slow-selling models at a discount before introducing new generations of PCs—for instance, Hewlett-Packard's retail dealers had an average of 43 days of HP products in stock as of October 2004. Direct sales eliminated retailer costs and markups; retail dealer margins were typically in the range of 4–10 percent.

Because of Dell's success in using its business model and strategy to become the low-cost leader, most other PC makers had tried to emulate various aspects of Dell's strategy, but with only limited success. Nearly all vendors were trying to cut days of inventory out of their supply chains and reduce their costs of goods sold and operating expenses to levels that would make them more cost-competitive with Dell. In an effort to cut their assembly costs, several others (including HP) had begun outsourcing assembly to contract manufacturers and refocusing their internal efforts on product design and marketing. Virtually all PC vendors were trying to minimize the amount of finished goods in dealer/distributor inventories and shorten the time it took to replenish dealer stocks. Collaboration with contract manufacturers was increasing to develop the capabilities to build and deliver PCs equipped to customer specifications within 7 to 14 days, but these efforts were hampered by the use of Asia-based contract manufacturers—delivering built-to-order PCs to North American and European customers within a two-week time frame required the use of costly air freight from assembly plants in Asia.

While most PC vendors would have liked to adopt Dell's sell-direct strategy for at least some of their sales, they confronted big channel conflict problems: If they started to push direct sales hard, they would almost certainly alienate the independent dealers on whom they depended for the bulk of their sales and service to customers. Dealers saw sell-direct efforts on the part of a manufacturer whose brand they represented as a move to cannibalize their business and to compete against them. However, Dell's success in gaining large enterprise customers with its direct sales force had forced growing numbers of PC vendors to supplement the efforts of their independent dealers with direct sales and service efforts of their own. During 2003–2007, several

of Dell's rivals were selling 15 to 25 percent of their products direct.

HEWLETT-PACKARD: DELL'S CHIEF RIVAL IN PCS AND X86 SERVERS

In one of the most contentious and controversial acquisitions in U.S. history, Hewlett-Packard shareholders in early 2002 voted by a narrow margin to approve the company's acquisition of Compaq Computer, the world's second largest full-service global computing company (behind IBM), with 2001 revenues of $33.6 billion and a net loss of $785 million. Compaq had passed IBM to become the world leader in PCs in 1995 and remained in first place until it was overtaken by Dell in late 1999. Compaq had acquired Tandem Computer in 1997 and Digital Equipment Corporation in 1998 to give it capabilities, products, and service offerings that allowed it to compete in every sector of the computer industry—PCs, servers, workstations, mainframes, peripherals, and such services as business and e-commerce solutions, hardware and software support, systems integration, and technology consulting.[24] In 2000, Compaq spent $370 million to acquire certain assets of Inacom Corporation that management believed would help Compaq reduce inventories, speed cycle time, and enhance its capabilities to do business with customers via the Internet. Nonetheless, at the time of its acquisition by HP, Compaq was struggling to compete successfully in all of the many product and service arenas where it operated.

Carly Fiorina, who became HP's CEO in 1999, explained why the acquisition of Compaq was strategically sound:[25]

> With Compaq, we become No. 1 in Windows, No. 1 in Linux and No. 1 in Unix . . . With Compaq, we become the No. 1 player in storage, and the leader in the fastest growing segment of the storage market—storage area networks. With Compaq, we double our service and support capacity in the area of mission-critical infrastructure design, outsourcing and support. . . . Let's talk about PCs. . . . Compaq has been able to improve their turns in that business from 23 turns of inventory per year to 62—100 percent improvement year over

year—and they are coming close to doing as well as Dell does. They've reduced operating expenses by $130 million, improved gross margins by three points, reduced channel inventory by more than $800 million. They ship about 70 percent of their commercial volume through their direct channel, comparable to Dell. We will combine our successful retail PC business model with their commercial business model and achieve much more together than we could alone. With Compaq, we will double the size of our sales force to 15,000 strong. We will build our R&D budget to more than $4 billion a year, and add important capabilities to HP Labs. We will become the No. 1 player in a whole host of countries around the world—HP operates in more than 160 countries, with well over 60 percent of our revenues coming from outside the U.S. The new HP will be the No. 1 player in the consumer and small- and medium-business segments. . . . We have estimated cost synergies of $2.5 billion by 2004. . . . It is a rare opportunity when a technology company can advance its market position substantially and reduce its cost structure substantially at the same time. And this is possible because Compaq and HP are in the same businesses, pursuing the same strategies, in the same markets, with complementary capabilities.

However, going into 2005 the jury was still out on whether HP's acquisition of Compaq was the success that Carly Fiorina had claimed it would be. The company's only real bright spot was its $24 billion crown jewel printer business, which still reigned as the unchallenged world leader. But the rest of HP's businesses (PCs, servers, storage devices, digital cameras, calculators, and IT services) were underachievers. Its PC and server businesses were struggling, losing money in most quarters and barely breaking even in others—and HP was definitely losing ground to Dell in PCs and low-priced servers. In servers, HP was being squeezed on the low end by Dell's low prices and on the high end by strong competition from IBM. According to most observers, IBM overshadowed HP in corporate computing—high-end servers and IT services. HP had been able to grow revenues in data storage and technical support services, but profit margins and total operating profits were declining. While HP had successfully cut annual operating costs by $3.5 billion—beating the $2.5 billion target set at the time of the Compaq acquisition, the company had missed its earnings forecasts in 7 of the past 20 quarters.

With HP's stock price stuck in the $18–$23 price range, impatient investors in 2004 began clamoring for the company to break itself up and create two separate companies, one for its printer business and one for all the rest of the businesses. While HP's board of directors had looked at breaking the company into smaller pieces, Carly Fiorina was steadfastly opposed, arguing that HP's broad product/business lineup paid off in the form of added sales and lower costs. But in February 2005, shortly after HP released disappointing financials for 2004 (the company's earnings per share total of $1.16 in 2004 was substantially below the earnings per share total of $1.80 reported in 2000), Carly Fiorina resigned her post as HP's CEO amid mounting differences between herself and members of HP's board of directors about what actions were needed to revive HP's earnings.

Mark Hurd, president and CEO of NCR (formerly National Cash Resister Systems), was brought in to replace Fiorina, effective April 1, 2005; Hurd had been at NCR for 25 years in a variety of management positions and was regarded as a no-nonsense executive who underpromised and overdelivered on results.[26] Hurd immediately sought to bolster HP's competitiveness and financial performance by bringing in new managers and attacking bloated costs. In his first seven months as CEO, the results were encouraging. HP posted revenues of $86.7 billion and net profits of $2.4 billion for the fiscal year ending October 31, 2005. HP had the number one ranking worldwide for server shipments (a position it had held for 14 consecutive quarters) and disk storage systems, plus it was the world leader in server revenues for Unix, Windows, and Linux systems. During the first seven months that Hurd was HP's CEO, the company's stock price rose about 25 percent.

With Hurd at the helm, Hewlett-Packard continued to gain traction in the marketplace in the next two fiscal years. For example, HP's sales of laptop computers increased 47 percent in fiscal 2007 and its PC business in China nearly doubled, making China HP's third biggest market for PCs. The company posted revenues of $91.7 billion in fiscal 2006 and $104.3 billion in fiscal 2007. Earnings climbed from $2.4 billion in 2005 to $6.2 billion in 2006 (equal to a diluted earnings per share of $2.18) and to $7.3 billion in 2007 (equal to a diluted earning per share of $2.68). By late fall 2007, HP's stock price was more than double what it had been during Carly Fiorina's last days as CEO. The company's 2007 share of the estimated $1.2 trillion global IT market was almost 9 percent. It was the global leader in both PCs and x86 servers running on Windows and Linux operating systems. About 67 percent of HP's sales were outside the United States. In May 2008, HP announced that it was expecting fiscal 2008 revenues of about $114 billion and a diluted earnings per share in the range of $3.30 to $3.34. Exhibit 9 shows the performance of Hewlett-Packard's four major business groups for fiscal years 2001–2007.

HP's strategy in PCs and servers differed from Dell's in two important respects:

1. Although HP had a direct sales force that sold direct to large enterprises and select other customers, a very sizable share of HP's sales of PCs were made through distributors, retailers, and other channels. These included:

- Retailers that sold HP products to the public through their own physical or Internet stores.

- Resellers that sold HP products and services, frequently with their own value-added products or services, to targeted customer groups.

- Distribution partners that supplied HP products to smaller resellers with which HP had no direct relationships.

- Independent distributors that sold HP products into geographic areas or customer segments in which HP had little or no presence.

Exhibit 9   Performance of Hewlett-Packard's Four Major Business Groups, Fiscal Years 2001–2007 (in millions)

Fiscal Years Ending October 31	Printing and Imaging	Personal Computing Systems	Enterprise Systems and Software	HP Services
2007				
Net revenue	$28,465	$36,409	$21,094	$16,646
Operating income	4,315	1,939	2,327	1,829
2006				
Net revenue	$26,786	$29,169	$18,609	$15,617
Operating income	3,978	1,152	1,531	1,507
2005				
Net revenue	$25,155	$26,741	$17,878	$15,536
Operating income	3,413	657	751	1,151
2004				
Net revenue	$24,199	$24,622	$16,074	$13,778
Operating income	3,847	210	28	1,263
2003				
Net revenue	$22,569	$21,210	$15,367	$12,357
Operating income (loss)	3,596	22	(48)	1,362
2002*				
Net revenue	$20,358	$21,895	$11,105	$12,326
Operating income (loss)	3,365	(372)	(656)	1,369
2001*				
Net revenue	$19,602	$26,710	$20,205	$12,802
Operating income (loss)	2,103	(728)	(579)	1,617

*Results for 2001 and 2002 represent the combined results of both HP and Compaq Computer.
Source: Company 10-K reports 2003, 2004, and 2007.

- Independent software vendors that often assisted HP in selling HP computers, servers, and other products/services to their software clients.
- Systems integrators that helped large enterprises design and implement custom IT solutions and often recommended that these enterprises purchase HP products when such products were needed to put a customized IT solution in place.

Much of HP's global market clout in PCs and servers came from having the world's biggest and most diverse network of distribution partners. The percentage of PCs and servers sold by its direct sales force and by its various channel partners varied substantially by geographic region and country, partly because customer buying patterns and different regional market conditions made it useful for HP to tailor its sales, marketing, and distribution accordingly.

2. While in-house personnel designed the company's PCs and x86 servers, the vast majority were assembled by contract manufacturers located in various parts of the world. Big-volume orders from large enterprise customers were assembled to each customer's particular specifications. The remaining units were assembled and shipped to HP's retail and distribution partners; these were configured in a variety of ways (different microprocessor speeds, hard drive sizes, display sizes, memory size, and so on) that HP and its resellers thought would be attractive to customers and then assembled in large production runs to maximize manufacturing efficiencies.

During 2005–2007, after replacing a number of HP's senior executives, Mark Hurd engineered several strategic moves to strengthen HP's competitiveness and ability to deliver better financial performance to shareholders:

- Top executives charged each HP business with identifying and implementing opportunities to boost efficiency and lower costs per unit. Every aspect of the company's supply chain and internal cost structure was scrutinized for ways to become more efficient and reduce costs. The costs of each value chain component—from real estate to procurement

to IT to marketing—were examined so that managers could know costs by business group, region, country, site, product, and employee; these levels of cost analysis were then used to scrutinize how each expense supported HP's strategy and whether there were opportunities for cost savings. Corporate overheads were trimmed, negotiations with suppliers were conducted to be sure that HP was getting the best terms and best prices on its purchases, steps were taken to trim HP's workforce by about 15,000 people worldwide, the organizational structure was streamlined resulting in three layers of management being removed, and the company's very complicated IT operations were simplified and the expenses reduced—the objective was to engineer HP's IT architecture and operations to be the world's best showcase for the company's technology. In 2008, HP began trimming the number of sites worldwide at which it conducted activities by 25 percent. The resulting improvements in operating expenses paved the way for HP to price its products more competitively against those of Dell and other rivals.

- Company personnel began working more closely with large enterprise customers to find ways to simplify their experience with information technology.

- A number of new products and services were introduced.

- HP spent close to $7 billion to acquire more than a dozen software, technology, and service companies that management believed would add significant capabilities and technology to HP's portfolio and help fuel revenue growth.

- The company prepared to capitalize on three big growth opportunities that top management saw emerging over the next four or five years: (1) next-generation data center architecture; (2) growing consumer interest in always-ready, always-on mobile computing; and (3) digital printing. Mark Hurd believed that HP had important strengths in all three of these high-growth market arenas but needed to be more adept in getting new products into the marketplace. He directed company personnel to develop a better "go-to-market" model and to arm the sales force with the tools needed to "get quotes and proposals in front of customers as fast as anybody on the planet." HP added 1,000 people to its sales force in 2007 to expand its coverage of key accounts and geographic markets; an additional 1,000 salespeople were added through acquisitions.

Soon after becoming CEO in 2005, Mark Hurd concluded that HP needed to beef up its IT services business in order to go head-to-head against IBM, the unquestioned worldwide leader in IT services; IBM had 2007 revenues of about $54 billion and an estimated 7.2 percent global share of a $748 billion market. Hurd took a major step in that direction in May 2008, making his first really big strategic move as HP's CEO by cutting a deal to acquire Electronic Data Systems (EDS) for a cash price of $13.25 billion. According to Gartner (one of the world's leading technology research firms), EDS had IT service revenues of $22.1 billion in 2007, equal to a global share of 3.0 percent—ahead of HP with revenues of $17.3 billion and a 2.3 percent share (see Exhibit 10 for the sales and market shares of the world's top six IT service providers). While a combined HP/EDS would have IT service revenues of more than $49 billion and market share of 5.3 percent—sufficient for a strong second place in the global market—industry observers were not enamored with the ability of HP/EDS to compete with IBM for high-end, high-profit buyers of IT services. IBM's profit margin in IT services was almost double EDS's 6 percent profit margin, partly because IBM catered to the needs of high-end customers and partly because IBM had about 74,000 employees in India, where wages for IT professionals were considerably lower—only 27,000 of EDS's 140,000 employees were in India.

EDS, founded in 1962, was best known for its capabilities in running clients' mainframe systems, operating help desks to support personal computer users, developing and running business software for its clients, and handling such automated IT processes as billing and payments for clients.[27] In contrast, HP's IT service business revolved around managing infrastructure—such as back-office server systems—for its large enterprises. There was relatively little overlap between

Exhibit 10   **Estimated Sales and Market Shares of the World's Six Leading Providers of Information Technology Services, 2007**

Company	2007 Revenues (in Billions)	Market Share
IBM	$ 54.1	7.2%
Electronic Data Systems (EDS)	22.1	3.0
Accenture	20.6	2.8
Fujitsu	18.6	2.5
Hewlett-Packard	17.3*	2.3
Computer Sciences Corp. (CSC)	16.3	2.2
All others	599.0	80.0
Totals	$748.0	100.0%

*Gartner's $17.3 billion estimate of for HP's 2007 revenues in IT services exceeds the $16.6 billion reported by HP in its 2007 10-K report and shown in Exhibit 9.

Source: Gartner, as reported in Justin Scheck and Ben Worthen, "Hewlett-Packard Takes Aim at IBM," *The Wall Street Journal*, May 14, 2008, p. B1.

the customer bases of the two companies. HP executives believed there was plenty of opportunity to cut costs at EDS and that there were clear revenue-boosting opportunities, such as expanding sales of managed printing services. Even so, HP's shareholders were unenthusiastic about the EDS acquisition—HP's stock price fell more than $10 per share in the two days following news of the acquisition but recovered $2.50 of the drop within a week.

DELL'S FUTURE PROSPECTS

In a February 2003 article in *Business 2.0,* Michael Dell said, "The best way to describe us now is as a broad computer systems and services company. We have a pretty simple system. The most important thing is to satisfy our customers. The second most important thing is to be profitable. If we don't do the first one well, the second one won't happen."[28] For the most part, Michael Dell was not particularly concerned about the efforts of competitors to copy many aspects of Dell's build-to-order, sell-direct strategy. He explained why on at least two occasions:

> The competition started copying us seven years ago. That's when we were a $1 billion business. . . . And they haven't made much progress to be honest with you. The learning curve for them is difficult. It's like going from baseball to soccer.[29]
>
> I think a lot of people have analyzed our business model; a lot of people have written about it and tried to understand it. This is an 18½-year process. . . . It comes from many, many cycles of learning. . . . It's very, very different than designing products to be built to stock. . . . Our whole company is oriented around a very different way of operating. . . . I don't, for any second, believe that they are not trying to catch up. But it is also safe to assume that Dell is not staying in the same place.[30]

On other occasions, Michael Dell spoke about the size of the company's future opportunities:

> When technologies begin to standardize or commoditize, the game starts to change. Markets open up to be volume markets and this is very much where Dell has made its mark—first in the PC market in desktops and notebooks and then in the server market and the storage market and services and data networking. We continue to expand the array of products that we sell, the array of services and, of course, expand on a geographic basis. The way we think about it is that there are all of these various technologies out there. . . . What we have been able to do is build a business system that takes those technological ingredients, translates them into products and services, and gets them to the customer more efficiently than any company around.[31] There are enormous opportunities for us to grow across multiple dimensions in terms of products, with servers, storage, printing and services representing a huge realm of expansion for us. There's geographic expansion and market share expansion back in the core business. The primary focus for us is picking those opportunities, seizing on them, and making sure we have the talent and the leadership growing inside the company to support all that growth. And there's also a network effect here. As we grow our product lines and enter new markets, we see a faster ability to gain share in new markets versus ones we've previously entered.[32]
>
> A great portion of our growth will come from key markets outside the U.S. We have about 10 percent market share outside the United States,

so there's definitely room to grow. We'll grow in the enterprise with servers, storage, and services. Our growth will come from new areas like printing. And, quite frankly, those are really enough. There are other things that I could mention, other things we do, but those opportunities I mentioned can drive us to $80 billion and beyond.[33]

That Dell had ample growth opportunities was indisputable—in 2007, it only had a minuscule 2 percent share of the $1.2 trillion global market for IT products and services. Exhibit 11 shows Dell's principal competitors in each of the industry's major product categories and its estimated 2007 market shares in each category.

In 2008, despite near-term prospects of sluggish economic growth in the United States and perhaps elsewhere, Michael Dell remained enthusiastic about the unrivaled opportunity for the company's business given that the number of people online globally (via PCs, cell phones, and other devices with Internet connectivity) was expected to increase from just over 1 billion in 2008 to over 2 billion by 2011:

> The world is witnessing the most exciting and promising period for technology ever seen. We call it the "Connected Era." The second billion people coming online, many from the world's fast growing and emerging economies, expect a different technology experience to the first. The Internet has unleashed billions of new conversations and made it possible for people to connect in new ways. The emergence of this connected era is arguably the most influential single trend remodeling the world today.[34]

In May 2008, the latest sales and market share data indicated that Dell might be closing the gap on Hewlett-Packard and on the verge of mounting another run at being the global leader in PC sales. Exhibit 12 shows the sales and market shares of the world's top five PC vendors in the first quarter of 2008 as compared to the fourth quarter of 2007. Moreover, Dell's senior executives believed that their aggressive moves to reduce costs would help restore profit margins, given that there seemed to be some modest relief from having to contend with eroding average revenues per unit sold (see Exhibit 7).

However, by late Fall 2008, Dell's prospects for overtaking HP were looking more bleak. Global recessionary forces had caused a significant

Exhibit 11   **Dell's Principal Competitors and Dell's Estimated Market Shares by Product Category, 2007**

Product Category	Dell's Principal Competitors	Estimated Size of Worldwide Market, 2007	Dell's Estimated Worldwide Share, 2007
PCs	Hewlett-Packard (maker of both Compaq and HP brands), Lenovo, Apple, Acer, Toshiba, Sony, Fujitsu-Siemens (in Europe and Japan)	$375 billion	~15%
Servers	Hewlett-Packard, IBM, Sun Microsystems, Fujitsu	$ 60 billion	~11%
Data storage devices	Hewlett-Packard, IBM, EMC, Hitachi	$ 48 billion	~5%
Networking switches and related equipment	Cisco Systems, Broadcom, Enterasys, Nortel, 3Com, Airespace, Proxim	~$ 65 billion	~2%
Printers and printer cartridges	Hewlett-Packard, Lexmark, Canon, Epson	~$ 50 billion	~5%
Services	Accenture, IBM, Hewlett-Packard, Fujitsu, EDS, many others	$748 billion	<1%

Source: Compiled by the case authors from a variety of sources, including International Data Corporation, www.dell.com, and *The Wall Street Journal,* May 14, 2008, p. B1.

Exhibit 12   **Worldwide Unit Sales and Market Shares of Top Five PC Manufacturers, First Quarter 2008 versus Fourth Quarter 2007**

Rank	Company	Q1, 2008 Shipments	Market Share	Q4, 2007 Shipments	Market Share	Percentage Growth in Shipments
1	Hewlett-Packard	13,251,000	19.1%	11,291,000	18.6%	17.4%
2	Dell	10,913,000	15.7	8,971,000	14.8	21.6
3	Acer*	6,914,000	9.9	4,164,000	6.9	66.0
4	Lenovo	4,814,000	6.9	3,980,000	6.6	21.0
5	Toshiba	3,069,000	4.4	2,544,000	4.2	20.6
	All Others	30,537,000	43.9	29,674,000	48.9	2.9
	Total	69,498,000	100.0%	60,624,000	100.0%	14.6%

*Figures for Acer include shipments of Gateway, which was acquired by Acer in 2007.
Source: International Data Corporation, as per posting at www.dell.com (accessed May 12, 2008).

slowdown in global IT spending during 2008 and even larger cutbacks were being forecast for at least the first half of 2009 in light of the global financial crisis that emerged in Fall 2008. Still, HP reported a 5 percent increase in revenues for its 2008 fourth quarter ending October 31 (excluding the effect of its recent acquisition of EDS) versus the year earlier 2007 fourth quarter and a 2008 fourth quarter earnings increase of 4 percent; moreover HP was forecasting that fiscal 2009 revenues would be in the $127.5 to $130 billion range, up from $118.4 billion in 2008. Dell's sales revenues in the third quarter of 2008 were 3 percent below those in the 2007 third quarter on unit-shipment growth of 3 percent; Dell's third quarter 2008 net profits were down 5 percent.

The Wall Street Journal reported in September 2008 that Dell was trying to sell its worldwide network of computer factories in an effort to reduce production costs; the apparent plan was to enter into agreements with contract manufacturers to produce its PCs. While Dell had for many years been the industry leader in lean manufacturing approaches and cost-efficient build-to-order production methods and was still the low-cost leader in producing desktop PCs, it had fallen behind contract manufacturers in producing notebook PCs cost efficiently—and there was a pronounced shift among individual consumers to purchase laptop PCs instead of desktops. Laptop PCs were more complex and labor-intensive to assemble than were desktops. To help contain the assembly costs of laptops, Dell had already begun having Asian contract manufacturers partially assemble its laptops; these partly assembled laptop units were then shipped to Dell's own plants where assembly was completed. Because each laptop was produced at two factories, Dell referred to its assembly of laptops as a "two-two" system. But the two-touch system was more costly than simply having a contract manufacturer in Asia perform the entire assembly: hence, Dell's interest in abandoning in-house production altogether and shifting to 100 percent outsourcing.

As of late November 2008, Dell had found no buyers for its plants. But the company had nonetheless begun outsourcing the full assembly of some laptop models to contract manufacturers (such as Taiwan's Foxconn Group) to eliminate the extra costs of the two-touch system, and it had made significant progress in cutting operating expenses elsewhere—operating expenses were 12.1 percent of revenues in the 2008 third quarter versus 12.8 percent in the 2007 third quarter. There were some other positives. In the 2008 third quarter, Dell's Global Consumer business posted a 10 percent revenue gain on a 32 percent increase in unit shipments—Dell's revenue growth was double the industry average and the profitability of this business was the highest in 13 quarters. Dell consumer products won 41 awards in the 2008 third quarter—the Inspiron Mini 9 notebook was selected as one of *Time Magazine's* "Best Inventions of 2008" and as one of CNET's "10 Most Cutting Edge Products of 2008."

ENDNOTES

1 As quoted in "Dell Puts Happy Customers First," *Nikkei Weekly,* December 16, 2002.

2 "Michael Dell: On Managing Growth," *MIS Week,* September 5, 1988, p. 1.

3 "The Education of Michael Dell," *Business-Week,* March 22, 1993, p. 86.

4 Dell's 2005 10-K report, pp. 1–2.

5 Remarks by Kevin Rollins in a speech at Peking University, November 2, 2005, and posted at www.dell.com.

6 As quoted in Joan Magretta, "The Power of Virtual Integration: An Interview with Dell Computer's Michael Dell," *Harvard Business Review,* March–April 1998, p. 74.

7 Ibid., p. 75.

8 Speech by Michael Dell at University of Toronto, September 21, 2004, www.dell.com (accessed December 15, 2004).

9 Ibid., p. 76.

10 Remarks by Michael Dell, Gartner Symposium, Orlando, FL, October 20, 2005, www.dell.com.

11 Quoted in Neel Chowdhury, "Dell Cracks China," *Fortune,* June 21, 1999, p. 121.

12 Remarks by Michael Dell, Gartner Fall Symposium, Orlando, FL, October 9, 2002, www.dell.com.

13 Remarks by Michael Dell at the University of Toronto, September 21, 2004, www.dell.com.

14 Quoted in the *Financial Times* Global News Wire, October 10, 2002.

15 Remarks by Michael Dell, Gartner Symposium, Orlando, FL, October 20, 2005, www.dell.com.

16 Kevin Rollins, "Using Information to Speed Execution," *Harvard Business Review,* March–April 1998, p. 81.

17 As quoted in Don Tennant, "Dell Exec Addresses Service Woes in Run-up to IT-as-a-Service Launch," *Computerworld,* March 17, 2008, www.computerworld.com (accessed May 12, 2008).

18 Ibid.

19 Magretta, "The Power of Virtual Integration," p. 79.

20 "Michael Dell Rocks," *Fortune,* May 11, 1998, p. 61

21 Quoted in Kathryn Jones, "The Dell Way," *Business 2.0,* February 2003.

22 Company press release, April 6, 2008.

23 Much of this paragraph was developed by the case authors from information in Hewlett-Packard's 2007 annual report.

24 "Can Compaq Catch Up?" *BusinessWeek,* May 3, 1999, p. 163.

25 Company press release and speech posted at www.hp.com, accessed December 11, 2004.

26 Louise Lee and Peter Burrows, "What's Dogging Dell's Stock," *BusinessWeek,* September 5, 2005, p. 90.

27 Justin Scheck and Ben Worthen, "Hewlett-Packard Takes Aim at IBM," *The Wall Street Journal,* May 14, 2008, p. B1.

28 *Business 2.0,* February 2003, www.business2.com.

29 Comments made to students at the University of North Carolina and reported in the *Raleigh News & Observer,* November 16, 1999.

30 Remarks by Michael Dell, Gartner Fall Symposium, Orlando, FL, October 9, 2002, www.dell.com.

31 Remarks by Michael Dell, MIT Sloan School of Management, September 26, 2002, www.dell.com.

32 Remarks by Michael Dell, University of Toronto, September 21, 2004, www.dell.com.

33 Remarks by Michael Dell, Gartner Symposium, Orlando FL, October 20, 2005, www.dell.com.

34 Remarks by Michael Dell to reporters in Dubai, company press release, April 6, 2008.

Atlassian: Supporting the World with Legendary Service

Tatiana Zalan[1]
University of South Australia, Australia

Olga Muzychenko
University of Adelaide, Australia

Sam Burshtein
Swinburne University of Technology, Australia

INTRODUCTION

In late February 2009, Mike Cannon-Brookes and Scott Farquhar, co-founders of Atlassian Software, a global technology company, were sipping beer on the deck of their office in downtown Sydney. Only days ago Mike was chosen by the World Economic Forum from a world-wide pool of 5,000 candidates as one of the 230 Young Global Leaders for his professional accomplishments, commitment to society and potential to contribute to shaping the future of the world. Mike and Scott, both in their late 20s, had all the reasons to feel proud that their efforts had been validated. Starting in 2002 as a consulting business, the founders, then fresh IT graduates, soon realised that they needed an issue and task tracking tool enabling them to manage their own consulting projects effectively. JIRA, Atlassian's first product, was soon to be followed by several other team collaboration products.

By 2009, Atlassian had become one of Australia's fastest growing technology ventures, had revenues of $35 million (nearly all of them outside Australia), in excess of 15,000 customers in some 110 countries and nearly 200 employees worldwide, with offices in Sydney, San Francisco, Amsterdam, Kuala Lumpur and Poland. Throughout the years Atlassian remained highly profitable and privately owned with no institutional or venture capital investment and spent 40% of its revenues on R&D. The company was equally well known for its transparent, vibrant and informal, yet highly professional culture. It received a sweep of industry and business awards (see Exhibit 1—Atlassian's awards), and in 2006, Mike and Scott became the youngest entrepreneurs to ever win the prestigious Ernst & Young's Entrepreneur of the Year Award for Australia.

Nevertheless, the current revenues and customer base were still a far cry from the founders' intent to grow a $100 million company with 50,000 customers worldwide. As Mike and Scott pondered the future of Atlassian, they wondered whether they could scale the business in a way that did not diminish the creative vitality, enthusiasm, and customer focus that had gotten them so far.

ATLASSIAN'S EARLY YEARS

The Founders

Mike and Scott met in 1998 as recipients of the prestigious Business IT Co-op Scholarship at the University of New South Wales (UNSW). The program was set up by industry and the UNSW to provide financial reward and industrial training for undergraduate students in the disciplines of Commerce, Science and Engineering.

Apart from this licenced copy, none of the material protected by the copyright notice can be reproduced or used in any form either electronic or mechanical, including photocopying, recording or by any other information recording or retrieval system, without prior written permission from the owner(s) of the copyright.
© NeilsonJournals Publishing 2011.

Exhibit 1   Atlassian's Awards

Read Write Web's Top 10 Enterprise Web Products (2008)

Part of its series of top products for 2008, ReadWriteWeb named Confluence to its list of Top 10 Enterprise Web Products. We are honored to be part of this year's list which includes the likes of Amazon, Google and SalesForce.com. As RWW says: "We are seeing major wiki adoption in the enterprise. It is simply a much easier way to collaborate than by putting lots of complex technology under the general umbrella of the Intranet . . . Atlassian seems a safe bet for enterprise, having traction and a good breadth of products."

EContent 100 (2008)

Atlassian Confluence was selected for the EContent 100 awards in the Collaboration category. EContent writes, "Everyone knows they should play well with others. But frankly, that's tough enough for a lot of folks. When those others span the globe and never meet, things get a whole lot more complicated. Collaboration tools enable teamwork, web-style, which emphasizes shared knowledge and member contribution, regardless of proximity."

Deloitte Technology Fast 50 (2008, 2007, 2006, 2005)

For the fourth year in a row, Atlassian was named as one of the winners of the 2008 Deloitte Technology Fast 50. The Fast 50 ranks the fifty fastest growing technology companies, public or private, based on percentage revenue growth over three years (2006–2008). Atlassian achieved a staggering 255% growth in revenue over this period and was accordingly ranked #20 among the Fast 50.

City of Sydney Business Awards (2008)

Atlassian took home two awards from the City of Sydney Business Awards including being named winner of the City of Sydney's Business of the Year. The ceremony took place at Doltone House and was presided over by Lord Mayor Clover Moore MP. Atlassian competed with 260 other Sydney–based businesses to win the Information and Communication award, recognising Atlassian as a leader in business technology, as well as the overall honour of Business of the Year.

NSW Pearcey Award (2008)

The Pearcey Awards is an Australian State Award that is given to an individual early in their career. Atlassian's founders Mike Cannon-Brookes and Scott Farquhar were jointly awarded this honour for their demonstrated innovative and pioneering achievements, and their contributions to research and development within the ICT industry.

SDTimes 100 (2008, 2006)

Atlassian was once again named to the prestigious SDTimes 100 list, which recognizes those companies, organizations and individuals that most broadly "set the agenda" in the software industry. Atlassian won in the Application Lifecycle Management category which recognized solutions that supported the spectrum of collaboration workflow from start to finish.

SmartCompany Award (2007, 2008)

For the second year in a row Atlassian was named one of the Smart50 companies in Australia. SmartCompany spent months combing though hundreds of applications, from start-ups to companies with up to $200 million revenue, to reach this final 50, which are ranked on revenue growth over three years. Atlassian was ranked 17th on the Smart50 List and took out the Top Exporter award which is judged based on the company's profitability, growth and innovation.

BRW Fast 100 (2005, 2006, 2007)

For the third year in a row, Atlassian was selected for the BRW Fast 100. The BRW Fast 100 is a list of Australia's fastest-growing small and medium-sized businesses, ranking companies with up to 200 staff according to their average annual turnover growth over three years. Atlassian achieved 168% growth in the last year, ranking it the ninth fastest growing company in Australia.

Ernst & Young's Australian Entrepreneur of the Year (2006)

Atlassian's founders Mike Cannon-Brookes and Scott Farquhar were named Ernst & Young's Entrepreneur of the Year for Australia. After being named Young Entrepreneur of the Year, they qualified to be in the running for the top honours. At just 26 years of age each, Mike and Scott were the youngest winners of the overall category award which honours entrepreneurs who are building and leading successful, growing and dynamic businesses.

In addition, Atlassian's products won a number of industry awards.

Source: http://www.atlassian.com/about/awards.jsp, accessed 7 June 2009.

UNSW Co-op Program scholarship holders received a tax-free scholarship of $53,600 for a four-year degree and $67,000 for a five-year degree as well as structured industrial training (between nine and eighteen months), gaining valuable work experience with up to four different sponsor companies. In addition to exceptionally high entry requirements based on scores from high school, Mike and Scott were selected on the basis of their motivation, leadership potential, involvement in extra-curriculum activities and excellent communication skills. Mike commented on the program:[2]

> There were a very small number of places, $15,000 a year tax free, which when you're at University is a lot of beer. And it requires a more American-style large application for that they cull down with interviews to get in. . . . Everyone who gets in is very smart, very ambitious. You have to do computer science subjects and information systems subjects as well as finance and accounting, and commerce. It is really supposed to be business IT, technical and non-technical. . . . It was an amazing bunch of people, a really good environment and a really good time to do it. We started in 1998/1999.

Like many of the scholarship holders, Mike and Scott came from different backgrounds. Mike's father was a successful British banker whose career took him and the family around the world. Mike was born in the U.S. and attended an elite private school in Sydney. Scott came from an Australian family of more modest means and went through a prestigious public school in Sydney before joining the Business IT program. Avid readers, both were influenced by high-tech entrepreneurial success stories of the likes of Microsoft and HP and the rhetoric of magazines encouraging young people to ride on the Internet boom and embark on entrepreneurial careers.

Soon after a positive start in the program Mike became bored and restless, largely due to one of his first internships with an industry sponsor who had given very little thought to how they would utilise the bright student more effectively. Mike began spending a lot of time working on an online book-marking start-up with another scholarship student. They realised that people used different PCs to store their bookmarks (at home, university and work), which in the end could become a nuisance. Once the founders had collected all of their favorite sites, they flipped

the service around to provide an efficient search engine of user-contributed links.

Firmly believing in the idea's potential, Mike and his partner, still only in their late teens, made the controversial decision to drop out of the prestigious program. The founders turned the start-up (called Bookmark Box) into a "mild success" and contemplated raising additional funds to grow the business, but were eventually outcompeted by cash-rich and aggressive American start-ups. After nine months of operation the founders sold their company to an American dot.com, staying on for three months.

Following this initial foray into business venturing, Mike went on to work for another NASDAQ-listed research firm while enrolled in night classes, and Scott took the more traditional BIT route which provided job placements of three to six months with established companies. A key element of Mike's job was to evaluate the business prospects and viability of other Internet start-ups, during which time he learnt "a lot of lessons about how not to run a business."[3] His 18-month stint at the company proved to be an exciting time: he earned a decent salary for a twenty-one year old and traveled extensively to Singapore, Hong Kong, Malaysia and China, where the Internet was just exploding. The good life came to an end in 2001 with the dot.com crash, when the company started shutting down its Asian offices. As Scott still had six months to graduate, Mike resigned and went back to the university full-time to finish off the loose ends and "get a piece of paper."

The Opportunity

In late 2001, Mike and Scott sat down to flesh out the foundations of their venture. Unimpressed by what they had seen in the corporate world and pre-revenue dot.com start-ups, who appeared to be interested more in quickly gaining market share than having a sustainable business model, they hatched the idea of a venture underpinned by an entirely different philosophy:[4]

> Australians definitely build real businesses. We don't have this build and flip mentality that the [Silicon] Valley has. Australians are typically very good managers because we are used to dealing with scarce resources in the true sense of the word.

Business is pretty simple. At some point we've got to have a product that people like and buy, and we've got to get more money when we sell it than it costs to make it. There are businesses that don't operate that way. There are some that need to lose money to grow, but we didn't have the resources to build one of those businesses, so we didn't.

We didn't have a formal business plan . . . we knew what we wanted to do, and we had a massive dose of common sense and reality.

By the New Year they were generating some cash flow with software service and consulting for a small Swedish company. Although the application server the company developed was, in Mike and Scott's judgment, "excellent," the company had no real interest in customers, resulting in poor support. So Mike and Scott set themselves up as third-party support experts for the server selling annual subscriptions and trying to make some money until they could carve their own niche.

In February 2002, the entrepreneurs moved into a simple office in downtown Sydney. They named their company Atlassian, after the ancient Greek Titan Atlas, the first person to fulfill the new venture's mission to provide legendary service while supporting the world.[5] With a modest initial start-up cost, total expenses of around $5,000 per month and a steady average monthly consultancy income of $18,000, they had enough funds and time to work on improving their own business processes, such as managing the flow of various leads and commitments. Once the entrepreneurs had the program—named JIRA—up and running, they quickly realised they had found their niche and their first product. JIRA helped project managers monitor the progression and completion of individual tasks. It was by no means a novel concept—in fact, JIRA was addressing a problem that had been solved a thousand times over the years, with plentiful solutions already available. The first few copies of JIRA were sold to clients Mike and Scott knew personally.

At the time of JIRA's launch, enterprise software companies sold software that was "heavy"—expensive (frequently costing over $200,000), difficult to use and taking months or even years to deploy. On the technical side, industry analysts were becoming increasingly critical of enterprise software in large organisations, which largely failed to fully integrate and intelligently control complex businesses processes while remaining

adaptive to changing business needs. Enterprise systems, they argued, brought high risks, uncertainty and a high level of complexity, and the way forward was to emphasise simplicity and efficiency in software development and implementation.[6] Purchasing in large user organisations was centralised with the IT department, who strived to ensure new software compatibility with the overall corporate network, and typically involved a protracted decision-making process. Customisation, service contracts and staff training added on thousands of dollars, and a trailing fee of 18% of the license fee for regular software updates was the industry norm. A significant proportion of these costs were built in from the sales model. A typical software company would have a world-wide network of distributors, and a direct sales force who sold in the vicinity of one in every one hundred leads. Needless to say, such software was out of reach of small and medium-sized businesses or individual consumers.

With JIRA Mike and Scott broke away from the mold, creating a new market niche between free open source software and expensive commercial software:[7]

> We sold copies to a couple of our clients for $800. The clients got back to us saying "It sort of does what we need, but it could use one or two other components." Being small, being keen, we fixed it up in a week and shipped them out a new version. They said "Great, now it does what we want." We sold ten or more versions to people we already knew. We were not looking at what competitors were offering; unless somebody asked for a change—or we identified a need for something among ourselves—it didn't get built in.

Committed to providing legendary service, the entrepreneurs strived to respond to customer queries within an hour. Not having any sales experience probably helped: they simply tried to answer their customers' queries intelligently and as quickly as possible. In an effort to break further away from competition, Atlassian adopted an open-pricing model. While the usual industry practice for enterprise software firms was to have an online form to fill in or a number to call for price quotes, the entrepreneurs did not believe in discounting, having differentiated pricing or giving credit terms to customers. They did, however, provide JIRA (and all subsequently developed programs) free of charge to non-profits and half price to academia.

As project management software was usually sold on a per user basis, enterprise software firms designed their systems with limited features and number of users. Atlassian, however, made very different choices. Atlassian's products could be bought by the actual user using a credit card and put onto a workgroup's machine. While in the early days configurability and scalability proved problematic, with further software development these issues were partially resolved, and a customer could run multiple projects on one higher-end version. Nevertheless, because Atlassian's software was so keenly priced, large users preferred to buy multiple copies for different functional departments or different cities around the world.

The entrepreneurs acknowledged their customers saw considerable value in their products, many of them admitting that Atlassian sold their software so inexpensively that they would gladly pay ten times more for it. Mike and Scott reasoned:[8]

> That's good to know. But in reality, this is probably classic supply and demand, because as long as we are at a price that is cheaper than what most people regard the value to be, we'll keep on selling heaps of copies and upgrades. If we can get 100 customers at $5,000, that's much better than five customers using us at $100,000. If one of them leaves, you're in big trouble.
>
> Our pricing also lowers the cost of selling upgrades. If we talk to them from time to time, they'll buy it. A thousand bucks? No problem, here you go. But thousands of dollars—thousands of times—means than we have lots of cash coming in the door every year for free.

ATLASSIAN'S BUSINESS MODEL AND FUNDING

Atlassian's business model was based on a few simple principles. Mike explained the early thinking behind their venture:[9]

> Our business is based on a few premises. One is that we foresaw—foresaw seems a bit glamorous, doesn't it—but we guessed that basically the price of software was going to keep coming down for a number of reasons. One, the price of producing software—although producing scalable software is still quite high—the cost of some componentry,

tooling and building has come down, maybe it's halved in the past ten years. So we could build stuff a lot more cheaply.

The second linchpin was related to Atlassian's choice of the global distribution platform, the Internet. Despite their young age, both founders were well-versed in the web-based tools and had the confidence that their fairly sophisticated customers would have little problem downloading software from the Internet. In addition, Mike and Scott figured out that they did not need salespeople to sell their inexpensive software, nor could they afford them:[10]

> This has always been a common sense business. We couldn't afford to have huge spikes in sales, or pay commissions and huge annual bonuses to a rep in the hope of making the big sales during the year. To keep our cash flow going, we had to have small, incremental sales that came without big marketing expenses.

The entrepreneurs were also trying to leverage the trend to 'software as a service' (or usage-based) business models to essentially convert the 18% maintenance trailing fee (the industry standard) into an ongoing 50% support fee.

As a result of its positioning, JIRA quickly gained a strong word-of-mouth following that spread across the IT community, enabling the entrepreneurs to raise its price to $1,200. Mike and Scott's ultimate ambition was to create a mass market enterprise software firm—a notion which, by their own admission, seemed almost oxymoronic:[11]

> One of our goals from day one has been to build a $100 million business with 50,000 customers. Why? Because that's a big number. Doing the math, we figured an average price of $2,000. This fits with our concept of selling high-quality enterprise software, with high-quality service, at very low price. To build that sort of business, we had to go to the mass market.

The broader business environment's conditions in the early 2000s, particularly the dot.com bubble and the 9/11 terrorist attacks in the U.S., helped to define Atlassian's funding and growth strategies. In addition, the Australian context in general and a lack of venture funding in particular was not conducive to entrepreneurship

Exhibit 2   The Australian Entrepreneurial Environment in 2001 (GEM Australia)

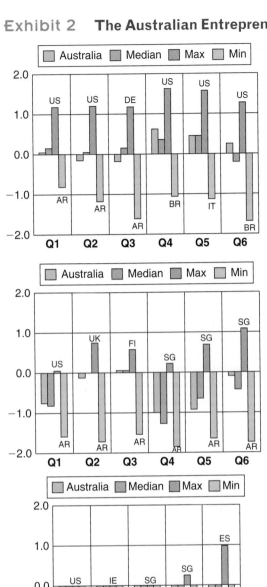

In my country:

1. There is sufficient equity funding for new and growing businesses.
2. There is sufficient debt funding for new and growing businesses.
3. There are sufficient government subsidies available for new and growing businesses.
4. Private individuals (other than founders) are an important source of finance for new and growing businesses.
5. Venture capitalists are an important source of private support for new and growing businesses.
6. IPOs are an important source of equity for new and growing businesses.

In my country:

1. Government policies (e.g. public procurement) consistently favour new and growing businesses.
2. The support of new and growing businesses is a high priority for policy at federal governmental level.
3. The support of new and growing businesses is a high priority for policy at state and local government level.
4. New businesses can get most of the permits and licences they need easily and rapidly.
5. The amount of taxes is NOT a burden for new and growig businesses.
6. Taxes and other regulations are applied to new and growing businesses in a predictable and consistent way.

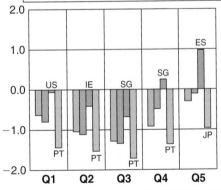

In my country:

1. Teaching in primary and secondary education encourages creativity, self-sufficiency and initiative.
2. Teaching in primary and secondary education provides adequate instruction in market economic principles.
3. Teaching in primary and secondary education provides adequate attention to entrepreneurship and business creation.
4. Colleges and universities have enough courses on entrepreneurship.
5. The level of business and management education is truly world class.

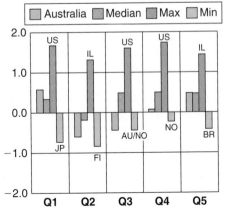

In my country:

1. The creation of new ventures is considered an appropriate way to become rich.
2. Most people consider becoming an entrepreneur a desirable career choice.
3. Successful entrepreneurs have a high level of status and respect.
4. You will often see stories in the public media about successful entrepreneurs.
5. Most people DO NOT think that people start new businesses only if they cannot find a good job.

Exhibit 2   *(Concluded)*

ITEM	Australia		All GEM Countries		
	Rank	Score	Mean	High Score (Country*)	Low Score (Country*)
Entrepreneurial Activity Indicators (Source: Adult pop'n survey; Scale: Percent of pop'n participating)					
Start-ups overall	4	9.0%	6.2%	12.7% (MX)	1.2% (IL)
Independent start-ups	3	7.1%	4.0%	11.2% (MX)	0.8% (FR)
Company-sponsored start-ups	5	1.9%	1.2%	3.7% (MX)	0.1% (FR)
Male participation rate in start-ups	4	11.1%	7.5%	16.6% (MX)	1.7% (IL)
Female participation rate in start-ups	6	5.9%	4.0%	9.4% (MX)	0.4% (IL)
New businesses (<42 months old)	1	7.2%	3.4%	7.2% (AU)	0.8% (JP)
Infant businesses (<18 months old)	1	4.1%	1.8%	4.1% (AU)	0.1% (JP)
Male particiaption rate in new firms	2	9.9%	4.5%	10.4% (KO)	0.6% (FR)
Female particiaption rate in new firms	2	4.3%	2.1%	5.4% (NZ)	0.4% (JP)
Total Entrepreneurial Activity	3	16.2%	9.7%	18.7% (MX)	4.6% (BE)
TEA – Opportunity	2	12.5%	6.6%	12.8% (NZ)	2.1% (IL)
TEA – Necessity	8	3.2%	2.5%	7.4% (IN)	0.2% (NO)
TEA – Percent Opportunity	10	77.0%	67.9%	88.9% (US)	33.8% (IN)
Risk Capital Investment Indicators					
Pct. of pop'n business angels last 3 years	6=	3.8%	2.9%	6.2% (NZ)	0.9% (BR)
Classic Venture Capital (pct of GDP)	16 (of 24)	0.12%	0.23%	1.2% (IL)	0.04% (JP)
Classic Venture Capital (US$ per person)	14 (of 24)	$32.23%	$72.03%	$504.83 (US)	$0.82 (IN)
Informal Venture Capital (pct of GDP)	3 (of 15)	1.45%	1.12%	3.66% (KR)	0.26% (FI)
Informal Venture Capital (US$ per person)	5 (of 28)	$450.38	$229.06	$969.92 (ES)	$5.39 (IN)

* See References for list country codes.

Source: Yellow Pages GEM Australia 2001, pp. 31–42.

(see Exhibit 2—the Australian Entrepreneurial Environment in 2001):[12]

> For IT purposes, we started the company right in the perfect storm. In 2002, everything was tight, budgets had been cut, and no one was buying much of anything. If we had gone to [potential investors] saying we have no experience in the industry but we're going to start a mass-volume software company and we're going to go into markets where there are already 10 to 20 other products, they would have shown us the door in 30 seconds—and probably rightly so from their understanding of how things should work.
>
> We knew we weren't going to raise any money, so we focused on making cheap stuff that was really good. We were talking with a lot of people who still didn't have budgets. They'd say "I don't have the bucks right now, I'll have to wait until next month." It may sound insane, but we were like—great, sounds like they're going to buy!

RAPID GROWTH

Innovation and Customer Service

Fuelled by JIRA's success, by 2004 Atlassian had grown to six developers. Unhappy with the bevy of wikis on the market, the team created Confluence, an enterprise wiki, Atlassian's second biggest product after JIRA. By 2006, Atlassian's customers ranged from very small two-person start-ups to very big enterprises like Cisco, Oracle and The World Bank, with half of *Fortune 500* companies reportedly using an Atlassian product.[13] In January 2007, the company doubled the number of products when it released Bamboo and Crowd. The acquisition, in August 2007, of Cenqua, a Sydney-based supplier of market leading software engineering tools FishEye, Crucible and

Exhibit 3   Description of Atlassian's Products

JIRA
JIRA lets you prioritise, assign, track, report and audit your "issues," whatever they may be—from software bugs and help-desk tickets to project tasks and change requests.

Confluence
Confluence is a simple, powerful wiki that lets you create and share pages, documents and rich content with your teammates.

FishEye
FishEye opens your source code repository and helps development teams keep tabs on what's going on using a web interface.

Bamboo
Bamboo automates the process of compiling and testing source code, saving time and instantly alerting you of build problems.

Clover
Clover measures code coverage generated by system tests, functional tests or unit tests, allowing you to improve test quality and find bugs sooner.

Crowd
Crowd is a single sign-on (SSO) application for as many users, web applications and directory servers as needed — all through a single, intuitive web interface.

Crucible
Crucible is a peer code review tool that allows teams to review, edit, comment and record outcomes.

JIRA Studio
JIRA Studio combines Atlassian's bug tracker, wiki, and development tools with Subversion source control to deliver an integrated development suite.

Source: http://www.atlassian.com/software/ accessed 7 June 2009.

Clover, further expanded Atlassian's portfolio of products (see Exhibit 3—Description of Atlassian's Products). Early in 2008 Atlassian released JIRA Studio, a hosted version of its product suite.[14] All Mike and Scott's ideas were developed into products to address their own "pain point" following essentially the same pattern:[15]

> We haven't really built anything without having the fundamental problem ourselves and actually trying to solve it, which makes what we're trying to do a lot easier. If you're solving your own problems, it's a lot easier to build something good.

Originally chalking up customer wins one at a time on a whiteboard, Atlassian started to gain hundreds of new customers per month. Its customer base and revenue quadrupled and tripled during the first few years (see Exhibit 4—Atlassian's Customers and Exhibit 5—Atlassian's Milestones). One of the best customer testimonials was posted on the company's website: "We now have a pretty simple rule for products from Atlassian—if they've built it, we'll buy it."[16]

Atlassian's transparent approach extended beyond its original pricing model to the software development process. Customers could raise feature requests as well as see what bugs had been reported. All customers received full source code, allowing them to customise Atlassian's products to suit their own environment. Atlassian worked closely with the open source software community in an admittedly "symbiotic" relationship. All products were built using open source components many of which had been developed by Atlassian and donated back to the community, enabling much faster product development at a lower cost.[17]

As the company grew, answering customer queries within an hour of the initial call became a difficult goal, but the entrepreneurs had not pulled back from their service commitments. All incoming communications were answered within 24 hours,

Exhibit 4   **Atlassian's Customers**

Atlassian has over 15,200 customers from more than 113 countries around the world (June 2009). A representative customer list broken down by industry sector includes:

Technology & electronics	**Retail & food**	**Health & biotechnology**
Cisco	Abercrombie & Fitch	Becton, Dickinson and Company
Dolby Laboratories	Best Buy	Cambridge Antibody Technology
Fujitsu	IKEA	CIGNA
Hewlett-Packard	KFC	Cochlear
Logitech	McDonalds	GlaxoSmithKline
Motorola	Miller Brewing Company	Imclone
Nikon	Office Depot	Kaiser Permanente
NEC	Procter & Gamble	Lexicon Genetics
Palm, Inc.	Target	McKesson
Panasonic	TetraPak	Novartis Pharmaceutical
Qualcomm	The Home Depot	Pfizer
Samsung		ResMed
Siemens		Roche Diagnostics
Sony		
Toshiba		
Universities & academia	**Internet & software**	**Entertainment & media**
Australian National University	Adobe	Associated Newspapers
Carnegie Mellon	AutoTrader.com	BBC
Cornell University	Borland	Bertelsmann Media Group (BMG)
Harvard University	eBay, Inc.	Disney
Hong Kong University of Science	Expedia	eMusic.com
& Technology	Intuit	GoTV Networks
MIT	JBoss	HBO
National Library of Medicine	Jive Software	Los Angeles Times
New York University	LinkedIn	MusicNet
Stanford University	Microsoft	ational Hockey League
University of California	Novell	Oxford University Press
University of Cambridge	Oracle	O'Reilly Media, Inc.
Yale University	Real Networks, Inc.	Pixar Animation Studio
	SAP	The Financial Times
	Yahoo!	
Engineering & aerospace	**Banking & finance**	**Science & research**
Airbus	ABN AMRO	CSIRO
Air Canada	American Express	European Space Agency
All Nippon Airways	Barclays Capital	Gemini Observatory
American Airlines	BNP Paribas	Lawrence Livermore National
Boeing	Citigroup	Laboratory
Caterpillar	Credit Suisse	NASA
Emirates Airlines	Dow Jones & Company	New Scientist
Lockheed Martin	Deutsche Bank	Norwegian Institute for Air Research
Lufthansa	E*TRADE	Software Engineering Institute
Mott MacDonald	Fidelity	
Northrop Grumman	First Gulf Bank	
Raytheon	HSBC	
Thales	Merrill Lynch	
	Reserve Bank of NZ	
	Western Union	
	World Bank	

(Continued)

Exhibit 4   *(Concluded)*

Automotive & travel	Consulting & services	Government
BMW	Accenture	Bundespolizei - German Federal
BP	AES	Police
DaimlerChrysler	ADP Employer Services	Department of Agriculture and Food
Hertz	BHP Billiton	(Ireland)
Honda	Booz Allen Hamilton	European Commission
John Deere	Digitas	European Parliament
Peugeot Citroen	Fannie Mae	FBI
Sabre	GE	Ministry of Health Singapore
Shell	Hoovers	National Library of Australia
Thomas Cook	Lehman Brothers	National Police
Toyota	PricewaterHouseCoopers	Port of Seattle
Volvo	The Gallup Organization	Swedish Armed Forces HQ
	Toll Solutions	United Nations
	TransCanada	USAID
		US Department of Energy
		US Environmental
		US Navy

Source: http://www.atlassian.com/about/customers.jsp accessed 7 June 2009.

Exhibit 5   Atlassian's Milestones

2002
- Mike and Scott invest $10,000 to start Atlassian with one product, Jira

2004
- Atlassian employs 6 software developers, Confluence is released

2005
- 3500 customers in approximately 50 countries

2006
- 3 years revenue growth reaches 945%
- the company records 197% annual revenue increase
- 5000 customers in more than 60 countries

2007
- Revenue for fiscal year 2006/07 reaches $ 22.5 million
- the number of products is doubled with the release of Bamboo and Crowd
- acquisition of Cenqua (developers of Fish Eye, Crucible and Clover)
- over 100 employees worldwide

2008
- Revenue for fiscal year 2007/08 reaches $ 35.5 million (74.5% annual growth)
- Jira Studio is released
- Amsterdam office opens
- Polish partnership

2009
- More than 15,200 customers in 113 countries
- 195 employees worldwide

Sources: Company website accessed 7 June 2009; *Business Wire,* 6 November, 2006; Press Release News Wire 16 January, 2006; *Smart Company,* 3 March 2009.

and customers could call and speak directly to the person who could help, from a customer service representative through to senior software developers. By late 2008, Atlassian had several dedicated people in support, and a pre-sales team responded to the many hundreds of email queries on a daily basis. This side of business was difficult to scale fast enough. The entrepreneurs believed that their ability to scale up was related to their proven talent for proactive problem-solving:[18]

> Perfect support means if someone asks a question, we take time to ensure that no one ever has to ask that same question again—whether through improvements to the system, or with better documentation. This is because by the time we have 50,000 customers, we want to eliminate the need for support. Okay, in reality, this is never going to happen, but the support team needs to have that sort of mindset. . . . We ought to be able to handle support for 50,000 customers with a dedicated team of around 100. That would represent an efficiency gain, but we have been getting efficiency gains in support all along. That's because our products continue to get better, and because we do more than just answer the query, we really extend the effort.

Mike and Scott considered Atlassian a product- and service-driven company, with the creation of new and innovative products being Atlassian's utmost business objective:[19]

> If you divide companies into single categories you'd have product companies, marketing companies, sales-oriented companies, and we're without doubt a product-oriented company. You'd probably also have engineering companies, and I would say we're an engineering company. Product is our main strength due to the founders, the way we set up the business and also largely due to the business model that we have.

The company did not practice marketing in a conventional sense (as anyone in the world could order the product off the web) and spent very little on advertising or sales support, relying mostly on word of mouth. While in the early years marketing was everybody's job—particularly that of the founders, the Sales Director and developers—in 2006 Mike and Scott realised that hiring a Marketing Director could help to professionalise the business and propel further growth. An experienced VP Marketing joined Atlassian a year later, and by 2008 the marketing team had grown to well above 20 people.

HR Practices

Finding technical talent had proved to be a major constraint on Atlassian's long term growth, despite it being Atlassian's priority. Atlassian spent very little money on recruiters, with the majority of new hires coming from staff referrals or from the website. The website openly declared: "HELP WANTED! Check out our current openings, we're always hiring!"[20] On occasions, Mike and Scott had to source talent outside Australia and closely followed Andrew Bassat's advice (the co-founder of the highly successful Australian online recruitment company Seek) that it is better to wait for good staff than hire the wrong ones out of desperation.[21] The founders explained how they tried to keep top talent:[22]

> We pay people very well. We spend a lot of money on offices—internal offices, not external. Our reception area isn't very flashy, our meeting rooms are basic, but we make sure everyone has a large flat screen on their desk. We spend a lot of money on filling the fridge with anything they might need. We take people out to nice parties, and work on maintaining a good office culture. I'm sure we could certainly save heaps by moving out of the central business district, but I know of at least three good people that would quit immediately if we did . . . We are very aware of not cutting costs where we actually make money from spending.

The choice of the head office premises in downtown Sydney reinforced Atlassian's commitment to attracting talented people. The leased 1877 heritage-listed building was extensively renovated and cleverly refurbished to give it a quirky and modern but not over-designed look. It was one of the few office buildings in the area that had a large deck to hold staff functions.

In 2005–2006, Atlassian appointed an HR director to improve recruitment, leadership development and training systems. The founders hoped that the number of customers would increase faster than the number of staff, as each employee developed multiple skills across operations, invoicing or sales. Atlassian's staff turnover was generally small and close to zero in some years.

Despite its exponential growth, Atlassian managed to retain an entrepreneurial spirit and create an organisation with distinctive culture. The founders were mindful of not stifling the early start-up stage excitement with excessive structures and processes so as not to lose the best people. As one of the elements of the organisational culture that did not scale were the founders themselves, in 2007–2008 Atlassian's founders and employees worked hard on codifying Atlassian's corporate values (see Exhibit 6—Atlassian's Corporate Values). These values became enshrined on the glass wall in the front office. Other ways of preserving the organisational fabric included founders' lunches (where Mike and Scott took every new employee out for lunch), various corporate parties and events, and "FedEx Day" and "lab days" aimed to promote creativity. For example, during FedEx Day (introduced in 2006) Atlassian developers would create something of their choice and "ship" it in 24 hours. This concept was subsequently copied by other companies, including Yahoo![23]

Global Reach

By their own admission, Atlassian's founders had global orientation from day one, as their business could not survive if it focused solely on the

Exhibit 6   **Atlassian's Corporate Values**

Mike Cannon-Brookes (left) and Scott Farquhar (right)

Open company, no bullshit
Atlassian embraces transparency wherever at all practical, and sometimes where impractical. All information, both internal and external, is public by default. We are not afraid of being honest with ourselves, our staff and our customers.

Build with heart and balance
Everyday we try to build products that are useful and that people lust after. Building with heart means really caring about what we're making and doing — it's a mission, not just a job. When we build with balance we take into account how initiatives and decisions will affect our colleagues, our customers and our stakeholders.

Don't #@!% the customer
When we make internal decisions we ask ourselves "how will this affect our customers?" If the answer is that it would "screw" them, or make life more difficult, then we need to find a better way. We want the customer to respect us in the morning.

Play, as a team
We want all Atlassians to feel like they work with Atlassian, not for Atlassian. We think it's important to have fun with your workmates while working and contributing to the Atlassian team.

Be the change you seek
We think Gandhi had it pretty right when he said "We need to be the change we wish to see in the world." At Atlassian we encourage everyone to create positive change—we're constantly looking for ways to improve our company, our products and our environment.

Disclaimer: We realise that some people might find our values offensive. Please be assured that we are not out to offend/shock/irritate you. Atlassian got where it is today by being openly and publicly ourselves. All these values have evolved from phrases and principles that we use and live everyday.

Source: http://www.atlassian.com/about/values.jsp accessed 7 June 2009.

Exhibit 7   **Atlassian's Offices and Functions, Late 2008**

Offices	No of employees	Functions
San Fransisco (US)	60	Marketing and support
Kuala Lumpur	20	Customer 24/7 support
Amsterdam	N/a	Sales and support, a potential European hub. Established in mid 2008
Poland	N/a	R&D and engineering

Source: Interviews and Atlassian's company website.

Australian market. In 2009, Atlassian had about 200 employees worldwide in Sydney, San Francisco, Amsterdam, Kuala Lumpur and Poland. While most of the engineering, R&D, customer support and corporate functions were centralized in Sydney, other overseas offices had a number of different functions (see Exhibit 7—Offices and Functions). The San Francisco office (in effect, Atlassian's second main office) provided Atlassian with access to marketing talent not available in Australia, and other offices were established mainly for "time zone reasons" to ensure 24/7 support. Atlassian aimed at four hours response for every interaction with the customers around the globe, be it by email, online, phone or chat.

Most of Atlassian's senior management team had some international experience: for example, Head of Engineering started in the Silicon Valley, and the CFO had worked in Hong Kong and the U.S. The founders traveled extensively between Australia, the U.S. and Europe, sometimes spending as much as a fortnight per month away from the Sydney office. Ensuring coordination in what was quickly becoming a medium-sized multinational enterprise proved a continuing challenge.

Social Contribution[24]

Since it opened its doors, Atlassian had donated over 2,500 licenses to charities and not-for-profits. Some well-known charities that used Atlassian software included World Vision, The United Nations, The Fox Chase Cancer Center, The Sierra Club, The MS Society, The National Breast Cancer Foundation, The Red Cross, UNICEF and Amnesty International. In late 2006, Atlassian created a nonprofit foundation to focus the charitable giving that had previously been ad-hoc by the founders. The Foundation adopted a '1%' model: 1% of staff time (up to six days per employee per year), 1% of revenue and 1% of equity were donated to its Foundation. While some employees chose to work in soup kitchens for their six days a year, many opted to put their technical skills to good use, helping charities build the websites or internal systems.

Recognising the importance of education in its success, Atlassian annually sponsored US$60,000 worth of scholarships at the University of NSW. These scholarships encouraged students to enter the IT profession, and were often awarded to country students who otherwise could not afford to move to the city for university.

NEW CHALLENGES

Throughout the years, Mike and Scott shared the same mentality of growing their business conservatively and hedging their bets carefully. They only funded out of retained earnings, and hired people when they could afford them. Atlassian still did not have a Board, because in the past Mike and Scott would not have attracted the people of the caliber needed to grow Atlassian to a $100 million company. The founders continued to eschew the typical sales, consulting and professional services revenue streams that diverted focus away from customers, maintaining their focus instead on creating innovative software. While in the relatively short span of seven years of its existence Atlassian had become very successful by Australian standards, its achievements looked modest compared to U.S. start-ups: Google, for example, turned over US$6 billion at the end of its seventh year (2005). The founders wondered whether the time had finally come for Atlassian to become more aggressive in its growth strategy.

ENDNOTES

[1] The authors would like to acknowledge the contribution of Carl Hedberg of Babson College who collected the interview and other data in 2006. The authors prepared this case solely as the basis for class discussion, rather than to illustrate an effective or ineffective handling of a business situation.

[2] Interview with Mike Cannon-Brookes and Scott Farquhar, 6 September, 2006.

[3] Ibid.

[4] Ibid.

[5] Atlassian company website, www.atlassian.com/about, accessed on 15 May 2009.

[6] See Cynthia Rettig (2007), "The Trouble with Enterprise Software", *MIT Sloan Management Review,* Fall, pp. 21–27.

[7] Interview with Mike Cannon-Brookes and Scott Farquhar, 6 September, 2006.

[8] Ibid.

[9] Interview with Mike Cannon-Brookes, 8 December, 2008.

[10] Interview with Mike Cannon-Brookes and Scott Farquhar, 6 September, 2006.

[11] Ibid.

[12] Ibid.

[13] http://itsinder.com/2006/10/26/atlassian-why-i-luvem, accessed 18 May 2009.

[14] Atlassian company website, www.atlassian.com/about, accessed on 15 May 2009.

[15] Interview with Mike Cannon-Brookes, 8 December, 2008.

[16] Atlassian company website, www.atlassian.com/about/press/backgroundd.jsp, accessed on 15 May 2009. All customer testimonials are unsolicited.

[17] Atlassian company website, www.atlassian.com/about, accessed on 15 May 2009.

[18] Interview with Mike Cannon-Brookes and Scott Farquhar, 6 September, 2006.

[19] Interview with Mike Cannon-Brookes, 8 December, 2008.

[20] Tim Treadgold (2006), "The Best of the Fast", 12 October, *Business Review Weekly*.

[21] Interview with Mike Cannon-Brookes and Scott Farquhar, 6 September, 2006.

[22] Atlassian company website, www.atlassian.com/about, accessed on 15 May 2009.

[23] Atlassian company website, www.atlassian.com/about, accessed on 2 June 2009.

[24] Atlassian company website, www.atlassian.com/about/press/background.jsp, accessed on 18 June 2009.

Nintendo's Strategy in 2009: The Ongoing Battle with Microsoft and Sony

Lou Marino
The University of Alabama

Sally Sarrett
The University of Alabama

The battle for market supremacy in the console segment of the video game industry began in earnest during the 2006 holiday retail season when Sony and Nintendo launched their latest-generation consoles to compete with the Xbox 360, which came to market in time for the 2005 Christmas shopping season. Video game analysts and writers for gaming magazines and Web sites marveled at the graphics-rendering capabilities of the Sony PlayStation 3 (PS3), which boasted a 3.2 GHz microprocessor, 550 MHz graphics card, 1080p HD resolution, Wi-Fi capabilities, a 60 GB hard drive and an HDBlu-ray optical drive. The PS3 matched the Microsoft Xbox 360 feature-by-feature and its Blu-ray drive was far superior to the standard DVD optical drive utilized by the Xbox 360. The only criticism of the PS3 was its astronomical introductory retail pricing of $499 to $599.

With Sony and Microsoft fully engaged in a technology war, video game analysts and writers were shocked by the technological limitations of the Nintendo Wii, which did not even match the graphics and processing capabilities of Microsoft's first-generation Xbox and had only slightly more computing power than the sixth-generation PlayStation 2 (PS2). Many industry analysts and hard-core gamers viewed the Wii as a toy, deriding the system for its weak graphics, lack of DVD playback, and childish name. Some video game industry analysts viewed the Wii as the last-ditch effort of a struggling company that had once dominated the global video game industry and then become increasingly irrelevant after Sony entered the market with its first PlayStation.

Interestingly enough, Nintendo didn't disagree that the Wii did not offer the best-quality graphics and did not include an extensive array of features and capabilities. In fact, while the Wii was in the developmental stage, Nintendo's CEO Satoru Iwata preferred not to speak of the Wii as a "next-generation" video game console, since this implied it would be an evolutionary improvement over the Game Cube, which had achieved a small global market share against the wildly popular PS2 and the modestly popular Xbox. Given Nintendo's declining sales and market share in the video game console segment since 2000, Iwata wanted to totally change the market's perception of the Wii by providing an entirely different video game playing experience that would be less intimidating to casual gamers and to people who had not previously played video games. The concept underlying the Wii—with its innovative and distinctively different controller—was to build on the company's success with the innovative user interface on the popular handheld Nintendo DS video game player.

While Nintendo's strategy for the Wii of concentrating on pioneering a daringly different video game controller (as opposed to building a raft of new graphics features and technological capability into the console itself) was viewed as very risky, it had proved to be spectacularly

Copyright © 2010 by Lou Marino. All rights reserved.

successful through 2009. Indeed, Nintendo quickly sold out of Wiis in the 2006 holiday season and sold all the Wiis it could produce throughout 2007 and 2008. Going into the 2009 holiday retail season, Nintendo's cumulative sales of the Wii far surpassed those of the PS3 and the Xbox 360. Nintendo's Wii, to the surprise of most everyone, was the market leader in sales of seventh-generation video game consoles.

While Nintendo's strategy for the Wii of concentrating on pioneering a daringly different video game controller (as opposed to building a raft of new graphics features and technological capability into the console itself) was viewed as very risky, it had proved to be spectacularly successful through 2009. Indeed, Nintendo quickly sold out of Wiis in the 2006 holiday season and sold all the Wiis it could produce throughout 2007 and 2008. Going into the 2009 holiday retail season, Nintendo's cumulative sales of the Wii far surpassed those of the PS3 and the Xbox 360. Nintendo's Wii, to the surprise of most everyone, was the market leader in sales of seventh-generation video game consoles.

Both Microsoft and Sony launched counterattacks against the Wii in 2008 and early 2009, including software releases targeting casual gamers, new controllers that allowed gamers to play in ways similar to Nintendo's controllers, and price cuts. Perhaps Nintendo's biggest threat was the international recession that began in late 2007 and was affecting many developed countries, including the United States. Video game console and software sales had been relatively unaffected by the recession until mid-2009. Video game industry revenues of $1.2 billion during the month of June 2009 were 31 percent less than the revenues of $1.7 billion recorded in June 2008. The quarterly decline in industry revenues was the steepest decline in industry sales since September 2000. Sales of consoles were affected the greatest by the recession, with June 2009 console sales falling by 38 percent to $382.6 million compared to June 2008 revenues of $617.3 million. The sales of Nintendo Wii units declined from 5.17 million during the quarter ended June 30, 2008, to 2.23 million during the quarter ended June 30, 2009. In addition, worldwide sales of Nintendo DS handheld gaming systems declined by 14 percent during the quarter and Nintendo's sales of video game software declined from 40.41 million units in the quarter ended June 30, 2008, to 31.07 million units in same quarter in 2009. The worsening economy and fresh attacks from Nintendo's chief rivals called for the company's senior managers to evaluate the company's strategy to avoid continuing declines in profits, which had fallen by 61 percent during its most recent quarter.

COMPANY HISTORY AND BACKGROUND

The playing card manufacturer founded in 1889 in Kyoto, Japan, eventually became known as the Nintendo Company Ltd. in 1963 when it expanded outside playing cards to other types of games. The company had produced electronic toys as early as 1970, but its 1981 introduction of a coin-operated video game called Donkey Kong transformed the company into a household name in North America, Asia, and Europe. The company formed a North American subsidiary headquartered in Seattle, Washington, in 1982 and, in 1983, launched the Family Computer home video gaming system in Japan along with adaptations of many of its most popular arcade titles. In 1985, the Family Computer home video gaming system was released in the United States as the Nintendo Entertainment System (NES); one of the video games available for play on the new NES system was the home version of Super Mario Brothers arcade game, a title that went on to rank as one of Nintendo's top-selling games of all time.

Nintendo introduced a handheld Game Boy device in 1989 that quickly became one of the world's best-selling video game playing systems. In 1991, Nintendo introduced the Super Nintendo Entertainment System (SNES); it had better graphics and stereo sound and was accompanied by a bigger selection and variety of games. The Nintendo 64 gaming system, a third-generation gaming system, was introduced in 1996; the N64's immense popularity drove Nintendo's revenues to record highs. It was followed by the also successful Game Boy Advance (2001) and a fourth-generation console system called GameCube (2001); while world-wide sales of the GameCube totaled 21.7 million units, it was considered by most video game enthusiasts as inferior to Sony's wildly popular PlayStation and PS2 and Microsoft's new Xbox.

Exhibit 1   **Estimated Total Sales of Nintendo Video Game Systems as of July 31, 2009**

Gaming System	Date First Released	Cumulative Units Sold (In Millions)
Video Game Consoles		
Nintendo Entertainment System (NES)	July 15, 1983	61.90
Super Nintendo Entertainment System (SNES)	November 21, 1990	49.10
Nintendo 64 (N64)	June 23, 1996	32.90
Nintendo GameCube (GCN)	September 14, 2001	21.74
Nintendo Wii	November 19, 2006	51.60
Handheld Game Systems		
Game Boy and Game Boy Color	April 21, 1989 and October 21, 1998	118.70
Game Boy Advance	March 21, 2001	81.06
Game Boy Advance SP	February 14, 2003	43.23
Game Boy Micro	September 13, 2005	2.50
Nintendo DS/DS Lite	November 21, 2004	107.24

Source: Compiled by the case researchers from a variety of sources.

Nintendo introduced the Nintendo Dual Screen (DS) in 2004 to combat increasing competition within the handheld video gaming console market segment. Sales of the DS quickly took off, with sales surpassing 50 million units worldwide by September 2007—a sales volume that made it the fastest-selling handheld video game console of all time. Nintendo introduced the DS Lite—a sleeker redesigned version of the DS—in 2006; it, too, was a market success. But Nintendo's major new product introduction in 2006 was the Wii, with its highly innovative wireless remote controller. Exhibit 1 provides the release dates and total units sold as of July 31, 2009, for Nintendo consoles and handheld systems launched between 1983 and 2006. Nintendo's consolidated statements of income for the fiscal year ending March 31, 2005, through fiscal year ending March 31, 2009, are presented in Exhibit 2 . Its consolidated balance sheets for fiscal 2005 through fiscal 2009 are presented in Exhibit 3.

NINTENDO 'S HANDHELD GAME SYSTEMS

Handheld game systems were portable, light-weight electronic devices that included built-in speakers and displays designed largely for playing video games. The first handheld systems were introduced in the 1970s and 1980s, but the market had been largely dominated by Nintendo since its release of the Game Boy in 1989. The two main competitors in handheld game players in 2008 were the Nintendo DS and the Sony PlayStation Portable (PSP).

Nintendo Game Boy

The Nintendo Game Boy was Nintendo's first handheld video gaming device; it was conceptualized and developed by Gunpei Yokoi, a long-time Nintendo employee. Yokoi's goal was to create a product (1) that was lightweight, durable, inexpensive, and small in overall size and (2) that had its own spectrum of recognizable games. The Game Boy could be powered with either disposable or rechargeable batteries. Nintendo's Tetris game—specially designed for the Game Boy—proved quite popular and was a factor in making the Game Boy a resounding market success. Game Boy's success in the handheld market soon led Nintendo to introduce many new versions: Game Boy Pocket (a smaller, lighter unit requiring fewer batteries); Game Boy Light (with a backlight); Game Boy Color (with a color screen); Game Boy Advance (with a higher-resolution screen and improved visual technology); Game Boy Advance SP (with backlighting, a flip-up screen, and

Exhibit 2   **Nintendo's Consolidated Statements of Income, Fiscal 2005–Fiscal 2009 (in millions of U.S. dollars)**

	3/31/2009	3/31/2008	3/31/2007	3/31/2006	3/31/2005
Total Revenues	$19,308.1	$16,557.0	$9,568.7	$5,041.6	$5,098.4
Cost of Sales	10,973.8	9,626.4	5,630.3	2,911.9	2,946.4
Gross Profit	8,334.3	6,930.6	3,938.3	2,129.6	2,152.0
Selling, General, and Administrative Expenses	2,503.3	2,105.4	1,697.3	1,225.6	1,028.8
Operating Income	5,831.0	4,825.2	2,241.0	904.1	1,123.2
Other Income (Interest and Other)	337.7	437.2	336.5	222.7	133.8
Currency Exchange Gains (Loss)	1,406.2	(914.2)	254.8	450.6	216.3
Other Nonoperating Income (Expenses)	50.7	17.5	30.5	23.7	(17.8)
EBT, Excluding Unusual Items	4,711.9	4,365.7	2,862.8	1,601.1	1,455.5
Gain (Loss) on Sale of Investments	(7.9)	(107.7)	5.5	35.0	(16.0)
Gain (Loss) on Sale of Assets	(0.6)	36.3	(1.3)	(0.2)	—
Other Unusual Items	2.6	—	—	12.2	—
Unusual Items, Total	(5.9)	—	—	12.2	—
EBT, Including Unusual Items	4,706.0	4,294.4	2,867.0	1,648.1	1,439.5
Income Tax Expense	1,776.1	1,747.7	1,141.9	674.6	573.8
Minority Interest in Earnings	(1.0)	1.0	0.4	0.5	(0.2)
Net Income	$ 2,930.8	$ 2,547.7	$1,725.5	$ 973.9	$ 865.4

Source: Nintendo Company Limited Annual Reports and financial releases.

rechargeable batteries as well as other solutions to problems with the original Game Boy Advance model); and Game Boy Micro (the third version of the Game Boy Advance system, the smallest Game Boy created, with the same resolution but higher visual quality).

Nintendo DS

In 2004, Nintendo released the Nintendo DS, a handheld video gaming system with a clamshell casing similar to that of the Game Boy Advance. The Nintendo DS had "dueling" screens on the top and bottom of the shell, and the bottom display was an LCD touch screen. The lower screen of the Nintendo DS was a touch-sensitive LCD designed to be pressed with a stylus, a user's finger, or a special thumb pad (a small plastic pad attached to the console's wrist strap that could be affixed to the thumb to simulate an analog stick). The DS was also equipped with a built-in microphone and Wi-Fi capability, which allowed its players to connectively network with one another's handheld systems to create a more interactive gaming experience.

Nintendo viewed the DS as a "third pillar" product with features that set it apart from the Game Boy Advance and the GameCube and that provided players with a unique entertainment experience. Nintendo President Satoru Iwata said:

> We believe that the Nintendo DS will change the way people play video games and our mission remains to expand the game play experience. Nintendo DS caters for the needs of all gamers whether for more dedicated gamers who want the real challenge they expect, or the more casual gamers who want quick, pick up and play fun.[1]

After its launch in November 2004, the Nintendo DS did remarkably well due to superior marketing and growing demand for the product, significantly boosting the company's overall revenues and profits. The Nintendo DS system had achieved about a 70 percent market share of all handheld video game players. By August 2009, Nintendo had sold more than 107 million DS handheld game systems units since its introduction. Additionally, Nintendo had sold more than 500 million copies of video games for its DS game systems.

Exhibit 3   **Nintendo's Consolidated Balance Sheets, Fiscal 2005–Fiscal 2009 (in millions of U.S. dollars)**

	3/31/2009	3/31/2008	3/31/2007	3/31/2006	3/31/2005
Assets					
Cash and Equivalents	$ 7,941.2	$10,925.1	$ 6,818.5	$ 6,109.7	$ 7,848.0
Short-Term Investments	4,872.1	1,472.9	3,855.4	2,566.2	538.7
Accounts Receivable	1,461.5	1,441.5	869.0	418.9	487.7
Inventory	1,520.1	1,037.9	877.2	305.3	492.6
Deferred Tax Assets, Current	463.7	376.5	352.7	239.3	193.2
Other Current Assets	1,055.2	1,049.7	1,034.4	446.1	279.3
Total Current Assets	17,313.9	16,303.7	13,807.3	10,085.4	9,839.5
Net Property Plant and Equipment	746.3	546.0	570.2	554.1	538.8
Long-Term Investments	574.7	730.2	914.9	596.1	726.6
Deferred Tax Assets, Long Term	310.5	233.1	142.7	102.1	100.5
Other Intangibles	22.8	19.9	5.0	3.2	—
Other Long-Term Assets	47.5	11.9	158.3	150.1	6.2
Total Assets	$19,015.6	$17,844.7	$15,598.4	$11,491.0	$ 11,211.7
Liabilities & Equity					
Accounts Payable	3,746.6	3,324.6	2,980.7	829.8	1,271.5
Accrued Expenses	20.3	18.3	17.6	17.1	—
Current Income Taxes Payable	877.4	1,113.3	891.1	525.1	514.3
Other Current Liabilities, Total	1,036.0	1,159.3	748.1	432.5	248.2
Total Current Liabilities	5,680.4	5,615.5	4,637.5	1,804.5	2,034.0
Pension & Other Post-Retirement Benefits	107.6	44.6	44.0	32.7	48.4
Other Noncurrent Liabilities	59.6	8.8	8.3	10.3	6.8
Total Liabilities	5,847.5	5,668.9	4,689.8	1,847.5	2,089.1
Common Stock	105.7	99.6	99.6	99.6	99.6
Additional Paid in Capital	123.1	115.2	114.7	114.7	114.7
Retained Earnings	15,048.1	13,666.3	12,080.9	10,851.1	10,225.1
Treasury Stock	(1,643.6)	(1,546.2)	(1,538.4)	(1,535.6)	(1,286.0)
Comprehensive Income and Other	—	(159.2)	151.8	113.6	(30.9)
Total Equity	13,633.3	12,175.8	10,908.6	9,643.5	9,122.5
Total Liabilities and Equity	$19,015.6	$17,844.7	$15,598.4	$11,491.0	$11,211.7

Source: Nintendo Company Limited Annual Reports and financial releases.

NINTENDO'S VIDEO GAME CONSOLES

A video game console was an electronic device designed to be used with an external display device (e.g., a television or a monitor) that enabled people to play a variety of games stored on external media (e.g., cartridges or discs). The most recent consoles included hard drives that could be used to download and store games. Consoles were larger and more powerful than handheld systems. Personal computers could also be used to play video games, as could arcade machines designed for commercial use. Over the years, Nintendo had introduced five generations of consoles: the Nintendo Entertainment System (NES), the Super Nintendo Entertainment System (SNES), Nintendo 64 (N64), the Nintendo GameCube (GCN), and the Nintendo Wii.

Nintendo Entertainment System

The Nintendo Entertainment System (NES) was the most successful gaming system of its time, selling almost 62 million NES units worldwide (see Exhibit 1). The system proved a tremendous success for Nintendo while simultaneously revitalizing the video gaming industry, which had taken a serious downturn in the early 1980s. The NES system was Nintendo's first cartridge-based home gaming console, although the company had developed several models of successful arcade gaming systems.

Super Nintendo Entertainment System

The Super Nintendo Entertainment System (SNES) was Nintendo's second home gaming console and appeared on the market as part of the fourth generation of video game consoles that various companies had introduced throughout the industry's history. SNES, with its vastly upgraded graphics and sound capabilities, was the most successful 16-bit gaming console manufactured in its generation, selling over 49 million units worldwide despite having a relatively slow central processing unit (CPU) in comparison to rival game-playing systems.

Nintendo 64

The video game industry's fifth-generation home game consoles included the Sega's Saturn, Sony's PlayStation, and the Nintendo 64 (N64). In terms of the number of units sold, the N64 with cumulative sales of nearly 33 million units ranked second in its generation behind the PlayStation with cumulative sales of 102.5 million units. Nintendo's developers struggled with the question of whether the N64 should have a cartridge-based memory or a disc-based memory. Their choice of sticking with a traditional cartridge-based system was said to be one of the major reasons why the N64 was unable to compete effectively with Sony's highly popular PlayStation.

Nintendo GameCube

Nintendo's GameCube console gaming system was first introduced in Japan in September 2001.

It was less expensive and more compact than Microsoft's Xbox and Sony's PS2, but lacked many of the graphics capabilities that attracted gamers to the Xbox and PS2. The GameCube was Nintendo's first system that did not use a cartridge storage method—instead it used optical discs. But it had disappointing global sales of only 21.72 million units.

Nintendo Wii

The Wii was Nintendo's latest gaming console system. Sales of the Wii exceeded all expectations. As of July 31, 2009, Nintendo had sold a total of 51.6 million Wii cosoles. Sales of the Wii were well above the Xbox 360's cumulative sales of 31.35 million units and the PlayStation 3's cumulative sales of 23 million. Nintendo's sales of games for the Wii exceeded 150 million units.

Nintendo engineers began designing the Wii gaming system in 2001, the same year that Nintendo introduced the GameCube. Originally referred to by its code name of Revolution, the Wii gaming system quickly became the benchmark for the Nintendo product line, bringing together research, innovation, technology, and functionality to create a revolutionary Bluetooth-activated wireless controller that provided a wide range of motion possibilities and allowed game players to control a game's characters through comparable movements of their own. Thus, players playing tennis imagined that the controller was their racket and the swinging motion with their arm triggered the character to act simultaneously. Indeed, the driving concept for the development of the Wii was to allow users to get up, move around the room, interact, and become a physical part of the game they were playing. "By giving players the ability to physically interact with a virtual world, Nintendo has significantly changed the experience of video gaming. It's suddenly more immersive, more compelling and potentially more appealing to consumers who have never considered buying a videogame console before," said David M. Ewalt, a writer who reviewed the Wii after its release. The inspiration and capabilities for Nintendo's new user interface came, at least partially, from Nintendo's success with the DS, the company's successes with games such as

Nintendo Duck Hunt, which used a gun controller, and Track and Field, which employed an exercise mat to allow users to participate in athletic events on their SNES consoles.

Nintendo developers chose the name *Wii* for the gaming system because it was a phonic allegory that linked the name of the system to its intended user. One member of the development team for the Wii system was quoted as saying, "Wii sounds like 'we,' which emphasizes this console is for everyone. People around the world can easily remember Wii no matter what language they speak. No confusion. Wii has a distinctive 'ii' spelling that symbolizes both the unique controllers and the image of people gathering to play." The two *i*s in *Wii* were also a visual representation meant to resemble the system's controller design, as well as two people standing side by side, insinuating interaction and play together.

Nintendo marketers carefully analyzed rival products, trends in the video game marketplace, and their targeted segments of the population. Several characteristics stood out. As competition had increased and the market for video game products had become more saturated, Nintendo marketers paid particular attention to the fact that the concept, design, and functionality of rival video game consoles had become increasingly similar and offered increasingly similar game-playing experiences. As a consequence of weakening differentiation among new game playing devices, marketing strategies for gaining sales and market share became priceoriented. The penetration pricing strategies of the major rivals took on a "price war" character that squeezed profit margins and limited the potential for market share gains. When any particular company announced a new product and market entry strategy, it could expect a competitor to release a relatively similar product, usually within several months. In order to significantly grow the company's market share, Nintendo's executives believed that it had to focus on creating product differentiation advantages over competitors— typically by assessing what competitors were doing and generating ways to accomplish the same thing "better." The gaming market had become an arena for companies to "try to outperform their rivals to grab a greater share of existing demand."[2]

Thus, the marketers with Nintendo began developing a new strategy for the Wii system, and when the development of the Wii gaming system began, Nintendo designers had a new market in mind to appeal to. According to Shugery Miyamoto, a member of Nintendo's Wii development team, "We started with the idea that we wanted to come up with a unique game interface. The consensus was that power isn't everything for a console. Too many powerful consoles can't coexist. It's like having only ferocious dinosaurs. They might fight and hasten their own extinction."[3] Accordingly, the team decided to develop a system to attract people who generally did not play video games. This new market segment included populations of people who had been disregarded by gaming efforts: the elderly, women, and so on. According to Nintendo's CEO Iwata, "Women are the most prized targets but this untapped market spans a vast swath of the population— everybody, actually, bar fast-thumbed teen-aged boys."[4] The view was that by marketing to segments of the consumer population currently not reached, Nintendo could create for itself infinite possibilities for profitable growth. Ultimately by taking its product outside the realms of the established demand, Nintendo intended to become its sole competitor. Mr. Iwata insisted that "having a unique product is more important than an attractive price point."[5]

By appealing to "ordinary" consumers, developers of the gaming console were able to simplify its design, focusing less on hyperrealistic graphics and more on artistic elements. Because of the intense competition within the gaming market, gaming systems had become extremely technologically complex. This factor alone was the cause for the large quantity of uncontested consumers who were either unable to learn or uninterested in learning to use such advanced systems for recreational entertainment. By simplifying the design and use of the Wii system, the developers created the perfect entry strategy for their new target market. The success and the challenges associated with this strategy were reflected by two comments that appeared on a blog in response to an article published by *Fortune* on CNNMoney.com in October 2008. One of the bloggers representative of the hard-core gaming segment, identified as "Former Nintendo Fan," commented:

As a gamer, I have never disliked a console more than the Wii. How it continues to dominate in sales is beyond me when there's very little quality games to play on it. I guess Nostalgia (outdated graphics, simple game-play etc.) really does sell.[6]

However, in response to this comment, a blogger who identified herself as Cheryl from Pittsburgh, Pennsylvania, and was more consistent with Nintendo's new target market replied:

See, that's what nobody gets—it's not the gamers that are buying Wii. It's moms, families, grandparents. They're after an interactive game that anyone can figure out in a few minutes, not intricate games with awesome graphics.[7]

Nintendo personnel believed that by creating an innovative product that would appeal to an entirely new demographic and engage new players of video games with its innovative remote controllers, the company could avoid a protracted battle with Sony and Microsoft to win added sales and market share for the Wii. Moreover, Nintendo decided to introduce the Wii with an innovative marketing strategy. The strategy called for using commercials featuring the slogan "Wii would like to play" and exhibiting a varied collection of people as users of the gaming system (grandparents, teens, urban families, etc.).

Nintendo sourced components for the Wii from a number of manufacturers to ensure product quality and to control distribution. Nintendo originally engaged a single manufacturer, Taiwan-based Foxconn Precision Components, which also manufactured the Apple iPhone, Sony's PS3, and personal computers. However, as the company's inability to keep up with demand continued, Nintendo announced in July 2007 that it would diversify its manufacturing base and formed additional partnerships for the manufacturing and supply of key components, such as controller chips, and for assembly of the Wii systems. In the months leading up to the 2008 holiday retail season, Nintendo increased production of the Wii by 50 percent to 2.4 million consoles per month in an attempt to keep up with retailer orders. While these tactics did help increase the supply of Wiis, the systems were still hard to find during the 2008 holiday retail season and into the spring of 2009. Wii's total sales through July 31, 2009, are shown in Exhibit 4.

Exhibit 4   **Total Nintendo Wii Unit Sales as of July 31, 2009**

Region	Total Units Sold (In Millions)	First Available
Europe	16.67	December 8, 2006
Japan	8.27	December 2, 2006
America	23.91	November 19, 2006
Other regions	2.75	December 8, 2006
Worldwide	51.60	

Source: www.vgchartz.com (accessed August 3, 2009).

COMPETITION IN THE CONSOLE SEGMENT OF THE VIDEO GAME INDUSTRY

Sales of video game consoles, software, and accessories reached a record high of $23.1 billion in 2008, which was 19 percent greater than 2007 industry revenues. Growth in the industry had fluctuated significantly over the past few decades and had been driven by technological advancements and societal trends, among other factors. The industry had also been impacted by the increase in the number of competitors, consolidation, and the continuous development of new products as competitors fought to capture a larger share of the core gamers in the market. Despite the increasing intensity of competition, the video gaming industry as a whole had continued to grow through the end of 2008 in the face of the downturn in the general world economy. However, as the recession lingered into 2009, the video game industry became affected, with industry revenues declining from $1.7 billion recorded in June 2008 to $1.2 billion in June 2009. The quarterly decline in industry revenues was the steepest decline in industry sales since September 2000. Sales of consoles were affected the greatest by the recession, with console sales falling from $617. 3 million in June 2008 to $382.6 million in June 2009.

Since the inception of the video gaming industry, companies producing video gaming consoles had attempted to win market share by developing products that were technologically superior and more powerful than the offerings of rivals. Sixth-generation consoles such as Nintendo's Game-Cube, Sega's Dreamcast, Sony's PlayStation 2, and Microsoft's Xbox began the century with considerable development in the realm of home video gaming technology. Nintendo became the first to use optical discs rather than game cartridges for gaming storage. Sega's Dreamcast, the first console of the sixth generation, introduced Internet gaming as a standard feature through its built-in modem and a corresponding Web browser. The Dreamcast was also the first home gaming console to fully display in standard definition (SD) resolution. With the PS2, consumers were able to play DVDs through their console, which was also backward-compatible with games made for its predecessor, PlayStation. Microsoft's Xbox continued Dreamcast's idea of online game playing by including a feature called Xbox Live, Microsoft's online gaming community that became a success because of the utilization of PC-style features such as a broadband connection and a hard disk drive available for memory storage, which connected Xbox players all over the world together in one place.

The seventh generation of home video gaming consoles contributed significantly to advancement in video gaming technology. Each new console introduced a new type of breakthrough technology. For example, Microsoft's Xbox 360 and Sony's PS3 offered the first ever high-definition graphics. The Nintendo Wii offered the integration of controllers and motion sensors to create a completely new arena of player control based on the individual player's own movements. Additionally, all three of the seventh-generation consoles employed wireless controllers. With regard to handheld gaming systems, the seventh-generation Nintendo DS perfected the use of Wi-Fi wireless technology. Sony developed the PlayStation Portable (PSP) with great multimedia capabilities, connectivity with the PS3, and other PSP consoles through Internet connectivity.

While overall technology had continued to advance as companies built on one another's progress, the current generation of consoles had leveraged advances in both technology and social trends in an attempt to establish a competitive advantage over rivals. Developers of video gaming consoles looked to changes in social trends in order to better target an appropriate market and capture considerable market share. As the focus on social trends had grown, developers such as Nintendo had shifted their focus to attempting to target *new* customers rather than fighting with competitors over the *old* customers. Competitors were actively seeking to develop new ways of attracting first-time video gaming consumers to their particular product but did not want to forget or neglect their loyal fan base.

When Nintendo released the Wii gaming console on September 14, 2006, the company was already facing significant competition from Microsoft's Xbox 360, which was released on November 22, 2005. Due to its early launch, the Xbox 360 had a one-year lead over both the Nin-tendo Wii and the Sony PS3; however, because of its new gaming concept, developers at Nintendo did not consider this a major setback. The target market they were aiming to pursue was completely different from that of Sony or Microsoft.

When launched, the Xbox 360 retailed at $299 to $399, PlayStation 3 at $499 to $599, and the Wii at $249. The Wii had generated monthly sales higher than those of competing products across the globe. According to the National Purchase Diary, a leading global market research company, in the first half of 2007, the Nintendo Wii sold more units in the United States than the Xbox 360 and PS3, fellow seventh-generation gaming consoles. This lead was even larger in the Japanese market, where the Wii led in total sales, having outsold both consoles by factors of 2:1 and 6:1 nearly every week from its launch until November 2007.

Over the long term, both Microsoft and Sony had traditionally been operating at a loss in hopes of making significant profit gain in software and game sales, especially when the systems were first launched. For example, it was estimated that PS3 in particular was generating a $250 loss with each unit sold. According to the *Financial Times*, however, the Wii was earning a profit per console sold estimated at around $13 in Japan, $50 in the United States, and $79 in parts of Europe.[8] The differences in gains and loss were attributed to the Wii's low cost of production and the extensive amount of money and resources Nintendo's competitors expended upon development. However, by October 2008, it was estimated that Microsoft had reduced its production costs on some of its Xbox models so that the company was making a profit on some of these models, and that Sony was also taking steps to reduce its production costs.

Another one-up for the Wii—neither Sony nor Microsoft had made any significant developments with regard to their controller, which-was one of the main differentiating features of the Wii gaming system. "Microsoft and Sony spend a lot of time developing cutting-edge technology. Nintendo is not a technology company—it is a toy company. It is not interested in bleeding-edge electronics and graphics," said In-Stat videogame analyst Brian O'Rourke.[9] Even considering this, comparing the three consoles was very difficult. Both the Xbox 360 and the PS3 were high-definition (HD) consoles with quality graphics and games specifically designed for HD output, while the Wii was an experimental, next-generation technology gaming console. A list of the most important game consoles of each technological generation is shown in Exhibit 5.

Exhibit 5   Evolution of the Home Gaming Console Industry

First generation	Magnavox Odyssey Atari Pong Coleco Telstar
Second generation	Atari 2600 Atari 5200 Coleco Vision
Third generation	Nintendo Entertainment System Atari 7800
Fourth generation	Sega Genesis Super Nintendo Entertainment System System
Fifth generation	Sony PlayStation Sega Saturn Nintendo 64
Sixth generation	Sega Dreamcast Sony PlayStation 2 Nintendo GameCube Microsoft Xbox
Seventh generation	Sony PlayStation 3 Nintendo Wii Microsoft Xbox 360

Sony PlayStation 3

Sony's seventh-generation video gaming console was the PlayStation 3. This model followed its similar predecessors—the PlayStation (fifth generation) and the PlayStation 2 (sixth generation). The PS3 separated itself from the previous systems through its unique feature of unified online gaming via the PlayStation Network. Other distinguishing features of the PS3 included connectivity with the PlayStation Portable, the inclusion of a high-definition Blu-ray optical drive, and various multimedia capabilities. Sony justified the PS3's exceptionally high price by pointing out that the PS3 was the only game console including a high-definition Blu-ray drive. Two initial versions of the PS3 were backward-compatible with many of the PlayStation and PS2 games. However, in August 2008, in an effort to reduce production costs, Sony announced that new versions of the console would no longer be backward-compatible with the PlayStation and PlayStation 2 discs, although many of the most popular titles would be available for download at the PlayStation Store.

First released on November 11, 2006, the PlayStation 3 proved relatively unprofitable for Sony despite its sales of 23 million units worldwide as of July 31, 2009. Shortly after its November 2006 launch, the production cost for the PlayStation 3 was said to be as high as $805.85. Even with a launch pricing of $499–$599, the high production costs of the PS3 led to an operating loss of ¥232.3 billion (U.S. $1.97 billion) in the fiscal year ending March 2007. The PS3's outlook with regard to its consumer reception wasn't much better than its financial performance. Initially, the PlayStation 3 received generally critical reviews from customers, with many noting its unreasonably high retail price and the lack of games equivalent in quality to those of its competitors. However, after Sony made several cuts in the retail price and developed a handful of successful games, the console proceeded to receive more positive reviews. However, in early 2009, unit sales for the $130 PS2 were nearly 60 percent as high as PS3 unit sales as many consumers looked for low-priced alternatives to seventh-generation game consoles. At the conclusion of the 2008 holiday retail season, more than 50 million PS2 consoles had been sold in North America and Sony management had commented that the company intended to promote the development of new PS2 games. Sony's PSP had sold nearly 49 million units worldwide by July 31, 2009.

Sony PS3 users with broadband Internet access had free access to the online PlayStation Network. The PlayStation Network provided users with an Internet browser, video and voice chat, and access to the PlayStation Store. The PlayStation Store allowed users to download both free and premium content, including full games, game demos, additional game content, and movies and television shows from major producers such as Sony Pictures, MGM, and Disney. Sony launched PlayStation Home in 2008, which allowed users to join a 3D virtual community in which they could create an avatar that would have its own home space that could be decorated with items that players could either acquire in games or purchase. Users in this virtual world could interact with others in a number of ways, including playing games. Unit sales by geographic region for the PS3 through July 31, 2009, are provided in Exhibit 6.

Microsoft Xbox 360

At its launch, Nintendo Wii's other main competitor was Microsoft's Xbox 360. This seventh-generation console was the second system manufactured by Microsoft following its predecessor Xbox (released in 2001). A distinguishing feature of the Xbox 360 was the ability to access its online multiplayer gaming network, Xbox Live. Microsoft's online gaming community became a success because of the utilization of PC-style features such as a broad-band connection and a hard drive disk available for memory storage, which con-

nected Xbox players all over the world. Inside, the Xbox 360 used the triple-core Xenon, designed by IBM, as its central processing unit (CPU). However, the Xbox 360 had suffered from a higher than average number of technical issues, which had resulted in Microsoft extending the warranty to three years for "general hardware failures."

When released, the Xbox 360 was available in four different variations: (1) the entry-level option named the Xbox 360 Core, which had since been discontinued and replaced by the Xbox 360 Arcade, which featured a wireless controller, a 256 MB memory unit, a composite AV cable, HDMI 1.2 output, and five Xbox Live Arcade titles; (2) the Xbox 360 Premium, which included all the features of the Arcade as well as a hybrid composite and component cable with optional optical out instead of a composite cable; (3) the Xbox 360 Premium, which also included a detachable 20 GB hard disk drive to store downloaded content; and (4) the Xbox 360 Elite, the most expensive variation of the console, priced at $449.99, which included a 120 GB hard drive and a matte black finish. The Elite retail package also included an HDMI 1.2 cable and a controller and headset that matched the console's black finish.

A key component of Microsoft's strategy involved its Xbox Live service. This service allowed users to access a number of features depending on their choice of the free Silver level of service or the Gold level, which cost approximately $50.00 per year. Services at the Silver level included online voice chat; the opportunity to download new content for video games such as new levels; and access to the XboxLive Marketplace, which had both free and premium content, including Xbox games, new game demos, and Xbox Live Arcade titles. Users who opted for the Gold level of service could play multiplayer games, had early access to downloadable content, and could use live video chat. In November 2008, Microsoft expanded Xbox Live with the New Xbox Experience, which allowed users to stream programming from Netflix's library of 30,000 movies and TV episodes and added enhanced multiplayer gaming capabilities. In early 2009 Xbox Live had more than 1 million Gold members. The combination of Xbox 360 sales, software sales and royalties, and Xbox Live subscriptions helped Microsoft's entertainment and devices division earn its first ever profit

Exhibit 6 **Total Sony PlayStation 3 Unit Sales as of July 31, 2009**

Region	Total Units Sold (In Millions)	First Available
Europe	9.28	March 23, 2007
Japan	3.31	November 11, 2006
America	8.95	November 17, 2006
Other regions	1.46	
Worldwide	23.00	

Source: www.vgchartz.com (accessed August 3, 2009).

Exhibit 7   **Total Microsoft Xbox 360 Unit Sales as of July 31, 2009**

Region	Total Units Sold (in Millions)	First Available
Europe	9.78	November 22, 2005
Japan	1.11	December 10, 2005
United States	17.82	November 22, 2005
Other regions	2.64	
Worldwide	31.35	

Source: www.vgchartz.com (accessed August 3, 2009).

in 2008. The division was expected to report a loss in 2009 as the economy continued to struggle and consumers cut back on discretionary spending. Unit sales by geographic region for the Xbox 360 through July 31, 2009, are shown in Exhibit 7.

NINTENDO'S SITUATION IN MID-2009

Nintendo had ended an extraordinary year in 2008 setting new revenue and earnings records and selling more than 31 million Nintendo DS handheld game systems and nearly 26 million Wii consoles during the year. However, with the company's sales of Wii consoles falling from 5.17 million units during the quarter ending June 30, 2008, to 2.23 million during the quarter ending June 30, 2009, and sales of DS systems falling 14 percent during the quarter to 5.97 million units, Nintendo management was forced to evaluate its strategic situation. Upon examining the company's performance that included a 40 percent year-over-year decline in quarterly revenues and a 61 percent year-over-year decline in quarterly profits, management had concluded that the poor quarterly performance was primarily related to the recession impacting many developed countries and its own inability to launch new blockbuster game titles to compete with new games introduced for the Sony PS3 and Microsoft Xbox 360.

Analysts believed that the effect of the recession brought on by rising oil prices and the credit crisis caused by the subprime home mortgage crisis in the U.S. would have a continuing effect on the producers of nonessential goods and services, but nevertheless also believed that Nintendo must continue to expand its customer base and defend its market from its rivals. Both Microsoft and Sony had announced intentions to create a broader variety of ways for users to interact with games on their respective systems and to pursue the casual gamer market. However, analysts who closely monitored the progression of the Wii noted that the only limitations of the system were the limitations of the designer and the user—leading most to believe they considered the possibilities endless. With that in mind, analysts suggested that Nintendo should continue to launch innovative products such as the Wii Fit to add to the company's already expansive repertoire of gaming possibilities with the console and continue to expand the video game market.

ENDNOTES

[1] Craig Harris, "Europe DS Launch Title Details," January 27, 2007, accessed at www.subgamers.com on October 1, 2008.

[2] "A Conversation with W. Chan Kim and Renee Mauborgne, authors of Blue Ocean Strategy," accessed at http://www.insead.edu/alumni/newsletter/February2005/Interview.pdf on September 22, 2008.

[3] Kenjii Hall, "The Big Ideas Behind Nintendo's Wii," *BusinessWeek*, November 16, 2006, www.businessweek.com/technology/content/nov2006/tc20061116_750580.htm (accessed October 10, 2008).

[4] Rhys Blakely, "Wii Are Swimming in a Clear Blue Ocean: Nintendo President Talks About Reinventing the Gaming Industry," July 12, 2007, http://business.timesonline.co.uk/tol/business/industry_sectors/technology/article2063714.ece?token=null&offset=0 (accessed on September 24, 2008).

[5] Ibid.

[6] Posted at http://techland.blogs.fortune.cnn.com/2008/10/06/no-slowdown-for-wii-and-ds-says-nintendo-prez/ in response to "No Slowdown for Wii and DS, Says Nintendo Prez," October 6, 2008.

[7] Ibid.

[8] James Brightman, "Report: Nintendo Makes About $49 Per Wii Sold in U.S.," GamingDaily. BIZ, September 17, 2007.

[9] "Nintendo Chief Confident in Wii's Long Term Success," TechNewsWorld.com, July 6, 2006.

TomTom: New Competition Everywhere!

Alan N. Hoffman

Rotterdam School of Management, Erasmus University and Bentley University

TomTom is one of the largest producers of satellite navigation systems in the world, comprised of both standalone devices and applications. It leads the navigation systems market in Europe while it stands second in the United States. TomTom attributes its position as a market leader to the following factors: the size of its customer and technology base; its distribution power; and its prominent brand image and recognition.[1]

With the acquisition of Tele Atlas, TomTom has become vertically integrated and also controls the map creation process now. This has helped TomTom establish itself as an integrated content, service and technology business. The company is Dutch by origin and has its headquarters based in Amsterdam, Netherlands. In terms of geography, the company's operations span from Europe to Asia Pacific, covering North America, Middle East and Africa.[1]

TomTom is supported by a workforce of 3,300 employees from 40 countries. The diverse workforce enables the company to compete in international markets.[2] The company's revenues have grown from €8 million in 2002 to €1.674 billion in 2008. However, more recently, because of the Tele Atlas acquisition and the current economic downturn the company has become a cause of concern for investors. TomTom reported a net loss of €37 million in the first quarter of 2009.[3]

TomTom is in the business of navigation based information services and devices. The company has been investing structurally and strategically in Research and Development to bring new and better products and services to its customers. The company's belief in radical innovation has helped it remain at the cutting edge of innovation within the navigation industry.

The vision of TomTom is to improve people's lives by transforming navigation from a don't-get-lost solution into a true travel companion that gets people from one place to another safer, faster, cheaper and better informed. This vision has helped the company to be a market leader in every market place in the satellite navigation information services market.

The objectives of the company focus around radical advances in three key areas:[4]

Better Maps: This objective is achieved by maintaining TomTom's high quality map data base that is continuously kept up to date by a large community of active users who provide corrections, verifications and updates to TomTom. This is supplemented by inputs from TomTom's extensive fleet of surveying vehicles.

Better Routing: TomTom has the world's largest historical speed profile data base IQ Routes™ facilitated by TomTom HOME, the company's user portal.

The author would like to thank Will Hoffman, Mansi Asthana, Aakashi Ganveer, Hing Lin, and Che Yii for their research. Printed by permission of Dr. Alan N. Hoffman and www.ecch.com.
Copyright © 2010 Alan N. Hoffman. No part of this publication may be copied, stored, transmitted, reproduced or distributed in any form or medium whatsoever without the permission of the copyright owner.

Better Traffic Information: TomTom possesses unique real time traffic information service TomTom HD traffic™ which provides users with high quality, realtime traffic updates.[4] These three objectives form the base of satellite navigation, working in conjunction to help TomTom achieve its mission.

TOMTOM'S PRODUCTS

TomTom offers a wide variety of products ranging from portable navigation devices to software navigation applications and digital maps. The unique features in each of these products make them truly "the smart choice in personal navigation."[1] Some of these products are described below.

TomTom Go and TomTom One   These
devices come with a LCD screen that makes it easy to use with fingertips while driving. They provide 1,000 Points of Interests (POI) that help in locating petrol stations, restaurants and places of importance. A number of other POIs can also be downloaded. Precise, up to minute traffic information, jam alerts and road condition alerts are provided by both these devices.[5]

TomTom Rider   These are portable models
especially for bikers. The equipment consists of an integrated GPS receiver that can be mounted on any bike and a wireless headset inside the helmet. Similar to the car Portable Navigation Devices (PNDs), the TomTom Rider models have a number of POI applications. The interfaces used in TomTom Rider are user friendly and come in a variety of languages.[5]

TomTom Navigator and TomTom
Mobile   These applications provide navigation software along with digital maps. Both of
these applications are compatible with most mobiles and PDAs, provided by companies like Sony, Nokia, Acer, Dell and HP. These applications come with TomTom HOME which can be used to upgrade to the most recent digital maps and application versions.[5]

TomTom for iPhone

On August 17, 2009, TomTom released TomTom for the iPhone. "With TomTom for iPhone, millions of iPhone users can now benefit from the same easy-to-use and intuitive interface, turn-by-turn spoken navigation and unique routing technology that our 30 million portable navigation device users rely on every day," said Corinne Vigreux, Managing Director of TomTom. "As the world's leading provider of navigation solutions and digital maps, TomTom is the most natural fit for an advanced navigation application on the iPhone."[4]

The TomTom app for iPhone 3G and 3GS users includes a map of the U.S. and Canada from Tele Atlas, and is available for $99.99 USD.

The TomTom app for iPhone includes the exclusive IQ Routes™ technology. Instead of using travel time assumptions, IQ Routes bases its routes on the actual experience of millions of TomTom drivers to calculate the fastest route and generate the most accurate arrival times in the industry. TomTom IQ Routes empowers drivers to reach their destination faster up to 35% of the time.

COMPANY BACKGROUND

Company History

TomTom was founded as Palmtop in 1991 by Peter-Frans Pauwels and Pieter Geelen, two graduates from Amsterdam University, Netherlands. Palmtop started out as a software development company and was involved in producing software for handheld computers, one of the most popular devices of the 90s. In the following few years the company diversified into producing commercial applications including software for personal finance, games, a dictionary and maps. In the year 1996, Corinne Vigreux joined Palmtop as the third partner. In the same year, the company announced the launch of Enroute and RouteFinder, the first navigation software titles. As more and more people using PCs adopted Microsoft's operating system, the company developed applications which were compatible with it. This helped the company increase its market share. The year 2001 marks the turning point in the history of

TomTom. It was in this year that Harold Goddijn, the former Chief Executive of Psion joined the company as the fourth partner. Not only did Palmtop get renamed to TomTom, but it also entered the satellite navigation market. TomTom launched TomTom Navigator, the first mobile car satnav system. Since then, as can be seen in Exhibit 1, the company has celebrated the successful launch of at least a product each year.[5]

In 2002, the company generated revenue of €8 million by selling the first GPS-linked car navigator, the TomTom Navigator to PDAs. The upgraded version, Navigator 2 was released in early 2003. Meanwhile, the company made efforts to gain technical and marketing personnel. TomTom took strategic steps to grow its sales. The former CTO of Psion, Mark Gretton, led the hardware team while Alexander Ribbink, a

former top marketing official looked after sales of new products introduced by the company.

TomTom Go, an all-in-one car navigation system, was the next major launch of the company. With its useful and easy to use features TomTom Go was included in the list of successful products of 2004. In the same year, the company launched TomTom Mobile, a navigation system which sat on top of smart phones.[5]

TomTom completed its IPO on the Amsterdam Stock Exchange in May 2005. It raised €469 million ($587 million) from this offer. The net worth of the company was nearly €2 billion after the IPO. A majority of the shares were with the four partners.[6] From the years 2006 to 2008, TomTom strengthened itself by making three key strategic acquisitions. Datafactory AG was acquired to power TomTom WORK through WEBfleet

Exhibit 1   Company history

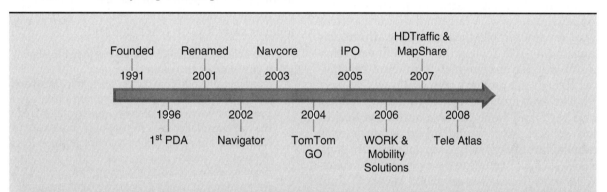

Year	Historical Event
1991	Palmtop founded by Harold Goddijn, Peter-Frans Pauwels and Pieter Geelen.
1994	Corinne Vigreux joined the Company to sell Palmtop applications in Europe.
1996	First navigation software for PDAs, EnRoute and RouteFinder launched.
2001	Palmtop renamed TomTom. Harold Goddijn joins TomTom as CEO. Number of employees 30.
2002	First GPS-linked car navigation product for PDAs, TomTom NAVIGATOR shipped. €8 million revenue.
2003	NavCore Software Architecture developed, on which all TomTom products are still based. Number of employees 90.
2004	First portable navigation device shipped, the TomTom GO. 248,000 PND units sold.
2005	TomTom listed on Euronext Amsterdam. €720 million revenue.
2006	TomTom WORK and TomTom Mobility Solutions launched. Number of employees 818.
2007	TomTom makes offer for Tele Atlas. TomTom HD Traffic and TomTom MapShare launched. 9.6 million PND units sold.
2008	TomTom acquired Tele Atlas.

Source: http://investors.tomtom.com/overview.cfm

technology, while Applied Generics gave its technology for Mobility Solutions Services. However, the most prominent of these three was the acquisition of Tele Atlas.[6]

In July of 2007, TomTom bid for Tele Atlas, a company specializing in digital maps. The original bid price of €2 billion was countered by a €2.3 billion offer from Garmin, TomTom's biggest rival. With TomTom raising the bid price to €2.9 billion, the two companies had initiated a bidding war for Tele Atlas. Although there was speculation that Garmin would further increase its bid price, in the end they decided not to pursue Tele Atlas any further. Rather, Garmin struck a content agreement with Navteq. Finally, TomTom's shareholders approved the takeover in December, 2007.[7]

TomTom's Customers

TomTom is a company that has a wide array of customers each with their own individual needs and desires. TomTom has a variety of products to meet the requirements of a large and varied customer base. As an example, their navigational products range from $100–$500 in the United States, ranging from lower end products with fewer capabilities, to high end products with advanced features.

The first group is the individual consumers who buy stand-alone portable navigation devices and services. The second group is automobile manufacturers. TomTom has teamed up with companies such as Renault to develop built-in navigational units to install as an option in cars. A third group of customers is the aviation industry and pilots with personal planes. TomTom produces navigational devices for air travel at affordable prices. Another group of customers is business enterprises. Business enterprises refers to companies such as Walmart, Target, or Home-Depot, huge companies with large mobile workforces. To focus on these customers, TomTom formed a strategic partnership with a technology company called "Advanced Integrated Solutions" to "optimize business fleet organization and itinerary planning on the TomTom pro series of navigation devices." This new advanced feature on PNDs offers ways for fleet managers and route dispatchers to organize, plan and optimize routes and to provide detailed mapping information about the final destination. "Every day, companies with mobile workforces are challenged to direct all their people to all the places they need to go. Our customers appreciate having a central web repository to hold and manage all their location and address information," says Scott Wyatt, CEO of Advanced Integrated Solutions.[8] TomTom's last group of customers is the coast guards. They are able to use Tom-Tom's marine navigational devices for their everyday responsibilities.

Mergers and Acquisitions

TomTom has made various mergers and acquisitions as well as partnerships that have positioned the company well. In 2008 TomTom acquired a digital mapping company called Tele Atlas. The acquisition has significantly improve TomTom customers' user experience and created other benefits for the customers and partners of both companies, including more accurate navigation information, improved coverage, and new enhanced features such as map updates and IQ routes which will be discussed in the scarce/unique resource section of the paper. Commenting on the proposed Offer, Alain De Taeye, Co-founder and CEO of Tele Atlas said:

> ". . . the TomTom-Tele Atlas partnership signals a new era in the digital mapping industry. The combination of TomTom's customer feedback tools and Tele Atlas' pioneering map production processes allows Tele Atlas to dramatically change the way digital maps are continuously updated and enhanced. The result will be a completely new level of quality, content and innovation that helps our partners deliver the best navigation products. This transaction is not only very attractive to our shareholders but demonstrates our longstanding commitment towards all of our partners and customers to deliver the best digital map products available."[9]

TomTom also formed a partnership with a company called Advanced Integrated Solutions, adding an itinerary planning and route guidance feature to the pro series of navigation devices to help businesses enterprises with large mobile workforces. A few years ago they also partnered with Avis, adding their user-friendly navigation system to all Avis rental cars. This partnership began in Europe and recently the devices have made their way into Avis rental cars in North America as well many other countries where Avis operates. Harold Goddijn, chief executive officer of TomTom commented:

> "Any traveler can relate to the stress of arriving in a new and unfamiliar city and getting horribly lost,

with the availability of the TomTom GO 700 we're bringing unbeatable, full feature car navigation straight into the hands of Avis customers."[10]

TomTom has acquired several patents for all of their different technologies. By having these patents for each of its ideas, the company has protected itself against its competition and other companies trying to enter into the market.

TomTom prides itself on being the innovator in its industry and always being a step ahead of the competition in terms of its technology. On their website they say, "TomTom leads the navigation industry with the technological evolution of navigation products from static find-your-destination devices into products and services that provide connected, dynamic find-the-optimal-route-to-your-destination, with time-accurate travel information. We are well positioned to maintain that leading position over the long term because of the size of our customer and technology base, our distribution power, and our prominent brand image and recognition. By being vertically integrated and also control the map creation process TomTom is in a unique position to evolve into an integrated content, service and technology business."[4]

TomTom has a strong brand name/image. TomTom has positioned itself well throughout the world as the leader in portable navigation devices. It markets its products through its very user-friendly online website and also through large companies such as Best Buy and Walmart. Recently TomTom teamed up with Locutio Voice Technologies and Twentieth Century Fox Licensing & Merchandising to bring the original voice of Homer Simpson to all TomTom devices via download. "Let Homer Simpson be your TomTom co-pilot" is just one of the many interesting ways TomTom markets its products and its name to its consumers.[11]

TomTom's Resources and Capabilities

The company believes that there are three fundamentals to a navigation system—digital mapping, routing technology and dynamic information. Based on these requirements three key resources can be identified that really distinguished TomTom from its competition.

The first of these resources is their in-house *routing algorithms*. These algorithms enable them to introduce technologies like-IQ Routes, that provides "community based information database." IQ Routes calculate your routes based on the real average speeds measured on roads at that particular time. Their website says, "The smartest route hour-by-hour, day-by-day, saving you time, money and fuel."[6]

The second unique resource identified was Tele Atlas and the *digital mapping technology* that the TomTom group specializes in. Having the technology and knowledge in mapping that the company brought to TomTom has allowed them to introduce many unique features to their customers. Firstly, TomTom recently came out with a map update feature. The company recognizes that roads around the world are constantly changing and because of this they used the technology to come out with four new maps each year, one per business quarter. This allows their customers to always have the latest routes to incorporate into their everyday travel. A second feature they recently introduced is their MapShare program. The idea behind this is that customers of TomTom who notice mistakes in a certain map are able to go in and request a change be made. The change is then verified and checked directly by TomTom and is shared with the rest of their global user community. "One and a half million map corrections have been submitted since the launch of TomTom Map Share™ in the summer of 2007."[6]

The third unique resource identified was *automotive partnerships* with two companies in particular: Renault and Avis. At the end of 2008, TomTom reached a deal with Renault to offer its navigation devices installed in their cars as an option. An article in AutoWeek Magazine said the following about the deal: "Renault developed its new low-cost system in partnership with Amsterdam-based technology company TomTom, the European leader in portable navigation systems. The system will be an alternative to the existing satellite navigation devices in Renault's upper-end cars."[12] The catch here is the new price of the built-in navigation units. The cost of a navigation device installed in Renault's cars before TomTom was €1,500. Now with TomTom system it costs only €500. As talked about earlier in the paper, TomTom also partnered with Avis back in 2005 to offer its navigation devices, specifically the model GO700 in all Avis rental cars, first starting in Europe and expanding into other countries where Avis operates.

COMPETITION FACING TOMTOM

Traditional Competition

TomTom faces competition from two main companies. The first of these is Garmin which holds 45% of the market share, by far the largest and double TomTom's market share (24%). Garmin was founded in 1989 by Gary Burrell and Min H. Kao. The company is known for their on-the-go directions since its introduction into GPS navigation in 1989. At the end of 2008, Garmin reported annual sales of $3493.1 million. Last year Garmin competed head-to-head with TomTom in trying to acquire Tele Atlas for their mapmaking. Garmin withdrew their bid when it became evident that it was becoming too expensive to own Tele Atlas. Garmin executives made a decision that it was cheaper to work out a long-term deal with its current supplier than to try to buy out a competitor. Garmin's current supplier for map services is Navteq which was also acquired by Nokia in 2008.

The second direct competitor is Magellan, which holds 15% of the market share. Magellan is part of a privately held company under the name of MiTac Digital Corporation. Similar to Garmin, Magellan products use Navteq based maps. Magellan was the creator of Magellan NAV 100 that was the world's first commercial handheld GPS receiver which was created in 1989. The company is also well known for their award-winning RoadMate and Maestro series portable car navigation systems.

Together these three dominant players account for about 85% of the total market. Other competitors in the personal navigation device market are Navigon, Nextar, and Nokia. Navigon and Nextar compete in the personal navigation devices with TomTom, Magellan, and Garmin who are the top three in the industry. But Navigon competes in the high-end segment which retails for more than any of the competitors but offer a few extra features in their PNDs. Nextar competes in the low-end market and its strategy is low cost. Finally, Nokia is mentioned as a competitor

in this industry because they recently acquired Navteq who is a major supplier of map services in this industry. Along with that, Nokia has a big market share in the cell phone industry and plans on incorporating GPS technology in every phone making them a potential key player to look at in the GPS navigation industry.

New Competition

Cell Phones   Cell phones are a widely used technology by people all around the world. With the 2005 FCC mandate that requires the location of any cell phone used to call 911, phone manufacturers have now included GPS receiver in almost every cell phone. Due to this mandate, cell phone manufacturers and cellular services are now able to offer a GPS navigation service through the cell phone for a fee.

In the cell phone industry, Nokia is leading the charge in combining cell phone technology with GPS technology. They have a plan to put GPS technology in all their phones. Around the same time TomTom acquired Tele Atlas, Nokia also purchased Navteq, a competitor to Tele Atlas. With the acquisition of Navteq, Nokia hopes to shape the cell phone industry by merging cell phone, Internet, and GPS technology together.

ATT Navigator   As we see the smart phone industry emerging with the iPhone and the Palm Pre, we also see a shift in how people are able to utilize these technologies as a navigation tool. A big trend in smartphones these days are applications. Because of the ease of developing software on platforms for smart phones, more and more competitors are coming to the forefront and developing GPS navigation applications.

GPS Navigation with AT&T Navigator and AT&T Navigator Global Edition feature real-time GPS enabled turn-by-turn navigation on AT&T mobile smartphones (iPhone and Blackberry) or static navigation and Local Search on a non-GPS AT&T mobile smartphone.

ATT Navigator features Global GPS turn-by-turn navigation—Mapping and Point of Interest content for three continents, including North America (U.S., Canada, and Mexico), Western Europe, and China where wireless coverage is available from AT&T or its roaming providers.

The ATT Navigator is sold as a subscription service and costs $9.99 per month.

Online Navigation Applications
Online navigation websites that are still popular amongst many users for driving directions and maps are MapQuest, Google Maps, and Yahoo Maps. Users are able to use this free site to get detailed directions on how to get to their next destination. In today's economic downturn many people are looking for cheap, or if possible free solutions to solve their problems. These online websites offer the use of free mapping and navigation information that will allow them to get what they need at no additional cost. However, there are down-sides to these programs, "such as they are not portable and may have poor visualization designs (such as vague image, or text-based)."[13]

Built-In Car Navigation Devices
In-car navigation devices first came about in more luxury, high-end vehicles. In today's market it has become more mainstream and now being offered in mid to lower tier vehicles. These built-in car navigation devices offer similar features to the personal navigation device but don't have the portability so you won't have to carry multiple devices but come with a hefty cost. Some examples of these are Kenwood, Pioneer, and Eclipse units all installed into your car. These units tend to be expensive and over-priced because of the fact that they are brand name products and require physical installation. For example, the top of the line Pioneer unit is $1,000 for the monitor and then another $500 for the navigation device plus the physical labor. When buying such products, a customer is spending a huge amount of money on a product that is almost identical to a product TomTom offers at significantly lower prices.

Physical Maps
Physical maps have been the primary option for navigating for decades until technology came around. Physical maps provide detailed road information to help a person get from point A to point B. Although cumbersome to use than some of the modern technology alternatives, it is an alternative for people who are not technically savvy or for whom navigation device is an unnecessary luxury that they do not feel the need to spend money on.

POTENTIAL ADVERSE LEGISLATION AND RESTRICTIONS

In the legal and political realm, TomTom is facing two issues that are not critical now, but may have significant ramifications to not only TomTom in the future, but also the entire portable navigation device industry. TomTom's reactions to each of these issues will determine whether or not there is an opportunity for gain or a threat of a significant loss will occur.

The most important issue deals with the possible legislative banning of all navigational devices from automobiles. In Australia, there is growing concern over the distraction caused by PNDs and the legislature has taken the steps toward banning these devices entirely from automobiles.[14] There is a similar sentiment in Ontario, Canada, where a law that is currently under review would ban all PNDs that were not mounted either to the dashboard or to the windshield itself.[15]

With the increase in legislation adding to the restrictions placed on PND devices, the threat that the PND market in the future will be severely limited cannot be ignored. All of the companies within the PND industry, not just TomTom, must create a coordinated and united effort to stem this tidal wave of restrictions as well as provide reassurance to the public that they are also concerned with the safe use of their products. An example of this opportunity comes from the toy industry where safety regulations are fast and furious at times. Many companies within the toy industry have combined to form the International Council of Toy Industries[16] to be proactive in regards to safety regulations as well as lobby governments on behalf of the toy industry against laws that may unfairly threaten the toy industry.[16]

The other issue within the legal and political spectrum that TomTom must focus on is the growing use of GPS devices as tracking devices. Currently, law enforcement agents are allowed to use their own GPS devices to track the movements and locations of individuals they deem to be suspicious, but how long will it be before budget cuts reduce the access to these GPS devices and then the simple solution will be to use the PND devices already installed in many automobiles?

This issue also requires the industry as whole to proactively work with the consumers and the government to come to an amicable resolution. The threat of having every consumer's GPS information at the fingertips of either the government or surveillance company will most certainly stunt or even completely halt any growth within the PND industry and that is why the industry must be on the offensive and not become a reactor.

Another alarming trend is the rise in PND thefts around the country.[17] With the prices for PNDs at a relatively high level, thieves are targeting vehicles that have visible docking stations for PNDs either on the dashboard or windshield. The onus will be on TomTom to create new designs that will help not only hide PNDs from would-be thieves but also deter them from ever trying to steal one. Consumers who are scared to purchase PNDs because of this rise in crime will become an issue if this problem is not resolved.

There is also a trend currently that is labeled the GREEN movement,[18] that aims to reduce any activities that will endanger the environment. This movement is a great opportunity for TomTom to tout its technology as the smarter and more environmentally safe tool if driving is an absolute necessity. Not only can individuals tout this improved efficiency, but more importantly on a larger scale, businesses that require large amounts of materials to be transported across long stretches can show activists that they too are working to becoming a green company.

It is ironic that the core technology used in TomTom's navigation system, the GPS system, is proliferating into other electronic devices at such a rapid pace that it is causing serious competition to the PND industry. GPS functionality is virtually a requirement for all new smart phones that enter the market and soon will become a basic functionality in regular cellular phones. TomTom will be hard pressed to compete with these multi-functional devices unless they can improve upon their designs and transform themselves into just a single focused device.

Another concern not only for TomTom, but for every company that relies heavily on GPS technology, is the aging satellites that support the GPS system. Analysts predict that these satellites will be either replaced or fixed before there are any issues, but this issue is unsettling due to the fact that TomTom has no control over it.[19]

TomTom will have to devise contingency plans in case of catastrophic failure of the GPS system much like what happened to Research in Motion when malfunctioning satellites caused disruption in their service.

Currently TomTom is one of the leading companies in the PND markets in both Europe and the United States. Although they are the leader in Europe, that market is showing signs of becoming saturated, and even though the U.S. market is currently growing, TomTom should not wait for the inevitable signs of that market's slowdown as well. TomTom needs to be proactive to the next big market instead of using its large resources to become a *fast follower*.

The two main opportunities for TomTom to expand, creating digital maps for developing countries and creating navigational services can either be piggybacked one on top of each other or can be taken in independent paths. The first-mover advantage for these opportunities will erect a high barrier of entry for any companies that do not have large amounts of resources to invest in the developing country. TomTom is already playing catch-up to Garmin and their already established service in India. Being proactive is an important and valuable opportunity that TomTom should take advantage of.

Globalization of any company's products does not come without a certain set of issues. For TomTom, the main threat brought on by foreign countries is twofold. The first threat which may be an isolated instance, but could also be repeated in many other countries is the restriction of certain capabilities for all of TomTom's products. Due to security and terrorism concerns, GPS devices are not allowed in Egypt since 2003.[20] In these times of global terrorism TomTom must be vigilant of the growing trend for countries to become overly protective of foreign companies and their technologies.

INTERNAL ENVIRONMENT

Finance

TomTom's current financial objectives are to diversify and become a broader revenue based company. The company not only seeks to increase the revenue base in terms of geographical expansion but also wants to diversify its product and service portfolio. Additionally, another important goal the company strives to achieve is to reduce its operating expenses.

Sales Revenue and Net Income

In Exhibit 2 it can be observed that from 2005 to 2007 there is a consistent growth in sales revenue and a corresponding increase in net income too. However, year 2008 is an exception to this trend. In this year sales revenue decreased by 3.7% and the net income decreased by 136%. In fact, in the first quarter the net income is actually negative totaling −€37 million. The decrease in sales can be accounted by the downturn in the economy. Actually, according to their 2008 annual report, the sales are in line with their expectations from

the market. However, the net income plummeted much more than the decrease in sales. This was actually triggered by its acquisition of a digital mapping company—Tele Atlas—which was funded by both cash assets and debt.

1. **Quarterly sales**—In second quarter of 2009 TomTom received sales revenue of €368 million compared to €213 million in first quarter and €453 million in the same quarter last year (Exhibit 3). By evaluating quarterly sales for a three year period from 2007 till present, it is apparent that the sales do follow a seasonal trend in TomTom. With highest sales in last quarter and lowest in the first quarter. However, focusing on just the first and

Exhibit 2   Sales Revenue and Net Income (€)

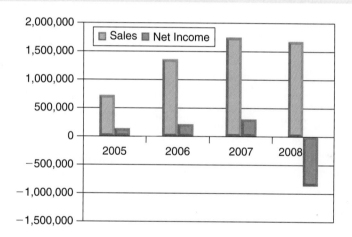

Exhibit 3   Quarterly sales (in millions €)

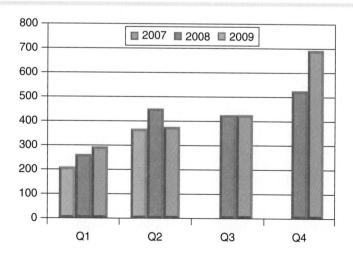

Exhibit 4   **Revenue per segment**

(in € millions)	Q1'09	Q1'08	y.o.y.	Q4'08	q.o.q
Revenue	172	264	−35%	473	−64%
PNDs	141	234	−40%	444	−68%
Others	31	29	5%	29	5%
# of PNDs sold (in thousands)	1,419	1,997	−29%	4,443	−68%
Average selling price (€)	99	117	−15%	100	−1%

second quarter for three years one can infer that the sales revenue as a whole is also going down year after year. To investigate further the causes of this scenario we will have to delve deeper into its revenue base. TomTom's sources of revenue can be broadly grouped into two categories—market segment and geographic location.

Revenue per segment: TomTom's per segment revenue stream can be divided into PNDs and others, where others consist of services and content. Evaluating first quarter of 2008 against that of 2009 and last quarter of 2008, TomTom experienced steep decline of 40% and 68% (Exhibit 4). This could be a consequence of the compounded effect of the following: Firstly, the number of devices (PNDs) decreased by a similar amount both the time periods. And secondly, the average selling price of PNDs has also been decreasing consistently. In a technology company a decrease in average selling price is a part and parcel of doing business in a highly competitive and dynamic market place. Nevertheless, the revenue stream from business units other than PNDs has seen a steady increase in both the scenarios.

Revenue per region: TomTom's per region revenue stream can be further divided into Europe, North America and the rest of the world. Comparing first quarter of 2009 against 2008 it can be seen that revenue from both Europe and North America are on decline, with a decrease of 22% and 52% respectively (Exhibit 5). At the same time, revenue from the rest of the world has seen a huge increase of 90%. Both of these analyses support TomTom's current objective to

Exhibit 5   **Revenue per region**

(in € millions)	Q1'08	Q1'09	Difference
Europe	178,114	146,549	−22%
North America	84,641	55,558	−52%
Rest of world	1,087	10,976	90%
Total	263,842	213,083	−24%

increase their revenue base and is aligned with their long-term strategy of being a leader in navigation industry.

2. **Long term debt**—In 2005 TomTom was cash-rich company but the recent acquisition of Tele Atlas, which amounted to €2.9 billion and was funded by cash, release of new shares as well as long term debt, which is in this case a borrowing of €1.2 billion. Currently, Tom-Tom's debt is €1,006 million.

3. **Operating Margin**—TomTom saw a consistent increase in operating margin till 2006 (Exhibit 7). But since 2007 operating margin has been decreasing for the firm. In fact, by the end of 2008 it came down to 13% compared to 26% in 2006.

Marketing

Traditionally high quality and ease of use of solutions have been of utmost importance to TomTom. In 2006, in an interview, TomTom's Marketing Head Anne Louise Hanstad, could not have emphasized more on the importance

Exhibit 6 **Cash versus Long term debt (in thousand €)**

	12/31/2005	12/31/2006	12/31/2007	12/31/2008	6/30/2009
Long Term Debt	301	338	377	4,749	4,811
Cash Assets	178,377	437,801	463,339	321,039	422,530
Borrowings	0	0	0	1,241,900	1,195,715

of simplicity and ease of use of their devices. (Hanstad) This underlines the TomTom's belief that "People prefer fit for purpose devices that are developed and designed to do one specific thing very well." At that time both of these were core to TomTom's strategy as their targeted customers were *early adopters*, but now as navigation industry has moved from embryonic to a growth industry TomTom's current customers are *early majority*, and hence, simplicity and ease alone could no longer provide it with competitive advantage.

Recently, to be in line with its immediate goal of diversifying into different market segment, TomTom is more focused on strengthening its brand name. In December 2008, TomTom's CEO stated ". . . we are constantly striving to increase awareness of our brand and strengthen our reputation for providing smart, easy-to-use, high-quality portable navigation products and services."[1]

Along with Tele Atlas the group has gained the depth and breadth of expertise over the last 30 years, and this makes it a trusted brand. Three out of four people are aware of the brand of the TomTom business across the markets. The TomTom group has always been committed to three fundamentals of navigation—mapping, routing algorithm and dynamic information. Tele Atlas' core competency is the digital mapping database and TomTom's is routing algorithms and guidance services using dynamic information, and the group together create synergies that enable them to introduce products almost every year advancing on one or a combination of these three elements. Acquiring their long time supplier of digital maps, Tele Atlas, in 2008 gives them an edge with in-house digital mapping technology.

TomTom provides a range of PND devices like TomTom One, TomTom XL and TomTom Go Series. Periodically, it tries to enhance those devices with new features and services, that they build based on the feedback from customers. Examples of services are IQ routes and LIVE services. While IQ routes provides drivers with the most efficient route planning, accounting for situations as precise as speed bumps and traffic lights, LIVE services forms a range of information services delivered directly to the LIVE devices. The LIVE services

Exhibit 7 **Operating Margin**

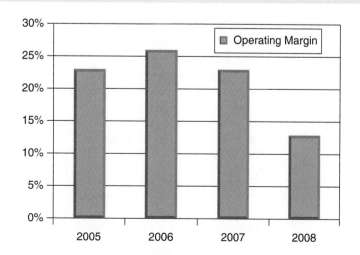

bundle includes Map Share and HD Traffic—that is bringing the content collected from vast driving community directly to the end user.

These products and services accentuate effective designs and unique features, and require TomTom to work along with its customers to share precise updates and also get feedback for future improvements. Hence, effective customer interaction becomes essential to its long term goal of innovation. In 2008, J.D. Power associates recognized TomTom for providing outstanding customer service experience.[21] Although, it awarded TomTom for customer service satisfaction, J.D. Power and associates ranked Garmin highest in overall customer satisfaction. TomTom followed Garmin in the ranking, performing well in the routing, speed of system and voice direction factors.[22]

As mentioned previously, when the navigation industry was still in its embryonic stages-Feature ease of use and high quality of its solutions gave TomTom products a competitive edge. Eventually, the competition increased in the navigation industry and even substitutes pose substantial threat to market share now. Currently, TomTom offers PNDs in different price ranges, broadly classified into high-range and mid-range PNDs, with an average selling price of €99. There are entry-level options that allow a savvy shopper to put navigation in his/her car for just over $100. Higher-end models add advanced features and services previously described.

TomTom sells its PNDs to consumers through retailers and distributors. After acquiring Tele Atlas it is strategically placed to gain the first mover advantage created by its rapid expansion of geographical coverage.[1] This is of key importance when it comes to increasing the global market share.

TomTom directs its marketing expenditure towards B2B advertising that is direct to retailers and distributors. TomTom also invested in an official blog website as well as search optimization which places it in premium results in online searches. This has enabled TomTom to do effective word-of-mouth promotion while keeping flexible marketing spending, in accordance to changes in the macroeconomic environment or seasonal trends.[1] Although, this approach gives it spending flexibility, it lacks a direct B2C approach. Currently only 21% of U.S. adults own PNDs while 65% of U.S. adults neither own nor use navigation.[23] By not spending on B2C marketing TomTom is discounting on the opportunity both to attract first-tier noncustomers and glean an insight of needs of second-tier noncustomers.[24]

Operations

The focus of operations has always been on innovation. More recently, TomTom's operational objective is to channel all the resources and core capabilities to create economies of scale so as to be aligned with their long term strategy. TomTom aims to focus and centralize R&D resources to create scale economies to continue to lead the industry in terms of innovation.[1]

Implementation of this strategy is well underway and the changes are visible. By second quarter of 2009 mid-range PNDs were introduced with capabilities from high-range devices, 50% of PNDs were sold with IQ Routes Technology, first in-dash product was also launched in alliance with Renault and TomTom iPhone application was also announced.[1]

After acquiring Tele Atlas, to better support the broader navigation solutions and content and

TOMTOM GROUP

TOMTOM B2C	TELE ATLAS B2B	WORK B2B	AUTOMOTIVE B2B
→ Consumers	→ PND → Automotive → Mobile → Internet → GIS	→ Commercial fleets	→ Car industry → Car industry suppliers

DYNAMIC CONTENT & PUBLISHING

SHARED TECHNOLOGIES

services, the group underwent restructuring. New organization structure consists of four business units that have clear focus on a specific customer group and are supported by two shared development centers.

TomTom's supply chain and distribution model is outsourced. This increases TomTom's ability to scale up or down the supply chain, while limiting capital expenditure risks. But, at the same time, it depends on a limited number of third parties and in certain instances sole suppliers for component supply and manufacturing, which increases its dependency on these suppliers.

TomTom's dynamic content sharing model uses high quality digital maps along with the connected services, like HD Traffic, Local Search with Google and weather information; provides our customers with relevant real-time information at the moment they need it; and this is helping them deliver the benefits of innovative technology directly to the end user and that to now at affordable prices. Although, the network externalities previously mentioned are one of the advantages of TomTom's LIVE, it has also increased TomTom's dependency on the network of the connected driving community. Bigger the network will be, the more effective would be the information from the guidance services.

Furthermore, in order to reduce operating expenses and strengthen the balance sheet, undue emphasis has been placed on the cost cutting program. Currently the cost reductions are made up of Reduction of staff, Restructuring and integration of Tele Atlas, Reduced discretionary spending and Reduction in the number of contractors and in marketing expenditures. However, if not executed wisely it could hamper TomTom's long term objective of being a market leader. For example one of the core capabilities of any technology company is its staff; reducing it can hinder future innovative projects. Likewise, reducing the marketing expenditures in a market which still holds rich prospects of high growth. There are still 65% of U.S. adults who don't own any kind of navigation system, either a device, in-car, or phone.[23]

Human Resources

Like any other technology company success of individual employees is very important to TomTom. Additionally, TomTom has a vision that success for TomTom as a business should also mean success for the individual employee. Therefore, at TomTom, employee competency is taken very seriously and talent development programs are built around it. There is a personal navigation plan that provides employees with a selection of courses based on competencies in their profile. In 2008 TomTom completed its Young Talent Development Program which was aimed at broadening the participants' knowledge, while improving their technical and personal skills.

TomTom's motto is to do business efficiently and profitably as well as responsibly. This underlines its corporate social responsibility. TomTom's headquarters is one of the most energy efficient buildings in Amsterdam. As mentioned before, earlier navigation was oriented towards making the drivers arrive at their destination without getting lost. TomTom was the pioneer in introducing different technology that actually helps drivers to make their journeys safer and more economical. This shows their commitment to their customer base as well as to the community as a whole.

ISSUES OF CONCERN FOR TOMTOM

First, TomTom is facing increasing competition from other platforms using GPS technology. Two main areas that come to mind are cell phones and smartphones. For TomTom, both of these sectors might signal major change is on the horizon and that there is no longer a need for hardware for GPS navigation devices. And that we are heading towards a culture where consumers want an all-in-one device such as cell phone or smartphone that will do everything they need including a GPS navigation services. TomTom and its main competitor, Garmin, have come under pressure since Google and Nokia started offering free turn-by-turn navigation on smartphones earlier 2010.[3] Analysts predicted that by 2013 phone-based navigation will dominate the industry.[23]

The other problem TomTom is facing is a mature U.S. and European personal navigation device market. After three years of steady growth in the PND market, TomTom has seen decreasing growth rate for PND sales. There could be many factors that are causing this such as the worldwide recession but we felt that based on sales figure we're seeing the same trend in the U.S. market as we have seen in the European market for TomTom. Initially entering the European market 12 months before entering the U.S. market, TomTom has seen a 21% dip in sales for the European market. Although, TomTom experienced some growth in the U.S. market for 2008, they are noticing the growth rate has not been as good as the prior years.

TomTom has responded to these problems by shifting its business mix toward value-added services, making its PND a smaller portion of total revenue. During the first quarter of 2010, PNDs only made up about 50 percent of the company's sales as a result of a rise in revenue from other products, compared with 2009, when PND sales contributed 70 percent to its total revenue.[3]

APPENDIX

Google Drives into Navigation Market

RUETERS
Wed Oct 28, 2009 11:30 AM EDT

SAN FRANCISCO (Reuters)—Google Inc. is adding Garmin Ltd and TomTom to its growing list of rivals as the Internet search giant weaves technology for driving directions into new versions of its smartphone software.

Google said its new Google Maps Navigation product will provide real-time, turn-by-turn directions directly within cell phones that are based on the new version of its Android software.

The navigation product, which features speech recognition and a visual display that incorporates Google's online archive of street photographs, marks the latest step by Google to challenge Apple Inc.'s iPhone and Microsoft Corp's Windows Mobile software with its Android smartphone software.

It also represents a direct competitive threat to companies like Garmin and TomTom which sell specialized hardware navigation devices. TomTom also makes a software navigation app for the iPhone that sells for $99.99 in the U.S.

Google executives told reporters at a press briefing on Tuesday ahead of the announcement that the company decided to offer turn-by-turn driving directions in its four-year-old maps product because it was the most requested feature by users.

CEO Eric Schmidt said that expanding into a new market with new competitors was not a part of Google's motivation.

"Those are tactical problems that occur after the strategic goal which is to offer something which is sort of magical on mobile devices using the cloud," Schmidt said.

The new navigation service will work with Google's forthcoming Android 2.0 software, the next version of the smartphone operating system developed by Google. The company announced development tools for Android 2.0 on Tuesday, but a spokeswoman said specific details about when Android 2.0 will be available should be directed to phone-makers and wireless carriers.

Google said the product, which will initially be limited to driving directions in the U.S., will be free for consumers.[25]

ENDNOTES

[1] TomTom AR-08. TomTom Annual Report 2008. December 2008.

[2] TomTom Challenge. <http://www.tomtomchallenge.nl/resources/AMGATE_400083_1_TICH_R76719135691/>.

[3] TomTom Move Away from PNDs Nets Strong Q1 Results. REUTERS. 26 April 2010.

[4] TomTom. TomTom, Portable GPS Car Navigation Systems. <http://investors.tomtom.com/overview.cfm>.

[5] Compare GPS Sat Nav Systems. <http://www.satellitenavigation.org.uk/gps-manufacturers/tomtom/>. Daniel, Robert. TomTom Net Fell 61%, Revenue Off 19%. <http://www.foxbusiness.com/story/markets/industries/telecom/tomtom-net-fell–revenue/>.

[6] TomTom NV. <http://www.answers.com/topic/tomtom-n-v>.

[7] Thomson Reuters. TomTom Launches 2.9 bln Euro Bid for Tele Atlas. 19 November 2007. <http://www.reuters.com/article/technology-media-telco-SP/idUSL1839698320071119>.

[8] Advanced Integrated Solutions. TomTom and Advantage Integrated Solutions Partner to Deliver an Intelligent Fleet Routing Solution for Businesses. March 2009. <http://www.highbeam.com/doc/1G1-196311252.html>.

[9] TeleAtlas press release. <http://www.teleatlas.com/WhyTeleAtlas/Pressroom/PressReleases/TA_CT015133>.

[10] TomTom press release. TomTom and Avis Announce the First Pan-European Deal to Provide TomTom GO.

[11] *Boston Business.* <http://www.boston.com/business/ticker/2009/06/let_homer_simps.html)>.

[12] *Auto-Week.* Renault, TomTom Promise Cheap Navigation. <http://www.autoweek.com/article/20080929/free/809299989#ixzz0MQ8bKdYo>.

[13] Magellan website. <http://www.magellangps.com/about/>.

[14] Richards, David. *Smarthouse.* 17 June 2009. 29 July 2009 <http://www.smarthouse.com.au/Automotive/Navigation/P4P3H9J8>.

[15] Talaga, Tanya and Rob Ferguson. *TheStar.com.* 28 Oct 2008. 29 July 2009 <http://www.thestar.com/News/Ontario/article/525697>.

[16] ICTI. 29 July 2009 <http://www.toy-icti.org/>.

[17] *GPS Magazine.* 23 September 2007. 29 July 2009 <http://gpsmagazine.com/2007/09/gps_thefts_rise.php>.

[18] Webist Media. Web Ecoist. 17 August 2008. 29 July 2009 <http://webecoist.com/2008/08/17/a-brief-history-of-the-modern-green-movement/>.

[19] Jones, Nick. Gartner. 5 January 2009. 29 July 2009 <http://www.gartner.com/resources/168400/168438/findings_risks_of_gps_perfor_168438.pdf>.

[20] *US News.* 14 October 2008. 29 July 2009 <http://usnews.rankingsandreviews.com/cars-trucks/daily-news/081014-GPS-Devices-Banned-in-Egypt/>.

[21] Reuters. TomTom Inc. Recognized for Call Center Customer Satisfaction Excellence by J.D. Power. 7 January 2008. <http://www.reuters.com/article/pressRelease/idUS141391+07-Jan-2008+PRN20080107>.

[22] J.D. Power and Associates. Garmin Ranks Highest in Customer Satisfaction with Portable Navigation Devices. 23 October 2008. <http://www.jdpower.com/corporate/news/releases/pressrelease.aspx?ID=2008221>.

[23] Forrestor Research. Phone-Based Navigation Will Dominate By 2013. 27 March 2009.

[24] Kim, W. Chan and Mauborgne. *Blue Ocean Strategy.* Boston: Harvard Business School Press, 2005.

[25] © Thomson Reuters 2009. All rights reserved. Reporting by Alexei Oreskovic; editing Bernard Orr.

Apple Inc. in 2010

Lou Marino
The University of Alabama

John E. Gamble
University of South Alabama

Despite the effects of ongoing poor economic conditions in the United States, Apple Inc. celebrated record quarterly revenues and unit sales of computers during its third quarter of 2010. In addition, the company's newly released iPad tablet computer had sold 3.3 million units between its April 3, 2010, launch and the June 26, 2010, quarter end. The company also sold 8.4 million iPhones during the quarter. Most of the smartphone units sold during the third quarter of 2010 were iPhone 3GS models since the new iPhone 4 launched only four days prior to the close of the quarter. Although there had been some criticism of the antenna design of the iPhone 4, more than 3 million iPhone 4 units had been purchased by July 16, 2010, with only 1.7 percent being returned by dissatisfied customers. By comparison, the iPhone 3GS had a 6 percent return rate.

Apple's chief operating officer, Tim Cook, commented to the *Wall Street Journal* that the company was selling iPads and iPhones "as fast as we can make them" and was "working around the clock to try to get supply and demand in balance."[1] Some analysts were projecting that Apple would sell nearly 12 million iPad tablet computers by year-end 2010. However, others were concerned that once Apple aficionados had purchased an iPad to complement their iPhone, iPod, or Mac, further sales growth might be difficult to achieve. A former Apple executive commented, "The first five million will be sold in a heartbeat. But let's see: you can't make a phone call with it, you can't take a picture with it, and you have to buy content that before now you were not willing to pay for. That seems tough to me."[2]

Analysts were also concerned with the general decline in iPod unit sales and worried that Apple might have to struggle to sustain its growth in the smartphone market. The iPod had been important in the company's resurgence in the past decade, but sustained growth in iPhone sales were critical to the company's financial performance, since iPhone sales accounted for $5.33 billion of the company's third-quarter 2010 revenues of $15.7 billion. Research in Motion (RIM) had been known for innovative smartphones since it introduced the BlackBerry in 1999, but Google's development of the Android operating system for smartphones had allowed HTC, LG, Nokia, and Samsung to introduce smartphones that matched many of the iPhone's best features. In addition, Microsoft's Windows Mobile 7 operating system, planned for a late-2010 launch, was expected to surpass some of the capabilities of the iPhone operating system. Google was also a growing threat to Apple, since many computer makers were developing new tablet computers similar to the iPad that would run the Android operating system; the two companies seemed to be headed for a future battle in mobile ads.

COMPANY HISTORY AND FINANCIAL PERFORMANCE

Steven Wozniak and Steven Jobs founded Apple Computer in 1976 when they began selling a crudely designed personal computer called the

Copyright © 2010 by Lou Marino. All rights reserved.

Apple I to Silicon Valley computer enthusiasts. Two years later, the partners introduced the first mass-produced personal computer (PC), the Apple II. The Apple II boasted the first color display and eventually sold more than 10,000 units. While the Apple II was relatively successful, the next revision of the product line, the Macintosh (Mac), would dramatically change personal computing through its user-friendly graphical user interface (GUI), which allowed users to interact with screen images rather than merely type text commands.

The Macintosh that was introduced in 1984 was hailed as a breakthrough in personal computing, but it did not have the speed, power, or software availability to compete with the PC that IBM had introduced in 1981. One of the reasons the Macintosh lacked the necessary software was that Apple put very strict restrictions on the Apple Certified Developer Program, which made it difficult for software developers to obtain Macs at a discount and receive informational materials about the operating system.

With the Mac faring poorly in the market, founder Steve Jobs became highly critical of the company's president and CEO, John Sculley, who had been hired by the board in 1983. Finally, in 1985, as Sculley was preparing to visit China, Jobs devised a boardroom coup to replace him. Sculley found out about the plan and canceled his trip. After Apple's board voted unanimously to keep Sculley in his position, Jobs, who was retained as chairman of the company but stripped of all decision-making authority, soon resigned. During the remainder of 1985, Apple continued to encounter problems and laid off one-fifth of its employees while posting its first ever quarterly loss.

Despite these setbacks, Apple kept bringing innovative products to the market, while closely guarding the secrets behind its technology. In 1987, Apple released a revamped Macintosh computer that proved to be a favorite in K–12 schools and with graphic artists and other users needing excellent graphics capabilities. However, by 1990, PCs running Windows 3.0 and Word for Windows were preferred by businesses and consumers and held a commanding 97+ percent share of the market for personal computers.

In 1991, Apple released its first-generation notebook computer, the PowerBook and, in 1993, Apple's board of directors opted to remove Sculley from the position of CEO. The board chose to place the chief operating officer, Michael Spindler, in the vacated spot. Under Spindler, Apple released the PowerMac family of PCs in 1994, the first Macs to incorporate the PowerPC chip, a very fast processor co-developed with Motorola and IBM. Even though the PowerMac family received excellent reviews by technology analysts, Microsoft's Windows 95 matched many of the capabilities of the Mac OS and prevented the PowerMac from gaining significant market share. In January 1996, Apple asked Spindler to resign and chose Gil Amelio, former president of National Semiconductor, to take his place.

During his first 100 days in office, Amelio announced many sweeping changes for the company. He split Apple into seven distinct divisions, each responsible for its own profit or loss, and he tried to better inform the developers and consumers of Apple's products and projects. Amelio acquired NeXT, the company Steve Jobs had founded upon his resignation from Apple in 1985. Steve Jobs was rehired by Apple as part of the acquisition. In 1997, after recording additional quarterly losses, Apple's board terminated Amelio's employment with the company and named Steve Jobs interim CEO.

Apple introduced the limited feature iMac in 1998 and the company's iBook line of notebook computers in 1999. The company was profitable in every quarter during 1998 and 1999, and its share price reached an all-time high in the upper $70 range. Jobs was named permanent CEO of Apple in 2000 and, in 2001, oversaw the release of the iPod. The iPod recorded modest sales until the 2003 launch of iTunes—the online retail store where consumers could legally purchase individual songs. By July 2004, 100 million songs had been sold and iTunes had a 70 percent market share among all legal online music download services. The tremendous success of the iPod helped transform Apple from a struggling computer company into a powerful consumer electronics company.

By 2005, consumers' satisfaction with the iPod had helped renew interest in Apple computers, with its market share in personal computers growing from a negligible share to 4 percent. The company also exploited consumer loyalty and satisfaction with the iPod to enter the market for smartphones with the 2007 launch of the iPhone.

Much of Apple's turnaround could be credited to Steve Jobs, who had idea after idea for how to improve the company and turn its performance around. He not only consistently pushed for innovative new ideas and products but also enforced several structural changes, including ridding the company of unprofitable segments and divisions.

The success of the turnaround could also be attributed to the efforts of Tim Cook, Apple's chief operating officer. While Jobs provided the vision for the organization, Cook and the other members of the executive staff and the board of directors were responsible for ensuring that all operations of Apple ran efficiently and smoothly. Between mid-2008 and mid-2009, when Steve Jobs took a leave of absence to receive a liver transplant, Cook took on the role of acting CEO.

A summary of Apple's financial performance for fiscal years 2005 through 2009 is provided in Exhibit 1. The company's net sales by operating segment and product line and unit sales by product line for 2005 through 2009 are provided in Exhibit 2.

OVERVIEW OF THE PERSONAL COMPUTER INDUSTRY

The personal computer industry was relatively consolidated, with five sellers accounting for 78.5 percent of the U.S. shipments and 60.3 percent of worldwide shipments in 2009—see Exhibit 3. Prior to the onset of the recession that began in 2008, the PC industry was expected to grow at a rate of 5–6 percent, to reach $354 billion by 2012. However, the effects of the recession caused a dramatic decline in industry revenues in 2008 and 2009.

PC industry shipments grew by a healthy 22.4 percent during the second quarter of 2010 as businesses were forced to replace aging computers. The sharp spike in shipments was not expected to continue throughout the year, with analysts expecting a 12.6 percent increase in worldwide shipments for the full year 2010. PC shipments in emerging markets were expected to grow at 18.5 percent to allow demand in emerging markets to overtake demand for PCs in developed countries by the end of 2010. Shipments of PCs in developed countries were expected to increase by only 7.2 percent in 2010 and were not expected to reach double-digit rates until 2011. Industry revenues were projected to grow more slowly than shipments because average selling prices had declined steadily since 2008.

Both businesses and consumers were tending to replace desktop PCs with portable PCs such as laptops and netbooks. Total shipments of portable PCs grew by 18.4 percent in 2009, with consumer purchases of portable PCs growing by 38 percent during the year. Low-end laptops and netbooks accounted for the majority of consumer portable PC sales in 2009. The sale of desktop computers was expected to decline in all country markets except emerging markets in Asia, which would allow portable PCs to make up 70 percent of industry shipments by 2012.

APPLE'S COMPETITIVE POSITION IN THE PERSONAL COMPUTER INDUSTRY

Even though a larger percentage of Apple's revenues were increasingly coming from noncomputer products, the company still saw computers as its core business. Apple's proprietary operating system and strong graphics-handling capabilities differentiated Macs from PCs, but many consumers and business users who owned PCs were hesitant to purchase a Mac because of Apple's premium pricing and because of the learning curve involved with mastering its proprietary operating system. The company's market share in the United States had improved from 4 percent in 2005 to 8 percent in 2009 primarily because of the success of the iPod and iPhone. These products created a halo effect whereby some consumers (but not business users) switched to Apple computers after purchasing an iPod or iPhone.

Apple's computer product line consisted of several models in various configurations. Its desktop lines included the Mac Pro (aimed at professional and business users); the iMac (targeted toward consumer, educational, and business use); and Mac mini (made specifically for consumer use). Apple had three notebook product

Exhibit 1   Summary of Apple, Inc.'s Financial Performance, 2005–2009 ($ millions, except share amounts)

Income Statement Data	2009	2008	2007	2006	2005
Net Sales					
Domestic	$ 19,870	$ 18,469	$ 14,128	$ 11,486	$ 8,334
International	16,667	14,010	9,878	7,829	5,597
Total net sales	36,537	32,479	24,006	19,315	13,931
Costs and Expenses					
Cost of sales	23,397	21,334	15,852	13,717	9,889
Research and development (R&D)	1,333	1,109	782	712	535
Selling, general and administrative (SG&A)	4,149	3,761	2,963	2,433	1,864
Total operating expenses	5,482	4,870	3,745	3,145	2,399
Operating income	7,658	6,275	4,409	2,453	1,643
Other income and expense	326	620	599	365	165
Income before provision for income taxes	7,984	6,895	5,008	2,818	1,808
Provision for income taxes	2,280	2,061	1,512	829	480
Net income	$ 5,704	$ 4,834	$ 3,496	$ 1,989	$ 1,328
Earnings per common share—diluted	$6.29	$5.36	$3.93	$2.27	$1.55
Shares used in computing earnings per share—diluted (in thousands)	907,005	902,139	889,292	877,526	856,878

Balance Sheet Data (as of September 30)					
Cash, cash equivalents, and short-term investments	$ 23,464	$ 24,490	$ 15,386	$ 10,110	$ 8,261
Accounts receivable, net	3,361	2,422	1,637	1,252	895
Inventories	455	509	346	270	165
Property, plant, and equipment, net	2,954	2,455	1,832	1,281	817
Total assets	53,851	39,572	25,347	17,205	11,516
Current liabilities	19,284	14,092	9,299	6,443	3,487
Noncurrent liabilities	6,737	4,450	1,516	778	601
Shareholders' equity	$ 27,832	$ 21,030	$ 14,532	$ 9,984	$ 7,428

Source: Apple Inc., 2007 and 2009 10-K reports.

Exhibit 2   Apple, Inc.'s Net Sales by Operating Segment, Net Sales by Product, and Unit Sales by Product, 2005–2009 ($ millions)

	2009	2008	2007	2006	2005
Net Sales by Operating Segment					
Americas net sales	$16,142	$14,573	$11,596	$ 9,415	$ 6,950
Europe net sales	9,365	7,622	5,460	4,096	3,073
Japan net sales	1,831	1,509	1,082	1,211	920
Retail net sales	6,574	6,315	4,115	3,246	2,350
Other Segments net sales [a]	2,625	2,460	1,753	1,347	998
Total net sales	$36,537	$32,479	$24,006	$19,315	$13,931
Net Sales by Product					
Desktops [b]	$ 4,308	$ 5,603	$ 4,020	$ 3,319	$ 3,436
Portables [c]	9,472	8,673	6,294	4,056	2,839
Total Macintosh net sales	13,780	14,276	10,314	7,375	6,275
iPod	8,091	9,153	8,305	7,375	4,540
Other music related products and services [d]	4,036	3,340	2,496	1,885	899
iPhone and related products and services [e]	6,754	1,844	123	—	—
Peripherals and other hardware [f]	1,470	1,659	1,260	1,100	1,126
Software, service, and other sales [g]	2,406	2,207	1,508	1,279	1,091
Total net sales	$36,537	$32,479	$24,006	$19,315	$13,931
Unit Sales by Product:					
Desktops [b]	3,182	3,712	2,714	2,434	2,520
Portables [c]	7,214	6,003	4,337	2,869	2,014
Total Macintosh unit sales	10,396	9,715	7,051	5,303	4,534
Net sales per Macintosh unit sold [h]	$1,326	$1,469	$1,463	$1,391	$1,384
iPod unit sales	54,132	54,828	51,630	39,409	22,497
Net sales per iPod unit sold [i]	$149	$167	$161	$195	$202
iPhone unit sales	20,731	11,627	1,389	—	—

[a]Other segments include Asia Pacific and FileMaker.

[b]Includes iMac, eMac, Mac mini, Power Mac, and Xserve product lines.

[c]Includes MacBook, MacBook Pro, iBook. and PowerBook product lines.

[d]Consists of iTunes Music Store sales, iPod services, and Apple-branded and third-party iPod accessories.

[e]Derived from handset sales, carrier agreements, and Apple-branded and third-party iPhone accessories.

[f]Includes sales of Apple-branded and third-party displays, wireless connectivity and networking solutions, and other hardware accessories.

[g]Includes sales of Apple-branded operating system, application software, third-party software, AppleCare, and Internet services.

[h]Derived by dividing total Macintosh net sales by total Macintosh unit sales.

[i]Derived by dividing total iPod net sales by total iPod unit sales.

Source: Apple Inc., 2007 and 2009 10-K reports.

Exhibit 3 U.S. and Global Market Shares of Leading PC Vendors, 2000 and 2005–2009

A. U.S. Market Shares of the Leading PC Vendors, 2000 and 2005–2009

2009 Rank	Vendor	2009 Shipments (in 000s)	2009 Market Share	2008 Shipments (in 000s)	2008 Market Share	2007 Shipments (in 000s)	2007 Market Share	2006 Shipments (in 000s)	2006 Market Share	2005 Shipments (in 000s)	2005 Market Share	2000 Shipments (in 000s)	2000 Market Share
1	Hewlett Packard[1]	18,781	26.9%	16,218	24.7%	16,759	23.9%	11,600	21.5%	12,456	19.5%	5,630	11.5%
2	Dell	17,099	24.5	19,276	29.4	19,645	28.0	20,472	31.2	21,466	33.6	9,645	19.7
	Compaq[1]	—		—		—		—		—		7,761	15.9
3	Acer[1]	7,983	11.4	6,106	9.3	3,860	5.5	1,421	2.2	n.a.	n.a.	n.a.	n.a.
4	Apple	5,579	8.0	5,158	7.9	4,081	5.8	3,109	4.7	2,555	4.0	n.a.	n.a.
5	Toshiba	5,379	7.7	3,788	5.8	3,509	5.0	2,843	4.3	2,327	3.6	n.a.	n.a.
	Others	15,008	21.5	15,026	22.9	22,235	31.7	23,350	35.7	25,070	39.2	18,959	38.8
	All vendors	69,829	100.0%	65,571	100.0%	70,088	100.0%	65,481	100.0%	63,874	100.0%	48,900	100.0%

B. Worldwide Market Shares of the Leading PC Vendors, 2000 and 2005–2009

2009 Rank	Vendor	2009 Shipments (in 000s)	2009 Market Share	2008 Shipments (in 000s)	2008 Market Share	2007 Shipments (in 000s)	2007 Market Share	2006 Shipments (in 000s)	2006 Market Share	2005 Shipments (in 000s)	2005 Market Share	2000 Shipments (in 000s)	2000 Market Share
1	Hewlett Packard[1]	59,942	20.3%	54,293	18.9%	50,526	18.8%	38,838	16.5%	32,575	15.7%	10,327	7.4%
2	Dell	38,416	13.1	42,388	14.7	39,993	14.9	39,094	16.6	37,755	18.2	14,801	10.6
	Compaq[1]	—		—		—		—		—		17,399	12.5
3	Acer[2]	38,377	13.0	31,377	10.9	21,206	7.9	13,594	5.8	9,845	4.7	n.a.	n.a.
4	Lenovo/IBM[3]	24,887	8.5	21,870	7.6	20,224	7.5	16,609	7.1	12,979	6.2	9,308	6.7
5	Toshiba	15,878	5.4	13,727	4.8	10,936	4.1	9,292	3.9	7,234	3.5	n.a.	n.a.
	Others	116,709	39.7	123,910	43.1	126,075	46.9	117,971	50.1	107,450	51.7	80,640	58.0
	All vendors	294,208	100.0%	287,566	100.0%	268,960	100.0%	235,397	100.0%	207,837	100.0%	139,057	100.0%

n.a. = not available; sales and market shares for these companies in the years where n.a. appears are included in the "Others" category because the company was not in the top 5 in shipments or market share.

[1]Compaq was acquired by Hewlett-Packard in May 2002.

[2]Acer acquired Gateway in 2007 and Packard Bell in 2008. Data for Acer includes shipments for Gateway starting in Q4 2007 and shipments for Packard Bell starting in Q1 2008, and only Acer data for prior periods.

[3]Lenovo, a Chinese computer company, completed the acquisition of IBM's PC business in 2005. The numbers for Lenovo/IBM for 2000 reflect sales of IBM branded PCs only; the numbers for 2005–2009 reflect their combined sales beginning in the second quarter of 2005. In 2007, Lenovo rebranded all IBM PCs as Lenovo.

Source: International Data Corp.

lines as well: MacBook Pro (for professional and advanced consumer users), the MacBook (designed for education users and consumers), and the MacBook Air (designed for professional and consumer users).

The MacBook Air was Apple's most recent notebook introduction. The MacBook Air was designed to target users who valued both portability and power. The notebook featured a 13.3-inch screen, a full-size keyboard, a built-in video camera, and cutting-edge wireless connectivity. This sleek notebook measured only 0.76 inches at its maximum height when closed and weighed only three pounds. The MacBook Air had won critical acclaim for both its design and its ease of use, and was one of the products helping Apple gain ground in the competitive computer industry. All Apple computers were priced at a steep premium compared to PCs and laptops offered by Dell, HP, and other rivals. The company lowered the prices of all its computer models by 10 percent or more in June 2009, with the price of the MacBook Pro falling to $1,199 and the MacBook Air getting a $300 price cut, to $1,499.

APPLE'S RIVALS IN THE PERSONAL COMPUTER INDUSTRY

Hewlett-Packard

Hewlett-Packard (HP) was broadly diversified across segments of the computer industry with business divisions focused on information technology consulting services, large enterprise systems, software, personal computers, printers and other imaging devices, and financial services. The company's Personal Systems Group (PSG), which manufactured and marketed HP and Compaq desktop computers and portable computers, was its largest division, accounting for revenues of $35.3 billion in 2009. HP recorded total net revenues of $114.6 billion in 2009, with information technology services contributing nearly $34.7 billion, imaging and printing devices contributing $24 billion, and enterprise systems accounting for about $15.4 billion. The company's financial services and software business units accounted for sales of about $6 billion in 2009.

HP's sales of personal computers declined by 16.5 percent between 2008 and 2009 as the recession forced consumers and businesses to reduce expenditures and capital investments. Handheld computers and workstations were affected most by the recession, with sales declining by 52.2 percent and 33.7 percent, respectively, during 2009. The company's sales of desktop computers were affected not only by the recession but also by business users' and consumers' growing preference for portable computers over desktop models. HP portable computers were harmed least by the recession, with a 10.8 percent decline in sales between 2008 and 2009. HP did sustain some growth in emerging markets despite the recession in developed countries. Exhibit 4 provides the revenue contribution by PSG product line for 2005 through 2009.

Dell Inc.

Dell Inc. was the world's second-largest seller of personal computers, with revenues of $52.9 billion for the fiscal year ending January 29, 2010.

Exhibit 4   **Hewlett-Packard Personal Systems Group, Net Revenue ($ millions)**

Product	2009	2008	2007	2006	2005
Notebooks	$20,210	$22,657	$17,650	$12,005	$ 9,763
Desktop PCs	12,864	16,626	15,889	14,641	14,406
Workstations	1,261	1,902	1,721	1,368	1,195
Handhelds	172	360	531	650	836
Other	798	750	618	502	541
Total	$35,305	$42,295	$36,409	$29,166	$26,741

Source: Hewlett-Packard, 2007 and 2008 10-K reports.

Exhibit 5 **Dell's Revenues by Product Category, Fiscal 2008–Fiscal 2010 ($ millions)**

Fiscal Year Ended	January 29, 2010		January 30, 2009		February 1, 2008	
	Dollars	% of Revenue	Dollars	% of Revenue	Dollars	% of Revenue
Servers and networking	$ 6,032	11%	$ 6,512	11%	$ 6,486	11%
Storage	2,192	4	2,667	4	2,429	4
Services	5,622	11	5,351	9	4,980	8
Software and peripherals	9,499	18	10,603	17	9,927	16
Mobility	16,610	31	18,604	30	17,961	29
Desktop PCs	12,947	25	17,364	29	19,350	32
Totals	$52,902	100%	$61,101	100%	$61,133	100%

Source: Dell Inc., 2010 10-K report.

Exhibit 5 presents Dell's revenues by product category for fiscal 2008 through fiscal 2010. The recession significantly affected Dell's financial performance in late 2008, when its fourth-quarter sales declined by 48 percent from the same period in the prior year. The revenue decline was a result of an overall decline in unit sales and strong price competition in both desktop PCs and portables. In addition, Dell's net earnings fell from $2.9 billion in fiscal 2008 to $2.5 billion in fiscal 2009 to $1.4 billion in fiscal 2010. The company offered a wide range of desktop computers and portables, ranging from low-end, low-priced models to state-of-the-art, high-priced models. The company also offered servers; workstations; peripherals such as printers, monitors, and projectors; and Wi-Fi products.

Acer

Taiwan-based Acer was the world's second-largest portable computer provider and third-largest desktop computer manufacturer in 2010. Acer's 2009 consolidated revenues rose by approximately 13 percent from the previous year to reach $18.3 billion, while operating income increased by 17 percent to reach $488 million. Its 40.5 percent annual growth in global PC shipments between 2005 and 2009 ranked first among the industry's leading sellers. The company's largest and one of its fastest-growing geographic segments was the Europe/Middle East/Africa segment, which accounted for 52 percent of the company's PC, desktop, and notebook sales. A summary of the company's financial performance between 2006 and 2009 is presented in Exhibit 6.

Exhibit 6 **Financial Summary for Acer Incorporated, 2006–2009 ($ thousands)**

	2009	2008	2007	2006
Revenue	$18,264,125	$16,186,102	$15,252,801	$10,577,113
Gross profit	1,855,993	1,697,374	1,565,278	1,150,865
Operating income	488,102	416,962	336,211	224,993
Operating margin	2.7%	2.6%	2.2%	2.1%
Income before income taxes	476,759	438,723	498,736	408,481
Net income	$361,248	$347,919	$427,774	$308,080

Source: Acer Incorporated Financial Snapshot, http://www.acer-group.com/public/Investor_Relations/financial_snapshot.htm.

Acer's multibrand strategy—which positioned Acer, Gateway, eMachines, and Packard Bell at distinct price points in the market for PCs—had helped it become one of the fastest-growing vendors in the United States. The company based its competitive strategy on its four pillars of success: a winning business model, competitive products, an innovative marketing strategy, and an efficient operation model. The company's computer offering included desktop and mobile PCs, LCD monitors, servers and storage, and high-definition TVs and projectors. In 2009, the company entered the market for smartphones with the launch of its Liquid line of stylish, high-end smartphones, which used Google's Android operating system.

APPLE'S COMPETITIVE POSITION IN THE PERSONAL MEDIA PLAYER INDUSTRY

Although Apple didn't introduce the first portable digital music player, the company held a 73 percent market share digital music players in 2010 and the name iPod had become a generic term used to describe digital media players. When Apple launched its first iPod, many critics did not give the product much of a chance for success, given its fairly hefty price tag of $399. However, the iPod's sleek styling, ease of use, and eventual price decreases allowed it to develop such high levels of customer satisfaction and loyalty that rivals found it difficult to gain traction in the marketplace.

The most popular portable players in 2010 not only played music but could be connected to Wi-Fi networks to play videos, access the Internet, view photos, or listen to FM high-definition radio. The iPod Touch was the best-selling media player in 2010, but electronics sector reviewers generally agreed that Microsoft's Zune, Archos's Vision models, and Sony's X-series media players compared quite favorably to the iPod Touch. In addition, electronics reviewers found that inexpensive MP3 music players offered by SanDisk, Creative, iRiver, and others generally performed as well as Apple's more basic iPod models. However, none of Apple's key rivals in the media player industry

had been able to achieve a market share greater than 5 percent in 2010. Most consumers did not find many convincing reasons to consider any brand of media player other than Apple.

In 2010, Apple offered four basic styles in the iPod product line:

- *The iPod Shuffle*—a basic flash-based player with no screen, FM radio, or voice recorder. The 4 gigabyte (GB) model was capable of storing 1,000 songs, and its rechargeable lithium polymer battery provided up to 10 hours of playback time.

- *The iPod Nano*—a multimedia player offered in 8 GB (8 hours of video or 2,000 songs) and 16 GB (16 hours of video or 4,000 songs) sizes that used a click wheel interface to navigate the player's controls. It allowed users to view photos and videos as well as to listen to music in Apple's Advanced Audio Coding (AAC) format, and it provided up to 24 hours of music playback and 5 hours of video playback on a single charge.

- *The iPod Classic*—a hard-drive-based click-wheel-controlled multimedia player offered with a 160 GB hard drive that, similar to the smaller Nano, played music in Apple's AAC format and showed videos and photos. The 160 GB player held up to 40,000 songs or 200 hours of video and provided up to 36 hours of audio playback or 6 hours of video playback on a single charge.

- *The iPod Touch*—a multimedia flash memory player controlled though an innovative touch screen interface that was a feature of the iPhone. It was offered in 8 GB (1,750 songs, 10 hours of video), 32 GB (7,000 songs, 40 hours of video), and 64 GB (14,000 songs, 80 hours of video) sizes, and provided up to 30 hours of music playback and 6 hours of video playback on a single charge. This multimedia player featured a wide 3.5-inch screen and built-in Wi-Fi, which allowed users to connect to the Internet and access e-mail, buy music from the iTunes store, and surf the Web from wireless hotspots. Touch users also had access to maps, the weather, and stocks, and the ability to write notes to themselves. The Touch featured an accelerometer that detected when the Touch rotated and automatically changed the display from portrait to landscape.

iTunes

Aside from the iPod's stylish design and ease of use, another factor that contributed to the popularity of the iPod was Apple's iPod/iTunes combination. In 2010, more than 50 million customers visited the iTunes Store to purchase and download music, videos, movies, and television shows that could be played on iPods, iPhones, or Apple TV devices. (Apple TV was a device that allowed users to play iTunes content on televisions.) Also in 2010, Apple's iTunes Store recorded its 10-billionth download since its launch in 2003. Additionally, iTunes was the world's most popular online movie store, with customers purchasing and renting more than 50,000 movies each day. Apple did not offer an iTunes subscription service, although a July 2010 survey by research firm NPD Group found that 7 to 8 million iPod owners would have a strong interest in subscribing to a service that would allow them to stream iTunes music and videos.

The success of the iPod/iTunes combination gave iTunes a 69 percent share of the U.S. digital music market in 2010. Since downloads accounted for about 40 percent of all music sales in the United States, iTunes' commanding share of the digital music sales also gave it a 27 percent share of total U.S. music sales. Amazon.com was the second-largest seller of digital music in the United States, with an 8 percent share of the market. Amazon.com and Walmart were tied for second in total U.S. music sales, with 12 percent market shares.

APPLE'S COMPETITIVE POSITION IN THE MOBILE PHONE INDUSTRY

The first version of the iPhone was released on June 29, 2007, and had a multitouch screen with a virtual keyboard, a camera, and a portable media player (equivalent to the iPod) in addition to text messaging and visual voice mail. It also offered Internet services including e-mail, Web browsing (using access to Apple's Safari Web browser), and local Wi-Fi connectivity. More than 270,000 first-generation iPhones were sold during the first 30 hours of the product's launch. The iPhone was named *Time* magazine's Invention of the Year in 2007.

The iPhone 3G was released in 70 countries on July 11, 2008, and was available in the United States exclusively through AT&T Mobility. The iPhone 3G combined the functionality of a wireless phone and an iPod, and allowed users to access the Internet wirelessly at twice the speed of the previous version of the iPhone. Apple's new phone also featured a built-in global positioning system (GPS) and, in an effort to increase adoption by corporate users, was compatible with Microsoft Exchange.

The iPhone 3GS was introduced on June 19, 2009, and included all of the features of the iPhone 3G but could also launch applications and render Web pages twice as fast as the iPhone 3G. The iPhone 3GS also featured a 3-megapixel camera, video recording, voice control, and up to 32 GB of flash memory. The iPhone 4 was launched on June 24, 2010, with the 16 GB model priced at $199 on a two-year AT&T contract and the 32 GB model priced at $299 on a two-year AT&T contract. Upgrades over the 3GS included video-calling capabilities (only over a Wi-Fi network), a higher resolution display, a 5-megapixel camera including flash and zoom, 720p video recording, a longer-lasting battery, and a gyroscopic motion sensor to enable an improved gaming experience. The iPhone 4 sold more than 1.7 million units within three days of its launch.

Similar to the iTunes/iPod partnership, Apple launched the App Store for the iPhone. The App Store allowed developers to build applications for the iPhone and to offer them either for free or for a fee. In January 2010, more than 3 billion apps had been downloaded by iPhone and iPod Touch users. Both Apple and Google had begun to embed ads into mobile apps to both create additional revenue sources and to allow app developers to earn revenues from apps that could be downloaded free of charge.

While worldwide shipments of mobile phones declined from 1.19 billion in 2008 to 1.27 billion in 2009 because of poor economic conditions in the United States and many other major country markets, worldwide sales of mobile phones grew by 21.7 percent during the first quarter of 2010 as economies in most countries began to improve. However, industry analysts did not expect the 21.7 percent year-over-year sales increase during the first quarter of 2010 to continue throughout the year and projected annual sales growth of about 11 percent for 2010. The growth in shipments of smartphones during the first quarter of 2010 outpaced the growth in basic-feature phone shipments by a considerable margin. The shipments of smartphones grew by 56.7 percent during the first quarter of 2010, while shipments of basic-feature phones increased by 18.8 percent between the first quarter of 2009 and the first quarter of 2010. The rapid growth in demand for smartphones during early 2010 allowed Research in Motion (RIM) to become the first company producing only smartphones to become a Top 5 vendor in the industry—see Exhibit 7.

Developing countries such as China offered the greatest growth opportunities but also presented challenges to smartphone producers. For example, there were 700 million mobile phone users in China, but popular-selling models were quickly counterfeited, it was difficult to develop keyboards that included the thousands of commonly used characters in the Chinese language, and most consumers preferred inexpensive feature phones over smartphones. Nevertheless, many analysts expected China to account for 10 percent of worldwide smartphone shipments within the near term. Apple planned to begin selling the iPhone in China in 2010 through a network of 25 flagship stores located in the country's largest cities. The iPhone would be available in 80 countries by year-end 2010.

With the market for smartphones growing rapidly and supporting high average selling prices, competition was becoming more heated. Google's entry into the market with its Android operating system had allowed vendors such as HTC, Motorola, Acer, and Samsung to offer models that matched many of the features of the iPhone. In addition, Microsoft's Windows Mobile 7, which was planned for a late-2010 launch, was expected to exceed the capabilities of the iPhone operating system with live tiles of rotating pictures, e-mail messages, and social-networking feeds. In addition, smartphones operating on Windows Mobile 7 would have all of the functionality of a Zune media player just as the iPhone included all of the functionality of the iPod Touch. While iPhones and Android phones primarily targeted consumers enthralled with clever and helpful Web apps, RIM had built a number one position in the smartphone market by appealing to businesspeople who needed the ability to check e-mail; maintain appointment calendars; receive fax transmissions; and open, edit, and save Microsoft Office and Adobe PDF files. Hewlett-Packard entered the market for smartphones in May 2010 with its $1.2 billion acquisition of Palm. However, Palm had lost its edge in innovation years before and was primarily popular with users who had purchased Palm Pilots in the company's heyday. Exhibit 8 presents market shares for the leading smartphone brands between 2006 and the first quarter of 2010.

APPLE'S ENTRY INTO THE MARKET FOR TABLET COMPUTERS

Apple entered the market for tablet computers with its April 3, 2010, launch of the iPad. Tablet computers such as the iPad allowed users to access the Internet, read and send e-mail, view photos, watch videos, listen to music, read e-books, and play video games. In addition, Apple's iPad could run 11,000 apps developed specifically for the iPad and most of the 225,000-plus apps developed for the iPhone and iPod Touch. Apple sold more than 3 million iPads within the first 90 days the product was on the market. Industry analysts expected that 13 million tablet computers would be sold in 2010, with Apple accounting for almost all shipments of tablet computers. The market for tablet computers was expected to increase to 46 million units by 2014. By comparison, the market for portable PCs was expected to grow to 398 million units by 2014.

Tablet computers had been on the market since the late 1990s, but only Apple's version had gained any significant interest from consumers and business users. Previous-generation tablet computers required the use of a stylus to launch applications and enter information. Most users found the stylus interface to be an annoyance and preferred to use a smartphone or laptop when portability was required. Dell, Acer, Hewlett-Packard, and Nokia were all racing to get touch-screen tablet computers to market but would be unable to do so until very late 2010 or early 2011 because of the technological differences between tablet computers and PCs. Tablet computers were technologically similar to smartphones and

Exhibit 7   **Worldwide Market Shares of Leading Mobile Phone Vendors, 2000 and 2005–2009**

Q1 2010 Rank	Vendor	Q1 2010		2009		2008		2007	
		Shipments (in millions)	Market Share	Shipments (in millions)	Market Share	Shipments (in millions)	Market Share	Shipments (in millions)	Market Share
1	Nokia	107.8	36.6%	431.8	38.3%	468.4	39.4%	437.1	38.3%
2	Samsung	64.3	21.8	227.2	20.1	196.8	16.5	161.1	14.1
3	LG	27.1	9.2	117.9	10.5	100.8	8.5	80.5	7.1
4	RIM	10.6	3.6	n.a.	n.a.	n.a.	n.a.	n.a.	n.a.
5	Sony Ericsson	10.5	3.6	57.0	5.1	96.6	8.1	103.4	9.1
	Others	74.6	25.3	293.8	26.0	327.7	27.5	358.8	31.4
	All vendors	294.9	100.0%	1,127.8	100.0%	1,190.1	100.0%	1,140.9	100.0%

n.a. = not available; sales and market shares for these companies in the years where n.a. appears are included in the "Others" category because the company was not in the top 5 in shipments or market share.

Source: International Data Corp.

Exhibit 8   **U.S. Smartphone Platform Market Share Rankings, Selected Periods, September 2009–May 2010**

Smartphone Platform	Share of Smartphone Subscribers			
	September 2009	December 2009	February 2010	May 2010
RIM (BlackBerry)	42.6%	41.6%	42.1%	41.7%
Apple iPhone	24.1	25.3	25.4	24.4
Microsoft Windows Mobile	19.0	18.0	15.1	13.2
Google Android	2.5	5.2	9.0	13.0
Palm	8.3	6.1	5.4	4.8
Others	3.5	3.8	3.0	2.9
Total	100.0%	100.0%	100.0%	100.0%

Source: ComScore.com.

shared almost no components with PCs. The primary reason tablet computers could not use PC components was that the small size of tablet computers limited battery size. The small battery size prevented the use of energy-hungry PC components and required that tablet computers run the limited-capability microprocessors and operating systems found in smartphones. This minimal processing capability made tablet computers suitable only for viewing information and prevented the devices from running applications such as Microsoft Word, Excel, or PowerPoint.

Intel's new Atom microprocessor and Microsoft's Windows Mobile 7 would both be suitable for use in tablet computers and were expected to arrive to market in late 2010. PC manufacturers unwilling to wait for the development of the Atom and Windows Mobile 7 were designing tablet computers that used smartphone microprocessors and Google's Android operating system. Analysts believed that HP's 2010 acquisition of Palm was motivated more by the desire to use the Palm operating system in HP tablet computers than the company's interest in entering the smartphone market. Smartphone manufacturer Archos was the only vendor offering a viable competing product to the iPad in mid-2010. E-readers such as Amazon's Kindle were not considered direct competitors to the iPad since dedicated reading devices could not browse the Internet, view videos, play music, or perform other media tasks. In addition, e-readers carried prices in the $99–$189 range, which was considerably lower than the $499–$829 range charged by Apple for various iPad models.

APPLE'S PERFORMANCE GOING INTO THE FOURTH QUARTER OF 2010

Apple set a number of records with its third-quarter 2010 performance. The company's quarterly revenue of 15.7 billion was its highest-ever quarterly sales figure, and the company set a new record for quarterly shipments of computers, with 3.47 million Macs shipped during the quarter. The company also sold 3.3 million iPads by the June 26, 2010, close of the quarter. By comparison, it took the first iPod 20 months to reach 1 million units in sales—the iPad hit the 1-million-unit mark within 30 days of its April 3, 2010, launch. In addition, Apple sold 8.4 million iPhones during the third quarter of 2010, which was 61 percent more than what was sold during the same period in 2009. The increase in iPhone sales came primarily from sales of iPhone 3GS models since the iPhone 4 launched only four days before the quarter end. Unit sales for the iPod declined by 8.6 percent between the third quarter of 2009 and the third quarter of 2010, although iPod revenues increased by 4 percent to reach $1.5 billion as consumers purchased a higher percentage of iPod Touch models rather than lower-priced iPod Shuffle, iPod Nano, and iPod Classic models.

However, the company did face some concerns going into the fourth quarter of 2010. The U.S. Justice Department had launched a preliminary inquiry into the company's tactics in the digital music industry. Specifically, the government was investigating reports that Apple had discouraged music labels from participating in an Amazon promotion by threatening to withdraw marketing support for songs included in Amazon's promotion that were also sold by the iTunes Store. Also, Steve Jobs was called upon to personally intervene in a flap involving the antenna design of the iPhone 4. Shortly after the iPhone 4 launch, the media widely reported that the iPhone 4's antenna design

caused calls to be dropped if users touched the lower edges of the phone. The company reported that the company had received fewer returns of iPhone 4s than iPhone 3GS models at its launch. To calm the media frenzy that he dubbed "Antennagate," Steve Jobs called a press conference to announce that the company would provide free bumper cases to iPhone 4 buyers concerned with reception problems caused by touching the metal edge of the phone.

ENDNOTES

1 Quoted in "New Gadgets Power Apple Sales," *Wall Street Journal Online*, July 21, 2010.

2 Quoted in "Doing the iPad Math: Utility + Price + Desire," *New York Times*, April 2, 2010, p. B1.

Google's Strategy in 2010

John E. Gamble

University of South Alabama

Google was the leading Internet search firm in 2010, with 60+ percent market shares in both searches performed on computers and searches performed on mobile devices. Google's business model allowed advertisers to bid on search terms that would describe their product or service on a cost-per-impression (CPI) or cost-per-click (CPC) basis. Google's search-based ads were displayed near Google's search results and generated advertising revenues of nearly $22.9 billion in 2009. The company also generated revenues of $761 in 2009 from licensing fees charged to businesses that wished to install Google's search appliance on company intranets and from a variety of new ventures. New ventures were becoming a growing priority with Google management since the company dominated the market for search based ads and sought additional opportunities to sustain its extraordinary growth in revenues, earnings, and net cash provided by operations.

In 2008, Google had launched its Android operating system for mobile phones, which allowed wireless phone manufacturers such as LG, HTC, and Nokia to produce Internet-enabled phones boasting features similar to those available on Apple's iPhone. Widespread use of the Internet-enabled Android phones would not only help Google solidify its lead in mobile search but also allow the company to increase its share of banner ads and video ads displayed on mobile phones. Google had also entered into alliances with Intel, Sony, DISH Network, Logitech, and other firms to develop the technology and products required to launch Google TV. Google TV was scheduled for a fall 2010 launch and would allow users to search live network and cable programming; streaming videos from providers such as Netflix, Amazon Video On Demand, and YouTube; and recorded programs on a DVR. Perhaps the company's most ambitious strategic initiative in 2010 was its desire to change the market for commonly used business productivity applications such as word processing, spreadsheets, and presentation software from the desktop to the Internet. Information technology analysts believed that the market for such applications—collectively called cloud computing—could grow to $95 billion by 2013.

While Google's growth initiatives seemed to take the company into new industries and thrust it into competition with companies ranging from AT&T to Microsoft to Apple, its CEO, Eric Schmidt, saw the new ventures as natural extensions of the company's mission to "organize the world's information and make it universally accessible and useful."[1] In a July 2010 interview with the *Telegraph,* Schmidt commented that Google's new ventures into mobile devices, television search, and cloud computing would allow the company to "organize the world's information on any device and in any way that we can figure out to do it."[2] In July 2010, it was yet to be determined to what extent Google's new initiatives would contribute to the company's growth. Some industry analysts preferred that Google focus on improving its search technology to protect its competitive advantage in search and thereby its key revenue source. There was also a concern among some that, as the company pushed harder

Copyright © 2011 by John E. Gamble. All rights reserved.

to sustain its impressive historical growth rates, it had backed away from its commitment to "make money without doing evil."[3] While free-speech advocates had criticized Google for aiding China in its Internet censorship practices since its 2006 entry into China, authorities in the United States, Canada, Australia, Germany, Italy, the United Kingdom, and Spain were conducting investigations into Google's Street View data collection practices. It had been discovered that while Google's camera cars photographed homes and businesses along city streets, the company also captured personal data from Wi-Fi networks in the photographed homes and businesses. In addition, the U.S. House Oversight Committee was in the first phase of an investigation into Google's lobbying efforts to encourage the Obama administration to institute new policies and regulations that would be favorable to the company and the development of its new ventures.

COMPANY HISTORY

The development of Google's search technology began in January 1996 when Stanford University computer science graduate students Larry Page and Sergey Brin collaborated to develop a new search engine. They named the new search engine BackRub because of its ability to rate websites for relevancy by examining the number of back links pointing to the website. The approach for assessing the relevancy of websites to a particular search query used by other websites at the time was based on examining and counting metatags and keywords included on various websites. By 1997, the search accuracy of BackRub had allowed it to gain a loyal following among Silicon Valley Internet users. Yahoo cofounder David Filo was among the converted, and in 1998 he convinced Brin and Page to leave Stanford to focus on making their search technology the backbone of a new Internet company.

BackRub would be renamed Google, which was a play on the word *googol*—a mathematical term for a number represented by the numeral 1 followed by 100 zeros. Brin and Page's adoption of the new name reflected their mission to organize a seemingly infinite amount of information on the Internet. In August 1998, a Stanford professor arranged for Brin and Page to meet at his home with a potential angel investor to demonstrate the Google search engine. The investor, who had been a founder of Sun Microsystems, was immediately impressed with Google's search capabilities but was too pressed for time to hear much of their informal presentation. The investor stopped the two during the presentation and suggested, "Instead of us discussing all the details, why don't I just write you a check?"[4] The two partners held the investor's $100,000 check, made payable to Google Inc., for two weeks while they scrambled to set up a corporation named Google Inc. and open a corporate bank account. The two officers of the freshly incorporated company went on to raise a total of $1 million in venture capital from family, friends, and other angel investors by the end of September 1998.

Even with a cash reserve of $1 million, the two partners ran Google on a shoestring budget, with its main servers built by Brin and Page from discounted computer components and its four employees operating out of a garage owned by a friend of the founders. By year-end 1998, Google's beta version was handling 10,000 search queries per day and *PC Magazine* had named the company to its list of "Top 100 Web Sites and Search Engines for 1998."

The new company recorded successes at a lightning-fast pace, with the search kernel answering more than 500,000 queries per day and Red Hat agreeing to become the company's first search customer in early 1999. Google attracted an additional $25 million in funding from two leading Silicon Valley venture capital firms by mid-year 1999 to support further growth and enhancements to Google's search technology. The company's innovations in 2000 included wireless search technology, search capabilities in 10 languages, and a Google Toolbar browser plug-in that allowed computer users to search the Internet without first visiting a Google-affiliated Web portal or Google's home page. Features added through 2004 included Google News, Google Product Search, Google Scholar, and Google Local. The company also expanded its index of Web pages to more than 8 billion and increased its country domains to more than 150 by 2004. Google also further expanded its products for mobile phones with a short message service (SMS) feature that allowed mobile phone users to send a search request to Google as a text message. After submitting the search request to 466453 (google), a mobile phone user would receive a text message from Google providing results to his or her query.

The Initial Public Offering

Google's April 29, 2004, initial public offering (IPO) registration became the most talked-about planned offering involving an Internet company since the dot-com bust of 2000. The registration announced Google's intention to raise as much as $3.6 billion from the issue of 25.7 million shares through an unusual Dutch auction. Among the 10 key tenets of Google's philosophy (presented in Exhibit 1) was "You can make money without doing evil."[5] The choice of a Dutch auction stemmed from this philosophy, since Dutch auctions allowed potential investors to place bids for shares regardless of size. The choice of a Dutch auction was also favorable to Google since it involved considerably lower investment banking and underwriting fees and few or no commissions for brokers.

At the conclusion of the first day of trading, Google's shares had appreciated by 18 percent to make Brin and Page each worth approximately $3.8 billion. Also, an estimated 900 to 1,000 Google employees were worth at least $1 million, with 600 to 700 holding at least $2 million in Google stock. On average, each of Google's 2,292 staff members held approximately $1.7 million in company stock, excluding the holdings of the top five executives. Stanford University also enjoyed a $179.5 million windfall from its stock holdings granted for its early investment in Brin and Page's search engine. Some of Google's early contractors and consultants also profited handsomely from forgoing fees in return for stock options in the company. One such contractor was Abbe Patterson, who took options for 4,000 shares rather than a $5,000 fee for preparing a PowerPoint presentation and speaking notes for one of Brin and Page's first presentations to venture capitalists. After two splits and four days of trading, her 16,000 shares were worth $1.7 million.[6] The company executed a second public offering of 14,159,265 shares of common stock in September 2005. The number of shares issued represented the first eight digits to the right of the decimal point for the value of π (pi). The issue added more than $4 billion to Google's liquid assets.

Exhibit 2 tracks the performance of Google's common shares between August 19, 2004, and July 2010.

Google Feature Additions between 2005 and 2010

Google used its vast cash reserves to make strategic acquisitions that might lead to the development of new Internet applications offering advertising opportunities. Google Earth was launched in 2005 after the company acquired Keyhole, a digital mapping company, in 2004. Google Earth and its companion software Google Maps allowed Internet users to search and view satellite images of any location in the world. The feature was enhanced in 2007 with the addition of street-view images taken by traveling Google camera cars. Digital images, webcam feeds, and videos captured by Internet users could be linked to locations displayed by Google Maps. Real estate listings and short personal messages could also be linked to Google Maps locations. In 2010, Google further enhanced Google Maps with the inclusion of an Earth View mode that allowed users to view 3D images of various locations from the ground level. Other search features added to Google between 2005 and 2010 that users found particularly useful included Book Search, Music Search, Video Search, and the expansion of Google News to include archived news articles dating to 1900.

Google also expanded its website features beyond search functionality to include its Gmail software, a Web-based calendar, Web-based document and spreadsheet applications, its Picasa Web photo albums, and a translation feature that accommodated 51 languages. The company also released services for mobile phone uses such as Mobile Web Search, Blogger Mobile, Gmail, Google News, and Maps for Mobile. A complete list of Google services and tools for computers and mobile phones in 2010 is presented in Exhibit 3.

GOOGLE'S BUSINESS MODEL

Google's business model had evolved since the company's inception to include revenue beyond the licensing fees charged to corporations needing search capabilities on company intranets or

Exhibit 1   **The 10 Principles of Google's Corporate Philosophy**

1. **Focus on the user and all else will follow.**

   From its inception, Google has focused on providing the best user experience possible. While many companies claim to put their customers first, few are able to resist the temptation to make small sacrifices to increase shareholder value. Google has steadfastly refused to make any change that does not offer a benefit to the users who come to the site:

   - The interface is clear and simple.
   - Pages load instantly.
   - Placement in search results is never sold to anyone.
   - Advertising on the site must offer relevant content and not be a distraction.

   By always placing the interests of the user first, Google has built the most loyal audience on the web. And that growth has come not through TV ad campaigns, but through word of mouth from one satisfied user to another.

2. **It's best to do one thing really, really well.**

   Google does search. With one of the world's largest research groups focused exclusively on solving search problems, we know what we do well, and how we could do it better. Through continued iteration on difficult problems, we've been able to solve complex issues and provide continuous improvements to a service already considered the best on the web at making finding information a fast and seamless experience for millions of users. Our dedication to improving search has also allowed us to apply what we've learned to new products, including Gmail, Google Desktop, and Google Maps.

3. **Fast is better than slow.**

   Google believes in instant gratification. You want answers and you want them right now. Who are we to argue? Google may be the only company in the world whose stated goal is to have users leave its website as quickly as possible. By fanatically obsessing on shaving every excess bit and byte from our pages and increasing the efficiency of our serving environment, Google has broken its own speed records time and again.

4. **Democracy on the web works.**

   Google works because it relies on the millions of individuals posting websites to determine which other sites offer content of value. Instead of relying on a group of editors or solely on the frequency with which certain terms appear, Google ranks every web page using a breakthrough technique called PageRank™. PageRank evaluates all of the sites linking to a web page and assigns them a value, based in part on the sites linking to them. By analyzing the full structure of the web, Google is able to determine which sites have been "voted" the best sources of information by those most interested in the information they offer.

5. **You don't need to be at your desk to need an answer.**

   The world is increasingly mobile and unwilling to be constrained to a fixed location. Whether it's through their PDAs, their wireless phones or even their automobiles, people want information to come to them.

6. **You can make money without doing evil.**

   Google is a business. The revenue the company generates is derived from offering its search technology to companies and from the sale of advertising displayed on Google and on other sites across the web. However, you may have never seen an ad on Google. That's because Google does not allow ads to be displayed on our results pages unless they're relevant to the results page on which they're shown. So, only certain searches produce sponsored links above or to the right of the results. Google firmly believes that ads can provide useful information if, and only if, they are relevant to what you wish to find.

   Advertising on Google is always clearly identified as a "Sponsored Link." It is a core value for Google that there be no compromising of the integrity of our results. We never manipulate rankings to put our partners higher in our search results. No one can buy better PageRank. Our users trust Google's objectivity and no short-term gain could ever justify breaching that trust.

7. **There's always more information out there.**

   Once Google had indexed more of the HTML pages on the Internet than any other search service, our engineers turned their attention to information that was not as readily accessible. Sometimes it was just a matter of integrating new databases, such as adding a phone number and address lookup and a business directory. Other efforts required a bit more creativity, like adding the ability to search billions of images and a way to view pages that were originally created as PDF files. The popularity of PDF results led us to expand the list of file types searched to include documents produced in a dozen formats such as Microsoft Word, Excel and PowerPoint. For wireless users, Google developed a unique way to translate HTML formatted files into a format that could be read by mobile devices. The list is not likely to end there as Google's researchers continue looking into ways to bring all the world's information to users seeking answers.

(Continued)

Exhibit 1   *(Concluded)*

8. The need for information crosses all borders.

Though Google is headquartered in California, our mission is to facilitate access to information for the entire world, so we have offices around the globe. To that end we maintain dozens of Internet domains and serve more than half of our results to users living outside the United States. Google search results can be restricted to pages written in more than 35 languages according to a user's preference. We also offer a translation feature to make content available to users regardless of their native tongue and for those who prefer not to search in English, Google's interface can be customized into more than 100 languages.

9. You can be serious without a suit.

Google's founders have often stated that the company is not serious about anything but search. They built a company around the idea that work should be challenging and the challenge should be fun. To that end, Google's culture is unlike any in corporate America, and it's not because of the ubiquitous lava lamps and large rubber balls, or the fact that the company's chef used to cook for the Grateful Dead. In the same way Google puts users first when it comes to our online service, Google Inc. puts employees first when it comes to daily life in our Googleplex headquarters. There is an emphasis on team achievements and pride in individual accomplishments that contribute to the company's overall success. Ideas are traded, tested and put into practice with an alacrity that can be dizzying. Meetings that would take hours elsewhere are frequently little more than a conversation in line for lunch and few walls separate those who write the code from those who write the checks. This highly communicative environment fosters a productivity and camaraderie fueled by the realization that millions of people rely on Google results. Give the proper tools to a group of people who like to make a difference, and they will.

10. Great just isn't good enough.

Always deliver more than expected. Google does not accept being the best as an endpoint, but a starting point. Through innovation and iteration, Google takes something that works well and improves upon it in unexpected ways. Google's point of distinction however, is anticipating needs not yet articulated by our global audience, then meeting them with products and services that set new standards. This constant dissatisfaction with the way things are is ultimately the driving force behind the world's best search engine.

Source: Google.com.

Exhibit 2   **Performance of Google's Stock Price, August 19, 2004, to July 2010**

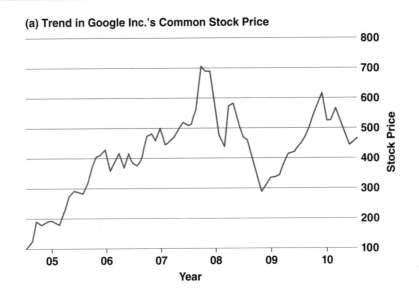

(a) Trend in Google Inc.'s Common Stock Price

(b) Performance of Google Inc.'s Stock Price Versus the S&P 500 Index

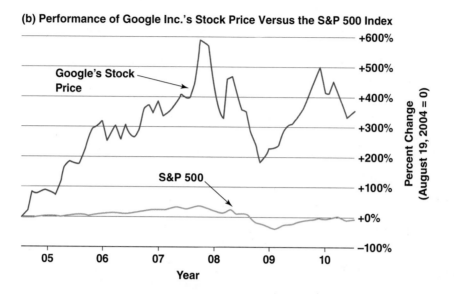

Exhibit 3 **Google' Services and Tools in 2010**

Search Features	
	Alerts Get email updates on the topics of your choice
	Blog Search Find blogs on your favorite topics
	Books Search the full text of books
	Checkout Complete online purchases more quickly and securely
	Google Chrome A browser built for speed, stability and security
	Custom Search Create a customized search experience for your community
	Desktop Search and personalize your computer
	Directory Search the web, organized by topic or category
	Earth Explore the world from your computer
	Finance Business info, news, and interactive charts

(Continued)

Search Features

GOOG-411
Find and connect with businesses from your phone

Google Health
Organize your medical records online

iGoogle
Add news, games and more to your Google homepage

Images
Search for images on the Web

Maps
View maps and directions

News
Search thousands of news stories

Patent Search
Search the full text of US Patents

Product Search
Search for stuff to buy

Scholar
Search scholarly papers

Toolbar
Add a search box to your browser

Trends
Explore past and present search trends

Videos
Search for videos on the Web

Web Search
Search billions of Web pages

Google Tools and Web Applications

Code
Developer tools, APIs and resources

Labs
Explore Google's technology playground

Blogger
Share your life online with a blog—it's fast, easy, and free

Google Tools and Web Applications

Calendar

Organize your schedule and share events with friends

Docs

Create and share your online documents, presentations, and spreadsheets

Google Mail

Fast, searchable email with less spam

Groups

Create mailing lists and discussion groups

Knol

Share what you know

orkut

Orkut

Meet new people and stay in touch with friends

Picasa

Find, edit and share your photos

Reader

Get all your blogs and news feeds fast

Sites

Create Web sites and secure group wikis

SketchUp

Build 3D models quickly and easily

Talk

IM and call your friends through your computer

Translate

View Web pages in other languages

YouTube

Watch, upload and share videos

Google Mobile Applications

Maps for mobile

View maps, your location and get directions on your phone

Search for mobile

Search Google wherever you are

Source: Google.com.

websites. The 2000 development of keyword-targeted advertising expanded its business model to include revenues from the placement of highly targeted text-only sponsor ads adjacent to its search results. Google was able to target its ads to specific users based on the user's browsing history. The addition of advertising-based revenue allowed Google to increase annual revenues from $220,000 in 1999 to more than $86 million in 2001. A summary of Google's financial performance between 2001 and 2009 is presented in Exhibit 4. The company's balance sheets for 2008 and 2009 are presented in Exhibit 5.

Google Search Appliance

Google's search technology could be integrated into a third party's website or intranet if search functionality was important to the customer. Google's Site Search allowed enterprises ranging from small businesses to public companies to license Google's search appliance for use on their websites for as little as $100 per year. The Google Search Appliance was designed for use on corporate intranets to allow employees to search company documents. The Search Appliance included a variety of security features to ensure that only employees with proper authority were able to view restricted documents. The Google Mini Search Appliance was designed for small businesses with 50,000 to 300,000 documents stored on local PCs and servers. The Google Mini hardware and software package could be licensed online (at www.google.com/enterprise/mini) at prices ranging from $2,990 to $9,900, depending on document count capability. Google's more robust search appliance had a document count capability of up to 30 million documents and was designed for midsized to global businesses. Licensing fees for the Google Search appliance ranged from $30,000 to $600,000, depending on document count capability.

AdWords

Google AdWords allowed advertisers, either independently through Google's automated tools or with the assistance of Google's marketing teams, to create text-based ads that would appear alongside Google search results. AdWords users could evaluate the effectiveness of their advertising expenditures with Google through the use of performance reports that tracked the effectiveness of each ad. Google also offered a keyword targeting program that suggested synonyms for keywords entered by advertisers, a traffic estimator that helped potential advertisers anticipate charges, and multiple payment options that included charges to credit cards, debit cards, and monthly invoicing.

Larger advertisers were offered additional services to help run large, dynamic advertising campaigns. Such assistance included the availability of specialists with expertise in various industries to offer suggestions for targeting potential customers and identifying relevant keywords. Google's advertising specialists helped develop ads for customers that would increase click-through rates and purchase rates. Google also offered its large advertising customers bulk posting services that helped launch and manage campaigns including ads using hundreds or thousands of keywords.

Google's search-based ads were priced using an auction system that allowed advertisers to bid on keywords that would describe their product or service. Bids could be made on a cost-per-impression (CPI) or cost-per-click (CPC) basis. Most Google advertisers placed bids based on CPC frequency rather than how many times an ad was displayed by Google. Google's auction pricing model assigned each bidder a Quality Score, which was determined by the advertiser's past keyword click-through rate and the relevance of the ad text. Advertisers with high Quality Scores were offered lower minimum bids than advertisers with poor quality scores.

Google allowed users to pay a CPC rate lower than their bid price if their bid was considerably more than the next highest bid. For example, an advertiser who bid $0.75 per click for a particular keyword would be charged only $0.51 per click if the next highest bid was only $0.50. The AdWords discounter ensured that advertisers paid only 1 cent more than the next highest bid, regardless of the actual amount of their bid.

AdSense

Google's AdSense program allowed Web publishers to share in the advertising revenues generated by Google's text ads. The AdSense program served content-relevant Google text ads to pages

Exhibit 4   **Financial Summary for Google, 2001–2009 ($ thousands, except per share amounts)**

	2009	2008	2007	2006	2005	2004	2003	2002	2001
Revenues	$23,650,563	$21,795,550	$16,593,986	$10,604,917	$ 6,138,560	$3,189,223	$1,465,934	$439,508	$86,426
Costs and expenses:									
Cost of revenues	8,844,115	8,621,506	6,649,085	4,225,027	2,577,088	1,457,653	625,854	131,510	14,228
Research and development	2,843,027	2,793,192	2,119,985	1,228,589	599,510	225,632	91,228	31,748	16,500
Sales and marketing	1,983,941	1,946,244	1,461,266	849,518	468,152	246,300	120,328	43,849	20,076
General and administrative	1,667,294	1,802,639	1,279,250	751,787	386,532	188,151	286,060	45,935	24,658
Contribution to Google Foundation	—	—	—	—	90,000	—	—	—	—
Non-recurring portion of settlement of disputes with Yahoo	—	—	—	—	—	201,000	—	—	—
Total costs and expenses	15,338,377	15,163,581	11,509,586	7,054,921	4,121,282	2,549,031	1,123,470	253,042	75,462
Income (loss) from operations	8,312,186	6,631,969	5,084,400	3,549,996	2,017,278	640,192	342,464	186,466	10,964
Impairment of equity investments	—	(1,094,757)	—	—	—	—	—	—	—
Interest income (expense) and other, net	69,003	316,384	589,580	461,044	124,399	10,042	4,190	-1,551	-896
Income (loss) before income taxes	8,381,189	5,853,596	5,673,980	4,011,040	2,141,677	650,234	346,654	184,915	10,068
Provision for income taxes	1,860,741	1,626,738	1,470,260	933,594	676,280	251,115	241,006	85,259	3,083
Net income (loss)	$ 6,520,448	$ 4,226,858	$ 4,203,720	$ 3,077,446	$ 1,465,397	$ 399,119	$ 105,648	$ 99,656	$ 6,985
Net income (loss) per share:									
Basic	$20.62	$13.46	$13.53	$10.21	$5.31	$2.07	$0.77	$0.86	$0.07
Diluted	$20.41	$13.31	$13.29	$9.94	$5.02	$1.46	$0.41	$0.45	$0.04
Number of shares used in per share calculations: (in thousands)									
Basic	316,220	314,031	310,806	301,403	275,844	193,176	137,697	115,242	94,523
Diluted	319,473	317,570	316,210	309,548	291,874	272,781	256,638	220,633	186,776
Net cash provided by operating activities	$ 9,316,198	$ 7,852,857	$ 5,775,410	$ 3,580,508	$ 2,459,422	$ 977,044	$ 395,445	$155,265	n/a
Net proceeds from public offerings	—	—	—	2,063,549	4,287,229	1,161,466	—	—	—
Cash, cash equivalents, and marketable securities	24,484,775	15,845,771	14,218,613	11,243,914	8,034,247	2,132,297	334,718	146,331	n/a
Total assets	40,496,778	31,767,575	25,335,806	18,473,351	10,271,813	3,313,351	871,458	286,892	n/a
Total long-term liabilities	1,745,087	1,226,623	610,525	128,924	107,472	43,927	33,365	n/a	n/a
Total stockholders' equity	36,004,224	28,238,862	22,689,679	17,039,840	9,418,957	2,929,056	588,770	173,953	n/a

Source: Google, Form S-1, filed April 29, 2004; Google, 2009 10-K report.

Exhibit 5   **Google's Balance Sheets, 2008–2009 ($ thousands, except per share amounts)**

	As of December 31	
	2009	2008
Assets		
Current assets:		
Cash and cash equivalents	$10,197,588	$ 8,656,672
Marketable securities	14,287,187	7,189,099
Accounts receivable, net of allowance of $16,914 and $32,887	3,178,471	2,642,192
Deferred income taxes, net	644,406	286,105
Income taxes receivable	23,244	—
Prepaid revenue share, expenses and other assets	836,062	1,404,114
Total current assets	29,166,958	20,178,182
Prepaid revenue share, expenses and other assets, non-current	416,119	433,846
Deferred income taxes, net, non-current	262,611	—
Non-marketable equity securities	128,977	85,160
Property and equipment, net	4,844,610	5,233,843
Intangible assets, net	4,774,938	996,690
Goodwill	4,902,565	4,839,854
Total assets	$40,496,778	$31,767,575
Liabilities and Stockholders' Equity		
Current liabilities:		
Accounts payable	$ 215,867	$ 178,004
Accrued compensation and benefits	982,482	811,643
Accrued expenses and other current liabilities	570,080	480,263
Accrued revenue share	693,958	532,547
Deferred revenue	285,080	218,084
Income taxes payable, net	—	81,549
Total current liabilities	2,747,467	2,302,090
Deferred revenue, long-term	41,618	29,818
Income taxes payable, long-term	1,392,468	890,115
Deferred income taxes, net, non-current	—	12,515
Other long-term liabilities	311,001	294,175
Commitments and contingencies		
Stockholders' equity:		
Convertible preferred stock, $0.001 par value, 100,000 shares authorized; no shares issued and outstanding	—	—
Class A and Class B common stock, $0.001 par value per share: 9,000,000 shares authorized; 315,114 (Class A 240,073, Class B 75,041) and par value of $315 (Class A $240, Class B $75) and 317,772 (Class A 243,611, Class B 74,161) and par value of $318 (Class A $244, Class B $74) shares issued and outstanding, excluding 26 and zero Class A shares subject to repurchase at December 31, 2008 and 2009	318	315
Additional paid-in capital	15,816,738	14,450,338
Accumulated other comprehensive income	105,090	226,579
Retained earnings	20,082,078	13,561,630
Total stockholders' equity	36,004,224	28,238,862
Total liabilities and stockholders' equity	$40,496,778	$31,767,575

Source: Google, 2009 10-K report.

on Google Network websites. For example, an Internet user reading an article about the state of the economy at Reuters.com would see Google text ads by investment magazines and companies specializing in home business opportunities. Google Network members shared in the advertising revenue whenever a site visitor clicked on a Google ad displayed on their sites. The more than 1 million Google Network members did not pay a fee to participate in the program and received about 60 percent of advertising dollars generated from the ads. Google's AdSense program also allowed mobile phone operators to share in Google revenues if text and image ads were displayed on mobile handsets. Also, owners of dormant domain names, Web-based game sites, video sites, and news feed services could also participate in the AdSense program. The breakdown of Google's revenues by source for 2003 through 2009 is presented in Exhibit 6.

Other Revenue Sources

The company's 2006 acquisition of YouTube allowed it to receive advertising revenues for ads displayed during Internet videos, while its 2008 acquisition of DoubleClick allowed the company to generate advertising revenues through banner ads. The company's 2008 launch of Google Checkout generated fees of as much as 2 percent of the transaction amount for purchases made at participating e-retailer sites. Google's business model was further expanded in 2008 to include licensing fees paid by users of its Web-based Google Apps document and spreadsheet software.

GOOGLE'S STRATEGY AND COMPETITIVE POSITION IN 2010

Google's Strategies to Dominate Internet Advertising

Google's multiple acquisitions since its 2004 IPO, and its research and development activities, were directed at increasing the company's dominance in Internet advertising. The addition of Google Maps, local search, airline travel information, weather, Book Search, Gmail, Blogger, and other features increased traffic to Google sites and gave the company more opportunities to serve ads to Internet users. Also, the acquisition of Double-Click in 2008 allowed Google to diversify its Internet advertising beyond search ads to include banner ads. However, not all of Google's acquisitions and innovations had resulted in meaningful contributions to the company's revenues. Even though more than 12 billion videos were watched on YouTube each month, the online video site's advertising revenues in 2009 were estimated at less than $300 million. Also, the company's internally developed social networking site, Orkut, had failed to match the success of competing social networking sites Facebook.com and MySpace.com.

Google's strategy to dominate Internet advertising also entailed becoming the number one search engine used not only in the United States but also across the world. In 2010, Google's search-based ads could be delivered to Internet users

Exhibit 6   Google's Revenues by Source, 2003–2009 ($ thousands)

	2009	2008	2007	2006	2005	2004	2003
Advertising revenues:							
Google websites	$15,722,486	$14,413,826	$10,624,705	$ 6,332,797	$3,377,060	$1,589,032	$ 792,063
Google Network websites	7,166,318	6,714,688	5,787,938	4,159,831	2,687,942	1,554,256	628,600
Total	22,888,804	21,128,514	16,412,643	10,492,628	6,065,002	3,143,288	1,420,663
Licensing and other revenues	761,759	667,036	181,343	112,289	73,558	45,935	45,271
Total revenues	$23,650,563	$21,795,550	$16,593,986	$10,604,917	$6,138,560	$3,189,223	$1,465,934

Source: Google, 2007 and 2009 10-K reports.

in 41 different languages. More than 50 percent of the company's 2009 revenues and traffic were generated from outside the United States, and the percentage of sales from outside the United States was expected to grow as Google entered emerging markets like Russia and China. China was a particularly attractive market for Google since it had more Internet users (300+ million) than any other country in the world. However, Google's 2006 entry into China was accompanied by challenges, including strong competition from local search provider Baidu and requirements by the Chinese government to censor search results that were critical of the government. Google complied with government censorship requirements until early 2010, when cyberattacks originating in China stole proprietary computer code from Google and information from the Gmail accounts of several Chinese human rights activists. Google first responded to the hacking incidents by stating that it would withdraw from the Chinese search market and then shifted to a strategy of redirecting users of its censored Google.cn site in China to its uncensored Hong Kong search site, Google.com.hk. The Chinese government was able to block search results from Google's Hong Kong site, but the new policy ended Google's involvement in China's censorship practices. To avoid breaking Chinese law prohibiting the distribution of information not authorized by the government,

Google agreed in June 2010 to stop the automatic redirects to its Hong Kong site. Instead, it presented Google.cn users with a link to Google.com.hk. In 2009, 64 percent of Internet searches in China were performed by Baidu, while Google held a 31 percent share of searches in that country. A breakdown of Google's revenues and long-lived assets by geographic region for 2006 through 2009 is presented in Exhibit 7.

Mobile Search and Google's Entry into the Market for Smartphones

In 2010, 234 million Americans ages 13 and older owned and used mobile phones. More than 30 percent of mobile phone users accessed the Internet from mobile devices, and a rapidly growing number of mobile phone users were exchanging basic mobile phones for smartphones. Smartphones like Research in Motion's Blackberry and Apple's iPhone could connect to the networks of wireless carriers to make phone calls, access the Internet, or run various Internet applications. Between February 2010 and May 2010, the number of smartphone users had grown by 8.1 percent to reach 49.1 million.

The company's introduction of its Android operating system for smartphones in 2008 was expected to allow it to increase its 60-plus percent

Exhibit 7   **Google's Revenues and Long-Lived Assets by Geographic Region, 2006–2009 (in thousands)**

Revenues	Year Ended December 31			
	2009	2008	2007	2006
United States	$11,193,557	$10,635,553	$ 8,698,021	$ 6,030,140
United Kingdom	2,986,040	3,038,488	2,530,916	1,603,842
Rest of the world	9,470,966	8,121,509	5,365,049	2,970,935
Total revenues	$23,650,563	$21,795,550	$16,593,986	$10,604,917

Long-Lived Assets	As of December 31			
	2009	2008	2007	2006
United States	$ 9,432,113	$ 9,782,825	$ 7,334,877	$ 5,070,694
Rest of the world	1,897,707	1,806,568	711,791	362,810
Total long-lived assets	$11,329,820	$11,589,393	$ 8,046,668	$ 5,433,504

Source: Google, 2007 and 2009 10-K reports.

Exhibit 8   **U.S. Smartphone Platform Market Share Rankings, Selected Periods, September 2009–May 2010**

Smartphone Platform	Share of Smartphone Subscribers			
	September 2009	December 2009	February 2010	May 2010
RIM (Blackberry)	42.6%	41.6%	42.1%	41.7%
Apple iPhone	24.1	25.3	25.4	24.4
Microsoft Windows Mobile	19.0	18.0	15.1	13.2
Google Android	2.5	5.2	9.0	13.0
Palm	8.3	6.1	5.4	4.8
Others	3.5	3.8	3.0	2.9
Total	100.0%	100.0%	100.0%	100.0%

Source: ComScore.com.

share of mobile searches and expand the market for other types of Internet ads delivered on mobile devices. Android was not a phone, but an operating system that Google made available free of charge to any phone manufacturer wishing to market mobile devices with Internet capability. Android's core applications included Wi-Fi capability, e-mail, a Web-based calendar, Google Earth maps, a browser, and GPS. T-Mobile was the first wireless provider to market an Android phone. Its $179 G1 was launched in September 2008 and included essentially the same features found on the more expensive Apple iPhone. By 2010, all major mobile phone providers had added smartphone models running Android software to its lineup of handsets. In addition, Google marketed its own Nexus One smartphone, which was produced by HTC and was compatible with all major wireless carrier 3G and 4G networks. Google was also collaborating with Verizon to develop a tablet computer similar to Apple's iPad that would run on Verizon's wireless networks.

Google's Android software had achieved remarkable success, despite its late entry into the market, with its market share increasing from zero in 2008 to 13.0 percent in May 2010—see Exhibit 8. Google also allowed mobile apps developers to use the Android operating system free of licensing fees. The worldwide market for mobile apps was expected to increase from $4.1 billion in 2009 to $17.5 billion by 2012. In 2010, more than 10,000 free and paid apps were available at Google's Android Market and more than 60 percent of mobile developers were actively working on new

apps for Android. About 50 percent of mobile developers were developing new apps for the iPhone and phones running Microsoft's Windows Mobile platform. Also in 2010, Google acquired AdMob, which had developed technology to deliver banner ads to smartphones and other mobile phones able to connect to the Internet. The transaction provided AdMob stockholders with Google shares worth $750 million.

Google's Strategic Offensive to Control the Desktop

Google's senior management believed that, in the very near future, most computer software programs used by businesses would move from local hard drives or intranets to the Internet. Many information technology analysts agreed that cloud computing would become a common software platform and could grow to a $95 billion market by 2013. Moving software applications to the cloud offered many possible benefits to corporate users, including lower software acquisition costs, lower computing support costs, and easier collaboration among employees in different locations. The beta version of Google Apps was launched in 2006 as a free word processing and spreadsheet package for individuals, but was relaunched in 2008 as a competing product to Microsoft Office. Google Apps was hosted on computers in Google's data centers and included Gmail, a calendar, instant messaging, word processing, spreadsheets, presentation software, and file storage space. Google Apps could be licensed by corporate customers at $50 per user per year. The licensing fee for the Microsoft Office and Outlook package was typically $350 per user per year. Industry analysts estimated Google Apps users at about 25 million and paid subscribers at about 1.5 million in 2010. Microsoft estimated Microsoft Office users at about 500 million in 2010.

Google's Chrome browser, which was launched in September 2008, and Chrome operating system (OS) launched in July 2009 were developed specifically to accommodate cloud computing applications. The bare-bones Chrome browser was built on a multiprocessor design that would allow users to operate spreadsheets, word processing, video editing, and other applications on separate tabs that could be run simultaneously. Each tab operated independently so that if one tab crashed, other applications running from Google's data centers were not affected. The Chrome browser also provided Google with a defense against moves by Microsoft to make it more difficult for Google to deliver relevant search-based ads to Internet users. Microsoft's Internet Explorer 8 allowed users to hide their Internet address and viewing history, which prevented Google from collecting user-specific information needed for ad targeting. Mozilla's Firefox browser employed a similar feature that prevented third parties from tracking a user's viewing habits. The clean-running Chrome OS was an open source operating system specifically designed as a platform for cloud computing applications.

Late in 2009, Google entered into agreements with Acer, Hewlett-Packard, and Lenovo to begin producing netbooks that would use the Chrome OS and Chrome browser to access the cloud-based Google Apps productivity software. Chrome OS netbooks were expected to be available for purchase by consumers and businesses in late 2010. Worldwide market share statistics for the leading browsers in September 2008 and June 2010 are presented in Exhibit 9.

Google's Initiatives to Expand Search to Television

In mid-2010, Google entered into an alliance with Intel, Sony, Logitech, Best Buy, DISH Network, and Adobe to develop Google TV. Google TV would be built on the Android platform and would run the Chrome browser software to search live network and cable programming; streaming

Exhibit 9 **Worldwide Browser Market Share Rankings, September 2008 and June 2010**

Browser	September 2008	June 2010
Internet Explorer	74%	60%
Firefox	19	24
Chrome	1	7
Safari	3	5
Opera	2	3
Others	1	1
Total	100%	100%

Source: "Google Rekindles Browser War," *Wall Street Journal Online,* July 7, 2010.

videos from providers such as Netflix, Amazon Video On Demand, and YouTube; and recorded programs on a DVR. Google TV users would also be able to use their televisions to browse the Web and run cloud-based applications such as Google Apps. Google TV was expected to be integrated into DISH Network's satellite service by fall 2010, while Sony was on schedule for fall 2010 shipments of Google TV–compatible high-definition televisions (HDTVs). Logitech was also on track for fall 2010 shipments of Google TV set-top boxes that would be compatible with all brands of HDTVs and Google TV accessories such as HD cameras that could be used for video chats.

Google acquired On2 Technologies, which was the leading developer of video compression technology, in February 2010 in a $124 million stock and cash transaction. The acquisition of On2 was expected to improve the video streaming capabilities of Google TV. Google also lobbied heavily during 2009 and 2010 to encourage the Obama administration to adopt a "Net neutrality" policy that would require Internet providers to manage traffic in a manner that would not restrict high-bandwidth services such as Internet television. The company was also testing an ultrafast broadband network in several cities across the United States that was as much as 100 times faster than what was offered by competing Internet providers. Google management had stated that the company did not intend to launch a nationwide Internet service, but did want to expose consumers to Internet applications and content that would be possible with greater bandwidth and faster transmission speeds.

GOOGLE'S INTERNET RIVALS

Google's ability to sustain its competitive advantage among search companies was a function of its ability to maintain strong relationships with Internet users, advertisers, and websites. In 2010, Google was the world's most-visited Internet site, with nearly 147 million unique Internet users going to Google sites each month to search for information. Google management believed its primary competitors to be Microsoft and Yahoo. A comparison of the percentage of Internet searches among websites offering search capabilities in July 2006, June 2009, and May 2010 is shown in Exhibit 10.

Exhibit 10 U.S. Search Engine Market Share Rankings, July 2006, June 2009, and May 2010

Search Entity	Percent of Searches		
	July 2006	June 2009	May 2010
Google Sites	43.7%	65.0%	63.7%
Yahoo Sites	28.8	19.6	18.3
Microsoft Sites	12.8	8.4	12.1
Ask.com	5.4	3.9	3.6
AOL	5.9	3.1	2.3
Others	3.4	n.m.	n.m.
Total	100.0%	100.0%	100.0%

n.m. = not material.

Source: ComScore.com.

Yahoo

Yahoo was founded in 1994 and was the third-most-visited Internet destination worldwide in 2010, with 130.5 million unique visitors each month. Facebook was the second-most-visited website, with 132 million unique visitors each month in 2010. Almost any information available on the Internet could be accessed through Yahoo's Web portal. Visitors could access content categorized by Yahoo or set up an account with Yahoo to maintain a personal calendar and e-mail account, check the latest news, check local weather, obtain maps, check TV listings, watch a movie trailer, track a stock portfolio, maintain a golf handicap, keep an online photo album, or search personal ads or job listings.

Yahoo also hosted websites for small businesses and Internet retailers and had entered into strategic partnerships with 20 mobile phone operators in the United States and Europe to provide mobile search and display ads to their customers. Yahoo accounted for about 35 percent of searches performed on mobile phones in 2010. Yahoo's broad range of services allowed it to generate revenues from numerous sources—it received fees for banner ads displayed at Yahoo.com, Yahoo! Messenger, Yahoo! Mail, Flickr, or mobile phone customers; it received listing fees at Yahoo! Autos, Cars.com, and Yahoo! Real Estate; it received revenues from paid search results at Yahoo! Search; it shared in travel agency booking fees made at Yahoo! Travel; and it received subscription fees from its registered users at Rivals.com, Yahoo! Games, Yahoo! Music, and Yahoo! Personals.

Yahoo's relationship with Google dated to 2000 and, since that time, had oscillated between cooperative and adversarial. Yahoo was among Google's earliest customers for its search appliance, but Yahoo began to distance itself from Google in 2002 when it began acquiring companies with developed search technologies. Yahoo replaced Google with its own search capabilities in February 2004. Yahoo later levied a patent infringement charge against Google that resulted in a settlement that gave Google ownership of the technology rights in return for 2.7 million shares of Google stock. Yahoo attempted to renew its relationship with Google in 2008 in hopes of reversing a decline in profitability and liquidity that began in 2006. After averting a hostile takeover by Microsoft in June 2008, Yahoo reached an agreement with Google that would allow Yahoo to host Google search ads. The partnership would provide Yahoo with an estimated $800 million in additional revenues annually, most of which would go directly to its bottom line. However, Google withdrew from the agreement in November 2008 after receiving notification from the U.S. Justice Department that the alliance would possibly violate antitrust statutes. Shortly after being notified that Google was withdrawing from the deal, Yahoo's chief managers told business reporters that the company was "disappointed that Google has elected to withdraw from the agreement rather than defend it in court."[7] In July 2009, Microsoft and Yahoo finally came to an agreement that would make Microsoft Bing Yahoo's imbedded search engine for a period of 10 years. A summary of Yahoo's financial performance between 2003 and 2009 is presented in Exhibit 11.

Microsoft Online Services

Microsoft Corporation recorded fiscal 2009 revenues and net income of approximately $58.4 billion and $14.6 billion, respectively, through the sales of computer software, consulting services, video game hardware, and online services. Windows 7 and Microsoft Office accounted for more than one-half of the company's 2009 revenues and nearly all of its operating profit. The company's online services business recorded sales of nearly $3.1 billion and an operating loss of almost $2.3 billion during fiscal 2009. Microsoft's online services business generated revenues from banner ads displayed at the company's MSN Web portal and its affiliated websites, search-based ads displayed with Bing results, and subscription fees from its MSN

dial-up service. A financial summary for Microsoft Corporation and its Online Services Division is provided in Exhibit 12.

Microsoft's search business was launched in November 2004 as Live Search to compete directly with Google and slow whatever intentions Google might have to threaten Microsoft in its core operating system and productivity software businesses. Microsoft's concern with threats posed by Google arose shortly after Google's IPO, when Bill Gates noticed that many of the Google job postings on its site were nearly identical to Microsoft job specifications. Recognizing that the position announcements had more to do with operating-system design than search, Gates e-mailed key Microsoft executives, warning, "We have to watch these guys. It looks like they are building something to compete with us."[8] Gates later commented that Google was "more like us than anyone else we have ever competed with."[9]

Gates speculated that Google's long-term strategy involved the development of Web-based software applications comparable to Word, Excel, PowerPoint, and other Microsoft products. Microsoft's strategy to compete with Google was keyed to making Live Search more effective than Google at providing highly relevant search results. Microsoft believed that any conversion of Google users to Live Search would reduce the number of PC users who might ultimately adopt Google's Web-based

Exhibit 11   Selected Financial Data for Yahoo, 2003–2009 ($ thousands)

	2009	2008	2007	2006	2005	2004	2003
Revenues	$ 6,460,315	$ 7,208,502	$ 6,969,274	$ 6,425,679	$ 5,257,668	$3,574,517	$1,625,097
Income from operations	386,692	12,963	695,413	940,966	1,107,725	688,581	295,666
Net income	597,992	418,921	639,155	731,568	1,877,407	839,553	237,879
Cash and cash equivalents	1,275,430	2,292,296	1,513,930	1,569,871	1,429,693	823,723	415,892
Marketable securities	3,242,574	1,229,677	849,542	1,967,414	2,570,155	2,918,539	2,150,323
Working capital	2,877,044	3,040,483	937,274	2,276,148	2,245,481	2,909,768	1,013,913
Total assets	14,936,030	13,689,848	12,229,741	11,513,608	10,831,834	9,178,201	5,931,654
Long-term liabilities	699,666	715,872	384,208	870,948	1,061,367	851,782	822,890
Total stockholders' equity	12,493,320	11,250,942	9,532,831	9,160,610	8,566,415	7,101,446	4,363,490

Source: Yahoo, 2007 and 2009 10-K reports.

Exhibit 12   Selected Financial Data for Microsoft Corporation and Microsoft's Online Services Business Unit, 2006–2009 ($ millions)

Microsoft Corporation	Fiscal Year Ended June 30			
	2009	2008	2007	2006
Revenue	$58,437	$60,420	$51,122	$44,282
Operating income	20,363	22,492	18,524	16,472
Net income	14,569	17,681	14,065	12,599
Cash, cash equivalents, and short-term investments	$31,447	$23,662	$23,411	$34,161
Total assets	77,888	72,793	63,171	69,597
Long-term obligations	11,296	6,621	8,320	7,051
Stockholders' equity	39,558	36,286	31,097	40,104
Microsoft's Online Services Business Unit	**2009**	**2008**	**2007**	**2006**
Revenue	$ 3,088	$ 3,214	$ 2,441	$ 2,296
Operating income (loss)	(2,253)	(1,233)	(617)	5

Source: Microsoft, 2007 and 2009 annual reports.

word processing, spreadsheet, and presentation software packages. In 2008, Microsoft paid more than $100 million to acquire Powerset, which was the developer of a semantic search engine. Semantic search technology offered the opportunity to surpass the relevancy of Google's search results since semantic search evaluated the meaning of a word or phrase and considered its context when returning search results. Even though semantic search had the capability to answer questions stated in common language, semantic search processing time took several seconds to return results. The amount of time necessary to conduct a search had caused Microsoft to limit Powerset's search index to only articles listed in Wikipedia. Microsoft's developers were focused on increasing the speed of its semantic search capabilities so that its search index could be expanded to a greater number of Internet pages. The company's developers also incorporated some of Powerset's capabilities into its latest-generation search engine, Bing, which was launched in June 2009.

Microsoft's search agreement with Yahoo was engineered to allow the company to increase its Internet search market share and achieve advertising scale necessary to make its online services business profitable. The addition of Yahoo's 130.5 million unique monthly users was expected to double exposure for Microsoft's banner ads to more than 200 million unique monthly users. Banner ads comprised the bulk of Microsoft's online advertising revenues, since its Bing search engine accounted for only 12 percent of online searches in 2010. Even though the market for display ads was only about one-half the size of the search ad market in 2009, the advertising spending on banner ads was expected to double by 2012 to reach $15 billion.

Microsoft was also moving forward with its own approach to cloud computing. The company's 2008 launch of Windows Live allowed Internet users to store files online at its password-protected SkyDrive site. SkyDrive's online file storage allowed users to access and edit files from multiple locations, share files with coworkers who might need editing privileges, or make files available in a public folder for wide distribution. Azure was Microsoft's most ambitious cloud computing initiative in 2010 and was intended to allow businesses to reduce computing costs by allowing Microsoft to host its operating programs and data files. In addition to reducing capital expenditures for software upgrades and added server capacity, Azure's offsite hosting provided data security in the event of natural disasters such as fires or hurricanes.

ISSUES CONCERNING GOOGLE'S PERFORMANCE AND BUSINESS ETHICS IN 2010

During its first quarter of fiscal 2010, Google had been able to achieve year-over-year revenue growth of 23 percent, while most companies in almost every industry struggled as the U.S. economy continued to falter. So far, it appeared that Google's business model and strategy had insulated it from the effects of the recession and it was in position to pursue its growth strategies. The company's strategic priorities in 2010 focused on expanding its share of mobile search and smartphone platforms, pushing forward with its plans to become the dominant provider of cloud computing solutions, increasing search advertising revenues from markets outside the United States, and extending search to television. Some analysts believed the company's priorities should also include the development of semantic search capabilities, while others were concerned that the company had strayed from its 10 Principles—specifically, Principle 6, "You can make money without doing evil."

Free-speech advocates had criticized Google for its complicity in China's censorship of Internet content since it launched its Chinese site in 2006, while privacy advocates complained that Google Map's street view mode violated privacy rights. The New Zealand government addressed privacy rights by requiring Google to blur the faces of all individuals photographed by its camera cars. The most serious issue involving Google's Street View involved Google management's decision to allow the company's camera cars to capture Wi-Fi data emitted from homes and businesses while photographing the route. In May 2010, authorities in the United States, Canada, Australia, Germany, Italy, the United Kingdom, and Spain were conducting investigations into Google's data collection activities to determine if prosecution of company managers was

warranted. Google cofounder Sergey Brin said the company "screwed up" by collecting personal data through wireless networks in an attempt to improve its mapping system.[10]

Also, the company's lobbying efforts to encourage the Obama administration to institute policies to promote Net neutrality had drawn the scrutiny of the U.S. House Oversight Committee. The primary concern of the House Oversight Committee involved communications between the company and its former head of public policy and government affairs, Andrew McLaughlin, who had been appointed to the position of White House deputy chief technology officer. Ethics rules created by an executive order signed by President Obama barred all White House officials from communicating with lobbyists or a company potentially affected by pending policy matters. A Freedom of Information Act (FOIA) request by a consumer group found that McLaughlin regularly communicated with Google executives to discuss the administration's push to have the Internet regulated by the Federal Communications Commission to promote Net neutrality. McLaughlin's e-mails could be obtained under the FOIA since all White House e-mail accounts were required to be archived under federal law. The House Oversight Committee was particularly disturbed by McLaughlin's alleged use of a personal Gmail account to avoid having his communications with Google executives archived and subject to FOIA requests.

Some analysts believed that pressure to achieve the revenue and earnings growth necessary to maintain Google's lofty stock price may have caused Google management to make decisions that pushed the bounds of its corporate philosophy. The company's revenues and earnings growth had begun to slow in recent years, and the sluggish U.S. economy seemed unlikely to give Google a dramatic boost in revenues in 2010. It remained to be determined if Google's strategies could sustain its growth and stock performance in a manner that would adhere to the company founders' early beliefs.

ENDNOTES

1 Google, www.google.com/corporate/, accessed July 13, 2010.

2 Quoted in "Google's Eric Schmidt: You Can Trust Us with Your Data," *UK Telegraph*, July 1, 2010.

3 Google, www.google.com/corporate/tenthings.html, accessed July 13, 2010.

4 Quoted in Google's Corporate Information, www.google.com/corporate/history.html.

5 Google, "Our Philosophy," www.google.com/corporate/tenthings.html.

6 "For Some Who Passed on Google Long Ago, Wistful Thinking," *Wall Street Journal Online,* August 23, 2004.

7 Quoted in "With Google Gone, Will Microsoft Come Back to Yahoo?" *Fortune,* November 5, 2008.

8 Quoted in "Gates vs. Google," *Fortune,* April 18, 2005.

9 Ibid.

10 Quoted in "Google Faces European Probes on Wi-Fi Data," *Wall Street Journal Online,* May 20, 2010.

Research In Motion: Managing Explosive Growth

Rod White
University of Western Ontario

Paul Beamish
University of Western Ontario

Daina Mazutis
University of Western Ontario

In early January 2008, David Yach, chief technology officer for software at Research In Motion (RIM), had just come back from Christmas break. Returning to his desk in Waterloo, Ontario, relaxed and refreshed, he noted that his executive assistant had placed the preliminary holiday sales figures for BlackBerry on top of his in-box with a note that read "Meeting with Mike tomorrow." Knowing 2007 had been an extraordinarily good year, with the number of BlackBerry units sold doubling, Dave was curious: Why did Mike Lazaridis, RIM's visionary founder and co–chief executive officer, want a meeting? A sticky note on page three flagged the issue. Mike wanted to discuss Dave's research and development (R&D) plans—even though R&D spending was up $124 million from the prior year, it had dropped significantly as a percentage of sales. In an industry driven by engineering innovations and evaluated on technological advances, this was an issue.

Ivey
Richard Ivey School of Business
The University of Western Ontario

Daina Mazutis wrote this case under the supervision of Professors Rod White and Paul W. Beamish solely to provide material for class discussion. The authors do not intend to illustrate either effective or ineffective handling of a managerial situation. The authors may have disguised certain names and other identifying information to protect confidentiality. Ivey Management Services prohibits any form of reproduction, storage or transmittal without its written permission. Reproduction of this material is not covered under authorization by any reproduction rights organization. To order copies or request permission to reproduce materials, contact Ivey Publishing, Ivey Management Services, c/o Richard Ivey School of Business, The University of Western Ontario, London, Ontario, Canada, N6A 3K7; phone (519) 661-3208; fax (519) 661-3882; e-mail cases@ivey.uwo.ca.

Copyright © 2008, Ivey Management Services
Version: (A) 2008-05-13.

R&D was the core of the BlackBerry's success—but success, Dave knew, could be a double-edged sword. Although RIM's engineers were continually delivering award-winning products, explosive growth and increased competition were creating pressures on his team to develop new solutions to keep up with changes in the global smartphone marketplace. With 2007 revenue up 98 percent from the previous year, his team of approximately 1,400 software engineers should also have doubled—but both talent and space were getting increasingly scarce. The current model of "organic" growth was not keeping pace, and his engineers were feeling the strain. As the day progressed, Dave considered how he should manage this expansion on top of meeting existing commitments, thinking: "How do you change the engine, while you're speeding along at 200 kilometers per hour?" As his BlackBerry notified him of dozens of other urgent messages, he wondered how to present his growth and implementation plan to Mike the next morning.

RESEARCH IN MOTION LTD. (RIM)

RIM was a world leader in the mobile communications market. Founded in 1984 by 23-year-old University of Waterloo student Mike Lazaridis, RIM designed, manufactured, and marketed the very popular line of BlackBerry products that had recently reached 14 million subscribers worldwide and had just over $6 billion in revenue (see Exhibits 1 and 2). In early 2008, RIM was

Exhibit 1   **BlackBerry Subscriber Account Base (in millions)**   **RIM Annual Revenue (in millions of U.S. dollars)**

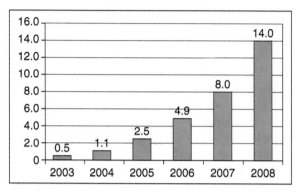
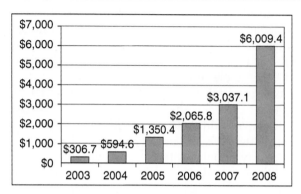

Note: RIM Fiscal year ends in March (Fiscal 2008 is the year ending March 31, 2008).

Source: RIM Fiscal 2007 annual report and Fiscal 2008 press release (April 2, 2008).

Exhibit 2   **Consolidated Statement of Operations, Research in Motion, Ltd., 2004–2008 (in thousands of U.S. dollars, except per share data)**

	For the Year Ended				
	Mar. 1, 2008 (Projected)	Mar. 3, 2007	Mar. 4, 2006	Feb. 26, 2005	Feb. 28, 2004
Revenue	$6,009,395	$3,037,103	$2,065,845	$1,350,447	$594,616
Cost of sales	2,928,814	1,379,301	925,598	636,310	323,365
Gross margin	3,080,581	1,657,802	1,140,247	714,137	271,251
Gross margin %	51.30%	54.60%	55.20%	52.88%	45.62%
Expenses					
Research and development	359,828	236,173	158,887	102,665	62,638
Selling, marketing, & admin.	881,482	537,922	314,317	193,838	108,492
Amortization	108,112	76,879	49,951	35,941	27,911
Litigation			201,791	352,628	35,187
	1,349,422	850,974	724,946	685,072	234,228
Income from operations	1,731,159	806,828	415,301	29,065	37,023
Investment income	79,361	52,117	66,218	37,107	10,606
Income before income taxes	1,810,520	858,945	481,519	66,172	47,629
Provision for income taxes					
Current	587,845	123,552	14,515	1,425	
Deferred	(71,192)	103,820	92,348	(140,865)	
	516,653	227,373	106,863	(139,440)	−4,200
Net Income	$1,293,867	$ 631,572	$ 374,656	$ 205,612	$ 51,829
Earnings per share					
Basic	$2.31	$1.14	$1.98	$1.10	$0.33
Diluted	$2.26	$1.10	$1.91	$1.04	$0.31

Source: Company annual reports; fiscal 2008 form; press release, April 2, 2008, "Research in Motion Reports Fourth Quarter and Year-End Results for Fiscal 2003," http://www.rim.com/news/press/2008/pr-02_04_2008-01.shtml.

one of Canada's largest companies with a market capitalization of $69.4 billion.[1]

The BlackBerry wireless platform and line of handhelds could integrate e-mail, phone, Instant Messaging (IM), Short Message Service (SMS), Internet, music, camera, video, radio, organizer, Global Positioning System (GPS), and a variety of other applications in one wireless solution that was dubbed "always on, always connected." These features, especially the immediate pushed message delivery, in addition to the BlackBerry's small size, long battery life, and ease of use, made the product extremely popular with busy executives who valued the safe and secure delivery of corporate mail and seamless extension of other enterprise and Internet services.

In particular, organizations that relied on sensitive information, such as the U.S. government and large financial institutions, were early and loyal adopters of BlackBerry and RIM's largest customers. RIM's enterprise e-mail servers, which were attached to the customer's e-mail and IM servers behind company firewalls, encrypted and redirected e-mail and other data before forwarding the information to end consumers through wireless service providers (see Exhibit 3). Having been the first to market with a "push" e-mail architecture and a value proposition built on security, RIM had more than 100,000 enterprise customers and an estimated 42 percent market share of converged devices, and significantly higher market share of data-only devices, in North America.[2]

RIM generated revenue through the "complete BlackBerry wireless solution," which included wireless devices, software, and services. Revenues, however, were heavily skewed to handheld sales (73 percent), followed by service (18 percent), software (6 percent) and other revenues (3 percent). In handhelds, RIM had recently introduced the award-winning BlackBerry Pearl and BlackBerry Curve, which were a significant design departure from previous models and for the first time targeted both consumer and business professionals (see Exhibit 4). RIM had accumulated a wide range of product design and innovation awards, including recognition from Computerworld as one of the Top 10 Products of the Past 40 Years.[3] Analysts and technophiles eagerly awaited the next-generation BlackBerry series expected for release in 2008.

Although originally built for busy professionals, BlackBerry had made considerable headway in the consumer market and had become something of a social phenomenon. Celebrity sightings put the BlackBerry in the hands of Madonna and Paris Hilton among others. The term "crackberry," used to describe the addictive or obsessive use of the BlackBerry, was added to Webster's New Millennium dictionary. Just six months after launching Facebook for BlackBerry, downloads of the popular social networking software application had topped one million, indicating that younger consumers were gravitating toward the popular handhelds.[4] RIM also actively sought partnerships with software developers to bring popular games such as Guitar Hero III to the BlackBerry mobile platform,[5] suggesting a more aggressive move to the consumer, or at least prosumer,[6] smartphone space.

Wireless carriers, such as Rogers in Canada and Verizon in the United States, were RIM's primary direct customers. These carriers bundled BlackBerry handhelds and software with airtime and sold the complete solution to end users. In 2007, RIM had over 270 carrier partnerships in more than 110 countries around the world. Through the BlackBerry Connect licensing program other leading device manufacturers such as Motorola, Nokia, Samsung, and Sony Ericsson could also equip their handsets with BlackBerry functionality, including push technology to automatically deliver e-mail and other data. Expanding the global reach of BlackBerry solutions was therefore a fundamental part of RIM's strategy. In 2007, 57.9 percent of RIM's revenues were derived from the United States, 7.3 percent from Canada and the remaining 34.8 percent from other countries. To date, RIM had offices in North America, Europe, and Asia Pacific; however, it had only three wholly owned subsidiaries—two in Delaware and one in England.

THE WIRELESS COMMUNICATIONS MARKET AND SMARTPHONES

Mobile wireless communication involved the transmission of signals using radio frequencies between wireless networks and mobile access

Exhibit 3 BlackBerry Enterprise Solution Architecture

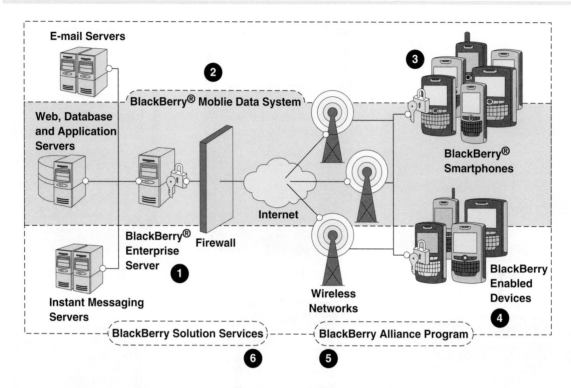

1. BlackBerry® Enterprise Server: Robust software that acts as the centralized link between wireless devices, wireless networks, and enterprise applications. The server integrates with enterprise messaging and collaboration systems to provide mobile users with access to e-mail, enterprise instant messaging and personal information management tools. All data between applications and BlackBerry® smartphones flows centrally through the server.

2. BlackBerry® Mobile Data System (BlackBerry MDS): An optimized framework for creating, deploying and managing applications for the BlackBerry Enterprise Solution. It provides essential components that enable applications beyond e-mail to be deployed to mobile users, including developer tools, administrative services, and BlackBerry® Device Software. It also uses the same proven BlackBerry push delivery model and advanced security features used for BlackBerry e-mail.

3. BlackBerry® Smartphones: Integrated wireless voice and data devices that are optimized to work with the BlackBerry Enterprise Solution. They provide push-based access to e-mail and data from enterprise applications and systems in addition to web, MMS, SMS, and organizer applications.

4. BlackBerry® Connect™ Devices: Devices available from leading manufacturers that feature BlackBerry push delivery technology and connect to the BlackBerry Enterprise Server.

5. BlackBerry® Alliance Program: A large community of independent software vendors, system integrators, and solution providers that offer applications, services, and solutions for the BlackBerry Enterprise Solution. It is designed to help organizations make the most of the BlackBerry Enterprise Solution when mobilizing their enterprises.

6. BlackBerry Solution Services: A group of services that include: BlackBerry® Technical Support Services, BlackBerry® Training, RIM® Professional Services, and the Corporate Development Program. These tools and programs are designed to help organizations deploy, manage, and extend their wireless solution.

Source: http://na.blackberry.com/eng/ataglance/solutions/architecture.jsp.

Exhibit 4   The Evolution of the BlackBerry Product Line (Select Models)

RIM Inter@ctive Pager 850

RIM 957

BlackBerry 6200

BlackBerry 8820

BlackBerry Pearl 8110

BlackBerry Curve 8330

Source: http://www.rim.com/newsroom/media/gallery/index.shtml and Jon Fortt, "BlackBerry: Evolution of an Icon," *Fortune,* Sept. 21, 2007 (accessed April 7, 2008), http://bigtech.blogs.fortune.cnn.com/blackberry-evolution-of-an-icon-photos-610/.

devices. Although RIM was one of the first to market with two-way messaging, recent technological developments had encouraged numerous handheld and handset vendors to go beyond traditional "telephony" and release new "converged"[7] devices including smartphones, Personal Digital Assistants (PDA), phone/PDA hybrids, converged voice and data devices, and other end-to-end integrated wireless solutions. A shift in the telecommunication industry was moving demand beyond just cellphones to smartphones—complete communications tools that marry all the functions of mobile phones with fully integrated e-mail, browser, and organizer applications. In 2007, key competitors to RIM's BlackBerry line-up included the Palm Treo 700 and 750, Sony Ericsson P900 Series, the Nokia E62, Motorola Q, and the Apple iPhone.

Exhibit 5 **Mobile Telephone Users Worldwide (in millions)**

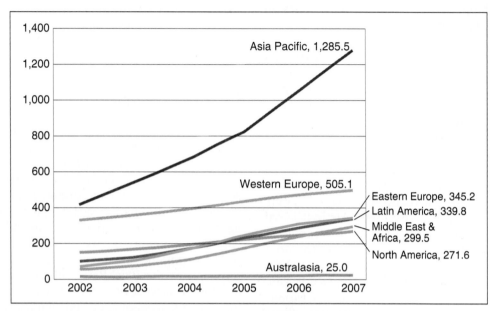

Source: Created from data accessed from the Global Market Information Database, April 4, 2008,
http://www.donal.suromonitor.com.proxy1lb.uo.ca.2048/portal/server.pt?control=SetCommunity&CommunityID=207&PageID
=720&cached=false&space=CommunityPage.

The number of wireless subscriber connections worldwide had reached 3 billion by the end of 2007. China led with over 524 million subscribers, followed by the United States at 254 million, and India with 237 million (see Exhibit 5). Year over year growth in the United States, however, was only 9.5 percent, with an already high market penetration rate (87 percent). In contrast, China's growth was 18.3 percent with only 39 percent penetration. In sheer numbers, India was experiencing the fastest growth rate with a 60 percent increase and room to grow with 21 percent market penetration. To put that into context, in late 2007 there were almost 300,000 new wireless network subscribers in India every day.[8]

Since the launch of Apple's iPhone in June 2007, competition in the smartphone segment of the mobile telecommunications industry had intensified. The iPhone "set a new standard for usability."[9] In 2007, smartphones represented only 10 percent of the global mobile phone market in units. However, this segment was projected to reach over 30 percent market share within five years.[10] In the U.S. the number of smartphone users had doubled in 2007 to about 14.6 million[11]

while global shipments of smartphones rose by 53 percent worldwide, hitting 118 million in 2007.[12] Some analysts saw the opportunity for smart phones as "immense," predicting that during 2008 and 2009, 500 million smart devices would be sold globally and cumulative global shipments would pass the one billion mark by 2012.[13]

Worldwide demand for wireless handhelds had been fueled by several global trends, including the commercial availability of high-speed wireless networks, the emergence of mobile access to corporate intranets, and the broad acceptance of e-mail and text messaging as reliable, secure, and indispensable means of communication. Coupled with the growth of instant messaging as both a business and personal communications tool, the demand for wireless handhelds and smartphones was robust.

COMPETING PLATFORMS

Symbian, a proprietary Operating System (OS) designed for mobile devices and jointly owned by Nokia, Ericsson, Sony Ericsson, Panasonic,

Siemens AG, and Samsung, held an estimated 65 percent worldwide share of the converged devices, shipping 77.3 million smartphones in 2007 (up 50 percent from 2006).[14] This was significantly ahead of Microsoft's Windows Mobile OS (12 percent) and RIM's BlackBerry OS (11 percent). However, in North America, RIM led with 42 percent of shipments, ahead of Apple (27 percent), Microsoft (21 percent) and Palm (less than 9 percent and shrinking).[15]

However, RIM could not afford to rest on its laurels. In the North American marketplace, Apple had recently announced that it would be actively pursuing the business segment. Conceding that push e-mail and calendar integration were key to securing enterprise users, Apple licensed ActiveSync Direct Push, a Microsoft technology. Apple hoped to entice corporate users to adopt the iPhone as their converged device of choice.[16] Similarly, Microsoft, which had struggled to gain widespread acceptance for its Windows Mobile OS, had recently revamped its marketing efforts and announced an end-to-end solution for enterprise customers as well as desktop-grade web browsing for Windows Mobile enabled phones.[17] Even Google had entered the fray with Android, an open and free mobile platform which included an OS, middleware and key applications. Rivalry, it seemed, was intensifying.

In early 2008, an analyst commented about the increasing competition in the converged device (smartphone and wireless handheld) segment:

> Apple's innovation in its mobile phone user interface has prompted a lot of design activity among competitors. We saw the beginnings of that in 2007, but we will see a lot more in 2008 as other smart phone vendors try to catch up and then get back in front. Experience shows that a vendor with only one smart phone design, no matter how good that design is, will soon struggle. A broad, continually refreshed portfolio is needed to retain and grow share in this dynamic market. This race is a marathon, but you pretty much have to sprint every lap.[18]

Another analyst observed:

> The good news for RIM? There still aren't many trusted alternatives for business-class mobile e-mail. This company could be one of the world's biggest handset manufacturers one day. It's hard for me to believe there won't be e-mail on every phone in the world. RIM is going to be a major force in this market.[19]

Given the rapid advances in the mobile communications industry, no technological platform had become the industry standard. In light of the dynamic market situation, RIM needed to ensure that its investment in R&D kept up with the pace of change in the industry.

R&D AT RIM

R&D and engineering were the heart and soul of RIM. In March 2007, RIM employed just over 2,100 people with different R&D areas of expertise: radio frequency engineering, hardware and software design, audio and display improvement, antenna design, circuit board design, power management, industrial design, and manufacturing engineering, among others. R&D efforts focused on improving the functionality, security, and performance of the BlackBerry solution, as well as developing new devices for current and emerging network technologies and market segments. The ratio of software to hardware developers was approximately 2:1, and about 40 percent of the software engineers were involved in core design work while another 40 percent were engaged in testing and documentation (the remaining 20 percent were in management, and support functions like documentation and project management).

R&D had increased significantly both in terms of the total number of employees as well as the geographic scope of its operations. Since 2000, the R&D group had grown more than tenfold, from 200 to 2,100 people and expanded to two more locations in Canada (Ottawa and Mississauga), several in the United States (Dallas, Chicago, Atlanta, Seattle, and Palo Alto) and one in England. Waterloo was still the principal location—home to a vibrant and collaborative culture of young and talented engineers.

RIM's cryptographic and software source code played a key role in the success of the company, delivering the safe and secure voice and data transmission on which the BlackBerry reputation was built. Chris Wormald, vice president of strategic alliances, who was responsible for acquisitions, licensing, and partnerships, described the challenge as follows:

> At the end of the day, our source code is really among our few enduring technical assets. We have gone through extraordinary measures to protect

Exhibit 6   **Competitive R&D Spend, Select Competitors (in millions of US$)**

Nokia		Dec. 31/04	Dec. 31/05	Dec. 31/06	Dec. 31/07
Revenue		$46,606	$54,022	$64,971	$80,672
R&D		$ 5,784	$ 6,020	$ 6,157	$ 8,229
% of Revenue		12.41%	11.14%	9.48%	10.20%
Microsoft	June 30/03	June 30/04	June 30/05	June 30/06	June 30/07
Revenue	$32,187	$36,835	$39,788	$44,282	$51,122
R&D	$ 6,595	$ 7,735	$ 6,097	$ 6,584	$ 7,121
% of Revenue	20.49%	21.00%	15.32%	14.87%	13.93%
Motorola	Dec. 31/03	Dec. 31/04	Dec. 31/05	Dec. 31/06	Dec. 31/07
Revenue	$23,155	$29,663	$35,310	$42,847	$36,622
R&D	$ 2,979	$ 3,316	$ 3,600	$ 4,106	$ 4,429
% of Revenue	12.87%	11.18%	10.20%	9.58%	12.09%
Apple	Sept. 27/03	Sept. 25/04	Sept. 24/05	Sept. 30/06	Sept. 29/07
Revenue	$ 6,207	$ 8,279	$13,931	$19,315	$24,006
R&D	$ 471	$ 491	$ 535	$ 712	$ 782
% of Revenue	7.59%	5.93%	3.84%	3.69%	3.26%
RIM	Feb. 28/04	Feb. 26/05	Mar. 4/06	Mar. 3/07	Proj. Mar./08
Revenue	$ 595	$ 1,350	$ 2,066	$ 3,037	$ 6,009
R&D	$ 63	$ 103	$ 159	$ 236	$ 360
% of Revenue	10.59%	7.63%	7.70%	7.77%	5.99%
Palm	May 31/03	May 31/04	May 31/05	May 31/06	May 31/07
Revenue	$ 838	$ 950	$ 1,270	$ 1,578	$ 1,561
R&D	$ 70	$ 69	$ 90	$ 136	$ 191
% of Revenue	8.35%	7.26%	7.09%	8.62%	12.24%

Note: Nokia 2007 includes Nokia Siemens.

Source: Company annual reports.

it. Extraordinary is probably still too shallow of a word. We don't give anyone any access under any circumstances. RIM was founded on a principle of "we can do it better ourselves"—it is a philosophy that is embedded in our DNA. This vertical integration of technology makes geographic expansion and outsourcing of software development very difficult.

Intellectual property rights were thus diligently guarded through a combination of patent, copyright, and contractual agreements. It was also strategically managed through a geography strategy that divided core platform development from product and technology development, with most of the core work (on the chip sets, software source code, product design) still occurring in Waterloo.

However, the exponential growth in sales, competition, and industry changes was placing tremendous pressures on the R&D teams at the Canadian headquarters.

Similar to other players in the telecommunications industry (see Exhibit 6), it was RIM's policy to maintain its R&D spending as a consistent percentage of total sales. Investment analysts often looked to this number to gauge the sustainability of revenue growth. R&D expenses were seen as a proxy for new product or service development and therefore used as a key indicator of future revenue potential. Human capital represented the bulk of R&D dollars, and the organizational development team in charge of hiring at RIM was working overtime to try to keep up with

Exhibit 7   Employee Growth at RIM

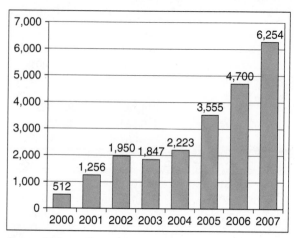

Source: RIM annual reports.

the growing demand for the qualified engineers needed to deliver on both customer and investor expectations.

ORGANIZATIONAL DEVELOPMENT FOR R&D AT RIM

The 2,100 R&D employees made up about 35 percent of RIM's 6,254 employees.[20] Total headcount had also been growing in double digits over the last five years (see Exhibit 7). However, if investment analysts were correct and sales grew by almost 70 percent again in 2008,[21] the large numbers involved could hinder RIM's ability to rely on its historic growth strategy: sourcing from the local talent pool, through employee referrals and new graduate recruitment, and making selective acquisitions of small technology companies. It needed to find upwards of 1,400 new software developers just to maintain the status quo in R&D. And not only did they have to find large numbers of talented individuals, they also had to figure out where they would be located and how to integrate them into RIM's culture.

The culture at RIM headquarters was seen as one of its differentiators and was a key factor in RIM's low employee turnover rate. In fact, the company had recently been recognized as one of "Canada's 10 Most Admired Corporate

Cultures."[22] In describing the way things worked in the software development group at RIM, Dayna Perry, director of organizational development for R&D, commented:

> What we have here is flexibility, adaptability, and the ability to work collaboratively and collegially. We haven't had a lot of process or the kind of bureaucracy that you may see in other larger organizations. . . . It is what has allowed us to be very responsive to market opportunities. It is sort of the "magic" or the "secret sauce" of how things just work and we get things done.

A software developer leading a team working on BlackBerry's many multilingual devices agreed, saying:

> RIM, in comparison to some of its competitors, is a nice and dynamic environment . . . RIM is a place engineers like to work. Some of our competitors treat their engineers as something unimportant. They don't participate in decisions. They are interchangeable. There is a very very strong bureaucracy . . . it's crazy. RIM is very different.

Maintaining its unique culture was a priority for RIM. Remaining centered in Waterloo nurtured this ability. But it was becoming clear that growing mostly in Waterloo was going to become increasingly difficult. Not only did RIM already employ most of the best developers in the area, it already attracted the best and brightest of the nearby University of Waterloo's engineering and computer science graduates. About 300 students came on board every semester through the company's coveted co-op program and many were asked to remain with RIM after graduation. In fact, the talent at the University of Waterloo was so widely recognized that even Bill Gates made frequent visits to the university to court the best students[23] and Google had recently opened facilities there, acknowledging that "Waterloo is an incredible pool of talent"[24] and that it was ready to start hiring the best and the brightest "as quickly as possible."[25]

Attracting outside talent to Waterloo was difficult given the competitive nature of the global software development industry. Most of the big players in the smartphone space were also ramping up. For example, Sony Ericsson had posted 230 design and engineering jobs in Sweden, China, and the United States. Nokia was looking for 375 R&D employees in Finland, the United States, India, and Germany, among other development sites. In California's Silicon Valley, Apple and Google had scooped up many of the top mobile browser developers in a technology cluster famous for its exaggerated employee benefits and unbeatable climate. Motorola could be the exception to the rule, having announced layoffs of engineers. Although Waterloo, Ontario, had recently been named ICF's "Intelligent Community of the Year," the city of 115,000 people[26] might not be perceived by some candidates to be as attractive as other high tech centers which were more cosmopolitan, for example: Silicon Valley, or previous winners of the ICF, Taipei (2006), Mitaka (2005), or Glasgow (2004).[27]

Compounding the problem was a shortage of physical space at RIM's Waterloo campus that was a running joke around headquarters. Even company founder Mike Lazaridis had to laugh about it—responding to a reporter's question about his most embarrassing moment, Lazaridis replied: "Scraping my Aston Martin in RIM's driveway. I was leaving a space and a car came from nowhere. The scratches have been fixed, but not the too-busy parking lot. It's a hazard of a growing company."[28]

On top of it all, RIM was looking to hire a very particular mix of engineers. Although new graduates were essential, to be ahead of the game a good proportion of the incoming employees was going to have to be senior hires. RIM needed people who could fit with the culture and hit the ground running. Dayna noted: "We just don't have the luxury of time to grow all our own talent. We do that in parallel and do a lot of internal promotion, but that is an investment you make in the future, it is not going to help you solve your problem today." And it wasn't just a question of the number of engineers. In software, breakthrough innovations often came from small teams led by a visionary. Many at RIM believed that "software is as much about art as it is about engineering." And in the dynamic wireless communications market, exceptional software developers were scarce.

MANAGING EXPLOSIVE GROWTH

The approach to growth used by RIM in the past would not deliver the scale and scope of R&D resources required to maintain its technical superiority. RIM had several options.

Do What We Do Now, Only More of It

RIM had been very successful in its local recruiting strategy as well as nationwide campus recruitment drives. It relied heavily on the personal and professional networks of existing employees as an ear-on-the-ground approach to finding new talent. One option was to expand co-op programs to other universities as well as increase the frequency and intensity of its new graduate recruitment efforts. Microsoft's intern program, for example, included subsidized housing and transportation (car rental or bike purchase plan), paid travel to Redmond, health club memberships, and even subsidized housecleaning![29]

Likewise, RIM could follow Microsoft's lead and form a global scouting group dedicated to finding the best talent worldwide and bringing them into RIM. Canada ranked as one of the best countries in the world to live in terms of life expectancy, literacy, education, and other standards of living.[30] These and other benefits could attract young developers particularly from emerging markets. As well, the stronger dollar made Canada more attractive.

Similar to other players in the industry (e.g., Apple, Motorola, Sony Ericson, Nokia), RIM posted many of its job openings online and potential employees searched and applied for the positions best suited for their skills and interests. However, with over 800 worldwide job postings, finding the right job was often a daunting task. RIM also had no formal way to manage qualified candidates that may have simply applied to the wrong team and hence good leads were potentially lost. Some competitors allowed candidates to build an open application (similar to Monster or Workopolis) that could then be viewed by anyone in the organization looking for talent. Revamping the careers website and being more creative in the way in which they structured recruiting was being considered.

Some competitors had also formalized hiring and the onboarding processes of computer scientists by hiring in "waves." Rather than posting individual job openings, Symbian, for example, solicited résumés once a year, which were then reviewed, and successful candidates invited to the London, U.K.-based head office to attend one of nine Assessment Days. If the attendees passed a series of tests and interviews, they were then inducted into the company during a formal "bootcamp" training session that lasted five weeks.[31] Symbian had also set up extensive collaborations with 44 universities in 17 countries including China, Russia, and India as well as Ethiopia, Kuwait, Lebanon, Thailand, and the United States. Dubbed The Symbian Academy, this network allowed partners and licensees to post jobs for Symbian Academy students and for professors to collaborate on the research and development of innovative applications such as pollution monitors on GPS-enabled Symbian smartphones.[32] Although RIM enjoyed an excellent relationship with the University of Waterloo, it did not currently have a recruiting strategy of this scope.

Grow and Expand Existing Geographies

RIM had established R&D operations beyond Waterloo, in Ottawa, Mississauga, Dallas, and Chicago over the last five years. It was also expanding the number of product and technology development facilities in locations such as Fort Lauderdale by recruiting through general job fairs. This strategy, however, had to be balanced with a number of trade-offs. First, RIM wanted to ensure that its geographic expansion was not haphazard, but rather strategically executed. Second, the cost of talent in various locations had to be considered. Software engineers in Palo Alto, for example, commanded much higher wages than in Waterloo and the competition there was even more intense, with high turnover costs incurred when employees were wooed away by the many other high tech companies in the area.

There was also some internal resistance to expanding R&D to locations outside of Waterloo. Although there was a growing realization that RIM could no longer continue to grow locally, one senior executive commented:

> There are people here, even leaders and senior people, who have said: "What? Products being built elsewhere? No! We can't do that! Then we won't have any control!" So some of it is a cultural shift and a mind shift for the people that have been here and it is hard for them to let go and to be part of a really big company. And RIM is getting to be a big company now. And for some

people, from an organizational culture perspective, it just doesn't resonate well with them.

This sentiment was not uncommon among software-centric organizations. Despite some geographic expansion, Microsoft, for example, had recently recommitted to its Redmond, Washington, campus, spending over $1 billion on new and upgraded facilities there with room to house an additional 12,000 employees.[33] Google was also strongly committed to maintaining its Mountain View, California, headquarters, with only a few satellite offices. Its unique company culture, built on attracting and keeping the best talent in a young and fun environment, was part of Google's incredible success story and helped it achieve the status of the number one company to work for, according to *Fortune* magazine.[34] Other large software companies such as Oracle and Apple also kept their software developers in one location to foster innovation. In some ways, RIM was already more geographically distributed than many larger software organizations.

Although establishing a geographic expansion plan posed difficulties, RIM had nevertheless laid out several criteria for selecting new locations for product and technology development sites. First, the area had to already have a pool of talent that housed a mature skill set; the city or region had be home to an existing base of software or hardware companies, thus ensuring that a critical mass of highly skilled employees was available. RIM's strategic expansion into Ottawa, for example, was influenced by the availability of talented software engineers in the area in the wake of Nortel's massive layoffs.[35] Lastly, the city or region had to have universities with strong technical programs. This allowed RIM to expand on its successful co-op programs and graduate recruitment initiatives. Once a satellite development site was set up, however, there was still the issue of how to transfer RIM's young and dynamic corporate culture to these locations.

Increase Acquisitions

RIM had success in bringing people on board through acquisition. Several years earlier, RIM had acquired Slangsoft, a high tech start-up in Israel that was developing code which allowed for the ability to display and input Chinese characters—key to tailoring BlackBerry for Asian and other foreign markets. As part of the acquisition, RIM worked with Immigration Canada to relocate 11 of the engineers to Waterloo, 10 of whom were still with RIM more than six years later.

Growth by acquisition was a common practice in the high tech and telecommunications sectors. Google had made its initial move to Waterloo in 2006, for example, through the acquisition of a small wireless software company, subsequently discontinuing the company's web browser product, making it a purchase of talent and intellectual property.[36] Other companies had also made strategic acquisitions of technology. In 2002, Apple, for example, purchased EMagic, a small German company whose software was then used in the development of the popular Mac program Garage Band.[37] In larger and more public acquisitions, Nokia and Motorola had both recently acquired software companies in the hopes of gaining faster access to the growing smartphone market. In 2006, Nokia purchased Intellisync Corporation, a wireless messaging and mobile-software developer, for $430 million, creating Nokia's "business mobility solutions" group.[38] Also in 2006, Motorola purchased Good Technology for a rumored $500 million and released Good 5.0, allowing for secure access to corporate intranets so enterprise users could download, edit, and send documents remotely.[39]

Given the depressed economic climate in the United States in early 2008, many smaller firms and technology start-ups were struggling financially, as were some larger competitors. There were persistent rumors that Palm, for example, was in severe financial trouble.[40] Further, growth by acquisition could also allow for the tactical expansion in other strategic markets.

The European mobile telecommunications market, in particular, was highly "nationalistic," with end users favoring home-grown companies over foreign solutions. Establishing a presence there through acquisition could buy RIM goodwill and serve as a portal to this lucrative market. The economic downturn in the United States and recent competitor plant closures in Europe presented RIM with the potential for opportunistic acquisitions, either of technology or of software engineering talent.

Go Global

In early 2008, most of the R&D was still done in Waterloo, with some core work also being done in Ottawa and product and technology sites throughout the United States and in the United Kingdom. RIM was exploring a broader global expansion. It already had customer service operations in Singapore and sales & marketing representative offices in France, Germany, Italy, Spain, China, Australia, Hong Kong, and Japan. Yet it had stopped short of establishing core research and development sites outside of Canada. Nonetheless, despite a strong desire to keep R&D close to home, RIM estimated that of all the new hires in 2008, likely half would have to be outside of Canada. In addition to the United States, it was looking to Europe, the Middle East, and Africa (EMEA) and Eastern Europe. The same selection criteria of a mature skill set and strong technological universities applied to choosing R&D sites outside North America.

Some of RIM's key competitors had a long history of global expansion of their R&D activities. Symbian, for example, opened an R&D center in Beijing in August 2007, already having three others in the United Kingdom and India.[41] Motorola, had been present in China since 1993 when it established its first R&D center there as part of its Global Software Group (GSG). It had since set up R&D activities in Beijing, Tianjin, Shanghai, Nanjing, Chengdu, and Hangzhou, investing an estimated US $800 million and employing more than 3,000 R&D staff in China. In 2007, Motorola added R&D sites in Vietnam and South Korea[42] and announced it would open an additional R&D complex in Wangjing, China, with another 3,000 employees.[43]

China in particular was beginning to gain worldwide recognition as a center for innovation. The number of patent applications was doubling every two years and the R&D to GDP ratio had also doubled in the last decade. In addition to Motorola, Nokia had set up a number of research bases in China.[44] In 2005, Nokia had five R&D units there, employing more than 600 people; an estimated 40 percent of its global Mobile Phones Business Group handsets were designed and developed in the Beijing Product Creation Center.[45] The company had also recently announced a long-term joint research program with Tsinghua

University in Beijing that would see 20 Nokia researchers working alongside 30 professors and associates and up to 50 students.[46] Globally, Nokia Research Centers (NRC) described its R&D strategy as follows:

> NRC has a two-fold approach to achieving its mandate of leading Nokia into the future. The work for core technology breakthroughs supporting Nokia's existing businesses takes place in the Core Technology Centers, the CTCs. More visionary, exploratory systems research that goes well beyond any current business model is conducted at the many System Research Centers, the SRCs.[47]

Nokia's core technology centers were in Finland, with the SRCs in China, Germany, the United Kingdom, the United States, Finland, and Japan. The company employed 112,262 people, of which 30,415, or 27 percent, were in R&D.[48]

The Motorola Global Software Group (GSG) was more decentralized. In addition to China it had R&D centers in Australia, Singapore, Mexico, Argentina, the United Kingdom, Poland, Russia, Italy, Canada, and India, among others, and employed approximately 27,000 R&D employees worldwide. The Motorola GSG in India had nearly 3,500 engineers and was responsible for designing 40 percent of the software used in Motorola phones worldwide, including the MOTORAZR and MOTO Q. However, Motorola was not noted for having world-class smartphone software. The GSG structure was speculated to have contributed to Motorola's inability to deliver a successful follow-up product to the RAZR as well as to have precipitated the company's recent financial downturn.[49]

Nonetheless, partnering with major research institutes to source top talent appeared to be a fairly common strategy. Motorola India collaborated with six of the seven Indian Institutes of Technology (IIT), as well as the Indian Institute of Science (IISC) and the Indian Institute of Information Technology (IIIT).[50] Other technology firms were also partnering with emerging market governmental and educational institutions to secure a foothold in future markets. Cisco Systems, for example, a leading manufacturer of network equipment, had recently announced a US$16 billion expansion plan into China, including investments in manufacturing,

venture capital and education. Working with China's Ministry of Education, Cisco had established 200 "Networking Academies" in 70 cities in China and had trained more than 90,000 students.[51]

These types of collaborations and international research consortiums, however, raised not only logistical but also legal issues. Source code loss, software piracy, and product imitations were more common in developing countries where IP protection laws (or enforcement) lagged the United States or Canada, leading to both explicit and tacit knowledge "leakage." For example, despite its strong commitment to China, Nokia was recently forced to file suit against two Beijing firms for manufacturing and selling mobile phones that were a direct copy of its proprietary and legally protected industrial designs.[52] Other large high tech companies such as Cisco and Microsoft had also suffered source code breaches. In late 2006, China Unicom, the state-run telecommunications company, had launched its own wireless e-mail service, which it boldly named the Redberry, announcing that their Redberry brand not only continued the already familiar "BlackBerry" image and name, it also fully reflected the symbolic meaning of China Unicom's new red corporate logo.[53] For much of East Asia, reverse engineering and copying foreign products were important sources of learning, helping to transition these markets from imitators of technology to innovators and competitive threats.[54]

Wormald described the difficulties with emerging market dynamics as follows:

> I was just talking to a Fortune 500 CEO the other day who is closing up shop in India. This company had a 45 percent employee turnover rate. They just walk down the street and go work for his competitor and he was tired of his source code just walking out the door.

For RIM, going global was therefore problematic on a number of fronts, most notably because the BlackBerry source code had to be protected. In addition, expanding to emerging markets was also complicated by restrictions regarding cryptographic software. Most governments, including those of Canada and the United States, along with Russia and China, regulated the import and export of encryption products due to national security issues. Encryption was seen as a "dual-use technology" which could have both commercial and military value and was thus carefully monitored. The U.S. government would not purchase any product that had not passed the Federal Information Processing Standard (FIPS) certification tests. This would preclude any product that had encrypted data in China because "if you encrypt data in China, you have to provide the Chinese government with the ability to access the keys."[55] India had also recently notified RIM that it planned to eavesdrop on BlackBerry users, claiming that terrorists may be hiding behind the encrypted messages to avoid detection.[56]

Even if these hurdles could be overcome, going global also brought with it additional challenges of organizational design, communication, and integration between head office and other geographically dispersed locations. Some competitors had chosen to expand globally by product line, while others had outsourced less sensitive functions such as testing and documentation. Eastern European countries such as Poland and Hungary, for example, were emerging as strong contenders for quality assurance testing. The lower cost of labor in developing and transitional economies, however, was showing signs of inflationary pressures in some locales and any planned savings might be somewhat offset by the increased monitoring, coordination, and integration costs. Furthermore, RIM was not set up to manage a multicountry research consortium and the mindset in Waterloo was still very much such that core engineers needed to be seen to be perceived as valuable. On the other hand, the potential could not be ignored. In China, where the penetration rate was only 38 percent, the Symbian OS system used in Nokia, Samsung, Sony Ericsson, and LG smartphones enjoyed a 68.7 percent share, and iPhone sales had reached 400,000 "unlocked" units.[57] In India, where the penetration rate stood at 21 percent, Virgin Mobile had recently struck a brand franchise agreement with Tata Teleservices, announcing plans to gain at least 50 million young subscribers to its mobile services, generating estimated revenues of US$350 billion.[58] The sheer number of potential new users was overwhelming.

CONCLUSION

Looking at the holiday sales numbers and the projected growth for 2008, Yach took a minute to think about the path he was on. He knew that first-quarter revenue projections alone were estimated at $2.2 billion to $2.3 billion and that RIM was expecting to add another 2.2 million BlackBerry subscribers by the end of May 2008.[59] At that rate, analysts projected that 2008 would bring at least another 70 percent growth in sales.[60] Furthermore, Mike Lazaridis had recently said in an interview:

> If you really want to build something sustainable and innovative you have to invest in R&D. If you build the right culture and invest in the right facilities and you encourage and motivate and inspire both young and seasoned people and put them all in the right environment—then it really performs for you. It's what I call sustainable innovation. And it's very different from the idea that you come up with something and then maximize value by reducing its costs. But building a sustainable innovation cycle requires an enormous investment in R&D. You have to understand all the technologies involved.[61]

Yach knew that his software developers were key to RIM's continued success; he was committed to delivering on the expectations for continued and sustainable growth in 2008 and beyond. Although he wanted to keep growing organically, sourcing talent locally and bringing his engineers into the cultural fold of RIM in Waterloo, he suspected this era was ending. In light of the unprecedented and exponential growth of the last year, coupled with the increasing competition and untapped global opportunities, he needed a plan.

Leaving the office after a hectic and frenetic first day back, Yach thought to himself: "How can I plan for this growth when it is just one of 10 burning issues on my agenda? We can't take a time-out to decide how to execute the growth." Grabbing the sales numbers to prepare for tomorrow's meeting, Yach knew he had the evening to consider the way ahead. The vacation was definitely over.

ENDNOTES

[1] D. George-Cosh, "Analysts cheer RIM results, hike targets," *Financial Post*, April 4, 2008, http://www.nationalpost.com/scripts/story.html?id=420318 (accessed April 22, 2008).

[2] Of converged device shipments (smartphones and wireless handhelds). Canalys Smart Mobile Device Analysis service, Press Release, February 5, 2008, http://www.canalys.com/pr/2008/r2008021.htm (accessed April 2, 2008).

[3] http://www.rim.com/newsroom/news/awards/index.shtml.

[4] AFX International Focus, "RIM: Facebook for BlackBerry downloads top 1M," April 1, 2008, http://global.factiva.com (accessed April 1, 2008).

[5] Business Wire, "Guitar Hero II Mobile will rock your BlackBerry Smartphone," April 1, 2008, http://global.factiva.com (accessed April 1, 2008).

[6] Prosumer refers to "professional consumers," customers that use their mobile devices for both business and personal communications.

[7] "Converged" refers to the convergence of the digital wireless communication industry (cellular telephony) and information technology industries, signaled by the arrival of 2G networks which merged voice and data transmissions.

[8] GSMA 20 year factsheet, http://www.gsmworld.com/documents/20_year_factsheet.pdf (accessed April 5, 2008).

[9] P. Svensson, "Microsoft Upgrades Windows Mobile," Associated Press Newswire, April 1, 2008, http://global.factiva.com (accessed April 1, 2008).

[10] Esmerk Finish News, "Global: Survey: Nokia has best innovation strategy," March 25, 2008, http://global.factiva.com (accessed April 1, 2008).

[11] N. Gohring, "Smartphones on the rise? Thank the iPhone, panel says," *Washington Post*, March 31, 2008, http://www.washingtonpost.com/wp-dyn/content/article/2008/03/31/AR2008033102392.html (accessed April 1, 2008).

[12] Canalys Smart Mobile Device Analysis service, Press Release, February 5, 2008, http://www.canalys.com/pr/2008/r2008021.htm (accessed April 2, 2008).

[13] Chris Ambrosio, Strategy Analytics, January 2008 and Pete Cunningham, Canalys, as quoted on www.symbian.com (accessed April 3, 2008).

[14] www.symbian.com (accessed April 3, 2008).

[15] Canalys Smart Mobile Device Analysis service, Press Release, February 5, 2008, http://www.canalys.com/pr/2008/r2008021.htm (accessed April 2, 2008).

[16] A. Hesseldahl, "How the iPhone is suiting up for work," *BusinessWeek*, March 6, 2008, www.businessweek.com (accessed March 21, 2008).

[17] "Microsoft unveils smartphone advancements to improve ability to work and play with one phone," April 1, 2008, Press Release; and "Microsoft announces enterprise-class mobile solution," April 1, 2008, Press Release, www.microsoft.com/prespass/press/2008/apr08.

[18] Canalys Smart Mobile Device Analysis service, Press Release, February 5, 2008, http://www.canalys.com/pr/2008/r2008021.htm (accessed April 2, 2008).

[19] Ken Dulaney of Gartner, as quoted in A. Hesseldahl, "RIM: Growth rules the day," February 22, 2008, www.businessweek.com.

[20] The remaining groups included 836 in sales, marketing and business development; 1,098 in customer care and technical support; 1,158 in manufacturing; and 1,002 in administration, which included information technology, BlackBerry network operations and service development, finance, legal, facilities, and corporate administration.

[21] http://finance.yahoo.com/q/ae?s=RIMM.

[22] Canada's 10 Most Admired Corporate Cultures for 2006, www.waterstonehc.com (accessed April 5, 2008).

[23] D. Friend, "Microsoft hunting IT grads," *London Free Press*, March 22, 2008.

[24] "Google expands Waterloo base," http://atuw.ca/feature-google-expands-waterloo-base/ (accessed April 11, 2008).

[25] A. Petroff, "A Recruiter's Waterloo?" http://www.financialpost.com/trading_desk/technology/story.html?id=389305 (accessed April 11, 2008).

[26] The greater Kitchener-Waterloo area had approximately 450,000 inhabitants.

[27] Intelligent Community Forum, 2007 Intelligent Community of the Year Awards, press release May 18, 2007, http://www.intelligentcommunity.org/displaycommon.cfm?an=1&subarticlenbr=221 (accessed April 5, 2008).

[28] J. Shillingford, "A life run by BlackBerry," *Financial Times*, March 19, 2008, http://global.factiva.com (accessed on April 1, 2008).

[29] http://www.microsoft.com/college/ip_overview.mspx.

[30] United Nations Human Development Index 2007/2008.

[31] http://www.symbian.com/about/careers/graduate%20program/index.html (accessed April 3, 2008).

[32] www.symbian.com (accessed April 3, 2008).

[33] B. Romano, "Microsoft campus expands, transforms, inside out," *Seattle Times*, November 23, 2007, http://seattletimes.nwsource.com/cgi-bin/PrintStory.pl?document_id=2004007121&zsection_id=2003750725&slug=microsoft11&date=20071111 (accessed April 22, 2008).

[34] http://money.cnn.com/magazines/fortune/bestcompanies/2007/snapshots/1.html (accessed April 22, 2008).

[35] Estimated at over 15,000 total jobs in the last eight years; B. Hill, "Nortel to keep Ottawa as main R&D centre," April 4, 2008, *The Montreal Gazette*, http://www.canada.com/montrealgazette/news/business/story.html?id=24aa8d53-154a-4d88-aa9d-593ce9794e10 (accessed April 11, 2008).

[36] M. Evans, "Waterloo gets Googled," January 6, 2006, http://www.financialpost.com/story.html?id=c4f6f084-d72f-43ea-8a82-affe38df3830&k=58579 (accessed April 11, 2008).

[37] A. Hesseldahl, "What to do with Apple's cash," *BusinessWeek*, March 1, 2007, http://www.businessweek.com/technology/content/mar2007/tc20070301_402290.htm (accessed April 11, 2008).

[38] TelecomWeb News Digest, "Nokia completes Intellisync purchase," February 10, 2006, http://global.factiva.com (accessed April 11, 2008).

[39] RCR Wireless News, "Motorola set to leverage Good in competitive e-mail market," June 25, 2007, http://global.factiva.com (accessed April 11, 2008).

[40] S. Weinberg, "Palm acquisition not considered threat to RIM," Dow Jones Newswire, http://global.factiva.com (accessed April 11, 2008).

[41] Business Monitor International, Asia Pacific Telecommunications Insight, April 2008, Issue 24.

[42] Business Monitor International, Asia Pacific Telecommunications Insight, January 2008, Issue 21.

[43] Press Release, "Twenty years' commitment ensures a more successful future," November 8, 2007, http://www.motorola.com/mediacenter/news/detail.jsp?globalObjectId=8923_8852_23&page=archive.

[44] Business Monitor International, Asia Pacific Telecommunications Insight, November 2007, Issue 19.

[45] Press Release, May 21, 2004, "Nokia Expands R&D in China," http://press.nokia.com/PR/200405/946603_5.html.

[46] Press Release, May 28, 2007, "Nokia and Tsinghua University announce new research framework," http://www.nokia.com/A4136001?newsid=1129236.

[47] http://research.nokia.com/centers/index.html..

[48] Nokia annual report 2007.

[49] "What's on Motorola's agenda?" *BusinessWeek*, January 9, 2008, http://www.businessweek.com/innovate/content/jan2008/id2008014_304911_page_2.htm (accessed April 16, 2008).

[50] Motorola 2007 10-K and http://www.motorola.com/mot/doc/6/6294_MotDoc.pdf.

[51] Business Monitor International, Asia Pacific Telecommunications Insight, January 2008, Issue 21.

[52] "Nokia files suit over alleged copy of model," *Shanghai Daily*, June 29, 2006, http://global.factiva.com (accessed April 16, 2008).

[53] A. Hesseldahl, "BlackBerry vs. Redberry in China," *BusinessWeek*, September 25, 2006, http://www.businessweek.com/technology/content/apr2006/tc20060413_266291.htm?chan=search (accessed April 16, 2008).

[54] United Nations World Investment Report 2005, "Transnational Corporations and the Internationalization of R&D," New York and Geneva, 2005, p. 165.

[55] E. Messmer, "Encryption restrictions" and "Federal encryption purchasing requirements," *Network World,* March 15, 2004, http://www .networkworld.com/careers/2004/0315man .html?page=1 (accessed April 22, 2008).

[56] N. Lakshman, "India wants to eavesdrop on BlackBerrys," *BusinessWeek,* April 1, 2008,

http://global.factiva.com (accessed April 7, 2008).

[57] Business Monitor International, Asia Pacific Telecommunications Insight, April 2008, Issue 24.

[58] Ibid.

[59] Press Release, April 2, 2008: http://www .rim.com/news/press/2008/pr-02_04_ 2008-01.shtml.

[60] http://finance.yahoo.com/q/ae?s=RIMM.

[61] A. Hesseldahl, "BlackBerry: Innovation behind the icon," *Business Week*, April 4, 2008, http://www.businessweek.com/inno- vate/content/apr2008/id2008044_416784. htm?chan=search (accessed April 6, 2008).

Problems at China Airlines

Debapratim Purkayastha
IBS Center for Management Research

Monjori Samanta
IBS Center for Management Research

Hadiya Faheem
IBS Center for Management Research

"It's [China Airlines Ltd.] a company that has come through years of external shocks and storms, probably shaken but still fighting."[1]

Derek Sadubin, airline analyst, Center for Asia Pacific Aviation,[2] **in December 2009.**

"We will do what we can to map out new operation strategies in order to increase the company's business and fight for its continued survival."[3]

Philip Wei, Chairman, China Airlines Limited, in July 2008.

INTRODUCTION

In January 2010, Taiwan-based full service airline, China Airlines Ltd. (CAL), announced that it had recorded sales of US$ 358.49 million for the month of December 2009.[4] This was attributed to the increasing cargo sales that offset the losses incurred by the airline in the previous three quarters of financial year (FY) 2009.

Founded in 1959, CAL was the flagship carrier of the Republic of China (ROC). However, it was not completely state-owned. The China Aviation Development Foundation[5] (CADF) had a nearly 54 percent stake in CAL. The airline faced turbulence in its initial years of operations. Its

ICMR
IBS Center for Management Research
www.icmrindia.org

© 2010, IBS Center for Management Research. All rights reserved. This case was written by *Monjori Samanta* and *Hadiya Faheem* under the direction of *Prof. Debapratim Purkayastha,* IBS Center for Management Research. It was prepared from primary sources, and is intended to be used as a basis for class discussion rather than to illustrate either effective or ineffective handling of a management situation.

To order copies, call +91-8417-236667/68 or write to IBS Center for Management Research (ICMR), IFHE Campus, Donthanapally, Sankarapally Road, Hyderabad 501 504, Andhra Pradesh, India or email: info@icmrindia.org.

poor safety record in the 1990s severely tarnished its brand image besides lowering passenger traffic. Analysts felt that faulty pilot recruitment policies, lax maintenance systems, high cost operational structure, inefficient corporate culture, etc. had only added to its troubles. Moreover, the strained political relations between mainland China and Taiwan, which prohibited the airline from launching flights to routes in China, made things worse for it.

The airline's mounting problems prompted it to look for ways to restore its image. Its initial efforts were focused on improving its brand image and regaining consumer confidence. The airline sought to pursue stringent safety norms, increase its maintenance facilities, and hire trained and experienced pilots from foreign countries. The airline also focused on improving cross-strait[6] relations between Taiwan and mainland China since the Chinese aviation market offered tremendous opportunity to it.

To some extent, CAL was successful in revamping its image as was evident from the fact that passenger traffic increased from the late 1990s. The growth in passenger numbers continued through the 2000s. Analysts attributed the growth to the airline's revival efforts that restored consumer confidence. In addition to this, with the improvement of the cross-strait relations between mainland China and Taiwan, the airline could enhance its prospects by tapping the cross-strait passenger traffic, experts pointed out.

Industry observers appreciated the efforts taken by CAL. According to Debbie Wu, a public relations expert at Fu-Jen Catholic University, "China Airlines has undergone many changes ranging from organizational reconstruction to buying new jets and designing new uniforms—changes that consumers have noticed. The public is forgetful, and the airline has diverted attention from the negative news by creating new topics with these moves. It has successfully turned its image around."[7] Estimates by Thomson-Reuters[8] in 2009 predicted a NT\$ 762 million profit in 2010 for the airline.[9,10] On the other hand, some experts felt that the growth outlook for the global aviation industry in 2009–2010 was quite gloomy in light of the rising oil prices and the declining demand for cargo and freight services due to the economic recession.

Some critics opined that while improved cross-strait relations offered CAL an opportunity, it also meant increased competition from low cost mainland China airlines, which might hamper CAL's prospects in the long run. The airline, however, remained positive and expected to return to profitability in 2010. "There is potential for us to swing from loss [this year] to profit next year if the international economy continues improving,"[11] said Philip Wei (Wei), Chairman, CAL.

BACKGROUND NOTE

China Airlines Limited (CAL) was started on December 10, 1959, by some Chinese ex-Air Force officers in Taiwan with an initial fund of NT\$ 400,000.[12] The airline operated with just 26 employees and the limited resources of two PBY-5A Catalina flying boats.[13,14] Initially, the airline undertook mostly military contract work.

From December 1966, the airline started its first international service to Saigon,[15] Vietnam. It also started flights from Japan to Taipei and Hong Kong. In May 1968, CAL was declared as the official airlines of Taiwan and it started operating domestic services across the island. In January 1969, the airline was enlisted by the International Air Transport Association[16] (IATA). During the

first quarter of 1970, CAL started a passenger service to San Francisco.

In 1971, CAL's international operations suffered a major blow when the United Nations[17] (UN) officially accepted the communist People's Republic of China (PRC) as Taiwan's legal government and the airline's membership of the International Civil Aviation Organization[18] (ICAO) was revoked. Following the cancellation by the UN, the carrier lost its international contracts with Japan, Malaysia, and Korea. Its significant air route to Saigon was also lost after the collapse of the South Vietnam government. To make matters worse, the 1973 oil crisis halted its soaring profits. In 1974, CAL started a freight service to Los Angeles in view of the growing exports from Taiwan to America. The airlines also bought a Boeing 747 for the trans-Pacific flight and three Boeing 737s for flying major regional routes in 1975. In 1975, CAL regained permission to fly to Tokyo. In the same year, the airline signed an agreement with Saudi Arabian Airlines to connect with Middle East destinations.

In 1980, CAL's domestic operations suffered and for the first time it registered losses when the rail and road services network improved on the island. Thereafter, the airline concentrated most of its efforts on increasing international passenger and freight services. CAL introduced a passenger and freight service route that went around the world via New York and Amsterdam in 1984. By the end of the 1980s, Taiwanese got permission to travel to mainland China and CAL carried passengers to Hong Kong or Tokyo. From there, mainland Chinese operators like Air China Ltd.,[19] China Eastern Airlines Corporation Limited,[20] and China Southern Airlines Company Limited[21] carried passengers to China.

However, the relations between mainland China and Taiwan remained strained due to the disagreement regarding the political status of Taiwan. While the ROC maintained that it was the valid government ruling both Taiwan and mainland China, most countries held the PRC as the legitimate government following the UN's recognition of it. To escape the diplomatic threat to its operation, CAL entered into a joint venture with Koos Development Corporation to form Mandarin Airlines in 1991. This was a bid to carry out its services in countries such as Canada and Australia where the carrier was banned from operating due to their diplomatic ties with PRC.

In 1991, CAL became a registered corporation but the government still had an 84 percent stake holding through the CADF. In 1993, CAL was listed on the Taipei Stock Exchange and registered a profit of US$ 125 million on revenues of US$ 1.7 billion, to rank as the fifth most profitable carrier in the world.[22] Cargo services accounted for 20 percent of the total revenue. In the same year, CAL also built a massive maintenance facility at Chiang Kai Shek Airport and expanded into other areas like hotels.

In the mid-1990s, CAL felt that the national flag of ROC in its symbol was controversial and so decided to change its logo. The airline felt that the logo would annoy countries favoring the PRC. Thus to revamp its image, the carrier went in for rebranding and unveiled a new brand logo, replacing the previous symbol of Taiwanese flags with pink plum blossoms.[23] The new brand slogan was 'blossom every day'. Analysts felt that the neutral corporate brand image helped CAL gain landing rights in many European cities like Amsterdam, Rome, Frankfurt, and Vienna.

In December 1995, CAL spent NT$ 750 million on procuring 15 advanced Boeing 737 medium-haul jets as part of its expansion strategy. In 1996, to improve its business prospects further, CAL took over one-third of Formosa Airlines[24] and went in for a code-sharing arrangement with American Airlines[25] for trans-Pacific routes. With all these efforts, CAL was able to register a higher profit of US$ 90 million in 1996.[26] In 1997, the carrier secured a place among the top ten cargo airlines. However, the Asian financial crisis of 1997–98 led to CAL incurring losses of US$ 92.6 million in 1998 on sales of US$ 1.61 billion.[27]

In 2004, the carrier started passenger flights to Seattle, Houston, and Hiroshima. In 2006, the Taiwanese government advocated the need to change the airline's name. They felt that it was controversial and misleading as many customers thought that it was a China-based airline. CAL hired international brand analysts, marketers, and accountants to analyze its existing brand value and estimated the costs the airline would have to bear if it went in for rebranding. The rebranding costs were estimated at US$ 10 billion.[28] However, analysts pointed out that renaming would reduce CAL's brand value as initially many customers would be unaware of the name change. While searching online they might end up selecting Air China, which sounded similar. Moreover, the cost of repainting its fleet of 67 airlines was estimated at a whopping amount of NT$ 13.4 million in addition to the labor charges. Since renaming appeared to be a costly exercise for the company, CAL continued with the same name.

By 2007, CAL had captured one fourth of the total aviation market in Taiwan to become the country's biggest airline. By 2008, its main areas of operation included airlines, cargo, and postal services. CAL's other businesses included repair and maintenance of airplanes, ground services, freight logistics, travel and tourism services, information networking, in-flight catering, laundry and cleaning, aerospace technology, and investment and leasing. The carrier also sold airplane spare parts and aviation equipment and dealt with renting and selling airplanes.

For the FY 2008, CAL's operating revenue stood at NT$125.22 billion (refer to Exhibit I for financial highlights of CAL from 2002–2008).

Exhibit I Financial Highlights (2002–2008) (in million NT$)

Years	2002	2003	2004	2005	2006	2007	2008
Operating Revenue	78,937	75,859	96,175	108,688	121,995	126,993	125,221
Passenger Revenue	41,971	36,565	48,595	55,656	63,062	67,207	68,546
Cargo Revenue	32,858	34,891	41,873	47,304	53,093	53,650	50,902
Other Revenue	4,108	4,402	5,706	5,727	5,840	6,136	5,773
Total cost	61,120	60,470	76,273	91,391	104,329	110,241	121,253
Operating Expenses	67,841	12,571	90,554	105,333	119,161	125,642	136,839
Gross Profits	17,817	15,388	19,901	17,295	17,665	16,751	3,967

Source: Annual Reports of China Airlines Limited from 2002–2008.

Exhibit II   CAL's International Routes

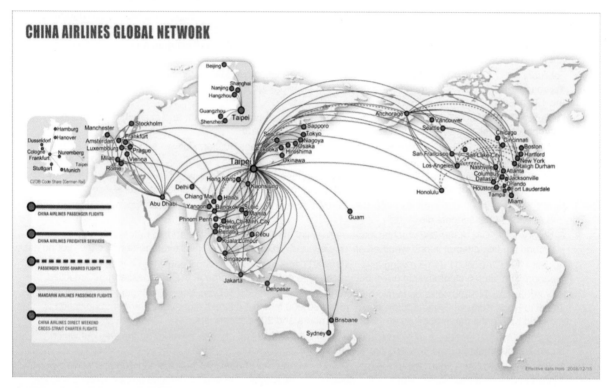

Source: www.checkusouttravel.com.au.

Its aviation network included Taiwan, Northeast Asia, Southeast Asia, the United States of America, Europe and Australia (refer to Exhibit II for CAL's International Routes). In 2008, CAL operated with a fleet of 66 airplanes and its network covered 76 destinations in 27 countries.

CAL'S DIFFICULTIES

Industry observers felt that the airline's poor reputation could be attributed to its safety record. In addition to this, CAL's recruitment policies, corporate culture, and the strained political relations between mainland China and Taiwan were blamed for its troubles. The rising fuel prices and the global economic slowdown only added to its woes.

Dreadful Safety Record

CAL's history of 50 years of operations was marred by several and frequent airlines disasters (refer to Exhibit III for Plane Crashes and Significant Safety Events of CAL). The unfortunate disaster record of almost 12 fatal events in its operations history had severely tarnished the image of the carrier.

The airlines crash history dated back to 1980, when one of its airliners crashed in Manila, the Philippines. The pilot made a risky landing and touched the ground even before it had reached the runway. The aircraft bounced and finally came to a halt on the runway, damaging two outboard engines and parts of a wing and killing two people among the 122 on board.[29] In 1986, a CAL airliner crashed into an island in Taiwan killing all the passengers on board when the pilot reportedly made an error in judgment and attempted to go around[30] before landing. In 1989, another pilot error led to an air crash. The pilot executed a wrong take-off, and killing all passengers on board.

Another go-around approach taken by a pilot went wrong in 1994, killing 264 people in

Exhibit III   Plane Crashes and Significant Safety Events of CAL

1. August 1970: The CAL YS11 runs into bad weather minutes before landing in Taipei and hits a ridge 800 meters from the runway. Two of the five crew members and 12 of the 26 passengers are killed.

2. November 1971: CAL Caravelle is bombed over the Formosa Strait. All 17 passengers and eight crew members are killed.

3. February 1980: CAL 707-300 again runs into trouble before landing in Manila Airport in a "steep and de-stabilized approach" and touches the ground short of the runway. Two engines and parts of a wing get damaged and two of the 122 passengers die.

4. February 1986: CAL 737-200 aborts landing in the Pescadores Islands, Taiwan, and in a failed go around attempt, kills all six passengers and seven crew members on board.

5. October 1989: CAL 737-200 makes incorrect takeoff procedure near Hualien, Taiwan and hits clouds at 2130 meters in sky. All seven crew members and 49 passengers are killed.

6. November 1993: Another CAL 747 touches down more than two-thirds of the way down the runway at Hong Kong's old Kai Tak Airport and lands in water. All 396 aboard who suffered the ordeal are alive.

7. April 1994: CAL A300-600 crashes because of crew errors during approach to Nagoya, Japan. All 15 crew and 249 of the 264 passengers die.

8. February 1998: CAL A300-600 crashes into a residential area in Taoyuan after landing before the runway during a second landing attempt in bad weather. All 15 crew and 182 passengers plus seven persons on the ground die.

9. August 1999: CAL MD11 drags a wing and crashes at Chek Lap Kok in Hong Kong when it tries to land in a typhoon. The aircraft stops upside down but catches fire. Luckily, only three of the 300 passengers are killed.

10. May 2002: CAL 747-200 splits up in mid air near the Penghu Islands, Taiwan, after 20 minutes during a flight from Taipei to Hong Kong while the aircraft is just above 30,000 feet. No distress signal or other communication is received before the crash that kills all 19 crew members and 206 passengers.

11. May 2002: A CAL flight takes off from a taxiway in Alaska and strikes an embankment on the way out which damages the landing gear. However, it manages to land safely later.

12. August 20, 2007: CAL Flight 120, a Boeing 737-800 inbound from Taipei, catches fire after landing at Naha Airport in Okinawa Prefecture, Japan. After stopping on the tarmac, the engine catches fire, and later explodes after all the passengers have been evacuated.

Source: http://www.airsafe.com/events/airlines/taiwan.htm.

Nagoya, Japan.[31] This incident led to a decrease in the airline's passenger traffic, bringing down its profits to US$ 24 million.[32] Investigations revealed that the pilot had accidentally kept the computerized "touch and go" mode on, which automatically pulled the aircraft up and away before landing. According to World Net Daily,[33] "The pilot, determined to land the aircraft, engaged in a battle for control of the plane. The result was a classic computer "loop." Each time the pilot pushed the airliner down to land, the computer obediently pulled the jet back up to go around. On the third try, the entire system, including the airliner, crashed."[34]

In 1996, a CAL aircraft caught fire. It was found that CAL had ignored Boeing Corporation's[35] (Boeing) recommendation that airlines should stop the cost-cutting measure of flying with empty fuel tanks on all older 747 models. This was the reason behind the aircraft disaster of CAL in 1996. As revealed by investigation reports, the aircraft's center fuel tank was half empty and hence had caught fire. CAL's vice president of flight safety, Samson Yeh, admitted that the aircraft had taken off with a half empty fuel tank. However, he also defended the airline's actions saying that it had "put some insulation on the wiring [of the fuel pumps]"[36] to prevent gases inside the empty tank from catching fire from any short circuit.

A CAL pilot also admitted that the airline had disregarded Boeing's instructions "because here in Taiwan everything is about money."[37] The pilot also claimed that many other pilots knew CAL was ignoring Boeing's recommendation but did not report it to the state Civil Aeronautics Administration[38] (CAA). According to the pilot, both the CAA and the company were owned by the government. Thus he feared that any report against the malpractices of CAL to the CAA would ultimately reach the government. If such reports were lodged, they would further jeopardize the image of the carrier. The pilot also feared that the government, to protect its image, would purposely fail the pilot and cancel his license to penalize him for complaining against CAL. Industry observers pointed out that such incidents pointed to the airline's faulty maintenance procedures for cost cutting that put passengers' lives at stake.

Some experts pointed out that CAL continued to neglect pilot training issues as was observed in a similar incident in 1998 when due to rains and reduced visibility, the pilot was ordered to go around and abort landing. But the pilot was unable to do so and this led to a crash landing during the second attempt, which killed all the passengers on board as well as people on the ground. This severely dented the image of the airline. David Learmount (Learmount) of *Flight International*[39] said, "After the 1998 crash we saw a mass boycott of CAL by the Taiwanese. It seems most people in Taiwan would prefer to travel on other airlines with better safety records."[40]

In February 1998, another CAL jet crashed in Taipei, killing 203 people. In the same year, Formosa Airlines also suffered a crash. About 130 flight attendants resigned from CAL after the crash. CAL's image took a severe beating after these accidents as also that of Taiwan's airlines industry as a whole. The Taiwanese government, with a 71 percent stake in the carrier, decided to disinvest 16 percent ownership to a foreign equity partner.

Despite receiving criticism from several quarters, the airline didn't improve its safety standards and witnessed another disaster in 2002, when a Boeing 747 crashed, killing all on board. Of those killed, 190 were from Taiwan, 14 from Hong Kong and Macau, nine from mainland China, and one from Switzerland.[41] To protect itself from public wrath, the airline initially passed on the blame to mainland China and issued a press statement accusing them of intentionally attacking the plane with a missile. These allegations were later refuted both by the Chinese authorities and the National Security Bureau of Taiwan. Preliminary investigations brought out the fact that the aircraft had been damaged in 1980 and only an aluminum patch had been used to repair an area near the rear cargo door. Aviation experts pointed

out that the crash was the result of CAL's wrong policies and technical defects in Boeing 747 aircraft. Learmount questioned the airline's safety procedures and said that, "It (aluminum patch) does look like a highly inadvisable piece of engineering. Either that or the hull was not inspected fully for a pattern of progressive cracking, which caused the plane to disintegrate in mid-air. The fact that either of these occurred speaks for itself when reflecting on CAL safety record, which is exceptionally bad when compared to other oriental airlines."[42]

The low standards of maintenance at CAL again came to light in the 2007 disaster. The aircraft caught fire immediately after landing in Okinawa, Japan. Moments after passengers were evacuated, the plane broke up into two parts. The investigation committee found that fuel had been leaking from a hole created by a loose bolt. Investigating officials said, "The bolt that came loose and damaged the fuel tank of the CAL jet that burst into flames at Okinawa's Naha Airport last Monday likely was incorrectly installed, as a washer and other parts that should have been installed with it have not been found."[43] According to them, this might have happened during a routine maintenance check up. According to The BBC's Jonathan Marcus, "Keeping older aircraft flying is not a problem in itself, but it clearly requires operators to maintain the highest levels of maintenance and to ensure that repair work is carried out to the standards recommended by the manufacturer."[44] Another fact which further damaged the airline's reputation was that it had offered an instant compensation amount of US$ 800–900 at the accident site. Industry observers described this as a desperate attempt by the airline to save its image. The step was strongly criticized by the passengers. In addition to this, passengers also complained that the airline crew was insufficiently trained to handle such an emergency situation. According to them, the crew wasn't alert enough and saw the fire only after some passengers had started screaming. They also failed to give proper instructions during evacuation and the passengers were not guided properly while opening emergency exits or while they were standing outside the aircraft after evacuation, some passengers charged. CAL was also criticized for whitening the name and logo of the aircraft to prevent these from appearing in news videos or photos. CAL justified its act and said that it had got the required permission for such an action from the Land, Infrastructure, and Transport Ministry's Aircraft and Railway Accidents Investigation Commission. The commission had permitted it to paint over the name as it would not affect the process of investigation of the accident, it said. However, all such attempts to save its image went in vain as it only succeeded in generating even more negative publicity for the carrier.

From 1970–2009, the average number of fatal events per million flights for CAL was estimated by Airsafe.com foundation[45] at 6.44, much higher than the worldwide average score of less than 1.5.[46]

Industry experts felt that the poor safety record of the airline could be attributed to several factors including neglect of aircraft maintenance, bad hiring policies for captains and co-pilots, a lenient flight crew training process, and cost-cutting policies of the management, which sacrificed safety standards. They also suggested that the airline was careless regarding flight simulators and training time of pilots. Another major reason pointed out by industry experts was the ex–air force background of a majority of the airline's pilots. Airline analysts reported that these pilots were known to have a tendency to take risks that other trained pilots would not take. Industry analysts also suggested that the airline's laidback attitude in matters of safety followed from the fact that it was a government-owned airline. According to Bruce Tsao (Tsao), an analyst with Capital Securities,[47] "Their staffs are more like government employees than their counterparts in other companies. It's an old company with a government background. That mentality may be related to its safety track record."[48]

Strained Political Relations

While most of its troubles were attributed to its poor safety record, hostile cross-strait relations between mainland China and Taiwan added to the airline's troubles. From 1949, mainland China carriers had been prohibited from operating services to Taiwan and it was mandatory for all Taiwanese planes to land in the airspace of a third country such as Hong Kong or Macau before flying to mainland China. Such transfer of flights and cargo in Hong Kong or Macau wasted both time (about three times more than the direct route across the 150-km long Taiwan Strait) and money and increased the cost burden for all Taiwanese carriers including CAL.

Over the years, the political relations between Taiwan and mainland China had become more strained due to the growing dispute regarding the political status of Taiwan, despite the existence of strong economic ties between both the countries. Industry observers felt that the strained relations hampered trade and commerce between mainland China and Taiwan since the economic prosperity of mainland China offered Taiwanese businesses a prospective market to carry on trade relations. It was reported that Taiwan had US$ 70 billion worth of business ventures with mainland China ranging from manufacturing electronics, toys, and textiles to real estate projects, in different provinces of China in 2007. It was also noted that around 1 million Taiwanese travelled from Taiwan to important cities of mainland China for their businesses.[49] However, the direct flight restrictions from Taiwan to mainland China had led to Taiwan's airlines incurring losses amounting to US$ 33 billion from 1998 to 2008, according to the Taipei Airline Association.[50]

In addition to this, experts pointed out that Taiwanese airlines also suffered because tourists from mainland China were not allowed to travel to Taiwan individually but only in groups. Moreover, cargo transshipment services were also not allowed between Taiwan and mainland China. Such restrictive rules had for long handicapped the expansion of CAL's services not only in the cross-strait region but also on the international flight routes to Europe. Taiwanese airlines travelling to Europe usually had to go via a southern route through Southeast Asia and the Middle East due to these restrictions. Instead, a northern route through mainland China was expected to reduce the flight time between Taipei and Europe by 3 hours.

Thus the opening up of relations between mainland China and Taiwan was expected to expand CAL's potential markets for both passenger and cargo services, according to CAL. CAL also pointed out the tremendous potential offered by the Chinese aviation market. Wei added, "There are about 1 million Taiwanese businesspeople doing business in China. They constantly go back and forth between the two sides. Their increasing investment in the Chinese market has given a boost to our cargo sector. We also value China's market potential, given its population of 1.3 billion and its substantial economic growth in recent years. Therefore, lifting the ban on cross-strait transportation would surely benefit the industry."[51]

The airline was also hopeful that improved cross-strait relations would offset the threat of competition it faced from Chinese carriers. According to Wei, "We definitely can compete. Our products, including our aircraft, our service, and our flight networks, are superior to those of our Chinese counterparts. In addition to a huge number of Taiwanese businesspeople, we also target Chinese visitors and other foreign passengers. If the government gives the green light to direct traffic, we will be able to fly the routes instantly with our flexible flight deployment and with our crews stationed in main cities, ready to serve."[52]

In addition, due to political pressure from the PRC, many countries had restricted the carrier from operating in their lands. The political environment too had limited CAL's growth since countries such as Canada and Australia had an agreement with the PRC which required them to ban CAL from operating in their territory. Traditionally, most Taiwanese carriers worked under bilateral air service agreements with other countries which had proved to be restrictive. To get out of the clutches of the restrictive authority of CADF, the airline had decided to transfer the ownership to some private hands. But investors had not shown much interest in buying out the company in face of the global recession and low yielding airline stocks.

The Low Cost Threat

The carrier faced competition from both Taiwanese carriers as well as China's aggressive government-owned budget airlines. These China-based Low Cost Carriers (LCCs) not only captured CAL's market for short-haul flights in the region, but also a significant proportion of its international market of operating nonstop flights to Europe, across the Pacific Ocean. CAL could not adopt an LCC model since the already low labor costs meant less

scope for reducing costs further. However, analysts felt that the "regulatory and interfering regime" of Taiwan had been responsible for restricting CAL's global expansion as an LCC. While much of the threat was from LCCs, CAL also faced competition from Taiwan-based EVA Airways, an FSA which operated on domestic as well as international routes.

Other Problems

In addition to the air crashes, strained political relations between mainland China and Taiwan, and competition from LCCs, there were other problems plaguing the company. The impact of the September 11, 2001, terrorist attacks[53] on the U.S. continued to hamper the airline's business. America constituted CAL's main operational market in relation to both cargo and passenger services. However, after the attacks, CAL had suffered major losses of US$ 2.3 billion due to a 5 percent drop in passenger traffic.

CAL's problems were compounded by the rise in fuel costs and the reduced passenger volumes due to the global economic slowdown. For the first quarter of 2008, CAL incurred losses of US$ 98 million. The airline adopted various strategies to lower operational costs like reducing the number of flights by 150 per month and allowing employees to take leave without pay. About 100 passenger services catering to destinations in the U.S. and Asia and 50 cargo services were reduced per month. The saturation of the main airport hubs in Asia and a dearth of secondary airports also posed some operational problems for CAL.

REVIVAL EFFORTS

CAL adopted various steps over the years to revive its image after several fatal air disasters happened due to pilot errors and poor maintenance procedures. The company diligently pursued a policy of retraining pilots and redesigning its safety procedures. As a first step toward improving its flight safety, the airline started reforming and standardizing its flight procedures in 2000. It diligently pursued a policy of recruiting experienced pilots from international airlines and retraining its own pilots.

Simple Fleet

One of the steps taken by CAL was to cut costs. It simplified its fleet by reducing the kinds of aircraft it operated. According to Wei, "By reducing the types of aircraft we have, we can improve our cost controls even more than through training our pilots and maintenance crews."[54] CAL reported that fleet renewal and aircraft type streamlining had always been one of the important cost-saving strategies of the airline. In 2007, the average age of the aircraft was only 5.6 years, with only three aircraft types, making it one of the youngest fleets in the world. In 2008, CAL removed two Boeing B747-400s and added a new Airbus A330-300. With this, CAL's average fleet age was just 6.2 years.

Continuing its Business Model

Since its inception, CAL had operated as an FSA and it continued with this business model rather than going in for an LCC model. The airline felt that the LCC model would not work out for it in view of the restrictive operating environment for Taiwan-based carriers. In addition, its fares were quite low and competitive. There was little scope for further reducing operational costs by lowering the fares even more and thereby increasing demand and total revenues. Thus to beat the competition from other Taiwanese operators and LCCs of mainland China, CAL pursued a different set of strategies to control operational costs and garner profits. It procured new aircraft, entered into alliances with important international airlines to expand its global networks, introduced new routes, expanded cargo business, enhanced in-flight services, and developed its maintenance and safety facilities. According to industry experts, all these steps helped the airline to streamline costs and boost sales.

While the airline continued with its business model, it planned to adopt some characteristics of LCCs to lower operational costs. It introduced a series of e-services on its website www.China-airlines.com, providing on-line booking, on-line individual and group check-in, and on-line baggage tracking services to customers. For business travelers who wanted quick service, it started express passenger check-in service kiosks at two important airports in Taiwan.

Revamping its HR Policies

Since the airline's image had taken a beating due to the culture prevailing in the organization, particularly among pilots, the carrier decided to go in for a revamp of its HR policies, according to experts. As a first step, the airline brought about a change in management. Chen Shui-bian, President of ROC, removed managers at the top-level and hired a woman chief executive, Christine Tsai-yi Tsung. The company also decided to reduce hiring pilots with a military background as they had become infamous as an "ex air-force flying club."[55] Instead, it started employing pilots who had worked with renowned international airlines like Singapore Airlines, United Airlines, Cathay Pacific Airways, etc.

The recruitment procedure at CAL was made stringent. The recruits had to undergo a strict screening process which ensured that the minimum qualification criteria of the pilots were met. This was a bid to curb the rising objections regarding the airlines' safety record. To offer training to the new recruits, CAL employed a military flight training method, developed by 'BAE Systems'[56] to train pilots. Besides regular training programs, CAL also started regular flight simulator tests once in three months. These tests included testing the pilot's skill under simulated emergency situations. For instance, pilots had to perform a successful landing operation in a simulated situation when the plane failed to function due to bad weather. They also tested a pilot's skill to control nonscheduled raid situations and emergency situations. During this process, the pilots' actions were monitored by a system that recorded any unacceptable behavior on their part. According to Young, "Pilots failing to pass the tests are required to enhance their skills until they can handle all kinds of critical situations without endangering a single life on board."[57] The company also took severe disciplinary action against pilots who failed to observe the rules laid down by the company. For instance, it immediately removed a pilot whose blood-alcohol level was 0.087 percent (more than the permitted level of 0.04 percent) before he boarded a flight that was leaving for the U.S. This prevented pilots from consuming alcohol 12 hours prior to any flight duty.

CAL also arranged for a training program for recruits in the U.S. and Australia to help build up their skills, language ability, and discipline. During the initial years, these newly recruited pilots had to work as co-pilots under the captaincy of the senior pilots who had a military background. An analyst said that one such co-pilot had revealed that "you have to remember at all times that the guy in the right-hand seat is trying to kill you."[58] However, this initiative led to the pilots complaining that, "they were frustrated when they came back because seniority kept them in the co-pilot's seat."[59]

From 2005, CAL started an online education system with the launch of the 'Enterprise Information Portal System'. The portal had up-to-date information regarding services and also served as a platform for employees to share useful experiences with their co-workers. The new e-Learning system gave the employees the option of studying and improving their aptitude irrespective of time and space. A similar skill enhancing e-management program was also started for administrative workers. The airline signed up a new safety consultant Lufthansa Technik[60] in 1995 for training its pilots and engineers to ensure higher aviation safety standards.

Experts commended CAL's efforts at improving its abysmal safety record when the airline initiated a practical safety awareness training program "China Airlines and I," for newly recruited pilots and cabin crew. In addition, CAL had established an E-Safety Report system, and arranged seminars for FOQA/FORAS[61] case study. An annual 'Safety Composition' contest was held for all employees where the winner was crowned Air Safety Model Worker.

In 2006, CAL introduced tougher selection procedures for pilots. All pilots underwent a basic training that was customized according to the personnel's background. They had to pass civil aviation exams, and get aircraft specific training. Their skills were reviewed regularly during each flight, and in addition simulator examinations were held every six months and route examinations were taken annually, to ensure the highest standards of piloting skills and to enhance flight safety.

In 2008, in keeping with the worldwide policy, CAL formulated the Multi-crew Pilot License training program for new pilots. At the same time to ensure best teaching practices, it developed 'Instructor Monitoring Guidelines' for the annual appraisal process of instructors. All these efforts helped the airline pass the prestigious and strict "IOSA-IATA Operational Safety Audit," done by IATA. To cut costs, the airline also offered pension packages to employees willing to retire voluntarily.

Promotional Efforts

In a bid to improve its brand image, the company continued with its Dynasty Flyer Program (DFP) launched in 1989 (refer to Exhibit IV for details of CAL's Dynasty Flyer program). In 2005, CAL launched the Dynasty Package program[62] and introduced 140 travel tour packages covering 17 countries and 13 cities including popular foreign tourist places of the Taiwanese. Such a program helped to increase the Dynasty Package sales by 132 percent in 2005. Dynasty tour sales in 2006 increased by 55 percent compared to the previous year. This was attributed to the introduction of an online system for Dynasty Packages which included product/price information, online payment, and E-vouchers.

CAL's promotional efforts led to the airline flying 80,000 travelers in 2008, a rise of 12 percent from 2007, despite the global economic slowdown.[63] Industry observers pointed out that the promotional efforts had helped to offset some of the effects of the negative image it had built in the minds of customers, who were wary of flying CAL.

e-Ticketing

While CAL took steps to revive its image, it also focused on offering benefits to consumers that would attract them to the airline. In 2005, it initiated an "Online ATM" with e-ticketing technology, in collaboration with Cathay United Bank[64] to reduce operational costs as well as provide consumers an easy payment option. Taiwanese consumers could purchase air tickets from the CAL website for international flights using these ATM cards. A Taipei Warehousing Integration Operation System was also launched that provided warehouses, freight forwarders, and airlines with a digital platform to exchange information, shorten procedures, increase cost efficiency, and ensure better service quality to customers.

Exhibit IV   CAL'S Dynasty Flyer Program

Started in 1989, CAL's Dynasty Flyer Program (DFP) offered its members various value added services as per the mileage earned by a passenger when he/she used CAL or any of its participating partner services. The program included four tiers: Dynasty Flyer, Gold, Emerald, and Paragon. Elite members enjoyed better amenities like the VIP Lounge facility and more allowance for checked baggage. Such members also had the option of upgrading their booking for a better cabin.

Analysts commended the program as it applied even to budget travelers, offering full mileage earning on most fares with only a few exceptions, as against other Asian carriers which focused mostly on higher class members. Moreover, its association with various partners like other airlines, banks, and hotels helped its members collect more mileage points and redeem them.

Members of the DFP had the convenient option of transferring awards to nominated relatives and friends, who were also members of the program. CAL permitted up to six nominations for each member. Passengers also were happy that membership expired after six years as compared to the normal period of two years offered by other airlines. However, passengers remained unhappy about the huge amount of mileage points they had to collect for elite class membership. Critics also opined that partners should include more internationally reputed hotel chains.

As of 2007, 1.6 million members had registered for DFP. By 2007, they added two further destinations under the Dynasty Package to Abu Dhabi and Dubai, offering about 150 products covering 37 destinations.

In 2008, CAL started a B2B2C system and XML data transfer system that helped agents and also customers to get the latest information about Dynasty tours. CAL also added many e-services on their website so that Dynasty fliers could avail of the program benefits online as for example purchasing online tickets, redeeming points, upgrading tickets, etc. In that year, CAL also started a joint loyalty program with Czech Airlines and Hainan Airlines of mainland China, so that passengers could add more mileage points by flying any of them.

Source: "Unstoppable and Irreversible: LCCs Spread Around the World: Regional Round-Up," www.centreforaviation.com, December 2, 2009.

CAL continuously improved its e-services and from 2007, a B2B2C system Axess[65] was also started that connected the CAL computer reservation system to ticket agencies. This enabled agents all over the world to issue e-tickets to travelers within a few minutes. According to experts, implementation of such an efficient and transparent transaction system for the benefit of customers to select tours, not only improved CAL's image but also increased its sales potential. E-service upgrades also helped agents to provide Dynasty Package products to frequent flyer members. An inter-airline e-ticket facility was also started between CAL and 54 major airlines such as British Airways, Cathay Pacific, KLM, US Airways, JAL, Singapore Airlines, Alitalia, China Southern Airlines, China Eastern Airlines, and EVA Airways. Experts opined that such a move to improve e-ticketing procedures would bring down check-in times and reduce the chances of tickets getting lost. This would benefit passengers and at the same time lower operating costs for the company.

Other Initiatives

In 2006, as part of its 47th anniversary celebration, CAL introduced new uniforms for its employees that were fashionable yet traditional, to reflect its corporate spirit and image. The airline, together with the CAA, also set up new operation headquarters, the "Taoyuan International Airport Airlines Operation Center." The center included CAL's corporate headquarters, as well as a crew training and dispatch center and a four-star international brand hotel Novotel. The airline's maintenance and flight operations and in-flight service functions were also integrated into a single location. According to Wei, "This is the first time ever for China Airlines to build a corporate compound, opening a new chapter in company history. The relocation of its corporate premises will boost CAL's corporate image and work efficiency, and will help reduce costs."[66]

In 2006, CAL joined Boeing's cutting-edge Maintenance Plan and Boeing E-One control system "to integrate airplane maintenance plans, airplane configuration management, and digital worksheet editing for aircraft maintenance control."[67] In 2007, the company started a 120,000-pound engine test cell in this regard and included Boeing's Maintenance Performance Toolbox to help the on-board inspection of maintenance and repairs.

CAL also entered into code sharing agreements with reputed airlines such as Continental Airlines, Delta Airlines, Thai Airways International (Star Alliance), Korean Air, Alitalia, Garuda Indonesia Airlines, Vietnam Airlines, etc. According to experts, this not only extended CAL's operating network but also improved its image and restored consumer confidence as it implied that these airlines had acknowledged CAL's safety and service record.

In 2007, CAL underwent a corporate reorganization anticipating improvements in cross-strait relations and also in global aviation markets. The company unveiled its new corporate vision and added 'Team Spirit'[68] to one of its earlier four core values, which were "Safety, Discipline, Innovation, and Service" in respect of in-flight and ground services, as well as on-the-job safety. The chairman of the board and the then president of CAL, Chao Kuo-Shui, said this reorganization outlined, "Strict discipline and a line of responsibility for every action, a new method for streamlining procedures, and an outline of appropriate attitudes toward customers and coworkers. CAL will strive to become one of the world's most trustworthy airlines through reorganization, innovation of corporate culture, and improvements in maintenance."[69] This included some personnel changes in the higher posts to implement higher standards in aircraft maintenance such as hiring a new Senior VP of Engineering and Maintenance and two new managers for the Engineering and Maintenance Division and the Maintenance Quality Management Division. The company's Senior VPs were entrusted with the task of forming a maintenance improvement policy committee whose job was to develop and execute the improvement plan.

As part of CAL's continuous efforts to implement safety measures, the year 2008 was declared as the "Safety Management System" promotion year by CAL. According to CAL, the "Safety Management System and efficient management of aviation risks relating to flight operations, engineering, and maintenance, and ground services have become part of our corporate culture, and will help us achieve our 'Zero Accident' objective."[70]

IMPROVING CROSS-STRAIT RELATIONS

From 1949, when the PRC government came to power, till 1979, relations between mainland China and Taiwan had remained practically frozen. Initiatives to relax the tension began from as early as 1979, but restrictive and non-cooperative political relations had mostly dampened the efforts to improve trade and transport between Taiwan and mainland China. The situation worsened in 2000 when the then President of Taiwan, Chen Shui-bian, who supported Taiwan's independence from China, came to power. Under his presidency, no progress was made on improving economic ties against the background of strained political relations, with Beijing being totally opposed to his advocacy for independent Taiwan. Experts pointed out that though political relations had worsened, the economic rise in mainland China had had a greater impact on Taiwan than on any other country. In 2007, it was reported that cross-strait trade stood at US$ 130.2 billion and mainland China was their highest contributor.[71] Even in terms of exports, mainland China was Taiwan's primary market, accounting for 40.7 percent of their total exports worth US$ 100.4 billion in 2007.[72] Industry experts felt that the removal of cross-strait trade restrictions would give a further boost to Taiwan's business prospects. The easing of cross-strait relations was also expected to reduce operational costs and increase the profits for both mainland China and Taiwan-based airlines.

In May 2008, Ma Ying-jeou (Ying-jeou) took office as the president of Taiwan. Ying-jeou took significant steps toward improving the economic ties of Taiwan with mainland China. He initiated efforts to remove policy restrictions and normalize trade relations across the Taiwan Strait after assessing the response from the Chinese government. The governments of Taiwan and mainland China sought to improve relations in the areas of commerce, finance, and transportation.

From July 2008, direct charter passenger flights were allowed across the Taiwan Strait on a regular basis. Eight airports of Taiwan and five of mainland China were opened up for flight operations. This helped to reduce operational costs for the Taiwanese carriers by reducing the total flight time. It was also estimated that passengers were able to save NT$ 3 billion a year due to the direct flights between both the countries.

By October 2008, 11 airlines from Taiwan and mainland China were operating 18 flights in each direction, linking Taoyuan International Airport in northern Taiwan and Taipei Songshan Airport in downtown Taipei city with airports in Beijing, Shanghai, Nanjing, Xiamen, and Guangzhou in mainland China.[73]

In 2008, CAL entered into an agreement with China Cargo Airlines and China Southern Airlines to exchange cargo space, for the benefit of cargo customers. China Southern agreed to endorse CAL's move to join the SkyTeam[74] alliance. CAL also teamed up with Chunghwa Post Co.[75] to transport daily mail and postal goods to China on passenger as well as freight charter flights.

The opening of direct cross-strait routes helped CAL take advantage of the thriving aviation market in China by introducing daily passenger flights as well as cargo services. As per the expanded cross-strait flight agreement signed on April 24, 2009, the number of passenger flights per week was increased from 108 in 2008 to 270 (or 135 for airline per side) in April 2009. The number of cargo flights allowed increased from 30 to 112 return services per month (28 per week, or 14 per side).[76] CAL also started 55 scheduled direct flights to 13 cities in mainland China whereas earlier it had had 22 charter flights to mainland China.[77] Bruce Chen (Chen), vice president of CAL's public relations division, said that with the opening of the cross-strait between mainland China and Taiwan, Taiwan would become the major transfer hub for cargo services from China to the rest of the world.

Critics, however, pointed out that even though routes had opened up to mainland China, CAL would face increased competition from both Taiwanese and mainland China carriers. However, CAL felt that it would be able to take advantage of the fact that foreign airlines could not operate on such routes as per government regulations.

Airline analyst Derek Sadubin added, "Without that pressure valve it would have been a disastrous environment for them, but it's not a panacea for the Taiwanese carriers."[78]

THE BENEFITS

Analysts felt that CAL's revival efforts had started to pay off. CAL also felt that its focus on revamping HR polices had begun to reap benefits. In 2004, CAL reported that several people had shown an interest in taking up a career with the airline. Wei added, "In terms of flight crew training, we've implemented stricter controls on both foreign and domestic pilots. We acknowledge that we have had a poor safety record in the past. However, after years of consistent effort, we've made significant progress. [. . .] Recently we started a recruiting program and received about 700 applications, showing that people are regaining confidence and trust in us."[79]

Industry observers felt that CAL's revival efforts had helped it to restore its image and confidence in consumers as depicted by a continuous increase in passenger and cargo revenue starting from 2004 to 2008 (refer to Exhibit V for growth in passenger and cargo revenue from 2004–2008). In June 2004, the airline received the 'Best Overall Airlines' and 'Best Cargo Airlines' categories in the 2003 Skyliners Awards awarded by the Manchester Airport.

In 2005, CAL passed the "IATA Operational Safety Audit", showing that the airline's continuous efforts to improve safety standards had helped it to achieve universal standards in flight safety. Moreover, in the Airline & Airport Customer Satisfaction Surveys conducted by Skytrax Research,[80] CAL ranked the highest worldwide for its "First Class" service, second runner-up for "Economy Class," and the "BestCabin Staff" for both Business and Economy Class. CAL registered an increase in revenue of 14.5 percent and 13 percent in passenger and cargo service respectively in 2005. As compared to 2004, CAL's total operational revenue increased by 13 percent in 2005 and reached NT$108.6 billion. In 2006, CAL's insurance fees were reduced by insurance companies by 45 percent, reflecting the fact that the airline had been able to win back trust by its all-round efforts.

Exhibit V   CAL: Growth in Passenger and Cargo Revenue (2004–2008)

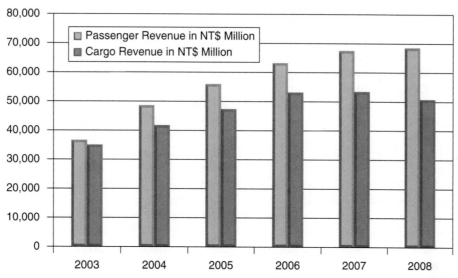

Adapted from Annual Reports of China Airlines Limited from 2004–2008.

With the easing of cross-strait relations in 2008, CAL's operational prospects improved considerably. Though the airlines had registered a net loss of NT$ 2.96 billion (US$89.4 million) in the first quarter of 2008, it was less than the loss of NT$ 2.971 billion experienced in the same quarter in 2007. For the first quarter of 2009, CAL reported an increase in operating profit to NT$ 0.6 billion, a noteworthy improvement from a net deficit of NT$ 2.4 billion in the same quarter in 2008. This was attributed to the increased direct links with mainland China, lower fuel prices, and the constant cost reduction strategies adopted by the airline.[81]

In May 2009, in light of the improved cross-strait relations between Taiwan and mainland China, Wei predicted that CAL would turn profitable in spite of the recession and the high crude oil prices of US$ 60 a barrel.[82] In October 2009, CAL reported a profit of NT$ 150 million and a further high of NT$ 900 million in November 2009. Experts attributed the airline's success to increased direct cross-strait flights and unprecedented recovery in the cargo business. The airline expected to break even in the last quarter of 2009, due to a boost in cargo transport and better cross-strait trade prospects. Chen added, "Our cargo figures were extremely weak last year, and if there's a rebound there we should be able

to break even."[83] The news came as a surprise to industry analysts since several competing airlines like Singapore Airlines and Cathay Pacific, which were witnessing declining profits, did not foresee such a turnaround for themselves. Investors too remained optimistic and CAL shares went up by 15 percent during the period 2008–2009.

THE OTHER VIEW

Industry observers applauded CAL's efforts to revamp its image and reduce its operating costs. They, however, suggested that CAL could further simplify fare structures by charging lower fares from price-sensitive travelers and higher fares from business travelers. They also opined that the typical no-frill operating model of budget airlines may not work out for a traditional airline like CAL. Analysts advised that the airlines should have different service quality management for short-haul and long-haul flights. For shorter flights, it could offer different fare choices to passengers depending on the level of service offered. Moreover, they stressed the fact that with the increase in passenger demand across Taiwan Straits, CAL should go in for both the hub-and-spoke networks[84] and point-to-point[85] services. This would help reduce operational costs and increase flight network as there were many regional airports in Taiwan that had the potential to serve as secondary airports after the upgrading of certain airport facilities.[86]

Industry observers opined that once CAA permitted the use of secondary airports and relaxed its controls over airfare policies, there was a huge scope for CAL to reduce operational costs by using these new air bases for international short-haul flights.

LOOKING AHEAD

On December 17, 2009, CAL celebrated its 50th anniversary. During the event, Wei said that CAL had managed to recover its costs despite the global economic slowdown. He added that the increase in revenues from cargo services and improved cross-strait relations had helped it maintain its position. Speaking on the occasion, Sun Huang-hsiang (Huang-hsiang), president of CAL, said that the airline would never compromise on safety and would continue to offer the best service while maintaining low operating costs in future.

CAL was optimistic that the increase in passenger and cargo services to mainland China would push its revenue up even in 2010. It aimed to improve its business prospects from the agreement between Taipei and Tokyo in December 2009. As per the agreement, both Taipei and Tokyo would be able to operate four daily round-trip flights between Tokyo International Airport and Taipei Songshan Airport beginning October 2010. CAL also started a non-stop service between London and Taipei thrice a week in January 2010. Anticipating the rising demand for passenger services in the future, CAL felt the need to expand its fleet and decided to lease one Airbus 330 jet in 2010. It had also placed an order for 14 new planes, which were expected to be delivered in the 2015–2018 period. Besides, the company planned to add newer direct routes to mainland China and expected more mainland Chinese tourists to Taiwan.

CAL was upbeat about registering profits in 2010, as a result of cost saving measures, network expansion, capacity regulation, and a wide ranging financial improvement program adopted in 2009. Huang-hsiang added, "The worst has passed [. . .] We hope for a profitable 2010 [. . .] We not only have confidence for 2010, but also for the next five decades"[87]

ENDNOTES

[1] "Dark Business Clouds Ahead for Taiwan's China Airlines," www.chinadaily.com.cn, December 15, 2009.
[2] Center for Asia Pacific Aviation is a global agency providing data services and analytical research on the aviation industry.
[3] "New Head of Taiwan's China Airlines Vows to Overcome Hard Times," www.earthtimes.org, July 10, 2008.
[4] "CAL, EVA See Sales Growth in December 2009," www.cens.com, January 14, 2010.
[5] Established in 1988, the China Aviation Development Foundation is a quasi-governmental holding company, owned by the People's Republic of China.
[6] Cross-Strait is a term that denotes the diplomatic relationship between mainland China and Taiwan situated on either side of Taiwan Strait. After October 1949, the Communist Party of China defeated the ruling party Republic of China (ROC) in China's civil war to establish the People's Republic of China in Beijing. From 1949, relations had been strained between the two governments regarding the political status of Taiwan. From 2008, a fresh round of discussions began to establish economic ties

as regards transportation, commerce, and communications between the two sides.
[7] "Dark Business Clouds Ahead for Taiwan's China Airlines," www.chinadaily.com.cn, December 15, 2009.
[8] Thomson Reuters is a provider of information services to companies. Reuters Estimates are real-time forecasts compiled by Thomson Reuters, required in research and analytic financial services, and also used by the media and corporate businesses.
[9] "Mainland Flights Lift Taiwan's China Airlines," www.avbuyer.com.cn, August 21, 2009.
[10] The New Taiwan Dollar also known as the Taiwanese Dollar is the currency in Taiwan. The symbol for TWD is either NT$, NTD, or NT. As of December 2009, US$1 = NT $ 32.328.
[11] "China Airlines Taking off Amid Economic Rebound," www.taiwantoday.tw, December 31, 2009.
[12] "China Airlines," www.fundinguniverse.com/company-histories/China-Airlines-Company-History.html.
[13] Manufactured by Consolidated Aircraft, the PBY Catalina flying boat was an aircraft used in the 1930s. During World War II,

these aircrafts were used for patrol bombing, anti-submarine warfare, air-sea search and rescue jobs, convoy escorts, and cargo transport.
[14] "At Age 50, China Airlines Faces a Turbulent Future," www.taipeitimes.com, December 14, 2009.
[15] From 1954 to 1975, Saigon was the capital of South Vietnam. But in 1976, it was joined with the adjacent province of Gia Đnh and renamed as Hồ Chí Minh City.
[16] The International Air Transport Association (IATA) is a representative body of the global aviation industry. It had 230 airlines as its members as of February 2009.
[17] Established in 1945, the United Nations Organization (UNO) or United Nations (UN) is a global organization that works with the stated goal of bringing about social progress, economic development, and world peace and ensuring human rights. In addition, it also helps the member countries to cooperate in matters of international law and international security.
[18] Headquartered in Montreal, Canada, the International Civil Aviation Organization (ICAO) is an organization operating under the

[18] United Nations that formulates the principles and techniques of international air navigation.

[19] Founded in 1988, Air China Limited is a state-owned major carrier based in Beijing. At the end of 2008, the company operated with a fleet of 243 aircraft.

[20] Founded in 1988, China Eastern Airlines Corporation Limited is a Shanghai-based major carrier that operates domestic, regional, and international flights. As of July 30, 2009, the airline operated with a fleet of 238 aircraft.

[21] Founded in 1989, China Southern Airlines Company Limited is a Guangzhou-based major air carrier that operates domestic, regional, and international flights. As of December 31, 2008, the airline operated with a fleet of 348 aircraft.

[22] "China Airlines," http://www.answers.com/topic/China-airlines.

[23] "China Airlines," http://en.wikipedia.org/wiki/China_Airlines.

[24] Formosa Airlines was a Taiwan-based airline founded in 1987. In 1999, CAL merged its subsidiary, Mandarin Airlines, with Formosa Airlines under the name Mandarin. Formosa's domestic operations were taken over by Mandarin Airlines and international flights were taken over by CAL.

[25] American Airlines, Inc. (AA) is a U.S.-based airline company headquartered in Fort Worth, Texas.

[26] "China Airlines," http://www.answers.com/topic/China-airlines.

[27] Ibid.

[28] Wei Hsiang, "What's in a Name? Companies Respond to Rebranding in Taiwan," www.webershandwick.com.

[29] "Plane Crashes and Significant Safety Events Since 1970 for China Airlines," www.airsafe.com/events/airlines/taiwan.htm.

[30] A go-around is an aborted landing of an aircraft when it is near landing.

[31] "Plane Crashes and Significant Safety Events Since 1970 for China Airlines," www.airsafe.com/events/airlines/taiwan.htm.

[32] "China Airlines," www.answers.com/topic/China-airlines.

[33] WorldNetDaily (WND) is an online news web site operating from Washington, DC.

[34] "Flying the Deadly Skies," www.wnd.com, October 18, 2000.

[35] Based in U.S., Boeing Corporation is the world's largest company manufacturing commercial jets for airline industry.

[36] "Questions over the Crash of China Airlines Flight 611," www.wsws.org, June 1, 2002.

[37] Ibid.

[38] The Civil Aeronautics Administration (CAA) is a government owned civil aviation regulatory body of Taiwan.

[39] *Flight International* is a UK-based, international aviation magazine published weekly that reports global news regarding general aviation, business aviation, defense air transport, and spaceflight.

[40] "China Airlines Back in The Dock," http://news.bbc.co.uk, June 3, 2003.

[41] "Plane Crashes and Significant Safety Events Since 1970 for China Airlines," www.airsafe.com/events/airlines/taiwan.htm.

[42] "China Airlines Back in The Dock," http://news.bbc.co.uk, June 3, 2003.

[43] "Bolt Put in Wrong in China Airways Jet That Burned," http://seattletimes.nwsource.com, August 27, 2007.

[44] "China Airlines Back in The Dock," http://news.bbc.co.uk, June 3, 2003.

[45] The AirSafe.com Foundation (ASF) is a non-profit corporation founded in December 2003 in the State of Washington.

[46] "Fatal Events and Fatal Event Rates of Airlines in Asia and Australasia Since 1970," http://www.airsafe.com/events/regions/asia.htm.

[47] Capital Securities Corporation is a Taiwan-based financial company headquartered in Taipei.

[48] "Dark Business Clouds Ahead for Taiwan's China Airlines," www.chinadaily.com.cn, December 15, 2009.

[49] "China's Ties with Taiwan Thaw," www.businessweek.com, April 14, 2008.

[50] "A China Lifeline for Taiwan's Airlines?" www.businessweek.com, June 23, 2008.

[51] "China Airlines Tries to Repair Its Image," www.taipeitimes.com, May 3, 2004.

[52] Ibid.

[53] On September 11, 2001, the Twin Towers of the World Trade Center (WTC) located in the US were attacked by terrorists. The attacks were coordinated by members of the militant Islamic group Al-Qaida. In addition to the loss of life and property, this attack had an adverse impact on the U.S. economy.

[54] "China Airlines Tries to Repair Its Image," www.taipeitimes.com, May 3, 2004.

[55] "Taiwan's Unfriendly Skies," www.asiasentinel.com, August 20, 2007.

[56] BAE Systems is Australia's largest defense company.

[57] Jessie Ho, "China Airlines Takes Air Safety to New Levels," www.taipeitimes.com, December 20, 2004.

[58] "Taiwan's Unfriendly Skies," www.asiasentinel.com, August 20, 2007.

[59] Ibid.

[60] Lufthansa Technik, a subsidiary of Lufthansa German Airlines, is a renowned global company providing maintenance, repair, overhaul, and modification services to the civil aviation industry.

[61] FOQA is Flight Operations Quality Assurance and FORAS is Flight Operations Risk Assessment System. Both are sophisticated systems that help an airline to check and ensure that correct safety procedures are maintained on every flight.

[62] Dynasty Packages referred to special discounted travel packages including airfares, accommodation, etc. offered to Dynasty members initially created by one of CAL's subsidiaries Yes Trip Co. Ltd.

[63] "Annual Report 2008," http://www.china-airlines.com/en/about/97ap.pdf.

[64] Headquartered in Taipei, Taiwan, Cathay United Bank was formed when two subsidiaries of Cathay Financial Holding Company, United World Chinese Commercial Bank and Cathay United Bank, were combined.

[65] "Annual Report 2007," www.china-airlines.com/en/about/96ap.pdf.

[66] "China Airlines Celebrates 47th Anniversary," www.china-airlines.com, December 4, 2006.

[67] "Annual Report 2006," www.china-airlines.com/en/about/95ap.pdf.

[68] In 2008, the word "Team Spirit" that was included in CAL's core vision was changed to "Team" to signify that the word also covered team spirit, teamwork, and team values for its workforce.

[69] "Annual Report 2008," www.china-airlines.com/en/about/97ap.pdf.

[70] Ibid.

[71] "Shin-Yuan Lai, The New Situation of Cross-Strait Relations," www.carnegieendowment.org, December 2, 2008.

[72] Ibid.

[73] Oscar Chung, "The Effort to Normalize Cross-Strait Transportation Links Is Picking up," http://taiwanreview.nat.gov.tw, December 1, 2008.

[74] Founded in June 2000, SkyTeam is an association of eleven airlines comprising Aeroflot, Aeromexico, Air France, Alitalia, China Southern Airlines, CSA Czech Airlines, Delta Air Lines, KLM Royal Dutch Airlines, Korean Air, Air Europa, Kenya Airways.

[75] Chunghwa Post Co. is the official postal mail service company serving areas governed by the ROC.

[76] "Cross-Strait Flights Boosted, Even More to Come?" www.centreforaviation.com, May 6, 2009.

[77] "Mainland Flights Lift Taiwan's China Airlines," www.avbuyer.com.cn, August 21, 2009.

[78] "Dark Business Clouds Ahead for Taiwan's China Airlines," www.chinadaily.com.cn, December 15, 2009.

[79] "China Airlines Tries to Repair Its Image," www.taipeitimes.com, May 3, 2004.

[80] Skytrax is a research agency based in the United Kingdom that carries on traveler surveys regarding various aspects of commercial airlines such as airport, airline, standard of cabin staff services and airline lounge services, in-flight entertainment, on-board catering, etc.

[81] "CAL Announces Q1 Results," www.china-airlines.com, April 30, 2009.

[82] "China Airlines Can Make Profit with US$60 Oil: Wei," www.taipeitimes.com, May 19, 2009.

[83] "China Airlines Sees '09 Break Even," www.reuters.com, July 15, 2009.

[84] The hub-and-spoke network refers to a transport system in which traffic moves along the spokes of a wheel linked to a hub at the center of the wheel.

[85] Point-to-point transit refers to a travel system where a vehicle moves directly from one destination to another, without travelling through a central hub.

[86] "The Low Cost Model and Strategies for Taiwanese Airlines," www.aerlines.nl/issue_34/34_Lu_et-al_LCCs_Strategies_for_Taiwanese_Airlines.pdf, Issue 31.

[87] "China Airlines Taking off Amid Economic Rebound," http://taiwantoday.tw, December 12, 2009.

REFERENCES AND SUGGESTED READINGS

"Flying the Deadly Skies," www.wnd.com, October 18, 2000.

"Questions over the Crash of China Airlines Flight 611," www.wsws.org, June 1, 2002.

"China Airlines Back in The Dock," http://news.bbc.co.uk, June 3, 2003.

"China Airlines Tries to Repair Its Image," www.taipeitimes.com, May 3, 2004.

Jessie Ho, "China Airlines Takes Air Safety to New Levels," www.taipeitimes.com, December 20, 2004.

"China Airlines Celebrates 47th Anniversary," www.china-airlines.com, December 4, 2006.

"Bolt Put in Wrong in China Airways Jet That Burned," http://seattletimes.nwsource.com, August 27, 2007.

"Taiwan's Unfriendly Skies," www.asiasentinel.com, August 20, 2007.

"New Head of Taiwan's China Airlines Vows to Overcome Hard Times," www.earthtimes.org, July 10, 2008.

Oscar Chung, "The Effort to Normalize Cross-Strait Transportation Links Is Picking up," http://taiwanreview.nat.gov.tw, December 1, 2008.

"CAL Announces Q1 Results," www.china-airlines.com, April 30, 2009.

"Cross-Strait Flights Boosted, Even More to Come?" www.centreforaviation.com, May 6, 2009.

"China Airlines Sees'09 Break Even," www.reuters.com, July 15, 2009.

"Mainland Flights Lift Taiwan's China Airlines," www.avbuyer.com.cn, August 21, 2009.

"China Airlines Taking off Amid Economic Rebound," http://taiwantoday.tw, December 12, 2009.

"At Age 50, China Airlines Faces a Turbulent Future," www.taipeitimes.com, December 14, 2009.

"Dark Business Clouds Ahead for Taiwan's China Airlines," www.chinadaily.com.cn, December 15, 2009.

"China Airlines Taking off Amid Economic Rebound," www.taiwantoday.tw, December 31, 2009.

"CAL, EVA See Sales Growth in December 2009," www.cens.com, Taipei, January 14, 2010.

"China Airlines," http://www.answers.com/topic/China-airlines.

"China Airlines," http://en.wikipedia.org/wiki/China_Airlines.

Wei Hsiang, "What's in a Name? Companies Respond to Rebranding in Taiwan," www.webershandwick.com.

"China Airlines," www.fundinguniverse.com/company-histories/China-Airlines-Company-History.html.

"Plane Crashes and Significant Safety Events Since 1970 for China Airlines," www.airsafe.com/events/airlines/taiwan.htm.

"Fatal Events and Fatal Event Rates of Airlines in Asia and Australasia Since 1970," http://www.airsafe.com/events/regions/asia.htm.

"Airlines in Asia and Australasia Since 1970," http://www.airsafe.com/events/regions/asia.htm.

"Annual Report 2008," http://www.china-airlines.com/en/about/97ap.pdf.

"Annual Report 2007," www.china-airlines.com/en/about/96ap.pdf.

"Annual Report 2006," www.china-airlines.com/en/about/95ap.pdf.

"Annual Report 2008," www.china-airlines.com/en/about/97ap.pdf.

"The Low Cost Model and Strategies for Taiwanese Airlines," www.aerlines.nl/issue_34/34_Lu_et-al_LCCs_Strategies_for_Taiwanese_Airlines.pdf, Issue 31.

Jordan Mitchell
University of Western Ontario

Paul W. Beamish
University of Western Ontario

INTRODUCTION

In late September 2009, Dr. Shawn Qu, CEO, president, chairman and founder of Canadian Solar, was constantly on the move. His company, a Nasdaq-traded solar cell and module manufacturer, had grown at a compound annual growth rate (CAGR) of 135.7 percent over the last five years from $9.7 million in revenues in 2004 to $705 million in 2008 (see Exhibit 1 for key financials). The strong growth had been spurred by an increasing number of government incentive programs to encourage the adoption of solar photovoltaic (PV)[1] technology. For the past couple of years, solar energy was seen to be the world's fastest-growing industry. However, the credit crunch and global economic downturn combined with changes to Spain's incentive program had put the worldwide PV industry into oversupply for the first half of 2009. During the summer, demand changed again. Forecasts were exceeded, causing a temporary undersupply of ready-to-install solar modules. The fluctuating

solar demand had caused analysts to change their financial outlook for Canadian Solar several times throughout 2009. A Deutsche Bank analyst had predicted full-year 2009 sales to come in at $395 million with net losses at −$18 million during the month of June 2009, only to revise the outlook two months later to sales of $574 million and net income of $49 million.

Part of the increasing positive outlook was attributed to government incentive programs in several geographies. Of particular interest to many players, including Canadian Solar, were proposed incentive programs in China and Canada. In Ontario, for example, the details of the provincial government's incentive program for green energy—the Feed-in Tariff (FIT) program—had just been released with specific requirements for domestic content. Although registered as a Canadian company, Canadian Solar had the bulk of its production operations in China; namely, seven facilities dedicated to the manufacture of different solar PV components. And, even though the company's "bases" were in China and Canada, 89.5 percent of 2008 revenues came from Europe. Company management expected that to change rapidly. Already, the first six months of 2009 had substantially changed the international configuration of Canadian Solar given that the company was planning or had already established new sales offices in South Korea, Japan, China, Italy, Spain, Germany, the United States and Canada.

When looking at the relatively nascent and rapidly growing solar PV industry replete with a mix of diverse competitors, Qu and other Canadian Solar senior managers wondered how best to compete in the increasingly "global" PV industry.

Ivey
Richard Ivey School of Business
The University of Western Ontario

Jordan Mitchell wrote this case under the supervision of Professor Paul W. Beamish solely to provide material for class discussion. The authors do not intend to illustrate either effective or ineffective handling of a managerial situation. The authors may have disguised certain names and other identifying information to protect confidentiality.

Ivey Management Services prohibits any form of reproduction, storage or transmittal without its written permission. Reproduction of this material is not covered under authorization by any reproduction rights organization. To order copies or request permission to reproduce materials, contact Ivey Publishing, Ivey Management Services, c/o Richard Ivey School of Business, The University of Western Ontario, London, Ontario, Canada, N6A 3K7; phone (519) 661-3208; fax (519) 661-3882; e-mail cases@ivey.uwo.ca.

Copyright © 2010, Ivey Management Services
Version: (A) 2010-04-05

SOLAR ENERGY

Solar energy was divided into three main categories: solar electric, solar thermal and concentrating solar. Solar electric converted the sun's energy into electricity and solar thermal used the sun for heating or cooling. Concentrating solar power mixed solar electric and solar thermal as it used small optical mirrors to collect solar energy and convert the sunlight to heat. The heat was then applied to a liquid or gas to turn a turbine, thereby creating electricity.

The other important distinction in solar energy was between "grid-tied" and "off-grid" applications. Grid-tied applications were solar-electric systems that were connected to an electricity utility grid (in nearly all jurisdictions, electricity utility grids were heavily regulated by government bodies and were often separate from electricity providers). Grid-tied applications were either "ground mount" or "rooftop"—ground mount applications were typically in a field or desert area and were either solar PV or concentrating solar power. Grid-tied rooftop projects ranged from one kilowatt to 10 kilowatts (kW) on residential homes to larger projects of 10 kilowatts to five megawatts (MW) on commercial buildings.

Off-grid applications were defined as a system completely independent of the main electricity grid. Off-grid applications ranged from tiny solar cells in pocket calculators to solar-thermal systems for hot water tanks in residential homes. In the last few years, off-grid applications had become popular for road lights, signs and parking meters whereby a solar module was placed on top of the apparatus to provide power at night through a battery. Off-grid applications were also seen as one solution to providing power in isolated rural areas.

Exhibit 1   Canadian Solar Financials

USD million, Years ended Dec. 31	2006	2007	2008
Net Revenues	**68.2**	**302.8**	**705.0**
Cost of revenues	55.9	279.0	634.0
Gross Profit	**12.3**	**23.8**	**71.0**
Operating expenses:	0.0	0.0	0.0
Selling expenses	2.9	7.5	10.6
General and administrative expenses	7.9	17.2	34.5
Research and development expenses	0.4	1.0	1.8
Total operating expenses	11.2	25.7	46.9
Income (loss) from operations	**1.1**	**−2.0**	**24.1**
Other income (expenses):			
Interest expense	−2.2	−2.4	−11.3
Interest income	0.4	0.6	3.5
Loss on change in fair value of derivatives	0.0	0.0	0.0
related to convertible notes	−8.2	0.0	0.0
Gain on foreign currency derivative assets	0.0	0.0	14.5
Debt conversion inducement expense	0.0	0.0	−10.2
Foreign exchange gain (loss)	−0.5	2.7	−20.1
Other - net	0.4	0.7	0.0
Income (loss) before income taxes	−9.0	−0.4	0.5
Income tax benefit (expense)	−0.4	0.2	−9.9
Net loss	−9.4	−0.2	−9.4
Loss per share - basic and diluted	−0.5	0.0	−0.3
Shares used in computation - basic and diluted	19.0	27.3	31.6

Source: Canadian Solar Annual Report, 20-F, www.sec.gov, December 31, 2008, p. 54.

Exhibit 1   *(Continued)*

USD million, Years ended Dec. 31	2007	2008
Assets		
Current assets		
Cash and cash equivalents	37.7	115.7
Restricted cash	1.6	20.6
Accounts receivable[1]	58.6	51.6
Inventories	70.9	92.7
Value added tax recoverable	12.2	15.9
Advances to suppliers	28.7	24.7
Foreign currency derivative assets		7.0
Prepaid expenses and other current assets	10.1	10.9
Total current assets	219.9	339.0
Property, plant and equipment, net	51.5	165.5
Deferred tax assets	4.0	7.0
Advances to suppliers	4.1	43.1
Prepaid land use right	1.6	12.8
Investment		3.0
Other non-current assets	3.4	0.3
TOTAL ASSETS	284.5	570.7
Liabilities and Stockholders' equity		
Current liabilities		
Short-term borrowings	40.4	110.7
Accounts payable	8.3	30.0
Amounts due to related parties	0.2	0.1
Other payables	6.2	24.0
Advances from customers	2.0	3.6
Other current liabilities	2.3	4.3
Total current liabilities	59.2	172.7
Accrued warranty costs	3.9	10.8
Convertible notes	75.0	1.0
Long-term borrowings	17.9	45.4
Liability for uncertain tax positions	2.3	8.7
TOTAL LIABILITIES	158.2	238.6
Stockholders' equity:		
Common shares - no par value: unlimited authorized shares, 27,320,389 and 35,744,563 shares issued and outstanding at Dec. 31, 2007, and 2008 respectively	97.5	294.7
Additional paid-in capital	26.4	35.5
Accumulated deficit	−3.6	−13.0
Accumulated other comprehensive income	6.0	14.9
Total stockholders' equity	126.3	332.2
TOTAL LIABILITIES AND STOCKHOLDERS' EQUITY	284.5	570.7

[1] Net allowance for doubtful accounts of $0.4 and $5.6 million on Dec 31, 2007 and 2008 respectively.

Source: Canadian Solar Annual Report, 20-K, December 31, 2008, p. F-3.

PHOTOVOLTAIC CELLS[2]

The main tenet of solar-electric power was the photovoltaic (PV) cell, which used the "photovoltaic effect" to generate electricity. When sunlight hit a PV cell, electrons bounced from negative to positive, thus producing electricity. In order to generate electricity, a PV cell required a semiconductor material and positive and negative poles.[3]

The most common semiconductor material for PV cells was silicon.[4] For most solar applications, the silicon was refined to 99.9999 percent purity, which was known as 6N silicon (the number "6" referred to the number of "9s"). Companies such as Canadian Solar had commercialized products with lower grades of silicon for solar applications. For example, upgraded metallurgical-grade silicon (UMG-Si) was one such type of lower grade silicon. It was 99.999 percent pure (or 5N for five "9s"). UMG-Si was a bi-product of the aluminum smelting business and historically had been less expensive than 6N silicon.

The three types of PV cells were polycrystalline ("poly"), monocrystalline ("mono") and amorphous ("thin-film"). Poly PV cells used silicon in its refined state whereas mono took the refinement a step further, thus creating higher efficiency (the drawback with mono PV was the higher cost of production vs. poly). The third type, thin-film, was substantially different in that it did not have crystalline silicon, but rather a painted or printed semi-conductor. There were six main types of materials used in thin-film, although three had not yet been proven to be commercially viable.[5]

The basic process of constructing a crystalline PV cell began by forming cylindrical ingots from the semi-conductor material. The ingots were then cut into very thin disc-shaped wafers. The wafer was etched with hydrofluoric acid and washed with water, creating a PV cell. To create a usable "solar module" (also called a "solar panel"), a series of PV cells were placed in between a sheet of glass held in by an aluminum frame and plastic backing connected to a cable plug. In most installations, a number of modules were used to make up an array. The array was then connected to an inverter (to convert the electricity from direct current (DC) to alternating current (AC)).

Solar modules were rated by their capacity in watts (W). Most solar PV modules were rated between 80W and 250W. Larger solar modules (200W+) weighed approximately 20 kilograms and were sized 1.6 meters long, one meter wide and four to five centimeters thick. Solar efficiency—the amount of sunlight energy converted to electricity—ranged between 12 and 18 percent for most PV modules. However, breakthroughs were constantly being achieved—as of mid-2009, the highest PV cells had efficiency ratings slightly above 23 percent. As a general rule of thumb, one to two percent efficiency was deducted from the rating of the cell to determine the rating of the module (i.e. an 18 percent efficient cell would have a 16–17 percent efficient module).

The cost of PV cells was a constantly moving target. In securing contracts with large volumes, it was common for PV manufacturers to offer substantial discounts, between 10 and 30 percent on the price of a module. In large-scale projects, many buyers saw PV modules more as a commodity product and were largely concerned with the price per watt. From 2007 to 2009, the selling price of a solar PV (from a PV module manufacturer to a customer) had increased slightly from $3.50 per watt to around $4 before dropping to approximately $2.50 per watt (put another way, the price for one 200W solar PV crystalline module was about $500 as of mid-2009).

One of the major drivers behind the price of solar PV was the price of silicon. A temporary silicon shortage around mid-2008 pushed the spot price of silicon to over $500 per kilogram (up from around $25 per kilogram in 2004). However, by mid-2009, that price had fallen to around $60 per kilogram.[6] As the supply for silicon increased along with greater manufacturing efficiencies, the manufactured cost for crystalline PV modules was expected to fall below $1 per watt in two to three years.

Many industry insiders debated whether thin-film modules held more promise given their lower cost versus poly and mono modules. As of August 2009, the price of thin-film was reported at $1.76 per watt versus $2.50 per watt for silicon modules.[7] Despite silicon's current higher price, crystalline silicon supporters often pointed to the fact that thin-film would have trouble competing as the price of crystalline modules dropped.

Additionally, poly and mono crystalline silicon modules typically enjoyed higher efficiencies than thin-film and required less space, fewer mounting systems and less cabling for the same power output.

In addition to the cost of the module itself, the cost of installation ranged from $4 to $8 per watt. On top of these costs, developers of utility-scale PV projects also had to be mindful of the real estate cost and electricity transmission costs. All tallied, the cost of solar PV was between 0.15 and 0.35 per kilowatt-hour (kWh) versus non-renewable sources of energy between 0.03 and 0.15 per kWh. As scale efficiencies grew along with technological breakthroughs, many insiders felt that the cost of solar would be competitive with non-renewable sources in a three to five year time horizon (this was referred to in the industry as reaching "grid parity").

THE GLOBAL SOLAR INDUSTRY

In 2008, solar PV experienced its largest increase to date by growing 5.6 gigawatts (60.8 percent) to 14.73 gigawatts (GW) in 2008.[8] (On a global level, solar power accounted for under one percent of all electricity generation.) Geographically, total installed capacity was split: 65 percent in Europe, 15 percent in Japan and eight percent in the United States. In 2008, the strongest market was Spain, which represented nearly half of the installations due to its aggressive Renewable Energy Feed-in Tariff (referred to as REFIT or FIT) program, which guaranteed electricity rates for certain renewable projects. Even though Spain dominated the PV market in 2008, the Spanish government had placed a 500MW cap on annual installations for the next two years, given uncontrollable growth. Thus, Spanish PV installations were expected to drop substantially in 2009. Germany was the second largest market, capturing 26.7 percent of worldwide installations during the year (Germany was one of the first countries in the world to introduce a FIT program). Other leading solar countries were the United States (six percent of worldwide installations), South Korea (five percent), Italy (4.9 percent) and Japan

(four percent). See Exhibit 2 for more information on the current state of the global PV market.

The future development of the global PV market largely hinged on government initiatives and renewable support schemes. Moving forward, the European Photovoltaic Industry Association (EPIA) predicted two scenarios: a moderate scenario without heavy government incentives; and a policy-driven scenario with some support initiatives present. Under the first scenario, EPIA projected that cumulative solar PV power would equate to 54.8GW in 2013 (representing a CAGR of 30 percent). The second scenario resulted in global installed PV power being 85.8GW by 2013 (CAGR of 42.3 percent). Exhibit 3 shows some highlights from different world markets and Exhibit 4 gives EPIA's moderate and policy-driven scenarios for the top 13 markets.

Germany was expected to be the top market for the next few years, given the government's continuing Renewable Energy Law (Erneuerbare-Energien-Gesetz or EEG). As a successor to an earlier law passed in 1991, the EEG came into effect in 2000 as part of Germany's aim to derive 12.5 percent of the country's energy from renewable sources by 2010 (the goal was surpassed in 2007 when Germany reached 14 percent and was modified to reach a new goal of 27 percent renewable by 2020). In 2009, the EEG was updated—for PV solar, the feed-in rates were between €0.33 and €0.43 per kWh ($0.46 to $0.60 per kWh) depending on the size of the project. The EEG called for those rates to decrease by eight to 10 percent in 2010 and nine percent after 2011 but guaranteed the rates for a period of 20 years.[9] Despite the decreasing feed-in rates over the next few years, the EPIA believed that the rates were sufficient to encourage installations. Furthermore, PV solar was expected to remain strong as a result of high public awareness and support of renewables, the skilled PV industry and accessible financing opportunities through Kreditanstalt für Wiederaufbau (KfW).[10]

The story of Spain's boom and subsequent bust had become a hot topic in the solar industry. Through laws in 2004 and 2007, the Spanish government created an attractive Feed-in Tariff (FIT) giving up to €0.44 per kWh ($0.62 per kWh) for solar projects installed before September 2008.

Exhibit 2   **Statistics on the Global PV Industry**

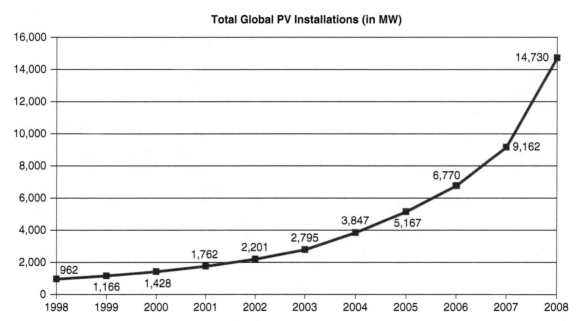

Total Global PV Installations (in MW)

Source: European Photovoltaic Industry Association (EPIA), "Global Market Outlook for Photovoltaics until 2013," March 2009, p. 3 and p. 14.

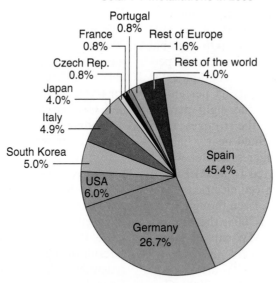

Solar PV Installations in 2008

In spite of the original cap of 400MW, the country was flooded with demand for projects and in an 18-month period (from the passing of the 2007 law to September 2008), about 3GW of PV solar energy were installed. The heavily unanticipated installations were estimated to cost taxpayers about $26.4 billion, causing a public backlash against the government.[11] In 2008, the Spanish government placed a new cap of 500MW on installations and backed off the Feed-in Tariffs to €0.32 to €0.34 per kWh ($0.45 to $0.48 per kWh).[12] Despite the new cap, Spain was seen as a key market in the long term due to its government's high renewable target (the government

Exhibit 3   Highlights From World Markets

Country	Comments
Germany	• Leading market for solar PV with strong financing available • Over 40,000 people were employed in the PV sector • The Renewable Energy Law (Erneuerbare-Energien-Gesetz or EEG) promised rates of $0.46 to $0.60 per kWh for solar PV with digression in 2010 and 2011 • The country had some of the world's largest solar parks (e.g. the 40MW Waldpolenz Solar Park) • Over 100,000 roof-top solar PV applications had been installed
Spain	• Historical strength had been on utility-scale solar parks • The Spanish market would undergo a major decrease in 2009 and 2010 due to the government's cap of 500MW • Potential growth beyond 2013 was still seen to be strong due to experience with renewables and long-term targets
Japan	• Historical strength had been with solar PV on residential homes due to the "Residential PV System Program," which ended supplying subsidies in 2006 • In December 2008, the government was renewing its focus on solar with the aim to have solar power installed on 70 percent of new homes. Furthermore, it wanted 14GW of installed PV power by 2020
United States	• The Investment Tax Credit (ITC), state programs and the potential of a federal-level FIT were expected to boost solar PV in 2010 and beyond • The challenge was seen to be a lack of financing • The United States had some of the world's largest solar PV parks (e.g. Nellis Solar Power Plant, NV 15MW) • California was the leading state for solar roof installations due to programs such as the "Million Solar Roofs" vision and the "California Solar Initiative"
Italy	• The country had a competitive FIT program and a net-metering scheme (allowing PV system owners to get credits for their produced electricity) • Italy had no cap for PV installations
South Korea	• The country's FIT program was seen as promising; however, the devaluation of the Korean currency and the placement of a cap of 500MW on the FIT in October 2008 were expected to dampen the number of installations • Observers believed that strong political support for solar PV still existed and expected the market to grow in 2010
France	• The government had a favorable FIT program for BIPV; however, the growth had been stalled by long administrative procedures to connect the systems to the grid • France was expected to adopt a FIT program for non-BIPV applications for commercial roofs, which would be the source of its growth over the next few years
Czech Republic	• The Czech government introduced a FIT program in 2008 and was one of the premiere Eastern European growth countries for solar PV
Portugal	• Portugal had several large-scale PV and concentrating solar power plants but had not yet introduced a FIT program or similar incentive scheme
Greece	• Greece was seen to have one of the most favorable FIT programs in Europe • The country had a pipeline of 3.5GW of PV projects • Bureaucracy and lengthy administrative procedures were seen to be barriers for installations in 2008
Israel	• Solar-thermal (solar water heaters) were very popular, being present in 90 percent of Israeli homes • Israel was extensively used for research and development due to the country's high level of solar irradiance • A FIT scheme was passed in 2008 and the market was expected to grow

(Continued)

Exhibit 3   *(Concluded)*

Country	Comments
India	• India was expected to develop slowly but held great potential due to efforts for both on and off-grid projects (off-grid projects were a specialty area for project developers—e.g. Shell Solar had had a division dedicated to off-grid solar PV development in India)
China	• The new incentive program was expected to boost solar PV applications both for residential, commercial and utility-scale applications
Canada	• Ontario's solar PV applications were expected to grow under the proposed FIT program
	• The FIT program required that for projects up to 10kW, the minimum domestic content was 40 percent and for projects greater than 10kW, the domestic content was 50 percent for projects with a commercial operation date prior to January 1, 2011. For projects thereafter, domestic content needed to be 60 percent

Source: Compiled by case writer.

wanted 20 percent of consumed energy to come from renewables by 2020).[13]

Prior to the boom in Germany and Spain, Japan had one of the strongest solar PV markets in the world up until 2006, when the government stopped supplying subsidies. The majority of its PV installations were in residential applications (different from other markets where commercial applications were the norm). Recently, the government had set new targets of reaching over 50GW of installed PV power by 2030 and had implemented national and regional support mechanisms. The country's Feed-in Tariff schemes promised an initial rate of 50 yen per kWh ($0.50 per kWh) for solar installations.[14]

The U.S. market also held great promise given President Obama's support of renewable energy and several state programs targeted at rolling out renewables. California, Arizona, New Mexico, Texas, Vermont and several other states had or were in the process of enacting incentives and stimulus programs. In 2010 many expected that the United States would enact a federal incentive program—one source suggested that the bill would guarantee a 10 percent return over 20 years for renewable projects under 20MW.[15] Nearly all of the PV manufacturers had set up offices in the United States given the future potential in what many believed would become the world's largest market by the middle of the next decade.

In several geographies around the world, a number of other policies and support mechanisms

had also been implemented or were in the design phase in countries as far-reaching as Italy, Greece, France, Israel, South Korea, China and Canada.

In Canada, the main program was Ontario's FIT, announced in early 2009 with a start date of October 1, 2009. Ontario's FIT would replace the 2006 Standard Offer Program, which gave PV solar rates of C$0.42 per kWh and other renewable sources rates of C$0.11 per kWh.[16] As North America's first FIT program, renewables could garner between Cdn$0.08 and Cdn$0.802 per kWh depending on the scale of the project. Smaller-scale solar rooftop systems for residential homes would receive the highest rates, between Cdn$0.539 and Cdn$0.802 per kWh. Larger-scale solar (less than 10MW) would receive Cdn$0.443 per kWh. The program called for domestic content to make up 40 percent on projects less than 10kW and 50 percent of the project cost on projects over 10kW (after January 1, 2011, domestic requirements would rise to 60 percent). See Exhibit 5 for more details on Ontario's FIT program.

In July 2009, the Chinese government announced major subsidies for utility-scale solar projects. The conditions of receiving the subsidies required that the project have a minimum of 300kW peak, and be built in one year with longevity of 20 years. The subsidy would be 20 yuan ($4) per watt with the overall goal of reaching 10GW of installed power by 2020.[17]

Exhibit 4   **EPIA Predictions by Market**

Country	Type	2006	2007	2008	2009E	2010E	2011E	2012E	2013E
Belgium	EPIA Moderate	2	18	48	100	70	80	90	100
	EPIA Policy-Driven				175	125	130	140	160
Czech Republic	EPIA Moderate	0	3	51	80	90	110	140	170
	EPIA Policy-Driven				100	160	200	220	240
France	EPIA Moderate	8	11	46	250	340	600	900	1,000
	EPIA Policy-Driven				300	500	850	1,200	1,400
Germany	EPIA Moderate	850	1,100	1,500,	2,000	2,000	2,300	2,600	3,000
	EPIA Policy-Driven				2,500	2,800	3,200	3,600	4,000
Greece	EPIA Moderate	1	2	11	35	100	100	100	100
	EPIA Policy-Driven				52	200	450	700	900
Italy	EPIA Moderate	13	42	258	400	600	750	950	1,250
	EPIA Policy-Driven				500	800	1,100	1,400	1,600
Portugal	EPIA Moderate	0	14	50	40	50	100	160	230
	EPIA Policy-Driven				50	80	180	350	500
Spain	EPIA Moderate	88	560	2,511	375	500	500	550	800
	EPIA Policy-Driven				375	500	600	650	1,500
Rest of Europe	EPIA Moderate	12	17	28	120	140	200	300	450
	EPIA Policy-Driven				250	325	400	525	625
Japan	EPIA Moderate	287	210	230	400	500	700	1,000	1,100
	EPIA Policy-Driven				500	1,000	1,200	1,500	1,700
USA	EPIA Moderate	145	207	342	340	1,000	1,200	1,500	2,000
	EPIA Policy-Driven				1,200	3,000	3,400	3,900	4,500
China	EPIA Moderate	12	20	45	80	100	300	600	1,000
	EPIA Policy-Driven				100	150	600	1,200	2,000
India	EPIA Moderate	12	20	40	50	60	80	120	300
	EPIA Policy-Driven				100	200	250	300	600
South Korea	EPIA Moderate	20	43	274	100	150	220	300	400
	EPIA Policy-Driven				200	350	450	700	1,000
Rest of the World	EPIA Moderate	153	125	126	250	300	300	300	350
	EPIA Policy-Driven				400	600	800	1,000	1,600
TOTAL	**EPIA Moderate**	**1,603**	**2,392**	**5,559**	**4,620**	**6,000**	**7,540**	**9,610**	**12,250**
	EPIA Policy-Driven				**6,802**	**10,790**	**13,810**	**17,385**	**22,325**
CUMULATIVE	**EPIA Moderate**	**6,770**	**9,162**	**14,730**	**19,350**	**25,350**	**32,890**	**42,500**	**54,750**
	EPIA Polici-Driven				**21,532**	**32,322**	**46,132**	**63,517**	**85,842**

Source: European Photovoltaic Industry Association (EPIA), "Global Market Outlook for Photovoltaics until 2013," March 2009, p. 6.

PLAYERS IN THE GLOBAL PV MARKET

Globally, there were hundreds of PV cell and module manufacturers. On the supply side of PV manufacturers, there were raw material suppliers for goods such as silicon, glass, substrates, metal and cables as well as specialized equipment manufacturers to make solar components such as furnaces, sawing machines, printing machines and laminators. On the buyer side of PV manufacturers, there were several potential customers. Consumer electronics, automotive and industrial product companies integrated solar cells into their products for resale (examples ranged from

Exhibit 5   Ontario's Feed-in Tariff Program

Renewable Fuel	Size Tranches	Contract Price cent/kWh
Biomass	≤ 10MW	13.8
	> 10MW	13.0
Biogas		
On-farm	≤ 100kW	19.5
On-farm	> 100kW ≤ 250kW	18.5
Biogas	≤ 500kW	16.0
Biogas	> 500kW ≤ 10MW	14.7
Biogas	> 10MW	10.4
Waterpower	≤ 10MW	13.1
	> 10MW ≤ 50MW	12.2
Landfill gas	≤ 10MW	11.1
	> 10MW	10.3
Solar PV		
Any type	≤ 10kW	80.2
Rooftop	> 10kW ≤ 250kW	71.3
Rooftop	> 250kW ≤ 500kW	63.5
Rooftop	> 500kW	53.9
Ground mounted	≤ 10MW	44.3
Wind		
Onshore	Any size	13.5
Offshore	Any size	19.0

Domestic Content Requirements: The minimum requirements of Ontario-based content: 40% for MicroFIT (projects less than 10kW) and 50% for FIT (projects over 10kW) for projects reaching commercial operation by the end of 2010. For projects with commercial operation after January 1, 2011, domestic content increases to 60%.

Designated Activity	Qualifying Percentage
1. Silicon that has been used as input to solar photovoltaic cells manufactured in an Ontario refinery.	10%
2. Silicon ingots and wafers, where silicon ingots have been cast in Ontario and wafers have been cut from the casting by a saw in Ontario.	12%
3. The crystalline silicon solar photovoltaic cells, where their active photovoltaic layer(s) have been formed in Ontario.	10%
4. Solar photovoltaic modules (i.e. panels), where the electrical connections between the solar cells have been made in Ontario, and the solar photovoltaic module materials have been encapsulated in Ontario.	13%
5. Inverter (to convert the electricity from direct current (DC) to alternating current (AC)), where the assembly, final wiring and testing have been done in Ontario	9%
6. Mounting systems, where the structural components of the fixed or moving mounting systems have been entirely machined or formed or cast in Ontario. The metal for the structural components may not have been pre-machined outside Ontario other than peeling/roughing of the part for quality control purposes when it left the smelter or forge. The machining and assembly of the mounting system must entirely take place in Ontario (i.e. bending, welding, piercing, and bolting).	9%
7. Wiring and electrical hardware that is not part of other designated activities (i.e. items 1, 2, 3, and 5 of this table), sourced from an Ontario supplier.	10%
8. All on- and off-site labour and services. For greater certainty, this designated activity shall apply in respect of all contract facilities.	27%
Total	**100%**

Source: Ontario Power Authority, http://fit.powerauthority.on.ca, accessed October 30, 2009.

solar cells in garden lamps through to cells used on marine buoys). For grid-tied applications, the typical customers were project developers, utility companies, solar installation companies, distributors, wholesalers, governments, construction companies and building owners.

Barriers to entry were considered fairly low due to the low capital requirements and medium-low technological know-how to make a PV module. However, product warranties were one barrier that was becoming more important. For example, smaller manufacturers struggled to sell modules for use in bank-financed large-scale projects because of requirements from the banks for greater assurances that 25-year product performance warranties would be upheld. Some analysts also predicted more vertical integration both from silicon producers, specialized suppliers of PV cells and customers (such as project developers). Complementary players such as inverter manufacturers or rack suppliers were not considered to pose an immediate vertical integration threat.

The top 10 producers accounted for 55.3 percent of PV module sales in 2008. Exhibit 6 shows the market shares of both PV module and PV cell producers. Some observers divided the market into three groups based on geography, market strength, size and quality perception. The first group competed on the basis of price and used China as a manufacturing base, the second was made up of up-start companies with a point of technological differentiation, and the third consisted of Japanese electronic firms with established brand names. The market could also be divided simply into: more recent start-ups and established incumbents. Exhibit 7 shows highlights of selected competitors.

One of the most powerful contingents of emerging PV module companies were the following four companies which used China as their primary manufacturing base: Suntech, Yingli Green, Trina Solar and Canadian Solar. The four competitors were vertically integrated in that they produced ingots, wafers, cells and modules and used their access to low-cost labor for a cost advantage. Canadian Solar's management believed its company to be unique in that it combined elements of Western management and engineering with a low-cost Chinese production base.

Of the specialized start-ups, two main groups of companies existed: those producing complete PV modules and those focusing on the production of PV cells only. PV module start-ups competed more on tailored propositions, customer relationships and service, technological differences and price. For example, First Solar was different from other module producers in that it used Cadmium Telluride as a semi-conductor, which allowed it to deliver a lower price per watt. The other notable U.S. competitor, SunPower, competed in a different way by offering solar systems complete with inverters for easy residential and commercial installation. Both U.S. companies had the majority of their production in low-cost Asian countries, namely Malaysia and the Philippines.

Up-starts such as Germany's Q-Cells and Solar World, Taiwan's Motech and Gintech and China's JA Solar produced PV cells only and sold the cells to module producers. Q-Cells had surpassed Sharp in terms of total PV cell production in the last couple of years. The five PV cell companies competed on technology, relationships with module producers and price.

Of the incumbents, Japanese electronics multinationals such as Sharp, Kyocera and Sanyo all had long histories developing PV solar. Japanese electronics companies typically competed on the strength of their brand recognition, research and development, strong distribution and in some cases, exclusive rights with large-scale customers.

Sharp had begun developing PV solar in 1959 and had dominated the world market for much of the last 50 years. While Sharp had historically sold mono and poly crystalline PV, the company had begun investing in thin-film technology in 2005, resulting in a fully-dedicated plant in Japan. In addition to its four plants in Japan, the company produced PV solar products in the United States, the United Kingdom and Thailand. To expand production even further, Sharp was seeking joint venture partners to build solar module factories in other countries (in late 2008, the company inked a deal with Italy's Enel for a joint venture plant in Italy).

Japan's second largest PV solar producer, Kyocera, also had a global footprint, producing a range of PV products in a network of factories split between Japan, China, the Czech Republic and Mexico. Japan's third major player, Sanyo, produced nearly all of its PV offerings in its home country. It had invested heavily in developing its own thin-film technology (called HIT for Heterojunction with Intrinsic Thin-layer), which it claimed had the highest efficiency of any solar

Exhibit 6   Market Shares by PV Module Producers

2008 Rank	PV Supplier	HQ	2008 % of Total MW Shipments
1	Suntech	China	7.2%
2	Sharp	Japan	7.2%
3	First Solar	U.S.	6.9%
4	Yingli Green Energy	China	4.4%
5	Kyocera	Japan	4.2%
6	Sunpower	U.S.	3.4%
7	Trina Solar	China	3.3%
8	Sanyo	Japan	2.8%
9	Canadian Solar	Canada/China	2.6%
10	Solar World	Germany	2.6%
	Top 10 Total		**44.7%**
	Others		**55.3%**
	Total Module Shipments in GWs		**6.3**

Source: IMS Research and company files.

Market Shares PV Cell Producers

2008 Rank	2007 Rank	PV Supplier	HQ	2007 % of Total MW	2008 % of Total MW	08/07 % Change	2007 % of Total $	2008 % of Total $	08/07 % Change
1	1	Q-Cells	Germany	10.9%	9.4%	48%	14.5%	12.2%	43%
2	4	First Solar	U.S.	5.8%	8.3%	144%	6.2%	9.0%	147%
3	2	Suntech	China	10.2%	8.2%	37%	9.0%	7.2%	36%
4	3	Sharp	Japan	9.0%	8.0%	51%	8.0%	7.3%	56%
5	6	Motech	Taiwan	4.9%	4.8%	67%	4.1%	4.0%	70%
6	5	Kyocera	Japan	5.7%	4.6%	37%	5.0%	4.0%	38%
7	10	JA Solar	China	3.7%	4.6%	108%	4.6%	5.8%	117%
8	9	Yingli Green Energy	China	4.0%	4.5%	93%	3.3%	3.8%	95%
9	12	Gintech Energy	Taiwan	3.1%	4.4%	144%	2.6%	3.6%	141%
10	8	Solar World	Germany	4.7%	4.0%	44%	4.9%	3.8%	32%
		Top 10 Total		**62.0%**	**60.8%**	**67.0%**	**62.0%**	**60.6%**	**67.0%**
		Others		**38.0%**	**39.2%**	**75%**	**38.0%**	**39.4%**	**77%**
		Cell & Panel PV Total		**3.57GW**	**6.0GW**	**70%**	**$8.1b**	**$13.85b**	**71%**

Source: "Japanese solar cell manufacturers losing market share, says IC Insights," July 22, 2009, www.pv-tech.org/news/_a/
japanese_solar_cell_manufacturers_losing_market_share_says_ic_insights.

PV cell in the world (its efficiency was 23 percent).[18] Sanyo sold its complementary batteries with its PV solar products and had reorganized its business to satisfy its master plan of becoming a "leading provider of environment and energy-related products."[19] Sanyo's strong position in PV solar and related products was one of the key reasons for Panasonic taking a key ownership stake in Sanyo in late 2008.[20]

In addition to the above mix of players, other multinationals participated in PV solar, namely, Japan's Mitsubishi, Britain's BP and U.S. companies General Electric and Chevron. Mitsubishi began developing PV solar technology in the 1970s and offered complete packages including the PV module and inverter. As of 2009, Mitsubishi claimed to have one of the highest efficiencies of any poly PV cell (18.9 percent).[21] Its

Exhibit 7   Selected Solar PV Competitors

Company Name	Head Office	Year Founded	Manufacturing Sites	Sales Offices and/or Subsidiaries	R&D Centers	Production Capacity Estimate (MW)	Revenues (US$ in millions)	Gross Profit %	Net Income (US$ in millions)	% of Revenues in Solar (Est)
Suntech	Wuxi, China	2001	Wuxi, China (PV cell and module); Shanghai, China (thin film); Suzhou, China (equipment design and manufacturing); Luoyang, China (PV cell); Yangzhou, China (PV cell, planned for 2010); Dauchingen, Germany (equipment design & manufacturing); and, Nagano.	Dubai, UAE; Madrid, Spain; Milan, Italy; Munich, Germany; San Francisco, CA, U.S.; Schaffhausen (outside of Zurich), Switzerland; Seoul, Korea; Sydney, Australia; and Tokyo, Japan	Wuxi, China; Dauchingen, Germany; Nagano, Japan	1,000MW	$1,923.5 in 2008	23.7% in 2008; 25.9% in 2007	$88.2 in 2008; $171.3 in 2007	100%
Sharp	Tokyo, Japan	1912	Osaka, Japan (PV module); Tochigi, Japan (PV module); Nara, Japan (PV cell and module); Nakornpathom, Thailand (PV module); Wrexham, UK (PV module); Memphis, TN, U.S. (PV module). Sakai City, Osaka plant in process (thin-film)	Offices in 30 countries	Osaka, Japan	2,000MW + 1,000MW in 2010	$27,618.1 in 2008; $29,050.8 in 2007	16% in 2008; 22.1% in 2007	($1,220.4) in 2008; $866.3 in 2007	7%
First Solar	Tempe, AZ, U.S.	1999	Four factories (16 lines) in Kulim, Malaysia; Perrysburg, U.S. (3 lines); Frankfurt/Oder, Germany (4 lines)	New York, NY, U.S.; Bridgewater, NJ, U.S.; Perrysburg, OH, U.S.; Denver, CO, U.S.; Mountain View, CA, U.S.; Berlin, Germany; Mainz, Germany; Brussels, Belgium; Paris, France; Madrid, Spain; and, Amsterdam, Netherlands	Perrysburg, OH, U.S.	1,145MW by 2010	$1,246.3 in 2008; $504.0 in 2007	54.4% in 2008; 49.9% in 2007	$348.3 in 2008; $158.4 in 2007	100%
Yingli Green Energy	Boading, China	1998	Boading, China	Chengdu, China; Lhasa (Tibet), China	Boading, China	600MW by end of 2009	$1,091.4 in 2008; $529.7 in 2007	21.9% in 2008; 23.8% in 2007	$97.7 in 2008; $51.3 in 2007	100%

(Continued)

Exhibit 7 (Continued)

Company Name	Head Office	Year Founded	Manufacturing Sites	Sales Offices and/or Subsidiaries	R&D Centers	Production Capacity Estimate (MW)	Revenues (US$ in millions)	Gross Profit %	Net Income (US$ in millions)	% of Revenues in Solar (Est)
Kyocera	Kyoto, Japan	1959	Higashi-Ohmi, Shiga, Japan (PV cells and modules); Tianjin, China (PV modules); Lanskroun, Czech Republic (PV modules); Tijuana, Mexico (PV modules)	Offices in 30 countries	Japan	1,000MW approx.	$11,399.9 in 2008; $11,288.9 in 2007	25.9% in 2008; 31.5% in 2007	$298 in 2008; $938.2 in 2007	12%
SunPower	San Jose, CA, U.S.	1985	Philippines (PV cell and modules); Malaysia (PV cells); joint venture in South Korea for ingot production	San Jose, CA, U.S.; Richmond, CA, U.S.; Irvine, CA, U.S.; Trenton, NJ, U.S.; Waikoloa, HI, U.S.; Toronto, Canada; Belmont, Australia; Geneva, Switzerland; Frankfurt, Germany; Faenza, Italy; Milan, Italy; Madrid, Spain; Seoul, South Korea	San Jose, CA, U.S.	400MW	$1,434.9 in 2008; $774.8 in 2007	25.3% in 2008; 19.1% in 2007	$92.3 in 2008; $9.2 in 2007	100%
Trina Solar	Changzhou, China	1997	Changzhou, China (14 lines)	Shanghai, China; Munich, Germany; Barcelona, Spain; Rotterdam, Netherlands (warehouse); San Francisco, CA, U.S.; Seognam, South Korea	China	550MW by end of 2009	$831.9 in 2008; $301.8 in 2007	19.7% in 2008; 22.4% in 2007	$61.4 in 2008; $35.7 in 2007	100%
Sanyo	Osaka, Japan	1947	Kaizuka City (Osaka), Japan; Unnan City (Shimane), Japan	Offices in 25 countries	Japan	600MW by end of 2010	$20,178.2 in 2008; $16,002.2 in 2007	15.8% in 2008; 15.5% in 2007	$287 in 2008; ($385.6) in 2007	6–8%
Canadian Solar	Kitchener, Canada/ Suzhou, China	2001	4 factories in Changshu (solar modules); 2 factories in Suzhou (cells and modules); 1 factory in Luoyang (ingots, wafers and modules)	Kitchener, Canada; Ottawa, Canada; San Ramon, CA, U.S.; Babenhausen, Germany; Seoul, South Korea; Tokyo, Japan	China	620MW in module production	$705 in 2008; $302.8 in 2007	10.7% in 2008; 7.9% in 2007	($9.4) in 2008; ($0.2) in 2007	100%
Solar World	Bonn, Germany	1998	Freiburg, Germany (integrated); Camarillo, CA, U.S. (PV modules), Hillsboro, OR, U.S. (solar wafers and cells); Vancouver, WA, U.S.	Bonn, Germany; Spain; Italy; France; CA, U.S.; South Africa; Singapore	Freiburg, Germany; Camarillo, CA, U.S.					100%

Company Name	Head Office	Year Founded	Manufacturing Sites	Sales Offices and/or Subsidiaries	R&D Centers	Production Capacity Estimate (MW)	Revenues (US$ in millions)	Gross Profit %	Net Income (US$ in millions)	% of Revenues in Solar (Est)
PV CELL PRODUCERS										
Q-Cells	Thalheim, Germany	1999	One factory (6 lines) at Thalheim, Germany; new plant planned for Malaysia	Rome, Italy; Madrid, Spain; Fremont, CA, U.S.; Mexicali, Mexico. Holdings in additional companies: Ayers & Martone (Spain), Becerril (Spain), Calyxo (Germany), Sontor (Germany) and VHF (Switzerland)	Thalheim, Germany	950MW	$1,831 in 2008; $1,175.3 in 2007	31.2% in 2008; 36.7% in 2007	$278.9 in 2008; $203.1 in 2007	100%
Motech	Taipei, Taiwan	1981	Three factories in Tainan, Taiwan; Kunshan, China	No foreign offices	Taiwan	700MW–800MW approx.	$725.8 in 2008; $474.2 in 2007	15.3% in 2008; 19.2% in 2007	$73.1 in 2008; $74.3 in 2007	70% approx.
JA Solar	Shanghai, China	2005	Ningjin, Hebei, China (23 lines); Yangzhou, China (12 lines); Donghai, China	Milpitas, CA, U.S.	Yangzhou, China; Donghai, China	875MW by end of 2009	$800 in 2008; $355.3 in 2007	18.2% in 2008; 22.3% in 2007	$70.2 in 2008; $52.8 in 2007	100%
Gintech Energy	Taipei, Taiwan	2005	Jhunan, Taiwan; Taipei, Taiwan	Taipei, Taiwan	Taipei, Taiwan	600MW by end of 2009	$502.5 in 2008; $207.9 in 2007	16.9% in 2008; $12% in 2007	$60.6 in 2008; $14.8 in 2007	100%

Source: Case writer from company websites and annual reports.

production capacity was about 200MW. BP Solar also had about 30 years of history in the solar industry. With a capacity of 200MW, it produced poly and mono PV cells and modules in five plants located in Sydney, Australia; Madrid, Spain; Frederick, Maryland, United States; Bangalore, India; and Xian, China. However, in a recent move to focus on its core business of petroleum, its parent company, BP, had announced that it would be closing factories in Australia, Spain and the United States and shifting to a mix of its lower cost plants and sub-contractors in China.[22] (Shell completely divested its solar operations in 2006 and 2007—the majority of the assets were purchased by Germany's SolarWorld.[23])

BACKGROUND ON CANADIAN SOLAR

Canadian Solar was established by Dr. Shawn Qu in October 2001 in Markham, Ontario. In tandem, a production facility in Changshu, China, registered as CSI Solartronics was set up as a wholly owned subsidiary of Canadian Solar. Qu, a graduate of applied physics at Tsinghua University (B.Sc.) and the University of Manitoba (M.Sc.), had completed a doctoral degree in material science from the University of Toronto (Ph.D) and extensive post-doctorate work on semiconductor optical devices and solar cells. In 1996, he joined Ontario Hydro (now Ontario Power Generation) as a research scientist, where he worked on the development of a next-generation solar technology called Spheral Solar™. In 1998, he joined ATS (Automation Tooling Systems), working in several capacities such as product engineer, director for silicon procurement, solar product strategic planning as well as technical vice president for one of ATS's subsidiaries.

Qu left ATS to establish Canadian Solar; he commented on the opportunity he saw at the time:

> In 2001, solar was still a very small industry. A lot of my colleagues from the PhD program in applied physics were involved in fibre optics for the telecommunications industry. I believed that solar had great prospects and I thought to myself, "Hmm, I could easily spend my career in the solar industry." Because solar was such a small part of ATS, it did not get a lot of management attention. Around 2000, I started thinking of starting my

own company and worked on the business plan. At that time, the major players were small solar divisions in multinationals like BP, Siemens, Shell and Sharp. My idea largely focused on areas that I felt they were not addressing: rural electrification with solar, the low-cost production of solar cells and solar modules, building integrated solar products and consumer solar products. It just so happened the first product was a consumer solar product for the automotive industry.

Canadian Solar's first contract was to manufacture and sell a solar charger to Audi-Volkswagen for use in its automobiles being manufactured in Mexico. Audi-Volkswagen required that Canadian Solar became ISO9001 and ISO16949 certified. Management saw the certification as an essential part of raising Canadian Solar's quality credibility in the early stages of the company. Canadian Solar established two additional solar module manufacturing plants in Suzhou, China, incorporated as separate companies: CSI Solar Technologies in August 2003; and CSI Solar Manufacturing in January 2005. The company purchased solar cells and silicon raw materials from a small group of companies such as Swiss Wafers (Switzerland), Kunical (United States), Luoyang Zhong Gui (China) and LDK (China).

While continuing to supply Audi-Volkswagen (eventually receiving the accolade of class A supplier), Canadian Solar's management saw a great opportunity to develop solar modules for electricity generation for residential and commercial applications in 2004. Qu commented:

> In early 2004 with the change of Germany's FIT program, I identified a major increase in demand for solar PV modules for buildings. Within three to four months, we were able to switch gears to large solar modules. When I think back now, the decision to spin-off the company from ATS in 2001 when we did was vital—had I waited until 2004, I would not have had the time to build the team and capabilities to make this switch into larger solar modules.

By the end of 2004, nearly three-quarters of Canadian Solar's sales were derived from selling standard solar modules to distributors and system integrators based in Germany, Spain and China. The company made initial contact with its customers through international trade shows such as Intersolar in Munich, Germany. By the end of 2005, the top five customers accounted for

68.2 percent of total sales. The majority of the sales were made with non-exclusive, three-month sales contracts. It was normal that the customer paid 20 to 30 percent of the purchase as prepayment and the remainder in advance of the shipment from China. In China, sales of solar modules were associated with development projects in conjunction with Chinese governmental organizations and the Canadian International Development Agency (CIDA)—for example, in the spring of 2005, the company installed a demonstration power plant in a rural area of the province of Jiangsu.

With sales of standard solar modules accelerating, Canadian Solar turned to venture capital (VC) funding. Qu stated: "Up until 2005, we had grown without any VC involvement. We received an investment from HSBC and Jafco Ventures [a VC from Japan with $350 million under management] and then started preparing for an IPO." In November 2006, the company listed on the Nasdaq, raising $115.5 million. The proceeds were to be used to purchase and prepay for solar cells and silicon (35 percent); expansion into solar cell manufacturing (45 percent); and general funding purposes (20 percent). The initial public offering (IPO) enabled it to expand into solar cell manufacturing, resulting in the following facilities: CSI Solarchip for solar cells and modules; and CSI Advanced and CSI Luoyang for solar modules. By the end of 2007, the company had established four solar cell production lines, taking total cell capacity to 120MW.

Canadian Solar's management established a sales office of two people in Phoenix, Arizona, and a European office of three people in Babenhausen, Germany (outside of Frankfurt), in December 2007. All sales in Spain were done through an independent distributor. As Qu said: "We serviced these growing markets from China and Canada. The decision to open up the offices in 2007 was a logical move given that the majority of sales were coming from those markets." On the production side, the company expanded to seven factories including a solar module manufacturing site in Changshu and an ingot and wafer manufacturing site in Luoyang. The continued expansion in China was complemented by a high-profile BIPV (Building Integrated Photovoltaic) module roof project as part of the Beijing 2008 Olympic Games. At the close of 2008, the company was recognized as one of the top 10 fastest-growing companies in China by Deloitte Asia, given its

sales had more than doubled from $302.8 million in 2007 to $705 million in 2008.

To usher in 2009, the company underwent a number of changes in its international configuration. To respond to market opportunity in South Korea, it established a two-person sales office. In Canada, the company established an international development office of three people in Ottawa to focus specifically on projects in Latin America and the Middle East, given its working history with CIDA. In the United States, the company moved the Phoenix office to San Ramon, California, to be located closer to the heart of the U.S. solar movement and to take advantage of the favorable Californian incentives. It opened a warehouse at the office site to store finished solar modules. In China, it opened a PV research and development facility at its head office in Suzhou. As of the end of 2008, the company had 3,058 employees of which 2,742 were in manufacturing, 251 in general and administrative, 36 in research and development and 29 in sales and marketing.[24]

CANADIAN SOLAR'S MODEL

The company described itself as an "inverted flexible vertical integration business model." This meant that the company had higher capacity as it went further downstream in the manufacturing process of each component of a solar module. The inverted vertical integration model is graphically illustrated on page C-206.

The rationale behind the "inverted vertical integration" model was to allow for flexibility in short-term demand shifts by purchasing ingots, wafers and cells from other manufacturers and to free the company from the capital investment required to have equal capacity of each component. The company believed that it would lead to a lower manufacturing cost base in the long term as well as superior production yields, better inventory control and efficient cash management.

Canadian Solar also had been one of the first solar companies to initiate a recycling process for reclaimable silicon from discarded, broken or unused silicon wafers and ingots at two of its plants in Suzhou and Changshu. The process involved a substantial amount of labour and analysts believed that Canadian Solar had a competitive advantage in recycling silicon. However,

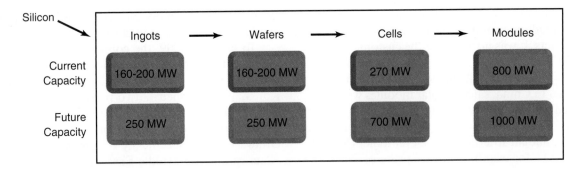

in the 2008 Annual Report, the company stated: "As a result of the oversupply of silicon materials that developed in the fourth quarter of 2008, we expect this aspect of our operation to be less significant in the foreseeable future."[25]

In addition to recycling reclaimed silicon, the company became a member of the Belgian organization PV CYCLE in mid-2009. PV CYCLE promoted a take-back and recycling of PV modules that had reached the end of their useful life.[26]

Products

Canadian Solar offered a portfolio of products ranging from 0.3W to 300W. It split its offerings into two main divisions: standard and specialty. The company used both its own branding and manufactured white label products for other OEMs. See Exhibit 8 for a sample product information sheet. With a few exceptions, all products were standardized for the global market.

The company offered three types of products:

1. Standard: Standard modules were used for both ground mount and rooftop systems and were available in both mono and poly.
2. e-Modules: e-Modules were a recent product introduction which were aimed at providing a lower-cost product for smaller roof-top systems. e-Modules were lower cost because they used upgraded metallurgical-grade silicon (Umg Si) instead of pure silicon.
3. BIPV (Building Integrated Photovoltaic). Finally, BIPV were intended to be used as a building material in a roof, skylight or façade.

Standard modules were all tested and certified by various international standards. Product performance warranties were normally 25 years depending on the product. Prices were negotiated on the quantity ordered but were between $2 and $3 per watt. Margins ranged from 13 to 18 percent for standard and e-Modules and were 15 to 20 percent on BIPV products. Canadian Solar's strategy was to maintain comparable prices to its primary Chinese competitors.

Specialty products included items to be used in battery chargers, GPS tracking systems, street and traffic lights, garden lights, marine lights and other home systems. Prices varied greatly depending on the level of customization—margins were usually around 15 to 20 percent for specialty items.

Production Facilities

The company produced all of its products in its seven plants in China. The seven factories had been set up because of Chinese government incentives to establish operations in specific jurisdictions. For example, the Luoyang factory, located approximately eight hours by road from the central offices of Suzhou, was set up at the request of the government-owned silicon supplier in Luoyang.

In late 2008, in a trade show interview, Canadian Solar's then vice president of corporate and production development, Robert Patterson, was asked if production facilities would be opened closer to areas of demand:

> Not yet. We got our hands full in terms of how fast we're growing and also our capital requirements going into our current plants. We'd probably have to stabilize our current supply stream and then we would address whether we'd want to do assembly plants in various locations. If you're based in China, you have an advantage on an assembly basis, mainly because of the labour content of a solar cell or solar module. So, it would be a future thing, not ruled out.[27]

Exhibit 8   Product Information Sheet—CS6P—Module (210W To 250W)

CanadianSolar

CS6P
210/220/230/240/250P

On-grid Module

CS6P is a robust solar module with 60 solar cells. These modules can be used for on-grid solar applications. Our meticulous design and production techniques ensure a high-yield, long-term performance for every module produced. Our rigorous quality control and in-house testing facilities guarantee Canadian Solar's modules meet the highest quality standards possible.

Key Features

- 6 years product warranty (materials and workmanship); 25 years module power output warranty

- Industry leading power tolerance: ±5W (±2%)

- Strong framed module, passing mechanical load test of 5400Pa to withstand heavier snow load

- The 1st manufacturer in PV industry certified for ISO:TS16949 (The automotive quality management system) in module production since 2003

- ISO17025 qualified manufacturer owned testing lab, fully complying to IEC, TUV, UL testing standards

Applications

- On-grid residential roof-tops
- On-grid commercial/industrial roof-tops
- Solar power stations
- Other on-grid applications

Quality Certificates

- IEC 61215, IEC61730, UL1703, CEC Listed, CE
- ISO9001: 2008: Standards for quality management systems
- ISO/TS16949:2009: The automotive quality management system
- QC080000 HSPM: The Certification for Hazardous Substances Regulations

Source: Company files.

Sales Offices

Canadian Solar had seven sales offices outside of China (domestic Chinese sales were done primarily from Suzhou and Shanghai). In the summer of 2009, the company had opened an office in Kitchener, Ontario, and shifted its official headquarters from Markham to Kitchener. The Kitchener office (eight people) was responsible for the development of Canadian sales with a focus on the Ontario market, given the recently introduced FIT program. The Ottawa office (four people) was the international sales office for projects in the Middle East and Latin America and initially also housed the company's investor relations manager. Opportunities in the Middle East and Latin America were developed through a combination of trade shows, bids on public tenders and CIDA-sponsored development projects.

The United States was primarily covered through the 10-person facility in San Ramon, California, which included business development managers and a warehouse. Additionally, there was a sales representative located in a satellite office in New York State.

The company's office in Munich, Germany, was responsible for the coordination of all sales efforts in Europe. The top five German customers accounted for just over half of the company's corporate sales. The customers were utility-scale developers and distributors of roof-top solar projects. With a total of 15 people, the office was responsible for managing the independent sales agent in Spain as well as establishing new offices.

Canadian Solar served the Asian market through its sales forces at the principal Chinese office in Suzhou as well as recently established offices in Seoul, South Korea (two people), and Tokyo, Japan (eight people). In Japan, due to the popularity of solar PV in residential applications, Canadian Solar was developing a complete systems package, which included the solar PV modules, racking systems, inverter and monitoring devices.

Marketing

Due to the small size of the PV industry, the company focused on building its brand through industry tradeshows and publications such as Photon International and PV Technology. In early 2009, the company had recently re-branded itself to emphasize its "Canadian" roots by changing its logo to read "Canadian Solar" instead of the previous "CSI" (standing for "Canadian Solar International"). Hanbing Zhang, the company's director of global marketing, explained:

> No one really understood what CSI meant—with Canadian Solar, we don't need to explain. As a country, Canada is well received around the world. People from all over have a connection to Canada;

for example, Koreans send their kids to learn English in Canada and many Europeans have relatives in Canada. It is seen as a peaceful and environmentally aware country. By emphasizing the Canadian image, we can further differentiate from the other Chinese manufacturers.

Development Projects

In addition to its role as a producer, Canadian Solar was becoming more active in the development of both ground-mount and rooftop commercial projects. Typically, Canadian Solar partnered with a solar developer, system integrator or utility to carry out the tasks involved in commercial solar development such as engineering, construction, financing, negotiation of the power purchase agreements (PPAs) and the operation of the solar project.

In its largest project to date in 2009, Canadian Solar had formed a strategic alliance with Chinese-based Guodian Power Development to build and operate two 50MW PV power plants in China. Historically, most of Canadian Solar's development projects had been focused on providing power to rural areas in China.[28]

Financials

For the past three years, Canadian Solar posted losses. In 2008, the net loss was $9.4 million. The global economic crisis caused the company to have higher than normal interest expenses on short-term loan facilities, increases in the allowance for doubtful accounts and a major inventory write-down (caused by both a weakening in demand and the rapidly declining price of silicon).

In June 2009, Deutsche Bank analysts projected Canadian Solar's revenues to be $395 million with a loss of $18 million (see Exhibit 9). In June 2009, an analyst wrote:

> [Canadian Solar] is a smaller, upstream solar PV company, struggling with weak fundamentals in a highly competitive industry where capital is still a constraint for its solar PV customers amidst a credit contraction environment. Upside risks include: a rapid demand rebound, minimal average sales price declines, a weakening U.S. dollar and more favorable policy and incentive programs. Downside risks include: gauging end demand for company products amidst industry

Exhibit 9   **Deutsche Bank's Pro-Forma Financials for Canadian Solar June 2009 & August 2009**

US$ millions	2005	2006	2007	2008	June Forecast		Aug. Forecast	
					2009E	2010E	2009E	2010E
Income Statement								
Sales	18	68	303	705	395	538	574	794
EBITDA	5	1	−1	46	21	45	80	128
EBIT	5	1	−2	24	−11	14	44	80
Pre-tax profit	5	−1	0	11	−15	−2	53	71
Net income	4	−10	−1	−9	−18	−2	49	62
Cash Flow								
Cash flow from operations	−5	−46	−93	53	6	26	50	114
Net capex	−1	−7	−35	−151	−90	−30	−115	−119
Free cash flow	−5	−53	−128	−98	−84	−3	−65	−5
Equity raised/(bought back)	0	83	0	204	0	0	0	0
Dividends paid	0	0	0	0	0	0	0	0
Net inc/(dec) in borrowings	9	5	130	24	97	0	141	0
Other investing/financing cash flows	0	0	−5	−52	−97	0	−128	0
Net cash flow	4	35	−3	78	−84	−3	−51	−5
Change in working capital	−9	−52	−102	24	−13	−5	−38	2
Balance Sheet								
Cash and cash equivalents	6	41	38	116	31	28	64	59
Property, plant and equipment	1	8	52	166	231	229	243	314
Goodwill	0	0	0	0	0	0	0	0
Other assets	20	81	195	289	424	431	543	540
Total assets	27	130	284	570	686	688	851	914
Debt	5	3	133	157	254	254	298	298
Other liabilities	16	13	25	81	113	115	162	161
Total liabilities	20	17	158	238	367	369	461	459
Total shareholders' equity	7	113	126	332	319	319	386	451
Net debt	−2	−38	96	41	223	226	234	239

Source: Deutsche Bank, "Canadian Solar: Notes from the Deutsche Bank alternative energy conference," June 10, 2009, p. 2.

August forecast from Deutsche Bank, "Canadian Solar: New market penetration drives solid shipments," August 6, 2009, p. 2.

demand destruction, rapid average sales price declines/high input costs dislocating business model assumptions, capital constraints hindering operational flexibility and managing currency dislocations.[29]

However, by August 2009, Deutsche Bank had raised its estimates to revenues of $574 million and net income of $49 million for 2009, stating:

Canadian Solar posted 2Q09 results well ahead of expectations on strong shipments growth [in markets like the Czech Republic, Korea and Italy], further aided by favorable FX trends (i.e., $0.14 contribution to EPS) and prior inventory writedowns . . . we believe the company is gaining share in new markets.[30]

Deutsche Bank rated the stock a "hold" and Oppenheimer rated it an "outperform." As of September 25, 2009, Canadian Solar's stock price closed at $16.74 (the 52-week range was from $3.00 to $19.91).

CONSIDERATIONS GOING FORWARD

Some industry observers believed that the solar PV industry needed to regroup and get back to basics. Consultants from BCG wrote:

> In order to thrive in and not merely survive the harsh reality of today's market, PV suppliers need to take a critical look at their business model and operations . . . To negotiate this far more challenging environment, PV suppliers will need to refocus their attention on the basics: relative cost position, go-to-market effectiveness, and an understanding of key market segments and channels.[31]

Having been on a track of dynamic growth since inception, it was now Canadian Solar's opportunity to strategically think about any changes to its international strategy. Qu stated:

> In terms of the solar industry, the first step is to determine the market and follow the renewable policies closely. For the next two to three years, we've determined that we will be focusing on 10 countries: Canada, China, Germany, Spain, Italy, France, Czech Republic, South Korea, Japan and the United States.

There is plenty of competition. First, the established players such as Sharp and Sanyo have powerful brands. From a technology standpoint, a company like FirstSolar clearly has a different product with their thin-film technology and the question is, "Which technology wins?" The other U.S. competitor is SunPower, which has high efficiency and a high price premium. Out of the Chinese producers, Suntech is slightly different than others since they combine Australian engineering with Chinese production much like we combine Canadian engineering with Chinese production. The other potential threat is the possibility that some upstream silicon makers will adapt their business models to start producing modules downstream. After the financial crisis, I think the industry realizes that silicon is not precious and there could be an increasing trend for silicon producers to move downstream to capture more value.

When I look back at my original business plan, we've greatly exceeded our initial revenue projections. The business has changed substantially from its initial focus—this illustrates that one of the key skills in this industry, and any start-up for that matter, is the ability to see changes in the marketplace and adapt the business accordingly.

ENDNOTES

[1] Solar photovoltaic (PV) technology is one of the main types of solar electric power. It is the main focus of this case.

[2] This section draws upon descriptions in: *SBI,* "The U.S. Solar Energy Market in a World Perspective," March 2008, pp. 2–30.

[3] Phosphorous was often used as the negative pole and boron was often used as the positive pole.

[4] Silicon was found in sand, rocks or soil as silicon oxide (SiO_2); the process for manufacturing silicon involved heating silicon oxide with a carbon material like coke or coal at high temperatures to remove the oxygen.

[5] The six types of materials used in thin-film technology were: amorphous silicon (a-Si); copper indium diselenide (CIS); copper indium gallium diselenide (CIGS); cadmium telluride (CdTe); gallium arsenide (GaAs); and thin-film silicon.

[6] Edgar Gunther, "Solar Polysilicon Oversupply until 2013?" August 3, 2009, http://guntherportfolio.com/2009/08/solar-polysilicon-oversupply-until-2013, accessed August 18, 2009.

[7] Quote from www.solarbuzz.com, accessed August 11, 2009.

[8] By comparison, the global installed capacity of wind power grew by 29 percent from 93.9GW in 2007 to 121.2GW in 2008.

[9] "Act Revising the Legislation on Renewable Energy Sources in the Electricity Sector and Amending Related Provisions—Renewable Energy Sources Act—EEG 2009," www.erneuerbare-energien.de/inhalt/42934/3860, accessed August 18, 2009.

[10] European Photovoltaic Industry Association (EPIA), "Global Market Outlook for Photovoltaics until 2013," March 2009, p. 7.

[11] Paul Voosen, "Spain's Solar Market Crash Offers a Cautionary Tale About Feed-In Tariffs," August 18, 2009, www.nytimes.com/gwire/2009/08/18/18greenwire-spains-solar-market-crash-offers-a-cautionary-88308.html?pagewanted=2, accessed August 18, 2009.

[12] "Spain Makes Changes to Solar Tariff," September 29, 2008, www.renewableenergyworld.com/rea/news/article/2008/09/spain-makes-changes-to-solar-tariff-53698, accessed August 18, 2009.

[13] "Plan de Energías Renovables 2011–2020," http://www.plane.gob.es/plan-de-energias-renovables-2011-2020, accessed August 17, 2009.

[14] *Energy Matters,* "Japan Announces Solar Feed In Tariffs," February 25, 2009, www.energymatters.com.au/index.php?main_page=news_article&article_id=335, accessed August 17, 2009.

[15] James Murray, "US lawmakers outline plan for feed-in tariff bill," *Business Green,* August 5, 2009, http://www.businessgreen.com/business-green/news/2247352/lawmakers-outline-plan-feed, accessed August 19, 2009.

[16] "Ontario's Standard Offer Contracts," March 22, 2006, www.energyalternatives.ca/content/SOC.htm, accessed August 18, 2009.

[17] Jim Bai and Leonora Walet, "China offers big solar subsidy, shares up," *Reuters,* July 21, 2009.

[18] "Sanyo Develops HIT Solar Cells with World's Highest Energy Conversion Efficiency of 23.0%," May 21, 2009, http://us.sanyo.com/News/SANYO-Develops-HIT-Solar-Cells-with-World-s-Highest-Energy-Conversion-

Efficiency-of-23-0-, accessed August 16, 2009.

[19] Sanyo Annual Report 2008, December 31, 2008, p. 9.

[20] "Panasonic and SANYO Agree to Capital and Business Alliance," http://sanyo.com/news/2008/12/19-1.html, accessed August 17, 2009.

[21] "Mitsubishi Electric Breaks Own Record With World's Highest Conversion Efficiency Rate Of 18.9% For Multi-Crystalline Silicon Photovoltaic Cells," February 18, 2009, www.mitsubishielectricsolar.com/news, accessed August 19, 2009.

[22] Ed Crooks, "Back to petroleum," *Financial Times*, July 7, 2009.

[23] Terry Macalister, "Big Oil lets sun set on renewables," *The Guardian*, December 11, 2007, www.guardian.co.uk/business/2007/dec/11/oil.bp, accessed August 19, 2009.

[24] Canadian Solar Annual Report 2008, 20-F, www.sec.gov, December 31, 2008, p. 74.

[25] Canadian Solar Annual Report 2008, 20-F, www.sec.gov, December 31, 2008, p. 30.

[26] "Canadian Solar Becomes Member of PV Cycle," July 21, 2009, http://phx.corporate-ir.net/phoenix.zhtml?c=196781&p=irol-news, accessed November 20, 2009.

[27] Interview with Robert Patterson, VP corporate & production development, by Mark Osborne, Photovoltaics International, December 3, 2008, www.pv-tech.org/solar_leaders_video_clips/_a/canadian_solar_vp_robert_patterson_talks_umg_si_product_lines_150mw_plus.

[28] Canadian Solar Prospectus, October 12, 2009, www.sec.gov, p. 5.

[29] "Canadian Solar: Notes from the Deutsche Bank alternative energy conference," Deutsche Bank, June 10, 2009, p. 3.

[30] "Canadian Solar: New market penetration drives solid shipments," *Deutsche Bank*, August 6, 2009, p. 1.

[31] "Back to the Basics: How Photovoltaic Suppliers Can Win in Today's Solar Market," *The Boston Consulting Group*, p. 1.

Cemex's Cost of 'Globalised' Growth—The Cash Crunch?

M.V. Vivek Gonela
IBSCDC

Saradhi Kumar Gonela
IBSCDC

Nagendra V. Chowdary
IBSCDC

In two decades, Cemex, the Mexican building materials major, has grown to be the world's largest cement trader and the third-largest producer through an array of global acquisitions. Since 1992, Cemex acquired many companies across North America, Latin America, Europe and Asia and spread its operations to more than 50 countries. These acquisitions helped the company in reducing its dependency on domestic market—in 2008. Mexico accounted for just one-third of its revenues—but substantially increased its debt burden, which stood at $19.4 billion by mid-2009 or more than six times its EBITDA.[1] In the wake of the global recession, Cemex had to grapple with a paradox—scouting for debt restructuring or selling assets—to honour impending debts. Given the nature and intensity of U.S. Financial Crisis, would banks allow it to come to negotiations or would it be forced to offload some of its acquired assets in distressed markets?

www.ibscdc.org This case study was written by M.V. Vivek and Saradhi Kumar Gonela under the guidance of Dr. Nagendra V. Chowdary, IBSCDC. It is intended to be used as the basis for class discussion rather than to illustrate either effective or ineffective handling of a management situation. The case was compiled from published sources.

© 2010, IBSCDC.

No part of this publication may be copied, stored, transmitted, reproduced or distributed in any form or medium whatsoever without the permission of the copyright owner.

CEMEX UNDER ZAMBRANO—CEMENTING ITS POSITION

Cemex' growth, since established as Cementos Hidalgo in 1906 in Mexico, has been an ordeal. Cementos Hidalgo merged with Cementos Portland Monterrey in 1931 to form Cementos Mexicanos (Cemex). Cemex grew to be a national player by acquiring a plant in Mérida, Yucatán, in 1960s from Cementos Maya and by constructing new plants in Ciudad Valles, San Luis Potosí and Torreón, Coahuila. It further expanded in early 1970s by installing new kilns in Mérida and Monterrey and acquiring a plant in Central Mexico. During 1976, it was listed on the Mexican *Bolsa* (stock exchange) and also became leading cement producer in Mexico by acquiring three plants owned by Cementos Guadalajara.

During early 1980s, Cemex diversified into unrelated businesses like petrochemicals, tourism, hotels and mining to reduce its dependence on the cement industry. However, in 1985 when Lorenzo Zambrano (Zambrano) became the CEO, he decided to divest non-cement holdings as, on one hand, petroleum prices fell sharply in the international markets and on the other, devaluation of Mexican Peso (in 1982) pushed the economy into recession. In later years, Zambrano's refusal to operate in non-cement industries proved to be the base of Cemex's success. Though started as a cement manufacturer, Cemex developed its expertise in distribution, marketing and sale of cement, ready-mix concrete, aggregates[2] and clinker. By the end of 1980s, having secured a domestic market share of 65%, Cemex became one of the 10 largest cement companies in the world.[3] Although Cemex was making rapid progress, Mexican cement industry was operating at only 50% capacity by the end of 1980s.[4]

Cemex improved its efficiency by using Information Technology (IT). In 1987, Zambrano hired a cyber-visionary Gelacio Iiguez, who created an information network system, by installing satellite dishes for voice and data transmission among all its plants. In 1994, a Cemex team visited FedEx, Exxon and 9-1-1 centre (Emergency Communication Centre) in Houston and on the same lines developed an integrated dispatching system, centralising dispersed operations by a satellite. Often, trucks failed to reach customers in time and orders were either cancelled or re-scheduled, resulting in losses. To avoid this, Cemex equipped their ready-mix delivery trucks with satellite connection, which enabled customers to track the trucks by global positioning system. This technology also helped in re-directing trucks on orders cancellation, through a central monitoring system. It drastically reduced the delivery time and 70 trucks could deliver same quantity as 100 trucks did in previous method. The technology resulted in huge savings of fuel, maintenance, payroll and an enormous increase in goodwill. "We have been able to run the company with a very small number of managers because of very sophisticated information systems,"[5] Zambrano quipped.

In 1995, Cemex launched one of the first wide-ranged corporate websites, featuring up-to-date financial information for investors and analysts, as well as catalogues of products for clients. Further, Zambrano launched a logistics system that allowed clients to track shipments online. "The Internet is changing the way we do business, but that doesn't change the traditional strategy of the past," Zambrano said, referring to Cemex's swift move towards IT and added, "We're investing in Internet-related businesses to strengthen our core business, which we define not as selling cement, but as selling service with certain attributes, like timeliness."[6] On IT focus Zambrano said, "A cement company is not supposed to be high-tech, but we showed it can be. It is supposed to be boring, but we showed it is not."[7]

Cemex's CxNetworks, based in Miami was formed in 2000 as a subsidiary to manage Cemex's various e-business efforts. Among these were *Construmex,* a construction industry online marketplace aimed at small- and medium-sized contractors in Latin America and Latinexus, an online exchange for indirect goods and services created in partnership with other leading companies in Mexico and Brazil. Cemex renamed its technological arm Cemtec as Neoris and spun it into an independent company to provide e-consulting, front-end web designing, web architecture and related services to various firms beyond Cemex. According to Zambrano, the company's e-business strategy is premised on five inter-related business realities to free the most valuable human assets (Annexure I).

While IT supported the growth of Cemex, an otherwise commodity was elevated into a product with unique marketing strategies and further made it into a successful brand with extraordinary

Annexure I   Basis of Cemex's e-Business Strategy

- The boundaries between companies and between industries are increasingly blurring.
- The relationships between companies and their markets have changed. In a world of mass customisation, Cemex's ability to brand cement and other products is a valuable asset.
- Time has sped up. Since information is everywhere, readily available and virtually free, companies like Cemex are differentiating themselves through the speed of their decision making and develop new business strategies.
- There has been a shift in the source of value creation from owning assets to leveraging assets through networks.
- Internet is changing the nature of work. As Cemex increasingly digitises its global network, the company is able to remove hands and minds from routine tasks throughout the organisation, replacing them with computers and networks.

  "This frees our most valuable resources—our people—to undertake information intensive activities that create more value for all our stakeholders," Zambrano says.

Source: "Cemex leverages clicks and mortar solutions", http://www.cemex.com/mc/rn/mc_rn_ms2001.asp, 2001.

consumer care service support. In Mexico, cement was sold in retail bags as a cheap commodity to average do-it-yourself customers that represented 85% of the total cement business.[8] However, the market was unattractive as home constructions and additions were passive. It was largely because the Mexicans spent savings heavily on local festivals, *Quinceañera* or *Quince años* (girls' 15th birthday celebrations) and weddings, denying Mexican families savings for building materials—a cement house remained a dream. Cemex solved this through *Patrimonio Hoy* programme launched in 1998. It shifted the image of cement from being a bag of white powder to a gift of dreams and blended the programme with traditional Mexican *tandas,* a community savings scheme, in which the winning family would spend the amount in festive seasons. Cemex, brought in *supertandas* which directed the family towards building additional rooms to the home. The *Patrimonio Hoy* programme consisted of roughly 70 people, each contributing 120 pesos for 70 weeks. Every week lots would be drawn and winners would get building materials worth the total money. Along with the prize, Cemex complemented winners with delivery of cement, organising classes on effective construction and a technical advisor to maintain relations with participants during the project.

Many Mexican families waited for their migrated relatives to U.S., to transfer money for building or remodelling homes, but huge commissions discouraged money transfers. Even when money reached, incomplete knowledge hampered construction. Another problem was that most of the time, money was spent on some unimportant matters instead of construction. To solve this, Cemex initiated a programme called *Construmex,* in 2001, targeting Mexican migrants to U.S. The *Construmex* programme, enabled customers in U.S. to buy, construct or remodel their home in Mexico. Initially, Cemex had to face challenges in gaining trust of migrants. Cemex realised the importance of gaining trust and establishing strong relations with customers rather than selling material and thus has altered its programme. Mexicans in U.S. could walk to a local Cemex office and select a plan. As soon as the money was paid in U.S., Cemex delivered the construction materials to the concerned families in Mexico. Credit facilities were also available for

the needy. *Construmex*'s catchy Spanish tagline *Hazla, Paisano,* which translates to 'You can do it, Compatriot,' was very effective in attracting the U.S.-based Mexicans.

Competitors sold bags of cement whereas Cemex sold a dream with a business model that involved innovative financing and construction expertise. Cemex went a step further through organising celebrations in the town whenever a room was finished, adding to shared happiness. This emotional positioning of cement helped to increase demand for cement in Mexico. More families started building additional rooms and demand for cement in Mexico tripled. Cemex could charge a relatively higher price and grew at a monthly growth of 15%.[9]

Success in the homeland did not take Cemex' attention away from global industry trends during late 1980s. It was the time when globalisation was attaining prominence and cement industry was consolidating along with other industries. Zambrano observed, "We suddenly found ourselves competing with very large international companies at a time of consolidation in the world cement industry. There were few independent players left. Either we became large and international or we would end up being purchased by a bigger player."[10] And that was the time when multinationals like Holcim of Switzerland were competing for a better market share in Mexico's developing economy (Annexure II) and a much bigger threat was from North American Free Trade Agreement (NAFTA) accord that would be implemented from 1994. This made Zambrano to look outside Mexico and strategise plans to go global (Annexure III). He muscled his way into more than 50 countries and became an inspirational leader as *The Wall Street Journal* described, "Lorenzo Zambrano is a poster boy for globalisation, a swashbuckling executive who turned a sleepy local cement maker into Mexico's first true multinational, with holdings on five continents. For many in Latin America, in particular, he became an inspiration, showing how to not just survive in a competitive world but dominate."[11] Zambrano became the face of calculated globalisation and Cemex was rated as the region's most admired company in a survey of Latin American business people in 2000 conducted by PricewaterhouseCoopers.

Annexure II   Globalisation Moves of the Major Three Firms of Cement Industry

Cemex

From a modest domestic player to a mighty multinational

- 1906: Cementos Hidalgo is established near Monterrey in Northern Mexico and begins operating a cement plant
- 1920: Lorenzo Zambrano opens a cement plant in Monterrey through his newly founded firm, Cementos Portland Monterrey
- 1931: The two companies merge to form Cementos Mexicanos, later known as Cemex; firm is based in Monterrey
- 1976: Cemex goes public; it becomes the largest cement maker in Mexico following the acquisition of Cementos Guadalajara's three plants
- 1985: The founder's grandson, also named Lorenzo Zambrano, is named chairman and CEO; the new leader embarks on an ambitious programme of expansion
- 1989: Acquisition of Cementos Tolteca, the number two cement producer in Mexico, gives Cemex 65% of the Mexican market and makes it one of the 10 largest cement companies in the world
- 1992: The company buys the two largest cement companies in Spain, Valenciana and Sanson, for $1.84 billion
- 1994: A controlling stake in Vencemos, the largest cement company in Venezuela, is acquired
- 1995: Expands to Dominican Republic and expands in Caribbean market
- 1996: Expands to Columbia and Panama to consolidate the Caribbean market
- 1997: Cemex makes its first direct investment in Asia, purchasing a 30% stake in Rizal Cement Company, Inc. of the Philippines
- 1999: A majority stake in Assiut Cement Company, the leading cement maker in Egypt, is acquired. Further expansions in India and South America follows.
- 2000: The second-largest U.S. cement producer, Houston-based Southdown Inc., is acquired for $2.63 billion
- 2002: A write-down from currency-hedging operations foreshadows the losses company will face in this years credit crisis. Expands to Puerto Rico
- 2005: Cemex acquires RMC for $5.8 billion, which enhanced its position to world's third-largest producer of cement
- 2007: Cemex acquires Rinker, an Australian company with its major operations in U.S., for a huge amount of $15.3 billion, loading up the debt
- 2008: Cemex stocks crumble as cement sales decline, flight to the dollar causes currency-hedging losses and the company is in huge debt crisis trying to refinance and come out of the cash crunch

Lafarge

From a family limestone business to the world leader in building materials

- 1833: Creation of Lafarge in France
- 1864: 1st major international contract. The company delivers 110,000 tonnes of lime for the construction of the Suez Canal
- 1866: First operations in Algeria and development in North Africa
- 1887: Lafarge opens its 1st laboratory, the Teil Laboratory, in the South of France
- 1926: Lafarge enters UK
- 1956: Lafarge enters U.S. and builds its 1st cement works in Canada, at Richmond
- 1959: Lafarge enters Brazil
- 1980: Lafarge enters Belgium through merging with Coppée
- 1980s: Lafarge expands to other European countries Germany, Spain, Turkey and Austria
- 1985: First operations in Cameroon and sub-Saharan Africa
- 1989: Expands to Kenya, acquires Cementia and thus expands to Switzerland. Expanded to Spain, Turkey and Austria through acquiring brands
- 1990: Expands to East Germany
- 1992: Expands to Czech Republic
- 1994: Lafarge enters the Chinese market through Chinefarge, a JV
- 1995: Starts operations in Poland
- 1996: Starts operations in Russia

(Continued)

Ānnexure II   (Concluded)

- 1997: Lafarge acquires the British firm, Redland. The Group becomes No. 1 in the aggregates market and enters the roofing market. Starts operations in Romania
- 1998: Expands to South Africa. Starts operations in South Korea, Indonesia and the Philippines
- 1999: Expands to India. Starts operations in Ukraine. Starts operations in Mexico
- 2001: Acquisition of the British cement company, Blue Circle Industries Plc. (B.C.I.), propels Lafarge to the rank of No. 1 global cement manufacturer. Starts operations in Malaysia. Expands to Zimbabwe, Tanzania, Malawi, Nigeria and Zambia
- 2006: Lafarge acquires 100% ownership of Lafarge North America. Starts plant in Bangladesh
- 2007: Lafarge acquires Orascom Cement, the leader in the Middle East and the Mediterranean Basin, marks a real acceleration in the Group's development strategy and turns Lafarge into the leader building materials in emerging markets
- 2008: The Excellence 2008 strategic plan is a success and Lafarge announces new ambitions and clear priorities. Lafarge is the world leader in building materials, with presence in 76 countries.

Holcim

From a humble beginning in a Swiss village to a global leader

- 1912: Holcim was founded in 1912 in the village of Holderbank, Canton Aargau, Switzerland.
- 1920's: By the early 1920's, the company began investing in cement businesses in other European countries. This trend was quickly followed by investments in Egypt, Lebanon and South Africa
- 1945–1970: In the years following 1945 and particularly in the fifties and sixties, a network of Group companies began to develop in North and Latin America (Holcim entered Mexican market in 1964)
- 1970's: The group ventures into the emerging markets of the Asia-Pacific began
- 1980's: In the 1980's, Holcim continued to expand into new markets, including Eastern Europe. A greater focus on aggregates and ready-mixed concrete production strengthened the company's position as a vertically integrated market leader
- 1990's: A strong focus on core business activities in cement, concrete and aggregates characterised Holcim's activities during the 1990's. Entry into new markets, particularly within Asia, expanded opportunities for the Group
- 2001: The name of the Group was changed from 'Holderbank' Financière Glaris Ltd. to Holcim Ltd. in May 2001
- 2005: In 2005, Holcim entered into a strategic alliance with Gujarat Ambuja Cements to participate in the growth market of India. Holcim also acquired Aggregate Industries, thus entering the UK market and strengthening its aggregates and ready-mix concrete businesses in North America
- 2008: Holcim became the single biggest shareholder of Huaxin Cement Co. Ltd., the Group's strategic partner in China, holding a 39.9% stake in the company

Holcim is one of the world's leading suppliers of cement and aggregates (crushed stone, gravel and sand) as well as further activities such as ready-mix concrete and asphalt including services. The Group holds majority and minority interests in more than 70 countries.

Compiled by the authors from www.cemex.com, www.lafarge.com, www.holcim.com.

CEMEX'S GLOBALISATION MOVES: GROWING THROUGH ACQUISITIONS

With excess capacity gained through acquisitions during 1980s, Cemex started exporting cement to U.S., a fragmented market with supposedly stable demand. By the end of 1980s, Cemex bought distribution facilities in U.S. and formed JVs with U.S. firms to sell the imported product under Sun Belt brand. Detecting a threat from Cemex, American cement makers, including two trade unions, filed an anti-dumping suit against Cemex. Eventually, Cemex was forced to pay anti-dumping duties in U.S. Hector Medina, executive vice president for Planning and Finance recalled, "The antidumping ruling and being blocked from the U.S. market made us realise the U.S. was not the whole world."[12]

Determined to go international, in 1991, Cemex invested in port facilities in Southeastern Spain through which it could gain a toehold in Europe. The following year, Cemex outplayed competitor

Annexure III   **Cemex: Major Acquisitions**

SL. No.	Target Company	Country	Year	Target Company's Product Portfolio	Cost of Acquisition	Area of Operations	The Acquisition Impact
1.	Sanson and Compania Valenciana	Spain	1992	Cement and related Products	$1.84 billion	Spain, US	Positive (In 1994 Cemex' net profit in Spain jumped to $95.5 million, up from $37.7 million in 1993)
2.	Vencemos	Venezuela	1994	Cement and related Products	$550 million	Venezuela	Positive (Cemex becomes largest cement producer in Venezuela)
3.	Cementos Nacionale	Dominican Republic	1995	Cement, Ready mix concrete, Aggregates		Caribbean	Positive (Expansion of Caribbean Market)
4.	Scancem Industries (50%)	Caribbean	1995	Cement, Ready mix concrete, Aggregates	$23 million	Caribbean	Positive (Cemex accounted for approximately 50% of the imported cement consumption in 5 Caribbean Countries)
5.	Cementos Diamante and Cementos Samper	Columbia	1996	Cement, Ready mix concrete, pre-fabricated concrete, Aggregates	$700 million	Caribbean	Positive (Cemex Grabs one-third share of Colombian Market and becomes third largest cement producer in the world)
6.	Cementos	Panama	1996	Cement, Ready mix concrete, Aggregates	$60 million	Caribbean	Positive (Enhanced presence in Caribbean Market)
7.	Rizal Cement (30%)	Philippines	1997	Cement, concrete, Aggregates	$93 million	Philippines	Positive (Initiation of business in Asia)
8.	APO Cement Corporation (99.9%)	Philippines	1999	Cement, concrete, Aggregates	$400 million	Philippines	Positive (Expansion of Asian Business)
9.	Cementos del Pacifico	Costa Rica	1999	Cement, Ready mix concrete	$72 million	Costa Rica	Positive (More profits as Costa Rica is predominently a retail market in case of cement)
10.	Semen Gresik (25%)	Indonesia	1999	Cement	$241 million	Indonesia	Negative (Employees were reluctant to accept a foreign company's indulgence in the state business)
11.	Cementos Bio (11.92)	Chile	1999	Cement, concrete, lime, mortar, aggregates, ceramics	$34 million	South America	Positive (Cementos Bio Bio is South America's largest cement maker)

(Continued)

Annexure III   *(Concluded)*

SL. No.	Target Company	Country	Year	Target Company's Product Portfolio	Cost of Acquisition	Area of Operations	The Acquisition Impact
12.	Assiut Cement Company (77%)	Egypt	1999	Cement, Clinker, Services	$319 million	Egypt and some African countries	Positive (Entry to Africa, increased logistics capabilities)
13.	Southdown	US	2000	Cement and readymix Concrete	$2.63 billion	US	Positive (Cemex Becomes Largest Cement Company in North America)
14.	Saraburi Cement Company	Thailand	2001	Cement, Construction equpment, Construction services	$73 million	Thailand	Positive (Enhancement of position in Asia)
15.	Puerto Rican Cement Company	Puerto Rica	2002	Cement, readymix concrete Aggregates	$180 million	Puertorica	Positive (Enhancement of position in Caribbean Market)
16.	RMC	UK	2005	Aggregates, Cement, ready mix concrete, roadstone, lime, aerated concrete	$5.8 million	Europe	Positive (Increased Synergies, doubled the size and expanded market reach in Europe)
17.	Rinker	Australia	2007	Aggregates Cement, ready mix concrete, concrete pipes, concrete Construction services	$14.3 billion	US, Australia China	Negative (Global Financial crisis and credit crunch affects Cemex badly as it becomes unable to deliver the expected results from the acquisition)

Compiled by the authors.

Holcim by acquiring two largest Spanish firms, Sanson and Compania Valenciana, by borrowing more than $1 billion. The two firms together accounted for 28% of the Spanish market and helped Cemex to restart the export programme to U.S. as Spain was exempted from anti-dumping duties.

To strengthen its presence in Latin America, in 1994 Cemex bought 60% of Vencemos, Venezuela's largest cement company, for $550 million.[13] The acquisition helped Cemex to export to Northern Brazil, Panama and the Caribbean. Expansion in Europe, North and Latin America was welcomed by the share market and in Mexican stock exchange its share value grew nearly 300% by 1994.[14]

Cemex purchased Cementos Nacionales in the Dominican Republic in 1995 along with Scancem Industries Ltd., that operated in five countries in the Caribbean region. It purchased controlling stake in two Colombian cement makers, Cementos Diamante, S.A. and Industrias e Inversiones Samper, in 1996. These acquisitions gave Cemex one-third share of the Colombian market and also made Cemex the third-largest cement company in the world. Further continuing consolidation in Caribbean market, Cemex acquired Cementos Bayano, a Panamanian government company, for a price of $60 million.[15] By this time Cemex's overseas sales soared up over 30% of total sales, de-risking the company from Mexican related uncertainties and enabling to borrow much cheaply compared to other Mexican companies.

Cemex made its first direct investment in Asia, in 1997, by purchasing a 30% stake in Rizal Cement Company of the Philippines. In 1998, it acquired 14% stake in Semen Gresik, a government-owned cement company in Indonesia and later increased the stake to 25%. However, Cemex failed to acquire it fully due to protest against foreign ownership. For financing its growing presence in Asia, Cemex created an investment holding company called Cemex Asia Holdings Ltd., in 1999.

Further, strengthening its presence in South America, Cemex acquired a 12% stake in the largest cement producer of Chile, Cementos Bio Bio, in 1999. It also acquired Cementos del Pacífico, Costa Rica's largest cement company and purchased two terminals in Haiti that supplied 70% of the cement to the Central American and Caribbean markets. Cemex also acquired APO Cement Corporation of the Philippines in 1999 and became the largest cement manufacturer in the country. In the same year, Cemex made its first acquisition in Middle East, acquiring 77% stake in Assiut Cement Company, a major cement producer in Egypt and by 2000 the control increased to 90%.

Even when it was away from U.S. throughout the 1990s, Cemex had plans ready for the entry when time was ripe. In 2000, it acquired the largest independent cement producer in the U.S., Houston-based Southdown Inc., for $2.8 billion. Acquisition of a large and well-performing cement producer in a developed market was entirely different from its previous strategy, where it acquired underperforming companies in developing markets. Southdown's highly decentralised system was reframed to match the standards of Cemex. In 2000, Cemex's credit rating was promoted to 'investment grade' by Standard and Poor. After the Southdown acquisition, Cemex acquired facilities in Thailand and Puerto Rico in 2001 and 2002 respectively. Though it had huge opportunity of acquisitions, as top 10 companies together were producing about one third of the global cement supply, Cemex reduced the pace of acquisitions to concentrate on debt repayment.

In 2005, it acquired UK-based RMC, world's largest ready-mix concrete maker for $6.5 billion. It was "a very compelling strategic opportunity, RMC's strong positions in cement, aggregates and ready-mixed concrete will add to our existing operations in these areas and enhance our leading position in the global building material market,"[16] Zambrano observed. Though analysts were sceptical about Cemex's statement that it will achieve synergies of $200 million within 6 months after acquisitions, the company managed to generate $360 million.[17] Barely a year after closing the deal, Cemex's ratio of net debt had fallen to 2.3 times of EBITDA, easily surpassing its target of 2.7.[18]

Boosted by the success of acquisitions hitherto, Cemex embarked on its biggest acquisition in 2007 by acquiring Rinker Materials Corporation (Rinker), an Australian building materials company serving majorly the U.S. market, for a mammoth $15.3 billion through leveraged buyout. "Cemex has a proven track record of disciplined acquisitions and successful integrations. Combining Rinker with Cemex will generate value for shareholders of both companies. Rinker's strong presence in key U.S. regions will significantly strengthen our ability to serve customers in the world's largest and most dynamic building materials market and extend our global network into Australia,"[19] said Zambrano. He explained the six success factors of Cemex, which helped it to become a global leader, during the Annual Investors and Analysts Meeting 2008 (Annexure IV). "At Cemex, consistently generating solid returns for our shareholders has always been a top priority, since 2000, Cemex has evolved from a cement company to a global integrated building materials company, all the while maintaining our commitment to our core strategies—operational excellence, industry-leading integration capabilities, driving cost efficiency, rigorous investment discipline and attracting and retaining the best talent. We believe we have the right operating and financial strategies in place and the right people to execute on those strategies to ensure the continued success of Cemex."[20] These standards have helped Cemex to generate half of its sales from countries other than Mexico.

Annexure IV   Efforts for Profitable Growth (An Excerpt from Lorenzo Zambrano's Speech)

At CEMEX, we produce profitable growth through several inter-related efforts:

- *First, constant commitment to operational excellence.*

  At the core, ours is a culture of engineers, and we pride ourselves on efficient, effective management of our productive assets.

- *Second, cost efficiency.*

  We want to be the most efficient global building materials company. That means managing our costs throughout the business cycle, not just when weakening demand puts pressure on margins.

- *Third, nurturing strong customer relationships.*

  We aim to be the supplier of choice in our key markets. That means understanding and segmenting our customers, developing new strategies, and constantly improving our service.

- *Fourth, industry-leading integration capabilities.*

  Our post merger integration process—what we call the PMI—is designed to extract value from every acquisition, quickly and efficiently. But the PMI is also designed to assure that our whole network benefits from newly identified best practices as well as newly acquired management talent.

- *Fifth, rigorous investment discipline.*

  Whether we are investing in acquisitions or in growth cap ex, we apply disciplined, return driven criteria. Every investment we make flows through the same process, and we allocate capital based on return, not geography or business line.

- *Sixth, attracting, investing in, and retaining the best people.*

  Most of our new talent comes to us through the acquisitions we make. We work very hard to identify the best people and to assure that they stay with CEMEX. We also work every bit as hard to identify and promote the best people within legacy CEMEX. And we succeed on both counts.

Source: Zambrano Lorenzo H. "CEMEX DAY", 2008.

THE GLOBALISATION AND POST-MERGER INTEGRATION: THE CEMEX WAY

Apart from considering the strategic geographic location of the target company that provides potential customer base in close vicinity, Cemex focussed on three conditions to acquire a company. First, the acquisition should provide return on investment well above the cost of capital; second, it should enable Cemex to maintain its financial strength and credit quality. Third, the management expertise of Cemex should be able to increase acquired company's value. It acquired only those companies that met these criteria. While the first was almost a prerequisite for acquisition, the second condition guided Cemex to minimise the financial burden of any new acquisition and to maintain a healthy balance sheet. The third assessing parameter enabled Cemex to identify the companies that possessed

a similar management philosophy to mitigate the danger of culture clash after acquisition.

In the integration process, Cemex decided on the operations that are to be decentralised and the ones that required centralised decision making. Cemex retained umbrella brand, for brand was one of its major assets. It sourced people and facilities internationally and standardised management practices throughout its manufacturing units. It also standardised local practices if they were found effective. All this helped Cemex in developing an efficient integration strategy, by stressing on standardisation of processes.

The integration of acquired firms was the decisive part of success. Even though cultural and regulatory differences always threatened the cross-border deals, Cemex has built a standard *modus operandi* for post-merger integration, often called as the 'Cemex Way'—documented in 2000. The 'Cemex Way' also is the way in which 'business process gap analysis' was done for every acquisition. Cemex Way has three main components: Systems and process standardisation, a new governance model and e-enabling process.

The decision to enter the global markets in early 1990s coincided with IT revolution and consolidation spree in global markets. The main competitors of Cemex—Lafarge and Holcim, which began global acquisitions much earlier, adopted decentralised approach. Predictably, Holcim and Lafarge had trouble unifying their diverse corporate cultures and systems.[21] Cemex, on the other hand, has been able to integrate its acquisitions within months, through its IT expertise and process standardisation.

To support and guarantee permanent standardisation, eight so called 'e-groups' were made responsible for the process effectiveness. Each e-group consisted of a business expert, who heads the group, along with HR and IT experts who extended support in relevant areas. All eight standardisation groups report to a vice president or above level, with senior executives taking responsibility for more than one group as business experts. Each group works closely with teams from the acquired company to compare their processes with those encoded in Cemex Way. The goal of this association would be to identify areas where Cemex Way processes can be adopted by the local company to speed integration and boost economies of scale, while also figuring out which practices can be left out to meet local cultural or regulatory demands. About 20% of an acquired company's practices are typically retained, remaining local practices are replaced by Cemex Way standards. To mitigate the danger of cultural clash, instead of scrapping 80% of local practices, the groups catalogue all practices and store them in a centralised database. Further, these processes are benchmarked against internal and external practices to choose the better of the two. Cemex Way is a method of systematically mapping, cataloguing and disseminating acquired business processes across the global enterprise—a highly centralised but flexible model.

More than the corporate brand name, processes or IT systems, Cemex's success lies in its people. Zambrano says that he likes to personally interview the candidates to ensure the exact fit in the company. Cemex has installed a clear career path to ensure the best of the new hires move up in the company. To make certain they understand Cemex's goals and philosophies, every new employee attends an induction course, tailored to each employee's level. It contains basics of the Cemex Way and tutorial on the technical and market aspects of the business. Beyond that, new employees are expected to attend several programmes designed to maintain a spirit of professional growth and competition. Young managers are encouraged to take international positions and the learning process continues beyond a new hire's early days. Employees have access to 261 e-learning courses which cover both Cemex operations and general business and managerial skills[22] (Exhibit I).

Branding and customer satisfaction are other two aspects that helped Cemex lead the industry.

Exhibit I   Human Capital Development at Cemex

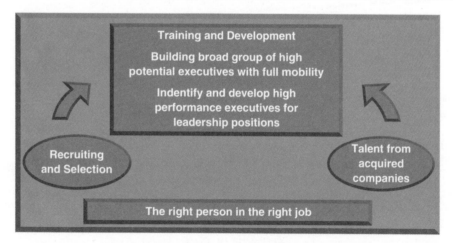

Source: Medina Hector, "Company Information", http://www.cemex.com/pdf/ir/am2006/Hector-Medina.pdf.

Under the umbrella brand of Cemex, there are many product brands, tailored to suit the needs of the customer. "At Cemex, the corporate brand is not just a logo, tagline or mission statement. It is a promise the company makes to its customers: a promise to deliver superior customer service and outstanding product quality in every market it serves. Because cement is essentially a consumer product in many of Cemex's developing markets, the company has a large opportunity to gain a competitive advantage by differentiating its brand and increasing customer loyalty,"[23] emphasised the company. To identify consumer preferences and serve them accordingly, Cemex followed innovative consumer interaction methods, like, 'Throw and Win' marketing campaign in Mexico.[24] It was awarded the Silver Promo Award for this innovative method of scrutinising consumer tastes. Cemex recognised the need to develop a brand to maintain customer trust. It always tries to match the needs of the customer. In UK, one of the Cemex brands, Rugby+ gave a product application chart to the customers giving them the chance to identify the best brand for their purpose (Annexure V). Cemex's ready-mix concretes are also highly customised to suit the needs of the customer, which gave competitive advantage in every market it entered.

By managing all the critical factors—IT, people, innovative marketing methods and effective customer support—Cemex delivered superior value to all its stakeholders (Exhibit II).

CEMEX' COST OF GLOBALISED GROWTH: THE CASH CRUNCH

Acquiring all companies during boom times Cemex grew optimistic after each acquisition. Cemex was warned about excessive debts during the acquisition of Rinker in 2007, but optimism, proven track record and debt clearance guided the acquisition. As demand in the U.S. market slowed down, where Rinker had most of its operations, Cemex's hopes were shattered. As the company was highly leveraged, a large amount of free cash flow went to debt services. Consequently, Cemex's net-debt-to-EBITDA increased.

The Annual Report (2007) states, "free cash flow after maintenance capital expenditures

Annexure V   Product Application Chart for Rugby+

	Rugby+ Cement	Rugby+ Premium	Rugby+ Sulfate	Rugby High Strength	Rugby Fast Set	Rugby White	Rugby Hydrated Lime
General purpose Concrete	R	S		S			
Below Ground Concrete/DPC	S	S	R	S			
Cold Weather Concreting			S	R		S	
Precasting						S	
Mortar	S	R	S	S		S	SM
Screeding	S	S	S	S			
Render	S	R	S	S		S	SM
Enhanced Sulfate Resistance			R				
Enhanced Freezed/Thaw Durability			R				
Decorative Light/Finishes						R	
Concrete/Mortar Repair Work	S	S			R		
Fixing Fence Posts					R		
High Strength				R		S	
Key   **R-** Recommended for best performance   **S-** Suitable for this application   **M-** Mix with Rugby Cements

Source: "Product application chart", www.cemex.co.uk/ce/pdf/15720_DL_Cement_Leaflet_v5.pdf.

Exhibit II   **Value Creation in Cemex**

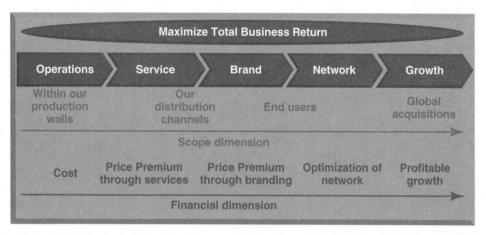

Source: Medina Hector, "Value Creation in Cemex", http://www.cemex.com/pdf/ir/03_ValueCreationCEMEX.pdf, July 2nd 2003.

decreased 4% to $2.58 billion, which we used primarily for expansion capital expenditures of $1.43 billion and to reduce debt. Net debt was $18.90 billion at the end of 2007 compared with $5.81 billion at year-end 2006. At the end of 2007, our net-debt-to-EBITDA ratio stood at 3.6 times, up from 1.4 times for 2006".[25] Cemex's 2007 Financial Report shows a decline in the free cash flow (Annexure VI). The situation further worsened in 2008 and the annual cash flows reduced to 17% of debt, well below its historic average of 30%.[26]

Analysts believe that Rinker was overvalued. In October 2006, Cemex made an unsolicited $12.8 billion offer to acquire Rinker, which rejected the offer on the grounds that the offer grossly undervalued its assets. Further, through a target statement, it requested its shareholders not to sell the shares to Cemex and Cemex increased the bid. Had Rinker remained independent, it would probably be worth around half of the $15.3 billion purchase price considering the global financial crisis. [27]

Rinker's acquisition helped Cemex only in the short-term revenue increment. During the first and second quarter of 2008, the sales and EBITDA of Cemex increased compared to those in 2007. But in the third quarter, things were different. The net sales in the third quarter 2008, decreased by 5% and EBITDA was down 4% (Annexure VII). Net income decreased by 74% to $200 million in the third quarter of 2008 from

$780 million in the same period a year ago. The net-debt-to-EBITDA ratio reached 3.4 times for the third quarter 2008 compared with 3.5 times in the second quarter 2008. Interest coverage reached 4.8 times during the third quarter, up from 4.6 in the second quarter.[28]

At the end of the third quarter of 2008, Cemex's net debt was $16.4 billion, out of which over $5.7 billion was due for 2009 and about another $8 billion matures by mid-2010. Compounding problems, in addition to the credit freeze, three of Cemex's main markets—the U.S., the UK and Spain are experiencing a slowdown in demand and are moving into recession. Mexican economy was no exception.

Cemex's leverage ratio and other financial ratios show the concern about debt payment and free cash flow (Annexure VIII). Shares crumbled after the debt repayment became doubtful (Annexure IX). The highest and lowest ADR value of Cemex were $32.61 on May 19th 2008 and $4.01 on November 21st 2008 respectively.[29] By the same period the falling dollar value forced a loss of around $711 million on the company due to its huge currency swaps and related derivatives.

The Davenport plant in California, which produces just less than 1 million tonnes of cement a year, has been hurt by a sharp decline in new home construction in the state. Cemex had no option but to close it and lay off the workers.[30] There were reports that Cemex will cut its worldwide staff of 60,000 by 10% and put $2 billion in

	1999	2000	2001	2002	2003	2004	2005	2006	2007
Net Sales	4,827,965	5,620,822	6,923,320	6,543,110	7,164,384	8,149,360	15,320,958	18,249,361	21,672,990
Cost of Sales	(2,689,914)	(2,902,840)	(3,738,349)	(3,655,513)	(4,130,046)	(4,586,349)	(9,271,197)	(11,648,475)	(14,441,027)
Gross Profit	2,138,051	2,717,982	3,184,972	2,887,597	3,034,338	3,563,011	6,049,761	6,600,886	7,231,963
Selling, General and Administrative Expenses	(701,556)	(1,064,151)	(1,531,632)	(1,577,196)	(1,579,134)	(1,711,334)	(3,563,102)	(3,655,059)	(4,260,499)
Operating Income	1,436,494	1,653,831	1,653,339	1,310,401	1,455,204	1,851,677	2,486,659	2,945,827	2,971,464
Financial Expenses	(487,829)	(466,868)	(411,742)	(332,524)	(380,684)	(372,230)	(526,168)	(493,908)	(806,642)
Financial Income	31,465	24,588	40,733	44,605	16,691	23,421	39,262	45,713	78,690
Exchange Gain (Loss), Net	27,599	(30,092)	153,799	(77,102)	(171,589)	(23,565)	(78,816)	20,296	(22,240)
Monetary Position Gain (Loss)	390,533	306,259	282,158	352,145	327,667	385,868	418,831	409,438	630,921
Gain (Loss) on Marketable Securities	9,304	(7,697)	199,719	(316,486)	(59,570)	119,844	386,201	(13,683)	218,560
Total Comprehensive Financing Cost (Income)	(28,928)	(173,810)	264,667	(329,362)	(267,499)	133,339	239,310	(32,144)	99,559
Other Expenses, Net	(296,858)	(234,287)	(416,970)	(389,277)	(456,737)	(483,861)	(317,494)	(34,172)	(278,017)
Net income Before Income Taxes	1,110,707	1,245,733	1,501,037	591,762	731,017	1,501,155	2,408,475	2,879,511	2,793,005
Income Tax	(68,383)	(157,944)	(166,811)	(54,836)	(89,612)	(183,451)	(330,260)	(497,302)	(439,204)
Employees' Statutory Profit Sharing	(38,285)	(35,807)	(23,620)	(10,299)	(16,989)	(29,637)	1,063	(15,687)	(22,503)
Total Income Tax and Profit Sharing	(106,667)	(193,751)	(190,431)	(65,135)	(106,601)	(213,088)	(329,197)	(512,989)	(461,707)
Net Income before Participation of Unconsolidated Subsidiaries	1,004,040	1,051,983	1,310,606	526,627	624,416	1,288,067	2,079,278	2,366,522	2,331,298
Participation in Unconsolidated Subsidiaries	24,878	25,294	20,516	30,703	34,768	40,061	87,352	121,690	136,198
Consolidated Net Income	1,028,918	1,077,277	1,331,122	557,330	659,184	1,328,128	2,166,630	2,488,212	2,467,496
Net Income Attributable to Minority Interest	56,358	77,959	153,306	37,061	30,412	20,932	55,041	110,282	76,670
Majority Interest Net Income	972,560	999,318	1,177,816	520,268	628,772	1,307,196	2,111,588	2,377,930	2,390,826
Earning per ADR (NYSE:CX)	3.87	3.65	4.14	1.74	1.99	3.93	6.10	3.31	3.22
EBITDA	1,791,447	2,029,707	2,255,671	1,917,070	2,108,028	2,538,260	3,557,099	4,137,681	4,586,114
Free Cash Flow	860,000	886,000	1,145,000	948,000	1,143,000	1,478,000	2,013,000	1,943,000	1,144,000

Source: http://www.cemex.com/ic/files/Financial_History.xls.

Annexure VII **Third Quarter Financials of Cemex ($'000s, Except Earnings per ADR)**

	Third Quarter			Third Quarter	
	2008	2007	% Var.	2008	2007
Net sales	5,787	6,101	(5%)	% of Net Sales	
Gross profit	1,930	2,017	(4%)	33.3%	33.1%
Operating income	818	940	(13%)	14.1%	15.4%
Majority net income	200	780	(74%)	3.5%	12.7%
EBITDA	1,303	1,361	(4%)	22.5%	22.3%
Free cash flow after maintenance capital expenditures	957	964	(1%)	16.5%	15.8%
Net debt	16,393	19,156	(14%)		
Net debt/EBITDA	3.4	3.6			
Interest coverage	4.8	6.9			
Earnings per ADS	0.26	1.04	(75%)		
Average ADSs outstanding	777.4	750.9	4%		

In millions of US dollars, except ratios and per-ADS amounts.
Average ADSs outstanding are presented in millions.

Source: "2008 Third Quarter Results", http://www.cemex.com/ic/PDF/2008/CXING08-3.pdf.

Annexure VIII **Financial Ratios of Cemex**

	Q3 2009
Leverage Ratio	2.7
Working Capital per Share	−$4.10
Cash Flow per Share	$1.46
Free Cash Flow per Share	$1.24
Price/Cash Flow Ratio	8.3
Price/Free Cash Flow Ratio	9.8

Source: "CEMEX S.A.B. DE C.V. Ratios and Returns", http://finapps.forbes.com/finapps/jsp/finance/compinfo/Ratios.jsp?tkr=CX.

assets up for sales as profits reduced and demand slowed.[31] "We are increasing the list of asset disposal so we can face this challenging environment,"[32] said Hector Medina. However, the initial asset sales were quite discouraging. In November 2008, Cemex's Spanish unit offloaded operations in the Canary Islands for $211 million, grossly undervalued according to industry analysts. During the same time, Cemex also sold assets in Hungary and Austria for $400 million—about $100 million less than expected or 25% less.

Cemex was in continuous talks with five major banks—Citi group Inc., Banco Bilbao Vizcaya Argentaria SA, Banco Santander SA, HSBC Holdings and Royal Bank of Scotland Group—for refinancing the large debt. With new terms, banks have agreed to refinance nearly $2.2 billion in debt maturing in 2009 through 2010. Cemex said creditors also agreed to extend $1.5 billion of the total $3 billion due in December 2009.

Another blow that Cemex had to take on its weakening finance during the recession was nationalisation in Venezuela. President Hugo Rafael Chávez (Chavez) took oil, steel and telephone companies from private owners. "These are all steps towards socialism,"[33] Chavez said. Cemex asked for $1.3 billion in compensation and the state offered only $650 million.[34] Cemex rejected the offer stating that the offer highly undervalued its operations in Venezuela (Annexure X). The government seized Cemex's assets. The dip in the company's net income was more than anybody could imagine (Annexure XI).

However, Cemex was not ready to budge back because of the financial issues. In 2009, it agreed to sell some of its Australian operations to competitor Holcim for a consideration of $1.62 billion to serve its payments till mid-2011.

Annexure IX   **Cemex Share Values**

Price history - CX (9/15/1999 – 1/21/2009)

■ Cemex ADR Repstg Ten Ord Participation Share Certificates

Source: "Cemex ADR repstg ten ord participation share certificates", http://moneycentral.msn.com/investor/charts/chartdl.aspx?D5=
0&D4=1&ViewType=0&D3=0&CE=0&Symbol=CX&ShowChtBt=Refresh+Chart&DateRangeForm=1&C9=2&DisplayForm=1&
ComparisonsForm=1&CP=0&PT=10.

Annexure X   **Cemex's Assets in Venezuela (As on December 31st 2007)**

Cement plants	3
Cement production capacity (mmt/year)	4.6
Ready-mix plants	33
Aggregate quarries	7
Land distribution centres	10
Marine terminals	2.8

Source: http://www.cemex.com/gl/ww_venezuela.asp.

Annexure XI   **Drop in Cemex' Net Income**

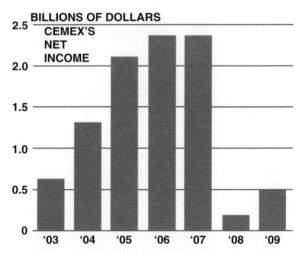

Source: Smith Geri, "Hard Times Ease for a Cement King", *Business Week,* November 5th 2009.

It was constantly negotiating for credit restructuring with a group of creditor banks including Citi group Inc., Banco Bilbao Vizcaya Argentaria SA, Banco Santander SA, HSBC Holdings and Royal Bank of Scotland Group to gain new credit line. All the negotiations paid off as these banks agreed to restructure the debt of approximately $4 billion in January 2009 and further $15.5 billion in August 2009. Though, "the refinancing removes the risk of a near-term insolvency, but with net debt of $18.3 billion and operating cash flow expected to fall this year to $3.1 billion from $4.3 billion in 2008, Cemex still faces a rocky road ahead."[35] Even with asset sale and debt restructuring, the company would still require additional refinancing in near future. However, its huge debts are blessing in disguise as they make Cemex unappealing for would-be acquirers.

ENDNOTES

[1] Hammond Ed, "Cemex moves tolay foundations for UK market offensive", *Financial Times,* September 30th 2009, page 15.

[2] Aggregates are granular materials such as sand, gravel, or crushed stone that are essential ingredients in concrete.

[3] "CEMEX S.A. de C.V.", www.fundinguniverse. com/company-histories/CEMEX-SA-de-CV-Company-History.html.

[4] Ibid.

[5] Dolan Kerry A., "Cyber-Cement", http://www. forbes.com//forbes/1998/0615/6112060a. html, June 15th 1998.

[6] Lorenzo Zambrano and Daniel J. McCosh, "Concrete results", http://findarticles.com/p/ articles/mi_m0OQC/is_9_1/ai_100439592/ pg_1?tag=artBody;col1, October 2000.

[7] Millman Joel, "Hard Times for Cement Man", http://online.wsj.com/article/ SB122894691555195919.html, December 11th 2008.

[8] Kim Chan W. and Mauborgne Renee, "Reconstructing market boundaries" (an excerpt from *Blue Ocean Strategy: Formulating Blue Ocean Strategy* by Kim Chan W. and Mauborgne Renee), Harvard Business School Press, 2005.

[9] Ibid.

[10] Podolny Joel and Roberts John, "Cemex Global Competition in a Local Business", http://gsbapps.stanford.edu/cases/ documents/Restricted/IB17.pdf, Sepember 7th 1999 (Rev. June 11th 2007), page 5.

[11] "Hard Times for Cement Man", op.cit.

[12] "Cemex Global Competition in a Local Business", op.cit., page 7.

[13] "CEMEX S.A. de C.V.", op.cit.

[14] Flaherty Francis, "Investing: Bright skies in Mexico bode well for ADRs", http://query. nytimes.com/gst/fullpage.html?res=9F0DE0D 71739F933A05754C0A962958260&scp= 16&sq=cemex&st=nyt, July 30th 1994.

[15] "A new foundation", http://www. thefreelibrary.com/ Growth+factors.-a017353395.

[16] "Mexican firm bids £2.3bn for RMC", http:// news.bbc.co.uk/2/hi/business/3692604.stm, September 27th 2004.

[17] Thomson Adam and Minder Raphael, "Cemex clinches $14.2bn Rinker takeover", http://www.ft.com/cms/s/0/0ce1f5de-1540-11dc-b48a-000b5df10621.html, June 7th 2007.

[18] Thomson Adam, "Cemex preparing for entry in to Chinese market", http://www. ft.com/cms/s/0/2a64e802-d63d-11da-8b3a-0000779e2340.html, April 27th 2006.

[19] "Cemex clinches $14.2bn Rinker takeover", op.cit.

[20] "Cemex Announces Increased Synergies from Rinker Integration", http://www.reuters. com/article/pressRelease/idUS173428+05-Mar-2008+BW20080305, March 5th 2008.

[21] Lichfield Gideon. "Cemex", http://www. wired.com/wired/archive/10.07/Cemex.html, July 2002.

[22] "Taking the high road", http://www.nyse .com/pdfs/NYSE_Oct_Nov_2006.pdf, October–November 2006.

[23] "CEMEX en los medios", http://www.cemex .com/espa/mc/rn/mc_rn_bf2001.asp.

[24] Through dart board game conducted in jobsites and questioning the participant at regular intervals during the game, Cemex gathered data about the products from the end users to realise the customers' needs and wants.

[25] "2007 annual report", http://www.cemex .com/CEMEX_AR2007/ENG/default.html.

[26] "Hard Times for Cement Man", op.cit.

[27] Beveridge John, "Rinker cements itself as a great deal", http://www.news.com.au/ heraldsun/story/0,,24144602-5014150,00 .html, August 8th 2008.

[28] "CEMEX's Third Quarter 2008 Net Sales Decrease 5%; EBITDA Down 4%", http:// www.finanznachrichten.de/nachrichten-2008-10/12036394-cemex-s-third-quarter-2008-net-sales-decrease-5-ebitda-down-4-004.htm, October 16th 2008.

[29] "Cemex, S.A.B. de C.V.", http://www.nyse .com/about/listed/lcddata.html?ticker=CX&fq =D&ezd=1Y&index=5.

[30] "Mexico's Cemex closes U.S. plant, lays off workers", http://www.reuters. com/article/rbssConstructionMaterials/ idUSN0929222120090109, January 9th 2009.

[31] Stevenson Mark, "Cemex to cut staff, sell assets as profits decline", http://au.ibtimes .com/articles/20081016/cemex-to-cut-staff-sell-assets-as-profits-decline.htm, October 17th 2008.

[32] Ibid.

[33] Enrique Andres Pretel, "Venezuela seizes cement plants in socialist drive", http://www .reuters.com/article/companyNewsAndPR/ idUSN1925911020080819, August 19th 2008.

[34] "Mexico says talks advance between Cemex and Caracas", http://www.reuters.com/ article/rbssIndustryMaterialsUtilitiesNews/ idUSN1750564120080917, September 17th 2008.

[35] Harrup Anthony, "Cemex gains bank accord to reschedule $15 billion in debt", *The Wall Street Journal,* August 13th 2009, page 16.

Corona Beer: Challenges of International Expansion

Ashok Som
ESSEC Business School

It's a typical Friday afternoon in 2007, and Carlos Fernandez, chairman of Grupo Modelo's board since 1997, was making an unexpected stop at one of his company's brewing facilities in Zacatecas, Mexico, where the plant was going through major renovations to increase capacity. Grupo Modelo S.A. de C.V. (Modelo) was Mexico's largest beer producer and distributor. It was expanding production capabilities across the board. Among the company's many brands was Corona Extra, which had been the world's fourth best selling beer in terms of volume (see Exhibit 1 for world ranking). With an investment of more than $300 million to renovate its facilities, Modelo aimed to increase production to face growing international demand. Carlos Fernandez clarified his ambition soon after his appointment as CEO in 1997:

> [I want] Modelo to leapfrog the competition and catapult itself into the ranks of the world's top five brewers.

And they did that when Grupo Modelo surpassed Heineken for bragging rights as the number one selling import in the United States in 1997. Yet competitors did not let that happen without reacting, and Grupo Modelo soon faced tough times both in its domestic market and abroad.

How did Modelo build up its domestic power? How did it consider the attack on the U.S. market? Could the company sustain its success trend against competition? Those were some of the questions analysts asked at the time.

Exhibit 1   **World's Top 10 Beer Brands, 2005 and 2006 (Millions of barrels—shipments)**

Brands	2005	2006	2006 Market Share
1. Bud Light	39.3	41.1	3.0%
2. Budweiser	34.6	33.7	2.5
3. Skol	27.9	28.6	2.1
4. Snow	13.5	25.9	1.9
5. Corona	24.5	25.6	1.9
6. Brahma Chopp	20.6	21.6	1.6
7. Heineken	20.0	21.4	1.6
8. Miller Lite	18.2	18.2	1.3
9. Coors Light	16.5	16.8	1.2
10. Asahi Super Dry	15.0	14.8	1.1
Total top 10	229.9	247.6	18.2%

Source: Grupo Modelo annual report, 2007.

This case was written by Ashok Som, Professor, Management Area at ESSEC Business School. The author gratefully acknowledges the contribution of George M. Skarpathiotakis, ESSEC MBA Exchange student and Guillaume Poutrel, ESSEC MBA student for their research help. The case was based on published sources and generalized experience. It was developed as a basis for class discussion rather than to illustrate either effective or ineffective handling of an administrative situation. Reproduction or distribution of this case is strictly prohibited without the prior permission of the author. To obtain reprints of this case, ECCH Reference number 308-110-1, please contact the ECCH at http://www.ecch.com.
©2011 Ashok Som. All Rights Reserved.

THE GRUPO MODELO STORY: BUILT TO BE A LOCAL LEADER

Cervecería Modelo S.A. was formed on March 8, 1922, and officially opened its first brewery three years later, with a strategic aim to focus on Mexico City and the surrounding areas. Modelo was the first brand to be produced by the group, followed a month later by Corona.

Headed in the early days by Pablo Diez Fernandez, Braulio Iriarte, and Martin Oyamburu, the company was soon controlled by Diez and Oyamburu after Iriarte died in 1932. Under the operational direction of Diez, Cervecia Modelo started producing Corona in clear quarter bottles in response to consumers' preference for clear glasses. Diez oversaw the expansion of the group's brewing capabilities that would turn it into Mexico's largest and most modern producer.

The 1930s were trying years for Modelo. After surviving the prohibition policy and the death of the company's president during the early 1930s, Diez bought Oyamburu's shares and became sole owner of the company in 1936, with financial help from Banco Nacional de Mexico. The company has remained under the majority ownership of the Fernandez family ever since.

In 1935, once financial stability was restored to the company, Cerveceria Modelo bought the brands and assets of the Toluca y México Brewery. From then on, Victoria, the country's oldest established brand of beer, would spearhead the company's fight to dominate the popular market. With these acquisitions, the 1940s proved to be a period of strong growth for the company, with production sky-rocketing as did its popularity. While most Mexican companies were focusing on selling beer to the American army for WWII efforts, Diez decided to concentrate domestically and improve distribution methods and production facilities within Mexico.

As Mexico became industrialized, the country's infrastructure allowed for large scale distribution. The key element behind the rapid growth domestically during the post-WWII era was a new way of distribution: direct with profit sharing.

Modelo's sales were revolutionized by the idea of direct distribution with the executive in charge getting a share of profits. A key element of this second stage was specialized concessions. In other words, splitting beer from groceries and making it an exclusive business gave rise to direct distributors—sometimes run by the concessionaire or his successors, or sometimes by a person sent from head office, a traveling agent, supervisor, or manager who would be moved from area to area.

In 1971, Antonino Fernandez was appointed CEO of Modelo. He was the husband of Pablo's niece. Under his control, Corona was listed on the Mexican Stock exchange in 1994. At that time, Anheuser-Busch acquired 17.7 percent of the equity and had an option to increase its ownership to 50.2 percent over time. The 50.2 percent represented only 43.9 percent of voting rights in order to preserve the ownership of the Diez family over Grupo Modelo S.A.

A LOCAL LEADER GOING ABROAD

Modelo's first entry into the U.S. beer market came in 1979 with Corona distributed by Amalgamated Distillery Products Inc. (later renamed Barton Beers Ltd.). Due to its nonrefundable policy, its clear and unique bottle, and different marketing, Corona quickly distinguished itself from the competition and gained popularity in southern states. Corona's sales experienced rapid growth throughout the 1980s and by 1988 it had become the second most popular imported beer in the United States. It wasn't until late 1991, with the doubling of federal excise tax on beer, that Corona's rise to the top of America's import beer market was slowed considerably (a decrease of 15 percent). An important change in the pricing strategy by Corona's distributor, namely to absorb the tax rather than pass it on to consumers, in 1992 rectified the downward trend, and Modelo has experience increasing sales of Corona ever since.

In 1997, with his grandfather still chairman of the board and taking over for his uncle, Carlos Fernandez was appointed the new chief executive office of the company. At the young age of 29, Carlos encompassed all the attributes needed to take the company into the new millennium. Not only had the young man dedicated himself to the family business since he was 13, when he

Exhibit 2   Total Imported Beers in the United States, 2006–2007 (thousands of cases)

Brand	2006	2007*
1. Corona Extra	116,155	115,060
2. Heineken	68,790	68,100
3. Modelo	19,605	22,404
4. Tecate	17,480	19,050
5. Guinness	12,725	13,360
6. Corona Light	11,055	12,207
7. Labatt Blue	12,500	12,000
8. Heineken Light	7,520	9,775
9. Stella Artois	6,175	8,335
10. Amstel Light	8,900	8,188
Total top 10	280,905	288,479

*Estimate.

Source: Grupo Modelo's annual report, 2007.

first started working at the company, but he carried with him a vision of an international business model—one that had the company expand internationally in order to capitalize on the newly introduced North American Free Trade Agreement (NAFTA) and streamline the company's focus. In just 12 years since his appointment, Carlos accomplished one of his more ambitious goals of leapfrogging his international competitors to become one of the top five beer companies in the world.

In 1997, at 37 years of age, Carlos Fernandez was named chairman when his grandfather stepped aside. In 2007, Grupo Modelo was exporting five kinds of beer to the United States: Corona Extra, Corona Light, Modelo Especial, Pacifico Clara, and Negra Modelo. These exports represented 131 million cases in 2005 and three Grupo Modelo brands ranked among eight firsts in the United States (see Exhibit 2 for detailed rankings).

THE BEER MARKET, A PROGRESSIVE CONSOLIDATION

Modern beer was first brewed in Europe in the 14th century. The industry developed differently in every country in order to address local tastes and specific recipes. This resulted in a clustered industry with many local breweries. The lack of a transportation network made exportation impossible for centuries and brewing remained a local and then a national domain for a long time. The first steps of national consolidation were carried out in the 19th century in the United Kingdom and the United States to achieve economies of scale. In other, smaller countries, with several mid-size players, the consolidation process was lighter and local breweries survived and became specialists. One determining factor behind the type of domestic beer was the national taste of the particular country. Some countries have distinct cultural tastes, where beer is not the alcoholic drink of preference. In countries such as Italy and France, wine outperforms beer for consumption per capita, whereas in countries like Germany and Ireland, the reverse is true. Whereas Italy and France have a few national beer brands, Germany and Ireland both have numerous medium brewing companies that are well respected domestically and internationally.

In the 1990s, a new phenomenon appeared whereby national leaders began expanding abroad. For example, the Belgian company Interbrew acquired breweries in 20 countries and expanded its sales to 110 countries, leaving local managers controlling the local brands while enjoying their presence to develop sales of its flagship brand: Stella Artois. This trend also might be due to the fact that initial startup costs of a brewery have always been extremely high and the need for a constant cash flow for maintenance and the fluctuating price of resources. That structure of the industry supported concentration.

Other companies followed the same strategy and the consolidation process led to a small number of global players. On March 3, 2004, the world's third largest brewery company, Belgium-based Interbrew, and the world's fifth largest brewery, Brazil-based AmBev, announced plans to merge their operations. In a deal valued at $12.8 billion, the merger created the world's largest brewing company in terms of volume. In 2007, the panorama of the brewing industry was clear, showing the top players as Inbev, Anheuser-Bush, SABMiller, and Heineken ranking as the market leaders. See Exhibit 3 for the top six global producers as of 2005.

Exhibit 3 **Top Brewing Companies (in millions of hectaliters)**

In 2000	In 2005
1. Anheuser-Busch—121	1. InBev—233.5
2. Heineken—74	2. Anheuser-Busch—152
3. Ambev—63	3. SABMiller—135
4. Miller Brewing—53	4. Heineken—107
5. SAB (South Africa Breweries)—43	5. Carlsberg—78
6. Interbrew—87	6. Scottish & Newcastle—52

Exhibit 4 **Beer Consumption around the World**

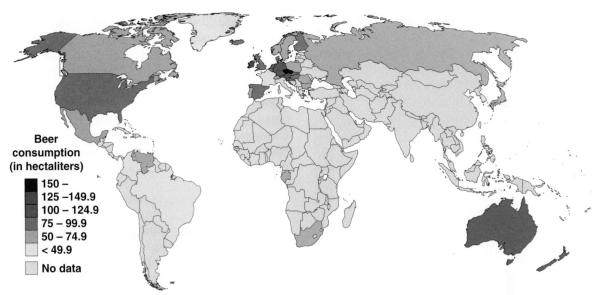

Beer consumption (in hectaliters)

- 150 –
- 125 –149.9
- 100 – 124.9
- 75 – 99.9
- 50 – 74.9
- < 49.9
- No data

Source: http://upload.wikimedia.org/wikipedia/commons/9/99/Map_of_world_by_world_by_beer_consumption.png.
Note: Chinese beer consumption was allegedly 16 liters in 2003.

KEY WORLD MARKETS

The United States had the largest beer market in the world until China surpassed it in 2003. Yet the consumption per capita remained almost six times higher in the United States than it was in China at the time (see Exhibit 4 for global beer consumption). The growth expectations were significantly reduced in the United States, but performance was not consistent across the clusters.

The top three breweries controlled almost 80 percent of the U.S. market, with 45 percent for Anheuser-Busch, 23 percent for Miller Brew and 10 percent for Adolph Coors. That being said, 300 breweries remained in the country thanks to a dense network of regional craft brewing. These companies struggled to find profitability since vertical integration and economies of scale were the main drivers to operating margins. The fact that Anheuser-Bush could capture 75 percent of the industry's total operating profits emphasized the volume effect in the industry.

Mexico, the world's 11th most populated country, was one of the largest beer markets in the world. This is impressive considering that Mexico is the birthplace and still home of the most affluent tequila market in the world. For a country that has a large proportion of its alcoholic industry split between beer and another beverage, Mexico is an anomaly considering the variety of beers it has to offer. Mexico has a large variety of brands with a vast array of tastes, from the darker and more sophisticated tastes of Dos Equis to the light and citrus flavor of Corona. However, even with this diversity, the market is essentially a duopoly split among two producers with very few microbreweries. Those two companies are Grupo Modelo and FEMSA. In 2007, Grupo Modelo captured 62.8 percent of the Mexican market (compared with 50 percent in 1989) and FEMSA owned the rest of the market.

In addition to owning the main beer brands of the domestic market (Corona, Dos Equis, and Sol) FEMSA and Grupo Modelo had built up strategic alliances with some major distributors that were enjoying the NAFTA environment. Grupo Modelo could enjoy the link with Anheuser-Busch to broaden its international impact, while FEMSA was distributing Coca-Cola products in Mexico and decided to have a partnership with Heineken to attack the U.S. market. To sum it up, the two Mexican players decided to attack the U.S. market but could not do it alone considering entrance barriers. FEMSA's CEO presented it this way in 2006:

> It was an exceptional year for exports. We continued to attract new consumers, and our volume growth exceeded expectations, up to 15.3 percent. Through our distribution agreement with Heineken USA, we significantly expanded our brands' availability and developed our brands' value across our U.S. market territories.

GRUPO MODELO EXPANDING ABROAD

Corona and the Early Successes

Since its entrance into the American beer market, Corona had built a marketing campaign around the idea of "fun in the sun." A myth surrounding the beer was that it was discovered by Californian surfers while traveling the Mexican Pacific coast looking for the next big wave. Amid mixed reviews among beer enthusiasts, Corona's ascent to stardom could be attributed to its brilliant and unique marketing campaign which was a direct result of the international strategy undertaken by Grupo Modelo when it expanded into the United States. While continuing to produce the beer domestically, Modelo entered into distribution contracts with companies that had local knowledge of the market and gave them autonomy to market the product fittingly, yet maintained an active involvement in the decision making. The result was the rise of Corona from a beer sold

primarily in the states bordering Mexico, to the number one imported beer in America. An analyst underlined:

> In recognition of the outstanding performance of Corona, Modelo Especial, and Negra Modelo in the U.S. import segment, they have been included in the *Impact Magazine* "Hot Brands" list. This happened 10 times in the last 11 years.

International Expansion through Competitive Distribution Channels

When Corona first entered the American beer market, it chose Chicago-based Barton Beers Ltd. as its distributor. According to Modelo executives, the choice to align itself with Barton Beers was an easy one because it was the largest beer importer in the 25 western states and was experienced in the marketing and sales of imported, premium beers. It was through Barton that the marketing image of "fun in the sun" was born. In 1986, to continue its growth within the United States and to supply the eastern states, Modelo decided to select a second distributor, Gambrinus Inc., which was headed by a former Modelo executive. Each company was responsible for its own 25 states and, according to Valentin Diez, Modelo's vice chairman and chief sales officer:

> There was a healthy competition that existed between the two of them, even if they didn't cover the same geographic area.

Modelo's agreement with its distributors was that each importer would be responsible for essentially all activities involving the sale of the beer, except its production, which took place in Modelo factories in Mexico. Everything—including transportation of the beer, insurance, custom clearance, pricing strategy, and creativity of the advertising campaigns—was the importers' responsibility. Although the importers were essentially autonomous to make these decisions, Modelo always took an active role in the decision making and maintained the final say on anything involving the brand image of its beers. In order to oversee all operations in the United States, Modelo set up Procermex Inc., a subsidiary whose purpose was to coordinate, support, and supervise the two distributors. The strength of the relationship between the importers and

Modelo was very strong, as evidenced with the tax increase in 1991. After talks with Modelo, Grambrinus, followed shortly by Barton Beers, decided to absorb the increase instead of passing it on to customers (while all other imported beers did) after being reassured by the Mexican producer that they would be subsidized.

Marketing, the Other Key Leading to Success

Ironically, the key to Modelo's success had been foreseen by the main casualty of that success story when Michael Foley, Heineken's president, said in 1993:

> There's no mystery about brewing beer. Everyone can do it . . . Beer is all marketing. People don't drink beer, they drink marketing.

Corona's ingenious marketing philosophy, which was born out of Modelo's international expansion strategy of giving autonomous control to experienced, local distributors, focused on "fun in the sun" and quickly saw Corona in an ever-increasing number of bars and restaurants in the United States. The marketing campaign's distinguishing feature was that it did not focus on the classical target market for beer drinkers, which were males between the ages of 25 and 45. Campaigns geared toward this target market had historically been testosterone driven, focused on attractive women and party scenes. Premium imported beers differed slightly as they focused on the beers' distinguished quality, usually as a result of superior brewing and rich heritage.

Corona did away with this status quo. It needed to develop an image of a beer that would attract everyone, yet position itself as a premium import, necessary due to the import taxes and resultant higher price paid for the beer. With the "fun in the sun" campaigns, it sold the idea of escape and the idea of leaving behind everyday life for one that is relaxing. Whereas taste and quality are subjective and different for each consumer, general guidelines and surveys consistently and accurately show quality brewing standards. Undeniably, images of escape, enjoyment and relaxation are even more free-form, allowing the customers to make what they will about the image of the brand. From the beginning, Corona's advertising accented this image as it focused on minimalist and often humorous, scenes of escape. Common to all advertisements was that these scenes of escape come in the form of relaxing on the beach. The advertisements never had a lot of action (in fact, most had little to no human action), and if there were people enjoying their time at the beach, their faces were never shown. The Corona bottle was always in the center of the screen, with no soundtrack other then the sounds of the sea and surrounding nature.

The most recent advertising slogan ("Miles away from ordinary") associated with Corona continues to conjure ideas of removing oneself from daily activities. In one advertisement, the scene shows a person relaxing by the beach on a slightly rainy day. In order to protect his Corona, he places his cellular phone above the bottle's neck so as not to allow water to drip in. By focusing on this image of escape, and not following the trend of testosterone-driven campaigns, Corona found a following like no other beer before it. Coupled with the fact that it had an unobtrusive or bland taste (a fact that beer enthusiasts continue to laud), Corona was able to get the non-beer-drinking population to drink beer, specifically, females. Eager to please the new market for beer drinkers, bars and restaurants decided to sell the beer, increasing its consumer reach. And because of its availability, it became a dependable second choice for beer drinkers who were frustrated with not having their favorite beer sold at the current establishment.

A good advertisement is not enough without the budgets to broadcast it widely. In 1996, Modelo spent $5.1 million in the United States, compared with $600,000 in 1985. Yet the same year Heineken spent $15.1 million and Anheuser-Busch spent $192 million. It must be précised that in the case of imported beers, advertising costs are shared by the producer and its distributors, the repartition being negotiated according to the campaign. Considering the performances of Heineken and Corona in 1996, the impact of the message was able to overcome a relative financial weakness.

THE 21ST-CENTURY CHALLENGES

Grupo Modelo had rarely played the role of the established brewery, or having one of its brands define a category. Even from its entrance into the

Mexican beer market in 1925, it was a startup company that sought to focus on Mexico City and the surrounding areas, competing against the already established breweries for market share. When Corona was introduced into the international market, more specifically the U.S. beer market, it paled in comparison to the then-established import leader, Heineken. However, this status as the beer industry's underdog soon shifted.

Since 1997, Corona has been the best-selling import beer in the United States. In 2004, Corona outsold the former number one by about 50 percent. And with a 56 percent market share of the domestic Mexican market, Grupo Modelo is the undisputed leader in one of the world's largest beer markets. And this success can be seen worldwide as well. Not only is Corono Extra the fourth best-selling beer in the world (by quantity) but Grupo Modelo is one of the top 10 biggest breweries in the world.

Remain Mexican Leader . . .

According to surveys, the top seven best-tasting beers in Mexico are produced by a subsidiary of FEMSA, Mexico's second largest beer company in terms of market share (see Exhibit 5 for details). Until recently, FEMSA had been a distant second in the duopoly that is the Mexican beer industry.

Exhibit 5   Taste Test Results for Mexican Beers

The following are the highest rated beers brewed in Mexico as they appear in the ranks at RateBeer.com. A minimum of 10 ratings is required to make the list. Beer scores are weighted means so that more ratings for a beer increase the score's tendency to the beer's actual mean.

	Name	Brewer	Ratings	Score
1	Casta Unica	Especialidades Cerveceras (FEMSA)	29	3.61
2	Casta Milenia	Especialidades Cerveceras (FEMSA)	73	3.59
3	Casta Urilca Castana	Especialidades Cerveceras (FEMSA)	17	3.48
4	Casta Morena	Especialidades Cerveceras (FEMSA)	142	3.45
5	Casta Dorade	Especialidades Cerveceras (FEMSA)	80	3.13
6	Casta Bruna	Especialidades Cerveceras (FEMSA)	105	3.12
7	Potro	Cerveceria Mexicana S.A. De C.V	18	3.09
8	Iodio	Femsa	18	2.86
9	Casta Triguera	Especialidades Cerveceras (FEMSA)	89	2.83
10	Noche Buena	Femsa	24	2.83
11	Negra Modelo	Grupo Modelo (Corona)	618	2.82
12	Dos Equis XX Amber	Femsa	616	2.55
13	Leon Negra	Grupo Modelo (Corona)	21	2.55
14	Victoria	Grupo Modelo (Corona)	23	2.42
15	Bohemia (Mexico)	Femsa	252	2.41
16	Dos Equis XX Special Lager	Femsa	405	2.24
17	Superior	Femsa	25	2.15
18	Pacifico Clara	Grupo Modelo (Corona)	350	2.13
19	Montejo	Grupo Modelo (Corona)	19	2.10
20	Modelo Especial	Grupo Modelo (Corona)	226	2.01
21	Carta Blanca	Femsa	154	2.01
22	Tecate	Femsa	369	1.86
23	Corona Extra	Grupo Modelo (Corona)	1245	1.72
24	Sol	Femsa	318	1.67
25	Chihuahua	Femsa	17	1.65
26	Tecate Light	Femsa	12	1.49
27	Corona Light	Grupo Modelo (Corona)	300	1.35

Source: www.ratebeer.com/Ratings/TopBeersByCountry.asp?CountryID=133.

In an industry so heavily dependent on distribution channels, FEMSA decided it wanted to control its beer from production to point of purchase. Not only did FEMSA produce all its beer domestically in Mexico, but it also owns Oxxo, Central America's largest chain of convenient stores (and one of the biggest in North America). Supplementing its beverage portfolio is the fact that FEMSA is the exclusive distributor of Coca-Cola products in Mexico and Central America.

The investment in a quality beer product, associated with the ownership of the complete distribution channel, has paid off with respect to the Mexican beer market. From 1997 to 2004, FEMSA continuously took more of the domestic beer market for Grupo Modelo. More significant is the fact that while domestic sales were decreasing for Modelo, FEMSA continued to experience steady growth which was in line with industry averages.

However, despite FEMSA's strength in the domestic market, it did not experience the same in the international arena. FEMSA beers are not nearly as popular as Modelo's in the United States. It launched a large marketing campaign in the mid-1990s, but failed to capture the imagination of the American customers and barely made an impact on the market. However, as economic conditions of the company improved, FEMSA decided to re-attempt to mass-market its beers north of the Mexican border. FEMSA recently entered into a marketing agreement with Heineken USA. With the expertise of one of the largest and most recognizable brands in the market leading the charge, FEMSA (and Heineken) hoped to dethrone Corona as the best-selling import in the United States. So far, exports for FEMSA's top three beers have greatly improved; in the 3rd quarter of 2005, the company realized an 18.7 percent growth in exports mainly driven by the U.S. market's demand.

Although Mexico's domestic beer market is one of the largest in the world, Carlos Fernandez knew that the future of Grupo Modelo was to go international. Mexico had the most trade agreements than any other country in the world, and the introduction of NAFTA in 1994 further reinforced the vision for Mexican companies that they had to have a global focus. However, with the opening of the international markets for Mexican companies comes the fact that the Mexican markets are also open to international companies. Specifically, with NAFTA and the beer market in Mexico, the newly introduced agreement opened the door for Canadian and American beer companies to operate in a previously highly protected market. Although their domestic market was now threatened by international companies, the years following 1994 showed that imported beer accounted for only 1 percent of beer sales in Mexico. Of that, half were sales from Anheuser-Busch products, which is distributed by Modelo. (Although the Fernandez family is still the primary stock holder of the company, Anheuser-Busch has a significant stake in the company, owning 50.6 percent of the available stock.)

The volatility of the Mexican economy was another reason to seek international markets for stability. With the devaluation of the Mexican peso in 1995, exporting became increasingly expensive, which led to a large decrease in sales. By having more operations internationally, Modelo would be able to rid itself of the dependency on the unstable peso for its profits. The proximity to the world's largest economy and the size of its beer market offered an opportunity for Modelo to create a beachhead for further international expansion.

Whereas Modelo sought to hedge its risk against the devaluating peso by pursuing international revenues, FEMSA went about doing the same by focusing on its core competency within Mexico. With the failed attempt to gain American market share in the 1990s, FEMSA realized it had a competitive advantage in Mexico through its distribution channel, namely OXXO, its chain of convenient stores. By owning the complete distribution channel for its different brands (therefore not having to exchange currency to transport or sell its products), coupled with the fact that its beers were made domestically, FEMSA's profits would not be significantly affected by a devaluated currency. Helping to stabilizing the company was the fact that it had the exclusive rights to Coca-Cola in Mexico. By distributing one of the most desired brands in the world, FEMSA held in its portfolio a brand that would not be susceptible to economic conditions.

. . . to Be a Global Player

Since the end of prohibition in the United States in 1935 and the introduction of imported beers shortly thereafter, the Dutch import Heineken was the undisputed best-selling import in the United States, which was consistent with its reputation for being among the top-selling beers in the world. Heineken did not see the introduction of Modelo's Corona in the United States in 1979 as threatening to its market share, nor did it see that Corona could eventually compete with it for pole position as the best-selling import. In fact, Heineken executives mocked the golden beer, saying it was nothing more than a novelty drink.

Like Modelo, Heineken decided that it would produce all its beer domestically in Holland and export to foreign markets. In contrast, Anheuser-Busch produced its beers in the foreign markets. Heineken did invest locally in its distribution channels as contracts were signed with local distributors for functions such as importing, distribution, and marketing. However, even here, Heineken headquarters remained in control as the companies that had the contracts were owned and operated by the Heineken parent company. This was the case in the United States, where Heineken USA (formerly known as Van Munching & Company) had the distribution contract for the Dutch beer but was owned and ultimately operated by executives from Holland.

Heineken's reputation throughout the years was built around marketing campaigns developed on positioning the beer as a premium import with superior taste. Because imports were subject to import taxes, distributors usually passed this tax on to their consumers to protect their profit margins, necessitating the need for the image of a premium product. To create this premium image, advertising for Heineken almost always focused on its superior quality, with little attention devoted to any other aspect of its brand.

However, this narrow-sighted vision of the beer eventually opened the door to other competitors, such as Corona, to create innovative campaigns that created more intangible myths surrounding their beers. By 1996, Corona had reached an import volume that was almost equal to Heineken's. Its "fun in the sun" advertising campaign paid no attention to taste.

Even Heineken's executives realized this issue. In reference to their declining sales in the 1990s, the new head of Heineken USA decided the company needed a new approach to marketing. Foley said:

There aren't many brands with myths in any segment of business. I think Heineken has a myth . . . that's almost intangible.

He continued to say that all that was needed was for Heineken to market that myth differently than they had in the past in order to turn the tide of decreasing sales. Over the next few years, Heineken repositioned its image through its marketing. After a few failed attempts at harnessing what they thought were their strengths in their brand image, i.e., focusing on the red star as the focal point of the brand, market share continued to decline, and in 1997 Corona surpassed Heineken as America's top imported beer. This trend continued with Corona's import volume through 2003 growing at a double-digit pace, and in 2004 it outsold Heineken by 50 percent. However, Heineken was determined to become number one again with respect to the U.S. market and had approved a new marketing budget that would see an aggressive campaign in the United States. Results came soon, and in 2006 the CEO could assert:

In particular, our growth has been driven by the USA, where the introduction of Heineken Premium Light has made a major contribution to overall performance.

FUTURE CHALLENGES

In 2007, Corona was Mexico's best-selling beer, the top-selling imported beer in the United States, and the world's fourth best-selling beer. It propelled Modelo into the elite class of being among the top 10 beer producers in the world. Grupo Modelo's CEO could proudly claim in the annual report (see Exhibit 6 for financials of Grupo Modelo):

Grupo Modelo is a growth company. Net sales have risen 7.8 percent on a compounded basis over the last 10 years, demonstrating solid performance in the domestic market and the growing export market year after year . . . The total volume of beer sold in 2005 was 45.5 million hectoliters, an increase of 6.4 percent compared with the previous year. This reflected growth of 4.0 percent in the domestic market and 12.3 percent in the export market. Export sales comprised 30.2 percent of total volume for the year, compared to 28.6 percent in 2004.

Exhibit 6   Grupo Modelo's Financial Highlights, 2004–2005

Grupo Modelo, S.A. de C.V. and Subsidiaries Figures in millions of constant Mexican pesos as of December 31, 2005 except sales of beer, per share data and employees.

	Year ended December		
	2005	2004	Change
Sales of Beer (millions of hectaliters)			
Domestic market	31.80	30.59	4.0%
Export market	13.74	12.23	12.3%
Total market	45.54	62.82	6.4%
Net sales	49,551	46,307	7.0%
Gross profit	26,776	26,082	2.7%
Operating income	13,773	13,588	1.4%
Net majority income	7,291	6,389	14.1%
Total assets	80,281	75,914	5.8%
Total liabilities	12,169	13,075	−6.9%
Majority stockholders' equity	52,365	48,283	8.5%
Funds provided by operating activities	10,292	10,486	−1.9%
ebitda	15,817	15,418	2.6%
Capital expenditures	4,027	4,444	9.4%
Return on equity	13.9%	13.2%	
Outstanding shares at year end (millions)	3,252	3,252	0.0%
Earnings per share	2.24	1.96	14.1%
Dividend per common share	1.07	0.91	17.8%
Closing stock price	38.50	30.66	25.6%
Number of employees and workers	40,617	44,591	−8.9%

This feat was accomplished by Modelo as it sought to expand internationally through smart strategic partnerships with experienced distributors that knew the local market, and wisely differentiated Corona from other imported beers through its marketing. But faced with increasing competition domestically and internationally as other top international brands gained momentum by spending more on media budgets, Corona's sales were decreasing domestically and in the United States. Corona's position as the world's most recognizable Mexican beer was becoming threatened.

Yet organic growth seemed to have limits, and global players aimed at more spectacular moves, as the *Financial Times* revealed on April 2:

> There was one question on everyone's mind when Carlos Brito, InBev's chief executive, presented

the brewer's annual earnings last month—was the group in preliminary merger talks with U.S. rival Anheuser-Busch? Such an alliance would form a brewing colossus with more than one-fifth of the world beer market by volume and could transform the sector.

Rumors of mergers and acquisitions deals in the beer industry are a dime a dozen at present amid speculation that mid-tier brewers such as Anheuser, Scottish & Newcastle, Carlsberg, Heineken, and Molson Coors will all be forced to consolidate to compete with industry behemoths InBev and SAB Miller, which have been expanding globally.

Hence, many expectations and challenges were in store for Grupo Modelo, which had to face its new status on the market in order to make its success story a sustainable one.

REFERENCES

"Mexico: 'Distrust' in Light Beers." Probrewery.com. Sept. 17, 2004. http://probrewery.com/news/news-002325.pho.

"U.S. Free-Trade Law Seen Aiding Mexican Beers; Cinqo de Mayo Highlights Popularity of South-of-the-Border Brews." MSNBC.com. May 5, 2005. http://msnbc.msn.com/id/7746223.

http://www.baramerica.com/bsreview/lager/014.html.

Beamish, Raul, and Goerzen, Anthony. "The Global Branding of Stella Artois." Ivey Management Services (Ivey Publishing), London. Reference #: 9B00A019.

CIA Fact book: Mexico. http://www.ciafactbook.com.

Herrero, Gustavo. "Corona Beers (A)." Harvard Business School. Harvard Business School Publishing, Boston, Jan. 23, 2003. Reference #: 9-502-023.

FEMSA.com. www.femsa.com Annual and Quarterly reports.

Gard, Lauren, Smith, G., and Weber, J. "Life's a Beach for Corona—Or Is It? Sales Growth Is Slowing in the U.S., So Grupo Modelo Is Searching for Better Margins and New Customers." *Business Week Online.* Feb. 7, 2005. http://www.businessweek.com/magazine/content/05_06/b3919098_mz058.htm.

www.heineken.com Annual report.

http://www.anheuser-busch.com/ Annual report.

http://www.inbev.com Annual report.

http://www.ratebeer.com/Ratings/TopBeers-ByCountry.asp?CountryID=133.

Scheinman, Marc N. "Beer Baron: Grupo Modelo CEO Carlos Fernandez Sets a Deadline for Catapulting His Company into the World's Top 5 Beer Brewers—2004." Find Articles, Jan.–Feb. 2000. http://www.findarticles.com/p/articles/mi_m0OQC/is_2_1/ai_100541553.

"InBev May Slake the Thirst for Consolidation; Sarah Laitner, Jenny Wiggins and Jonathan Wheatley Examine the Options Facing the World's Largest Brewer in a Sector Ripe for Change." *Financial Times,* April 2, 2007.

Globalization of Komatsu: Digging Out of Trouble

Nadine Khayat,
INSEAD

J. Stewart Black,
INSEAD

The 2008 recession hit Komatsu especially hard. From a peak of ¥4,000 per share in October 2007, Komatsu executives watched the share price plummet 80% over the next 12 months to a low of ¥786. Over the next two years, as the world avoided a financial system meltdown and a 1930s-type depression, the general economic outlook stabilized. With this, Komatsu's financial prospects improved somewhat, as did its stock price. From its October 2008 low, the stock price recovered some lost ground and crept back up to ¥1,700 by July 2010. While Komatsu executives could take some comfort in this, the fact that the share price was still down 55% from its peak while arch-rival Caterpillar was down less than half that at 25% was less comforting. Was this disparity just a momentary fluke or did it foreshadow a more troubling systemic issue that a recent study had revealed about many Japanese multinationals as they made the move from domestic player and exporter to global competitor?

Looking forward, Komatsu's current senior executives faced some tough questions. Why did growth strategies in different geographical locations succeed at times and fail at others? What were the implications for Komatsu's management policies as they responded to changing domestic and global market conditions? Was a lack of a diversified top leadership inhibiting sustained growth in the global market, especially as it pushed further into emerging markets in Asia, Latin America and the Middle East? How could they ensure that Komatsu was the exception rather than the rule to the pattern of early domestic and export success followed by international stumbles and a continued struggle to compete globally?

A TROUBLING PATTERN FOR LARGE JAPANESE MULTINATIONALS

In the late 1980s and early 1990s it seemed that Japanese firms were destined to take over the world. They were buying up iconic real estate in the USA, such as the Rockefeller Center in New York and Pebble Beach Golf Resort in California, and topping global business rankings such as the *Fortune* Global 500. During one five-year period in the mid-1980s no fewer than 36 different articles appeared in the *Harvard Business Review* either praising the Japanese or fretting about the power of Japanese companies.

However, a recently published study had found a troubling pattern among large Japanese multinational companies (MNCs) that kept them from sustaining this success.[1] The authors compared this to the $280 million NASA rocket carrying the Orbiting Carbon Observatory satellite that in February 2009 had a brilliant liftoff but failed to launch into global orbit and crashed back to earth. Japanese firms had experienced a fantastic liftoff in the 1960s through the 1980s due to meteoric domestic growth and skyrocketing exports. But while having a large, protected

08/2010-5721

This case was written by Nadine Khayat, case writer, under the supervision of Professor J. Stewart Black, Associate Dean of Executive Development Programs, INSEAD. It is intended to be used as a basis for class discussion rather than to illustrate either effective or ineffective handling of an administrative situation.

This case was developed with the financial contribution of the Abu Dhabi Education Council, whose support is gratefully acknowledged.
Copyright © 2010 INSEAD

domestic market, a homogeneous workforce and leadership team, and a consistent company "way" had helped to create many domestic powerhouses and export juggernauts, these same factors seemed to inhibit success when Japan's MNCs moved to the next stage of development—international expansion by setting up operations overseas. The study argued that these initial positive factors further hobbled Japanese MNCs when they subsequently tried to compete globally and to find the optimal configuration of globally-integrated and locally-responsive functional as well as business activities.

As evidence of the failure of Japanese MNCs to sustain their global launch, the study pointed to a disturbing and significant trend. In 1995, Japanese firms topped *Fortune*'s Global 500 with 35.2% of total Global 500 revenues; the top three firms were all Japanese; U.S. firms came in second with a 28.4% share. But over the next 15 years the picture changed dramatically. Specifically, Japanese firms saw their share of global revenues drop from 35.2% in 1995 to 20.8% by 2000, to 14.2% by 2005, and to an all-time low of 11.8% in 2009. During the same 15-year period, the market share of U.S. firms rose from 28% to 30%, and that of European (including Swiss) firms went from 31% to 36%. Companies from the BRIC countries (Brazil, Russia, India, and China) saw their share increase from 0.9% to 10.4%.

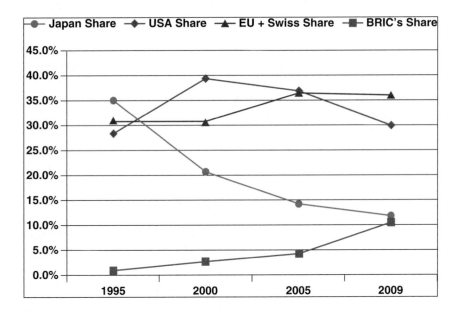

Was Komatsu treading the same path? And if it were, could management ignite a new trajectory that would put them into sustainable global orbit? Looking back over Komatsu's history might provide some insight to answer these questions.

KOMATSU'S DOMESTIC FOCUS 1921–1964

Komatsu Ltd. was founded in 1921 by Maitaro Takeuchi in Osaka, Japan. The company started out as a specialized mining equipment manufacturer, then expanded its operations into agricultural machinery in the 1930s and subsequently provided military equipment during World War II.

Yoshinari Kawai, who headed Komatsu from 1947 to 1964, shifted the emphasis towards applying new technology to civil engineering and towards manufacturing construction equipment in Japan.[2] Accordingly, by the 1950s Komatsu's production and sales revenues mainly came from industrial earth moving equipment (see Exhibit 1 for a sample of its current products).

Kawai recognized that if he wanted to substantially grow Komatsu's position in Japan he would have to increase product quality. Therefore, in 1961 he launched a company-wide quality control programme.[3] This focus on quality was pushed into a higher gear in 1963 when the Japanese Ministry of International Trade and Industry (MITI) decided to open the earth moving

Exhibit 1 A Selection of Komatsu Products

Construction and Mining Equipment

Minimal rear-swing radius hydraulic excavator

Hydraulic excavator [PC200

Super-large hydraulic excavator [PC2000]

Wheel loader [WA600]

Bulldozer [D51PX]

Micro excavator [PC05]

Crawler carrier [CD110R]

Dump truck [HD785]

Electric forklift truck

Machine Tools

Motor grader [GD655]

Crankshaft miller

(Continued)

Exhibit 1   *(Concluded)*

Recycling Equipment

On-site recycling method   Mobile soil recycler

Tunnelling Machines

Slurry shield

Sheet Metal Machines

3D Laser cutting machine

Engines

"ecot3" engine

Forest Machines

Harvester

Forwarder

Other

Light armoured vehicle

Excimer lasers

Source: Komatsu 2010 Annual report. www.komatsu.com. Accessed July 2010.

equipment (EME) market to foreign capital investment. This meant that after 42 years of protection from foreign firms, Komatsu would have to compete in Japan with the likes of Caterpillar (Cat), leader in the heavy construction industry since the 1920s. With the change in regulation, Cat in fact decided to enter the Japanese market via a joint venture with Mitsubishi, thereby bringing new competition and higher quality products to the Japanese market. This worried Kawai because at the time Komatsu held a 50% domestic market share and he was determined to defend it.

DOMESTIC AND EXPORT PHASE 1964–1982

It was in this context that Yoshinari Kawai passed the leadership baton to his son, Ryoichi Kawai, in 1964. The newly appointed president pursued what he called "management by policy," a concept meant to help management focus on what he saw as the strategic priorities:

- Upgrade product quality—Obtain international certification for Komatsu products from Cummins, International Harvester and Bucyrus-Erie to raise production standards.
- Enhance efficiency—Slash costs by scrutinizing all aspects of production, and launch "World A" campaign to ensure Komatsu was internationally recognized for quality and competitive prices.
- Acquire advanced technology—Leverage technology for improved manufacturing and product performance.

Kawai's strategies proved successful and the company recorded increased sales and a rise in its domestic market share from 50% to 65%, just as Cat entered the Japanese market.

Exports and Product Growth

Having secured Komatsu's position in the Japanese market and raised the standard of its products, the younger Kawai recognized that given such a high domestic market share and a more mature and slower-growing domestic market he would have to push exports if he wanted to continue to increase Komatsu's overall sales. Kawai's

export push found its footing in the early 1970s, and exports accounted for nearly 50% of total sales by 1975. From 1963 (just before the younger Kawai took over) through 1982, sales exploded from $168 million to $3.4 billion.[4] However, as sales in Japan grew only modestly from 1970 through 1982, the bulk of the increase came from exports. By 1982, exports accounted for nearly 75% of total sales.[5] Despite this, Komatsu's international growth was held in check because the best dealerships were already locked into contracts with its competitors. Komatsu had little choice but to settle for second-class dealers.

INTERNATIONALIZATION 1982–1989

In 1982, Shoji Nogawa, an engineer, took over the company's operational leadership. Unfortunately, the recession in the U.S. and the slump in global construction market demand hit about the same time. Decline in demand led to price wars and fierce competition as Komatsu and others struggled to hang on to market share and keep their factories open. Nogawa initially adopted a strategy focused on centralized international production facilities, cost cutting and aggressive export sales.[6] His rigid, autocratic managerial style, very high expectations, and relentless pressure on managers to achieve their goals were well suited to the tough times and Komatsu's performance initially improved.

However, Nogawa's strategy proved short-lived because the global market went into even greater turmoil in 1985–1986. The yen rapidly appreciated against the dollar, recording a 25% rise in nine months (see Exhibit 2). Consequently, products exported from Japan became less competitive in overseas markets. This forced Nogawa to somewhat de-emphasize exports and shift production overseas. Under normal market conditions, such a shift (often referred to as internationalization) typically involves moving production to foreign markets with lower costs and/or capturing additional sales beyond exports by adjusting products to fit the customized needs of the local market.[7]

In the late 1980s, Nogawa established two key overseas production plants: one in Tennessee (U.S.) and the other in Newcastle (UK). However,

Exhibit 2   Japan/U.S. Foreign Exchange Rate

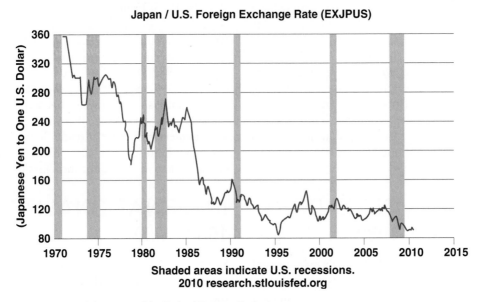

Japan / U.S. Foreign Exchange Rate (EXJPUS)

Shaded areas indicate U.S. recessions.
2010 research.stlouisfed.org

Source: Board of Governors of the Federal Reserve System.

he did not fully align the plants with local needs, in part because the "Komatsu way" was well established in Japan and believed to be the source of its past success. This perspective was noted in an article in *Forbes* in 1988 with reference to the newly established Tennessee plant:

> The plant had new management, a new workforce, new tools and techniques, robots and flexible manufacturing centres. The plan was to assemble a wide variety of products in a small location. "We intended to produce products exactly the way Komatsu does in Japan."[8]

Diversification

In addition to expanding the geographic base of production facilities, Nogawa also expanded the product line into non-construction machinery production to reduce dependence on the cyclical construction sector. These new products included laser machines, robots and power tools, as well as machines for plastics manufacturing.[9] However, the vast majority of this product diversification was done organically or through small acquisitions and therefore was simply not large enough to have an immediate impact on the revenue mix or mitigate the swings in the construction equipment demand cycle.

Price Hikes

Until 1986, Komatsu had only moderately increased wholesale prices in its international markets. However, with the significant appreciation of the yen, Komatsu was forced to increase prices in key foreign markets, such as the U.S. Not only were their fully assembled exports out of Japan more expensive due to the yen's appreciation, but also their own and their Japanese suppliers' exported component parts sent to Komatsu's overseas assembly plants were more costly. As a consequence, between 1985 and 1988 Komatsu implemented seven U.S. price increases, resulting in a total aggregate increase of 40%. This in turn led to a drop in Komatsu's North American market share from 12% in 1986 to 9% in 1988.[10]

Unfortunately these efforts to deal with the difficult times proved 'too little too late,' as continuing turbulent economic times coupled with Nogawa's rigid management style, belated international expansion and non-adapted foreign affiliate production resulted in Komatsu's construction equipment sales dropping each year beginning in 1985. As a result, in 1988 Chairman Kawai dismissed Nogawa.

That same year, under Kawai's direction, an international business division was set up in

Komatsu's Tokyo headquarters. The goals of the division included development of joint ventures around the world and overseas purchase of parts. One of the first major joint ventures was struck in 1988 with Dresser Industries—'Komatsu Dresser.' This was intended to sharpen Komatsu's competitive edge in the U.S. and help it better adjust its products to the differentiated needs of the U.S. market. Included within the venture were Komatsu's two existing U.S. subsidiaries and Dresser's construction machinery division. Together they formed the second-largest maker of construction machinery in the United States. The combination enabled Komatsu to reduce its exports to the U.S., increase its construction equipment assembly in the U.S. and make better use of Dresser's plants, which had been running at 50% capacity. In the same year, in response to the Japanese government's commitment to reduce its trade surplus by importing more foreign products, Kawai established Komatsu Trading International in order to increase imports to Japan.

REGIONALIZATION AND LOCALIZATION 1987–1995

In 1988, Kawai filled the spot vacated by Nogawa by promoting Masao Tanaka as the new CEO. Previously, Tanaka had held the position of Overseas General Manager and was known for his flexible managerial approach. The outlook during that year was bleak as sales were at their lowest point in four years. Tanaka set out to address the problem of Komatsu's less competitive products in the global market. He "emphasized the need to end price discounting and high-pressure sales practices."[11] His response to the rising yen and global market competition was to increase regional capacity by having autonomous bases of operations, including finance, manufacturing and sales in the three core markets: Japan, U.S. and Europe.[12]

In order to further combat the surging yen, the company shifted to outsourcing equipment such as mini excavators, engines and dump trucks from the UK, Germany and Italy, marketing them globally under its own brand name.

Komatsu Dresser Joint Venture

Executives at Komatsu saw the joint venture formed with Dresser, which included a $300 million investment, as a means of expanding production without having to build factories from scratch. External perceptions were less positive, as reflected in a *Forbes* article at the time:

> "It is a marriage of desperation. Dresser's construction equipment plants are running at half capacity, and Komatsu has lost three-fourths of its profits thanks to the strong yen."[13]

Though much of the manufacturing was done jointly, Komatsu and Dresser opted for separate dealer networks. This proved problematic as Komatsu and Dresser dealers started competing against each other. In addition, the venture was headed by a Dresser executive. This was a first for Komatsu; prior to that it had operated wholly owned subsidiaries with Japanese management running its operations.[14] Lack of cross-cultural experience was evident from the outset as Komatsu executives communicated in their native language and excluded their U.S. counterparts from major decisions.[15]

These leadership and facility problems contributed to the joint venture losing $125 million during the first years. To stop the loss, Komatsu invested in improving and reorganizing the production lines and also in cross-cultural training for both Komatsu and Dresser leaders. As the global market improved in 1989, and as the joint venture's initial production problems were resolved, Komatsu's overall financial picture improved.

Tetsuya Katada 1989–1995

After a little over a year at the helm, Tanaka was replaced by Tetsuya Katada, former Vice President of Corporate Planning and the man behind the international expansion and localization policies pursued under Tanaka. When Katada took over he continued the push for regionalization and tried to change the way Komatsu was managed. He believed that the traditional company policy of total control of subsidiaries would not work. Accordingly, his policy was to introduce further local participation in the different subsidiaries to raise their effectiveness in their respective geographical contexts.

3 G's: Growth, Global, Groupwide

Katada recognized that Komatsu's past obsession with trying to run everything from Japan and in a Japanese way was simply not going to propel the company forward. As a consequence he created the 3 G's: Growth, Global, Groupwide. Through this he aimed to double sales over the next five years. Growth would come from continued support of Komatsu's main focus on mining and construction equipment but would take on a more global perspective by pushing further autonomous regional production in Europe and the U.S. The company expanded the roles of all of its offshore facilities to include manufacturing, purchasing, development and sales, thus developing a worldwide network of state-of-the-art facilities. Under Katada's leadership, Komatsu purchased 64% of Hanomag, a German producer of construction equipment that held a 20% share of the German market. Komatsu also signed a supply agreement with FAI, an Italian producer of mini excavators. Additionally, Komatsu Europe International SA was formed to coordinate the company's operations and distribution in Europe. With this it slowly moved away from its centralized system and began delegating clear responsibilities to the regional centres. For example, European management was given full responsibility for developing and distributing all small wheel loaders across Europe to the Hanomag plant.[16]

By 1993 (after about five years of operation), the joint venture was doing well enough that in September of that year Komatsu increased its stake to 81%. The next year it purchased the remaining stake and took full control of Komatsu Dresser. In January 1996, the U.S. subsidiary was renamed Komatsu America International Company.[17]

Localizing Management

Katada believed that Komatsu was limited by its bureaucratic, top-down management style. He realized that the changing global environment required greater empowerment of both management and operations across all geographical locations. He also realized that for a meaningful delegation of authority to occur the company would need to commit to the development of local managers across geographies. In 1989, he changed global HR policy, requiring a substantial increase in the number of foreigners in managerial positions. As a result, between 1986 and 1992 the number of European employees in Komatsu Europe rose from 180 to 260, while the number of Japanese expatriate managers was reduced from 26 to 13.[18]

However, localizing management across its international operations presented many of the general cross-cultural communication problems Komatsu had experienced during its early days in its joint venture with Dresser. Now, however, the cross-cultural problems increasingly arose not just within local affiliates but between local leaders and regional Japanese expatriates and between local leaders and Japanese managers at headquarters. For example, Japanese managers focused on revenue growth and market share, while Komatsu's non-Japanese leaders tended to focus on profits.

Even when these cross-cultural communication and style differences could be resolved, Katada and other executives were often frustrated by the lack of initiative they saw in many local leaders. Some back in Japan wondered if foreigners were just not as hardworking or proactive as the Japanese. Others speculated that Komatsu's historical top-down approach inhibited the effective delegation of responsibility to local management because after following directions from Tokyo for so long many local leaders were reluctant to take initiative or conditioned not to. Others speculated that the problem stemmed from the type of managers Komatsu selected when it set up its initial operations— managers who were ready and willing to conform to the Komatsu Way rather than take initiative and show how and why things should be done differently in their market.

Product Diversification

In addition to geographic expansion, Katada pushed for greater product diversification than the company had ever experienced before. During the 1990s, Komatsu executed several alliances and acquisitions that allowed it to further diversify its products. The company targeted growth in mechatronics, electronics, material engineering and systems engineering. For example, Katada pursued a strategic alliance in 1993 with U.S.-based Applied Materials Inc., a company specialized in computer display panels, and formed Applied

Komatsu Technology Inc. This alliance made electronics Komatsu's second-largest business segment. Moreover, Komatsu targeted several acquisitions and strategic alliances to expand further into manufacturing robotics, plastics, injection moulding machinery and various components of local area network (LAN) equipment.[19]

Komatsu enjoyed four years of growth and an increase in sales and revenues. However, in 1993 net sales declined along with worldwide demand as a function of the global recession that began in 1992. Komatsu's difficulty in aligning its joint ventures and acquisitions also contributed to its problems. This was complicated by the cultural and communication challenges the company encountered as it diversified its workforce and the leadership within its foreign affiliates.

The global economy recovered in 1995 and demand for construction equipment rebounded, moving past the levels enjoyed in 1992. With the economic upturn, Komatsu's financial picture also improved. However, Katada realized that Komatsu would have to not only improve the quantity and quality of its local leaders in its foreign affiliates but would also have to internationalize top management in order to compete in the global market down the road. How could you have more than 50% of your revenues coming from outside Japan and yet have no senior managers from those markets? How could you continue to succeed internationally if none of your senior regional executives were from the region? How could non-Japanese leaders' voices be heard by executives back at Komatsu headquarters in Japan if they occupied no significant leadership positions in the markets? Some saw this as a major challenge in the coming years as Komatsu strove to become a truly global player.

GLOBALIZATION
1995–2007

Some of these concerns faded as the economic climate improved. In 1995, Satoru Anzaki took over the leadership, while Katada became chairman. Over the next three years, Komatsu enjoyed rising profits, aided by a flourishing U.S. economy and booming construction sector. On this enhanced financial base, Anzakis' strategy was to move Komatsu further along the path to globalization.

Because globalization does not mean centralizing everything or doing things only one way, executives moving deeper into globalization try to find the optimal configuration of globally integrated and locally responsive activities. As a consequence, during the globalization stage of development, they try to place segments of the value chain in specific geographies to optimize complex and sometimes competing criteria such as cost, quality, reliability, proximity to customers, transshipment and coordination costs, and time lags between links in the value chain. They often discover that activities such as purchasing, IT, finance, HR, etc., that were allowed to be differentiated during the internationalization stage—when they focused on customizing products to different markets—now create levels of duplication and incompatibility that, with the increased size of the company, are too great to be ignored. In many cases these activities need to be harmonized, standardized and integrated—though that integration need not be located at the company's headquarters.

For activities such as research and development, executives typically find that a limited number of centres located in parts of the world that have supportive ecosystems around a given topic are best. For others, such as government relations, labour relations and even aspects of product design, they often find that it is best to locate activities close to markets and differentiate them by market in order to respond effectively to market differences. In addition, during the globalization stage companies often not only try to consolidate and strengthen their position in developed markets but make major moves into developing markets.

All of this was the case for Komatsu during the period of Anzaki's leadership.

Geographic Expansion

Eager to take advantage of the emerging and rapidly expanding Asian market, Komatsu established two production bases in Singapore and Indonesia. The company also created Komatsu Asia & Pacific Pte Ltd in Singapore to coordinate its Asian operations.

Komatsu continued to expand its core businesses through joint ventures. The company expanded its mining business through the acquisition of Mannesmann Demag AG and Modular Mining Systems, Inc. in Germany. In 1997,

Komatsu further expanded its mining business and made Vernon Hills in Illinois its international headquarters for the mining equipment business.

In early 1998, it joined with Larsen & Toubro Ltd. of India to form Bangalore-based L&T-Komatsu Limited, which would make Komatsu hydraulic excavators and sell them in India and neighbouring countries. Komatsu was unlucky in the timing of its expansion in Asia. Not long after its push into Singapore, Indonesia and India, the Asian economic and currency crisis of 1997 rippled through the region and continued over the next three years. As a result, Asia as percentage of total global demand declined from about 25% in 1997 to about 15% by 1999. To make matters worse, during this same period Japan's share of global demand also declined from about 30% to 20%. In combination this had a devastating impact: in 1999 Komatsu experienced its first-ever net income loss of ¥12.3 billion (approximately $102 million) on net sales of ¥1,061.5 billion (approximately $8.8 billion).[20]

Internal Restructuring

In response to this sharp decline, between 1999 and 2000 Komatsu restructured its domestic operations. The restructuring was primarily aimed at reducing fixed costs by consolidating factories. Three factories were closed in Japan resulting in a 20% reduction in production floor space.

At the same time, declines in semiconductor prices hit Komatsu's electronics business. As a consequence, it closed a major plant in the U.S. and refocused production on Japan and Taiwan. In a further pullback in its electronics business, in November 1999 Komatsu sold its stake in Applied Komatsu Technology, the flat panel display joint venture, to its partner Applied Materials.

In an effort to improve internal leadership and decision-making, Anzaki reduced the number of board directors from 26 to eight. He attempted to diversify top management by appointing a four-member International Advisory Board (AIB), all of whom were foreigners. Jim Henderson, former chairman of Cummins, a U.S. diesel engine supplier, who sat on the AIB, commented in support of Anzaki's initiative:

> "He has clear objectives about trying to improve value for shareholders and maintaining Komatsu's commitment to globalization."[21]

In 2000, in a further effort to internationalize top management, Anzaki announced that Keith Sheldon, a General Motors veteran, would take up the new position of Global Financial Officer. Sheldon was entrusted with listing Komatsu on the New York Stock Exchange, overhauling the company's finances and preparing for a series of takeovers and spinoffs in non-core operations. Although appointing a foreigner to a top management position was unusual for a Japanese company, Anzaki was determined to pursue a more Western-style approach to management.[22]

Anzaki's globalization strategy was successful to an extent but was dampened by an ailing Japanese domestic market and declining demand for construction machinery. As a consequence, the company suffered its second net loss of ¥852 billion ($710 million) nine months after the new president, Masahiro Sakane, took over.

Masahiro Sakane 2001–2007

In 2001, Masahiro Sakane succeeded Anzaki as president. Sakane had worked at Komatsu since 1963 and was formerly COO of Komatsu Dresser in the U.S. He inherited a challenging situation. In 2001, the Japanese government drastically reduced spending on infrastructure and public works, which significantly reduced the demand for heavy construction machinery. Japan's share of the global construction equipment industry declined from a peak of 42% in 1990 to just 17% by 2002. On top of this, the recession of 2000 in the U.S. had spread to Europe and had been amplified by the terrorists' attacks on the U.S. in September 2001. Given these unfavourable global market conditions, if he were to restart revenue growth and return the company to profitability in 2002 and beyond, Sakane had to move quickly and decisively.

Company Restructuring

In 2001, Sakane announced a major company restructuring, focused on optimizing production and cutting costs. He explained:

> "We want to cut fixed costs by ¥30 billion by fiscal 2003; the rest we must absorb through growth. If we fail to do this, the additional 3% to be absorbed will be waiting for us."[23]

Accordingly, he set out to reduce the workforce by 10% (2,200 workers), consolidate businesses and affiliated companies both in Japan and abroad, and increase competitiveness in manufacturing. In 2003, further restructuring occurred when Sakane announced that he would increase the number of external directors:

> "To further enhance the neutrality, transparency and fairness of the Board of Directors based on our previous reorganization, we have decided to increase the number of external directors from one to two."[24]

Sakane also called for the promotion of human resource development throughout Komatsu's global operations. He focused on cross-cultural education initiatives to enhance communication. He also started an initiative to form cross-organizational teams involving key people from various Komatsu groups to tackle global challenges for the company.

Globalization Efforts

With the U.S. and Europe in recession and Japan in the middle of the "lost decade" in which it fluctuated between stagnation and decline, Komatsu had little choice but to focus on growth in emerging markets. Consequently, Sakane aggressively pursued joint ventures, production facilities, and sales and distribution facilities in the fast-growing markets of Brazil, China, India and Russia.[25] In 2003, Komatsu Forklift (Shanghai) Co., Ltd. was established in China for the sale of forklift trucks. In 2004, the company acquired Partek Forest AB, a manufacturer and distributor of forestry equipment in Sweden, and through this acquisition established Komatsu Forest AB in order to supply logging companies with heavy equipment across the global customer base.

In a bid to expand core construction and mining equipment, Sakane launched a "Global Cycling System for Construction Equipment." This initiative included establishing a new rental business model, which took advantage of Komatsu's originality and superiority as a manufacturer without requiring customers to commit upfront capital to equipment purchases. It also included the creation of a new "certified" used equipment market, much like that in the automotive industry.[26] Generally, analysts made positive comments on the new rental and refurbishing business:

> "Given Komatsu's very strong franchise, market share and distribution network, I think it's the right strategy."[27]

In order to further enhance its global position as a quality producer, in 2003 Komatsu launched its "Dantotsu strategy," which called for concentrating company resources on overwhelmingly differentiating specific features of Komatsu products. Products with the Dantotsu (unrivalled) designation were considered vastly superior to competitors' products. Another initiative was the Komtrax system, designed as a revolutionary new way to track equipment over the Internet, which utilized rugged hardware, GPS positioning systems and powerful management software so that distributors and their customers could know exactly where the machines were operating, when they were in use, how often, and for how long.

Sakane's efforts, along with a global market recovery, helped turn Komatsu's fortunes around. The company recorded an impressive increase in its net income from ¥3,009 billion in 2003 to ¥114,290 billion in 2006.

KUNIO NOJI 2007–2010

In 2007, Kunio Noji succeeded Sakane, who was appointed chairman. Noji had previously held the position of President of Construction & Mining Equipment Marketing Division at Komatsu Ltd. Anticipating increased global demand of 6% in construction and mining machinery until 2010, Noji focused on growth in the core business of industrial machinery (including construction, mining and utility equipment as well as industrial machinery) and strengthening workplace capability.[28] In 2007, Komatsu recorded a 17% increase in net sales to ¥1,893 billion and a 44% increase in net income to ¥164 billion.

Global Growth Efforts

Construction and mining equipment had consistently constituted the majority of Komatsu's revenues and were 85% of total revenues by the end of 2008. However, the geographical mix was significantly different in 2008 from just four years earlier. Noji believed that the change in geographic mix would better enable Komatsu to capture growth opportunities and weather any downturns in the business cycle, which consistently plagued the construction and mining industries globally.

Change in Komatsu's Geographic Mix 2004–2008			
Region	2004	2008	Percentage Change
Japan	30.2%	15.2%	−49.7%
North America	21.2%	15.6%	−26.4%
Europe & CIS	16.0%	21.9%	36.9%
Asia & Oceania	12.0%	16.7%	39.2%
China	8.7%	9.3%	6.9%
Middle East & Africa	6.7%	11.6%	73.1%
Latin America	5.2%	9.7%	86.5%

Five Principles	Seven Ways of Komatsu
1. Vitalize the functions of the board of directors.	1. Commitment to quality and reliability
2. Take the initiative in communicating with all our stakeholders.	2. Customer oriented
3. Comply with the rules of the business community.	3. Defining the root cause
4. Never put off responses to risks.	4. Workplace (*genba*) philosophy
5. Keep thinking about your successor.	5. Policy deployment
	6. Collaboration with business partners
	7. Human resource development

Source: Komatsu Annual Report 2007.

Strengthening Organizational and Leadership Capability

Although finding the optimal configuration for globally integrated and standardized activities, as well as locally responsive and differentiated activities, was an ongoing challenge, some aspects of the optimal configuration were coming into focus. For example, on the financial reporting, IT and resource planning side, Komatsu implemented an enterprise resource planning system (ERP). Komatsu selected "iBaanERP" from Baan Japan Co., Ltd. as its ERP package and utilized "IBM@serverz Series" by IBM Japan, Ltd. as the enterprise server platform for this system. At the time it was the largest ERP implementation in Japan's manufacturing industry, involving approximately 5,000 users at nine sites in eight countries across planning, procurement, manufacturing, sales, logistics and accounting. This system allowed Komatsu to launch new products in Japan, the United States, Europe and Asia simultaneously.

In order to address different cultures, Noji personally set about raising internal awareness and conducting presentations of "the Komatsu Way", a set of core values aimed at strengthening corporate governance within Komatsu globally. The table below depicts the Five Principles and Seven Ways of Komatsu:

Noji conducted over 65 presentations throughout the company on the Komatsu Way. The intent was to create a unifying culture globally, while promoting understanding of different styles of management and communication.[29]

Komatsu's International Advisory Board was seen by many as an important step on its path to globalization. Since its inception more than a decade earlier, the AIB had met twice a year and provided outside advice to the Komatsu Board of Directors. In 2008, the IAB consisted of four members: Yukio Okamoto, specialist in international affairs and President of Okamoto Associates Inc, Dr. Lawrence J. Lau, Vice Chancellor, President, and the Ralph and Claire Landau Professor of Economics at the Chinese University of Hong Kong, Dr. Juergen M. Geissinger, President and CEO of INA-Holding Schaeffler KG, and Travis Engen, former President and CEO of Alcan Inc.

Despite Komatsu's successes in many aspects of globalization, there was one glaring failure: after 25 years of efforts to increase the percentage of local leaders in foreign affiliates, none of the 22 listed executive officers in 2008 were foreigners—all were Japanese and male. Komatsu's Board of Directors consisted of 10 individuals, seven were internal executives, three were external directors and all were Japanese and male.[30]

Dealing with the Financial Crisis and Global Recession

The financial crisis that began in late 2008 and swept the world in 2009 continued to hamper economic growth across virtually every market in 2010, but the downturn had a particularly harsh impact on Komatsu. Because much of the crisis was concentrated in the residential and commercial real estate industries, the collapse in demand for construction equipment was severe. Prior to the recession, Komatsu's revenues and profits peaked in 2008 at ¥2,243 billion and ¥209 billion respectively.[31] The following table illustrates the impact of the recession on revenues and profits in 2009 and 2010 compared with 2008.

Figures in billions of yen	2008	2009	2010	2008–2010 Change
Net Sales	¥2,243	¥2,022	¥1,432	−36.02%
Net Income	¥209	¥79	¥34	−83.7%

The decline between 2008 and 2010 was spread across virtually all of Komatsu's regions, with the exception of China. Over the two-year period, sales in China increased by nearly 43% and in 2010 constituted nearly 19% of all Komatsu's sales. Declines in the other regions ranged from a high of 70% in Europe and CIS to a low of just over 4% in Latin America.

However, while sales were growing in China, so too were its leadership and labour problems. In 2010, Komatsu faced various strikes in its Chinese plants due to the lack of local ties with the plant workforce; most of the key leaders in China were Japanese expatriates. Komatsu was not alone in failing to develop local Chinese leadership. The *Financial Times* noted its promise to fix the problem in the future:

> "A number of Japanese manufacturers . . . said they were planning to promote more foreign executives to top positions at their overseas operations, opening the way for potentially significant cultural changes. Komatsu, which makes heavy equipment for the building and mining industries, . . . said it planned to install Chinese managers as the top executives of all 16 of its subsidiaries in China by 2012."[32]

Only time would tell if Komatsu would be successful in identifying and developing local leaders in China when it had largely failed elsewhere. But the fact that the company had still not succeeded in moving non-Japanese into its corporate executive ranks, even from developed markets such as the U.S. and Germany where it had had significant operations for decades, was not encouraging. According to its 2010 Annual Report, Komatsu's Board of Directors consisted of seven members from Komatsu and three from outside organizations—all of them Japanese and male. Of the 25 listed executive officers, all were Japanese and male. Of the six regional executive officers listed, all were Japanese and male.[33]

A New Mid-term Plan

In April 2010, Komatsu announced a new mid-range management plan: "Global Teamwork for Tomorrow" to come into effect until March 2013.[34] The company indicated that it expected an upturn in market demand for construction and mining equipment in China and other emerging countries in Asia and Latin America over the next three years. With more than 50% of its revenues coming from emerging markets, Komatsu anticipated that growth in these markets would have a positive impact on its overall financial performance. The mid-term plan called for similar financial targets to the previous plan, including return on equity of 20% and an operating income ratio of 15% or higher.

The mid-term plan called for strengthening the company's focus on IT applications, including Komtrax (Komatsu Machine Tracking System) for construction equipment and Autonomous Haulage System for use in large-scale mines. It emphasized investments in product development that would help customers reduce CO_2 emissions from equipment and that would advance Komatsu's hybrid and HST (hydrostatic transmission) technologies for construction equipment and forklift trucks. It also emphasized the firm's continuing efforts to anchor the Komatsu Way. Finally, the plan stated: "We are going to materialize these . . . efforts in the form of human resource development needed for global business expansion."

Would Komatsu's fortunes recover with the economy from 2010 to 2013? Some were sceptical. Komatsu's history showed some troubling similarities with the overall pattern among many Japanese MNCs of failure to successfully launch globally.[35] Its sales had exploded during the 1960s, from ¥9 billion in 1960 to ¥260 billion by 1970—an explosion driven almost exclusively by domestic success. In the 1970s, sales had more than doubled, but nearly 40% of that growth came from the addition of exports. In the 1980s, Komatsu had begun to set up operations overseas. Sales had increased 38%, although almost all of the increase came from domestic sales and exports, not from overseas operations. In the 1990s, Komatsu had continued expanding its international operations, but total sales only increased 17%. During the last decade (2000–2010), sales had increased by a total of 35%. Importantly, all of the increase came from exports and international operations; absolute domestic Japanese sales declined from about ¥550 billion to ¥324 billion. Some felt that this was proof that Komatsu's investments in overseas operations over the last 10–20 years were finally gaining traction and paying off. Others felt this perspective had to be tempered with the fact that, as a percentage of sales, Komatsu's exports from 2004 through 2010 had increased by about 50% compared with the 1990s, signalling a return to the company's past dependence on exports.

Other signs that it was falling victim to the failure to launch globally syndrome were more troubling. For example, Komatsu had ranked #424 on the *Fortune* Global 500 list in 1995 but had dropped to #460 by 2009. In contrast, Caterpillar was #233 on the list in 1995 but had risen to #144 by 2009. Komatsu's stock was down 55% from July 2007 to July 2010, while Caterpillar was down only 25% over the same period.

Some argued that the contrast in the global fate of these two competitors was in large part due to the differences in leadership. Even though Caterpillar and Komatsu had very similar product portfolios and geographic coverage, they diverged in terms of their senior leadership. In 2010, 100% of Komatsu's senior leaders were Japanese and male, and with the exception of Keith Sheldon ten years before this had always been the case. In contrast, of Caterpillar's five group presidents, one was a non-U.S. national, and of the 28 listed vice presidents, six were non-U.S. nationals. In addition, of the 22 vice presidents that were U.S. nationals, three were women.[36]

While some questioned whether diversity of leadership really affected a firm's performance as it tried to become a global player, there was mounting empirical evidence of a direct and significant link.[37] But even if Komatsu's leaders accepted this evidence, the question still remained—what should they do differently to ensure that they didn't keep moving backwards? Could they ignite a new strategy that would help them rocket ahead, break free from the gravitational pull of their past, and get into sustainable global orbit?

Exhibit 3   Company Financials

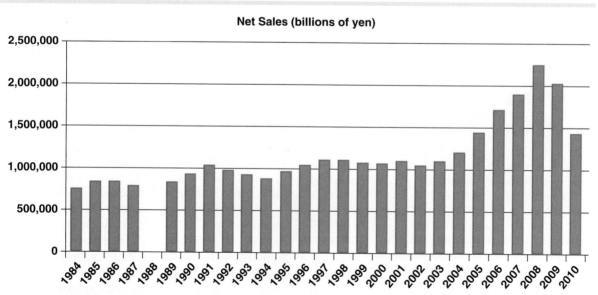

Source: Capital IQ-Compustat.

(Note: in 1988 Komatsu changed its fiscal calendar.)

Exhibit 3 *(Concluded)*

Net Income (millions JPY)

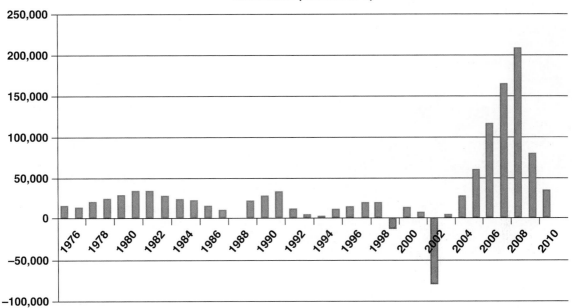

Source: Capital IQ-Compustat.

Sales by Region (billions of yen)

☐ Japan ☐ America ☐ Europe & CIS ☐ China ☐ Asia* ☐ Middle East and Africa

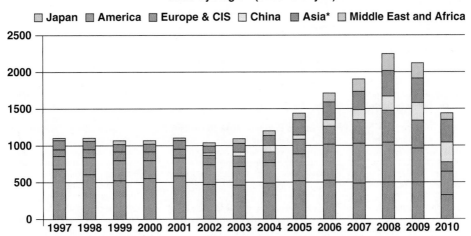

Source: Komatsu annual reports.

*China is included in Asia 1997–2001.

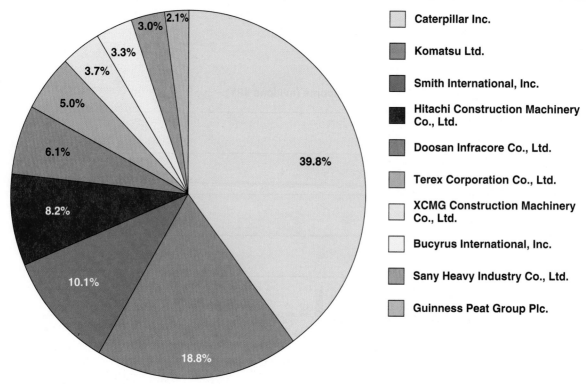

Source: Factiva, Dow Jones; Caterpillar Inc. Company Report 2010.

ENDNOTES

[1] Black Stewart and Allen Morrison. *Sunset in the Land of the Rising Sun: Why Japanese Firms Will Struggle in a Global Future.* London: Palgrave Macmillan, 2010.
[2] www.komatsu.com/ technical report (accessed June 2010).
[3] www.komatsu.com/ Komatsu History (accessed June 2010).
[4] Komatsu 2007 Annual Report.
[5] Ibid.
[6] Bartlett, Christopher. "Komatsu Ltd.: Project G's Globalization." Harvard Business School. 1997. p. 3.
[7] Black, Stewart and Allen Morrison. "Failure to Launch Globally: A Cautionary Tale from Japan to the World," *Harvard Business Review,* forthcoming-September 2010. p. 6.
[8] Flint, Jerry. "The Enemy of My Enemy," *Forbes,* November 14, 1988, Vol. 142, Issue 10. p. 43.
[9] www.komatsu.com/ Komatsu History (accessed June 2010).
[10] Allen, Stephen. "Caterpillar and Komatsu in 1988". ECCH 1990. p. 5.
[11] Bartlett. "Komatsu Ltd.: Project G's Globalization." p. 4.
[12] www.komatsu.com/ Komatsu History (accessed June 2010).
[13] Flint. "The Enemy of My Enemy." p. 42.
[14] Ibid.
[15] Levenson, Georgia and Ashish Nanda. "Komatsu and Dresser: Putting Two plus Two

Together." Harvard Business School. October 16, 1998. pp. 6–7.
[16] Ibid.
[17] www.komatsu.com/ Komatsu History (accessed June 2010).
[18] Bartlet. "Komatsu Ltd.: Project G's Globalization." p. 10.
[19] www.komatsu.com/ Komatsu History (accessed June 2010).
[20] Komatsu Annual Report 1999.
[21] Marsh, Peter. "Inside Track—Digging for Ideas in the West". *The Financial Times.* May 2, 2000.
[22] *Bloomberg BussinessWeek* 50 Leaders. "No. 20: Komatsu" http://www.businessweek.com/magazine/content/05_43/b3956420.htmhttp://www.businessweek.com/magazine/content/05_43/b3956420.htm (accessed July 2010).
[23] Ibid.
[24] www.komatsu.com. (accessed July 2010).
[25] Company history, www.komatsu.com/ (accessed July 2010).
[26] www.komatsu.com. (accessed July 2010).
[27] Kruger, David and Ichiko Fuyuno. "Komatsu Heads For the Trenches." *Far Eastern Economic Review,* November 22, 2001.
[28] Komatsu Annual report. 2007. www.komatsu.com. (accessed July 2010).
[29] Komatsu Annual Report 2007.
[30] Komatsu Annual Report 2008.

[31] Note: Komatsu's annual financial results are from April 1 to March 31 and therefore 2008 annual results are from March 2007 through March 2008. Therefore, Komatsu's 2008 annual results were complete before the financial market meltdown that began in the fall of 2008.
[32] Soble, Jonathan. "Japanese Groups Seek Leaders Abroad." *The Financial Times,* June 29, 2010.
[33] Komatsu Annual Report 2010.
[34] Komatsu press release (http://www.komatsu.com/CompanyInfo/press/2010042715561427585.html).
[35] Komatsu Annual Report 2007.
[36] http://www.cat.com/corporate-overview/governance/officers (accessed July 2010).
[37] Nielsen, Sabina and Bo Bernhard Nielsen. 'The Effects of Top Management Team and Board Nationality Diversity and Compensation Systems on Firm Performance,' *Academy of Management Proceedings,* 2006; Carpenter, Mason and James Fredrickson, 'Top Management Teams, Global Strategic Posture, and the Moderating Role of Uncertainty,' *Academy of Management Journal,* 44 (3), pp. 533–545, 2001; Carpenter, Mason A. Wm. Gerard Sanders, and Hal B. Gregersen, 'Internationalization and Firm Governance,' *Academy of Management Journal,* 44 (3), pp. 493–511, 2001.

PepsiCo's Diversification Strategy in 2008

John E. Gamble
University of South Alabama

PepsiCo was the world's largest snack and beverage company, with 2007 net revenues of approximately $39.5 billion. The company's portfolio of businesses in 2008 included Frito-Lay salty snacks, Quaker Chewy granola bars, Pepsi soft drink products, Tropicana orange juice, Lipton Brisk tea, Gatorade, Propel, SoBe, Quaker Oatmeal, Cap'n Crunch, Aquafina, Rice-A-Roni, Aunt Jemima pancake mix, and many other regularly consumed products. Gatorade, Propel, Rice-A-Roni, Aunt Jemima, and Quaker Oats products had been added to PepsiCo's arsenal of brands through the $13.9 billion acquisition of Quaker Oats in 2001. The acquisition was the final component of a major portfolio restructuring initiative that began in 1997. Since the restructuring, the company had increased revenues and net income at annual rates of 7 percent and 12 percent, respectively. A summary of PepsiCo's financial performance is shown in Exhibit 1.

Through 2007, the company's top managers were focused on sustaining the impressive performance that had been achieved since its restructuring through strategies keyed to product innovation, close relationships with distribution allies, international expansion, and strategic acquisitions. Newly introduced products such as Gatorade G2, Tiger Woods signature sports drinks, and Quaker Simple Harvest multigrain hot cereal had accounted for 15–20 percent of all new growth in recent years. New product innovations that addressed consumer health and wellness concerns were the greatest contributors to

the company's growth, with PepsiCo's better-for-you and good-for-you products accounting for 16 percent of its 2007 snack sales in North America, 70 percent of net beverage revenues in North America during 2007, and more than 50 percent of its 2007 sales of Quaker Oats products in North America. The company also increased the percentage of healthy snacks in markets outside North America since consumers in most developed countries wished to reduce their consumption of saturated fats, cholesterol, trans fats, and simple carbohydrates.

The company's Power of One retailer alliance strategy had been in effect for more than 10 years and was continuing to help boost PepsiCo's volume and identify new product formulations desired by consumers. Under the Power of One strategy, PepsiCo marketers and retailers collaborated in stores and during offsite summits to devise tactics to increase consumers' tendency to purchase more than one product offered by PepsiCo during a store visit. In addition, some of PepsiCo's most successful new products had been recommended by retailers.

PepsiCo's international sales had grown by 22 percent during 2007, but the company had many additional opportunities to increase sales in markets outside North America. The company held large market shares in many international markets for beverages and salty snacks, but it had been relatively unsuccessful in making Quaker branded products available outside the United States. In 2006, 75 percent of Quaker Oats' international sales of $500 million was accounted for by just six countries. In addition, PepsiCo's international

Copyright © 2008 by John E. Gamble. All rights reserved.

Exhibit 1   **Financial Summary for PepsiCo Inc., 1998–2007 (in millions, except per share amounts)**

	2007	2006	2005	2004	2003	2002	2001	2000	1999	1998
Net revenue	$39,474	$35,137	$32,562	$29,261	$26,971	$25,112	$23,512	$20,438	$20,367	$22,348
Net income	5,599	5,065	4,078	4,212	3,568	3,000	2,400	2,183	2,050	1,993
Income per common share—basic, continuing operations	$3.38	$ 3.00	$2.43	$2.45	$2.07	$1.69	$1.35	$1.51	$1.40	$1.35
Cash dividends declared per common share	$1.42	$1.16	$1.01	$0.85	$0.63	$0.60	$0.58	$0.56	$0.54	$0.52
Total assets	$34,628	$29,930	$31,727	$27,987	$25,327	$23,474	$21,695	$18,339	$17,551	$22,660
Long-term debt	4,203	2,550	2,313	2,397	1,702	2,187	2,651	2,346	2,812	4,028

Source: PepsiCo 10-Ks, various years.

operations were much less profitable than its businesses operating in North America. While the operating profit margins of PepsiCo's international division had ranged from 13.4 to 15.6 percent between 2004 and 2007, operating profit margins for its Frito-Lay and North American beverage business ranged from 21.3 to 25 percent during the same time period. Quaker Foods' sales of Cap'n Crunch, Life cereal, Quaker oatmeal, Chewy granola bars, Aunt Jemima, and Rice-A-Roni produced the highest profit margins among all PepsiCo brands, with operating profits exceeding 30 percent each year between 2004 and 2007.

PepsiCo management developed a new organizational structure in 2008 to address the low relative profitability of its international operations and to produce even faster growth in international markets. The new structure that would place all brands sold in the United Kingdom, Europe, Asia, the Middle East, and Africa into a common division was expected to aid the company in its ability to capture strategic fits between its various brands and products. It was also quite possible that PepsiCo management needed to consider restructuring its lineup of snack and beverage businesses to improve overall profitability and reverse the downturn in its stock price that began in 2008. Exhibit 2 tracks PepsiCo's market performance between 1998 and October 2008.

COMPANY HISTORY

PepsiCo Inc. was established in 1965 when Pepsi-Cola and Frito-Lay shareholders agreed to a merger between the salty snack icon and soft drink giant. The new company was founded with annual revenues of $510 million and such well-known brands as Pepsi-Cola, Mountain Dew, Fritos, Lay's, Cheetos, Ruffles, and Rold Gold. PepsiCo's roots can be traced to 1898, when New Bern, North Carolina, pharmacist Caleb Bradham created the formula for a carbonated beverage he named Pepsi-Cola. The company's salty-snack business began in 1932 when Elmer Doolin of San Antonio, Texas, began manufacturing and marketing Fritos corn chips and Herman Lay started a potato chip distribution business in Nashville, Tennessee. In 1961, Doolin and Lay agreed to a merger between their businesses to establish the Frito-Lay Company.

During its first five years as a snack and beverage company, PepsiCo introduced new products such as Doritos and Funyuns; entered markets in Japan and Eastern Europe; and opened, on average, one new snack food plant per year. By 1971, PepsiCo had more than doubled its revenues to reach $1 billion. The company began to pursue growth through acquisitions outside snacks and beverages as early as 1968, but its 1977

Exhibit 2   Monthly Performance of PepsiCo Inc.'s Stock Price, 1998 to March 2008

(a) Trend in PepsiCo, Inc.'s Common Stock Price

(b) Performance of PepsiCo, Inc.'s Stock Price versus the S&P 500 Index

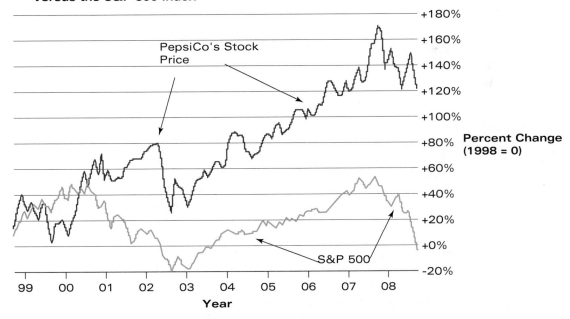

acquisition of Pizza Hut significantly shaped the strategic direction of PepsiCo for the next 20 years. The acquisitions of Taco Bell in 1978 and Kentucky Fried Chicken in 1986 created a business portfolio described by Wayne Calloway (PepsiCo's CEO between 1986 and 1996) as a balanced three-legged stool. Calloway believed the combination of snack foods, soft drinks, and fast food offered considerable cost-sharing and skills-transfer opportunities, and he routinely shifted managers between the company's three divisions as part of the company's management development efforts.

PepsiCo also strengthened its portfolio of snack foods and beverages during the 1980s and 1990s with acquisitions of Mug root beer, 7UP International, Smartfood ready-to-eat popcorn, Walker's Crisps (UK), Smith's Crisps (UK), Mexican cookie company, Gamesa, and SunChips. Calloway also added quick-service restaurants Hot-n-Now in 1990, California Pizza Kitchens in 1992, and East Side Mario's, D'Angelo Sandwich Shops, and Chevy's Mexican Restaurants in 1993. The company expanded beyond carbonated beverages with a 1992 agreement with Ocean Spray to distribute single-serving juices, the introduction of Lipton ready-to-drink teas in 1993, and the introduction of Aquafina bottled water and Frappuccino ready-to-drink coffees in 1994.

By 1996, it had become clear to PepsiCo management that the potential strategic-fit benefits existing between restaurants and PepsiCo's core beverage and snack businesses were difficult to capture. In addition, any synergistic benefits achieved were more than offset by the fast-food industry's fierce price competition and low profit margins. In 1997, CEO Roger Enrico spun off the company's restaurants as an independent, publicly traded company to focus PepsiCo on food and beverages. Soon after the spin-off of PepsiCo's fast-food restaurants was completed, Enrico acquired Cracker Jack, Tropicana, Smith's Snackfood Company in Australia, SoBe teas and alternative beverages, Tasali Snack Foods (the leader in the Saudi Arabian salty snack market), and the Quaker Oats Company.

The Quaker Oats Acquisition

At $13.9 billion, Quaker Oats was PepsiCo's largest acquisition and gave it the number one brand of oatmeal in the United States, with a 60+ percent category share; the leading brand of rice cakes and granola snack bars; and other well-known grocery brands such as Cap'n Crunch, Rice-A-Roni, and Aunt Jemima. However, Quaker's most valuable asset in its arsenal of brands was Gatorade.

Gatorade was developed by University of Florida researchers in 1965 but was not marketed commercially until the formula was sold to Stokely–Van Camp in 1967. When Quaker Oats acquired the brand from Stokely–Van Camp in 1983, Gatorade gradually made a transformation from a regionally distributed product with annual sales of $90 million to a $2 billion powerhouse. Gatorade was able to increase sales by more than 10 percent annually during the 1990s, with no new entrant to the isotonic beverage category posing a serious threat to the brand's dominance. PepsiCo, Coca-Cola, France's Danone Group, and Swiss food giant Nestlé all were attracted to Gatorade because of its commanding market share and because of the expected growth in the isotonic sports beverage category. PepsiCo became the successful bidder for Quaker Oats and Gatorade with an agreement struck in December 2000 but would not receive U.S. Federal Trade Commission (FTC) approval until August 2001. The FTC's primary concern over the merger was that Gatorade's inclusion in PepsiCo's portfolio of snacks and beverages might give the company too much leverage in negotiations with convenience stores and ultimately force smaller snack food and beverage companies out of convenience store channels. In its approval of the merger, the FTC stipulated that Gatorade could not be jointly distributed with PepsiCo's soft drinks for 10 years.

Acquisitions after 2001

After the completion of the Quaker Oats acquisition in August 2001, the company focused on integration of Quaker Oats' food, snack, and beverage brands into the PepsiCo portfolio. The company made a number of "tuck-in" acquisitions of small, fast-growing food and beverage companies in the United States and internationally to broaden its portfolio of brands. Tuck-in acquisitions in 2006 included Stacy's bagel and pita chips, Izze carbonated beverages, Duyvis nuts (Netherlands), and Star Foods (Poland). Acquisitions made during 2007 included Naked Juice fruit beverages, Sandora juices (Ukraine), Bluebird snacks (New Zealand), Penelopa nuts and seeds (Bulgaria), and Lucky snacks (Brazil). The company also entered into a joint venture with the Strauss Group in 2007 to market Sabra, the top-selling and fastest-growing brand of hummus in the United States and Canada.

PepsiCo's acquisitions in 2007 totaled $1.3 billion, whereas the company had made

Exhibit 3 **PepsiCo Inc.'s Consolidated Statements of Income, 2005–2007 (in millions, except per share amounts)**

	2007	2006	2005
Net revenue	$39,474	$35,137	$32,562
Cost of sales	18,038	15,762	14,176
Selling, general, and administrative expenses	14,208	12,774	12,314
Amortization of intangible assets	58	162	150
Operating profit	7,170	6,439	5,922
Bottling equity income	560	616	557
Interest expense	(224)	(239)	(256)
Interest income	125	173	159
Income before income taxes	7,631	6,989	6,382
Provision for income taxes	1,973	1,347	2,304
Net income	$ 5,658	$ 5,642	$ 4,078
Net income per common share—basic	$ 3.48	$ 3.42	$ 2.43
Net income per common share—diluted	$ 3.41	$ 3.34	$ 2.39

Source: PepsiCo Inc., 2007 10-K report.

acquisitions totaling $522 million in 2006 and $1.1 billion in 2005. The combination of acquisitions and the strength of PepsiCo's core snacks and beverages business allowed the company's revenues to increase from approximately $20 billion in 2000 to more than $39.5 billion in 2007. Exhibit 3 presents PepsiCo's consolidated statements of income for 2005–2007. The company's balance sheets for 2005–2007 are provided in Exhibit 4. The company's calculation of management operating cash flow for 2004–2007 is shown in Exhibit 5.

BUILDING SHAREHOLDER VALUE IN 2008

Three people had held the position of CEO since the company began its portfolio restructuring in 1997. Even though Roger Enrico was the chief architect of the business lineup as it stood in 2007, his successor, Steve Reinemund, and the company's CEO in 2007, Indra Nooyi, were both critically involved in the restructuring. Nooyi joined PepsiCo in 1994 and developed a reputation as a tough negotiator who engineered the 1997 spin-off of Pepsi's restaurants, spearheaded the 1998 acquisition of Tropicana, and played a critical role in the 1999 initial public offering of Pepsi's bottling operations. After being promoted to chief financial officer, Nooyi was also highly involved

in the 2001 acquisition of Quaker Oats. Nooyi was selected as the company's CEO upon Reinemund's retirement in October 2006. Nooyi had emigrated to the United States in 1978 to attend Yale's Graduate School of Business and worked with Boston Consulting Group, Motorola, and Asea Brown Boveri before arriving at PepsiCo in 1994.

In 2008, PepsiCo's corporate strategy had diversified the company into salty and sweet snacks, soft drinks, orange juice, bottled water, ready-to-drink teas and coffees, purified and functional waters, isotonic beverages, hot and ready-to-eat breakfast cereals, grain-based products, and breakfast condiments. Most PepsiCo brands had achieved number one or number two positions in their respective food and beverage categories through strategies keyed to product innovation, close relationships with distribution allies, international expansion, and strategic acquisitions. A relatively new element of PepsiCo's corporate strategy was product reformulations to make snack foods and beverages healthier. The company believed that its efforts to develop "good-for-you" or "better-for-you" products would create growth opportunities from the intersection of business and public interests.

The company was organized into four business divisions, which all followed the corporation's general strategic approach. Frito-Lay North America manufactured, marketed, and

11 percent during first six months of 2009 when compared to the same period in 2008 as volume declined, materials prices increased, and more promotions were needed to generate sales.

A summary of adidas' financial performance for 1998 through 2008 is presented in Exhibit 1. The performance of the company's common shares between October 1999 and August 2009 is provided in Exhibit 2. Exhibit 3 presents balance sheets for adidas for 2007 and 2008.

COMPANY HISTORY

The history of adidas can be traced to 1920, when German baker Adolph (nicknamed Adi) Dassler began trying his hand at designing and producing footwear for athletes competing in soccer, tennis, and track and field events. In 1924, Adolph Dassler's brother, Rudolph, joined him in the shoemaking venture to establish Gebrüder Dassler Schuhfabrik (translated in English as Dassler Brothers Shoe Factory). The Dasslers made their first major innovation in athletic shoe design in 1925 when they integrated studs and spikes into the soles of track and field shoes. The Dassler brothers continued to develop key innovations in athletic footwear such as the arch support. Many of the standard features of today's athletic footwear were developed by the Dassler brothers, with Adi Dassler alone accumulating 700 patents and property rights worldwide by the time of his death in 1978.

The Dasslers were also innovators in the field of marketing—giving away their shoes to German athletes competing in the 1928 Olympic Games in Amsterdam. By the 1936 Olympic Games in Berlin, most athletes would compete only in Gebrüder Dassler shoes, including Jesse Owens who won four gold medals in the Berlin games. By 1937, the company was making 30 different styles of shoes for athletes in 11 sports. All of the company's styles were distinguished from other brands by two stripes applied to each side of the shoe.

The Dasslers' sports shoe production ceased during World War II when Gebrüder Dassler Schuhfabrik was directed to produce boots for the armed forces of Nazi Germany. Adi Dassler was allowed to remain in Herzogenaurach to run the factory, but Rudolph (Rudi) Dassler was drafted into the army and spent a year in an Allied prisoner-of-war camp after being captured. Upon the

conclusion of the war, Rudi Dassler was released by the Allies and returned to Herzogenaurach to rejoin his family. The Dasslers returned to production of athletic shoes in 1947, but the company was dissolved in 1948 after the two brothers entered into a bitter feud. Rudi Dassler moved to the other side of the small village to establish his own shoe company, Puma Schuhfabrik Rudolph Dassler. With the departure of Rudi Dassler, Adi renamed the company adidas—a combination of his nickname and the first three letters of his last name. Adi Dassler applied a third stripe to the sides of adidas shoes and registered the three stripe trademark in 1949.

The nature of the disagreement between the two brothers was never known for certain, but the two never spoke again after their split and the feud became the foundation of both organizations' cultures while the two brothers were alive. The two rival companies were highly competitive and both companies discouraged employees from fraternizing with cross-town rivals. An adidas spokesperson described the seriousness of the feud: "Puma employees wouldn't be caught dead with adidas employees. . . . It wouldn't be allowed that an adidas employee would fall in love with a Puma employee."[2]

Adi Dassler kept up his string of innovations with molded rubber cleats in 1949, and in 1952 he developed track shoes with screw-in spikes. He expanded the concept to soccer shoes in 1954 with screw-in studs, which has been partially credited for Germany's World Cup Championship that year. By 1960, adidas was the clear favorite among athletic footwear brands with 75 percent of all track and field athletes competing in the Olympic Games in Rome wearing adidas shoes. The company began producing soccer balls in 1963 and athletic apparel in 1967. The company's dominance in the athletic footwear industry continued through the early 1970s with 1,164 of the 1,490 athletes competing in the 1972 Olympic Games in Munich wearing adidas shoes. As jogging developed into a popular recreational activity in the early 1970s, adidas became the leading brand of consumer jogging shoe in the United States. Also, T-shirts and other apparel bearing adidas' three-lobed trefoil logo were popular wardrobe items for U.S. teenagers during the 1970s.

At the time of Adi Dassler's death in 1978, adidas remained the worldwide leader in athletic footwear, but the company was rapidly losing

Exhibit 1   Financial Summary for adidas AG, 1998–2008 (in millions except per share data)

	2008	2007	2006	2005	2004	2003	2002	2001	2000	1999	1998
Net sales	€ 10,799	€ 10,299	€ 10,084	€ 6,636	€ 5,860	€ 6,267	€ 6,523	€ 6,112	€ 5,835	€ 5,354	€ 5,065
Cost of sales	5,543	5,417	5,589	3,439	3,047	3,453	3,704	3,511	3,307	3,002	2,941
Gross profit	5,256	4,882	4,495	3,197	2,813	2,814	2,819	2,601	2,528	2,352	2,124
Royalty and commission income	89	102	90	47	42	42	46	42	43	35	45
Operating expenses	4,275	4,035	3,704	2,537	2,236	2,324	2,343	2,126	2,091	1,870	1,698
Operating profit	1,070	949	881	707	584	490	477	475	437	482	416
Financial expenses, net	166	135	158	52	59	49	87	102	94	84	115
Income before taxes	904	815	723	655	526	438	390	376	347	398	319
Income taxes	260	260	227	221	193	167	148	147	140	153	105
Minority interests	2	4	13	8	7	11	14	21	25	18	9
Net income	€ 642	€ 551	€ 483	€ 426	€ 326	€ 260	€ 228	€ 208	€ 182	€ 227	€ 205
Basic earnings per share	€ 3.25	€ 2.71	€ 2.37	€ 2.05	€ 1.72	€ 1.43	€ 1.26	€ 1.15	€ 1.00	€ 1.26	€ 1.13
Diluted earnings per share	€ 3.07	€ 2.57	€ 2.25	€ 1.93	€ 1.64	€ 1.43	€ 1.26	€ 1.15	€ 1.00	€ 1.26	€ 1.16
Dividends per share	€ 0.50	€ 0.50	€ 0.42	€ 0.33	€ 0.33	€ 0.25	€ 0.25	€ 0.23	€ 0.23	€ 0.23	€ 0.21
Number of shares outstanding at year-end	193,516	203,629	203,537	203,047	183,436	181,816	181,692	181,396	181,396	181,396	181,396

Source: adidas AG Annual Reports, various years.

Exhibit 2   Performance of adidas AG's Stock Price, October 1999–August 2009

(a) Trend in adidas AG's Common Stock Price

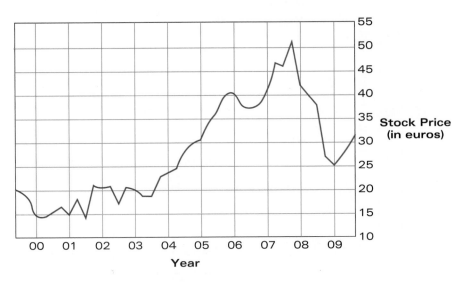

**(b) Performance of adidas AG's Stock Price
versus the DAX Index**

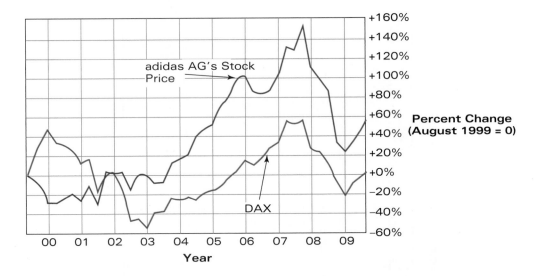

market share in the United States to industry newcomer Nike. The first Nike shoes appeared in the 1972 U.S. Olympic Trials in Eugene, Oregon, and had become the best-selling training shoe in the United States by 1974. Both Adi Dassler and his son Horst, who took over as adidas' chief manager after Adi Dassler's death, severely underestimated the threat of Nike. With adidas perhaps more concerned with cross-town adversary Puma, Nike pulled ahead of its European rivals in the U.S. athletic footwear market by launching new styles in a variety of colors and by signing recognizable sports figures to endorsement contracts. Even though Nike was becoming the market leader in U.S. athletic footwear market, adidas was able to retain its number-one ranking among competitive athletes, with 259 gold medal winners in the 1984 Olympic Summer

Exhibit 3 **Adidas AG Balance Sheets, 2007–2008 (in millions)**

	December 31, 2008	December 31, 2007
Assets		
Cash and cash equivalents	€ 244	€ 295
Short-term financial assets	141	86
Accounts receivable	1,624	1,459
Inventories	1,995	1,629
Other current assets	930	669
Total current assets	4,934	4,138
Property, plant and equipment, net	886	702
Goodwill, net	1,499	1,436
Trademarks	1,390	1,291
Other intangible assets, net	204	194
Long-term financial assets	96	103
Deferred tax assets	344	315
Other noncurrent assets	180	147
Total noncurrent assets	4,599	4,188
Total assets	€ 9,533	€ 8,325
Liabilities, minority interests and shareholders' equity		
Short-term borrowings	€ 797	€ 186
Accounts payable	1,218	849
Income taxes	321	285
Accrued liabilities and provisions	1,008	1,025
Other current liabilities	301	270
Total current liabilities	3,645	2,615
Long-term borrowings	1,776	1,960
Pensions and similar obligations	132	124
Deferred tax liabilities	463	450
Other noncurrent liabilities	117	142
Total noncurrent liabilities	2,488	2,676
Minority interests	14	11
Shareholders' equity	3,386	3,023
Total liabilities, minority interests and shareholders' equity	€ 9,533	€ 8,325

Source: Adidas AG 2008 Annual Report.

Games in Los Angeles wearing adidas products. Only 65 Olympic athletes wore Nike shoes during the 1984 Summer Games, but the company signed up-and-coming NBA star Michael Jordan to a $2.5 million endorsement contract after adidas passed on the opportunity earlier in the year. At the time of Horst Dassler's unexpected death in 1987, Nike was the undisputed leader in the U.S. athletic footwear market with more than $1 billion in annual sales.

Adidas' performance spiraled downward after the death of Horst Dassler, with no clear direction from the top and quality and innovation rapidly deteriorating. By 1990, adidas had fallen to a number-eight ranking in the U.S. athletic footwear market and held only a 2 percent share of the market. A number of management and ownership changes occurred between Horst Dassler's death in 1987 and 1993, when a controlling interest in the company was acquired by a group of investors led by French advertising executive Robert Louis-Dreyfus. Louis-Dreyfus launched a dramatic turnaround of the company—cutting costs, improving styling, launching new models, and signing endorsement contracts with popular athletes such as Kobe Bryant, Anna Kournikova, and David Beckham. At year-end 1994, adidas had increased its annual sales in the United States by 75 percent from the prior year and improved its market share enough to become the third largest seller of athletic footwear in the United States, trailing only Nike and Reebok.

THE 1998 SALOMON SA ACQUISITION

Even though the company's turnaround had produced outstanding results with sales and earnings growing at annual rates of 38.3 percent and 37.5 percent, respectively, between 1995 and 1997, the company was a distant number three in the worldwide athletic footwear and apparel industry. Nike's 1997 revenues of $9.2 billion were nearly three times greater than that of adidas, and Nike continued to grow at a fast pace as it expanded into more international markets. In late 1997, Louis-Dreyfus and the family owners of Salomon SA, a French sports equipment manufacturer, agreed to a €1.5 billion merger that would diversify adidas beyond footwear and apparel into ski equipment, golf clubs, bicycle components, and winter sports apparel. Salomon's business lineup contained a large number of strong businesses—its Salomon ski division was the leading producer of ski equipment; TaylorMade Golf was the second largest seller of golf equipment; and Mavic was the leading producer of high-performance bicycle wheels and rims. Other Salomon businesses included Bonfire snowboard apparel and Cliché skateboard equipment.

Adidas' €1.5 billion acquisition of Salomon SA allowed it to surpass Reebok to become the world's second largest sporting goods company with 1998 sales of nearly €5.1 billion. The price of adidas' shares fell upon the announcement of the acquisition over concerns about the high price adidas agreed to pay for Salomon and how the company might finance the acquisition. There was also some concern among investors that adidas did not have expertise in manufacturing sports equipment since its apparel and footwear were produced by contract manufacturers. A Merrill Lynch analyst suggested the Salomon acquisition might prove troublesome for adidas since other athletic shoe companies had "dabbled in the hard goods segment, but they have been unsuccessful to date in making inroads."[3]

Louis-Dreyfus expected the Salomon acquisition to boost the company's pretax profits by 20–25 percent annually through 2000. However, Louis-Dreyfus' projections never materialized with adidas taking control of Salomon just as the winter sports equipment and golf equipment industries were becoming less attractive. The poor performance of Salomon and TaylorMade in 1998 led to a net loss of $164 million for adidas-Salomon during the first nine months of its fiscal year. To make matters worse, the integration of Salomon's bicycle components, skateboard, winter sports, and golf equipment businesses did not go as smoothly as Louis-Dreyfus and adidas' shareholders had expected.

By summer 1999, adidas-Salomon's share price had declined by more than a third from its early 1998 high, and most large investors believed adidas had "bitten off more than it could chew" with the acquisition.[4] Robert Louis-Dreyfus announced in early 2000 that he would step down from adidas-Salomon and rejoin his family's business in France in early 2001. Herbert Hainer, the company's head of marketing in Europe and Asia, was tapped as his replacement to run the diversified sporting goods company. Under Hainer's leadership, the company cut costs, introduced new apparel and footwear products, increased the company's advertising, signed additional athletes to endorsement contracts, and opened extended retail distribution to company-owned stores.

ADIDAS' BROAD CORPORATE RESTRUCTURING PLAN

Adidas' 1998 acquisition of diversified sporting goods producer Salomon was expected to allow the athletic footwear company to vault over Nike to become the leader of the global sporting goods industry. But almost as soon as the deal was consummated, it looked doubtful that the €1.5 billion acquisition of Salomon would help adidas achieve its strategic intent. Chief concerns with the acquisition were the declining attractiveness of the winter sports industry and integration problems between the adidas footwear and apparel business and Salomon's business units. Not until 2003, five years after the acquisition, had adidas' earnings per share returned to the level that shareholders enjoyed in 1997. In addition, the company's stock price failed to return to its 1998 trading range until 2004. The Salomon winter sports business had contributed very little operating profit to the company's overall financial performance since its acquisition, and the TaylorMade-adidas Golf division had struggled at various times to deliver good earnings. However, TaylorMade seemed to have turned the corner in 2005 with sales and operating earnings finally improving after a three-year decline.

The 2005 Divestiture of Salomon Business Units

The company divested all of its winter sports brands and Mavic bicycle components business in October 2005 to Amer Sports Corporation for €485 million. Amer Sports was the maker of Atomic skis and Wilson sporting goods. The divestiture of Salomon's winter sports and bicycle

components business would make TaylorMade Golf the lone business retained from the company's 1998 acquisition of Salomon SA. Upon the completion of the Salomon divestiture, adidas-Salomon's shareholders approved a resolution to change the company's name to adidas AG.

The 2006 Acquisition of Reebok International Ltd.

With the Salomon divestiture to Amer Sports all but consummated, adidas management announced in August 2005 that it would acquire Reebok International Ltd. for €3.1 billion. The acquisition of Reebok would be the final component of a restructuring initiative that would focus the company's business lineup primarily on athletic footwear and apparel and golf equipment by 2006. In addition to Reebok-branded athletic footwear and apparel, Reebok International also designed, marketed, and sold Rockport footwear, Greg Norman apparel, and CCM hockey equipment. In 2004, Rockport and Reebok's hockey brands contributed $377.6 million and $146.0 million, respectively, to the company's total sales of nearly $3.8 billion. The company's sales of Greg Norman golf apparel approximated $50 million in 2004. Exhibit 4 provides

Exhibit 4 Reebok International Net Sales, 2002–2004

Reebok International's net sales by product type:			
	2004	**2003**	**2002**
Net sales:			
Footwear	$ 2,430,311	$ 2,226,712	$ 2,060,725
Apparel	1,354,973	1,258,604	1,067,147
	$ 3,785,284	$ 3,485,316	$ 3,127,872

Reebok International's net sales by geographic region:			
	2004	**2003**	**2002**
Net sales:			
United States	$ 2,069,055	$ 2,021,396	$ 1,807,657
United Kingdom	474,704	444,693	416,775
Europe	810,418	692,400	607,381
Other countries	431,107	326,827	296,059
	$ 3,785,284	$ 3,485,316	$ 3,127,872

Source: Reebok International, Ltd. 2004 10-K.

Reebok International's sales by product line and by geographic region for 2002 through 2004.

The Reebok acquisition, which was finalized in 2006, increased the company's revenues from €5.8 billion in 2005 to €10.1 in 2006 and allowed sales in North America to more than double between 2005 and 2006. In addition, adidas expected to capture annual cost-sharing benefits of approximately €125 million within three years of the closing date. The company's post-merger branding strategy would position adidas as a technologically superior shoe designed for serious athletes, while Reebok would be positioned as a leisure shoe that would sell at middle price points. Adidas divested the Greg Norman golf apparel line shortly after the completion of the Reebok acquisition.

Performance Expectations for Adidas' Restructured Business Lineup

Even though the restructured lineup of businesses offered adidas an improved chance of catching Nike in its race to be the world's largest sporting goods company, some observers were not convinced the move would prove to be any more successful than the company's 1998 acquisition of Salomon. The president of a sports marketing firm doubted adidas' "German mentality of control, engineering, and production" would prove to be compatible with Reebok's "U.S. marketing-driven culture" and added "in reality, I don't think [the merged company] is going to dent the market, because Nike is already too far ahead."[5] A Goldman Sachs analyst added "We fail to see how this combo will erode Nike's franchise as the global brand leader."[6]

ADIDAS' CORPORATE STRATEGY IN 2009

In 2009, adidas' businesses were organized under three units based around the company's core brands—adidas, Reebok, and Taylor Made-adidas Golf. The company's corporate strategy was focused on extending its leadership in product innovation, creating a differentiated image for the products offered by each of its three business segments, expanding controlled retail space

through its network of company-owned stores, and achieving efficiencies in its global supply chain processes and activities. The relative performance of adidas' business units during 1998 through 2008 is presented in Exhibit 5.

Adidas' corporate focus on product design and innovation contributed to the differentiation strategies employed in each of its businesses. Each business unit was expected to develop at least one major product innovation per year in each product category. In 2009, TaylorMade Golf introduced its r9 driver that incorporated nine movable weights and an adjustable shaft. The movable weights and adjustable shaft allowed golfers to create 24 different configurations to produce over 1,000 different ball flight trajectories. In 2008, the adidas athletic footwear and apparel division introduced its innovative SelectRide running shoe and F50 Tunit soccer shoe families and a Cirque du Soleil gym and yoga apparel collection. Reebok's most notable product launch in 2008 was its EasyTone women's walking shoe line that utilized spongy balance pods in the sole to encourage leg toning while walking or exercising. The company also improved the comfort of its Rockport footwear collection in 2008 by incorporating its Torsion system developed for adidas running shoes.

Adidas also relied heavily on ongoing brand-building activities to further differentiate adidas, Reebok, and TaylorMade from competing brands of sporting goods. Partnerships with major sporting events around the world and with notable athletes competing in track and field, soccer, basketball, tennis, and golf were critical to creating a distinctive image with consumers. The company also attempted to provide its retailers with superior customer service, including on-time deliveries, since retailer activities were such important elements of the sporting goods industry value chain.

Adidas management believed that controlled retail space would provide customers with a thorough understanding of product features and offer consumers a rewarding point-of-sale experience. In 2009, the company's controlled space included mono-branded retail stores, shop-in-shop locations, factory outlet stores, team apparel stores located in stadiums and arenas, and e-commerce sites. Adidas had opened company-owned retail stores in the United States and Europe and such emerging markets as Russia and China. Adidas management expected its company-owned retail

Adidas AG Financial Data by Operating Segment, 1998–2008 (in millions)

Business Segment	2008	2007	2006	2005	2004	2003	2002	2001	2000	1999	1998
Adidas											
Sales	€7,821	€7,133	€6,626	€5,861	€5,174	€4,950	€5,105	€4,825	€4,672	€4,427	€4,316
Gross profit	3,802	3,370	3,059	2,654	2,284	2,008	2,004	1,845	1,907	1,827	1,818
Operating profit	1,098	920	788	693	564	365	343	352	391	431	412
Operating assets	3,872	3,329	3,211	2,526	2,089	2,172	2,294	1,954	2,286	1,987	1,730
Capital expenditures	189	150	135	138	85	63	84	113	93	105	102
Amortization and depreciation	117	104	91	69	56	56	63	57	52	45	48
Reebok[1]											
Sales	€2,148	€2,333	€2,473	—	—	—	—	—	—	—	—
Gross profit	795	902	863	—	—	—	—	—	—	—	—
Operating profit	(7)	109	86	—	—	—	—	—	—	—	—
Operating assets	3,033	2,913	3,217	—	—	—	—	—	—	—	—
Capital expenditures	53	57	72	—	—	—	—	—	—	—	—
Amortization and depreciation	60	60	53	—	—	—	—	—	—	—	—
TaylorMade-adidas Golf											
Sales	€812	€804	€856	€709	€633	€637	€707	€545	€441	€327	€263
Gross profit	359	360	376	312	298	290	345	281	221	160	118
Operating profit	78	65	73	50	48	67	74	63	44	30	20
Operating assets	748	629	656	692	619	391	433	316	219	156	99
Capital expenditures	15	12	13	17	9	12	49	16	12	10	16
Amortization and depreciation	11	12	13	13	11	9	7	6	4	4	2
Salomon											
Net sales	—	—	—	—	€653	€658	€684	€714	€703	€587	€487
Gross profit	—	—	—	—	259	264	279	313	296	233	188
Operating profit	—	—	—	—	9	35	39	63	61	32	6
Operating assets	—	—	—	—	505	521	581	679	566	533	598
Capital expenditures	—	—	—	—	19	18	18	38	24	17	20
Amortization and depreciation	—	—	—	—	7	7	7	7	7	5	7
Corporate/Consolidation											
Sales	€18	€49	€129	€66	€53	€22	€27	€28	€19	€10	—
Gross profit	300	250	195	232	232	252	191	162	104	—	—
Operating profit	(99)	(145)	(66)	(36)	(27)	23	21	(3)	(59)	(14)	(22)
Operating assets	1,880	1,454	1,295	2,532	1,072	1,104	953	1,234	947	903	782
Capital expenditures	123	70	57	45	27	29	22	20	16	—	—
Amortization and depreciation	33	25	25	30	28	17	26	25	23	6	6

[1] 2006 financial data is for an 11-month period because of the closing date of the Reebok International acquisition by adidas AG.

Source: adidas AG 2005, 2007, and 2008 Annual Reports.

stores to generate at least 35 percent of its revenues by 2012. Exhibit 6 presents the number of adidas and Reebok locations in 2007 and 2008.

Efficient supply chain management was critical to adidas' profitability because of the importance of getting new styles to market quickly and because of the importance of low-cost manufacturing. Adidas kept its production costs low by outsourcing more than 97 percent of its footwear and 83 percent of its apparel production requirements to contract manufacturers located throughout Asia. In 2005, the company launched a "World Class Supply Chain" initiative to improve coordination with its contract manufacturers, get new products to market more quickly, and lower costs. The initiative allowed adidas to reduce its number of contract manufacturers from 547 in 2005 to 300 in 2008, thereby reducing complexities in its procurement planning. The reduced number of suppliers also allowed the company to better respond to rapid changes in the marketplace that called for certain styles to be discontinued or production of others to be increased. The fewer number of contract manufacturers also allowed Adidas to speed its product design-to-market cycle times. Adidas management also reengineered replenishment activities to improve product availability to retailers without

Exhibit 6   Number of Company-Owned adidas and Reebok Retail Stores, 2007, 2008

Company-Owned adidas Retail Stores	2008	2007
Sport Performance stores	652	459
Originals stores	140	83
Sport Style stores	4	—
Factory outlets	381	317
Concession sales locations	150	142
Consumer e-commerce sites	5	2
Total U.S. Retail Locations	1,332	1,003
Company-Owned Reebok Retail Stores	**2008**	**2007**
Factory outlets	327	287
Concept stores	253	164
Concession sales locations	67	73
	647	524

substantially boosting its inventories of footwear, apparel, and sporting goods hardware.

Adidas Footwear and Apparel

Adidas' core footwear and apparel business competed in the $125 billion sports apparel and footwear industry. The annual growth rate for the global athletic footwear and apparel industry had slowed from 6.8 percent in 2005 to 3.3 percent in 2007. At about $42.5 billion, North America was the largest market for athletic apparel and footwear, but its 3 percent annual growth rate was greater than only Europe's 2 percent annual growth rate among all developed and emerging markets for athletic apparel and footwear. Markets in Eastern Europe, South and Central Asia, and China grew at rates of 20 percent, 13 percent, and 15 percent, respectively, between 2006 and 2007.

In 2008, however, worldwide athletic footwear and apparel industry sales failed to grow, with the global economy for all goods and services expanding by only 2 percent compared to a 4 percent increase in global gross domestic product (GDP) in 2007. Adidas' largest markets were most affected by the global economic slowdown—GDP declined by 1.3 percent in the United States and grew by just 0.9 percent in Europe during 2008. Latin America and Asia had been less affected by the recession with the GDPs of both Asia and Latin America increasing by 4.2 percent in 2008. Industry revenues grew by 4 percent in Asia and 7 percent in the Middle East/Africa in 2008 and declined in North America and Europe by 1 percent during 2008. The international economic slowdown had intensified in 2009 and had led to steeper drops in industry revenues. Most industry analysts did not expect industry sales to grow through 2010.

Adidas footwear and apparel was organized under two categories which were based upon the clothing needs of the consumer. The adidas Sport Performance group developed sports shoes and attire that was suitable for use by athletes in four key sports categories—running, soccer, basketball, and general training. The Sport Style product line was marketed to those who enjoyed the comfort of athletic apparel.

Soccer was adidas' strongest product category where it held market shares greater than 50 percent in Europe and North America. Adidas was runner-up to Nike in most other athletic categories where it competed. It maintained its advantage over other sporting attire and footwear producers primarily through innovations like its AdiSTAR cushion system for running shoes and its TECHFIT athletic apparel designed to increase blood flow during athletic activity and through endorsements by individual athletes or league sponsorships. Kevin Garnett, Dwight Howard, and Tracy McGrady were among the latest NBA athletes to endorse adidas footwear and apparel. In soccer, players such as David Beckham, Lionel Messi, and entire clubs endorsed adidas soccer shoes and clothing. Adidas was the official sponsor for the German national women's team and UEFA European soccer league teams in Munich, Amsterdam, Milan, and Madrid. Also, the adidas Roteiro was the Official Match Ball for all UEFA games. Adidas was also the official sportswear partner of the 2008 Beijing Olympics and the London Olympics set for 2012. The Sport Performance group accounted for 80 percent of adidas-branded apparel and footwear sales in 2008. Sport Performance sales increased by 15 percent between 2007 and 2008.

The company's Sport Style streetwear and lifestyle fashion group represented a relatively small fraction of adidas' overall apparel and footwear sales, but offered high profit margins because of the small research and development budget needed to design such items. Another attractive aspect of adidas' lifestyle apparel group was that the market for sports lifestyle apparel and footwear was growing at a faster rate than the market for actual sports products. The Sport Style group included two segments—adidas Originals and Y-3. Adidas Originals targeted consumers in three distinct categories—hip hop, surfers and skateboarders, and young metropolitan consumers. Adidas Originals products designed for the hip hop and surfer/skater lifestyle included items such as warm-up suits, T-shirts, and updated versions of classic adidas court shoes. The company's products targeted toward young metropolitan consumers included a jeans line developed in collaboration with Diesel and its Grün footwear collection made from recycled materials. Adidas Y-3 ready-to-wear fashion collection was developed in collaboration with designer Yohji Yamamoto. Y-3 line included apparel items such as women's tights, skirts, blouses, and leather jackets. Y-3 apparel for men included jeans, coats, leather jackets, polo shirts, and stretch pants. The Sport Style group accounted

for 20 percent of adidas-branded apparel and footwear sales in 2008. Sport Style sales improved by 10 percent between 2007 and 2008.

In 2008, Europe accounted for 50 percent of adidas-branded sales of footwear and apparel, North America accounted for 15 percent of adidas' total sales of athletic gear, Asia accounted for 27 percent of adidas-branded apparel and footwear sales, and Latin America accounted for 8 percent of the division's sales. Adidas had long held the title of market share leader in Europe's developed country markets for athletic footwear and apparel, but the company was intent to also hold leading positions in emerging markets in Eastern Europe and Asia. Sales had grown by as much as 50 percent annually in Russia and other former Soviet states such the Ukraine, Armenia, and Belarus to give it a 2-to-1 margin over runner-up Nike. Adidas management expected Russia to become its largest and most profitable market in Europe by 2010.

Asia was projected to become adidas' largest market overall within the near term because of the strong demand for athletic footwear and apparel in Asia and the vast numbers of consumers living in Asian country markets. Asia made up more than two-thirds of the world's population in 2008, and was projected to grow from 3.2 billion people in 2008 to 3.6 billion people by 2028. Adidas' emphasis on emerging markets had made it the largest seller of athletic gear in Asia in 2008 and the company expected to displace Nike as market leader in Latin America by 2010. The share of the North American athletic footwear market held by adidas-branded athletic footwear had declined from 10.62 percent in 2006 to 5.86 percent in 2008. Exhibit 7 presents

Exhibit 7 U.S. Retail Market Shares for the Leading Sellers of Athletic Footwear, 2006–2008

Brand	2006	2007	2008
Nike*	29.73%	31.52%	34.61%
New Balance	9.26	8.03	6.26
Adidas	10.62	6.93	5.86
Reebok	4.68	4.43	2.66

*Does not include the Nike-owned Jordan or Converse brands.

Source: SportsOneSource.

market shares for the largest sellers of athletic footwear in the United States for 2006 through 2008. Exhibit 8 presents a summary of adidas AG's geographic financial performance for 1998 through 2008.

Reebok

The Reebok brand was acquired by adidas AG in 2006 to boost the company's sales in North America. Approximately $2 billion of Reebok International's 2004 sales of $3.7 billion were generated in North America from the sale of Reebok athletic footwear and apparel; Reebok and CCM hockey skates, uniforms, and gear; Rockport men's shoes; and Greg Norman golf apparel. Adidas divested the Greg Norman apparel line soon after the completion of the 2006 acquisition of Reebok International.

At the time of its acquisition by adidas, the Reebok brand suffered from a poor reputation for quality, innovation, and styling. The company had struggled to develop a strong image with it changing marketing campaigns on a regular basis. Since Nike's launch of its "Just Do It" advertising campaign in 1988, Reebok had launched campaigns keyed to the taglines, "Time to Play," "Life is Short—Play Hard," "Pump Up," "Air Out," "Wear the Vector— Outperform," "Defy Convention," "Are You Feeling It?" "Planet Reebok," "Reebok Lets UBU," "Run Easy," and "I Am What I Am." Even though its most recent campaigns acknowledged its failure to appeal to athletically minded consumers, the brand did, however, have a loyal following among women participating in general fitness training, walking, and aerobics. In 2009, adidas management had chosen to use the Reebok brand of athletic footwear to focus on beginning and recreational runners and women athletes participating in running, aerobics, walking, and training. Reebok athletic shoes were also frequently purchased by women looking for comfortable casual shoes. The company developed a variety of new styles such as its EasyTone walking shoes that were intended to appeal to women and developed a partnership with the Avon Walk Around the World for Breast Cancer charitable organization to increase awareness of the Reebok brand among women.

Adidas management had also undertaken efforts to improve Reebok's image in men's sports with endorsements from such professional athletes as Peyton and Eli Manning, Allen Iverson, Yao Ming, David Ortiz, and Vince Young. Reebok was also the official outfitter of the National Football League and was an apparel partner with Major League Baseball. Its relationship with the National Hockey League, the American Hockey League, and the Canadian Hockey League helped solidify Reebok-CCM as the number-one seller of hockey skates and gear. Reebok and CCM both offered complete head-to-toe product lines for hockey, but in 2008 the company had begun to position CCM as a premium skate brand and Reebok as general hockey equipment and apparel brand. Adidas' strategic priority for the Rockport line of casual men's shoes was to increase the brand's sales outside of North America. Adidas management expected that more than 50 percent of Rockport's sales would be generated in Europe, Asia, and Latin America by 2010.

Adidas management had also expanded Reebok's distribution beyond its historical focus on specialty athletic footwear stores and discount family footwear retailers to both improve its image and make Reebok shoes available to a wider range of consumers. Beginning in 2008, the company increased Reebok's distribution network to include a greater number of large sporting goods stores and department stores. Distribution was also improved by the addition of 95 additional concept stores and 52 additional factory outlet stores during 2008. Adidas also moved to control distribution of Reebok in emerging markets by purchasing distribution rights in Russia, Brazil, and China, which had been sold to third parties by Reebok International management. Adidas also began purchasing distribution rights for Rockport in emerging markets, which too had been sold to third parties by Reebok International management.

Reebok's net sales declined by 2 percent between 2007 and 2008, with sales of Reebok-branded shoes and apparel remaining unchanged between 2007 and 2008, Reebok-CCM hockey revenues declining by 6 percent during the year and Rockport sales declining by 10 percent between 2007 and 2008. Between 2006 and 2007, the sales of Reebok branded athletic footwear and

Exhibit 8   Adidas AG Financial Data by Geographic Region, 1998–2008 (in millions)

Regions	2008	2007	2006	2005	2004	2003	2002	2001	2000	1999	1998
Europe											
Net sales	€ 4,665	€ 4,369	€ 4,162	€ 3,166	€ 3,068	€ 3,365	€ 3,200	€ 3,066	€ 2,860	€ 2,723	€ 2,774
Operating assets	2,319	1,819	1,808	1,376	1,461	1,428	1,396	1,419	1,107	1,167	1,114
Capital expenditures	102	105	84	57	46	44	56	74	55	40	35
North America											
Net sales	€ 2,520	€ 2,929	€ 3,234	€ 1,561	€ 1,332	€ 1,562	€ 1,960	€ 1,818	€ 1,907	€ 1,826	€ 1,784
Operating assets	1,659	1,489	1,564	325	768	778	969	945	862	848	666
Capital expenditures	45	34	49	51	27	22	82	68	54	26	29
Asia											
Net sales	€ 2,662	€ 2,254	€ 2,020	€ 1,523	€ 1,192	€ 1,116	€ 1,166	€ 1,010	€ 875	€ 663	€ 383
Operating assets	962	772	719	617	480	447	505	743	455	390	201
Capital expenditures	61	49	74	37	23	12	16	15	17	18	9
Latin America											
Net sales	€ 893	€ 657	€ 499	€ 319	€ 224	€ 179	€ 163	€ 178	€ 171	€ 126	€ 112
Operating assets	547	285	217	176	56	93	79	98	109	75	66
Capital expenditures	29	10	7	5	1	1	1	2	3	3	2
Headquarters/consolidation											
Net sales	€ 59	€ 89	€ 169	€ 66	€ 47	€ 45	€ 34	€ 40	€ 23	€ 34	€ 12
Operating assets	4,046	3,960	4,071	3,256	1,601	1,442	1,312	978	1,485	1,108	1,162
Capital expenditures	143	91	63	50	43	43	15	28	16	45	63

Source: Adidas AG 2005, 2007, and 2008 Annual Reports.

apparel declined by 7 percent, sales of hockey equipment increased by 3 percent, and Rockport sales improved by 1 percent. Net sales during the 2007 fiscal year were also negatively affected by the divestiture of its Greg Norman apparel line, which had 2006 net sales of approximately $50 million. Operating profit margins for the Reebok division decreased from a positive 4.7 percent in 2007 to a negative 0.3 percent in 2008 (see Exhibit 5).

TaylorMade-adidas Golf

TaylorMade Golf was the third largest producer of golf equipment in the $2.8 billion industry. The industry had struggled to find growth during the late 2000s as the number of golfers in the U.S. declined from more than 27 million in 1998 to 25.6 million in 2008. Also, rounds played had not grown appreciably between 2004 and 2007 and had declined by 1.8 percent during 2008 as consumers reacted to economic uncertainty by shifting discretionary income from spending to savings. Sales of golf equipment declined by 5.7 percent during 2008 and it appeared that 2009 industry sales would decline by an additional 15 to 20 percent.

TaylorMade-adidas Golf management expected to increase sales primarily through market share gains since they had concluded that it would be unwise to count on growth of the game. TaylorMade believed it could increase market share through endorsement contracts with touring professionals on the PGA Tour and other professional tours and through new product innovations like the movable weight and adjustable shaft systems used in its r9 driver. TaylorMade management also wished to achieve revenue growth by increasing sales in Asia. The company had successfully increased its sales in Asia from 13 percent of sales in 1999 to 37 percent of sales in 2008, and the United States accounted for less than 50 percent of sales in 2008 versus 69 percent of sales in 1999.

In 2009, TaylorMade was the largest seller of drivers, fairway woods, and hybrid clubs. Taylor-Made maintained its lead in the driver category of the golf equipment industry with updated models that were launched at 12–18 month intervals. In 2009, the company's flagship r9 driver was among the most innovative in the industry and sold at a

price point of $500. TaylorMade offered drivers at four different price points, with two r9 sub-models selling for $400 and $300, two r7 models selling for $300 and $200, and three Burner models selling at price points of $400, $300, and $200.

Even though TaylorMade achieved the number-one ranking in metalwoods, its market share in irons was about one-half that of industry leader Callaway Golf Company, and its market share in wedges and putters was negligible. TaylorMade also produced and marketed a line of golf balls, but had not achieved any significant market success in the product category.

The sales of TaylorMade's adidas-branded golf apparel and golf shoes had grown at compounded annual rates of 23 percent and 13 percent, respectively, between 2004 and 2008 through the continued introduction of new styles and exposure on the professional tours by such well-known golfers as Sergio Garcia, Natalie Gulbis, Paula Creamer, and Retief Goosen. In all, TaylorMade-adidas Golf had signed endorsement contracts with 70 golfers on the men's and women's professional tours. The heavy reliance on endorsements by touring professionals made adidas the most widely worn apparel brand on the professional tours. Some of its touring staff was also compensated to use TaylorMade's TP Red or TP Black golf balls during tournaments. TaylorMade also had limited contracts with an additional 40 golfers to use TaylorMade drivers during professional tournaments. Exhibit 9 presents the TaylorMade-adidas Golf division's sales by product category for 2004–2008.

Exhibit 9   TaylorMade-adidas Golf Sales Contribution by Product Line, 2004–2008 (in millions)

	2008	2007	2006	2005	2004
Metalwoods	€ 309	€ 338	€ 325	€ 319	€ 304
Apparel	162	145	197	99	70
Footwear	73	72	60	50	44
Other hardware*	268	249	274	255	215

*Other hardware includes irons, putters, golf balls, golf bags, gloves, and other accessories.

Source: adidas AG annual reports, various years.

ADIDAS AG'S PERFORMANCE IN 2009

At mid-year 2008, there were signs that adidas AG's corporate strategies were bringing about the hoped-for improvement in the company's financial performance. During the first six months of 2008, corporate revenues increased by 12 percent, with sales for the adidas business unit growing by 16 percent during the six-month period and sales at TaylorMade-adidas Golf growing by 11 during the first six months of 2008. Sales at Reebok declined by 2 percent during the first six months of 2008. The revenue growth and cost savings resulting from the Reebok integration allowed adidas AG's gross margins and operating margins to improve by 2.5 percentage points and 1.1 percentage points, respectively, during the first half of 2008. Earnings per share increased by 25 percent during the first half of 2008 and the company's improvement in free cash flow allowed the company to buy back nearly 7.7 million shares at an average price of €41.35 per share. The company also used its free cash flows in 2008 to fund the acquisitions of Saxon Athletic Manufacturing for $4.2 million and Textronics for $35 million. Textronics was the developer and manufacturer of wearable sensors used for fitness and health monitoring, and Saxon Athletic designed, manufactured, and marketed team uniforms worn by various sports teams throughout North America.

However, the effects of the international recession had severely damaged the company's 2009 performance and raised concerns about the long-term effectiveness of its 2005–2006 corporate restructuring plan. The company's total revenues during the first six months of 2009 declined by 7 percent when compared to the same period in 2008, and its net income for the six-month period declined by 95 percent when compared to the first six months of 2008. Sales during the first half of 2009 declined in all geographic regions except Latin America, with sales in North America declining by 10 percent, sales in Europe declining by 8 percent, and sales in Asia falling by 9 percent. Total revenues in Latin America increased by 24 percent during the first six months of 2009. Adidas-branded apparel and footwear remained the strength of the company's portfolio, with operating profits increasing by 7.2 percent between the second quarter of 2008 and the second quarter of 2009. Operating profits at TaylorMade-adidas Golf fell by 89 percent between the first half of 2008 and the first half of 2009 and the company's Reebok division recorded operating losses of nearly €150 million during the first six months of 2009. Adidas management expected its ongoing restructuring efforts would result in cost savings of €100 million by year-end 2009.

ENDNOTES

[1] As quoted in "Reebok and adidas: A Good Fit," *BusinessWeek Online*, August 4, 2005.

[2] As quoted in "The Brothers Dassler Fight On," *Deutsche Welle*, dw-world.de.

[3] As quoted in "Sporting Goods Consolidation off to the Races," *Mergers & Acquisitions Report*, November 10, 1997.

[4] As quoted in "Sports Goods/Shareholders Criticize Salomon Takeover," *Handesblatt*, May 21, 1999.

[5] As quoted in "Reebok and adidas: A Good Fit."

[6] Ibid.

Robin Hood

Joseph Lampel
New York University

It was in the spring of the second year of his insurrection against the High Sheriff of Nottingham that Robin Hood took a walk in Sherwood Forest. As he walked he pondered the progress of the campaign, the disposition of his forces, the Sheriff's recent moves, and the options that confronted him.

The revolt against the Sheriff had begun as a personal crusade. It erupted out of Robin's conflict with the Sheriff and his administration. However, alone Robin Hood could do little. He therefore sought allies, men with grievances and a deep sense of justice. Later he welcomed all who came, asking few questions and demanding only a willingness to serve. Strength, he believed, lay in numbers.

He spent the first year forging the group into a disciplined band, united in enmity against the Sheriff and willing to live outside the law. The band's organization was simple. Robin ruled supreme, making all important decisions. He delegated specific tasks to his lieutenants. Will Scarlett was in charge of intelligence and scouting. His main job was to shadow the Sheriff and his men, always alert to their next move. He also collected information on the travel plans of rich merchants and tax collectors. Little John kept discipline among the men and saw to it that their archery was at the high peak that their profession demanded. Scarlock took care of the finances, converting loot to cash, paying shares of the take, and finding suitable hiding places for the surplus. Finally, Much the Miller's son had the difficult task of provisioning the ever-increasing band of Merrymen.

Copyright © 1991, by Joseph Lampel.

The increasing size of the band was a source of satisfaction for Robin, but also a source of concern. The fame of his Merrymen was spreading, and new recruits were pouring in from every corner of England. As the band grew larger, their small bivouac became a major encampment. Between raids the men milled about, talking and playing games. Vigilance was in decline, and discipline was becoming harder to enforce. "Why," Robin reflected, "I don't know half the men I run into these days."

The growing band was also beginning to exceed the food capacity of the forest. Game was becoming scarce, and supplies had to be obtained from outlying villages. The cost of buying food was beginning to drain the band's financial reserves at the very moment when revenues were in decline. Travelers, especially those with the most to lose, were now giving the forest a wide berth. This was costly and inconvenient to them, but it was preferable to having all their goods confiscated.

Robin believed that the time had come for the Merrymen to change their policy of outright confiscation of goods to one of a fixed transit tax. His lieutenants strongly resisted this idea. They were proud of the Merrymen's famous motto: "Rob the rich and give to the poor." "The farmers and the townspeople," they argued, "are our most important allies. How can we tax them, and still hope for their help in our fight against the Sheriff?"

Robin wondered how long the Merrymen could keep to the ways and methods of their early days. The Sheriff was growing stronger and becoming better organized. He now had the money and the men and was beginning to harass the band, probing for its weaknesses. The tide of events was beginning to turn against the Merrymen. Robin felt that the campaign must be decisively concluded before the Sheriff had a chance to deliver a mortal blow. "But how," he wondered, "could this be done?"

Robin had often entertained the possibility of killing the Sheriff, but the chances for this seemed increasingly remote. Besides, killing the Sheriff might satisfy his personal thirst for revenge, but it would not improve the situation. Robin had hoped that the perpetual state of unrest, and the Sheriff's failure to collect taxes, would lead to his removal from office. Instead, the Sheriff used his political connections to obtain reinforcement. He had powerful friends at court and was well regarded by the regent, Prince John.

Prince John was vicious and volatile. He was consumed by his unpopularity among the people, who wanted the imprisoned King Richard back. He also lived in constant fear of the barons, who had first given him the regency but were now beginning to dispute his claim to the throne. Several of these barons had set out to collect the ransom that would release King Richard the Lionheart from his jail in Austria. Robin was invited to join the conspiracy in return for future amnesty. It was a dangerous proposition. Provincial banditry was one thing, court intrigue another. Prince John had spies everywhere, and he was known for his vindictiveness. If the conspirators' plan failed, the pursuit would be relentless, and retributions swift.

The sound of the supper horn startled Robin from his thoughts. There was the smell of roasting venison in the air. Nothing was resolved or settled. Robin headed for camp promising himself that he would give these problems his utmost attention after tomorrow's raid.

Shangri-La Hotels

Dennis Campbell
Harvard Business School

Brent Kazan
Harvard Business School

I n November 2006, Symon Bridle, the newly appointed chief operating officer of Shangri-La Hotels and Resorts, was reviewing the progress the Hong Kong–based company had made over the previous 10 years as it grew from a regionally focused business into a rapidly expanding international deluxe hotel group. With 18,400 employees, 50 hotels, and $842 million in revenues, Shangri-La Hotels and Resorts (Shangri-La) was a leading player in the luxury hotel industry. The company was growing rapidly to satisfy increased demand for deluxe hotels and resorts in Asia, Europe, and North America and Bridle was in charge of ensuring that Shangri-La's signature standards of "Shangri-La Hospitality," a service model based on traditional Asian hospitality, were maintained during this expansion.

For the past two weeks, Bridle and a task force of his top managers had been discussing a number of organizational issues that presented challenges to Shangri-La's rapid expansion strategy. There were three major issues at hand: (1) the company was expanding into high-wage economies in Europe and North America; (2) the company was expanding its presence in China— a country where front-line employees were not used to exercising decision-making authority; and (3) newcomers in the Chinese hotel market were poaching Shangri-La's staff and driving up wages in historically low-wage markets.

All of these issues weighed on Bridle's mind as he wondered what he should do next. "How do you still articulate your brand in tight labor markets with these pressure points?" he pondered.

CORPORATE BACKGROUND

Shangri-La Hotels and Resorts, a deluxe Asian hotel chain, was founded in 1971 in Singapore by the Malaysian-Chinese tycoon Robert Kuok. Inspired by British author James Hilton's legendary novel *Lost Horizon,* the name "Shangri-La" meant "eternal youth, peace and tranquility" and embodied the serenity and service for which the hotel chain was renowned throughout the world.

With its first and flagship hotel in Singapore, the company quickly differentiated itself from the competition and provided distinctive Asian standards of hospitality and service. Within a decade, Hong Kong–based Shangri-La established a world-class reputation and became one of the world's finest hotel management companies, garnering international awards and recognition from prestigious publications and industry partners—"Best Business Hotel Chain in Asia Pacific" by *Business Traveler* (U.K. and Germany) and "Best Hotel Chain" by *Chinese Hurun Report* (China)[1]—along the way.

HARVARD|BUSINESS|SCHOOL

9-108-006

Copyright © 2008 by the President and Fellows of Harvard College. Harvard Business School Case 9-108-006. This case was prepared by Professor Dennis Campbell and Research Associate Brent Kazan as the basis for class discussion rather than to illustrate either effective or ineffective handling of an administrative situation. Reprinted by permission of Harvard Business School.

As of 2006, Shangri-La had four main business segments: hotel ownership and operations, property development including commercial buildings and serviced apartments, hotel management services to group-owned and third-party hotels, and spas.

Expansion History

In the early 1980s, Shangri-La went through a period of rapid expansion in Asia and built 29 hotels over the next decade. The hotel chain continued to prosper throughout the 1990s, in step with Asia's economic boom. By 1999, Shangri-La had a total of 35 hotels and resorts located in Asia's most sought-after leisure destinations. In the following years, the company continued to grow. To raise funds for expansion, Shangri-La subsidiaries in various countries, including Malaysia and Thailand, were incorporated and listed on local stock exchanges between 1982 and 2002, under Shangri-La Asia.

In the early 2000s, Shangri-La began expanding beyond its core Asian markets through both management contracts and owner/operator developments. The Shangri-La Dubai, in the United Arab Emirates, opened in July 2003, followed a year later by the Traders Hotel Dubai, and a destination Shangri-La & Spa Resort in Muscat, Oman. Opportunities were also taken in Sydney (2003) and Cairns (2004) in Australia, while contracts were signed for upcoming properties in North America (Vancouver, Chicago, Las Vegas, Toronto, Miami, New York) and Europe (London, Paris, Vienna).

As of 2006, Shangri-La was the largest Asian-based deluxe hotel group in Southeast Asia. The company managed a total of 50 hotels under two brands: the five-star Shangri-La and the four-star Traders—a sister brand established in 1989 to deliver high value, mid-range, quality accommodation to the business traveler—with total inventory of over 23,000 rooms across 39 locations (see Exhibit 1 for locations).[2] As of November 2006, the company still had over 40 projects under development worldwide (see Exhibit 2).

Despite its aggressive expansion elsewhere, the company remained focused on business and capital investments in the Asia-Pacific region, in particular China. The primary reason for this decision was the fact that China's successive relaxation of travel restrictions dating back to the late 1980s, coupled with rising urban incomes, had created a boom in Chinese domestic and outbound travel. In addition, inbound international travel was also increasing. The country had recently entered into the World Trade Organization and its capital, Beijing, was selected as the host of the 2008 Olympics. With an additional role as the host of the World

Exhibit 1 Shangri-La Hotels and Resorts Growth Timeline

1971	April	Shangri-La Hotel, Singapore, opens (managed by Westin until January 1983)
1979		Kuok Hotels established to manage three properties:
		Rasa Sayang (2004 November) temporarily closed for re-development and re-opened in September 2006
		Golden Sands
		The Fijian
1981	April	Kowloon Shangri-La opens (managed by Westin until April 1991)
1983	January	Shangri-La International Hotel Management Limited (management takeover of Shangri-La Hotel, Singapore)
1984	November	Shangri-La Hotel, Hangzhou (management takeover of Hangzhou Hotel)
1985	April	Shangri-La Hotel, Kuala Lumpur opens
1986	March	Shangri-La Hotel, Bangkok opens
	April	Shangri-La Hotel, Penang opens
	October	Shangri-La Hotel, Beijing opens

(Continued)

Exhibit 1   *(Concluded)*

1988	December	Shangri-La's Tanjung Aru Resort, Kota Kinabalu (management takeover)
1989	December	Traders Hotel, Beijing opens
1990	July	China World Hotel, Beijing opens
1991	March	Island Shangri-La, Hong Kong opens
	April	Kowloon Shangri-La, Hong Kong (Shangri-La assumes management)
1992	August	Edsa Shangri-La, Manila opens
	September	Shangri-La Hotel, Shenzhen opens
1993	March	Rasa Sentosa Resort, Singapore opens
	April	Makati Shangri-La, Manila opens
	June	Shangri-La Golden Flower, Xian (management takeover)
	October	Shangri-La's Mactan Island Resort & Spa, Cebu opens
1994	March	Shangri-La Hotel, Jakarta opens
	March	Shangri-La's Far Eastern Plaza Hotel, Taipei opens
1995	January	Rebranding of Traders Hotel, Manila
	January	Shangri-La Hotel, Surabaya opens
	April	Traders Hotel, Singapore opens
1996	April	Shangri-La Hotel, Beihai opens
	June	Shangri-La's Rasa Ria Resort, Kota Kinabalu opens
	August	Traders Hotel, Shenyang opens
	August	Shangri-La Hotel, Changchun opens
	November	Traders Hotel, Yangon opens
1997	August	Shangri-La Hotel, Qingdao opens
	December	Shangri-La Hotel, Dalian opens
1998	August	Pudong Shangri-La, Shanghai opens
1999	April	Shangri-La Hotel, Wuhan opens
	April	Shangri-La Hotel, Harbin opens
	August	The Kerry Centre Hotel, Beijing opens
2003	February	Putrajaya Shangri-La Hotel opens
	July	ANA Harbour Grand Hotel rebrands as Shangri-La Hotel, Sydney, Australia
	July	Shangri-La Hotel, Dubai opens
2004	January	Shangri-La Hotel, Zhongshan opens
	July	Traders Hotel, Dubai opens
	August	Shangri-La Hotel, The Marina, Cairns re-branding
2005	January	Traders Hotel, Changzhou opens
	January	Shangri-La Hotel, Fuzhou opens
	September	Shangri-La Hotel, New Delhi opens
	October	Traders Hotel, Kunshan opens
2006	February	Shangri-La's Barr Al Jissah Resort and Spa, Muscat opens
	July	Traders Hotel, Kuala Lumpur opens
	July	Shangri-La Hotel, Suzhou opens
2007	January	Shangri-La Hotel, Guangzhou opens

Source: Shangri-La Hotels and Resorts, http://www.shangri-la.com/en/home.aspx (accessed February 5, 2007).

Exhibit 2   Ongoing Shangri-La Developments

Hotel Name	Hotel Location	Expected Opening Date
Shangri-La Hotel, Chiang Mai	Chiang Mai, Thailand	2007
Shangri-La Hotel, Xian	Xian, China	2007
Shangri-La Hotel, Baotou	Baotou, China	2007
Futian Shangri-La, Shenzhen	Futian, China	2008
Shangri-La Hotel, Huhhot	Huhhot, China	2007
Shangri-La Hotel, Chengdu	Chengdu, China	2007
Shangri-La Hotel, Qaryat Al Beri, Abu Dhabi	Abu Dhabi, UAE	2007
Shangri-La Hotel, Bangalore	Bangalore, India	2008
Traders Hotel, Bangalore	Bangalore, India	2009
Shangri-La's Phuket Resort and Spa, Thailand	Phuket, Thailand	2009
Shangri-La Hotel, Manzhouli	Manzhouli, China	2008
Shangri-La Hotel, Doha	Doha, Qatar	2008
Palm Retreat Shangri-La, Bangalore	Bangalore, India	2008
Shangri-La Hotel, Ningbo	Ningbo, China	2008
Shangri-La Hotel, Vancouver	Vancouver, Canada	2009
Shangri-La Hotel, Wenzhou	Wenzhou, China	2008
Shangri-La Hotel, Macau	Macau	2009
Traders Hotel, Macau	Macau	2009
Shangri-La's Villingili Resort and Spa, Maldives	Villingili Island, Maldives	2008
Traders Hotel, Urumqi	Urumqi, China	2009
Shangri-La's Boracay Resort and Spa, Philippines	Boracay, Philippines	2008
Shangri-La Hotel, Palais d'Iena, Paris	Paris, France	2009
Shangri-La Resort and Spa, Seychelles	Mahe, Seychelles	2009
Shangri-La Hotel, Chicago	Chicago, U.S.	2009
Shangri-La Hotel, Guilin	Guilin, China	2009
Shangri-La Hotel, Tokyo	Tokyo, Japan	2009
Shangri-La Hotel, Miami	Miami, U.S.	2010
Shangri-La Hotel, Dongguan	Dongguan, China	2009
Shangri-La Hotel, Las Vegas	Las Vegas, U.S.	2010
Shangri-La West, Jingan, Shanghai	Jingan, China	2010
Shangri-La Hotel, at London Bridge Tower, London	London, United Kingdom	2011
Shangri-La Vienna	Vienna, Austria	2010

Source: Shangri-La Hotels and Resorts, http://www.shangri-la.com/en/home.aspx, accessed February 5, 2007.

Expo 2010, Shangri-La planned to capitalize on China's economic advancement and expand its hotels in China from 17 to over 30 by 2008.[3]

Financials

Shangri-La's early focus on the Chinese market helped the company shield itself from the worst of the Asian economic crisis of 1997–98, which hit Southeast Asia hard but left China relatively unscathed. In 2005, the company benefited from continuing robust travel demand in Hong Kong and China to post revenues of $842 million (see Exhibit 3 and Exhibit 4 for financials). Both room and food and beverage revenues continued to improve and occupancy rates of Shangri-La hotels increased to 73 percent in 2005, compared with 71 percent for 2004 (see Exhibit 5 for hotel

Exhibit 3   **Shangri-La Asia Ltd., Annual Income Statements, 2002–2006***
(in USD millions)

	2006	2005	2004	2003	2002
Filed currency	USD	USD	USD	USD	USD
Net sales	$1,002.9	$ 842	$725.5	$540.4	$600.5
Revenue	1,002.9	842	725.5	540.4	600.5
Total revenue	1,002.9	842	725.5	540.4	600.5
Cost of revenue	408.8	345.6	308.5	234.4	248.8
Cost of revenue, total	408.8	345.6	308.5	234.4	248.8
Gross profit	594.1	496.4	417	306	351.8
Selling/general/ administrative expense	121.3	114.3	90.5	77.4	80.1
Total selling/general/ administrative expenses	121.3	114.3	90.5	77.4	80.1
Other operating expense	279.8	238.4	209.9	116.3	155.8
Other, net	−80.3	−44.7	−26	−23.7	−6.9
Other operating expenses, total	199.5	193.7	183.8	92.6	149.0
Total operating expense	729.6	653.6	582.8	404.4	477.8
Operating income	273.3	188.4	142.7	136	122.8
Interest expense— non-operating	−32.5	−39.9	−52.7	−48.6	−43.8
Interest capitalized— non-operating	—	7	4.4	2.3	1.7
Interest expense, Net non-operating	−32.5	−32.9	−48.3	−46.4	−42.1
Investment income—non-operating	42.0	64.3	41.0	38.8	41.7
Interest/investment income—non-operating	42.0	64.3	41.0	38.8	41.7
Interest income (expense)—net non-operating	9.5	31.5	−7.3	−7.6	−0.4
Income before tax	282.8	219.8	135.4	128.4	122.4
Total income tax	63.5	52.3	12.9	46.4	49.7
Income after tax	219.3	167.5	122.5	82	72.7
Minority interest	−17.2	−16.5	−9.0	−9.3	−9.3
Net income before extraord items	202.2	151.0	113.5	72.7	63.4
Net income	$ 202.2	$151.0	$113.5	$ 72.7	$ 63.4

*2006 projected.

Source: Shangri-La Asia Ltd. Financial Report (Reuters), via OneSource, accessed February 26, 2008.

operating statistics). While hotel operating costs were market-specific, labor, utilities, and maintenance costs together accounted for approximately 32 percent of gross operating revenue in a typical Shangri-La property in Asia with 20 percent due to labor costs and the remaining 12 percent due to utilities (7 percent) and maintenance (5 percent) costs.

Exhibit 4   **Shangri-La Asia Ltd., Summary of Balance Sheet, 2002–2006***
             (in USD millions)

	2006	2005	2004	2003	2002
Cash and short term investments	$ 380.3	$ 313.8	$ 223.9	$ 199.1	$ 164.8
Total receivables, net	112.0	126.9	157.4	152.9	166
Total inventory	22.0	20.7	18.9	17.4	15.7
Total current assets	627.6	492.1	417.2	369.4	346.4
Property/plant/equipment—net	3045	2,508.6	2,393.7	3,761.6	3,605.1
Goodwill, net	75.8	76.8	−109.0	−116.3	−122.1
Intangibles, net	393.1	385.0	379.5	—	—
Long-term investments	925.7	790.5	626.4	723.4	725.5
Other long-term assets, total	4.6	6.6	7.6	4.3	4.6
Total assets	5,075.7	4,263.1	3,720.1	4,742.5	4,559.5
Accounts Payable	107.1	213.2	150.9	331.5	266.5
Other current liabilities, total	248.3	205.2	169.1	1.7	4.9
Total current liabilities	355.4	418.4	320.0	333.2	271.4
Long-term debt	1,506.4	990.4	952.7	1,037.2	1,010.9
Total long-term debt	1,506.4	990.4	952.7	1,037.2	1,010.9
Total debt	1,549.3	1,143.3	1,056.6	1,215.2	1141.0
Deferred income tax	211.9	202.2	189.5	356.6	339.8
Other liabilities, total	26.6	21.8	92.5	—	—
Total liabilities	2,376.5	1882.0	1,742.4	2,118.5	2,004.4
Common stock	330.7	326.4	310.6	282.0	281.8
Other equity, total	108.6	−39.6	−43.9	56.5	27.1
Total equity	2,699.2	2381.0	1,977.7	2624.0	2,555.1
Total liabilities and shareholders' equity	5,075.7	4,263.1	3,720.1	4,742.5	4,559.5
Total common shares outstanding	2,560.8	2,527.4	2,404.3	2,181.3	2,179.7

*2006 projected.

Source: Shangri-La Asia Ltd. Financial Report (Reuters), via OneSource (accessed February 26, 2008).

SERVICE MODEL: "SHANGRI-LA HOSPITALITY"

Starting with its first hotel, Shangri-La Hotel-Singapore, Shangri-La built its brand on service excellence with a stated mission to "delight customers each and every time" (see Exhibit 6). The core of the Shangri-La brand was steeped in offering customers an unforgettable experience by blending local cultures, exotic art, and lively ambience.

With its Asian foundations, Shangri-La's service model of "Shangri-La Hospitality" was built around five core principles: respect, humility, courtesy, helpfulness, and sincerity. With properties spanning geographic and cultural boundaries, implementing these principles consistently was challenging and affected everything from staffing and amenities to customer–employee interactions. For example, certain service principles (i.e., respect) meant different things to different customers in different markets.

Greg Dogan, regional vice president, explained:

Shangri-La Hospitality basically covers what we do in Asia. Within each country, you need to adapt to the local requirements whether it is Myanmar, Philippines, or Indonesia. In Thailand

Exhibit 5 Shangri-La Asia Limited Occupancy and Rates Statistics (June 2006)

Hotel	Current Month Rooms Available		Occupancy YTD June				Average Room Rates YTD June				Revenue per Available Room YTD June			
	2006 Actual	2005 Actual	2006 Actual %	Budget %	2005 L-Year %	INC/(DEC) 06 vs 05 %	2006 Actual US$	Budget US$	2005 L-Year US$	INC/(DEC) 06 vs 05 %	2006 Actual US$	Budget US$	2005 L-Year US$	INC/(DEC) 06 vs 05 %
1. Kowloon Shangri-La Hotel	700	700	78%	76%	73%	5%	$236	$238	$214	10%	$180	$176	$151	19%
2. Island Shangri-La Hotel	565	565	83	79	76	7	324	311	273	19	263	240	224	17
Total Hong Kong average (1–2)	1,265	1,265	80	77	74	6	277	271	241	15	217	204	182	19
3. Shangri-La Hotel, Beijing	528	528	73	76	69	4	117	114	102	15	82	83	67	22
4. China World Hotel, Beijing	716	716	75	80	81	(6)	196	188	164	19	147	149	132	11
5. Traders Hotel, Beijing	570	570	84	86	86	(2)	104	95	91	14	87	81	78	12
6. Portman Ritz Carlton Hotel, Shanghai	506	488	77	80	81	(4)	220	221	204	8	169	178	165	2
7. Shangri-La Hotel, Hongzhou	383	383	71	73	74	(2)	120	122	117	2	80	84	81	(0)
8. Shangri-La Hotel, Shenzhen	522	522	74	72	67	8	101	98	91	10	74	67	60	25
9. Shangri-La Golden Flower Hotel, Xian	416	416	65	73	75	(10)	69	65	62	11	44	46	45	(1)
10. Shangri-La Hotel Changchun	458	458	71	72	71	0	83	85	77	8	56	60	58	(5)
11. Traders Hotel Shenyang	588	588	60	64	62	(2)	44	46	42	5	25	28	25	1
12. Shangri-La Hotel Beihai	362	362	31	34	32	(1)	50	48	44	13	15	16	14	12
13. Shangri-La Hotel, Qingdoo	501	501	70	78	77	(7)	103	99	87	19	78	85	67	16
14. Shangri-La Hotel, Dalian	562	562	63	68	71	(8)	92	98	85	8	56	65	59	(5)
15. Shangri-La Hotel, Pudong	957	606	68	73	78	(10)	225	231	187	20	148	165	139	6
16. Shangri-La Hotel, Wuhan	448	468	75	68	66	9	72	70	66	9	52	49	42	24
17. Shangri-La Hotel, Harbin	340	342	66	66	64	2	80	80	73	9	52	52	59	(12)
18. Beijing Kerry Centre Hotel	487	487	75	79	80	(5)	170	167	138	23	126	131	109	15
19. Shangri-La Hotel, Zhongshan	458	426	50	59	58	(7)	83	81	69	21	41	47	39	6
20. Shangri-La Hotel, Fuzhou	414	367	64	64	63	2	80	78	67	20	50	49	39	27
Total China average (3–20)	9,217	8,790	68	71	71	(3)	125	124	108	16	84	87	75	11
21. Shangri-La Hotel, Makati, Manila	697	693	89	86	84	5	136	128	121	12	118	106	98	20
22. Shangri-La's Edsa Plaza Hotel, Manila	620	651	69	76	71	(2)	87	76	72	21	67	62	49	36
23. Shangri-La's Moctan Island Resort, Cebu	543	543	65	62	79	(14)	137	134	126	8	117	109	96	21
Total Philippines average (21–23)	1,860	1,887	75	75	78	(3)	121	112	107	13	101	92	81	25

Hotel	Current Month Rooms Available		Occupancy YTD June				Average Room Rates YTD June				Revenue per Available Room YTD June			
	2006 Actual	2005 Actual	2006 Actual %	2006 Budget %	2005 L-Year %	INC/(DEC) 06 vs 05 %	2006 Actual US$	2006 Budget US$	2005 L-Year US$	INC/(DEC) 06 vs 05 %	2006 Actual US$	2006 Budget US$	2005 L-Year US$	INC/(DEC) 06 vs 05 %
24. Shangri-La Hotel, Jakarta	668	668	52%	63%	55%	(3)%	$109	$114	$103	6%	$51	$70	$49	4%
25. Fijian Resort	436	436	71	71	63	8	144	132	133	9	101	92	116	(13)
Total Philippines, Jakarta & Fiji average (21–25)	2,964	2,991	69	72	71	(1)	123	116	110	12	89	87	77	16
Original group average (1–25)	13,446	13,046	70	72	71	(1)	142	137	122	16	98	99	86	14
26. Shangri-La Hotel, Singapore	750	750	78	80	80	(1)	198	174	162	23	153	138	127	21
27. Shangri-La's Rosa Sentosa Resort	459	459	82	80	81	1	114	101	99	16	92	79	77	19
28. Traders Hotel, Singapore	546	546	77	85	83	(6)	115	97	87	33	88	82	71	24
Total Singapore average (26–28)	1,755	1,755	79	82	81	(2)	150	130	121	24	117	105	96	21
29. Shangri-La Hotel, Bangkok	799	799	80	79	77	3	130	124	118	11	101	95	87	17
30. Traders Hotel, Yangon	385	403	51	49	47	4	35	36	33	8	18	17	15	20
31. Shangri-La Hotel, Kuala Lumpur	694	695	69	73	68	1	94	93	87	9	63	66	56	11
32. Traders Hotel, Penang	441	441	79	71	67	13	49	48	43	14	38	33	29	31
33. Shangri-La's Golden Sands Resort, Penang	395	395	78	76	64	14	82	80	71	14	62	59	45	40
34. Shangri-La's Tanjung Aru Resort	495	495	84	81	80	4	90	87	74	22	72	68	56	29
35. Shangri-La's Rasa Ria Resort	330	328	80	76	72	8	80	78	64	25	63	58	54	16
Total Malaysia average (31–35)	2,355	2,354	77	75	70	7	80	79	70	14	60	58	49	23
Total other area average (21–35)	8,258	8,302	74	75	72	2	115	107	100	14	85	80	71	19
Total group average (1–35)	18,740	18,357	72%	73%	72%	(0)%	$132	$127	$114	16%	$93	$92	$81	16%

Note: Portman Ritz-Carlton is undergoing major renovation. Available rooms, occupancy %, average room rates, and revenue per available room are based on saleable rooms. Rasa Sayang Resort ceased operations in Dec 04 for redevelopment. Fiji Mocambo was disposed in Dec 05.

*Decrease in RevPar due to renovation in 2005, i.e. lower saleable roomnights.

Source: Shangri-La Investors Relations, http://www.ir.shangri-la.com/en/hoteloperatingstatistics/ (accessed January 31, 2008).

methodologies, such as role playing, to create the circumstances employees would face. "In our training facility we tried to simulate interaction with customers. For instance, in our training lounge—used as a restaurant in our restaurant simulation—we would have people pose as customers. They would come as guests, order food and beverages, and go through the whole service sequence. And our employees would get a chance to interact with them and practice what they learned in the classroom," said Perry, Director of the Room programs at the Shangri-La Academy.

In these interactive modules, a work situation scenario was taught with emphasis on common mistakes and best practices, so that trainees would learn to examine and question why "things were done in a certain way." Classes were often videotaped and analyzed for employee body language and manner with "customers." "What was their body language? Did they smile? Was the hand in the pocket when they served the customers? We would look at things like that," added Perry.

Tay Beng Koon, Director of Academic Development, added:

> One of our challenges was that our employees could see the immediate costs, as in I am giving up

this room, but could not easily see the long-term implications. The issue was very tangible on one side and intangible on the other. To emphasize the future benefits, we developed and focused on company-wide guiding principles.

SHANGRI-LA CARE

Shangri-La's employee philosophy was to develop local talent to world class expectations. The company had already launched its culture training program, Shangri-La Care, in 1996 to ensure that each global employee delivered service "the Shangri-La Way" (see Exhibit 7). Shangri-La Care 1 focused on the five core values of Shangri-La Hospitality: respect, humility, courtesy, helpfulness and sincerity. The program was strongly supported by the top management and continuously cascaded through the organization. All hotels were required to allocate a specific budget for training and development, and the general manager of each hotel was personally responsible for ensuring that all the allocated funds were spent year after year.

As the company grew, Shangri-La added new modules to its culture program. In 1998,

Exhibit 7 **The Shangri-La Care (also known as the Shangri-La Way)**

Care Module 1: Shangri-La Hospitality from Caring People (Launched in 1996)

Addresses how to make our guests feel special and important by focusing on the five core values of Shangri-La Hospitality: Respect, Humility, Courtesy, Helpfulness and Sincerity. It also imbues the value of "Pride Without Arrogance" as the service hallmark.

Care Module 2: Delighting Customers (Launched in 1998)

Focuses on the importance of guest loyalty and how it can only be achieved by delighting our guests not just the first time but every single time. Employees must be guest obsessed, doing more for guests by "going the extra mile," being flexible and never saying no, anticipating and responding quickly, and recognizing the guest's individual needs.

Care Module 3: Recover to Gain Loyalty (Launched in 2003)

Highlights the importance of recovery when a mistake is made. When recovery is done well, it may be an opportunity to gain further commitment and loyalty but if there is no or poor recovery the lifetime value of the guest is lost in addition to at least 25 others who may hear of the incident through word of mouth. The module teaches the five steps to recovery—Listen, Apologize, Fix the Problem, Go the Extra Mile and Follow Up.

Care Module 4: Take Ownership (Launched in 2005)

Addresses the importance of our employees taking ownership—to show care for our customers, colleagues and company. The driver of ownership is "SELF," which means S—Show commitment, E—Eager to take initiative, L—Lead ourselves and F—Filled with passion. This module attempts to create in our employees the mind-set to live in an environment that is filled with Care for guests, Compassion for colleagues and Pride in our Company.

Source: Shangri-La Hotels and Resorts, http://www.shangri-la.com/en/home.aspx (accessed February 5, 2007).

Shangri-La Care 2 was launched. In Module 2, the company focused on retention and guest loyalty. Going the extra mile, pleasing guests not just the first time but every single time, being flexible and never saying no, anticipating and responding quickly to customer requests, and recognizing the guest's individual needs were emphasized.

In 2003, the company launched Shangri-La Care 3 to emphasize the importance of recovery when a mistake was made. In Module 3, the company focused on the five steps to recovery—Listen, Apologize, Fix the Problem, Go the Extra Mile, and Follow Up. In 2005, Shangri-La announced its fourth Shangri-La Care module, addressing the need of employees to take responsibility for customer satisfaction.

COMPENSATION AND CAREER GROWTH

By investing heavily in employee development, the company was not only making its employees valuable to Shangri-La but also to its competitors. "Retention became a big problem," said Tan Eng-Leong. "Traditionally, our turnover had always been low, 19–20 percent, compared to the industry norm, 27–28 percent, but the competition was offering 35 to 50 percent higher salaries."

Shangri-La had a three-tier compensation system. The company's level 1 employee—typically division heads and hotel general managers (GMs)—were paid a base salary and a bonus based on the hotel's overall performance. Overall, GM compensation was heavily geared towards the financial results (Gross Operating Profit and Gross Operating Revenue attainment).* Compensation for level 2 and 3 employees (e.g., property line managers) was similar to the level 1 structure—salary and bonus pay—with the exception that factors such as customer loyalty and employee satisfaction scores were also linked to employees' bonus awards. Employees at levels 4 and 5 typically enjoyed a common bonus incentive which was linked to property overall performance, but not to individual goals.

*RevPar (Revenue Per Available Room) = A (Average Price Per Room) × O% (Rate of Occupancy)

Bridle explained Shangri-La's compensation structure:

We almost have a three-tier type of approach to it. We award our GMs very much based on the financial results: against budget and last year's financial performance. And there is a discretionary element based on their leadership competency. Level 2–3 compensation is also linked directly to GM's financial goals—everyone's compensation is—but at that level bonus numbers start breaking down to additional goals that reflect customer loyalty and employee satisfaction. All these things come in below the GM level. So, if you are at a level 3, you have more of directly measurable items like customer loyalty, quality standards, and audit standards. As you move up to Level 1 and 2, the compensation becomes more financial results oriented. However, even though our GM compensation doesn't have a direct link to customer satisfaction, they still have incentives to make sure that those goals are met. I think our senior management, as in level 1 and 2, sees this. They see that the performance is bottom-up; they know without customer satisfaction they would not achieve financial results.

He continued:

It is becoming more transparent now. I think the important step for us is to move customer satisfaction, employee satisfaction and some compliance goals into the performance review scoring system, still with its key emphasis on financial results, to allow bonus/incentive numbers to move up and down. And indirectly it may influence your salary increment potential as well.

At individual properties, incentive pay did not typically vary across employees within each level. Increasingly, Shangri-La corporate executives moved to standardize pay practices across properties.

Dogan elaborated:

In our old system, we had a lot of variation in compensation across properties. For instance, when people moved from one property to another, sometimes their compensation went down. That was not fair. We realized that we needed to reform our incentive pay model immediately.

To retain its workforce, the company also focused on creating transparent, well-defined career paths (see Exhibit 8). "Employees felt that an opportunity for professional growth was a

Exhibit 8   **Career Path in Shangri-La**

Source: Shangri-La Academy Beijing, http://www.shangri-la-academy.com/careerpath/en/index.aspx (accessed January 21, 2008).

key motivator," said Tan Eng-Leong. "So we created a lot of opportunities for our staff. We were expanding and we promoted from within. Our expansion gave huge opportunities to a lot of young people. People frequently got promoted to another property. We wanted to give our employees career paths and opportunities outside of their areas that other companies could not provide." Shangri-La's growth created a lot of opportunities for advancement. Within one to two years, most Shangri-La Service Associates were promoted to be Service Leaders. Another two years on the job would get them a managerial position and if they worked four years as a Senior Service Manager they became Service Executives.

Shangri-La staff could also move laterally from property to property. "Our expansion gave huge opportunities for our employees. Not only were there opportunities to move up within the property, there were also opportunities to transfer to other Shangri-La properties in exotic locations like Dubai. Basically, if our staff decided to stay with our company, we gave them a future," Dogan added.

The company also tried alternative methods, including non-pay recognition (i.e., contests, awards, etc.) to motivate employees. Dogan recalled: "When I had the staff assembly with 2,000 people in the ballroom, I used to get out there with a $100 bill and say 'Anybody who has the guts to come up here, from each department, and recite the guiding principle and tell me what it means, come up here.' People would storm the stage. It was a lot of fun, everyone was cheering for their department, and it was a simple, non-stressful way of getting them to make sure that they knew it, understood it, and practiced it. It became a real culture."

EXPANSION TO THE EAST: CHINA'S HOTEL MARKET

As Shangri-La trained its employees, fixed cultural issues, and expanded its operations in China, the company faced additional challenges. After 20 years of rapid economic growth, China in 2006 had become the world's fourth largest economy and one of the world's most attractive destinations for tourists, which meant significant opportunities for hotel development.[4] According to industry analysts, China would be Asia's hottest spot for hotel development in 2006, accounting for nearly half of all new projects in the region.[5] Of the 386 hotels actively in development throughout Asia in 2006, 188 were in China, and 134 of those were rated four- or five-star.[6]

Competition

With growth slowing in Europe and North America, hotel chains were targeting Asia—China in particular—for their new growth. Soon after the International Olympic Committee announced Beijing as the 2008 Olympics' host, premium hotels started to pop up all over Shanghai, Beijing and other Chinese cities as Regent, Ritz-Carlton, Hyatt, Sheraton and others poured billions of dollars into expansion.[7]

By 2001, the U.K.-based InterContinental Hotel Group (IHG), which also operated the Crowne Plaza and Holiday Inn chains, was the most ambitious player in the Chinese market. IHG had a portfolio of 51 hotels in China and planned to develop an additional 74 by 2008.[8] The U.S.-based Marriott chain, which operated the Ritz-Carlton, Renaissance, and Courtyard brands, had 26 hotels in China and planned to expand its portfolio to 100 by 2010. France's Accor had 30 hotels under development in China, all scheduled to open before 2008.[9] Wyndham Hotel Group, which also owned the Ramada and Wingate Inn brands, had a portfolio of 60 hotels in China in 2006 and planned to expand its China business at an annual rate of 40 percent in anticipation of the 2008 Olympics.[10]

Local Hotels

Local hotels had poor brand recognition relative to their overseas rivals. Some thought that the influx of foreign capital and brands would force the local hotels to improve their establishments and services. However, none of the Chinese hotel chains could match the name recognition and service standards of Hilton, Hyatt, InterContinental, or Marriott. Some local hotel groups considered forming alliances with international brands, in which the local partner would be responsible for funding the construction of the hotel, while the foreign partner took on the management and operation of the business.

Pressure on Wages

Asia's low labor costs boosted hotel gross profits significantly. In 2001, China's average cost of manual labor averaged less than $1 per hour, while the U.S. averaged $16 per hour (see Exhibit 9). As a result, the hotel industry was more profitable in Asia than in the West. A typical four- or five-star luxury hotel in Asia achieved gross profit margins of 35 to 45 percent, compared with 20 to 25 percent in the West.[11]

In 2001, several major international hotel chains entered the Chinese deluxe (four- and five-star) hotel market, creating sudden demand for skilled hotel workers. Newcomers either poached Shangri-La's trained staff or offered higher than average industry wages to attract their own. Shangri-La, the only major player in China up until that point, found it difficult to keep up with the competition. "Consider Beijing," Bridle said. "A half-dozen five-star hotels coming into the

Exhibit 9 Hourly Wages by Country

Country	Dollars per Hour
Japan	$16.46
United States	16.14
Europe	14.13
Singapore	6.72
Korea	5.69
Taiwan	5.18
Mexico	2.08
Brazil	2.04
China	0.61

Source: Bureau of Labor Statistics; China Statistical Yearbook, http://www.bls.gov/opub/cwc/content/articles.stm (accessed March 28, 2007).

market . . . Our reservation managers are being offered 35 percent higher salary by our competitors. Our security managers are being offered 50 percent higher!" Shangri-La's low annual turnover rates of 19 to 20 percent—versus 27 to 28 percent for the industry as a whole—were under threat.

Dogan commented:

> With China coming onto the world stage, what I am finding out is that some of our staff is like "gold dust" to outside industry. Our trained, English speaking front office staff is whisked away when the multinationals come in to set up their company. That is our biggest challenge.

EXPANSION TO THE WEST

China was not Shangri-La's only focus. The company was about to launch multiple hotels in Europe, Australia, and North America. These countries had relatively more expensive labor markets, where trained hotel staff was in short supply. In Sydney, for instance, the typical staff-to-guest ratio was 0.8 (compared to Shangri-La's 1.5). Chicago, Miami, Las Vegas, Vancouver, and Toronto—some of the locations Shangri-La targeted for expansion—all had similar labor markets. The only exception was Paris, with a staff-to-guest ratio of 2.1 or higher, but this was driven by Paris' comparatively high hotel prices. A typical five-star hotel room in Paris usually went for €600 or €700. "Unfortunately, this pricing strategy cannot necessarily be translated into other markets where new Shangri-La's were coming," Bridle said. "Charging more for rooms could not really be considered as an option in new high-wage markets, since pricing is dictated by the market."

He continued:

> During our expansion, our main concern is to maintain worldwide service quality standards and deliver excellent service to customers. An immediate, and long-term, challenge is to ensure that signature Shangri-La quality and service standards are translated to new hotels in new markets. It's been said that you only have one chance to make a first

impression and guests must know they will experience the essence of Shangri-La hospitality wherever one of its hotels opens its doors. And when loyal Shangri-La guests travel outside the region, they must experience the same level and style of service they have come to expect at Shangri-La hotels and resorts in Asia-Pacific and the Middle East. We need to maintain control and translate our Asian service model into tighter labor markets in the western world.

Superior customer care was typical of many luxury Asian hotels and was definitely a standard at Shangri-La and to deliver a consistent experience of Asian grace, warmth, and care—what Shangri-La called "Shangri-La Hospitality"—all of its hotels maintained a high staff-to-guest ratio. In Hong Kong and Singapore, for example, this ratio was close to 1.25 to 1.5 staff per guest. In developing countries it could be as high as 2.5 to 3.0 staff per guest.[12] Keeping a high ratio of staff-to-guests, which ensured better service and attention to detail, had never been an issue for Shangri-La in low-wage countries like Malaysia or China; however, the practice was not easily transferable to high-wage countries such as the U.S., Australia, or Canada—at least not without creating unacceptably high payroll costs.

LOOKING AHEAD

As Bridle grabbed the phone to call his assistant to schedule another executive meeting, a stream of questions rushed through his mind. Did Shangri-La need to alter its strategy? Could they maintain their unique brand of Shangri-La Hospitality as they moved into tighter labor markets? They were battling high-end Western hotel chains at home and abroad and needed to overcome wage and cultural issues in their properties across the globe.

Bridle wanted to ensure that Shangri-La maintained its service model as they continued to expand. "We need to have a consistent platform and consistent service quality," thought Bridle. With the first of the new slate of hotels scheduled to open in 2007, time was running out.

ENDNOTES

1 "Shangri-La Hotels and Resorts," http://www.shangri-la.com/en/home.aspx (accessed February 5, 2007).

2 "Tej Company Profile—Shangri-La Asia Ltd," *Taiwan Economic Journal,* available via Factiva (accessed February 2, 2007).

3 "Shangri-La Hotels Opens The Shangri-La Academy to Provide Chinese Students Hospitality Tools and Training," http://www.hotel-online.com/News/PR2004_4th/Dec04_ShangriLaAcademy.html (accessed April 18, 2007).

4 "China, India to Drive Strong Growth in Emerging Asia: IMF," *Agence France Presse,* April 11, 2007, available via Factiva (accessed April 11, 2007).

5 "First-ever Lodging Development Pipeline for Asia Reveals China as Having the World's Largest Development Activity Outside the U.S.," *Lodging Econometrics,* June 2, 2006 (accessed April 18, 2007).

6 "InterContinental Ramps Up China Growth Pace," *Reuters News,* October 17, 2006, available via Factiva (accessed March 12, 2007).

7 "China Hotel and Tourism News," http://www.chinaeconomicreview.com/hotels/2006/08/ (accessed April 10, 2007).

8 "Intercontinental Hotels Transcript of Preliminary Results Conference," http://www.ihgplc.com/files/presentations/prelims05/conference_call_transcription.pdf (accessed April 18, 2007).

9 "Competition Heats Up in Hotel Market," *China Daily,* September 27, 2006, available via Factiva (accessed March 12, 2007).

10 "Wyndham Plans Rapid China Hotel Growth, Eyes India," *New Zealand Press Association,* October 12, 2006, available via Factiva (accessed March 29, 2007).

11 "A Tasteful Host," *Forbes,* July 28, 1997, available via ProQuest (accessed April 10, 2007).

12 "Shangri-La Hotels to Spread Their Allure to Vancouver," *Sun,* September 24, 2004 (accessed April 12, 2007).

Toyota Motor Company: Losing Its Quality Edge?

Debapratim Purkayastha

IBS Center for Management Research

Syeda Maseeha Qumer

IBS Center for Management Research

"The recalls and sales and production suspension cast a negative light on Toyota's reputation for quality, just as the company emerges from an unprecedented downturn in the auto industry. This could hamper the company's potential sales and profitability recovery, especially in the U.S. market."[1]

—Jeong Min Pak, senior director, Fitch Ratings Ltd,[2] in 2010.

"[The lean production system] runs too deep in the Toyota culture and has been too successful and too effective. I would anticipate Toyota is going to get through this with a weakened reputation—but since the company made great cars for a great price for 50 years, they are on a much better platform for restoring the luster of their reputation because the platform was so strong to begin with."[3]

—Michael Useem, a management professor at Wharton Business School,[4] in 2010.

INTRODUCTION

On January 21, 2010, Toyota Motor Corporation (Toyota) recalled 2.3 million select Toyota Division vehicles in the U.S. The recall was done to fix sticking accelerator pedals which caused unintended acceleration, leading to accidents. Earlier in November 2009 too, the company had recalled 4.2 million cars in the U.S. to rectify accelerator pedals which were getting lodged under the floor mats of the vehicles. Subsequently on February 1, 2010, Toyota suspended the sales of eight of its popular car models involved in the recall and discontinued production at six of its North American car-assembly plants in response to growing customer concerns. The eight car models represented 57% of Toyota's sales in the U.S. in 2009.[5] Talking about the recalls, Japanese Trade Minister Masayuki Naoshima said, "The scale of the recalls is huge. The situation is serious. It points to the possible dangers a global economy can bring. I would like Toyota to respond properly to secure consumer confidence."[6]

Toyota, an iconic car maker founded in 1937, was known for its innovations, quality, and global competitiveness. Its business segments mainly included automotive operations, financial services operations, and other business operations.[7] Automotive operations accounted for 89% of Toyota's total revenues in 2008. The company manufactured vehicles at 53 production sites in 27 countries around the globe. In the fiscal year 2008,[8] Toyota sold approximately 8.91 million vehicles in 170 countries and regions under the Toyota, Lexus, Daihatsu, and Hino brands. North America was its biggest market followed by Japan, Europe, and Asia. For the third quarter ended December 31, 2009, Toyota's net revenues totaled 5.3 trillion yen, an increase of 10.2% compared to the corresponding period of 2008. Vehicle sales during the same quarter amounted

ICMR
IBS Center for Management Research
www.icmrindia.org

© 2010, IBS Center for Management Research. All rights reserved. This case was written by Syeda Maseeha Qumer, under the direction of Prof. Debapratim Purkayastha, IBS Center for Management Research. It was compiled from published sources, and is intended to be used as a basis for class discussion rather than to illustrate either effective or ineffective handling of a management situation. To order copies, call +91-08417-236667/68 or write to IBS Center for Management Research (ICMR), IFHE Campus, Donthanapally, Sankarapally Road, Hyderabad 501 504, Andhra Pradesh, India or email: info@icmrindia.org.

to 2.07 million units, an increase of 227 thousand units over the same period of 2008.[9]

According to analysts, delivering quality was one of the most fundamental principles of Toyota and the company's success was led by unusual quality delivered at very competitive prices. The company recognized quality as one of the most important factors affecting customer satisfaction and strove to achieve excellence in manufacturing quality products. The foundation of Toyota's strong quality was its efficient and much emulated manufacturing system known as the Toyota Production System (TPS). Through its well-organized production system, Toyota rapidly captured market share, controlled cost, and launched better car models. Toyota employees world over practiced philosophies such as *Kaizen* (continuous improvement), PDCA (plan, do, check, action), *Pokayoke* (mistake-proofing), and Just-in-Time (JIT) to achieve excellence in production. To ensure zero defects in the finished product, Toyota set up quality assurance systems across various divisions, including development, purchasing, and production. Because of its competent quality process system, the Toyota brand had become synonymous with quality, reliability, and durability, experts said.

However, some analysts felt that the Japanese company had succumbed to the pressures of rapid globalization and sacrificed its legendary quality to reach the goal of becoming the number one auto maker in the world. According to them, a series of recalls in the U.S., China, and Europe had tainted the automaker's image of manufacturing reliable cars and trucks. According to Maryann Keller, senior adviser at Casesa Shapiro Group LLC,[10] Toyota's "reputation for long-term quality is finished. People aren't going to buy Toyotas, period. It doesn't matter which model. What's happened is sufficient to keep people out of the stores."[11]

However, some analysts were positive that Toyota would not lose its quality edge. According to them, the fact that the car maker had discontinued sales of the affected models until the recall issues were resolved was proof of its commitment to quality. They felt that in order to retain its reputation as a quality car maker, Toyota should try to gain the confidence of its customers and concentrate on the quality of its products rather than expanding its business and gaining market share. "They need to do something warmer, something that demonstrates caring. I think they can recover, but that window is closing. They will have to do something big and fast,"[12] said Maurice E. Schweitzer, an associate professor of operations and information management at the Wharton School.

BACKGROUND NOTE

Toyota was founded by Kiichiro Toyoda (Kiichiro) in 1937. The history of Toyota goes back to 1897, when Sakichi Toyoda (Sakichi), father of Kiichiro, diversified into the textile machinery business from the traditional family business of carpentry. In 1926, Sakichi founded the Toyoda Automatic Loom Works, Ltd (TALW) which manufactured automatic power looms. The looms stopped automatically when any of the threads snapped. This concept of designing equipment to stop so that defects could be immediately fixed formed the basis of the TPS.

Kiichiro, an engineer from Tokyo University, was more interested in automobiles and engines than the family's textile business. In 1929, he traveled to the U.S. and Europe to study the manufacturing processes in car factories there. After returning to Japan, he spent his time studying car engines and experimenting with better ways to manufacture them. In the early 1930s, Kiichiro convinced his father to launch an automobile business and in 1933, Sakichi established an automobile department within TALW. Kiichiro developed the first passenger car prototype A1 in 1935.

In 1936, Sakichi sold the patent rights of his automatic loom to a company in England to raise money to set up a new automobile business. With the £100,000 that Sakichi received from the sale, Kiichiro laid the foundations of the company. The company named Toyota was established on August 28, 1937, with a capital of 12 million yen. The name 'Toyota' was used instead of 'Toyoda' as it took eight pen strokes to write 'Toyota' in Japanese and eight was considered a lucky number in Japan. Kiichiro was made the managing director of the company. In the late 1930s, Kiichiro traveled to the U.S. to study the manufacturing processes at Ford Motor Company (Ford).[13] Armed with strong knowledge about the Ford production system, Kiichiro returned to

Japan determined to adapt the system to smaller production quantities, more suitable to Japan.

Following World War II, international manufacturers had begun concentrating on medium-sized and larger cars but Toyota kept its focus on small cars. Toyota faced tough competition from Ford and General Motors Company, LLC[14] (GM), which were the top car manufacturers in Japan at that time. In 1950, after a major strike by labor unions, Kiichiro was forced to step down and his cousin Eiji Toyoda (Eiji), who was also an engineer from Tokyo University, was made managing director. In 1957, Eiji renamed Toyota 'The Toyota Company'.

Due to World War II, there was severe shortage of raw material in Japan and Toyota did not have enough capital to carry huge inventories. The main challenge for the company was to produce the maximum units possible, given financial and other constraints and to reduce manufacturing inefficiencies. To overcome these problems, the TPS was put in place by the then production chief of Toyota, Taiichi Ohno (Ohno). Ohno traveled to the U.S. in 1956 and came back with several ideas on which he based the TPS. The objective of TPS, also referred to as the lean manufacturing system, was to manufacture vehicles ordered by customers in the quickest and most efficient way and to deliver them as quickly as possible. Though the TPS was not the handiwork of Ohno alone as it included concepts developed by Sakichi, Kiichiro, and Eiji, it was Ohno who streamlined the concepts and developed them into a formal system. He was also responsible for training a number of Toyota's engineers on how to use and implement the system.

The TPS overcame limitations of production, while making the most of the available resources. It made use of concepts like Just-in-Time (JIT), *Kaizen, Kanban,* and *Jidoka*[15] to reach a high level of efficiency in production. The system formally came to be known as the TPS in 1977. Quality management experts opined that over the years, TPS had developed into a model of industrial excellence, leading to the company's manufacturing methods being emulated by other players in the automobile sector. The TPS enabled Toyota to come out with many innovative models in a cost-efficient way, they added.

The company started its globalization in the 1950s and entered the U.S. market in 1957.

It established its first overseas production unit in Brazil in 1959 followed by its entry into the European market in 1963. Besides manufacturing, Toyota started a global network of design and R&D facilities covering the three major car markets of Japan, North America, and Europe. The company underwent rapid expansion in the 1960s and 1970s and exported fuel-efficient small cars to many foreign markets. It focused on lowering its production costs and on developing more sophisticated cars. The Toyota Corolla, which went on sale in 1966, became Japan's most popular family car.

Toyota received a major boost in the late 1970s, when the oil crisis resulted in many people shifting to Toyota's fuel-efficient cars. The crisis also sent Japan into recession and most of the auto makers suffered losses. However, the efficiency and flexibility of the TPS helped Toyota bounce back. In 1978, a group of engineers from Toyota, under the guidance of Ohno, gave a presentation at Tokyo on the TPS. This further sparked interest in the system and many expressed keenness to learn more about it. Toyota brought TPS to the U.S. in the 1980s, when it set up a joint venture with GM called New United Motor Manufacturing Inc. (NUMMI).

By the early 1970s, Toyota's production was behind that of only GM and Ford. It also began to tap the markets in the Middle East. By 1974, Toyota Corolla had become the largest selling car in the world, and a decade later, Toyota ranked second only to GM in the total number of cars produced. By the end of the 1980s, Toyota began to build new brands and the luxury division, Lexus, was launched. During this period, Toyota continued to strive for improvements and its manufacturing processes served as a model for other companies. In 1983, the company's name was changed to Toyota Motor Corporation. In 1988, Toyota opened its own production plant in Georgetown, Kentucky.

In 1990, to provide safe and innovative products and safeguard the environment and culture of the local communities in which it operated, Toyota established the 'Guiding Principles at Toyota'. These principles highlighted the management philosophy, values, and methods that the company had embraced since its foundation. (Refer to Exhibit I for 'Guiding Principles at Toyota'). The Toyota Guiding Principles,

Exhibit I   Principles of Toyota

Guiding Principles of Toyota*

1. Honor the language and spirit of the law of every nation and undertake open and fair corporate activities to be a good corporate citizen of the world.
2. Respect the culture and customs of every nation and contribute to economic and social development through corporate activities in the communities.
3. Dedicate ourselves to providing clean and safe products and to enhancing the quality of life everywhere through all our activities.
4. Create and develop advanced technologies and provide outstanding products and services that fulfill the needs of customers worldwide.
5. Foster a corporate culture that enhances individual creativity and teamwork value, while honoring mutual trust and respect between labor and management.
6. Pursue growth in harmony with the global community through innovative management.
7. Work with business partners in research and creation to achieve stable, long-term growth and mutual benefits, while keeping ourselves open to new partnerships.

Five Main Principles of Toyota

1. Always be faithful to your duties, thereby contributing to the Company and to the overall good.
2. Always be studious and creative, striving to stay ahead of the times.
3. Always be practical and avoid frivolousness.
4. Always strive to build a homelike atmosphere at work that is warm and friendly.
5. Always have respect for God, and remember to be grateful at all times.

---

*Established in 1990, revised in 1997.

Source: http://www2.toyota.co.jp/en/vision/philosophy/.

considered as the foundation of the company's corporate management philosophy, were revised in 1997. In the early 1990s, as Toyota expanded its overseas operations, excessive capital spending affected its profit margins. Tatsuro Toyoda (Tatsuro) took over as the company's President in 1992. In 1995, after Tatsuro resigned due to health reasons, Hiroshi Okuda (Okuda) became Toyota president. After some setbacks in the early 1990s, the company began to grow further under the leadership of Okuda, who focused on international expansion and localization of production. He also developed a strong dealership network and increased advertising. This resulted in a significant increase in sales. In 1996, Toyota consolidated its production in the North American production units into the Cincinnati-based Toyota Motor Manufacturing (North America). One of Toyota's major innovations was the Prius, a gasoline-electric car and the world's first mass-produced hybrid car launched in 1997. The Prius, which was successful in the U.S., further consolidated the company's position in the country. Toyota's overseas production increased from

1.22 million units per year in 1994 to 1.54 million units per year in 1998.

In 1999, Okuda replaced Chairman Shoichiro Toyoda while Fujio Cho (Cho) became the president of the company. Besides increasing manufacturing centers and expanding sales networks worldwide, Cho focused on localizing design, development, and purchasing in every country. In 1999, Toyota listed its shares on both the New York and London stock exchanges. During the 2000s, Toyota registered strong sales in the U.S. and Japan. In 2000, for the first time ever, Toyota's total worldwide production exceeded five million vehicles. In 2001, Toyota started two new plants in Europe and in 2002 it established Toyota Motor Manufacturing Turkey to manufacture Corolla sedans for export markets.

In April 2002, Toyota announced a new corporate strategy, the '2010 Global Vision', to achieve a 15% market share of the global automobile market by early 2010. By mid-2003, Toyota had a presence in almost all the major segments of the automobile market that included small cars, luxury sedans, full-sized pickup trucks, SUVs, small trucks, and crossover vehicles. In 2005, Katsuaki Watanabe[16](Watanabe) was appointed President of the company. In the first quarter of 2007, Toyota replaced GM as the world's leading automaker, breaking the latter's 77-year reign. The company sold about 2.35 million vehicles compared to GM's 2.26 million. Based on the market capitalization, Toyota was valued at almost 12 times GM's value (Refer to Exhibit II for a timeline of the company).

Exhibit II   **Toyota Milestones**

Year	Event
	1930s
1935	Completion of A1 prototype passenger car
1936	Launch of AA passenger car
1937	Establishment of Toyota Motor Co., Ltd.
1938	Production began at Koromo plant (now Honsha plant)
	1940s
1947	Domestic production reached 100 thousand vehicles
	1950s
1950	Establishment of Toyota Motor Sales Co., Ltd.
1955	Launch of the Toyopet Crown
1957	Export of the first made-in-Japan passenger car to the U.S. (the Crown). Establishment of Toyota Motor Sales, U.S.A., Inc.
	1960s
1961	Launch of the Publica
1966	Launch of the Corolla
	1970s
1972	Cumulative total domestic production reaches 10 million vehicles
1973	Establishment of Calty Design Research, Inc.
1977	Establishment of Toyota Technical Center, U.S.A., Inc.
	1980s
1982	Toyota Motor Co., Ltd., and Toyota Motor Sales Co., Ltd., merge to become Toyota Motor Corporation
1984	Joint venture company (NUMMI) established with General Motors begins production in the United States
1987	Establishment of Toyota Technical Center of Europe
1988	Kentucky plant (now TMMK) begins production in the United States
1989	Launch of Lexus in North America
	1990s
1992	Establishment of Toyota Supplier Support Center in the United States U.K. plant (TMUK) begins production
1997	Launch of the Prius hybrid vehicle
1999	Toyota Motor Corporation lists on the New York and London stock exchanges cumulative total domestic production reaches 100 million vehicles
	2000s
2002	Establishment of the Toyota Institute, a personnel training facility Toyota Motor Corporation participates in F1, the pinnacle of motorsports
2005	Joint venture company established with PSA Peugeot Citroën begins production in the Czech Republic launch of Lexus in Japan
2007	Global cumulative sales of Toyota hybrid vehicles top 1 million
2008	Worldwide Prius sales top 1-million mark

Source: 2008 Annual Report, Toyota Motors Corporation.

Analysts felt that the global financial crisis[17] had had its impact on the world's largest automaker and it became difficult for the company to cope with a shift in the global automobile industry. As the global financial crisis deepened in 2008, the consumer demand for cars and other goods plummeted, especially in the U.S. and European markets. Because of the credit crunch, automobile sales dropped significantly as consumers stopped buying new cars. This led to a fall in the vehicle sales of auto companies. In 2008, Toyota's sales were down 4% from 2007 and the company sold about 8.97 million vehicles.[18] In North America, which accounted for a third of Toyota's worldwide revenues, sales fell 15.4% to 2,217,660 vehicles in 2008. The sales of large pickups were down about 25% and the sales of SUVs fell by 30%.[19] The company's sales were also affected in Europe and Japan (Refer to Exhibit III for Vehicle Production, Sales and Exports of Toyota in 2008).

In early 2009, Toyota projected a loss of ¥450 billion (US$5 billion) for the fiscal year 2009 in its vehicle-manufacturing operations, the first annual net loss reported by the company in six decades. Consolidated sales totaled 7.57 million units, a decrease of 1.34 million units compared to the previous year[20] (Refer to Exhibit IV for the income statement of Toyota). Toyota then began to look for a leader who would steer the company back to profits. In January 2009, the company announced that it had selected Akio Toyoda (Akio), grandson of Kiichiro Toyoda, to lead the company and manage a turnaround. On June 23, 2009, Akio took over as President of Toyota. The challenge before Akio was to bring the automaker back to profits. Akio embraced a traditional Toyota practice called *genchi genbutsu*,[21] meaning "go and see for yourself" to resolve the problems at Toyota.

QUALITY MANAGEMENT AT TOYOTA

Analysts were of the view that Toyota recognized quality as an important aspect of customer satisfaction and strove to deliver quality products to the market. Experts opined that quality, considered as the DNA of Toyota, was inbuilt into each process. By focusing on smaller production lots based on demand rather than on capacity, Toyota had set a standard for manufacturing, product development, and process excellence in the automotive industry, they said.

The quest for superior quality was evident in the TPS which focused on eliminating variability from the production process so that quality products were offered to the customer. Toyota's commitment to manufacturing world class and quality automobiles was entrenched in its entire manufacturing philosophy right through the development stages to manufacturing. At Toyota, quality was improved through collaboration and communication among personnel in development, purchasing, production, and after-sales service divisions. "Delivering quality is one of the most fundamental responsibilities that Toyota has to customers. Toyota must aim to achieve zero customer complaints,"[22] said Shinichi Sasaki (Sasaki), chief quality officer at Toyota.

Exhibit III   **Vehicle Production, Sales and Exports of Toyota (2008)**

	Toyota	Daihatsu	Hino	Total
Japanese Production	4,012	793	106	4,912
Overseas Production	4,198	115	–	4,313
Total Global Production	8,211	908	106	9,225
Sales in Japan	1,470	642	41	2,153
Overseas Sales	6,526	224	69	6,819
Total Global Sales	7,996	866	110	8,972
Exports	2,586	130	67	2,783

(Figures rounded to the nearest hundred.)
(In units, 1 unit = 1000 vehicles.)

Source: Toyota in the world 2009.

Exhibit IV   Income Statement of Toyota Motors

(All amounts in millions of US Dollars except per share data)	03/2009	03/2008	03/2007	03/2006
Operating Revenue	207,852.28	262,394.00	202,864.00	179,083.00
Total Revenue	207,852.28	262,394.00	202,864.00	179,083.00
Adjustment to Revenue	0.00	0.00	0.00	0.00
Cost of Sales	171,718.44	199,912.00	151,171.00	133,938.00
Cost of Sales with Depreciation	186,856.33	214,795.00	162,883.00	144,249.00
Gross Margin	0.00	0.00	0.00	0.00
Gross Operating Profit	36,133.85	62,482.00	51,693.00	45,145.00
R&D	0.00	0.00	0.00	0.00
SG&A	25,663.47	24,938.00	21,017.00	18,844.00
Advertising	0.00	0.00	0.00	0.00
Operating Profit	−4,667.52	22,661.00	18,964.00	15,990.00
Operating Profit before Depreciation (EBITDA)	10,470.38	37,544.00	30,676.00	26,301.00
Depreciation	15,137.90	14,883.00	11,712.00	10,311.00
Depreciation Unreconciled	0.00	0.00	0.00	0.00
Amortization	0.00	0.00	0.00	0.00
Amortization of Intangibles	0.00	0.00	0.00	0.00
Operating Income After Depreciation	−4,667.52	22,661.00	18,964.00	15,990.00
Interest Income	1,401.91	1,654.00	1,118.00	800.00
Earnings from Equity Interest	2,121.24	2,696.00	1,775.00	1,399.00
Other Income, Net	−3,622.01	471.00	518.00	1,163.00
Income Acquired in Process R&D	0.00	0.00	0.00	0.00
Interest Restructuring and M&A	0.00	0.00	0.00	0.00
Other Special Charges	0.00	0.00	0.00	0.00
Total Income Avail for Interest Expense (EBIT)	−4,766.38	27,482.00	22,375.00	19,352.00
Interest Expense	474.66	460.00	418.00	184.00
Income Before Tax (EBT)	−5,241.04	27,022.00	21,957.00	19,168.00
Income Taxes	−571.45	9,098.00	7,609.00	6,769.00
Minority Interest	−245.80	778.00	421.00	718.00
Preferred Securities of Subsidiary Trust	0.00	0.00	0.00	0.00
Net Income from Continuing Operations	−4,423.78	17,146.00	13,927.00	11,681.00
Net Income from Discontinued Ops.	0.00	0.00	0.00	0.00
Net Income from Total Operations	−4,423.78	17,146.00	13,927.00	11,681.00
Extraordinary Income/Losses	0.00	0.00	0.00	0.00
Income from Cum. Effect of Acct Chg	0.00	0.00	0.00	0.00
Income from Tax Loss Carryforward	0.00	0.00	0.00	0.00
Other Gains (Losses)	0.00	0.00	0.00	0.00
Total Net Income	−4,423.78	17,146.00	13,927.00	11,681.00
Normalized Income	−4,423.78	17,146.00	13,927.00	11,681.00
Net Income Available for Common	−4,423.78	17,146.00	13,927.00	11,681.00
Preferred Dividends	0.00	0.00	0.00	0.00
Excise Taxes	0.00	0.00	0.00	0.00

(Continued)

Exhibit IV *(Concluded)*

(All amounts in millions of US Dollars except per share data)	03/2009	03/2008	03/2007	03/2006
Per Share Data				
Basic EPS from Continuing Ops.	−2.82	5.40	8.68	7.18
Basic EPS from Discontinued Ops.	0.00	0.00	0.00	0.00
Basic EPS from Total Operations	−2.82	5.40	8.68	7.18
Basic EPS from Extraordinary Inc.	0.00	0.00	0.00	0.00
Basic EPS from Cum Effect of Accounting Chg	0.00	0.00	0.00	0.00
Basic EPS from Other Gains (Losses)	0.00	0.00	0.00	0.00
Basic EPS Total	−2.82	5.40	8.68	7.18
Basic Normalized Net Income/Share	−2.82	5.40	8.68	7.18
Diluted EPS from Continuing Ops.	−2.82	5.39	8.68	7.18
Diluted EPS from Discontinued Ops.	0.00	0.00	0.00	0.00
Diluted EPS from Total Operations	−2.82	5.39	8.68	7.18
Diluted EPS from Extraordinary Inc.	0.00	0.00	0.00	0.00
Diluted EPS from Cum Effect of Accounting Chg	0.00	0.00	0.00	0.00
Diluted EPS from Other Gains (Losses)	0.00	0.00	0.00	0.00
Diluted EPS Total	−2.82	5.39	8.68	7.18
Diluted Normalized Net Income/Share	−2.82	5.39	8.68	7.18
Dividends Paid per Share	2.49	2.16	0.00	1.26

*Toyota's financial year ends on March 31.

Source: http://www.marketwatch.com/investing/stock/tm/financials.

According to some analysts, TPS enhanced flexibility and production capacity which allowed the company to make the best use of its resources. The focus of the TPS was to reduce cost through elimination of waste or *Muda*.[23] The company believed that waste not only raised cost, but also concealed problems within the system, leading to more serious repercussions at a later stage. Toyota practiced the principle of lean thinking which allowed workers to become independent goal seekers and encouraged them to apply their problem-solving skills to fixing defects during the production process and reducing wastes in all transactions. Experts opined that Toyota implemented lean production techniques through continuous improvement and learning, eliminating waste, getting quality right the first time, empowering employees to become problem solvers, and satisfying customers.

In June 1960, Eiji laid down the guiding principles for quality control at Toyota and introduced the concept of building quality into processes. These guiding principles were formulated in response to the deteriorating quality of products caused by insufficiently trained staff at Toyota plants. For instance, the pressure to launch the second generation Corona into the market as quickly as possible in order to meet market demand led to some early product defects. Though the defects were rectified later, the issue affected the image of the company. In June 1961, Toyota adopted a system of Total Quality Control (TQC) to modernize management operations. This system analyzed the cause of defects that occurred during production and developed measures to prevent their recurrence. In addition to this, quality control teams were formed at all levels to promote company-wide participation. Toyota's TQC efforts were officially recognized in 1965, when the company was awarded the Deming Application Prize[24] for quality control management.

To manufacture world-class, quality automobiles at competitive prices, Toyota incorporated several operational concepts into its production system. The TPS was built on two main principles, Just-in-Time (JIT) production and *Jidoka*.

JUST-IN-TIME

Ohno implemented the concept of JIT in Toyota's manufacturing operations during the early 1970s. The JIT system comprised a set of activities aimed at increasing production volume through the optimum use of inventories of raw materials, work-in-process, and finished goods. The objective of the JIT system was to avoid waste, reduce inventories, and increase production efficiency. It was based on the principle of producing only the required products in specific quantities at a given point in time thereby eliminating waste of all kinds and reducing cost. JIT was based on the 'pull' system of manufacturing wherein products were manufactured on demand as against the commonly used 'push' system,[25] where each process manufactured components based on capacity regardless of the demand. The 'push' system often created excess inventory and blocked the production line.

At Toyota JIT was used not only in manufacturing but also in product development, supplier relations, and distribution. It helped the company respond quickly to changing customer needs and offered high quality products at low costs, thereby enhancing customer satisfaction. Implementing JIT was a complex procedure for Toyota as thousands of components were involved and it was difficult for preceding processes to correctly anticipate the exact demand of the subsequent processes. In order to overcome this difficulty, Ohno developed the *Kanban* system.

Kanban

Kanban (meaning 'signboard' in Japanese) was an essential component of JIT. The concept was used in the TPS to effectively control production quantities. The idea was devised by Ohno based on the system followed by supermarkets in the U.S. for replenishment of store shelves based on the quantities picked by the customers. The essence of *Kanban* was that a supplier delivered components to the production line only when required, thus eliminating storage in the production area. People working on a certain process of the production line withdrew units in required quantities from the preceding process on the line at a given point of time.

In the *Kanban* system, workers of a process listed the number of components required on a card called the *Kanban*. A worker would take the card to the preceding process and withdraw the amount required from it. The system was made up of a fixed number of containers, each holding a certain fixed quantity of parts. Each container had a set of *Kanbans* attached to it. Each set comprised two types of *Kanbans*— the 'Withdrawal *Kanban*' and the 'Production *Kanban*'. A Withdrawal *Kanban* detailed the kind and quantity of product that the subsequent process should withdraw from the preceding process. The Production-ordering *Kanban* specified the kind and quantity of the product that the preceding process must produce. The total number of containers and the number of parts each container would hold was calculated using a formula to arrive at the maximum amount of inventory that could be present in the system to hold the process together.

Jidoka

Another important operational principle of the TPS was *Jidoka* (self-regulation), which focused on empowerment of workers. The company believed that people were an important element of the TPS and that without their support the system would not work efficiently. To ensure smooth and quality production, Toyota encouraged its workers to play an active role in quality control and implement their ideas and opinions in production processes. Workers were given the responsibility of ensuring the quality of their own work and were instructed not to pass on poor quality to the next stage. Through visible control, any employee at any level of the hierarchy had a right to make improvements in processes or eliminate any waste that they identified.

Jidoka promoted worker participation and empowered workers to stop the equipment or operations in a line any time during the production process if they spotted a problem in the line. Whenever a worker detected an abnormality or problem in the production line, or was unable to keep pace with the line, he/she could stop the operation by pulling a cord called the 'andon' cord located next to the assembly line. Pulling the cord set off an alarm system, and illuminated the color coded andon electric light board, and alerted supervisors to the presence of a problem in the line. Until the problem was resolved, the line was not restarted.

Experts pointed out that the *Jidoka* system helped direct attention to a problem as soon as it occurred, thus preventing further complications and breakdown of equipment. The process involved every team member in monitoring and checking the quality of cars produced which helped the company in achieving high levels of efficiency. Implementing *Jidoka* helped make problems transparent and the production process saw a lot of improvement.

In addition to JIT and *Jidoka*, Toyota adopted many other operational principles such as *Kaizen* which became benchmarks for production practices across the global corporate world.

Kaizen

Kaizen, which meant 'continuous improvement,' was adopted by Toyota in the early 1950s to improve the production processes, increase efficiency, and reduce waste. Some analysts opined that *Kaizen* was the major contributor to the company's global success. Kaizen required all employees to participate in eliminating all activities that were classified as 'waste', from the production system and improve plant layout, machine design, or process flow. At Toyota, *Kaizen* was not used just to identify a problem and develop a solution, but was viewed as a corporate philosophy. The 'five whys' were an important part of *Kaizen.* Ohno insisted that workers at Toyota should ask 'why' five times when confronted with any problem. This way one would get to the root of the problem, eliminate it, and prevent its recurrence. "He wanted us to watch and ask 'why' over and over again. If we did that, he knew that better ideas would come. Mr. Ohno realized new thoughts and new technologies do not come out of the blue—they come from true understanding of the process,"[26] said Teruyuki Minoura, former president and CEO, Toyota Motor Manufacturing North America Inc.

At Toyota, team leaders and supervisors followed *Kaizen* seriously and were on the constant lookout for problems and ways to improve productivity. They observed workers and their work processes so that problems could be detected on the spot. Through quality circles[27] and a reward system, team members strove to achieve *Kaizen.* Ohno believed that to achieve *Kaizen,* it was important for employees at Toyota to be in touch with *gemba* or the place where the action was (in this case the manufacturing plant) and come up with at least one idea for *Kaizen.*

An important element in *Kaizen* was *Poka-yoke* or error proofing. *Pokayoke* involved the creation of processes that moved smoothly from step to step, without giving room for errors to creep in. At Toyota, processes were often created in such a way as to make it impossible to assemble a product in any way other than the correct one, to eliminate the chance of error. According to experts, *Kaizen* played a vital role in the application of TPS, JIT, *Kanban,* and *Jidok*a (Refer to Figure I for an outline of the Toyota Production System).

As a company committed to quality, Toyota established an efficient development and production system which handled complex automobile functions and systems and met the goals of design, cost, and production volume. During the planning stage, Toyota designed quality into the automobile and ensured that the end product was defect free. At the beginning of the development stage, the design staff worked along with the production team to incorporate easy-to-manufacture features into design drawings. The purchasing division communicated Toyota's quality guidelines to the suppliers through presentations and meetings related to the quality of purchased parts. Personnel from Toyota's development and production divisions too visited suppliers to check the quality of components. The company conducted quality audits to check the reliability of its vehicles. These audits included testing exhaust systems, maintaining mass production quality control levels, identifying improvements for quality assurance methods, and carrying out detailed vehicle evaluations. At the end of the final assembly, the vehicles were put through functional inspection wherein every aspect of the vehicle was subjected to a series of tests. During the final inspection, the functional and physical aspects of the vehicles were examined. Test tracks were conducted for a check of road performance and customer satisfaction drive tests were done.

Exhibit VII   World's Top 10 Auto Groups by 2009 H1 Sales

Rank	Company	Sales (US$ million)
1	Toyota Motor Corp	3.564
2	General Motors Co	3.553
3	*Volkswagen AG	3.265
4	#Hyundai Motor Co	2.153
5	**Ford Motor Co	2.145
6	PSA Peugeot Citroen	1.587
7	Honda Motor Co	1.586
8	Nissan Motor Co	1.546
9	Suzuki Motor Corp	1.15
10	Renault SA	1.107

*Excludes Scania.
**Ford publishes wholesale, not retail, figures.
#Including Kia Motors Corp (000270.KS).

Source: www.reuters.com.

on being the biggest instead of the best, and that's a shame,"[44] said Jake Fisher (Fisher), senior engineer at the nonprofit Consumer Union, which publishes *Consumer Reports*.

Despite the recalls, in 2008, Toyota realized its goal and surpassed GM as the world's largest car maker in terms of sales volume (Refer to Exhibit VII for World's Top 10 Auto Groups by 2009 H1 Sales). Critics alleged that Toyota had had to compromise on quality to achieve the number one spot in the auto industry. The ranking came at the expense of the company's engineering and quality control prowess, they said.

MORE PROBLEMS IN 2009

In mid-2009, after reporting its first losses due to the global financial crisis, Toyota was taking some urgent steps to bring the automaker back into profits under the new President, Akio, who adopted the traditional Toyota practice *genchi genbutsu* to solve problems. Just then, Toyota received another setback. The company's handling of safety issues came under scrutiny because of the increase in incidents of sudden acceleration in Toyota and Lexus vehicles, which had caused accidents resulting in 19 fatalities since 2001.[45] Experts said that there were faults with the Toyota's vehicle throttle systems[46] which caused

accelerators to stick at high speeds, thereby causing accidents. In 2009, Toyota recalled about 4 million Toyota and Lexus cars for faulty gas pedals that stuck in floor mats, resulting in sudden acceleration. The recall came after a family of four was killed in California as the Lexus in which they were traveling reportedly accelerated on its own. The pedal parts were manufactured by a supplier, CTS Corp,[47] in North America. However, Toyota's Japanese models which sourced the same parts from a different supplier were not affected. Also in November 2009, Toyota recalled 110,000 Tundra pick-up trucks due to rust-prone frames which caused the spare tire to fall into the roadway, posing a danger to other vehicles.

As the intensity of the recalls increased, experts began to question Toyota's reputation as a quality automaker. Toyota's position began to slip in consumer satisfaction surveys too. In the Insurance Institute for Highway Safety's tests of 2010 model cars and light trucks, none of Toyota's vehicles were named top picks. "It takes a very long time to establish a reputation for safety and reliability. It doesn't take very long to lose it,"[48] said Fisher. According to a study carried out by U.S. Global Quality Research System[49] in April 2009, Toyota lost its top position as a quality car maker and was tied with Ford. According to Martin Zimmerman, a staff writer at *Los Angeles Times*, "It's a humbling comedown for an automaker that in the early years of this decade routinely had the fewest recalls among the six largest players in the U.S. auto market. In 2000, for example, Toyota recalled a mere 8,379 vehicles, according to government data."[50]

On January 21, 2010, Toyota recalled approximately 2.3 million select Toyota Division vehicles in the U.S. due to a faulty gas pedal that stuck and caused acceleration without warning. Toyota also suspended the sales of eight of its most popular models involved in the recall. The suspended models contributed to 57% of Toyota's sales in the U.S. in 2009. (Refer to Box I for Toyota vehicles affected by the recall).

Soon after the recalls, Toyota announced that it would discontinue production of the affected vehicles at six North American plants for a week starting February 1, 2010. The automaker said the move would affect plants in Princeton, (Indiana), Lafayette (Indiana), Georgetown (Kentucky), San Antonio (Texas), Cambridge (Ontario), and

Box I **Toyota Models Affected by the Recall**

1	Certain 2009–2010 RAV4
2	Certain 2009–2010 Corolla
3	2009–2010 Matrix
4	2005–2010 Avalon
5	Certain 2007–2010 Camry
6	Certain 2010 Highlander
7	2007–2010 Tundra
8	2008–2010 Sequoia

Source: http://pressroom.toyota.com.

Woodstock (Ontario). However, the Lexus Division or Scion vehicles, Toyota Prius, the Tacoma, the Sienna, the Venza, the Solara, the Yaris, the 4Runner, the FJ Cruiser, the Land Cruiser, Highlander hybrids, and certain Camry models, including Camry hybrids were available for sale. The recall also widened to Europe and China where a similar accelerator part was used in the vehicles. In Europe, Toyota was expected to recall two million vehicles and was evaluating the models to be recalled. In China, Toyota was expected to start a recall in February 2010 for 75,500 RAV4 SUVs that were manufactured in China between March 2009 and January 2010.

WHAT WENT WRONG?

According to analysts, as the company was aggressively expanding globally, it lost its focus on quality and failed to maintain quality standards at its overseas plants. After becoming the president of Toyota in June 2009, Akio accepted that the company in a bid to become the world's largest car maker, had drifted away from its core value of focusing on the customer. "I do not think we were wrong to expand our business to meet the needs of customers around the world, but we may have stretched more than we should have. Rather than asking, 'How many cars will we sell?' or 'How much money will we make by selling these cars?' we need to ask ourselves, 'What kind of cars will make people happy?' as well as, 'What pricing will attract them in each region?' Then we must make those cars," he said.[51]

Some experts were of the opinion that Toyota's very success had contributed to some of its failures and that the company had only itself to blame. They pointed out that Toyota's global growth pressured the automaker's resources. Analysts said that quality suffered as Toyota began chasing sales to increase its market share and gain market dominance and profitability. The company's pursuit of cost-savings may have seen those values compromised, they added. According to Michelle Krebs, a senior analyst at Edmunds .com[52], "Toyota has been the favored child for a long time. Now, all of a sudden, they're just like the rest of the auto companies: They make mistakes. We've always wondered if they've stretched their resources too thin. Engineering, marketing, manufacturing—they're doing a lot more with the same amount of people."[53]

Experts were of the view that the company's cost-cutting measures had also contributed to the fall in quality. In order to save money, Toyota used an increasing number of common parts across a number of its car models. For instance, Toyota used the same accelerator pedal made by supplier CTS Corp in the eight different car models whose production was halted in February 2010. Experts said that generally big car companies used this kind of platform sharing to reduce costs but this, in turn, exposed them to risk as even a small defect could lead to big problems for the companies. According to some analysts, the quality failure at Toyota was due to a greater emphasis being placed on costs, which was creating a wedge between the company and its suppliers. "They're not keeping as close a watch on how suppliers are performing and they're not letting suppliers know how they are performing. They're a malaise in the Toyota way. There's an increasing number of recalls and we're hearing it from suppliers about how Toyota treats them. Toyota is becoming just another automaker,"[54] said John W. Henke Jr., president of Planning Perspectives, Inc.[55]

Some analysts also said that the automaker had set aside its "Toyota way" of quality and become more aggressive in its sales in order to topple GM. The management even failed to anticipate looming problems and expanded too quickly, ignoring Toyota's style of disciplined growth, they added. Some analysts were of the view that though its profits had grown, it had spent less wisely. John R. Harris, a Tokyo-based communications consultant specializing in the auto industry, said,

"It's hubris, in a word. A cloak of false humility. Toyota secretly set its sights on catching General Motors as the world's top-selling carmaker. They snuck up behind GM, all while keeping their head down. But as they got closer, they got caught by this desire to be No. 1. But behind it all was this huge ambition. As the ambition got a hold of them, they overreached."[56]

Some experts opined that outsourcing may have also played a part in the carmaker's problems. Initially, the company purchased parts from Japanese suppliers. But as it began to expand, Toyota outsourced most of its manufacturing and production. It begun to source parts locally, changed its raw materials suppliers, and opened plants nearer to its markets. It was reported that during recession, the company demanded that suppliers make parts cheaply. According to an executive at a major U.S. supplier, Toyota insisted that his firm make each group of parts 10% cheaper.[57] Analysts said that a fewer number of Toyotas were built in Japan and the company had not maintained the same quality levels at its overseas plants. Some experts were of the opinion that the quality of Toyota cars had slipped after the company began its expansion in North America. In Japan, quality control was not an issue as executives could go to the sites to help train workers and impart the firm's values for building vehicles. "Production was expanding so fast that there was a lack of trained mechanics to teach the new ones. Those mechanics teaching were doing so with a bit of concern about their expertise,"[58] said Masahiro Fukuda, a senior analyst at Fourin, Inc.[59]

According to Hiroyuki Yokoyama (Yokoyama), the company's general manager for quality, at Toyota, quality had suffered for a number of internal and external reasons such as a rapid increase in production, a proliferation of model types, more electronic controls, swelling global ranks of employees, and customers' heightened quality expectations. "Internally, we were not able to keep up with the external changes, and some of those results showed up in quality,"[60] said Yokoyama.

Some analysts opined that Toyota had deliberately overlooked issues related to the quality of its vehicles. The company delayed recalls and tried to blame human error in cases where owners claimed vehicle defects. According to an investigation carried out by the *Los Angeles Times* in December 2009, Toyota had concealed safety issues on several occasions in an effort to keep its name clean and allegedly paid out cash settlements to people who had sued the company after serious accidents.[61] Even customers who complained of acceleration problems with their vehicles received buybacks under lemon laws[62] from Toyota. In both cases, the owners were forced to sign non-disclosure agreements. The paper reported that the sudden-acceleration issue had existed for years, leading to several recalls since 2000. Several incidents of Toyota concealing defects or delaying recalls even after receiving several complaints were reported. For instance, in 1994, National Highway Traffic Safety Administration (NHTSA)[63] slapped a US$ 250,000 fine on Toyota, for providing misleading information about a fuel leak in Land Cruisers and waiting for two years to fix the problem. Some analysts felt that though Toyota had been facing quality problems since the 2000s, the company had reacted to the situation strongly only in the end of 2009.

Some analysts blamed Watanabe for the lapse in quality as he was at the helm in 2006 when recalls mounted to more than 1 million a year. In pursuing the company's goal of becoming a market leader, Watanabe had taken some missteps, they added. For instance, in order to gain a stronghold of profits and a market share in Detroit's car market, the company built a US$ 1.3 billion plant in November 2006 in San Antonio to manufacture its largest pick-up, the Tundra, just before cracks emerged in the U.S. subprime-mortgage market. Analysts felt that the opening of the Texas plant just when the market had fallen apart was a big mistake on Toyota's part. In his speech to Japan's National Press Club in 2008, Watanabe said that Toyota was a victim of the "big company disease."[64]

HAS TOYOTA LOST ITS QUALITY EDGE?

Some analysts expected Toyota's quality problems and the subsequent recalls to affect the brand image of the company in the long run and lead to a short-term effect on earnings. Toyota dealers would suffer losses and brand loyalty would get eroded, they said. Moreover, experts felt that constant recalls by Toyota would hurt the reputation of the automotive industry of Japan in general. "Automaking is perhaps Japan's premier industry, and the perception here is that one of our national champions has embarrassed us,"[65] said Christopher Richter, senior research analyst at Calyon Capital Markets Asia.[66]

Analysts were of the view that Toyota's decision to stop selling some of its top-selling models in the U.S. would cost the carmaker dearly as these models accounted for 70% of Toyota-brand sales and about 56% of overall U.S. sales. In December 2009, Toyota sold more than 34,000 Camrys in America, which made it the best-selling car in the country. According to IHS Global Insight[67] Toyota would lose 20,000 vehicle sales a week till it resumed sales and production of the eight car models.[68] According to Tatsuo Yoshida, an auto analyst at UBS Securities Japan Ltd.,[69] lost sales were costing Toyota US $155 million a week and the cost of the recalls was likely to total about US$ 900 million.[70] On February 2, 2010, the company reported a 16% decline in sales to a 10-year low of 98,796 vehicles.[71] According to John Paul MacDuffie, co-director of the International Motor Vehicle Program,[72] "It's a huge threat to their reputation. Now, Toyota is having to stop the line at the corporate level in a big way."[73]

On the other hand, some analysts felt that the recalls would not affect the reputation of Toyota, which had been known for years for manufacturing quality vehicles. They opined that the recalls might actually end up being positive for the brand as the company had taken the responsibility for the fault, halted production, and addressed the issue in the best interests of its customers. Some experts said that Toyota had been proactive by taking responsibility and fixing the quality related problems. Even though other manufacturers had faced similar problems, none of them had pulled the models out from the market as Toyota had done, they added. Analysts were of the view that despite the recalls, Toyota's reputation as a quality car maker remained unscathed. In 2009, 10 of the J.D. Power Initial Quality Study (IQS)[74] awards for the best vehicles in a segment were given to Toyota or its Lexus unit. This was more than any other automaker had received (Refer to Exhibit VIII for 2009 nameplate IQS rankings).

Exhibit VIII   2009 J.D. Power Initial Quality Study (IQS) Rankings

Brand	Problems per 100 Vehicles*	Brand	Problems per 100 Vehicles
Lexus	84	Audi	118
Porsche	90	Pontiac	118
Cadillac	91	Scion	118
Hyundai	95	Volvo	118
Honda	99	Saturn	120
Mercedes-Benz	101	Mazda	123
Toyota	**102**	Lincoln	129
Ford	102	Subaru	130
Chevrolet	103	Dodge	134
Suzuki	103	Jaguar	134
Infiniti	106	Mitsubishi	135
Mercury	106	Chrysler	136
Nissan	110	HUMMER	136
Acura	111	Jeep	137
BMW	112	SAAB	138
Kia	112	Smart	138
Volkswagen	112	Land Rover	150
GMC	116	MINI	165
Buick	117		

*The industry average is 108.

Source: J.D Power & Associates 2009 Initial Quality Study.

Toyota's assembly plant in Higashi-Fuji, Japan, received the Platinum Plant Quality Award for manufacturing vehicles with fewest defects and malfunctions. In January 2010, the brand also topped *Consumer Reports* magazine's annual survey of automotive brand perceptions.

Some experts felt that the issues related to quality would be resolved quickly and that it would not be fair to question the reputation of a company which had been viewed as the leader in automotive quality for years. For instance, during the recession, Toyota had no involuntary layoffs and employed extra people to focus intensely on quality and safety. At some of the Toyota's plants, 40% of workers who were not needed for production were paid full-time to learn its famous production system and point out problems during production. Jeffrey K. Liker, professor of industrial and operations engineering at the University of Michigan and writer of the international best seller *The Toyota Way* (McGraw-Hill, 2004), said, "Before all of the recent negative news—about unintended acceleration, recalls of millions of vehicles, and a shutdown of U.S. production—I was working on a book extolling the virtues of this great company, which was using the recession to retain employees, not lay them off, and teach them *kaizen* (the Japanese philosophy of continuous improvement). So what happened that is causing the media to write off 60 years of progress in a company that has become a model of operational excellence. It seems to me that the inferences about Toyota's quality problems are emotional and have little to do with actual facts."[75]

Some experts opined that though the parts of the recalled vehicles had been supplied by an American company, it was Toyota's responsibility to ensure that they worked properly before they were installed. Critics alleged that Toyota had stopped sales as it was not able to fix the problem and not because of its concern for customers. It might take a significant amount of time for the company to address the quality issues across all its vehicle models, they said. According to John Wolkonowicz, (Wolkonowicz), an analyst at IHS Global Insight, "This is the biggest crisis in the auto industry since the bankruptcies of GM and Chrysler. Toyota is not going to be able to contain this problem in a short period of time."[76]

Some industry observers opined that quality was one of the biggest strengths of Toyota and if that itself deteriorated, the brand would lose its value. "There's nothing else to the brand [Toyota]. It's not built on eye-catching design. It's not built on a cutting-edge driving experience. It's not built on performance. It's built on quality and low-cost of ownership,"[77] said Wolkonowicz. Experts were of the view that if consumers lost their confidence in Toyota cars, they might switch to other brands. According to research by Art Spinella, president of CNW Marketing Research, Inc.[78] in 2004, 92% of first-year Toyota owners were willing to recommend their car to a friend, while the recommendation percentage dropped to 88% in 2009 behind Ford, Chevrolet, Honda, Volkswagen, and Hyundai. Analysts felt that Toyota's quality woes had also opened the doors for its competitors. For instance, in the U.S., Ford, GM, and Hyundai started offering interest-free loans and additional trade-in incentives to owners of Toyota vehicles. These companies also offered US$1,000 to customers who were willing to trade in any Toyota. According to Peter DeLorenzo, editor of AutoExtremist.com,[79] "Toyota is in serious trouble, because now there are too many competitive models from savvy competitors—Ford and Hyundai for instance—that are presenting a real alternative to the consumer. The days of Toyota being automatically successful with everything it touches are well and truly over."[80]

Industry insiders were also speculating on whether Toyota's quality troubles might spell the end for the company's president, Akio. He had been under pressure to improve quality since he had taken the helm and recall setbacks may add to the strain, they said. Analysts felt that Akio's ability to steer Toyota through a crisis would decide his legacy at Toyota. However, some analysts opined that with a spate of recalls and issues related to quality, a tough road lay ahead for Akio. Commenting on the crisis, Sean Kane, president of Safety Research & Strategies, Inc.[81] said, "It is a perfect storm for Toyota. I don't think they're unfairly being targeted. I think they're finally being targeted."[82]

OUTLOOK

Experts felt that in order to prevent its image from slipping further, Toyota had to focus on its quality aspect. The company needed to closely monitor quality and overhaul its design, engineering, and manufacturing operations. Toyota should reorganize its production plants, switch suppliers, and ship in parts from Japan. The company should retrain its North American assembly workers by following a "back to basics" approach to identify and correct defective working practices and highlight the need for increased front line vigilance, they said.

According to industry analysts, Toyota, known for its reputation for quality, had to effectively communicate its strategy to customers to retain its position as one of the biggest auto makers in the world. In order to maintain its position in the market, the company should contact owners individually in order to get them into dealerships for repairs, and then compensate them by offering a rebate or another free service. Toyota must avoid creating more bad feelings among consumers, they said. According to Schweitzer, "If I were advising Toyota, I'd tell them this is an opportunity to regain trust, to demonstrate unparalleled commitment to its customers. The company should show that it is willing to do what it takes to make sure [its] customers are driving safe vehicles. If they miss this opportunity, it will be very costly. The politicians will be trying to score political points by raking some [Toyota officials] over the coals and painting them as profit-hungry executives. It's going to be a tough crowd."[83]

On January 31, 2010, in order to rebuild its decades-long reputation for quality and to promote the reliability and safety of its vehicles, Toyota launched a major public relations campaign. The company ran a full-page print ad in major newspapers explaining its decision to halt production of the defective cars. The black-and-white ads featured a large image of a 'pause' button with the caption "A temporary pause," "To put you first." A top executive from the company was likely to appear on television to discuss the recalls. George Peterson, an analyst at AutoPacific, Inc.,[84] said, "What they absolutely have to do is convince people that they are working on this and are going to do the right thing for cars on the road, at dealerships and in production."[85]

In the fiscal year through March 2010, Toyota expected a net loss of 200 billion yen despite efforts to cut costs by 440 billion yen during the year. It was reported that global recalls of about 8 million vehicles would reduce the demand by 100,000 vehicles and cost the company 100 billion yen.[86] In the three months ending March 31, 2010, sales of 503,000 vehicles were predicted in North America. However, analysts felt that the company would not be able to achieve the sales target as customers were reluctant to buy Toyota vehicles due to quality problems. "There's a huge possibility that Toyota won't meet this forecast. The recalls will damage their reputation and if they widen, there will be costs which Toyota has not yet taken into account,"[87] said Koji Endo, managing director of Advanced Research Japan Co.[88]

In order to uphold the reputation of Toyota, Akio planned to set up a global quality special task force that would conduct regional quality improvement activities around the world. The committee headed by the president was to inspect every process—quality in design, quality in production, quality in sales, and quality in service and provide customers with satisfying products in each and every region. *Genchi-genbutsu* activities would be encouraged and the company would enhance the frequency of communication between itself and regional authorities. To develop quality-management professionals, Toyota would start an "Automotive Center of Quality Excellence" in key regions. Based on the improvements, Akio planned to seek evaluation from outside experts regarding its newly improved quality-control management and listen to each and every customer and improve quality. Talking about his initiatives, Akio said, "Under the banner, "Let's build better cars", we will go back to the basics of "customer first" and "*genchi genbutsu*", and once more, deeply consider what "customer first" really means. All our employees around the world, all of our dealers, and all of our suppliers will unify in their utmost efforts to regain the trust of our customers as soon as possible."[89]

ENDNOTES

[1] Yuri Kageyama, "Toyota Recalls Show Price of Too Rapid Growth," www.miamiherald.com, January 28, 2010.

[2] Fitch Ratings is a global rating agency which provides credit markets with independent and prospective credit opinions, research, and data. Headquartered in New York and London, the agency has 50 offices worldwide.

[3] "Quality on the Line: The Fallout from Toyota's Recall," http://knowledge.wharton.upenn.edu, February 3, 2010.

[4] The University of Pennsylvania's Wharton School of Business is one of the top business schools in the U.S.

[5] Kate Linebaugh and Norihiko Shirouzu, "Toyota Halts Sales over Safety Issue," http://online.wsj.com, January 26, 2010.

[6] Yuri Kageyama, "Toyota Recalls Show Price of Too Rapid Growth," www.miamiherald.com, January 28, 2010.

[7] Other business operations of Toyota include intelligent transport systems, IT and telecommunications, housing, motorboat manufacturing, and biotechnology and afforestation businesses.

[8] Toyota's financial year ends on March 31.

[9] "Toyota Announces Third-quarter Financial Results," www.toyota.co.jp, February 4, 2010.

[10] Based in New York, Casesa Shapiro Group LLC is an independent advisory firm specializing in the auto industry.

[11] Alan Ohnsman and Mike Ramsey, "Toyota Quality Image May Be 'Finished' as Sales, Output Halted," www.businessweek.com, January 27, 2010.

[12] "Quality on the Line: The Fallout from Toyota's Recall," http://knowledge.wharton.upenn.edu, February 3, 2010.

[13] Founded in 1903, Ford Motor Company is one of the largest automakers in the world. For the year ended 2008, its revenues were US$ 146.277 billion.

[14] General Motors Company, LLC (earlier General Motors Corporation) based in Detroit, is the second-largest automaker in the world. In June 2009, the company filed for Chapter 11 bankruptcy protection. The bankruptcy filing was a dramatic downfall for GM, which was founded in 1908 by William C. Durant. For the year ended 2008, the company reported revenues of US$ 148.979 billion.

[15] Jidoka means that when a problem occurs, the equipment stops immediately, preventing defective products from being produced.

[16] Katsuaki Watanabe served as the president of Toyota from 2005 to mid-2009. He led Toyota on an aggressive and a largely successful growth track. He joined Toyota in 1964 and gained experience primarily in corporate planning and administrative affairs. In 1999, Watanabe was appointed as senior managing director, after which he assumed the position of executive vice-president in 2001. In June 2005, he was appointed as the president of Toyota.

[17] The global financial crisis refers to the credit, banking, trade, and currency crisis that emerged in 2007–2008. This was the result of the failure of several U.S.-based investment companies, mortgage companies, and insurance companies due to the sub-prime crisis in the country. The sub-prime crisis was the result of mortgage delinquencies and foreclosures, which had an impact on banks and markets around the world.

[18] Nick Bunkley, "Toyota Ahead of G.M. in 2008 Sales," www.nytimes.com, January 21, 2009.

[19] Bill Vlasic and Nick Bunkley, "Toyota Scales Back Production of Big Vehicles," www.nytimes.com, July 11, 2008.

[20] www2.toyota.co.jp/en/news/09/0508_1.html.

[21] Genchi Genbutsu means "Go and See the problem first hand" The Company believed that practical experience is valued over theoretical knowledge.

[22] "Aiming to Achieve Zero Customer Complaints," www.toyota.co.jp, 2007.

[23] Muda was identified as any material or action that did not add value to the final product. It was assumed that any equipment, materials, parts, and workers (working time), that exceeded the minimum amount that was absolutely essential to production, was surplus and resulted in increased cost.

[24] The Deming Application Prize is an annual award presented to a company that has achieved distinctive performance improvements through the application of TQM in any industry.

[25] In 'pull'-based manufacturing, products and components are pulled through the system on demand. In contrast, in 'push'-based manufacturing, products are manufactured and then pushed through the system from preceding levels to subsequent levels.

[26] http://akseli.tekes.fi/opencms/opencms/.../ohjelmat/...ja.../NUMMI.pdf.

[27] Quality circle is a group of employees who perform similar duties and meet regularly to identify, analyze, and solve the problems that arise during the course of their work. The basic objectives of quality circles are to develop and utilize human resources effectively, to develop quality products, to improve the quality of work life, and to sharpen and utilize an individual's creative abilities.

[28] The Toyota Way is a management philosophy used by Toyota to communicate the company's corporate philosophy and work culture to its employees. The Toyota Way consists of 14 foundational principles of the Toyota culture, which allows the TPS to function effectively.

[29] Toyota City is located, in the Mikawa region of Aichi, east of Nagoya, Japan. From the time Toyota started the first automobile factory in the city in 1937, it developed rapidly and was named after the auto maker. Toyota's global headquarters are located in this city.

[30] "Aiming to Achieve Zero Customer Complaints," www.toyota.co.jp, 2007.

[31] Norihiko Shirouzu, Mariko Sanchanta and Yoshio Takahashi, "WSJ: Toyota Sales Halt Raises Quality Questions," www.nni.nikkei.co.jp, January 31, 2010.

[32] Micheline Maynard and Martin Fackler, "A Dent in Toyota Quality?–Business–International Herald Tribune," www.nytimes.com, August 4, 2006.

[33] Chrysler Group, LLC is an American automobile manufacturer headquartered in Detroit. On April 30, 2009, Chrysler filed for Chapter 11 bankruptcy protection and announced a plan for a partnership with Italian automaker Fiat.

[34] David Olive, "Toyota's Reputation for Quality Went Long Ago," www.thestar.com, January 29, 2010.

[35] "Toyota's Reputation Takes Some Hard Hits," www.post-gazette.com, August 2, 2006.

[36] Power Information Network (PIN), a subsidiary of J.D. Power and Associates, provides automotive solutions and services to about 7,500 franchise dealerships throughout the U.S. and Canada.

[37] "Toyota's reputation Takes Some Hard Hits," www.post-gazette.com, August 2, 2006.

[38] Micheline Maynard and Martin Fackler, "A Dent in Toyota Quality?–Business–International Herald Tribune," www.nytimes.com, August 4, 2006.

[39] Ibid.

[40] David Olive, "Toyota's Reputation for Quality Went Long Ago," www.thestar.com, January 29, 2010.

[41] Headquartered in Westlake Village, California, J.D. Power and Associates is a global marketing information services company operating in key business sectors including market research, forecasting, performance improvement, Web intelligence, and customer satisfaction. The firm conducts surveys based on customer satisfaction, product quality, and buyer behavior for industries ranging from automobiles to advertising firms. The firm is best known for its customer satisfaction research on new-car quality and long-term dependability.

[42] Headquartered in Seoul, South Korea, Hyundai Motor Co is one of the largest automakers in the world. In the year 2008, the company's net income was KRW 1,447,904 million.

[43] David Olive, "Toyota's Reputation for Quality Went Long Ago," www.thestar.com, January 29, 2010.

[44] Martin Zimmerman "Recall Another Blow to Toyota's Reputation," http://articles.latimes.com, November 26, 2009.

[45] Ken Bensinger and Ralph Vartabedian, "Toyota Found to Keep Tight Lid on Potential Safety Problems," www.latimes.com, December 23, 2009.

[46] A throttle system comprises principal and supplementary throttle valves which control air flow through an engine air induction passage and regulates the supply of fuel to the engine.

[47] Based in Elkhart, Indiana, CTS Corp designs and manufactures electronic components and sensors for the automotive,

computer, communications, medical, defense, aerospace, and industrial markets. The company supplies accelerator pedals to Toyota, Honda, Mitsubishi, Nissan, and Chrysler.

[48] Martin Zimmerman "Recall Another Blow to Toyota's Reputation," http://articles.latimes.com, November 26, 2009.

[49] The U.S. Global Quality Research System is the automotive industry's primary third-party assessment of quality.

[50] Thomas Sloma-Williams, "The Last Word: 'Big' Problems for Toyota," www.qualitymag.com, December 22, 2009.

[51] John Murphy, "Toyota Boss Vows to Change Priorities," http://online.wsj.com, June 26, 2009.

[52] Edmunds.Com is an online resource for automotive consumer information.

[53] Yuri Kageyama, "Toyota Recalls Show Price of too Rapid Growth," www.miamiherald.com, January 28, 2010.

[54] Dave Hannon, "Toyota Quality Concerns Shut Down North American Production," www.purchasing.com, January 27, 2010.

[55] Planning Perspectives, Inc. is a US based management consulting firm specializing in business-to-business marketing, purchasing, and buyer-supplier relations.

[56] John M. Glionna and Coco Masters, "Toyota Recalls Undermine Japanese Confidence in an Industrial Titan," http://m.latimes.com, January 29, 2010.

[57] David Welch, "Toyota's Recalls: A Tough Road Back," www.businessweek.com, February 3, 2010.

[58] Blaine Harden, "Analysts Say Toyota's Push for Growth Caused Faults in Cars," www.contracostatimes.com, January 28, 2010.

[59] Fourin, Inc. is an automobile research and publishing company based in Nagoya, Japan.

[60] Hans Greimel, "Toyota Faces Major Repair Work on its Ailing Image," www.tirebusiness.com, January 18, 2010.

[61] Chris Shunk, "LA Times details Toyota History of Concealing Safety Issues," www.autoblog.com, December 24, 2009.

[62] Lemon laws are American state or federal laws that protect consumers when the automobile they purchase fails to meet quality and performance standards on a consistent basis. Buybacks under lemon laws refer to

those automobiles which the manufacturer has purchased back from an individual under the lemon law. The manufacturer then fixes the problem and sells them at auto auctions as used cars.

[63] The National Highway Traffic Safety Administration (NHTSA) is an agency of the U.S. Department of Transportation (DOT). Its objective is to save lives, prevent injuries, and reduce economic costs due to road traffic crashes through education, research, safety standards, and enforcement activity.

[64] Husna Haq, "Toyota Recall: Did Rapid Growth Hurt the Carmaker's Quality?" www.csmonitor.com, January 28, 2010.

[65] John M. Glionna and Coco Masters, "Toyota Recalls Undermine Japanese Confidence in an Industrial Titan," http://articles.latimes.com, January 29, 2010.

[66] Calyon Calyon Capital Markets Asia is a brokerage house in Hong Kong.

[67] IHS Global Insight provides economic and financial analysis, forecasting, and market intelligence of countries, regions, and industries. Based in the U.S., IHS Global Insight serves more than 170 industries in over 200 countries.

[68] Makiko Kitamura and Tetsuya Komatsu, "Toyoda Shrinks Biggest Carmaker for Quality Control (Update1)," www.businessweek.com, January 28, 2010.

[69] UBS Securities Japan Ltd, a subsidiary of UBS AG, is an investment banking and securities firm.

[70] Yuri Kageyama, "Hurt by Recalls, Toyota Expected to Lose US sales," www.forbes.com, January 29, 2010.

[71] Alan Ohnsman and Keith Naughton, "Toyota's U.S. Sales Decline Signals 'Uphill Battle' (Update1)," www.bloomberg.com, February 3, 2010.

[72] The International Motor Vehicle Program (IMVP) is one of the largest international research groups studying and reporting on the global automobile industry.

[73] "Quality on the Line: The Fallout from Toyota's Recall," http://knowledge.wharton.upenn.edu, February 3, 2010.

[74] The Initial Quality Study serves as the industry benchmark for new-vehicle quality measured at 90 days of ownership. The study

is used by auto makers worldwide to help them design and build better vehicles and by consumers to help them in their vehicle purchase decisions.

[75] Jeffrey Liker, "Toyota's Lost Its Quality Edge? Not So Fast," www.businessweek.com, January 28, 2010.

[76] Alan Ohnsman and Makiko Kitamura, "Toyota Falls as Widening Recalls, Sales Halt Tarnish Reputation," www.bloomberg.com, January 28, 2010.

[77] Martin Zimmerman "Recall Another Blow to Toyota's Reputation," http://articles.latimes.com, November 26, 2009.

[78] CNW Marketing Research, Inc. is a U.S.-based automotive marketing research company.

[79] Autoextremist.com is a weekly online magazine which publishes news, commentaries, and analyses of the auto industry.

[80] James R. Healey and Sharon Silke Carty, "Toyota Recall: Gas Pedal Issue Affects More than 2M vehicles," www.usatoday.com, January 22, 2010.

[81] Safety Research & Strategies Inc. is a U.S.-based auto safety research group which provides analysis, strategies, and advocacy on motor vehicle and product safety issues.

[82] Hans Greimel, "Toyota Faces Major Repair Work on its Ailing Image," www.tirebusiness.com, January 18, 2010.

[83] "Quality on the Line: The Fallout from Toyota's Recall," http://knowledge.wharton.upenn.edu, February 3, 2010.

[84] AutoPacific, Inc. is a California-based automotive-specialist research firm.

[85] Roger Vincent and Ken Bensinger, "Toyota Works to Save Face," http://m.latimes.com, February 1, 2010.

[86] Makiko Kitamura and Tetsuya Komatsu, "Toyota Expects to Return to Full-Year Profit amid Recall Crisis," www.bloomberg.com, February 4, 2010.

[87] Ibid.

[88] Advanced Research Japan Co. is an equity research firm in Tokyo.

[89] "Address by TMC President Akio Toyoda," www.toyota.co.jp, February 5, 2010.

beans and make their own freshly brewed coffee at home. Baldwin, Siegel, and Bowker were well acquainted with Peet's expertise, having visited his store on numerous occasions and listened to him expound on quality coffees and the importance of proper bean-roasting techniques.

The Pikes Place store featured modest, hand-built, classic nautical fixtures. One wall was devoted to whole bean coffees, while another had shelves of coffee products. The store did not offer fresh-brewed coffee sold by the cup, but tasting samples were sometimes available. Initially, Siegel was the only paid employee. He wore a grocer's apron, scooped out beans for customers, extolled the virtues of fine, dark-roasted coffees, and functioned as the partnership's retail expert. The other two partners kept their day jobs but came by at lunch or after work to help out. During the start-up period, Baldwin kept the books and developed a growing knowledge of coffee; Bowker served as the "magic, mystery, and romance man."[2] The store was an immediate success, with sales exceeding expectations, partly because of interest stirred by a favorable article in the *Seattle Times*. For most of the first year, Starbucks ordered its coffee beans from Peet's, but then the partners purchased a used roaster from Holland, set up roasting operations in a nearby ramshackle building, and came up with their own blends and flavors.

By the early 1980s, the company had four Starbucks stores in the Seattle area and had been profitable every year since opening its doors. But then Zev Siegel experienced burnout and left the company to pursue other interests. Jerry Baldwin took over day-to-day management of the company and functioned as chief executive officer; Gordon Bowker remained involved as an owner but devoted most of his time to his advertising and design firm, a weekly newspaper he had founded, and a microbrewery that he was launching known as the Redhook Ale Brewery.

Howard Schultz Enters the Picture

In 1981, Howard Schultz, vice president and general manager of U.S. operations for a Swedish maker of stylish kitchen equipment and coffee-makers, decided to pay Starbucks a visit—he was curious about why Starbucks was selling so many of his company's products. When he arrived at the Pikes Place store, a solo violinist was playing Mozart at the door (his violin case open for donations). Schultz was immediately taken by the powerful and pleasing aroma of the coffees, the wall displaying coffee beans, and the rows of coffeemakers on the shelves. As he talked with the clerk behind the counter, the clerk scooped out some Sumatran coffee beans, ground them, put the grounds in a cone filter, poured hot water over the cone, and shortly handed Schultz a porcelain mug filled with freshly brewed coffee. After taking only three sips of the brew, Schultz was hooked. He began asking questions about the company, the coffees from different parts of the world, and the different ways of roasting coffee.

Later, when he met with Jerry Baldwin and Gordon Bowker, Schultz was struck by their knowledge of coffee, their commitment to providing customers with quality coffees, and their passion for educating customers about the merits of dark-roasted coffees. Baldwin told Schultz, "We don't manage the business to maximize anything other than the quality of the coffee."[3] The company purchased only the finest arabica coffees and put them through a meticulous dark-roasting process to bring out their full flavors. Baldwin explained that the cheap robusta coffees used in supermarket blends burned when subjected to dark-roasting. He also noted that the makers of supermarket blends preferred lighter roasts because it allowed higher yields (the longer a coffee was roasted, the more weight it lost).

Schultz was also struck by the business philosophy of the two partners. It was clear that Starbucks stood not just for good coffee but also for the dark-roasted flavor profiles that the founders were passionate about. Top-quality, fresh-roasted, whole-bean coffee was the company's differentiating feature and a bedrock value. It was also clear to Schultz that Starbucks was strongly committed to educating its customers to appreciate the qualities of fine coffees. The company depended mainly on word of mouth to get more people into its stores, then built customer loyalty cup by cup as buyers gained a sense of discovery and excitement about the taste of fine coffee.

On his return trip to New York, Howard Schultz could not stop thinking about Starbucks and what it would be like to be a part of the Starbucks enterprise. Schultz recalled, "There was something magic about it, a passion and authenticity I had never experienced in business."[4] The appeal of living in the Seattle area was another strong plus. By the time he landed at Kennedy Airport, he knew in his heart he wanted to go to work for Starbucks. At the first opportunity, Schultz asked Baldwin whether there was any way he could fit into Starbucks. While he and Baldwin had established an easy, comfortable personal rapport, it still took a year, numerous meetings at which Schultz presented his ideas, and a lot of convincing to get Baldwin, Bowker, and their silent partner from San Francisco to agree to hire him. Schultz pursued a job at Starbucks far more vigorously than Starbucks pursued hiring Schultz. The owners were nervous about bringing in an outsider, especially a high-powered New Yorker who had not grown up with the values of the company. Nonetheless, Schultz continued to press his ideas about the tremendous potential of expanding the Starbucks enterprise outside Seattle and exposing people all over America to Starbucks coffee.

At a meeting with the three owners in San Francisco in the spring of 1982, Schultz once again presented his ideas and vision for opening Starbucks stores across the United States and Canada. He thought the meeting went well and flew back to New York, believing a job offer was in the bag. However, the next day Jerry Baldwin called Schultz and indicated that the owners had decided against hiring him because geographic expansion was too risky and they did not share Schultz's vision for Starbucks. Schultz was despondent, seeing his dreams of being a part of Starbucks' future go up in smoke. Still, he believed so deeply in Starbucks' potential that he decided to make a last-ditch appeal; he called Baldwin the next day and made an impassioned, reasoned case for why the decision was a mistake. Baldwin agreed to reconsider. The next morning Baldwin called Schultz and told him the job of heading marketing and overseeing the retail stores was his. In September 1982, Howard Schultz took over his new responsibilities at Starbucks.

Starbucks and Howard Schultz, 1982–1985

In his first few months at Starbucks, Schultz spent most of his waking hours in the four Seattle stores—working behind the counters, tasting different kinds of coffee, talking with customers, getting to know store personnel, and learning the retail aspects of the coffee business. By December, Jerry Baldwin concluded that Schultz was ready for the final part of his training: actually roasting the coffee. Schultz spent a week getting an education about the colors of different coffee beans, listening for the telltale second pop of the beans during the roasting process, learning to taste the subtle differences among the various roasts, and familiarizing himself with the roasting techniques for different beans.

Schultz made a point of acclimating himself to the informal dress code at Starbucks, gaining credibility and building trust with colleagues, and making the transition from the high-energy, coat-and-tie style of New York to the more casual, low-key ambience of the Pacific Northwest. Schultz made real headway in gaining the acceptance and respect of company personnel while working at the Pike Place store one day during the busy Christmas season that first year. The store was packed and Schultz was behind the counter ringing up sales of coffee when someone shouted that a shopper had just headed out the door with two coffeemakers. Without thinking, Schultz leaped over the counter and chased the thief, yelling, "Drop that stuff! Drop it!" The thief dropped both pieces and ran. Schultz returned to the store, holding the coffeemakers up like trophies. Everyone applauded. When Schultz returned to his office later that afternoon, his staff had strung up a banner that read: "Make my day."[5]

Schultz was overflowing with ideas for the company. Early on, he noticed that first-time customers sometimes felt uneasy in the stores because of their lack of knowledge about fine coffees and because store employees sometimes came across as a little arrogant or superior to coffee novices. Schultz worked with store employees on customer-friendly sales skills and developed brochures that made it easy for customers to learn about fine coffees. However, Schultz's biggest inspiration and vision for Starbucks' future came during the spring of 1983 when the company sent him to Milan, Italy, to attend an international housewares show. While walking from his hotel to the convention center, he spotted an espresso bar and went inside to look around. The cashier beside the door nodded and smiled. The barista behind the counter greeted Schultz cheerfully and began pulling a shot of espresso for one customer and handcrafting a foamy cappuccino for another, all the while conversing merrily with patrons standing at the counter. Schultz thought the barista's performance was great theater. Just down the way on a side street, he entered an even more crowded espresso bar, where the barista, which he surmised to be the owner, was greeting customers by name; people were laughing and talking in an atmosphere that plainly was comfortable and familiar. In the next few blocks, he saw two more espresso bars. That afternoon when the trade show concluded for the day, Schultz walked the streets of Milan to explore more espresso bars. Some were stylish and upscale; others attracted a blue-collar clientele. Most had few chairs, and it was common for Italian opera to be playing in the background. What struck Schultz was how popular and vibrant the Italian coffee bars were. They seemed to function as an integral community gathering place, and energy levels were typically high. Each bar had its own unique character, but they all had a barista that performed with flair and established a camaraderie with the customers.

Schultz remained in Milan for a week, exploring coffee bars and learning as much as he could about the Italian passion for coffee drinks. Schultz was particularly struck by the fact that there were 1,500 coffee bars in Milan, a city about the size of Philadelphia, and a total of 200,000 in all of Italy. In one bar, he heard a customer order a *caffelatte* and decided to try one himself—the barista made a shot of espresso, steamed a frothy pitcher of milk, poured the two together in a cup, and put a dollop of foam on the top. Schultz liked it immediately, concluding that lattes should be a feature item on any coffee bar menu even though none of the coffee experts he had talked to had ever mentioned them.

Schultz's 1983 trip to Milan produced a revelation: the Starbucks stores in Seattle completely missed the point. There was much more to the coffee business than just selling beans and getting people to appreciate grinding their own beans and brewing fine coffee in their homes. What Starbucks needed to do was serve fresh-brewed coffee, espressos and cappuccinos in its stores (in addition to beans and coffee equipment) and try to create an American version of the Italian coffee bar culture. Going to Starbucks should be an experience, a special treat, a place to meet friends and visit. Re-creating the authentic Italian coffee bar culture in the United States could be Starbucks' differentiating factor.

Schultz Becomes Frustrated

On Schultz's return from Italy, he shared his revelation and ideas for modifying the format of Starbucks' stores with Baldwin and Bowker. But instead of winning their approval for trying out some of his ideas, Schultz encountered strong resistance. Baldwin and Bowker argued that Starbucks was a retailer, not a restaurant or coffee bar. They feared that serving drinks would put them in the beverage business and diminish the integrity of Starbucks' mission as a purveyor of fine coffees. They pointed out that Starbucks had been profitable every year and there was no reason to rock the boat in a small, private company like Starbucks. But a more pressing reason not to pursue Schultz's coffee bar concept emerged shortly—Baldwin and Bowker were excited by an opportunity to purchase Peet's Coffee and Tea. The acquisition was finalized in early 1984, and to fund it Starbucks had to take on considerable debt, leaving little in the way of financial flexibility to support Schultz's ideas for entering the beverage part of the coffee business or expanding the number of Starbucks stores. For most of 1984, Starbucks managers were dividing their time between operations in Seattle and the Peet's enterprise in San Francisco. Schultz found himself in San Francisco every other week supervising the marketing and operations of the five Peet stores. Starbucks employees began to feel neglected and, in one quarter, did not receive their usual bonus due to tight financial conditions. Employee discontent escalated to the point where a union election was called. The union won by three votes. Baldwin was shocked at the results, concluding that employees no longer trusted him. In the months that followed, he began to spend more of his energy on the Peet's operation in San Francisco.

It took Howard Schultz nearly a year to convince Jerry Baldwin to let him test an espresso bar. Baldwin relented when Starbucks opened its sixth store in April 1984. It was the first Starbucks store designed to sell beverages, and it was the first located in downtown Seattle. Schultz asked for a 1,500-square-foot space to set up a full-scale Italian-style espresso bar, but Baldwin agreed to allocating only 300 square feet in a corner of the new store. The store opened with no fanfare as a deliberate experiment to see what would happen. By closing time on the first day, some 400 customers had been served, well above the 250-customer average of Starbucks' best-performing stores. Within two months, the store was serving 800 customers per day. The two baristas could not keep up with orders during the early-morning hours, resulting in lines outside the door onto the sidewalk. Most of the business was at the espresso counter, while sales at the regular retail counter were only adequate.

Schultz was elated at the test results, expecting that Baldwin's doubts about entering the beverage side of the business would be dispelled and that he would gain approval to pursue the opportunity to take Starbucks to a new level. Every day he went into Baldwin's office to show him the sales figures and customer counts at the new downtown store. But Baldwin was not comfortable with the success of the new store, believing that it felt wrong and that espresso drinks were a distraction from the core business of marketing fine arabica coffees at retail. Baldwin rebelled at the thought that people would see Starbucks as a place to get a quick cup of coffee to go. He adamantly told Schultz, "We're coffee roasters. I don't want to be in the restaurant business. . . . Besides, we're too deeply in debt to consider pursuing this idea."[6] While he didn't deny that the experiment was succeeding, he didn't want to go forward with introducing beverages in other Starbucks stores. Schultz's efforts to persuade Baldwin to change his mind continued to meet strong resistance, although to avoid a total impasse Baldwin finally did agree to let Schultz put espresso machines in the back of one or two other Starbucks stores.

Over the next several months, Schultz made up his mind to leave Starbucks and start his own company. His plan was to open espresso bars in high-traffic downtown locations, serve espresso drinks and coffee by the cup, and try to emulate the friendly, energetic atmosphere he had encountered in Italian espresso bars. Baldwin and Bowker, knowing how frustrated Schultz had become, supported his efforts to go out on his own and agreed to let him stay in his current

job and office until definitive plans were in place. Schultz left Starbucks in late 1985.

Schultz's Il Giornale Venture

With the aid of a lawyer friend who helped companies raise venture capital and go public, Schultz began seeking out investors for the kind of company he had in mind. Ironically, Jerry Baldwin committed to investing $150,000 of Starbucks' money in Schultz's coffee bar enterprise, thus becoming Schultz's first investor. Baldwin accepted Schultz's invitation to be a director of the new company, and Gordon Bowker agreed to be a part-time consultant for six months. Bowker, pumped up about the new venture, urged Schultz to make sure that everything about the new stores—the name, the presentation, the care taken in preparing the coffee—was calculated to elevate customer expectations and lead them to expect something better than competitors offered. Bowker proposed that the new company be named II Giornale Coffee Company (pronounced *il jor NAHL ee*), a suggestion that Howard accepted. In December 1985, Bowker and Schultz made a trip to Italy, where they visited some 500 espresso bars in Milan and Verona, observing local habits, taking notes about decor and menus, snapping photographs, and videotaping baristas in action.

About $400,000 in seed capital was raised by the end of January 1986, enough to rent an office, hire a couple of key employees, develop a store design, and open the first store. But it took until the end of 1986 to raise the remaining $1.25 million needed to launch at least eight espresso bars and prove that Schultz's strategy and business model were viable. Schultz made presentations to 242 potential investors, 217 of whom said no. Many who heard Schultz's hour-long presentation saw coffee as a commodity business and thought that Schultz's espresso bar concept lacked any basis for sustainable competitive advantage (no patent on dark roast, no advantage in purchasing coffee beans, no ways to bar the entry of imitative competitors). Some noted that coffee couldn't be turned into a growth business—consumption of coffee had been declining since the mid-1960s. Others were skeptical that people would pay $1.50 or more for a cup of coffee, and the company's hard-to-pronounce name turned some off. Being rejected by so many potential investors was disheartening—some who listened to Schultz's presentation didn't even bother to call him back; others refused to take his calls. Nonetheless, Schultz maintained an upbeat attitude and displayed passion and enthusiasm in making his pitch. He ended up raising $1.65 million from about 30 investors; most of the money came from 9 people, 5 of whom became directors.

The first Il Giornale store opened in April 1986. It had 700 square feet and was located near the entrance of Seattle's tallest building. The decor was Italian, and there were Italian words on the menu. Italian opera music played in the background. The baristas wore white shirts and bow ties. All service was stand-up; there were no chairs. National and international papers were hung on rods on the wall. By closing time on the first day, 300 customers had been served—mostly in the morning hours.

But while the core idea worked well, it soon became apparent that several aspects of the format were not appropriate for Seattle. Some customers objected to the incessant opera music, others wanted a place to sit down, and many did not understand the Italian words on the menu. These "mistakes" were quickly fixed, but an effort was made not to compromise the style and elegance of the store. Within six months, the store was serving more than 1,000 customers a day. Regular customers had learned how to pronounce the company's name. Because most customers were in a hurry, it became apparent that speedy service was essential.

Six months after the first Il Giornale opened, a second store was opened in another downtown building. In April 1987, a third store was opened in Vancouver, British Columbia, to test the transferability of the company's business concept outside Seattle. Schultz's goal was to open 50 stores in five years, and he needed to dispel his investors' doubts about geographic expansion early on to achieve his growth objective. By mid-1987, sales at the three stores were running at a rate equal to $1.5 million annually.

Il Giornale Acquires Starbucks

In March 1987, Jerry Baldwin and Gordon Bowker decided to sell the whole Starbucks operation in Seattle—the stores, the roasting plant, and the Starbucks name. Bowker wanted to cash out his coffee business investment to concentrate on his other enterprises; Baldwin, who was tired of commuting between Seattle and San Francisco, wanted to concentrate on the Peet's operation. As he recalls, "My wife and I had a 30-second conversation and decided to keep Peet's. It was the original and it was better."[7]

Schultz knew immediately that he had to buy Starbucks; his board of directors agreed. Schultz and his newly hired finance and accounting manager drew up a set of financial projections for the combined operations and a financing package that included a stock offering to Il Giornale's original investors and a line of credit with local banks. While a rival plan to acquire Starbucks was put together by another Il Giornale investor, Schultz's proposal prevailed and within weeks Schultz had raised the $3.8 million needed to buy Starbucks. The acquisition was completed in August 1987. The new name of the combined companies was Starbucks Corporation. Howard Schultz, at the age of 34, became Starbucks' president and CEO.

STARBUCKS AS A PRIVATE COMPANY, 1987–1992

The following Monday morning, Howard returned to the Starbucks offices at the roasting plant, greeted all the familiar faces, and accepted their congratulations. Then he called the staff together for a meeting on the roasting plant floor:

> All my life I have wanted to be part of a company and a group of people who share a common vision. . . . I'm here today because I love this company. I love what it represents. . . . I know you're concerned. . . . I promise you I will not let you down. I promise you I will not leave anyone behind. . . . In five years, I want you to look back at this day and say "I was there when it started. I helped build this company into something great."[8]

Schultz told the group that his vision was for Starbucks to become a national company with values and guiding principles that employees could be proud of. He indicated that he wanted to include people in the decision-making process and that he would be open and honest with them.

Schultz believed that building a company that valued and respected its people, that inspired them, and that shared the fruits of success with those who contributed to the company's long-term value was essential, not just an intriguing option. His aspiration was for Starbucks to become the most respected brand name in coffee and for the company to be admired for its corporate responsibility. In the next few days and weeks, Schultz came to see that the unity and morale at Starbucks had deteriorated badly in the 20 months he had been at Il Giornale. Some employees were cynical and felt unappreciated. There was a feeling that prior management had abandoned them and a wariness about what the new regime would bring. Schultz decided to make building a new relationship of mutual respect between employees and management a priority.

The business plan Schultz had presented investors called for the new 9-store company to open 125 stores in the next five years—15 the first year, 20 the second, 25 the third, 30 the fourth, and 35 the fifth. Revenues were projected to reach $60 million in 1992. But the company lacked experienced management. Schultz had never led a growth effort of such magnitude and was just learning what the job of CEO was all about, having been the president of a small company for barely two years. Dave Olsen, a Seattle coffee bar owner whom Schultz had recruited to direct store operations at Il Giornale, was still learning the ropes in managing a multistore operation. Ron Lawrence, the company's controller, had worked as a controller for several organizations. Other Starbucks employees had only the experience of managing or being a part of a six-store organization. When Starbucks' key roaster and coffee buyer resigned, Schultz put Dave Olsen in charge of buying and roasting coffee. Lawrence Maltz, who had 20 years' experience in business and 8 years' experience as president of a profitable public beverage company, was hired as executive vice president and charged with heading operations, finance, and human resources.

In the next several months, a number of changes were instituted. To symbolize the merging of the two companies and the two cultures, a new logo was created that melded the designs of the Starbucks logo and the Il Giornale logo. The Starbucks stores were equipped with espresso machines and remodeled to look more Italian than Old World nautical. Il Giornale green replaced the traditional Starbucks brown. The result was a new type of store—a cross between a retail coffee bean store and an espresso bar/café—that became Starbucks' signature.

By December 1987, the mood of the employees at Starbucks had turned upbeat. They were buying into the changes that Schultz was making, and trust began to build between management and employees. New stores were on the verge of opening in Vancouver and Chicago. One Starbucks store employee, Daryl Moore, who had started working at Starbucks in 1981 and who had voted against unionization in 1985, began to question the need for a union with his fellow employees. Over the next few weeks, Moore began a move to decertify the union. He carried a decertification letter around to Starbucks' stores securing the signatures of employees who no longer wished to be represented by the union. He got a majority of store employees to sign the letter and presented it to the National Labor Relations Board. The union representing store employees was decertified. Later, in 1992, the union representing Starbucks' roasting plant and warehouse employees was also decertified.

Market Expansion Outside the Pacific Northwest

Starbucks' entry into Chicago proved far more troublesome than management anticipated. The first Chicago store opened in October 1987, and three more stores were opened over the next six months. Customer counts at the stores were substantially below expectations. Chicagoans did not take to dark-roasted coffee as fast as Schultz had anticipated. The first downtown store opened onto the street rather than into the lobby of the building where it was located; in the winter months, customers were hesitant to go out in the wind and cold to acquire a cup of coffee. It was expensive to supply fresh coffee to the Chicago stores out of the Seattle warehouse (the company solved the problem of freshness and quality assurance by putting freshly roasted beans in special FlavorLock bags that used vacuum packaging techniques with a one-way valve to allow carbon dioxide to escape without allowing air and moisture in). Rents were higher in Chicago than in Seattle, and so were wage rates. The result was a squeeze on store profit margins. Gradually, customer counts improved, but Starbucks lost money on its Chicago stores until, in 1990, prices were raised to reflect higher rents and labor costs, more experienced store mangers were hired, and a critical mass of customers caught on to the taste of Starbucks products.

Portland, Oregon, was the next market entered, and Portland coffee drinkers took to Starbucks products quickly. By 1991, the Chicago stores had become profitable and the company was ready for its next big market entry. Management decided on California because of its host of neighborhood centers and the receptiveness of Californians to innovative, high-quality food. Los Angeles was chosen as the first California market to enter, principally because of its status as a trendsetter and its cultural ties to the rest of the country. L.A. consumers embraced Starbucks quickly, and the *Los Angeles Times* named Starbucks as the best coffee in America before the first store opened. The entry into San Francisco proved more troublesome because San Francisco had an ordinance against converting stores to restaurant-related uses in certain prime urban neighborhoods; Starbucks could sell beverages and pastries to customers at stand-up counters but could not offer seating in stores that had formerly been used for general retailing. However, the city council was soon convinced by café owners and real estate brokers to change the code. Still, Starbucks faced strong competition from Peet's and local espresso bars in the San Francisco market.

Starbucks' store expansion targets proved easier to meet than Schultz had originally anticipated, and he upped the numbers to keep challenging the organization. Starbucks opened 15 new stores in fiscal 1988, 20 in 1989, 30 in 1990, 32 in 1991, and 53 in 1992—producing a total of 161 stores, significantly above his original 1992 target of 125 stores.

From the outset, the strategy was to open only company-owned stores; franchising was avoided so as to keep the company in full control of the quality of its products and the character and location of its stores. But company ownership of all stores required Starbucks to raise new venture capital to cover the cost of new store expansion. In 1988, the company raised $3.9 million; in 1990, venture capitalists provided an additional $13.5 million; and, in 1991, another round of venture capital financing generated $15 million. Starbucks was able to raise the needed funds despite posting losses of $330,000 in 1987, $764,000 in 1988, and $1.2 million in 1989. While the losses were troubling to Starbucks' board of directors and investors, Schultz's business plan had forecast losses during the early years of expansion. At a particularly tense board meeting where directors sharply questioned him about the lack of profitability, Schultz said:

> Look, we're going to keep losing money until we can do three things. We have to attract a management team well beyond our expansion needs. We have to build a world-class roasting facility. And we need a computer information system sophisticated enough to keep track of sales in hundreds and hundreds of stores.[9]

Schultz argued for patience as the company invested in the infrastructure to support continued growth well into the 1990s. He contended that hiring experienced executives ahead of the growth curve, building facilities far beyond current needs, and installing support systems laid a strong foundation for rapid, profitable growth down the road. His arguments carried the day with the board and with investors, especially since revenues were growing by approximately 80 percent annually and customer traffic at the stores was meeting or exceeding expectations.

Starbucks became profitable in 1990. Profits had increased every year since 1990 except for fiscal year 2000 (because of a $58.8 million in investment write-offs in four dot-com enterprises) and for fiscal year 2008 (when the sharp global economic downturn hit the company's bottom line very hard). Because of the economic downturn in 2008–2009, Howard Schultz believed that new strategic initiatives and rejuvenated strategy execution efforts were very much needed at Starbucks. Exhibit 2 provides a summary of the company's financial performance for fiscal years 2005–2009. Exhibit 3 shows the long-term performance of the company's stock price; the stock had split 2-for-1 five times.

Exhibit 2   **Financial Summary for Starbucks Corporation, Fiscal Years 2005–2009 ($ billions, except for per share amounts)**

	Fiscal Years Ending*				
	Sept. 27, 2009	Sept. 28, 2008	Sept. 30, 2007	Oct. 1, 2006	Oct. 2, 2005
Results of Operations Data					
Net revenues:					
Company-operated retail store revenues	$8,180.1	$ 8,771.9	$7,998.3	$6,583.1	$5,391.9
Specialty revenues:					
Licensing	1,222.3	1,171.6	1,026.3	860.6	673
Foodservice and other	372.2	439.5	386.9	343.2	304.4
Total specialty revenues	1,594.5	1,611.1	1,413.2	1,203.8	977.4
Total net revenues	$9,774.6	$10,383.0	$ 9,411.5	$7,786.9	$6,369.3
Cost of sales, including occupancy costs	4,324.9	4,645.3	3,999.1	3,178.8	2,605.2
Store operating expenses	3,425.1	3,745.3	3,215.9	2,687.8	2,165.9
Other operating expenses	264.4	330.1	294.2	253.7	192.5
Depreciation and amortization expenses	534.7	549.3	467.2	387.2	340.2
General and administrative expenses	453.0	456.0	489.2	479.4	361.6
Restructuring charges	332.4	266.9	—	—	—
Total operating expenses	9,334.5	9,992.7	8,465.6	6,986.9	5,665.4
Income from equity investees	121.9	113.6	108.0	93.9	76.6
Operating income	$ 562.0	$ 503.9	$1,053.9	$ 894.0	$ 780.5
Earnings before cumulative effect of change in accounting principle	390.8	315.5	672.6	581.5	494.4
Cumulative effect of accounting change for asset retirement obligations, net of taxes	—	—	—	17.2	—
Net earnings	$ 390.8	$ 315.5	$ 672.6	$ 564.3	$ 494.4
Net earnings per common share—diluted	$0.52	$0.43	$0.87	$0.71	$0.61
Balance Sheet Data					
Current assets	$2,035.8	$ 1,748.0	$1,696.5	$1,529.8	$1,209.3
Current liabilities	1,581.0	2,189.7	2,155.6	1,935.6	1,227.0
Total assets	5,576.8	5,672.6	5,343.9	4,428.9	3,513.7
Short-term borrowings	—	713	710.3	700	277
Long-term debt (including current portion)	549.5	550.3	550.9	2.7	3.6
Shareholders' equity	$3,045.7	$ 2,490.9	$2,284.1	$2,228.5	$2,090.3
Cash Flow Data					
Net cash provided by operating activities	$1,389.0	$1,258.7	$ 1,331.2	$ 1,131.6	$922.9
Capital expenditures (net additions to property, plant and equipment)	$445.6	$984.5	$1,080.3	$771.2	$643.3

*The company's fiscal year ended on the Sunday closest to September 30.
Source: Starbucks, 2009, 2007 and 2005 10-K reports.

Exhibit 3   The Performance of Starbucks' Stock, 1993–2010

Source: Wall Street Journal, http://online.wsj.com, accessed June 18, 2010.

STARBUCKS STORES: DESIGN, AMBIENCE, AND EXPANSION OF LOCATIONS

Store Design

Starting in 1991, Starbucks created its own in-house team of architects and designers to ensure that each store would convey the right image and character. Stores had to be custom-designed because the company didn't buy real estate or build its own freestanding structures; rather, each space was leased in an existing structure, making each store differ in size and shape. Most stores ranged in size from 1,000 to 1,500 square feet and were located in office buildings, downtown and suburban retail centers, airport terminals, university campus areas, and busy neighborhood shopping areas convenient for pedestrian foot traffic and/or drivers. Only a select few were in suburban malls.

A "stores of the future" project team was formed in 1995 to raise Starbucks' store design to a still higher level and come up with the next generation of Starbucks stores. The team came up with four store designs—one for each of the four stages of coffeemaking: growing, roasting, brewing, and aroma—each with its own color combinations, lighting scheme, and component materials. Within each of the four basic store templates, Starbucks could vary the materials and details to adapt to different store sizes and settings (downtown buildings, college campuses, neighborhood shopping areas). In late 1996, Starbucks began opening new stores based on one of four formats and color schemes.

But as the number of stores increased rapidly between 2000 and 2003, greater store diversity and layout quickly became necessary. Some stores had special seating areas to help make Starbucks a desirable gathering place where customers could meet and chat or simply enjoy a peaceful interlude in their day. Flagship stores in high-traffic, high-visibility locations had fireplaces, leather chairs, newspapers, couches, and lots of ambience. The company also experimented with drive-through windows in locations where speed and convenience were important to customers and with kiosks in supermarkets, building lobbies, and other public places. In recent years, Starbucks had begun emphasizing drive-through retail stores in order to provide a greater degree of access and convenience for nonpedestrian customers. At the end of fiscal 2009, Starbucks had around 2,650 drive-through locations.[10]

In June 2009, Starbucks announced a new global store design strategy. Each new store was to be a reflection of the environment in which it operated and was to be environmentally friendly. In 2010, Starbucks began an effort to achieve Leadership in Energy and Environmental Design (LEED) certification for all new company-owned stores. (LEED certification was a program that used independent third parties to certify that a building incorporated green building design, construction, operations, and maintenance solutions.)[11] Core characteristics of each new store included celebration of local materials and craftsmanship, a focus on reused and recycled elements, exposure of structural integrity and authentic roots, elevation of coffee and removal of unnecessary distractions, storytelling and customer engagement through all five senses, and flexibility to meet the needs of many customer types.[12] Exhibit 4 shows the diverse nature of Starbucks stores.

To better control average store opening costs, the company centralized buying, developed standard contracts and fixed fees for certain items, and consolidated work under those contractors who displayed good cost-control practices. The retail operations group outlined exactly the minimum amount of equipment each core store needed so that standard items could be ordered in volume from vendors at 20 to 30 percent discounts, then delivered just in time to the store site either from company warehouses or the vendor. Modular designs for display cases were developed. The layouts for new and remodeled stores were developed on a computer, with software that allowed the costs to be estimated as the design evolved. All this cut store opening and remodeling costs significantly and shortened the process to about 18 weeks.

Store Ambience

Starbucks management viewed each store as a billboard for the company and as a contributor to building the company's brand and image. The company went to great lengths to make sure that store fixtures, merchandise displays, colors, artwork, banners, music, and aromas all blended to create a consistent, inviting, stimulating environment that evoked the romance of coffee; that signaled the company's passion for coffee; that enhanced the mood and ambience of the store; and that rewarded customers with ceremony, stories, surprise, and a satisfying experience. The thesis was that every detail mattered in making Starbucks stores a welcoming and pleasant "third place" (apart from home and work) where people could meet friends and family, enjoy a quiet moment alone with a newspaper or book, or simply spend quality time relaxing.

To try to keep the coffee aromas in the stores pure, Starbucks banned smoking and asked employees to refrain from wearing perfumes or colognes. Prepared foods were kept covered so that customers would smell coffee only. Colorful banners and posters were used to keep the look of Starbucks stores fresh and to highlight seasons and holidays. Company designers came up with artwork for commuter mugs and T-shirts in different cities that were in keeping with each city's personality (peach-shaped coffee mugs for Atlanta, pictures of Paul Revere for Boston and the Statue of Liberty for New York).

In August 2002, Starbucks teamed up with T-Mobile USA to experiment with providing Internet access and enhanced digital entertainment to patrons at more than 1,200 Starbucks locations. The objective was to heighten the "third place" Starbucks experience, entice customers into perhaps buying a second latte or espresso while they caught up on e-mail, listened to digital music, put the finishing touches on a presentation, or surfed the Internet. Since the August 2002 introduction of Wi-Fi at Starbucks, wireless Internet service had been added at most company-operated stores in the United States. In an effort to better bridge Starbucks' "third place" coffeehouse experience with digital and social media, Starbucks announced that, beginning July 1, 2010, it would provide free Wi-Fi one-click Internet service through AT&T in all company-operated stores in the United States. There were also plans for a new online customer experience called the Starbucks Digital Network, in partnership with Yahoo, to debut in the fall of 2010 in U.S. company-operated Starbucks stores. This online experience would provide customers with free unrestricted access—via laptop, e-reader, or smartphone—to various paid sites and services such as the *Wall Street Journal*'s site

Exhibit 4   **Scenes from Starbucks Stores**

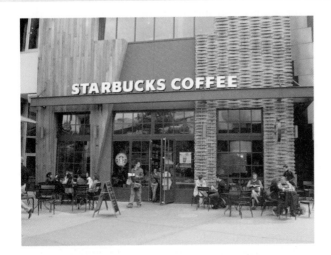

(www.wsj.com), exclusive content and previews, free downloads, and local community news and activities.

Store Expansion Strategy

In 1992 and 1993, Starbucks developed a three-year geographic expansion strategy to target areas that not only had favorable demographic profiles but also could be serviced and supported by the company's operations infrastructure. For each targeted region, Starbucks selected a large city to serve as a "hub"; teams of professionals were located in hub cities to support the goal of opening 20 or more stores in the hub in the first two years. Once a number of stores were opened in a hub, then additional stores were opened in smaller, surrounding "spoke" areas in the region. To oversee the expansion process, Starbucks had zone vice presidents who oversaw the store expansion process in a geographic region and instilled the Starbucks culture in the newly opened stores.

In recent years, Starbucks' strategy in major metropolitan cities had been to blanket major cities with stores, even if some stores cannibalized a nearby store's business. While a new store might draw 30 percent of the business of an existing store two or so blocks away, management believed that a "Starbucks everywhere" strategy cut down on delivery and management costs, shortened customer lines at individual stores, and increased foot traffic for all the stores in an area. In 2002, new stores generated an average of $1.2 million in first-year revenues, compared with $700,000 in 1995 and only $427,000 in 1990. The steady increases in new-store revenues were due partly to growing popularity of premium coffee drinks, partly to Starbucks' growing reputation, and partly to expanded product offerings. But the strategy of blanketing metropolitan areas with stores had cannibalized sales of existing stores to such an extent that average sales per store in the United States had dropped to around $1 million annually. Starbucks' long-term profitability target for its retail stores in the United States was an operating profit margin in the high teens—the operating margin was 14.3 percent in fiscal 2007, but declining store sales and depressed economic conditions had driven the margins down to 6.0 percent in fiscal 2008 and 7.5 percent in fiscal 2009.

One of Starbucks' core competencies was identifying good retailing sites for its new stores. The company was regarded as having the best real estate team in the coffee bar industry and a sophisticated system for identifying not only the most attractive individual city blocks but also the exact store location that was best; it also worked hard at building good relationships with local real estate representatives in areas where it was opening multiple store locations.

Licensed Retail Stores In 1995, Starbucks began entering into licensing agreements for store locations in areas where it did not have ability to locate its own outlets. Two early licensing agreements were with Marriott Host International to operate Starbucks retail stores in airport locations and with Aramark Food and Services to put Starbucks stores on university campuses and other locations operated by Aramark. Very quickly, Starbucks began to make increased use of licensing, both domestically and internationally. Starbucks preferred licensing to franchising because licensing permitted tighter controls over the operations of licensees.

Starbucks received a license fee and a royalty on sales at all licensed locations and supplied the coffee for resale at these locations. All licensed stores had to follow Starbucks' detailed operating procedures, and all managers and employees who worked in these stores received the same training given to managers and employees in company-operated Starbucks stores. As of 2009, there were 4,364 licensed stores in the United States and 3,439 licensed stores internationally.

International Expansion In markets outside the continental United States (including Hawaii), Starbucks had a two-pronged store expansion: either open company-owned and -operated stores or else license a reputable and capable local company with retailing know-how in the target host country to develop and operate new Starbucks stores. In most countries, Starbucks used a local partner/licensee to help it recruit talented individuals, set up supplier relationships, locate suitable store sites, and cater to local market conditions. Starbucks looked for partners/licensees that had strong retail/restaurant experience, had values and a corporate culture compatible with Starbucks, were committed to good customer service, possessed talented management and strong financial resources, and had demonstrated brand-building skills. In those foreign countries where business risks were deemed relatively high, most if not all Starbucks stores were licensed rather than being company-owned and operated. As of September 2009, Starbucks had company-operated and licensed stores in 50 countries (see Exhibit 5) and expected to open 200 new stores internationally in fiscal 2010.

Starbucks' long-term profitability target for its international operations was an operating profit margin in the mid-to-high teens. But the margins in recent years had been far below the

Exhibit 5   Company-Operated and Franchised Starbucks Stores

A. Number of Starbucks Store Locations Worldwide, 1987–March 2010 (selected years)

End of Fiscal Year*	Company-Operated Store Locations		Licensed Store Locations		Worldwide Total
	United States	International	United States	International	
1987	17	0	0	0	17
1990	84	0	0	0	84
1995	627	0	49	0	676
2000	2,446	530	173	352	3,501
2005	4,918	1,217	2,435	1,671	10,241
2006	5,728	1,457	3,168	2,087	12,440
2007	6,793	1,743	3,891	2,584	15,011
2008	7,238	1,979	4,329	3,134	16,680
2009	6,764	2,068	4,364	3,439	16,635
March 28, 2010	6,736	2,076	4,385	3,467	16,664

B. International Starbucks Store Locations at End of Fiscal Year 2009

International Locations of Company-Operated Starbucks Stores		International Locations of Licensed Starbucks Stores					
		Americas		Asia-Pacific		Europe/Africa/Middle East	
Canada	775	Canada	262	Japan	875	Turkey	123
United Kingdom	666	Mexico	261	South Korea	288	United Arab Emirates	91
China	191	Other	69	China	283	Spain	76
Germany	144			Taiwan	222	Greece	69
Thailand	131			Philippines	160	Saudi Arabia	68
Singapore	64			Malaysia	118	Kuwait	62
Australia	23			Indonesia	74	France	52
Other	74			New Zealand	42	Switzerland	47
Total	2,068					United Kingdom	46
						Other	151
						Licensed total worldwide	3,439

*Starbucks' fiscal year ended on the Sunday closest to September 30.

Source: Starbucks, 10-K reports, various years, and company records.

target: 8.1 percent in fiscal 2007, 5.2 percent in fiscal 2008, and 4.5 percent in fiscal 2009.

STARBUCKS' STRATEGY TO EXPAND ITS PRODUCT OFFERINGS AND ENTER NEW MARKET SEGMENTS

In the mid-1990s, thinking it was time for Starbucks to move out into mainstream markets, Howard Schultz led what proved to be an ongoing series of initiatives to expand Starbucks' product offerings beyond its retail stores and to pursue sales of Starbucks products in a wider variety of distribution channels and market segments. The strategy was to make Starbucks products more accessible to both existing and new customers where they worked, traveled, shopped, and dined and to find and promote new occasions for enjoying Starbucks products. The strategic objectives were to capitalize on Starbucks' growing brand awareness and brand-name strength and create a broader foundation for sustained long-term growth in revenues and profits.

The first initiative involved the establishment of an in-house specialty sales group to begin marketing Starbucks coffee products to restaurants, airlines, hotels, universities, hospitals, business offices, country clubs, and select retailers. Early users of Starbucks coffee included Horizon Airlines, a regional carrier based in Seattle, and United Airlines. There was much internal debate at Starbucks about whether it made sense for Starbucks coffee to be served on all United flights (since there was different coffeemaking equipment on different planes) and the possible damage to the integrity of the Starbucks brand if the quality of the coffee served did not measure up. It took seven months of negotiations for Starbucks and United to arrive at a mutually agreeable way to handle quality control on United's various types of planes. The specialty sales group also won accounts at Hyatt, Hilton, Sheraton, Radisson, and Westin hotels, resulting in packets of Starbucks coffee being in each room with coffeemaking equipment. Starbucks entered into an agreement with Wells Fargo to provide coffee ser-

vice at some of the bank's locations in California. Later, the specialty sales group began working with leading institutional foodservice distributors, including Sysco Corporation and US Foodservice, to handle the distribution of Starbucks products to hotels, restaurants, office coffee distributors, educational and health care institutions, and other such enterprises. In fiscal 2009, Starbucks generated revenues of $372.2 million from providing whole bean and ground coffees and assorted other Starbucks products to some 21,000 food service accounts.

The second initiative came in 1994 when PepsiCo and Starbucks entered into a joint venture (now called the North American Coffee Partnership) to create new coffee-related products in bottles or cans for mass distribution through Pepsi channels. Howard Schultz saw the venture with PepsiCo as a major paradigm shift with the potential to cause Starbucks' business to evolve in heretofore unimaginable directions. The joint venture's first new product, Mazagran, a lightly flavored carbonated coffee drink, was a failure. Then, at a meeting with Pepsi executives, Schultz suggested developing a bottled version of Frappuccino, a new cold coffee drink that Starbucks had begun serving at its retail stores in the summer of 1995 and that quickly became a big hot-weather seller. Pepsi executives were enthusiastic. After months of experimentation, the joint venture product research team came up with a shelf-stable version of Frappuccino that tasted quite good. It was tested in West Coast supermarkets in the summer of 1996; sales ran 10 times projections, with 70 percent being repeat business. Sales of Frappuccino ready-to-drink beverages reached $125 million in 1997 and achieved national supermarket penetration of 80 percent. Starbucks' management believed that the market for Frappuccino would ultimately exceed $1 billion. The company began selling ready-to-drink Frappuccino products in Japan, Taiwan, and South Korea in 2005 chiefly through agreements with leading local distributors; the ready-to-drink beverage market in these countries represented more than $10 billion in annual sales.[13] In 2007, the PepsiCo-Starbucks partnership introduced a line of chilled Starbucks Doubleshot espresso drinks in the United States. Also in 2007, PepsiCo and Starbucks entered into a second joint venture called the International Coffee Partnership (ICP) for the purpose of introducing Starbucks-related beverages in country markets outside North America; one of the ICP's early moves was to begin marketing Frappuccino in China.[14] As of 2010, sales of Frappuccino products worldwide had reached $2 billion annually.[15]

In 2008, Starbucks partnered with Suntory to begin selling chilled ready-to-drink Doubleshot drinks in Japan. In 2010, Starbucks partnered with Arla Foods to begin selling Doubleshot products and Starbucks Discoveries chilled cup coffees in retail stores (as well as in Starbucks retail stores) across the United Kingdom.

In October 1995, Starbucks partnered with Dreyer's Grand Ice Cream to supply coffee extract for a new line of coffee ice cream made and distributed by Dreyer's under the Starbucks brand. By July 1996, Starbucks coffee-flavored ice cream was the number-one-selling superpremium brand in the coffee segment. In 2008, Starbucks discontinued its arrangement with Dreyer's and entered into an exclusive agreement with Unilever to manufacture, market, and distribute Starbucks-branded ice creams in the United States and Canada. Unilever was considered the global leader in ice cream, with annual sales of about $6 billion; its ice cream brands included Ben & Jerry's, Breyers, and Good Humor. Seven flavors of Starbucks ice cream and two flavors of novelty bars were marketed in 2010. Pints were available in the freezer sections at supermarkets for a suggested retail price of $3.99; the novelty bars sold for a suggested retail price of $2.49 and were also available in many convenience stores.

In 1997, a Starbucks store manager who had worked in the music industry and selected the music Starbucks played as background in its stores suggested that Starbucks begin selling the background music on tapes (and later on CDs as they become the preferred format). The manager had gotten compliments from customers wanting to buy the music they heard and suggested to senior executives that there was a market for the company's handpicked music. Research through two years of comment cards turned up hundreds asking Starbucks to sell the music it played in its stores. The Starbucks tapes/CDs proved a significant seller as an addition to the company's product line. In 2000, Starbucks acquired Hear Music, a San Francisco–based company, to give it added capability in enhancing its music CD offerings. In 2004, Starbucks introduced Hear Music media bars, a service that offered custom CD burning at select Starbucks stores. Later, Starbucks began offering customers the option of downloading music from the company's 200,000+ song library and, if they wished, having the downloaded songs burned onto a CD for purchase.

In the spring of 2008, Starbucks, in partnership with Apple's iTunes, began offering a Pick of the Week music card at its 7,000 stores in the United States that allowed customers to download each week's music selection at iTunes.[16] In 2010, Starbucks was continuing to offer CDs with handpicked music and new CDs featuring particular artists, all managed by Starbucks Entertainment in conjunction with Concord Music Group (which began managing the Hear Music Record Label in 2008); the CDs were typically priced at $12.95. Starbucks also had established a relationship with the William Morris Agency to identify books that it could offer for sale in its stores. Over the years, Starbucks' successes in music and books had included eight Grammy Awards and three number one books on the *New York Times* best-seller list.

In 1998, Starbucks licensed Kraft Foods to market and distribute Starbucks whole bean and ground coffees in grocery and mass-merchandise channels across the United States. Kraft managed all distribution, marketing, advertising, and promotions and paid a royalty to Starbucks based on a percentage of net sales. Product freshness was guaranteed by Starbucks' FlavorLock packaging, and the price per pound paralleled the prices in Starbucks' retail stores. Flavor selections in supermarkets were more limited than the varieties at Starbucks stores. The licensing relationship with Kraft was later expanded to include the marketing and distribution of Starbucks coffees in the United Kingdom and Europe. Going into 2010, Starbucks coffees were available in some 33,500 grocery and warehouse clubs in the United States and 5,500 retail outlets outside the United States; Starbucks' revenues from these sales were approximately $370 million in fiscal 2009.[17]

In 1999, Starbucks purchased Tazo Tea for $8.1 million. Tazo Tea, a tea manufacturer and distributor based in Portland, Oregon, was founded in 1994 and marketed its teas to restaurants, food stores, and tea houses. Starbucks proceeded to introduce hot and iced Tazo Tea drinks in its retail stores. As part of a long-term campaign to expand the distribution of its line of superpremium Tazo teas, Starbucks expanded its agreement with Kraft to market and distribute Tazo teas worldwide. In August 2008, Starbucks entered into an agreement with PepsiCo and Unilever (Lipton Tea was one of Unilever's leading brands) to manufacture, market, and distribute Starbucks' superpremium Tazo Tea ready-to-drink beverages (including iced teas, juiced teas, and herbal-infused teas) in the United States and Canada. The Tazo line of ready-to-drink beverages was to become part of an existing venture between PepsiCo and Unilever (the Pepsi/Lipton Tea partnership) that was the leading North American distributor of ready-to-drink teas.

In 2001, Starbucks introduced the Starbucks Card, a reloadable card that allowed customers to pay for their purchases with a quick swipe at the cash register and also to earn and redeem rewards. In 2009, about 15 percent of customer purchases at Starbucks stores were made on Starbucks cards.

In 2003, Starbucks acquired Seattle's Best Coffee, an operator of Seattle's Best coffee shops and marketer of Seattle's Best whole bean and ground coffees, for $70 million. Starbucks continued to operate Seattle's Best as a separate subsidiary. As of May 2008, there were more than 540 Seattle's Best cafés in the United States (a number of which were in Borders book and music stores) and 86 Seattle's Best Coffee Express espresso bars. The Seattle's Best product line included more than 30 whole bean and ground coffees (including flavored, organic, and Fair Trade Certified coffees), espresso beverages, signature handcrafted JavaKula blended beverages, OvenSong bakery food and sandwiches, and select merchandise. Shortly after the acquisition, Starbucks expanded its licensing arrangement with Kraft Foods to include marketing and distributing Seattle's Best whole bean and ground coffees in grocery and mass merchandise channels in North America, with Starbucks to receive a royalty on all such sales. In 2009, Seattle's Best whole bean and ground coffee blends were available nationwide in supermarkets and were being served at more than 15,000 food service locations (college campuses, restaurants, hotels, airlines, and cruise lines). A new Seattle's Best line of ready-to-drink iced lattes was introduced in April 2010 in major grocery and convenience stores in

the western United States; the manufacture, marketing, and distribution of the new Seattle's Best beverages was managed by PepsiCo as part of the long-standing Starbucks-PepsiCo joint venture for ready-to-drink Frappuccino products. In May 2010, Starbucks announced that it would relaunch Seattle's Best Coffee with new distinctive red packaging and a red logo, boost efforts to open more franchised Seattle's Best cafés, and expand the availability of Seattle's Best coffees to 30,000 distribution points by October 2010. By July 2010, freshly brewed and iced Seattle's Best Coffee drinks were being sold at 7,250 Burger King outlets in the United States, 9,000 Subway locations, and some 299 AMC movie theaters in five countries.

In 2004 Starbucks teamed with Jim Beam Brands to invent a Starbucks Coffee Liqueur that would be sold be sold in bars, liquor stores, and restaurants; projections were for systemwide gross sales of more than $8 million annually. Launched in February 2005, Starbucks Coffee Liqueur was the number-one-selling new spirit product year-to-date through August 2005, according to Nielsen. In October 2005, again collaborating with Jim Beam Brands, Starbucks introduced Starbucks Cream Liqueur, a blend of cream, spirits, and a hint of Starbucks coffee. There were an estimated 22 million cordial consumers in the U.S. market, making the cream liqueur category nearly three times the size of coffee liqueur category. Both Starbucks Coffee Liqueur and Starbucks Cream Liqueur were packaged in 750 milliliter bottles priced at $22.99.

In April 2005, Starbucks acquired Ethos Water for $8 million in cash. The acquisition was made to expand the line of beverages in Starbucks stores in the United States. Following the acquisition, the brand also became known for its campaign to raise $10 million by donating $0.05 of the retail price of each bottle sold to a charitable organization working to increase access to clean drinking water and conduct sanitation and hygiene education programs in developing countries in Africa and Asia; in 2010, more than $6 million had been raised.[18] The production, distribution, and marketing of Ethos water products was handled by PepsiCo, as part of its long-standing joint venture with Starbucks.

In response to customer requests for more wholesome food and beverage options and also to bring in business from non–coffee drinkers, Starbucks in 2008 began offering fruit cups, yogurt parfaits, skinny lattes, banana walnut bread (that was nearly 30 percent real banana), a 300-calorie farmer's market salad with all-natural dressing, and a line of "better-for-you" smoothies called Vivanno Nourishing Blends. Each Vivanno smoothie averaged 250 calories and consisted of one serving of fruit, 16 grams of protein, and 5 grams of fiber.[19] Additionally, in 2009, healthier, lower-calorie selections were included in the bakery cases at Starbucks stores, and the recipes for several other food items on the menu at Starbucks stores were reformulated to include whole grains and dried fruits and to cut back on or eliminate the use of artificial flavorings, dyes, high-fructose corn syrup, and artificial preservatives.[20]

In 2008, Starbucks introduced a new coffee blend called Pike Place Roast that would be brewed every day, all day in every Starbucks store.[21] Before then, Starbucks rotated coffees through its brewed lineup, sometimes switching them weekly, sometimes daily. While some customers liked the ever-changing variety, the feedback from a majority of customers indicated a preference for a consistent brew that customers could count on when they came into a Starbucks store. This reinvention of brewed coffee returned the company to the practice of grinding the beans in the store. Pike Place Roast was brewed in small batches in 30-minute intervals to ensure that customers were provided the freshest coffee possible. The Pike Place Roast was created by Starbucks' master blenders and coffee quality team using input from nearly 1,000 customers—it was smoother than any other Starbucks coffee and tasted great either black or with cream and sugar.

In the fall of 2009, Starbucks introduced Starbucks VIA Ready Brew—packets of roasted coffee in an instant form. VIA was made with a proprietary microground technology that Starbucks claimed represented a breakthrough.[22] Simply adding a packet of VIA to a cup of hot or cold water produced an instant coffee with a rich, full-bodied taste that closely replicated the taste, quality, and flavor of traditional freshly brewed coffee. Initially, VIA was introduced in Starbucks stores in the United States and Canada and select food service accounts; Starbucks stores held a four-day Starbucks VIA Taste Challenge

promotional during which customers were invited to compare the difference between Starbucks VIA and fresh-brewed Starbucks coffee. During the 2009 holiday season, Starbucks VIA Ready Brew was one of the top-selling coffee products at Amazon.com. Encouraged by favorable customer response, in mid-2010 Starbucks expanded the distribution of VIA to include 25,000 grocery store, mass-merchandise store, and drugstore accounts, including Kroger, Safeway, Walmart, Target, Costco, and CVS. VIA was available in three roasts—Colombian, Italian Roast, and Decaffeinated Italian Roast; the suggested retail price for Starbucks VIA was $2.95 for three servings and $7.49 for eight servings. Starbucks executives saw VIA as a promising vehicle for entering the instant coffee market and attracting a bigger fraction of on-the-go and at-home coffee drinkers. Instant coffee made up a significant fraction of the coffee purchases in the United Kingdom (80 percent), Japan (53 percent), Russia (85 percent), and other countries where Starbucks stores were located—in both the UK and Japan, sales of instant coffee exceeded $4 billion annually. Globally, the instant and single-serve coffee category was a $23 billion market. In March 2010, Starbucks made VIA available in all of its Starbucks stores in the UK. In April 2010, Starbucks introduced VIA in all of Japan's 870 Starbucks stores under the name Starbucks VIA Coffee Essence.[23]

The company's overall retail sales mix in 2009 was 76 percent beverages, 18 percent food items, 3 percent coffeemaking equipment and other merchandise, and 3 percent whole bean coffees.[24] However, the product mix in each store varied, depending on the size and location of each outlet. Larger stores carried a greater variety of whole coffee beans, gourmet food items, teas, coffee mugs, coffee grinders, coffeemaking equipment, filters, storage containers, and other accessories. Smaller stores and kiosks typically sold a full line of coffee beverages, a limited selection of whole bean and ground coffees and Tazo teas, and a few coffee-drinking accessories. Moreover, menu offerings at Starbucks stores were typically adapted to local cultures; for instance, the menu offerings at stores in North America included a selection of muffins, but stores in France had no muffins and instead featured locally made French pastries.

Starbucks' Consumer Products Group

All distribution channels for Starbucks products outside both licensed and company-operated retail stores were collectively referred to by Starbucks executives as "specialty operations." In 2010, Starbucks formed its Consumer Products Group (CPG) to manage all specialty operations activities. CPG was responsible for selling a selection of whole bean and ground coffees as well as a selection of premium Tazo teas outside Starbucks retail stores through licensing and distribution arrangements with Kraft, PepsiCo, Unilever, and others that covered both the United States and international markets. CPG also oversaw production and sales of ready-to-drink beverages (including bottled Frappuccino beverages, Starbucks Doubleshot espresso drinks, and Discoveries chilled cup coffee) as well as Starbucks superpremium ice creams and Starbucks liqueurs through the company's marketing and distribution agreements and joint ventures with PepsiCo, Unilever, and others. And it managed the sales of various Starbucks products to both food service accounts and the vast majority of the company's partnerships and licensing arrangements with prominent third parties.

Exhibit 6 shows the recent performance of the Consumer Products Group. Starbucks executives considered CPG's specialty operations attractive from the standpoint of both long-term growth and profitability. In fiscal 2007–2009, the company's operating profit margins from specialty operations were higher than the long-term target of 35 percent and vastly superior to the operating profit margins for the company's U.S. and international operations, as the following table shows:

	Operating Profit Margins		
	FY 2009	**FY 2008**	**FY 2007**
Consumer Products Group	39.6%	37.3%	35.9%
U.S. operations	7.5	6.0	14.3
International operations	4.8	5.2	8.1

Advertising

So far, Starbucks had spent relatively little money on advertising, preferring instead to build the brand cup by cup with customers and depend on word of mouth and the appeal of its storefronts. Advertising expenditures were $126.3 million in fiscal 2009, versus $129.0 million in fiscal 2008, $103.5 million in 2007, and $107.5 million in 2006. Starbucks stepped up advertising efforts in 2008 to combat the strategic initiatives of McDonald's and several other fast-food chains to begin offering premium coffees and coffee drinks at prices below those charged by Starbucks. In 2009, McDonald's reportedly spent more than $100 million on television, print, radio, billboard, and online ads promoting its new line of McCafé coffee drinks. Starbucks countered with the

Exhibit 6 **Performance of Starbuck's Consumer Products Group, Fiscal Years 2007–2009**

	Fiscal Year		
Consumer Product Group Operations	**2009**	**2008**	**2007**
Licensing revenues	$427.2	$392.6	$366.3
Foodservice revenues	322.4	355.0	326.1
Total revenues	$749.6	$747.6	$692.4
Operating income	$296.3	$279.2	$248.9
Operating income as a percent of total revenues	39.5%	37.3%	35.9%

Source: Starbucks, 2009 10-K report, p. 76.

biggest advertising campaign the company had ever undertaken.[25]

Vertical Integration

Howard Schultz saw Starbucks as having a unique strategy compared to the strategies pursued by its many coffeehouse competitors. He observed:

> People sometimes fail to realize that almost unlike any retailer or restaurant, we are completely vertically integrated. We source coffee from 30 countries. We have a proprietary roasting process. We distribute to company owned stores, and finally serve the coffee. Others are resellers of commodity-based coffees.[26]

HOWARD SCHULTZ'S EFFORTS TO MAKE STARBUCKS A GREAT PLACE TO WORK

Howard Schultz deeply believed that Starbucks' success was heavily dependent on customers having a very positive experience in its stores. This meant having store employees who were knowledgeable about the company's products, who paid attention to detail in preparing the company's espresso drinks, who eagerly communicated the company's passion for coffee, and who possessed the skills and personality to deliver consistent, pleasing customer service. Many of the baristas were in their 20s and worked part-time, going to college on the side or pursuing other career activities. The challenge to Starbucks, in Schultz's view, was how to attract, motivate, and reward store employees in a manner that would make Starbucks a company that people would want to work for and that would generate enthusiastic commitment and higher levels of customer service. Moreover, Schultz wanted to send all Starbucks employees a message that would cement the trust that had been building between management and the company's workforce.

Instituting Health Care Coverage for All Employees

One of the requests that employees had made to the prior owners of Starbucks was to extend health insurance benefits to part-time workers. Their request had been turned down, but Schultz believed that expanding health insurance coverage to include part-timers was something the company needed to do. His father had recently passed away from cancer and he knew from having grown up in a family that struggled to make ends meet how difficult it was to cope with rising medical costs. In 1988, Schultz went to the board of directors with his plan to expand the company's health insurance plans to include part-timers who worked at least 20 hours per week. He saw the proposal not as a generous gesture but as a core strategy to win employee loyalty and commitment to the company's mission. Board members resisted because the company was unprofitable and the added costs of the extended coverage would only worsen the company's bottom line. But Schultz argued passionately that it was the right thing to do and wouldn't be as expensive as it seemed. He observed that if the new benefit reduced turnover, which he believed was likely, then it would reduce the costs of hiring and training—which equaled about $3,000 per new hire; he further pointed out that it cost $1,500 a year to provide an employee with full benefits. Part-timers, he argued, were vital to Starbucks, constituting two-thirds of the company's workforce. Many were baristas who knew the favorite drinks of regular customers; if the barista left, that connection with the customer was broken. Moreover, many part-time employees were called on to open the stores early, sometimes at 5:30 or 6:00 a.m.; others had to work until closing, usually 9:00 p.m. or later. Providing these employees with health insurance benefits, he argued, would signal that the company honored their value and contribution.

The board approved Schultz's plan, and starting in late 1988, part-timers working 20 or more hours were offered the same health coverage as full-time employees. Starbucks paid 75 percent of an employee's health insurance premium; the employee paid 25 percent. Over the years, Starbucks extended its health coverage to include preventive care, prescription drugs, dental care, eye care, mental health, and chemical dependency. Coverage was also offered for unmarried partners in a committed relationship. Since most Starbucks employees were young and comparatively healthy, the company had been able to provide broader coverage while keeping monthly payments relatively low. Even when the company fell on lean times in 2008–2009, Starbucks refrained from making cuts in employee health insurance benefits; company expenditures for employee health insurance were $300 million in fiscal 2009, more than the company spent on its purchases of coffee beans.[27]

A Stock Option Plan for Employees

By 1991, the company's profitability had improved to the point where Schultz could pursue a stock option plan for all employees, a program he believed would have a positive, long-term effect on the success of Starbucks.[28] Schultz wanted to turn all Starbucks employees into partners, give them a chance to share in the success of the company, and make clear the connection between their contributions and the company's market value. Even though Starbucks was still a private company, the plan that emerged called for granting stock options to every full-time and part-time employee in proportion to his or her base pay. In May 1991, the plan, dubbed Bean Stock, was presented to the board. Though board members were concerned that increasing the number of shares might unduly dilute the value of the shares of investors who had put up hard cash, the plan received unanimous approval. The first grant was made in October 1991, just after the end of the company's fiscal year in September; each partner was granted stock options worth 12 percent of base pay. When the Bean Stock program was initiated, Starbucks dropped the term *employee* and began referring to all of its people as *partners* because every member of Starbucks' workforce became eligible for stock option awards after six months of employment and 500 paid work hours.

Starbucks went public in June 1992, selling its initial offering at a price of $17 per share. Starting in October 1992 and continuing through October 2004, Starbucks granted each eligible employee a stock option award with a value equal to 14 percent of base pay. Beginning in 2005, the plan was modified to tie the size of each employee's stock option awards to three factors: (1) Starbucks' success and profitability for the fiscal year, (2) the size of an employee's base wages, and (3) the price at which the stock option could be exercised. The value of the stock options exercised by

Starbucks partners was $44 million in fiscal 2009, $50 million in fiscal 2008, and $274 million in fiscal 2007. As of September 27, 2009, Starbucks partners held 63.6 million shares in stock option awards that had a weighted-average contractual life of 6.7 years; these shares had a weighted-average exercise price of $14.75 and an aggregate value of $442.4 million.[29]

Starbucks Stock Purchase Plan for Employees

In 1995, Starbucks implemented an employee stock purchase plan that gave partners who had been employed for at least 90 days an opportunity to purchase company stock through regular payroll deductions. Partners who enrolled could devote anywhere from 1 to 10 percent of their base earnings (up to a maximum of $25,000) to purchasing shares of Starbucks stock. After the end of each calendar quarter, each participant's contributions were used to buy Starbucks stock at a discount of 5 percent of the closing price on the last business day of the each calendar quarter (the discount was 15 percent until March 2009).

Since inception of the plan, some 23.5 million shares had been purchased by partners; roughly one-third of Starbucks partners participated in the stock purchase plan during the 2000–2009 period.

The Workplace Environment

Starbucks' management believed that the company's competitive pay scales and comprehensive benefits for both full-time and part-time partners allowed it to attract motivated people with above-average skills and good work habits. An employee's base pay was determined by the pay scales prevailing in the geographic region where an employee worked and by the person's job skills, experience, and job performance. About 90 percent of Starbucks' partners were full-time or part-time baristas, paid on an hourly basis. After six months of employment, baristas could expect to earn $8.50 to $9.50 per hour. In 2009, experienced full-time baristas in the company's U.S. stores earned an average of about $37,800; store managers earned an average of $44,400.[30] Voluntary turnover at Starbucks was 13 percent in 2009.[31] Starbucks executives believed that efforts to make the company an attractive, caring place to work were responsible for its relatively low turnover rates. Starbucks received 225,000 job applications in 2008 and 150,000 job applications in 2009.

Surveys of Starbucks partners conducted by *Fortune* magazine in the course of selecting companies for inclusion on its annual list "100 Best Companies to Work For" indicated that full-time baristas liked working at Starbucks because of the camaraderie, while part-timers were particularly pleased with the health insurance benefits (those who enrolled in Starbucks' most economical plan for just routine health care paid only $6.25 per week).[32] Starbucks had been named to *Fortune*'s list in 1998, 1999, 2000, and every year from 2002 through 2010. In 2010, Starbucks was ranked 93rd, down from 24th in 2009 and 7th in 2008.

Starbucks' management used annual Partner View surveys to solicit feedback from its workforce, learn their concerns, and measure job satisfaction. The 2002 survey revealed that many employees viewed the benefits package as only "average," prompting the company to increase its match of 401(k) contributions for those who had

been with the company more than three years and to have these contributions vest immediately. In a survey conducted in fiscal 2008, 80 percent of Starbucks partners reported being satisfied.[33]

Schultz's approach to offering employees good compensation and a comprehensive benefits package was driven by his belief that sharing the company's success with the people who made it happen helped everyone think and act like an owner, build positive long-term relationships with customers, and do things efficiently. Schultz's rationale, based on his father's experience of going from one low-wage, no-benefits job to another, was that if you treated your employees well, they in turn would treat customers well.

Exhibit 7 contains a summary of Starbucks' fringe benefit program.

Employee Training and Recognition

To accommodate its strategy of rapid store expansion, Starbucks put in systems to recruit, hire,

Exhibit 7 Starbucks' Fringe Benefit Program, 2010

- Medical insurance
- Sick time
- Dental and vision care
- Paid vacations (up to 120 hours annually for hourly workers with five or more years of service at retail stores and up to 200 hours annually for salaried and nonretail hourly employees with five or more years of service)
- Six paid holidays
- One paid personal day every six months for salaried and nonretail hourly partners
- A 30 percent discount on purchases of beverages, food, and merchandise at Starbucks stores
- Mental health and chemical dependency coverage
- 401(k) retirement savings plan—the company matched from 25% to 150%, based on length of service, of each employee's contributions up to the first 4% of compensation
- Short- and long-term disability
- Stock purchase plan—eligible employees could buy shares at a discounted price through regular payroll deductions
- Life insurance
- Short- and long-term disability insurance
- Accidental death and dismemberment insurance
- Adoption assistance
- Financial assistance program for partners that experience a financial crisis
- Stock option plan (Bean stock)
- Pre-tax payroll deductions for commuter expenses
- Free coffee and tea products each week
- Tuition reimbursement program

Source: Starbucks, "Careers," www.starbucks.com, accessed June 7, 2010.

and train baristas and store managers. Starbucks' vice president for human resources used some simple guidelines in screening candidates for new positions: "We want passionate people who love coffee. . . . We're looking for a diverse workforce, which reflects our community. We want people who enjoy what they're doing and for whom work is an extension of themselves."[34]

All partners/baristas hired for a retail job in a Starbucks store received at least 24 hours training in their first two to four weeks. The topics included classes on coffee history, drink preparation, coffee knowledge (four hours), customer service (four hours), and retail skills, plus a four-hour workshop called "Brewing the Perfect Cup." Baristas spent considerable time learning about beverage preparation—grinding the beans, steaming milk, learning to pull perfect (18- to 23-second) shots of espresso, memorizing the recipes of all the different drinks, practicing making the different drinks, and learning how to customize drinks to customer specifications. There were sessions on cash register operations, how to clean the milk wand on the espresso machine, explaining the Italian drink names to customers, selling home espresso machines, making eye contact with customers and interacting with them, and taking personal responsibility for the cleanliness of the store. And there were rules to be memorized: milk must be steamed to at least 150 degrees Fahrenheit but never more than 170 degrees; every espresso shot not pulled within 23 seconds must be tossed; never let coffee sit in the pot more than 20 minutes; always compensate dissatisfied customers with a Starbucks coupon that entitled them to a free drink.

Management trainees attended classes for 8 to 12 weeks. Their training went much deeper, covering not only coffee knowledge and information imparted to baristas but also details of store operations, practices and procedures as set forth in the company's operating manual, information systems, and the basics of managing people. Starbucks' trainers were all store managers and district managers with on-site experience. One of their major objectives was to ingrain the company's values, principles, and culture and to pass on their knowledge about coffee and their passion about Starbucks.

When Starbucks opened stores in a new market, it sent a Star Team of experienced managers and baristas to the area to lead the store opening effort and to conduct one-on-one training following the company's formal classes and basic orientation sessions at the Starbucks Coffee School in San Francisco. From time to time, Starbucks conducted special training programs, including a coffee masters program for store employees, leadership training for store managers, and career programs for partners in all types of jobs.

To recognize partner contributions, Starbucks had created a partner recognition program consisting of 18 different awards and programs. Examples included Coffee Master awards, Certified Barista awards, Spirit of Starbucks awards for exceptional achievement by a partner, a Manager of the Quarter for store manager leadership, Green Apron Awards for helping create a positive and welcoming store environment, Green Bean Awards for exceptional support for company's environmental mission, and Bravo! Awards for exceeding the standards of Starbucks customer service, significantly increasing sales, or reducing costs.

STARBUCKS' VALUES, BUSINESS PRINCIPLES, AND MISSION

During the early building years, Howard Schultz and other Starbucks senior executives worked to instill some key values and guiding principles into the Starbucks culture. The cornerstone value in their effort "to build a company with soul" was that the company would never stop pursuing the perfect cup of coffee by buying the best beans and roasting them to perfection. Schultz was adamant about controlling the quality of Starbucks products and building a culture common to all stores. He was rigidly opposed to selling artificially flavored coffee beans, saying that "we will not pollute our high-quality beans with chemicals"; if a customer wanted hazelnut-flavored coffee, Starbucks would provide it by adding hazelnut syrup to the drink rather than by adding hazelnut flavoring to the beans during roasting. Running flavored beans through the grinders would result in chemical residues being left behind to alter the flavor of beans ground afterward; plus, the chemical smell given off by artificially flavored beans was absorbed by other beans in the store.

Starbucks' management was also emphatic about the importance of employees paying attention to what pleased customers. Employees were trained to go out of their way and to take heroic measures, if necessary, to make sure customers were fully satisfied. The theme was "just say yes" to customer requests. Further, employees were encouraged to speak their minds without fear of retribution from upper management—senior executives wanted employees to be straight with them, being vocal about what Starbucks was doing right, what it was doing wrong, and what changes were needed. The intent was for employees to be involved in and contribute to the process of making Starbucks a better company.

Starbucks' Mission Statement

In early 1990, the senior executive team at Starbucks went to an off-site retreat to debate the company's values and beliefs and draft a mission statement. Schultz wanted the mission statement to convey a strong sense of organizational purpose and to articulate the company's fundamental beliefs and guiding principles. The draft was submitted to all employees for review, and several changes were made based on employee comments. The resulting mission statement and guiding principles are shown in Exhibit 8. In 2008, Starbucks partners from all across the company met for several months to refresh the mission statement and rephrase the underlying guiding principles; the revised mission statement and guiding principles are also shown in Exhibit 8.

STARBUCKS' COFFEE PURCHASING STRATEGY

Coffee beans were grown in 70 tropical countries and were the second-most-traded commodity in the world after petroleum. Most of the world's coffee was grown by some 25 million small farmers, most of whom lived on the edge of poverty. Starbucks personnel traveled regularly to coffee-producing countries, building relationships with growers and exporters, checking on agricultural conditions and crop yields, and searching out varieties and sources that would meet Starbucks' exacting standards of quality and flavor. The coffee-purchasing group, working with Starbucks

personnel in roasting operations, tested new varieties and blends of green coffee beans from different sources. Sourcing from multiple geographic areas not only allowed Starbucks to offer a greater range of coffee varieties to customers but also spread the company's risks regarding weather, price volatility, and changing economic and political conditions in coffee-growing countries.

Starbucks' coffee sourcing strategy had three key elements:

- Make sure that the prices Starbucks paid for green (unroasted) coffee beans were high enough to ensure that small farmers were able to cover their production costs and provide for their families.
- Use purchasing arrangements that limited Starbucks' exposure to sudden price jumps due to weather, economic and political conditions in the growing countries, new agreements establishing export quotas, and periodic efforts to bolster prices by restricting coffee supplies.
- Work directly with small coffee growers, local coffee-growing cooperatives, and other types of coffee suppliers to promote coffee cultivation methods that protected biodiversity and were environmentally sustainable.

Pricing and Purchasing Arrangements

Commodity-grade coffee was traded in a highly competitive market as an undifferentiated product. However, high-altitude arabica coffees of the quality purchased by Starbucks were bought on a negotiated basis at a substantial premium above commodity coffee. The prices of the top-quality coffees sourced by Starbucks depended on supply and demand conditions at the time of the purchase and were subject to considerable volatility due to weather, economic and political conditions in the growing countries, new agreements establishing export quotas, and periodic efforts to bolster prices by restricting coffee supplies.

Starbucks typically used fixed-price purchase commitments to limit its exposure to fluctuating coffee prices in upcoming periods and, on occasion, purchased coffee futures contracts to provide price protection. In years past, there had been times when unexpected jumps in coffee

Exhibit 8   Starbucks' Mission Statement, Values, and Business Principles

Mission Statement, 1990–October 2008

Establish Starbucks as the premier purveyor of the finest coffee in the world while maintaining our uncompromising principles as we grow.

The following six guiding principles will help us measure the appropriateness of our decisions:

- Provide a great work environment and treat each other with respect and dignity.
- Embrace diversity as an essential component in the way we do business.
- Apply the highest standards of excellence to the purchasing, roasting, and fresh delivery of our coffee.
- Develop enthusiastically satisfied customers all of the time.
- Contribute positively to our communities and our environment.
- Recognize that profitability is essential to our future success.

Mission Statement, October 2008 Forward

Our Mission: To inspire and nurture the human spirit—one person, one cup, and one neighborhood at a time.

Here are the principles of how we live that every day:

Our Coffee

It has always been, and will always be, about quality. We're passionate about ethically sourcing the finest coffee beans, roasting them with great care, and improving the lives of people who grow them. We care deeply about all of this; our work is never done.

Our Partners

We're called partners, because it's not just a job, it's our passion. Together, we embrace diversity to create a place where each of us can be ourselves. We always treat each other with respect and dignity. And we hold each other to that standard.

Our Customers

When we are fully engaged, we connect with, laugh with, and uplift the lives of our customers—even if just for a few moments. Sure, it starts with the promise of a perfectly made beverage, but our work goes far beyond that. It's really about human connection.

Our Stores

When our customers feel this sense of belonging, our stores become a haven, a break from the worries outside, a place where you can meet with friends. It's about enjoyment at the speed of life—sometimes slow and savored, sometimes faster. Always full of humanity.

Our Neighborhood

Every store is part of a community, and we take our responsibility to be good neighbors seriously. We want to be invited in wherever we do business. We can be a force for positive action— bringing together our partners, customers, and the community to contribute every day. Now we see that our responsibility—and our potential for good—is even larger. The world is looking to Starbucks to set the new standard, yet again. We will lead.

Our Shareholders

We know that as we deliver in each of these areas, we enjoy the kind of success that rewards our shareholders. We are fully accountable to get each of these elements right so that Starbucks—and everyone it touches—can endure and thrive.

Source: Starbucks, "Our Starbucks Mission," www.starbucks.com, accessed March 7, 2010.

prices had put a squeeze on Starbucks' margins, forcing an increase in the prices of the beverages and beans sold at retail. During fiscal 2008, Starbucks more than doubled its volume of its fixed-price purchase commitments compared with fiscal 2007 because of the risk of rising prices for green coffee beans. Starbucks bought 367 million pounds of green coffee beans in fiscal 2009, paying an average of $1.47 per pound. At the end of fiscal 2009, the company had purchase commitments totaling $238 million, which, together with existing inventory, were expected to provide an adequate supply of green coffee through fiscal 2010.[35]

Starbucks and Fair Trade Certified Coffee

A growing number of small coffee growers were members of democratically run cooperatives that were registered with the Fair Trade Labeling Organizations International; these growers could sell their beans directly to importers, roasters, and retailers at favorable guaranteed fair trade prices. The idea behind guaranteed prices for fair trade coffees was to boost earnings for small coffee growers enough to allow them to invest in their farms and communities, develop the business skills needed to compete in the global market for coffee, and afford basic health care, education, and home improvements.

Starbucks began purchasing Fair Trade Certified coffee in 2000, steadily increasing its purchasing and marketing of such coffees in line with growing awareness of what Fair Trade Certified coffees were all about and consumer willingness to pay the typically higher prices for fair trade coffees. In 2008, Starbucks announced that it would double its purchases of Fair Trade Certified coffees in 2009, resulting in total purchases of 39 million pounds in 2009 (versus 19 million pounds in 2008 and 10 million pounds in 2005) and making Starbucks the largest purchaser of Fair Trade Certified coffee in the world. Starbucks marketed Fair Trade Certified coffees at most of its retail stores and through other locations that sold Starbucks coffees.

Best-Practice Coffee Cultivation and Environmental Sustainability

Since 1998, Starbucks had partnered with Conservation International's Center for Environmental Leadership to promote environmentally sustainable best practices in coffee cultivation methods and to develop specific guidelines—called Coffee and Farmer Equity (C.A.F.E.) Practices—to help farmers grow high-quality coffees in ways that were good for the planet. The C.A.F.E. Practices covered four areas: product quality, the price received by farmers/growers, safe and humane working conditions (including compliance with minimum wage requirements and child labor provisions), and environmental responsibility.[36] In addition, Starbucks operated Farmer Support Centers in Costa Rica and Rwanda that were staffed with agronomists and experts on environmentally responsible coffee growing methods; staff members at these two centers worked with coffee farming communities to promote best practices in coffee production and improve both coffee quality and production yields. During 2008–2009, approximately 80 percent of the coffee beans purchased by Starbucks came from suppliers whose coffee-growing methods met C.A.F.E. standards. In those instances where Starbucks sourced its coffee beans from non-grower C.A.F.E. Practices suppliers, it required suppliers to submit evidence of payments made through the coffee supply chain to demonstrate how much of the price Starbucks paid for green coffee beans got to the farmer/grower.

A growing percentage of the coffees that Starbucks purchased were grown organically (i.e., without the use of pesticides, herbicides, or chemical fertilizers); organic cultivation methods resulted in clean ground water and helped protect against degrading of local ecosystems, many of which were fragile or in areas where biodiversity was under severe threat. Starbucks purchased 14 million pounds of certified organic coffee in fiscal 2009.

COFFEE ROASTING OPERATIONS

Starbucks considered the roasting of its coffee beans to be something of an art form, entailing trial-and-error testing of different combinations of time and temperature to get the most out of each type of bean and blend. Recipes were put together by the coffee department, once all the components had been tested. Computerized roasters guaranteed consistency. Highly trained and experienced roasting personnel monitored the process, using both smell and hearing, to help check when the beans were perfectly done—coffee beans make a popping sound when ready. Starbucks' standards were so exacting that roasters tested the color of the beans in a blood-cell analyzer and discarded the entire batch if the reading wasn't on target. After roasting and cooling, the coffee was immediately vacuum-sealed in bags that preserved freshness for up to 26 weeks. As a matter of policy, however, Starbucks removed coffees on its shelves after three months and, in the case of coffee used to prepare beverages in stores, the shelf life was limited to seven days after the bag was opened.

Starbucks had roasting plants in Kent, Washington; York, Pennsylvania; Minden, Nevada; Charleston, South Carolina; and The Netherlands. In addition to roasting capability, these plants also had additional space for warehousing and shipping coffees. In keeping with Starbucks' corporate commitment to reduce its environmental footprint, the new state-of-the-art roasting plant in South Carolina had been awarded LEED Silver certification for New Construction by the U.S. Green Building Council. Twenty percent of materials used in the construction of the building were from recycled content and more than 75 percent of the waste generated during construction was recycled. In addition, the facility used state-of-the-art light and water fixtures and was partly powered by wind energy. Some of the green elements in the South Carolina plant were being implemented in the other roasting plants as part of the company's initiative to achieve LEED certification for all company-operated facilities by the end of 2010.[37] In May 2010, Starbucks announced the opening of its first LEED-certified store in Asia. Located in Fukuoka, Japan, the new store was designed to serve as an extension of the existing landscape and to preserve the surrounding trees.[38]

STARBUCKS' CORPORATE SOCIAL RESPONSIBILITY STRATEGY

Howard Schultz's effort to "build a company with soul" included a long history of doing business in ways that were socially and environmentally responsible. A commitment to do the right thing had been central to how Starbucks operated as a company since Howard Schultz first became CEO in 1987. The specific actions comprising

Starbucks' social responsibility strategy had varied over the years, but the intent of the strategy was consistently one of contributing positively to the communities in which Starbucks had stores, being a good environmental steward, and conducting its business in ways that earned the trust and respect of customers, partners/employees, suppliers, and the general public.

The Starbucks Foundation was set up in 1997 to orchestrate the company's philanthropic activities. Starbucks stores participated regularly in local charitable projects and community improvement activities. For years, the company had engaged in efforts to reduce, reuse, and recycle waste, conserve on water and energy usage, and generate less solid waste. Customers who brought their own mugs to stores were given a $0.10 discount on beverage purchases—in 2009, some 26 million beverages were served in customers' mugs. Coffee grounds, which were a big portion of the waste stream in stores, were packaged and given to customers, parks, schools, and plant nurseries as a soil amendment. Company personnel purchased paper products with high levels of recycled content and unbleached fiber. Stores participated in Earth Day activities each year with in-store promotions and volunteer efforts to educate employees and customers about the impacts their actions had on the environment. Suppliers were encouraged to provide the most energy-efficient products within their category and eliminate excessive packaging; Starbucks had recently instituted a set of Supplier Social Responsibility Standards covering the suppliers of all the manufactured goods and services used in the company's operations. No genetically modified ingredients were used in any food or beverage products that Starbucks served, with the exception of milk (U.S. labeling requirements do not require milk producers to disclose the use of hormones aimed at increasing the milk production of dairy herds). In 2005, Starbucks made a $5 million, five-year commitment to long-term relief and recovery efforts for victims of hurricanes Rita and Katrina and committed $5 million to support educational programs in China. In 2010, the Starbucks Foundation donated $1 million to the American Red Cross efforts to provide aid to those suffering the devastating effects of the earthquake in Haiti; in addition, Starbucks customers were invited to make cash donations to the Haitian relief effort at store registers.[39]

In 2008–2010, Starbucks' corporate social responsibility strategy had four main elements:

1. *Ethically sourcing all of the company's products.* This included promoting responsible growing practices for the company's coffees, teas, and cocoa and striving to buy the manufactured products and services it needed from suppliers that had a demonstrated commitment to social and environmental responsibility. Starbucks had a 2015 goal of purchasing 100 percent of its coffees through sources there were either Fair Trade Certified or met C.A.F.E. Practices guidelines.

2. *Community involvement.* This included engaging in a wide variety of community service activities, Starbucks Youth Action Grants to engage young people in community improvement projects (in fiscal 2009, Starbucks made 71 grants totaling $2.1 million), a program to provide medicine to people in Africa with HIV, the Ethos Water Fund, and donations by the Starbucks Foundation. The company had a goal of getting Starbucks partners and customers to contribute more than 1 million hours of community service annually by 2015; service contributions totaled 246,000 hours in 2008 and 186,000 hours in 2009.

3. *Environmental stewardship.* Initiatives here included a wide variety of actions to increase recycling, reduce waste, be more energy-efficient and use renewable energy sources, conserve water resources, make all company facilities as green as possible by using environmentally friendly building materials and energy-efficient designs, and engage in more efforts to address climate change. The company had immediate objectives of achieving LEED certification globally for all new company-operated stores beginning in late 2010, reducing energy consumption in company-owned stores by 25 percent by the end of fiscal 2010, and purchasing renewable energy equivalent to 50 percent of the electricity used in company-owned stores by the end of fiscal 2010. Management believed that the company was on track to achieve all three targets.

In 2009, Starbucks became a member of the Business for Innovative Climate Change and Energy Policy coalition, which sought to spur a clean energy economy and mitigate global warming by advocating strong legislation by the U.S. Congress. Starbucks was also collaborating with Earthwatch Institute on replanting rain forests, mapping water resources and biodiversity indicators, and sharing sustainable agriculture practices with coffee growers. Starbucks had goals to implement front-of-store recycling in all company-owned stores by 2015, to ensure that 100 percent of its cups were reusable or recyclable by 2015, to serve 25 percent of the beverages made in its stores in reusable containers by 2015, and to reduce water consumption in company-owned stores by 25 percent by 2015. In 2009 the company made progress toward achieving all these goals but still faced significant challenges in implementing recycling at its more than 16,000 stores worldwide because of wide variations in municipal recycling capabilities.

4. *Farmer loans.* Because many of the tens of thousands of small family farms with less than 30 acres that grew coffees purchased by Starbucks often lacked the money to make farming improvements and/or cover all expenses until they sold their crops, Starbucks provided funding to organizations that made loans to small coffee growers. Over the years, Starbucks had committed more than $15 million to a variety of coffee farmer loan funds. The company boosted its farmer loan commitments from $12.5 million to $14.5 million in 2009 and had a goal to commit a total of $20 million by 2015.

In 2010, Starbucks was named to *Corporate Responsibility Magazine*'s list "The 100 Best Corporate Citizens" for the 10th time. The "100 Best Corporate Citizens" list was based on more than 360 data points of publicly available information in seven categories: Environment, Climate Change, Human Rights, Philanthropy, Employee Relations, Financial Performance, and Governance. In addition, Starbucks had received over 25 awards from a diverse group of organizations for its philanthropic, community service, and environmental activities.

TOP MANAGEMENT CHANGES: CHANGING ROLES FOR HOWARD SCHULTZ

In 2000, Howard Schultz decided to relinquish his role as CEO, retain his position as chairman of the company's board of directors, and assume the newly created role of chief strategic officer. Orin Smith, a Starbucks executive who had been with the company since its early days, was named CEO. Smith retired in 2005 and was replaced as CEO by Jim Donald, who had been president of Starbucks' North American division. In 2006, Donald proceeded to set a long-term objective of having 40,000 stores worldwide and launched a program of rapid store expansion in an effort to achieve that goal.

But investors and members of Starbucks' board of directors (including Howard Schultz) became uneasy about Donald's leadership of the company when customer traffic in Starbucks' U.S. stores began to erode in 2007, new store openings worldwide were continuing at the rate of six per day, and Donald kept pressing for increased efficiency in store operations at the expense of good customer service. Investors were distressed with the company's steadily declining stock price during 2007. Schultz had lamented in a 2007 internal company e-mail (which was leaked to the public) that the company's aggressive growth had led to "a watering down of the Starbucks experience."[40] In January 2008, Starbucks' board asked Howard Schultz to return to his role as CEO and lead a major restructuring and revitalization initiative.

HOWARD SCHULTZ'S TRANSFORMATION AGENDA FOR STARBUCKS, 2008–2010

Immediately upon his return as Starbucks CEO, Schultz undertook a series of moves to revamp the company's executive leadership team and change the roles and responsibilities of several key executives.[41] A former Starbucks executive was hired for the newly created role of chief creative officer responsible for elevating the in-store experience of customers and achieving new levels of innovation and differentiation.

Because he believed that Starbucks in recent years had become less passionate about customer relationships and the coffee experience that had fueled the company's success, Schultz further decided to launch a major campaign to retransform Starbucks into the company he had envisioned it ought to be and to push the company to new plateaus of differentiation and innovation—the transformation effort instantly became the centerpiece of his return as company CEO. Schultz's transformation agenda for Starbucks had three main themes: strengthen the core, elevate the experience, and invest and grow. Specific near-term actions that Schultz implemented to drive his transformation of Starbucks in 2008–2010 included the following:

- Slowing the pace of new store openings in the United States and opening a net of 75 new stores internationally.

- Closing 900 underperforming company-operated stores in the United States, nearly 75 percent of which were within three miles of an existing Starbucks store. It was expected that these closings would boost sales and traffic at many nearby stores.

- Raising the projected return on capital requirements for proposed new store locations.

- Restructuring the company's store operations in Australia to focus on three key cities and surrounding areas—Brisbane, Melbourne, and Sydney—and to close 61 underperforming store locations (mostly located in other parts of Australia).

- Coming up with new designs for future Starbucks stores. The global store design strategy was aimed at promoting a reinvigorated customer experience by reflecting the character of each store's surrounding neighborhood and making customers feel truly at home when visiting their local store. All of the designs had to incorporate environmentally friendly materials and furnishings.

- Enhancing the customer experience at Starbucks stores, including the discontinuance of serving warmed breakfast sandwiches in North American stores (because the scent of warmed sandwiches interfered with the coffee aroma) and a program to develop best-in-class baked goods and other new menu items that would make Starbucks a good source of a healthy breakfast for people on the go and better complement its coffee and espresso beverages. These efforts to improve the menu offerings at Starbucks stores were directly responsible for (1) the recent additions of fruit cups, yogurt parfaits, skinny lattes, the farmer's market salad, Vivanno smoothies, and healthier bakery selections, (2) the reformulated recipes to cut back on or eliminate the use of artificial flavorings, dyes, high-fructose corn syrup, and artificial preservatives, and (3) all-day brewing of Pikes Place Roast.

- A program to share best practices across all stores worldwide.

- Additional resources and tools for store employees, including laptops, an Internet-based software for scheduling work hours for store employees, and a new point-of-sale system for all stores in the United States, Canada, and the United Kingdom.

- Rigorous cost-containment initiatives to improve the company's bottom line, including a 1,000-person reduction in the staffing of the company's organizational support infrastructure to trim administrative expenses at the company's headquarters and regional offices.

- Renewed attention to employee training and reigniting enthusiasm on the part of store employees to please customers. In February 2008, Schultz ordered that 7,100 U.S. stores be temporarily closed for three regularly operating business hours (at 5:30 p.m. local time) for the purpose of conducting a special training session for store employees. The objectives were to give baristas hands-on training to improve the quality of the drinks they made, help reignite the emotional attachment of store employees to customers (a long-standing tradition at Starbucks stores), and refocus the attention of store employees on pleasing customers. Schultz viewed the training session as a way to help the company regain its "soul of the past" and improve the in-store Starbucks experience for customers.[42] When several major shareholders called Schultz to get his take on why he was closing 7,100 stores for three hours, he told them, "I am doing the right thing. We are retraining our people because we have forgotten what we stand for, and that is the pursuit of an unequivocal, absolute commitment to quality."[43]

Schultz's insistence on more innovation had also spurred the recent introduction of the Starbucks VIA instant coffees.

Howard Schultz believed that the turning point in his effort to transform Starbucks came when he decided to hold a leadership conference for 10,000 store managers in New Orleans in early 2008. According to Schultz:

> I knew that if I could remind people of our character and values, we could make a difference. The conference was about galvanizing the entire leadership of the company—being vulnerable and transparent with our employees about how desperate the situation was, and how we had to understand that everyone must be personally accountable and responsible for every single customer interaction. We started the conference with community service. Our efforts represent the largest single block of community support in the history of New Orleans, contributing more than 54,000 volunteer hours and investing more than $1 million in local projects like painting, landscaping, and building playgrounds.
>
> If we had not had New Orleans, we wouldn't have turned things around. It was real, it was truthful, and it was about leadership. An outside CEO would have come into Starbucks and invariably done what was expected, which was cut the thing to the bone. We didn't do that. Now we did cut $581 million of costs out of the company. The cuts targeted all areas of the business, from supply chain efficiencies to waste reduction to rightsizing our support structure. But 99 percent were not consumer-facing, and in fact, our customer satisfaction scores began to rise at this time and have continued to reach unprecedented levels. We reinvested in our people, we reinvested in innovation, and we reinvested in the values of the company.

In 2010, as part of Schultz's "invest and grow" aspect of transforming Starbucks, the company was formulating plans to open "thousands of new stores" in China over time.[44] Japan had long been Starbucks' biggest foreign market outside North America, but Howard Schultz said that "Asia clearly represents the most significant growth opportunity on a go-forward basis."[45]

Schultz also indicated that Starbucks was anxious to begin opening stores in India and Vietnam, two country markets that Starbucks believed were potentially lucrative.

Exhibit 9 is a letter that Howard Schultz sent to customers on the day he reassumed the position of Starbucks' chief executive officer. Exhibit 10 is a letter that Howard Schultz sent to all Starbucks partners three weeks after he returned as company CEO.

STARBUCKS' FUTURE PROSPECTS

In April 2010, halfway through the fiscal year, Howard Schultz continued to be pleased with the company's progress in returning to a path of profitable, long-term growth. Following five consecutive quarters of declining sales at stores open 13 months or longer (beginning with the first quarter of fiscal 2008), sales at Starbucks' company-operated stores worldwide had improved in each of the most recent five consecutive quarters—see Exhibit 11. Moreover, traffic (as measured by the number of cash register transactions) increased by 3 percent in the company's U.S. stores in the second quarter of fiscal 2010, the first positive increase in the last 13 quarters. Net revenues increased 8.6 percent in the second quarter of fiscal 2010 compared with the same quarter in fiscal 2009, while net income jumped from $25.0 million in the second quarter of fiscal 2009 to $217.3 million in the second quarter of fiscal 2010.

Exhibit 9 **Letter from Howard Schultz to Starbucks Customers, January 7, 2008**

To Our Customers:

Twenty-five years ago, I walked into Starbucks' first store and I fell in love with the coffee I tasted, with the passion of the people working there, and with how it looked, smelled and felt. From that day, I had a vision that a store can offer a welcoming experience for customers, be part of their community, and become a warm "third place" that is part of their lives everyday and that it can provide a truly superior cup of coffee.

Based on that vision, I, along with a very talented group of people, brought Starbucks to life. We did it by being creative, innovative and courageous in offering coffee products that very few in America had ever tasted; by celebrating the interaction between us and our customers; by developing a store design unlike any that existed before; and by bringing on board an exceptionally engaged group of partners (employees) who shared our excitement about building a different kind of company.

In doing this, we developed a culture based on treating each other, our customers and our coffee growers with respect and dignity. This includes embracing diversity, committing ourselves to ethical sourcing practices, providing health care and stock options to all of our eligible full- and part-time partners, supporting the communities we serve, and, most of all, ensuring that we are a company you can be proud to support.

I am writing today to thank you for the trust you have placed in us and to share with you my personal commitment to ensuring that every time you visit our stores you get the distinctive Starbucks Experience that you have come to expect, marked by the consistent delivery of the finest coffee in the world. To ensure this happens, in addition to my role as chairman, I am returning to the position of chief executive officer to help our partners build upon our heritage and our special relationship with you, and lead our company into the future.

We have enormous opportunity and exciting plans in place to make the Starbucks Experience as good as it has ever been and even better. In the coming months, you will see this come to life in the way our stores look, in the way our people serve you, in the new beverages and products we will offer. That is my promise to you. Everyone at Starbucks looks forward to sharing these initiatives with you.

Onward,

Howard Schultz

Source: Starbucks, press release, January 7, 2008, www.starbucks.com, accessed June 17, 2010.

Exhibit 10   **Communication from Howard Schultz to All Starbucks Partners, February 4, 2008**

What I Know to Be True

Dear Partners,

As I sit down to write this note (6:30 a.m. Sunday morning) I am enjoying a spectacular cup of Sumatra, brewed my favorite way—in a French press.

It has been three weeks since I returned to my role as CEO of the company I love. We have made much progress as we begin to transform and innovate and there is much more to come. But this is not a sprint—it is a marathon—it always has been. I assure you that when all is said and done, we will, as we always have, succeed at our highest potential. We will not be deterred from our course—we are and will be a great, enduring company, known for inspiring and nurturing the human spirit.

During this time, I have heard from so many of you; in fact, I have received more than 2,000 emails. I can feel your passion and commitment to the company, to our customers and to one another. I also thank you for all your ideas and suggestions . . . keep them coming. No one knows our business and our customers better than you. I have visited with you in many of your stores, as well as stopping by to see what our competitors are doing as well.

It's been just a few days since my last communications to you, but I wanted to share with you

what I know to be true:

- Since 1971, we have been ethically sourcing and roasting the highest quality *Arabica* coffee in the world, and today there is not a coffee company on earth providing higher quality coffee to their customers than we are. Period!

- We are in the people business and always have been. What does that mean? It means you make the difference. You are the Starbucks brand. We succeed in the marketplace and distinguish ourselves by each and every partner embracing the values, guiding principles and culture of our company and bringing it to life one customer at a time.

  Our stores have become the Third Place in our communities—a destination where human connections happen tens of thousands of times a day. We are not in the coffee business serving people. We are in the people business serving coffee. You are the best people serving the best coffee and I am proud to be your partner. There is no other place I would rather be than with you right here, right now!

- We have a renewed clarity of purpose and we are laser-focused on the customer experience. We have returned to our core to reaffirm our coffee authority and we will have some fun doing it. We are not going to embrace the status quo. Instead, we will be curious, bold and innovative in our actions and, in doing so, we will exceed the expectation of our customers.

- There will be cynics and critics along the way, all of whom will have an opinion and a point of view. This is not about them or our competitors, although we must humbly respect the changing landscape and the many choices facing every consumer. We will be steadfast in our approach and in our commitment to the *Starbucks Experience*—what we know to be true. However, this is about us and our customers. We are in control of our destiny. Trust the coffee and trust one another.

- I will lead us back to the place where we belong, but I need your help and support every step of the way. My expectations of you are high, but higher of myself.

- I want to hear from you. I want to hear about your ideas, your wins, your concerns, and how we can collectively continue to improve. Please feel free to reach out to me. I have been flooded with emails, but believe me, I am reading and responding to all of them.

As I said, I am proud to be your partner. I know this to be true.

Onward . . .

Howard

P.S. Everything that we do, from this point on (from the most simple and basic), matters.

Master the fundamentals. Experience Starbucks.

Source: Starbucks, press release, February 4, 2008, www.starbucks.com, accessed June 17, 2010.

Exhibit 11 **Quarterly Sales Trends at Starbucks Company-Operated Stores, Quarter 1 of Fiscal 2008 through Quarter 2 of Fiscal 2010**

Sales at Company-Operated Starbucks Stores	Five Quarters of Deteriorating Sales				
	Q1 2008	Q2 2008	Q3 2008	Q4 2008	Q1 2009
United States	(1%)	(4%)	(5%)	(8%)	(10%)
International	5%	3%	2%	0%	(3%)

Sales at Company-Operated Starbucks Stores	Five Quarters of Improving Sales				
	Q2 2009	Q3 2009	Q4 2009	Q1 2010	Q2 2010
United States	(8%)	(6%)	(1%)	4%	7%
International	(3%)	(2%)	0%	4%	7%

In commenting on the company's earnings for the second quarter of fiscal 2010, Schultz said:

> Starbucks second quarter results demonstrate the impact of innovation and the success of our efforts to dramatically transform our business over the last two years. Much credit goes to our partners all around the world who continue to deliver an improved experience to our customers. In addition, new products like Starbucks VIA, the opening of exciting new stores in Asia, Europe and the U.S., and expanded distribution outside our retail stores all represent opportunities for future growth.[46]

In March 2010, Starbucks announced its first-ever cash dividend of $0.10 per share to be paid quarterly starting with the second quarter of fiscal 2010.

The company's updated targets for full-year 2010 were as follows:

- Mid-single-digit revenue growth world-wide, driven by mid-single-digit sales growth at company-operated stores open at least 13 months.
- Opening approximately 100 net new stores in the United States and approximately 200 net new stores in international markets. Both the U.S. and international net new additions were expected to be primarily licensed stores.
- Earnings per share in the range of $1.19 to $1.22.
- Non-GAAP earnings per share in the range of $1.19 to $1.22, excluding approximately $0.03 of expected restructuring charges and including approximately $0.04 from the extra

week in the fiscal fourth quarter, as fiscal 2010 was a 53-week year for Starbucks.
- Capital expenditures are expected to be approximately $500 million for the full year.
- Cash flow from operations of at least $1.5 billion, and free cash flow of more than $1 billion.

Long term, the company's objective was to maintain Starbucks' standing as one of the most recognized and respected brands in the world. To achieve this, Starbucks executives planned to continue disciplined global expansion of its company-operated and licensed retail store base, introduce relevant new products in all its channels, and selectively develop new channels of distribution.

Schultz's long-term vision for Starbucks had seven key elements:

- Be the undisputed coffee authority.
- Engage and inspire Starbucks partners.
- Ignite the emotional attachment with our customers.
- Expand our global presence—while making each store the heart of the local neighborhood.
- Be a leader in ethical sourcing and environmental impact.
- Create innovative growth platforms worthy of our coffee.
- Deliver a sustainable economic model.

Schultz believed that Starbucks still had enormous growth potential. In the United States, Starbucks had only a 3 percent share of the estimated

37 billion cups of coffee served to on-the-go coffee drinkers, only a 4 percent share of the 25 billion cups of coffee served at home, and only a 13 percent share of the 3.7 billion cups of coffee served in restaurants and coffeehouses.[47] Internationally, Starbucks' shares of these same segments were smaller. According to Schultz:

> The size of the prize is still huge. We sell less than 10 percent of the coffee consumed in the U.S. and less than 1 percent outside the U.S.

The momentum will come from international. Slower growth in the U.S., accelerating growth overseas. The response to the Starbucks brand has been phenomenal in our international markets.[48]

Nonetheless, since his return as CEO in January 2008, Schultz had been mum about whether and when the company would aggressively pursue former CEO Jim Donald's lofty goal of having 40,000 stores worldwide.

ENDNOTES

[1] Starbucks, 2009 annual report, "Letter to Shareholders," p.1.
[2] Howard Schultz and Dori Jones Yang, *Pour Your Heart into It* (New York: Hyperion, 1997), p. 33.
[3] Ibid., p. 34.
[4] Ibid., p. 36.
[5] As told in ibid., p. 48.
[6] Ibid., pp. 61–62.
[7] As quoted in Jennifer Reese, "Starbucks: Inside the Coffee Cult," *Fortune,* December 9, 1996, p.193.
[8] Schultz and Yang, *Pour Your Heart Into It,* pp. 101–2.
[9] Ibid., p. 142.
[10] Starbucks, 2009 annual report, p. 3.
[11] Starbucks, "Global Responsibility Report," 2009, p. 13.
[12] "Starbucks Plans New Global Store Design," *Restaurants and Institutions,* June 25, 2009, www.rimag.com, accessed December 29, 2009.
[13] Starbucks, press releases, May 31, 2005, and October 25, 2005.
[14] Starbucks, press release, November 1, 2007.
[15] As stated by Howard Schultz in an interview with *Harvard Business Review* editor-in-chief Adi Ignatius; the interview was published in the July–August 2010 of the *Harvard Business Review*, pp. 108–15.
[16] Starbucks, "Starbucks and iTunes Bring Complimentary Digital Music and Video Offerings with Starbucks Pick of the Week," April 15, 2008, http://news.starbucks.com/article_display.cfm?article_id=93, accessed June 8, 2010.

[17] Starbucks, 2009 annual report, p. 5.
[18] Starbucks, "Starbucks Foundation," www.starbucks.com, accessed June 18, 2010.
[19] Starbucks, press release, July 14, 2008.
[20] Starbucks, press release, June 30, 2009.
[21] Starbucks, press release, April 7, 2008.
[22] Starbucks, press release, February 19, 2009.
[23] Starbucks, press release, April 13, 2010.
[24] Starbucks, 2009 annual report, p. 4.
[25] Claire Cain Miller, "New Starbucks Ads Seek to Recruit Online Fans," *New York Times,* May 18, 2009, www.nytimes.com, accessed January 3, 2010.
[26] Andy Server, "Schultz' Plan to Fix Starbucks," *Fortune,* January 18, 2008, www.fortune.com, accessed June 21, 2010.
[27] Beth Cowitt, "Starbucks CEO: We Spend More on Healthcare Than Coffee," *Fortune,* June 7, 2010, http://money.cnn.com/2010/06/07/news/companies/starbucks_schultz_healthcare.fortune/index.html, accessed June 8, 2010.
[28] As related in Schultz and Yang, *Pour Your Heart Into It,* pp. 131–36.
[29] Starbucks, 2009 10-K report, p. 68.
[30] "100 Best Companies to Work For," *Fortune,* http://money.cnn.com/magazines/fortune/bestcompanies/2010/snapshots/93.html, accessed June 9, 2010.
[31] Ibid.
[32] Starbucks, press release, May 21, 2009, www.starbucks.com, accessed June 14, 2010.
[33] Starbucks, "Global Responsibility Report," 2008.

[34] Kate Rounds, "Starbucks Coffee," *Incentive* 167, no. 7, p. 22.
[35] Starbucks, 2009 10-K report, p. 6.
[36] Starbucks, "Corporate Responsibility," www.starbucks.com, accessed June 18, 2010.
[37] Starbucks, press release, February 19, 2009.
[38] Starbucks, press release, May 26, 2010.
[39] Starbucks, press release, January 18, 2010.
[40] "Shakeup at Starbucks," January 7, 2008, www.cbsnews.com, accessed June 16, 2010.
[41] Transcript of Starbucks Earnings Conference Call for Quarters 1 and 3 of fiscal year 2008, http://seekingalpha.com, accessed June 16, 2010.
[42] "Coffee Break for Starbucks' 135,000 Baristas," CNN, http://money.cnn.com, February 26, 2008, accessed December 28, 2009, and "Starbucks Takes a 3-Hour Coffee Break," *New York Times,* February 27, 2008, www.nytimes.com, accessed June 15, 2010.
[43] Quoted in Adi Ignatius, "We Had to Own the Mistakes," *Harvard Business Review* 88, no. 7/8 (July–August 2010), p. 111.
[44] Mariko Sanchanta, "Starbucks Plans Major China Expansion," *Wall Street Journal,* April 13, 2010, http://online.wsj.com, accessed June 10, 2010.
[45] Ibid.
[46] Starbucks, press release, April 21, 2010.
[47] Management presentation to Barclays Capital Retail and Restaurants Conference, April 28, 2010, www.starbucks.com, accessed June 21, 2010.
[48] Server, "Schultz' Plan to Fix Starbucks."

Rhino Capture in Kruger National Park

A. J. Strickland
The University of Alabama

William E. Mixon
The University of Alabama
MBA Candidate

Dr. Markus Hofmeyr, head of Veterinary Wildlife Services for South African National Parks (SANParks), returned from another rhino capture with his team. They had captured their 252nd rhino for the year before the rainy season set in, with heat and rain making it almost impossible to continue the capture program. As Hofmeyr and his team were winding down another successful year, given that each rhino was worth between $30,000 and $35,000,[1] he began to reflect on next year's game capture. Hofmeyr faced the daunting question of how to continue to supplement the funding for SANParks' Park Development Fund. Over the years, the budget for his unit had been reduced, and pressure for self-funding of SANParks was increasing.

Some of the funding for SANParks' operations had long been provided by the South African national government in the form of an annual grant. That began to change in 2010, however, when a budget shortfall forced the government to initiate the removal of the grant over three years. The South African government shifted its strategy toward building a new South Africa, focused on providing additional funds for education, job creation through infrastructure expansions, better health care for all South Africans, and economic prosperity. Funding cuts outside of these priority areas threatened the ability of SANParks' Veterinary Wildlife Services to continue delivering normal veterinary and operational services—services that were beneficial to all SANParks wildlife and the habitat in which the wildlife had roamed for centuries. SANParks' budget allocation is shown in Exhibit 1.

KRUGER NATIONAL PARK

Kruger National Park was established in South Africa in 1898 to protect the nation's fast-dwindling wildlife areas. By the turn of that century, it was estimated that white rhinos were extinct in Kruger. The first translocation of white rhinos to Kruger National Park occurred in 1961, and a total of 345 white rhinos had been relocated from the parks in Kwa Zulu Natal by the mid-1970s. In 2007, an assessment by the African Rhino Specialist Group estimated that 15,000 white rhinos and 1,500 black rhinos existed in South Africa. As of 2009, research indicated that 10,000 white rhinos and 500 black rhinos existed within Kruger National Park, making it home to the largest rhino population in the world. Population estimates for rhinos in South Africa are shown in Exhibit 2.

Kruger National Park covered 7,722 square miles (20,000 square kilometers) of conservation area, with eight gates that controlled the flow of

Exhibit 1 SANParks Budget Allocation (in U.S. dollars)

Kruger National Park Budget	$4,951,900
Poaching	$ 275,100
Infrastructure	$ 275,100

Copyright © 2010 by A. J. Strickland. All rights reserved.

unauthorized traffic into the park. Since its establishment, it had become known for its unrivaled wildlife diversity and easy viewing and for its world leadership in advanced environmental management techniques, research, and policies. Many viewed Kruger as the best national park in all of Africa in all aspects—management, infrastructure, and, of course, biodiversity. The flagship of South Africa's 22 national parks, Kruger held a variety of species: 336 trees, 49 fish, 34 amphibians, 114 reptiles, 507 birds, and 147 mammals. Over time, the park had developed into a tourist attraction because of the wildlife and the beautiful scenery, which was representative of South Africa's Lowveld region. (The Lowveld consisted of areas around the eastern part of the country where the altitude was about 1,000 feet.)

Tourist operations at Kruger were quite large, with the park offering 21 rest camps, 7 private lodge concessions, and 11 private safari lodges. Lodges that previously had been private were operated in partnership between communities and private companies, which provided concessions for parcels of land. The concessions were placed on tender, and areas were allocated for 25- to 30-year leases, during which operational activities linked with tourism were allowed. At the end of the period, the fixed assets became the property of SANParks, which could decide to extend the lease or retender the concession. An integral part of Kruger National Park's conservation effort was game capture. Traditionally, capturing game allowed Kruger to reintroduce certain species to previously uninhabited areas of the park, as well as to introduce rhino to the other national parks in South Africa and neighboring countries.

Game capture also enabled the park to better manage rare species by placing them in breeding enclosures. In some instances, game capture was used to reduce populations where that goal was impeded by natural regulatory mechanisms.

Exhibit 2   **Rhino Population in South Africa**

	2007	2010
White rhinos	15,000	17,500
Black rhinos	1,500	4,200

Traditional game capture evolved into an income-generating operation as the demand for rhinos increased.

INCOME GENERATION FROM GAME CAPTURE

The sale of wildlife for income generation was accepted and supported by South Africa's National Environmental Management Act (2004). SANParks maximized income from wildlife sales by concentrating on selling high-value species. The two species sold without clearly required ecological reasons for their sale were white rhinos from Kruger National Park and disease-free buffalos from other parks. The only condition required when an animal was sold was that its removal could not negatively impact the populations from which it came. In 2009, 500 rhinos were sold in South Africa. Kruger National Park claimed 252 of these transactions; the others were sold from provincial parks and the private sector. A flow chart of sales transactions is shown in Exhibit 3. The average selling price for a white rhino was $30,300. Many wildlife biologists and other experts feared that these rhinos would eventually fall into the hands of private game hunters. Rhino hunting and rhino breeding for future sales or hunting were driving up the price for a rhino. SANParks accepted hunting as a legal form of wildlife utilization but did not support unethical put-and-take hunting practices because it was very difficult to determine what happened to a rhino after leaving SANParks. SANParks was not responsible for enforcing hunting regulations on wildlife; instead, this responsibility was passed on to each respective South African province. However, many provinces were understaffed, which weakened the regulation of hunting activities.

The most common method for selling rhinos outside Kruger National Park was through provincial and private-sector auctions. In 2009, 45 auctions accounted for most rhino sales outside SANParks. During that year, 252 rhinos on a direct tender were captured in the bush and sold at three auctions held by SANParks. The revenue generated from rhino sales in 2009 totaled $7,033,400. These revenue sales supplemented the conservation budget for SANParks' Park

Exhibit 3   **Flow Chart of Sales Transactions**

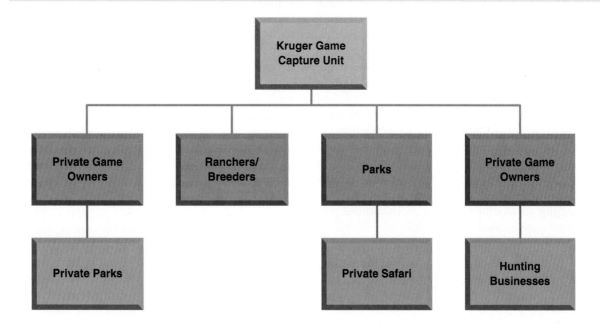

Development Fund. The buyers of the live rhinos were dealers who specialized in wild game or private owners who bought directly from SANParks. Rhinos were typically sold to a private game reserve for either tourist viewing or hunting. Rhinos were also sold or donated by SANParks to neighboring countries. Rhinos purchased in the private sector were sometimes sold internationally to zoos or to buyers who dealt in wild game.

Typically, white rhinos were sold more often than black rhinos, since black rhinos were rarer and much more aggressive. SANParks had sold only two black rhino bulls; the other black rhinos moved from Kruger were donated as part of conservation efforts to reestablish them in countries where they had gone extinct. The private sector bought black rhinos from Kwa Zulu Natal Wildlife, where the remaining black rhinos survived with white rhinos at the turn of the twentieth century. Kwa Zulu Natal moved from completely selling black rhinos to retaining full ownership of the adults and partial ownership of the offspring. Offspring were placed into a custodianship program that split the rights between two or more parties. North West Province sold black rhinos, as did the private sector. Compared with white rhinos, black rhinos were more difficult to introduce and had a higher intraspecies mortality rate from fighting. The tendency to fight made black rhinos a riskier investment than white rhinos, which bred and coexisted much better than black rhinos. The majority of white rhinos were purchased in cow/calf combinations, which were not hunted. White rhino bulls were much more likely than white rhino cows to be purchased for hunting. However, most provinces had regulations that limited the number of rhinos eligible to be hunted. Before a rhino was killed, it had to have lived on the current property for more than two years; however, this regulation was very difficult to enforce. Park Services was a critical component of conservation for rhinos and other animals within the park.

PARK SERVICES

Veterinary Wildlife Services (VWS) offered a variety of operational and veterinary services for Kruger National Park. Veterinarian operations were critical to the conservation of wildlife within and outside the park. The service's operations included wildlife capture, holding, and translocation; park development; species conservation management; wildlife sales; animal exchanges and contractual commitments; regional cooperation; and research. VWS's aims and objectives and responsibilities are shown in Exhibit 4. Game capture operations began in the 1980s for Kruger National Park; Kruger had also operated game capture in other parks. In the 1990s, a second unit was established for operations outside Kruger. Both units were combined to form VWS in 2002, ensuring that the service was serving SANParks' objectives and not just those of Kruger. Kruger aimed for VWS to "provide ethical and professional services relating to capture, holding, translocation and research pertaining to wildlife."[2] Some of the values and functions associated with VWS are shown in Exhibit 5.

SANPARKS' GAME CAPTURE UNIT

SANParks' game capture unit had branch offices in three locations in South Africa: Kruger, Kimberley, and Port Elizabeth. The capture, translocation and reestablishment functions of SANParks' Veterinary Wildlife Services are shown in Exhibit 6.

Population growth, sex and age structure, spatial use, natural dispersal, resource distribution, and population dynamics were considered when making the decision to sell an animal to a private buyer. According to SANParks' chief executive officer, Dr. David Mabunda, "SANParks, by selling or donating rhino, is assisting in the process of recolonization of the range in the country and outside. It should be noted that it would be foolhardy if South Africa were to have its only rhino population residing in the Kruger, because we run the danger of losing them should there be a major outbreak of disease or rampant poaching. We would be sitting ducks." Bovine tuberculosis and anthrax were two diseases being monitored by VWS in efforts to better understand how to contain them, which in turn would lead to better decisions about disease management where required. Intervention was not always needed in wildlife populations, but an understanding of how a disease influenced population dynamics was. VWS disease management services are shown in Exhibit 7. In addition to these issues, SANParks concerned itself with

Kruger National Park's capability to assess and evaluate financial implications and the risks imposed to its white rhino population by intense localized removals and emerging diseases.[3]

CAPTURING A RHINO

The rhino capture process involved the use of state-of-the-art equipment accompanied by a team of experts. A game capture team included a helicopter pilot, a veterinarian, an operational coordinator, a veterinary technician, five capture staff personnel, and two drivers for the translocation and crane trucks. Selected operating expenses of a rhino capture are shown in Exhibit 8.

Once a rhino was located, the capture process consisted of darting it with a drug combination from a helicopter. The fast-acting drug combination made the whole capture process less dangerous to the capture unit by rendering the rhino unconscious for evaluation before relocation. Once the rhino was unconscious, a team from the game capture unit moved in to examine it. The game capture unit conducted a medical examination of the rhino by taking blood samples to test for any signs of disease. At this point in the game capture process, three radio-frequency identification (RFID) microchips were tagged on the rhino for identification purposes. Inserting an RFID microchip involved drilling into the horn, which is made of keratin, a material similar to that which human hair and fingernails are composed of. Photos of the game capture process are shown in Exhibit 9.

Park officials used tagging as a method to better understand the rhinos' movement within their landscape. South African law mandated the tagging of any rhino darted as well. Park services were also looking at ways to place tracking devices on rhinos to increase the capability of understanding rhino movements within their landscape. Prevention was the main emphasis of the rhino poaching counteroffensive in Kruger. It was thought that these potential tracking devices would help deter poaching, but the main deterrent was gaining information from informants on possible plans for rhino poaching.

After the evaluation and tagging process, a partial antidote was administered to partially wake up the rhino but keep it in a semi-anesthetized state. Partial antidotes were necessary to protect

Exhibit 4 **Aims, Objectives, and Responsibilities of SANParks' Veterinary Wildlife Services**

The SANParks Strategic Organizational Objectives Framework

Prioritization of services according to resources, ethical and legal constraints

Optimal utilization of resources

Development and training of the wildlife profession

Recognition that SANParks concerns itself with populations rather than individuals

The leveraging of information and skills developed in SANParks to the benefit of the SADC region

The recognition of the importance of the wildlife and ecological socio-interfaces

Coordination of research on wildlife diseases and their impact on human livelihoods, wildlife itself, and livestock

Implementation of wildlife capture and translocation programs

Reintroducing populations into national parks

Enhancing the conservation status of rare and threatened species

Controlling over-abundant wildlife populations to avert the threats of habitat degradation and loss of biodiversity

Generating revenue for SANParks through wildlife sales

Enhancing breeding projects involving valuable and rare species

Building capacity in the veterinary and wildlife capture fields, particularly in persons from historically disadvantaged population groups

Exhibit 5   Veterinary Wildlife Services' Values and Functions

Veterinary Wildlife Values

VWS is a service delivery department for SANParks, providing specialist veterinary and wildlife handling and translocation support.

The SANParks strategic organizational objectives framework of bio-diversity, balancing, people and enabling systems will guide these services.

The resource, ethical, and legal constraints as well as other drivers will make it necessary to prioritize the services that can be delivered. (Guided by the Wildlife Management Commitee recommendations)

Optimal utilitization of resources.

The leveraging of information and skills developed in SANParks to the benefit of the SADEC region, particularly in SANParks TFC involment.

Development and training of the wildlife profession.

The recognition of the importance of wildlife and ecological and diagnostic test development.

Veterinary Wildlife Functions

Service to scientific services and park management with regard to implementing veterinary aspects of removals and introductions into our parks, collar fitting, sample taking and any other activities that require handling of wildlife.

Disease monitoring, management and surveillance (including sample taking, storing and distribution aid research).

Development of current veterinary aspects of capture, translocation and animal husbandry techniques.

Veterinary support to special species management related to approved plans (e.g., predator management plans).

Conservation medicine (implementing and integrating disease and ecological principles in our function).

Veterinary research relevant to the service delivery component of VWS.

Liaison and education at the appropriate national and international level.

Exhibit 6 The Capture, Translocation and Reestablishment Functions of SANParks' Veterinary Wildlife Services

Capture, Translocation and Reestablishment Functions

Operational capture, care and translocation of wildlife species aligned with SANParks requirements

Import species and disease-free breeding projects

Coordination of game sales

Transfrontier developemt

International translocations

Coordination of capture by external entities

Exhibit 7 Veterinary Wildlife Service's Disease Management Services

Disease Management Services

BTB monitoring in Buffalo and Lion within Kruger

Monitoring in all parks when opportunities arise

Sarcoid research in Mountain Zebra in Bontebok NP

Disease prevention principles applied to animal movements and quarantine facilities both in Kruger and Kimberely

Exhibit 8   Selected Operating Expenses of Rhino Capture

Game Capture Operating Expenses	Cost per Rhino	Cost per Hour	Cost per Day	Cost per Year	Unit Cost
Helicopter	N/A	$800	N/A	N/A	N/A
Transportation of rhino	$300	N/A	N/A	$11,000	N/A
Truck	N/A	N/A	$ 300	N/A	N/A
Boom	N/A	N/A	$ 300	N/A	N/A
Capture team	N/A	$200	$1,400	N/A	N/A
RFID microchip	$ 50	N/A	N/A	N/A	$17

the game capture team while walking the rhino into the transportation crate. After the rhino was successfully loaded into a transportation crate, a boom truck lifted the crate onto the translocation truck. A boom truck was needed since an average rhino weighed 3,300 pounds (1,500 kilograms). Typically, the average distance traveled by a rhino captured from Kruger National Park was 50 miles (80 kilometers), at a cost of $300 per rhino per 16 miles. The next translocation process was maintenance in holding facilities (see Exhibit 10). Rhinos were placed in *bomas* (holding pens). *Bomas* allowed a rhino to become accustomed to a new habitat by slowly facilitating a passive release. Once released, the rhino was typically still confined to a larger pen or fenced-in area, depending on the buyer's intentions. It was estimated that 50 percent of the bulls transferred to private hunting companies were killed within two years, at a price of $2,800 per inch of rhino horn.

RHINO HUNTING

A typical rhino hunt could cost $82,400 per hunter. In 2009, South Africa generated an estimated $6.9 billion in revenues from tourist attractions; of that amount, hunting accounted for about 70 percent, or about $4.8 billion.[2] The cost of booking a rhino hunt varied depending on the safari company, as detailed in Exhibit 11. Most safari companies required a deposit of 50 percent of the basic cost of a safari, which was fully refundable until within three months of the contracted safari date. Accommodations varied according to packages offered by each safari company and were considered comparable to those of

any other tourist attraction in the world. Some safari companies offered photo safaris and wedding packages, in addition to hunting services, to further generate revenue for operations.

Typically, each safari company recommended certain equipment and clothing for hunters to bring along with them. This list varied by season, since temperatures could range between 30°F (low) in the winter and 90°F (high) in the wet summer season. Expenses also varied according to the specific details of a trip such as length of stay, trophy fees, number of hunters and observers, and the daily rate charged per hunter. Airfare to and from South Africa also varied depending on how far in advance travel arrangements were made and whether the flight was direct. Typically, coach seating ranged from $800 to $1,100, whereas first-class price ranges easily approached $3,000. Rifles, bows, and darting weapons were offered in some packages, but rifles could be imported into South Africa under strict guidelines and regulations. However, hunters were not allowed to import automatic or semiautomatic weapons.

Some companies charged high trophy fees and low daily rates, in contrast to low trophy fees and high daily rates. Trophy fees varied according to the specific animal wounded or killed and were typically not paid until the end of the safari. Daily rates depended on the services offered and could include or exclude a number of amenities necessary to hunt in South Africa. In general, some safari companies offered a lower daily rate as a marketing tool to increase their customer base; a large trophy fee reflected the fact that a safari company's profits depended on a successful hunt by the customer. As Zingeli Safaris stated in its

Exhibit 9 The Game Capture Process

The game capture unit follows the helicopter in pursuit of a rhino.

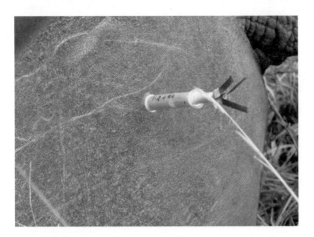

The dart shot from the helicopter is inspected by game capture personnel.

Game capture unit personnel inspect the sedated rhino.

Game capture personnel drill a hole in the rhino's horn to insert the RFID microchip.

Game capture personnel inspect the sedated rhino.

Boom trucks are needed to load the rhino.

After the antidote is given, the staff helps the rhino stand up.

Exhibit 10   Dr. Markus Hofmeyr Standing above Several *Bomas* (Holding Pens)

brochure, "If you don't get your animal we lose; this is your guarantee that we will do our best to find you your dream trophy!" Customers incurred taxidermist fees, in addition to trophy fees, if they desired to have something tangible to take home.

POACHING

Demand for rhino horn in emerging markets such as Asia and India made rhino poaching highly profitable. In 2009, rhino horn was sold on the black market at $3,600 per pound, but by 2010 the price was reported to be $7,200 per pound. An average rhino horn weighed six to eight pounds. Businesses with ties to political insiders were entering the market to supply and sell rhino horn as wealth creation resulted from the growth of Asia's and India's economies.

Exhibit 11   Selected Company Safari Expenses and Trip Details

Africa Sport Hunting Safaris

Services Offered

– First-class rifle and bow hunting

– Ethical, professional hunters

– Personal attention to all our clients

– Family and photographic tours

– Specialized, well-maintained vehicles

– Luxury accommodation

– Excellent cuisine

– Dedicated staff

Firearms and Calibers

– Rhino legal minimum .375 caliber and 3-9 × 40 variable-power telescope

– Ammunition recommended minimum of 40 full metal jacket/solids in addition to soft point bullets

Travel Information

– Valid passport required

Trophy Handling

– All animals will be skinned by our very experienced skinners, as well as marked, salted, and dried prior to being sent to a taxidermist. All documentation will be handled by Africa Sport Hunting Safaris.

Clothing and Other Requirements

– Three sets of hunting clothing: long pants (zip-offs), long-sleeve shirts, socks, and underwear

– Hunting boots/shoes—comfortable

– Casual/running shoes

– Sweater/warm jacket

– Flip flops/sweat suit

Africa Sport Hunting Safaris	

– Cap/wide-brimmed hat

– Casual clothes

– Adjust your clothing to the time of year your hunt takes place.

– Winter May–August (35–70°F)

– Summer September–April (50–90°F)

Personal

– Personal medical kit

– Sunblock—minimum 30 SPF

– Mosquito repellent

– Pair of sunglasses

– Toiletries

Additional Equipment

– Small day pack

– Flashlight with spare batteries

– Binoculars

– Camera with spare film and batteries

– Pocket knife

Accommodation: Luxury Thatched Chalets with a True African Ambience

– Private rooms with ensuite bathrooms

– Running hot and cold water

– Electricity with converters

– Flush toilets

Food and Beverages

– Traditional South African cuisine. For dietary requirements such as diabetes and high cholesterol, please make arrangements on booking of the safari.

Additional Services

– Facials and full body massages

– Manicures and pedicures

– Day excursions

South African Hunting Areas Price List Limpopo Province 2010

– White Rhino	$45,000
– White Rhino (Green-Hunt)	$13,000

Daily Rate: South Africa

– Dangerous Game	$ 800
– Plains Game	
– 1 Hunter × 1 Professional Hunter:	$ 400
– 2 Hunters × 1 Professional Hunter:	$ 300
– All non-hunters are welcome at:	$ 200

Included in Daily Rate

– Pick up and drop off at Polokwane International Airport

(Continued)

Exhibit 11   *(Continued)*

– Hunting licenses and fees

– Transportation to and from hunting concessions

– Field preparation of trophies

– Professional hunters, trackers, skinners, and camp staff

– Fully equipped hunting vehicles

– Luxury accommodation and meals

– Drinks and beverages in moderation

– Daily laundry services

Excluded from Daily Rates

– Flights: international and domestic

– Charter flights where applicable

– All animals shot and wounded will be charged per price list

– Dipping, packing, taxidermy cost

– Non-hunting, traveling days at $150 per day

– Accommodation before and after hunt

– Any additional tours or excursions

Methods of Payment Accepted

– U.S. currency

– Traveler's checks

– Wire transfers

– Credit cards

– Personal checks with prior approval

Members Of:

– Professional Hunters Association South Africa

– Accredited Tour Guides

– Safari Club International

– North American Hunters Association

– National Rifle Association

Chattaronga Safaris	

Daily Fees Hunter

1	$400
2	$350
3	$300
4	$300
Observer	$200

Included Tariffs

– Accommodation including full board

– Liquor and beverages served in camp

– Full-time service of experienced professional hunter.

– Trained staff

– Trackers

– Skinners

Chattaronga Safaris

– Field preparation of trophies

– All transportation within hunting areas

– All hunting licenses

– Pickup and drop-off at international airport: Limpopo-Polokwane, Kwa-Zulu Natal-Johannesburg, Mpumalanga-Johannesburg

Excluded Tariffs

– International and domestic flights

– Traveling day (non-hunting days) at $180 per day

– Trophy fees of animal shot or wounded

– Rifle hire (firearms may be rented at $80 per day)

– Ammunition is available at cost

– Dipping, packing, taxidermy, and shipping

– Air charters and accommodation before and after safari

– Tips for staff, telephone calls, and curio purchases

Rhino Safari

7 Day 1 × 1	$60,000

Includes representative 20" fake horn (because it is not standard practice to cut off the horn of a rhino).

Dumukwa

Daily Rates

1 hunter/1 professional hunter	$ 400
2 hunters/1 professional hunter	$ 300
Non-hunters/observers	$ 200
Rhino dart	$ 8,500

5 day 1 × 1 Hunt

Included in Daily Rates

– Full accommodation, meals, and use of camp facilities

– All liquid refreshments including wine, beer, bottled water, and sodas

– Daily laundry

– Service of professional hunter with his team of skinners and trackers

– Field preparation of trophies

– Transport of raw trophies to local taxidermist for the area you in hunt in

– All transportation during the safari including from and to the airport

– 14 percent value added tax (VAT) on all packages

Excluded in Daily Rates

– Internet, faxes, and telephone calls

– Airfare

– Hotel accommodation before and after the contracted safari

– Dipping and packing or mounting of trophies

– Shipping of trophies back to your country

– Optional hire of firearms

(Continued)

Exhibit 11   *(Concluded)*

Zingeli Safaris

Included in Daily Rates

– Full board and lodging with traditional catering

– South African wines and beer in moderation, and soft drinks

– Experienced professional hunter and trained staff

– Trackers and skinners

– Field preparation, salting and packing

– Transportation of trophies to reliable and qualified taxidermist who will follow your instructions and fulfill the necessary requirements

– Use of hunting vehicle

– Laundry services

– Transportation to the ranch and return to Johannesburg International Airport or charter plane

Excluded in Daily Rates

– Air travel before, during and after the contracted period of the safari

– Accommodation and travel charges incurred before and after the contracted period of the safari

– Trophy fees for animals taken or wounded

– Value added tax (VAT) 14 percent on daily rates

– Air charters

– Gratuities to professional hunters and staff

– Preparation, packing, documentation, and export of trophies from South Africa

The market for raw rhino horn was mainly driven by demand in China and Vietnam. Cultural beliefs, combined with increasing wealth, were creating a strong foundation for the demand of rhino horn. Asians believed that rhino horn was a very beneficial aphrodisiac, and Indians desired rhino horn daggers. These beliefs and desires were strong enough to produce enough capital to entice the illegal killing of rhinos without regard to law enforcers such as the SANParks Environmental Crimes Unit, South African Police Service, and park rangers.

Poachers were well equipped with highly sophisticated transportation such as helicopters and the latest military weaponry available in the region. They were able to strike fast within even the most protected game conservation areas. Poaching was even a problem in Kruger National Park, home to what some considered the best antipoaching unit in South Africa. In 2006, two rhinos were even poached by staff members employed by SANParks. In 2009 alone, there were about 50 rhinos poached in Kruger

and 100 poached in South Africa as a whole. As of January 22, 2010, poachers had killed 14 rhinos in Kruger National Park as well.

Poachers were ruthless in the slaughtering of rhinos. They typically cut off the rhino's horns after darting it with a deadly poison (see Exhibit 12). Poachers also darted rhinos with an immobilizing antidote that sometimes left the rhino helpless in the wild to be eaten by other game. SANParks' CEO, Dr. David Mabunda, described poachers as "dangerous criminals." Their exploits were not limited to killing rhinos, but also included human trafficking, arms smuggling, prostitution, and drug trafficking.

"Poachers must beware," Mabunda said in a statement announcing a $250,000 funding boost, in addition to the $5.2 million allocated to train and prepare the SANParks Environmental Crimes Unit and South African Police Service. Fifty-seven rangers equipped with night vision goggles and high-powered motorbikes had been dispatched to guard highly poached areas of the park day and night. Said Mabunda, "This war

Exhibit 12 **Rhino Left to Die after Poachers Cut Off Horn**

we plan on winning." In addition to the funding boost, plans were considered to guard the porous border near Kruger National Park with military personnel. Elisabeth McLellan, a species expert with the World Wildlife Foundation (WWF), was quoted as saying, "The situation is bad for rhino worldwide, in terms of poaching." Conservationists were facing an environment that had evolved into an industry, as world trade had reached a 15-year high for illegal rhino horn trading.

Kenyan authorities at Jomo Kenyatta International Airport had seized a 662-pound load of elephant tusk and rhino horn believed to have come from South Africa. It was speculated that the load, valued at approximately $1 million, was destined for China. Industry experts suggested that the high value placed on elephant tusk and rhino horn by consumers was driving the demand for both substances.

ANIMAL SUPERMARKET

Kruger National Park was determined to win the war against poaching, but determination alone wasn't enough to protect the rhino. Primary-market transactions involved buyers that protected the rhino—such as other national parks, private game farms, game dealers, and photography safari business owners—but secondary markets from the sale of captured rhinos had also developed. Hunters had become the most numerous buyers in the secondary market, which wasn't aligned with Kruger National Park's mission. Animal rights activists dubbed the sale of animals at Kruger National Park an "animal supermarket." Many believed that the commercial trade posed a greater threat than poaching did. Many also felt it was fundamentally wrong to herd animals from a popular wildlife reserve and sell them in efforts at "conservation." Wildlife activists accused SANParks of misusing the park by serving as nothing more than a private game breeder, and experts feared that the vast majority of the rhinos sold by SANParks would fall into the hands of private hunters.

SANPARKS' JUSTIFICATION

SANParks was guided in its decision to sell wildlife by Clause 55(2)(b) of the Protected Areas Act No. 57 of 2003 (as amended), which stated that "SANParks may, in managing national parks, sell, exchange or donate any animal, plant, or other organism occurring in a park, or purchase, exchange or otherwise acquire any indigenous species which it may consider desirable to reintroduce into a specific park." SANParks believed that it was critical to its conservation efforts to maintain the sale of animals to private entities. For years, SANParks had sold animals to fund conservation efforts, and in many cases the park had traded animals to obtain other species. Also, SANParks screened animals and buyers to ensure that animals were released not arbitrarily, but to buyers with the proper permits and intentions. Decisions to sell or donate wildlife were scientifically determined according to population dynamics, sex and age structure, spatial use, natural dispersal, and resource distribution.

SANParks' strategy was informed by the following objectives: population control, broadening of the range for populations, spreading the risk of managing wildlife, making the populations more resilient and viable, and fund-raising for specific conservation and land-expansion programs. The responsibilities of SANParks' conservation biologists are shown in Exhibit 13. The challenge facing SANParks was how to effectively communicate that selling rhinos was for the greater good.

Exhibit 13   Responsibilities of Conservation Biologists

Identify key research themes necessary for national parks to achieve their conservation objectives.

Conduct research on key themes.

Coordinating research projects conducted by external scientific institutions in national parks.

Integrating best available biodiversity data into park management through interactions with external researchers and research institutions.

Maintaining inventories of biodiversity in national parks, including species checklists for vertebrates and higher plants and the mapping of landscape. Geology, soil and vegetation.

Identifying and averting threats to biodiversity in national parks, including overabundance of certain wildlife populations, invasive alien plant and animal species, pollutants, human development, excessive resource exploitation or other factors.

Ensuring that development within parks takes place in a manner that does not compromise biodiversity conservation.

Conservation for rare and threatened species.

Provide scientific inputs on the rehabilitation of degraded landscapes.

Providing scientific inputs on biodiversity aspects of park management plans and activities.

Building capacity in conservation biology and related sciences, particularly in persons from historically disadvantaged population groups.

ENDNOTES

[1] All monetary amounts in this case are in U.S. dollars.
[2] *Wildlife Research Magazine.*
[3] Sam Ferreira & Travis Smith Scientific Services, SANParks, Skukuza, South Africa.

Coca-Cola India's Corporate Social Responsibility Strategy

Debapratim Purkayastha
IBS Center for Management Research

Hadiya Faheem
IBS Center for Management Research

"Coca-Cola India undertakes a diverse range of activities for the benefit of the community across the country. As part of our CSR strategy, sustainable water management remains our top priority."[1]

—Deepak Kaul, Regional Vice-President, South, The Hindustan Coca-Cola Beverages Pvt. Ltd., in 2007.

"It is in India where the company's abuse of water resources have been challenged vociferously, and communities across India living around Coca-Cola's bottling plants have organized in large numbers to demand an end to the mismanagement of water. . . . In response to the growing Indian campaigns against Coca-Cola, the company has decided to promote rainwater harvesting—a traditional Indian practice—in and around its bottling plants in India. Touting rainwater harvesting initiatives is now central to Coca-Cola's public relations strategy in India."[2]

—Amit Srivastava, Coordinator of India Resource Center,[3] in 2007.

INTRODUCTION

On February 18, 2008, leading beverage company in India, The Hindustan Coca-Cola Beverages Pvt. Ltd (Coca-Cola India), was awarded the Golden Peacock award[4] for Corporate Social Responsibility (CSR) for the several community initiatives it had taken and its efforts toward conservation of water. The award recognizes companies for their commitment toward business, their employees, local communities, and the society. Atul Singh (Singh),

ICMR
IBS Center for Management Research
www.icmrindia.org

This case is a runner-up in the oikos Global Case Writing Competition 2009 (Corporate Sustainability track), organized by oikos Foundation for Economy and Ecology, University of St. Gallen, Switzerland.

© 2009, IBS Center for Management Research. All rights reserved. This case was written by Hadiya Faheem, under the direction of Prof. Debapratim Purkayastha, IBS Center for Management Research. It was compiled from published sources, and is intended to be used as a basis for class discussion rather than to illustrate either effective or ineffective handling of a management situation.

To order copies, call +91-8417-236667/68 or write to IBS Center for Management Research (ICMR), IFHE Campus, Donthanapally, Sankarapally Road, Hyderabad 501 504, Andhra Pradesh, India or email: info@icmrindia.org.

CEO, Coca-Cola India, said, "Coca-Cola India has always placed high value on good citizenship and has undertaken several initiatives for community development and inclusive growth. We are gratified to receive this global award and are humbled at being recognized for the little contributions that we have been able to make to preserve and protect the environment and toward community development."[5]

Coca-Cola India was established as the Indian subsidiary of the U.S.-based Coca-Cola Company (Coca-Cola) in 1993. As of 2008, Coca-Cola India had 24 bottling operations of its own and 25 bottling operations owned by its franchisees.[6] In addition to beverage brands like Coke, Fanta, Sprite, etc., Coca-Cola India had a strong local cola brand Thums Up, the Kinley brand of mineral water, energy drinks, and powdered concentrates.

Keeping in mind the fact that it was one of the largest beverage companies in India, Coca-Cola India said it had made CSR an integral part of its corporate agenda. According to the company, it was aware of the environmental, social, and economic impact caused by a business of its scale and therefore it had taken up a wide range of initiatives to improve the quality of life of its customers, the workforce, and society at large. Since the company used large amounts of water and energy in its beverage production and tons of packaging material for its products, it had taken up several initiatives to act as a responsible company and reduce its environmental impact, it said. In addition to water, energy, and sustainable packaging, Coca-Cola India also focused on several community initiatives in India as part of its social responsibility initiatives.

Coca-Cola India's CSR initiatives came in for a lot of commendation, but this wasn't true of all its actions. The company had to face plenty of criticism on several fronts. In the southern Indian state of Kerala, it was severely criticized for depleting groundwater, a major resource for farmers and villagers who resided in the vicinity. The company was also criticized for allegedly supplying toxic materials as fertilizers to farmers in the region. Moreover, a report released by the Center for Science and Environment[7] (CSE) in 2003 revealed that 12 soft drink brands sold by Coca-Cola and PepsiCo. Inc.[8] (Pepsi) in India had pesticide levels far higher (almost 36 times more) than what was permitted by the European Economic Commission[9] (EEC). It was believed that the use of groundwater which had high pesticide residues and which had not been properly treated by the companies was the main reason for such high pesticide levels. These residues could cause cancer, damage to the nervous and reproductive systems, birth defects, and severe disruption of the immune system in the long run. The same study stated that no such residues were found in the same brands sold in the U.S. This issue cropped up again in 2006, leading to considerable erosion in the company's revenue and a hit to its image.

The company was vehement in its denial of all the criticism and described the charges as completely false. In addition to increasing the amount to be spent on CSR initiatives and initiating several projects like rainwater harvesting, watershed protection (globally) for restoring the groundwater it had utilized for beverage production, and other community development initiatives, Coca-Cola India made an endeavor to communicate to the public that it was a socially responsible company. However, critics were of the view that the company was engaged in various unethical practices, and that its claims of being socially responsible were nothing short of greenwashing.[10]

BACKGROUND NOTE

The Coca-Cola drink, popularly referred to as 'Coke,' is a kind of cola, a sweet carbonated[11] drink containing caramel[12] and other flavoring agents. It was invented by Dr. John Smith Pemberton (Pemberton) on May 8, 1886, at Atlanta, Georgia, in USA. The beverage was named Coca-Cola because at that time it contained extracts of Coca leaves and Kola nuts.[13]

Pemberton later sold the business to a group of businessmen, one of whom was Griggs Candler (Candler). By 1888, several cola brands were in the market competing against each other. Candler acquired these businesses from the other businessmen and established Coca-Cola in 1892. He aggressively marketed the product through advertising and distribution of coupons and souvenirs, and promoted the brand name Coca-Cola. Sales grew rapidly and by 1895, the product was being sold across the U.S.

In the initial years, Coca-Cola was sold through soda fountains[14] wherein the Coca-Cola syrup, carbon dioxide, and water were mixed and given to customers. In 1894, a fountain seller named Joseph A. Biedenharn introduced the concept of selling the prepared drink in bottles. He thus became the first bottler for Coca-Cola. There was no looking back after that. The Coca-Cola bottling system grew to become one of the largest and widest production and distributions networks in the world.

In 1919, a group of investors headed by Ernest Woodruff and W. C. Bradley purchased Coca-Cola from Candler for US$ 25 million.[15] In 1923, Robert Winship Woodruff (Woodruff), son of Ernest Woodruff, was elected as company president. He is widely credited with making Coca-Cola, one of the world's most recognized brands and a multinational company with huge revenues and profits.

The period 1940 to 1970 was one of rapid international growth and Coca-Cola became a symbol of friendliness and refreshment across the world. It entered India during the 1970s. In 1977, the Janata Party, the then ruling party in India, made it mandatory for foreign firms in the consumer sector to divest a majority stake in favor of Indian partners. Rather than dilute its stake, Coca-Cola India opted to close down its operations in India and exited the market in 1977.

In 1993, as part of India's liberalization policy, the market was opened up to foreign companies to establish their operations in India. The same year, Coca-Cola India staged a re-entry into the country through a strategic alliance with Parle Exports[16] (Parle). The alliance gave Coca-Cola India ownership of five of Parle's popular brands (Thums Up, Limca, Maaza, Citra, and Gold Spot) with a market share of around 60 percent, and a well-established network of 56 bottlers.[17]

Since its inception, the company had endeavored to touch the lives of people and communities in a positive way. This was in line with the parent company's CSR strategy. For instance, in 2006, E. Neville Isdell (Isdell), Chairman and Chief Executive Officer, Coca-Cola, said, "As we create value for our shareowners and other stakeholders by running a successful business, we must also be a force for positive global change—one community at a time. We must help create economic and social value, protect the environment, and contribute to the long-term sustainability of every community we serve."[18] (Refer to Figure 1 for Coca-Cola's CSR model).

Coca-Cola India undertook several initiatives like waste management, water conservation management, etc. in an attempt to improve the life of communities in its areas of operation. Its environmental responsibility initiatives included assessing the environmental impact on sites before the commencement of any project, a survey of groundwater resources before the selection of a site, training personnel on wastewater treatment, and several energy conservation programs. The company engaged in rainwater harvesting projects to restore the depleted levels of groundwater. It also focused on providing education and

Figure 1   Coca-Cola's CSR Model

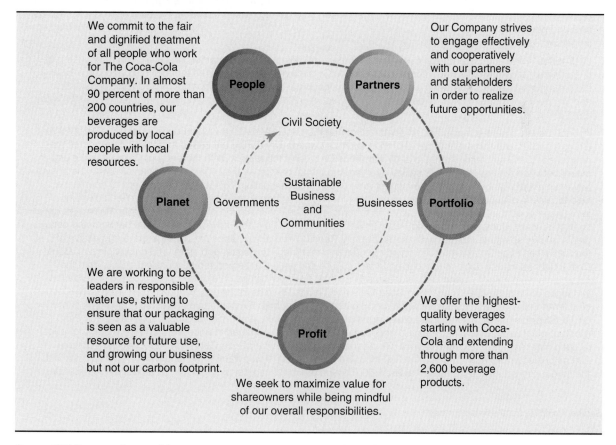

Source: 2006 Corporate Responsibility Review, www.thecoca-colacompany.com, 2006.

healthcare in what it described as an attempt to build stronger communities. The company set up education projects for children residing in villages and urban slums. It also conducted health camps in partnership with the government and non-governmental organizations[19] (NGOs) for providing healthcare benefits to the poor.

Ever since its re-entry into India, the company had experienced sound growth in revenues. In 2002, Coca-Cola India achieved a volume growth of 39 percent.[20] Between September 2002 and March 2003, it doubled its capacity by making investments of US$ 125 million.[21] From 1993 to 2003, the company had made investments of around US$ 1 billion in India, making it one of the country's biggest international investors.

Despite growth in revenues, India was a difficult market for Coca-Cola to crack since its business broke even in early 2007 (Refer to Exhibit I for a note on the Indian soft drink beverages market). Irial Finan, Head, Coca-Cola's worldwide bottling operations, added, "In bottling operations, the business will move into profitability next year. In one of the months in 2007, we broke even but on the full year basis we are expecting to be in profits in 2008."[22] In 2007, the company planned to make investments of around US$ 250 million over the next three years in an attempt to enhance its business operations in India. Venkatesh Kini (Kini), Vice-President, marketing, Coca-Cola India, said, "We will be spending around $250 million in the next three years for

Exhibit I A Note on the Indian Soft Drink Beverage Market

The Indian soft drink beverage market can be classified into soft drinks and fruit drinks. Soft drinks consist of carbonated and non-carbonated drinks. Carbonated drinks include cola, orange, and lemon drinks while non-carbonated drinks include mango drinks. The market can also be segmented based on the type of products such as cola and non-cola products. In 2000, cola drinks accounted for around 61–62 percent of the total soft drinks market in India while non-cola drinks accounted for 36 percent.[1]

Until 1990s, Parle Group, a domestic player, dominated the Indian soft drink market. However, with the opening up of the Indian economy for entry by foreign players, MNCs such as PepsiCo entered India in 1991 and Coca-Cola India re-entered in 1993. The rising population in India coupled with growing number of middle class consumers and low per capita consumption of aerated drinks (which signified huge growth potential) prompted these MNCs to enter India.

Though PepsiCo led the Indian soft drink market during the mid-1990s, Coca-Cola through its acquisition of Parle Group's brands and some international brands such as Canada Dry during the 1990s and 2000, emerged as the new leader in the soft drink market in 2001 with PepsiCo closely following it. With the entry of Coca-Cola the global rivalry between the two cola giants spilled over into the Indian market as they competed aggressively on the pricing, advertising and distribution front. The biggest area of conflict was bottling. This was because bottling operations held the key to distribution, an extremely important feature for soft drink marketing. Both companies took pains to maintain good relationships with bottlers, in order to avoid defections to the other camp. Another major area of conflict between Coca-Cola India and PepsiCo was advertising. The global advertisement wars between the cola giants quickly spread to India as well. Internationally, PepsiCo had always been seen as the more aggressive of the two. While PepsiCo always relied on advertisements featuring films stars, pop stars, and cricket players, Coca-Cola India had initially decided to focus on Indian culture and jingles based on Indian classical music. Both the cola giants were quick to launch ad campaigns to counter any new campaign of their rival. While there were many instances of PepsiCo directly attacking Coca-Cola and Thums Up in its Pepsi and Mountain Dew ads, Coca-Cola countered these ads with its ads for Sprite and Thums Up. While both the companies invested huge sums of money on TV advertising, they also adopted other forms of advertising such as print, billboards, banner ads, and POP (point-of-purchase) advertising. PepsiCo and Coca-Cola India also engaged in price wars and were quick to react to each other's price changes. The price war aggravated in 2000, when Coca-Cola India launched Mini Coke in 200 ml bottles priced at Rs. 5 since the 300 ml bottle priced at Rs. 9 was hampering its growth. Pepsi hit back with the introduction of its 200 ml version at Rs. 4.50. Though the initial campaign said 'Offer till stocks last,' Pepsi later

Source: Compiled from various sources.

[1] "Soft Drinks," www.agriculture-industry-india.com.

Exhibit I   *(Concluded)*

decided to continue with the offer to retain its customer base until the increase in excise duties in 2000, forced both the companies to increase prices. Experts felt that both the companies were investing heavily in their operations in India, sacrificing short term interest in their endeavor to dominate the Indian soft drink beverage market and for long term profitability.

The period between 1998 and 2002 was characterized by increase in soft drink sales by 76 percent from 5,670 million bottles to more than 10,000 million bottles.[2] In 2002, the combined sales of Coca-Cola India and PepsiCo in the soft drinks market accounted for Rs. 62.47 billion.[3] Moreover, the market was expected to grow by 10 percent per year till 2012.[4] Despite this positive growth, the per capita consumption of soft drinks in India remained among the lowest in the world—6 bottles per annum compared to 17 bottles per annum in Pakistan, 173 in Philippines, and 800 in the U.S.[5] In a bid to increase its volumes, both Coca-Cola India and PepsiCo started targeting the rural segment considering its huge untapped potential in early 2000s. According to industry estimates, rural market had immense potential to tap with a population of 74 percent of the country, 41 percent of its middle-class consumers and 58 percent of its disposable income.[6] By the end of 2003, PepsiCo and Coca-Cola India had sales of 91 percent from rural segments.[7]

In 2003, both the companies faced allegations that their products contained harmful levels of pesticides. The companies had earlier come under criticism for allegedly depleting groundwater levels and causing pollution across their bottling plants. Amidst all these controversies, Coca-Cola India and PepsiCo continued their dominance in the Indian soft drink market with a combined market of over 95 percent in 2005.[8] The pesticide issue cropped up again in 2006, leading to considerable erosion in the revenue and image of both the companies. The companies also faced temporary bans imposed by various state governments and both the companies had to undertake extensive public relations efforts to get the bans revoked and earn back the confidence of the consumers.

As of 2008, the Indian beverage market was estimated at US$ 3.8 billion with an annual growth rate of 6.5 percent.[9] The carbonated beverages contributed to a major portion of the sales followed by bottled water. India was seen as the country that offered maximum potential for the growth of the beverage industry since it accounted for 10 percent of global beverage consumption, which made it third largest consumer of beverages after US and China.[10] Coca-Cola India and PepsiCo continued to dominate the Indian soft drink market with market share of 57.8 percent and 35.6 percent respectively, in 2008.[11] In 2008, the demand for aerated drinks stood at 373 million unit cases and was expected to reach 479 million unit cases by 2014–15. Moreover, the market was expected to grow at a rate of 3.5 percent from 2009–2010 to 2014–2015.[12] With the high growth potential of the market, experts expected both Coca-Cola India and PepsiCo to go all out in their effort to garner a bigger share of the market.

---

[2] "Coca-Cola in Rural India–Presentation Transcript," www.slideshare.net.

[3] "Analysis of Pesticide Residues in Soft Drinks," http://www.cseindia.org, August 2, 2006.

[4] "Coca-Cola in Rural India–Presentation Transcript," www.slideshare.net.

[5] "Coca-Cola in Rural India - Presentation Transcript," www.slideshare.net.

[6] "Coca-Cola in Rural India - Presentation Transcript," www.slideshare.net.

[7] Sunita, "The World is being Drowned in Cola," http://you.liveoncampus.com, January 30, 2009.

[8] "Coca-Cola in Rural India - Presentation Transcript," www.slideshare.net.

[9] "India Path to Innovation," www.thefoodworld.com, October 15, 2008.

[10] "For the Beverage Industry, India is the Country that Offers the Greatest Potential," www.21food.com, August 1, 2008.

[11] Surbhi Goel, "Adding Fizz: Coca-Cola India, Pepsico," http://economictimes.indiatimes.com, October 26, 2008.

[12] Sunita, "The World is being Drowned in Cola," http://you.liveoncampus.com, January 30, 2009.

---

setting up of infrastructure and strengthening sales and distribution activities."[23]

In August 2007, the company planned to expand its product portfolio by launching brands from its parent company, Coca-Cola. The products included energy drinks, sports drinks, and juices. "We are anticipating the future needs and exploring a wide range of products such as flavored water and teas. The company is also evaluating getting into categories such as energy drinks, sports drink, and juices,"[24] added Kini.

For the fourth quarter ending December 2007, Coca-Cola India reported a growth of 18 percent in unit sales volume.[25] The company saw India's 1.1 billion population as a major growth driver for its brand in the future.

CORPORATE SOCIAL RESPONSIBILITY INITIATIVES IN INDIA ENVIRONMENTAL RESPONSIBILITY INITIATIVES

Environmental responsibility was a key aspect of Coca-Cola India's CSR initiatives. Since Coca-Cola India was involved in beverage production, its operations affected the environment in many ways such as through excessive levels of water consumption, wastewater discharge, high energy consumption, discharge of effluents, and greenhouse gas[26] (GHG) emissions due to the use of refrigeration, vending machines, air conditioning equipment, etc. Its business operations were also criticized as having an adverse impact on the environment (Refer to Exhibit II for criticisms against Coca-Cola India). Coca-Cola India said that since its operations had such an impact on the environment, it felt it had to focus on sustainable efforts to minimize the impact on the communities and the markets it served.

Water

To counter the criticism against it, Coca-Cola India decided that it had to take steps to conserve water. The company implemented several water conservation initiatives like watershed protection, rainwater harvesting projects, and community initiatives in several places in India (Refer to

Exhibit II   Criticisms against Coca-Cola India

In 2002, Coca-Cola India was severely criticized for overexploiting groundwater resources in its bottling facility located at Plachimada, Kerala. The communities residing in nearby villages were severely affected since they depended heavily on the groundwater for water consumption and farming. In addition to this, a BBC[1] report in 2003 revealed that Coca-Cola India was distributing improperly treated sludge containing toxic carcinogens and heavy metals like cadmium and lead as fertilizer to farmers in the region. Coca-Cola India shut down this plant in March 2004 owing to mounting pressure. The company then decided to shift its operations to a nearby industrial zone, the Kanjikode Industrial Area.

There were also protests at Coca-Cola India's Mehdiganj plant in North India over similar issues. In addition to these accusations, in 2003, the CSE made public the findings of its study wherein it reported that the products of both Coca-Cola India and Pepsi that were sold in India had a cocktail of harmful pesticide residues in them.

Coca-Cola India came under scrutiny for its water consumption since its estimated water usage in 2004 was 283 billion liters, which was equal to the world's consumption of water for a period of ten days. Moreover, the company used 2.7 liters of water for the production of a single beverage bottle of one liter, with 1.7 liters being discarded as waste after being used in the manufacturing processes in 2004.[2]

In 2005, it was reported that Coca-Cola India had been drawing around 225,000 liters of water per day in Khammam district of Andhra Pradesh for its Kinley brand of mineral water. This excessive water usage had led to the drying up of wells, resulting in the local communities facing a severe water shortage. In the same year, the company released saline effluents into a water body in a village near Chennai, South India. The saline effluent made the water brackish and unsafe for drinking.

In August 2006, the pesticide issue cropped up again when CSE tested around 57 samples of carbonated drinks of Coca-Cola and Pepsi in India. The CSE found pesticides in all the samples. Moreover, the pesticide residues were 24 times more than the standards proposed by the European Union[3] and the Bureau of Indian Standards.[4,5]

Source: Compiled from various sources.

[1] The British Broadcasting Corporation (BBC) is a publicly funded radio and television broadcasting corporation of the UK.

[2] "Coca-Cola Essay," http://sgu05ysw.wordpress.com.

[3] The European Union is comprised of 27 member states located in Europe and was formed to enhance the social, political, and economic co-operation among member nations.

[4] The Bureau of Indian Standards is the national body that sets standards related to product quality and management system, consumer affairs, and technical standards in India.

[5] "Dangerous Pesticides in Coca-Cola and Pepsi in India," www.indiaresource.org, August 3, 2006.

Exhibit III for Coca-Cola's global water conservation goals; Refer to Box I for Coca-Cola India's water sustainability initiatives). The company in partnership with the government, NGOs, and several communities, actively participated in educating communities and personnel of its bottling facilities on the significance of preserving watersheds. In 2005, Coca-Cola initiated a Community Watershed Partnership (CWP) program for all its global operations, focusing on watershed protection, access to safe water and sanitation, water for productive use, and education and awareness (Refer to Exhibit IV for Coca-Cola's global community watershed program).

Coca-Cola India claimed that its water sustainability initiatives had helped it to reduce its water consumption by 35 percent between 1999 and 2006 and that by 2009, it would curb its groundwater usage even more and reach zero water balance.[27] The company aimed to achieve zero water balance by focusing on core areas such as curbing water usage in the production of beverages, recycling the water it used for the purpose of manufacturing beverages, reusing water, and finally, replenishing water for returning to the environment.

The company also aimed at efficient treatment of its wastewater and at reaching a 100 percent standard by 2010.[28] According to Isdell, "By 2010, we will return all water that we use in our manufacturing processes to the environment at a level that supports aquatic life and agriculture."[29]

Exhibit III   Coca-Cola's Global Water Conversation Goals

Reduce, Recycle, and Replenish

In June 2007, Coca-Cola aimed to focus on three core objectives of reducing, recycling, and replenishing water used in its beverage production.

Reduce

Coca-Cola planned to set targets for water efficiency. Between 2002 and 2007, its unit case volume was augmented by over 21 percent while its global consumption of water went down by over 2 percent. The company's water use efficiency was around 2.47 liters for every liter of product it produced in 2007.[1] Around 1 liter of water was used in the beverage while the remaining 1.47 liters was used in the manufacturing processes.

Recycle

The water used in the company's manufacturing operations was recycled in a bid to return it to the environment. The company had to abide by the laws and regulations while treating this wastewater. The company had a standard that would ensure water treatment to the extent it would support aquatic life. However, in certain communities, wastewater treatment was not practiced or the water could not be treated to an acceptable standard. In such cases, the bottling partners created their own water treatment system that cleaned the water and discharged it in a polluted waterway. In 2007, around 85 percent of the bottling partners met the acceptable level of standards. However, the company planned to adopt stringent water standards and comply with 100 percent recycling by 2010.[2]

Replenish

In 2007, Coca-Cola had utilized around 122 billion liters of water. In a bid to counterbalance, Coca-Cola planned to launch several projects that helped in water conservation and improvement in sanitation and access to safe and clean water. These projects were carried out with the help of initiatives like agriculture water use efficiency, rainwater harvesting, reforestation, watershed protection, etc. By 2007, Coca-Cola had launched more than 120 community water projects in over 50 countries. These projects were conducted in partnership with organizations like the U.S. Agency for International Development[3] (USAID), WWF, CARE,[4] The United Nations Development Program[5] (UNDP), governments, NGOs, and several local communities.

Adapted from "The Coca-Cola Company Pledges to Replace the Water It Uses in Its Beverages and their Production," www.thecoca-colacompany.com, June 5, 2007, and "Our Water Conservation Goal," www.thecoca-colacompany.com, 2007.

[1] 2007/2008 Sustainability Review, www.thecoca-colacompany.com.

[2] 2007/2008 Sustainability Review, www.thecoca-colacompany.com.

[3] Launched in 2001, USAID is the key federal agency in the U.S. that provides humanitarian assistance. USAID supports long-term economic growth, global health, trade and agriculture, conflict prevention, etc.

[4] CARE is a humanitarian organization that was formed with the stated objective of working for serving the poor communities.

[5] The United Nations Development Programme is the United Nations' global development network. It works with local governments to meet development challenges and develop local capacity.

Box I   Coca-Cola India's Water Sustainability Initiatives

- In January 2006, Coca-Cola India, as part of its commitment to water conservation, restored a 400-year old *Kale Hanuman Ki Bawari*[1] in Rajasthan. This initiative was implemented in conjunction with the Rajasthan Ground Water Department, several NGOs, local communities, and villagers. Around 10,000 local people were benefited by this initiative.

- In 2006, the company completed a rainwater recharge initiative at its Kaladera plant in Rajasthan. As part of the project, the company built around 110 recharge shafts that collected rainwater. The collected rainwater was passed back to the ground through a reverse filter system. This process helped in restoring depleted groundwater tables.

- In March 2007, Coca-Cola India launched a rooftop rainwater harvesting initiative at Varanasi. This project was expected to recharge more than 4,900 cubic meters of groundwater.[2]

- In March 2007, Coca-Cola India in association with the Forum of Recyclers' Communities and Environment[3] (FORCE) organized an event called *Jal Tarang* as part of the company's initiative to commemorate World Water Day.[4] The event announced the launch of a rainwater harvesting project at Greater Kailash, in New Delhi. The project aimed to recharge around 4 million liters of water every year.[5]

- In June 2007, Coca-Cola India in association with Rotary International[6] (Rotary) announced the establishment of 10 rainwater harvesting projects in different schools of Jamshedpur city.[7]

- In June 2007, Coca-Cola India in association with the Associated Chambers of Commerce & Industry[8] (ASSOCHAM) organized a program that focused on environment education. The program also initiated a campaign "Think Green, Go Green" to raise awareness among the public for being environmentally responsible.

- In June 2007, the company launched a film in conjunction with BAIF Development Research Foundation, a non-profit organization that focused on protection and enhancement of the environment. The film was to be showcased to over 5,000 children across India.[9]

- In 2007, the company initiated drinking water projects in Maharashtra and Gujarat to provide potable water to the local communities.

Source: Compiled from various sources.

[1] Bawari is a watering hole that collects water.

[2] "Hindustan Coca-Cola Unveils Its Water Initiatives for 2007," www.thecoca-colacompany.com, March 19, 2007.

[3] Founded in October 2000, the Forum of Recycler's Communities and Environment is an NGO that was formed as a forum for the communities of recyclers in India. It also dealt with issues related to the environment.

[4] In 1992, the United Nations General Assembly conceded a resolution that observed March 22 as World Water Day. This day was observed to draw the people's attention to the plight of over 1 billion people worldwide who had little or no access to potable water (Source: www.worldwaterday.net).

[5] "FORCE in Association with Coca-Cola India and GKII Welfare Association Organizes Jal Tarang as Part of World Water Day Celebrations," www.thecoca-colacompany.com, March 24, 2007.

[6] Rotary International is an organization that consists of Rotary Clubs that are located worldwide. These service clubs provide humanitarian service to professional and business leaders all over the world and encourage people to follow ethical standards in all occupations.

[7] "Hindustan Coca-Cola Celebrates World Environment Day," www.thecoca-colacompany.com, June 5, 2007.

[8] Established in 1920, The Associated Chambers of Commerce and Industry of India (ASSOCHAM) is a representative body of Indian companies aiming to impact the policy and legislative environment for balanced economic, social, and industrial development (Source: www.assocham.org).

[9] "Coca-Cola India Celebrates World Environment Day through a Slew of Initiatives to Preserve, Protect and Enhance the Environment," www.thecoca-colacompany.com, June 5, 2007.

In 2007, Coca-Cola launched a global water project in a bid to restore all the depleted groundwater tables and return the water it utilized in its beverage production to the environment.

In 2008, as part of its water management initiatives, Coca-Cola India in collaboration with the International Crops Research Institute for the Semi-Arid Tropics[30] (ICRISAT), and Confederation of Indian Industry[31] (CII) undertook several initiatives like rural water resources infrastructure and other natural resources management (NRM) for sustaining watershed in the districts of Rajasthan and Tamil Nadu. With this initiative, Coca-Cola India aimed to generate a source of income for poor farmers residing in villages in those districts and to develop interventions for agricultural production, soil and water conservation, rural income, etc. CII felt that such a private-public partnership model could help improve the livelihoods of the Bottom of the Pyramid (BOP) populations.

Exhibit IV Coca-Cola's Global Community Watershed Program

In 2005, Coca-Cola in partnership with the USAID initiated a 'Global Community—Watershed Partnerships Program' (GCWPP) in a bid to support water-related programs in developing nations. Commenting on USAID's partnership with Coca-Cola, Andrew S. Natsios, USAID Administrator, said, "Water projects help improve access to safe and adequate water supply and sanitation, improve irrigation technology, enhance natural environments, and develop better institutional capacity for water resources management. When we work together with our partners in the private sector, this important work can benefit even more people in developing nations."[1] The USAID and Coca-Cola worked in conjunction with the Global Environment and Technology Foundation[2] to curb the impact of problems related to water in developing countries worldwide.

The GCWPP benefited from the strength of the partner during the water project implementation. For instance, in Mali, the alliance supported activities such as agriculture, water supply, and sanitation by utilizing recycled wastewater released from the company's bottling plant.

In the first year of operations, the community watershed programs involved combined investments of more than US$ 3.5 million.[3] The community projects were funded by Coca-Cola, USAID, and the Water and Development Alliance[4] (WADA). Between 2005 and early 2008, the combined investment was around US$ 13.8 million. With this investment, WADA had successfully improved the lives of local communities in nearly 14 countries of Africa, Asia, and Latin America.[5] In addition to these, the WADA had other funding sources (Refer to Table for WADA funding sources).

WADA Funding Sources

Sources	Funding (in %)
Coca-Cola Bottling partners	2
Coca-Cola Africa Foundation	34
Coca-Cola Atlanta Foundation	11
Coca-Cola Corporate	3
USAID/Washington (GDA, Africa, LAC)	39
USAID/Missions	11

Adapted from "Coca-Cola and USAID: A Global Partnership on Water," www.thecoca-colacompany.com, March 18, 2008.

[1] USAID and Coca-Cola Announce Global Watershed Partnership Agreement," www.cokefacts.com, September 14, 2005.

[2] The Global Environment and Technology Foundation promotes sustainable development in energy and water sectors by entering into partnerships with several institutions, promotes environmental practices and builds communities using information technology, and promotes installation of new technology for the improvement and security of the environment (Source: www.getf.org).

[3] "USAID and Coca-Cola Announce Global Watershed Partnership Agreement," www.cokefacts.com, September 14, 2005.

[4] In November 2005, the WADA was founded by Coca-Cola and USAID in conjunction with the Global Environment and Technology Foundation. WADA supported initiatives like protection of watersheds, improved sanitation and water supply, and encouraged local communities to productively use water.

[5] Partnership with USAID," www.thecoca-colacompany.com.

Energy

Since Coca-Cola India was involved in the production of beverages, its operations required refrigeration equipment, coolers, and vending machines that resulted in the emission of GHGs. Coca-Cola India therefore focused on reducing energy consumption and emission of GHGs by concentrating on areas such as refrigeration and cold drink equipment that used a high amount of energy.

In 2000, Coca-Cola India launched an eKO-freshment cooler that used technologies devoid of hydrofluorocarbons[32] (HFCs). This initiative helped it curb its emission of GHGs.

At a global level Coca-Cola converted over 1,300 models of refrigeration equipment to HFC-free refrigeration in June 2006. In contrast to its old equipment, the new insulation provided in the equipment cut down the GHG emission by three-fourths when compared to the old equipment. However, the company continued to make investments in carbon dioxide refrigeration. By the end of 2006, Coca-Cola had placed 6,000 units with carbon dioxide refrigeration in several countries worldwide. In 2006, it developed an Energy Management System (EMS) that curbed energy consumption by 35 percent.[33] By mid-2007, the Coca-Cola system had installed over half a million units of EMS. The company claimed that this had helped it in reducing energy consumption by 640 million kilowatt-hours as a result of which there was a reduction of 300,000 metric tons of GHGs.[34]

By 2007, Coca-Cola along with its bottling partners had installed over 8,500 units of HFC-free equipment. The company planned to install nearly 30,000 units by the end of 2008.[35] In addition to the cold drink equipment, the company aimed to enhance its energy efficiency and curb its GHG emissions from its manufacturing operations at various bottling facilities. For this, it launched an initiative called Project esKO in 2007. This initiative aimed to reduce Coca-Cola's carbon footprint at a global level by improving its driving and manufacturing operations. With this initiative, Coca-Cola aimed to curb its carbon dioxide emissions by 10,000 metric tons every year.

Coca-Cola India also increased its energy efficiency by fixing insulating pipes, leaks, optimizing the temperature, and reducing the pressure. Besides, the company made investments in heat recovery, efficient lighting, and optimization of compressors. The company also planned to make investments in renewable energy and combined power and heat systems. By 2010, the company aimed to increase the energy efficiency of its equipment by 40 to 50 percent.[36]

Fuel

Though Coca-Cola had the largest distribution system in the world, its kept its transportation footprint low since it had local operations for production, bottling, and delivery in each country of operation.

Packaging and Recycling

Being a beverage company, it depended heavily on packaging to deliver the product to the consumer. The packaging was in the form of aluminum cans, Polyethylene terephthalate[37] (PET) bottles, glass bottles, etc. Coca-Cola India believed that packaging had several environmental impacts. The company focused on developing a packaging framework that planned to use packaging material as a useful resource that could be used in future rather than being considered as a waste.

In 2005, Coca-Cola India initiated a PET recycling project in Mumbai in partnership with Brihan Mumbai Municipal Corporation, (BMC), Municipal Corporation of Mumbai, and FORCE. This initiative aimed to reduce the impact of these PET bottles on the environment and raise the income of around 100 PET crusaders[38] by 50 percent.[39] Commenting on the launch of the project, Datta Dalvi, Mayor, Delhi said, "We welcome private participation in keeping Mumbai clean and provide better work opportunities to a neglected section of the society. We are happy that Coca-Cola is the first corporate house in Mumbai to put together a PET Recycling Project. I am hopeful that other corporate houses will also come forward to transform the Mumbai landscape."[40] The company also aimed to conduct several awareness campaigns to educate people about the significance of solid waste recycling.

In June 2006, Coca-Cola India in partnership with the Delhi government and Indian Association of Plastic Manufacturers[41] (IAPM), launched a film on PET recycling called, '*Abhiyan—The Movement*'. The film focused on the need for and significance of recycling PET bottles, an important packaging material. By the end of 2006, Coca-Cola India had established PET recycling projects at over 100 locations in India. The company built a capacity to collect and recycle nearly 80 percent of the waste generated from the PET.[42]

Coca-Cola India's strategy for sustainable packaging focused on reduction, recovery, and reuse of the packaging material. The company aimed to reduce its packaging by using minimum resources while maintaining the quality of the product. It had several innovative teams which continuously tested and designed innovative ways of packaging that would help in reducing the quantity of raw material required while decreasing costs related to packaging for the company. In 2006, Coca-Cola started an initiative called e3 that focused on eco-innovation, improving efficiency, and life-cycle effectiveness. This initiative helped the company redesign its trademarked bottle, resulting in the reduction of its weight and impact on the environment. This initiative helped

Coca-Cola save 89,000 metric tons of glass in 2006 at a global level.[43]

Coca-Cola India developed several packaging management systems that collected the company's packaging material consisting of glass bottles, cans, etc. after they were disposed of by the consumer. The packaging material was recovered by the company and recycled for reuse. Most of the packaging material used by Coca-Cola India was 100 percent recyclable. Around 85 percent of the global unit case volume of Coca-Cola was delivered in materials that were 100 percent recyclable.[44] The company invested millions of dollars on collecting and recovering packaging materials used for the beverages. It worked in partnership with several local communities to develop environmentally and economically viable solutions. It also worked on improving the quality of life of collectors who collected the waste. Besides, it used refillable containers that it took back and reused.

It purchased products that were made from recycled packaging material and also made efforts to enhance the efficiency of its refillable bottles.

Despite Coca-Cola India's efforts to have a strong sustainable packaging strategy, it faced problems related to litter which was found along waterways, beaches, and roadsides. The company initiated several community recycling programs in addition to educating the local communities on ways to prevent litter.

COMMUNITY DEVELOPMENT INITIATIVES

Communities

A commitment to the community was part of Coca-Cola India's CSR. The company's community initiatives focused on water conservation, education, health, etc. for serving the underserved communities. In 2003, Coca-Cola India launched Jagriti Learning Centers to provide education facilities to more than 1,800 children residing near its bottling facilities in Pune.[45] These centers were managed by NGOs like Literacy India, Prayas, Child Relief & You (CRY), and Pratham. In the same year, in conjunction with Literacy India, it initiated a community

awareness program at Gurgaon that focused on the importance of education.

In March 2007, Coca-Cola India in association with Rotary launched a project called, 'Elixir for Life' for providing potable water to underprivileged children in Chennai. This initiative aimed to curb waterborne diseases among children by providing them with access to clean drinking water. Coca-Cola India in association with UN-HABITAT[46] also launched several projects in West Bengal for providing clean drinking water and access to improved sanitation services in around 150 schools.[47] The company in partnership with several local communities, government, and NGOs planned to supply clean drinking water to children in around 1,000 schools across India by 2010.[48]

As part of its social responsibility initiatives, Coca-Cola India established several education projects for children residing in villages. It set up around 2,000 schools for children residing near its bottling plants with the aim of providing free education to them. It provided scholarships to poor children to help them pursue further education. Coca-Cola India's bottling partners provided health facilities, books, and stationery items to nearly 16 schools in the Wada district of Maharashtra.

Health

Coca-Cola India's community initiatives also focused on organizing several camps that provided health checkups, medicine, and education to rural communities on health-related topics. In 2003, Coca-Cola India in association with the Delhi government and the Indian Red Cross initiated a health education camp that aimed to raise awareness among the poorer communities living in slum areas on key aspects like hygiene and sanitation, HIV/AIDS, immunization, communicable diseases, reproductive and child health.

Coca-Cola India also funded polio eradication camps in several parts of India. In a few districts of Andhra Pradesh, it conducted camps for Hepatitis B vaccinations, eye checkups, and malaria eradication. In addition, the company conducted blood donation camps and supported a 24-hour emergency service for children. Coca-Cola India in partnership with several organizations provided health facilities to people who could not afford medical facilities.

ECONOMIC RESPONSIBILITY INITIATIVES

According to Coca-Cola India, it had made strong efforts to contribute to overall economic growth and development in and around all of its bottling facilities across India. It had played an active role in providing employment and giving the community opportunities to expand and grow, it said. The company claimed that to contribute to the communities that it served, it employed local people. A few studies in the past had estimated that for every job in the Coca-Cola system, 10 more jobs were created indirectly along the value chain for people belonging to the local communities through its multiplier effect.[49,50]

The company supported retailers operating on a small scale to build their businesses and become its business partners. It initially bought equipment from these retailers and later encouraged them to become its business partners. In 2007, Coca-Cola India launched an initiative called *Parivartan* (Change) for training small retailers in India. The program, launched in Agra by the Coca-Cola University,[51] enabled small retailers to learn the tools, techniques, and skills needed to establish their retail operations and succeed in India's lucrative retail market. The retailers learned the intricacies of retailing through sessions and presentations in the Hindi language.

THE 5 PILLAR GROWTH STRATEGY

In August 2007, Coca-Cola India launched a 5 pillar growth strategy to strengthen its relationship with India. This strategy focused on people, planet, portfolio, partners, and performance (Refer to Exhibit V for Coca-Cola India's 5 pillar

Exhibit V   Coca-Cola India's 5 Pillar Growth Strategy

People
- The Coca-Cola System aimed to provide global services in several areas such as Marketing, Technical R&D, Engineering, and Finance.
- Coca-Cola aimed to set up the Coca-Cola University in India to help marketers learn skills and techniques to win in the marketplace.
- An equipment testing facility was set up at Hyderabad, South India for testing the quality standards in coolers.

Planet
- By 2009, the company aimed to become water neutral and reach a zero water balance. The company's approach to water management included a 4R program of reducing, reusing, recycling, and recharging water.
- The company aimed to supply drinking water solutions to over 1000 schools by 2010.
- By 2009, the company planned to study around 10 watershed areas and implement water conservation initiatives accordingly.

Portfolio
- Coca-Cola India planned to expand its product portfolio by launching flavored water and juices, sports drinks, and energy drinks. A few instances included launch of Minute Maid Pulpy Orange, a juice drink in North and South India, and a strong tasting Fanta in South India.

Partners
- With the changing retail environment, Coca-Cola India set up a Retail University to provide training to several Indian retailers. The retailers would be taught the skills, techniques, and tools to operate in the retail environment and win in the market.

Performance
- By August 2007, Coca-Cola had made investments of more than US$ 1.2 billion. Over the next three years, the company planned to further invest around US$ 250 million.
- In the second quarter of 2007, the company's unit case volume increased by 12 percent compared to the same quarter of 2006.

Adapted from "Coca-Cola Strengthens Its Bonds with India, Launches "Little Drops of Joy," www.coca-colaindia.com, August 17, 2007.

growth strategy). While announcing the 5 pillar growth strategy, Singh said, "It gives me great joy to announce the 5 Pillar strategic framework which focuses on Portfolio, People, Planet, Partners, and Performance. Each initiative that we are announcing today are drops of a larger vision aimed at mutual growth and development. Over the last few years, we have continuously engaged with a large number of stakeholders and have incorporated their learnings in refining our strategy for India."[52]

CRITICISMS

Though Coca-Cola India claimed that it had taken several such efforts, it continued to attract criticism from several quarters. The company was censured for depleting groundwater tables, leaving the local communities with no access to drinking water and water for farming which was their primary source of income. In fact, data collected by the government agency the Ground Water Board seemed to confirm that groundwater levels had dropped in the first seven years of the company's operations, from 1999 to 2006. Even in 2008, the company continued to face mass demonstrations from local communities who demanded that the company shut down its bottling operations.

There were also allegations that the company had seized land from farmers and that it had discharged hazardous material and sludge in the areas surrounding its plants in India. The India Resource Center (IRC) also accused Coca-Cola India of releasing wastewater into the surrounding agricultural fields near its bottling facilities at several locations in India. IRC's Amit Srivastava (Srivastava) said, "The Coca-Cola Company is announcing to the world that it is an environmentally responsible company, and it has partnered with UN agencies and NGOs to paint a pretty green picture of itself. But all that is corporate social responsibility gone wrong because the reality on the ground is different. It is littered with toxic waste and a complete disregard and destruction of the way of life as many people in rural India know it."[53]

Critics alleged that Coca-Cola India's rhetoric regarding its plans to conserve the water resources near its bottling facilities and return all the water it used in beverage production to the environment was just a move to silence the growing criticism

against it. The company said that it was implementing several rainwater harvesting projects in India to replenish all the depleted groundwater tables. Moreover, the parent company had initiated various water sustainability initiatives globally including in 2007 when it announced a three-year, US$ 20 million partnership with the World Wildlife Fund[54] (WWF) on water conservation. Reacting to these moves, Srivastava said, "We call this 'greenwashing.' An attempt by the Coca-Cola company to manufacture a green image of itself that it clearly is not, as their practice in India shows."[55] Critics pointed out that the rainwater harvesting initiative in India which the company was touting was already a common practice in many places in India. In any case, the water replenished through this method was too little to offset the water used up by Coca-Cola India's operations, they said.

Many critics also pointed out that an investment of US$ 20 million for its water conservation projects was just 1 percent of the company's annual advertising budget, which stood at US$ 2.4 billion,[56] Coca-Cola would spend more money on advertising its efforts at water conservation than on water resource management, they charged.

And the criticism against the company's business practices in India was not restricted to the country alone. Several student activists at the University of Michigan were up in arms over the way in which the company had been functioning in India since 2004. The students alleged that to run its business, Coca-Cola India had depleted groundwater levels in areas around its factories, thus destroying the livelihood of farmers residing in nearby localities.[57] To quell these criticisms, Coca-Cola in conjunction with the University of Michigan initiated a third-party assessment of its bottling facilities in India. On January 14, 2008, The Energy and Resource Institute[58] (TERI) released a report on Coca-Cola India's environmental practices. The report concluded that no traces of pesticide had been found in the treated water and intake water that the company used to make beverages. The report also said that the company had complied with the norms of the Indian regulatory environment. However, TERI recommended that Coca-Cola India take steps in areas such as water resource management and to curb the presence of bacteria in effluent water. An official at Coca-Cola India said, "The TERI report confirms that we meet Indian regulations and on an overall basis, the Coca Cola Company's standards are often more stringent. However, it identified some areas where we can do better."[59]

Even after the TERI report was published, the company continued to receive negative publicity, with critics pointing out that the report had itself been commissioned by Coca-Cola. A few activists of the Plachimada Solidarity Committee[60] said Coca-Cola India's plans to revive its tarnished image by gaining a clean chit from TERI had backfired since the study that surveyed only six plants out of the 60 bottling facilities the company had in India, had concluded that two bottling facilities located at Kaladera and Nabipur fell in the overexploited zones of groundwater depletion; three facilities located at Mehdiganj, Pirangut, and Sathupalle fell in the safe zones, while one facility Nemam fell in the critical zone. The report also said that Coca-Cola India had exploited the groundwater resources by giving precedence to its company's business over the rights of farmers. The soil quality at its plant locations had also exceeded parameters related to alkalinity and the content of lead, coliforms, iron, fluorides, etc. A few plants also had a high content of nitrates, aluminum, manganese, chloride, nickel, turbidity, etc. The bottling facilities at Kaladera also reported that the groundwater contained pesticides. The local communities had asked the company to shut down its plant since it was affecting the farmers. The TERI report also highlighted the fact that some of the bottling facilities of Coca-Cola India had failed to maintain the mandatory standards concerning waste management.

A few critics came down heavily on Coca-Cola's much acclaimed TCCC standards[61] for waste management. According to the TERI report, none of the six plants surveyed met the TCCC standards. The critics also raised questions over Coca-Cola India being conferred the Golden Peacock award for its CSR initiatives. They pointed out that the award had been conferred by the World Environment Foundation[62] (WEF) and that Coca-Cola was the only sponsor for the WEF. The critics charged that Coca-Cola wanted to paint a green picture of itself by receiving awards for its environmental practices. They also said that the award had been received by Coca-Cola India just a few weeks after it was advised by TERI to shut down its bottling facilities in Rajasthan for continuing to deplete the groundwater tables, in 2008.

In March 2008, Isdell in an article for a leading Indian daily titled 'A New Model for Sustainability' said that for any business to be sustainable, the communities the business served should be sustainable. Critics were of the view that a company like Coca-Cola did not even qualify to talk about the ways to build sustainable communities considering its track record related to CSR in India. "The fact is that the Coca-Cola company has located many of its bottling plants in India strictly from a business and profit motivated principle, and has given scant, if any, attention to the impacts on the community. Such a company cannot and must not be allowed to talk about new models of sustainability,"[63] wrote Srivastava.

Many critics were of the view that since Coca-Cola's environmental practices in India had tarnished its brand image, the company had started making claims of working meticulously toward becoming a water neutral company and had launched several water sustainability initiatives. They felt that these initiatives were part of Coca-Cola's public relations (PR) strategy in India and were aimed at misleading the various stakeholders. "Coke has done 'greenwashing' very well. They shifted their image to one of a green and socially responsible organization, but they're not changing their operations,"[64] said Richard Girard, researcher, Polaris Institute[65] (Polaris). In April 2007, the Polaris presented Coca-Cola with the First Corporate Greenwashing Award.[66,67]

Critics also contended that Coca-Cola's sustainability review report for the year 2007–2008 was aimed at painting a green image of itself rather than at narrating the challenges it had faced related to its business practices in India. Srivastava added, "The media, the corporate social responsibility movement, and everyone concerned with transparency and good corporate practices needs to take a good look at Coca-Cola's Sustainability Review. What kind of a review has Coca-Cola conducted by conveniently forgetting to mention its ongoing trouble spots where its operations are hugely unsustainable? This is an attempt by the company, once again, to mislead the public."[68]

COCA-COLA INDIA'S RESPONSE

Coca-Cola opened an exclusive website, www. cokefacts.org, which addressed the allegations related to India and other countries. In another official statement, Coca-Cola rebutted the charges against its bottling plant at Plachimada, Kerala. The company said the plant was not responsible for the depletion of the underground water table. It quoted a study conducted in October 2002 by Dr. R.N. Athvale, emeritus scientist at the National Geophysical Research Institute[69] (NGRI), which had concluded that there was no field evidence of overexploitation of the groundwater reserves in the area surrounding the plant. The report had added that any underground depletion could not be attributed to water extraction in the plant area.

Coca-Cola also quoted another report prepared by the Palakkad District Environmental Protection Council and Guidance Society in June 2002. The report had concluded that the factory had not caused any environmental damage at any level. Coca-Cola alleged that over the previous two years, the rainfall in Kerala had decreased by 60 percent and that this was the reason for depletion of the water tables.[70] The company said a report prepared by the Kerala State Groundwater Department too had rejected these allegations and attributed the depletion to a decrease in rainfall over the years. It also rejected the allegation that its factory had released un-treated industrial effluents. Coca-Cola stated that the technology used for wastewater treatment at the plant was among the most advanced in the world, equivalent to the technology used at its bottling plants in America and Europe. Moreover, the procedures for treatment and discharge of effluents complied with the standards and norms set by the Kerala State Pollution Control Board[71] (KSPCB). Coca-Cola said it had set up a few standards for water management that enabled it to take measures to sustain water and set up its plant after assessing whether the region was water-stressed. The company also said that it had standards to treat wastewater effluents.

Strongly refuting the allegations that it had supplied toxic sludge to farmers as fertilizer, Coca-Cola claimed that the dry sediment slurry waste or sludge, a by-product of its operations, was not harmful. The sludge was made up of organic and inorganic material that would not contaminate the land. The sludge was used around the world, including by Coca-Cola, as a soil enhancer, it said. The generation of sludge in all the company's plants was monitored for composition and was disposed of properly. Further, the KSPCB had concluded in a detailed study that the concentration of cadmium and other heavy metals in the sludge were below prescribed limits and therefore could not be considered hazardous, it said.

The company also quoted a study conducted by the Department of Family and Child Welfare, Central Government of India, after the allegations regarding high pesticide level in its beverages were made in August 2003. It said the study had found that the products sold by the company were perfectly safe. It also provided scientific data on the safety of its beverages when the issue cropped up in 2006 and with the help of these, managed to get the temporary ban imposed on its beverages in some states of India revoked.

Coca-Cola maintained that most of the allegations leveled against it were false and were not supported by reliable data. It alleged that it was being targeted as it was the leading beverage company. The company also rebutted the allegations that its own report (TERI report) had implicated the company. Deepak Jolly (Jolly), Vice President, Public Affairs and Communication, Coca-Cola India said, "It doesn't blame us even once. It blames the farmers and agriculture. It also does not even once suggest that we should pack up and leave those areas. It says that there are four or five options for [bringing] up the water levels and if nothing is possible then alone we should go. These options are helping farmers with reducing water consumption, or creation of ponds, and so on. Anything but closure."[72] Critics opined that Coca-Cola India's agreement with the University of Michigan for publishing the TERI report on its website was nothing short of a PR fiasco. But Jolly said that publishing the TERI report only showed how transparent the company was in its operations. He added, "Which company would commission a 600-page study on its own plants and then put it on its website?"[73]

Coca-Cola said that it was a responsible corporate citizen in India and mentioned that it had won many awards with regard to its CSR initiatives in the country (Refer to Exhibit VI for a list of awards and recognition of Coca-Cola India).

Exhibit VI   List of Awards and Recognition Received by Coca-Cola India*

2008	Coca-Cola India was awarded the Golden Peacock Global CSR Award for 2008, in recognition of its water conservation/management and community development initiatives.
	In 2008, Singh was conferred the distinguished fellowship by the Institute of Directors (IOD) for outstanding business leadership and contribution to society.
	For four consecutive years, Coca-Cola India received the "Bhagidari Award" from the Delhi government for its water conservation and community development initiatives.
	Coca-Cola India received community recognition from the villagers of Kaladera in Rajasthan for various citizenship initiatives. The projects included restoration of ancient step wells—*Sarai Bawri* & *Kale Hanuman ki Bawri*, 140 recharge shafts being set up and the setting up of rainwater harvesting projects, providing infrastructure support, and introducing initiatives in primary health and education.
2007	The Confederation of Indian Industries (CII) recognized Coca-Cola India's Kaladera plant as a "Water Efficient Unit" across industries at the National Award for Excellence in Water Management. The Kaladera plant also won the Innovative Project Award for its contribution to reducing specific water consumption.
	Coca-Cola India was recognized by the Cultural Council of the Kaladera Community in Rajasthan for outstanding citizenship initiatives.
2006	The Golden Peacock Environment Management Commendation was given to the Coca-Cola India bottling facility in Varanasi.
	The Pollution Control Excellence Award was given to the Coca-Cola India bottling facility at Khurda, Orissa, by the Orissa State Pollution Control Board.
2005	Coca-Cola India, Jalpaiguri unit received the Environment Appreciation Certificate 2005 in recognition of its efforts to protect and preserve the environment through proactive environmental practices.
	The Best Management Award was given to Coca-Cola India by the Government of Andhra Pradesh for its people management practices.
	It received the Best Organization Award from the Government of Uttar Pradesh in 2005.
2004	The Corporate Social Responsibility Award was given to the Coca-Cola bottling facility at Patna by J.M. Institute of Speech and Hearing in 2004–05.
	The Golden Peacock Award was given by the World Environment Foundation for effective environmental management at the Coca-Cola India plant at Ameenpur Village, near Hyderabad, India.
2003	Coca-Cola India bottling plant at Atmakuru, Andhra Pradesh, received the Golden Peacock National Quality Award.

*The list is not exhaustive.

Adapted from "Coca-Cola Awards & Recognition," www.cokefacts.com, 2008.

OUTLOOK

As of February 2008, Coca-Cola India had carried out its CSR activities across 45 bottling plants at an annual spend of Rs. 40 to 50 million on activities such as water conservation management, health, and education.[74]

By February 2008, the company had installed around 350 rainwater harvesting projects in several states of India. By the end of 2008, the company planned to add 80 more rainwater harvesting structures in India. Coca-Cola India said, "As a business that depends on water, and has expertise in water

resource management, we are already making a net positive contribution to the water levels through the rainwater harvesting structures that we have installed. We have already created a potential to recharge 15 times more water than we use. Going forward, we are exploring ways we can contribute to more efficient use of water in irrigation."[75] The company aimed to pump in an additional investment of US$ 25 to 30 million to install water conservation projects that included checking and cleaning of dams and rainwater harvesting. The company said its water conservation efforts had helped it save around 2.7 mcm[76] water in early 2008.[77]

As mentioned in its 5 pillar growth strategy, the company planned to reach a zero water balance by 2009. The company also planned to implement water solutions in 1,000 schools in India by 2010.[78]

Some critics opined that Coca-Cola India's rhetoric of working toward becoming a water neutral company was nothing more than PR and aimed at exploiting the opportunity provided by a growth in green consumerism. "Coca-Cola has jumped on this opportunity because the term water neutral has tremendous marketing opportunities and the potential to deflect attention away from the water crisis that the company is a significant part of. No matter that scientifically speaking, it is impossible to be water neutral,"[79] said Srivastava. He said that the IRC would be watching closely to see how Coca-Cola India achieved its aim of becoming water neutral by 2009.

Analysts felt that Coca-Cola's problems in India had had an impact on the image of the company not only in India but also globally. Coca-Cola India had recognized the need to communicate to the various stakeholders what it was doing on the CSR front. In August 2007, when it announced the company's 5 pillar growth strategy, it also launched an integrated marketing communication campaign, 'Little Drops of Joy' in a bid to connect with its multiple stakeholders. The campaign was integrated with Coca-Cola India's 5 pillar growth strategy.

The campaign aimed to project the company as a responsible corporate citizen that worked to bring joy into the lives of the people and its efforts to establish a connection with its stakeholders. Jolly said, "Nowadays, stakeholders, including consumers, evaluate companies not only on their financial success but more on what they do for the community at large."[80] (Refer to Exhibit VII for print ad of Coca-Cola India's Little Drops of Joy campaign). The primary aim of the campaign was to change its corporate brand image of a single brand to a portfolio of brands (Refer to Box II for Coca-Cola India's Manifesto). Through this campaign, the company also planned to change its image from that of a multinational company to that of a modest and approachable company.

In February 2008, in what analysts viewed as a significant move, Coca-Cola India announced its plans to set up a fund for its CSR activities in India with an investment of US\$ 10 million.[81] The fund was established to support projects related to wetland management, water management, environmental campaigns, water conservation, etc.

Exhibit VII   **Print Ad of Coca-Cola India's 'Little Drops of Joy' Communication Campaign**

Source: "Coca Cola India: Little Drops of Joy," http://marketing-practice.blogspot.com, September 8, 2007.

Box II   **Coca-Cola India's Manifesto**

> A mighty ocean we're not. But we are the little drops that make one. Because small things go a long way. At Coca-Cola India, we believe that there's more to a little sip. It's the moment of truth. A second of satisfaction. An instant of happiness. A bubble of hope. Because we don't quench your thirst. We recharge your soul. For one moment. One drop at a time.

Source: "Coca Cola India: Little Drops of Joy," http://marketingpractice.blogspot.com, September 8, 2007.

ENDNOTES

1 "Coca-Cola Reaffirms Its Commitment to Water Stewardship and Community Development in India," www.thecoca-colacompany.com, October 6, 2007.

2 Amit Srivastava, "Indian Campaign Forces Coca-Cola to Announce Ambitious Water Conservation Project," www.indiaresource.org, July 30, 2007.

3 India Resource Center is an organization that keeps track of activities related to corporate globalization in India. As of 2008, Amit Srivastava is the director of IRC.

4 The Golden Peacock Awards were instituted by the Institute of Directors (a non-profit association of company directors) in 1991 to recognize corporate excellence in areas of quality, innovation, training, governance, environment management, and corporate social responsibility.

5 "Coca-Cola India Wins the Golden Peacock Global Award for Corporate Social Responsibility 2008," www.andhranews.net, 2008.

6 www.cokefacts.org.

7 The Center for Science and Environment (CSE) is an independent, non-governmental organization with the stated aim of increasing public awareness about science, technology, environment, and development. CSE was established in 1980 and is based in New Delhi.

8 Headquartered in New York, PepsiCo. Inc. was founded in 1965 through a merger between Pepsi Cola and Frito Lay. Its products include beverages, snacks, juices, etc. For the financial year 2007, it had global revenues of US$ 39 billion.

9 The European Economic Commission is a branch of the governing body of the European Union (EU) possessing executive and some legislative powers. It is located in Brussels, Belgium.

10 The 10th edition of the Concise Oxford English Dictionary defines greenwash as "disinformation disseminated by an organization so as to present an environmentally responsible public image."

11 Carbonation, which involves dissolving carbon dioxide, is used in aqueous solutions like soft drinks to make them effervescent.

12 Caramel is a food which has a brown colour and a sweet toasted flavour. Caramel can be made from sugar by heating it slowly to around 170°C.

13 The kola nut is a kind of a nut with a bitter flavor and high caffeine content, and is primarily obtained from some West African or Indonesian trees.

14 Soda fountains used to refer to soda shops and the part of a drugstore (pharmacy) where sodas, ice creams, sundaes, hot beverages, iced beverages, baked goods, and light meals were prepared and served. Now the term refers to the carbonated drink dispensers found in fast food restaurants and convenience stores in the U.S. and Canada.

15 "W.C. Bradley Co.," www.fundinguniverse.com.

16 Parle Exports is one of the largest confectioners and biscuit manufacturers in India.

17 Shefali Rekhi, "Cola Quarrels," www.india-today.com, May 4, 1998.

18 2006 Corporate Responsibility Review, www.thecoca-colacompany.com, 2006.

19 A non-governmental organization is a legal organization set up by private companies or public having no contribution from the government or any representative of the government.

20 "History of Coke," http://mba.tuck.dartmouth.edu, 2004.

21 Ibid.

22 "Coca-Cola to Invest US$250 mln in India in Next Three Years," www.antara.co.id, May 29, 2007.

23 Sagar Malviya, "Coca-Cola Bets Big on India, Plans to Enter Newer Segments," www.livemint.com, August 18, 2007.

24 Ibid.

25 "Coca-Cola India Sees 18% Growth in Unit Case Volume," www.thehindubusinessline.com, February 16, 2008.

26 The greenhouse gases are carbon dioxide, nitric oxide, and chlorinated fluoro carbons which trap the sun's heat in the atmosphere, thereby, leading to global warming.

27 "The Facts: The Coca-Cola Company and India," www.cokefacts.com, 2008.

28 "Coca-Cola Joins International Water Conservation Campaign," www.huliq.com, June 5, 2007.

29 Ibid.

30 ICRISAT is a non-profit organization that focuses on capacity building and agricultural research in association with several partners across the world (Source: www.icrisat.org).

31 CII is a non-profit, non-governmental organization based in Delhi. It focuses on business promotion, industry development, and small and medium enterprise services in India (Source: www.ciionline.org).

32 Hydrofluorocarbons are compounds consisting of fluorine, hydrogen, and carbon. They emit GHGs that cause global warming.

33 2006 Corporate Responsibility Review, www.thecoca-colacompany.com, 2006.

34 Ibid.

35 2007/2008 Sustainability Review, www.thecoca-colacompany.com.

36 Neil Merrett, "Coca-Cola Calls on Peers for Cooler Commitment," www.foodproductiondaily.com, June 9, 2008.

37 PET is a thermoplastic polymer used for storage of food, beverage, and other liquids.

38 Crusaders are rag-pickers who picked up metal scraps, paper, plastic bags, etc., for recycling. Like the human scavengers in any other country, they make a living from the waste thrown out by others and also act as informal recyclers.

39 "Coca-Cola India Joins Hands with BMC and FORCE to Initiate PET Recycling Projects in Mumbai," www.thecoca-colacompany.com, September 19, 2005.

40 Ibid.

41 Established in 1945, IAPM is an association of 2,600 members with an additional 12,000 affiliated members as of 2008. IAPM is responsible for conducting seminars, publishing news related to the plastic industry, and organizing exhibitions.

42 "Coca-Cola Celebrates World Environment Day through a Slew of Initiatives to Preserve & Protect the Environment," www.thecoca-colacompany.com, June 5, 2006.

43 2006 Corporate Responsibility Review, www.thecoca-colacompany.com, 2006.

44 Ibid.

45 Aparna Mahajan and Kate Ives, "Enhancing Business-Community Relations," www.worldvolunteerweb.org, October 2003.

46 UN-HABITAT is a United Nations-owned agency responsible for helping policymakers and local communities to make settlements related to human issues and find lasting solutions (Source: www.unhabitat.org).

47 "Coca-Cola Announces Setting up of the Coca-Cola India Foundation," www.cokecfacts.com.

48 "Coca-Cola Renews its Commitment to Water Stewardship in India," www.thecoca-colacompany.com, September 7, 2007.

49 Coca-Cola through the multiplier effect provided jobs to people residing nearby its bottling facilities with the stated aim to improve the livelihood of poor people across the world while sustaining its business.

50 "Our Economic Impact," www.thecoca-colacompany.com.

51 The Coca-Cola University is a virtual university that enables people to gain knowledge and acquire skills to succeed in the marketplace. The employees of Coca-Cola could enroll themselves for courses in several areas such as Customer/Commercial Leadership, People Leadership, Franchise Leadership, and Consumer Marketing (Source: www.thecoca-colacompany.com).

52 "Coca-Cola Strengthens Its Bonds with India, Launches "Little Drops of Joy"," www.coca-colaindia.com, August 17, 2007.

53 "WWF and Coca-Cola Embark on Water Conservation Initiative," www.ens-newswire.com, June 5, 2007.

54 On September 11, 1961, the World Wildlife Fund was established for the protection of nature. The WWF was also responsible for sustaining natural resources, promoting efficient utilization of resources, and provides approaches to curb the level of pollution.

55 "Coke Faces New Charges in India, Including 'Greenwashing'," www.polarisinstitute.org, June 11, 2007.

56 "Indian Campaign Forces Coca-Cola to Announce Ambitious Water Conservation Project," www.indiaresource.org, July 30, 2007.

57 In fact, Coca-Cola had been facing campaigns against it by several students in the UK, Canada, and the U.S. in the 2000s. More than 20 universities and colleges had imposed a ban on Coca-Cola and its products

within their campuses protesting against the company's allegedly unethical practices in different parts of the world.

[58] Based in India, The Energy and Resource Institute was established in 1974 to deal with the issues of depletion of earth's resources and develop solutions to problems related to environment, energy, etc.

[59] "TERI Gives Clean Chit to Coca Cola," www.saharasamay.com, January 14, 2008.

[60] Plachimada Solidarity Committee was established by 32 organizations based in Kerala for fighting against a just issue.

[61] TCCC standards are Coca-Cola's standards related to waste management.

[62] World Environment Foundation is a non-profit organization registered in India and the UK.

[63] Amit Srivastava, "Coca-Cola: A Model for Good Public Relations, Not Sustainability," www.indiaresource.org, March 28, 2008.

[64] Ling Woo Liu, "Water Pressure," www.time.com, June 12, 2008.

[65] Launched in 1997, the Polaris Institute empowers the movement of citizens in the direction of democratic social change (Source: www.polarisinstitute.org).

[66] According to the Polaris Institute, the 'award is presented to companies that have pushed profits higher while investing millions of dollars into covering up environmentally damaging practices with corporate social responsibility projects'.

[67] "Coca-Cola Company Wins Corporate Greenwashing Award," www.polarisinstitute.org, April 16, 2007.

[68] "Coca-Cola Omits Issues in Sustainability Review," www.scoop.co.nz, October 29, 2008.

[69] NGRI, based in Hyderabad, India, is an institute dedicated to basic and applied research in the field of geophysics, groundwater exploration, environmental information, etc.

[70] Jonathan Hills and Richard Welford, "Coca-Cola and Water in India," *Corporate Social Responsibility & Environmental Management*, September 2005.

[71] The Kerala State Pollution Control Board is an agency in the Department of Health and Family Welfare under the government of Kerala. The responsibility of the board includes enforcement of laws related to the protection of the environment.

[72] "Coke Gets CSR Award Amidst Protests," www.business-standard.com, February 19, 2008.

[73] Ibid.

[74] Sohini Das, "Coca-Cola to Set up $10 Mn Trust for CSR," http://in.rediff.com, February 20, 2008.

[75] "Coke Blamed for Depleting Water Resources," http://southasia.oneworld.net, February 22, 2008.

[76] Million Cubic Meters (MCM) is a unit of volume.

[77] Sohini Das, "Coca-Cola to Set up $10 Mn Trust for CSR," http://in.rediff.com, February 20, 2008.

[78] "Coca-Cola Strengthens Its Bonds with India, Launches "Little Drops of Joy"," August 17, 2007.

[79] "Coca-Cola Omits Issues in Sustainability Review," www.scoop.co.nz, October 29, 2008.

[80] Priyanka Mehra and Rajeshwari Sharma, "CSR Advertising: Doing Good to Look Good," www.livemint.com, January 13, 2008.

[81] Sohini Das, "Coca-Cola to Set up $10 Mn Trust for CSR," http://in.rediff.com, February 20, 2008.

Detecting Unethical Practices at Supplier Factories: The Monitoring and Compliance Challenges

Arthur A. Thompson
The University of Alabama

Importers of goods from Bangladesh, Cambodia, China, the Dominican Republic, Honduras, India, Indonesia, Korea, Malaysia, Pakistan, Peru, the Philippines, Sri Lanka, Tunisia, Vietnam, and several other countries in Latin America, Eastern Europe, the Middle East, and Africa have long had to contend with accusations by human rights activists that they sourced goods from sweatshop manufacturers who paid substandard wages, required unusually long work hours, used child labor, exposed workers to toxic chemicals and other safety hazards, failed to provide even minimal fringe benefits, and habitually engaged in assorted other unsavory practices. Exhibit 1 provides a sample of the problems in eight countries. Factories in China were particularly in the spotlight because of China's prominence as the largest single source of goods imported into both the United States and the 25 countries comprising the European Union; U.S. imports from Chinese manufacturers amounted to about $320 billion in 2007. Political support in many countries for growing trade ties with countries where low-cost manufacturers were located, especially China, often hinged on the ability of companies with global sourcing strategies to convince domestic governmental officials, human rights groups, and concerned citizens that they were doing all they could do to police working conditions in the plants of suppliers in low-wage, poverty-stricken countries where sweatshop practices were concentrated.

Starting in the 1990s, companies began countering these criticisms by instituting elaborate codes of conduct for suppliers and by periodically inspecting supplier facilities to try to eliminate abuses and promote improved working conditions. A strong program of auditing labor practices and working conditions in supplier factories was a way for a company to cover itself and negate accusations that it was unfairly exploiting workers in less-developed countries. By 2008, hundreds of companies that sourced goods from factories in less-developed parts of the world had instituted strict codes for suppliers and either had an internal staff to conduct audits of supplier factories or used the services of recognized third parties with auditing expertise to inspect supplier factories. Most companies focused their efforts on improving working conditions at supplier factories, preferring to help suppliers comply with the expected standards rather than to impose penalties for violations and perhaps abruptly and/or permanently cutting off purchases.

However, in November 2006, *BusinessWeek* ran a cover story detailing how shady foreign manufacturers were deliberately deceiving inspection teams and concealing violations of supplier codes of conduct.[1] According to the *BusinessWeek* special report, Ningbo Beifa Group—a top Chinese supplier of pens, mechanical pens, and highlighters to Wal-Mart, Staples, Woolworth, and some 400 other retailers in 100 countries—was alerted in late 2005 that a Wal-Mart inspection team would soon be visiting the company's factory in the coastal city of Ningbo. Wal-Mart was Beifa's largest customer, and on three previous occasions Wal-Mart inspectors had caught Beifa paying its 3,000 workers less than the Chinese minimum-wage and violating overtime rules.

Copyright © 2008 by Arthur A. Thompson. All rights reserved.

Exhibit 1   Comparative Labor and Workplace Conditions in Eight Countries, 2006

Country	Labor and Workplace Overview
Brazil	The primary problems in the manufacturing workplace are forced labor, inadequate occupational safety (work accidents are common in several industries), and wage discrimination (wages paid to females are 54% to 64% of those paid to males).
China	Factories are most prone to ignore minimum-wage requirements, underpay for overtime work, subject workers to unsafe and unhealthy working conditions, and suppress worker attempts to join independent unions.
India	The most common issues concern underpayment of minimum wages, overtime pay violations, use of child labor (according to one estimate some 100 million children ages 5 to 14 work and at least 12.6 million work full-time), the use of forced labor (perhaps as many as 65 million people), and inattention to occupational safety.
Indonesia	The stand-out issues concern weak enforcement of minimum-wage rules and work hours in factories, overtime pay violations in factories, subpar occupational safety (especially in mining and fishing), and use of underage labor (particularly in domestic service, mining, construction, and fishing industries).
Mexico	Problem areas include sweatshop conditions in many assembly plants near U.S. border and elsewhere, fierce opposition to unions, insistence on pregnancy tests for female job applicants of child-bearing age, and use of child labor in non-export economic sectors.
Peru	The worst workplace conditions relate to lack of enforcement of wage and overtime provisions in factories, mandatory overtime requirements for many workers, and inattention to occupational safety.
South Africa	The most frequent offenses entail failure to observe minimum-wage and overtime pay rules (particularly in the garment industry), use of child labor, occupational safety violations (especially in non-export sectors where outside monitoring is nonexistent), and low pay for women.
Sri Lanka	The most frequent violations relate to underpayment of wages, forced overtime requirements, compulsory work on Sundays and holidays, and inattention to worker health and safety (such as excessive noise, blocked exits, and disregard for worker safety—one study found 60% of grain and spice mill workers lost fingers in work-related accidents and/or contracted skin diseases).

Source: Compiled by the author from information in "How China's Labor Conditions Stack Up Against Those of Other Low-Cost Nations," *BusinessWeek Online,* November 27, 2006, www.businessweek.com (accessed January 26, 2007). The information was provided to *BusinessWeek* by Verité, a Massachusetts-based nonprofit social auditing and research organization with expertise in human rights and labor abuses in supplier factories around the world.

A fourth offense would end Wal-Mart's purchases from Beifa. But weeks prior to the audit, an administrator at Beifa's factory in Ningbo got a call from representatives of Shanghai Corporate Responsibility Management & Consulting Company offering to help the Beifa factory pass the Wal-Mart inspection.[2] The Beifa administrator agreed to pay the requested fee of $5,000. The consultant advised management at the Beifa factory in Ningbo to create fake but authentic-looking records regarding pay scales and overtime work and make sure to get any workers with grievances out of the plant on the day of the audit. Beifa managers at the factory were also coached on how to answer questions that the auditors would likely ask. Beifa's Ningbo factory reportedly passed the Wal-Mart inspection in

early 2006 without altering any of its practices.[3] A lawyer for Beifa confirmed that the company had indeed employed the Shanghai consulting firm but said that factory personnel engaged in no dishonest actions to pass the audit; the lawyer indicated that the factory passed the audit because it had taken steps to correct the problems found in Wal-Mart's prior audits.

WAGE AND EMPLOYMENT PRACTICES IN CHINA

Minimum-wage rules in China were specified by local or provincial governments and in 2007 ranged from $36 to $105 per month, which equated to hourly rates of $0.21 to $0.61 based on a 40-hour workweek.[4] In recent years, governments in most Chinese locales had boosted minimum-wage requirements annually so as to preserve worker purchasing power in light of the 5–7 percent annual rates of inflation experienced in China. A comprehensive study involving 57 million employees of larger Chinese manufacturing enterprises revealed average hourly compensation of $0.98 as of 2004, but there were big variations from sector to sector (in textiles and apparel wages averaged about $0.70 per hour, whereas the hourly average was $1.35 in transportation equipment and $1.59 in petroleum processing).[5] Using more recent but somewhat sketchy Chinese government income data compiled by the U.S. Bureau of Labor Statistics and a Beijing consulting firm, another study showed the average manufacturing wage in China in 2005 was $0.64 per hour (again assuming a 40-hour workweek). While the standard workweek in Chinese provinces officially ranged from 40 to 44 hours, there were said to be numerous instances where plant personnel worked 60 to 100 hours per week, sometimes with only one or two days off per month. Such long work hours meant that the actual average manufacturing wage in China was likely well below the levels based on a 40-hour workweek. According to estimates made by a veteran inspector of Chinese factories, employees at garment, electronics, and other plants making goods for export typically worked more than 80 hours per week and earned an average of $0.42 per hour.[6]

Overtime pay rules in Chinese provinces officially called for time-and-a-half pay for all work over eight hours per day and between double and triple pay for work on Saturdays, Sundays, and holidays. However, it was commonplace for Chinese employers to disregard overtime pay rules, and governmental enforcement of minimum-wage and overtime requirements by both Beijing officials and officials in local Chinese provinces was often minimal to nonexistent. At a Hong Kong garment plant where 2,000 employees put in many overtime hours operating sewing and stitching machines, worker pay averaged about $125 per month—an amount which the owner acknowledged did not meet Chinese overtime pay requirements. The owner said the overtime rules were "a fantasy" and added: "Maybe in two or three decades we can meet them."[7] Many young Chinese factory workers were tolerant of long

hours and less than full overtime pay because they wanted to earn as much as possible, the idea being to save enough of their income to return to their homes in the countryside after a few years of factory employment.

Chinese export manufacturing was said to be rife with tales of deception to frustrate plant monitoring and escape compliance with local minimum-wage and overtime rules and supplier codes of conduct. Indeed, a new breed of consultants had sprung up in China to aid local manufacturers in passing audits conducted both by customer companies and industry alliance groups.[8]

GROWING USE OF STRATEGIES TO DELIBERATELY DECEIVE PLANT INSPECTORS

The efforts of unscrupulous manufacturers in China and other parts of the world to game the plant-monitoring system and use whatever deceptive practices it took to successfully pass plant audits had four chief elements:

1. *Maintaining two sets of books*—Factories generated a set of bogus payroll records and time sheets to show audit teams that their workers were properly paid and received the appropriate overtime pay; the genuine records were kept secret. For example, at an onsite audit of a Chinese maker of lamps for Home Depot, Sears, and other retailers, plant managers provided inspectors with payroll records and time sheets showing that employees worked a five-day week from 8:00 a.m. to 5:30 p.m. with a 30-minute lunch break and no overtime hours; during interviews, managers at the plant said the records were accurate. But other records auditors found at the site, along with interviews with workers, indicated that employees worked an extra three to five hours daily with one or two days off per month during peak production periods; inspectors were unable to verify whether workers at the plant received overtime pay.[9] According to a compliance manager at a major multinational company who had overseen many factory audits, the percentage of Chinese employers submitting

false payroll records had risen from 46 percent to 75 percent during the past four years; the manager also estimated that only 20 percent of Chinese suppliers complied with local minimum-wage rules and that just 5 percent obeyed hour limitations.[10]

2. *Hiding the use of underage workers and unsafe work practices*—In some instances, factories in China, parts of Africa, and select other countries in Asia, Eastern Europe, and the Middle East employed underage workers. This was disguised either by falsifying the personnel records of underage employees, by adeptly getting underage employees off the premises when audit teams arrived, or by putting underage employees in back rooms concealed from auditors. A memo distributed in one Chinese factory instructed managers to "notify underage trainees, underage full-time workers, and workers without identification to leave the manufacturing workshop through the back door. Order them not to loiter near the dormitory area. Secondly, immediately order the receptionist to gather all relevant documents and papers."[11] At a toy plant in China, a compliance inspector, upon smelling strong fumes in a poorly ventilated building, found young female employees on a production line using spray guns to paint figurines; in a locked back room that a factory official initially refused to open, an apparently underage worker was found hiding behind coworkers.[12]

3. *Meeting requirements by secretly shifting production to subcontractors*—On occasion, suppliers met the standards set by customers by secretly shifting some production to subcontractors who failed to observe pay standards, skirted worker safety procedures, or otherwise engaged in abuses of various kinds.

4. *Coaching managers and employees on answering questions posed by audit team members*—Both managers and workers were tutored on what to tell inspectors should they be interviewed. Scripting responses about wages and overtime pay, hours worked, safety procedures, training, and other aspects related to working conditions was a common tactic for thwarting what inspectors could learn from interviews. However, in instances where plant inspectors were able to speak confidentially with employees away from the worksite, they often got information at variance with what they were told during onsite interviews—plant personnel were more inclined to be truthful and forthcoming about actual working conditions and pay practices when top-level plant management could not trace the information given to inspectors back to them.

There was a growing awareness among companies attempting to enforce supplier codes of conduct that all factories across the world with substandard working conditions and reasons to hide their practices from outside view played cat-and-mouse games with plant inspectors. In many less-developed countries struggling to build a manufacturing base and provide jobs for their citizens, factory managers considered deceptive practices a necessary evil to survive, principally because improving wages and working conditions to comply with labor codes and customers' codes of conduct for suppliers raised costs and imperiled already thin profit margins. Violations were said to be most prevalent at factories making apparel, but more violations were surfacing in factories making furniture, appliances, toys, and electronics.

However, large global corporations such as General Electric, Motorola, Dell, Nestlé, and Toyota that owned and operated their own offshore manufacturing plants in China and other low-wage countries had not been accused of mistreating their employees or having poor working conditions. The offshore factories of well-known global and multinational companies were seldom subject to monitoring by outsiders because the workplace environments in their foreign plants were relatively good in comparison to those of local manufacturing enterprises that made a business of supplying low-cost components and finished goods to companies and retailers in affluent, industrialized nations.

Corporate sensitivity to charges of being socially irresponsible in their sourcing of goods from foreign manufacturers had prompted hundreds of companies to establish supplier codes of conduct and to engage in compliance monitoring efforts of one kind or another. The clothing retailer Gap had an internal compliance team of more than 90 people to audit approximately 2,000 factories of its garment suppliers; Gap's team conducted 4,316 inspections in 2005.[13]

The retailing giant Target had 40 full-time compliance employees, including more than 20 foreign-based auditing staff, and conducted 100 percent of its factory audits unannounced. Hewlett-Packard had a program to monitor conduct at some 550 supplier factories. Moreover, an increasing number of companies, many with common suppliers, had begun collaborating to establish standards for suppliers and to conduct factory audits. For example, in 2004, Hewlett-Packard, Dell, IBM, and five other electronics companies that relied heavily on outside manufacturers to supply components or assemble products had created the Electronics Industry Code of Conduct; the new code replaced individual codes used by these companies and sought to establish industrywide standards for supplier factories regarding labor and employment practices, worker health and safety, ethics, and environmental protection. Other electronics companies were invited to voluntarily adopt the same standards, because it was simpler for supplier factories to comply with a single set of standards as opposed to scrambling to satisfy the different code requirements of different companies.

FOREIGN SUPPLIER COMPLIANCE PROGRAMS AT NIKE AND WAL-MART

Nike and Wal-Mart were two companies with supplier codes of conduct and rather extensive programs to monitor whether suppliers in low-wage, low-cost manufacturing locations across the world are complying with those codes. Both companies initiated such efforts in the 1990s because they came under fire from human rights activist groups for allegedly sourcing goods from sweatshop factories in China and elsewhere.

Nike's Supplier Code of Conduct and Compliance Monitoring Program

Nike was the world's leading designer, distributor, and marketer of athletic footwear, sports apparel, sports equipment and accessories, but it did no manufacturing. All of Nike products were sourced from contract manufacturers. In 2007, Nike reported that it had almost 700 factories in 52 countries actively engaged in manufacturing its products; of these, about 148 were in China (including Hong Kong and Macau); 63 in Thailand, 35 in Indonesia, 29 in Korea, 35 in Vietnam, 34 in Malaysia, 18 in Sri Lanka, 18 in India, 26 in Brazil, and 9 in Honduras.[14] Nike's contract factories employed roughly 800,000 workers, an estimated 80 percent of whom were women ages 18 to 24 performing entry-level, low-skill jobs. In fiscal year 2006, Nike approved 81 new contract factories for the Nike brand, down from 83 in 2005 and 122 in 2004. Of the new contract factories, 11 were in the Americas, 6 in the Europe/Middle East/Africa region, and 64 in Asia.

Nike drafted a code of conduct for its contract factories in 1991, distributed the code to all of its contract factories in 1992, and directed them to post the code in a visible place and in the appropriate local language. The code had been modified and updated over the years, and in 2007 also included a set of leadership standards that was adopted in 2002. Nike's code of conduct is presented in Exhibit 2. In 1998, in a move to strengthen its opposition to the use of child labor in factories, Nike directed its contract factories to set age standards for employment at 16 for apparel and 18 for footwear; these age standards were more demanding than those set in 1991 and exceeded the International Labor Organization's age minimum of 15.

Nike's System for Monitoring Contract Manufacturers   During 2003–2006, Nike used four approaches to plant monitoring:[15]

- *Basic monitoring or SHAPE inspections:* SHAPE inspections, used since 1997, sought to gauge a factory's overall compliance performance, including environment, safety, and health. They were typically performed by Nike's field-based production staff and could be completed in one day or less. Nike's stated goal was to conduct two SHAPE audits on each active factory each year, but the actual number of such audits had fallen short of that target.
- *In-depth M-Audits:* The M-Audit was designed to provide a deeper measure of the working

Exhibit 2   Nike's Code of Conduct for Its Suppliers and Contract Manufacturers, 2006

Nike, Inc. Was Founded on a Handshake

Implicit in that act was the determination that we would build our business with all of our partners based on trust, teamwork, honesty and mutual respect. We expect all of our business partners to operate on the same principles.

At the core of the NIKE corporate ethic is the belief that we are a company comprised of many different kinds of people, appreciating individual diversity, and dedicated to equal opportunity for each individual.

NIKE designs, manufactures, and markets products for sports and fitness consumers. At every step in that process, we are driven to do not only what is required by law, but what is expected of a leader. We expect our business partners to do the same. NIKE partners with contractors who share our commitment to best practices and continuous improvement in:

1. Management practices that respect the rights of all employees, including the right to free association and collective bargaining
2. Minimizing our impact on the environment
3. Providing a safe and healthy work place
4. Promoting the health and well-being of all employees

Contractors must recognize the dignity of each employee, and the right to a work place free of harassment, abuse or corporal punishment. Decisions on hiring, salary, benefits, advancement, termination or retirement must be based solely on the employee's ability to do the job. There shall be no discrimination based on race, creed, gender, marital or maternity status, religious or political beliefs, age or sexual orientation.

Wherever NIKE operates around the globe we are guided by this Code of Conduct and we bind our contractors to these principles. Contractors must post this Code in all major workspaces, translated into the language of the employee, and must train employees on their rights and obligations as defined by this Code and applicable local laws.

While these principles establish the spirit of our partnerships, we also bind our partners to specific standards of conduct. The core standards are set forth below.

Forced Labor

The contractor does not use forced labor in any form—prison, indentured, bonded or otherwise.

Child Labor

The contractor does not employ any person below the age of 18 to produce footwear. The contractor does not employ any person below the age of 16 to produce apparel, accessories or equipment. If at the time Nike production begins, the contractor employs people of the legal working age who are at least 15, that employment may continue, but the contractor will not hire any person going forward who is younger than the Nike or legal age limit, whichever is higher. To further ensure these age standards are complied with, the contractor does not use any form of homework for Nike production.

Compensation

The contractor provides each employee at least the minimum wage, or the prevailing industry wage, whichever is higher; provides each employee a clear, written accounting for every pay period; and does not deduct from employee pay for disciplinary infractions.

Benefits

The contractor provides each employee all legally mandated benefits.

Hours of Work/Overtime

The contractor complies with legally mandated work hours; uses overtime only when each employee is fully compensated according to local law; informs each employee at the time of hiring if mandatory overtime is a condition of employment; and on a regularly scheduled basis provides one day off in seven, and requires no more than 60 hours of work per week on a regularly scheduled basis, or complies with local limits if they are lower.

Environment, Safety and Health (ES&H)

The contractor has written environmental, safety and health policies and standards, and implements a system to minimize negative impacts on the environment, reduce work-related injury and illness, and promote the general health of employees.

Documentation and Inspection

The contractor maintains on file all documentation needed to demonstrate compliance with this Code of Conduct and required laws; agrees to make these documents available for Nike or its designated monitor; and agrees to submit to inspections with or without prior notice.

Source: www.nike.com (accessed January 25, 2007).

conditions within contract factories. As a general rule, Nike focused its plant inspection efforts on factories where noncompliance was most likely to occur. Factories located in highly regulated countries where workers were more informed about their rights and workplace laws and regulations were enforced were deemed less likely to be out of compliance. In 2003, Nike focused its M-Audits on factories presumed to have the highest risk of noncompliance and the greatest size (as measured by worker population). In 2004, M-Audits were focused on factories believed to be of medium risk for noncompliance. Nike's stated goal was to conduct M-Audits for approximately 25–33 percent of its active factory base each year. The M-Audit included four major categories of inquiry (hiring practices, worker treatment, worker-management communications, and compensation) and covered more than 80 labor-management issues.

In 2004 Nike had 46 employees who regularly conducted M-Audits. The typical M-Auditor was under the age of 30, and 74 percent were women. Nike tried to hire auditors who were local nationals and understood the local language and culture. In 2003–2004, more than 9,200 factory workers were individually interviewed as part of the M-Audit process. Each interview took approximately 30 minutes. The typical M-Audit took an average of 48 hours to complete, including travel to and from the factory—travel hours accounted for between 25 and 30 percent of total M-Audit time.

- *MAV Audits:* Starting in fiscal year 2006, Nike introduced a new audit focused on finding root causes of noncompliance issues that most impacted workers, specifically work hours, wages/benefits, grievance systems, and freedom of associations. Prior audit experience had led Nike's staff to believe that root cause identification would help supplier factories remediate the problems that were identified. Nike conducted 42 MAV audits through fiscal year 2006.

- *Independent external monitoring:* Beginning in 2003, Nike became a member of the Fair Labor Association (FLA), an organization that conducted independent audits of factories that provided goods to members. The FLA applied a common set of compliance standards in all of its factory audits.

In 2004, Nike's compliance team consisted of 90 people based in 24 offices in 21 countries. The typical Nike compliance team in each country spent about one-third of their time on monitoring and auditing activities, about half their time assisting and tracking factory remediation activities, and the remainder of their time on troubleshooting and collaboration/outreach work.[16] In its 2004 Corporate Responsibility Report, Nike said:

> With an average of one compliance staff for more than 10 factories—some of which are remote and some of which are large and complex businesses with 10,000 or more employees—tracking and assisting factory remediation is at times an overwhelming and incomplete body of work.[17]

Nike's 2003–2004 factory audits were announced rather than unannounced because "much of the information we require in our evaluation of a factory is dependent upon access to relevant records and individuals within factory management."[18] When a factory was found to be out of compliance with the code of conduct, Nike's compliance team worked with factory management and the Nike business unit for which products were being manufactured to develop a master action plan (MAP) that specified the factory's needed remediation efforts. The Nike production manager responsible for the business relationship with the contract factory monitored MAP progress and exchanged information about progress or obstacles with Nike's country compliance team. The Nike general manager for production monitored the progress of all factories within his or her purview and weighed in when factory remediation progress was too slow.

To further facilitate factory compliance with Nike's code of conduct for suppliers, the company conducted or sponsored training and education programs for factory personnel. In 2004, more than 16,500 factory managers and workers attended programs relating to labor issues, worker health and safety, and environmental protection.[19]

Nike's Compliance Rating System

Nike's factory ratings for SHAPE and M-Audits resulted in numeric scores ranging from 0 to 100 (a score of 100 indicated full compliance); these numeric scores were then converted to one of four overall grades (see table below).[20]

Exhibit 3 presents a summary of Nike's factory ratings for fiscal years 2003–2004. Exhibit 4 shows the ratings for fiscal years 2005 and 2006.

Grade	Criteria
A	Isolated violations of standards, but none considered serious or critical; no more than 5 minor issues outstanding on a factory's master action plan (MAP) for improving working conditions and achieving higher levels of compliance with Nike's code of conduct
B	Isolated violations of standards, but none considered serious or critical; more than 5 minor issues outstanding on the MAP, but none considered serious or critical
C	Noncompliant with serious failures and making little progress in remedying them. Examples of C-level issues include: • Factory does not provide basic terms of employment (contracts, documented training on terms, equal pay, discriminatory employment screening). • More than 10 percent of employees work between 60 and 72 hours each week. • More than 10 percent of employees exceed annual legal limits. • More than 10 percent of employees work seven or more consecutive days without a break. • Factory violates local migrant labor laws. • Non-income-related benefits fall short of legal provisions. • Some evidence of verbal or psychological harassment or abuse. • One or more serious issues on MAP, but none considered critical.
D	Noncompliant; general disregard for Nike's code of conduct; and evidence of deliberately misleading auditors. Examples of D-level issues and problems include: • Management refuses or continues to demonstrate unwillingness to comply with Nike standards. • Management provides false information (statements, documents or demonstrates coaching). • Factory fails to provide verifiable timekeeping system to accurately record work hours. • Factory fails to pay legally mandated minimum wage. • More than 10 percent of employees work more than 72 hours each week. • More than 10 percent of employees exceed daily work hour limits. • More than 10 percent of employees work 14 or more consecutive days without a break. • Factory requires pregnancy testing as condition of employment. • Factory uses workers under the minimum legal age. • Factory uses bonded, indentured or prison labor. • Factory uses force to compel illegal work hours. • Audit finds confirmed evidence of physical or sexual abuse. • Factory management denies access to authorized compliance inspectors. • Factory denies freedom of association for workers, including demotion or dismissal of workers seeking to exercise their rights. • Factory provides no benefits tied to security (workers' compensation, medical coverage, social security, retirement funds). • Factory outsources to unauthorized facilities or issues homework to employees.
E	Not enough information to measure compliance

Exhibit 3   Summary of Nike's Audits of Supplier Factories, Fiscal Years 2003 and 2004

	Geographic Region				
	Americas	Europe, Middle East, Africa	Northern Asia	Southern Asia	Worldwide Total
Number of SHAPE* audits in 2004	178	157	378	303	1,016
Number of M-Audits† in 2003 and 2004	148	56	198	167	569
M-Audit numeric scores in 2003–2004					
Lowest score	46	49	25	20	20
Average score	78	70	58	58	65
Highest score	94	96	95	95	99
Compliance ratings for contact factories as of June 2004					
Grade of A	32	15	34	25	106 (15%)
Grade of B	64	40	147	76	327 (44%)
Grade of C	18	7	33	65	123 (17%)
Grade of D	5	35	14	8	62 (8%)
Grade of E	18	7	22	70	117 (16%)

*SHAPE audits were a monitoring tool used by Nike since 1997 and provided a basic gauge of a factory's compliance performance.
†M-Audits, Nike's main auditing tool in 2003–2004, provided a deeper assessment of a factory's management practices. Worker population in M-Audited factories was 375,000 in fiscal year 2003 and 213,000 in fiscal year 2004.

Source: Nike's 2004 Corporate Responsibility Report, pp. 20, 34, and 35.

Nike's Corrective Actions to Deal with Noncomplying or Nonperforming Suppliers

A factory was cut from Nike's supplier base when, over a period of time, Nike management determined that factory management lacked the capacity or the will to correct serious issues of noncompliance. One supplier in China, for example, was cited for repeated violations of overtime standards and falsification of records. The compliance team established action plans, which three different Nike business units worked with the factory to implement. After six months of continuous efforts and no improvement, the factory was dropped. In November 2006, Nike severed its business relationship with a Pakistani supplier of soccer balls that failed to correct serious code of conduct violations.

More typically, Nike's decisions to end a business relationship with problem suppliers was based on a "balanced scorecard" of factory performance that took into account labor code compliance along with such measures such as price, quality, and delivery time. For example, a manufacturing group in South Asia had performed poorly on a range of issues, from overtime and worker–management communication to the quality of product and shipping dates. After a series of performance reviews, Nike management informed the factory group that it would not be placing orders for the next season. Nike did not report on factories dropped solely from noncompliance reasons related to its code of conduct because management said "it is often difficult to isolate poor performance on compliance as the sole reason for terminating a business relationship."[21]

To give its contract manufacturers greater incentive to comply with Nike's workplace standards and expectations, during crunch production periods Nike management and plant auditors had given some factories latitude to institute long workweeks (above 72 hours) and not hold them

Exhibit 4 **Summary Results of Nike's Audit Grades for Contract Factories, Fiscal Years 2005–2006**

Factory Rating Trends FY2005

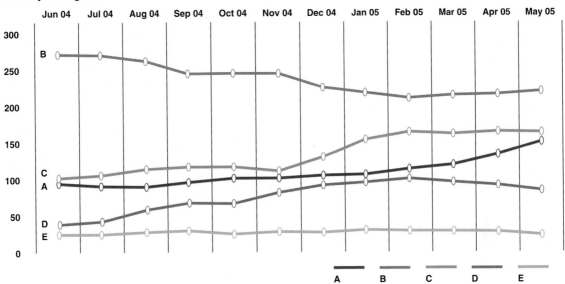

Factory Rating Trends FY2006

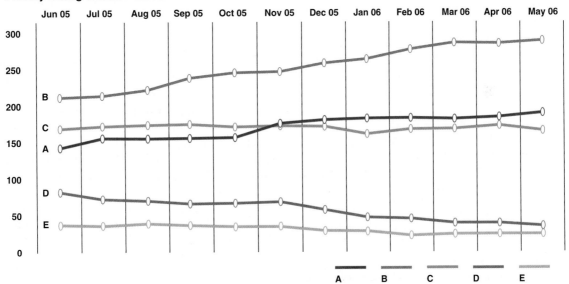

Note: Of the 42 M-Audits that Nike conducted through fiscal year 2006, 7 supplier factories received a grade of A and 13 factories received a D rating; Nike found the two big drivers of noncompliance were ignorance of the law or Nike standards and a lack of systems to manage people and processes.

Source: Nike fiscal year 2005–2006 Corporate Responsibility Report, pp. 30 and 31.

to a strict standard of 1 day off out of every 14 days if the employer gave workers more days off during slack production periods. Nike was also working to streamline its methods of designing shoes and placing orders with key suppliers and helping foreign factories develop more efficient production techniques, so as to help contract factories eliminate the need to institute long work-weeks and excessive overtime. According to Nike's vice president for global footwear operations, "If you improve efficiency and innovation, it changes the cost equation" for factories.[22]

In 2008, Nike discovered serious breaches of conduct involving unacceptable living conditions, withholding of worker passports, and garnishing of wages at a contract factory in Malaysia. To correct the problem, Nike announced that it was requiring the supplier to immediately make the following non-negotiable changes:[23]

1. All current migrant workers will be reimbursed for fees associated with employment including but not limited to recruiting fees paid to agents and worker permit fees.

2. Going forward, any and all fees associated with employment will be paid by the factory as a cost of doing business.

3. Any worker who wishes to return home will be provided with return airfare, irrespective of their contract requirements.

4. The majority of housing has been found to be unacceptable. All workers will be transitioned into new Nike-inspected and approved housing within 30 days. This transition has already begun.

5. All workers will have immediate and total free access to their passports. No restrictions.

6. Workers will have access to a 24-hour Nike hotline should they be denied access to their passports by factory management. All claims will be promptly investigated.

7. Communication to the workers of these changes will be delivered verbally as well as posted in all communal areas in all appropriate languages.

Nike also announced that during the next 10 days, it would review its entire Malaysian contract factory base and require factories to institute these same policies.

Wal-Mart's Supplier Code of Conduct and Compliance Monitoring Program

In 1992 Wal-Mart established a set of standards for its suppliers and put in place an ethical standards program to monitor supplier compliance with these standards.[24] Since then, Wal-Mart's standards for suppliers had been periodically evaluated and modified based on experience and feedback from the ethical sourcing community. The company's standards for suppliers covered compensation, working hours, forced labor, underage labor, discrimination, compliance with applicable national laws and regulation, health and safety practices, environmental abuse, freedom of association and collective bargaining, rights concerning foreign contract workers, and the right of audit by Wal-Mart.

Prior to contracting with any supplier, Wal-Mart required suppliers to review and sign a supplier agreement, which incorporated an expectation that the supplier would comply with Wal-Mart's standards for suppliers. In addition, it was mandatory that all suppliers display Wal-Mart's "Standards for Suppliers" poster in all of the suppliers' factories. Factory management was required to sign that it had read and fully understood the "Standards for Suppliers" poster, and a copy of the poster in the relevant language had to be posted in a public place within the factory. Wal-Mart's "Standards for Suppliers" poster was available in 25 languages.

In February 2002, Wal-Mart created an entity called the Global Procurement Services Group (GPSG), which was charged with identifying new suppliers, sourcing new products, building partnerships with existing suppliers, managing Wal-Mart's global supply chain of direct imports, providing workplace standards training to suppliers, and enforcing compliance with Wal-Mart's supplier standards. All Wal-Mart personnel engaged in monitoring supplier compliance became part of the GPSG. In 2008, the GPSG consisted of about 1,700 people working from offices in 25 countries, including China, Indonesia, India, Pakistan, Sri Lanka, Bangladesh, Honduras, Nicaragua, Guatemala, Mexico, Brazil, and Turkey (countries where supplier compliance presented big challenges).

In 2005–2007, Wal-Mart purchased goods from close to 9,000 factories in some 60 countries; about 2,500 of the 9,000 factories had recently come into Wal-Mart's compliance and factory audit system due to mergers, acquisitions, and new factory construction. About 200 Wal-Mart personnel scattered across the GPSG's offices in all 25 countries were engaged in monitoring suppliers for compliance with Wal-Mart's standards for suppliers. Suppliers covered by Wal-Mart ethical standards program had to disclose the factory (or factories) used to fulfill each order placed by Wal-Mart.

Wal-Mart's Supplier Auditing Program and Compliance Rating System
During 2006, Wal-Mart audited more factories than any other company in the world, performing 16,700 initial and follow-up audits of 8,873 factories. In 2005, Wal-Mart conducted 13,700 initial and follow-up audits of 7,200 supplier factories; in 2004, Wal-Mart conducted 12,561 initial and follow-up audits at 7,600 factories. The company's audit methodology and factory rating system is described in Exhibit 5. A summary of Wal-Mart's audit findings for 2004–2006 is contained in Exhibit 6. According to Wal-Mart management, the lower number of disapproved factories in 2005 and 2006 relative to 2004 was chiefly due to extending the disapproval period from 90 days to one year for factories receiving four Orange ratings within a two-year period; other contributing factors were a revision of the ratings and Wal-Mart's public announcement that it was expanding the percentage of unannounced audits to 20 percent in 2005 and as many as 30 percent in 2006. Also, starting in 2004, more rigorous supplier standards were instituted, certain types of violations were reclassified to increase their severity, and audits were conducted by two-person teams instead of just a single individual. Increases in the number of audits had also resulted in Wal-Mart's auditors becoming more familiar with the factories and their workers. About 52 percent of the supplier factories audited in 2005 were not included in the 2006 audit program because of supplier turnover, disapproved factories, permanently banned factories receiving Red ratings, and the two-year re-audit cycle for supplier factories receiving a Green

Rating. Rather than promptly banning the placement of orders at supplier factories receiving Yellow and Orange ratings, Wal-Mart's policy was to work with supplier factories to reduce violations and achieve steady improvement of workplace conditions, a position widely endorsed by most human rights activists, concerned citizens groups, and nongovernmental agencies striving for better factory conditions for low-wage workers. To help promote higher levels of supplier compliance, Wal-Mart trained more than 8,000 supplier personnel in 2004, 11,000 suppliers and members of factory management in 2005, and 5,000 suppliers and members of factory management in 2006. The training focused on increasing supplier familiarity with Wal-Mart's standards for suppliers and encouraging an exchange of information about factory operating practices. Wal-Mart actively worked with its foreign suppliers on ways to do better production planning, enhance plant efficiency, better educate and train workers, make supply chain improvements, and adopt better factory operating practices. Wal-Mart also consulted with knowledgeable outside experts and organizations on ways to accelerate ethical compliance and the achievement of better working conditions in supplier factories.

Upon learning of the incident in the *BusinessWeek* report cited in the opening of this case, Wal-Mart began an investigation of the Beifa factory in Ningbo. Wal-Mart acknowledged that some of its suppliers were trying to deceive plant monitors and avoid complying with Wal-Mart's standards for suppliers.

Audit Fatigue on the Part of Supplier Factories
In 2008, supplier monitoring had become a standard practice for many retailers and brand owners that sourced their goods from factories in foreign locations where working conditions were often less than satisfactory. It was not uncommon for the audit teams of different companies to be in some supplier factories as often as 10 times each month, leading not only to duplication of audit efforts but also to audit fatigue and frustration on the part of factory managers. While the supplier codes of conduct of various retailers and brand owners tended to be similar, the interpretation of standards and local laws frequently varied by company, thus resulting

Exhibit 5   Wal-Mart's Factory Audit Methodology and Factory Ratings System, 2006

- **Opening Meeting**—The Opening Meeting consisted of (1) confirmation of the factory and its information, (2) an introduction by the Wal-Mart auditors to factory management and supplier representatives, (3) a presentation and signing of the Wal-Mart Gifts & Gratuity Policy (which forbids any offer or receipt of gifts or bribes by the factory or the auditor), and (4) a request by the auditors of factory documentation related to personnel, production, time and pay records.

- **Factory Tour**—The auditors conducted a factory walk-through to examine factory conditions. The walk-through had minimal factory managers present because auditors asked production employees questions about machinery operation and other working conditions. Auditors also followed up with workers interviewed in previous audits about conditions since the last audit. The tour lasted up to three hours, depending on the size of the factory.

- **Worker Interviews**—During factory tours, auditors typically choose workers off the shop floor to interview, although additional workers could be requested to verify factory records during the documentation review process. Factory management had provide a private location for interviews, and under no circumstances were interviews conducted with factory management or supplier representatives present. Workers were interviewed in same-sex groups. The objectives of the interviews were to discover what interviewees had to say relevant to the audit, verify findings and observations made by the auditors, and ensure that workers understood their rights. A minimum of 15 workers were interviewed. The number of workers interviewed depended on the size of the factory.

- **Factory Documentation Review**—Auditors conducted an on-site inspection of payroll records, time cards, personnel files, and other pertinent production documents. For Initial and Annual audits, document review required records dating back at least three months and up to one year. Follow-up audits not only included reviewing findings from the previous audit, but also always included review of hours and compensation. Any factory that failed or refused to comply with this requirement was subject to immediate cancellation of any and all outstanding orders.

- **Closing Meeting**—Auditors summarized the audit findings, described any violations found, made recommendations to remedy the violations, and gave factory management a chance to ask any questions about the audit. Factory management and the auditor both signed the on-site audit report. Auditors left a copy of the signed audit findings and recommendations. Factory management was expected to act on all the recommendations in the on-site report and to present a completed action plan to the auditor during the follow-up audit opening meeting so auditors could validate that the actions were taken. Suppliers and factory management were encouraged to contact the regional Wal-Mart Ethical Standards office to discuss any concerns or questions about the on-site report and recommendations.

- **Factory Ratings**—Factories were rated Green, Yellow, Orange, or Red.

  A Green rating was assigned for factories having no or only minor violations

  A Yellow rating signified medium-risk violations.

  An Orange rating entailed high-risk violations (an Orange-Age rating was automatic for factories where the use of one or two underage workers was discovered). Factories receiving four Orange ratings within a two-year period were disapproved for producing goods for Wal-Mart for one year; after a year, the factory could be approved to supply Wal-Mart if it achieved a Yellow or Green rating.

  A Red rating indicated failure to pass the audit because of such egregious violations as use of prison or forced labor, extremely unsafe working conditions, employing more than two underage workers, serious worker abuse, or exceptionally long work hours. Red-rated factories were immediately and permanently banned from producing merchandise for Wal-Mart.

Starting in 2006, Green-rated factories had re-audits every two years instead of annually. Yellow- and Orange-rated factories had follow-up audits after 120 days to allow time for corrections and verification that corrective actions had been implemented. Factories rated Orange with underage labor violations for only one or two workers were an exception to the timeline for re-audits; such factories were re-audited within 30 days. If the follow-up audit for these factories indicated that the use of underage labor had been corrected, the factory could continue production for Wal-Mart; a failure on the follow-up 30-day audit resulted in a Red rating and a permanent order ban. A factory receiving an Orange assessment four times in a two-year period was banned from producing for Wal-Mart for up to one year (the ban on orders for such factories was extended from 90 days to one year starting January 1, 2005, in order to strengthen the seriousness of program noncompliance).

- **Use of Outside Auditors**—When Wal-Mart sourced goods for its foreign stores from suppliers in the same country in which the foreign stores were located, it used outside auditors to check supplier compliance. In 2005–2007, the outside auditing firms performing audits for some supplier factories included Accordia, Bureau Veritas, Cal Safety Compliance Corporation (CSCC), Global Social Compliance, Intertek Testing Services, and Société Générale de Surveillance.

Source: Wal-Mart's Report on Ethical Sourcing, 2005 and 2006, posted at www.walmart.com (accessed January 25, 2007, and September 18, 2008).

Exhibit 6　**Comparison of Wal-Mart's Factory Audit Results for 2004, 2005, and 2006**

	2004	2005	2006
Total number of factory audits	12,561 (8% were unannounced)	13,600 (20% were unannounced)	16,700 (26% were unannounced)
Number of factories audited	7,600	7,200	8,873
Audits resulting in Green ratings (re-audited after 2 years)	19.1%	9.6%	5.4%
Audits resulting in Yellow ratings (re-audited after 120 days*)	38.8%	37.0%	51.6%
Audits resulting in Orange ratings (re-audited after 120 days)	32.5%	52.3%	40.3%
Audits resulting in Orange-Age ratings (re-audited after 30 days)	—	0.8%	0.4%
Factories disapproved for producing for one year—four Orange assessments in a two-year period	8.8%	0.1%	2.1%
Audits resulting in Red ratings—factories permanently banned from receiving orders	0.8%	164 (141 of these related to the use of underage labor)	0.2%

*In 2007, the re-audit period for Yellow-rated factories was changed to 180 days.

Source: Wal-Mart's Report on Ethical Sourcing, 2005 and 2006, www.walmart.com (accessed January 25, 2007, and September 18, 2008).

in situations where factory managers were asked to comply with a variety of interpretations.

Wal-Mart recognized that multiple audits by multiple companies with varying standards and interpretations needed to be addressed. Its response had been to increase its collaboration with other companies and organizations that were engaged in monitoring to work toward a convergence of supplier codes of conduct and common interpretation of standards and local laws; Wal-Mart's goal was to develop a unified and credible certification program for factories that would both facilitate compliance and reduce audit fatigue.

Toward this end, Wal-Mart had begun working closely with the International Council of Toy Industries (ICTI) CARE Process and the Global Social Compliance Program. ICTI consisted of toy trade associations from 21 countries and was engaged in promoting toy safety standards, fair labor treatment and safe working conditions in toy factories, and a responsible approach in advertising and marketing toys to children. ICTI had developed a code of business practices that included high standards for labor practices and employee health and safety. Its CARE Process

was aimed at providing a single, thorough, and consistent audit program for monitoring toy factories compliance with the code; most of ICTI's auditing activities were concentrated in China, where 70 percent of the world's toy volume was manufactured. Wal-Mart had begun accepting ICTI's audit results in lieu of conducting its own audits.

Wal-Mart was a cofounder of the Global Social Compliance Program (GSCP). The GSCP was an initiative to promote uniform global standards for supplier conduct and acceptable factory working conditions, particularly as concerned health and safety, child labor, discrimination, and compensation. Factory monitoring was an important component of the program. Although much of the work to put the program in place was being done by CIES, an international association of food retailers and suppliers, the scope of the GSCP covered both food and nonfood production. While the current members of GSCP were companies, it was envisioned that there would be extensive collaboration with trade unions, governmental organizations, and nongovernmental organizations.

In July 2008, Wal-Mart announced that Intertek Group, PLC, an independent supplier monitoring organization with 25 offices in China, would begin conducting audit of Wal-Mart's supplier factories in China. Intertek was among the several outside groups that Wal-Mart used to help conduct audits of its supplier factories.

COMPLIANCE EFFORTS OF INDUSTRY GROUPS AND NONGOVERNMENTAL ORGANIZATIONS

Some companies, rather than conducting their own supplier monitoring and compliance effort, had banded together in industry groups or multi-industry coalitions to establish a common code of supplier conduct and to organize a joint program of factory inspections and compliance efforts. For example, Hewlett-Packard, Dell, and other electronics companies that relied heavily on Asian-based manufacturers to supply components or else assemble digital cameras, handheld devices, and PCs had entered into an alliance to combat worker abuse and poor working conditions in the factories of their suppliers.

The Fair Labor Association

One of the most prominent and best organized coalitions was the Fair Labor Association (FLA), whose members and affiliates included 194 colleges and universities, a number of concerned nongovernmental organizations, and a group of 35 companies that included Nike, the Adidas Group (the owner of both Reebok and Adidas brands), Puma, Eddie Bauer, Liz Claiborne, Patagonia, Cutter & Buck, Russell Corporation, and Nordstrom. As part of its broad-based campaign to eliminate human rights abuses and improve global workplace conditions, the FLA had established its Workplace Code of Conduct, a document to which all members and affiliates had subscribed. To aid in winning supplier compliance with the Workplace Code of Conduct, the FLA conducted unannounced audits of factories across the world that supplied its members and affiliates.

In 2006, FLA's teams of independent plant monitors conducted inspections at 147 factories in 18 countries, the results of which were published in FLA's 2007 annual public report. The audits, all of which involved factories that were supplying goods to one or more FLA members, revealed 2,511 instances of noncompliance with FLA's Workplace Code of Conduct, an average of 18.2 violations per factory (versus averages of 15.1 per factory in 2003 and 18.2 per factory in 2004).[25] The violations included excessive work hours, underpayment of wages and overtime, failure to observe legal holidays and grant vacations (27.5 percent); health and safety problems (44 percent); and worker harassment (5.1 percent). The FLA concluded that the actual violations relating to underpayment of wages, hours of work, and overtime compensation were probably higher than those discovered because "factory personnel have become sophisticated in concealing noncompliance relating to wages. They often hide original documents and show monitors falsified books."[26]

In its 2006 public annual report, the FLA said that accredited independent monitors conducted unannounced audits of 99 factories in 18 countries in 2005; the audited factories employed some 77,800 workers.[27] The audited factories were but a small sample of the 3,753 factories employing some 2.9 million people from which the FLA's 35 affiliated companies sourced goods in 2005; however, 34 of the 99 audited factories involved facilities providing goods to 2 or more of FLA's 35 affiliated companies. The 99 audits during 2005 revealed 1,587 violations, an average of 15.9 per audit. The greatest incidence of violations was found in Southeast Asia (chiefly factories located in China, Indonesia, Thailand, and India), where violations averaged about 22 violations per factory audit. As was the case with the audits conducted in 2004, most of the violations related to health and safety (45 percent); wages, benefits, hours of work, and overtime compensation (28 percent); and worker harassment and abuse (7 percent). The FLA stated in its 2006 report that the violations relating to compensation and benefits were likely higher than those detected in its 2005 audits: "Factory personnel have become accustomed to concealing real wage documentation and providing falsified records at the time of compliance audits, making any noncompliances difficult to detect."[28]

In its 2007 public annual report, the FLA said that accredited independent monitors conducted unannounced audits of 147 factories in 30 countries in 2006; the audited factories employed some 110,000 workers.[29] The audited factories were but a small sample of the 5,178 factories employing some 3.8 million people from which the FLA's affiliated companies sourced goods in 2006; however, 24 of the audited factories involved facilities providing goods to 2 or more of FLA's affiliated companies. The 147 audits during 2006 revealed 2,511 violations, an average of 17.1 per audit. Over 80 percent of all the reported violations were in Asian countries; there was an average of 37.4 violations per factory visited in South Asia. Most of the 2006 violations related to health and safety (46 percent); wages, benefits, hours of work, and overtime compensation (30 percent); and code awareness (9 percent). Once again, the FLA stated in its report that the violations relating to compensation and benefits were likely higher than those detected in its prior-year audits because "Factory personnel have become accustomed to concealing real wage documentation and providing falsified records at the time of compliance audits, making noncompliances difficult to detect."[30]

The Fair Factories Clearinghouse

The Fair Factories Clearinghouse (FFC), formed in 2004, was a collaborative effort to create a system for managing and sharing factory audit information that would facilitate detecting and eliminating sweatshops and abusive workplace conditions in foreign factories. Members as of 2008 included ASICS America, L. L. Bean, Timberland, Hudson's Bay Company, Levi Strauss & Co., Macy's Merchandising Group, Mark's Work Wearhouse, Nike Inc., Patagonia, Starbucks Coffee Company, and VF Corporation. Membership fees were based on a company's annual revenues, with annual fees ranging from as little as $5,000 to as much as $75,000 (not including one-time initiation fees of $2,500 to $11,500). The idea underlying the FFC was that members would pool their audit information on offshore factories, creating a database on thousands of manufacturing plants. As of October 2007, FFC's database included 25,000 audits of 13,000 factories. Once a plant was certified by a member company or organization, other members could accept the results without having to do an audit of their own. One benefit of collaborative audit-sharing via an organization like FFC was that members sourcing goods from the same factories could band together and apply added pressure on a supplier to improve its working conditions and comply with buyers' codes of supplier conduct.[31]

Aside from the audit-sharing appeal of making factory audit programs less expensive, audit-sharing had the additional appeal of lessening the time that factory managers had to spend dealing with the audit teams of many different customer companies that conducted their own audits, thereby reducing "audit fatigue." Some large plants with big customer bases were said to undergo audits as often as weekly and occasionally even daily; in addition, they were pressured into having to comply with varying provisions and requirements of each auditing company's code of supplier conduct—being subject to varying and conflicting codes of conduct was a factor that induced cheating.

THE OBSTACLES TO ACHIEVING SUPPLIER COMPLIANCE WITH CODES OF CONDUCT IN LOW-WAGE, LOW-COST COUNTRIES

Factory managers subject to inspections and audits of their plants and work practices complained that strong pressures from their customers to keep prices low gave them a big incentive to cheat on their compliance with labor standards. As the general manager of a factory in China that supplied goods to Nike said, "Any improvement you make costs more money. The price [Nike pays] never increases one penny but compliance with labor codes definitely raises costs."[32]

The pricing pressures from companies sourcing components or finished goods from offshore factories in China, India, and other low-wage, low-cost locations were acute. Since 1996, the prices paid for men's shirts and sweaters sourced in China were said to have dropped by 14 percent, while the prices of clocks and lamps had dropped 40 percent and the prices of toys and games had fallen 30 percent.[33] Such downward pressure on prices made it financially difficult for foreign manufacturers to improve worker compensation and benefits, make their workplaces safer and more pleasant, introduce more efficient production methods, and overhaul inefficient plant layouts. Many factory managers believed that if they paid workers a higher wage, incurred other compliance costs, and then raised their prices to cover the higher costs that their customers would quickly cut and run to other suppliers charging lower prices. Hence the penalties and disincentives for compliance significantly outweighed any rewards.

The CEO of the Fair Labor Association, Auret van Heerden, in a 2006 interview with *BusinessWeek,* offered a number of reasons why underpayment of wages and excessive overtime in supplier factories in China were such difficult problems to resolve:

> The brands book and confirm orders really late. And they often change their orders after booking. The brands want to order later and they don't want to hold product. Then you add price

pressures into that and it is really tough for the supplier [to not overwork its workers].

> But the factory often doesn't order the materials until too late and they are often delivered late [to the factory], too. The factory production layout is often a mess, so the supplier gets behind schedule and over budget even before they know it. Then they have to catch up. And to save money, they extend hours, but don't pay overtime premiums. And the suppliers also lack proper training. The styles [of clothing and footwear] are becoming more complicated and are changing more frequently.

> Multiple codes are a big problem. The classic example is the height that a fire extinguisher should be kept off the ground—how high varies according to different codes. Companies like McDonald's, Disney, and Wal-Mart are doing thousands of audits a year that are not harmonized. That's where audit fatigue comes in.

> And auditing in itself tells you a little about the problem, but not enough, and not why there is a problem. So you have an overtime problem, but you don't know why. Is it because of electricity shortages, labor shortages, or a shorter order turnaround time? You don't know.[34]

ENDNOTES

[1] Dexter Roberts and Pete Engardio, "Secrets, Lies, and Sweatshops," *BusinessWeek,* November 27, 2006, pp. 50–58.

[2] Ibid., p. 50.

[3] Ibid.

[4] www.chinatownconnection.com (accessed September 17, 2008).

[5] Judith Bannister, "Manufacturing in China Today: Employment and Labor Compensation," *Conference Board,* November 2007, p. 22.

[6] Roberts and Engardio, "Secrets, Lies, and Sweatshops," p. 54.

[7] Ibid., p. 54.

[8] Ibid., p. 50.

[9] Ibid., p. 55.

[10] Ibid., p. 53.

[11] Ibid., pp. 55–56.

[12] Ibid., p. 53.

[13] Lisa Roner, "Wal-Mart's Ethical Sourcing: Green Does Not Mean Ethical," October 19, 2007, www.ethicalcorp.com (accessed September 22, 2008).

[14] Nike FY2005–06 Corporate Responsibility Report, www.nike.com/nikebiz (accessed September 19, 2008), p. 28.

[15] Information posted at www.nikebiz.com (accessed on January 26, 2007); Nike's 2004 Fiscal Year Corporate Responsibility Report, pp. 21–24.

[16] Nike's 2004 Fiscal Year Corporate Responsibility Report, p. 28.

[17] Ibid., p. 29.

[18] Ibid., p. 20.

[19] Ibid., p. 30.

[20] Ibid., p. 25.

[21] Ibid., p. 26.

[22] Pete Engardio and Dexter Roberts, "How to Make Factories Play Fair," *BusinessWeek,* November 27, 2007, p. 58.

[23] Company press release, August 1, 2008.

[24] The content of this section was developed by the case author from information posted in the supplier section at www.walmartstores.com (accessed January 25, 2007).

[25] Fair Labor Association, 2005 annual public report, www.fairlabor.org (accessed January 23, 2007).

[26] Ibid., p. 38; also quoted in Roberts and Engardio, "Secrets, Lies, and Sweatshops," p. 54.

[27] Fair Labor Association, 2006 annual public report, www.fairlabor.org (accessed January 23, 2007).

[28] Ibid., p. 40.

[29] Fair Labor Association, 2007 annual public report, www.fairlabor.org (accessed September 19, 2008).

[30] Ibid., p. 48.

[31] Roberts and Engardio, "Secrets, Lies, and Sweatshops," p. 58.

[32] As quoted in ibid., p. 53.

[33] Ibid., p. 58.

[34] As quoted in Dexter Roberts, "A Lion for Worker Rights," *BusinessWeek* Online Extra, November 27, 2006, www.businessweek.com (accessed on January 23, 2007).

COMPANY INDEX

A

A. T. Kearney, 163
A&E networks, 335
A&W, 282
ABB, 250
ABC network, 199, 335
Aber Diamond, 230
Accenture, 163, 267, 286, C-79
 market share, C-77
Accor, 205
Acer Inc., 192, C-51, C-79, C-108, C-132, C-150
 competition with Apple, C-129–C-130,
  C-148–C-149
 financial performance, C-129
 global market share, C-127
 market share, C-52
 multibrand strategy, C-130
 revenues, C-129
 U.S. market share, C-127
ACNielsen Corporation, C-261
Acushnet Company, C-46
Adams Golf, C-41
Adelphia Communications, 347, 450
Adgator, C-2
Adidas Group, 86, 362, C-45, C-410
Adidas Group, case, C-271–C-285
 acquisition(s), C-261
  Salomon, C-276
  Saxon Athletic Manufacturing, C-285
  of Textronics, C-285
 balance sheets 2007–2008, C-275
 brand-building, C-278
 business units
  financial data for, C-279
  footwear and apparel, C-280–C-282
  Reebok, C-282–C-284
  TaylorMade Golf, C-284
 company history, C-272–C-276
 controlled retail space, C-278–C-280
 differentiation strategy, C-278
 divestiture of Salomon, C-261
 in financial crisis of 2008, C-285
 financial performance 1998–2008, C-273
 financial performance by region, C-283
 market share, C-281
 versus Nike, C-261
 number of retail outlets, C-280
 performance in 2009, C-285
 regional sales comparison, C-281–C-282
 restructuring failure, C-271–C-272
 restructuring plan, C-276–C-278
  acquisition of Reebok, C-277–C-278
  divestiture of Salomon, C-277
  performance expectations, C-278
 stock price performance, C-274
 strategy in 2009, C-278–C-284
 supply chain management, C-280
Adobe, C-132, C-150

Adolph Coors, 117, C-228, C-231
Advanced Integrated Solutions, C-110
Advanced International Multitech Company,
 C-39
Advanced Research Japan Company, C-323
Aer Lingus, 217
Aerospatiale, 267, 392
Affiliated Computer Services, 297
AFL Pvt. Ltd., 403
Africa Sport Hunting Safaris, C-370–C-372
AfriData, C-7
Afrigator, case, C-2–C-14
 acquisition by Naspers, C-8–C-9
 advertising, C-7
 beta version features, C-4
 business model, C-7–C-8
 company business, C-3
 competitors, C-9–C-11
 content features, C-5–C-7
 founding of, C-3–C-5
 future of, C-14
 growth of, C-5
 mobile version, C-4
 monthly traffic, C-12
 and Online Publishers Association, C-2
 partnerships, C-13–C-14
 product launch, C-4
 ranking, C-2
 restructuring, C7
 and social media, C-3
 statistics on, C-12
 success of, C-11–C-13
 users by country, C7
Afrigator Mobile, C-4
Agilent Technologies, 328
Ahold, 116
AIG (American International Group), 347
Airbus Industrie, 259, 267, C-180
Air China Ltd., C-173
Airespace, C-79
Air France–KLM, 362
Airsafe.com, C-178
Alberto-Culver Company, 438
 corporate culture, 439
Alcan Aluminum, 416, C-250
Aldi, 116
Aldila, C-39
Alitalia, C-182, C-183
Allegro Manufacturing, 305
Allstate Insurance, 232
Amalgamated Distillery Products Inc., C-229
Amatomu, C-11
Amazon.com, 194, 382, 384, 416, 421, 423, 448,
 455, C-61, C-82, C-131, C-135, C-138,
 C-344
 first-mover advantage, 224
Amazon Kindle, C-134, C-153
Amazon Video on Demand, C-136, C-150
AmBev, C-230, C-231

Amerada Hess, C-69–C-70
America Movil, 51, 214
American Airlines, 239, C-174
American Brands, C-46
American Express, 236
American Hockey League, C-282
American Lock, 309
American Productivity and Quality Center,
 164, 413
American Red Cross, C-353
Amer Sports Corporation, C-271, C-277
AM-FM, Inc., 230
Amgen, motivation and rewards at, 427
Amnesty International, C-92
Am Tran Technology, 203
Anaheim Angels, 335
Anheuser-Busch, 117, 186, C-24, C-28, C-229,
 C-230, C-231, C-232, C-233, C-235, C-237
Animal Compassion Foundation, 365
APO Cement Corporation, C-217, C-219
Apple Inc., 51, 56, 57, 82, 145, 148, 152, 157,
 198, 216, 231–232, 236, 301, 340, 448,
 C-51, C-120, C-136, C-148, C-162, C-165,
 C-166, C-167
 market share, C-52
 revenues, C-163
 Supplier Code of Conduct, 341
 supplier problems, 341
 value chain, C-59
Apple Inc., case, C-122–C-135
 company history, C-122–C-124
 competition, C-122
 competitive position
  in mobile phones industry, C-131–C-132
  in personal computer industry, C-124–C-128
  in personal media player industry,
   C-130–C-131
 entry into tablet computer business,
  C-132–C-134, C-151–C-153
 financial performance, C-122–C-124
 financial performance 2005–2009, C-125
 management change, C-123
 market share, C-127
 new product launches, C-122
 performance in 2010, C-134–C-135
 product line, C-122–C-124
 rivals in PC industry, C-128–C-130
 sales by product, C-126
 turnaround, C-124
Apple iPad, 152
Apple iPhone, 152, 194, C-4, C-102, C-112,
 C-149, C-160, C-161, C-169
Apple iPod, 152, C-53, C-62
Apple iTunes, C-342
Applied Generics, C-109
Applied Komatsu Technology Inc., C-248, C-249
Applied Materials Inc., C-246, C-248
App Store, C-131
Aprica strollers, 310

Aquafina, C-24
Aramark Food and Services, C-339
Archos, C-130
Arsenal Digital Solutions, 267
Arthur Andersen, 349
Asahi, C-228
ASAP Software, C-68
Asea Brown Boveri, C-259
ASICS America, C-411
Assiut Cement Company, C-215, C-218, C-219
Aston Martin, 201
Atari Pong, C-104
Atlassian, case, C-81–C-93
    awards to, C-82
    business model, C-86–C-87
    customer service, C-87–C-91
    customers worldwide, C-89–C-90
    early years, C-81–C-83
    financing, C-85–C-87
    global distribution platform, C-85
    global reach, C-92–C-93
    growth, C-81
    human resources practices, C-91–C-92
    innovation at, C-87–C-91
    marketing by, C-91
    milestones, C-90
    new challenges foe, C-93
    office locations and functions, C-93
    philanthropic activities, C-93
    product line, C-88
    rapid growth, C-87–C-93
    revenues in 2009, C-81
AT&T, 295, C-136, C-337
AT&T Mobility, C-131
AT&T Navigator, C-112–C-113
Audi, 207
Audi-Volkswagen, C-204
AutoExtremist.com, C-322
Automation Tooling Systems, C-204
AutoPacific, Inc., C-323
Avis Rent-a-Car, C-110, C-111–C-112
Avon Products, Inc., 82, 198, 457
    financial statements, 176–178
Avon Walk Around the World for Breast
    Cancer, C-282
Avusa Limited, C-2, C-3

B

Baan Japan Company, Ltd., C-250
Baidu, C-148
Banana Republic, 127
Banco Bilbao Vizcaya Argentaria SA, C-225,
    C-226
Banco Nacional de Mexico, C-229
Banco Santander SA, C-225, C-226
B&Q, 358
Bank of America, 227, 229, 236, 299, 416
Bank of China, 93
Banyan Tree Hotels, C-296
Barton Beers Ltd., C-229, C-232, C-233
BASF, 93
Bata, 192
BBC, 198
Beaird-Poulan, 304
Beijing Product Creation Center, C-167
Bell helicopters, 309

Ben & Jerry's Homemade, 151, 366, C-342
Benchmarking Exchange, 163, 412
Benchnet, 163
Berkshire Hathaway, 311
Bernard L. Madoff Investment Securities, 349
    investment fraud, 350–351
Bernzomatic, 310
Best Buy, 203, 427, C-54, C-62, C-111, C-150
Best Practices, LLC, 163, 412–413
BHP Billiton, 51
Bic Camera, C-63
Bihran Mumbai Municipal Corporation, C-386
Bing, C-152, C-153
Biotherm, 334
Black & Decker, 305
BlackBerry, C-156, C-158; *see also* Research in
    Motion
    enterprise solution architecture, C-159
    evolution of, C-160
    subscriber base, C-157
Bluebird snacks, C-258
Blue Circle Industries, C-216
Blueworld, C-11
BMW, 75, 145, 194, 207, 212, 252, 362, 416,
    C-321
Body Shop, 366
Boeing Company, 267, 392, 416, C-173, C-174,
    C-176, C-177, C-180, C-182–C-183
Bonefish Grill, 334
Bookmark Box, C-83
Borders, C-343
Boston Beer Company, 231
Boston Consulting Group, 418, C-210, C-259
BP Amoco, 261
BP Solar, C-200, C-204
Braun, 328
Breyer's, C-342
Bridgestone Corporation, 246
Bridgestone/Firestone, 116
Bright House Networks, 238
British Aerospace, 267
British Airways, 217, 420, C-182
British Petroleum (BP), 422
British Sky Broadcasting, 228
British Telecommunications, 295, 357
Broadcom, 391, C-79
BRW, C-82
BTR, 324
Bucyrus Erie, C-243
Bucyrus International, Inc., C-254
Burger King, C-343
Burghy, 299
Business for Innovative Climate Change and
    Energy Policy Coalition, C-354
Business Roundtable, 356
Business 2.0, C-77

C

Cadillac, 207
California Pizza Kitchen, C-258
Callaway Golf Company, 168, C-30, C-35, C-36,
    C-37, C-38, C-39, C-44, C-45, C-46, C-48,
    C-49, C-50, C-284
    financial performance, C-43
    net sales, C-43
    products, C-40–C-42

Calphalon, 310
Canadian Hockey League, C-282
Canadian Solar, case, C-189–C-210
    business model, C-205–C-209
    company history, C-204–C-205
    competitors, C-201–C-203
    development projects, C-208
    and feed-in tariff program, C-189, C-193,
        C-198, C-204
    financial performance, C-190–C-191,
        C-208–C-209
    in global solar industry, C-193–C-197
    government support schemes, C-193–C-196
    growth 2004–2008, C-189
    initial public offering, C-205
    international strategy changes, C-210
    inverted vertical integration, C-205
    joint venture programs, C-189
    low barriers to entry, C-199
    marketing by, C-208
    market share, C-200
    photovoltaic cells, C-192–C-193
    players in global market, C-197–C-204
    production facilities, C-206–C-207
    products, C-206
    sales offices worldwide, C-205, C-207–C-208
    and solar energy, C-190
    venture capital funding, C-205
Canon, 386, C-79
Capital Securities, C-178
CareerJunction, C-3
Carlsberg, C-231, C-237
Carphone Warehouse, C-62
Carrabba's Italian Grill, C-333
Carrefour, 115, 116, 167, C-62
Carrier, 334
Casesa Shapiro Group LLC, C-305
Castrol, 261, 269
Caterpillar, 79, 362, 416, C-239, C-243, C-254
    strategic vision, 73
Cathay Pacific Airways, C-180, C-182, C-185
Cathay United Bank, C-181
CBS network, 199
Cementia, C-215
Cementos Bayano, C-219
Cementos Bio Bio, C-217, C-219
Cementos del Pacifico, C-217, C-219
Cementos Diamente SA, C-217, C-218
Cementos Guadalajara, C-212
Cementos Hidalgo, C-212, C-215
Cementos Maya, C-212
Cementos Mexicanos, C-212, C-215
Cementos Nacionales, C-217, C-218
Cementos Portland Monterrey, C-212
Cementos Samper, C-217
Cementos Tolteca, C-215
Cemex, case, C-212–C-226
    bank negotiations, C-225, C-226
    branding, C-221–C-222
    cash flow decline, C-224
    customer satisfaction, C-221–C-222
    debt burden 2009, C-212
    debt increase, C-224
    diversification, C-212
    e-business strategy, C-213
    financial performance 1993–2007,
        C-224–C-225
    financial rations, C-225

globalization
   through acquisitions, C-216–C-220
   and cash crunch, C-222–C-226
   moves 1906–2008, C-215
   post-merger integration, C-220–C-222
growth by acquisition, C-212
growth efforts, C-220
human capital development, C-221
and immigrants to U.S., C-214
information technology at, C-212–C-213,
   C-221
joint ventures, C-214–C-216
major acquisitions, C-217–C-218
marketing by, C-213–C-214
net income decline, C-226
and North American Free Trade Agreement,
   C-214
problems in Venezuela, C-225
Rugby+ brand, C-222
stock price performance, C-226
value creation, C-223
CEMIG, 362
Cenqua, C-87
Ceridian Corporation, 338
Cerveceria Modelo S.A., C-229
Cessna, 309
Chanel, 127, 194, 275
Chattaronga Safaris, C-372–C-373
Cheetos, C-24
Chevrolet Volt, 367
Chevron, 94, 392, C-200
Chevy's Mexican Restaurants, C-258
Chicago Tribune, 56
Chik-Fil-A, 365
Chinaairlines.com, C-180
China Airlines Ltd., case, C-172–C-186
   company history, C-173
   crashes 1970–2001, C-176–C-177
   and cross-strait relations, C-183–C-184
   financial performance, C-174
   frequent disasters, C-175–C-178
   future prospects, C-186
   image restoration, C-172–C-173
   international routes, C-175
   losses in 2008, C-179
   loss of international contracts, C-173
   low-cost threat, C-179
   low maintenance standards, C-177–C-178
   mounting problems, C-172
   opinions of analysts on, C-185–C-186
   ownership, C-172
   rebranding, C-174
   relations with mainland China, C-173
   revenue growth 2004–2009, C-185
   revenues in 1993, C-174
   revival efforts
      benefits of, C-184–C-185
      business model, C-180
      code sharing agreement, C-183
      Dynasty Flyer Plan, C-181, C-182
      e-ticketing, C-181–C-182
      human resources policies, C-180–C-181
      maintenance plan, C-182–C-183
      promotion, C-181
      recruitment procedures, C-180
      reorganization, C-183
      simplified fleet, C-179–C-180
      training program, C180–C-181

sales in 2009, C-172
strained political relations, C-178–C-179
Taiwan-China relations, C-178–C-179
China Aviation Development Foundation,
   C-172, C-174
China Cargo Airlines, C-184
China Eastern Airlines Corporation Limited,
   C-173, C-182
China Southern Airlines Company Limited,
   C-173, C-182, C-184
China Unicom, C-168
Chopin Vodka, 167
Chrome browser, C-150
Chrysler Corporation, 229, 239, 259, C-317,
   C-322
Chunghwa Post Company, C-184
Ciba Vision, 418
Cirque du Soleil, 219
Cisco-Nokia-Siemens alliance, 267
Cisco Systems, 228, 237, 244, 267, 274, 328, 362,
   382, 384, 448, C-53, C-64, C-79, C-87,
   C-168
Citigroup, 324, 347, C-225, C-226
Citizen Holding Company, 302
Classic Sports Network, 335
Clear Channel Communications, 239
   mergers and acquisitions, 230
Clear Channel Worldwide, 229
Clearwire, 238
Cleveland Golf, C-38, C-47
CNET, C-80
CNNMoney.com, C-101
CNW Marketing Research, Inc., C-322
Coach, 232, 236
Cobra Golf, 168, C-37, C-38, C-41, C-49, C-50
   products, C-46–C-48
Coca-Cola Company, 51, 145, 196, 228, 229,
   358, 362, 363, 367, C-17–C-29, C-232,
   C-235, C-258, C-266, C-267, C-377
   alternative beverages, C-26
   company history, C-378
   financial performance, C-27
   overseas brands, C-26
   sales and brands, C-25–C-26
Coca-Cola India, case, C-377–C-393
   awards and recognitions, C-392
   company background, C-378–C-380
   corporate social responsibility
      awards for, C-377
      community development initiatives, C-387
      in corporate agenda, C-377–C-378
      criticisms of, C-378, C-382, C-389–C-390
      early initiatives, C-379–C-380
      economic responsibility initiatives, C-388
      environmental responsibility initiatives,
         C-381–C-387
      funding of, C-393
      Global Community Watershed Program,
         C-385
      model, C-379
      recent initiatives, C-392–C-393
      response to criticism, C-391
      water conservation goals, C-383
      water sustainability initiatives, C-384
   establishment of, C-377
   five pillar growth strategy, C-388–C-389
   in Indian soft drink market, C-380–C-381
   manifesto, C-393

market difficulty, C-380–C-381
outlook for future, C-392–C-393
revenue growth, C-380
Coleco, C-104
Colgate-Palmolive, 235
Comcast Corporation, 238
Compania Valencia, C-217, C-218
Compaq Computer, C-61, C-64, C-72
   acquired by Hewlett-Packard, C-73–C-74
   global market share, C-127
   market share, C-52
   U.S. market share, C-127
CompUSA, C-54
Computer Sciences Corporation, market share,
   C-77
Conair Corporation, 305
Concha y Toro, 289
Concord Music Group, C-342
Confederation of Indian Industry, C-384
Conservation International, C-352
Consumer Union, C-318
Continental Airlines, 239, 430, C-183
Continental Tires, 116
Coors, 117
Corning, 302
Corona beer; see Grupo Modelo case
Costco Wholesale, 203, C-54, C-344
Countrywide Financial Corporation, 450
Courts, C-63
Courtyard by Marriott, C-301
Courvoisier, 309
Cracker Jack, C-24, C-258
Craftsman, 109
Cray, 386
Creative, C-130
Credit Suisse, 416
Crowne Plaza, C-301
CSI Solar Manufacturing, C-204
CSI Solar Technologies, C-204
CSREurope, 360
Ctrip, defense against rivals, 285
CTS Corporation, C-318
Cummins, C-243, C-248
Cutter & Buck, C-410
CVS Pharmacies, 201, C-344
CxNetworks, C-213
Czech Airlines, C-182

D

Daimler AG, 79, 229, 237, 239, 388
Daimler-Benz Aerospace, 267
DaimlerChrysler, 237, 266
D'Angelo Sandwich Shops, C-258
Danone Group, C-258
Dassler Brothers Shoe Factory, C-271
Datafactory AG, C-109
DeBeers Group, 230, 299
Deer Park Refinery, 237
Dell Direct Store kiosks, C-62
Dell Inc., 94, 121, 188, 197, 214, 236, 239, 286,
   304, 349, 382–384, 392, C-108, C-132,
   C-399, C-400, C-410
   in China, 282–283
   competition with Apple, C-128–C-129
   global market share, C-127
   impact of financial crisis, C-129

Dell Inc.—*Cont.*
  revenues 2008–2010, C-130
  U.S. market share, C-127
Dell Inc., case, C-51–C-80
  acquisitions 2007–2008, C-67–C-68
  advertising, C-70
  average revenue per unit sold, C-66
  business model, C-57–C-71
  company background, C-55–C-57
  cost reductions, C-70–C-71
  customer service and support
    for large companies, C-68–C-69
    listening to customers, C-69
    number of service centers, C-66–C-67
    online product reviews, C-69
    premier pages, C-67
    product design services, C-67
  customer service and support
    value added services, C-67–C-68
  direct sales approach, C-53–C-54
  early business concept, C-51
  financial performance, C-55
  future prospects, C-77–C-80
  geographic area performance, C-56
  and information technology marketplace,
    C-71–C-72
  just-in-time system, C-60–C-61
  loss of global leadership, C-51
  low-cost leader, C-54
  market share
    trends in PCs and servers, C-65
    United States, C-52
    worldwide, C-52
  new product categories, C-53
  new products, C-63–C-66
  number of employees, C-54
  principal competitors, C-79
  research and development, C-69–C-70
  revenue by product category, C-65
  revenues in 2008, C-54
  rivalry with Hewlett-Packard, C-73–C-77
  sale of factories, C-80
  sales and marketing
    customer-based sales, C-61–C-62
    direct sales, C-61–C-62
    retail store sales, C-62–C-63
    website strategy, C-61
  and server technology, C-51
  strategy
    build-to-order, C-58–C-61
    main tenets, C-57
    ongoing assembly improvements, C-58–C-60
    quality control, C-60
    supplier partnerships, C-60
    value chain activities, C-59
  unbranded PCs, C-70
  worldwide sales, C-79
Deloitte Asia, C-205
Deloitte Technology, C-82
Delta Air Lines, 239, C-183, C-206
DePuy International, 343
Deutsche Bank, 227, C-189, C-208–C-209
DHL, 420
Diamonds.com, C-138
Dick's Sporting Goods, C-45
Diesel, C-281
Digg, C-14
Digital Equipment Corporation, C-73

Dillard's, 127
DISH Network, C-136, C-150
Disney Automation, 239
Disney Channel, 335
Disney Cruise Line, 335
Disneyland Paris, 272
Disney Radio, 335
Disney Store chain, 335
Dollar Rent-a-Car, 228
Dollar Thrifty, 228
Domino's Pizza, 203
Doosan Infracore Company, Ltd., C-254
Doritos, C-24
DoubleClick, C-147
Dresser Industries, C-245, C-246, C-248
Dreyer's Grand Ice Cream, C-342
DSGi, C-62
Ducati Motorcycles, 194, 197, 232, 255, 401
Dumukwa, C-373
Dunkin' Donuts, 56
Du Pont Corporation, 416
Duracell, 305, 328
Duyvis, C-258

E

E. & J. Gallo Winery, 391
Earthwatch Institute, C-354
East Side Marino's, C-258
eBay, 56, 201, 421, 448, C-37, C-61
Eclipse, C-113
EContent, C-82
Eddie Bauer, C-410
Edmunds.com, C-319
Edwin Watts, C-40
Electronic Arts, 146
Electronic Data Systems, 286, 382, C-56, C-79
  market share, C-77
eMachines, C-130
EMagic, C-167
EMC, C-53, C-79
Emerge Logistics, 284
Emerson Electric, 304, 416
Energy Brands, C-17
Enron Corporation, 91, 347, 348–349, 351–352,
  450
Enterasys, C-79
Entergy Corporation, 436
Epson, 60, C-79
EqualLogic, C-68
Ericsson, C-161
Ernst & Young, 364, C-81, C-82
ESPN, 335
ESPN2, 335
Etap Hotels, 205
Ethos Water, C-343
Ethos Water Fund, C-354
European Aeronautic Defense and Space
  Company, 267
European Photovoltaic Industry Association,
  C-193
EVA Airways, C-179, C-182
Everdream Corporation, C-67–C-68
Expedia, 239, 285
Exxon, C-213
ExxonMobil, 261
EzTravel, 285

F

Facebook, 201, C-71, C-151
FAI, C-246
Fannie Mae, 89
  failure of corporate governance, 90–91
Federal Express, 57, 75, 167, 194, 219, 403, 416,
  420, 442, C-92, C-212
Feedburner, C-12
FEMSA, C-232
  competitor for Grupo Modelo, C-234–C-235
Fendi, 127
Ferrari, 202, 203, 255
Fiat, 259
Fiat-Chrysler, 229
Finance Week, C-3
Firefox, C-150
First Solar, C-200, C-201, C-210
Flat Earth, C-264–C-265
Fleming's Prime Steakhouse & Wine Bar, 334
Flickr, C-13, C-14, C-151
Flight International, C-177
Focus Media, 286
Folgers, 305
FootJoy, 309, C-46
Ford Motor Company, 207, 218, 229, 259, 281,
  388, C-305–C-306, C-318
Formosa Airlines, C-174, C-177
Formule1 Hotels, 205
Forrester Research, C-71
Fortune Brands, 309, C-38, C-46, C-47
  financial summary, C-48
Four Seasons Hotels and Resorts, 57
Fox Chase Cancer Center, C-92
Foxconn Group, C-80
Foxconn Precision Components, C-102
Fox network, 199, 228, 331
Fox News, 228
Fox Sports, 228
Fox Studios, 228
FOXTEL, 228
Freddie Mac, 89
  failure of corporate governance, 90–91
Frito-Lay Company, 442, C-256, C-267, C-268,
  C-270
Frito-Lay North America, C-259, C-270
  description, C-261–C-265
  financial data, C-263–C-264
Fujikura, C-39
Fujitsu, market share, C-77
Fujitsu-Siemens, C-72, C-79
Fuji-Xerox, 162
FX, 228

G

Gambrinus Inc., C-232
Gamesa, C-258
Gap Inc., 127, C-399
Garmin Ltd., C-110, C-112, C-114, C-118,
  C-119, C-120
Garner, 334
Gartner Research, C-71, C-77
Garuda Indonesia Airlines, C-183
Gateway Computer, C-51, C-61, C-72, C-130
  market share, C-52

Gatorade, C-21, C-22, C-24, C-25, C-258, C-268, C-270
Gatorpeeps, C-3, C-5
Gebrüder Dassler Schuhfabrik, C-271
GEM Australia, C-86
Genentech, 239
General Electric, 82, 89, 155, 292, 309, 311, 312, 352, 362, 367, 382, 413–414, 416, 417, 425, 438, 455, 457, C-48, C-62, C-200, C-399
  corporate culture, 353–354
  talent development, 383–384
General Electric Capital, 309
General Electric Capital Mortgage, 416
General Electric Healthcare, 331
General Electric Leadership Development Center, 383
General Mills, 148, 302, 358, C-261, C-269
General Motors, 207, 218, 259, 267, 287, 386, 388, 395, 449, C-248, C-308, C-317, C-318, C-319–C-320, C-321, C-322
  joint venture with Toyota, C-306
Giant Mistake, C-14
Gilbey's gin, 309
Gillette Company, 60, 305, 328
Gintech Energy, C-199, C-200, C-203
Giorgio Armani, 334
Glaceau, 228
GlaxoSmithKline, 357, C-29
Global Crossing, 91
Global Reporting Initiative, 361
Global Software Group, C-167
Godiva Chocolates, 54, 202
Goldman Sachs, 382, C-278
Golfcraft, Inc., C-46
Gome, C-63
Good Humor, C-342
Good Technology, C-167
Goodyear, 116, 232
Google AdSense, C-144–C-147
Google AdWords, C-144
Google Android, C-149
Google Earth, C-138
Google Inc., 51, 216, 238, 382, 384, 416–417, 438, 448, 460, C-61, C-82, C-92, C-119, C-122, C-131, C-162, C-164, C-165, C-167
  corporate culture, 439
  motivation and rewards at, 426
  in navigation market, C-120
  smartphone ranking, C-134
Google Inc., case, C-136–C-154
  alliances, C-136
  Android launch, C-136
  balance sheets, C-146
  business ethics, C-154
  business model
    AdSense, C-144–C-147
    AdWords, C-144
    search appliance, C-144
  company history, C-137–C-138
  competitors, C-136
  corporate philosophy, C-139–C-140
  features and additions 2006–2010, C-138
  financial performance, C-145
  growth strategies, C-136–C-137
  initial public offering in 2004, C-138
  Internet rivals

    Microsoft, C-152–C-153
    Yahoo!, C-151–C-152
  overseas problems, C-137, C-154
  performance in 2010, C-154
  revenues by region, C-148
  revenues in 2009, C-136
  revenue sources, C-147
  search engine market share, C-151
  services and tools, C-141–C-143
  smartphone market share, C-149
  stock price performance, C-140–C-141
  strategies
    to control desktop, C-149–C-150
    for Internet advertising, C-147–C-148
    market for smartphones, C-148–C-149
    TV initiatives, C-150–C-151
Google Maps, C-113, C-138, C-154
Google Maps Navigator, C-120
Google News, C-3
Google Reader, C-12
Google Street View, C-154
Google TV, C-136
Go2Web20.net, C-12
Grabble, C-3
Grand Mercure Hotels, 205
Graphite Designs, C-39
Green Bay Packers, C-24
Green Mountain Coffee Roasters, 364
Greenpeace, 73
Grupo Bimbo, 158
Grupo Modelo, case, C-228–C-237
  and beer market, C-230–C-231
  company history, C-229
  competition from FEMSA, C-234–C-235
  competition from Heineken, C-236
  competitive position, C-228–C-230
  entry into U.S. market, C-229
  expansion abroad
    competitive distribution channels, C-232–C-233
    early success, C-232
    marketing, C-233
  financial performance, C-237
  globalization, C-229–C-230
  key world markets, C-231–C-232
  Mexican peso problem, C-235
  and North American Free Trade Agreement, C-230, C-235
  21st century challenges, C-233–C-236
    future, C-236–C-237
    as global player, C-235–C-236
    remaining Mexican leader, C-234–C-235
Gucci, 127, 194
Guinness Peat Group Plc., C-254
Gujarat Ambuja Cements, C-216
Guodian Power Development, C-208

H

H. J. Heinz Company, 117
Häagen-Dazs, 202
Haier, 192, 211–212
Hainan Airlines, C-182
Hallmark, 413
Hamilton Sundstrand, 334
Handy Dan Home Improvement, 217
Hanomag, C-246

Hansen Natural Corporation, C-17, C-23, C-27–C-28, C-266
  alternative beverages, C-27
  competition with Red Bull, C-28
  financial performance, C-28
  outsourcing by, C-28
  product line in 2910, C-28
  sales and profits, C-27
Hanson Trust, 310
Harley-Davidson, 166, 232, 300
Harris Corporation, 408
Hartman Productions, C-3
HealthSouth, 347, 349, 450
Heat Music Record Label, C-342
Heineken, C-228, C-230, C-231, C-233, C-234, C-236, C-237
Helena Rubinstein, 334
Hero Group, 289
Hershey Foods, C-261
Hertz Rent-A-Car, 228
Hess Corporation, C-70
Hewlett-Packard, 60, 76, 236, 239, 286, 328, 410, C-51, C-62, C-64, C-65, C-69, C-70, C-72, C-78, C-79, C-108, C-132, C-150, C-400, C-410
  acquisition of Compaq, C-73–C-74
  in China, C-74
  competition with Apple, C-128
  financial performance, C-75
  global market share, C-127
  information technology services, C-77
  management change, C-74–C-75
  management change 2005, C-74
  market share, C-52, C-77
    information technology, C-77
    personal computer, C-79
    by product category, C-79
  net revenues, C-128
  revenue and profits 2005, C-74
  rivalry with Dell, C-73–C-77
  sales decline 2008–2009, C-128
  stock price increase, C-75
  strategy, C-75–C-77
  U.S. market share, C-127
  value chain, C-59
Hillenbrand, 217
Hilton Hotels Corporation, 79, 93, 261, 264, C-301, C-341
HiMart, C-63
Hindalco, 286
Hindustan Coca-Cola Beverages Pvt. Ltd., C-377
Hitachi, C-79
Hitachi Construction Machinery Company, Ltd., C-254
Holcim, C-214, C-216, C-220, C-225
Holiday Inn, C-301
Hollinger International, 450
Home Depot, 187, 212, 217, 283–284, 358, C-110, C-398
Hometel, 201
Honda Motor Company, 109, 194, 207, 222, 252, 276, 386, 408, C-318, C-321, C-322
Honeywell International, 374
Hontu, C-63
Horizon Airlines, C-341
Hotmail, 225
HSBC Holdings, 324, C-205, C-225, C-226

HTC, C-122, C-132, C-136, C-149
Huaxin Cement Company Ltd., C-216
Hudson's Bay Company, C-411
Hugo Boss, 392
Huiyuan Juice Group, 229
Hulu, 239
Hyatt Hotels Corporation, C-301, C-341
Hyundai Heavy Industries, 51, 57
Hyundai Motor Company, C-317, C-318,
     C-321, C-322

I

iBlog, C-11
IBM, 182, 235, 236, 239, 286, 362, 421, C-53,
     C-69, C-70, C-72, C-73, C-79, C-123, C-400
     market share, C-77
IBM Japan, Ltd., C-252
IHS Global Insight, C-322
iJol, C-11
IKEA, 51, 64, 167, 194, 214, 370
iLab, C-3
Il Giornale Coffee Company, C-331–C-332, C-333
INA-Holding Schaeffler KG, C-252
InBev, C-231, C-237
Independent Online, C-2
Indian Association of Plastic Manufacturers,
     C-386
Indian Red Cross, C-387
Inditex, 232
Information Resources Inc., C-261
Infosys Technologies, 286
ING Insurance, 194, 392
Innovative Beverage Group, C-24
Inside the USGA, C-47
In-Stat, C-104
Insurance Institute for Highway Safety, C-318
Intel Corporation, 94, 113, 238, 239, 362, 382,
     460, C-60–C-61, C-134, C-136, C-150
Intellisync Corporation, C-167
Interbrew, C-230, C-231
InterContinental Hotel Group, C-301
Interface, C-2
International Coffee Partnership, C-341–C-342
International Council of Industries, C-113
International Council of Toy Industries, C-409
International Crops Research for the Semi-Arid
     Tropics, C-384
International Data Corporation, C-71
International Harvester, C-243
International Paper Company, 232
International (Star Alliance), C-183
Internet Explorer, C-150
Internet Security Systems, 267
Internet World Statistics, C-9
Intertek Group PLC, C-410
iRiver, C-130
iTunes Store, C-135
Izze, C-258

J

J. D. Power & Associates, 207, C-118, C-317
     Initial Quality Study, C-321
J. D. Power Asia Pacific, 283
Jafco Ventures, C-205

Jaguar, 207, 229
Jani-King International, 264
Japan Airlines (JAL), 261, 392, C-182
JA Solar, C-199, C-200, C-203
Jiffy Lube International, 56–57
Jim Beam Brands, 309, C-343
JM Family Enterprises, 426
John Deere, 109, 358
     corporate social responsibility, 359–360
John F. Welch Leadership Development Center,
     383
John Reuter, Jr., C-46
Johnson & Johnson, 56, 194, 328, 343, 357,
     362, 460
     managing diversification, 329
     product lines, 334
Jollibee Foods, 286
Just Coffee, 158, 175–176
     value chain, 160

K

Kaiser Permanente, 421
Karsten Manufacturing, C-48
Kellogg's, 281, C-261, C-269
Kentucky Fried Chicken, 80, 113, 264, 272, 282,
     392, C-257
Kenwood, C-113
Keyhole, C-138
Kia Motors, C-321
Kiehl's, 334
KillerStartups.com, C-12
KLM Royal Dutch Airlines, 266, 362, C-182
Kmart, 57, 127
Koch Industries, 68
Kohl's, 127
Komatsu, case, C-239–C-254
     versus Caterpillar, C-239, C-254
     change in geographic mix, C-250
     company restructuring, C-248–C-249
     core values and principles, C-250
     diversification, C-244
     domestic and export phase 1964–1982,
         C-243
     domestic focus 1921–1964, C-240–C-243
     economic turmoil 1985–86, C-243
     in financial crisis of 2008, C-239, C-251
     financial performance, C-251–C-252
     geographic expansion, C-247–C-248
     global growth efforts, C-249–C-250
     globalization 1995–2007, C-247–C-249
     internal restructuring, C-248
     internationalization, C-243–C-245
     and Japan's multinational problems,
         C-239–C-240
     joint venture, C-245
     management change, C-245, C-250,
         C-251
     market share, C-249
     new management plan, C-251–C-252
     organizational and leadership capability,
         C-250
     overseas production, C-243–C-244
     price increases, C-244–C-245
     problems in China, C-253
     product diversification, C-248
     product line, C-241–C-242

regionalization and localization,
     C-245–C-247
     sales by region, C-253
     stock price performance, C-239
     strategic alliance, C-246–C-247
     strategic priorities, C-243
Komatsu America International Company,
     C-246
Komatsu Asia & Pacific Pte Ltd, C-247
Komatsu Dresser, C-250
Komatsu Europe International SA, C-246
Komatsu Forest AB, C-249
Komatsu Forklift Company, C-249
Komatsu Trading International, C-245
Koos Development Corporation, C-173
Korean Air, C-183
Kraft Foods, 227, C-261, C-342, C-343, C-345
Krating Daeng, C-26
Kreditanstalt für Wiederaufbau, C-193
Kroger, 116, 191, C-344
Kruger National Park, C-361–C-376
     animal rights activists, C-375
     income from animal capture, C-362–C-363
     justification to sell wildlife, C-375
     park services, C-363–C-364
     poaching problem, C-370–C-378
     rhino capturing, C-364–C-370
     sales transactions, C-363
Kunical, C-204
Kyocera, C-199, C-200, C-202

L

L. L. Bean, C-411
Ladies Professional Golf Association, C-35
Lafarge, C-215–C-216, C-220–C-221
Lancôme, 334
Land Rover, 229
L&T Komatsu Limited, C-248
La Roche–Posay, 334
Larsen & Tonbro Ltd., C-248
Latin American Foods, C-270
Lay's Potato Chips, C-24
LDK, C-204
Lenovo, 286, C-62, C-150
Lenovo/IBM, C-51
     global market share, C-127
     market share, C-52
     value chain, C-59
Lenox, 310
Levelor, 310
Levi Strauss & Company, 73, C-411
Lexmark, 60, C-65, C-79
LG (Lucky Goldstar), C-122, C-136, C-169
     market share, C-133, C-152
LGT Asset Management, 338
Lifetime channel, 335
Lincoln automobile, 207
Lincoln Electric Company, 149, 222
     motivation and rewards at, 426
Lipton Iced Tea, C-24
Lipton Tea, 364, C-343
Living Essentials, C-17, C-23
Liz Claiborne, Inc., 460, C-410
Logitech, C-136, C-150
Long John Silver's, 80, 282
L'Oréal, 302, 334, 403

Lotus Connections, 421
Louis Vuitton, 167
Lowe's, 212, 239
Lucent Technologies, 344
Lucky snacks, C-258
Lufthansa, 94, 420
Lufthansa Technik, C-181
Luoyang Zhong Gui, C-204
LVMH, 299

M

Macy's, Inc., 127
Macy's Merchandising Group, C-411
Magellan, C-112
Magnavox, C-104
Mahindra and Mahindra, 283
Mail & Guardian Online, C-2
Major League Baseball, C-282
Mandarin Airlines, C-173
Mandarin Oriental Hotels, C-296
Mannesmann Demag AG, C-247
Maple Leaf Foods, 230
MapQuest, C-113
Mark's Work Wearhouse, C-411
Marriott Host International, C-339
Marriott Hotels, 158, 261, C-301
Marriott International, 365, 456
Marsh & McLennan, 450
Maruti-Suzuki, 281
Marvel Comics, 301
Mary Kay Cosmetics, 68
Maserati, 255
Master Foods, C-261
Mavic, C-276, C-277
Maybelline, 334
Mayo Clinic, 73
McAfee, 57
McDonald's Corporation, 51, 53, 64, 75, 113,
    252, 263, 264, 272, 281, 283, 286, 299, 357,
    392, 410, 456, 458, C-345, C-412
  company objectives, 80
  strategy, 55–56
McKinsey & Company, 382, 425
Media24, C-2, C-3
Mercantec, 267
Mercedes-Benz, 56, 194, 207, 229
Mercure Hotels, 205
Merrill Lynch, 229, 299, C-276
MessageOne Inc., C-68
Metro AG, 115, 395
Mexx chain, 460
MGallery resorts, 205
MGM, C-105
Michelin, 116, 194, 252
Microsoft Corporation, 51, 65, 74–75, 113, 226,
    228, 239, 267, 357, 370, 382, 408, 442,
    C-102, C-108, C-120, C-122, C-130, C-132,
    C-136, C-150, C-151, C-162, C-165, C-166,
    C-168
  company objectives, 80
  competition with Red Hat, 61
  financial performance, C-153
  revenues, C-163
  smartphone ranking, C-134, C-153
Microsoft Exchange, C-131
Microsoft Office, 194, 198

Microsoft Online Services, competitor for
    Google, C-152–C-153
Microsoft TV Internet Protocol Television,
    228
Microsoft Windows, 148
Microsoft Windows Mobile, C-149
Microsoft Xbox, 217, C-95, C-96, C-100, C-103,
    C-104, C-105–C-106
Mighty Ducks NHL franchise, 335
MIH Print Africa (Pty) Ltd., C-8
Miller Brewing, C-228, C-231
MillerCoors, C-24
Minute Maid, 228, C-26, C-267
Mr. Rooter, 113
MiTac Digital Corporation, C-112
Mitsubishi, 266, C-200, C-243
Modular Mining Systems, Inc., C-247
Moen faucets, 309
Molson Coors, C-237
Monitor Consulting, 96, 182
Motech, C-199, C-200, C-203
Motel 6, 205
Motobecane, 201
Motorola, 285, 416, C-132, C-158, C-160,
    C-165, C-167, C-259, C-399
  revenues, C-163
Motorola Global Software Group, C-168
Mountain Dew, C-24
Mozilla, C-150
MSN, C-2, C-152
MS Society, C-92
Mug root beer, C-258
Muti, C-11
MWEB, C-2
MyBroadcast.co.za, C-2
MyGenius, C-11
Myopia Hunt Club, C-47
MySpace, 239, C-71, C-147

N

Naked Juice, C-258
Naspers Limited, C-8
National Breast Cancer Foundation, C-92
National Cash Register Systems, C-74
National Golf Foundation, C-37
National Hockey League, 214, C-282
National Semiconductor, C-123
National Tyre Services, 324
Navigon, C-112
Navteq, C-110–C-112
NBC network, 199, 331
Neiman Marcus, 127, 128
Neoris, C-213
Nestlé, 146, 202, 227, 252, 370, C-258, C-399
  differentiation strategy, 204–205
Nestlé Research Center, 74
Netflix, C-105, C-136, C-150
Netvibes, C-12
Networked Storage Company, C-68
Nevada Bob's, C-40
New Balance, C-271, C-281
Newell Company, 388
Newell Rubbermaid, 310
NewsCorp, 228, 232, 250
New United Motor Manufacturing Inc., C-306
NeXT, C-123

Nextar, C-112
Nextel, 229, 238
Nickent Golf, C-39
Nielsen Online, C-2
Nike, Inc., 73, 86, 361, 366, 382, 391, C-271,
    C-274, C-275, C-276, C-278, C-280–C-281,
    C-411
  audit grades for supplier factories, C-405
  audits of supplier factories, C-404
  compliance rating system, C-403
  corrective actions for suppliers,
      C-404–C-406
  non-negotiable changes ordered, C-406
  supplier code of conduct and compliance
      monitoring program, C-400–C-406
  system for monitoring contract
      manufacturers, C-400–C-402
Nike Golf, C-36, C-37, C-38, C-39, C-45, C-46
  products, C-49–C-50
Nikki, 261
Ningbo Beifa Group, C-396–C-397
Nintendo, 51, 75, 246
Nintendo, case, C-95–C-106
  balance sheets, C-99
  battle for market supremacy, C-95
  company history, C-96–C-97
  competitors, C-102–C-106
  counterattack against, C-96
  handheld game systems, C-97–C-98
  income statements, C-98
  production for, C-102
  sales by 2009, C-97
  sales of Wii, C-102
  strategy for Wii, C-95–C-96
  video game consoles, C-99–C-102
Nintendo DS, C-98
Nintendo Entertainment System, C-96, C-99,
    C-100, C-104
Nintendo Game Boy, C-97–C-98
Nintendo GameCube, C-99, C-100, C-104
Nintendo 64, C-99, C-100, C-104
Nintendo Wii, 217, 246, C-95–C-96,
    C-100–C-102, C-104
Nissan Motor Company, 82, 239, C-318,
    C-321
Nokia, 75, 239, 252, 285, 362, 416, C-108,
    C-112, C-119, C-122, C-132, C-136, C-158,
    C-160, C-161, C-164, C-165, C-167, C-168,
    C-169
  market share, C-133
  revenues, C-163
Nokia Research Center, C-168
Nokia Siemens Networks, 267
Nordstrom, 127, 134, 410, 438, 442, C-410
  motivation and rewards at, 426
Nortel, C-79
North American Coffee Partnership, C-341
Northrup Grumman Corporation, 267
Northwest Airlines, 239, 266
Northwest Water, 414
Norwest Corporation, 228
Novartis, 362
Novotel, 205, C-182
NPD Group, C-131
NTT Communications, 267, 295
Nucor Steel Corporation, 167, 188, 190, 430,
    453
  incentives and strategy, 429

O

Oakland Raiders, C-24
Ocean Spray, C-258
Odwalla, 228
Officeworks, C-63
Okamoto Associates Inc., C-250
Online Publishers Association, C-2, C-13
Ontario Hydro, C-204
Ontario Power Generation, C-204
On2 Technologies, C-150
Opera browser, C-150
Oppenheimer, C-209
Oracle Corporation, 229, 267, C-87, C-166
Orascom Cement, C-216
Orbitz, 239
Orkut, C-147
OSI Restaurants, 333–334
Otis Elevator, 272, 334, 421
Otsuka Pharmaceutical, C-29
Outback Steakhouse, 333
Owens Corning, 416
Oxxo, C-235

P

Pacific Gas & Electric, 363
Packard Bell, C-130
Palm, C-132, C-149
    revenues, C-163
    smartphone ranking, C-134
Palm Pro, C-112
Palmtop, C-108, C-109
Palm Treo, C-160
Panasonic, C-161, C-200
Pandora, 239
Papa John's Pizza, 203
Parmalat, 347, 450
Partek Forest AB, C-249
Patagonia, 366, C-410, C-411
PC Magazine, C-70
PCs Ltd., C-53
PC World, C-70
Peet's Coffee and Tea, C-327, C-328, C-330,
    C-333, C-334
Pemex, 237, 347
Penelopa, C-258
Pennzoil, 261
Pepperidge Farm, 232
PepsiCo, 145, 186, 187, 196, 329, 362, 363, 367,
    382, 436, C-341, C-343, C-345, C-378,
    C-381
    alternative beverages, C-25
    financial performance, C-25
    sales and brands, C-24–C-25
PepsiCo, case, C-255–C-270
    acquisitions after 2001, C-258–C-259
    acquisitions 1980s–1990s, C-258
    balance sheets 2005–2007, C-260
    brands, C-262–C-263
    building shareholder value, C-259–C-270
    business units, C-259–C-269
        financial data, C-263–C-264
        Frito-Lay North America, C-261–C-265
        PepsiCo Beverage North America,
            C-265–C-267

PepsiCo International, C-267–C-269
        Quaker Foods North America, C-269
    carbonated soft drink business, C-266
    company history, C-256–C-259
    diversification strategy, C-255–C-270
    financial performance 1998–2007, C-256
    focus of strategy, C-258
    income statements 2006–2007, C-259
    international beverage sales, C-267–C-268
    international sales growth, C-255–C-256
    International sales/long-lived assets, C-269
    international snack food sales, C-268–C-269
    market share
        versus competitors, C-261
        snack foods, C-268
        soft drinks, C-267
    new organizational structure, C-256
    new product innovations, C-255
    noncarbonated soft drink brands, C-266–C-267
    portfolio in 2008, C-258
    Quaker Oats acquisition, C-258
    stock price performance, C-257
    strategic fit, C-270
    strategy diversification 2008, C-259
    strategy realignment 2008, C-270
    value chain activities, C-270
PepsiCo Americas Foods, C-270
PepsiCo Beverages North America, C-270
    carbonated soft drinks, C-266
    description, C-265–C-267
    financial data, C-263–C-264
    market share, C-265
    noncarbonated soft brands, C-266–C-267
PepsiCo International, C-270
    beverage sales in international markets,
        C-267–C-268
    description, C-267–C-270
    financial data, C-263–C-264
    international sales of Quaker Oats, C-269
    snack food sales in International markets,
        C-268–C-269
Pepsi-Gemex SA de CV, C-268
Perrigo Company, 201
Pets.com, 224
Pfizer, Inc., 150
PGA European Tour, C-35
PGA Magazine, C-36
PGA Tour, C-34, C-39, C-284
Philips Electronics, 416
Pillsbury, 148, 302
Ping Golf, 168, C-30, C-37, C-38, C-44, C-50
    founding of, C-48
    products, C-48–C-49
Pioneer, C-113
Pirelli, 116
Pizza Hut, 80, 113, 263–264, 282, C-257
PlayStation Store, C-105
Polaris Institute, C-390
Polo/Ralph Lauren, 127
Pontofrio, C-62
Porsche, 203, C-321
Powerade, C-21
Power Information Network, C-317
Practiv, 292
Prada, 197
Pratt & Whitney, 334
Price Club, C-54
Procermex Inc., C-232

Procter & Gamble, 51, 75, 188, 227, 304, 305,
    328, 360, 362, 382, C-261
    supplier to Walmart, 191
Professional Golfers Association, C-34
Proxim, C-79
PSA Peugeot Citroen, C-318
Psion, C-108–C-109
Puerto Rican Cement Company, C-218
Pullman resorts, 205
Puma, 366, C-410
Puma Schuhfabrik Rudolph Dassler, C-271,
    C-274

Q

Q-Cells, C-199, C-200, C-203
Quaker Foods North America, C-261, C-270
    financial data, C-263–C-264
Quaker Oats Company, C-24, C-255, C-267
    acquired by PepsiCo, C-258
    brands, C-262–C-263
    international sales, C-269
Quaker Oats North America, C-269
Quaker State, 261
Qualserve Benchmarking Clearinghouse, 164
Qwest Communications, 91, 450

R

Radisson Hotels, 113, C-341
Rainforest Alliance Certified Farms, 364
Ralph Lauren, 127, 197, 232, 334, C-37
ReadWriteWeb, C-6, C-12, C-13, C-82
Red Bull GmbH, 194, 201, C-17–C-29, C-266
    company history, C-26
    energy drinks, C-26
    product line, C-27
    sponsorship of events, C-26–C-27
Red Cross, C-92
Red Hat, 60, C-137
    competition with Microsoft, 61
Redhook Ale Brewery, C-328
Redland, C-216
Reebok International, C-271, C-276, C-280,
    C-281, C-285, C-410
    acquired by Adidas, C-277–C-278
    description, C-282–C-284
Refco, 450
Regent Hotels, C-301
Renaissance Hotels, C-301
Renault SA, C-110, C-111, C-318
Research in Motion, C-122, C-132, C-148, C-149
    market share, C-133
    smartphone ranking, C-134
Research in Motion, case, C-156–C-169
    annual revenues, C-157
    BlackBerry wireless platform, C-158
    company background, C-156–C-158
    competing platforms, C-161–C-162
    competitive research and development, C-163
    competitors worldwide, C-167–C-168
    consumer market, C-158
    and emerging market dynamics, C-168
    evolution of product line, C-160
    geographic expansion, C-166

globalization challenge, C-169
going global, C-167–C-169
increased acquisitions, C-166–C-167
intellectual property rights, C-163
licensing program, C-158
managing growth, C-165–C-169
organizational culture, C-164
organizational development, C-164–C-165
planning for growth, C-169
recruiting strategy, C-165–C-166
research and development, C-162–C-164
research and development spending, C-156
search for talent, C-164–C-165
smartphones, C-158–C-161
source code protection, C-168–C-169
statement of operations, C-157
subscriber base, C-157
and wireless carriers, C-158
wireless communications market, C-158–C-161
workforce growth 2000–2007, C-164
Reuters.com, C-147
Rinker Materials Corporation, C-215, C-219,
    C-222, C-223
Rio Tinto, 94
Rite-Aid, 201, 347, 450
Ritz-Carlton Hotels, 57, 167, C-301
Rizal Cement Company, C-217, C-218
RMC, C-215, C-218, C-219
Robin Hood, case, C-286–C-287
Roche AG, 362
Rockstar, Inc., C-17
Rogers, C-158
Rolex, 56, 128, 194, 197, 275, C-37
Rolls-Royce, 197, 202
Ronald McDonald House, 357
Roto-Rooter, 264
Royal Bank of Scotland, 324, C-225, C-226
Royal Dutch Shell, 76, 347, 352, 365
mission and core values, 77–78
Roy's Restaurant, 334
Rubbermaid, 388
Rugby+, C-222
Russell Corporation, C-410
Ryanair, 167, 217

S

SABMiller, C-230, C-231, C-237
Sabra, C-258
SAB (South Africa Breweries), C-231
Safari browser, C-150
Safety Research & Strategies, Inc., C-322
Safeway, 191, 201, C-344
SAIC-GM-Wulung Automotive Company, 267
SAIC (Shanghai Automotive Industrial
    Corporation), 267
Saks Fifth Avenue, 127, 128, 158
SalesForce Products, C-82
Salomon SA, C-44, C-271
acquired by Adidas, C-276
divested by Adidas, C-277
Sam's Club, 203, C-54
Samsonite, 232
Samsung Electronics, 75, 239, 243, 274, 285,
    362, C-122, C-158, C-162, C-169
market share, C-133
strategic vision, 73

Samsung Group, 243
Samuel Adams, 231
SanDisk, C-130
Sandora, C-258
Sanson, C-216, C-217
Sany Heavy Industry Company, Ltd., C-254
Sanyo, C-199, C-200, C-202
SAP, 414
Saraburi Cement Company, C-218
Satyam Computer Services, 286
Saxon Athletic Manufacturing, C-285
Scancem Industries Ltd., C-217, C-218
Schneiders, 230
Scottish & Newcastle, C-231, C-237
Scotty Cameron, 309
SDTimes, C-82
Sears, 127
Seattle's Best Coffee, C-343
Seek, C-91
Sega Dreamcast, C-103, C-104
Sega Genesis, C-104
Sega Saturn, C-100, C-104
Semen Gresik, C-217, C-218
7-Eleven Stores, 113, 264
7UP International, C-258
Shanda, 284
Shanghai Corporate Responsibility
    Management & Consulting Company,
    C-396–C-397
Shangri-La Academy, C-297–C-298
Shangri-La Asia Ltd., C-292, C-293
Shangri-La Hotels and Resorts, case,
    C-288–C-302
balance sheet, C-293
business philosophy, C-298–C-299
career growth, C-299–C-300
company background, C-288–C-293
compensation plan, C-299–C-300
competitors, C-301
delegation of authority, C-296–C-297
expansion history, C-289–C-291
expansion in China, C-301–C-302
expansion in West, C-302
financial performance, C-291–C-293
future of, C-302
growth 1996–2006, C-288
income statement, C-292
mission statement, C-296
occupancy rate statistics, C-294–C-295
organizational culture, C-293–C-296
organizational design, C-296–C-297
pressure on wages, C-301–C-302
training program, C-297–C-298
workforce retention, C-299–C-300
Sharp, C-199, C-200, C-201
Sharpie, 310
Shell Oil Company, 75, 237, 261
Sheraton Hotels, 261, C-301, C-341
Shu Uemura, 334
Siemens AG, 79, 267, 343, 416, 450, C-162
Sierra Club, C-92
Sikorsky, 334
SilverBack Technologies Inc., C-68
Singapore Airlines, 178, 420, C-180, C-182,
    C-185
Sky Deutschland, 228
Sky Italia, 228
Sky News, 198

SkyTeam, C-184
Skytrax Research, C-184
Slangsoft, C-166–C-167
Smart cars, 229
Smartfood, C-258
Smith International, Inc., C-254
Smith's Crisps, C-258
Smith's Snackfood Company, C-258
Smucker's, 304
Snapper, 109
SoBe, C-17, C-21, C-24, C-25, C-255, C-258,
    C-261–C-262, C-265–C-266
Sofitel, 205
Soft Warehouse Superstores, C-54
Solar World, C-199, C-200, C-202, C-204
Sony Corporation, 74, 239, 301, 362, C-72,
    C-79, C-95, C-102, C-108, C-130, C-136
value chain, C-59
Sony Ericsson, C-133, C-158, C-160, C-161,
    C-164, C-165, C-169
Sony PlayStation, C-100
Sony PlayStation home, C-105
Sony PlayStation Portable, C-97
Sony PlayStation 3, 217, C-95, C-96, C-102,
    C-104–C-105, C-106
Sony PlayStation 2, C-103, C-104
South African National Parks, case, C-361–C-376
and animal rights activists, C-375
conservation biologists, C-376
Environmental Crimes Unit, C-374
game capture unit, C-364
income from captures, C-362–C-363
justification for animal sales, C-375
poaching problem, C-370–C-375
rhino capturing, C-364–C-368
rhino hunting, C-368–C-370
rhino population, C-362
safari companies, C-370–C-374
tour operations, C-362
Veterinary Wildlife Services, C-363–C-364,
    C-365–C-367
Southdown Inc., C-215, C-218, C-219
Southwest Airlines, 51, 56, 163, 188, 190, 382,
    420, 443
Spheral Solar, C-204
Sphinx Search, C-7
Sprint, 229, 238
St. Jude Children's Research Hospital, 351
Stacy's, C-258
Standard and Poor's, 368
Stanford Financial Group, 349, 450
investment fraud, 350–351
Stanford International Bank, 350–351
Staples, 361, 367, C-54, C-62, C-396
STAR, 283
Starbucks Corporation, 56, 82, 86, 196, 219,
    358, 367, 399, 456, C-411
Starbucks Corporation, case, C-326–C-360
advertising, C-345–C-346
business plan, C-333
coffee purchasing strategy
environmental sustainability, C-352
Fair Trade Labeling, C-352
key elements, C-350
pricing, C-350–C-352
company background, C-326–C-332
company-operated stores, C-340
consumer products group, C-345

Starbucks Corporation, case—*Cont.*
  core values, C-349–C-350, C-351
  corporate social responsibility, C-353–C-354
  expansion strategies
    acquisitions, C-342–C-344
    hub cities, C-339
    international expansion, C-339–C-341
    licensed retail stores, C-339
    licensing, C-341–C-343
    new offerings, C-342–C-344
    partnerships, C-341–C-343
  financial performance 2005–2009, C-335
  financing in 1980s, C-331–C-332
  and Howard Schultz, C-328–C-332
  human resources practices
    fringe benefits, C-348
    health care coverage, C-346–C-347
    stock option plan, C-347
    stock purchase plan, C-347
    training and recognition, C-348–C-349
    workplace environment, C-347–C-348
  and Il Giornale Coffee Co., C-331–C-332
  international locations, C-340
  layoffs, C-326
  LEED certified construction, C-353
  long-term vision, C-359
  management changes, C-355
  market expansion in 1980s, C-333–C-334
  mission statement, C-350, C-351
  number of stores worldwide, C-326
  operating statistics 2006–2009, C-327
  operations, C-352–C-353
  as private company, C-332–C-334
  prospects, C-357–C-360
  quarterly sales trends, C-359
  sales decline in 2009, C-326
  stock price performance, C-336
  store ambience, C-337–C-339
  store closings, C-326
  store design, C-336–C-337
  transformation agenda, C-355–C-357
  venture capital, C-334
  vertical integration, C-346
Starbucks Digital Network, C-337
Starbucks Foundation, C-353, C-354
Star Foods, C-258
Stihl, 212
Stokely–Van Camp, C-258
Strategic Planning Institute, 163
Strauss Group, C-258
Summers Group, 324
SunChips, C-258
Sundaram Fasteners, 286–287
Suning, C-63
Sun Microsystems, 229, 267, C-69, C-79, C-137
SunPower, C-199, C-200, C-202, C-210
Suntech, C-199, C-200, C-201, C-210
Suntory, C-342
Super Nintendo Entertainment System, C-99,
  C-100, C-104
SuperSport Zone, C-2
Suzuki, 283
Suzuki Motor Corporation, C-318, C-321
Swiss Wafers, C-204
Symbian, C-161, C-167, C-169
Symbian Academy, C-166
Synaptix (Pty) Ltd., C-3

Syndication Products, C-12–C-13
Sysco Corporation, C-341

T

T. C. Pharmaceutical, C-26
T. J. Maxx, 127
Taco Bell, 80, 264, 282
Taco Teas, C-342–C-343, C-344
Taipei Airline Association, C-178
Taiwan Semiconductor, 391
Tandem Computer, C-73
Target Stores, 57, 127, 157, 305, C-110, C-344,
  C-400
Tasali Snack Foods, C-258
Tata Motors, 94, 229
Tata Nano, 267
TATA SKY, 228
Tata Teleservices, C-169
TaylorMade-adidas Golf, C-277, C-278, C-285
  description, C-284
  financial performance, C-245
  products, C-44–C-46
TaylorMade Golf, C-30, C-37, C-38, C-39, C-41,
  C-47, C-48, C-49, C-50, C-271, C-278,
  C-284
Techmeme, C-6, C-12
Technorati, Inc., C-3, C-12
Telcel, 214
Tele Atlas, C-107, C-108, C-109–C-110, C-111,
  C-112, C-116, C-117, C-118, C-119
Televisa, 286
Telmex, 214
Tencent, 285
Terex Corporation Company, Ltd., C-254
Tesco, 115, 395, C-62
Tesla Motors, 239
Tesler Roadster, 367
Textron, 309
Textronics, C-285
TGW.com, C-40
Thai Airways, C-183
Thalassa sea & spa resorts, 205
Therma-Tru, 309
Thomson Reuters, C-173
3Com, C-79
3M Corporation, 150, 151, 167, 194, 362,
  417–418, 457
Thrifty Rent-a-Car, 228
Tiffany & Company, 157, 197, 230, 256, 275
Timberland, C-411
Time Warner, 331
Time Warner Cable, 238
Timex, 128
Titleist, 309, C-36, C-37, C-38, C-45, C-49, C-50
  products, C-46–C-48
T.J. Maxx, 127
T-Mobile USA, C-337
Toluca y Mexico Brewery, C-229
TomTom, case, C-107–C-120
  acquisition of Tele Atlas, C-107
  business concept, C-107
  company history, C-108–C-110
  competition for
    new types, C-112–C-113
    traditional, C-112

  competition from Google, C-120
  cost reductions, C-119
  customers, C-110
  finance
    objectives, C-114–C-115
    sales revenue and net income, C-115–C-116
  globalization problems, C-114
  human resources practices, C-119
  issues of concern for, C-119–C-120
  marketing by, C-116–C-118
  mergers and acquisitions, C-110–C-111
  operations, C-118–C-119
  potential adverse legislation, C-113–C-114
  product line, C-108
  resources and capabilities
    automotive partnerships, C-111–C-112
    digital mapping technology, C-111
    routing algorithms, C-111
  revenue growth, C-107
  vision and focus, C-107–C-108
  workforce, C-107
Toon Disney, 335
Top-Flite Golf, C-41
Toro, 109
Toshiba Corporation, 239, 436, C-51, C-72, C-79
  global market share, C-127
  market share, C-52
  U.S. market share, C-127
  value chain, C-59
Toyoda Automatic Loom Works Ltd., C-305
Toyota Motor Corporation, 163, 192, 206, 217,
  218, 239, 364, 386, 426, C-399
  best-cost provider strategy, 207
  joint venture with General Motors, C-306
  production system, 387–388
Toyota Motor Corporation, case, C-304–C-323;
  see also Toyota Production System
  company guidelines, C-314–C-316
  company history, C-305–C-309
  core values, C-307
  in financial crisis of 2008, C-309
  global expansion spree 2007, C-317
  global quality task force, C-323
  income statement, C-310–C-311
  milestones, C-308
  models affected by recalls, C-319
  net loss in 2010, C-323
  new strategy in 2002, C-307–C-309
  outlook for future, C-323
  outsourcing, C-320
  production, sales, and exports 2008, C-309
  public relations campaign 2010, C-323
  quality management, C-309–C-313
  quality principle, C-305
  quality problems, C-316–C-322
  reasons for problems, C-319–C-320
  recalls 2003–2007, C-317
  recalls of 2010, C-304
  reputation since 1937, C-304–C-305
  sales in 2008, C-318
Toyota Motor Manufacturing North America,
  C-207
Toyota Motor Manufacturing Turkey, C-207
Toyota Prius, 197
Toyota Production System, C-305, C-306, C-315
  jidoka (self-regulation) system, C-312–C-313
  just-in-time systems, C-312

kaizen (continuous improvement), C-313
kanban (signboard) system, C-312
  outline of, C-314
  for quality management, C-309–C-314
Trader Joe's, 202
Travelocity, 239, 285
Trina Solar, C-199, C-200, C-202
Tropicana, C-24, C-258, C-268, C-270
True Love Magazine, C-3
Tupperware, 457
Twentieth Century Fox, 228, 232
Twentieth Century Fox Licensing &
  Merchandising, C-111
Twitter, C-13, C-14
Tyco International, 347, 348, 450
Tyson Foods, 367

U

UBS, strategic vision, 73
UBS Securities Japan Ltd., C-321
Ukrop's Super Markets, 427
UNICEF, C-92
Unifreight India Pvt., 403
Unilever, 151, 227, 281–282, 363–364, C-342,
  C-343, C-345
United Airlines, 239, C-180, C-341
United-Continental merger, 226
United Parcel Service, 79, 420
United Parcel Service Store, 264
United States Golf Association, C-38, C-47
United Technologies, 334
uPlay, C-42
Upton RTD, C-268
US Airways, C-182
USA Today, C-70
US Foodservice, C-341
US Global Quality Research System, C-318
UST, C-39
UTC Fire & Security, 334
UTC Power, 334

V

Van Munching & Company, C-236
Vector Products, 305
Vencemos, C-215, C-217, C-218
VentureBeat, C-12
Verio, 267

Verizon Wireless, C-149, C-158
VF Corporation, C-411
Viacom, 331
Vichy Laboratories, 334
Vietnam Airlines, C-183
Virgin Mobile, C-169
Vivendi Universal Entertainment, 331
Vizio, Inc., 201
  low-cost strategy, 203
Vodafone, 392
Volkswagen, 259, 388, 416, C-318, C-321, C-322
Vottle, C-11

W

W. L. Gore, 202, 456
  motivation and rewards at, 427
Wachovia Bank, 229
Walgreens, 201
Walker's Crisps, C-258
Wall Street Journal, C-70
Walmart, 51, 54, 55, 56, 57, 115, 116, 127–128,
  149, 157, 188, 189, 190–192, 201, 203, 216,
  217, 252, 305, 358, 395, 438, 453, 455, 456,
  C-54, C-62, C-110, C-111, C-131, C-261,
  C-344, C-396–C-397, C-400, C-412
  and audit fatigue of suppliers, C-407–C-410
  compliance rating system, C-407
  factory audit methodology, C-408
  factory audit results, C-409
  Global Procurement Services Group,
    C-410–C-411
  Procter & Gamble as supplier to, 191
  supplier auditing program, C-407
  supplier code of conduct and compliance
    monitoring program, C-406–C-410
Walt Disney Company, 57, 272, 276, 292, 301,
  331, 456, C-105, C-412
  businesses owned by, 335
Weather Channel, 57
Wegmans, motivation and rewards at, 426
Wells Fargo & Company, 228–229, 364, C-341
Westin Hotels, C-341
Whirlpool Corporation, 275, 277, 392, 416
  Six Sigma at, 417
Whole Foods Market, 365
Wikipedia, C-153
William Morris Agency, C-342
Wingate Inn, C-301
Woolworth's, 115, C-396

WorldCom, 91, 349, 450
World Environment Foundation, C-390
World Net Daily, C-176
Worldvision, C-92
World Wildlife Fund, C-389
Wulung, 267
Wyndham Hotel Group, C-301

X

XCMG Construction Machinery Company,
  Ltd., C-254
Xerox Corporation, 162–163, 297, 416, C-54

Y

Yahoo!, C-12, C-61, C-153
  competitor for Google, C-151–C-152
  financial performance, C-152
Yahoo! Autos, C-151
Yahoo! Games, C-151
Yahoo! Mail, C-151
Yahoo! Maps, C-113
Yahoo! Messenger, C-151
Yahoo! Music, C-151
Yahoo! Personals, C-151
Yahoo! Real Estate, C-151
Yahoo! Travel, C-151
Yamaha, 301
Yingli Green Energy, C-199, C-200, C-201
Yola, C-11
YouTube, 203, C-6, C-13, C-14, C-136, C-147,
  C-150
Yum! Brands, 263–264, 281
  in China, 282
  company objectives, 80

Z

Zara, 225, 232
Zingeli Safaris, C-368, C-374
Zipcar Inc., 220
Zoho, C-12
Zoopy, C-11

NAME INDEX

A

Aaronson, Susan Ariel, 372
Abkowitz, Alysa, 351
Adams, Gary, C-44
Adamy, Janet, 56
Agle, Bradley R., 372
Ahlstrand, Bruce, 95
Ahuja, G., 336
Alexander, Marcus, 292, 336
Ambrosio, Chris, C-170
Ambroz, Milan, 433
Amelio, Gil, C-123
Amit, R., 179
Amsden, Davida M., 433
Amsden, Robert T., 433
Anand, J., 290
Anslinger, Patricia L., 336
Antony, Jiju, 433
Anzaki, Satoru, C-247
Appleby, Stuart, C-41
Argandoña, Antonio, 371
Arnold, David J., 291
Ascari, Alessio, 433
Ash, Mary Kay, 68
Asthana, Mansi, C-107
Athvale, R. N., C-391
Aulakh, P., 291

B

Badaracco, Joseph L., 461
Bai, Jim, C-210
Bailey, Wendy J., 371
Bain, J. S., 135
Baldwin, Jerry, C-326–C-327, C-328, C-329, C-330, C-331, C-332
Bamford, James, 248
Band, David C., 434
Bandler, James, 351
Bannister, Judith, C-412
Bareilles, Sara, 239
Barkema, H., 336, 405
Barney, Jay B., 179, 461
Barrett, Amy, 329
Barringer, Bruce, 95
Barthélemy, Jérôme, 248, 405
Bartlett, Christopher A., 179, 248, 291, 404, 405, 462, C-254
Bassat, Andrew, C-91
Basu, Kumal, 338
Baum, J., 405
Beamish, Paul W., C-189, C-238
Beauchamp, T. L., 371
Beckett, Ron, 433

Beckham, David, C-276, C-281
Beckhard, Richard, 405
Benner, Katie, 351
Bensinger, Ken, C-324, C-325
Bergen, Mark E., 179, 248
Bettcher, Kim Eric, 372
Beveridge, John, C-227
Bezos, Jeff, 224, 423, 455
Bhattacharya, Arindam K., 285, 291
Biedenbarn, Joseph A., C-378
Birchall, David W., 180
Birinyi, Laszlo, 96
Black, J. Stewart, C-239, C-254
Blakely, Rhys, C-106
Blank, Arthur, 217
Bleeke, Joel, 248, 291
Bluedorn, Allen C., 95
Blum, Justin, 351
Bogan, Christopher E., 433
Bommer, Fred, C-46
Bontis, Nick, 180
Boosie, Lil, C-24
Bossidy, Larry, 374, 404, 462
Bower, Joseph L., 248
Bowie, N. E., 371
Bowker, Gordon, C-327, C-328, C-329, C-330, C-331, C-332
Boyink, Jeffrey L., 384
Bradley, W. C., C-378
Brady, D., 384
Bridle, Symon, C-288, C-296–C-297, C-299, C-301–C-302
Brightman, James, C-106
Brin, Sergey, 439, C-137, C-138, C-154
Brinkman, Johannes, 372
Briscoe, Jason, 433
Brohan, Mark, 224
Bromley, Philip, 95
Brown, David, 372
Brown, Robert, 95
Brown, Shona L., 66
Brugmann, Jeb, 372
Brush, T., 336
Bryant, Kobe, C-276
Bryce, David J., 247
Buckley, P. J., 290
Bunkley, Nick, C-324
Burcher, Peter, 433
Burke, Doris, 351
Burke, Ronald J., 433
Burnah, Philip, 405, 434
Burns, Lawton R., 433
Burrell, Gary, C-112
Burrows, Peter, C-80
Burshstein, Sam, C-81
Burton, R. M., 405
Byrne, John, 404
Byrnes, N., 429

C

Caliguiri, Paula M., 434
Calkins, Laurel Brubaker, 351
Callaway, Ely Reeves, Jr., C-40–C-41
Calloway, Wayne, C-257
Cameron, Scotty, C-47
Camp, Robert C., 180
Campbell, Andrew, 292, 336, 405
Campbell, Denis, C-288
Candler, Griggs, C-378
Cannella, A., 336
Cannon-Brookes, Mike, C-81–C-85, C-88, C-90, C-91–C-94
Capron, L., 290, 404
Carasco, Emily F., 461
Carpenter, Mason A., C-254
Carroll, Archie B., 372
Carroll, Lewis, 68
Carter, John C., 462
Carty, Sharon Silke, C-325
Carver, John, 95
Cavanagh, Roland H., 433
Cha, Sandra E., 461
Chadha, A., 291
Champy, James, 213, 433
Chandler, Alfred D., Jr., 405
Chao Kuo-Shui, C-183
Charan, Ram, 374, 404, 462
Chatain, O., 248
Chatham, Jennifer A., 461
Chatterjee, S., 336
Chavez, Hugo Rafael, C-225
Che Yu, C-107
Chen Shui-ban, C-180, C-183
Chen, Bruce, C-184, C-185
Chen, C., 371
Chen, Ming-Jer, 248
Chen, R., 371
Cheney, Glenn, 372
Chittoor, R., 291
Cho, Fujio, C-207
Christensen, Clayton M., 66, 434
Chung, Oscar, C-187, C-188
Clark, Delwyn N., 179, 461
Clark, Robert C., 95
Collins, James C., 95, 374, 404
Collins, John, 214
Collis, David J., 66, 95, 336, 337
Cook, Tim, C-122, C-124
Cooper, Robin, 180
Copeland, Thomas E., 336
Cordon, Carlos, 405
Covin, Jeffrey G., 95, 248
Cowitt, Beth, C-360
Coyne, Kevin P., 248
Creamer, Paula, C-45, C-284

Cristie, James R., 91
Crooks, Ed, C-211
Crosby, Philip, 433
Cucuzza, Thomas G., 180
Cullen, J. B., 248
Cummins, Chip, 372
Cusumano, M. A., 248

D

D'Aveni, Richard, 247
Dalvi, Datta, C-386
Darr, Eric D., 434
Das, Sohini, C-395
Das, T. K., 248
Dash, Eric, 91
Dassler, Adolph "Adi," C-272, C-274
Dassler, Horst, C-274, C-275
Dassler, Rudolph, C-272
Davidson, Hugh, 72, 95
Davidson, Wallace N., 372
Davies, E., 434
Davis, Jim, C-271
Davis, Scott, 248
Dawar, Niroj, 291
Dayton, Nick A., 434
De Taeye, Alain, C-110
De Waal, Mandy, C-15, C-16
Deal, Terrence E, 461
DeCarlo, Scott, 91
Dechant, Kathleen, 372
Delios, A., 290
Dell, Michael, 214, C-51, C-53, C-54–C-57,
    C-60, C-61, C-63, C-64, C-68, C-69, C-70,
    C-77–C-78, C-80
DeLorenzo, Peter, C-322
Derfus, Pamela J., 135
Deshpardé, Rohit, 372
Devinney, Timothy M., 372
Dhanaraj, C., 290
Dhorat, Ismail, C-15, C-16
Dienhart, John W., 355
Diez, Valentin, C-232
DiMicco, Daniel, 429
Dinur, A., 290
Disney, Walt, 374
DJ Screw, C-24
Dogan, Greg, C-293–C-296, C-297, C-299,
    C-302
Dolan, Kerry A., C-227
Donald, Jim, C-355
Donaldson, Gordon, 95
Donaldson, Thomas, 371
Doolin, Elmer, C-256
Dosi, G., 404
Doz, Yves L., 248, 267, 291, 336
Dragonetti, Nicola C., 180
Dranikoff, Lee, 337
Drucker, Peter F., 138, 336, 337
Dulaney, Ken, C-170
Dunfee, Thomas W., 371, 372
Durant, William C., C-324
Dussauge, P., 290, 404
Dutta, Soumitra, 433
Dyer, Jeffrey H., 247, 248, 249, 291

E

Eichenwald, Kurt, 372, 462
Eisenhardt, Kathleen M., 66, 180, 249, 336
Eisenstat, Russell, 179, 404
Eisner, Michael, 292
El-Jelly, Abuzar, 372
Elfenbein, Hillary A., 372
Els, Enrie, C-41
Emerson, Ralph Waldo, 63
Eminem, C-24
Endo, Koji, C-323
Engardio, Pete, C-412
Engen, Travis, C-250
English, Michael J., 433
Enrico, Roger, 436, C-258, C-259
Ernst, David, 248, 291
Evans, M., C-170
Ewalt, David M., C-100

F

Fackler, Martin, C-324
Faheem, Hadiya, C-172, C-377
Fahey, Liam, 248
Farkas, Charles M., 462
Farquhar, Scott, C-81–C-85, C-88, C-90,
    C-91–C-94
Fastow, Andrew, 349–349
Fawcett, Stanley E., 405, 433, 434
Fernandez, Antonino, C-229
Fernandez, Carlos, C-228, C-229, C-230, C-235
Fernandez, Pablo Diez, C-229
Ferratt, Thomas W., 433
Ferrier, W. J., 247
Fiegenbaum, Avi, 136
Filo, David, C-137
Finan, Irial, C-380
Fiorina, Carly, C-73–C-74, C-75
Fisher, Jake, C-318
Flaherty, Francis, C-227
Flint, Jerry, C-254
Florentino, Amy E., 361
Floyd, Steven W., 404
Foley, Michael, C-233, C-236
Foley, Ryan, C-121
Foote, Nathaniel, 179, 404
Forbes, Malcolm, 406
Forrester, Mark, C-4, C-8, C-15
Franklin, Benjamin, 338
Franko, Lawrence G., 336
Fredrickson, James, C-254
Friend, D., C-170
Froese, F., 291
Frost, Tony, 291
Fukuda, Masahiro, C-320
Fuyuno, Ichiko, C-254

G

Galunic, Charles, 336
Gamble, John E., C-17, C-30, C-51, C-122,
    C-136, C-255, C-271

Ganveer, Aakashi, C-107
Garcia, Sergio, C-45, C-284
Gard, Lauren, C-238
Garnett, Kevin, C-281
Garrette, B., 290
Garvin, David A., 95
Gates, Bill, C-152, C-164
Gavetti, G., 213
Geelen, Peter, C-108, C-109
Geissinger, Juergen M., C-250
George, S., 433
George-Cosh, D., C-170
Ger, Guitz, 291
Geroski, Paul A., 248
Gerstner, Lou, 182
Ghemawat, Pankaj, 291
Ghoshal, Sumantra, 179, 248, 291, 404, 405, 462
Ghosn, Carlos, 82
Gibbon, Henry, 248
Girard, Richard, C-390
Glaister, K. W., 290
Glass, Kathryn, 351
Glionna, John M., C-325
Glover, J., 336
Goddjin, Harold, C-108–C-109, C-110–C-111
Goeritz, L., 291
Goerzen, Anthony, C-238
Goffee, Robert, 461
Gohring, N., C-170
Goizueta, Roberto, C-266
Golden, Timothy D., 372
Goldsmith, Marshall, 405
Goleman, Daniel, 462
Gonela, Saradhi Kumar, C-212
Goodland, Robert, 372
Goodman, Paul S., 434
Goold, Michael, 292, 336, 405
Goosen, Retief, C-45, C-284
Gordon, Joseph, 433
Gordon, M. Joseph, Jr., 433
Gordon, Mary Ellen, 136
Govindarajan, Vijay, 180
Graham, Jefferson, 427
Grant, R., 404, 405
Greenberg, Duncan, 351
Greenfield, W. M., 371
Gregersen, Hal B., C-254
Greimel, Hans, C-325
Grimm, Curtis M., 135, 247
Gulbis, Natalie, C-45, C-284
Gunnarson, Sarah K., 462
Gunther, Edgar, C-210
Gupta, Nandini Sen, 267

H

Hainer, Herbert, C-276
Hall, Gene, 433
Hall, Kenji, C-106
Hambrick, Donald C., 248, 336
Hamel, Gary, 182, 248, 267, 291, 336, 404
Hamm, Steve, 291
Hammer, Michael, 213, 433
Hammond, Ed, C-227
Hanbing Zhang, C-208

Hannon, Dave, C-325
Hansen, Hubert, C-27
Hanson, Hames, 310
Hanstad, Anne Louise, C-116, C-121
Haq, Husna, C-325
Harden, Blaine, C-325
Hariharan, S., 136
Harrigan, Kathryn R., 248
Harris, Craig, C-106
Harris, John R., C-319
Harrup, Anthony, C-227
Hartman, Justin, C-2–C-4, C-5–C-6, C-11–C-15
Haspeslagh, P., 336
Hayes, Robert H., 138, 404
Hayibor, Sefa, 372
Hayward, M. L. A., 336
Healey, James R., C-325
Hedberg, Carl, C-94
Heeley, Michael B., 248
Heifetz, Ronald A., 462
Heikkiiä, Jussi, 405
Hein, Lester, C-16
Heineman, Ben W., Jr., 354
Helfat, C., 180, 404
Henderson, Jim, C-248
Hendricks, Kevin B., 95
Henke, John W., Jr., C-319
Henriques, Adrian, 372
Herrera, Tilde, 372
Herrero, Gustavo, C-238
Herzberg, Frederick, 406
Heskett, James L., 434, 461, 462
Hess, David, 372
Hesselbein, Frances, 405
Hesseldahl, A., C-170, C-171
Hewlett, Bill, 76
Hill, Ronald Paul, 357
Hills, Jonathan, C-395
Hilmer, F., 405
Hilton, James, C-288
Hilton, Paris, C-158
Hindo, Brian, 433
Hing Lin, C-107
Ho, Jessie, C-187, C-188
Hodgetts, Richard M., 434
Hoffman, Alan N., C-107
Hoffman, Will, C-107
Hofmeyr, Markus, C-361, C-370
Holmes, J. B., C-47
Holpp, Larry, 433
Horn, John, 248
House, Charles H., 95
Hout, Thomas M., 462
Howard, Dwight, C-281
Hubbell, Victoria, 461
Hughes, Jonathan, 248, 249
Hull, G., 405
Humble, John, 461
Hurd, Jonathan, 248
Hurd, Mark, C-74, C-76–C-77
Hyland, Paul, 433

I

Iacobucci, Dawn, 180
Iansiti, Marco, 191
Ignatius, Adi, C-360

Iiguez, Gelacio, C-213
Immelt, Jeffrey, 331, 353, 383, 384
Inkpen, A. C., 248, 290, 291
Iriarte, Braulio, C-229
Isdell, E. Neville, C-379, C-383, C-390
Iverson, Allen, C-282
Ives, Kate, C-394
Iwata, Satoru, C-95, C-98, C-101

J

Jackson, David, 461
Jacobsen, Kristine, 179
James II of Scotland, C-30
James III of Scotland, C-30
James IV of Scotland, C-30
James VI of Scotland, C-30
James VII of Scotland, C-30
Jassawalla, Avan R., 461
Jemison, D., 336
Jenk, Justin, 248
Jickling, Mark, 91
Jobs, Steven, 82, C-122–C-124, C-135
John, Prince of England, C-287
Johnson, J. L., 248
Johnson, Mark W., 66
Jolly, Deepak, C-391, C-393
Jolly, Johnny, C-24
Jones, Del, 433
Jones, Gareth, 461
Jones, Kathryn, C-80
Jones, Mike, C-24
Jones, Nick, C-121
Jordan, Michael, C-275
Jung, Andrea, 82
Juran, Joseph M., 433

K

Kageyama, Yuri, C-324, C-325
Kahaner, Larry, 136
Kale, Prashant, 248, 249, 291
Kamprad, Ingvar, 214
Kanazawa, Michael T., 462
Kane, Sean, C-322
Kanter, Rosabeth Moss, 248, 291, 405, 462
Kao, Kin H., C-112
Kaplan, Nancy J., 248
Kaplan, Robert S., 95, 180
Karim, S., 404
Katada, Tetsuya, C-245–C-248
Katila, R., 336
Kaufman, Rhonda, 95
Kaufman, Stephen P., 95
Kaul, Deepak, C-377
Kawai, Ryoichi, C-240, C-243, C-244–C-245
Kawai, Yoshinari, C-240, C-243
Kazari, Brent, C-288
Keeble, Justin, 372
Keith, Jonathan D., 160
Keller, Maryann, C-305
Kennedy, Allan A., 461
Kerr, Steven, 434
Khanna, Tarun, 291
Khayat, Nadine, C-239

Kim, Chan W., C-227
Kim, Jane J., 351
Kim, W. Chan, 66, 95, 138, 248, C-106, C-121
Kimberly, John R., 433
Kini, Venkatesh, C-380, C-381
Kirkpatrick, Marshall, C-6
Kitamura, Makiko, C-325
Knight, Phil, 366
Koch, Charles G., 68
Kogut, B., 290, 404
Kolakowski, Nicholas, 341
Koller, Tim, 337
Komatsu, Tetsuya, C-325
Kotler, Philip P., 248
Kotter, John P., 72, 434, 461, 462
Kournikova, Anna, C-276
Koza, M., 248
Kramer, Mark R., 372
Krebs, Michelle, C-319
Kruger, David, C-254
Kulashekaran, Mukund, 267
Kumar, N., 291
Kuok, Robert, C-288
Kwak, M., 248
Kwak, Mary, 247

L

Lachenauer, Rob, 247, 248
Lakshman, N., C-171
Lampel, Joseph, 66, 95, C-286
Lanzolla, Gianvito, 248
Latner, Sarah, C-238
Latour, Almar, 372
Lau, Lawrence J., C-250
Laurie, Donald L., 462
Lawrence, Anne T., 371
Lawrence, Ron, C-333
Lay, Herman, C-256
Lazaridis, Mike, C-156, C-165, C-169
Learmount, David, C-177
Lee, Hau L., 180
Lee, Louise, C-80
Lee, Terry Nels, 433
Lee, Timothy E., 267
Lemak, David J., 434
Leonard, Wayne, 436
Leonard-Barton, D., 179
Levenson, Georgia, C-254
Levesque, Lynned C., 95
Levicki, C., 405
Levien, Roy, 191
Lewin, A., 248
Libby, Tom, C-317
Lichfield, Gideon, C-227
Lieberthal, K., 291
Liedtka, Jeanne M., 336, 405
Liker, Jeffrey W., C-315, C-322, C-325
Lil' Wayne, C-24
Lil' Wyte, C-24
Linebaugh, Kate, C-324
Ling Woo Liu, C-395
Little, Arthur D., 372
Little, Royal, 309
Logan, Amanda, C-50
Lorsch, Jay W., 95, 462
Louis-Dreyfus, Robert, C-276

Lubatkin, M., 336
Ludacris, C-24
Lyles, M. A., 290
Lynn, B. C., 136

M

Ma Ying-jeou, C-183
Mabunda, David, C-364, C-374
Macalister, Terry, C-211
MacDuffie, John Paul, C-321
MacMillan, Ian C., 248
Madhok, Anoop, 248
Madoff, Bernard L., 349, 350, 354
Madonna, C-158
Maggitti, Patrick G., 135
Magretta, Joan, 66, C-80
Mahajan, Aparna, C-394
Main, Jeremy, 180, 291
Majchrzak, Ann, 433
Maltz, Lawrence, C-333
Malviya, Sagar, C-394
Manning, Eli, C-282
Manning, Peyton, C-282
Mannix, E., 405
Marcus, Bernie, 217
Marcus, Jonathan, C-177
Margolis, Joshua D., 372
Marino, Lou, C-95, C-122
Markides, Constantinos C., 66, 138, 248, 336, 337
Marsh, Peter, C-254
Martin, J., 180
Martin, Karla L., 404
Marx, Matt, 434
Masters, Coco, C-325
Mateschitz, Dietrich, C-26
Mauborgne, Renée, 66, 95, 138, 248, C-106, C-121
Maynard, Micheline, C-324
Mays, Lowry, 230
Mazutis, Daina, C-156
McCawley, Tom, 372
McClellan, S., 439
McCombs, Billy Joe, 230
McGrady, Tracy, C-281
McGrath, Rita Gunther, 248
McIvor, Ronan, 248
McKay, Peter A., C-50
McLaughlin, Andrew, C-154
McLellan, Elisabeth, C-375
McNerney, James, 417–418
McQuillen, Bill, 351
Medina, Hector, C-216, C-221, C-223, C-225
Menkes, Justin, 404
Menor, Larry, 95
Merrett, Neil, C-394
Messi, Lionel, C-281
Messmer, E., C-171
Meyer, K. E., 291
Meyerson, Morton, C-56
Michael, David C., 285, 291
Mickelson, Phil, C-41
Miles, Morgan P., 95
Miles, Robert H., 462
Miller, Claire Cain, C-360
Miller, Danny, 179, 404

Millman, Joel, C-227
Milne, George R., 136
Minder, Raphael, C-227
Ming Zeng, 213
Minoura, Teruyuki, C-313
Mintz, Jenni, 434
Mintzberg, Henry, 66, 95, 338, 405
Mitchell, Jordan, C-189
Mitchell, W., 290, 404
Mixon, William E., C-361
Miyamoto, Shugery, C-101
Mizrahi, Isaac, 57
Mohammad, 344
Mokwa, Michael P., 136
Montgomery, Cynthia A., 66, 95, 136, 179, 336, 337
Montgomery, Joseph C., 434
Moore, Clover, C-82
Moore, Daryl, C-333
Moren, Dan, 341
Morgan, C. David, 80
Morrison, Allen, C-254
Morse, Andrew, 341
Mroz, John Edward, 405
Muller, Joanne, 267, 291
Murdoch, Rupert, 250
Murphy, John, C-325
Murphy, Patrick E., 461
Murray, James, C-210
Mustapha, Aishah, 434
Muzychenko, Olga, C-81

N

Nadler, David A., 95
Nanda, Ashish, C-254
Naoshima, Masayuki, C-304
Natsios, Andrew S., C-385
Naughton, Keith, C-325
Nazareth, Rita, 336
Neilson, Gary L., 404
Nelson, R., 404
Ness, Joseph A., 180
Neuman, Robert P., 433
Nichols, P. M., 372
Nicklaus, Jack, C-30
Nielsen, Bo Bernhard, C-254
Niles-Jolly, Kathryn, 462
Nilsen, Sabina, C-254
Noble, Charles H., 136
Nogawa, Shoji, C-240, C-244
Nohria, Nitin, 462
Noji, Kunio, C-249, C-250
Nooyi, Indra, C-259
Nordhielm, Christie, 180
Norman, Greg, C-271, C-277, C-278, C-282, C-284
Norton, David P., 95

O

Obama, Barack, C-38, C-154, C-196
O'Bannon, Douglas P., 372
Obel, B., 405
Ochoa, Lorena, C-49

Ohinata, Yoshinobu, 433
Ohmae, Kenichi, 96
Ohno, Taiichi, 388, C-305, C-312, C-313
Ohnsman, Alan, C-324, C-325
Okamoto, Yukio, C-250
Okamura, Tadashi, 436
Okuda, Hiroshi, C-207
Olian, Judy D., 434, 462
Olie, R., 291
Olive, David, C-324
Olsen, Dave, C-333
Olsen, E., 405
Olusoga, S. Ade, 136
O'Reilly, Charles A., 433
Oreskovic, Alexei, C-120
O'Rourke, Brian, C-104
Orr, Bernard, C-120
Ortiz, David, C-282
Osegowitsch, Thomas, 248
Ososo, Emi, 388
Oyamburu, Martin, C-229

P

Pablo, E., 291
Page, Larry, 439, C-137, C-138
Pagonis, William G., 406
Paine, Lynn Sharpe, 291, 372, 461
Pak, Jeong Min, C-304
Palepu, Krishna G., 291
Palmer, Arnold, C-30, C-35
Pan, Y. G., 249
Pande, Peter S., 433
Parise, Salvatore, 248
Parlotones, The, C-14
Patterson, Abbe, C-138
Patterson, George, C-30
Patterson, Robert, C-206, C-211
Pauwels, Peter-Frans, C-108, C-109
Peel, Michael, 371
Peet, Alfred, C-327
Pemberton, John Smith, C-378
Perlman, Lawrence, 338
Perry, Dayna, C-164, C-165
Peteraf, Margaret A., 66, 179, 180, 404
Peterson, George, C-323
Petroff, A., C-170
Pettit, A., 290
Pfeffer, Jeffrey, 434, 462
Phoenix, 239
Pisano, Gary P., 138, 180, 248, 404, 405
Player, Gary, C-30
Podolny, Joel, C-227
Porras, Jerry I., 95
Portanger, Erik, 371
Porter, Michael E., 66, 96, 103, 135, 136, 159, 162, 180, 182, 184, 187, 195, 213, 248, 254, 290, 291, 336, 372, 462
Post, James C., 371
Poulter, Ian, C-47
Poutrel, Guillaume, C-228
Powell, Thomas C., 434
Powers, Elizabeth, 404
Prahalad, C. K., 182, 248, 291, 372, 404, 405
Premji, Azim, 50
Pressel, Morgan, C-41

Preston, Lee E., 372
Pretel, Enrique Andres, C-227
Pretorius, Stiaan, C-4, C-8, C-15
Price, Raymond L., 95
Priem, Richard L., 213
Pruthi, S., 291
Purkayastha, Debapratim, C-2, C-172, C-304, C-377
Puterman, Simone, C-15, C-16

Q

Qu, Shawn, C-189, C-204, C-205, C-210
Quelch, John A., 291
Quinn, James Brian, 405, 433, 462
Quittner, Josh, 224
Qumer, Syeda Maseeha, C-2, C-304

R

Raines, Franklin, 90
Ramsey, Mike, C-324
Rao, Ashkay R., 248
Raubitschek, R., 404
Ray, S., 291
Reed, John, 371
Reed, Richard, 66, 434
Reese, Jennifer, C-360
Reid, Joanne, 461
Reinemund, Steve, C-259
Rekhi, Shefali, C-394
Rettig, Cynthia, C-94
Retton, Mark, C-109
Reuer, J. J., 249
Rhoads, Gary K., 405, 434
Ribbink, Alexander, C-109
Richard Lionheart, King, C-287
Richards, David, C-121
Richardson, Sandy, 95
Richter, Christopher, C-321
Ridderstråle, Jonas, 404
Rivkin, Jan, 66
Robert, Daniel, C-120
Robert, Michel, 72, 95
Roberts, Dexter, C-412
Roberts, John, C-227
Roberts, Sarah, 372
Robin Hood, C-286–C-287
Rock, Melinda, 433
Rockwood, K., 291
Rogovsky, Nikolai, 372
Roll, R., 336
Rollins, Kevin, C-57, C-70, C-80
Roman, Ronald M., 372
Romano, B., C-170
Roner, Lisa, C-412
Roos, Goran, 180
Rosenthal, Jim, 433
Rothschild, William E., 248
Rounds, Kate, C-360
Rui, H., 291
Rukstad, Michael G., 66, 95
Russell, JaMarcus, C-24
Rynes, Sara L., 434, 462

S

Sacks, Rodney, C-27
Sadubin, Derek, C-172
Sakane, Masahiro, C-250–C-251
Sakano, T., 248
Samanta, Monjori, C-172
Sanchanta, Mariko, C-324, C-360
Sanders, William Gerard, C-254
Sanyal, Rajib, 371
Sarkar, M. B., 291
Sarrett, Sally, C-95
Sasaki, Shinichi, C-309, C-316
Sashittal, Hemant C., 461
Sasson, Lisa, 248
Satchell, M. J., 371
Sathe, Vijay, 461
Scanlan, Gerald, 434
Schaal, Dennis, 285
Scheck, Justin, C-80
Scheinman, Marc N., C-238
Scherer, F. M., 135
Schermerhorn, John R., 355
Schlosberg, Hilton, C-27
Schmidt, Eric, 416–417, C-120, C-136, C-155
Schneider, Anton, 337
Schneider, Benjamin, 462
Schoemaker, P., 179
Schoonhoven, C. B., 249
Schultz, Howard, 82, C-326, C-328–C-334, C-341, C-346, C-347, C-349, C-353, C-355, C-356, C-357, C-358, C-359, C-360
Schupak, Adam, C-50
Schwartz, Mark S., 371, 461
Schweitzer, Maurice E., C-305, C-323
Sculley, John, C-123
Server, Andy, C-360
Seth, A., 290
Shah, Amit J., 372, C-326
Shank, John K., 180
Shaw, Gordon, 95
Shaw, Warren, 338
Sheldon, Keith, C-248, C-252
Shen-Yuan Lai, C-187
Shielfer, A., 336
Shih, Willy C., 248, 405
Shillingford, J., C-170
Shimizu, Norihiko, 388
Shin, Annys, 91
Shirouzu, Norihiko, C-324
Showdhury, Neel, C-80
Shuen, A., 180
Shunk, Chris, C-325
Simons, Robert, 338, 405, 434
Sims, Ronald R., 372
Singh, Atul, C-377
Singh, Harbir, 248, 249, 291
Sinha, Jayant, 291
Skarpathiotakis, George M., C-228
Slater, S., 405
Slevin, Dennis P., 248
Slim, Carlos, 214
Sloma-Williams, Thomas, C-325
Smith, G., C-238
Smith, Iain, 357
Smith, Ken G., 135, 247
Smith, Kennedy, 433

Smith, N. Craig, 372
Smith, Orin, C-355
Soble, Jonathan, C-254
Solheim, Karsten, C-48
Som, Ashok, C-228
Somerville, Iain, 405
Song, K., 290
Speth, J. G., 372
Spicer, Andrew, 371
Spindler, Michael, C-123
Spinella, Art, C-322
Srivastava, Amit, C-377, C-389, C-390, C-393, C-394, C-395
Stalk, George, Jr., 247, 248
Stanford, R. Allen, 350
Steensma, H. K., 290
Stephen, Allen, C-254
Stephens, Debra, 357
Stevenson, Howard, 434
Stevenson, Mark, C-227
Stone, Reuben E., 180
Stopforth, Mike, C-3, C-8, C-15
Strickland, A. J., C-361
Stroh, Linda K., 434
Stuckey, John, 248
Suarez, Fernando, 248
Sull, Donald, 180
Summers, Lawrence, C-38
Sun Huang-hsiang, C-186
Sundaram, A., 291
Svensson, P., C-170
Swift, Taylor, 239
Syron, Richard, 90–91
Szulanski, Gabriel, 290, 404

T

T. I., C-24
Takahashi, Yoshio, C-324
Takeuchi, Hirotaka, 388
Takeuchi, Maitaro, C-240
Tan Eng-Leong, C-297, C-299, C-300
Tanaka, Masao, C-245
Tay Beng Koon, C-298
Teece, David, 180
Teng, B. S., 248
Tennant, Don, C-80
Thomas, Howard, 136
Thomas, Terry, 355
Thompson, Arthur A., 372, C-51, C-326, C-396
Thomson, Adam, C-227
Thomson, Alan, 461
Three 6 Mafia, C-24
Tovstiga, George, 180
Toyoda, Akio, C-309, C-318, C-319, C-322, C-323
Toyoda, Eiji, C-306, C-311
Toyoda, Kiichiro, C-305, C-306
Toyoda, Sakichi, C-305, C-306
Toyoda, Tatsuro, C-207
Tsao, Bruce, C-177
Tse, D. K., 249
Tsung, Christine Tsai-yi, C-180
Tushman, Michael L., 433
Twer, Doran, 434

U

Uihlien, Wally, C-48
Ungan, Mustafa, 433
Upton, David M., 138, 404
Useem, Michael, C-304

V

Van Heerden, Auret, C-412
Van Marrewijk, Marcel N. A., 372
Van Putten, Alexander B., 248
Varchaver, Nicholas, 351
Vartabedian, Ralph, C-324
Veiga, John F., 372, 434
Vermeulen, F., 336
Vigreux, Corinne, C-108, C-109
Villegas, Camillo, C-47
Vincent, Roger, C-325
Vishny, R., 336
Vivek, M. V., C-212
Vlasic, Bill, C-324
Vogelstein, Fred, 434, 462
Vokey, Bob, C-47

W

Wade, Judy, 433
Wakean, Jason, 248
Walet, Leonora, C-210
Walker, Lee, C-54–C-56
Wally, S., 405
Walsh, J. P., 336
Walston, Stephen L., 433
Walton, M., 433
Walton, Sam, 455
Wambold, Richard, 292
Wang, Qianwei, 433

Watanabe, Katsuke, 387, C-308, C-317, C-320, C-324
Waterman, Robert H., Jr., 250
Waters, J. A., 66
Watson, Gregory H., 180
Webb, Allen P., 461
Weber, J., C-238
Weber, James, 371
Wei Hsiang, C-187, C-188
Wei, Philip, C-172, C-173, C-178–C-179, C-180, C-182, C-184, C-185
Weinberg, S., C-170
Weis, Jeff, 248
Weiss, Eric, 91
Weiss, Jeff, 248, 249
Welch, David, C-325
Welch, Jack, 50, 292, 383, 404, 455
Welch, Suzy, 404
Welford, Richard, C-395
Weller, Christian E., C-50
Wernerfelt, Birger, 136, 179, 336
Wesley, Norm, 309
Wessel, Godecke, 433
West, Kanye, C-24
Wetlaufer, Suzy, 462
White, David, 248
White, Gordon, 310
White, Mike, C-268
White, Rod, C-156
Wiedman, Christine, 95
William IV of England, C-30
Williamson, O., 405
Williamson, Peter J., 138, 213, 336
Wingfield, Nick, 341
Winter, Sidney G., 180, 290, 404
Wolkonowicz, John, C-322
Woodridge, Bill, 404
Woodruff, Ernest, C-378
Woodruff, Robert Winship, C-378
Woods, Tiger, 385, C-34, C-39, C-49, C-50, C-255, C-267

Wormald, Chris, C-162–C-163, C-168
Worrell, Dan L., 372
Worthern, Ben, C-80
Wozniak, Steve, C-122
Wright, M., 291
Wu, Debbie, C-173
Wyatt, Scott, C-110

Y

Yach, David, C-156, C-169
Yamamoto, Yohji, C-281
Yang, Dori Jones, C-360
Yao Ming, C-282
Yeh, Samson, C-176
Yip, George S., 136, 291
Yoffie, David B., 136, 213, 247, 248
Yokoi, Gunpei, C-97
Yokoyama, Hiroyuki, C-320
Yoon, Sangwon, 291
Yoshida, Tatsuo, C-321
Young, Philip, C-46
Young, Vince, C-282
Yoyoda, Shoichiro, C-207

Z

Zalan, Tatiana, C-81
Zambrano, Lorenzo, C-212–C-214, C-219, C-220, C-221
Zander, U., 404
Zbaracki, Mark J., 433
Zemsky, P., 248
Zetsloot, Gerald I. J. M., 372
Zimmerman, Martin, C-318, C-324, C-325
Zollo, M., 180, 249, 404
Zook, Chris, 336

SUBJECT INDEX

A

Abandoned strategy elements, 58–59
Ability, 386
Accounting fraud, 349–351
Acquisition(s), 226; *see also* Mergers and
        acquisitions
    to access resources and capabilities, 296
    to acquire capabilities, 388–389
    by Adidas, C-271, C-276, C-277–C-278
    by Apple Inc., C-167
    by Cemex, C-212, C-216–C-220
    cross-border, 252
    by Dell Inc., C-67–C-68
    for diversification, 296–297
    DoubleClick by Google, C-147
    by local companies, 286
    by Motorola, C-167
    necessitating restructuring, 331
    by Nokia, C-167
    by PepsiCo, C-255, C-256–C-259
    by Research in Motion, C-166–C-167
    by Starbucks, C-332, C-342–C-343
    Tele Atlas by TomTom, C-107
    that fail to deliver, 297
    transaction costs, 296, 299–300
    of undervalued companies, 310
Acquisition strategies, 264
Action agenda, 86–87
Action plan, 52
Activity-based costing, 160
Activity ratios, 143
Adaptive cultures
    accepting change, 447
    dominant traits, 447–448
    examples, 448
Adaptive strategies, 58–59
Advertising
    by Dell Inc., C-70
    Google and Internet, C-147–C-148
    by Grupo Modelo, C-233
    Starbucks, C-345–C-346
Africa, social media in, C-3–C-7, C-9–C-10
Aggressive price-cutting, 193
Airline industry, China Airlines Ltd.,
        C-172–C-186
Airplane crashes, C-175–C-176
Air pollution, 363
Al Qaeda, C-37
Ambidextrous organizations, 418
Analyze, 414
Animal rights activists, C-375
Assets, effects of value chain, 158–160
Athletic footwear industry
    Adidas, C-271–C-285
    main companies, C-271
    market share in U.S., C-281
    sales by Reebok 2002–2004, C-277

Audit committee, 91
Australia
    Atlassian in, C-81–C-93
    ban on China Airlines, C-179
    Cemex in, C-219
    concern over navigation devices, C-114
    entrepreneurial environment, C-86–C-87
    investigation of Google, C-154
    Shangri-La Hotels in, C-302
Authoritarian structure, 397–399
Automobile industry
    bargaining power, 116
    Initial Quality Study rankings, C-321
    recalls by Toyota, C-304, C-317–C-319
    top ten groups, C-318
    Toyota Motor Corporation, C-304–C-323
Automotive partnerships, C-111–C-112
Average collection period, 143
Awards, 424
    to Atlassian, C-82
    to Coca-Cola India, C-392

B

Backward integration
    cost-saving strategy, 231
    definition, 230
    differentiation-based advantage, 232
    to enhance competitiveness, 231–232
    in-house activities, 231–232
    and supplier bargaining power, 115
    threat by buyers, 117
Balanced scorecard
    definition, 79
    examples, 79
    for financial objectives, 78–79
Balance sheet
    Adidas, C-275
    Google Inc., C-146
    Nintendo, C-99
    PepsiCo, C-260
    Shangri-La Asia Ltd., C-293
Banking regulation, 328
Banks, in financial crisis of 2008, 309
Bargaining power; *see also* Buyer bargaining
        power; Supplier bargaining power
    in auto industry, 116
    of companies with suppliers, 187
    of retailers, 116
    of supermarkets, 116
Barriers to entry
    brand preferences, 108
    conditions for, 107
    cost advantage of incumbents, 108
    customer loyalty, 108
    distributor network, 108
    in diversification decisions, 299

economies of scale, 107
high capital requirements, 108
and industry growth rate, 121
learning curve advantage, 107
low in solar energy industry, C-199
network effects, 108
restrictive government policies, 108–109
securing retail space, 108
for start-up companies, 295–296
Barron's, 229
Beer industry, 131
    FEMSA, C-234–C-235
    Grupo Modelo expansion, C-232–C-233
    imports to U.S., C-230
    key world markets, C-231–C-232
    Mexican beer taste tests, C-234
    progressive consolidation, C-230
    top companies, C-231
    world consumption, C-231
    world's top brands, C-228
Beliefs, in corporate culture, 440
Below-market pricing, 279–280
Benchmarking
    for accessing costs of rivals, 163
    for assessing value chain activities, 162–163
    for best practices, 412–413
    capturing full value of, 419–420
    databases for, 412–413
    definition, 162
    and ethics, 164
    to focus on continuous improvement, 456
    inadequate for complete competitive
        situation, 168
    information sources for, 163
    objectives, 162
Best-cost provider strategies, 57
    definition and characteristics, 205–206
    distinguishing features, 208–209, 228–229
    as hybrid, 206
    versus low-cost providers, 206
    market position, 183
    resources and capabilities, 206
    risks, 207–208
    target market, 206
    at Toyota, 207
    when successful, 206
Best practices
    adapted to circumstances, 412
    benchmarking for, 412–413
    capturing full value of, 419–420
    definition, 411
    to focus on continuous improvement, 456
    identifying, 162–163, 411–413
Better-off test, 296
    for unrelated diversification, 307, 308
Beverage industry, C-17–C-29, C-255–C-270
    Asian market share, C-20
    Coca-Cola India, C-377–C-393

competition in, C-17
competitors, C-261
conditions in 2010, C-18–C-24
criticisms of, C-17–C-18
distribution and sales, C-20–C-21
dollar value and volume sales, C-18
European market share, C-20
geographic market share, C-19
global sales, C-19
impact of financial crisis, C-17
India's soft drink market, C-380–C-381
key competitive capabilities, C-22–C-23
leading producers
  Coca-Cola Company, C-25–C-26
  Hansen Natural Corporation, C-27–C-28
  PepsiCo, C-24–C-25
  Red Bull, C-25–C-27
market shares, C-265
number of brands, C-29
origin of Coca-Cola Company, C-378
Pepsi's product line, C-262–C-263
pharmaceutical companies, C-29
recent trends, C-23–C-24
Rockstar, C-29
sales in United States, C-19, C-20
shift in consumer preferences, C-18
suppliers, C-21–C-22
types of drinks, C-17
worldwide growth, C-18–C-19
worldwide market shares, C-21
Big-box discounters, 57
Blogging, C-9–C-11
Blue-ocean strategy
characteristics, 219
examples, 219–220
view of market space, 219
Board of directors
appraisal of company direction and strategy,
  88
audit committee, 91
compensation committee, 89
executive compensation plan, 89
fiduciary duty, 89
inside directors, 91
leadership evaluation, 88–89
negligent, 89
outside directors, 91
oversight of financial accounting and
  reporting, 89–91
qualities for effectiveness, 91
Bottom-of-the Pyramid populations, C-384
Boycotts, 366
Branding, by Cemex, C-221–C-222
Brand loyalty, for first-movers, 222
Brand management activities, 196
Brand names
exploiting common use of, 301
global, 271, 276
Brand preferences, as barrier to entry, 108
Brand recognition, establishing, 108
Brand reputation, in global competition, 261
Brands, 145–146
competing in alternative beverages, C-29
corporate, 309
and customer loyalty, 196
not transferable, 277

top beer brands, C-228
umbrella, 309
Brand switching, rivalry and cost of, 105
Brazil
exchange rates, 258
market growth potential, 286
working conditions, C-397
Bribes
payment of, 342–343
permitted or forbidden, 345
and social contract theory, 346
BRIC countries, share of global revenue, C-240
Brihan Mumbai Municipal Corporation, C-386
Broadly diversified companies, 313
Brutal rivalry, 106–107
Budget-conscious buyers, 206
Budget proposal reviews, 407
Budget reallocation, 408
Build-to-order manufacturing, C-58
Bureau of Labor Statistics, on wages in China,
  C-398
Business base, broadening, 327–328
Business ethics
bribes and kickbacks, 342–343
business case for, 354–355
and child labor, 342
context of generalized ethics, 339–340
and corporate social responsibility, 356–362,
  364–368
cosmetic approach to, 347
definition, 339
and drivers of unethical strategies, 348–352
and ethical relativism, 343–344
failure of suppliers at Apple, 341
Google Inc., C-154
implied social contract, 365
integrated social contracts theory, 345–346
and law, 347
moral case for, 354
and strategy, 346–347
sustainability strategies, 362–368
Business-level strategy
in diversified companies, 293
in multidivisional structure, 396
and scope of the firm, 226
Business model(s)
Afrigator, C-7–C-8
Atlassian, C-81–C-83
Canadian Solar
  development projects, C-208
  financing, C-208–C-209
  inverted flexible vertical integration, C-205
  marketing, C-208
  production facilities, C-206–C-207
  product line, C-206
  recycling program, C-205–C-206
  sales offices, C-207–C-208
China Airlines, C-180
Ctrip in China, 285
customer value proposition, 59
definition, 59
Dell Inc., C-57–C-71
examples, 60
Google Inc., C-138–C-147
for local companies, 284
Microsoft vs. Red Hat, 61

modified for developing countries, 282–283
profit formula, 59–60
relevance of, 60
Shangri-La Hotels, C-293–C-296
and strategy, 59–60
Business process reengineering
capturing full value of, 419–420
description, 413–414
focus on operating excellence, 455–457
Business risk
reduction in, 123
spread in foreign markets, 253
in vertical integration, 233
Business strategy, 83; *see also* Strategies/Strategy
definition, 84
single-business enterprise, 85
Business Traveler, C-288
Business 2.0, C-12
Business units
Adidas, C-278–C-284
cash cows, 323–324
cash hogs, 323–324
competitive strength
  calculating, 317–318
  interpreting scores, 318–319
  nine-cell matrix for portraying, 319–321
divesting, 325
PepsiCo, C-259–C-269
pressure to achieve excellence, 455–457
ranking performance prospects, 325–326
BusinessWeek, C-396, C-407, C-412
Buyer bargaining power
in auto industry, 116
conditions for, 115
determinants, 115–116
discretion to delay purchases, 117–118
factors affecting, 117
few relative to number of sellers, 116
increased by Internet, 122
lacking for individual consumers, 116
and low-cost providers, 192
low switching costs, 116
price sensitivity, 118
product information, 116–117
of retailers, 115–116
from shift in demographics, 121–122
standardized/weak differentiation, 116
of supermarket chains, 116
threat of backward integration, 117
and types of buyers, 118
weak demand, 116
Buyer demographics, 121–122
Buyer expectations, unmet, 223
Buyer patronage, increased, 366
Buyer-related activities, 274–275
Buyers
budget-conscious, 206
lower overall costs, 197
price-conscious, 206
unenthusiastic about differentiation, 200
value-conscious, 206
Buyer's market, 106
Buyer tastes or preferences
cross-border differences, 259–260
flexibility in shifting, 233
reduced risk exposure to, 236

C

Canada
  ban on China Airlines, C-179
  concern over navigation devices, C-114
  investigation of Google, C-154
  solar energy industry, C-196
Capabilities
  added by outsourcing, 392
  adequate for diversification, 325
  aggressive spending on, 191–192
  avoiding overtaxing, 325
  basis of competitive attack, 216
  for best-cost provider strategy, 206
  competitive assets, 141–150
  competitively superior, 149
  competitively valuable, 57
  cross-border sharing, 275–277
  cross-functional, 147
  cutting-edge, 150
  definition, 145
  diverse kinds of expertise, 237
  in diversification decisions, 298–299
  durable value, 150
  dynamic, 150, 385
  hollowing out, 237
  identifying, 137–147
  knowledge-based, 146
  at Komatsu, C-252
  of local companies to compete, 286–287
  needed in vertical integration, 234
  rare, 148
  reason for mergers and acquisitions, 229
  related to functions, 147
  relation to value chain, 167–168
  resource bundles, 147
  specialized vs. generalized, 301–303
  for successful differentiation, 198
  from testing resources, 146–147
  and threat of new entrants, 109
  at TomTom, C-111–C-112
  at Toyota, 387–388
  updating and remodeling, 386
  used in foreign markets, 252–253
Capabilities-based matrix structure, 397
Capabilities-motivated acquisitions, 388–389
Capacity, unused, 106
Capacity-matching problems, 144
Capacity utilization rate, 186–187
Capital, needed for exporting, 262–263
Capital requirements, as barrier to entry, 108
Career growth at Shangri-La Hotels, C-299–C-300
Car navigation devices, C-113
Cash cows, 323–324
  surplus funds from, 325–326
Cash flow
  in diversified company, 323–324
  from operations at PepsiCo, C-261
Cash hogs, 323–324
Causal ambiguity, 149
Cell phones, C-112–C-113; see also Mobile
    phones
  manufacturers, 196
Cement industry
  acquisitions by Cemex, C-212, C-216–C-220
  in financial crisis of 2008, C-222–C-226
  globalization, C-220–C-222
  globalization by major firms, C-215–C-216

Center for Science and Environment, C-378
Centralized decision making
  versus decentralized decision making, 398
  pros and cons, 397–399
CEOs; see also Managers; Top executives
  board of directors evaluation, 88–89
  leading strategy-making, 81–82
Ceremonies, 442
Change
  acceptance of, 447–448
  hostility to, 449
Change-resistant cultures, 448
Channel allies, coordinating with, 196
Channel conflict, 233
Charitable contributions, 357
Child labor, C-399
Child labor, extent of, 342
Child Relief and You, C-387
China
  Canadian Solar in, C-189
  counterfeit merchandise, C-37
  Dell's experience in, 283
  Dell's rivals in, C-62
  export strategies, 263
  factories in, C-396
  Google and censorship in, C-137, C-148,
    C-154
  Hewlett-Packard in, C-74
  hotel market, C-301–C-302
  labor problems, C-253
  largest economy, 281
  largest online travel agency, 285
  low-cost carriers, C-179
  market for rhino horn, C-374
  market growth potential, 286
  market potential, 259–260
  market size, 281
  mobile phone makers, C-167–C-168
  mobile phone users, C-132
  outdoor advertising in, 286
  population, 259, 281
  relations with Taiwan, C-178–C-179,
    C-183–C-184
  Shangri-La Hotels in, C-291–C-292
  solar energy industry, C-196
  and source code protection, C-168–C-169
  wage rates, C-301
  wages and employment in, C-397–C-398
  wireless subscribers, C-161
  working conditions, C-397
  Yum! Brands in, 282
China Learning Center, 384
Chinese Hurun Report, C-288
Civil Aeronautics Administration, C-176
Cloud computing, C-149, C-153
Code of Supplier Conduct, Nike, Inc.,
    C-400–C-402
Codes of ethics, 346–347
Coffee industry, 204–205
Collaboration with external partners, 400–401
Collaborative partnerships, to access
    capabilities, 389
Collateralized debt obligations, 347
Combination related-unrelated diversification,
    313
Combination structure, 396–397
Command-and-control paradigm, 397–399
Communication systems, for low-cost
    providers, 188

Community development initiatives, Coca-Cola
    India
  community commitment, C-387
  education, C-387
  health, C-387
Community involvement, at Starbucks, C-354
Community Watershed Partnership, C-383,
    C-385
Companies; see also Diversified companies
  ambidextrous organizations, 418
  assessing competencies, 151–152, 154
  bargaining with suppliers, 187
  benefits of profit sanctuaries, 277–279
  board responsibilities, 88–91
  business model and strategy, 59–60
  codes of ethics, 346–347
  competitively important resources and
      capabilities, 141–150
  competitiveness of prices and costs,
      156–168
  conclusions from SWOT analysis, 155–156
  conglomerate, 307
  corporate governance, 88–91
  corporate social responsibility strategies,
      358–360
  corrective adjustments, 87–88
  cost drivers, 186–187
  cost-shifting by, 368
  crafting strategy, 81–82
  diverse strategies, 53
  dominating depth, 276
  entry and exit of, 122–123
  future direction, 52
  game plan, 52
  global giants vs. local companies, 284–287
  going on the offensive, 215–216
  how strategy is working, 140–141
  with incompatible subcultures, 450
  internal universities, 389–390
  long-lived success, 51
  low-cost leadership, 185
  macroenvironment, 98–100
  mission statements, 74–75
  nullifying external threats, 150–156
  performance evaluation, 87–88
  present situation, 52
  recognized for triple bottom line, 362
  responsibilities of, 339
  restructuring, 310
  scope of the firm, 84, 225–226
  seizing market opportunities, 150–156
  set apart from rivals, 53
  setting objectives, 76–81
  strategic balance sheet, 152
  strategic intent, 86
  strategic issues to be addressed, 173
  strategic plan, 85–86
  strategic vision, 70–74
  strategies for competitive advantage, 54–57
  strategy execution, 86–87
  strategy-making hierarchy, 82–84
  stronger or weaker than rivals, 168–172
  SWOT analysis, 150–155
  timing of strategies, 221–225
  tradition-steeped, 441
  undervalued, 310
  value chain, 157–163, 165–167
  values, 75–76

winning strategy tests
  competitive advantage test, 61–62
  fit test, 60
  performance test, 62
Company culture, 146, 149, 188; *see also*
  Corporate culture
  driver of unethical strategies, 351–352
  at General Electric, 353–354
  with high ethical principles, 352
Company image, 145–146
Company opportunity, 153
Companywide restructuring, 330–332
Comparative advantage, 321–322
Comparative cost, 299–300
Compensation; *see also* Executive
  compensation; Incentive compensation
  lavish for executives, 349–351
  low-wage countries, 256
  at Shangri-La Hotels, C-299–C-300
  for top executives, 89
Compensation committee, 89
Competence, 151–152
Competencies
  assessing, 151–152
  conceptual differences among, 152
  core, 151–152
  distinctive, 151–152
Competition
  basis of competitive advantage, 54
  five-forces model, 102–103
  Hewlett-Packard vs. Dell, C-73–C-77
  increased by globalization, 121
  industry attractiveness and intensity of, 317
  and quality spectrum, 157
  in research and development on cell phones,
    C-163
  varying among strategic groups, 128
Competitive advantage
  connected to profitability, 57
  cost-based, 56, 167
  definition, 54
  differentiation-based, 167, 232
  in differentiation strategy, 198
  in diversified companies, 293
  from environmentally sustainable strategies,
    364–365
  in focused differentiation strategy, 201–202
  in focused low-cost strategy, 201
  in global competition, 261
  in international marketing
    cross-border coordination, 277
    sharing and transferring resources,
      275–277
    using location, 273–275
  limited in unrelated diversification, 311–312
  loss in strategic alliances, 268
  protecting
    blocking avenues open to challengers,
      220–221
    signaling retaliation, 221
  in related diversification, 306
  from resources and capabilities, 147–150
  strategic approaches
    best-cost provider, 57
    differentiation features, 56
    low-cost provider, 56
    market niche focus, 56–57
  strategy as quest for, 53–57
  from strategy execution, 390

sustainable, 54
  at Toyota, 387–388, C-315–C-316
  translating value chain activities into,
    166–167, 169
Competitive advantage test, 62
Competitive analysis
  costs of value chain activities, 161
  inadequate, 168
  key success factors, 170
  quantitative strength rankings, 169–170
  weighted assessment, 170–173
Competitive assets, 144, 152
  caliber of, 147–148
Competitive attack
  based on strategic assets, 216
  strategic options
    continuous innovation, 217
    cost-based advantages, 216–217
    hit-and-run guerrilla tactics, 217–218
    improving ideas of rivals, 217
    next-generation technologies, 217
    pre-emptive strike, 218
    time to yield results, 218
Competitive battles, 102–104
Competitive capabilities
  alternative beverage market, C-22–C-23
  building and straightening, 385–390
Competitive deficiency, 152
Competitive environment; *see also* Industry
  environment
  ideal for profits, 119
Competitive forces
  buyer bargaining power, 115–118
  effect of Internet, 122
  and industry change, 120
  key success factors, 130–131
  matching strategy to, 119
  price sensitivity, 115–118
  prospects for profitability, 118–119
  rivalry among competing sellers, 102–103
  sellers of substitutes, 111–112
  supplier bargaining power, 112–115
  threat of new entrants, 107–110
Competitive intelligence
  about rival's strategies, 129
  questions for managers, 129–130
Competitive liabilities, 152
Competitively superior strength, 151–152
Competitively unattractive industry, 118–119
Competitively valuable resources, 148
Competitiveness
  backward integration to enhance, 231–232
  effect of globalization, 251
  forward integration to enhance, 232–233
Competitive position
  of Apple Inc.
    in mobile phones, C-131–C-132
    in PC industry, C-124–C-128
    in personal media players, C-130–C-131
  defensive strategies
    blocking avenues open to challengers,
      220–221
    signaling retaliation, 221
  first-mover advantages, 221–223, 224
  first-mover disadvantages, 223
  horizontal merger and acquisitions strategies,
    226–229
  late-mover advantages, 223
  and mutual restraint, 280

options for improving, 214–220
  basis for competitive attack, 216–218
  blue ocean strategy, 219–220
  choosing rivals to attack, 218–219
  outsourcing strategies, 235–236
  pros and cons for first movers, 224–225
  strategic alliances/partnerships, 237–244
  strengthening scope of operations, 225–226
  vertical integration strategies, 229–235
Competitive pressures
  from existing industry members, 110
  favoring some/hurting others, 128
Competitive strategy, resource-based, 210
Competitive strength, 62
  business unit scores
    calculating, 317–318
    interpreting, 318–319
  of countries, 253
  nine-cell matrix for, 319–321
  quantifying factors, 318
  weighted scores, 318, 319
Competitive success, 53
Competitors
  for Afrigator, C-9–C-11
  for Apple Inc., C-128–C-130
  in athletic shoe industry, C-271
  bases for attack on, 216–220
  in construction machinery industry, C-254
  for Dell in Asia, C-62
  for Dell Inc., C-72–C-73, C-79
  in energy drink market, C-22
  exploiting weaknesses of, 216
  in golf equipment industry, C-38–C-39
  for Google Inc., C-151–C-153
  in hotel industry, C-301
  rivalry and diversity of, 106
  rivalry and number of, 106
  in solar energy industry, C-201–C-203
  for TomTom
    Google Inc., C-120
    new types, C-112–C-113
    traditional, C-112
  for Toyota, C-318
  in video game industry, C-102–C-106
Compliance rating system, Walmart, C-407
Components, self-manufacturing, 115
Composite structure, 396–397
Computer-aided design, 188
Conglomerate, 307
Conservation biologists, C-376
Construction machinery industry, C-240–C-254
  competitors, C-254
  in financial crisis of 2008, C-251
  market shares, C-254
  product line of Komatsu, C-241–C-242
Consumer Reports, C-317–C-318, C-322
Consumers; *see also* Buyer *entries;* Customer
  entries
  as buyer group, 116
  lack of bargaining power, 116
  selling direct to, 189
Consumer tastes/preferences
  global convergence, 262
  in local markets, 285
  shift in, C-18
Continuous improvement, 387, C-306
  at Dell Inc., C-58–C-60
  focus on, 456
  process management tools, 411–420

Continuous improvement—*Cont.*
  in quality, 195–196
  at Toyota, C-305, C-313, C-322
Continuous product innovation, 217
Contract manufacturers, monitoring system,
    C-400–C-402
Control, 415
  advantages in greenfield ventures, 264–265
  lacking in outsourcing, 237
Convenience stores, C-21
Copy cats, 199–200
Core business, concentration on, 237
Core competencies, 151–152
  building and straightening
    from acquisitions, 388–389
    through collaborative partnerships, 389
    internal development, 386–388
    upgrading, 389–390
  for foreign markets, 252
  leveraged across borders, 276
  preserved in outsourcing, 235
Core values; *see also* Values
  at Atlassian, C-92
  in corporate culture, 440–441
  definition, 75
  Komatsu, C-250
  number of, 75
  in practice, 75–76
  retention of, 442
  Royal Dutch Shell, 77
  at Shangri-La Hotels, C-298
  Toyota, C-307
  transformed into cultural norms, 441–442
Corporate brands, 309
Corporate citizenship, 358
Corporate culture; *see also* Company culture
  adaptive cultures, 447–448
  at Alberto-Culver, 439
  at Atlassian, C-92
  change-resistant, 448–449
  characteristics, 437
  core values and ethics in, 440–441
  definition, 438
  evolution of, 443
  in fast-growing companies, 443
  at Google, Inc., 439
  high-performance cultures, 446–447
  with incompatible subcultures, 450
  insular and inwardly focused, 449
  key features, 438–440
  leadership role in changing
    at Chrysler, 454
    making a case for change, 451–452
    substantive actions, 452–453
    symbolic actions, 453–454
    time it takes, 454
  matched to strategy execution, 445
  origin of, 440
  politicized, 449
  role of stories, 341
  in strategy-execution process, 445–450
  strong-culture companies, 443–444
  and total quality management, 414
  in tradition-steeped companies, 441
  transforming values into norms, 441–442
  unethical and greed-driven, 449–450
  ways of perpetuating, 442–443
  weak-culture companies, 444–445

Corporate governance; *see also* Business ethics
  basic principle, 89
  board of director roles, 88–91
  failure at Fannie Mae and Freddie Mac, 90
  financial scandals, 91
  versus self-dealing, 348
Corporate Knights, 360
Corporate parenting
  administrative resources, 309
  definition, 308
  examples, 309
  high-level oversight, 308–309
Corporate responsibility, 358
Corporate Responsibility Magazine, 360, C-354
Corporate restructuring, 330
Corporate scandals, 91, 347, 450
  Bernard L. Madoff Investment Securities, 350
  Dell Computer, 349
  Enron, 348–349, 352–353
  HealthSouth, 349
  Royal Dutch/Shell, 353
  Stanford Financial Group, 350–351
  Tyco International, 348
  WorldCom, 349
Corporate social responsibility
  at Coca-Cola India
    community development, C-387
    in corporate agenda, C-377–C-378
    criticisms of, C-389–C-390
    economic responsibility, C-388
    environmental responsibility initiatives,
        C-382–C-387
    initiatives, C-379–C-380
    model, C-379
    recent initiatives, C-392–C-393
    responses to criticism, C-391
  definition, 356
  diverse workforce, 358
  environmentally sustainable business
      practices, 365–368
  environmental protection, 358
  ethical strategy, 356
  at John Deere, 359–360
  philanthropic initiatives, 357
  at Starbucks
    community involvement, C-354
    environmental stewardship, C-354
    ethical sourcing, C-354
    farmer loans, C-354
    philanthropic activities, C-353
    responses to hurricanes, C-353–C-354
  and sustainability strategies, 364–365
  and triple bottom line, 360–362
  work environment, 358
Corporate social responsibility strategies,
    358–360
  reporting criticism of, 361
Corporate strategy; *see also* Strategies/Strategy
  definition, 82–84
  facets in diversified companies
    actions to boost combined performance,
        294
    cross-business value chain activities, 293
    investment priorities, 293–294
    picking industries to enter, 293
Corporate venturing, 297–298
Corrective adjustments
  challenges of, 458
  to strategy execution, 87–88

  success in, 457–458
  time frame, 457
Cost(s)
  of acquisitions, 296–297
  of acquisition strategies, 264
  in adjoining markets, 123
  competitive with rivals, 156–168
  effects of value chain, 158–160
  of rivals, 163
  of switching brands, 104
  of transferring resources and capabilities,
      276
  of unethical behavior, 354–355
  value chain analysis, 158–161
Cost advantage
  as barrier to entry, 107–108
  failing to recognize avenues of, 193
Cost-based advantages, 216–217
Cost-based competitive advantage, 56, 167
Cost competitiveness, 160
Cost-cutting methods
  advanced production technology, 188
  company bargaining power, 187
  economies of scale, 186
  full capacity operation, 186–187
  gaining advantages over rivals, 188–189
  information technology, 188
  learning-curve effects, 186
  lower input costs, 187
  motivating employees, 188
  outsourcing, 188
  supply chain efficiency, 187
  vertical integration, 188
Cost disadvantages, strategic options, 163–166
  improving distribution, 166
  improving internally performed activities, 165
  improving supplier-related activities, 165–166
Cost drivers
  definition, 186
  types of, 187
Cost information, and buyer bargaining power,
    116–117
Cost-of-entry test, 295–296, 299
  for unrelated diversification, 307
Cost reduction
  by Dell Inc., C-57–C-58, C-70–C-71
  in foreign markets, 252
  too fixated on, 193
Cost saving, in backward integration, 231
Cost-shifting, 368
Counterfeiting, golf equipment, C-37–C-38
Coverage ratio, 143
Creativity, stifled by Six Sigma, 416–418
Credit rating, 324
Cross-border acquisitions, 252
Cross-border alliances, 252
Cross-border coordination, 277
Cross-border subsidization
  definition, 279
  and price-cutting, 279–280
Cross-border tactics, 280
Cross-business allocation, 309–310
Cross-business strategic fit, 304, 329, 400
  competitive advantage potential, 321–322
Cross-business value chain activities, 293
Cross-country strategic fit, 315
Cross-country variations
  demand conditions, 253–254
  factor conditions, 254–255

firm strategy, structure, and rivalry, 255
related-and supporting industries, 255
Cross-functional capabilities, 147
Cross-functional teams, 413
Cultural clash, avoiding, C-221
Cultural differences, 242
in acquired companies, 450
ethical relativism, 342–345
integrated social contracts theory, 345–346
think-local, act-local approach, 270–271
Cultural due diligence, 450
Cultural fit, 329–330
Cultural norms
practicing and enforcing, 451–452
strictly enforced, 442
transforming values and ethics into, 441–442
Culture, cross-country variations, 259–260
Culture change; see Corporate culture
Culture-induced peer pressures, 445
Current ratio, 52
Customer demand; see Demand
Customer-first policy, Toyota, C-315
Customer loyalty
as barrier to entry, 108
to brands, 196
Customer needs
and differentiation strategy, 193–194, 197
in local markets, 285
meet efficiently and effectively, 54
Customers
of Atlassian, C-89–C-90
for TomTom, C-110
Customer satisfaction
Apple Inc., C-123–C-124
at Cemex, C-221–C-222
from intangible features, 197–198
from tangible features, 197
Customer service
at Atlassian, C-87–C-91
capability for, 386
Dell Inc., C-66–C-69
improvements, 195
strategic fit, 305
Customer value proposition
competitiveness in, 157
value chain analysis, 158
Custom fitting, C-40
Customization
for foreign markets, 260
in local markets, 285
Custom-order manufacturers, 195
Cut-rate pricing attack, 279
Cutthroat rivalry, 106–107
Czech Republic, solar energy industry, C-195

D

Data sharing, 188
Days of inventory ratio, 143
Debt, of Cemex, C-212, C-222–C-226
Debt-to-assets ratio, 143
Debt-to-equity ratio, 143
Decentralized decision making
capturing strategic fit, 400
versus centralized decision making, 398
pros and cons, 399–400

Decision making
centralized, 397–399
decentralized, 399–400
to empower employees, 425
in strategic alliances, 242
Defect-free process completion, C-315
Defects
dealing with, 387
Six Sigma for reducing, 415–418
Defensive strategies
blocking avenues open to challengers, 220–221
late-mover advantage, 223–224
signaling retaliation, 221
Define, 414
Delegation of authority, 456
centralized decision making, 397–399
decentralized decision making, 399–400
at Shangri-La Hotels, C-296–C-297
Deliberate strategy, 58–59
Delivery time, 189
Demand
and buyer bargaining power, 116
conditions in foreign markets, 253–254
cultural influences, 260
and exit barriers, 121
increased by globalization, 121
and rivalry, 105
and shift in buyer demographics, 121–122
for smartphones, C-161
strong network effects in, 108
Deming Application Prize, C-311
Demographic market segment, 101
Demographics
of buyers, 121–122
cross-country variations, 259–260
definition, 100
think-local, act-local approach, 270–271
Departmental structure, 395
Department of Family and Child Welfare, India, C-391
Department of Justice, and Google Inc., C-151–C-152
Design features, 194
Design for manufacture procedures, 188
Developing countries
local defenses against global giants
acquisitions and rapid-growth strategies, 286
business models, 284
cross-border transfer of expertise, 286–287
local workforce, 285–286
understanding customer needs, 285
major nations, 281
population of, 281
purchasing power, 259
strategies for competing in, 280–284
avoid impractical markets, 283–284
business model modification, 282–283
changing local market, 283
low-price basis, 281–282
tailoring products for, 281
Development projects, by Canadian Solar, C-208
Diamond model of national advantage, 251, 254
Differentiation
buyer bargaining power forcing, 116
in golf equipment, C-39–C-40
Differentiation-based competitive advantage, 167, 232

Differentiation strategies, 56; see also Focused differentiation strategy
best conditions for
diverse buyer needs, 199
fast-paced technological change, 199
followed by few rivals, 199
many ways of differentiating, 199
delivering superior value
approaches difficult to duplicate, 198
intangible features, 197–198
lowering buyer's costs, 197
from resources and capabilities, 198
signals of value, 198
tangible features, 197
distinguishing features, 208–209, 228–229
effects on firms, 194
enhancing profitability, 194
examples, 194
incentive system in, 428
managing value chain to create, 194–196
market position, 183, 184
pitfalls to avoid
overspending, 200
possible rapid imitation, 199–200
timidity, 200
too high a price, 200–201
too many features, 200
unenthusiastic buyers, 200
reasons for failure, 194
revamping value chain
coordinating with channel allies, 196
coordinating with suppliers, 197
strong vs. weak, 200
successful, 193–194
unique customer value proposition, 194
uniqueness drivers
continuous improvement, 195–196
high-quality inputs, 196
human resource management activities, 196
improved customer service, 195
innovation, 195
marketing and sales activities, 196
research and development, 195
superior features, design and performance, 194
technological advances, 195
Digital mapping technology, C-111
Direct selling, 189, 233
by Dell Inc., C-57, C-61–C-62
Discount stores; see Wholesale clubs
Disruptive environmental change, 150
Distinctive competencies, 198
Distribution
by Atlassian, C-85
definition, 159
by Grupo Modelo, C-232–C-233
by Reebok, C-282
strategic fit, 305
TomTom, C-119
value chain activities, 161
Distribution channels, low-cost, 189
Distribution networks
as barrier to entry, 108
local, 284
Distribution-related value chain activities, 166
Distributors
avoiding costs of, 189
coordinating with, 196
of golf equipment, C-40

Diverse workforce, 358
Diversification; *see also* Related diversification;
          Unrelated diversification
    to add shareholder value
        better-off test, 296
        cost-of-entry test, 295–296
        industry attractiveness test, 295
    Apple Inc., C-124–C-128, C-130–C-134
    barriers to entry, 299
    circumstances for, 295
    combination related-unrelated, 313
    comparative cost, 299–300
    critical resources and capabilities, 298–299
    four main options after, 327
    at Johnson & Johnson, 329
    by Komatsu, C-244
    by PepsiCo, C-255–C-270
    speed, 299
    strategies
        acquisition of existing business, 296–297
        corporate venturing, 297–298
        internal development, 297–298
        joint ventures, 298
    timing of, 294–295
Diversification strategy
    alternatives for using, 314
    and multidivisional structure, 395–396
Diversified companies, 293
    broadening business base, 327–328
    broadly diversified, 313
    conglomerates, 307
    crafting new strategy moves, 326–332
    divesting or retrenching, 328–330
    dominant-business enterprises, 313
    internal capital market, 323
    narrowly diversified, 313
    parenting advantage, 311
    ranking performance prospects, 325–326
    restructuring, 330–331
    sticking with existing business line, 326–327
    strategy analysis
        business unit competitive strength,
            317–321
        competitive advantage potential, 321–322
        industry attractiveness, 314–317
        resource fit, 322–325
        steps, 313–314
    turnaround capabilities, 310
    unrelated groups of related businesses, 313
Divesting, 294, 327
    candidates for, 331
    causes leading to, 330
    of marginal units, 325
    reasons for, 328–329
    of Salomon by Adidas, C-271, C-277
    useful guide for, 330
Dividend payout ratio, 144
Dividend yield on common stock, 143
Divisional structure, 395
DMADV (define, measure, analyze, design, and
        verify) Six Sigma, 415
DMAIC (define, measure, analyze, improve, and
        control) Six Sigma, 415–416
Domestic market, Komatsu 1921–1964,
        C-240–C-243
Dominant-business enterprise, 313
Dominating depth, 276
Domini 400 index, 368

Dot-com bubble, C-85
Dow Jones Large Cap Index, 368
Dow Jones Sustainability Index, 368
Dow Jones Sustainability World Index
    companies recognized by, 362
    composition of, 361
Dow Jones Total Market Index, 368
Dow Jones World Index, 361
Downstream partners, 196
Drivers of change
    assessing impact of, 124–125
    favoring some/hurting others, 128
    identifying, 120–124
    most common, 124
    strategy to deal with, 125
Dumping, 156–157
    definition, 279
    reason for appeal of, 279
    retaliation against, 279–280
    unfair, 279
    World Trade Organization on, 280
Dutch auction, C-138
Dynamic capabilities, 150, 385
Dynamic fit, 60
Dynamic industry analysis, 121, 122
    value of, 125
Dynamic management of resources, 149–150
Dynasty Flyer Program, C-181–C-182

E

Early adopters, C-116
Early majority, C-116
Earnings per share, 142
Economic conditions; *see also* Financial crisis
        of 2008
    banking crisis of 2008, 309
    definition, 100
    reason for broadening business base, 328
Economic indicators of growth opportunities,
        101
Economic responsibility initiatives, Coca-Cola
        India
    business partners, C-388
    employment, C-388
    training retailers, C-388
Economic risks, 257
Economies of scale
    as barrier to entry, 107
    from centralizing production, 263
    cost-cutting method, 186
    versus economies of scope, 306
    in foreign markets, 252
    location-based, 274
    from standardization, 260
    from technological change, 122
    and vertical integration, 144
Economies of scope, 306
Efficiency, in adjoining markets, 123
Electronic score cards, 422
Electronics Industry Code of Conduct, C-400
E-mail, and industry change, 122
Emergent strategy, 58–59
Empire-building managers, 449
Employee motivation, 188
Employee recruiting, 366–367

Employees; *see also* Human resource
        management
    acting on ideas from, 424–425
    developing capabilities in, 381–390
    in high-performance cultures, 447
    incentives extended to all, 428
    misconceptions about strategy, 375–376
    monitoring performance of, 423
    perpetuating corporate culture, 442–443
    recruiting and training, 382–385
    at Research in Motion, C-164
    rewards and incentives for, 423–430
    at Shangri-La Hotels, C-296–C-297
    sharing information with, 425
    in strong-culture companies, 445–446
    treated as valued partners, 456
    work environment, 358
Employee skills, 196
    upgrading, 389–390
Employment, in China, C-397–C-398
Empowerment, 387, 399, 423, 425, 456
Energy and Resource Institute, C-389–C-391
Energy efficiency at Coca-Cola India,
        C-385–C-386
Enterprise resource planning, 188
Enterprise Resource Planning software, 414
Entrepreneurship
    at Atlassian, C-81–C-93
    in Australia, C-86–C-87
    internal, 447
Entry of major firms, 122–123
Environment, 362
Environmentally sustainable strategies
    business case for, 366–368
    and buyer patronage, 366
    competitive advantage, 364–365
    and corporate social responsibility, 364
    and cost reductions, 366–367
    versus cost-shifting, 368
    definition, 363
    forms of, 364
    implied social contract, 365
    moral case for, 365
    and procurement policies, 365
    reducing risk of reputation-damaging
            incidents, 366
    revenue enhancement, 367
    shareholder interests, 367–368
    Starbucks, C-350–C-352
    workforce retention, 366–367
Environmental protection, 358
Environmental regulation, 358
Environmental responsibility initiatives,
        Coca-Cola India
    energy efficiency, C-385–C-386
    fuel efficiency, C-386
    packaging and recycling, C-386–C-387
    water conservation, C-382–C-385
Environmental stewardship, at Starbucks, C-354
Esprit de corps, 456
Ethical principles, 356
Ethical relativism
    breakdown of
        local standards, 344
        rudderless standards, 344
    bribes and kickbacks, 342–343
    definition, 342
    and multinational corporations, 344–345

multiple sets of standards, 343–344
use of underage labor, 342
Ethical sourcing, C-354
Ethical standards
conflicting for multinational corporations, 344–345
impact on strategy, 346–347
local, 344–345
multiple sets of, 344–345
rudderless, 344
Ethical strategy, 356
business case for, 354–355
moral case for, 354
reasons for, 352
Ethical universalism, 340–342
Ethics, 339
in benchmarking, 164
in corporate culture, 440–441
ethical relativism, 342–344
ethical universalism, 340–342
integrated social contracts theory, 345–346
transformed into cultural norms, 441–442
E-ticketing, C-181–C-182
Europe
Shangri-La Hotels in, C-302
telecommunications market, C-167
European Economic Commission, C-378
European Photovoltaic Industry Association (EPIA), C-193
European Union
imports from China, C-396
share of global revenue, C-240
Evolving strategy, 57–58
Exchange rates
decline of dollar, 258–259
favorable shift, 259
fluctuating, 258
Japan-U.S. 1970-2010, C-244
risks of adverse shifts, 257–259
strength of euro, 259
unpredictable, 259
Execution-critical activities, consistency in, 410
Executive compensation
board responsibility for, 89
incentive, 329
lavish, 349–351
need for reform, 89
Executives
as agents for shareholders, 89
board of directors evaluation, 88–89
Existing business lineup, sticking with, 326–327
Exit barriers
effect of demand, 121
and strength of rivalry, 106–107
Exit of major firms, 122–123
Expansion
by Research in Motion, C-166
by Shangri-La Hotels, C-289–C-291
Experience, benefits in single location, 274
Experience curve, 107, 186
Expertise
competitively valuable, 57
diverse kinds of, 237
transferred to cross-border markets, 286–287
transferring, 301
Exports
by Komatsu, C-243
by Toyota, C-309

Export strategies
and cost competitiveness, 263
disadvantages, 263
to enter foreign markets, 262–263
vulnerability, 263
External fit, 60

F

Factor conditions, foreign markets, 254–255
Factories, of Canadian Solar, C-206–C-207
Fair Factories Clearinghouse, C-411
Fair Labor Association, C-402, C-410–C-411, C-412
Fair Trade Certified coffee, C-352
Farmer loans, C-354
Fast-changing market, 153
Fast-growing market, and rivalry, 105
Faulty oversight, 348–349
Federal Communications Commission, and net neutrality, C-154
Federal Home Loan Mortgage Corporation; see Freddie Mac
Federal National Mortgage Association; see Fannie Mae
Feed-in Tariff program for solar energy, C-189, C-193, C-196, C-198, C-204
Fiduciary duty, 89
Fierce rivalry, 107
Financial accounting, board of directors oversight, 89–91
Financial crisis of 2008, 347
impact on Adidas, C-285
impact on beverage industry, C-17
impact on Cemex, C-222–C-226
impact on Dell Inc., C-129
impact on golf equipment industry, C-38
impact on Hewlett-Packard, C-127
impact on Komatsu, C-252–C-253
impact on Toyota, C-308
Financial incentives
at Amgen, 427
components, 424
fringe benefits, 424
high-powered motivation, 424
at Lincoln Electric, 426
major piece of total compensation, 428
at Nordstrom, 426
perks, 424
at Ukrop's Super Markets, 427
Financial Mail, C-12
Financial objectives, 76–78
Financial options for allocating financial resources, 326
Financial performance
Adidas, C-273, C-279
for Adidas by region, C-283
Apple Inc., C-122–C-124, C-125
benefits of sustainability strategies, 367–368
Callaway Golf Company, C-43
Canadian Solar, C-190–C-191, C-208–C-209
Cemex, C-225
China Airlines, C-174
Coca-Cola Company, C-27
Dell Inc., C-55

Fortune Brands Golf Division, C-48
Google Inc., C-145
Grupo Modelo, C-237
Hansen Natural Corporation, C-28
Hewlett-Packard, C-75
Komatsu, C-246–C-247
measures of
balanced scorecard, 78–79
lagging indicators, 78
leading indicators, 78
pursuing strategic outcomes, 79
MSN business unit, C-153
PepsiCo, C-25, C-256
PepsiCo business units, C-263–C-264
ratios for, 142–144
Research in Motion, C-157
of rivals, 129
Shangri-La Hotels, C-291–C-292
Starbucks, C-335
TaylorMade-adidas Golf, C-45
at TomTom
objectives, C-114–C-115
sales and net income, C-115–C-116
Yahoo!, C-152
Financial ratios
activity ratios, 143
for Cemex, C-223, C-225
dividend payout ratio, 144
dividend yield, 143
free cash flow, 144
internal cash flow, 144
leverage ratios, 143
liquidity ratios, 142
price-earnings ratio, 144
profitability ratios, 142
Financial reporting, 89–91
Financial resource fit
adequate financial strength, 324
business unit inadequacy, 324
cash flow considerations, 323–324
good credit rating, 324
internal capital market, 323
Financial resources, 145–146
cross-business allocation, 309–310
options for allocating, 326
Financial scandals, 91
Financial statements, for Cemex, C-224
Financial strain, 324
Financial strength, 324
Financial Times, C-103, C-251
Financial Week, C-12
Financing
of Atlassian, C-84, C-85–C-87
early Starbucks, C-331–C-332
venture capital, C-334
Firm strategy, structure, and rivalry, 255
First followers, C-114
First-mover advantages
at Amazon.com, 224
create brand loyalty, 221–222
create switching costs, 222
definition, 221
hard questions for, 223
learning curve, 222
property rights protection, 222
pros and cons, 224–225
requirements, 223
setting technical standard, 222–223

First-mover disadvantages
  costly pioneering, 223
  definition, 221
  market uncertainties, 223
  not meeting buyer expectations, 223
  opening for fast followers, 223
  rapid market evolution, 223
"First-order" ethical norms, 345
Fit test, 60
Five-forces model of competition
  as analytical tool, 103
  definition, 102
  using, 102
Five Pillar Growth Strategy, Coca-Cola India,
    C-388–C-389
Fixed costs, and intensity of rivalry, 106
Flat structure, 394
Flexible manufacturing systems, 195
Fluctuating exchange rates risks, 258–259
Focused differentiation strategy
  attractiveness, 202–203
  characteristics, 201–202
  distinguishing features, 208–209, 228–229
  at Nestlé, 204–205
  risks, 203–205
  at Vizio, Inc., 203
Focused low-cost strategy
  attractiveness, 202–203
  characteristics, 201
  distinguishing features, 208–209, 228–229
  risks, 203–205
Focused strategies, market position, 183
Focus strategy, 56–57
Food and Drug Administration, C-24, C-25
Forbes, 229, 350
Foreign Corrupt Practices Act, 343
Foreign markets
  in developing countries, 281–284
  exploit core competencies, 252
  impractical to enter, 283–284
  lower costs, 252
  options for entering
    acquisition strategies, 264
    export strategies, 262–263
    franchising, 263–264
    greenfield ventures, 264–265
    joint ventures, 265–269
    licensing strategies, 263
    risks of alliances, 266–268
    strategic alliances, 265–269
    when alliances are unnecessary, 268–269
  reason for broadening business base, 328
  reasons for entering
    access to new capabilities, 252–253
    access to new customers, 252
    spread business risk, 253
Foreign partners, risks of alliances with, 266–268
Foreign supplier compliance programs
  at Nike, Inc., C-400–C-406
  at Walmart, C-406–C-410
Fortune, 229, 331, 349, C-54, C-87, C-101,
    C-166, C-348
Forward integration
  and channel conflict, 243
  definition, 230
  direct selling, 243
  to enhance competitiveness, 232–233
France, solar energy industry, C-195

Franchised Starbucks stores, C-340
Franchising strategies, 263–264
Free cash flow, 144
  decline at Cemex, C-222–C-223
Freedom of Information Act, C-154
Free-speech advocates, C-137, C-154
Frills, stripping, 188–189
Fringe benefits, 424
  Starbucks, C-348
Frontline managers, 85
Fuel efficiency, at Coca-Cola India, C-386
Full capacity operations, 186–187
Full integration, 230–231
Functional-area strategies, 83, 84
Functional structure, 394–395
Functions related to capabilities, 147
Funding
  reallocating, 408
  too little or too much, 407

G

Gasoline prices, C-38
General administration, 159
Generalized resources and capabilities, 301–303
  low value, 312
  in unrelated diversification, 308
Generally accepted accounting principles, 89–91
Generic competitive strategies
  attractiveness of focused differentiation
      strategy, 202–203
  attractiveness of focused low-cost strategy,
      202–203
  best-cost provider strategy, 205–208
  contrasting features of, 197–210
  differentiation strategies, 193–201
  focused differentiation strategy, 201–202
  focused low-cost strategy, 201
  low-cost provider strategies, 184–193
  and market position, 184
  purpose, 183
  resource-based, 210
  risks in focused differentiation strategy,
      203–205
  risks in focused low-cost strategy, 203–205
Geographic boundary lines, 101
Geographic coverage, 227
Germany
  investigation of Google, C-154
  solar energy industry, C-193, C-195
Global brand names, 271, 276
Global Community Watershed Partnership
    Program, C-385
Global competition
  competitive advantage, 261
  convergence of tastes, 262
  definition, 261
  transition from multidomestic competition,
      261–262
  types of market segments, 261
Global forces, 100
Global giants
  versus competitive abilities of local
      companies, 286
  disadvantages in developing countries, 284
  lacking local workforce, 285–286

  and local company expertise, 286–287
  versus local orientation, 285
  strategies for local companies against, 284–287
Globalization
  accelerating pace of, 251
  by Cemex, C-216–C-219
  challenge for Research in Motion, C-169
  by Grupo Modelo, C-229–C-230, C-232–C-233
  by Komatsu, C-243–C-245, C-248–C-251
  leading to industry change, 121
  by Research in Motion, C-167–C-169
  solar energy industry, C-193–C-204
  started at Toyota, C-306
Global market leadership, 241
Global Social Compliance Program, C-409
Global strategy
  advantages/disadvantages, 273
  definition, 271
  drawbacks, 272
  standardization, 271–272
  think-global, act-global approach, 271
Global warming, 363
Glocalization, 272
Goal conflict, 398
Golf equipment industry, case, C-30–C-50
  Callaway Golf Company, C-40–C-43
  in crisis in 2009, C-30–C-31
  in financial crisis of 2008, C-38
  forces shaping competition
    competitive rivalry, C-38–C-39
    retailers and distributors, C-40
    suppliers, C-39–C-40
  game history, C-30
  industry conditions 2009
    counterfeiting problem, C-37–C-38
    decline in number of golfers, C-37
    limited innovation opportunities, C-34–C-37
  leading manufacturers, C-38
  Nike Golf, C-49–C-50
  participation rate, C-34
  Ping Golf, C-48–C-49
  rounds played 2001–2008, C-34
  TaylorMade-adidas Golf, C-44–C-46
  Titleist/Cobra Golf, C-46–C-48
  value and sales 1997–2008, C-31–C-33
Golf equipment industry, TaylorMade-adidas
    Golf, C-284
Government
  hostile to business, 257
  incentives for solar energy, C-189, C-196
  pro-business environment, 256
Government policies
  as barrier to entry, 108–109
  cross-country variations, 256–257
  and industry change, 123
Greece, solar energy industry, C-195
Greed-driven culture, 449–450
Greenfield ventures
  control advantage, 264–265
  learning by doing, 264
  problems, 264
Greenhouse gases, 363
Green movement, C-114
Gross profit margin, 142
Ground Water Board, India, C-389
Growth
  of Atlassian, C-87–C-93
  Canadian Solar, C-189

efforts by Cemex, C-220
long-term rate changes, 120–121
opportunities for, 101
of Research in Motion, C-165–C-169
of Shangri-La Hotels, C-289
wrong reason for diversification, 312
Growth rate, long-term changes, 120–121
Growth strategy
    Coca-Cola India, C-388–C-389
    Starbucks, C-359–C-360
Guerrilla offensive, 217–218
Guggenheim Museum, New York, 194
Guidelines for activities, 409–410

H

Haitian relief effort, C-353–C-354
Health care coverage, C-346–C-347
Health initiatives, by Coca-Cola India, C-387
Hezbollah, C-37
High-performance cultures, 446–447
High-powered motivation, 424
High-tech companies, 382–384
Hiring; see Recruitment
Hit-and-run guerrilla offensive, 217–218
Home mortgage problem, 347
Horizontal mergers and acquisitions, 226–227
Horizontal scope, 226
Hotel industry, C-288–C-312
    competition in, C-301
    hourly wages by country, C-301
    performance of major chains, C-301
Houston Post, C-53
Human assets, 145–146
Human capital, at Cemex, C-221
Human resource management
    at Atlassian, C-91–C-92
    at China Airlines, C-180–C-181
    and differentiation strategy, 196
    Starbucks
        fringe benefits, C-348
        health care coverage, C-346–C-347
        stock option plan, C-347
        stock purchase plan, C-347
        training and recognition, C-348–C-349
        workplace environment, C-347–C-348
    TomTom, C-119
    value chain activity, 159
Human rights, commitment to, 344
Hybrid strategy, 206

I

Imitation, rapid, 199–200
Immigrants, money transfers by, C-214
Implied social contract, 365
Imports, of beer into U.S., C-230
Improve, 415
Incentive compensation, 329
    communicating and explaining, 430
    guidelines
        extended to all employees, 428
        financial incentives, 428
        performance targets and outcomes, 429–430
        results not effort rewarded, 430

scrupulous administration, 429
timing of rewards, 430
high vs. average performance, 428
Incentives
    based on results, 427–430
    financial, 424
    for high-performance standards, 456–457
    nonmonetary, 424–425
    piece-rate plan, 429
    and strategy execution at Nucor, 429
    strategy execution objectives, 423
Incentive system, 145–146, 149, 187–188
Income statement
    Naspers Limited, C-8
    Nintendo, C-98
    PepsiCo, C-259
    Shangri-La Asia Ltd., C-292
    Toyota, C-310–C-311
Incompatible subcultures, 450
India
    market growth potential, 286
    products tailored for, 281–282
    soft drink market, C-380–C-381
    solar energy industry, C-196
    wireless subscribers, C-161
    working conditions, C-397
Indian Institute of Information technology,
    C-168
Indian Institute of Science, C-168
Indian Institute of Technology, C-168
Indian Red Cross, C-387
Indian Resource Center, C-389
Indoctrination of new employees, 442
Indonesia, working conditions, C-397
Industries/Industry
    changed conditions over time, 57–58
    competitively unattractive, 118–119
    convergence of, 228
    differences among, 101
    for diversified companies, 293
    globally competitive, 261
    high exit barriers, 106–107
    key success factors, 130–131
    profit prospects, 132–133
    strategic groups, 126
    supplier compliance efforts
        Fair Factories Clearinghouse, C-411
        Fair Labor Association, C-410–C-411
    value chain system for, 161–162
Industry attractiveness, 119
    cross-country strategic fit, 315
    and diversification strategy, 315
    evaluating
        questions required, 314–315
        scores for ranking, 315–317
    key indicators, 315
    nine-cell matrix for portraying, 319–321
    and profit prospects, 132–133
    resource requirements, 315
Industry attractiveness scores
    calculating, 315–316
    difficulties of calculating, 317
    interpreting, 316–317
    weighted, 316
Industry attractiveness test
    for related diversification, 295
    for unrelated diversification, 307

Industry change
    analyzing industry dynamics, 120
    effect of competitive forces, 120
    environmental scanning for, 120
    identifying drivers of change
        cost and efficiency in adjoining markets, 123
        diffusion of technological know-how, 123
        exit or entry of firms, 122–123
        globalization, 121
        Internet, 122
        lifestyle changes, 123–124
        long-term growth rate, 120–121
        product market innovation, 122
        reduction in uncertainty, 123
        regulatory influences, 123
        shift in buyer demographics, 121–122
        societal change, 123–124
        technological change, 122
    impact of drivers of change, 124–125
    most common drivers of, 124
    strategy to deal with, 125
Industry competitiveness, cross-country
        variations
    demand conditions, 253–254
    factor conditions, 254–255
    firm strategy, structure, and rivalry, 255
    related and supporting industries, 255
Industry environment; see also Competitive
        environment
    buyer bargaining power, 115–118
    characteristics, 58
    golf equipment, C-34–C-38
    growth opportunities, 101
    kinds of competitive forces
        rivalry among sellers, 102–107
        threat of new entrants, 107–110
    pressure from price sensitivity, 115–118
    profitability prospects, 118–119
    sellers of substitutes, 111–112
    strategic thinking about, 100–101
    supplier bargaining power, 112–115
Industry life cycle, 101
Industry opportunity, 153
Industry position, 241
Industry rivals
    competitive intelligence about, 129
    likely strategic moves, 128–130
    questions to ask about, 129–130
    strategic group mapping, 125–128
        assessing market position, 126–127
        benefits of using, 127–128
        definition of groups, 126
        guidelines, 126–127
        procedures, 126
        some positions more attractive, 128
        variables for, 126–127
        varying profit prospects, 128
Industry standard, 222–223
Information-sharing with employees, 425
Information systems
    areas covered by, 422
    electronic score cards, 422
    to monitor employees, 423
    real-time, 422
    for strategy execution, 420–422
Information technology
    at Cemex, C-212–C-213
    for low-cost providers, 188

Information technology industry
  Atlassian in, C-81–C-93
  Google Inc. in, C-136–C-154
  makeup of, C-71–C-72
  sales and market shares, C-77
Infrastructure, developing countries, 284
Initial public offering, Google Inc., C-138
Innovation
  at Atlassian, C-87–C-91
  limited in golf equipment, C-34–C-37
  loss in outsourcing, 237
  rapid, 199
  stifled by Six Sigma, 416–418
  striving for, 195
Inputs
  high-quality, 196
  lower-cost, 187
Inside directors, 91
Insular, inwardly-focused cultures, 449
Intangible assets, 145–146
Intangible features, 197–198
Integrated social contracts theory
  cross-cultural differences, 345–346
  guidance for managers, 346
  imposing limitations, 345
  and local standards, 345
  and major religions, 346
  and "second-order" norms, 346
  universal "first-order" norms, 345–346
Integration, post-merger, C-220–C-222
Intellectual capital, 145–146
Intellectual property rights, in smartphones,
    C-163
Intelligence Magazine, C-12
Internal capital market, 309, 323
Internal cash flow, 144
Internal cost structure, 160–161
Internal development
  of core competencies, 386–388
  diversification by, 297–298
Internal entrepreneurship, 447
Internal fit, 60
Internally performed value chain activities, 165
Internal universities, 389–390
International Air Transport Association, C-173
International Civil Aviation Organization, C-173
International expansion
  Atlassian, C-92–C-93
  Starbucks, C-339–C-341
International Labor Organization, 342
International marketing, 250–287
  cross-border subsidization, 279–280
  cross-border tactics, 280
  cross-country variations, 253–255
  demographic differences, 259–260
  in developing countries, 280–284
  economic risks, 257
  exchange rate risks, 257–259
  global competition, 262
  global strategy, 271–272
  impact of government policies, 256–257
  local defenses against global giants, 284–287
  locating value chain activities, 255–256
  multidomestic competition, 260–262
  multidomestic strategy, 269–271
  options for entering foreign markets, 262–269
  political risks, 257
  profit sanctuaries, 277–278

  quest for competitive advantage, 273–277
  reasons for entering foreign markets, 252–253
  strategy complexity, 253–260
  transnational strategy, 272–273
International rivals
  cross-border tactics against, 280
  mutual restraint, 280
International Standards Organization, 360
International strategy
  advantages and disadvantages, 273
  Atlassian, C-87–C-91, C-92–C-93
  Canadian Solar, C-207–C-208
  Cemex, C-212–C-222
  Coca-Cola Company, C-26
  definition, 269
  Dell Inc., C-62
  global, 270–272
  Google Inc., C-147–C-148
  Grupo Modelo, C-229–C-230, C-232–C-233
  Komatsu, C-243–C-249
  multidomestic, 269–271
  Red Bull, C-26
  Research in motion, C-165–C-169
  Shangri-La Hotels, C-289–C-291,
    C-301–C-302
  Starbucks, C-339–C-341
  transnational, 272
International trade
  dumping strategy, 279
  and exchange rates, 258–259
Internet
  effect on competitive forces, 122
  Google Inc., C-136–C-154
  and industry change, 122
  rivals for Google Inc., C-151–C-153
  use in China, 282–283
  Voice-over-Internet Protocol (VoIP), 122
Internet access at Starbucks, C-337–C-339
Internet browsers, ranking by publisher, C-2
Internet retailing; *see* Online retailing
Interpol, C-37
Introductory low prices, 192
Inventory turn cycle, by Dell Inc., C-61
Inventory turnover ratio, 143
Inverted flexible vertical integration business
    model, C-205
Investment
  industry attractiveness test, 295
  priorities for diversified companies, 293–294
  socially responsible, 368
Investment fraud, 350–351
Ireland, pro-business environment, 256
ISO 9000 standard, 196, 287
Israel, solar energy industry, C-195
Italy
  investigation of Google, C-154
  solar energy industry, C-195

J

J. D. Power Initial Quality Study ranking of
    automobiles, C-321
Japan
  Dell's rivals in, C-62
  export strategies, 263
  kaizen, 414
  problems at MNCs, C-239–C-240

  as profit sanctuary, 277–278
  share of global revenue, C-240
  solar energy industry, C-195
  solar producers, C-199–C-200
Jargriti Learning Centers, C-387
Jikoda (self-regulation), C-306, C-312–C-313
Job postings, at Research in Motion,
    C-164–C-165
Joint ventures
  to access capabilities, 389
  Cemex, C-214–C-216
  cross-border, 252
  definition, 239
  diversification by, 298
  to enter foreign markets, 265–269
  examples, 239–240
  facilitating resource and risk sharing, 265–266
  GM-Toyota, C-306
  Komatsu, C-249
  Komatsu Dresser, C-245
  learning and added expertise, 267
  risks
    conflicting objectives, 266
    loss of competitive advantage, 268
    overly dependent on partners, 268
    transaction costs, 266
  when unnecessary, 268–269
Just-in-time delivery, 189–190
Just-in-time systems, 274, 387
  by Dell Inc., C-60–C-61
  at Toyota, C-311

K

Kaizen (continuous improvement), 414, C-305,
    C-306, C-313, C-322
Kanban (signboard), C-306, C-312
Kerala State Groundwater Department, India,
    C-391
Kerala State Pollution Control Board, India,
    C-391
Key success factors
  in beer industry, 131
  and company strategy, 130–131
  for competitiveness analysis, 170
  correctly diagnosing, 130–131
  definition, 130
  number of, 131
  questions for, 131
Kickbacks
  payment of, 342–343
  permitted or forbidden, 345
  and social contract theory, 346
Kiosks, Dell Direct Store, C-62
Knowledge-based capabilities, 146
Knowledge resources, upgrading, 389–390

L

Labor costs, country differences, 121
Labor force
  underage workers, C-399
  unrest in China, C-253
Lagging indicators, 78
Land, Infrastructure and Transport Ministry,
    Taiwan, C-178

Late-mover advantages
  buyer expectations, 223
  and costly pioneering, 223
  market uncertainties, 223
  pros and cons, 224–225
  rapid market evolution, 223
Latin America, Cemex in, C-218–C-219
Lead by example, 453
Leadership; *see also* Management; Managers
  to change problem cultures
    difficulties, 450
    making a case for change, 451–452
    questions needed for, 450–451
    steps, 452
    substantive actions, 452–453
    symbolic actions, 453–454
    time it takes for, 454
  at Komatsu, C-252
  in strategy execution
    making corrective adjustments, 457–458
    management by walking around, 455
    managerial actions, 454–455
    pressure for excellence, 455–457
    role of top executives, 454–455
Leadership in Energy and Environmental
    Design standards; *see* LEED certified
    construction
Leading indicators of financial performance, 78
Leapfrogging competitors, 217
Learning curve, 107
  benefits in single location, 274
  from centralizing production, 263
  from foreign markets, 252
Learning-curve effects, 186
Learning process, in strategic alliances, 242
LEED certified construction
  definition, C-353
  at Starbucks, C-337, C-353
Legal factors, 100
Legislation, and TomTom, C-113–C-114
Leverage ratios, 143
Licensed retail stores, C-339
Licensing
  as barrier to entry, 108–109
  versus diversification, 300
Licensing strategies, 263
Lifestyles
  changes, 123–124
  national differences, 277
Line-and-staff structure, 394
Liquidity ratios, 142
Literacy India, C-387
Loans; *see* Farmer loans; Mortgage lending
Local companies, defenses against global
    giants
  acquisitions and rapid-growth strategies, 286
  business models, 284
  customized products, 285
  knowing customer needs, 285
  local workforce, 285–286
  transfer of company expertise, 286–287
Local-country ethical norms, 346
Local market, making changes in, 283
Local workforce, 285–286
Location, to build competitive advantage,
    273–275
  concentrated, 274
  dispersed, 274–275

Location-based economies of scale, 274
Lodging industry; *see* Hotel industry
Long-term debt, at TomTom, C-116, C-117
Long-term debt-to-capital ratio, 143
Long-term debt-to-equity ratio, 143
Long-term growth rate changes, 120–121
Long-term objectives, 79–81
Los Angeles Times, C-318, C-320
Lost Horizon (Hilton), C-288
Lowballing on price, 217–218
Low-cost advantage
  achieving, 185–186
  over rivals, 185
Low-cost carriers, China, C-179
Low-cost distribution channels, 189
Low-cost leadership, 185
Low-cost providers, 208–209
Low-cost provider strategies, 56
  to achieve cost leadership, 185
  advantages over rivals, 185
  avenues to achieving, 185–190
    cost-efficient value chain, 186–189
    revamp value chain, 189–190
  best conditions for
    buyer bargaining power, 192
    few ways to differentiate, 192
    low switching costs, 192
    price cuts, 192
    products identical, 192
    same product use, 192
    vigorous price-cutting, 192
  compared to best-cost providers, 216
  compared to focused low-cost strategy, 201
  corporate examples, 192
  distinguishing features, 228–229
  features and services, 185
  incentive system in, 428
  keys to success
    scrutinize cost-cutting activities, 190–191
    spend on resources and capabilities,
        191–192
  market position, 183
  pitfalls to avoid
    aggressive price-cutting, 193
    failure to emphasize cost advantage, 193
    fixation on cost reduction, 193
  strategic target, 185
Low-price strategy, for developing countries,
    281–282
Low-wage countries, 256

M

Macroenvironment
  components, 98–99
  demographics, 100
  general economic conditions, 100
  global forces, 100
  immediate and competitive environment, 99
  natural environment, 100
  political, legal, and regulatory forces, 100
  rapid or slow changes in, 99
  social forces, 100
  strategically relevant, 98–99
  technological factors, 100
Make-or-buy decision, 115

Management
  action agenda, 86–87
  demands on, in unrelated diversification, 311
  to develop core competencies, 388
  as good strategy execution, 62–63
  of greenfield ventures, 265
  localizing, C-246–C-248
  style in foreign markets, 255
Management by walking around, 455
Management change
  at Komatsu, C-243, C-245, C-248, C-250,
      C-251
  at Starbucks, C-355
Management team
  assembling, 381–382
  critical mass of talented managers, 382
  at General Electric, 383–384
  main considerations, 381–382
  situational differences, 381
Managerial motives, wrong reason for
    diversification, 312–313
Managers; *see also* Leadership
  empire-building, 449
  frontline, 85
  in high-performance cultures, 447
  involved in strategy-making, 81–86
  issues meriting attention of, 173
  pressure to meet short-term targets,
      349–351
  questions faced by, 52
  self-dealing, 348
  strategy execution procedures, 409–411
  in strong-culture companies, 443–444
  "worry list" of problems, 173
Managing by the numbers, 311
Manufacturing
  concentrated in few locations, 274
  country variations, 255–256
  cross-border coordination, 277
  dispersed, 274–275
  export strategies, 262–263
  global competition, 261–262
  incentive compensation, 329
  lower costs in some locations, 274
  multidomestic competition, 260–261
  strategic fit, 305
Manufacturing execution system, 188
Market(s)
  as competitive battleground, 102–103
  with growing demand, 104
  oversupplied, 106
  for smartphones, C-158–C-161
  worldwide beer industry, C-231–C-232
Market conditions
  cross-country variations, 259–260
  deterioration of, 328–329
  external fit, 60
  think-local, act-local approach, 270–271
Market demand, 109
Market evolution, rapid, 223
Market expansion, Starbucks
  international expansion, C-339–C-341
  licensed retail stores, C-339
  new market segments, C-341–C-344
  new product offerings, C-342–C-344
  outside Pacific Northwest, C-333–C-334
  partnerships, C-342–C-343
  strategy for, C-339–C-341

Marketing
  by Atlassian, C-91
  by Canadian Solar, C-208
  by Cemex, C-222
  by Dell Inc., C-61–C-63
  in differentiation strategy, 196
  by Grupo Modelo, C-233
  incentive compensation, 329
  strategic fit, 304–305
  by TomTom, C-116–C-118
  value chain activity, 159
Marketing innovation, 122
Marketing strategy, 84
Market leaders
  attack on, 218–219
  global vs. domestic, 251
Market niche focus, 56–57
Market niche strategy; *see* Focus strategies
Market opportunities
  emerging and fast-changing markets, 153
  factor in shaping strategy, 152–153
  identifying, 152–153
  industry vs. market opportunity, 153
  list of, 154
  new, 228
Market pioneers, 221–222
Market position
  and acquisition, 296
  defensive strategies, 220–221
  of generic competitive strategies, 184
  mergers and acquisitions, 226–229
  outsourcing strategies, 235–237
  reason for broadening business base, 328
  and scope of the firm, 225–226
  strategic alliances, 237–240
  strategic group mapping for, 125–128
  strategic offensives, 216–221
  and timing of strategies, 221–225
  vertical integration, 229–235
Market potential in China, 259–260
Market segments in global competition, 261–262
Market share
  in athletic shoe industry, C-281
  in construction machinery industry, C-250
  and costs, 157
  decline for Japanese MNCs, C-240
  energy drink brands, C-22
  Komatsu, C-254
  leading PC vendors
    United States, C-52
    worldwide, C-52
  major PC vendors, C-127
  PepsiCo, C-261
  PepsiCo carbonated drinks, C-267
  PepsiCo snack foods, C-268
  photovoltaic cell producers, C-200
  photovoltaic module producers, C-200
  reason for mergers and acquisitions, 227
  relative, 318
  search engine rankings, C-151
  smartphone makers, C-149
  soft drink industry, C-265
  and total profit, 193
  trends for Dell 1994–2007, C-63
Market shocks, 153–155
Market size, 101
Market space, types of, 219

Market standing, 62
Market uncertainties, 223
Mass-customization
  from technological change, 122
  in transnational strategy, 272
Massively multiplayer online role-playing games, 284
Materials handling, reducing, 189–190
Matrix structure
  advantages and disadvantages, 397
  capabilities-based, 397
  definition, 396
  modern form, 396
  multiple reporting relationships, 396
  terms for, 396–397
M-audits, C-400–C-402, C-403
MAV audits, C-402
Measure, 414
Merger, 226
Mergers and acquisitions; *see also* Acquisitions
  to acquire capabilities, 388–389
  benefits of, 227
  Clear Channel Communications, 230
  and cultural compatibility, 450
  horizontal, 226–229
  and horizontal scope, 226
  to increase scale and scope, 226–227
  market leadership from, 228–229
  much-used option, 226
  outcomes aimed at
    access to new technologies, 228
    convergence of industries, 228
    expanding geographic coverage, 227
    increasing market share, 227
    increasing scale of operations, 227
    new product categories, 227–228
    new resources and capabilities, 228
  reasons for failure, 229
  recent failures, 228–229
  versus strategic alliances, 237–238, 243–244
  to strengthen competitiveness, 227
  by TomTom, C-110–C-111
Mexico
  Cemex, C-212–C-226
  community savings scheme, C-214
  income from immigrants, C-24
  working conditions, C-397
M-forms, 395
Minimum wage in China, C-397–C-398
Ministry of International Trade and Industry, Japan, C-240
Mission statement
  definition, 74
  descriptive nature of, 75
  flawed examples, 75
  Microsoft, 75
  Royal Dutch Shell, 77
  Shangri-La Hotels, C-296
  Sony Corporation, 74
  Starbucks, C-350, C-351
Mistake-proofing at Toyota, C-305, C-313
Mobile phone industry
  Apple's competitive position, C-131–C-132
  in China, C-132
Mobile phones, 197, C-112–C-113; *see also* Smartphones
  Android, C-136

BlackBerry solution architecture, C-159
  competing platforms, C-161–C-162
  competitive research and development, C-163
  demand for, C-161
  global shipments in 2007, C-161
  market for, C-158–C-161
  number of BlackBerry subscribers, C-157
  number of users in U.S., C-161
  number of users worldwide, C-161
  from Research in Motion, C-156–C-169
  wireless communications, C-158–C-161
Moderate rivalry, 107
Moral free space, 345
Motivation
  at Amgen, 427
  of employees, 188
  from financial incentives, 424
  at Google, Inc., 426
  for high-performance standards, 456–457
  high-powered, 424
  at JM Family Enterprises, 426
  at Lincoln Electric, 426
  from nonmonetary incentives, 424–425
  at Nordstrom, 426
  at Ukrop's Super Markets, 427
  at W. L. Gore, 427
  at Wegmans, 426
Multibrand strategy, C-130
Multidivisional structure
  definition, 395
  and diversification strategy, 395–396
  versus functional structure, 396
  related diversification problems, 396
  vertically integrated firms, 396
Multidomestic competition
  features of, 260–261
  transition to global competition, 261–262
Multidomestic strategy
  advantages/disadvantages, 273
  definition, 269
  drawbacks, 271
  think-local, act-local approach, 269–271
Multinational corporations
  less need for alliances, 268–269
  payment of bribes and kickbacks, 342–343
  problems in Japan, C-239–C-240
Municipal Corporation of Mumbai, C-386
Mutual restraint, 280

N

Narrowly diversified companies, 313
National Geophysical Research Institute, C-391
National Highway Traffic Safety
  Administration, C-320
National Security Bureau, Taiwan, C-177
Natural environment, 100
Natural resources, 362, 363
Near-term performance targets, 86
Net income
  decline at Cemex, C-223, C-226
  at TomTom, C-115–C-116
Net neutrality, C-154
Net profit margin, 142
Net return on sales, 142
Network effects, barrier to entry, 108

Network structure, 401
New customers, in foreign markets, 252
New employees
    and corporate culture, 442–443
    screening, 442
New entrants
    and barriers to entry, 107–109
    competitive pressures from threat of, 107–110
    effect on market, 107
    existing industry members, 110
    factors affecting threat of, 110
    from growing demand, 109
    from high profit potential, 109
    from lower trade barriers, 121
    pool of potential entrants, 109–110
    quality level of products, 157
    reaction of incumbent firms, 106
    test of weakness or strength, 109
Newly emerging markets, 153
New product categories, 227–228
New products
    at Dell Inc., C-53, C-63–C-66
    speeding to market, 386
    Starbucks, C-344
New venture development, 297–298
New York Times, C-12
New Zealand, and Google, C-154
Next-generation products, 199, 237
Next-generation technologies, 217
Nine-cell matrix
    for competitive strength, 319–321
    to portray industry attractiveness, 319–321
Nonfinancial resource fit
    avoid overtaxing, 325
    resources and capabilities, 324–325
Nongovernmental organizations
    India, C-387
    supplier compliance efforts
        Fair Factories Clearinghouse, C-411
        Fair Labor Association, C-410–C-411
Nonmonetary incentives
    acting on employees' ideas, 424–425
    attractive office space, 425
    awards and recognition, 424
    information-sharing, 425
    promotion from within, 424
    strategic vision, 425
    work atmosphere, 425
Normal rivalry, 107
Norms, 340
    in corporate culture, 441–442
North America, Shangri-La Hotels in, C-302

O

Obama administration, C-137, C-150, C-154
Objectives
    at all organizational levels, 79–81
    balanced scorecard for, 78–79
    of benchmarking, 162
    characteristics, 76
    corporate examples, 91
    financial, 76–78
    long-term, 79–81
    merits of strategic objectives, 79
    setting, 76–81

    short-term, 79–81
    strategic, 78
    top-down process, 81
    as yardsticks, 76
Office of Federal Housing Enterprise Oversight,
    90
Office space, 425
Oil crisis of 1970s, C-306
Olympic Games of 2008, C-289
Online navigation websites, C-113
Online retailing
    advantages, 233
    and channel conflict, 233
    by Dell Inc., C-61
Online training, 390
Ontario, Feed-in Tariff program, C-198
Operating excellence, 455–457
Operating flexibility, 233
Operating funds, reallocating, 408
Operating income, Dell Inc., C-56
Operating margin, at TomTom, C-116, C-117
Operating profit margin, 142
Operating statistics, 423
Operating strategies, 83
    definition, 84–85
Operating systems
    corporate uses, 420–421
    for strategy execution, 422–423
Operations, 159
    business process reengineering, 413–414
    component of value chain, 158
    reason for mergers and acquisitions, 227
    TomTom, C-118–C-119
Opportunity; *see also* SWOT analysis
    for Atlassian, C-83–C-85
    industry vs. company, 153
    for related diversification, 301
Organizational bridges, 400–401
Organizational capabilities; *see* Capabilities
Organizational culture; *see* Company culture;
    Corporate culture
    Google Inc., C-139–C-140
    at Research in Motion, C-164
    at Shangri-La Hotels, C-298–C-299
    at Toyota, C-314–C-316
Organizational resources, 145–146
Organizational structure
    aligned with strategy, 393
    benefits of good design, 393
    centralized decision making, 397–399
    collaboration with external partners, 400–401
    decentralized decision making, 399–400
    definition, 393
    in foreign markets, 255
    functional, 394–395
    matrix, 396–397
    multidivisional, 395–396
    network structure, 401
    PepsiCo, C-256
    at Shangri-La Hotels, C-296–C-297
    simple, 394
    strategy-critical activities as building blocks,
        393–394
Organization-building activities
    core competencies, 380, 385–390
    organizing work effort, 380, 390–401
    staffing, 380–385

Organization for Economic Cooperation and
    Development antibribery standards, 343
Organizations
    need for objectives at all levels, 79–81
    strategy-making at all levels, 81–86
Outside directors, 91
Outside specialists, 235
Outsourcing
    to access capabilities, 389
    advantages of, 188
        concentration on core business, 237
        diverse kinds of expertise, 237
        not crucial for competitive advantage, 235
        outside specialists, 235
        reduced risk exposure, 236
        speed time to market, 235–236
    definition, 235
    by Dell Inc., C-80
    drawbacks, 392–393
    risks in
        hollowing out capabilities, 237
        lack of direct control, 237
        weakened innovation, 237
    by Toyota, C-320
    of value chain activities, 392–393
Outsourcing decisions, 226
Overspending, 200
Overtime pay rules, China, C-398

P

Packaging, Coca-Cola India, C-386–C-387
Palakkad District Environmental Protection
    Council and Guidance Society, India,
    C-391
Parenting advantage, 311
Parenting capabilities, 308
Partial integration, 231
Partnerships; *see also* Strategic alliances
    of Afrigator, C-13–C-14
    Google Inc., C-150
    of Motorola India, C-168
    with Starbucks, C-341–C-343
    for TomTom, C-111–C-112
Peer-based control, 423
Performance
    better-off test, 296
    combined, 294
    prospects for business units, 325–326
    rewards linked to, 427–430
    short-term earnings targets, 349
    short-termism, 351
    strategy moves to improve, 326–332
Performance evaluation, 87–88
Performance indicators
    competitive strength, 62
    market standing, 62
    profitability, 62
Performance measures
    for incentive compensation, 329
    triple bottom line, 361
Performance targets, 81, 428
    to enhance individual commitment, 429–430
    near-term, 86
    results vs. efforts rewarded, 430
    and timing of rewards, 430

Performance test, 62
Perks, 424
Personal computer industry
   Acer, C-129–C-130
   Apple's competitive position, C-124–C-128
   Apple's product line, C-122–C-124
   comparative value chains, C-53
   Dell Inc., C-51–C-73, C-77–C-80,
      C-128–C-129
   early years, C-72
   Hewlett-Packard, C-73–C-77, C-127
   market shares, C-52, C-127
   overview, C-124
   research and development, C-72–C-73
   specialization, C-72
   white-box PCs, C-70
   worldwide shipments 1980–2011, C-72
   worldwide unit sales, C-79
Personal media player industry, C-130–C-131
Personal navigation devices, C-108, C-112,
      C-113–C-114, C-116, C-117, C-118,
      C-119–C-120
Peru, working conditions, C-397
Pharmaceutical industry, energy drinks, C-29
Philanthropic activities, 357
Philanthropy
   by Atlassian, C-92–C-93
   by Starbucks, C-353
Photovoltaic cells (PV), C-192–C-193
Physical maps, C-113
Physical resources, 145–146
Piece-rate incentive plan, 429
Pioneering
   to build brand loyalty, 222
   for firm's reputation, 222
   more costly than imitation, 223
   risks in, 221
Plachimada Solidarity Committee, India,
      C-390
Plant inspectors, C-399
   strategies to deceive, C-398–C-400
Poaching, C-370–C-374
Pokayoke (mistake-proofing), C-305, C-313
Political factors, 100
Political risks, 257
Politicized cultures, 449
Ponzi scheme, 349, 350
Poor, the, Bottom-of-the Pyramid populations,
      C-384
Population
   cross-country variations, 259
   of developing countries, 281
Portfolio approach to financial fit, 323–324
Portugal, solar energy industry, C-195
Post-merger integration, C-219–C-220
Practices, in corporate culture, 440
Pre-emptive strike, 218
Press releases, 129
Pressure groups, 366
Price(s)
   below-market pricing, 279–280
   competitive with rivals, 156–168
   dumping strategies, 156–157
   lowballing, 217–218
   low introductory, 192
   of substitutes, 113
Price competition, 192
Price-conscious buyers, 206

Price-cutting
   aggressive, 193
   and cross-market subsidization, 279–280
Price-cutting offensive, 216–217
Price-earnings ratio, 144
Price gouging, 200
Price information, 116–117
Price premium, 200–201
Price sensitivity, and buyer bargaining power
   with low profit or income, 118
   product performance, 118
   purchase as large fraction of budget, 118
Price wars, video game industry, C-101
Pricing by Komatsu, C-244–C-245
Primary value chain activities, 157–158
   distribution, 159
   operations, 159
   sales and marketing, 159
   service, 159
   supply chain management, 159
Proactive strategies, 58–59
Pro-business environment, 256
Process innovation, 188
Process management tools
   benchmarking, 412–413
   best practices, 411–413
   business process reengineering, 413–414
   capturing benefits of, 419–420
   Six Sigma quality programs, 415–418
   total quality management, 414
Procurement policies, 365
Product(s)
   continuous innovation, 217
   diverse needs and uses of buyers, 199
   essentially identical, 192
   identical or differentiated, 104–105
   next-generation, 199, 237
   superior features, design, and performance,
      194
   tailored for developing countries, 281–282
   too many features, 200
   top international, of 2008, C-13
Product development strategy, 84; see also New
      product development
Product differentiation
   in beer industry, 131
   in best-cost provider strategy, 206
   and degree of rivalry, 104–105
   effect on switching costs, 106
   few ways of achieving, 192
   at Komatsu, C-249
   in multidomestic strategy, 269
   from technological change, 122
Product information, and buyer bargaining
      power, 116–117
Product innovation, 122
Production
   build-to-order manufacturing, C-58
   of Nike products, C-400
   for Nintendo, C-102
   at Starbucks, C-352–C-353
   by Toyota, C-309
Production capacity, 106
Production costs
   and industry change, 123
   lower costs in some locations, 274
Production research and development
      activities, 195

Production technology, advanced, 188
Product life cycle, extended in foreign markets,
      252
Product line
   Apple Inc., C-122–C-124
   Atlassian, C-88
   Canadian Solar, C-206
   Google Inc., C-141–C-143
   Komatsu, C-241–C-243
   limited, 189
   Nintendo, C-97–C-102
   PepsiCo, C-255, C-262–C-263
   personal media players, C-130–C-131
   Rugby+, C-222
   TaylorMade-adidas Golf, C-284
   TomTom, C-108
Product research and development, 159
Product "versioning," 195
Profitability, 62
   connected to competitive advantage, 57
   cost-of-entry test, 295–296
   enhanced by differentiation, 194
   eroded by overspending, 200
   identifying threats to, 153–155
   in related diversification, 307
   slow in developing countries, 284
   and strength of competitive forces, 118–119
Profitability ratios, 142
Profit margin, 158
Profit potential, and threat of new entrants,
      109
Profit prospects
   factors in analyzing, 132–133
   and industry attractiveness, 132–133
   varying among strategic groups, 128
Profits
   at Komatsu, C-252–C-253
   requirement in unrelated diversification, 308
Profit sanctuaries
   as competitive asset, 279
   and cross-market subsidization, 279–280
   definition, 277
   to deter rivals, 280
   domestic-only companies, 278
   Japan, 277–278
   part-international company, 278
   worldwide company, 278
Promotion, at China Airlines, C-181
Promotion (job)
   from within, 424
   at Shangri-La Hotels, C-300
Proprietary knowledge, 231–232
Pro shops, C-40
Protected Areas Act No. 57, South Africa,
      C-375
Public recognition, 424
Punishment, 425–427
Purchase, buyer discretion to delay, 115–118
Purchasing power
   in developing countries, 259
   in foreign markets, 252
Purchasing process, at Starbucks
   best practices cultivation, C-352
   environmental sustainability, C-352–C-353
   Fair Trade Certified coffee, C-352
   key elements, C-350
   pricing, C-350–C-352
Pursuit of personal gain, 348–349

Q

Quality
  ISO 9000 standard, 196
  problems at Toyota, C-316–C-322
  of products, 157
  at Toyota, C-305
Quality assurance, at Toyota, C-316
Quality circles, at Toyota, C-313
Quality control
  at Dell Inc., C-60
  in franchises, 264
  Six Sigma program, 415–418
  total quality management, 414
Quality control process, 195–196
Quality management, at Toyota, C-309–C-314
Quality spectrum, 157
Quantitative strength ratings, 169–170
Quick-service restaurant industry, 55

R

Radio frequency identification tags, on rhinos, C-364
Rapid-growth strategies, 286
Raw materials, 253
Realized strategy, 58–59
Recognition, C-349
  at Shangri-La Hotels, C-300
Recruitment
  at China Airlines, C-180
  at Research in Motion, C-165–C-166
Recycling
  at Canadian Solar, C-205–C-206
  Coca-Cola India, C-386–C-387
Reengineering
  value chain activities, 414
  work effort, 413
Regulatory factors
  definition, 100
  and industry change, 123
  and TomTom, C-113–C-114
Related and supporting industries
  in foreign markets, 255
  location near, 274
Related businesses, 300
Related diversification
  based on value chain matchup, 301
  definition, 300–301
  economies of scope, 306
  gains in shareholder value, 306–307
  and multidivisional structure, 395–396
  path to competitive advantage, 306
  satisfying better-off test, 307
  specialized resources and capabilities, 301–303
  strategic fit, 300–303
  value chain activities, 303
Relationship managers, 401
Relationships, 145–146
Relative market share, 318
Religious beliefs
  and bribery and corruption, 346
  and ethical standards, 342
Renewable Energy Law, Germany, C-193
Reorganization at China Airlines, C-183

Republic of China; see also Taiwan
  China Airlines, C-172
  dropped from United Nations, C-173
  relations with mainland China, C-178–C-179, C-183–C-184
Reputational assets, 145–146
Reputation-damaging incidents, 366
Reputation of firm, for first-movers, 222
Research and development
  Dell Inc., C-69–C-70
  Motorola Center, C-168
  Research in Motion, C-156, C-162–C-164
  strategic fit, 305, 400
  value chain activity, 159
Resource allocation, assigning priority for, 325–326
Resource and capability analysis, 168
  dynamic management, 149–150
  identifying resources and capabilities, 144–147
  to produce competitive advantage, 147–150
  purpose, 144
  tests of competitive power, 148–149
Resource-based competitive strategies, 210
Resource bundles, 147, 168
Resource fit
  definition, 322
  in diversified companies, 322–325
  financial, 323–324
  nonfinancial, 324–325
  related diversification, 322–323
  unrelated diversification, 322–323
Resources
  adequate for diversification, 324–325
  aggressive spending on, 191–192
  avoiding overtaxing, 325
  basis of competitive attack, 216
  for best-cost provider strategy, 206
  better in some locations, 274
  causal ambiguity, 149
  competitive assets, 141–150
  competitively superior, 149
  cross-border sharing, 275–277
  cutting-edge, 150
  definition, 148–149
  in diversification decisions, 298–299
  durable value, 150
  intangible, 145–146
  of local companies to compete, 286–287
  reason for mergers and acquisitions, 229
  relation to value chain, 167–168
  requirements for diversification, 315
  social complexity, 148–149
  specialized vs. generalized, 301–303
  for successful differentiation, 198
  tangible, 145–146
  tests of competitive power
    available substitutes, 149
    competitively valuable, 148
    hard to copy, 148–149
    rarity, 148
  at TomTom, C-111–C-112
  used in foreign markets, 252–253
Restructuring, 327
  companywide, 330
  corporate, 330
  through divesting and new acquisition, 330–332
  examples, 332
  failure at Adidas, C-271–C-272

following divestiture, 331
  at Komatsu
    company, C-248–C-249
    internal, C-248
  necessitated by large acquisition, 331
  plan at Adidas, C-276–C-278
  undervalued companies, 310
  at VF Corporation, 331
Results-oriented work climate, 456–457
Retailers
  Adidas, C-280
  bargaining power, 115–116
  coordinating with, 196
  franchising strategies, 263–264
  of golf equipment, C-40
  sales by Dell, C-62–C-63
Retail space, barrier to entry, 108
Retaliation
  for below-market pricing, 279–280
  signaling, 221
Retraining, 389–390
Retrenching, 327
  to narrow diversification base, 328–330
Return on invested capital, 142
Return on sales, 142
Return on total assets, 142
Revenue enhancement, 366–367
Revenues, C-189
  Acer 2006–2009, C-129
  Atlassian in 2009, C-81
  Dell Inc., C-56
  Dell Inc. 2006–2008, C-65, C-66
  Dell Inc. 2008–2010, C-129
  from energy shot brands, C-23
  of Google by source, C-147
  at Komatsu, C-251
  Microsoft in 1009, C-152
  Research in Motion, C-157
  of TomTom, C-107
  at Toyota, C-304–C-305
Rewards
  balanced with punishment, 425–427
  company examples, 426–427
  in corporate culture, 442
  linked to performance, 427–430
  scrupulous administration of, 429
  strategy execution objectives, 423
  for success, 457
Rhinos
  and animal rights activists, C-375
  capturing, C-364–C-368
  hunting, C-368–C-370
  income from captures, C-362–C-363
  number in South Africa, C-361
  poaching, C-370–C-374
  translocation 1961, C-361
Risk reduction, wrong reason for diversification, 312
Risks
  best-cost provider strategy, 207–208
  of exchange rate shifts, 257–259
  focused differentiation strategy, 203–205
  focused low-cost strategy, 206
  political, 257
Rivalry
  and buyer demand
    cost of brand switching, 104
    in fast-growing markets, 104

Rivalry—*Cont.*
  cutthroat, 107
  and diversity of competitors, 106
  factors affecting strength of, 105
  fierce or strong, 107
  in foreign markets, 255
  in globally competitive markets, 106
  and high exit barriers, 105–107
  identical vs. differentiated products, 104–106
  moderate or normal, 107
  as number of competitors increases, 106
  and unused production capacity, 106
  varying by industry, 103
  weak, 107
Rivals; *see also* Competitors; Industry rivals
  accessing costs of, 163
  adopting or improving ideas of, 217
  chosen for attack, 218–219
  competitive battles among, 102–104
  competitive intelligence on, 129–130
  competitive weapons, 104
  cost advantage over, 188–189
  costs and prices competitive with, 156–168
  deterred by profit sanctuaries, 280
  following differentiation, 199
  low-cost advantage over, 185
  signaling retaliation, 221
  strategy for competitive edge over, 102
  ways of competing, 102–103
Robotic production, 188
Routing algorithms, C-111
Royal and Ancient Golf Club of St. Andrews,
  C-30
Runner-up firms, attack on, 219
Russia, McDonald's experience in, 283

S

Safaris
  companies operating, C-370–C-373
  cost of, C-368
Sales
  by Adidas regionally, C-281
  Apple Inc. 2005–2009, C-126
  Asian beverage market, C-20
  Callaway Golf Company, C-43
  Canadian Solar, C-204–C-205
  Dell Inc., C-61–C-63
  in differentiation strategy, 196
  and distribution in beverage industry,
    C-20–C-21
  European beverage industry, C-20
  global beverage industry, C-18, C-19
  golf equipment 1997–2008, C-31–C-33
  incentive compensation, 329
  by Komatsu, C-247
  Microsoft Xbox, C-106
  Nintendo game systems, C-97
  Nintendo Wii, C-102
  PepsiCo, C-255–C-256
  PepsiCo beverages, C-267–C-268
  PepsiCo snack foods, C-268–C-269
  Quaker Oats products, C-269
  Reebok 2002–2004, C-277
  Six Sigma program for, 416
  Sony PlayStation 3, C-105
  strategic fit, 304–305

TomTom, C-115–C-116
  top ten auto groups, C-318
  Toyota, C-304–C-305, C-309
  U.S. beverage industry, C-19
  value chain activity, 159
Sales decline
  at Nintendo, C-96
  at Reebok, C-282–C-284
  for soft drinks, C-17
Sales offices, Canadian Solar, C-207–C-208
Sarbanes-Oxley Act, 346
Satellite navigation systems, C-107–C-120
Scope of the firm
  decisions, 225–226
  horizontal, 226
  outsourcing decisions, 226
  vertical, 226
Search engines
  Google Inc., C-136–C-154
  market share rankings, C-151
  MSN online services, C-152–C-153
  Yahoo!, C-151–C-152
"Second-order" ethical norms, 346
Securities and Exchange Commission, 90, 346
  failure in Madoff fraud, 349
  and Tyco International, 348
Self-dealing, 348
Self-managed work groups, 423
Self-manufacturing, 115
Self-regulation, at Toyota, C-306,
  C-312–C-313
Sellers, number of, in relation to buyers, 116
Serious Fraud Office, United Kingdom, 343
Service enterprises
  franchising strategies, 263–264
  value chain activity, 159
SHAPE inspections, C-402
Shareholders
  benefits of sustainability strategies, 367–368
  effect of unethical behavior, 355
  executive as agents for, 89
Shareholder value
  justification for diversification
    better-off test, 296
    cost-of-entry test, 295–296
    industry attractiveness test, 295
  PepsiCo, C-259–C-270
  in related diversification, 306–307
  from unrelated diversification
    acquiring undervalued companies, 310
    corporate parenting, 308–309
    cross-business allocation of financial
      resources, 309–310
    requirements, 310–311
    restructuring, 310
Short-term earnings targets, 349–351
Short-termism, 351
Short-term objectives, 79–81
Signaling retaliation, 221
Signaling value, 198
Simple structure, 394
Single-business company, 141
Six Sigma quality programs, 413
  blended approach, 418
  capturing full value of, 419–420
  companies using, 416–418
  compared to business process
    reengineering, 418

compared to total quality management, 418
  definition, 415
  DMADV type, 415
  DMAIC type, 415–416
  to focus on continuous improvement, 456
  innovation stifled by, 416–418
  underlying principles, 415
  at Whirlpool, 417
Skills
  needed in vertical integration, 234
  upgrading, 389–390
Slogan, vision expressed as, 73–74
Slotting fees, C-21
Small companies
  simple structure, 394
  strategic plans, 86
Small firms, attack on, 219
Smartphones, 199, C-112–C-113; *see also*
  Mobile phones
  Google in market for, C-148–C-149
  market shares, C-147
  number of subscribers, C-149
Snack food industry, C-255–C-270
  competitors, C-261
  market shares, C-265
  Pepsi's product line, C-262–C-263
Social complexity of resources, 148–149
Social conscience, 356
Social contract theory, 345–346
Social forces, 100
Socially responsible investments, 368
Social media
  in Africa, C-3–C-7, C-9–C-10
  and Afrigator, C-3–C-7
Societal concerns, changing, 123
Solar energy industry
  Canadian Solar, C-204–C-210
  categories of solar energy, C-190
  Feed-in Tariff program, C-189, C-193, C-196,
    C-204, C-298
  global industry, C-193–C-197
  global players, C-197–C-204
  government incentives, C-189, C-196
  main competitors, C-201–C-203
  market predictions, C-197
  market shares, C-200
  photovoltaic cells, C-192–C-193
  total installations 1998–2008, C-194
  world market highlights, C-195–C-196
Source code protection, C-168–C-169
South Africa, working conditions, C-397
South African Police Services, C-374
South Korea
  export strategies, 263
  solar energy industry, C-195
Spain
  investigation of Google, C-154
  solar energy industry, C-193–C-196
Specialized assets, 307
Specialized resources and capabilities, 301–303
Specifications, lower, 188
Speed, factor in diversification, 299
Sports participation rate 1998–2008, C-34
Sri Lanka, working conditions, C-397
SS United States, 344
St. Andrews, Scotland golf course, C-30
Stabilization, wrong reason for
  diversification, 312

Staffing
  recruiting and training employees, 382–385
  scope of, 380
  strong management team, 381–382
Stakeholders, 89
  benefits of sustainability strategies, 365
  and corporate social responsibility, 356
Standard and Poor's, and Cemex, C-219
Standard and Poor's index, 368
Standardization
  for foreign markets, 260
  in global strategy, 271–272
Standardized goods, 116
Star businesses, 324
Start-up companies, barriers to entry, 295–296
Start-ups
  Internet in Africa, C-11
  in solar energy industry, C-199
Stock option plan, Starbucks, C-347
Stock price performance
  Adidas, C-274
  Canadian Solar, C-209
  at Cemex, C-226
  Google Inc.
    at initial public offering, C-138
    versus Standard and Poor's 500 index,
      C-141
    from 2004–2010, C-140
  Hewlett-Packard, C-75
  PepsiCo, C-257
  Starbucks, C-336
Stock purchase plan, C-347
Storage costs, 106
Store ambiance, Starbucks, C-337–C-339
Store design, Starbucks, C-336–C-337
Stories, role in corporate culture, 442
Strategic alliances; see also Joint ventures;
    Partnerships
  to access capabilities, 389
  advantages over mergers and acquisitions,
    237–238
  advantages over vertical integration, 237–238,
    243–244
  capturing benefits of
    decision-making process, 242
    keeping commitments, 242
    managing learning process, 242
    mutual benefit, 242
    picking a good partner, 242
    sensitive to cultural differences, 242
  definition, 238
  and diversification costs, 300
  drawbacks
    culture clash, 243
    integration problems, 243
    losing proprietary knowledge, 243
  to enter foreign markets, 265–269
  examples, 239–240, 267–268
  facilitating resource and risk sharing,
    265–266
  for global market leadership, 241
  joint ventures, 239
  key advantages, 244
  learning and added expertise, 267
  long-lasting, 243
  number of failures, 244
  qualifications for, 239
  reasons for, 241
  requirements for effectiveness, 244–245

risks
  conflicting objectives, 266
  loss of competitive advantage, 268
  overly dependent on partners, 268
  transaction costs, 266
  for strong industry position, 241
  when unnecessary, 268–269
Strategically relevant environmental factors,
    98–100
Strategic assets, 216
Strategic balance sheet, 152
Strategic choices, 53
Strategic fit
  competitive advantage, 306
  cross-business, 321–322, 329
  cross-country, 315
  versus cultural fit, 329–330
  in decentralized structure, 400
  definition, 300–301
  economies of scope, 306
  examples of opportunities, 301
  lacking in unrelated diversification, 312
  profitability and shareholder value, 306–307
  specialized resources and capabilities, 301–303
  along value chain
    customer service, 305
    distribution, 305
    manufacturing-related, 304
    research and development, 304
    sales and marketing, 304–305
    supply chain activities, 304
    technology, 304
  value chain matchup, 301
Strategic group mapping, 125–128
  competing and noncompeting groups, 127–128
  definition of groups, 126
  example, 127
  prevailing competitive pressures, 128
  procedures, 126
  profit prospects, 128
  variables, 126–127
Strategic groups, 126
Strategic intent, 86
Strategic management process
  corrective adjustments, 87–88
  mission statement, 74–76
  performance evaluation, 87–88
  setting objectives, 76–81
  strategic vision, 70–74
  strategy execution, 86–87
  strategy-making, 81–86
Strategic objectives, 78
Strategic offensives
  basis for competitive attack, 216–218
  block avenues open to challengers, 220–221
  blue-ocean strategy, 219–220
  choosing rivals to attack, 218–219
  for competitive advantage, 216
  to exploit competitor weakness, 216
  first-mover advantages, 221–223
  late-mover advantage, 223–224
  principal options, 217–218
  principles for, 216
  signaling retaliation, 221
  timing of, 215–216
Strategic options
  for allocating financial resources, 326
  after diversification, 327
  for allocating financial resources, 326

Strategic plan, 85–86
Strategic vision
  communicating
    easily stated, 72
    expressed as slogan, 74
    to lower-level managers, 71
  corporate examples, 73
  definition, 70–71
  developing, 70–71
  distinctive, 71
  inspirational, 425
  and mission statement, 74–75
  payoffs, 74
  specific, 71
  winning support for, 71–72
Strategies/Strategy; see also Ethical strategy;
    Unethical strategies
  abandoned elements, 58–59
  adaptive reactions, 58–59
  at Adidas, C-278–C-284
  blue-ocean strategy, 219–220
  and business model, 59–60
  Cemex, C-213
  for competitive edge, 102
  complexity in international marketing
    cross-country variations, 253–255
    demographics, 259–260
    economic conditions, 256–257
    exchange rate risks, 257–260
    impact of government policies, 256–257
    locating value chain activities, 254–256
  components, 52
  components for single-business company, 141
  crafting and executing, 62
  definition, 52
  deliberate, 58–59
  Dell Inc.
    advertising, C-70
    build-to-order, C-58–C-61
    cost reductions, C-57–C-58, C-70–C-71
    customer service, C-66–C-69
    direct sales, C-61–C-63
    expansion into new products, C-63–C-66
    just-in-time systems, C-60–C-61
    main tenets, C-57
    ongoing assembly improvements,
      C-58–C-60
    quality control, C-60
    research and development, C-69–C-70
    retail store selling, C-62–C-63
    supplier partnerships, C-60
    technical support, C-66–C-69
    white-box segment, C-70
  emergent, 58–59
  employee misconceptions, 375–376
  evolution over time, 57–58
  Google Inc.
    control of desktop, C-149–C-150
    dominate Internet advertising,
      C-147–C-148
    expansion into TV, C-150–C-151
    smartphone market, C-148–C-149
  Hewlett-Packard, C-75–C-77
  indicators of success, 140–141
  issues meriting manager attention, 173
  key to successful, 57
  levels of
    business, 84
    corporate, 82–84

Strategies/Strategy—*Cont.*
  functional-area, 84
  operating, 84–85
  likely moves of rivals
    from financial performance, 129
    from press releases, 129
    from public documents, 129
    questions to ask about, 129–130
  for local companies against global giants, 284–287
  for long-lived success, 51
  market opportunity factor, 152–153
  matched to competitive conditions, 60, 119
  matched to industry, 60
  at McDonald's, 55–56
  multibrand, C-130
  needed changes at Toyota, C-323
  proactive, 58–59
  quest for competitive advantage, 53–57
  reactive, 58–59
  realignment at PepsiCo, C-270
  realized, 58–59
  revision at Komatsu, C-253–C-254
  revision at Toyota, C-307–C-308
  to set company apart, 53
  for small companies
    for competing in developing countries, 281–284
    in developing countries, 284–287
  stages in crafting and executing, 69–70
  tests for winning strategy
    competitive advantage test, 61–62
    fit test, 60
    performance test, 62
  types of action and approaches, 54
  what not to do, 53
  as work in progress, 58
  "worry list" of problems, 173
Strategy-critical activities
  benefits of focus on, 392
  building blocks of organizations, 393–394
  consistency in, 410
  hindrances to, 413
Strategy execution
  without added expense, 408
  building on capabilities, 379–380
  for competitive advantage, 390
  and corporate governance, 88–91
  devising action agenda, 378
  employee skills and knowledge for, 389–390
  framework for, 376–379
  and good management, 62–63
  impact of ethical standards, 346–347
  information systems for, 420–422
  internal fit, 60
  in large organizations, 378–379
  leadership roles, 454–458
  management challenges, 376
  operating systems for, 422–423
  operations-driven activity, 375
  organization-building activities
    core competencies, 380, 385–390
    organizing work effort, 380, 390–401
    staffing, 380–385
  paramount actions for, 390
  policies and procedures
    consistency in critical activities, 410
    prescribed vs. independent activities, 411

  top-down guidance, 409–410
  work climate, 410
  poor, 375
  principal aspects, 87
  principal components, 377–379
  prior requirements, 407
  process management tools, 411–420
  process steps, 454
  proficient, 88
  relevance of corporate culture
    adaptive cultures, 447–448
    change-resistant cultures, 448–449
    changing problem cultures, 450–454
    clash of culture with execution, 446
    high-performance cultures, 446–447
    incompatible subcultures, 450
    insular and inwardly focused cultures, 449
    politicized cultures, 449
    strong-culture companies, 445–446
    unethical greed-driven cultures, 449–450
    ways of implementation, 445–446
    weak-culture companies, 445
  resource allocation for, 407–408
  and resource shifts, 408
  in small organizations, 379–380
  summary on, 458
  ten basic tasks of, 378
  tied to rewards and incentives, 423–430
  time-consuming, 86
  for whole management team, 376
  work involved in, 376–377
Strategy-making, 52–53
  at all organizational levels, 81–85
  bases of, 375
  collaborative team effort, 85
  and corporate governance, 88–91
  diversity in, 53
  ethical, 354
  at General Electric, 82
  impact of ethical standards, 346–347
  led by CEOs, 81–82
  on-the-scene managers, 82
  in single-business enterprise, 85
  strategic plan from, 85–86
  summary of process, 81, 458
Strategy-making hierarchy, 83
Strategy options, to improve corporate performance
  broadening business base, 327–328
  divesting or retrenching, 328–330
  restructuring, 330–332
  sticking with business lineup, 326–327
Strengths, 151; *see also* SWOT analysis
Stretch objectives, 76, 79, 425, 456
Strikes, in Chinese plants, C-251
Strong-culture companies, 443–444
  effects on strategy execution, 445–446
  ingrained values and norms, 444
  senior management in, 444
Strong rivalry, 107
Strong vs. weak differentiation, 200
Struggling firms, attack on, 219
Subcultures, incompatible, 450
Subsidiaries, Coca-Cola India, C-377
Substantive culture-changing actions, 452–453
Substitutes
  available for resources, 149
  competitive pressure from sellers of, 111–112

  creating a price ceiling, 111
  factors affecting competition from, 112
  identifying, 113
  market indicators of competitive strength, 111–112
  pricing of, 111
  switching costs, 111
  from technological change, 122
Sudden-death threat, 153–155
Sunday Times of India, C-12
Supermarkets, bargaining power, 116
Supplier auditing program, Walmart, C-407
Supplier bargaining power
  competitive pressures from, 112–115
  decreased by globalization, 121
  determining strength of, 113–115
  factors affecting, 114
  Microsoft and Intel, 113
  versus small-scale retailers, 113
Supplier Code of Conduct, Apple, Inc., 341
Supplier factories' unethical practices, case, C-396–C-412
  audit fatigue, C-407–C-410
  compliance programs
    at Nike, Inc., C-400–C-406
    at Walmart, C-406–C-410
  industry and NGO compliance efforts, C-410–C-412
  obstacles to compliance, C-411–C-412
  reports on, C-396
  strategies to deceive inspectors, C-398–C-400
  wages and employment in China, C-397–C-398
Supplier partnerships, at Dell Inc., C-60
Supplier-related value chain activities, 165–166
Suppliers
  to beverage industry, C-21–C-22
  company bargaining power with, 187
  coordinating with, 189, 197
  expanding internationally, 253
  in golf equipment industry, C-39–C-40
  located near company, 189–190
  partnering with, 187
  value chain activities, 161
Supply chain, TomTom, C-119
Supply chain activities, 305
Supply chain efficiency, 187
Supply chain management, 159
  Adidas, C-280
Support value chain activities, 157–158
  general administration, 159
  human resource management, 159
  research and development, 159
  systems development, 159
  technology, 159
Sustainability, means of, 362
Sustainable business practices, 79
  definition, 363
  at Unilever, 363–364
Sustainable competitive advantage
  definition, 53, 148
  from resources and capabilities, 147–150
  strategic approaches for, 54–57
Sustainable differentiation advantage, 198
Switching costs
  and buyer bargaining power, 116
  created by first-movers, 222
  and differentiation strategy, 198
  kinds of, 104

and low-cost providers, 192
and product differentiation, 106
to substitutes, 113
Switzerland, share of global revenue, C-240
SWOT analysis
conclusions from, 155–156
definitions, 150–151
identifying opportunities, 152–153
identifying strengths, 151–152
identifying threats to profitability, 153–155
identifying weaknesses, 152
questions answered by, 156
steps involved, 155
what to look for, 154
Symbolic culture-changing actions
ceremonial events, 453–454
lead by example, 453
Synergy, 296
post-merger integration, C-220–C-222
Systems development, 159

T

Tacit knowledge, 146, 388
leakage, C-168
Taiwan, China's relations with, C-178–C-179,
C-183–C-184
Tangible assets, 145–146
Tangible features, 197
Tapered integration, 231
Target market
for best-cost provider strategy, 206
foreign, 252
Tariffs, barrier to entry, 109
Team leader system, at Toyota, C-315
Technical know-how
diffusion of, 123
in licensing strategies, 263
Technical support, Dell Inc., C-66–C-69
Technological advances/change
fast-paced, 199
and industry change, 122
striving for, 195
in vertical integration, 233
Technological assets, 145–146
Technological factors, 100
Technological standard, set by first-movers,
222–223
Technology
for decentralized decision making, 399
digital mapping, C-111
next-generation, 217
reason for mergers and acquisitions, 229
routing algorithms, C-111
strategic fit, 305
value chain activity, 159
Technology companies, adaptive cultures, 448
Television, Google's expansion into,
C-150–C-151
Terrorist attack of 2001, 153–155, C-85, C-179,
C-248
Think-global, act-global approach, 271
Think-global, act-local approach, 272
Think-local, act-local approach, 269–271
Threats; *see* SWOT analysis
Time, C-80, C-131

Time required for culture change, 454
Times interest earned ratio, 143
Time to market, 235–236
Timing of offensive or defensive strategies,
221–225
Top-down process of setting objectives, 81
Top executives
with centralized decision making, 397–399
with decentralized decision making, 399
incentive compensation, 329
role in strategy execution, 454–455
Total Quality Control, C-311
Total quality management, 413
capturing full value of, 419–420
compared to business process reengineering,
418
compared to Six Sigma, 418
description, 414
to focus on continuous improvement, 456
Toyota Way (Liker), C-322
Tracking devices, C-113–C-114
Trade barriers
and acquisition strategies, 264
as barrier to entry, 109
threat of entry from lowering, 121
Tradition-steeped companies, 441
Training, 389–390
at China Airlines, C-180–C-181
by Coca-Cola India, C-377
at Shangri-La Hotels, C-297–C-298
at Starbucks, C-348–C-349
Transaction costs
in acquisitions, 299–300
in strategic alliances, 266
Transformation agenda, Starbucks,
C-355–C-357
Transnational strategy
advantages/disadvantages, 273
definition, 272
drawbacks, 272
leveraging skills and capabilities, 272
mass-customization in, 272
Triple bottom line
companies recognized for, 362
and corporate social responsibility strategies,
361
definition and scope, 360–361
measures of performance, 361
mutual fund companies, 361
Triple-bottom-line reporting, 361
Turnaround capabilities, 310
Turnaround strategy
Apple Inc., C-124
Starbucks, C-355–C-357

U

U-forms, 395
Umbrella brands, 309
Uncertainty, reduction in, 123
Underage workers, 342
Undercapitalized firms, 324
Undervalued companies, 310
Unemployment, in recession of 2008, C-38
Unethical and greed-driven culture, 449–450
Unethical behavior, costs of, 354–355

Unethical behavior by supplier factories, case
breaches uncovered by Nike, C-406
compliance programs
at Nike, Inc., C-400–C-406
at Walmart, C-406–C-410
industry and NGO compliance efforts
Fair Factories Clearinghouse, C-411
Fair Labor Organization, C-410–C-411
obstacles to compliance, C-411–C-412
reports of, C-396–C-397
strategies to deceive inspectors, C-398–C-400
workplace conditions, C-397
Unethical strategies
corporate scandals, 347, 348–353
drivers of
company culture, 351–352
faulty oversight, 348–349
pressure to meet short-term targets, 349–351
pursuit of personal gain, 348–349
UN-HABITAT, C-387
Uniqueness drivers, 194; *see also* Differentiation
strategies
Unitary structure, 395
United Kingdom
Cemex in, C-219
investigation of Google, C-154
United Nations, revocation of Taiwan's
membership, C-173
United States
beverage industry, C-18
Cemex in, C-219
Foreign Corrupt Practices Act, 343
history of golf in, C-30–C-31
imports from China, C-396
investigation of Google, C-154
share of global revenue, C-240
solar energy industry, C-195, C-196
wireless subscribers, C-161
United States dollar, decline in value, 258–259
United States Golf Association
rules, C-35–C-36
and technology, C-36
United States House Oversight Committee,
C-137, C-154
University of Buffalo, C-69
University of Michigan, C-389, C-391
University of New South Wales, C-81–C-83,
C-93
Unrelated businesses, 300
Unrelated diversification
better-off test, 308
building shareholder value
acquisition of undervalued companies, 310
corporate parenting, 308–309
cross-business allocation of financial
resources, 309–310
generalized resources and capabilities, 308
requirements, 310–311
criteria for, 307
drawbacks
demands on management, 311
limited competitive advantage, 311–312
focus of, 307
inadequate reasons for
growth, 312
managerial motives, 312–313
risk reduction, 312
stabilization, 312

Unrelated diversification—*Cont.*
  and multidivisional structure, 395–396
  parenting advantage, 311
Unrelated groups of related businesses, 313
USAID, C-385

V

Value
  differentiating to add, 199
  from differentiation strategy, 197–198
  golf equipment 1997–2008, C-31–C-33
  provided to customers, 157
  signaling, 198
Value chain
  definition, 157
  at Just Coffee, 160
  managed for differentiation, 194–196
  operations component, 158
  profit margin component, 158
  raising costs, 158–160
  revamped to increase differentiation, 196–197
  tying up assets, 158–160
Value chain activities
  activity-based costing, 160
  benchmarking, 162–163
  for competitive advantage, 166–167, 169
  and competitiveness, 161
  cost-efficient management
    advanced production technology, 188
    company bargaining power, 187
    cost advantage over rivals, 188–189
    economies of scale, 186
    full capacity operation, 186–187
    information technology, 188
    learning-curve effects, 186
    lower input costs, 187
    motivating employees, 188
    outsourcing, 188
    supply chain efficiency, 187
    vertical integration, 188
  of distribution channel, 161
  in foreign markets, 255–256
  in global strategy, 271
  improving
    distribution-related activities, 166
    internally performed activities, 165
    supplier-related activities, 165–166
  kinds of primary activities, 159
  kinds of support activities, 159
  for low-cost providers, 186–189
  management at Walmart, 191
  in outsourcing, 235–237
  PC vendors, C-59
  performed internally vs. outsourcing, 392–393
  primary, 157–158
  realignment at PepsiCo, C-270
  reengineering, 414
  in related diversification, 303
  relation to resources and capabilities, 167–168
  revamped to lower costs
    coordination with suppliers, 189
    direct selling, 189
    nearby supplier location, 189–190
    at Nucor Corporation, 190
    at Southwest Airlines, 190

  of suppliers, 161
  support, 157–158
Value chain analysis
  comparison of rival companies, 158
  customer value proposition, 158
  inadequate for complete competitive
    situation, 168
  internal cost structure, 158–161
Value chain matchup, 293
  in related diversification, 301, 304–305
Value chain system
  for entire industry, 161–162
  scope of, 161
Value-conscious buyers, 206
Value creation, at Cemex, C-223
Values; *see also* Core values
  of companies
    definition, 75
    linked to vision and mission, 75–76
  in corporate culture, 440
  at Starbucks, C-349–C-350, C-351
Value statement, 76
  Royal Dutch Shell, 77
Variables in strategic group mapping, 126–127
Venezuela, problems for Cemex, C-225
Venture capital, C-334
Vertical integration, 229–235
  advantages, 188, 231–233
  at American Apparel, 236
  backward or forward, 230
  disadvantages
    capacity-matching problems, 234
    economies of scale unrealized, 234
    impair flexibility, 233
    increased business risk, 233
    less flexibility in buyer preferences, 233
    need for new business capabilities, 234
    need for new skills, 234
    slow to embrace technological advances, 233
  to expand activities, 230
  full integration, 230–231
  inverted flexible, C-205
  in multidivisional structure, 396
  partial integration, 231
  Starbucks, C-346
  versus strategic alliances, 237–238, 243–244
  tapered integration, 231
  weighing pros and cons, 234–235
Vertically integrated firm, 229
Vertical scope, 226
Veterinary Wildlife Services, South Africa,
    C-361, C-363–C-364
  aims and responsibilities, C-365
  values and functions, C-366–C-367
Videoconferencing, 122
Video game industry
  competition in, C-102–C-106
  evolution of, C-104
  market share goals, C-102–C-103
  Nintendo, C-95–C-106
  recent trends, C-102
  seventh generation, C-103
  technological advances, C-103
Vietnam, market for rhino horn, C-374
Vision
  Starbucks, C-359–C-360
  of TomTom, C-107–C-108

Vision statement
  dos and don'ts, 72
  purpose, 71
Voice-over Internet Protocol (VoIP), 122

W

Wages
  in China, C-397–C-398
  country comparisons, C-301–C-302
  country differences, 121
  low-wage countries, 256
Wall Street Journal, C-80, C-122, C-337–C-339
Waste reduction, at Toyota, C-311
Water and Development Alliance, C-385
Water conservation, by Coca-Cola India,
    C-382–C-385
Weak-culture companies
  lack of employee allegiance, 444
  and strategy execution, 445
Weakness, 151; *see also* SWOT analysis
Weak rivalry, 107
Weighted competitive strength assessment
  description, 168–171
  implications, 172
Weighted competitive strength scores, 318, 319
Weighted industry attractiveness scores, 316
White-box PCs, C-70
Wholesale distributors, 108
Winning strategy tests
  competitive advantage test, 61–62
  fit test, 60
  performance test, 62
Wireless communications, C-158–C-161
Work atmosphere, 425
Work climate, 410
  results-oriented, 456–457
Work effort
  aligning structure and strategy, 393–397
  collaboration with partners, 400–401
  delegation of authority, 397–400
  to fit business lineup, 401
  for good strategy execution, 390–391
  internal vs. outsourced value chain, 391–393
  reengineering, 413
Workforce; *see also* Employees; Human resource
    management
  empowerment, 456
  local, 285–286
Workforce diversity, 358
Workforce retention, 366–367
  at Shangri-La Hotels, C-299–C-300
Working capital ratio, 52
Working conditions, 358
  national comparisons, C-397
  Starbucks, C-347–C-348
Work organization, 387–388
World Bank, C-87
World Economic Forum, C-81
World Trade Organization, C-289
  and dumping, 280
World Wildlife Federation, C-375
"Worry list" of problems, 173